D0524144

Principles of Marketing

Principles of Marketing

15e

Philip Kotler
Northwestern University

Gary Armstrong
University of North Carolina

PEARSON

Boston Columbus Indianapolis New York San Francisco Upper Saddle River
Amsterdam Cape Town Dubai London Madrid Milan Munich Paris Montreal Toronto
Delhi Mexico City São Paulo Sydney Hong Kong Seoul Singapore Taipei Tokyo

Editor in Chief: Stephanie Wall
Director of Development: Stephen Deitmer
Director of Editorial Services: Ashley Santora
Editorial Project Manager: Meeta Pendharkar
Editorial Assistant: Jacob Garber
Executive Marketing Manager: Anne Fahlgren
Senior Managing Editor: Judy Leale
Senior Production Project Manager: Karalyn Holland
Operations Specialist: Cathleen Petersen
Creative Director: Blair Brown
Senior Art Director: Janet Slowik

Cover and Interior Designer: Karen Quigley
Cover Photo: Dave King/Dorling Kindersley/Getty
Cover Illustration: Artved/iStock
Senior Media Project Manager: Denise Vaughn
Media Project Manager: Lisa Rinaldi
Full-Service Project Management: Roxanne Klaas/ S4Carlisle Publishing Services
Composition: S4Carlisle Publishing Services
Printer/Binder: Courier/Kendallville
Cover Printer: Lehigh-Phoenix Color/Hagerstown
Text Font: 9/12.5 Palatino LT Std

Credits and acknowledgments borrowed from other sources and reproduced, with permission, in this textbook appear on the appropriate page within the text.

Microsoft and/or its respective suppliers make no representations about the suitability of the information contained in the documents and related graphics published as part of the services for any purpose. All such documents and related graphics are provided "as is" without warranty of any kind. Microsoft and/or its respective suppliers hereby disclaim all warranties and conditions with regard to this information, including all warranties and conditions of merchantability, whether express, implied, or statutory; fitness for a particular purpose; title; and non-infringement. In no event shall Microsoft and/or its respective suppliers be liable for any special, indirect, or consequential damages or any damages whatsoever resulting from loss of use, data, or profits, whether in an action of contract, negligence, or other tortious action, arising out of or in connection with the use or performance of information available from the services.

The documents and related graphics contained herein could include technical inaccuracies or typographical errors. Changes are periodically added to the information herein. Microsoft and/or its respective suppliers may make improvements and/or changes in the product(s) and/or the program(s) described herein at any time. Partial screen shots may be viewed in full within the software version specified.

Microsoft® and Windows® are registered trademarks of the Microsoft Corporation in the U.S.A. and other countries. This book is not sponsored or endorsed by or affiliated with the Microsoft Corporation.

Copyright © 2014, 2012, 2010 Pearson Education, Inc., One Lake Street, Upper Saddle River, New Jersey 07458. All rights reserved. Manufactured in the United States of America. This publication is protected by Copyright, and permission should be obtained from the publisher prior to any prohibited reproduction, storage in a retrieval system, or transmission in any form or by any means, electronic, mechanical, photocopying, recording, or likewise. To obtain permission(s) to use material from this work, please submit a written request to Pearson Education, Inc., Permissions Department, One Lake Street, Upper Saddle River, New Jersey 07458.

Many of the designations by manufacturers and sellers to distinguish their products are claimed as trademarks. Where those designations appear in this book, and the publisher was aware of a trademark claim, the designations have been printed in initial caps or all caps.

Library of Congress Cataloging-in-Publication Data
Kotler, Philip.
 Principles of marketing / Philip Kotler, Gary Armstrong.—15th ed.
   p. cm.
  ISBN-13: 978-0-13-308404-7
  ISBN-10: 0-13-308404-3
 1. Marketing.   I. Armstrong, Gary (Gary M.)   II. Title.
 HF5415.K636 2014
 658.8—dc23

                                  2012037271

10 9 8 7 6 5 4 3 2

ISBN 13: 978-0-13-308404-7
ISBN 10:   0-13-308404-3

Dedication

*To Kathy, Betty, Mandy, Matt, KC, Keri, Delaney, Molly, Macy, and Ben;
Nancy, Amy, Melissa, and Jessica*

About The Authors

As a team, Philip Kotler and Gary Armstrong provide a blend of skills uniquely suited to writing an introductory marketing text. Professor Kotler is one of the world's leading authorities on marketing. Professor Armstrong is an award-winning teacher of undergraduate business students. Together they make the complex world of marketing practical, approachable, and enjoyable.

Philip Kotler is S. C. Johnson & Son Distinguished Professor of International Marketing at the Kellogg School of Management, Northwestern University. He received his master's degree from the University of Chicago and his PhD from M.I.T., both in economics. Dr. Kotler is author of *Marketing Management* (Pearson Prentice Hall), now in its fourteenth edition and the most widely used marketing textbook in graduate schools of business worldwide. He has authored dozens of other successful books and has written more than 100 articles in leading journals. He is the only three-time winner of the coveted Alpha Kappa Psi award for the best annual article in the *Journal of Marketing*.

Professor Kotler was named the first recipient of two major awards: the Distinguished Marketing Educator of the Year Award given by the American Marketing Association and the Philip Kotler Award for Excellence in Health Care Marketing presented by the Academy for Health Care Services Marketing. His numerous other major honors include the Sales and Marketing Executives International Marketing Educator of the Year Award; the European Association of Marketing Consultants and Trainers Marketing Excellence Award; the Charles Coolidge Parlin Marketing Research Award; and the Paul D. Converse Award, given by the American Marketing Association to honor "outstanding contributions to science in marketing." A recent Forbes survey ranks Professor Kotler in the top 10 of the world's most influential business thinkers. In a recent *Financial Times* poll of 1,000 senior executives across the world, Professor Kotler was ranked as the fourth "most influential business writer/guru" of the twenty-first century. And he recently topped BusinessEducators .com's "Management A-List of Academics," based on outstanding achievements as well as Google global Web search interest.

Dr. Kotler has served as chairman of the College on Marketing of the Institute of Management Sciences, a director of the American Marketing Association, and a trustee of the Marketing Science Institute. He has consulted with many major U.S. and international companies in the areas of marketing strategy and planning, marketing organization, and international marketing. He has traveled and lectured extensively throughout Europe, Asia, and South America, advising companies and governments about global marketing practices and opportunities.

Gary Armstrong is Crist W. Blackwell Distinguished Professor Emeritus of Undergraduate Education in the Kenan-Flagler Business School at the University of North Carolina at Chapel Hill. He holds undergraduate and master's degrees in business from Wayne State University in Detroit, and he received his PhD in marketing from Northwestern University. Dr. Armstrong has contributed numerous articles to leading business journals. As a consultant and researcher, he has worked with many companies on marketing research, sales management, and marketing strategy.

But Professor Armstrong's first love has always been teaching. His long-held Blackwell Distinguished Professorship is the only permanently endowed professorship for distinguished undergraduate teaching at the University of North Carolina (UNC) at Chapel Hill. He has been very active in the teaching and administration of Kenan-Flagler's undergraduate program. His administrative posts have included Chair of Marketing, Associate Director of the Undergraduate Business Program, Director of the Business Honors Program, and many others. Through the years, he has worked closely with business student groups and has received several UNC campus-wide and Business School teaching awards. He is the only repeat recipient of the school's highly regarded Award for Excellence in Undergraduate Teaching, which he received three times. Most recently, Professor Armstrong received the UNC Board of Governors Award for Excellence in Teaching, the highest teaching honor bestowed by the 16-campus University of North Carolina system.

Brief Contents

Contents

4 Managing Marketing Information to Gain Customer Insights 100

5 Consumer Markets and Consumer Buyer Behavior 134

6 Business Markets and Business Buyer Behavior 166

Part 3: Designing a Customer-Driven Strategy and Mix 190

7 Customer-Driven Marketing Strategy: Creating Value for Target Customers 190

Preface

The Fifteenth Edition of *Principles of Marketing*! The World's Most-Trusted Undergraduate Marketing Text

Students across six continents, more than 40 countries, and 24 languages rely on Kotler/Armstrong's *Principles of Marketing* as the world's most-trusted source for learning about basic marketing concepts and practices. More than ever, the fifteenth edition introduces new marketing students to the fascinating world of modern marketing in an innovative, complete, and authoritative yet fresh, practical, and enjoyable way. We've poured over every page, table, figure, fact, and example in an effort to keep this the best text from which to learn about and teach marketing. Enhanced by MyMarketingLab, our online homework and personalized study tool, the fifteenth edition of *Principles of Marketing* remains the world standard in introductory marketing education.

Marketing: Creating Customer Value and Relationships

Top marketers at outstanding companies share a common goal: putting the consumer at the heart of marketing. Today's marketing is all about creating customer value and building profitable customer relationships. It starts with understanding consumer needs and wants, determining which target markets the organization can serve best, and developing a compelling value proposition by which the organization can attract and grow valued consumers. If the organization does these things well, it will reap the rewards in terms of market share, profits, and customer equity.

Five Major Customer Value Themes

From beginning to end, the fifteenth edition of *Principles of Marketing* develops an innovative framework of customer value and customer relationships that captures the essence of today's marketing. It builds on five major value themes:

1. *Creating value for customers in order to capture value from customers in return.* Today's marketers must be good at *creating customer value* and *managing customer relationships*. Outstanding marketing companies understand the marketplace and customer needs, design value-creating marketing strategies, develop integrated marketing programs that deliver customer value and delight, and build strong customer relationships. In return, they capture value from customers in the form of sales, profits, and customer loyalty.

   This innovative *customer-value framework* is introduced at the start of Chapter 1 in a five-step marketing process model, which details how marketing *creates* customer value and *captures* value in return. ● The framework is carefully developed in the first two chapters and then fully integrated throughout the remainder of the text.

2. *Building and managing strong, value-creating brands.* Well-positioned brands with strong brand equity provide the basis upon which to build customer value and profitable customer relationships. Today's marketers must position their brands powerfully and manage them well to create valued brand experiences. The fifteenth edition provides a

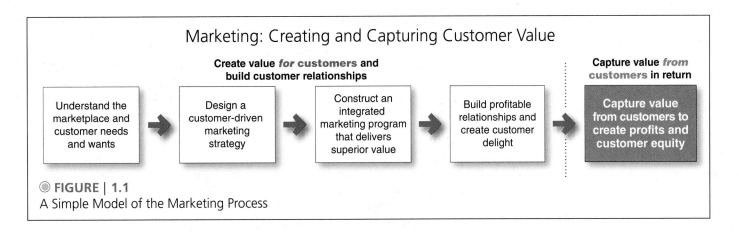

Marketing: Creating and Capturing Customer Value

Create value *for* customers and build customer relationships

Capture value *from* customers in return

| Understand the marketplace and customer needs and wants | → | Design a customer-driven marketing strategy | → | Construct an integrated marketing program that delivers superior value | → | Build profitable relationships and create customer delight | → | Capture value from customers to create profits and customer equity |

⦿ **FIGURE | 1.1**
A Simple Model of the Marketing Process

deep focus on brands, anchored by the Chapter 8 section "Branding Strategy: Building Strong Brands."

3. *Harnessing new marketing technologies.* New digital and other high-tech marketing developments are dramatically changing how consumers and marketers relate to one another. No other force is having more impact than technology on marketing strategy and practice. The fifteenth edition thoroughly explores the new technologies impacting marketing, from digital relationship-building tools in Chapter 1 to new digital marketing and online technologies in Chapters 15 and 17 to the exploding use of online social networks and consumer-generated marketing in Chapters 1, 5, 14, 15, 17—and just about everywhere else in the text.

4. *Measuring and managing return on marketing.* Especially in uncertain economic times, marketing managers must ensure that their marketing dollars are being well spent. In the past, many marketers spent freely on big, expensive marketing programs, often without thinking carefully about the financial returns on their spending. But all that has changed rapidly. "Marketing accountability"—measuring and managing return on marketing investments—has now become an important part of strategic marketing decision making. This emphasis on marketing accountability is addressed throughout the fifteenth edition.

5. *Sustainable marketing around the globe.* As technological developments make the world an increasingly smaller and more fragile place, marketers must be skilled at marketing their brands globally and in sustainable ways. New material throughout the fifteenth edition emphasizes the concepts of global marketing and sustainable marketing—meeting the present needs of consumers and businesses while also preserving or enhancing the ability of future generations to meet their needs. The fifteenth edition integrates global marketing and sustainability topics throughout the text. It then provides focused coverage of each topic in Chapters 19 and 20, respectively.

New in the Fifteenth Edition

We've thoroughly revised the fifteenth edition of *Principles of Marketing* to reflect the major trends and forces impacting marketing in this high-tech era of customer value and relationships. Here are just some of the major and continuing changes you'll find in this edition:

- More than any other developments, sweeping new digital and online technologies are now affecting the ways in which marketers and customers learn about and relate to each other. In recent years, nothing has had greater impact than technology on consumers and the marketers who serve them. Every chapter of the fifteenth edition features new, revised, and expanded discussions of the explosive impact of the exciting **new marketing technologies** shaping marketing strategy and practice—from online social networks and brand communities discussed in Chapters 1, 5, 14, 15, and 17; to "online listening" and Webnology research tools in Chapter 4, neuromarketing in Chapter 5, and location-based marketing in Chapter 7; to the use of social networks in business-to-business marketing and sales in Chapters 6 and 16; to Internet and mobile marketing and other new communications technologies in Chapters 1, 14, 15, 17, and throughout. The fifteenth edition is packed with new stories and examples illustrating how companies employ technology to gain competitive advantage—from traditional marketing all-stars such as P&G, McDonald's, and Nike to new-age digital competitors such as Apple, Google, Amazon.com, and Facebook.

- The fifteenth edition continues to build on and extend the innovative **customer-value framework** from previous editions. The customer-value model presented in the first chapter is fully integrated throughout the remainder of the book. No other marketing text presents such a clear and compelling customer-value approach.

- Throughout the fifteenth edition, you will find revised coverage of the rapidly **changing nature of customer relationships** with companies and brands. Today's marketers are creating deep consumer involvement and a sense of customer community surrounding their brands—making brands a meaningful part of consumers' conversations and lives. Today's new relationship-building tools include everything from Web sites, blogs, in-person events, and video sharing to online communities and social networks such as Facebook, YouTube, Pinterest, Twitter, or a company's own social networking sites. For just a few examples, see Chapter 1 (the section "The Changing Nature of Customer Relationships"); Chapter 4 (qualitative approaches to gaining deeper customer insights); Chapter 5 (managing online influence and marketing through social networks); Chapter 9 (customer-driven new-product development and co-creation); Chapters 14 and 15 (the shift toward more personalized, interactive communications); and Chapter 17 (online social networks, customer communities, and direct digital media).

- The fifteenth edition contains substantial new material on the continuing trend toward two-way interactions between customers and brands, including such topics as **customer-managed relationships, consumer empowerment, crowdsourcing, customer co-creation,** and **consumer-generated marketing**. Today's more empowered customers are giving as much as they get in the form of two-way relationships (Chapter 1), a more active role in providing customer insights (Chapter 4), crowdsourcing and co-creating new products (Chapter 8), consumer-generated marketing content (Chapters 1 and 15), developing or passing along brand messages (Chapters 1, 5, 8, 14, and 15), interacting in customer communities (Chapters 5, 15, and 17), and other developments.

- New coverage in every chapter of the fifteenth edition shows how companies and consumers are dealing with **marketing in an uncertain economy** in the lingering aftermath of the recent Great Recession. Starting with a section and feature in Chapter 1 and continuing with new sections, discussions, and examples integrated throughout the text, the fifteenth edition shows how now, even as the economy recovers, marketers must focus on creating customer value and sharpening their value propositions in this era of more sensible consumption.

- New material throughout the fifteenth edition highlights the increasing importance of **sustainable marketing**. The discussion begins in Chapter 1 and ends in Chapter 20, which pulls marketing concepts together under a sustainable marketing framework. In between, frequent discussions and examples show how sustainable marketing calls for socially and environmentally responsible actions that meet both the immediate and the future needs of customers, companies, and society as a whole.

- The fifteenth edition provides new discussions and examples of the growth in **global marketing.** As the world becomes a smaller, more competitive place, markets face new global marketing challenges and opportunities, especially in fast-growing emerging markets such as China, India, Brazil, Africa, and others. You'll find much new coverage of global marketing throughout the text, starting in Chapter 1 and discussed fully in Chapter 19.

- The fifteenth edition provides revised and expanded coverage of the developments in the fast-changing areas of **integrated marketing communications** and **direct and online marketing**. It tells how marketers are blending the new digital and direct technologies—everything from Internet and mobile marketing to blogs, viral videos, and online social networks—with traditional media to create more targeted, personal, and interactive customer relationships. Marketers are no longer simply creating integrated promotion programs, they are practicing *marketing content management* in paid, owned, earned, and shared media. No other text provides more current or encompassing coverage of these exciting developments.

- The fifteenth edition continues its emphasis on **measuring and managing return on marketing**, including many new end-of-chapter financial and quantitative marketing exercises that let students apply analytical thinking to relevant concepts in each chapter and link chapter concepts to the text's innovative and comprehensive Appendix 2: Marketing by the Numbers.
- The fifteenth edition continues to improve on its **innovative learning design**. The text's active and integrative presentation includes learning enhancements such as annotated chapter-opening stories, a chapter-opening objective outline, and explanatory author comments on major chapter figures. The chapter-opening layout helps to preview and position the chapter and its key concepts. Figures annotated with author comments help students to simplify and organize chapter material. End-of-chapter features help to summarize important chapter concepts and highlight important themes, such as marketing technology, ethics, and financial marketing analysis. This innovative learning design facilitates student understanding and eases learning.
- The fifteenth edition provides 20 new or revised end-of-chapter company cases by which students can apply what they learn to actual company situations. The fifteenth edition also features many new video cases, with brief end-of-chapter summaries and discussion questions. A **newly revised Appendix 1: Marketing Plan** presents a brand new marketing plan by which students can apply text concepts to a hypothetical brand and situation. Finally, all of the chapter-opening stories and Real Marketing highlights in the fifteenth edition are either new or revised for currency.

An Emphasis on Real Marketing

Principles of Marketing, fifteenth edition, takes a practical marketing-management approach, providing countless in-depth, real-life examples and stories that show concepts in action and reveal the drama of modern marketing. In the fifteenth edition, every chapter-opening vignette and Real Marketing highlight is new or revised, providing fresh insights into real marketing practices. Learn how:

- Amazon.com's deep-down passion for creating customer value and relationships has made it the world's leading online retailer.
- Giant social network Facebook promises to become one of the world's most powerful and profitable online marketers—but it's just getting started.
- Sony's dizzying fall provides a cautionary tale of what can happen when a company—even a dominant marketing leader—fails to adapt to its changing environment.
- Domino's Pizza turned a five-year revenue slide into a fresh, hot turnaround by simply listening to customers and using the insights gained to develop better products and marketing.
- Apple's customer-centered product leadership engenders a love affair with the brand that has produced stunning sales and profit results.
- Dunkin' Donuts successfully targets the "Dunkin' Tribe"—not the Starbucks snob but the average Joe.
- How "showrooming"—the common consumer shopping practice of coming into store showrooms to scope out merchandise but instead buying it from an online rival—has become the bane of store retailers.
- Chipotle's sustainability mission isn't an add-on, created just to position the company as "socially responsible"—doing good is ingrained in everything the company does.
- Walmart, the world's largest retailer, and Amazon.com, the planet's largest online merchant, are fighting it out online on price.
- Athletic shoe maker Converse transformed the classic yesteryear brand into a fresh, expressive lifestyle brand befitting current times.
- Southwest's new-age direct marketing capability for building up-close-and-personal interactions with customers makes the passenger-centered company the envy of its industry.
- For Coca-Cola, marketing in Africa is like "sticking its hand into a bees' nest to get some honey."
- The explosion of the Internet, mobile devices, and other technologies has some marketers asking: "Who needs face-to-face selling anymore?"
- Under its Sustainable Living Plan, Unilever plans to double its size by 2020 while at the same time reducing its impact on the planet.

Beyond these features, each chapter is packed with countless real, relevant, and timely examples that reinforce key concepts. No other text brings marketing to life like the fifteenth edition of *Principles of Marketing*.

Learning Aids That Create More Value for You

A wealth of chapter-opening, within-chapter, and end-of-chapter learning devices help you to learn, link, and apply major concepts:

- *Integrated chapter-opening preview sections.* The active and integrative chapter-opening spread in each chapter starts with a *Chapter Preview,* which briefly previews chapter concepts, links them with previous chapter concepts, and introduces the chapter-opening story. This leads to a chapter-opening vignette—an engaging, deeply developed, illustrated, and annotated marketing story that introduces the chapter material and sparks your interest. Finally, an *Objective Outline* provides a helpful preview of chapter contents and learning objectives, complete with page numbers.
- *Real Marketing highlights.* Each chapter contains two carefully developed highlight features that provide an in-depth look at real marketing practices of large and small companies.
- *Author figure annotations.* Each figure contains author comments that aid your understanding and help organize major text sections.
- *Reviewing Objectives and Key Terms.* A summary at the end of each chapter reviews major chapter concepts, chapter objectives, and key terms.
- *Discussion and Critical Thinking Questions and Exercises.* Sections at the end of each chapter help you to keep track of and apply what you've learned in the chapter.
- *Applications and Cases.* Brief *Marketing Technology, Marketing Ethics,* and *Marketing by the Numbers* sections at the end of each chapter provide short application cases that facilitate discussion of current issues and company situations in areas such as marketing technology, ethics, and financial marketing analysis. A *Video Case* section contains short vignettes with discussion questions to be used with a set of mostly new four- to seven-minute videos that accompany the fifteenth edition. End-of-chapter *Company Case* sections provide all-new or revised company cases that help you to apply major marketing concepts to real company and brand situations.
- *Marketing Plan appendix.* Appendix 1 contains a brand new sample marketing plan that helps you to apply important marketing planning concepts.
- *Marketing by the Numbers appendix.* An innovative Appendix 2 provides you with a comprehensive introduction to the marketing financial analysis that helps to guide, assess, and support marketing decisions. An exercise at the end of each chapter lets you apply analytical and financial thinking to relevant chapter concepts and links the chapter to the Marketing by the Numbers appendix.

More than ever before, the fifteenth edition of *Principles of Marketing* creates value for you—it gives you all you need to know about marketing in an effective and enjoyable total learning package!

Supplements for Instructors

The following supplements are available to adopting instructors at the Pearson Instructor Resource Center, http://www.pearsonhighered.com/kotler.

- **Instructor's Manual:** provides the following for every chapter in the book: overview, outline, end-of-chapter solutions, additional projects, and examples and Web resources.
- **Test Bank:** includes 3,000 questions, consisting of multiple-choice, true/false, short-answer, and essay questions.
- **Image Library:** access many of the images, ads, and illustrations from the text.
- **PowerPoint slides:** includes basic chapter outlines, key points from each chapter, advertisements and art from the text, and discussion questions.
- **Blackboard and WebCT courses.**

Acknowledgments

No book is the work only of its authors. We greatly appreciate the valuable contributions of several people who helped make this new edition possible. As always, we owe very special thanks to Keri Jean Miksza for her dedicated and valuable help in *all* phases of the project, and to her husband Pete and little daughters Lucy and Mary for all the support they provide Keri during this often-hectic project.

We owe substantial thanks to Andy Norman of Drake University, for his valuable revision advice and skillful contributions in developing chapter vignettes and highlights, company and video cases, the Marketing Plan appendix, and selected marketing stories. This edition has benefited greatly from Andy's assistance. We also thank Laurie Babin of the University of Louisiana at Monroe for her dedicated efforts in preparing end-of-chapter materials and keeping our Marketing by the Numbers appendix fresh. Additional thanks also go to Dr. Andrew Lingwall of the Clarion University of Pennsylvania for revising the Instructor's Manual, to Mary Albrecht of Maryville University for revising the PowerPoint sets, and to the team at ANSR Source Group for revising the Test Bank for the fifteenth edition, as well as to Carol Davis from California State University, Monterrey Bay, for accuracy checking the supplements for this edition.

Many reviewers at other colleges and universities provided valuable comments and suggestions for this and previous editions. We are indebted to the following colleagues for their thoughtful input:

Fifteenth Edition Reviewers

Greg Black, Metropolitan State University of Denver
Rod Carveth, Naugatuck Valley Community College
Linda Morable, Richland College
Randy Moser, Elon University

David Murphy, Madisonville Community College
Donna Waldron, Manchester Community College
Douglas Witt, Brigham Young University

Fourteenth Edition Reviewers

Rod Carveth, Naugatuck Valley Community College
Anindja Chatterjee, Slippery Rock University of Pennsylvania
Mary Conran, Temple University
Eloise Coupey, Virginia Tech
Alan Dick, University of Buffalo
Karen Gore, Ivy Tech Community College, Evansville Campus
Charles Lee, Chestnut Hill College
Samuel McNeely, Murray State University
Chip Miller, Drake University
David Murphy, Madisonville Community College

Esther Page-Wood, Western Michigan University
Tim Reisenwitz, Valdosta State University
Mary Ellen Rosetti, Hudson Valley Community College
William Ryan, University of Connecticut
Roberta Schultz, Western Michigan University
J. Alexander Smith, Oklahoma City University
Deb Utter, Boston University
Donna Waldron, Manchester Community College
Wendel Weaver, Oklahoma Wesleyan University

We also owe a great deal to the people at Pearson who helped develop this book. Senior Acquisitions Editor Erin Gardner provided fresh ideas and support throughout the revision. Project Manager Meeta Pendharkar provided valuable assistance in managing the many facets of this complex revision project. Senior Art Director Janet Slowik developed the fifteenth edition's exciting design, and Senior Production Project Manager Karalyn Holland helped guide the book through the complex production process. We'd also like to thank Stephanie Wall, Anne Fahlgren, Judy Leale, and Jacob Garber for their contributions. We are proud to be associated with the fine professionals at Pearson Education. We also owe a mighty debt of gratitude to Project Editor Roxanne Klaas and the fine team at S4Carlisle Publishing Services.

Finally, we owe many thanks to our families for all of their support and encouragement—Kathy, Betty, Mandy, Matt, KC, Keri, Delaney, Molly, Macy, and Ben from the Armstrong clan and Nancy, Amy, Melissa, and Jessica from the Kotler family. To them, we dedicate this book.

Gary Armstrong
Philip Kotler

Principles of Marketing

Marketing

Creating and Capturing **Customer Value**

Chapter Preview This chapter introduces you to the basic concepts of marketing. We start with the question: What is marketing? Simply put, marketing is managing profitable customer relationships. The aim of marketing is to create value for customers in order to capture value from customers in return. Next we discuss the five steps in the marketing process—from understanding customer needs, to designing customer-driven marketing strategies and integrated marketing programs, to building customer relationships and capturing value for the firm. Finally, we discuss the major trends and forces affecting marketing in this age of customer relationships.

Understanding these basic concepts and forming your own ideas about what they really mean to you will provide a solid foundation for all that follows.

Let's start with a good story about marketing in action at Amazon.com, by far the world's leading online marketer. The secret to Amazon's success? It's really no secret at all. Amazon is flat-out customer obsessed. It has a deep-down passion for creating customer value and relationships. In return, customers reward Amazon with their buying dollars and loyalty. You'll see this theme of creating customer value in order to capture value in return repeated throughout this chapter and the remainder of the text.

Amazon.com: Obsessed with Creating Customer Value and Relationships

When you think of shopping online, chances are good that you think first of Amazon. The online pioneer first opened its virtual doors in 1995, selling books out of founder Jeff Bezos's garage in suburban Seattle. Amazon still sells books—lots and lots of books. But it now sells just about everything else as well, from music, electronics, tools, housewares, apparel, and groceries to loose diamonds and Maine lobsters.

From the start, Amazon has grown explosively. Its annual sales have rocketed from a modest $150 million in 1997 to more than $48 billion today. During the past two years alone, despite a shaky economy, Amazon's revenues and profits both nearly doubled, growing by 40 percent annually. This past holiday season, at one point, Amazon.com's more than 173 million active customers worldwide were purchasing 110 items per second. Analysts predict that by 2015, Amazon will become the youngest company in history to hit $100 billion in revenues (it took Walmart 34 years). That would make it the nation's second largest retailer, trailing only Walmart.

What has made Amazon such an amazing success story? Founder and CEO

Bezos puts it in three simple words: "Obsess over customers." To its core, the company is relentlessly customer driven. "The thing that drives everything is creating genuine value for customers," says Bezos. Amazon believes that if it does what's good for customers, profits will follow. So the company starts with the customer and works backward. Rather than asking what it can do with its current capabilities, Amazon first asks Who are our customers? What do they need? Then, it develops whatever capabilities are required to meet those customer needs.

At Amazon, such words are more than just "customer-speak." Every decision is made with an eye toward improving the Amazon.com customer experience. In fact, at many Amazon meetings, the most influential figure in the room is "the empty

> Amazon.com's deep-down passion for creating customer value and relationships has made it the world's leading online retailer. Amazon has become the model for companies that are obsessively and successfully focused on delivering customer value.

chair"—literally an empty chair at the table that represents the all-important customer. At times, the empty chair isn't empty, but is occupied by a "Customer Experience Bar Raiser," an employee who is specially trained to represent customers' interests. To give the empty chair a loud, clear voice, Amazon relentlessly tracks performance against nearly 400 measurable customer-related goals.

Amazon's obsession with serving the needs of its customers drives the company to take risks and innovate in ways that other companies don't. For example, when it noted that its book-buying customers needed better access to e-books and other digital content, Amazon developed the Kindle e-reader, its first-ever original product. The Kindle took more than four years and a whole new set of skills to develop. But Amazon's start-with-the-customer thinking paid off handsomely. The Kindle is now the company's number one selling product, and Amazon.com now sells more e-books than hardcovers and paperbacks combined. What's more, the company's new Kindle Fire tablet now leads the market for low-priced tablet computers. Thus, what started as an effort to improve the customer experience now gives Amazon a powerful presence in the burgeoning world of digital media. Not only does the Kindle allow access to e-books, music, videos, and apps sold by Amazon, it makes interacting with the online giant easier than ever.

Perhaps more important than *what* Amazon sells is *how* it sells. Amazon wants to deliver a special experience to every customer. Most Amazon.com regulars feel a surprisingly strong relationship with the company, especially given the almost complete lack of actual human interaction. Amazon obsesses over making each customer's experience uniquely personal. For example, the Amazon.com site greets customers with their very own personalized home pages, and its "Recommendations for You" feature offers personalized product recommendations. Amazon was the first company to use "collaborative filtering" technology, which sifts through each customer's past purchases and the purchasing patterns of customers with similar profiles to come up with personalized site content. Amazon wants to personalize the shopping experience for each individual customer. If it has 173 million customers, it reasons, it should have 173 million stores.

Visitors to Amazon.com receive a unique blend of benefits: huge selection, good value, low prices, and convenience. But it's the "discovery" factor that makes the buying experience really special. Once on the Amazon.com site, you're compelled to stay for a while—looking, learning, and discovering. Amazon.com has become a kind of online community in which customers can browse for products, research purchase alternatives, share opinions and reviews with other visitors, and chat online with authors and experts. In this way, Amazon does much more than just sell goods online. It creates direct, personalized customer relationships and satisfying online experiences. Year after year, Amazon places at or near the top of almost every customer satisfaction ranking, regardless of industry.

To create even greater selection and discovery for customers, Amazon long ago began allowing competing retailers—from mom-and-pop operations to Marks & Spencer department stores—to offer their products on Amazon.com, creating a virtual shopping mall of incredible proportions. It even encourages customers to sell used items on the site. And with the recent launch of AmazonSupply.com, the online seller now courts business and industrial customers with products ranging from

Amazon.com does much more than just sell goods online. It creates satisfying online customer experiences. "The thing that drives everything is creating genuine value for customers," says Amazon founder and CEO Bezos, shown above.
Contour by Getty Images

office supplies to radiation detectors and industrial cutting tools. The broader selection attracts more customers, and everyone benefits. "We are becoming increasingly important in the lives of our customers," says an Amazon marketing executive.

Based on its powerful growth, many analysts have speculated that Amazon.com will become the Walmart of the Web. In fact, some argue, it already is. Although Walmart's total sales of $444 billion dwarf Amazon's $48 billion in sales, Amazon's Internet sales are 12 times greater than Walmart's. So it's Walmart that's chasing Amazon on the Web. Put another way, Walmart wants to become the Amazon.com of the Web, not the other way around. However, despite its mammoth proportions, to catch Amazon online, Walmart will have to match the superb Amazon customer experience, and that won't be easy.

Whatever the eventual outcome, Amazon has become the poster child for companies that are obsessively and successfully focused on delivering customer value. Jeff Bezos has known from the very start that if Amazon creates superior value for customers, it will earn their business in return, and if it earns their business, success will follow in terms of company profits and returns.[1]

Objective Outline

MyMarketingLab™
✪ Improve Your Grade!
Over 10 million students improved their results using the Pearson MyLabs. Visit **mymktlab.com** for simulations, tutorials, and end-of-chapter problems.

Today's successful companies have one thing in common: Like Amazon, they are strongly customer focused and heavily committed to marketing. These companies share a passion for understanding and satisfying customer needs in well-defined target markets. They motivate everyone in the organization to help build lasting customer relationships based on creating value.

Customer relationships and value are especially important today. Facing dramatic technological changes and deep economic, social, and environmental challenges, today's customers are spending more carefully and reassessing their relationships with brands. In turn, it's more important than ever to build strong customer relationships based on real and enduring value.

Objective 1 ┈┈➤
Define marketing and outline the steps in the marketing process.

What Is Marketing?

Marketing, more than any other business function, deals with customers. Although we will soon explore more-detailed definitions of marketing, perhaps the simplest definition is this one: *Marketing is managing profitable customer relationships.* The twofold goal of marketing is to attract new customers by promising superior value and to keep and grow current customers by delivering satisfaction.

For example, McDonald's fulfills its "i'm lovin' it" motto by being "our customers' favorite place and way to eat" the world over, giving it nearly as much market share as its nearest four competitors combined. Walmart has become the world's largest retailer—and the world's largest company—by delivering on its promise, "Save Money. Live Better."[2]

Sound marketing is critical to the success of every organization. Large for-profit firms, such as Google, Target, Procter & Gamble, Toyota, and Microsoft, use marketing. But so do not-for-profit organizations, such as colleges, hospitals, museums, symphony orchestras, and even churches.

You already know a lot about marketing—it's all around you. Marketing comes to you in the good old traditional forms: You see it in the abundance of products at your nearby shopping mall and the ads that fill your TV screen, spice up your magazines, or stuff your mailbox. But in recent years, marketers have assembled a host of new marketing approaches, everything from imaginative Web sites and smartphone apps to online social networks and blogs. These new approaches do more than just blast out messages to the masses. They reach you directly and personally. Today's marketers want to become a part of your life and enrich your experiences with their brands—to help you *live* their brands.

At home, at school, where you work, and where you play, you see marketing in almost everything you do. Yet, there is much more to marketing than meets the consumer's casual eye. Behind it all is a massive network of people and activities competing for your attention and purchases. This book will give you a complete introduction to the basic concepts and practices of today's marketing. In this chapter, we begin by defining marketing and the marketing process.

Marketing Defined

What *is* marketing? Many people think of marketing as only selling and advertising. We are bombarded every day with TV commercials, catalogs, sales calls, and e-mail pitches. However, selling and advertising are only the tip of the marketing iceberg.

Today, marketing must be understood not in the old sense of making a sale—"telling and selling"—but in the new sense of *satisfying customer needs*. If the marketer understands consumer needs; develops products that provide superior customer value; and prices, distributes, and promotes them effectively, these products will sell easily. In fact, according to management guru Peter Drucker, "The aim of marketing is to make selling unnecessary."[3] Selling and advertising are only part of a larger *marketing mix*—a set of marketing tools that work together to satisfy customer needs and build customer relationships.

Broadly defined, marketing is a social and managerial process by which individuals and organizations obtain what they need and want through creating and exchanging value with others. In a narrower business context, marketing involves building profitable, value-laden exchange relationships with customers. Hence, we define **marketing** as the process by which companies create value for customers and build strong customer relationships in order to capture value from customers in return.[4]

Marketing
The process by which companies create value for customers and build strong customer relationships in order to capture value from customers in return.

The Marketing Process

● **Figure 1.1** presents a simple, five-step model of the marketing process. In the first four steps, companies work to understand consumers, create customer value, and build strong customer relationships. In the final step, companies reap the rewards of creating superior customer value. By creating value *for* consumers, they in turn capture value *from* consumers in the form of sales, profits, and long-term customer equity.

In this chapter and the next, we will examine the steps of this simple model of marketing. In this chapter, we review each step but focus more on the customer relationship

This important figure shows marketing in a nutshell. By creating value for customers, marketers capture value from customers in return. This five-step process forms the marketing framework for the rest of the chapter and the remainder of the text.

Create value *for customers* and build customer relationships

Capture value *from customers* in return

| Understand the marketplace and customer needs and wants | → | Design a customer-driven marketing strategy | → | Construct an integrated marketing program that delivers superior value | → | Build profitable relationships and create customer delight | → | Capture value from customers to create profits and customer equity |

● **FIGURE | 1.1**
A Simple Model of the Marketing Process

steps—understanding customers, building customer relationships, and capturing value from customers. In Chapter 2, we look more deeply into the second and third steps—designing marketing strategies and constructing marketing programs.

Objective 2 ┈┈┈▶
Explain the importance of understanding the marketplace and customers and identify the five core marketplace concepts.

Understanding the Marketplace and Customer Needs

As a first step, marketers need to understand customer needs and wants and the marketplace in which they operate. We examine five core customer and marketplace concepts: (1) *needs, wants, and demands*; (2) *market offerings (products, services, and experiences)*; (3) *value and satisfaction*; (4) *exchanges and relationships*; and (5) *markets*.

Customer Needs, Wants, and Demands

The most basic concept underlying marketing is that of human needs. Human **needs** are states of felt deprivation. They include basic *physical* needs for food, clothing, warmth, and safety; *social* needs for belonging and affection; and *individual* needs for knowledge and self-expression. Marketers did not create these needs; they are a basic part of the human makeup.

Wants are the form human needs take as they are shaped by culture and individual personality. An American *needs* food but *wants* a Big Mac, french fries, and a soft drink. A person in Papua, New Guinea, *needs* food but *wants* taro, rice, yams, and pork. Wants are shaped by one's society and are described in terms of objects that will satisfy those needs. When backed by buying power, wants become **demands**. Given their wants and resources, people demand products with benefits that add up to the most value and satisfaction.

Outstanding marketing companies go to great lengths to learn about and understand their customers' needs, wants, and demands. They conduct consumer research and analyze mountains of customer data. Their people at all levels—including top management—stay close to customers. For example, Kroger chairman and CEO David Dillon regularly dons blue jeans and roams the aisles of local Kroger supermarkets, blending in with and talking to other shoppers. He wants to see his stores through customers' eyes and understand why they make the choices they do. Similarly, to stay closer to customers, successful Ford CEO Alan Mulally has been known to spend time selling cars at Ford dealerships.[5]

Needs
States of felt deprivation.

Wants
The form human needs take as they are shaped by culture and individual personality.

Demands
Human wants that are backed by buying power.

Market offerings
Some combination of products, services, information, or experiences offered to a market to satisfy a need or want.

Market Offerings— Products, Services, and Experiences

Consumers' needs and wants are fulfilled through **market offerings**—some combination of products, services, information, or experiences offered to a market to satisfy a need or a want. Market offerings are not limited to physical *products*. They also include *services*—activities or benefits offered for sale that are essentially intangible and do not result in the ownership of anything. Examples include banking, airline, hotel, retailing, and home repair services.

More broadly, market offerings also include other entities, such as *persons*, *places, organizations, information*, and *ideas*. ● For example, the "Pure Michigan" campaign markets the state of Michigan as a tourism destination that "lets unspoiled nature and authentic character revive your spirits." And the "Let's Move" public service campaign, jointly sponsored by

Let's catch up.
Not on the phone, online or over lunch.

Let's catch up when
we've got nothing but time,
and just the clear, fresh waters
of Michigan in front of us.

Off a dock. On a boat.
Or just offshore, we can catch more than fish.

Catch up on the kids, old friends,
the ones that got away,

And the ones waiting for us
in Pure Michigan.

PURE *M*ICHIGAN®
Your trip begins at michigan.org

● **Marketing offerings are not limited to physical products. The Pure Michigan campaign markets the idea of Michigan as a tourism destination that "lets unspoiled nature and authentic character revive your spirits."**
The Michigan Economic Development Corporation

the U.S. Department of Agriculture and the U.S. Department of Health & Human Services, markets the idea of reducing childhood obesity by urging kids and their families to make healthier food choices and increase their physical activity. One ad promotes "Family Fun Friday: Dance. Play. Go for a walk in the park. Make every Friday the day you and your family get moving."[6]

Marketing myopia

The mistake of paying more attention to the specific products a company offers than to the benefits and experiences produced by these products.

Many sellers make the mistake of paying more attention to the specific products they offer than to the benefits and experiences produced by these products. These sellers suffer from **marketing myopia**. They are so taken with their products that they focus only on existing wants and lose sight of underlying customer needs.[7] They forget that a product is only a tool to solve a consumer problem. A manufacturer of quarter-inch drill bits may think that the customer needs a drill bit. But what the customer *really* needs is a quarter-inch hole. These sellers will have trouble if a new product comes along that serves the customer's need better or less expensively. The customer will have the same *need* but will *want* the new product.

Smart marketers look beyond the attributes of the products and services they sell. By orchestrating several services and products, they create *brand experiences* for consumers. For example, you don't just visit Walt Disney World Resort; you immerse yourself and your family in a world of wonder, a world where dreams come true and things still work the way they should. You're "in the heart of the magic!" says Disney.

Even a seemingly functional product becomes an experience. HP recognizes that a personal computer is much more than just a cold collection of wires and electrical components. It's an intensely personal user experience. As noted in one HP ad, "There is hardly anything that you own that is *more* personal. Your personal computer is your backup brain. It's your life. . . . It's your astonishing strategy, staggering proposal, dazzling calculation." It's your connection to the world around you. HP's ads don't talk much about technical specifications. Instead, they celebrate how HP's technologies help create seamless connections in today's "instant-on world."[8]

Customer Value and Satisfaction

Consumers usually face a broad array of products and services that might satisfy a given need. How do they choose among these many market offerings? Customers form expectations about the value and satisfaction that various market offerings will deliver and buy accordingly. Satisfied customers buy again and tell others about their good experiences. Dissatisfied customers often switch to competitors and disparage the product to others.

Marketers must be careful to set the right level of expectations. If they set expectations too low, they may satisfy those who buy but fail to attract enough buyers. If they set expectations too high, buyers will be disappointed. Customer value and customer satisfaction are key building blocks for developing and managing customer relationships. We will revisit these core concepts later in the chapter.

Exchanges and Relationships

Exchange

The act of obtaining a desired object from someone by offering something in return.

Marketing occurs when people decide to satisfy their needs and wants through exchange relationships. **Exchange** is the act of obtaining a desired object from someone by offering something in return. In the broadest sense, the marketer tries to bring about a response to some market offering. The response may be more than simply buying or trading products and services. A political candidate, for instance, wants votes; a church wants membership; an orchestra wants an audience; and a social action group wants idea acceptance.

Marketing consists of actions taken to create, maintain, and grow desirable exchange *relationships* with target audiences involving a product, service, idea, or other object. Companies want to build strong relationships by consistently delivering superior customer value. We will expand on the important concept of managing customer relationships later in the chapter.

Markets

Market

The set of all actual and potential buyers of a product or service.

The concepts of exchange and relationships lead to the concept of a market. A **market** is the set of actual and potential buyers of a product or service. These buyers share a particular need or want that can be satisfied through exchange relationships.

● **FIGURE | 1.2**
A Modern Marketing System

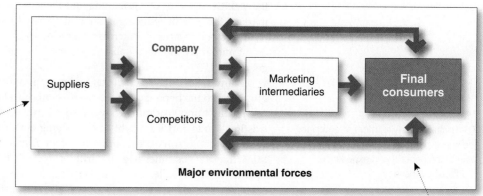

Each party in the system adds value. Walmart cannot fulfill its promise of low prices unless its suppliers provide low costs. Ford cannot deliver a high-quality car-ownership experience unless its dealers provide outstanding service.

Arrows represent relationships that must be developed and managed to create customer value and profitable customer relationships.

Marketing means managing markets to bring about profitable customer relationships. However, creating these relationships takes work. Sellers must search for buyers, identify their needs, design good market offerings, set prices for them, promote them, and store and deliver them. Activities such as consumer research, product development, communication, distribution, pricing, and service are core marketing activities.

Although we normally think of marketing as being carried out by sellers, buyers also carry out marketing. Consumers market when they search for products, interact with companies to obtain information, and make their purchases. In fact, today's digital technologies, from Web sites and online social networks to smartphones, have empowered consumers and made marketing a truly interactive affair. Thus, in addition to customer relationship management, today's marketers must also deal effectively with *customer-managed relationships*. Marketers are no longer asking only "How can we reach our customers?" but also "How should our customers reach us?" and even "How can our customers reach each other?"

● **Figure 1.2** shows the main elements in a marketing system. Marketing involves serving a market of final consumers in the face of competitors. The company and competitors research the market and interact with consumers to understand their needs. Then they create and send their market offerings and messages to consumers, either directly or through marketing intermediaries. Each party in the system is affected by major environmental forces (demographic, economic, natural, technological, political, and social/cultural).

Each party in the system adds value for the next level. The arrows represent relationships that must be developed and managed. Thus, a company's success at building profitable relationships depends not only on its own actions but also on how well the entire system serves the needs of final consumers. Walmart cannot fulfill its promise of low prices unless its suppliers provide merchandise at low costs. And Ford cannot deliver a high-quality car-ownership experience unless its dealers provide outstanding sales and service.

Objective 3 ┈┈▶
Identify the key elements of a customer-driven marketing strategy and discuss the marketing management orientations that guide marketing strategy.

Marketing management
The art and science of choosing target markets and building profitable relationships with them.

Designing a Customer-Driven Marketing Strategy

Once it fully understands consumers and the marketplace, marketing management can design a customer-driven marketing strategy. We define **marketing management** as the art and science of choosing target markets and building profitable relationships with them. The marketing manager's aim is to find, attract, keep, and grow target customers by creating, delivering, and communicating superior customer value.

To design a winning marketing strategy, the marketing manager must answer two important questions: *What customers will we serve (what's our target market)?* and *How can we serve these customers best (what's our value proposition)?* We will discuss these marketing strategy concepts briefly here and then look at them in more detail in Chapters 2 and 7.

Selecting Customers to Serve

The company must first decide *whom* it will serve. It does this by dividing the market into segments of customers (*market segmentation*) and selecting which segments it will go after (*target marketing*). Some people think of marketing management as finding as many customers as possible and increasing demand. But marketing managers know that they cannot serve all customers in every way. By trying to serve all customers, they may not serve any customers well. Instead, the company wants to select only customers that it can serve well and profitably. For example, Nordstrom profitably targets affluent professionals; Dollar General profitably targets families with more modest means.

Ultimately, marketing managers must decide which customers they want to target and on the level, timing, and nature of their demand. Simply put, marketing management is *customer management* and *demand management*.

Choosing a Value Proposition

The company must also decide how it will serve targeted customers—how it will *differentiate and position* itself in the marketplace. A brand's *value proposition* is the set of benefits or values it promises to deliver to consumers to satisfy their needs. Facebook helps you "connect and share with the people in your life," whereas YouTube "provides a place for people to connect, inform, and inspire others across the globe." BMW promises "the ultimate driving machine," whereas the diminutive Smart car suggests that you "Open your mind to the car that challenges the status quo." New Balance's Minimus shoes are "like barefoot only better"; and with Vibram FiveFingers shoes, "You are the technology."

Such value propositions differentiate one brand from another. They answer the customer's question, "Why should I buy your brand rather than a competitor's?" Companies must design strong value propositions that give them the greatest advantage in their target markets. For example, Vibram FiveFingers shoes promise the best of two worlds—running with shoes and without. "You get all the health and performance benefits of barefoot running combined with a Vibram sole that protects you from elements and obstacles in your path. With Vibram FiveFingers shoes "The more it looks like a foot, the more it acts like a foot."

● Value propositions: With Vibram FiveFingers shoes, "You are the technology."
Vibram USA, Inc.

Marketing Management Orientations

Marketing management wants to design strategies that will build profitable relationships with target consumers. But what *philosophy* should guide these marketing strategies? What weight should be given to the interests of customers, the organization, and society? Very often, these interests conflict.

There are five alternative concepts under which organizations design and carry out their marketing strategies: the *production, product, selling, marketing,* and *societal marketing concepts.*

The Production Concept

Production concept
The idea that consumers will favor products that are available and highly affordable; therefore, the organization should focus on improving production and distribution efficiency.

The **production concept** holds that consumers will favor products that are available and highly affordable. Therefore, management should focus on improving production and distribution efficiency. This concept is one of the oldest orientations that guides sellers.

The production concept is still a useful philosophy in some situations. For example, both personal computer maker Lenovo and home appliance maker Haier dominate the highly competitive, price-sensitive Chinese market through low labor costs, high production efficiency, and mass distribution. However, although useful in some situations, the production concept can lead to marketing myopia. Companies adopting this orientation run a major risk of focusing too narrowly on their own operations and losing sight of the real objective—satisfying customer needs and building customer relationships.

The Product Concept

Product concept

The idea that consumers will favor products that offer the most quality, performance, and features; therefore, the organization should devote its energy to making continuous product improvements.

The **product concept** holds that consumers will favor products that offer the most in quality, performance, and innovative features. Under this concept, marketing strategy focuses on making continuous product improvements.

Product quality and improvement are important parts of most marketing strategies. However, focusing *only* on the company's products can also lead to marketing myopia. For example, some manufacturers believe that if they can "build a better mousetrap, the world will beat a path to their doors." But they are often rudely shocked. Buyers may be looking for a better solution to a mouse problem but not necessarily for a better mousetrap. The better solution might be a chemical spray, an exterminating service, a house cat, or something else that suits their needs even better than a mousetrap. Furthermore, a better mousetrap will not sell unless the manufacturer designs, packages, and prices it attractively; places it in convenient distribution channels; brings it to the attention of people who need it; and convinces buyers that it is a better product.

The Selling Concept

Selling concept

The idea that consumers will not buy enough of the firm's products unless the firm undertakes a large-scale selling and promotion effort.

Many companies follow the **selling concept**, which holds that consumers will not buy enough of the firm's products unless it undertakes a large-scale selling and promotion effort. The selling concept is typically practiced with unsought goods—those that buyers do not normally think of buying, such as insurance or blood donations. These industries must be good at tracking down prospects and selling them on a product's benefits.

Such aggressive selling, however, carries high risks. It focuses on creating sales transactions rather than on building long-term, profitable customer relationships. The aim often is to sell what the company makes rather than making what the market wants. It assumes that customers who are coaxed into buying the product will like it. Or, if they don't like it, they will possibly forget their disappointment and buy it again later. These are usually poor assumptions.

The Marketing Concept

Marketing concept

A philosophy in which achieving organizational goals depends on knowing the needs and wants of target markets and delivering the desired satisfactions better than competitors do.

The **marketing concept** holds that achieving organizational goals depends on knowing the needs and wants of target markets and delivering the desired satisfactions better than competitors do. Under the marketing concept, customer focus and value are the *paths* to sales and profits. Instead of a product-centered *make and sell* philosophy, the marketing concept is a customer-centered *sense and respond* philosophy. The job is not to find the right customers for your product but to find the right products for your customers.

● **Figure 1.3** contrasts the selling concept and the marketing concept. The selling concept takes an *inside-out* perspective. It starts with the factory, focuses on the company's existing products, and calls for heavy selling and promotion to obtain profitable sales. It focuses primarily on customer conquest—getting short-term sales with little concern about who buys or why.

In contrast, the marketing concept takes an *outside-in* perspective. As Herb Kelleher, the colorful founder of Southwest Airlines, once put it, "We don't have a marketing department; we have a customer department." The marketing concept starts with a well-defined

● **FIGURE | 1.3**
The Selling and Marketing Concepts Contrasted

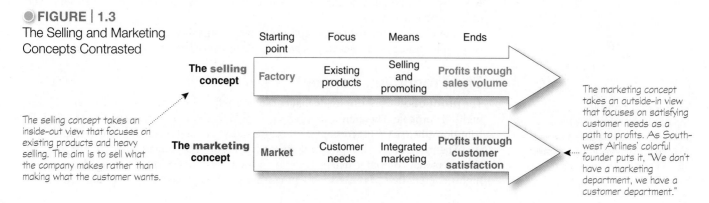

The selling concept takes an inside-out view that focuses on existing products and heavy selling. The aim is to sell what the company makes rather than making what the customer wants.

	Starting point	Focus	Means	Ends
The selling concept	Factory	Existing products	Selling and promoting	Profits through sales volume
The marketing concept	Market	Customer needs	Integrated marketing	Profits through customer satisfaction

The marketing concept takes an outside-in view that focuses on satisfying customer needs as a path to profits. As Southwest Airlines' colorful founder puts it, "We don't have a marketing department, we have a customer department."

market, focuses on customer needs, and integrates all the marketing activities that affect customers. In turn, it yields profits by creating relationships with the right customers based on customer value and satisfaction.

Implementing the marketing concept often means more than simply responding to customers' stated desires and obvious needs. *Customer-driven* companies research customers deeply to learn about their desires, gather new product ideas, and test product improvements. Such customer-driven marketing usually works well when a clear need exists and when customers know what they want.

In many cases, however, customers *don't* know what they want or even what is possible. As Henry Ford once remarked, "If I'd asked people what they wanted, they would have said faster horses."[9] For example, even 20 years ago, how many consumers would have thought to ask for now-commonplace products such as tablet computers, smartphones, digital cameras, 24-hour online buying, and GPS systems in their cars? Such situations call for *customer-driving* marketing—understanding customer needs even better than customers themselves do and creating products and services that meet both existing and latent needs, now and in the future. As an executive at 3M put it, "Our goal is to lead customers where they want to go before *they* know where they want to go."

The Societal Marketing Concept

Societal marketing concept
The idea that a company's marketing decisions should consider consumers' wants, the company's requirements, consumers' long-run interests, and society's long-run interests.

The **societal marketing concept** questions whether the pure marketing concept overlooks possible conflicts between consumer *short-run wants* and consumer *long-run welfare*. Is a firm that satisfies the immediate needs and wants of target markets always doing what's best for its consumers in the long run? The societal marketing concept holds that marketing strategy should deliver value to customers in a way that maintains or improves both the consumer's *and society's* well-being. It calls for *sustainable marketing,* socially and environmentally responsible marketing that meets the present needs of consumers and businesses while also preserving or enhancing the ability of future generations to meet their needs.

Even more broadly, many leading business and marketing thinkers are now preaching the concept of *shared value,* which recognizes that societal needs, not just economic needs, define markets.[10]

The concept of shared value focuses on creating economic value in a way that also creates value for society. A growing number of companies known for their hard-nosed approach to business—such as GE, Google, IBM, Intel, Johnson & Johnson, Nestlé, Unilever, and Walmart—have already embarked on important efforts to create shared economic and societal value by rethinking the intersection between society and corporate performance. They are concerned not just with short-term economic gains, but with the well-being of their customers, the depletion of natural resources vital to their businesses, the viability of key suppliers, and the economic well-being of the communities in which they produce and sell. One prominent marketer calls this *Marketing 3.0.* "Marketing 3.0 organizations are values-driven," he says. "I'm not talking about being value-driven. I'm talking about 'values' plural, where values amount to caring about the state of the world."

As **Figure 1.4** shows, companies should balance three considerations in setting their marketing strategies: company profits, consumer wants, *and* society's interests. UPS does this well.[11]

UPS seeks more than just short-run sales and profits. Its three-pronged corporate sustainability mission stresses *economic prosperity* (profitable growth through a customer focus), *social responsibility* (community engagement and individual well-being), and *environmental stewardship* (operating efficiently and protecting the environment). Whether it involves greening up its operations or urging employees to volunteer time in their communities, UPS proactively seeks opportunities to act responsibly. For example, UPS employees have volunteered millions of hours to United Way's Live United campaign to improve the education, income, and health of the nation's communities. UPS knows that doing what's right benefits both consumers and the company. By operating efficiently and acting responsibly, it can "meet the needs of the enterprise . . . while protecting and enhancing the human and natural resources that will be needed in the future." Social responsibility "isn't just good for the planet," says the company. "It's good for business."

The societal marketing concept: According to UPS, social responsibility "isn't just good for the planet. It's good for business."
Cheryl Gerber/AP Photo

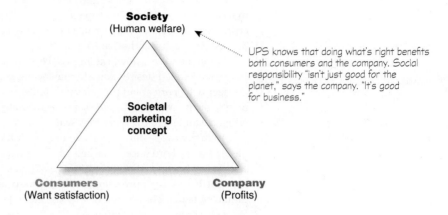

FIGURE | 1.4
The Considerations Underlying
the Societal Marketing Concept

Preparing an Integrated Marketing Plan and Program

The company's marketing strategy outlines which customers it will serve and how it will create value for these customers. Next, the marketer develops an integrated marketing program that will actually deliver the intended value to target customers. The marketing program builds customer relationships by transforming the marketing strategy into action. It consists of the firm's *marketing mix*, the set of marketing tools the firm uses to implement its marketing strategy.

　　The major marketing mix tools are classified into four broad groups, called the *four Ps* of marketing: product, price, place, and promotion. To deliver on its value proposition, the firm must first create a need-satisfying market offering (product). It must then decide how much it will charge for the offering (price) and how it will make the offering available to target consumers (place). Finally, it must communicate with target customers about the offering and persuade them of its merits (promotion). The firm must blend each marketing mix tool into a comprehensive *integrated marketing program* that communicates and delivers the intended value to chosen customers. We will explore marketing programs and the marketing mix in much more detail in later chapters.

Objective 4 ▸
Discuss customer relationship management and identify strategies for creating value *for* customers and capturing value *from* customers in return.

Building Customer Relationships

The first three steps in the marketing process—understanding the marketplace and customer needs, designing a customer-driven marketing strategy, and constructing a marketing program—all lead up to the fourth and most important step: building and managing profitable customer relationships.

Customer Relationship Management

Customer relationship management is perhaps the most important concept of modern marketing. Some marketers define it narrowly as a customer data management activity (a practice called *CRM*). By this definition, it involves managing detailed information about individual customers and carefully managing customer *touchpoints* to maximize customer loyalty. We will discuss this narrower CRM activity in Chapter 4, when dealing with marketing information.

　　Most marketers, however, give the concept of customer relationship management a broader meaning. In this broader sense, **customer relationship management** is the overall process of building and maintaining profitable customer relationships by delivering superior customer value and satisfaction. It deals with all aspects of acquiring, keeping, and growing customers.

Relationship Building Blocks: Customer Value and Satisfaction

The key to building lasting customer relationships is to create superior customer value and satisfaction. Satisfied customers are more likely to be loyal customers and give the company a larger share of their business.

Customer relationship management
The overall process of building and maintaining profitable customer relationships by delivering superior customer value and satisfaction.

Customer-perceived value
The customer's evaluation of the difference between all the benefits and all the costs of a marketing offer relative to those of competing offers.

Customer Value. Attracting and retaining customers can be a difficult task. Customers often face a bewildering array of products and services from which to choose. A customer buys from the firm that offers the highest **customer-perceived value**—the customer's evaluation of the difference between all the benefits and all the costs of a market offering relative to those of competing offers. Importantly, customers often do not judge values and costs "accurately" or "objectively." They act on *perceived* value.

To some consumers, value might mean sensible products at affordable prices. To other consumers, however, value might mean paying more to get more. For example, a top-of-the-line Weber Summit E-670 barbecue grill carries a suggested retail price of $2,600, more than five times the price of competitor Char-Broil's best grill. According to Weber, the stainless steel Summit grill "embraces true grilling luxury with the highest quality materials, exclusive features, and stunning looks." However, Weber's marketing also suggests that the grill is a real value, even at the premium price. For the money, you get practical features such as all-stainless-steel construction, spacious cooking and work areas, lighted control knobs, a tuck-away motorized rotisserie system, and an LED tank scale that lets you know how much propane you have left in the tank. Is the Weber Summit grill worth the premium price compared to less expensive grills? To many consumers, the answer is no. But to the target segment of affluent, hard-core grillers, the answer is yes.[12]

Customer satisfaction
The extent to which a product's perceived performance matches a buyer's expectations.

Customer Satisfaction. **Customer satisfaction** depends on the product's perceived performance relative to a buyer's expectations. If the product's performance falls short of expectations, the customer is dissatisfied. If performance matches expectations, the customer is satisfied. If performance exceeds expectations, the customer is highly satisfied or delighted.

Outstanding marketing companies go out of their way to keep important customers satisfied. Most studies show that higher levels of customer satisfaction lead to greater customer loyalty, which in turn results in better company performance. Smart companies aim to delight customers by promising only what they can deliver and then delivering more than they promise. Delighted customers not only make repeat purchases but also become willing marketing partners and "customer evangelists" who spread the word about their good experiences to others.

For companies interested in delighting customers, exceptional value and service become part of the overall company culture. ● For example, year after year, JetBlue ranks at or near the top of the airline industry in terms of customer satisfaction. The company's slogan—"JetBlue: YOU ABOVE ALL"—tells customers that they are at the heart of the company's strategy and culture:[13]

JetBlue has an evangelistic zeal for creating first-rate, customer-satisfying experiences. At JetBlue, customer care starts with basic amenities that exceed customer expectations, especially for a low-cost carrier—leather coach seats with extra leg room, free premium snacks, free satellite TV. But it's the *human* touch that really makes JetBlue special. JetBlue employees not only *know* the company's core values—safety, integrity, caring, passion, and fun—they *live* them. Those heart-felt values result in outstanding customer experiences, making JetBlue customers the most satisfied and enthusiastic of any in the airline industry.

In fact, JetBlue often lets its customers do the talking. For example, its "Experience JetBlue" Web site features real first-person testimonials from devoted fans. And in a former advertising campaign, called "Sincerely, JetBlue," actual customers gave voice to specific service heroics by dedicated JetBlue employees. For example, customer Brian related how a JetBlue flight attendant dashed from the plane just before takeoff to retrieve a brand-new iPod he'd left in a rental car. And the Steins from Darien, Connecticut, told how they arrived late at night for a family vacation in Florida with their three very tired small children only to learn that their

● Creating customer satisfaction: JetBlue creates first-rate, customer-satisfying experiences. Its slogan—JetBlue: YOU ABOVE ALL—tells customers that they are at the very heart of JetBlue's strategy and culture.

JetBlue Airways

hotel wouldn't take them in. "Out of nowhere we heard a voice from behind us, go ahead, take my room," the Steins recalled. "A superhero in a JetBlue pilot's uniform, who sacrificed his room graciously, saved our night. And we slept like babies. Thank you, JetBlue." So, JetBlue really means it when it tells customers, YOU ABOVE ALL. It "gets us back to our DNA, our original mission, bringing humanity back to air travel," says JetBlue's senior VP of marketing.

Other companies that have become legendary for their service heroics include Zappos.com, Ritz-Carlton Hotels, Amazon.com, and Nordstrom department stores (see Real Marketing 1.1). However, a company doesn't need to have over-the-top service to create customer delight. Customer satisfaction "has a lot more to do with how well companies deliver on their basic, even plain-vanilla promises than on how dazzling the service experience might be," says one expert. "To win [customers'] loyalty, forget the bells and whistles and just solve their problems."[14]

Although a customer-centered firm seeks to deliver high customer satisfaction relative to competitors, it does not attempt to *maximize* customer satisfaction. A company can always increase customer satisfaction by lowering its prices or increasing its services. But this may result in lower profits. Thus, the purpose of marketing is to generate customer value profitably. This requires a very delicate balance: The marketer must continue to generate more customer value and satisfaction but not "give away the house."

Customer Relationship Levels and Tools

Companies can build customer relationships at many levels, depending on the nature of the target market. At one extreme, a company with many low-margin customers may seek to develop *basic relationships* with them. For example, Nike does not phone or call on all of its consumers to get to know them personally. Instead, Nike creates relationships through brand-building advertising, public relations, and its numerous Web sites and apps. At the other extreme, in markets with few customers and high margins, sellers want to create *full partnerships* with key customers. For example, Nike sales representatives work closely with the Sports Authority, Dick's Sporting Goods, Foot Locker, and other large retailers. In between these two extremes, other levels of customer relationships are appropriate.

Beyond offering consistently high value and satisfaction, marketers can use specific marketing tools to develop stronger bonds with customers. For example, many companies offer *frequency marketing programs* that reward customers who buy frequently or in large amounts. Airlines offer frequent-flyer programs, hotels give room upgrades to frequent guests, and supermarkets give patronage discounts to "very important customers." These days almost every brand has a loyalty rewards program. ● For example, fast-casual restaurant Panera has a MyPanera loyalty program that surprises frequent customers with things like complimentary bakery-café items, exclusive tastings and demonstrations, and invitations to special events. Almost half of all Panera purchases are logged onto MyPanera cards. The program not only lets Panera track individual customer purchases, it also lets the company build unique relationships with each MyPanera member.[15]

Other companies sponsor *club marketing programs* that offer members special benefits and create member communities. For example, Apple encourages customers to form local Apple user groups. More than 800 registered Apple user groups worldwide offer monthly meetings, a newsletter, advice on technical issues, training classes, product discounts, and a forum for swapping ideas and stories with like-minded Apple fans. Similarly, buy one of those Weber grills and you can join the Weber Nation—"the site for real people who love their Weber grills." Membership gets you exclusive access to online grilling classes, an interactive recipe box, grilling tips and 24/7 telephone support, audio and video podcasts, straight-talk forums for interacting with other grilling fanatics, and even a chance to star in a Weber TV commercial. "Become a spatula-carrying member today," says Weber.[16]

● Relationship marketing tools: The MyPanera loyalty rewards program not only lets Panera track individual customer purchases, it also lets the company build unique relationships with each MyPanera member.

Photo courtesy of Gary Armstrong

Real Marketing 1.1

Nordstrom: Taking Care of Customers No Matter What It Takes

Nordstrom is legendary for outstanding customer service. The upscale department store chain thrives on stories about its service heroics, such as employees dropping off orders at customers' homes or warming up their cars on a cold day while customers spend a little more time shopping. Then there's the one about the Nordstrom employee who split pairs of shoes in order to fit a man with different sized feet, or the sales clerk who ironed a new shirt for a customer who needed it for a meeting that afternoon. In another case, a man reportedly walked into Nordstrom to return a set of tires that he insisted he'd bought there. Nordstrom doesn't sell tires. But without hesitation, even though his receipt clearly indicated a different store, the Nordstrom clerk refunded the man's money out of her own pocket. Later, on her lunch hour, she took the tires and receipt to the store where they'd been purchased and got her money back.

Whether factual or fictional, such stories are rooted in actual customer experiences at Nordstrom. It seems that almost everyone who shops regularly at Nordstrom has their own favorite story to tell. As one journalist noted after seeing the chain near the top of yet another Customer Service Hall of Fame list, "It almost gets old: Nordstrom and its legendarily good customer service." But such stories never get old at Nordstrom.

Superb customer service is deeply rooted in the 100-year-old Nordstrom's DNA, as summarized in its staunchly held mantra: Take care of customers no matter what it takes. Although many companies pay homage to similar pronouncements hidden away in their mission statements, Nordstrom really means it—and really makes it happen. Consider these customer-delight-inducing stories:

- One man tells a story about his wife, a loyal Nordstrom customer, who died with her Nordstrom account $1,000 in arrears. Not only did Nordstrom settle the account, it also sent flowers to the funeral.
- A woman had been shopping with her daughter at San Diego's ritzy Horton Plaza. After browsing in Nordstrom for a while and believing nobody was around, she said with an exhausted sigh, as if thinking out loud to herself, "I could sure use a Dr. Pepper." Sure

enough, within only a few short minutes, a Nordstrom employee appeared out of nowhere with an ice-cold can of Dr. Pepper.
- One late November, a woman buying a sweater as a Christmas present for her husband found just the one she wanted at Nordstrom, but not in the right color or size. No worries, said the Nordstrom manager. He'd find her one in plenty of time for the holidays. A week before Christmas, just as the woman was beginning to worry, the manager called ahead and delivered the sweater to her home, already beautifully gift wrapped. That's amazing enough, but here's the back story: The manager hadn't been able to find the right sweater after all. But while discussing the problem with his wife, he learned that she'd already bought that very sweater for *him* for Christmas, and that it was already wrapped and under their tree. The manager and his wife quickly agreed to pass his sweater along to the customer.

How does Nordstrom consistently exceed customer expectations? For starters, it hires people who truly enjoy serving other people. Then, it trains them thoroughly on the intricacies of providing customer care and turns them loose. Nordstrom trusts its employees to make the right judgments without bogging them down with procedures and policies. The famous Nordstrom employee "handbook" consists of a single card containing only 75 words, among them: "Rule #1: Use best judgment in all situations. There will be no additional rules." As a result, at Nordstrom, customer service doesn't come across as sales clerks reciting rehearsed scripts. Rather, it's about Nordstrom people genuinely connecting with and serving customers.

To motivate its employees even more, Nordstrom collects and recycles stories of customer service heroics. Every Nordstrom register supplies pens and paper with which customers can share their good experiences. Every morning, in the main lobby of each store, managers share some of the best customer stories from the previous day and reward the employees involved for their good deeds. In turn, the feel-good stories inspire everyone in the store to continue the cycle of pampering customers and making them feel special.

Founded in 1901 by Swedish immigrant John W. Nordstrom, the company is now run by the fourth generation of Nordstroms—brothers Blake, Pete, and Erik and second cousin Jamie Nordstrom—in a way that would make their great-great-grandfather proud. This team of young executives is giving Nordstrom's

Delighting customers: Customer service is deeply rooted in Nordstrom's DNA, as summarized in its staunchly-held mission: Take care of customers no matter what it takes.

Associated Press

ageless philosophy a dose of modern technology. For example, they recently restructured the chain's entire purchasing and inventory management system, making it easier for front-line employees to quickly find and obtain items that customers want. When the system went live, sales immediately surged. But more important, customer service improved dramatically. As Jamie Nordstrom puts it, "You are saying 'yes' to a customer more often."

Creating customer delight has been good for Nordstrom's bottom line over the years. Last year alone, even in the midst of a still-sluggish post-recession retailing economy, Nordstrom's sales grew 12 percent to a record $10.9 billion. And while rival department stores have grown little or not at all, Nordstrom continued to gain market share with 19 straight months of growth.

As Erik Nordstrom shared these and other good tidings with shareholders at the most recent Nordstrom annual meeting, he also shared yet another story of customer delight. He told of a woman in North Carolina who recently lost the diamond from her wedding ring while trying on clothes at a Nordstrom store. A store security worker saw her crawling on the sales floor under the racks and joined the search. When they came up empty, the security employee enlisted the help of two

building-services workers, who vacuumed the area and then opened the vacuum cleaner bags and painstakingly searched the contents, where they recovered the sparkling gem.

After showing a video clip featuring the delighted shopper, to thunderous applause, Erik Nordstrom introduced the three employees to the shareholders. Extending his hand to the three, Nordstrom proclaimed that when it comes to taking care of customers no matter what it takes, "this raises the bar."

Sources: Amy Martinez, "Tale of Lost Diamond Adds Glitter to Nordstrom's Customer Service," *Seattle Times*, May 11, 2011; Cotten Timberlake, "How Nordstrom Bests Its Retail Rivals," *Bloomberg Businessweek*, August 11, 2011, www.businessweek.com/magazine/how-nordstrom-bests-its-retail-rivals-08112011.html; "Legends of Unbelievable Nordstrom Service," Toddand.com, February 18, 2007, http://toddand.com/2007/02/18/legends-of-unbelievable-nordstrom-service/; Karen Aho, "The 2011 Customer Service Hall of Fame," *MSNMoney*, http://money.msn.com/investing/the-2011-customer-service-hall-of-fame.aspx?cp-documentid=6820771; and http://shop.nordstrom.com/c/company-history, accessed November 2012.

The Changing Nature of Customer Relationships

Significant changes are occurring in the ways companies relate to their customers. Yesterday's companies focused on mass marketing to all customers at arm's length. Today's companies are building deeper, more direct, and lasting relationships with more carefully selected customers. Here are some important trends in the way companies and customers are relating to one another.

Relating with More Carefully Selected Customers

Few firms today still practice true mass marketing—selling in a standardized way to any customer who comes along. Today, most marketers realize that they don't want relationships with every customer. Instead, they target fewer, more profitable customers. "Not all customers are worth your marketing efforts," states one analyst. "Some are more costly to serve than to lose."[17]

Many companies now use customer profitability analysis to pass up or weed out losing customers and target winning ones for pampering. One approach is to preemptively screen out potentially unprofitable customers. Progressive Insurance does this effectively. It asks prospective customers a series of screening questions to determine if they are right for the firm. If they're not, Progressive will likely tell them, "You might want to go to Allstate." A marketing consultant explains: "They'd rather send business to a competitor than take on unprofitable customers." Screening out unprofitable customers lets Progressive provide even better service to potentially more profitable ones.[18]

But what should the company do with unprofitable customers that it already has? If it can't turn them into profitable ones, the company may want to dismiss those customers who are too unreasonable or that cost more to serve than they are worth. "Save your company by firing your customers," advises one marketer. "Well, not all your customers—just the ones who ask for more than they give." Adds another marketer, "Firing the customers you can't possibly please gives you the bandwidth and resources to coddle the ones that truly deserve your attention and repay you with referrals, applause, and loyalty."[19] Consider this example:

Sprint sent out letters to about 1,000 people to inform them that they had been summarily dismissed—but the recipients were Sprint *customers*, not employees. For about a year, the

Memo To: **Unprofitable Customers**

You Are Fired!

● **Marketers don't want relationships with every possible customer. In fact, a company might want to "fire" customers that cost more to serve than to lose.**

wireless-service provider had been tracking the number and frequency of support calls made by a group of high-maintenance users. According to a Sprint spokesperson, "in some cases, they were calling customer care hundreds of times a month . . . on the same issues, even after we felt those issues had been resolved." Ultimately, the company determined it could not meet the needs of this subset of subscribers and, therefore, waived their termination fees and cut off their service. Such "customer divestment" practices were once considered an anomaly. But new segmentation approaches and technologies have made it easier to focus on retaining the right customers and, by extension, showing problem customers the door.

Relating More Deeply and Interactively

Beyond choosing customers more selectively, companies are now relating with chosen customers in deeper, more meaningful ways. Rather than relying on one-way, mass-media messages only, today's marketers are incorporating new, interactive approaches that help build targeted, two-way customer relationships.

Interactive Customer Relationships. New technologies have profoundly changed the ways in which people relate to one another. New tools for relating include everything from e-mail, Web sites, blogs, mobile phones, and video sharing to online communities and social networks, such as Facebook, YouTube, Pinterest, and Twitter.

This changing communications environment also affects how companies and brands relate to customers. The new communications approaches let marketers create deeper customer involvement and a sense of community surrounding a brand—to make the brand a meaningful part of consumers' conversations and lives. "Becoming part of the conversation between consumers is infinitely more powerful than handing down information via traditional advertising," says one marketing expert. It's no longer about "just pushing messages out," says another. "It's allowing the individual, the person, to really feel like they're part of your brand in a unique way."[20]

At the same time that the new technologies create relationship-building opportunities for marketers, however, they also create challenges. They give consumers greater power and control. Today's consumers have more information about brands than ever before, and they have a wealth of platforms for airing and sharing their brand views with other consumers. Thus, the marketing world is now embracing not only customer relationship management, but also **customer-managed relationships**.

Greater consumer control means that companies can no longer rely on marketing by *intrusion*. Instead, marketers must practice marketing by *attraction*—creating market offerings and messages that involve consumers rather than interrupt them. Hence, most marketers now augment their mass-media marketing efforts with a rich mix of direct marketing approaches that promote brand-consumer interaction.

For example, many brands are creating dialogues with consumers via their own or existing *online social networks*. To supplement their traditional marketing campaigns, companies now routinely post their latest ads and made-for-the-Web videos on video-sharing sites. They join social networks. Or they launch their own blogs, online communities, or consumer-generated review systems, all with the aim of engaging customers on a more personal, interactive level.

Take Twitter, for example. Organizations ranging from Dell, JetBlue Airways, and Dunkin' Donuts to the Chicago Bulls, NASCAR, and the Los Angeles Fire Department have created Twitter pages and promotions. They use "tweets" to start conversations with Twitter's more than 300 million registered users, address customer service issues, research customer reactions, and drive traffic to relevant articles, Web and mobile sites, contests, videos, and other brand activities. Similarly, almost every company has something going on Facebook these days. Starbucks has more than 29 million Facebook "fans"; Coca-Cola has more than 40 million. Social media such as Facebook, YouTube, Twitter, and e-mail can get consumers involved with and talking about a brand.

For example, ice cream retailer Cold Stone Creamery uses all of these media to engage customers:[21]

On YouTube, Cold Stone posts footage from events like its annual "World's Largest Ice Cream Social," which benefits Make-A-Wish Foundation. ● Cold Stone's Facebook page, with more than 1.8 million friends, constitutes a modern-day, online version of an ice cream social. Fans can

Customer-managed relationships
Marketing relationships in which customers, empowered by today's new digital technologies, interact with companies and with each other to shape their relationships with brands.

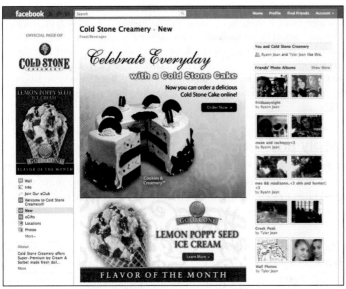

● **Online social networks: Cold Stone Creamery uses a variety of social media to engage customers on a more personal, interactive level. Its Facebook page constitutes a modern-day, online version of an ice cream social.**

Kahala Corp. Facebook is a trademark of Facebook, Inc.

post pictures of their favorite Cold Stone experiences, exchange views with the company and fellow ice cream lovers, and learn about new flavors and happenings. Social media help build both customer relationships and sales. In response to a recent 2-for-$5 coupon campaign using e-mail and Facebook, fans printed more than 500,000 coupons in just three weeks, redeeming an amazing 14 percent of them. A new-summer-flavors contest drew 4,000 entrants and 66,000 new fans in just eight weeks. According to Cold Stone, every social media campaign so far has brought a spike in store traffic and sales. More than half of the company's advertising budget is now dedicated to nontraditional activities like social media.

Most marketers are still learning how to use social media effectively. Using such media approaches calls for caution. Because consumers have so much control, even the seemingly most harmless social media campaign can backfire. For example, McDonald's recently launched a Twitter campaign using the hashtag #McDStories, hoping that it would inspire heart-warming stories about Happy Meals. Instead, the effort was hijacked by Twitter users, who turned the hashtag into a "bashtag" by posting less-than-appetizing messages about their bad experiences with the fast-food chain. McDonald's pulled the campaign within only two hours, but the hashtag was still churning weeks later. "You're going into the consumer's backyard. This is their place," warns one social marketer. "Social media is a pressure cooker," says another. "The hundreds of thousands, or millions, of people out there are going to take your idea, and they're going to try to shred it or tear apart and find what's weak or stupid in it."[22]

The key is to find unobtrusive ways to enter consumers' social conversations with engaging and relevant brand messages. Simply posting a humorous video, creating a social network page, or hosting a blog isn't enough. Successful social network marketing means making relevant and genuine contributions to consumer conversations. "Nobody wants to be friends with a brand," says an online marketing executive. "Your job [as a brand] is to be part of other friends' conversations."[23]

Consumer-Generated Marketing. A growing part of the new customer dialogue is **consumer-generated marketing**, by which consumers themselves are playing a bigger role in shaping their own brand experiences and those of others. This might happen through uninvited consumer-to-consumer exchanges in blogs, video-sharing sites, and other digital forums. But increasingly, companies are *inviting* consumers to play a more active role in shaping products and brand messages.

Some companies ask consumers for new product and service ideas. For example, at its My Starbucks Idea site, Starbucks collects ideas from customers on new products, store changes, and just about anything else that might make their Starbucks experience better. "You know better than anyone else what you want from Starbucks," says the company at the Web site. "So tell us. What's your Starbucks idea? Revolutionary or simple—we want to hear it." The site invites customer to share their ideas, vote on and discuss the ideas of others, and see which ideas Starbucks has implemented.[24]

Consumer-generated marketing
Brand exchanges created by consumers themselves—both invited and uninvited— by which consumers are playing an increasing role in shaping their own brand experiences and those of other consumers.

Other companies are inviting customers to play an active role in shaping ads. For example, PepsiCo, Southwest Airlines, MasterCard, Unilever, H. J. Heinz, Harley-Davidson, and many other companies have run contests for consumer-generated commercials that have been aired on national television. For the past several years, PepsiCo's Doritos brand has held a "Crash the Super Bowl" contest in which it invites 30-second ads from consumers and runs the best ones during the game. The consumer-generated ads have been a huge success. Last year, from more than 6,100 entries, Doritos aired two fan-produced ads during the Super Bowl. Amazingly, both ads grabbed first place in one or the other of *USA Today*'s two separate AdMeter rankings, earning each of their creators a cool $1 million cash prize from PepsiCo. A spot called "Man's Best Friend," featuring a dog that bribes a man to keep quiet about the dead cat it's burying in the yard, took first place in the traditional AdMeter ratings by people watching the big game. That ad cost all of $20 to make. The second ad, called "Sling Baby" and showing a woman slingshotting a baby across the

● **Harnessing consumer-generated marketing: When H.J. Heinz invited consumers to submit homemade ads for its ketchup brand on YouTube, it received more than 8,000 entries—some very good but most only so-so or even downright dreadful.**

AJ Mast/The New York Times/Redux Pictures

yard to nab a bag of Doritos from a taunting kid, grabbed first place in two-day online voting in the *USA Today*/Facebook social media AdMeter.[25]

However, harnessing consumer-generated content can be a time-consuming and costly process, and companies may find it difficult to glean even a little gold from all the garbage. ● For example, when Heinz invited consumers to submit homemade ads for its ketchup on its YouTube page, it ended up sifting through more than 8,000 entries, of which it posted nearly 4,000. Some of the amateur ads were very good—entertaining and potentially effective. Most, however, were so-so at best, and others were downright dreadful. In one ad, a contestant chugged ketchup straight from the bottle. In another, the would-be filmmaker brushed his teeth, washed his hair, and shaved his face with Heinz's product.[26]

Consumer-generated marketing, whether invited by marketers or not, has become a significant marketing force. Through a profusion of consumer-generated videos, reviews, blogs, and Web sites, consumers are playing an increasing role in shaping their own brand experiences. Beyond creating brand conversations, customers are having an increasing say about everything from product design, usage, and packaging to pricing and distribution. Brands need to accept and embrace the emergence of consumer power. Says one analyst, "Humans, formerly known as either consumers or couch potatoes, are now creators and thought leaders, passive no more."[27]

Partner Relationship Management

Partner relationship management
Working closely with partners in other company departments and outside the company to jointly bring greater value to customers.

When it comes to creating customer value and building strong customer relationships, today's marketers know that they can't go it alone. They must work closely with a variety of marketing partners. In addition to being good at *customer relationship management,* marketers must also be good at **partner relationship management**—working closely with others inside and outside the company to jointly bring more value to customers.

Traditionally, marketers have been charged with understanding customers and representing customer needs to different company departments. However, in today's more connected world, every functional area in the organization can interact with customers. The new thinking is that—no matter what your job is in a company—you must understand marketing and be customer focused. Rather than letting each department go its own way, firms must link all departments in the cause of creating customer value.

Marketers must also partner with suppliers, channel partners, and others outside the company. Marketing channels consist of distributors, retailers, and others who connect the company to its buyers. The *supply chain* describes a longer channel, stretching from raw materials to components to final products that are carried to final buyers. Through *supply chain management*, companies today are strengthening their connections with partners all along the supply chain. They know that their fortunes rest on more than just how well they perform. Success at delivering customer value rests on how well their entire supply chain performs against competitors' supply chains.

Capturing Value from Customers

The first four steps in the marketing process outlined in Figure 1.1 involve building customer relationships by creating and delivering superior customer value. The final step involves capturing value in return in the form of sales, market share, and profits. By creating superior customer value, the firm creates highly satisfied customers who stay loyal and buy more. This, in turn, means greater long-run returns for the firm. Here, we discuss the outcomes of creating customer value: customer loyalty and retention, share of market and share of customer, and customer equity.

Creating Customer Loyalty and Retention

Good customer relationship management creates customer satisfaction. In turn, satisfied customers remain loyal and talk favorably to others about the company and its products. Studies show big differences in the loyalty of customers who are less satisfied, somewhat satisfied, and completely satisfied. Even a slight drop from complete satisfaction can create an enormous drop in loyalty. Thus, the aim of customer relationship management is to create not only customer satisfaction but also customer delight.

The recent Great Recession and the economic uncertainty that followed it put strong pressures on customer loyalty. It created a new sensibility in consumer spending that will last well into the future. Recent studies show that, even in an improved economy, 55 percent of U.S. consumers say they would rather get the best price than the best brand. Some 50 percent of consumers now purchase store brands "all the time" as part of their regular shopping behavior, up from just 12 percent in the early 1990s. Nearly two-thirds say they will now shop at a different store with lower prices even if it's less convenient. Research also shows that it's five times cheaper to keep an old customer than acquire a new one. Thus, companies today must shape their value propositions even more carefully and treat their profitable customers well to keep them loyal.[28]

Losing a customer means losing more than a single sale. It means losing the entire stream of purchases that the customer would make over a lifetime of patronage. For example, here is a classic illustration of **customer lifetime value**:[29]

Customer lifetime value
The value of the entire stream of purchases a customer makes over a lifetime of patronage.

> Stew Leonard, who operates a highly profitable four-store supermarket in Connecticut and New York, once said that he sees $50,000 flying out of his store every time he sees a sulking customer. Why? Because his average customer spends about $100 a week, shops 50 weeks a year, and remains in the area for about 10 years. If this customer has an unhappy experience and switches to another supermarket, Stew Leonard's has lost $50,000 in lifetime revenue. The loss can be much greater if the disappointed customer shares the bad experience with other customers and causes them to defect.

● Customer lifetime value: To keep customers coming back, Stew Leonard's has created the "Disneyland of dairy stores." Rule #1—The customer is always right. Rule #2—If the customer is ever wrong, reread Rule #1.
Courtesy of Stew Leonard's

To keep customers coming back, Stew Leonard's has created what the *New York Times* has dubbed the "Disneyland of Dairy Stores," complete with costumed characters, scheduled entertainment, a petting zoo, and animatronics throughout the store. From its humble beginnings as a small dairy store in 1969, Stew Leonard's has grown at an amazing pace. It's built 29 additions onto the original store, which now serves more than 300,000 customers each week. This legion of loyal shoppers is largely a result of the store's passionate approach to customer service. ● "Rule #1: The customer is always right. Rule #2: If the customer is ever wrong, reread rule #1."

Stew Leonard is not alone in assessing customer lifetime value. Lexus, for example, estimates that a single satisfied and loyal customer is worth more than $600,000 in lifetime sales. And the estimated lifetime value of a young mobile phone consumer is $26,000.[30] In fact, a company can lose money on a specific transaction but still benefit greatly from a long-term relationship. This means that companies must aim high in building customer relationships. Customer delight creates an emotional relationship with a brand, not just a rational preference. And that relationship keeps customers coming back.

Growing Share of Customer

Share of customer
The portion of the customer's purchasing that a company gets in its product categories.

Beyond simply retaining good customers to capture customer lifetime value, good customer relationship management can help marketers increase their **share of customer**—the share they get of the customer's purchasing in their product categories. Thus, banks want to increase "share of wallet." Supermarkets and restaurants want to get more "share of stomach." Car companies want to increase "share of garage," and airlines want greater "share of travel."

To increase share of customer, firms can offer greater variety to current customers. Or they can create programs to cross-sell and up-sell to market more products and services to existing customers. For example, Amazon.com is highly skilled at leveraging relationships with its 173 million customers to increase its share of each customer's spending budget:[31]

> Once they log onto Amazon.com, customers often buy more than they intend. And Amazon does all it can to help make that happen. The online giant continues to broaden its merchandise assortment, creating an ideal spot for one-stop shopping. And based on each customer's purchase and search history, the company recommends related products that might be of interest. This recommendation system influences up to 30 percent of all sales. Amazon's ingenious Amazon Prime two-day shipping program has also helped boost its share of customers' wallets. For an annual fee of $79, Prime members receive delivery of all their purchases within two days, whether it's a single paperback book or a 60-inch HDTV. According to one analyst, the ingenious Amazon Prime program "converts casual shoppers, who gorge on the gratification of having purchases reliably appear two days after the order, into Amazon addicts." As a result, after signing up for Prime, shoppers more than triple their annual Amazon.com purchases. The shipping program is responsible for an estimated 20 percent of Amazon's U.S. sales.

Building Customer Equity

We can now see the importance of not only acquiring customers but also keeping and growing them. The value of a company comes from the value of its current and future customers. Customer relationship management takes a long-term view. Companies want not only to create profitable customers but also "own" them for life, earn a greater share of their purchases, and capture their customer lifetime value.

Customer equity
The total combined customer lifetime values of all of the company's customers.

● **Managing customer equity: To increase customer lifetime value, Cadillac is trying to make the Caddy cool again with edgier, high-performance designs that target a younger generation of consumers.**

© Michael Edwards. Courtesy Veda Partalo

What Is Customer Equity?

The ultimate aim of customer relationship management is to produce high *customer equity*.[32] **Customer equity** is the total combined customer lifetime values of all of the company's current and potential customers. As such, it's a measure of the future value of the company's customer base. Clearly, the more loyal the firm's profitable customers, the higher its customer equity. Customer equity may be a better measure of a firm's performance than current sales or market share. Whereas sales and market share reflect the past, customer equity suggests the future. ● Consider Cadillac:[33]

> In the 1970s and 1980s, Cadillac had some of the most loyal customers in the industry. To an entire generation of car buyers, the name *Cadillac* defined "The Standard of the World." Cadillac's share of the luxury car market reached a whopping 51 percent in 1976, and based on market share and sales, the brand's future looked rosy. However, measures of customer equity would have painted a bleaker picture. Cadillac customers were getting older (average age 60) and average customer lifetime value was falling. Many Cadillac buyers were on their last cars. Thus, although Cadillac's market share was good, its customer equity was not.

Compare this with BMW. Its more youthful and vigorous image didn't win BMW the early market share war. However, it did win BMW younger customers (average age about 40) with higher customer lifetime values. The result: In the years that followed, BMW's market share and profits soared while Cadillac's fortunes eroded badly. BMW overtook Cadillac in the 1980s. In recent years, Cadillac has struggled to make the Caddy cool again with edgier, high-performance designs that target a younger generation of consumers. The brand now positions itself as "The New Standard of the World" with marketing pitches based on "power, performance, and design." As a result, after a decades-long slide, Cadillac sales are up 36 percent over the past three years. The moral: Marketers should care not just about current sales and market share. Customer lifetime value and customer equity are the name of the game.

Building the Right Relationships with the Right Customers

Companies should manage customer equity carefully. They should view customers as assets that need to be managed and maximized. But not all customers, not even all loyal customers, are good investments. Surprisingly, some loyal customers can be unprofitable, and some disloyal customers can be profitable. Which customers should the company acquire and retain?

The company can classify customers according to their potential profitability and manage its relationships with them accordingly. ● **Figure 1.5** classifies customers into one of four relationship groups, according to their profitability and projected loyalty.[34] Each group requires a different relationship management strategy. *Strangers* show low potential profitability and little projected loyalty. There is little fit between the company's offerings and their needs. The relationship management strategy for these customers is simple: Don't invest anything in them.

Butterflies are potentially profitable but not loyal. There is a good fit between the company's offerings and their needs. However, like real butterflies, we can enjoy them for only a short while and then they're gone. An example is stock market investors who trade shares often and in large amounts but who enjoy hunting out the best deals without building a regular relationship with any single brokerage company. Efforts to convert butterflies into loyal customers are rarely successful. Instead, the company should enjoy the butterflies for the moment. It should create satisfying and profitable transactions with them, capturing as much of their business as possible in the short time during which they buy from the company. Then, it should cease investing in them until the next time around.

True friends are both profitable and loyal. There is a strong fit between their needs and the company's offerings. The firm wants to make continuous relationship investments to delight these customers and nurture, retain, and grow them. It wants to turn true friends into *true believers*, who come back regularly and tell others about their good experiences with the company.

Barnacles are highly loyal but not very profitable. There is a limited fit between their needs and the company's offerings. An example is smaller bank customers who bank regularly but do not generate enough returns to cover the costs of maintaining their accounts. Like barnacles on the hull of a ship, they create drag. Barnacles are perhaps the most problematic customers. The company might be able to improve their profitability by selling them more, raising their fees, or reducing service to them. However, if they cannot be made profitable, they should be "fired."

The point here is an important one: Different types of customers require different relationship management strategies. The goal is to build the *right relationships* with the *right customers*.

● **FIGURE** | 1.5
Customer Relationship Groups

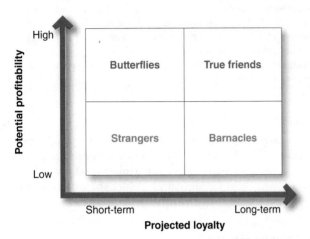

Objective 5 ⋯⋯▶

Describe the major trends and forces that are changing the marketing landscape in this age of relationships.

The Changing Marketing Landscape

Every day, dramatic changes are occurring in the marketplace. Richard Love of HP observed, "The pace of change is so rapid that the ability to change has now become a competitive advantage." Yogi Berra, the legendary New York Yankees catcher and manager, summed it up more simply when he said, "The future ain't what it used to be." As the marketplace changes, so must those who serve it.

In this section, we examine the major trends and forces that are changing the marketing landscape and challenging marketing strategy. We look at five major developments: the changing economic environment, the digital age, rapid globalization, and the call for more ethics and social responsibility.

The Changing Economic Environment

Beginning in 2008, the United States and world economies experienced a Great Recession, a stunning economic meltdown unlike anything since the Great Depression of the 1930s. The stock market plunged, and trillions of dollars of market value simply evaporated. The financial crisis left shell-shocked consumers short of both money and confidence as they faced losses in income, a severe credit crunch, declining home values, and rising unemployment.

The Great Recession caused many consumers to rethink their spending priorities and cut back on their buying. After two decades of overspending, consumers tightened their purse strings and changed their buying attitudes and habits. More than just a temporary change, the new consumer values and consumption patterns will likely remain for many years to come. Even as the economy strengthens, consumers continue to spend more carefully and sensibly (see Real Marketing 1.2).

In response, companies in all industries—from discounters such as Target to luxury brands such as Lexus—have aligned their marketing strategies with the new economic realities. More than ever, marketers are emphasizing the *value* in their value propositions. They are focusing on value-for-the-money, practicality, and durability in their product offerings and marketing pitches.

● For example, for years discount retailer Target focused increasingly on the "Expect More" side of its "Expect More. Pay Less." value proposition. Its carefully cultivated "upscale-discounter" image successfully differentiated it from Walmart's more hard-nosed "lowest-price" position. But when the economy soured, many consumers worried that Target's trendier assortments and hip marketing also meant higher prices, and Target's performance slipped. So Target shifted its balance more toward the "Pay Less" half of the slogan, making certain that its prices are in line with Walmart's and that customers know it. Although still trendy, Target's marketing now emphasizes more practical price and savings appeals. "We let too much space drift between 'Expect More' and 'Pay Less,'" says Target's chief marketing officer. Now, "we believe we've negated the price perception issues," says the executive.[35]

● In the current economic environment, companies must emphasize the value in their value propositions. Target has shifted the balance more toward the "Pay Less" half of its "Expect More. Pay Less." positioning.

Associated Press

In adjusting to the new economy, companies may be tempted to cut their marketing budgets and slash prices in an effort to coax more frugal customers into opening their wallets. However, although cutting costs and offering selected discounts can be important marketing tactics, smart marketers understand that making cuts in the wrong places can damage long-term brand images and customer relationships. The challenge is to balance the brand's value proposition with the current times while also enhancing its long-term equity.

"A recession creates winners and losers just like a boom," notes one economist. "When a recession ends, when the road levels off and the world seems full of promise once more, your position in the competitive pack will depend on how skillfully you managed [during the tough times]."[36] Thus, rather than slashing prices in difficult times, many marketers held the line on prices and instead explained why their brands were worth it. And rather than cutting their marketing budgets, companies such as McDonald's, Hyundai, and General Mills maintained or actually increased their marketing spending, leaving them stronger when the economy strengthened. The goal in uncertain economic times is to build market share and strengthen customer relationships at the expense of competitors who cut back.

The Digital Age

The explosive growth in digital technology has fundamentally changed the way we live—how we communicate, share information, learn, shop, and access entertainment. In turn, it has had a major impact on the ways companies bring value to their customers. For better or worse, technology has become an indispensable part of our lives:[37]

Karl and Dorsey Gude can remember simpler mornings when they used to chat as they ate breakfast and read the newspaper and competed only with the television for the attention of their two teenage sons. Today, Karl wakes and immediately checks his work e-mail and his Facebook and

Real Marketing 1.2

A New Era of More Sensible Consumption

The Great Recession of 2008 to 2009 and its aftermath hit American consumers hard. The housing bust, credit crunch, high unemployment, and plunging stock market blew away the savings and confidence of consumers who for years operated on a buy-now, pay-later philosophy, chasing bigger homes, bigger cars, and better brands. The new economic realities forced consumers to bring their excessive consumption back in line with their incomes and rethink buying priorities. People across all income segments reined in their spending, postponed big purchases, searched for bargains, and hunkered down to weather the worst economic crisis since the Great Depression rocked the worlds of their parents or grandparents.

In today's post-recession era, consumer incomes and spending are again on the rise. However, even as the economy strengthens, rather than reverting to their old free-spending ways, Americans are now showing an enthusiasm for frugality not seen in decades. Sensible consumption has made a comeback, and it might be here to stay. The behavioral shift isn't simply about spending less. The new consumption ethic emphasizes simpler living and more value for the dollar. It focuses on living with less, fixing something yourself instead of buying a new one, packing a lunch instead of eating out, spending more time in discount and dollar chains, or trading down to store brands. Despite their rebounding means, consumers are now clipping more coupons, swiping their credit cards less, and putting more in the bank.

For example, not that long ago, yoga teacher Gisele Sanders shopped at the Nordstrom in Portland, Oregon, and didn't think twice about dropping $30 for a bottle of Chianti to go with dinner. That was before the recession, when her husband, a real estate agent, began to feel the brunt of slowing home sales. Now, even with the improved economy, Sanders picks up grocery-store wine at $10 or less per bottle, shops for used clothes, and takes her mother's advice about turning down the thermostat during winter. "It's been a long time coming," she said. "We were so off the charts before."

Such new-found buying sensibilities are more than just a fad—most experts agree that the impact of the Great Recession will last well into the future. The new frugality appears to be a lasting lifestyle change based on a broad reassessment values. The old expression "Shop till you drop" has been replaced by "No, not today."

The pain of the Great Recession moved many consumers to reconsider their very definition of the good life, changing the way they buy, sell, and live in a post-recession society. "People are finding happiness in old-fashioned virtues—thrift, savings, do-it-yourself projects, self-improvement, hard work, faith, and community—and in activities and relationships outside the consumer realm," says John Gerzema, chief insights officer for ad agency Young & Rubicam, which maintains one of the world's largest databases of information about consumer attitudes. In what Gerzema calls the "spend shift," consumers have become uneasy with debt and excess spending and skeptical of materialistic values. "From now on, our purchases will be more considered. We are moving from mindless to mindful consumption."

Most consumers see the new frugality as a good thing. One recent survey showed that 78 percent of people believe the recession has changed their spending habits for the better. In another survey, 79 percent of consumers agreed with the statement, "I feel a lot smarter now about the way I shop versus two years ago." Some 65 percent of Americans feel that "since the recession I realize I am happier with a simpler more down-to-basic lifestyle." According to a researcher, "They look at their old spending habits and are a bit embarrassed by their behavior. So while consumption may [not] be as carefree and fun as it was before, consumers seem to like their new outlook, mindfulness, and strength."

For example, in Maine, Sindi Card says her husband's job is now secure. However, because the couple has two sons in college, even in the more buoyant economy, she fixed her broken 20-year-old clothes dryer herself. It was a stark change from the past, when she would have taken the old model to the dump and had a new one delivered. With help from an appliance-repair Web site, she saved hundreds of dollars. "We all need to find a way to live within our means," she said.

The new, more practical spending values don't mean that people have resigned themselves to lives of deprivation. As the economy has improved, consumers are indulging in luxuries and bigger-ticket purchases again, just more sensibly. "We're seeing an emergence in what we call 'conscious recklessness,' where consumers actually plan out frivolous or indulgent spending," says the researcher. It's like someone on a diet who saves up calories by eating

Even as the economy strengthens, rather than reverting to their old free-spending ways, Americans are now showing an enthusiasm for frugality not seen in decades. More sensible spending might be here to stay.

Igor Kisselev/Shutterstock.com

prudently during the week and then lets loose on Friday night. But "people are more mindful now and aware of the consequences of their (and others') spending. So luxury is [again] on the 'to-do' list, but people are taking a more mindful approach to where, how, and on what they spend."

What does the new era of consumer spending mean to marketers? Whether it's for everyday products like cereal and detergents or expensive luxuries like Starbucks coffee or diamonds, marketers must clearly spell out their value propositions: what it is that makes their brands worth a customer's hard-earned money. Frugality is in; value is under scrutiny. For companies, it's not about cutting costs and prices. Instead, they must use a different approach to reach today's more pragmatic consumers: Forego the flash and prove your products' worth. According to Starbucks CEO Howard Schultz:

There's been a real sea change in consumer behavior. And [companies] must appeal to the consumer in a different way today than they did two or three years ago. And it's not all based on value. Cutting prices or putting things on sale is not sustainable business strategy. . . . You can't cut enough costs to save your way to prosperity. I think the question is, What is your relevancy to the life of the new consumer, who is more discriminating about what they're going to spend money on?

Even diamond marketer De Beers has adjusted its longstanding "A diamond is forever" value proposition to these more sensible times. One ad, headlined "Here's to Less," makes that next diamond purchase seem—what else—downright practical. Although a diamond purchase might be spendy up front, it's something you'll never have to replace or throw away. As the old James Bond thriller suggests, a diamond is forever.

Sources: Extracts, quotes, and other information from Nin-Hai Tsneg, "Why Dollar Stores Are Thriving, Even Post-Recession," *Fortune,* April 2, 2012, http://finance.fortune.cnn.com/2012/04/02/dollar-stores/; Gregg Fairbrothers and Catalina Gorla, "The Decline and Rise of Thrift", *Forbes,* April 23, 2012, www.forbes.com; Mark Dolliver, "Will Traumatized Consumers Ever Recover?" *Adweek,* March 22, 2010, www.adweek.com; Dan Sewell, "New Frugality Emerges," *Washington Times,* December 1, 2008; John Gerzema, "How U.S. Consumers Are Steering the Spend Shift," *Advertising Age,* October 11, 2010, p. 26; Bobbie Gossage, "Howard Schultz, I'm Getting a Second Shot," *Inc.,* April 2011, pp. 52–53; and Kathleen Madigan, "For Lasting Recovery, Savings as Important as Spending," *Wall Street Journal,* March 1, 2012, http://blogs.wsj.com/economics/2012/03/01/for-lasting-recovery-savings-as-important-as-spending/.

⬤ **In this digital age, for better or worse, technology has become an indispensable part of our lives. The technology boom provides exciting new opportunities for marketers.**

David Sacks/Getty Images

Internet

A vast public web of computer networks that connects users of all types all around the world to each other and to an amazingly large information repository.

Twitter accounts. Dorsey cracks open her laptop right after breakfast. The Gudes' sons sleep with their phones next to their beds, starting each day with text messages from Karl in place of alarm clocks. "I could just walk up stairs, but they always answer their texts," says Karl. ⬤ Welcome to the digital age. By one account, digital communication is more valued than sanitation: There are now 5.3 billion mobile phones in use, compared to only 4.3 billion toilets.

The digital age has provided marketers with exciting new ways to learn about and track customers and create products and services tailored to individual customer needs. Digital technology has also brought a new wave of communication, advertising, and relationship-building tools—ranging from online advertising and video-sharing tools to online social networks and smartphone apps. The digital shift means that marketers can no longer expect consumers to always seek them out. Nor can they always control conversations about their brands. The new digital world makes it easy for consumers to take marketing content that once lived only in advertising or on an online brand site with them wherever they go and share it with friends. More than just add-ons to traditional marketing channels, the new digital media must be fully integrated into the marketer's customer relationship-building efforts.

The most dramatic digital technology is the **Internet**. Almost 78 percent of the U.S. adult population now has Internet access. Of all adults with Internet access, 91 check their e-mail, 84 percent search for maps or driving directions, 76 percent get the news, 64 percent keep in touch with friends on social-networking sites such as Facebook and LinkedIn, and 61 percent do online banking. By 2020, many experts believe, the Internet will be accessed primarily via a mobile device operated by voice, touch, and even thought or "mind-controlled human-computer interaction."[38]

Online marketing is now the fastest-growing form of marketing. These days, it's hard to find a company that doesn't use the Internet in a significant way. In addition to the click-only dot-coms, most traditional brick-and-mortar companies have now become *click-and-mortar* companies. They have ventured online to attract new customers and build stronger relationships with existing ones. Today, 71 percent of American online users use the Internet to shop. Last year, consumer online retail spending topped $161.5 billion, up more than 13 percent over the previous year.[39] Business-to-business (B-to-B) online commerce is also booming.

Thus, the technology boom is providing exciting new opportunities for marketers. We will explore the impact of digital marketing technologies in future chapters, especially Chapter 17.

The Growth of Not-for-Profit Marketing

In recent years, marketing has also become a major part of the strategies of many not-for-profit organizations, such as colleges, hospitals, museums, zoos, symphony orchestras, and even churches. The nation's not-for-profits face stiff competition for support and membership. Sound marketing can help them attract membership, funds, and support.

For example, not-for-profit St. Jude Children's Research Hospital has a special mission: "Finding cures. Saving children." Named the most-trusted charity in the nation by Harris Interactive, St. Jude serves some 5,700 patients each year and is the nation's top children's cancer hospital. What's even more special is that St. Jude does not deny any child treatment for financial reasons—families never have to pay for treatment not covered by insurance. So how does St. Jude support its $1.7 million daily operating budget? By raising funds through powerhouse marketing:[40]

> This past winter, you saw something about St. Jude Children's Hospital about anywhere you looked—in public service announcements (PSAs), on the Discovery Channel's "American Chopper," on the lapel pins of Fox Sports announcers, in Facebook new feeds, and at the checkout counters of major retailers ranging from Target and Williams-Sonoma to pizza peddler Domino's. None of this happened by chance. Rather, it resulted from high-powered marketing. St. Jude targets a broad range of consumers using a mix of event marketing, celebrity star power, and corporate partnerships. Fundraising efforts include everything from PSAs and a sophisticated Internet presence to Trike-a-thons, Math-a-thons, an Up `Til Dawn student challenge, and a Dream Home Giveaway. More than 50 corporate sponsors—including Target, Domino's, Williams-Sonoma, Regal Cinemas, and Expedia—participate in St. Jude's annual Thanks and Giving campaign,  which asks consumers to "give thanks for the healthy kids in your life, and give to those who are not." The companies donate a portion of their sales or ask customers to donate at the sales counter. Through its broad outreach, St. Jude raises hundreds of millions of dollars each year—nearly $700 million last year alone.

● **Not-for-profit marketing: St. Jude's annual Thanks and Giving campaign asks consumers to "give thanks for the healthy kids in your life, and give to those who are not."**

PR Newswire/Associated Press

Government agencies have also shown an increased interest in marketing. For example, the U.S. military has a marketing plan to attract recruits to its different services, and various government agencies are now designing *social marketing campaigns* to encourage energy conservation and concern for the environment or discourage smoking, excessive drinking, and drug use. Even the once-stodgy U.S. Postal Service has developed innovative marketing to sell commemorative stamps, promote its Priority Mail services, and lift its image as a contemporary and competitive organization. In all, the U.S. government is the nation's 28th largest advertiser, with an annual advertising budget of more than $1.1 billion.[41]

Rapid Globalization

As they are redefining their customer relationships, marketers are also taking a fresh look at the ways in which they relate with the broader world around them. Today, almost every company, large or small, is touched in some way by global competition. A neighborhood florist buys its flowers from Mexican nurseries, and a large U.S. electronics manufacturer competes in its home markets with giant Korean rivals. A fledgling Internet retailer finds itself receiving orders from all over the world at the same time that an American consumer-goods producer introduces new products into emerging markets abroad.

American firms have been challenged at home by the skillful marketing of European and Asian multinationals. Companies such as Toyota, Nokia, Nestlé, and Samsung have often outperformed their U.S. competitors in American markets. Similarly, U.S. companies in a wide range of industries have developed truly global operations, making and selling their products worldwide. Quintessentially American McDonald's now serves 68 million customers daily in more than 33,000 local restaurants in 119 countries worldwide—68 percent of its corporate revenues come from outside the United States. Similarly, Nike markets in more than 180 countries, with non-U.S. sales accounting for 65 percent of its worldwide sales.[42] Today, companies are not just selling more of their locally produced goods in international markets; they are also sourcing more supplies and components abroad.

Thus, managers in countries around the world are increasingly taking a global, not just local, view of the company's industry, competitors, and opportunities. They are asking: What is global marketing? How does it differ from domestic marketing? How do global competitors and forces affect our business? To what extent should we "go global"? We will discuss the global marketplace in more detail in Chapter 19.

Sustainable Marketing—The Call for More Social Responsibility

Marketers are reexamining their relationships with social values and responsibilities and with the very Earth that sustains us. As the worldwide consumerism and environmentalism movements mature, today's marketers are being called on to develop *sustainable marketing* practices. Corporate ethics and social responsibility have become hot topics for almost every business. And few companies can ignore the renewed and very demanding environmental movement. Every company action can affect customer relationships. Today's customers expect companies to deliver value in a socially and environmentally responsible way.

The social-responsibility and environmental movements will place even stricter demands on companies in the future. Some companies resist these movements, budging only when forced by legislation or organized consumer outcries. Forward-looking companies, however, readily accept their responsibilities to the world around them. They view sustainable marketing as an opportunity to do well by doing good. They seek ways to profit by serving immediate needs and the best long-run interests of their customers and communities.

Some companies, such as Patagonia, Ben & Jerry's, Timberland, Method, and others, practice *caring capitalism*, setting themselves apart by being civic minded and responsible. They build social responsibility and action into their company value and mission statements. ● For example, when it comes to environmental responsibility, outdoor gear marketer Patagonia is "committed to the core." "Those of us who work here share a strong commitment to protecting undomesticated lands and waters," says the company's Web site. "We believe in using business to inspire solutions to the environmental crisis." Patagonia backs these words with actions. Each year it pledges at least 1 percent of its sales or 10 percent of its profits, whichever is greater, to the protection of the natural environment.[43] We will revisit the topic of sustainable marketing in greater detail in Chapter 20.

● **Sustainable marketing: Patagonia believes in "using business to inspire solutions to the environmental crisis." It backs these words by pledging at least 1 percent of its sales or 10 percent of its profits, whichever is greater, to the protection of the natural environment.**

Patagonia, Inc.

So, What Is Marketing?
Pulling It All Together

At the start of this chapter, Figure 1.1 presented a simple model of the marketing process. Now that we've discussed all the steps in the process, ● **Figure 1.6** presents an expanded model that will help you pull it all together. What is marketing? Simply put, marketing is the process of building profitable customer relationships by creating value for customers and capturing value in return.

The first four steps of the marketing process focus on creating value for customers. The company first gains a full understanding of the marketplace by researching customer needs and managing marketing information. It then designs a customer-driven marketing strategy based on the answers to two simple questions. The first question is "What consumers will we serve?" (market segmentation and targeting). Good marketing companies know that they cannot serve all customers in every way. Instead, they need to focus their resources on the customers they can serve best and most profitably. The second marketing strategy question is "How can we best serve targeted customers?" (differentiation and positioning). Here, the marketer outlines a value proposition that spells out what values the company will deliver to win target customers.

With its marketing strategy chosen, the company now constructs an integrated marketing program—consisting of a blend of the four marketing mix elements—the four Ps—that transforms the marketing strategy into real value for customers. The company develops product offers and creates strong brand identities for them. It prices these offers to create real customer value and distributes the offers to make them available to target consumers. Finally, the company designs promotion programs that communicate the value proposition to target customers and persuade them to act on the market offering.

This expanded version of Figure 1.1 at the beginning of the chapter provides a good road map for the rest of the text. The underlying concept of the entire text is that marketing creates value for customers in order to capture value from customers in return.

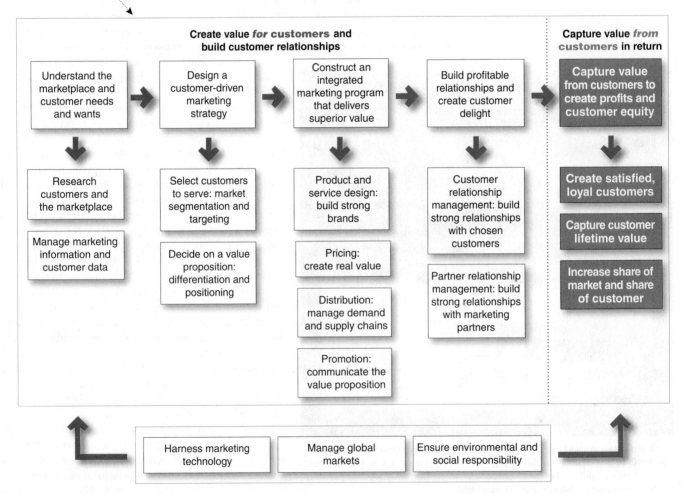

● **FIGURE** | **1.6**
An Expanded Model of the Marketing Process

Perhaps the most important step in the marketing process involves building value-laden, profitable relationships with target customers. Throughout the process, marketers practice customer relationship management to create customer satisfaction and delight. In creating customer value and relationships, however, the company cannot go it alone. It must work closely with marketing partners both inside the company and throughout its marketing system. Thus, beyond practicing good customer relationship management, firms must also practice good partner relationship management.

The first four steps in the marketing process create value *for* customers. In the final step, the company reaps the rewards of its strong customer relationships by capturing value *from* customers. Delivering superior customer value creates highly satisfied customers who will buy more and buy again. This helps the company capture customer lifetime value and greater share of customer. The result is increased long-term customer equity for the firm.

Finally, in the face of today's changing marketing landscape, companies must take into account three additional factors. In building customer and partner relationships, they must harness marketing technology, take advantage of global opportunities, and ensure that they act in an environmentally and socially responsible way.

Figure 1.6 provides a good road map to future chapters of this text. Chapters 1 and 2 introduce the marketing process, with a focus on building customer relationships and capturing value from customers. Chapters 3 through 6 address the first step of the marketing process—understanding the marketing environment, managing marketing information, and understanding consumer and business buyer behavior. In Chapter 7, we look more deeply into the two major marketing strategy decisions: selecting which customers to serve (segmentation and targeting) and determining a value proposition (differentiation and positioning). Chapters 8 through 17 discuss the marketing mix variables, one by one. Chapter 18 sums up customer-driven marketing strategy and creating competitive advantage in the marketplace. The final two chapters examine special marketing considerations: global marketing and sustainable marketing.

Reviewing the Concepts

MyMarketingLab™

Go to **mymktlab.com** to complete the problems marked with this icon .

Reviewing Objectives and Key Terms

Objectives Review

Today's successful companies—whether large or small, for-profit or not-for-profit, domestic or global—share a strong customer focus and a heavy commitment to marketing. The goal of marketing is to build and manage profitable customer relationships.

Objective 1 Define marketing and outline the steps in the marketing process. (pp 4–6)

Marketing is the process by which companies create value for customers and build strong customer relationships in order to capture value from customers in return.

The marketing process involves five steps. The first four steps create value *for* customers. First, marketers need to understand the marketplace and customer needs and wants. Next, marketers design a customer-driven marketing strategy with the goal of getting, keeping, and growing target customers. In the third step, marketers construct a marketing program that actually delivers superior value. All of these steps form the basis for the fourth step, building profitable customer relationships and creating customer delight. In the final step, the company reaps the rewards of strong customer relationships by capturing value *from* customers.

Objective 2 | **Explain the importance of understanding the marketplace and customers and identify the five core marketplace concepts.** (pp 6–8)

Outstanding marketing companies go to great lengths to learn about and understand their customers' *needs*, *wants*, and *demands*. This understanding helps them to design want-satisfying market offerings and build value-laden customer relationships by which they can capture *customer lifetime value* and greater *share of customer*. The result is increased long-term *customer equity* for the firm.

The core marketplace concepts are needs, wants, and demands; market offerings (products, services, and experiences); value and satisfaction; exchange and relationships; and markets. Wants are the form taken by human needs when shaped by culture and individual personality. When backed by buying power, wants become demands. Companies address needs by putting forth a value proposition, a set of benefits that they promise to consumers to satisfy their needs. The value proposition is fulfilled through a market offering, which delivers customer value and satisfaction, resulting in long-term exchange relationships with customers.

Objective 3 | **Identify the key elements of a customer-driven marketing strategy and discuss the marketing management orientations that guide marketing strategy.** (pp 8–12)

To design a winning marketing strategy, the company must first decide *whom* it will serve. It does this by dividing the market into segments of customers (*market segmentation*) and selecting which segments it will cultivate (*target marketing*). Next, the company must decide *how* it will serve targeted customers (how it will *differentiate and position* itself in the marketplace).

Marketing management can adopt one of five competing market orientations. The *production concept* holds that management's task is to improve production efficiency and bring down prices. The *product concept* holds that consumers favor products that offer the most in quality, performance, and innovative features; thus, little promotional effort is required. The *selling concept* holds that consumers will not buy enough of an organization's products unless it undertakes a large-scale selling and promotion effort. The *marketing concept* holds that achieving organizational goals depends on determining the needs and wants of target markets and delivering the desired satisfactions more effectively and efficiently than competitors do. The *societal marketing concept* holds that generating customer satisfaction *and* long-run societal well-being through sustainable marketing strategies is key to both achieving the company's goals and fulfilling its responsibilities.

Objective 4 | **Discuss customer relationship management and identify strategies for creating value *for* customers and capturing value *from* customers in return.** (pp 12–22)

Broadly defined, *customer relationship management* is the process of building and maintaining profitable customer relationships by delivering superior customer value and satisfaction. The aim of customer relationship management is to produce high *customer equity,* the total combined customer lifetime values of all of the company's customers. The key to building lasting relationships is the creation of superior *customer value* and *satisfaction*.

Companies want to not only acquire profitable customers but also build relationships that will keep them and grow "share of customer." Different types of customers require different customer relationship management strategies. The marketer's aim is to build the *right relationships* with the *right customers*. In return for creating value *for* targeted customers, the company captures value *from* customers in the form of profits and customer equity.

In building customer relationships, good marketers realize that they cannot go it alone. They must work closely with marketing partners inside and outside the company. In addition to being good at customer relationship management, they must also be good at *partner relationship management*.

Objective 5 | **Describe the major trends and forces that are changing the marketing landscape in this age of relationships.** (pp 22–29)

Dramatic changes are occurring in the marketing arena. The Great Recession left many consumers short of both money and confidence, creating a new age of consumer frugality that will last well into the future. More than ever, marketers must now emphasize the *value* in their value propositions. The challenge is to balance a brand's value proposition with current times while also enhancing its long-term equity.

The boom in digital technology has created exciting new ways to learn about and relate to individual customers. It has also allowed new approaches by which marketers can target consumers more selectively and build closer, two-way customer relationships in the digital era. In recent years, marketing also has become a major part of the strategies of many not-for-profit organizations, such as colleges, hospitals, museums, zoos, symphony orchestras, and even churches.

In an increasingly smaller world, many marketers are now connected *globally* with their customers and marketing partners. Today, almost every company, large or small, is touched in some way by global competition. Finally, today's marketers are also reexamining their ethical and societal responsibilities. Marketers are being called to take greater responsibility for the social and environmental impact of their actions.

Pulling it all together, as discussed throughout the chapter, the major new developments in marketing can be summed up in a single word: *relationships*. Today, marketers of all kinds are taking advantage of new opportunities for building relationships with their customers, their marketing partners, and the world around them.

Key Terms

Objective 1

Marketing (p 5)

Objective 2

Needs (p 6)
Wants (p 6)
Demands (p 6)
Market offerings (p 6)
Marketing myopia (p 7)
Exchange (p 7)
Market (p 7)

Objective 3

Marketing management (p 8)
Production concept (p 9)
Product concept (p 10)
Selling concept (p 10)
Marketing concept (p 10)
Societal marketing concept (p 11)

Objective 4

Customer relationship management (p 12)
Customer-perceived value (p 13)

Customer satisfaction (p 13)
Customer-managed relationships (p 17)
Consumer-generated marketing (p 18)
Partner relationship management (p 19)
Customer lifetime value (p 20)
Share of customer (p 20)
Customer equity (p 21)

Objective 5

Internet (p 25)

Discussion and Critical Thinking

Discussion Questions

1. Define marketing and outline the steps in the marketing process. (AACSB: Communication)

2. What is marketing myopia, and how can it be avoided? (AACSB: Communication; Reflective Thinking)

3. What is customer-perceived value, and what role does it play in customer satisfaction? (AACSB: Communication; Reflective Thinking)

✪ **4.** Discuss trends impacting marketing and the implications of these trends for how marketers deliver value to customers. (AACSB: Communication)

Critical Thinking Exercises

1. Form a small group of three or four students. Discuss a need or want you have that is not adequately satisfied by any offerings currently in the marketplace. Think of a product or service that will satisfy that need or want. Describe how you will differentiate and position your offering in the marketplace and develop the marketing program for your offering. Present your ideas to the other groups. (AACSB: Communication; Reflective Thinking)

2. Search the Internet for salary information regarding jobs in marketing from a Web site such as www.simplyhired.com/a/salary/search/q-marketing or a similar site. What is the national average salary for five different jobs in marketing? How do the averages compare in different areas of the country? Write a brief report on your findings. (AACSB: Communication; Use of IT; Reflective Thinking)

✪ **3.** Interview someone who works in a marketing job and ask him or her the following questions:
a. What does your job entail?
b. How did you get to this point in your career? Is this what you thought you'd be doing when you grew up? What influenced you to get into this field?
c. What education is necessary for this job?
d. What advice can you give to college students?
e. Add one additional question that you create.

Write a brief report of the responses to your questions and explain why you would or would not be interested in working in this field. (AACSB: Communication; Reflective Thinking)

Applications and Cases

 ## Marketing Technology Apple and Adobe—Flash Clash

Apple's iDevices are wildly popular, starting with the iPod followed by iPhones and iPads. But where's the flash? Adobe Flash, that is. Adobe's Flash, the long-standing multimedia platform behind approximately 75 percent of the animated and streaming audio and video on the Internet, is not supported by Apple's devices. Many purchasers were disappointed after spending hundreds of dollars on sleek iPads only to realize they couldn't play their favorite Internet game or watch that funny video on their device. And they still can't, even with the second-generation device, the iPad 3. It seems Apple's late founder and CEO, Steve Jobs, didn't like Flash and would not support it on Apple's devices. Instead, app developers must conform to Apple's operating system and existing applications on the Web must convert to HTML5 to play on an Apple product. Adobe's co-founders claim Apple is "undermining the next chapter of the Web" and bloggers exclaim this is not just an "Adobe/Apple problem . . . but an Apple/World problem."

⭐ **1.** Does Apple appear to embrace the marketing concept? (AACSB: Communication; Reflective Thinking)

2. Research the controversy surrounding this issue and debate whether Apple did the right thing for its customers by not including the ubiquitous Adobe Flash software on Apple's products. (AACSB: Communication; Reflective Thinking)

 ## Marketing Ethics Goodbye Big Gulp

With two-thirds of adults and one-third of school-aged children in the United States overweight or obese, New York City Mayor Michael Bloomberg is taking action against the soft drink industry. Mayor Bloomberg proposed a ban on big sugary drinks such as 7–11's mammoth 32-ounce "Big Gulp." The ban would put a 16-ounce cap on fountain and bottled drinks sold at restaurants, theaters, and sporting events. While it applies to drinks having more than 25 calories per 8 ounces, it does not apply to 100 percent juice or milk-based beverages. Establishments serving fountain drinks will see a significant revenue drop because these drinks are often marked up 10 to 15 times their cost. Many consumers oppose the ban because they perceive it as further encroachment of the "nanny state." Mayor Bloomberg has already banned smoking in public parks and trans fats in restaurant foods, as well as requiring chain restaurants to include calorie information on menus. This leads many to ask, "What's next?"

⭐ **1.** Is it fair to single out soda in such a ban? Debate this argument from all sides of this issue: government, soft drink marketers, and consumers. (AACSB: Communication; Reflective Thinking)

2. Should marketers embrace the societal marketing concept with respect to foods or products that could be harmful to consumers? Discuss an example of a company embracing the societal marketing concept with respect to the obesity epidemic. (AACSB: Communication; Ethical Reasoning)

 ## Marketing by the Numbers How Much Is Enough?

Marketing is expensive! A 30-second advertising spot during the 2012 Super Bowl cost $3.5 million, and that doesn't include the $500,000 or more to produce the commercial. Anheuser-Busch usually purchases multiple spots each year. Similarly, sponsoring one car during one NASCAR race costs $500,000. But Sprint, the sponsor of the popular Sprint Cup, pays much more than that. And what marketer sponsors only one car for only one race? Want customers to order your product by phone? That will cost you $8 to $13 per order. Or how about a sales representative calling on customers? That costs about $100 per sales call, and that's if the rep doesn't have to get on an airplane and stay in a hotel, which can be very costly considering some companies have thousands of sales reps calling on thousands of customers. And what about the $1-off coupon for Tropicana orange juice that you got in the Sunday newspaper? It costs Tropicana more than a $1 when you redeem it at the store. These are all examples of just one marketing element—promotion. Marketing costs also include the costs of product research and development, the costs of distributing products to buyers, and the costs of all the employees working in marketing.

1. Describe trends in marketing expenditures. What factors are driving these trends? (AACSB: Communication; Analytic Reasoning)

2. What percentage of sales should a business devote to marketing? Discuss the factors used in this decision. (AACSB: Communication; Analytic Reasoning)

Video Case Zappos

These days, online retailers are a dime a dozen. But in a short period of time, Zappos has become a billion-dollar e-tailer. How did it hit the dot-com jackpot? By providing some of the best service available anywhere. Zappos customers are showered with such perks as free shipping both ways, surprise upgrades to overnight service, a 365-day return policy, and a call center that is always open. Customers are also delighted by employees who are empowered to spontaneously hand out rewards based on unique needs.

With such attention to customer service, it's no surprise that Zappos has an almost cultlike following of repeat customers. But remaining committed to the philosophy that the customer is always right can be challenging. This video highlights some of the dilemmas that can arise from operating within a highly customer-centric strategy. Zappos also demonstrates the ultimate rewards it receives from keeping that commitment.

After viewing the video featuring Zappos, answer the following questions:

1. Describe Zappos' market offering.
2. What is Zappos' value proposition? How does it relate to its market offering?
3. How does Zappos build long-term customer relationships?

 # Company Case In-N-Out Burger: Customer Value the Old-Fashioned Way

In 1948, Harry and Esther Snyder opened the first In-N-Out Burger in Baldwin Park, California. It was a simple double drive-thru set up with the kitchen between two service lanes, a walk-up window, and outdoor seating. The menu consisted of burgers, shakes, soft drinks, and fries. This format was common for the time period. In fact, another burger joint that fit this same description opened up the very same year just 45 minutes away from the first In-N-Out Burger. It was called McDonald's. Today, McDonald's boasts over 33,500 stores worldwide that bring in more than $85 billion every year. In-N-Out has only 276 stores in five states, good for an estimated $550 million a year. Based on the outcomes, it would seem that McDonald's has emerged the clear victor.

But In-N-Out never wanted to be another McDonald's. And despite its smaller size—or perhaps because of it—In-N-Out's customers like the regional chain just the way it is. When it comes to customer satisfaction, In-N-Out beats McDonald's hands down. It regularly posts the highest customer satisfaction scores of any fast-food restaurant in its market areas. Compared to McDonald's customers, patrons of In-N-Out are *really* "lovin' it." Just about anyone who has been to an In-N-Out believes it's the best burger they've ever had. It comes as no surprise, then, that the average per-store sales for In-N-Out eclipse those of McDonald's and are double the industry average.

Breaking All the Rules

According to Stacy Perman, author of a definitive book on In-N-Out, the company has achieved unequivocal success by "breaking all the rules." By rules, Ms. Perman refers to the standard business practices for the fast-food industry and even retail in general. In-N-Out has maintained a tenacious focus on customer well-being, but it has done so by doing the unthinkable: not changing. The company's original philosophy is still in place today and best illustrates the basis for the company's rule breaking: "Give customers the freshest, highest quality foods you can buy and provide them with friendly service in a sparkling clean environment." The big burger giants might take exception to the idea that they aren't providing the same customer focus. But let's take a closer look at what these things mean to In-N-Out.

For starters, at In-N-Out, quality food means fresh food. Burgers are made from 100 percent pure beef—no additives, fillers, or preservatives. In-N-Out owns and operates its own patty-making commissaries, ensuring that every burger is fresh and never frozen. Vegetables are sliced and diced by hand in every restaurant. Fries are even made from whole potatoes. And, yes, milkshakes are made from real ice cream. In an industry that has progressively become more and more enamored with processing technologies such as cryogenically freezing foods and preparing all ingredients in off-site warehouses, In-N-Out is indeed an anomaly. In fact, you won't even find a freezer, heating lamp, or microwave oven in an In-N-Out restaurant. From the beginning, the company slogan has been "Quality you can taste." And customers are convinced that they can do just that.

In-N-Out hasn't changed its formula for freshness. But in another deviation from the norm, it hasn't changed its menu. Unlike McDonald's or Wendy's, which introduce a seemingly unending stream of new menu items, In-N-Out stays true to Harry Snyder's original mantra: "Keep it real simple. Do one thing and do it the best you can." This charge from the founder focuses on what the chain has always done well: making really good hamburgers, really good fries, and really good shakes—that's it. While others have focused on menu expansion in constant search of the next hit item to drive traffic, In-N-Out has tenaciously stuck to the basics. In fact, it took 60 years for the company to add 7up and Dr. Pepper to its menu.

Although the limited menu might seem restrictive, customers don't feel that way. In another demonstration of commitment to customers, In-N-Out employees will gladly make any of the menu items in a truly customized fashion. From the chain's earliest years, menu modifications became such a norm at In-N-Out that a "secret" menu emerged consisting of code words that aren't posted on regular menu boards. So customers in the know can order their burgers "animal style" (pickles, extra spread, grilled onions, and a mustard-fried patty). While the "Double-Double" (double meat, double cheese) is on the menu, burgers can also be ordered in 3×3 or 4×4 configurations. Fries can also be ordered animal style (two slices of cheese, grilled onions, and spread), well done, or light. A Neapolitan shake is a mixture of chocolate, vanilla, and strawberry shakes. The list goes on and on. Knowledge of this secret menu is yet another thing that makes customers feel special.

It's not just In-N-Out's food that pleases customers. The chain also features well-trained employees who deliver unexpectedly friendly service. In-N-Out hires and retains outgoing, enthusiastic, and capable employees and treats them very well. It pays new part-time staff $10 an hour and gives them regular raises.

Part-timers also receive paid vacations. General managers make over $100,000 a year plus bonuses and a full-benefit package that rivals anything in the corporate world. Managers who meet goals are sent on lavish trips with their spouses, often to Europe in first-class seats. For gala events, managers wear tuxedos. Executives believe that the men and women who run In-N-Out stores stand shoulder-to-shoulder with any blue-chip manager, and want them to feel that way. Managers are promoted from within. In fact, 80 percent of In-N-Out managers started at the very bottom. As a result, In-N-Out has one of the lowest turnover rates in an industry famous for high turnover.

Happy, motivated employees help create loyal, satisfied customers. In fact, words like *loyal* and *satisfied* don't do justice to how customers feel about In-N-Out Burger. The restaurant chain has developed an unparalleled cult following. When a new In-N-Out first opens, the line of cars often stretches out a mile or more, and people stand in line for an hour to get a burger, fries, and a shake. Fans have been known to camp overnight to be the first in line. When the first Arizona store opened in Scottsdale, people waited in line for as long as four hours while news helicopters buzzed above the parking lot.

Slow Growth Nurtures Fans

Some observers point out that it may be more than the food and the service that created In-N-Out's diehard customer base. In-N-Out's slow-growth expansion strategy means that you won't find one of the famous red-and-white stores with crisscrossed palm trees on every corner. By 1976, In-N-Out had grown to only 18 southern California stores, whereas McDonald's and Burger King had opened thousands of stores worldwide. It took the company 40 years to open its first non-California store in Las Vegas. And even as the company expands into Arizona, Utah, and Texas, it sticks tenaciously to its policy of not opening more than about 10 stores per year.

The lack of access to an In-N-Out in most states has created legions of cravers coast to coast. Countless Facebook pages have been created, filled with posts by consumers begging the family-owned corporation to bring In-N-Out to their states. But In-N-Out's policy is driven by its commitment to quality. It will open a new store only when it has trained management and company-owned distribution centers are in place.

The scarcity of In-N-Out stores only adds to its allure. Customers regularly go out of their way and drive long distances to get their fix. Driving a little further contributes to the feeling that going to In-N-Out is an event. Out-of-state visitors in the know often put an In-N-Out stop high on their list of things to do. Jeff Rose, a financial planner from Carbondale, Illinois, always stops at In-N-Out first when he visits Las Vegas to see his mother. "You have to pass it when you drive to her house," he says in his defense. "It's not like the time I paid an extra $40 in cab fare to visit an In-N-Out on the way to the San Diego airport."

Consistent with the other elements of its simple yet focused strategy, In-N-Out doesn't spend much on advertising—it doesn't have to. In fact, while the company doesn't release financial figures, some estimates place total promotional spending at less than 1 percent of revenues. McDonald's shells out 7 percent of its revenue on advertising. In-N-Out's small promotional budget is for local billboards and radio ads. But when it comes to really spreading the word, In-N-Out lets its customers do the heavy lifting. Customers truly are apostles for the brand. They proudly wear In-N-Out T-shirts and slap In-N-Out bumper stickers on their cars. Rabid regulars drag a constant stream of new devotees into restaurants, an act often referred to as "the conversion." They can't wait to pass along the secret menu codes and

share the sublime pleasures of diving into a 4 × 4 animal style. "When you tell someone else what 'animal style' means," says an analyst, "you feel like you're passing on a secret handshake. People really get into the whole thing."

In-N-Out doesn't use paid endorsers, but word-of-mouth messages regularly flow from A-list celebrities. When former *Tonight Show* host Conan O'Brien asked Tom Hanks what he recommended doing in Los Angeles, Hanks replied, "One of the true great things about Los Angeles is In-N-Out Burger." Paris Hilton famously claimed she was on her way to In-N-Out when she was pulled over for a DUI. And paparazzi have snapped shots of scores of celebrities getting an In-N-Out fix, including Miley Cyrus, Selena Gomez, Christian Slater, and Nick Jonas. The fact that such celebrities aren't paid to pay homage to the brand underscores that In-N-Out is truly a hip place.

A Questionable Future?

Many have questioned whether or not In-N-Out's unwavering 64-year run can be sustained. For example, the company that had been run only by Harry, Esther, or one of their two sons for its first 58 years hit a barrier in 2006 when Esther Snyder passed away. The only direct descendant of the Snyder family at that time was 23-year-old Lynsi Martinez, who was not yet in a position to take over the company. That left In-N-Out in the hands of Mark Taylor, the former vice president of operations. But as directed by Esther Snyder's will, granddaughter Lynsi took over as In-N-Out's sixth president in 2010 before her 28th birthday. Often described as shy, Martinez also progressively gained ownership of the company.

The fact that the changing of the executive guard has gone by unnoticed by customers and fans is an indication that the In-N-Out legacy carries on. With long lines snaking out the door of any location at lunchtime, demand seems as high as ever. "The more chains like McDonald's and Burger King change and expand, the more In-N-Out sticks to its guns," says the analyst. "In a way, it symbolizes the ideal American way of doing business: Treating people well, focusing on product quality, and being very successful." In-N-Out's customers couldn't agree more. When it comes to fast-food chains, delighted customers will tell you, "There's In-N-Out, and then there's everyone else."

Questions for Discussion

1. Describe In-N-Out in terms of the value it provides for customers.

2. Evaluate In-N-Out's performance relative to customer expectations. What is the outcome of this process?

3. Do you think In-N-Out should adopt a high-growth strategy? Why or why not?

4. With so many customers drawn in to In-N-Out's "no-change" philosophy, why don't more burger chains follow suit?

Sources: Jay Weston, "In-N-Out Burger's 'Secret Menu' Revealed," *Huffington Post*, April 6, 2012, www.huffingtonpost.com/jay-weston/in-n-out-burgers-secret-menu_b_1407388.html; Meredith Land, "Inside the In-N-Out Burger Empire," *NBCDFW*, November 17, 2011, www.nbcdfw.com/the-scene/food-drink/Inside-the-In-N-Out-Burger-Empire-134008293.html; Stacy Perman, "In-N-Out Burger: Professionalizing Fast Food," *Business Week*, April 9, 2009, www.businessweek.com/stories/2009-04-08/in-n-out-burger-professionalizing-fast-food; Dan Macsai, "The Sizzling Secrets of In-N-Out Burger," *Fast Company*, April 22, 2009; www.fastcompany.com/blog/dan-macsai/popwise/sizzling-secrets-n-out-burger-qa and www.in-n-out.com, accessed November 2012.

MyMarketingLab

Go to **mymktlab.com** for Auto-graded writing questions as well as the following Assisted-graded writing questions:

1-1. What is consumer-generated marketing? Describe examples of both invited and uninvited consumer exchanges. (AACSB: Communication; Reflective Thinking)

1-2. When implementing customer relationship management, why might a business desire fewer customers over more customers? Shouldn't the focus of marketing be to acquire as many customers as possible? (AACSB: Communication; Reflective Thinking)

1-3. Mymktlab Only – comprehensive writing assignment for this chapter.

References

1. See George Anders, "Inside Amazon's Idea Machine," *Forbes*, April 4, 2012, p. 1; David Welch, "Why Wal-Mart Is Worried About Amazon," *Bloomberg Businessweek*, April 2, 2012, pp. 25–26; Garrick Schmitt, "The :ast Campaign: How Experiences Are Becoming the New Advertising," *Advertising Age*, November 10, 2009, http://adage.com/article/digitalnext/experiences-advertising/140388/; Joe Nocera, "Put Customers First? What a Concept," *New York Times*, January 5, 2008, http://www.nytimes.com/2008/01/05/technology/05nocera.html?pagewanted=all&_r=0; Daniel Lyons, "The Customer Is Always Right," *Newsweek*, January 4, 2010, p. 85; Scott Davis, "Will Amazon Get Physical?" *Forbes*, March 19, 2012, www.forbes.com/sites/scottdavis/2012/03/19/will-amazon-get-physical/; George Anders, "Jeff Bezos's Top 10 Leadership Lessons," *Forbes*, April 4, 2012, www.forbes.com/sites/georgeanders/2012/04/04/bezos-tips/; and annual reports and other information found at www.amazon.com and http://local.amazon.com/businesses, accessed September 2012.

2. See Keith O'Brien, "How McDonald's Came Back Bigger Than Ever," *New York Times*, May 4, 2012, www.nytimes.com/2012/05/06/magazine/how-mcdonalds-came-back-bigger-than-ever.html?pagewanted=all.

3. See Philip Kotler and Kevin Lane Keller, *Marketing Management*, 14th ed. (Upper Saddle River, NJ: Prentice Hall, 2012), p. 5.

4. The American Marketing Association offers the following definition: "Marketing is the activity, set of institutions, and processes for creating, communicating, delivering, and exchanging offerings that have value for customers, clients, partners, and society at large." See www.marketingpower.com/_layouts/Dictionary.aspx?dLetter=M, accessed November 2012.

5. See Dan Sewell, "Kroger CEO Often Roams Aisles, Wielding Carte Blanche," *Journal Gazette* (Fort Wayne, IN), November 15, 2010, www.journalgazette.net/article/20101115/BIZ/311159958/-1/BIZ09. For another example, see Kevin Peters, "How I Did It: Office Depot's President on How 'Mystery Shopping' Helped Spark a Turnaround," *Harvard Business Review*, November 2011, pp. 47–49.

6. See www.michigan.org and www.adcouncil.org/default.aspx?id=602, accessed September 2012; and "Childhood Obesity—Let's Move," Ad Council, www.adcouncil.org/Our-Work/Current-Work/Health/Childhood-Obesity-Let-s-Move, accessed July 2012.

7. See Theodore Levitt's classic article, "Marketing Myopia," *Harvard Business Review*, July–August 1960, pp. 45–56. For more recent discussions, see Lance A. Bettencourt, "Debunking Myths About Customer Needs," *Marketing Management*, January/February 2009, pp. 46–51; N. Craig Smith, Minette E. Drumright, and Mary C. Gentile, "The New Marketing Myopia," *Journal of Public Policy & Marketing*, Spring 2010, pp. 4–11; and Roberto Friedmann, "What Business Are You In?" *Marketing Management*, Summer 2011, pp. 18–23.

8. Information from HP's recent "The Computer Is Personal Again" and "Everybody On" marketing campaigns. See www.hp.com/united-states/personal_again/index.html and www.hp.com/global/us/en/everybody-on/ribbons/passionTVSpot.html, accessed April 2012.

9. "Henry Ford, Faster Horses and Market Research," Research Arts, January 25, 2011, www.researcharts.com/2011/01/henry-ford-faster-horses-and-market-research/.

10. Adapted from information found in Michael E. Porter and Mark R. Kramer, "Creating Shared Value," *Harvard Business Review*, January–February 2011, pp. 63–77; Michael Krauss, "Evolution of an Academic: Kotler on Marketing 3.0," *Marketing News*, January 30, 2011, p. 12; and Vivian Gee, "Creating Shared Value," *Huffington Post*, January 29, 2012, www.huffingtonpost.com/vivian-gee/creating-shared-value_1_b_1240228.html.

11. Based on information from www.responsibility.ups.com/Sustainability; and www.responsibility.ups.com/community/Static%20Files/sustainability/Highlights.pdf, accessed July 2012.

12. Based on information from www.weber.com, accessed September 2012.

13. See "JetBlue, Southwest, Virgin America Get Top Customer-Service Marks," "The American Customer Satisfaction Index: Scores by Industry," *TravelKit MSNBC*, March 14, 2012, http://travelkit.msnbc.msn.com/_news/2012/03/14/10686622-jetblue-southwest-virgin-america-get-top-customer-service-marks; Kelly Liyakasa, "Customer Experience Is Critical in Net Promoter Benchmarks," *CRM Magazine*, June 2012, www.destinationcrm.com/Articles/Columns-Departments/Insight/Customer-Experience-Is-Critical-in-Net-Promoter-Benchmarks-82569.aspx; and http://experience.jetblue.com/ and www.jetblue.com/about/, accessed November 2012.

14. Matthew Dixon, Karen Freeman, and Nicholas Toman, "Stop Trying to Delight Your Customers," *Harvard Business Review*, July–August 2010, pp. 116–122. Also see Chris Morran, "Stop Treating Customers Like Liabilities, Start Treating Them Like People," *Advertising Age*, February 14, 2011, p. 10.

15. Ron Ruggless, "Panera Loyalty Program Approaches 10M Members," *Nation's Restaurant News*, March 8, 2012, http://nrn.com/article/panera-loyalty-program-approaches-10m-members; and http://mypanera.panerabread.com/, accessed November 2012.

16. For more information, see www.apple.com/usergroups/ and www.webernation.com, accessed November 2012.

17. Elizabeth A. Sullivan, "Just Say No," *Marketing News*, April 15, 2008, p. 17. Also see Raymund Flandez, "It Just Isn't Working? Some File for Customer Divorce," *Wall Street Journal*, November 16, 2009, p. B7.

18. Sullivan, "Just Say No," p. 17.

19. The following example is adapted from information found in Vikas Mittal, Matthew Sarkees, and Feisal Murshed, "The Right Way to Manage Unprofitable Customers," *Harvard Business Review*, April 2008, pp. 95–102; and K. Sudhir, "Firing Customers to

Flatten the Whale," *Huff Post Business,* February 6, 2012, www .huffingtonpost.com/k-sudhir/firing-customers-to-flatt_b_1258527 .html?view=print&comm_ref=false. Quotes from http://whitneyhess .com/blog/2010/02/21/fire-your-worst-customers/; and Jeff Schmidt, "Save Your Company by Firing Your Customers," *Bloomberg Businessweek,* April 5, 2011, www.businessweek.com/managing/content/ apr2011/ca2011045_952921.htm?campaign_id=rss_topStories.

20. Quotes from Andrew Walmsley, "The Year of Consumer Empowerment," *Marketing,* December 20, 2006, p. 9; and David Goetzi, "Coke Likes Social Media, Still Moves to Beat of TV," *MediaPost,* May 11, 2012, www.mediapost.com/publications/article/174483/ coke-likes-social-media-still-moves-to-beat-of-tv.html.

21. Casey Hibbard, "Cold Stone Transforms the Ice Cream Social with Facebook," *Social Media Examiner,* November 22, 2010, www .socialmediaexaminer.com/cold-stone-transforms-the-ice-cream-social-with-facebook/; Heba Hornsby, "Social Media Success Stories: See How Cold Stone Ice Cream Became So 'Hot' on Facebook," *Garious Blog,* February 10, 2011, http://garious.com/ blog/2011/02/cold-stone-creamery-success-story/; and www .facebook.com/coldstonecreamery, accessed August 2012.

22. Example and quotes from Kashmir Hill, "#McDStories: When a Hashtag Becomes a Bashtag," *Forbes,* January 24, 2012, www .forbes.com/sites/kashmirhill/2012/01/24/mcdstories-when-a-hashtag-becomes-a-bashtag/; Gabriel Beltrone, "Brand #Fail," *Adweek,* May 15, 2012, www.adweek.com/news/advertising-branding/brand-fail-140368; and Michael Bourne, "Sailing of 14 Social Cs," Mullen Advertising, February, 13, 2012, www.mullen.com/ sailing-the-14-social-cs/.

23. Elizabeth A. Sullivan, "We Were Right!" *Marketing News,* December 15, 2008, p. 17.

24. See mystarbucksidea.force.com, accessed November 2012.

25. "2012 USA Today Facebook Super Bowl Ad Meter," www.usatoday .com/superbowl46/admeter.htm, accessed March 2012; "Doritos Pays Double to 'Crash the Super Bowl' Winners," *Adweek,* February 8, 2012, www.adweek.com/adfreak/doritos-pays-double-crash-super-bowl-winners-138120; and www.crashthesuperbowl .com, accessed July 2012.

26. See Gavin O'Malley, "Entries Pour in for Heinz Ketchup Commercial Contest," August 13, 2007, http://publications.mediapost.com; and www.youtube.com/watch?v=JGY-ubAJSyI; accessed November 2012.

27. "Teaching Brands New Tricks," *Adweek,* April 4, 2011, pp. 12–13. Also see Steven Rosenbaum, *Curator Nation: How to Win in the World Where Consumers Are Creators* (New York: McGraw-Hill, 2011).

28. "Consumer 'New Frugality' May Be an Enduring Feature of Post-Recession Economy, Finds Booz & Company Survey," *Business Wire,* February 24, 2010; Ely Portillo, "In Weak Economy, Store Brands Prosper," *McClatchy-Tribune News Service,* March 18, 2011; and Christine Birkner, "The End of the Middle," *Marketing News,* January 31, 2012, pp. 22–23.

29. "Stew Leonard's," *Hoover's Company Records,* July 15, 2012, www.hoovers.com; and www.stew-leonards.com/html/about.cfm, accessed November 2012.

30. Graham Brown, "MobileYouth Key Statistics," March 28, 2008, www .mobileyouth.org/?s=MobileYouth+Key+Statistics. For interesting discussions of customer lifetime value, see Norman W. Marshall, "Commitment, Loyalty, and Customer Lifetime Value: Investigating the Relationships Among Key Determinants," *Journal of Business & Economics Research,* August 2010, pp. 67–85; V. Kumar and Denish Shah, "Can Marketing Lift Stock Prices?" *MITSloan Management Review,* Summer 2011, pp. 23–26; and Christian Gronroos and Pekka Helle, "Return on Relationships: Conceptual Understanding and Measurement of Mutual Gains from Relational Business Engagements," *Journal of Business & Industrial Marketing,* Vol. 27, Iss. 5, 2012, pp. 344–359.

31. Based on quotes and information from Heather Green, "How Amazon Aims to Keep You Clicking," *BusinessWeek,* March 2, 2009, pp. 34–40; Brad Stone, "What's in the Box? Instant Gratification," *Bloomberg BusinessWeek,* November 29–December 5, 2010, pp. 39–40; JP Mangalindan, "Amazon's Prime and Punishment," *CNNMoney,* February 21, 2012, http://tech.fortune.cnn .com/2012/02/21/prime-and-punishment/; and www.amazon.com/ gp/prime/ref=footer_prime, accessed July 2012.

32. For more discussions on customer equity, see Roland T. Rust, Valerie A. Zeithaml, and Katherine A. Lemon, *Driving Customer Equity* (New York: Free Press, 2000); Rust, Lemon, and Zeithaml, "Return on Marketing: Using Customer Equity to Focus Marketing Strategy," *Journal of Marketing,* January 2004, pp. 109–127; Dominique M. Hanssens, Daniel Thorpe, and Carl Finkbeiner, "Marketing When Customer Equity Matters," *Harvard Business Review,* May 2008, pp. 117–124; V. Kumar and Denish Shaw, "Expanding the Role of Marketing: From Customer Equity to Market Capitalization," *Journal of Marketing,* November 2009, p. 119; Crina O. Tarasi et al., "Balancing Risk and Return in a Customer Portfolio," *Journal of Marketing,* May 2011, pp. 1–17; and Christian Gronroos and Pekka Helle, "Return on Relationships: Conceptual Understanding and Measurement of Mutual Gains from Relational Business Engagements," *Journal of Business & Industrial Marketing,* Vol. 27, Iss. 5, 2012, pp. 344–359.

33. This example is adapted from information found in Rust, Lemon, and Zeithaml, "Where Should the Next Marketing Dollar Go?" *Marketing Management,* September–October 2001, pp. 24–28; with information from Dan Slater, "She Drives a Cadillac," *Fast Company,* February 2012, pp. 26–28.

34. Based on Werner Reinartz and V. Kumar, "The Mismanagement of Customer Loyalty," *Harvard Business Review,* July 2002, pp. 86–94. Also see Stanley F. Slater, Jakki J. Mohr, and Sanjit Sengupta, "Know Your Customer," *Marketing Management,* February 2009, pp. 37–44; and Crina O. Tarasi, et al., "Balancing Risk and Return in a Customer Portfolio," *Journal of Marketing,* May 2011, pp. 1–17.

35. Natalie Zmuda, "Why the Bad Economy Has Been Good for Target," *Advertising Age,* October 4, 2010, p. 1; Sharon Edelson, "Target Eying $100 Billion in Sales," *WWD,* February 25, 2011, p. 2; Matt Townsend, "Why Target's Cheap-Chic Glamour Is Fading," *Bloomberg Businessweek,* September 26, 2012, pp. 30–31; and "Our Mission," http://sites.target.com/site/en/company/page .jsp?contentId=WCMP04-031699, accessed November 2012.

36. Emily Thornton, "The New Rules," *BusinessWeek,* January 19, 2009, pp. 30–34. Also see Christine Birkner, "The End of the Middle," *Marketing News,* January 31, 2012, pp. 22–23.

37. Adapted from information in Brad Stone, "Breakfast Can Wait. Today's First Stop Is Online," *New York Times*, August 10, 2009, p. A1; with information from R. Gary Bridge, "Get Connected for Better Service," *Marketing Management,* Winter 2011, pp. 21–24.

38. Internet usage stats from www.internetworldstats.com/stats.htm, accessed July 2012; "Digital Hotlist: By the Numbers," *Adweek,* October 11, 2010, p. 20; and "Pew Internet and the American Life Project: Trend Data," http://pewinternet.org/Trend-Data/Online-Activites-Total.aspx, accessed June 2012.

39. "Pew Internet and the American Life Project: Trend Data," http://pewinternet.org/Trend-Data/Online-Activites-Total.aspx, accessed June 2012; and Anthony DeMarco, "Retail E-Commerce Spending Totals $161.5 Billion in 2011," *Forbes,* February 6, 2012, www.forbes.com/sites/anthonydemarco/2012/02/06/retail-e-commerce-spending-totals-161-5-billion-in-2011/.

40. See Natalie Zmuda, "St. Jude's Goes from Humble Beginnings to Media Ubiquity," *Advertising Age,* February 14, 2011, p. 37; and various pages at www.stjude.org, accessed November 2012.

41. "Leading National Advertisers," *Advertising Age*, June 20, 2011, pp. 8–24. For more on social marketing, see Philip Kotler, Ned Roberto, and Nancy R. Lee, *Social Marketing: Improving the Quality of Life*, 2nd ed. (Thousand Oaks, CA: Sage Publications, 2002).

42. www.aboutmcdonalds.com/mcd and www.nikeinc.com, accessed June 2012.

43. Quotes and information found at www.patagonia.com/web/us/contribution/patagonia.go?assetid=2329, accessed November 2012.

2

Company and Marketing
Strategy   Partnering to Build
Customer Relationships

Chapter Preview In the first chapter, we explored the marketing process by which companies create value for consumers to capture value from them in return. In this chapter, we dig deeper into steps two and three of that process: designing customer-driven marketing strategies and constructing marketing programs. First, we look at the organization's overall strategic planning, which guides marketing strategy and planning. Next, we discuss how, guided by the strategic plan, marketers partner closely with others inside and outside the firm to create value for customers. We then examine marketing strategy and planning—how marketers choose target markets, position their market offerings, develop a marketing mix,

and manage their marketing programs. Finally, we look at the important step of measuring and managing return on marketing investment (marketing ROI).

Let's begin by looking at McDonald's, a good company and marketing strategy story. When it burst onto the scene more than 55 years ago, McDonald's perfected the modern fast-food concept and grew rapidly. By the turn of the twenty-first century, however, McDonald's once-shiny Golden Arches seemed to be losing some of their luster. But thanks to a new customer-focused strategic blueprint—called the "Plan to Win"—McDonald's launched an amazing turnaround that once again has both customers and the company humming the chain's catchy jingle, "i'm lovin' it."

McDonald's: A Customer-Focused "Plan to Win" Strategy

More than half a century ago, Ray Kroc, a 52-year-old salesman of milkshake-mixing machines, set out on a mission to transform the way Americans eat. In 1955, Kroc discovered a string of seven restaurants owned by Richard and Maurice McDonald. He saw the McDonald brothers' fast-food concept as a perfect fit for America's increasingly on-the-go, time-squeezed, family-oriented lifestyles. Kroc bought the small chain for $2.7 million, and the rest is history.

From the start, Kroc preached a motto of QSCV—quality, service, cleanliness, and value. These goals became mainstays in McDonald's corporate and marketing strategy. By applying these values, the company perfected the fast-food concept—delivering convenient, good-quality food at affordable prices.

McDonald's grew quickly to become the world's largest fast-feeder. The fast-food giant now serves more than 68 million

customers each day through more than 33,000 restaurants in 118 countries, racking up system-wide sales of more than $85 billion annually. The Golden Arches are one of the world's most familiar symbols; other than Santa Claus, no character in the world is more recognizable than Ronald McDonald.

In the mid-1990s, however, McDonald's fortunes began to turn. The company appeared to fall out of touch with customers. Americans were looking for fresher, better-tasting food

> Fast-food giant McDonald's knows the importance of good strategic and marketing planning. Thanks to its new customer-focused strategic blueprint—called the Plan to Win—customers and the company alike are once again humming the chain's catchy jingle, "i'm lovin' it."

and more contemporary atmospheres. They were also seeking healthier eating options. In a new age of health-conscious consumers and $5 lattes at Starbucks, McDonald's strategy seemed a bit out of step with the times.

To fix the problem, the company tried new products, everything from pizza to toasted deli sandwiches (both failed). It acquired nonburger franchises, such as Boston Market (later sold). It continued opening thousands of new restaurants each year, but the new operations suffered from the same malaise as already existing ones. Meanwhile, McDonald's became an ever-more-popular target for social activists and nutritionists, who blamed the chain's fat- and sugar-laden menu for contributing to the nation's growing obesity crisis.

Although McDonald's remained the world's most visited fast-food chain, the once-shiny Golden Arches lost some of their luster. Sales growth slumped, and its market share fell by more than 3 percent by the early 2000s. In 2002, the company posted its first-ever quarterly loss. In the face of changing customer value expectations, the company had lost sight of its fundamental value proposition. McDonald's and its strategy needed to adapt.

In early 2003, McDonald's announced a new strategic blueprint—what it now calls its "Plan to Win." At the heart of this strategic plan was a new mission statement that refocused the company on its customers. No longer satisfied with being "the world's best quick-service restaurant," McDonald's changed its mission to "being our customers' favorite place and way to eat." In line with the new mission, the company built its Plan to Win around five basics of an exceptional customer experience: people, products, place, price, and promotion. This new focus profoundly changed McDonald's strategic direction and priorities. Rather than simply working to provide the cheapest, most convenient meals to customers, the Plan to Win, along with the seemingly simple shift in mission, motivated McDonald's and its employees to focus on quality and the overall customer restaurant experience.

Under the Plan to Win, McDonald's got back to the basic business of taking care of customers. The goal was to get "better, not just bigger." The company halted rapid expansion and instead poured money back into improving the food, the service, the atmosphere, and marketing at existing outlets. McDonald's redecorated its restaurants with clean, simple, more-modern interiors and amenities such as live plants, Wi-Fi access, and flat-screen TVs showing cable news. To make the customer experience more convenient, McDonald's stores now open earlier to extend breakfast hours and stay open longer to serve late-night diners—more than one-third of McDonald's restaurants are now open 24 hours a day.

McDonald's has had its share of product flops over the years (ever heard of the McLean, the Arch Deluxe, or McPizza?). But the company has learned from its past mistakes. Under the Plan to Win, McDonald's now pursues what the industry calls "platforms" rather than random, one-hit wonders. For example, chicken is a platform, and McNuggets, Chicken Selects, and Chicken McBites are products under that platform.

With platforms as a foundation, McDonald's has completely and successfully reworked its menu under the direction

McDonald's successful customer-focused strategy—called the Plan to Win—got the company back to the profitable basics of creating exceptional customer experiences.
Bloomberg via Getty Images

of Chef Daniel Coudreaut, a Culinary Institute of America graduate and former chef at the Four Seasons in Dallas. The new menu gives customers more variety and healthier options at the same time that it puts more money in the company's coffers. Within only a year of introducing its Premium Salads platform, McDonald's became the world's largest salad seller. And McCafé, the beverage platform that serves up coffee drinks and smoothies, became the company's biggest launch in 35 years, adding nearly $125,000 in annual sales per store and now accounting for more than 7 percent of total company sales.

McDonald's rediscovered dedication to customer value has resulted in nothing short of a Golden Age for the Golden Arches. Since announcing its Plan to Win, McDonald's total restaurant sales have increased by 87 percent, profits have nearly quadrupled, and McDonald's stock price has tripled. Over the past several years, even as the fast-food industry struggled through the Great Recession, McDonald's outperformed competitors by a sizable margin. Despite the tough times, from 2008 through the start of 2011, McDonald's achieved a lofty 12.7 percent compound annual return to investors versus the Standard & Poor's average—2.9 percent. The chain has enjoyed more than nine straight years of global same-store monthly sales increases.

Objective Outline

McDonald's revenues are now 20 percent greater than those of competitors Wendy's, Burger King, KFC, Pizza Hut, and Taco Bell *combined*.

Thus, McDonald's Plan to Win appears to be the right strategy for the times. Now, more than ever, when you think of McDonald's, you think of convenience and value. The contemporary menu features iconic favorites along with new products that today's consumer wants—whether it's Premium Salads, snack wraps, Angus Burgers, or McCafé coffees and smoothies. Newly renovated restaurants have a fresh, upbeat feel, and the cash registers keep ringing. And that has customers and the company alike humming the chain's catchy jingle, "i'm lovin' it."[1]

MyMarketingLab™

⭐ **Improve Your Grade!**

Over 10 million students improved their results using the Pearson MyLabs.
Visit **mymktlab.com** for simulations, tutorials, and end-of-chapter problems.

Like McDonald's, outstanding marketing organizations employ strongly customer-driven marketing strategies and programs that create customer value and relationships. These marketing strategies and programs, however, are guided by broader company-wide strategic plans, which must also be customer focused. To understand the role of marketing, we must first understand the organization's overall strategic planning process.

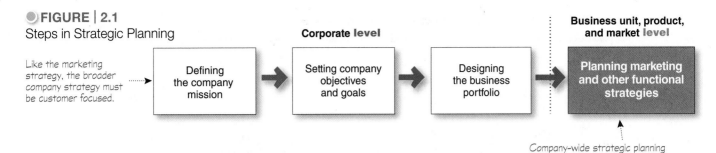

● FIGURE | 2.1
Steps in Strategic Planning

Like the marketing strategy, the broader company strategy must be customer focused. ······▶

Corporate level

Business unit, product, and market level

| Defining the company mission | ➡ | Setting company objectives and goals | ➡ | Designing the business portfolio | ➡ | **Planning marketing and other functional strategies** |

Company-wide strategic planning guides marketing strategy and planning.

Objective 1 ······▶

Explain company-wide strategic planning and its four steps.

Company-Wide Strategic Planning: Defining Marketing's Role

Each company must find the game plan for long-run survival and growth that makes the most sense given its specific situation, opportunities, objectives, and resources. This is the focus of **strategic planning**—the process of developing and maintaining a strategic fit between the organization's goals and capabilities and its changing marketing opportunities.

Strategic planning sets the stage for the rest of planning in the firm. Companies usually prepare annual plans, long-range plans, and strategic plans. The annual and long-range plans deal with the company's current businesses and how to keep them going. In contrast, the strategic plan involves adapting the firm to take advantage of opportunities in its constantly changing environment.

At the corporate level, the company starts the strategic planning process by defining its overall purpose and mission (see ● **Figure 2.1**). This mission is then turned into detailed supporting objectives that guide the entire company. Next, headquarters decides what portfolio of businesses and products is best for the company and how much support to give each one. In turn, each business and product develops detailed marketing and other departmental plans that support the company-wide plan. Thus, marketing planning occurs at the business-unit, product, and market levels. It supports company strategic planning with more detailed plans for specific marketing opportunities.

Strategic planning

The process of developing and maintaining a strategic fit between the organization's goals and capabilities and its changing marketing opportunities.

Mission statement

A statement of the organization's purpose—what it wants to accomplish in the larger environment.

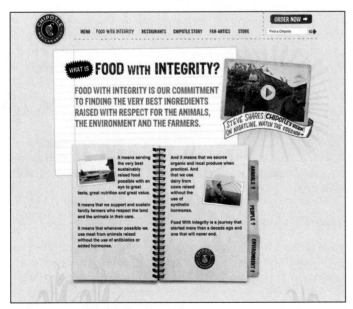

● **Market-oriented missions: Chipotle's mission isn't to sell burritos.** Instead, it promises "Food with Integrity," highlighting its commitment to good food made from natural, local, and sustainably raised ingredients.

© Chipotle Mexican Grill, Inc.

Defining a Market-Oriented Mission

An organization exists to accomplish something, and this purpose should be clearly stated. Forging a sound mission begins with the following questions: What *is* our business? Who is the customer? What do consumers value? What *should* our business be? These simple-sounding questions are among the most difficult the company will ever have to answer. Successful companies continuously raise these questions and answer them carefully and completely.

Many organizations develop formal mission statements that answer these questions. A **mission statement** is a statement of the organization's purpose—what it wants to accomplish in the larger environment. A clear mission statement acts as an "invisible hand" that guides people in the organization.

Some companies define their missions myopically in product or technology terms ("We make and sell furniture" or "We are a chemical-processing firm"). But mission statements should be *market oriented* and defined in terms of satisfying basic customer needs. Products and technologies eventually become outdated, but basic market needs may last forever. For example, Facebook doesn't define itself as just an online social network. Its mission is to connect people around the world and help them share important moments in their lives. ● Likewise, Chipotle's mission isn't to sell burritos. Instead, the restaurant promises "Food with Integrity," highlighting

● **Table 2.1** | **Market-Oriented Business Definitions**

Company	Product-Oriented Definition	Market-Oriented Definition
Facebook	We are an online social network.	We connect people around the world and help them share important moments in their lives.
Hulu	We are an online video service.	We help people enjoy their favorite video content anytime, anywhere.
Home Depot	We sell tools and home repair and improvement items.	We empower consumers to achieve the homes of their dreams.
NASA	We explore outer space.	We reach for new heights and reveal the unknown so that what we do and learn will benefit all humankind.
Revlon	We make cosmetics.	We sell lifestyle and self-expression; success and status; memories, hopes, and dreams.
Ritz-Carlton Hotels & Resorts	We rent rooms.	We create the Ritz-Carlton experience—a memorable stay that far exceeds guests' already high expectations.
Walmart	We run discount stores.	We deliver low prices every day and give ordinary folks the chance to buy the same things as rich people. "Save Money. Live Better."

its commitment to the immediate and long-term welfare of customers and the environment. To back its mission, Chipotle's serves only the very best natural, sustainable, local ingredients. ● **Table 2.1** provides several other examples of product-oriented versus market-oriented business definitions.[2]

Mission statements should be meaningful and specific yet motivating. Too often, mission statements are written for public relations purposes and lack specific, workable guidelines. Instead, they should emphasize the company's strengths and tell forcefully how it intends to win in the marketplace. For example, Google's mission isn't to be the world's best search engine. It's to give people a window into the world's information, wherever it might be found.[3]

Finally, a company's mission should not be stated as making more sales or profits; profits are only a reward for creating value for customers. Instead, the mission should focus on customers and the customer experience the company seeks to create. Thus, as discussed in our chapter-opening story, McDonald's mission isn't to be the world's best and most profitable quick-service restaurant; it's to provide customers with their favorite fast-dining experience." If McDonald's accomplishes this customer-focused mission, profits will follow.

Setting Company Objectives and Goals

The company needs to turn its mission into detailed supporting objectives for each level of management. Each manager should have objectives and be responsible for reaching them. For example, most Americans know H. J. Heinz for its ketchup—it sells more than 650 billion bottles of ketchup each year. But Heinz owns a breadth of other food products under a variety of brands, ranging from Heinz and Ore-Ida to Classico. Heinz ties this diverse product portfolio together under this mission: As the trusted leader in nutrition and wellness, Heinz—the original Pure Food Company—is dedicated to the sustainable health of people, the planet, and our company."

This broad mission leads to a hierarchy of objectives, including business objectives and marketing objectives. ● Heinz's overall objective is to build profitable customer relationships by developing foods "superior in quality, taste, nutrition, and convenience" that embrace its nutrition and wellness mission. It does this by investing heavily in research.

NO ONE GROWS KETCHUP LIKE HEINZ.

That's because every red, ripe tomato in every bottle is grown only from Heinz seeds. It's what helps us deliver the uniquely thick, rich flavor that America loves.

HEINZ. GROWN, NOT MADE.™

Learn more at www.heinzketchup.com.

● **Heinz's overall objective is to build profitable customer relationships by developing foods "superior in quality, taste, nutrition, and convenience" that embrace its nutrition and wellness mission.**

© 2007 H.J. Heinz Co., L.P.

Objective 2 ┈┈┈►
Discuss how to design business portfolios and develop growth strategies.

Business portfolio
The collection of businesses and products that make up the company.

Portfolio analysis
The process by which management evaluates the products and businesses that make up the company.

However, research is expensive and must be funded through improved profit, so improving profits becomes another major objective for Heinz. Profits can be improved by increasing sales or reducing costs. Sales can be increased by improving the company's share of domestic and international markets. These goals then become the company's current marketing objectives.

Marketing strategies and programs must be developed to support these marketing objectives. To increase its market share, Heinz might broaden its product lines, increase product availability and promotion in existing markets, and expand into new markets. For example, last year Heinz added breakfast wraps to its Weight Watchers Smart Ones product line. And it purchased an 80 percent stake in Quero, a Brazilian brand of tomato-based sauces, ketchup, condiments, and vegetables. Quero is expected to double Heinz's sales in Latin America this year and to serve as a platform to market Heinz in Brazil.[4]

These are Heinz's broad marketing strategies. Each broad marketing strategy must then be defined in greater detail. For example, increasing the product's promotion may require more advertising and public relations efforts; if so, both requirements will need to be spelled out. In this way, the firm's mission is translated into a set of objectives for the current period.

Designing the Business Portfolio

Guided by the company's mission statement and objectives, management now must plan its business portfolio—the collection of businesses and products that make up the company. The best **business portfolio** is the one that best fits the company's strengths and weaknesses to opportunities in the environment.

Most large companies have complex portfolios of businesses and brands. Strategic and marketing planning for such business portfolios can be a daunting but critical task. For example, ESPN's portfolio consists of more than 50 business entities, ranging from multiple ESPN cable channels to ESPN Radio, ESPN.com, *ESPN The Magazine*, and even ESPN Zone sports-themed restaurants (see Real Marketing 2.1). In turn, ESPN is just one unit in the even broader, more complex portfolio of its parent company, The Walt Disney Company. The Disney portfolio includes its many Disney theme parks and resorts; Disney studio entertainment (movie, television, and theatrical production companies such as Walt Disney Pictures, Pixar, Touchstone Pictures, and Hollywood Pictures); Disney consumer products (from apparel and toys to interactive games); and a sizable collection of broadcast, cable, radio, and Internet media businesses (including ESPN and the ABC Television Network).

Business portfolio planning involves two steps. First, the company must analyze its *current* business portfolio and determine which businesses should receive more, less, or no investment. Second, it must shape the *future* portfolio by developing strategies for growth and downsizing.

Analyzing the Current Business Portfolio

The major activity in strategic planning is business **portfolio analysis**, whereby management evaluates the products and businesses that make up the company. The company will want to put strong resources into its more profitable businesses and phase down or drop its weaker ones.

Management's first step is to identify the key businesses that make up the company, called *strategic business units* (SBUs). An SBU can be a company division, a product line within a division, or sometimes a single product or brand. The company next assesses the attractiveness of its various SBUs and decides how much support each deserves. When designing a business portfolio, it's a good idea to add and support products and businesses that fit closely with the firm's core philosophy and competencies.

Real Marketing 2.1

ESPN: A Real Study in Strategic and Marketing Planning

When you think about ESPN, you probably think of it as a cable TV network, or a magazine, or maybe a Web site. ESPN is all of those things. But over the years, ESPN has grown to become much more. Thanks to stellar strategic and marketing planning, the brand now consists of a vast array of sports-entertainment entities.

In 1979, entrepreneur Bill Rasmussen took a daring leap and founded the around-the-clock sports network ESPN (Entertainment and Sports Programming Network). The rest, as they say, is history. Despite many early skeptics—a 24-hour sports network?—ESPN is now a multibillion-dollar sports empire and a "can't-live-without-it" part of the daily routine for hundreds of millions of people worldwide. Here's a brief summary of the incredible variety of entities now tied together under the ESPN brand.

Television: From its original groundbreaking cable network, the ESPN brand has sprouted seven additional networks—ESPN3D, ESPN2, ESPN Classic, ESPNEWS, ESPNU, ESPN Deportes (Spanish-language), and the Longhorn Network. With its signal now flowing into more than 100 million U.S. households at an industry-topping cost of $4.69 per household per month—TNT is a distant second at $1.16—ESPN is by far the most sought cable network. Additionally, ESPN International serves fans through 48 international networks in more than 200 countries on every continent. ESPN is the home of the NBA Finals, WNBA, Monday Night Football, NASCAR, IndyCar, the NHRA, college football and the BCS, college basketball, tennis's Grand Slam events, golf's Masters, the U.S. Open and British Open, World Cup Soccer, the Little League World Series, and more. This list grows every year as ESPN outbids the major broadcast networks to capture the rights to major sports events. ESPN has certainly answered the question of whether cable TV has the mass appeal needed to support major sports events.

Radio: Sports radio is thriving, and ESPN operates the largest sports radio network, broadcasting more than 9,000 hours of content annually to 24 million listeners through 700 U.S. affiliates plus 45 Spanish-language ESPN Deportes stations in major markets. Overseas, ESPN has radio and syndicated radio programs in 11 countries.

Online: ESPN.com is the leading sports Web site with more than 41 million unique visitors spending 3.3 billion minutes on the site each month. Its video offerings capture 35 percent of all sports-related video streams. ESPNRadio.com is the most listened-to online sports destination, with 35 original podcasts each week.

With literally dozens of global and market-specific sites, ESPN more than dominates. With access to content from television, radio, and print, ESPN has a plentiful supply of material to feed its digital efforts. But ESPN is also leading the game in the exploding mobile arena. It employs a "mobile first" strategy, in which it orients all of its Web sites around mobile, thus optimizing performance. Now, ESPN delivers mobile sports content via all major U.S. wireless providers—including real-time scores, stats, late-breaking news, and video-on-demand. The digital strategy has led to ESPN3, a multi-screen live 24/7 sports network available at no cost to 70 million homes that receive their high-speed Internet connection from an affiliated service provider. ESPN3 viewers can stream ESPN

ESPN is more than just cable networks, publications, and other media. To consumers, ESPN is synonymous with sports entertainment, inexorably linked with consumers' sports memories, realities, and anticipations.
ZUMA Press/Newscom

coverage on their computers, tablets, or smartphones.

Publishing: When ESPN first published *ESPN The Magazine* in 1998, critics gave it little chance against mighty *Sports Illustrated*. Yet, with its bold look, bright colors, and unconventional format, the ESPN publication now serves more than 16 million readers each month and continues to grow. By comparison, a relatively stagnant *SI* is struggling to make the shift to a digital world.

As if all this weren't enough, ESPN also manages events, including the X Games, Winter X Games, ESPN Outdoors (featuring the Bassmaster Classic), the Skins Games, the Jimmy V Classic, and several football bowl games. It also develops ESPN-branded consumer products and services, including CDs, DVDs, video games, apparel, and even golf schools. If reading all this makes you hungry, you may be near an ESPN Zone, which includes a sports-themed restaurant, interactive games, and sports-related merchandise sales. You'll now find ESPN content in airports and on planes, in health clubs,

and even on gas station video panels. All this translates into annual revenues of $8.5 billion, making ESPN more important to the parent Walt Disney Company than the Disneyland and Disney World theme parks combined.

Managing this successful and growing brand portfolio is no easy proposition, but ESPN has been more than up to the task. What ties it all together? The brand's customer-focused mission: "To serve sports fans wherever sports are watched, listened to, discussed, debated, read about, or played." To most consumers, ESPN is a unified brand experience—a meaningful part of their lives that goes well beyond the cable networks, publications, and other entities it comprises.

Based on its customer-focused mission, ESPN has a philosophy known as "best available screen." It knows that when fans are at home, they'll watch the big 50-inch flat screen. But during the morning hours, smartphones

light up more. During the day, desktops dominate, and in the evening, tablet activity increases. ESPN is on a crusade to know when, where, and under what conditions fans will reach for which device, and to provide the most seamless, high-quality experience for them.

As a result, ESPN has become synonymous with sports entertainment, inexorably linked with consumers' sports memories, realities, and anticipations. No matter what your sport or where you are, ESPN probably plays a prominent part in the action. To fans around the world, ESPN means sports. Tech savvy, creative, and often irreverent, the well-managed, ever-extending brand portfolio continues to build meaningful customer experiences and relationships. If it has to do with your life and sports—large or small—ESPN covers it for you, anywhere you are 24/7. Perhaps the company should rename ESPN to stand for Every Sport Possible—Now.

Sources: See Anthony Kosner, "Mobile First: How ESPN Delivers to the Best Available Screen," *Forbes*, January 30, 2012, www.forbes.com/sites/anthonykosner/2012/01/30/mobile-first-how-espn-delivers-to-the-best-available-screen/2/; Nick Summers, "Big, Bigger, Biggest," *Newsweek*, January 23, 2012, p. 4; and information from http://mediakit.espn.go .com/home.aspx, http://espnmediazone.com/us/about-espn/, and www.espn.com, accessed November 2012.

The purpose of strategic planning is to find ways in which the company can best use its strengths to take advantage of attractive opportunities in the environment. For this reason, most standard portfolio analysis methods evaluate SBUs on two important dimensions: the attractiveness of the SBU's market or industry and the strength of the SBU's position in that market or industry. The best-known portfolio-planning method was developed by the Boston Consulting Group, a leading management consulting firm.[5]

The Boston Consulting Group Approach

Using the now-classic Boston Consulting Group (BCG) approach, a company classifies all its SBUs according to the **growth-share matrix**, as shown in Figure 2.2. On the

Growth-share matrix

A portfolio-planning method that evaluates a company's SBUs in terms of market growth rate and relative market share.

FIGURE | 2.2
The BCG Growth-Share Matrix

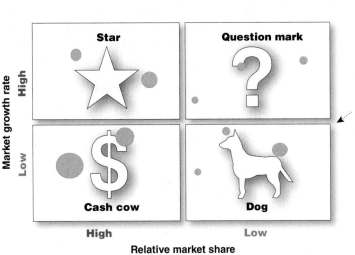

Under the classic BCG portfolio planning approach, the company invests funds from mature, successful products and businesses (cash cows) to support promising products and businesses in faster-growing markets (stars and question marks), hoping to turn them into future cash cows.

The company must decide how much it will invest in each product or business (SBU). For each SBU, it must decide whether to build, hold, harvest, or divest.

Star Question mark

Cash cow Dog

Market growth rate — High / Low

Relative market share — High / Low

vertical axis, *market growth rate* provides a measure of market attractiveness. On the horizontal axis, *relative market share* serves as a measure of company strength in the market. The growth-share matrix defines four types of SBUs:

1. *Stars.* Stars are high-growth, high-share businesses or products. They often need heavy investments to finance their rapid growth. Eventually their growth will slow down, and they will turn into cash cows.
2. *Cash cows.* Cash cows are low-growth, high-share businesses or products. These established and successful SBUs need less investment to hold their market share. Thus, they produce a lot of the cash that the company uses to pay its bills and support other SBUs that need investment.
3. *Question marks.* Question marks are low-share business units in high-growth markets. They require a lot of cash to hold their share, let alone increase it. Management has to think hard about which question marks it should try to build into stars and which should be phased out.
4. *Dogs.* Dogs are low-growth, low-share businesses and products. They may generate enough cash to maintain themselves but do not promise to be large sources of cash.

The 10 circles in the growth-share matrix represent the company's 10 current SBUs. The company has two stars, two cash cows, three question marks, and three dogs. The areas of the circles are proportional to the SBU's dollar sales. This company is in fair shape, although not in good shape. It wants to invest in the more promising question marks to make them stars and maintain the stars so that they will become cash cows as their markets mature. Fortunately, it has two good-sized cash cows. Income from these cash cows will help finance the company's question marks, stars, and dogs. The company should take some decisive action concerning its dogs and its question marks.

Once it has classified its SBUs, the company must determine what role each will play in the future. It can pursue one of four strategies for each SBU. It can invest more in the business unit to *build* its share. Or it can invest just enough to *hold* the SBU's share at the current level. It can *harvest* the SBU, milking its short-term cash flow regardless of the long-term effect. Finally, it can *divest* the SBU by selling it or phasing it out and using the resources elsewhere.

As time passes, SBUs change their positions in the growth-share matrix. Many SBUs start out as question marks and move into the star category if they succeed. They later become cash cows as market growth falls, and then finally die off or turn into dogs toward the end of their life cycle. The company needs to add new products and units continuously so that some of them will become stars and, eventually, cash cows that will help finance other SBUs.

Problems with Matrix Approaches

The BCG and other formal methods revolutionized strategic planning. However, such centralized approaches have limitations: They can be difficult, time-consuming, and costly to implement. Management may find it difficult to define SBUs and measure market share and growth. In addition, these approaches focus on classifying *current* businesses but provide little advice for *future* planning.

Because of such problems, many companies have dropped formal matrix methods in favor of more customized approaches that better suit their specific situations. Moreover, unlike former strategic planning efforts that rested mostly in the hands of senior managers at company headquarters, today's strategic planning has been decentralized. Increasingly, companies are placing responsibility for strategic planning in the hands of cross-functional teams of divisional managers who are close to their markets.

For example, consider The Walt Disney Company. ● Most people think of Disney as theme parks and wholesome family entertainment. But in the mid-1980s, Disney set up a powerful, centralized strategic planning group to guide its direction and growth. Over the next two decades, the strategic planning group turned The Walt Disney Company into a huge and diverse collection of media and entertainment businesses. The sprawling company grew to include everything from theme resorts and film studios (Walt Disney Pictures, Touchstone Pictures, Hollywood Pictures, Pixar, and others) to media networks

● **Managing the business portfolio: Most people think of Disney as theme parks and wholesome family entertainment, but over the past two decades, it's become a sprawling collection of media and entertainment businesses that requires big doses of the famed "Disney Magic" to manage.**

Martin Beddall/Alamy

(ABC Television plus ESPN, Disney Channel, parts of A&E and History Channel, and a half dozen others) to consumer products and a cruise line.

The newly transformed company proved hard to manage and performed unevenly. To improve performance, Disney disbanded the centralized strategic planning unit, decentralizing its functions to Disney division managers. As a result, Disney retains its position at the head of the world's media conglomerates. And even through the recently weak economy, Disney's sound strategic management of its broad mix of businesses has helped it fare better than rival media companies.[6]

Developing Strategies for Growth and Downsizing

Beyond evaluating current businesses, designing the business portfolio involves finding businesses and products the company should consider in the future. Companies need growth if they are to compete more effectively, satisfy their stakeholders, and attract top talent. At the same time, a firm must be careful not to make growth itself an objective. The company's objective must be to manage "profitable growth."

Marketing has the main responsibility for achieving profitable growth for the company. Marketing needs to identify, evaluate, and select market opportunities and establish strategies for capturing them. One useful device for identifying growth opportunities is the **product/market expansion grid**, shown in ● **Figure 2.3**.[7] We apply it here to Starbucks:[8]

Product/market expansion grid
A portfolio-planning tool for identifying company growth opportunities through market penetration, market development, product development, or diversification.

> In only three decades, Starbucks has grown at an astonishing pace, from a small Seattle coffee shop to a nearly $12 billion powerhouse with more than 17,000 retail stores in every state and 56 countries. In the United States alone, Starbucks serves more than 50 million espresso-dependent customers each week. Starbucks gives customers what it calls a "third place"—away from home and away from work. Growth is the engine that keeps Starbucks perking. However, in recent years, the company's remarkable success has drawn a full litter of copycats, ranging from direct competitors such as Caribou Coffee to fast-food merchants such as McDonald's McCafe. Almost every eatery, it seems, now serves its own special premium brew. To maintain its incredible growth in an increasingly overcaffeinated marketplace, Starbucks must brew up an ambitious, multipronged growth strategy.

Market penetration
Company growth by increasing sales of current products to current market segments without changing the product.

First, Starbucks' management might consider whether the company can achieve deeper **market penetration**—making more sales to current customers without changing its original products. It might add new stores in current market areas to make it easier for customers to visit. In fact, Starbucks is adding 300 net new stores each year. Improvements in advertising, prices, service, menu selection, or store design might encourage customers to stop by more often, stay longer, or buy more during each visit. For example, Starbucks is remodeling many of its stores to give them more of a neighborhood feel—with earth tones, wood counters, and handwritten menu boards. And it's adding beer, wine, cheeses, and premium

● **FIGURE | 2.3**
The Product/Market
Expansion Grid

Companies can grow by developing new markets for existing products. For example, Starbucks is expanding rapidly in China, which by 2015 will be its second-largest market, behind only the United States.

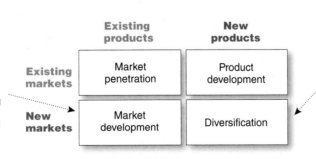

	Existing products	New products
Existing markets	Market penetration	Product development
New markets	Market development	Diversification

Through diversification, companies can grow by starting or buying businesses outside their current product/markets. For example, Starbucks is entering the "health and wellness" market with stores called Evolution By Starbucks.

● **Strategies for growth: To maintain its incredible growth, Starbucks has brewed up an ambitious, multipronged growth strategy.**

Bloomberg via Getty Images

Market development

Company growth by identifying and developing new market segments for current company products.

Product development

Company growth by offering modified or new products to current market segments.

Diversification

Company growth through starting up or acquiring businesses outside the company's current products and markets.

food to its menu in some markets with the goal of boosting business beyond the breakfast rush, which still constitutes the bulk of the company's revenue.

Second, Starbucks might consider possibilities for **market development**—identifying and developing new markets for its current products. For instance, managers could review new demographic markets. Perhaps new groups—such as seniors—could be encouraged to visit Starbucks coffee shops for the first time or to buy more from them. Managers could also review new geographic markets. Starbucks is now expanding swiftly in non-U.S. markets, especially Asia. The company recently opened its 1,000th store in Japan, expects to have 1,500 stores in China by 2015, and plans to more than double its number of stores in South Korea to 700 by 2016.

Third, Starbucks could consider **product development**—offering modified or new products to current markets. For example, Starbucks recently introduced its highly successful Via instant coffee. And it's now introducing a lighter-roast coffee called Blonde, developed to meet the tastes of the 40 percent of U.S. coffee drinkers who prefer lighter, milder roasts. Starbucks is also forging ahead into new product categories. For instance, it recently entered the $8 billion energy drink market with Starbucks Refreshers, a beverage that combines fruit juice and green coffee extract.

Finally, Starbucks might consider **diversification**—starting up or buying businesses beyond its current products and markets. For example, the company recently acquired Evolution Fresh, a boutique provider of super-premium fresh-squeezed juices. Starbucks intends to use Evolution as its entry into the "health and wellness" category, including standalone stores called Evolution By Starbucks. In recent years, Starbucks has also diversified into selling merchandise in categories ranging from coffee- and tea-brewing equipment to music and books.

Companies must not only develop strategies for growing their business portfolios but also strategies for *downsizing* them. There are many reasons that a firm might want to abandon products or markets. The firm may have grown too fast or entered areas where it lacks experience. The market environment might change, making some products or markets less profitable. For example, in difficult economic times, many firms prune out weaker, less-profitable products and markets to focus their more limited resources on the strongest ones. Finally, some products or business units simply age and die.

When a firm finds brands or businesses that are unprofitable or that no longer fit its overall strategy, it must carefully prune, harvest, or divest them. For example, P&G just recently sold off the last of its food brands, Pringles, to Kellogg, allowing the company to focus on household care and beauty and grooming products. And in recent years, GM has pruned several underperforming brands from its portfolio, including Oldsmobile, Pontiac, Saturn, Hummer, and Saab. Weak businesses usually require a disproportionate amount of management attention. Managers should focus on promising growth opportunities, not fritter away energy trying to salvage fading ones.

Objective 3 ·······▶

Explain marketing's role in strategic planning and how marketing works with its partners to create and deliver customer value.

Planning Marketing: Partnering to Build Customer Relationships

The company's strategic plan establishes what kinds of businesses the company will operate and its objectives for each. Then, within each business unit, more detailed planning takes place. The major functional departments in each unit—marketing, finance, accounting, purchasing, operations, information systems, human resources, and others—must work together to accomplish strategic objectives.

Marketing plays a key role in the company's strategic planning in several ways. First, marketing provides a guiding *philosophy*—the marketing concept—that suggests the company strategy should revolve around building profitable relationships with important consumer groups. Second, marketing provides *inputs* to strategic planners by helping to identify attractive market opportunities and assessing the firm's potential to take advantage of them. Finally, within individual business units, marketing designs *strategies* for reaching the unit's objectives. Once the unit's objectives are set, marketing's task is to help carry them out profitably.

Customer value is the key ingredient in the marketer's formula for success. However, as noted in Chapter 1, although marketing plays a leading role, it alone cannot produce superior value for customers. It can be only a partner in attracting, keeping, and growing customers. In addition to *customer relationship management*, marketers must also practice *partner relationship management*. They must work closely with partners in other company departments to form an effective internal *value chain* that serves customers. Moreover, they must partner effectively with other companies in the marketing system to form a competitively superior external *value delivery network*. We now take a closer look at the concepts of a company value chain and a value delivery network.

Partnering with Other Company Departments

Value chain

The series of internal departments that carry out value-creating activities to design, produce, market, deliver, and support a firm's products.

Each company department can be thought of as a link in the company's internal **value chain**.[9] That is, each department carries out value-creating activities to design, produce, market, deliver, and support the firm's products. The firm's success depends not only on how well each department performs its work but also on how well the various departments coordinate their activities.

For example, Walmart's goal is to create customer value and satisfaction by providing shoppers with the products they want at the lowest possible prices. Marketers at Walmart play an important role. They learn what customers need and stock the stores' shelves with the desired products at unbeatable low prices. They prepare advertising and merchandising programs and assist shoppers with customer service. Through these and other activities, Walmart's marketers help deliver value to customers.

● The value chain: Walmart's ability to help you "Save money. Live Better." by offering the right products at lower prices depends on the contributions of people in all of the company's departments.

© digitallife/Alamy

However, the marketing department needs help from the company's other departments. ● Walmart's ability to help you "Save Money. Live Better." depends on the purchasing department's skill in developing the needed suppliers and buying from them at low cost. Walmart's information technology (IT) department must provide fast and accurate information about which products are selling in each store. And its operations people must provide effective, low-cost merchandise handling.

A company's value chain is only as strong as its weakest link. Success depends on how well each department performs its work of adding customer value and on how the company coordinates the activities of various departments. At Walmart, if purchasing can't obtain the lowest prices from suppliers, or if operations can't distribute merchandise at the lowest costs, then marketing can't deliver on its promise of unbeatable low prices.

Ideally, then, a company's different functions should work in harmony to produce value for consumers. But, in practice, interdepartmental relations are full of conflicts and misunderstandings. The marketing department takes the consumer's point of view. But when marketing tries to develop customer satisfaction, it can cause other departments to do a poorer job *in their terms*. Marketing department actions can increase purchasing costs, disrupt production schedules, increase inventories, and create budget headaches. Thus, other departments may resist the marketing department's efforts.

Yet marketers must find ways to get all departments to "think consumer" and develop a smoothly functioning value chain. One marketing expert puts it this way: "True market orientation does not mean becoming marketing-driven; it means that the entire company obsesses over creating value for the customer and views itself as a bundle of processes that profitably define, create, communicate, and deliver value to its target customers. . . . Everyone must do marketing regardless of function or department." Says another, "Engaging customers today requires commitment from the entire company. We're all marketers now."[10] Thus, whether you're an accountant, an operations manager, a financial analyst, an IT specialist, or a human resources manager, you need to understand marketing and your role in creating customer value.

Partnering with Others in the Marketing System

In its quest to create customer value, the firm needs to look beyond its own internal value chain and into the value chains of its suppliers, distributors, and, ultimately, its customers. Again, consider McDonald's. People do not swarm to McDonald's only because they love the chain's hamburgers. Consumers flock to the McDonald's *system*, not only to its food products. Throughout the world, McDonald's finely tuned value delivery system delivers a high standard of QSCV—quality, service, cleanliness, and value. McDonald's is effective only to the extent that it successfully partners with its franchisees, suppliers, and others to jointly create "our customers' favorite place and way to eat."

More companies today are partnering with other members of the supply chain— suppliers, distributors, and, ultimately, customers—to improve the performance of the customer **value delivery network**. Competition no longer takes place only between individual competitors. Rather, it takes place between the entire value delivery networks created by these competitors. Thus, Toyota's performance against Ford depends on the quality of Toyota's overall value delivery network versus Ford's. Even if Toyota makes the best cars, it might lose in the marketplace if Ford's dealer network provides more customer-satisfying sales and service.

Value delivery network
The network made up of the company, its suppliers, its distributors, and, ultimately, its customers who partner with each other to improve the performance of the entire system.

Objective 4 ⸺▶
Describe the elements of a customer-driven marketing strategy and mix and the forces that influence it.

Marketing Strategy and the Marketing Mix

The strategic plan defines the company's overall mission and objectives. Marketing's role is shown in ● **Figure 2.4**, which summarizes the major activities involved in managing a customer-driven marketing strategy and the marketing mix.

Consumers are in the center. The goal is to create value for customers and build profitable customer relationships. Next comes **marketing strategy**—the marketing logic by which the company hopes to create this customer value and achieve these profitable relationships. The company decides which customers it will serve (segmentation and targeting) and how (differentiation and positioning). It identifies the total market and then divides it

● **FIGURE** | **2.4**
Managing Marketing
Strategies and the
Marketing Mix

Marketing strategy
involves two key questions:
Which customers will we
serve (segmentation and
targeting)? and How will
we create value for them
(differentiation and
positioning)? Then, the
company designs a
marketing program—the
four Ps—that delivers the
intended value to targeted
consumers.

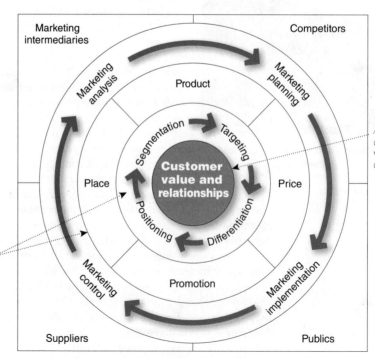

At its core, marketing is all about creating customer value and profitable customer relationships.

Marketing strategy

The marketing logic by which the company hopes to create customer value and achieve profitable customer relationships.

into smaller segments, selects the most promising segments, and focuses on serving and satisfying the customers in these segments.

Guided by marketing strategy, the company designs an integrated *marketing mix* made up of factors under its control—product, price, place, and promotion (the four Ps). To find the best marketing strategy and mix, the company engages in marketing analysis, planning, implementation, and control. Through these activities, the company watches and adapts to the actors and forces in the marketing environment. We will now look briefly at each activity. In later chapters, we will discuss each one in more depth.

Customer-Driven Marketing Strategy

As emphasized throughout Chapter 1, to succeed in today's competitive marketplace, companies must be customer centered. They must win customers from competitors and then keep and grow them by delivering greater value. But before it can satisfy customers, a company must first understand customer needs and wants. Thus, sound marketing requires careful customer analysis.

Companies know that they cannot profitably serve all consumers in a given market—at least not all consumers in the same way. There are too many different kinds of consumers with too many different kinds of needs. Most companies are in a position to serve some segments better than others. Thus, each company must divide up the total market, choose the best segments, and design strategies for profitably serving chosen segments. This process involves *market segmentation*, *market targeting*, *differentiation*, and *positioning*.

Market Segmentation

The market consists of many types of customers, products, and needs. The marketer must determine which segments offer the best opportunities. Consumers can be grouped and served in various ways based on geographic, demographic, psychographic, and behavioral factors. The process of dividing a market into distinct groups of buyers who have different needs, characteristics, or behaviors, and who might require separate products or marketing programs, is called **market segmentation**.

Market segmentation

Dividing a market into distinct groups of buyers who have different needs, characteristics, or behaviors, and who might require separate products or marketing programs.

Every market has segments, but not all ways of segmenting a market are equally useful. For example, Tylenol would gain little by distinguishing between low-income and high-income pain-relief users if both respond the same way to marketing efforts. A **market segment** consists of consumers who respond in a similar way to a given set of marketing efforts. In the car market, for example, consumers who want the biggest, most comfortable car regardless of price make up one market segment. Consumers who care mainly about price and operating economy make up another segment. It would be difficult to make one car model that was the first choice of consumers in both segments. Companies are wise to focus their efforts on meeting the distinct needs of individual market segments.

Market segment

A group of consumers who respond in a similar way to a given set of marketing efforts.

Market Targeting

After a company has defined its market segments, it can enter one or many of these segments. **Market targeting** involves evaluating each market segment's attractiveness and selecting one or more segments to enter. A company should target segments in which it can profitably generate the greatest customer value and sustain it over time.

Market targeting

The process of evaluating each market segment's attractiveness and selecting one or more segments to enter.

A company with limited resources might decide to serve only one or a few special segments or market niches. Such nichers specialize in serving customer segments that major competitors overlook or ignore. For example, Ferrari sells only 1,500 of its very-high-performance cars in the United States each year but at very high prices—such as its Ferrari 458 Italia at $255,000 or the 740-horsepower F-12 Berlinetta at an eye-opening $400,000. Most nichers aren't quite so exotic. WhiteWave Foods, the maker of Silk Soymilk, has found its niche as the nation's largest soymilk producer. And profitable low-cost airline Allegiant Air avoids direct competition with major airline rivals by targeting smaller, neglected markets and new flyers. Nicher Allegiant "goes where they ain't" (see Real Marketing 2.2).

Alternatively, a company might choose to serve several related segments—perhaps those with different kinds of customers but with the same basic wants. Abercrombie & Fitch, for example, targets college students, teens, and kids with the same upscale, casual clothes and accessories in three different outlets: the original Abercrombie

Real Marketing | 2.2

Nicher Allegiant Air: "Going Where They Ain't"

In July 2001, Maurice Gallagher wanted to start a new airline. Conventional wisdom suggested that, to be successful, a new airline needed to follow the JetBlue model: Invest a lot of cash and fly from a large urban hub with lots of brand-new planes. It needed to meet competitors head-on, wresting frequent flyers from rival airlines in the hypercompetitive commercial airspace. Unfortunately, Gallagher didn't have much cash, and he had only one aging, gas-guzzling, 150-seat MD-80 airplane. So he needed to find a different model—one that let him find his own special uncontested niche in the chronically overcrowded skies.

The result is Allegiant Air, arguably today's most successful American airline. As other airlines have struggled through the worst recession in recent history, Allegiant has seen nine straight years of profits—something no other airline can claim. Last year alone, Allegiant's revenue soared 17 percent, with gross margins of 51 percent—double those of industry darling Southwest. This financial performance has earned the upstart airline a place on *Fortune's* annual list of the 100 fastest-growing companies as well as boosting it into the top 10 on *Forbes'* annual list of top publicly traded small companies.

So, what makes Allegiant different? In an industry littered with failing low-cost initiatives, "we needed a strategy that was low-cost and could make money from day one," says Gallagher. "Slowly, we figured it out: Go where they ain't." By "go where they ain't," Gallagher means a new kind of airline—one that finds a whole new way to serve a customer niche now neglected by major competitors. According to one analyst, unlike other airlines, Allegiant "eschews business travelers, daily flights, even service between major cities." Allegiant is the "un-airline."

First, Allegiant looks for uncontested turf—routes neglected by larger, more established competitors. In their efforts to cut costs, the major airlines have abandoned many smaller markets, and Allegiant has moved in to fill the gap. It began by connecting its home city, Las Vegas—and later other popular tourist destinations such as Los Angeles, Orlando, and Phoenix—with dozens of otherwise empty airports in smaller cities such as Fresno, California; Sanford, Florida; and Mesa, Arizona; not to mention Bozeman, Montana; Peoria, Illinois; and Toledo, Ohio. These smaller markets around cities not served by any other scheduled airline welcome Allegiant with open arms and runways. "These small cities have been neglected over the years," Gallagher notes. "We're the circus coming to town, but we don't ever leave." As a result of flying where other airlines don't, Allegiant has direct competition on very few of its 176 routes.

Second, Allegiant doesn't just target the usual frequent business and leisure flyers coveted by rival airlines. Instead, rather than trying to steal competitors' passengers, Allegiant also targets customers who might not otherwise fly—those who are used to driving an hour or two to some vacation spot but now want to go on a real vacation. Allegiant's idea is to entice that person in Peoria, who doesn't fly all that much, to get off the couch and take a weekend vacation at a more distant destination, such as Las Vegas or Orlando. This approach appears to be working. Despite Allegiant's substantial success in almost every market it enters, it has had no measurable impact on competitor passenger loads or pricing structures. By stimulating incremental air travel, Allegiant flies under the radar and avoids direct competition.

To entice more-reluctant travelers, Allegiant offers rock-bottom fares and direct flights. It "provides a complete travel experience with great value and without all the hassle," says the airline. Allegiant lures passengers on board with really low teaser fares—as low as $9. Of course, you have to pay extra to book online or phone a call center. You also have to pay for bags—checked or carry-on—and for onboard snacks, priority boarding, or a reserved seat. On the front of its annual report, the company even states, "We'd charge you for this [report] if we could." But add it all up, and you'll still pay less than you would for a ticket on a competing airline. And Allegiant's à la carte pricing structure provides psychological advantages. "If I tried to charge you $110 up front, you wouldn't pay it," observes Gallagher. "But if I sell you a $75 ticket and you self-select the rest, you will."

What's more, Allegiant doesn't just sell airline tickets. It also encourages customers to buy an entire vacation package at its Web site. Last year, it sold hundreds of thousands of hotel rooms, along with extras such as rental cars, show tickets, and even beach towels and suntan oil. "Ancillary charges" and third-party product sales generate almost 30 percent of the airline's $133 average total fare.

To support its lower fares, Allegiant prides itself on being one of the industry's lowest-cost, most-efficient operators. With innovative methods like removing the unnecessary galley from its planes (Allegiant doesn't

SAVE $20* OFF YOUR FLIGHT WHEN YOU BOOK WITH HOTEL!

FLIGHTS START FEB. 18!

Now fly from **Moline/Quad Cities** to

TAMPA BAY
Via the St. Pete Airport

from $79 .99* each way

Only at an Allegiant airport ticket counter.

Easier.   **allegiant** Travel is our deal.

allegiant.com
call our travel experts at (702) 505-8888

VISIT St. Petersburg Clearwater

Introducing new nonstop flights to Tampa Bay from Moline/Quad Cities!
Save even more by booking your complete air, hotel and car rental package.

Nichers: Profitable low-cost airline Allegiant Air avoids direct competition with major airline rivals by targeting smaller, neglected markets and new flyers. Allegiant "goes where they ain't."

Allegiant Travel Company; (beach photo) Devon Stephens/iStockphoto.com

serve hot food), Allegiant can stuff an additional 16 seats on each plane. Even though its old MD-80 airplanes slurp gas, Allegiant buys used ones for as little as $4 million, a tenth of what it costs Southwest to buy a new 737. And rather than running three-times-a-day service to its smaller markets, Allegiant offers about three flights a week. Passengers don't seem to mind the less-frequent service, especially because they can fly nonstop. Whereas flying Allegiant nonstop from Peoria to Las Vegas takes right around three hours, the same trip using other airlines with connecting flights might take three times as long—and you pay more for the ticket.

Less frequent flights make for more efficient use of Allegiant's fleet. For example, the low-cost airline serves 47 destinations from Las Vegas with only 14 planes, with an average occupancy of 90 percent. Allegiant also limits each plane to no more than six hours of flying time per day, resulting in lower

maintenance costs and less downtime. The bottom line is that greater efficiency results in higher margins, despite lower fares.

Under its "go where they ain't" strategy, nicher Allegiant is thriving in an otherwise super-competitive airline environment. Whereas the major airlines are battling it out with one another for the same passengers in major markets, Allegiant has found its own uncluttered niche. In a mature industry that's struggling just to stay in the air, Allegiant has found a profitable place to land. And by quietly adding six Boeing 757s to its fleet, it has increased its

maximum nonstop range, putting even more routes within reach. The airline recently added routes from Stockton and Fresno, California, to Honolulu, Hawaii, and has identified 300 more potential routes in the United States, Canada, Mexico, and the Caribbean.

In all, nicher Allegiant is breaking the airline industry mold any way that it can. "They're very much one of a kind," says another analyst. Forget talk about milking secondary markets, cutting costs, or flying all-but-vintage airplanes. "The truth is, [Allegiant] is a totally new business model."

Sources: Quotes and other information from Richard N. Velotta, "Earnings Up 26.5 Percent at Las Vegas–Based Allegiant Travel," *McClatchy-Tribune Business News,* April 25, 2012; Jerome Greer Chandler, "Pledging Allegiant Ascendance of the Un-Airline," *Air Transport World,* February 2010, p. 60; Greg Lindsay, "Flying for Fun and Profit," *Fast Company,* September 2009, p. 48; "Is Allegiant Ready for Take Off?" *Forbes,* February 22, 2011, www.forbes.com/sites/investor/2011/02/22/airline-allegiant-southwest-ual-profits/; Jack Nicas, "Allegiant Air to Start Hawaii Flights," *Wall Street Journal,* April 10, 2012, http://online.wsj.com/article/SB10001424052702303815404577335950867973044.html; and www.allegiantair.com, accessed September 2012.

Positioning
Arranging for a product to occupy a clear, distinctive, and desirable place relative to competing products in the minds of target consumers.

Positioning: Burt's Bees offers "Earth friendly natural personal care products for The Greater Good."

BURT'S BEES® is a registered trademark of Burt's Bees, Inc. Used with permission. © 2012 Burt's Bees, Inc. Reprinted with permission.

& Fitch, Hollister, and Abercrombie. Or a large company (for example, car companies like Honda and Ford) might decide to offer a complete range of products to serve all market segments.

Most companies enter a new market by serving a single segment; if this proves successful, they add more segments. For example, Nike started with innovative running shoes for serious runners. Large companies eventually seek full market coverage. Nike now makes and sells a broad range of sports products for just about anyone and everyone, with the goal of "helping athletes at every level of ability reach their potential."[11] It designs different products to meet the special needs of each segment it serves.

Market Differentiation and Positioning

After a company has decided which market segments to enter, it must determine how to differentiate its market offering for each targeted segment and what positions it wants to occupy in those segments. A product's *position* is the place it occupies relative to competitors' products in consumers' minds. Marketers want to develop unique market positions for their products. If a product is perceived to be exactly like others on the market, consumers would have no reason to buy it.

Positioning is arranging for a product to occupy a clear, distinctive, and desirable place relative to competing products in the minds of target consumers. Marketers plan positions that distinguish their products from competing brands and give them the greatest advantage in their target markets.

BMW is "The ultimate driving machine"; Audi promises "Truth in Engineering." Neutrogena is "#1 Dermatologist Recommended"; ● Burt's Bees, Inc. offers "Earth friendly natural personal care products for The Greater Good."[12] At McDonald's you'll be saying "i'm lovin' it"; at Wendy's, "Quality is our recipe." Such deceptively simple statements form the backbone of a product's marketing strategy. For example, McDonald's designs its entire worldwide integrated marketing campaign—from television and print commercials to its Web sites—around the "i'm lovin' it" positioning.

In positioning its brand, a company first identifies possible customer value differences that provide competitive advantages on which to build the position. A company can offer greater customer value by either charging lower prices than competitors or offering more benefits to justify higher prices. But if the company *promises* greater value, it must then *deliver* that greater value. Thus, effective positioning begins with **differentiation**—actually *differentiating* the company's market offering so that it gives consumers more value. Once the company has chosen a desired position, it must take strong steps to deliver and communicate that position to target consumers. The company's entire marketing program should support the chosen positioning strategy.

Differentiation
Actually differentiating the market offering to create superior customer value.

Developing an Integrated Marketing Mix

After determining its overall marketing strategy, the company is ready to begin planning the details of the **marketing mix**, one of the major concepts in modern marketing. The marketing mix is the set of tactical marketing tools that the firm blends to produce the response it wants in the target market. The marketing mix consists of everything the firm can do to influence the demand for its product. The many possibilities can be collected into four groups of variables—the four Ps. ● **Figure 2.5** shows the marketing tools under each P.

Marketing mix
The set of tactical marketing tools—product, price, place, and promotion—that the firm blends to produce the response it wants in the target market.

- *Product* means the goods-and-services combination the company offers to the target market. Thus, a Ford Escape consists of nuts and bolts, spark plugs, pistons, headlights, and thousands of other parts. Ford offers several Escape models and dozens of optional features. The car comes fully serviced and with a comprehensive warranty that is as much a part of the product as the tailpipe.
- *Price* is the amount of money customers must pay to obtain the product. For example, Ford calculates suggested retail prices that its dealers might charge for each Escape. But Ford dealers rarely charge the full sticker price. Instead, they negotiate the price with each customer, offering discounts, trade-in allowances, and credit terms. These actions adjust prices for the current competitive and economic situations and bring them into line with the buyer's perception of the car's value.
- *Place* includes company activities that make the product available to target consumers. Ford partners with a large body of independently owned dealerships that sell the company's many different models. Ford selects its dealers carefully and strongly supports them. The dealers keep an inventory of Ford automobiles, demonstrate them to potential buyers, negotiate prices, close sales, and service the cars after the sale.

● **FIGURE | 2.5**
The Four Ps of the Marketing Mix

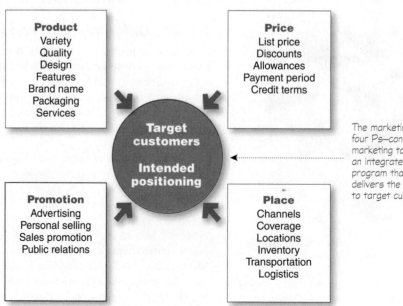

The marketing mix—or the four Ps—consists of tactical marketing tools blended into an integrated marketing program that actually delivers the intended value to target customers.

- *Promotion* refers to activities that communicate the merits of the product and persuade target customers to buy it. Ford spends more than $1.9 billion each year on U.S. advertising to tell consumers about the company and its many products.[13] Dealership salespeople assist potential buyers and persuade them that Ford is the best car for them. Ford and its dealers offer special promotions—sales, cash rebates, and low financing rates—as added purchase incentives.

An effective marketing program blends the marketing mix elements into an integrated marketing program designed to achieve the company's marketing objectives by delivering value to consumers. The marketing mix constitutes the company's tactical tool kit for establishing strong positioning in target markets.

Some critics think that the four Ps may omit or underemphasize certain important activities. For example, they ask, "Where are services?" Just because they don't start with a *P* doesn't justify omitting them. The answer is that services, such as banking, airline, and retailing services, are products too. We might call them *service products*. "Where is packaging?" the critics might ask. Marketers would answer that they include packaging as one of many product decisions. All said, as Figure 2.5 suggests, many marketing activities that might appear to be left out of the marketing mix are included under one of the four Ps. The issue is not whether there should be 4, 6, or 10 Ps so much as what framework is most helpful in designing integrated marketing programs.

There is another concern, however, that is valid. It holds that the four Ps concept takes the seller's view of the market, not the buyer's view. From the buyer's viewpoint, in this age of customer value and relationships, the four Ps might be better described as the four Cs:[14]

4Ps	4Cs
Product	Customer solution
Price	Customer cost
Place	Convenience
Promotion	Communication

Thus, whereas marketers see themselves as selling products, customers see themselves as buying value or solutions to their problems. And customers are interested in more than just the price; they are interested in the total costs of obtaining, using, and disposing of a product. Customers want the product and service to be as conveniently available as possible. Finally, they want two-way communication. Marketers would do well to think through the four Cs first and then build the four Ps on that platform.

Managing the Marketing Effort

Objective 5 ·······▶
List the marketing management functions, including the elements of a marketing plan, and discuss the importance of measuring and managing return on marketing investment.

In addition to being good at the *marketing* in marketing management, companies also need to pay attention to the *management*. Managing the marketing process requires the four marketing management functions shown in ● **Figure 2.6**—*analysis, planning, implementation,* and *control*. The company first develops company-wide strategic plans and then translates them into marketing and other plans for each division, product, and brand. Through implementation, the company turns the plans into actions. Control consists of measuring and evaluating the results of marketing activities and taking corrective action where needed. Finally, marketing analysis provides the information and evaluations needed for all the other marketing activities.

Marketing Analysis

SWOT analysis
An overall evaluation of the company's strengths (S), weaknesses (W), opportunities (O), and threats (T).

Managing the marketing function begins with a complete analysis of the company's situation. The marketer should conduct a **SWOT analysis** (pronounced "swat" analysis), by which it evaluates the company's overall strengths (S), weaknesses (W), opportunities (O), and threats (T) (see ● **Figure 2.7**). Strengths include internal capabilities, resources, and positive situational factors that may help the company serve its customers and achieve its objectives. Weaknesses include internal limitations and negative situational factors that may interfere with the company's performance. Opportunities are favorable factors or trends in the external environment that the company may be able to

FIGURE | 2.6
Managing Marketing:
Analysis, Planning,
Implementation,
and Control

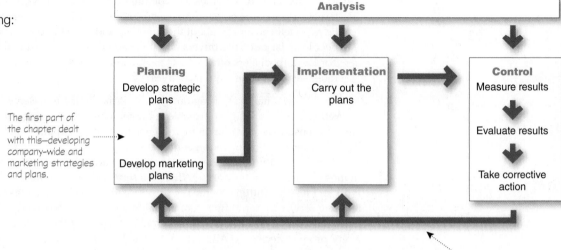

The first part of the chapter dealt with this—developing company-wide and marketing strategies and plans.

We'll close the chapter by looking at how marketers manage those strategies and plans—how they implement marketing strategies and programs and evaluate the results.

exploit to its advantage. And threats are unfavorable external factors or trends that may present challenges to performance.

The company should analyze its markets and marketing environment to find attractive opportunities and identify environmental threats. It should analyze company strengths and weaknesses as well as current and possible marketing actions to determine which opportunities it can best pursue. The goal is to match the company's strengths to attractive opportunities in the environment, while simultaneously eliminating or overcoming the weaknesses and minimizing the threats. Marketing analysis provides inputs to each of the other marketing management functions. We discuss marketing analysis more fully in Chapter 3.

Marketing Planning

Through strategic planning, the company decides what it wants to do with each business unit. Marketing planning involves choosing marketing strategies that will help the company attain its overall strategic objectives. A detailed marketing plan is needed for each business, product, or brand. What does a marketing plan look like? Our discussion focuses on product or brand marketing plans.

● **Table 2.2** outlines the major sections of a typical product or brand marketing plan. (See Appendix 1 for a sample marketing plan.) The plan begins with an executive summary that quickly reviews major assessments, goals, and recommendations. The main section of the plan presents a detailed SWOT analysis of the current marketing situation as well as potential threats and opportunities. The plan next states major objectives for the brand and outlines the specifics of a marketing strategy for achieving them.

FIGURE | 2.7
SWOT Analysis:
Strengths (S),
Weaknesses (W),
Opportunities (O),
and Threats (T)

The goal of SWOT analysis is to match the company's strengths to attractive opportunities in the environment, while eliminating or overcoming the weaknesses and minimizing the threats.

Internal

External

Strengths Internal capabilities that may help a company reach its objectives	**Weaknesses** Internal limitations that may interfere with a company's ability to achieve its objectives
Opportunities External factors that the company may be able to exploit to its advantage	**Threats** Current and emerging external factors that may challenge the company's performance

Positive   **Negative**

Hang on to this one! SWOT analysis (pronounced "swot" analysis) is a widely used tool for conducting a situation analysis. You'll find yourself using it a lot in the future, especially when analyzing business cases.

A *marketing strategy* consists of specific strategies for target markets, positioning, the marketing mix, and marketing expenditure levels. It outlines how the company intends to create value for target customers in order to capture value in return. In this section, the planner explains how each strategy responds to the threats, opportunities, and critical issues spelled out earlier in the plan. Additional sections of the marketing plan lay out an action program for implementing the marketing strategy along with the details of a supporting *marketing budget*. The last section outlines the controls that will be used to monitor progress, measure return on marketing investment, and take corrective action.

Marketing Implementation

Marketing implementation

Turning marketing strategies and plans into marketing actions to accomplish strategic marketing objectives.

Planning good strategies is only a start toward successful marketing. A brilliant marketing strategy counts for little if the company fails to implement it properly. **Marketing implementation** is the process that turns marketing *plans* into marketing *actions* to accomplish strategic marketing objectives. Whereas marketing planning addresses the *what* and *why* of marketing activities, implementation addresses the *who, where, when,* and *how.*

● **Table 2.2** | **Contents of a Marketing Plan**

Section	Purpose
Executive summary	Presents a brief summary of the main goals and recommendations of the plan for management review, helping top management find the plan's major points quickly.
Current marketing situation	Describes the target market and the company's position in it, including information about the market, product performance, competition, and distribution. This section includes the following: • A *market description* that defines the market and major segments and then reviews customer needs and factors in the marketing environment that may affect customer purchasing. • A *product review* that shows sales, prices, and gross margins of the major products in the product line. • A review of *competition* that identifies major competitors and assesses their market positions and strategies for product quality, pricing, distribution, and promotion. • A review of *distribution* that evaluates recent sales trends and other developments in major distribution channels.
Threats and opportunities analysis	Assesses major threats and opportunities that the product might face, helping management to anticipate important positive or negative developments that might have an impact on the firm and its strategies.
Objectives and issues	States the marketing objectives that the company would like to attain during the plan's term and discusses key issues that will affect their attainment.
Marketing strategy	Outlines the broad marketing logic by which the business unit hopes to create customer value and relationships and the specifics of target markets, positioning, and marketing expenditure levels. How will the company create value for customers in order to capture value from customers in return? This section also outlines specific strategies for each marketing mix element and explains how each responds to the threats, opportunities, and critical issues spelled out earlier in the plan.
Action programs	Spells out how marketing strategies will be turned into specific action programs that answer the following questions: *What* will be done? *When* will it be done? *Who* will do it? *How* much will it cost?
Budgets	Details a supporting marketing budget that is essentially a projected profit-and-loss statement. It shows expected revenues and expected costs of production, distribution, and marketing. The difference is the projected profit. The budget becomes the basis for materials buying, production scheduling, personnel planning, and marketing operations.
Controls	Outlines the controls that will be used to monitor progress, allow management to review implementation results, and spot products that are not meeting their goals. It includes measures of return on marketing investment.

THE RIGHT TIRE CHANGES EVERYTHING

Michelin makes some of the most fuel efficient†, longest lasting tires. Plus they offer more security with their incredible stopping power. See how the right tire changes everything at **michelinman.com/righttire**.

MICHELIN
a better way forward

†Based on comparative rolling resistance testing. Copyright ©2009 Michelin North America, Inc. All rights reserved. The Michelin Man is a registered trademark owned by Michelin North America, Inc.

● **Marketing implementation: At Michelin, marketing implementation requires that thousands of people inside and outside the company work together to convince customers that "The right tire changes everything."**

Michelin North America

Many managers think that "doing things right" (implementation) is as important as, or even more important than, "doing the right things" (strategy). The fact is that both are critical to success, and companies can gain competitive advantages through effective implementation. One firm can have essentially the same strategy as another, yet win in the marketplace through faster or better execution. Still, implementation is difficult—it is often easier to think up good marketing strategies than it is to carry them out.

In an increasingly connected world, people at all levels of the marketing system must work together to implement marketing strategies and plans. ● At Michelin, for example, marketing implementation for the company's original equipment, replacement, industrial, and commercial tires requires day-to-day decisions and actions by thousands of people both inside and outside the organization. Marketing managers make decisions about target segments, branding, product development, pricing, promotion, and distribution. They talk with engineering about product designs, with manufacturing about production and inventory levels, and with finance about funding and cash flows. They also connect with outside people, such as advertising agencies to plan ad campaigns and the news media to obtain publicity support. The sales force works closely with automobile manufacturers and supports independent Michelin dealers and large retailers like Walmart in their efforts to convince buyers of all types and sizes that "The right tire changes everything."

Marketing Department Organization

The company must design a marketing organization that can carry out marketing strategies and plans. If the company is very small, one person might do all the research, selling, advertising, customer service, and other marketing work. As the company expands, however, a marketing department emerges to plan and carry out marketing activities. In large companies, this department contains many specialists—product and market managers, sales managers and salespeople, market researchers, and advertising experts, among others.

To head up such large marketing organizations, many companies have now created a *chief marketing officer* (or CMO) position. This person heads up the company's entire marketing operation and represents marketing on the company's top management team. The CMO position puts marketing on equal footing with other "C-level" executives, such as the chief operating officer (COO) and the chief financial officer (CFO). As a member of top management, the CMO's role is to champion the customer's cause—to be the "chief customer officer."[15]

Modern marketing departments can be arranged in several ways. The most common form of marketing organization is the *functional organization*. Under this organization, different marketing activities are headed by a functional specialist—a sales manager, an advertising manager, a marketing research manager, a customer service manager, or a new product manager. A company that sells across the country or internationally often uses a *geographic organization*. Its sales and marketing people are assigned to specific countries, regions, and districts. Geographic organization allows salespeople to settle into a territory, get to know their customers, and work with a minimum of travel time and cost. Companies with many very different products or brands often create a *product management organization*. Using this approach, a product manager develops and implements a complete strategy and marketing program for a specific product or brand.

For companies that sell one product line to many different types of markets and customers who have different needs and preferences, a *market* or *customer management organization*

● **Marketers must continually plan their analysis, implementation, and control activities.**
© Yuri Arcurs/Shutterstock

might be best. A market management organization is similar to the product management organization. Market managers are responsible for developing marketing strategies and plans for their specific markets or customers. This system's main advantage is that the company is organized around the needs of specific customer segments. Many companies develop special organizations to manage their relationships with large customers. For example, companies such as P&G and Stanley Black & Decker have created large teams, or even whole divisions, to serve large customers, such as Walmart, Target, Safeway, or Home Depot.

Large companies that produce many different products flowing into many different geographic and customer markets usually employ some *combination* of the functional, geographic, product, and market organization forms.

Marketing organization has become an increasingly important issue in recent years. More and more, companies are shifting their brand management focus toward *customer management*—moving away from managing only product or brand profitability and toward managing customer profitability and customer equity. They think of themselves not as managing portfolios of brands but as managing portfolios of customers. And rather than managing the fortunes of a brand, they see themselves as managing customer-brand experiences and relationships.

Marketing Control

Marketing control

Measuring and evaluating the results of marketing strategies and plans and taking corrective action to ensure that the objectives are achieved.

Because many surprises occur during the implementation of marketing plans, marketers must practice constant **marketing control**—evaluating the results of marketing strategies and plans and taking corrective action to ensure that the objectives are attained. Marketing control involves four steps. Management first sets specific marketing goals. It then measures its performance in the marketplace and evaluates the causes of any differences between expected and actual performance. Finally, management takes corrective action to close the gaps between goals and performance. This may require changing the action programs or even changing the goals.

Operating control involves checking ongoing performance against the annual plan and taking corrective action when necessary. Its purpose is to ensure that the company achieves the sales, profits, and other goals set out in its annual plan. It also involves determining the profitability of different products, territories, markets, and channels. *Strategic control* involves looking at whether the company's basic strategies are well matched to its opportunities. Marketing strategies and programs can quickly become outdated, and each company should periodically reassess its overall approach to the marketplace.

Measuring and Managing Return on Marketing Investment

Marketing managers must ensure that their marketing dollars are being well spent. In the past, many marketers spent freely on big, expensive marketing programs, often without thinking carefully about the financial returns on their spending. They believed that marketing produces intangible creative outcomes, which do not lend themselves readily to measures of productivity or return. But in today's leaner economic times, all that has changed:[16]

> For years, corporate marketers have walked into budget meetings like neighborhood junkies. They couldn't always justify how well they spent past handouts or what difference it all made. They just wanted more money—for flashy TV ads, for big-ticket events, for, you know, getting out the message and building up the brand. But those heady days of blind budget increases are

fast being replaced with a new mantra: measurement and accountability. Marketing's days as a soft science are officially over. In its place, the concept of marketing performance—the practice of measuring, learning from, and improving upon marketing strategies and tactics over time—is taking hold. More companies are now working to connect the dots between marketing activities and results than ever before.

Return on marketing investment (or marketing ROI)
The net return from a marketing investment divided by the costs of the marketing investment.

One important marketing performance measure is **return on marketing investment** (or **marketing ROI**). *Marketing ROI* is the net return from a marketing investment divided by the costs of the marketing investment. It measures the profits generated by investments in marketing activities.

In one recent survey, 63 percent of chief marketing officers said marketing return on investment will be the most important measure of their success by 2015. However, another survey found that only 45 percent of organizations were satisfied with their measurement of marketing ROI. A startling 57 percent of CMOs don't take ROI measures into account when setting their marketing budgets, and an even-more startling 28 percent said they base their marketing budgets on "gut instinct." One analyst's conclusion: "Marketers must start thinking more strategically about how their programs impact their business's own revenue."[17]

Marketing ROI can be difficult to measure. In measuring financial ROI, both the *R* and the *I* are uniformly measured in dollars. For example, when buying a piece of equipment, the productivity gains resulting from the purchase are fairly straightforward. As of yet, however, there is no consistent definition of marketing ROI. For instance, returns like advertising and brand-building impact aren't easily put into dollar returns.

A company can assess marketing ROI in terms of standard marketing performance measures, such as brand awareness, sales, or market share. Many companies are assembling such measures into *marketing dashboards*—meaningful sets of marketing performance measures in a single display used to monitor strategic marketing performance. Just as automobile dashboards present drivers with details on how their cars are performing, the marketing dashboard gives marketers the detailed measures they need to assess and adjust their marketing strategies. For example, VF Corporation uses a marketing dashboard to track the performance of its more than 30 lifestyle apparel brands—including Wrangler, Lee, The North Face, Vans, Nautica, 7 For All Mankind, and others. VF's marketing dashboard tracks brand equity and trends, share of voice, market share, online sentiment, and marketing ROI in key markets worldwide, not only for VF brands but also for competing brands.[18]

Increasingly, however, beyond standard performance measures, marketers are using customer-centered measures of marketing impact, such as customer acquisition, customer retention, customer lifetime value, and customer equity. These measures capture not only current marketing performance but also future performance resulting from stronger customer relationships. ● **Figure 2.8** views marketing expenditures as investments that

● **FIGURE** | 2.8
Return on Marketing Investment
Source: Adapted from Roland T. Rust, Katherine N. Lemon, and Valerie A. Zeithaml, "Return on Marketing: Using Consumer Equity to Focus Marketing Strategy," *Journal of Marketing*, January 2004, p.112. Used with permission.

Beyond measuring return on marketing investment in terms of standard performance measures such as sales or market share, many companies are using customer-relationship measures, such as customer satisfaction, retention, and equity. These are more difficult to measure but capture both current and future performance.

produce returns in the form of more profitable customer relationships.[19] Marketing investments result in improved customer value and satisfaction, which in turn increases customer attraction and retention. This increases individual customer lifetime values and the firm's overall customer equity. Increased customer equity, in relation to the cost of the marketing investments, determines return on marketing investment.

Regardless of how it's defined or measured, the marketing ROI concept is here to stay. "In good times and bad, whether or not marketers are ready for it, they're going to be asked to justify their spending with financial data," says one marketer. Adds another, marketers "have got to know how to count."[20]

Reviewing the Concepts

MyMarketingLab™
Go to **mymktlab.com** to complete the problems marked with this icon .

Reviewing Objectives and Key Terms

 ## Objectives Review

In Chapter 1, we defined marketing and outlined the steps in the marketing process. In this chapter, we examined company-wide strategic planning and marketing's role in the organization. Then we looked more deeply into marketing strategy and the marketing mix and reviewed the major marketing management functions. So you've now had a pretty good overview of the fundamentals of modern marketing.

Objective 1 Explain company-wide strategic planning and its four steps. (pp 41–43)

Strategic planning sets the stage for the rest of the company's planning. Marketing contributes to strategic planning, and the overall plan defines marketing's role in the company.

Strategic planning involves developing a strategy for long-run survival and growth. It consists of four steps: (1) defining the company's mission, (2) setting objectives and goals, (3) designing a business portfolio, and (4) developing functional plans. The company's *mission* should be market oriented, realistic, specific, motivating, and consistent with the market environment. The mission is then transformed into detailed *supporting goals and objectives*, which in turn guide decisions about the business portfolio. Then each business and product unit must develop *detailed marketing plans* in line with the company-wide plan.

Objective 2 Discuss how to design business portfolios and develop growth strategies. (pp 43–48)

Guided by the company's mission statement and objectives, management plans its *business portfolio*, or the collection of businesses and products that make up the company. The firm wants to produce a business portfolio that best fits its strengths and

weaknesses to opportunities in the environment. To do this, it must analyze and adjust its *current* business portfolio and develop *growth* and *downsizing* strategies for adjusting the *future* portfolio. The company might use a formal portfolio-planning method. But many companies are now designing more-customized portfolio-planning approaches that better suit their unique situations.

Objective 3 Explain marketing's role in strategic planning and how marketing works with its partners to create and deliver customer value. (pp 48–50)

Under the strategic plan, the major functional departments—marketing, finance, accounting, purchasing, operations, information systems, human resources, and others—must work together to accomplish strategic objectives. Marketing plays a key role in the company's strategic planning by providing a *marketing concept philosophy* and *inputs* regarding attractive market opportunities. Within individual business units, marketing designs *strategies* for reaching the unit's objectives and helps to carry them out profitably.

Marketers alone cannot produce superior value for customers. Marketers must practice *partner relationship management*, working closely with partners in other departments to form an effective *value chain* that serves the customer. And they must also partner effectively with other companies in the marketing system to form a competitively superior *value delivery network*.

Objective 4 Describe the elements of a customer-driven marketing strategy and mix and the forces that influence it. (pp 50–55)

Customer value and relationships are at the center of marketing strategy and programs. Through market segmentation, targeting, differentiation, and positioning, the company divides the total market into smaller segments, selects segments it can best serve, and decides how it wants to bring value to target consumers in the selected segments. It then designs an *integrated marketing mix* to produce the response it wants in the target market. The marketing mix consists of product, price, place, and promotion decisions (the four Ps).

| Objective 5 | **List the marketing management functions, including the elements** |

of a marketing plan, and discuss the importance of measuring and managing return on marketing investment. (pp 55–61)

To find the best strategy and mix and to put them into action, the company engages in marketing analysis, planning, implementation, and control. The main components of a *marketing plan* are the executive summary, the current marketing situation, threats and opportunities, objectives and issues, marketing strategies,

action programs, budgets, and controls. Planning good strategies is often easier than carrying them out. To be successful, companies must also be effective at *implementation*—turning marketing strategies into marketing actions.

Marketing departments can be organized in one or a combination of ways: *functional marketing organization*, *geographic organization*, *product management organization*, or *market management organization*. In this age of customer relationships, more and more companies are now changing their organizational focus from product or territory management to customer relationship management. Marketing organizations carry out *marketing control*, both operating control and strategic control.

Marketing managers must ensure that their marketing dollars are being well spent. In a tighter economy, today's marketers face growing pressures to show that they are adding value in line with their costs. In response, marketers are developing better measures of *return on marketing investment*. Increasingly, they are using customer-centered measures of marketing impact as a key input into their strategic decision making.

 # Key Terms

Objective 1

Strategic planning (p 41)
Mission statement (p 41)

Objective 2

Business portfolio (p 43)
Portfolio analysis (p 43)
Growth-share matrix (p 45)
Product/market expansion grid (p 47)
Market penetration (p 47)
Market development (p 48)

Product development (p 48)
Diversification (p 48)

Objective 3

Value chain (p 49)
Value delivery network (p 50)

Objective 4

Marketing strategy (p 50)
Market segmentation (p 51)
Market segment (p 51)

Market targeting (p 51)
Positioning (p 53)
Differentiation (p 54)
Marketing mix (p 54)

Objective 5

SWOT analysis (p 55)
Marketing implementation (p 57)
Marketing control (p 59)
Return on marketing investment
    (marketing ROI) (p 60)

Discussion and Critical Thinking

 # Discussion Questions

1. Define strategic planning and briefly describe the four steps that lead managers and the firm through the strategic planning process. Discuss the role marketing plays in this process. (AACSB: Communication)

⊗ **2.** Name and describe the four product/market expansion grid strategies. Provide an example of a company implementing each strategy. (AACSB: Communication; Reflective Thinking)

⊗ **3.** Explain the roles of market segmentation, market targeting, differentiation, and positioning in implementing an effective marketing strategy. (AACSB: Communication)

⊗ **4.** Define each of the four Ps. What insights might a firm gain by considering the four Cs rather than the four Ps? (AACSB: Communication; Reflective Thinking)

⊗ **5.** Discuss the four marketing management functions. (AACSB: Communication)

Critical Thinking Exercises

1. Form a small group and conduct a SWOT analysis for a publicly traded company. Based on your analysis, suggest a strategy from the product/market expansion grid and an appropriate marketing mix to implement that strategy. (AACSB: Communication; Reflective Thinking)

2. Find the mission statements of two for-profit and two not-for-profit organizations. Evaluate these mission statements with respect to their market orientation. (AACSB: Communication; Reflective Thinking)

Applications and Cases

 ## Marketing Technology Google's Nexus 7 Tablet

Google is making a move into the consumer electronics market. In 2012, Google introduced the Nexus 7 tablet that runs on its popular Android operating system. Priced at $199 to $249, it is much cheaper than Apple's iPad but comparable to Amazon's Kindle Fire. In fact, it is very similar to the Kindle Fire in terms of size, weight, and features. The Kindle Fire also runs on Google's Android operating system, but the Nexus 7 runs on Google's newest version of Android called Jelly Bean. One feature the Nexus 7 has that the Kindle doesn't have is a voice-activated assistant, similar to Apple's Siri on the iPhone 4S. Google is also introducing Nexus Q, which is a $300 black ball-shaped home-entertainment amplifier that wirelessly streams content to other devices. For $1,500, Google offers Google Glass, which is an eyeglasses-like device that displays Internet information in front of the wearer's eyes. Google purchased Motorola Mobility, so keep your eye out for another entrant in the smartphone category.

1. Learn more about Google and its products/services and create a BCG growth-share matrix for this company. On which products and services should Google concentrate its marketing efforts? (AACSB: Communication; Reflective Thinking)

2. How is Google positioning the Nexus 7 tablet? Does this product offer significant differentiation from competing offerings so that consumers will perceive it to have higher value? (AACSB: Communication; Reflective Thinking)

 ## Marketing Ethics Tiny Hearts

You've probably heard of heart procedures such as angioplasty and stents that are routinely performed on adults. But such heart procedures, devices, and related medications are not available for infants and children, despite the fact that almost 40,000 children a year are born in the United States with heart defects that often require repair. This is a life-or-death situation for many young patients, yet doctors must improvise by using devices designed and tested on adults. For instance, doctors use an adult kidney balloon on an infant's heart because it is the appropriate size for a newborn's aortic valve. However, this device is not approved for the procedure. Why are specific devices and medicines developed for the multibillion-dollar cardiovascular market not also designed for kids? It's a matter of economics—this segment of young consumers is just too small. One leading cardiologist attributed the discrepancy to a "profitability gap" between the children's market and the much more profitable adult market for treating heart disease. Although this might make good economic sense for companies, it is of little comfort to the parents of these small patients.

1. Is it wrong for these companies to not address the needs of this segment? Suggest some arguments in defense of companies not offering products to meet these needs. (AACSB: Communication; Reflective Thinking; Ethical Reasoning)

2. Suggest some solutions to this problem. (AACSB: Communication; Reflective Thinking)

 ## Marketing by the Numbers Walmart vs. Target

For the period ending January 2012, Walmart reported profits of almost $16 billion on sales of just under $450 billion. For that same period, Target posted a profit of $3 billion on sales of almost $70 billion. Walmart is a better marketer, right? Sales and profits provide information to compare the profitability of these two competitors, but between these numbers is information regarding the efficiency of marketing efforts in creating those sales and profits. Appendix 2, Marketing by the Numbers, discusses other marketing profitability measures beyond the return on marketing investment (marketing ROI) measure described in this chapter.

Review Appendix 2 to answer the questions using the following information from Walmart's and Target's income statements (all numbers are in thousands):

Period Ending January, 2012	Walmart	Target
Sales	$446,950,000	$69,865,000
Gross Profit	$111,823,000	$22,005,000
Marketing Expenses	$ 63,948,750	$10,914,000
Net Income (Profit)	$ 15,699,000	$ 2,929,000

1. Calculate profit margin, net marketing contribution, marketing return on sales (or marketing ROS), and marketing return on investment (or marketing ROI) for both companies. Which company is performing better? (AACSB: Communication; Use of IT; Analytic Thinking)

2. Go to Yahoo! Finance (http://finance.yahoo.com/) and find the income statements for two other competing companies. Perform the same analysis for these companies that you performed in the previous question. Which company is doing better overall and with respect to marketing? For marketing expenses, use 75 percent of the company's reported "Selling General and Administrative" expenses. (AACSB: Communication; Analytic Reasoning; Reflective Thinking)

 # Video Case OXO

You might know OXO for its well-designed, ergonomic kitchen gadgets. But OXO's expertise at creating handheld tools that look great *and* work well has led it to expand into products for bathrooms, garages, offices, babies' rooms, and even medicine cabinets. In the past, this award-winning manufacturer has managed to move its products into almost every home in the United States by relying on a consistent and in some cases nontraditional marketing strategy.

But in a highly competitive and turbulent market, OXO has focused on evaluating and modifying its marketing strategy in order to grow the brand. This video demonstrates how OXO is using strategic planning to ensure that its marketing strategy results in the best marketing mix for the best and most profitable customers.

After viewing the video featuring OXO, answer the following questions:

1. What is OXO's mission?

2. What are some of the market conditions that have led OXO to reevaluate its marketing strategy?

3. How has OXO modified its marketing mix? Are these changes in line with its mission?

 # Company Case

Trap-Ease America: The Big Cheese of Mousetraps

Conventional Wisdom

One April morning, Martha House, president of Trap-Ease America, entered her office in Costa Mesa, California. She paused for a moment to contemplate the Ralph Waldo Emerson quote that she had framed and hung near her desk:

> If a man [can] . . . make a better mousetrap than his neighbor, the world will make a beaten path to his door.

Perhaps, she mused, Emerson knew something that she didn't. She *had* the better mousetrap—Trap-Ease—but the world didn't seem all that excited about it.

Martha had just returned from the National Hardware Show in Chicago. Standing in the trade show display booth for long hours and answering the same questions hundreds of times had been tiring. Yet, all the hard work had paid off. Each year, National Hardware Show officials held a contest to select the best new product introduced at that year's show. The Trap-Ease had won the contest this year, beating out over 300 new products.

Such notoriety was not new for the Trap-Ease mousetrap, however. *People* magazine had run a feature article on the trap, and the trap had been the subject of numerous talk shows and articles in various popular press and trade publications.

Despite all of this attention, however, the expected demand for the trap had not materialized. Martha hoped that this award might stimulate increased interest and sales.

Background

A group of investors had formed Trap-Ease America in January after it had obtained worldwide rights to market the innovative mousetrap. In return for marketing rights, the group agreed to pay the inventor and patent holder, a retired rancher, a royalty fee for each trap sold. The group then hired Martha to serve as president and to develop and manage the Trap-Ease America organization.

Trap-Ease America contracted with a plastics-manufacturing firm to produce the traps. The trap consisted of a square, plastic tube measuring about 6 inches long and 1-1/2 inches in diameter. The tube bent in the middle at a 30-degree angle, so that when the front part of the tube rested on a flat surface, the other end was elevated. The elevated end held a removable cap into which the user placed bait (cheese, dog food, or some other aromatic tidbit). The front end of the tube had a hinged door. When the trap was "open," this door rested on two narrow "stilts" attached to the two bottom corners of the door. (See Exhibit.)

The simple trap worked very efficiently. A mouse, smelling the bait, entered the tube through the open end. As it walked up the angled bottom toward the bait, its weight made the elevated end of the trap drop downward. This action elevated the open end, allowing the hinged door to swing closed, trapping the mouse. Small teeth on the ends of the stilts would catch in a groove on

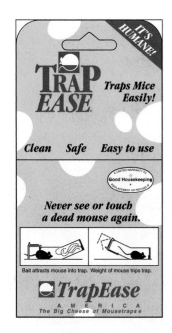

the bottom of the trap, locking the door closed. The user could then dispose of the mouse while it was still alive, or the user could leave it alone for a few hours to suffocate in the trap.

Martha believed the trap had many advantages for the consumer when compared with traditional spring-loaded traps or poisons. Consumers could use it safely and easily with no risk of catching their fingers while loading it. It posed no injury or poisoning threat to children or pets. Furthermore, with Trap-Ease, consumers avoided the unpleasant "mess" they often encountered with the violent spring-loaded traps. The Trap-Ease created no "clean-up" problem. Finally, the user could reuse the trap or simply throw it away.

Martha's early research suggested that women were the best target market for the Trap-Ease. Men, it seemed, were more willing to buy and use the traditional, spring-loaded trap. The targeted women, however, did not like the traditional trap. These women often stayed at home and took care of their children. Thus, they wanted a means of dealing with the mouse problem that avoided the unpleasantness and risks that the standard trap created in the home.

To reach this target market, Martha decided to distribute Trap-Ease through national grocery, hardware, and discount chains. She sold the trap directly to these large retailers, avoiding any wholesalers or other middlemen.

The traps sold in packages of two, with a suggested retail price of $5.99. Although this price made the Trap-Ease about five times more expensive than smaller, standard traps, consumers appeared to offer little initial price resistance. The manufacturing cost for the Trap-Ease, including freight and packaging costs, was about 59 cents per unit. The company paid an additional 19 cents per unit in royalty fees. Martha priced the traps to retailers at $2.38 per unit (two units to a package) and estimated that, after sales and volume discounts, Trap-Ease would produce net revenue from retailers of $1.50 per unit.

To promote the product, Martha had budgeted approximately $145,000 for the first year. She planned to use $100,000 of this amount for travel costs to visit trade shows and to make sales calls on retailers. She planned to use the remaining $45,000 for advertising. So far, however, because the mousetrap had generated so much publicity, she had not felt that she needed to do much advertising. Still, she had placed advertising in *Good Housekeeping* (after all, the trap had earned the *Good Housekeeping* Seal of Approval) and in other "home and shelter" magazines. Martha was the company's only salesperson, but she intended to hire more salespeople soon.

Martha had initially forecasted Trap-Ease's first-year sales at 5 million units. Through April, however, the company had only sold several hundred thousand units. Martha wondered if most new products got off to such a slow start, or if she was doing something wrong. She had detected some problems, although none seemed overly serious. For one, there had not been enough repeat buying. For another, she had noted that many of the retailers upon whom she called kept their sample mousetraps on their desks as conversation pieces—she wanted the traps to be used and demonstrated. Martha wondered if consumers were also buying the traps as novelties rather than as solutions to their mouse problems.

Martha knew that the investor group believed that Trap-Ease America had a "once-in-a-lifetime chance" with its innovative mousetrap, and she sensed the group's impatience with the company's progress so far. She had budgeted approximately $500,000 in administrative and fixed costs for the first year (not including marketing costs). To keep the investors happy, the company needed to sell enough traps to cover those costs and make a reasonable profit.

Back to the Drawing Board

In these first few months, Martha had learned that marketing a new product was not an easy task. Some customers were very demanding. For example, one national retailer had placed a large order with instructions that Trap-Ease America was to deliver the order to the loading dock at one of the retailer's warehouses between 1:00 and 3:00 p.m. on a specified day. When the truck delivering the order arrived after 3:00 p.m., the retailer had refused to accept the shipment. The retailer had told Martha it would be a year before she got another chance.

As Martha sat down at her desk, she realized she needed to rethink her marketing strategy. Perhaps she had missed something or made some mistake that was causing sales to be so slow. Glancing at the quotation again, she thought that perhaps she should send the picky retailer and other customers a copy of Emerson's famous quote.

Questions for Discussion

1. Martha and the Trap-Ease America investors believe they face a once-in-a-lifetime opportunity. What information do they need to evaluate this opportunity? How do you think the group would write its mission statement? How would *you* write it?

2. Has Martha identified the best target market for Trap-Ease? What other market segments might the firm target?

3. How has the company positioned the Trap-Ease for the chosen target market? Could it position the product in other ways?

4. Describe the current marketing mix for Trap-Ease. Do you see any problems with this mix?

5. Who is Trap-Ease America's competition?

6. How would you change Trap-Ease's marketing strategy? What kinds of control procedures would you establish for this strategy?

MyMarketingLab

Go to **mymktlab.com** for Auto-graded writing questions as well as the following Assisted-graded writing questions:

2-1. Explain why it is important for all departments of an organization—marketing, accounting, finance, operations management, human resources, and so on—to "think consumer." Why is it important that even people who are not in marketing understand it? (AACSB: Communication)

2-2. Marketers are increasingly held accountable for demonstrating marketing success. Research the various marketing metrics, in addition to those described in the chapter and Appendix 2, used by marketers to measure marketing performance. Write a brief report of your findings. (AACSB: Communication; Reflective Thinking)

2-3. Mymktlab Only – comprehensive writing assignment for this chapter.

References

1. Quotes, and other information found in Keith O'Brien, "How McDonald's Came Back Bigger Than Ever," *New York Times*, May 4, 2012; Andrew Martin, "McDonald's Maintains Momentum in Bad Times," *New York Times*, January 11, 2009; Beth Kowitt, "Why McDonald's Wins in Any Economy," *Fortune*, September 5, 2011, pp. 71–77; "McDonald's Stock: Can the New CEO Maintain the Incredible Focus on Incremental Improvement?" *Forbes*, March 22, 2012, www.forbes.com/sites/ycharts/2012/03/22/mcdonalds-stock-can-the-new-ceo-maintain-the-incredible-focus-on-incremental-improvement/; and financial and other company information and facts from www.aboutmcdonalds.com/mcd/media_center.html/invest.html and www.aboutmcdonalds.com/mcd, accessed September, 2012.

2. The NASA mission statement is from www.nasa.gov/about/highlights/what_does_nasa_do.html; accessed November 2012.

3. For more discussion of mission statements and examples, both good and bad, see Jack and Suzy Welch, "State Your Business; Too Many Mission Statements Are Loaded with Fatheaded Jargon. Play It Straight," *BusinessWeek*, January 14, 2008, p. 80, Piet Levy, "Mission vs. Vision," *Marketing News,* February 28, 2011, p. 10; Setayesh Sattari, et al., "How Readable Are Mission Statements? An Exploratory Study," *Corporate Communications*," 2011, p. 4; and www.missionstatements.com/fortune_500_mission_statements.html, accessed November 2012.

4. Information about Heinz and its mission from www.heinz.com/our-company/about-heinz/mission-and-values.aspx and www.heinz.com, accessed November 2012.

5. The following discussion is based in part on information found at www.bcg.com/documents/file13904.pdf, accessed November 2012.

6. Lisa Richwine, "Disney Earnings Beat Despite Shaky Economy," *Reuters.com*, February 8, 2012, www.reuters.com/article/2012/02/08/us-disney-idUSTRE8161TE20120208; and http://corporate.disney.go.com/investors/annual_reports.html, accessed September 2012.

7. H. Igor Ansoff, "Strategies for Diversification," *Harvard Business Review*, September–October 1957, pp. 113–124.

8. Facts in this and the following paragraphs are based on information found in Tess Steins, "Starbucks Details Plans for Energy Drink, International Expansion," *Wall Street Journal*, March 21, 2012, http://online.wsj.com/article/SB10001424052702304636404577295673557464182.html; David A. Kaplan, "Strong Coffee," *Fortune*, December 12, 2011, pp. 101–115; Jon Carter, "Starbucks: For Infusing a Steady Stream of New Ideas to Revise Its Business," *Fast Company*, March 2012, pp. 112+; and www.starbucks.com, accessed September 2012.

9. See Michael E. Porter, *Competitive Advantage: Creating and Sustaining Superior Performance* (New York: Free Press, 1985); and Michael E. Porter, "What Is Strategy?" *Harvard Business Review*, November–December 1996, pp. 61–78. Also see "The Value Chain," www.quickmba.com/strategy/value-chain, accessed July 2012; and Philip Kotler and Kevin Lane Keller, *Marketing Management*, 14th ed. (Upper Saddle River, NJ: Prentice Hall, 2012), pp. 34–35 and pp. 203–204.

10. Nirmalya Kumar, "The CEO's Marketing Manifesto," *Marketing Management*, November–December 2008, pp. 24–29; and Tom French and others, "We're All Marketers Now," McKinsey Quarterly, July 2011, www.mckinseyquarterly.com/Were_all_marketers_now_2834.

11. See http://nikeinc.com/pages/about-nike-inc, accessed September 2012.

12. BURT'S BEES® is a registered trademark of Burt's Bees, Inc. Used with permission.

13. "Advertising Spending," *Advertising Age*, December 19, 2011, p. 4.

14. The four Ps classification was first suggested by E. Jerome McCarthy, *Basic Marketing: A Managerial Approach* (Homewood, IL: Irwin, 1960). For the four Cs, other proposed classifications, and more discussion, see Robert Lauterborn, "New Marketing Litany: 4P's Passé C-Words Take Over," *Advertising Age*, October 1, 1990, p. 26; Phillip Kotler, "Alphabet Soup," *Marketing Management*, March–April 2006, p. 51; Nirmalya Kumar, "The CEO's Marketing Manifesto," *Marketing Management*, November/December 2008, pp. 24–29; and Roy McClean, "Marketing 101—4 C's versus the 4 P's of Marketing," www.customfitfocus.com/marketing-1.htm, accessed November 2012.

15. For more discussion of the chief marketing officer position, see Philip Kotler and Kevin Lane Keller, *Marketing Management*, 14th ed. (Upper Saddle River, NJ: Prentice Hall, 2012), p. 17; and Natalie Zmuda, "When CMOs Learn to Love Data, They'll Be VIPs," *Advertising Age*, February 13, 2012, p. 2.

16. Adapted from information found in Diane Brady, "Making Marketing Measure Up," *BusinessWeek*, December 13, 2004, pp. 112–113; and J. Mark Carr and Richard Schreuer, *Marketing Management*, Summer 2010, pp. 26–32.

17. Paul Albright, "Metrics Must Show Impact of Marketing on Revenue," *DM News*, December 1, 2011, p. 15; and "Study Finds Marketers Don't Practice ROI They Preach," *Advertising Age*, March 11, 2012, http://adage.com/article/233243/.

18. See "We Believe Research Should Lead to Action," *Marketing News*, November 15, 2009, p. 30; and http://marketingnpv.com/dashboard-platform, accessed September 2012.

19. For a full discussion of this model and details on customer-centered measures of return on marketing investment, see Roland T. Rust, Katherine N. Lemon, and Valerie A. Zeithaml, "Return on Marketing: Using Customer Equity to Focus Marketing Strategy," *Journal of Marketing*, January 2004, pp. 109–127; Roland T. Rust, Katherine N. Lemon, and Das Narayandas, *Customer Equity Management* (Upper Saddle River, NJ: Prentice Hall, 2005); Roland T. Rust, "Seeking Higher ROI? Base Strategy on Customer Equity," *Advertising Age*, September 10, 2007, pp. 26–27; Andreas Persson and Lynette Ryals, "Customer Assets and Customer Equity: Management and Measurement Issues," *Marketing Theory*, December 2010, pp. 417–436; and Kirsten Korosec, "'Tomāto, Tomäto'? Not Exactly," *Marketing News*, January 13, 2012, p. 8.

20. Elizabeth A. Sullivan, "Measure Up," *Marketing News*, May 30, 2009, pp. 8–17; and "Marketing Strategy: Diageo CMO: 'Workers Must Be Able to Count,'" *Marketing Week*, June 3, 2010, p. 5.

Analyzing the Marketing
Environment

Chapter Preview So far, you've learned about the basic concepts of marketing and the steps in the marketing process for building profitable relationships with targeted consumers. Next, we'll begin digging deeper into the first step of the marketing process—understanding the marketplace and customer needs and wants. In this chapter, you'll see that marketing operates in a complex and changing environment. Other actors in this environment—suppliers, intermediaries, customers, competitors, publics, and others—may work with or against the company. Major environmental forces—demographic, economic, natural, technological, political, and cultural—shape marketing opportunities, pose threats, and affect the company's ability to build customer relationships. To develop effective marketing strategies, a company must first understand the environment in which marketing operates.

To start, let's look at YouTube, the Internet video-sharing giant that burst onto the scene only a few short years ago. Last year, YouTube captured more than 1 trillion video views worldwide, giving it a 43 percent share of the online video market. To stay on top and grow profitably, however, YouTube will have to adapt nimbly to the fast-changing marketing environment.

YouTube: Adapting to the Fast-Changing Marketing Environment

Some 2,500 years ago, Greek philosopher Heraclitus observed, "Change is the only constant." That statement holds especially true today in the turbulent video entertainment industry. Today's environment is a far cry from the old days when you found video entertainment only on your TV from schedules set by the networks. Instead, consumers now face a bewildering array of choices about what they watch, when, and where. But if the fast-changing video environment befuddles consumers, it's doubly daunting for the companies that serve them.

Perhaps no company has navigated this changeable marketing environment better than Google-owned YouTube. YouTube's mission is to provide a distribution platform by which people can discover, watch, and share video entertainment. Last year, YouTube had more than 1 trillion video views worldwide—that's 140 views for every man, woman, and child on the globe. More video is uploaded to YouTube in one month than the three major U.S. networks created in 60 years. YouTube captures a stunning 43 percent of the online video market (number two is China's YouKu with only 2.3 percent). It's the third-most visited Web site on the Internet, trailing only Google (its parent company) and Facebook.

Rather than simply surviving in its chaotic environment, YouTube is thriving, leading the way in shaping how video is produced, distributed, and monetized. For the first several years, YouTube's revenues barely covered costs. Recently, however, the video-sharing site has reached the Valhalla of dot-coms. Not only is it generating mind-numbing traffic, it's also making money. With 98 of *Advertising Age's* top 100 advertisers now using YouTube as a promotional channel, the online video giant generates more than $1 billion in annual revenue for Google.

> Video-sharing giant YouTube dwarfs its competitors, capturing a 43 percent share of the online video market. But to stay on top, it will have to adapt nimbly to the turbulent marketing environment.

YouTube began as a place where regular folks could upload low-quality homemade video clips. But as the video industry has bolted forward, the company has adapted quickly. For example, YouTube's "Shows" now compete with video-streaming competitors such as Netflix and Hulu, offering an ever-expanding list of full-length films and television episodes accompanied by advertisements.

But more than just reacting to changes in the environment, YouTube wants to lead those changes. So rather than simply providing more access to traditional Hollywood-type content, YouTube created its Partner Program, which encourages aspiring Web video producers to create original new content for YouTube. In all, more than 30,000 partners in 27 countries now participate in the Partner Program, producing new content and sharing the revenue that YouTube generates from ads that accompany the videos.

Many YouTube partners have hit the big-time. As just one example, partner Ray William Johnson's channel, "=3" (Equals Three), is the most-viewed YouTube channel, with more than 5 million subscribers. The semi-weekly commentary on viral videos posted on YouTube has drawn more than 1.7 billion views, earning Johnson millions of dollars in YouTube revenue plus additional income from sales of merchandise such as Ray William Johnson bobbleheads and smartphone apps.

With all the channels now available on broadcast and cable television, you'd think there would be little need for even more video content. But YouTube sees things differently. It plans to employ the power of its vast social network by creating thousands, if not hundreds of thousands, of channels. YouTube wants to be a home for special-interest channels that have no place on network or cable TV. It aims to provide something for everyone. "On cable, there is no kitesurfing channel, no skiing channel, no piano channel," says YouTube CEO Salar Kamangar, an avid kitesurfer, skier, and pianist. "So . . . we're helping define a new way for content creators to reach an audience, and all the topics [an individual might] care about suddenly have a home."

Creating innovative content in the topsy-turvy video environment presents a big challenge. But finding new and better ways to distribute that content might be an even bigger one. YouTube's favorite distribution playground has been through PCs via the Internet. It has also expanded into mobile with a popular app that gives people full on-the-go access to YouTube. But with technology exploding, that model doesn't go far enough anymore. One YouTube executive sums up the company's broader distribution ambitions this way: "YouTube is emerging as the first global TV station, the living room for the world," taking video to people wherever they are, whenever they want it.

To become the living room for the world, however, YouTube needs to be on every available screen. Ultimately, in addition to having people access YouTube via their PCs, tablets, and phones, YouTube wants people to watch YouTube the same way they watch TV. For example, YouTube's personalized Leanback channel provides simple controls, full screen viewing, and easy browsing that "makes watching videos on YouTube as effortless as watching TV." But YouTube needs to do more if it wants to become a "most-viewed" big-screen option alongside the major TV networks and top cable channels. The average YouTube session lasts only 15 minutes, whereas the average television watcher

spends five hours a day in front of the television. To that end, YouTube is working feverishly to create an experience on the big screen that will attract more people and keep them watching longer. For example, its Personalized Channels provide dynamic streams of videos adjusted to an individual's viewing patterns, much as Pandora radio creates personalized music stations.

YouTube worked with Kraft's Philadelphia Cream Cheese brand to create an effective YouTube-based campaign, built around the Real Women of Philadelphia YouTube channel featuring Food Network chef Paula Deen.
Jarrod Weaton/Weaton Digital, Inc.

At the same time that YouTube is changing the way it produces and distributes video content, it's also trying to figure out the best way to monetize (or make money on) that content in an era when consumers still think that everything on the Internet should be free. To that end, YouTube is developing an advertising model that's built around the way people use the site, a model that best suits the needs of users, content providers, advertisers, and its own bottom line.

For example, YouTube worked with Kraft Food's Philadelphia Cream Cheese brand to create an award-winning YouTube-based campaign to show that the product is a versatile cooking ingredient and not just something you smear on bagels. Recognizing YouTube as a haven for how-to videos, the brand came up with a "Real Women of Philadelphia" (RWoP) community Web site, starring Food Network chef Paula Deen. The award-winning site and campaign revolves around YouTube-hosted videos, including Paula Deen videos posted by Kraft, "how-to" recipe videos, and cooking contests that invite users to submit their own cooking videos via YouTube.

On opening day of the first season, Kraft placed a commercial for RWoP featuring Paula Deen on YouTube's home page for $375,000. The goal was to drive traffic to the RWoP site and The Philadelphia Channel on YouTube. Although $375,000 might seem expensive, the Paula Deen commercial on YouTube was seen by 51 million people, making it much cheaper than an ad with comparable reach on primetime television. More important, 10 million people viewed the ad all the way through, and 100,000 people clicked through to the RWoP Web site. Ultimately, RWoP helped boost the brand's revenue by 35 percent,

Objective Outline

its first real sales lift in five years. "You look at those numbers; they almost don't even make sense," says Philadelphia's brand manager. "It's bigger than TV."

What does the future hold for YouTube? Stay tuned. But to remain on top, the company will have to be nimble in adapting to the ever-changing marketing environment—or better, in leading the change. To repeat the words of Heraclitus, change will be the only constant. A respected current marketing thinker puts it a little differently: "In five years, if you're still in the same business you're in now, you're going to be out of business."[1]

MyMarketingLab™

⊕ **Improve Your Grade!**

Over 10 million students improved their results using the Pearson MyLabs.
Visit **mymktlab.com** for simulations, tutorials, and end-of-chapter problems.

Marketing environment
The actors and forces outside marketing that affect marketing management's ability to build and maintain successful relationships with target customers.

A company's **marketing environment** consists of the actors and forces outside marketing that affect marketing management's ability to build and maintain successful relationships with target customers. Like YouTube, companies constantly watch and adapt to the changing environment—or, in many cases, lead those changes.

More than any other group in the company, marketers must be environmental trend trackers and opportunity seekers. Although every manager in an organization should watch the outside environment, marketers have two special aptitudes. They have disciplined methods—marketing research and marketing intelligence—for collecting information about the marketing environment. They also spend more time in customer and competitor environments. By carefully studying the environment, marketers can adapt their strategies to meet new marketplace challenges and opportunities.

The marketing environment consists of a *microenvironment* and a *macroenvironment*. The **microenvironment** consists of the actors close to the company that affect its ability to serve its customers—the company, suppliers, marketing intermediaries, customer markets, competitors, and publics. The **macroenvironment** consists of the larger societal forces that affect the microenvironment—demographic, economic, natural, technological, political, and cultural forces. We look first at the company's microenvironment.

The Microenvironment

Marketing management's job is to build relationships with customers by creating customer value and satisfaction. However, marketing managers cannot do this alone. ● **Figure 3.1** shows the major actors in the marketer's microenvironment. Marketing success requires building relationships with other company departments, suppliers, marketing intermediaries, competitors, various publics, and customers, which combine to make up the company's value delivery network.

The Company

In designing marketing plans, marketing management takes other company groups into account—groups such as top management, finance, research and development (R&D), purchasing, operations, and accounting. All of these interrelated groups form the internal environment. Top management sets the company's mission, objectives, broad strategies, and policies. Marketing managers make decisions within the broader strategies and plans made by top management. Then, as we discussed in Chapter 2, marketing managers must work closely with other company departments. With marketing taking the lead, all departments—from manufacturing and finance to legal and human resources—share the responsibility for understanding customer needs and creating customer value.

Suppliers

Suppliers form an important link in the company's overall customer value delivery network. They provide the resources needed by the company to produce its goods and services. Supplier problems can seriously affect marketing. Marketing managers must watch supply availability and costs. Supply shortages or delays, labor strikes, natural disasters, and other events can cost sales in the short run and damage customer satisfaction in the long run. Rising supply costs may force price increases that can harm the company's sales volume.

Most marketers today treat their suppliers as partners in creating and delivering customer value. For example, giant Swedish furniture retailer IKEA doesn't just buy from its suppliers. ● It involves them deeply in the process of delivering a stylish and affordable lifestyle to IKEA's customers:[2]

IKEA, the world's largest furniture retailer, is the quintessential global cult brand. Each year, customers from Beijing to Moscow to Middletown, Ohio, flock to the Scandinavian retailer's

Microenvironment

The actors close to the company that affect its ability to serve its customers—the company, suppliers, marketing intermediaries, customer markets, competitors, and publics.

Objective 1 ·····▶
Describe the environmental forces that affect the company's ability to serve its customers.

Macroenvironment

The larger societal forces that affect the microenvironment—demographic, economic, natural, technological, political, and cultural forces.

● **FIGURE | 3.1**
Actors in the Microenvironment

In creating value for customers, marketers must partner with other firms in the company's value delivery network.

Marketers must work in harmony with other company departments to create customer value and relationships.

Customers are the most important actors in the company's microenvironment. The aim of the entire value delivery system is to serve target customers and create strong relationships with them.

● **Giant Swedish furniture manufacturer IKEA doesn't just buy from suppliers. It involves them deeply in the process of delivering a stylish and affordable lifestyle to its customers worldwide.**

Used with the permission of Inter IKEA Systems B.V.

Marketing intermediaries
Firms that help the company to promote, sell, and distribute its goods to final buyers.

more than 300 huge stores in 38 countries, snapping up more than $32 billion worth of IKEA's trendy but simple and practical furniture at affordable prices. But IKEA's biggest obstacle to growth isn't opening new stores and attracting customers. Rather, it's finding enough of the right kinds of suppliers to help design and make all the products that customers will carry out of its stores. IKEA currently relies on more than 2,000 suppliers in 50 countries to stock its shelves. IKEA can't just rely on spot suppliers who might be available when needed. Instead, it must systematically develop a robust network of supplier-partners that reliably provide the more than 12,000 items it stocks. IKEA's designers start with a basic customer value proposition. Then they find and work closely with key suppliers to bring that proposition to market. Thus, IKEA does more than just buy from suppliers. It involves them deeply in questions of quality, design, and price to create the kinds of products that keep customers coming back again and again.

Marketing Intermediaries

Marketing intermediaries help the company promote, sell, and distribute its products to final buyers. They include resellers, physical distribution firms, marketing services agencies, and financial intermediaries. *Resellers* are distribution channel firms that help the company find customers or make sales to them. These include wholesalers and retailers who buy and resell merchandise. Selecting and partnering with resellers is not easy. No longer do manufacturers have many small, independent resellers from which to choose. They now face large and growing reseller organizations, such as Walmart, Target, Home Depot, Costco, and Best Buy. These organizations frequently have enough power to dictate terms or even shut smaller manufacturers out of large markets.

Physical distribution firms help the company stock and move goods from their points of origin to their destinations. *Marketing services agencies* are the marketing research firms, advertising agencies, media firms, and marketing consulting firms that help the company target and promote its products to the right markets. *Financial intermediaries* include banks, credit companies, insurance companies, and other businesses that help finance transactions or insure against the risks associated with the buying and selling of goods.

Like suppliers, marketing intermediaries form an important component of the company's overall value delivery network. In its quest to create satisfying customer relationships, the company must do more than just optimize its own performance. It must partner effectively with marketing intermediaries to optimize the performance of the entire system.

Thus, today's marketers recognize the importance of working with their intermediaries as partners rather than simply as channels through which they sell their products. For example, when Coca-Cola signs on as the exclusive beverage provider for a fast-food chain, such as McDonald's, Wendy's, or Subway, it provides much more than just soft drinks. It also pledges powerful marketing support.[3]

> Coca-Cola assigns cross-functional teams dedicated to understanding the finer points of each retail partner's business. It conducts a staggering amount of research on beverage consumers and shares these insights with its partners. It analyzes the demographics of U.S. zip code areas and helps partners determine which Coke brands are preferred in their areas. Coca-Cola has even studied the design of drive-through menu boards to better understand which layouts, fonts, letter sizes, colors, and visuals induce consumers to order more food and drink. Based on such insights, the Coca-Cola Food Service group develops marketing programs and merchandising tools that help its retail partners improve their beverage sales and profits. Its Web site, www.CokeSolutions .com, provides retailers with a wealth of information, business solutions, merchandising tips, and techniques on how to go green. "We know that you're passionate about delighting guests and enhancing their real experiences on every level," says Coca-Cola to its retail partners. "As your partner, we want to help in any way we can." Such intense partnering has made Coca-Cola a runaway leader in the U.S. fountain-soft-drink market.

Competitors

The marketing concept states that, to be successful, a company must provide greater customer value and satisfaction than its competitors do. Thus, marketers must do more than simply adapt to the needs of target consumers. They also must gain strategic advantage by positioning their offerings strongly against competitors' offerings in the minds of consumers.

No single competitive marketing strategy is best for all companies. Each firm should consider its own size and industry position compared to those of its competitors. Large firms with dominant positions in an industry can use certain strategies that smaller firms cannot afford. But being large is not enough. There are winning strategies for large firms, but there are also losing ones. And small firms can develop strategies that give them better rates of return than large firms enjoy.

Publics

Public

Any group that has an actual or potential interest in or impact on an organization's ability to achieve its objectives.

The company's marketing environment also includes various publics. A **public** is any group that has an actual or potential interest in or impact on an organization's ability to achieve its objectives. We can identify seven types of publics:

- *Financial publics:* This group influences the company's ability to obtain funds. Banks, investment analysts, and stockholders are the major financial publics.
- *Media publics:* This group carries news, features, and editorial opinion. It includes newspapers, magazines, television stations, and blogs and other Internet media.
- *Government publics:* Management must take government developments into account. Marketers must often consult the company's lawyers on issues of product safety, truth in advertising, and other matters.
- *Citizen-action publics:* A company's marketing decisions may be questioned by consumer organizations, environmental groups, minority groups, and others. Its public relations department can help it stay in touch with consumer and citizen groups.
- *Local publics:* This group includes neighborhood residents and community organizations. Large companies usually create departments and programs that deal with local community issues and provide community support. ● For example, the Life is good Company recognizes the importance of community publics. Its Life is good Playmakers program promotes the philosophy that "Life can hurt, play can heal." It provides training and support for child-care professionals to use the power of play to help children overcome challenges ranging from violence and illness to extreme poverty in cities around the world, from Danbury, Connecticut, to Port-au-Prince, Haiti. So far, the organization has raised more than $9 million to benefit children.[4]
- *General public.* A company needs to be concerned about the general public's attitude toward its products and activities. The public's image of the company affects its buying.
- *Internal publics.* This group includes workers, managers, volunteers, and the board of directors. Large companies use newsletters and other means to inform and motivate their internal publics. When employees feel good about the companies they work for, this positive attitude spills over to the external publics.

● Publics: The Life is good Company recognizes the importance of community publics. Its Life is good Playmakers program provides training and support for child-care professionals in cities around the world to use the power of play to help children overcome challenges ranging from violence and illness to extreme poverty.

The Life is good Company

A company can prepare marketing plans for these major publics as well as for its customer markets. Suppose the company wants a specific response from a particular public, such as goodwill, favorable word of mouth, or donations of time or money. The company would have to design an offer to this public that is attractive enough to produce the desired response.

Customers

As we've emphasized throughout, customers are the most important actors in the company's microenvironment. The aim of the entire value delivery network is to serve target customers and create strong relationships with them. The company might target any or all five types of customer markets. *Consumer markets* consist of individuals and households that buy goods and services for personal consumption. *Business markets* buy goods and services for further processing or use in their production processes, whereas *reseller markets* buy goods and services to resell at a profit. *Government markets* consist of government agencies that buy goods and services to produce public services or transfer the goods and services to others who need them. Finally, *international markets* consist of these buyers in other countries, including consumers, producers, resellers, and governments. Each market type has special characteristics that call for careful study by the seller.

The Macroenvironment

Objective 2 ➤
Explain how changes in the demographic and economic environments affect marketing decisions.

The company and all of the other actors operate in a larger macroenvironment of forces that shape opportunities and pose threats to the company. ● **Figure 3.2** shows the six major forces in the company's macroenvironment. Even the most dominant companies can be vulnerable to the often turbulent and changing forces in the marketing environment. Some of these forces are unforeseeable and uncontrollable. Others can be predicted and handled through skillful management. Companies that understand and adapt well to their environments can thrive. Those that don't can face difficult times (see Real Marketing 3.1). In the remaining sections of this chapter, we examine these forces and show how they affect marketing plans.

The Demographic Environment

Demography
The study of human populations in terms of size, density, location, age, gender, race, occupation, and other statistics.

Demography is the study of human populations in terms of size, density, location, age, gender, race, occupation, and other statistics. The demographic environment is of major interest to marketers because it involves people, and people make up markets. The world population is growing at an explosive rate. It now exceeds 7 billion people and is expected to grow to more than 8 billion by the year 2030.[5] The world's large and highly diverse population poses both opportunities and challenges.

Changes in the world demographic environment have major implications for business. Thus, marketers keep a close eye on demographic trends and developments in their markets. They analyze changing age and family structures, geographic population shifts, educational characteristics, and population diversity. Here, we discuss the most important demographic trends in the United States.

The Changing Age Structure of the Population

The U.S. population currently stands at more than 313 million and may reach almost 364 million by 2030.[6] The single most important demographic trend in the United States is the changing age structure of the population. The U.S. population contains several generational groups. Here, we discuss the three largest groups—the baby boomers, Generation X, and the Millennials—and their impact on today's marketing strategies.

Baby boomers
The 78 million people born during the years following World War II and lasting until 1964.

The Baby Boomers. The post–World War II baby boom produced 78 million **baby boomers**, who were born between 1946 and 1964. Over the years, the baby boomers have

● **FIGURE | 3.2**
Major Forces in the Company's Macroenvironment

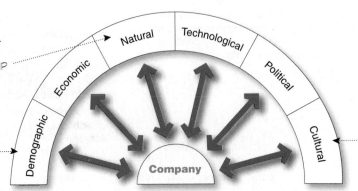

Concern for the natural environment has spawned a so-called green movement. For example, last year HP recovered and recycled 800 jumbo jets worth of electronics globally.

Changing demographics mean changes in markets and marketing strategies. For example, Merrill Lynch targets aging baby boomers to help them overcome the hurdles to retirement planning.

Marketers also want to be socially responsible citizens in their markets and communities. For example, shoe brand TOMS was founded on a cause: "No complicated formulas. It's simple," says the company's founder. "You buy a pair of TOMS and I give a pair to a child on your behalf."

Real Marketing 3.1

Sony: Battling the Marketing Environment's "Perfect Storm"

After a decade of struggle, the year 2011 was supposed to be a comeback year for Sony. The consumer electronics and entertainment giant had one its best batches of new products ever heading for store shelves. Even more important, Sony was heading back into the digital big leagues with the launch of an iTunes-like global digital network that would combine Sony's strengths in movies, music, and video games for all its televisions, PCs, phones, and tablets. Analysts forecasted a $2 billion profit. "I really and truly believed that I was going to have a year to remember," says Sony's chairman Sir Howard Stringer. "And I did, but in the wrong way."

Instead of a banner year, 2011 produced a near-perfect storm of environmental calamities for Sony. For starters, in March 2011, eastern Japan was devastated by a mammoth earthquake and tsunami. The disaster forced Sony to shutter 10 plants, disrupting operations and the flow of Sony products worldwide. In April, a hacking attack on the company's Internet entertainment services—the second-largest online data breach in U.S. history—forced the company to shut down its PlayStation Network. Only four months later, fires set by rioters in London destroyed a Sony warehouse and an estimated 25 million CDs and DVDs, gutting an inventory of 150 independent labels. To round out the year, floods in Thailand shut down component plants there.

When the rubble was cleared, Sony's projected $2 billion profit ended up as a $3.1 billion loss—the largest in 16 years. That loss marked a three-year streak of losses that had begun with yet another environmental upheaval—the Great Recession and global financial meltdown of 2008. In mid-2012, Sony's shell-shocked new CEO, Kazuo Hirai, spoke out publicly about Sony's "sense of crisis," projecting yet another annual loss in excess of a billion dollars.

There's no doubt that environmental unforeseeables have dealt Sony some heavy blows. But not all the blame for Sony's woes goes to uncontrollable environmental forces. Sony's current difficulties began long before the recent string of events. More to blame than any natural disaster has been Sony's longer-term inability to adapt to one of the most powerful environmental forces of our time—dramatic changes in technology.

Interestingly, it was Sony's magical touch with technology that first built the company into a global powerhouse. Only a dozen years ago, Sony was a high-tech rock star, a veritable merchant of cool. Not only was it the world's largest consumer electronics company, its history of innovative products—such as Trinitron TVs, Walkman portable music players, Handycam video recorders, and PlayStation video game consoles—had revolutionized entire industries. Sony's innovations drove pop culture, earned the adoration of the masses, and made money for the company. The Sony brand stood for innovation, style, and high quality.

Today, however, although still an $88-billion company, Sony is more a relic than a rock star, lost in the shadows of high-fliers such as Apple, Samsung, and Microsoft. Samsung overtook Sony as the world's largest consumer electronics maker nearly a decade ago. Samsung's sales last year bested Sony's by 50 percent, and Samsung earned profits of $14 billion while Sony lost $3.2 billion. Likewise, Apple has pounded Sony with one new product after another. "When I was young, I had to have a Sony product," summarizes one analyst, "but for the younger generation today it's Apple." Apple's zooming stock price has made it the most valuable company in history. Meanwhile, Sony's stock price recently hit a low of around $15, a stunning slide from its high of more than $300 just a decade ago. All of this has turned Sony's current "Make. Believe." brand promise into more of a "make-believe" one.

How did Sony fall so hard so fast? It fell behind in technology. Sony built its once-mighty empire based on the innovative engineering and design of standalone electronics—TVs, CD players, and video game consoles. As the Internet surged, however, creating a more connected and mobile world, standalone hardware was rapidly replaced by new connecting technologies, media, and content. As our entertainment lives swirled toward digital downloads and shared content accessed through PCs, iPods, smartphones, tablets, and Internet-ready TVs, Sony was late to adapt.

Behaving as though its superiority could never be challenged, an arrogant Sony clung to its successful old technologies rather than embracing the new. For example, prior to the launch of Apple's first iPod in 2001, Sony had already developed devices that would download and play digital music files. Sony had everything it needed to create an iPod device, including its own recording company. But it passed on that idea in favor of continued emphasis on its then-highly successful CD

The marketing environment: Environmental unforeseeables have dealt Sony some heavy blows. But the company's inability to adapt to the changing technological environment has turned Sony's current "Make. Believe." brand promise into more of a "make-believe" one.

Bloomberg via Getty Images

business. "[Apple's] Steve Jobs figured it out, we figured it out, we didn't execute," says Sony chairman Stringer. "The music guys didn't want to see the CD go away."

Similarly, as the world's largest TV producer, Sony clung to its cherished Trinitron cathode-ray-tube technology. Meanwhile, Samsung, LG, and other competitors were moving rapidly ahead with flat screens. Sony eventually responded. But today, both Samsung and LG sell more TVs than Sony. Sony's TV business, once its main profit center, has lost nearly $8.5 billion over the past eight years.

It was a similar story for Sony's PlayStation consoles, once the undisputed market leader and accounting for one-third of Sony's profits. Sony yawned when Nintendo introduced its innovative motion-sensing Nintendo Wii, dismissing it as a "niche game device." Instead, Sony engineers loaded up the PS3 with pricey technology that produced a loss of $300 per unit sold. Wii became a smash hit and the best-selling game console; the PS3 has lost billions for Sony, dropping it from first place to third.

Even as a money loser, the PS3 with its elegant blending of hardware and software had all the right ingredients to make Sony a leader in the new world of digital entertainment distribution and social networking. Executives inside Sony even recognized the PlayStation platform as the "epitome of convergence," with the potential to create "a fusion of computers and entertainment." But that vision never materialized, and Sony has lagged in the burgeoning business of connecting people to digital entertainment.

To his credit, Howard Stringer made a credible effort to reignite Sony. After taking over in 2005, he drew up a turnaround plan aimed at changing the Sony mind-set and moving the company into the new connected and mobile digital age. Under his early leadership, the consumer electronics giant began to show renewed life as revenues and profits rose. Then came the Great Recession, once again knocking the bottom out of profits. And just as Sony began digging out from that disaster, it was struck by the string of 2011 environmental calamities.

Thus, environmental forces—whether unforeseeable natural and economic events or more predictable turns in technology—can heavily impact company strategy. Sony's difficult times provide a cautionary tale of what can happen when a company—even a dominant market leader—fails to adapt to its changing marketing environment. Despite the setbacks, however, giant Sony still has a lot going for it. It recently announced new plans to revitalize its core electronics businesses through renewed innovation. Now, if Sony can just get the economy and Mother Nature to cooperate. . . .

Sources: Bryan Gruley and Cliff Edwards, "Sony Needs a Hit," *Bloomberg Businessweek*, November 21, 2011, pp. 72–77; Mariko Yasu and Cliff Edwards, "Sony's Hirai Vows to Deliver Stringer Vision with Cost Cuts," *Bloomberg Businessweek*, February 5, 2012, www.businessweek.com/news/2012-02-05/sony-s-hirai-vows-to-deliver-stringer-vision-with-cost-cuts.html, and information from www.sony.net/SonyInfo/IR/, accessed September 2012.

been one of the most powerful forces shaping the marketing environment. The youngest boomers are now moving into their fifties; the oldest are in their late sixties and entering retirement. The maturing boomers are rethinking the purpose and value of their work, responsibilities, and relationships.

After years of prosperity, free spending, and saving little, the Great Recession hit many baby boomers hard, especially the preretirement boomers. A sharp decline in stock prices and home values ate into their nest eggs and retirement prospects. As a result, many boomers are now spending more carefully and planning to work longer.

However, although some might be feeling the postrecession pinch, the baby boomers are still the wealthiest generation in U.S. history. Today's baby boomers account for about 25 percent of the U.S. population but control an estimated 80 percent of the nation's personal wealth. The 50-plus consumer segment now accounts for nearly half of all discretionary consumer spending.[7] As they reach their peak earning and spending years, the boomers will continue to constitute a lucrative market for financial services, new housing and home remodeling, new cars, travel and entertainment, eating out, health and fitness products, and just about everything else.

It would be a mistake to think of the older boomers as phasing out or slowing down. Today's boomers think young no matter how old they are. One study showed that boomers, on average, see themselves as 12 years younger than they actually are. And rather than viewing themselves as phasing out, they see themselves as entering new life phases. The more active boomers—sometimes called zoomers, or baby boomers with zip—have no intention of abandoning their youthful lifestyles as they age. For example, a recent study found that whereas 9 percent of baby boomers attended the symphony or opera during the previous 12 months, 12 percent attended a rock concert. "Baby Boomers represent a segment of the American population that has a thirst for adventure, and the financial freedom to explore that passion," notes one expert. Says another, "They are showing the nation that their heyday is far from over by taking pleasure in life's adventures."[8]

🔵 Targeting baby boomers: Travel companies such as ElderTreks target active boomers who have the time, resources, and passion for high-adventure travel but prefer to do it with others their own age—no young'uns allowed.

ELDERTREKS

Generation X

The 49 million people born between 1965 and 1976 in the "birth dearth" following the baby boom.

For example, many travel companies—such as ElderTreks, 50PlusExpeditions, and Row Adventures—now design adventure travel expeditions for active baby boomers. 🔵 ElderTreks, for instance, offers small-group, off-the-beaten-path tours designed exclusively for people 50 and over. Whether it's for wildlife and tribal African safari, active hiking in the Himalayas or Andes, or an expedition by icebreaker to the Artic or Antarctic, ElderTreks targets active boomers who have the time, resources, and passion for high-adventure travel but prefer to do it with others their own age—no young'uns allowed.[9]

Generation X. The baby boom was followed by a "birth dearth," creating another generation of 49 million people born between 1965 and 1976. Author Douglas Coupland calls them **Generation X** because they lie in the shadow of the boomers and lack obvious distinguishing characteristics.

Considerably smaller that the boomer generation that precedes them and the Millennials who follow, the Generation Xers are a sometimes overlooked consumer group. Although they seek success, they are less materialistic than the other groups; they prize experience, not acquisition. For many of the Gen Xers who are parents, family comes first—both children and their aging parents—and career second. From a marketing standpoint, the Gen Xers are a more skeptical bunch. They tend to research products before they consider a purchase, prefer quality to quantity, and tend to be less receptive to overt marketing pitches. They are more likely to be receptive to irreverent ad pitches that make fun of convention and tradition.

The first to grow up in the Internet era, Generation X is a highly connected generation that embraces the benefits of new technology. Some 49 percent own smartphones and 11 percent own tablets. Of the Xers on the Internet, 74 percent use the Internet for banking, 72 percent use it for researching companies or products, and 81 percent have made purchases online. Ninety-five percent have a Facebook page.

The Gen Xers have now grown up and are taking over. They are increasingly displacing the lifestyles, culture, and values of the baby boomers. They are moving up in their careers, and many are proud homeowners with growing families. They are the most educated generation to date, and they possess hefty annual purchasing power. They spend 62 percent more on housing, 50 percent more on apparel, and 27 percent more on entertainment than the average. However, like the baby boomers, the Gen Xers now face growing economic pressures. Like almost everyone else these days, they are spending more carefully.[10]

Still, with so much potential, many brands and organizations are focusing on Gen Xers as a prime target segment. 🔵 For example, Dairy Queen targets this segment directly, with a marketing campaign that fits the Gen Xer family situation and sense of humor:[11]

Generation X is Dairy Queen's new sweet spot. Its primary target market—parents roughly 34 to 44 years old with young children—falls squarely within the Gen X cohort. So what does that mean for DQ's marketing? A "So Good It's RiDQulous" advertising campaign loaded with irreverent Gen X humor—as in old-fashioned shaving bunnies, a guitar that sounds like a dolphin, fencing ninjas, and kittens in bubbles. In one ad, DQ's new pitchman—a mustachioed 30-something—touts Dairy Queen birthday cakes, then says, "And we don't just blow bubbles, we blow bubbles with kittens inside them [which he then does], because at Dairy Queen, good isn't good enough." In another ad, the DQ spokesperson exclaims, "We don't just have piñatas, we have piñatas filled with Mary Lou Retton." With a flair, he smashes the piñata and out falls Retton (a former

🔵 Targeting Gen Xers: Dairy Queen's "So Good It's RiDQulous" campaign targets Gen Xers with irreverent humor and online ad placements.

American Dairy Queen Corporation

Olympic gymnast and iconic Gen Xer). To reach Gen X consumers better, DQ has shifted a batch of its ads from TV to online sites such as Hulu. "We're going where our Gen X customers' eyeballs are," says DQ's chief brand officer. Gen Xers appear to like the "So Good It's RiDQulous" ads. An independent study last year found the ads to be the most effective in the quick service restaurant segment.

Millennials (or Generation Y)
The 83 million children of the baby boomers born between 1977 and 2000.

Millennials. Both the baby boomers and Gen Xers will one day be passing the reins to the **Millennials** (also called **Generation Y** or the echo boomers). Born between 1977 and 2000, these children of the baby boomers number 83 million or more, dwarfing the Gen Xers and becoming larger even than the baby boomer segment.[12] In the postrecession era, the Millennials are the most financially strapped generation. Facing higher unemployment and saddled with more debt, many of these young consumers have near-empty piggy banks. Still, because of their numbers, the Millennials make up a huge and attractive market, both now and in the future.

One thing that all Millennials have in common is their utter fluency and comfort with digital technology. They don't just embrace technology; it's a way of life. The Millennials were the first generation to grow up in a world filled with computers, mobile phones, satellite TV, iPods and iPads, and online social networks. As a result, they engage with brands in an entirely new way, such as with mobile or social media. "They tend to expect one-to-one communication with brands," says one analyst, "and embrace the ability to share the good and bad about products and services with friends and strangers."[13]

Rather than having mass-marketing messages pushed at them, the Millennials prefer to seek out information and engage in two-way brand conversations. Thus, reaching them effectively requires creative marketing approaches. ● For example, consider Keds, the 95-year-old sneaker brand, which recently launched an integrative marketing campaign aimed at reintroducing the iconic brand to young Millennial consumers.[14]

● Targeting Millennials: The Keds "How Do You Do?" campaign urges young Millennial consumers to engage, create, and collaborate, emphasizing Keds sneakers as a canvas used to express that creativity.
Xiao Chang/The Daily Pennsylvanian

The Keds campaign—called "How Do You Do?"—engages the Millennials firsthand through print ads, a micro Web site, YouTube videos, Twitter, Facebook, brand ambassadors, artists, and a mobile campus tour. At the heart of the campaign is a 32-foot white Keds shoebox on wheels, which is making a cross-country tour of college campuses. The arts-based campaign urges Millennials to engage, create, and collaborate, emphasizing Keds sneakers as a canvas for expressing that creativity. Inside the mobile shoebox, visitors can watch videos about the local artists, retail outlets, and charity organizations that Keds is working with in each city. They can also see a gallery of locally inspired Keds shoes or even use a touch-screen kiosk to customize and purchase their own sneakers at the Keds Web site. Other campaign elements expand on the "How Do You Do?" campaign slogan. As it tours from city to city, the campaign asks Millennials questions to tweet about, such as "How Do You Do Austin?" or "How Do You Do Inspiration?" or, simply, "How Do You Do Keds?" "We really feel that what's important to this consumer is to engage with a brand and experience [it] firsthand," says Keds president Kristin Kohler.

Generational Marketing. Do marketers need to create separate products and marketing programs for each generation? Some experts warn that marketers need to be careful about turning off one generation each time they craft a product or message that appeals effectively to another. Others caution that each generation spans decades of time and many socioeconomic levels. For example, marketers often split the baby boomers into three smaller groups—leading-edge boomers, core boomers, and trailing-edge boomers—each with its own beliefs and behaviors. Similarly, they split the Millennials into teens and young adults.

Thus, marketers need to form more precise age-specific segments within each group. More important, defining people by their birth date may be less effective than segmenting them by their lifestyle, life stage, or the common values they seek in the products they buy. We will discuss many other ways to segment markets in Chapter 7.

The Changing American Family

The traditional household consists of a husband, wife, and children (and sometimes grand-parents). Yet, the once American ideal of the two-child, two-car suburban family has lately been losing some of its luster.

In the United States today, married couples with children represent only 20 percent of the nation's 118 million households, half that of 1970. Married couples without children represent 29 percent, and single parents are another 17 percent. A full 34 percent are non-family households—singles living alone or adults of one or both sexes living together.[15] More people are divorcing or separating, choosing not to marry, marrying later, or marrying without intending to have children. Marketers must increasingly consider the special needs of nontraditional households because they are now growing more rapidly than traditional households. Each group has distinctive needs and buying habits.

The number of working women has also increased greatly, growing from under 40 per-cent of the U.S. workforce in the late 1950s to 59 percent today. Among households made up of married couples with children, 65 percent are dual-income households; only the husband works in 28 percent. Meanwhile, more men are staying home with their children and man-aging the household while their wives go to work. Four percent of married couples with children in the United States have a full-time stay-at-home dad.[16]

The significant number of women in the workforce has spawned the child day-care business and increased the consumption of career-oriented women's clothing, convenience foods, financial services, and time-saving services. Royal Caribbean targets time-crunched working moms with budget-friendly family vacations that are easy to plan and certain to wow the family. Royal Caribbean estimates that, although vacations are a joint decision, 80 percent of all trips are planned and booked by women—moms who are pressed for time, whether they work or not. "We want to make sure that you're the hero, that when your family comes on our ship, it's going to be a great experience for all of them," says a senior marketer at Royal Caribbean, "and that you, mom, who has done all the planning and scheduling, get to enjoy that vacation."[17]

Geographic Shifts in Population

This is a period of great migratory movements between and within countries. Americans, for example, are a mobile people, with about 12 percent of all U.S. residents moving each year. Over the past two decades, the U.S. population has shifted toward the Sunbelt states. The West and South have grown, whereas the Midwest and Northeast states have lost pop-ulation.[18] Such population shifts interest marketers because people in different regions buy differently. For example, people in the Midwest buy more winter clothing than people in the Southeast.

Also, for more than a century, Americans have been moving from rural to metropoli-tan areas. In the 1950s, they made a massive exit from the cities to the suburbs. Today, the migration to the suburbs continues. And more and more Americans are moving to "micropolitan areas," small cities located beyond congested metropolitan areas, such as Bozeman, Montana; Natchez, Mississippi; and Torrington, Connecticut. These smaller mi-cros offer many of the advantages of metro areas—jobs, restaurants, diversions, community organizations—but without the population crush, traffic jams, high crime rates, and high property taxes often associated with heavily urbanized areas.[19]

The shift in where people live has also caused a shift in where they work. For example, the migration toward micropolitan and suburban areas has resulted in a rapid increase in the number of people who "telecommute"—work at home or in a remote office and conduct their business by phone or the Internet. This trend, in turn, has created a booming SOHO (small office/home office) market. An increasing number of people are working from home with the help of electronic conveniences such as PCs, smartphones, and broadband Internet access. One recent study estimates that 24 percent of employed individuals did some or all of their work at home.[20]

Many marketers are actively courting the lucrative telecommuting market. For exam-ple, WebEx, the Web-conferencing division of Cisco, helps connect people who telecom-mute or work remotely. With WebEx, people can meet and collaborate online via computer or smartphone, no matter what their work location. ● Additionally, companies such as Regus or Grind rent out fully equipped shared office space by the day or month for telecom-muters and others who work away from the main office.[21]

● **Serving the telecommuter market: Companies such as Grind rent out shared office space by the day or month to telecommuters and others who work away from the main office.**

Grind, LLC

A Better-Educated, More White-Collar, More Professional Population

The U.S. population is becoming better educated. For example, in 2010, 87 percent of the U.S. population over age 25 had completed high school and 30 percent had completed college, compared with 66 percent and 16 percent, respectively, in 1980. Moreover, more than two-thirds of high school graduates now enroll in college within 12 months of graduating.[22] The workforce also is becoming more white collar. Job growth is now strongest for professional workers and weakest for manufacturing workers. Between 2010 and 2020, of 30 detailed occupations projected to have the fastest employment growth, 17 require some type of postsecondary education.[23] The rising number of educated professionals will affect not just what people buy but also how they buy.

Increasing Diversity

Countries vary in their ethnic and racial makeup. At one extreme is Japan, where almost everyone is Japanese. At the other extreme is the United States, with people from virtually all national origins. The United States has often been called a melting pot, where diverse groups from many nations and cultures have melted into a single, more homogenous whole. Instead, the United States seems to have become more of a "salad bowl" in which various groups have mixed together but have maintained their diversity by retaining and valuing important ethnic and cultural differences.

Marketers now face increasingly diverse markets, both at home and abroad, as their operations become more international in scope. The U.S. population is about 65 percent white, with Hispanics at about 16 percent and African Americans at about 13 percent. The U.S. Asian American population now totals 4.7 percent of the total U.S. population, with the remaining 1.3 percent being Native Hawaiian, Pacific Islander, American Indian, Eskimo, Aleut, or people of two or more races. Moreover, more than 40 million people living in the United States—about 13 percent of the population—were born in another country. The nation's ethnic populations are expected to explode in coming decades. By 2050, Hispanics will be an estimated 30 percent of the population, African Americans will hold steady at about 13 percent, and Asians will increase to 8 percent.[24]

Most large companies, from P&G, Walmart, Allstate, and Bank of America to Levi Strauss and Harley-Davidson, now target specially designed products, ads, and promotions to one or more of these groups. For example, Harley-Davidson recently launched a print and online campaign celebrating the dedication and pride of Hispanic Harley riders, or Harlistas, and their relationships with the brand. Harley even invited Hispanic riders to share their own experiences about what being a part of the Harlista community means to them. It showcases the passion and commitment of Harlistas in a documentary—*Harlistas: An American Journey*—directed by an award-winning director. "Being a Harlista," says one ad, "is about living fearlessly, overcoming obstacles, and experiencing the camaraderie of the open road." In addition, Harley-Davidson has long been a supporter of the Latin Billboard Music Awards, Lowrider Tours, Los Angeles' Fiesta Broadway, and one of the largest Hispanic motorcycle clubs in the United States, the Latin American Motorcycle Association (LAMA).[25]

Diversity goes beyond ethnic heritage. For example, many major companies explicitly target gay and lesbian consumers. According to one estimate, the 6 to 7 percent of U.S. adults who identify themselves as lesbian, gay, bisexual, and transgender (LGBT) have buying power of more than $790 billion.[26] As a result of TV shows such as *Modern Family* and *Glee*, movies like *Brokeback Mountain* and *The Kids Are All Right*, and openly gay celebrities and public figures such as Neil Patrick Harris, Ellen DeGeneres, David Sedaris, and Congressman Barney Frank, the LGBT community has increasingly emerged in the public eye.

A number of media now provide companies with access to this market. For example, Planet Out Inc., a leading global media and entertainment company that exclusively serves the LGBT community, offers several successful magazines (*Out*, *The Advocate*, *Out Traveler*) and Web sites (Gay.com and PlanetOut.com). In addition, media giant Viacom's

MTV Networks offer LOGO, a cable television network aimed at gays and lesbians and their friends and family. LOGO is now available in 46 million U.S. households. More than 100 mainstream marketers have advertised on LOGO, including Ameriprise Financial, Anheuser-Busch, Continental Airlines, Dell, Levi Strauss, eBay, J&J, Orbitz, Sears, Sony, and Subaru.

Companies in a wide range of industries are now targeting the LGBT community with gay-specific ads and marketing efforts. For example, American Airlines has a dedicated LGBT sales team, sponsors gay community events, and offers a special gay-oriented Web site (www.aa.com/rainbow) that features travel deals, an e-newsletter, podcasts, and a gay events calendar. The airline's focus on gay consumers has earned it double-digit revenue growth from the LGBT community each year for more than a decade.[27]

● Targeting consumers with disabilities: Samsung features people with disabilities in its mainstream advertising and signs endorsement deals with Paralympic athletes.

GEPA/Imago/Icon SMI/Newscom

Another attractive diversity segment is the 54 million U.S. adults with disabilities—a market larger than African Americans or Hispanics—representing more than $220 billion in annual spending power. Most individuals with disabilities are active consumers. For example, one study found that the segment spends $13.6 billion on 31.7 million business or leisure trips every year. And if certain needs were met, the amount spent on travel could double to $27 billion annually.[28]

How are companies trying to reach consumers with disabilities? Many marketers now recognize that the worlds of people with disabilities and those without disabilities are one in the same. Marketers such as McDonald's, Verizon Wireless, Nike, Samsung, and Honda have featured people with disabilities in their mainstream marketing. ● For instance, Samsung and Nike sign endorsement deals with Paralympic athletes and feature them in advertising.

As the population in the United States grows more diverse, successful marketers will continue to diversify their marketing programs to take advantage of opportunities in fast-growing segments.

The Economic Environment

Economic environment

Economic factors that affect consumer purchasing power and spending patterns.

Markets require buying power as well as people. The **economic environment** consists of economic factors that affect consumer purchasing power and spending patterns. Marketers must pay close attention to major trends and consumer spending patterns both across and within their world markets.

Nations vary greatly in their levels and distribution of income. Some countries have *industrial economies*, which constitute rich markets for many different kinds of goods. At the other extreme are *subsistence economies*; they consume most of their own agricultural and industrial output and offer few market opportunities. In between are *developing economies* that can offer outstanding marketing opportunities for the right kinds of products.

Consider India with its population of more than 1.2 billion people. In the past, only India's elite could afford to buy a car. In fact, only one in seven Indians currently owns one. But recent dramatic changes in India's economy have produced a growing middle class and rapidly rising incomes. Now, to meet the new demand, European, North American, and Asian automakers are introducing smaller, more affordable vehicles in India. But they'll have to find a way to compete with India's Tata Motors, which markets the least expensive car ever in the world, the Tata Nano. Dubbed "the people's car," the Nano sells for just over 158,000 rupees (about US$2,900). It can seat four passengers, gets 50 miles per gallon, and travels at a top speed of 65 miles per hour. The ultralow-cost car is designed to be India's Model T—the car that puts the developing nation on wheels. ● "Can you imagine a car within the reach of all?" asks a Nano advertisement. "Now you can," comes the answer. Tata hopes to sell 1 million of these vehicles per year.[29]

Changes in Consumer Spending

Economic factors can have a dramatic effect on consumer spending and buying behavior. For example, until fairly recently, American consumers spent freely, fueled by income

● **Economic environment: To capture India's growing middle class, Tata Motors introduced the small, affordable Tata Nano. "Can you imagine a car within the reach of all?" asks this advertisement. "Now you can."**

Tata Motors Ltd.

Natural environment
The physical environment and the natural resources that are needed as inputs by marketers or that are affected by marketing activities.

Objective 3 ┈┈►
Identify the major trends in the firm's natural and technological environments.

growth, a boom in the stock market, rapid increases in housing values, and other economic good fortunes. They bought and bought, seemingly without caution, amassing record levels of debt. However, the free spending and high expectations of those days were dashed by the Great Recession of 2008/2009.

As a result, as discussed in Chapter 1, consumers have now adopted a back-to-basics sensibility in their lifestyles and spending patterns that will likely persist for years to come. They are buying less and looking for greater value in the things that they do buy. In turn, *value marketing* has become the watchword for many marketers. Marketers in all industries are looking for ways to offer today's more financially frugal buyers greater value—just the right combination of product quality and good service at a fair price.

You'd expect value pitches from the sellers of everyday products. For example, as Target has shifted emphasis toward the "Pay less" side of its "Expect more. Pay less." slogan, the once-chic headlines at the Target.com Web site have been replaced by more practical appeals such as "Our lowest prices of the season," "Fun, sun, save," and "Free shipping, every day." However, these days, even luxury-brand marketers are emphasizing good value. For instance, upscale car brand Infiniti now promises to "make luxury affordable."

Income Distribution

Marketers should pay attention to *income distribution* as well as income levels. Over the past several decades, the rich have grown richer, the middle class has shrunk, and the poor have remained poor. The top 5 percent of American earners get nearly 22 percent of the country's adjusted gross income, and the top 20 percent of earners capture over 50 percent of all income. In contrast, the bottom 40 percent of American earners get just 12 percent of the total income.[30]

This distribution of income has created a tiered market. Many companies—such as Nordstrom and Neiman Marcus—aggressively target the affluent. Others—such as Dollar General and Family Dollar—target those with more modest means. In fact, dollar stores are now the fastest-growing retailers in the nation. Still other companies tailor their marketing offers across a range of markets, from the affluent to the less affluent. For example, Ford offers cars ranging from the low-priced Ford Fiesta, starting at $13,200, to the luxury Lincoln Navigator SUV, starting at $57,775.

Changes in major economic variables, such as income, cost of living, interest rates, and savings and borrowing patterns, have a large impact on the marketplace. Companies watch these variables by using economic forecasting. Businesses do not have to be wiped out by an economic downturn or caught short in a boom. With adequate warning, they can take advantage of changes in the economic environment.

The Natural Environment

The **natural environment** involves the physical environment and the natural resources that are needed as inputs by marketers or that are affected by marketing activities. At the most basic level, unexpected happenings in the physical environment—anything from weather to natural disasters—can affect companies and their marketing strategies. For example, a recent unexpectedly warm winter put the chill on sales of products ranging from cold-weather apparel to facial tissues and Campbell's soups. In contrast, the warmer weather boosted demand for products such as hiking and running shoes, house paint, and gardening supplies. Similarly, the damage caused by the recent earthquake and tsunami in Japan had a devastating effect on the ability of Japanese companies such as Sony and Toyota to meet worldwide demand for their products. Although companies can't prevent such natural occurrences, they should prepare contingency plans for dealing with them.[31]

At a broader level, environmental sustainability concerns have grown steadily over the past three decades. In many cities around the world, air and water pollution have reached dangerous levels. World concern continues to mount about the possibilities of global warming, and many environmentalists fear that we soon will be buried in our own trash.

Marketers should be aware of several trends in the natural environment. The first involves growing shortages of raw materials. Air and water may seem to be infinite resources, but some groups see long-run dangers. Air pollution chokes many of the world's large cities, and water shortages are already a big problem in some parts of the United States and the world. By 2030, more than one in three people in the world will not have enough water to drink.[32] Renewable resources, such as forests and food, also have to be used wisely. Nonrenewable resources, such as oil, coal, and various minerals, pose a serious problem. Firms making products that require these scarce resources face large cost increases, even if the materials remain available.

A second environmental trend is *increased pollution*. Industry will almost always damage the quality of the natural environment. Consider the disposal of chemical and nuclear wastes; the dangerous mercury levels in the ocean; the quantity of chemical pollutants in the soil and food supply; and the littering of the environment with nonbiodegradable bottles, plastics, and other packaging materials.

A third trend is *increased government intervention* in natural resource management. The governments of different countries vary in their concern and efforts to promote a clean environment. Some, such as the German government, vigorously pursue environmental quality. Others, especially many poorer nations, do little about pollution, largely because they lack the needed funds or political will. Even richer nations lack the vast funds and political accord needed to mount a worldwide environmental effort. The general hope is that companies around the world will accept more social responsibility and that less expensive devices can be found to control and reduce pollution.

In the United States, the Environmental Protection Agency (EPA) was created in 1970 to create and enforce pollution standards and conduct pollution research. In the future, companies doing business in the United States can expect continued strong controls from government and pressure groups. Instead of opposing regulation, marketers should help develop solutions to the material and energy problems facing the world.

Concern for the natural environment has spawned the so-called green movement. Today, enlightened companies go beyond what government regulations dictate. They are developing strategies and practices that support **environmental sustainability**— an effort to create a world economy that the planet can support indefinitely. Environmental sustainability means meeting present needs without compromising the ability of future generations to meet their needs.

Many companies are responding to consumer demands with more environmentally responsible products. Others are developing recyclable or biodegradable packaging, recycled materials and components, better pollution controls, and more energy-efficient operations. ● For example, Timberland's mission is about more than just making rugged, high-quality boots, shoes, clothes, and other outdoor gear. The brand is about doing everything it can to reduce the environmental footprint of its products and processes.[33]

> Timberland is on a mission to develop processes and products that cause less harm to the environment and to enlist consumers in the cause. For example, it has a solar-powered distribution center in California and a wind-powered factory in the Dominican Republic. It has installed energy-efficient lighting and equipment retrofits in its facilities and is educating workers about production efficiency. Timberland is constantly looking for and inventing innovative materials that allow it to reduce its impact on the planet while at the same time making better gear. Its Earthkeepers line of boots is made from recycled and organic materials, and the brand has launched footwear collections featuring outsoles made from recycled car tires. Plastic from recycled soda bottles goes into its breathable linings and durable shoe laces. Coffee grounds find a place in its odor-resistant jackets. Organic cotton without toxins makes it into its rugged canvas. To inspire consumers to make more sustainable decisions, Timberland puts Green Index tags on its products that rate each item's ecological footprint in terms of climate impact, chemicals used, and resources consumed. To pull it all together, Timberland launched an Earthkeeper's campaign, an online social networking effort that seeks to inspire people to take actions to lighten their environmental footprints.

Environmental sustainability

Developing strategies and practices that create a world economy that the planet can support indefinitely.

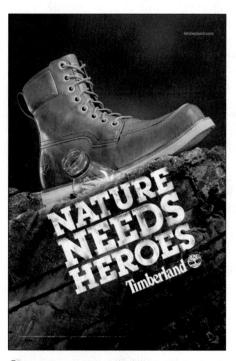

● **Environmental sustainability: Timberland is on a mission to do everything it can to reduce its impact on the planet while at the same time making better outdoor gear.**

The Timberland Company

Companies today are looking to do more than just good deeds. More and more, they are recognizing the link between a healthy ecology and a healthy economy. They are learning that environmentally responsible actions can also be good business.

The Technological Environment

Technological environment
Forces that create new technologies, creating new product and market opportunities.

The **technological environment** is perhaps the most dramatic force now shaping our destiny. Technology has released such wonders as antibiotics, robotic surgery, miniaturized electronics, smartphones, and the Internet. It also has released such horrors as nuclear missiles, chemical weapons, and assault rifles. It has released such mixed blessings as the automobile, television, and credit cards. Our attitude toward technology depends on whether we are more impressed with its wonders or its blunders.

New technologies can offer exciting opportunities for marketers. For example, what would you think about having tiny little transmitters implanted in all the products you buy, which would allow tracking of the products from their point of production through use and disposal? On the one hand, it would provide many advantages to both buyers and sellers. On the other hand, it could be a bit scary. Either way, it's already happening:

> Envision a world in which every product contains a tiny transmitter, loaded with information. As you stroll through supermarket aisles, shelf sensors detect your selections and beam ads to your smart phone, offering special deals on related products. As your cart fills, scanners detect that you might be buying for a dinner party; your phone lights up to suggest a wine to go with the meal you've planned. When you leave the store, exit scanners total up your purchases and automatically charge them to your credit card. At home, readers track what goes into and out of your pantry, updating your shopping list when stocks run low. For Sunday dinner, you pop a Butterball turkey into your "smart oven," which follows instructions from an embedded chip and cooks the bird to perfection. Seem far-fetched? Not really. In fact, it might soon become a reality, thanks to radio-frequency identification (RFID) transmitters that can be embedded in the products you buy.

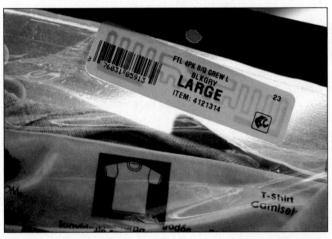

● **Technological environment: Envision a world in which every product contains a transmitter loaded with information. In fact, it's already happening on the back of RFID product labels like this one at Walmart.**

Marc F. Henning/Alamy

Many firms are already using RFID technology to track products through various points in the distribution channel. ● For example, Walmart has strongly encouraged suppliers shipping products to its distribution centers to apply RFID tags to their pallets. So far, more than 600 Walmart suppliers are doing so. And retailers such as American Apparel, Macy's, Bloomingdales, and JCPenney are now installing item-level RFID systems in their stores.[34]

The technological environment changes rapidly. Think of all of today's common products that were not available 100 years ago—or even 30 years ago. Abraham Lincoln did not know about automobiles, airplanes, radios, or the electric light. Woodrow Wilson did not know about television, aerosol cans, automatic dishwashers, air conditioners, antibiotics, or computers. Franklin Delano Roosevelt did not know about xerography, synthetic detergents, birth control pills, jet engines, or earth satellites. John F. Kennedy did not know about PCs, the Internet, or Google, and Ronald Reagan knew nothing about smartphones or Facebook.

New technologies create new markets and opportunities. However, every new technology replaces an older technology. Transistors hurt the vacuum-tube industry, digital photography hurt the film business, and MP3 players and digital downloads are hurting the CD business. When old industries fought or ignored new technologies, their businesses declined. Thus, marketers should watch the technological environment closely. Companies that do not keep up will soon find their products outdated. If that happens, they will miss new product and market opportunities.

As products and technology become more complex, the public needs to know that these items are safe. Thus, government agencies investigate and ban potentially unsafe products. In the United States, the Food and Drug Administration (FDA) has created complex regulations for testing new drugs. The Consumer Product Safety Commission (CPSC) establishes safety standards for consumer products and penalizes companies that fail to meet them. Such regulations have resulted in much higher research costs and longer times between new product ideas and their introduction. Marketers should be aware of these regulations when applying new technologies and developing new products.

Objective 4 ····►
Explain the key changes in the political and cultural environments.

Political environment

Laws, government agencies, and pressure groups that influence and limit various organizations and individuals in a given society.

The Political and Social Environment

Marketing decisions are strongly affected by developments in the political environment. The **political environment** consists of laws, government agencies, and pressure groups that influence or limit various organizations and individuals in a given society.

Legislation Regulating Business

Even the strongest advocates of free-market economies agree that the system works best with at least some regulation. Well-conceived regulation can encourage competition and ensure fair markets for goods and services. Thus, governments develop *public policy* to guide commerce—sets of laws and regulations that limit business for the good of society as a whole. Almost every marketing activity is subject to a wide range of laws and regulations.

Legislation affecting business around the world has increased steadily over the years. The United States and many other countries have many laws covering issues such as competition, fair trade practices, environmental protection, product safety, truth in advertising, consumer privacy, packaging and labeling, pricing, and other important areas (see ● **Table 3.1**).

Understanding the public policy implications of a particular marketing activity is not a simple matter. In the United States, there are many laws created at the national, state, and local levels, and these regulations often overlap. For example, aspirins sold in Dallas are governed by both federal labeling laws and Texas state advertising laws. Moreover, regulations are constantly changing; what was allowed last year may now be prohibited, and what was prohibited may now be allowed. Marketers must work hard to keep up with changes in regulations and their interpretations.

Business legislation has been enacted for a number of reasons. The first is to *protect companies* from each other. Although business executives may praise competition, they sometimes try to neutralize it when it threatens them. Therefore, laws are passed to define and prevent unfair competition. In the United States, such laws are enforced by the Federal Trade Commission (FTC) and the Antitrust Division of the Attorney General's office.

The second purpose of government regulation is to *protect consumers* from unfair business practices. Some firms, if left alone, would make shoddy products, invade consumer privacy, mislead consumers in their advertising, and deceive consumers through their packaging and pricing. Rules defining and regulating unfair business practices are enforced by various agencies.

The third purpose of government regulation is to *protect the interests of society* against unrestrained business behavior. Profitable business activity does not always create a better quality of life. Regulation arises to ensure that firms take responsibility for the social costs of their production or products.

International marketers will encounter dozens, or even hundreds, of agencies set up to enforce trade policies and regulations. In the United States, Congress has established federal regulatory agencies, such as the FTC, the FDA, the Federal Communications Commission, the Federal Energy Regulatory Commission, the Federal Aviation Administration, the Consumer Product Safety Commission, the Environmental Protection Agency, and hundreds of others. Because such government agencies have some discretion in enforcing the laws, they can have a major impact on a company's marketing performance.

New laws and their enforcement will continue to increase. Business executives must watch these developments when planning their products and marketing programs. Marketers need to know about the major laws protecting competition, consumers, and society. They need to understand these laws at the local, state, national, and international levels.

Increased Emphasis on Ethics and Socially Responsible Actions

Written regulations cannot possibly cover all potential marketing abuses, and existing laws are often difficult to enforce. However, beyond written laws and regulations, business is also governed by social codes and rules of professional ethics.

● **Table 3.1** | **Major U.S. Legislation Affecting Marketing**

Legislation	Purpose
Sherman Antitrust Act (1890)	Prohibits monopolies and activities (price-fixing, predatory pricing) that restrain trade or competition in interstate commerce.
Federal Food and Drug Act (1906)	Created the Food and Drug Administration (FDA). It forbids the manufacture or sale of adulterated or fraudulently labeled foods and drugs.
Clayton Act (1914)	Supplements the Sherman Act by prohibiting certain types of price discrimination, exclusive dealing, and tying clauses (which require a dealer to take additional products in a seller's line).
Federal Trade Commission Act (1914)	Established the Federal Trade Commission (FTC), which monitors and remedies unfair trade methods.
Robinson-Patman Act (1936)	Amends the Clayton Act to define price discrimination as unlawful. Empowers the FTC to establish limits on quantity discounts, forbid some brokerage allowances, and prohibit promotional allowances except when made available on proportionately equal terms.
Wheeler-Lea Act (1938)	Makes deceptive, misleading, and unfair practices illegal regardless of injury to competition. Places advertising of food and drugs under FTC jurisdiction.
Lanham Trademark Act (1946)	Protects and regulates distinctive brand names and trademarks.
National Traffic and Safety Act (1958)	Provides for the creation of compulsory safety standards for automobiles and tires.
Fair Packaging and Labeling Act (1966)	Provides for the regulation of the packaging and labeling of consumer goods. Requires that manufacturers state what the package contains, who made it, and how much it contains.
Child Protection Act (1966)	Bans the sale of hazardous toys and articles. Sets standards for child-resistant packaging.
Federal Cigarette Labeling and Advertising Act (1967)	Requires that cigarette packages contain the following statement: "Warning: The Surgeon General Has Determined That Cigarette Smoking Is Dangerous to Your Health."
National Environmental Policy Act (1969)	Establishes a national policy on the environment. The 1970 Reorganization Plan established the Environmental Protection Agency (EPA).
Consumer Product Safety Act (1972)	Establishes the Consumer Product Safety Commission and authorizes it to set safety standards for consumer products as well as exact penalties for failing to uphold those standards.
Magnuson-Moss Warranty Act (1975)	Authorizes the FTC to determine rules and regulations for consumer warranties and provides consumer access to redress, such as the class action suit.
Children's Television Act (1990)	Limits the number of commercials aired during children's programs.
Nutrition Labeling and Education Act (1990)	Requires that food product labels provide detailed nutritional information.
Telephone Consumer Protection Act (1991)	Establishes procedures to avoid unwanted telephone solicitations. Limits marketers' use of automatic telephone dialing systems and artificial or prerecorded voices.
Americans with Disabilities Act (1991)	Makes discrimination against people with disabilities illegal in public accommodations, transportation, and telecommunications.
Children's Online Privacy Protection Act (2000)	Prohibits Web sites or online services operators from collecting personal information from children without obtaining consent from a parent and allowing parents to review information collected from their children.
Do-Not-Call Implementation Act (2003)	Authorizes the FTC to collect fees from sellers and telemarketers for the implementation and enforcement of a National Do-Not-Call Registry.
CAN-SPAM Act (2003)	Regulates the distribution and content of unsolicited commercial e-mail.
Financial Reform Law (2010)	Created the Bureau of Consumer Financial Protection, which writes and enforces rules for the marketing of financial products to consumers. It is also responsible for enforcement of the Truth-in-Lending Act, the Home Mortgage Disclosure Act, and other laws designed to protect consumers.

Socially Responsible Behavior. Enlightened companies encourage their managers to look beyond what the regulatory system allows and simply "do the right thing." These socially responsible firms actively seek out ways to protect the long-run interests of their consumers and the environment.

Almost every aspect of marketing involves ethics and social responsibility issues. Unfortunately, because these issues usually involve conflicting interests, well-meaning people can honestly disagree about the right course of action in a given situation. Thus, many industrial and professional trade associations have suggested codes of ethics. And more companies are now developing policies, guidelines, and other responses to complex social responsibility issues.

The boom in Internet marketing has created a new set of social and ethical issues. Critics worry most about online privacy issues. There has been an explosion in the amount of personal digital data available. Users, themselves, supply some of it. They voluntarily place highly private information on social networking sites, such as Facebook or LinkedIn, or on genealogy sites that are easily searched by anyone with a computer or a smartphone.

However, much of the information is systematically developed by businesses seeking to learn more about their customers, often without consumers realizing that they are under the microscope. Legitimate businesses track consumers' Internet browsing and buying behavior and collect, analyze, and share digital data from every move consumers make at their online sites. Critics worry that these companies may now know *too* much and might use digital data to take unfair advantage of consumers. Although most companies fully disclose their Internet privacy policies and most try to use data to benefit their customers, abuses do occur. As a result, consumer advocates and policymakers are taking action to protect consumer privacy. In Chapter 20, we discuss these and other societal marketing issues in greater depth.

Cause-Related Marketing. To exercise their social responsibility and build more positive images, many companies are now linking themselves to worthwhile causes. These days, every product seems to be tied to some cause. For example, Toyota recently ran a "100 Cars for Good" program in which it gave a new car to a deserving nonprofit every day for 100 consecutive days based on consumer voting on its Facebook page. The P&G Tide Loads of Hope program provides mobile laundromats and loads of clean laundry to families in disaster-stricken areas—P&G washes, dries, and folds clothes for these families for free. ● Down the street, needy people will probably find the P&G Duracell Power Relief Trailer, which provides free batteries and flashlights as well as charging stations for phones and laptops. Walgreens sponsors a "Walk with Walgreens" program—do simple things like walk and log your steps, hit your goals, or just comment on other walkers' posts at the Web site and you'll be rewarded with coupons and exclusive offers from Bayer, Vaseline, Degree, Slimfast, Dr. Scholls, or another program partner.

Some companies are founded entirely on cause-related missions. Under the concept of "values-led business" or "caring capitalism," their mission is to use business to make the world a better place. For example, TOMS Shoes was founded as a for-profit company—it wants to make money selling shoes. But the company has an equally important not-for-profit mission—putting shoes on the feet of needy children around the world. For every pair of shoes you buy from TOMS, the company will give another pair to a child in need on your behalf.

Cause-related marketing has become a primary form of corporate giving. It lets companies "do well by doing good" by linking purchases of the company's products or services with benefiting worthwhile causes or charitable organizations. At TOMS Shoes, the "do well" and "do good" missions go hand in hand. Beyond being socially admirable, the buy-one-give-one-away concept is also a good business proposition. "Giving not only makes you feel good, but it actually is a very good business strategy," says TOMS founder Blake Mycoskie. "Business and charity or public service don't have to be mutually exclusive. In fact, when they come together, they can be very powerful."[35]

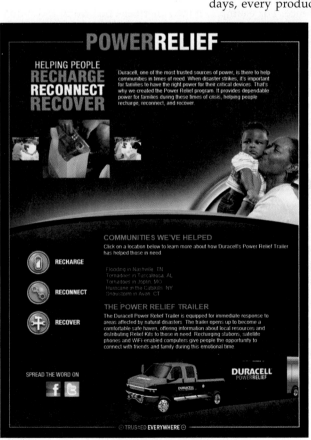

● **Cause-related marketing: The P&G Duracell Power Relief Trailer Program provides free batteries and flashlights as well as charging stations for phones and laptops to people in disaster-stricken areas.**

The Procter & Gamble Company

Cause-related marketing has stirred some controversy. Critics worry that cause-related marketing is more a strategy for selling than a strategy for giving—that "cause-related" marketing is really "cause-exploitative" marketing. Thus, companies using cause-related marketing might find themselves walking a fine line between increased sales and an improved image and facing charges of exploitation. For example, following the 2011 Japanese tsunami disaster, Microsoft's Bing search engine created a backlash when it posted a message on Twitter offering to donate $1 to Japan's relief efforts each time someone forwarded its message. The tweet set off a firestorm of complaints from Twitter users, who accused Bing of using the tragedy as a marketing opportunity. Microsoft quickly apologized.[36]

However, if handled well, cause-related marketing can greatly benefit both the company and the cause. The company gains an effective marketing tool while building a more positive public image. The charitable organization or cause gains greater visibility and important new sources of funding and support. Spending on cause-related marketing in the United States skyrocketed from only $120 million in 1990 to $1.73 billion in 2012.[37]

The Cultural Environment

Cultural environment

Institutions and other forces that affect society's basic values, perceptions, preferences, and behaviors.

The **cultural environment** consists of institutions and other forces that affect a society's basic values, perceptions, preferences, and behaviors. People grow up in a particular society that shapes their basic beliefs and values. They absorb a worldview that defines their relationships with others. The following cultural characteristics can affect marketing decision making.

The Persistence of Cultural Values

People in a given society hold many beliefs and values. Their core beliefs and values have a high degree of persistence. For example, most Americans believe in individual freedom, hard work, getting married, and achievement and success. These beliefs shape more specific attitudes and behaviors found in everyday life. *Core* beliefs and values are passed on from parents to children and are reinforced by schools, churches, business, and government.

Secondary beliefs and values are more open to change. Believing in marriage is a core belief; believing that people should get married early in life is a secondary belief. Marketers have some chance of changing secondary values but little chance of changing core values. For example, family-planning marketers could argue more effectively that people should get married later than not get married at all.

Shifts in Secondary Cultural Values

Although core values are fairly persistent, cultural swings do take place. Consider the impact of popular music groups, movie personalities, and other celebrities on young people's hairstyle and clothing norms. Marketers want to predict cultural shifts to spot new opportunities or threats. The major cultural values of a society are expressed in people's views of themselves and others, as well as in their views of organizations, society, nature, and the universe.

People's Views of Themselves. People vary in their emphasis on serving themselves versus serving others. Some people seek personal pleasure, wanting fun, change, and escape. Others seek self-realization through religion, recreation, or the avid pursuit of careers or other life goals. Some people see themselves as sharers and joiners; others see themselves as individualists. People use products, brands, and services as a means of self-expression, and they buy products and services that match their views of themselves.

For example, ads for Sherwin Williams paint—headlined "Make the most for your color with the very best paint"—seem to appeal to older, more practical do-it-yourselfers. By contrast, Benjamin Moore's ads, along with its Facebook and other social media pitches, appeal to younger, more outgoing fashion individualists. ● One Benjamin Moore print ad—consisting of a single long line of text in a crazy quilt of fonts—describes Benjamin Moore's Hot Lips paint color this way: "It's somewhere between the color of your lips when you go outside in December with your hair still wet and the color of a puddle left by

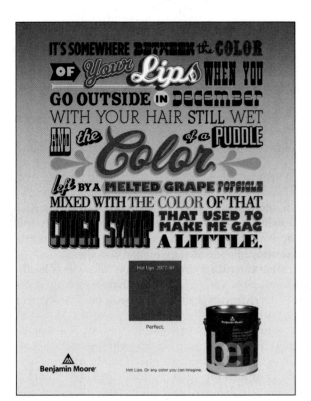

People's self-views: In its ads, Benjamin Moore appeals to people who view themselves as outgoing fashion individualists.

Courtesy of Benjamin Moore Paints

a melted grape popsicle mixed with the color of that cough syrup that used to make me gag a little. Hot lips. Perfect."

People's Views of Others. People's attitudes toward and interactions with others shift over time. In recent years, some analysts have voiced concerns that the Internet age would result in diminished human interaction, as people buried their heads in their computers or e-mailed and texted rather than interacting personally. Instead, today's digital technologies seem to have launched an era of what one trend watcher calls "mass mingling." Rather than interacting less, people are using online social media and mobile communications to connect more than ever. And, often, more online and mobile interactions result in more offline mingling:[38]

> More people than ever [are] living large parts of their lives online. Yet, those same people also mingle, meet up, and congregate more often with other "warm bodies" in the offline world. In fact, social media and mobile communications are fueling a *mass mingling* that defies virtually every cliché about diminished human interaction in our "online era." Ironically, the same technology that was once condemned for turning entire generations into mobile gaming zombies and avatars is now deployed to get people *out* of their homes.
>
> Basically, the more [people] date and network and twitter and socialize online, the more likely they are to eventually meet up with friends and followers in the real world. Thanks to social networking services such as Facebook (whose more than one billion fans spend more than 700 billion minutes a month on the site), people are developing more diverse social networks, defying the notion that technology pulls people away from social engagement. Rather than being more isolated, people today are increasingly tapping into their networks of friends.

This new way of interacting strongly affects how companies market their brands and communicate with customers. "Consumers are increasingly tapping into their networks of friends, fans, and followers to discover, discuss, and purchase goods and services in ever-more sophisticated ways," says one analyst. "As a result, it's never been more important for brands to make sure they [tap into these networks] too."[39]

People's Views of Organizations. People vary in their attitudes toward corporations, government agencies, trade unions, universities, and other organizations. By and large, people are willing to work for major organizations and expect them, in turn, to carry out society's work.

The past two decades have seen a sharp decrease in confidence in and loyalty toward America's business and political organizations and institutions. In the workplace, there has been an overall decline in organizational loyalty. Waves of company downsizings bred cynicism and distrust. In just the last decade, major corporate scandals, rounds of layoffs resulting from the recent recession, the financial meltdown triggered by Wall Street bankers' greed and incompetence, and other unsettling activities have resulted in a further loss of confidence in big business. Many people today see work not as a source of satisfaction but as a required chore to earn money to enjoy their nonwork hours. This trend suggests that organizations need to find new ways to win consumer and employee confidence.

People's Views of Society. People vary in their attitudes toward their society—patriots defend it, reformers want to change it, and malcontents want to leave it. People's orientation to their society influences their consumption patterns and attitudes toward the marketplace. American patriotism has been increasing gradually for the past two decades. It surged, however, following the September 11, 2001, terrorist attacks and the Iraq War. For example, the summer following the start of the Iraq War saw a surge of pumped-up Americans visiting U.S. historic sites, ranging from the Washington, D.C., monuments, Mount Rushmore, the Gettysburg battlefield, and the *USS Constitution* ("Old Ironsides") to Pearl Harbor and the Alamo. Following these peak periods, patriotism in the United States still remains high. A recent global survey on "national pride" found Americans tied for number one among the 17 democracies polled.[40]

Marketers respond with patriotic products and promotions, offering everything from orange juice to clothing to cars with patriotic themes. For example, ads for PepsiCo's Tropicana Pure Premium orange juice proclaim that the brand is "100% pure Florida orange juice—made from oranges grown, picked, and squeezed in Florida." Chrysler's "Imported from Detroit" campaign, which declared that "the world's going to hear the roar of our engines," resonated strongly with Americans consumers.[41] Although most of these marketing efforts are tasteful and well received, waving the red, white, and blue can sometimes prove tricky. Flag-waving promotions can be viewed as corny, or as attempts to cash in on the nation's triumphs or tragedies. Marketers must take care when responding to such strong national emotions.

People's Views of Nature. People vary in their attitudes toward the natural world—some feel ruled by it, others feel in harmony with it, and still others seek to master it. A long-term trend has been people's growing mastery over nature through technology and the belief that nature is bountiful. More recently, however, people have recognized that nature is finite and fragile; it can be destroyed or spoiled by human activities.

This renewed love of things natural has created a 63-million-person "lifestyles of health and sustainability" (LOHAS) market, consumers who seek out everything from natural, organic, and nutritional products to fuel-efficient cars and alternative medicine. This segment spends nearly $300 billion annually on such products.[42]

Tom's of Maine caters to such consumers with sustainable, all-natural personal care products—toothpaste, deodorant, mouthwash, and soap—made with no artificial colors, flavors, fragrances, or preservatives.[43] The products are also "cruelty-free" (no animal testing or animal ingredients). Tom's makes sustainable practices a priority in every aspect of its business and strives to maximize recycled content and recyclability of its packaging. Finally, Tom's donates 10 percent of its pretax profits to charitable organizations. ● In all, Tom's "makes uncommonly good products that serve the common good."

Food producers have also found fast-growing markets for natural and organic products. In total, the U.S. organic food market generated nearly $29 billion in sales last year, more than doubling over the past five years. Niche marketers, such as Whole Foods Market, have sprung up to serve this market, and traditional food chains, such as Kroger and Safeway, have added separate natural and organic food sections. Even pet owners are joining the movement as they become more aware of what goes into Fido's food. Almost every major pet food brand now offers several types of natural foods.[44]

People's Views of the Universe. Finally, people vary in their beliefs about the origin of the universe and their place in it. Although most Americans practice religion, religious conviction and practice have been dropping off gradually through the years. According to a recent poll, 16 percent of Americans now say they are not affiliated with any particular faith, almost double the percentage of 18 years earlier. Among Americans ages 18 to 29, 25 percent say they are not currently affiliated with any particular religion.[45]

However, the fact that people are dropping out of organized religion doesn't mean that they are abandoning their faith. Some futurists have noted a renewed interest in spirituality, perhaps as a part of a broader search for a new inner purpose. People have been moving away from materialism and dog-eat-dog ambition to seek more permanent values—family, community, earth, faith—and a more certain grasp of right and wrong. Rather than calling it "religion," they call it "spirituality."[46]

The **whitening** you want, **naturally!**

clinically proven | natural

SIMPLY WHITE®

whitening | cavity protection | fresh breath
fluoride toothpaste
clean mint

What makes a product good? At Tom's, it includes how we make it.

No animal testing or animal ingredients.

No artificial colors, flavors, fragrance, or preservatives.

Sustainable practices are a priority in every aspect of our business.

We share every ingredient, its purpose, and its source at www.tomsofmaine.com.

We strive to maximize recycled content and recyclability of our packaging.

5% (12 days) of employee time to volunteering. 10% of profits to human and environmental goodness.

Bring back the natural beauty of your smile! Try Simply white® today!

© 2011 Tom's of Maine

● Riding the trend toward all things natural: Tom's of Maine "makes uncommonly good products that serve the common good."
Tom's of Maine

This changing spiritualism affects consumers in everything from the television shows they watch and the books they read to the products and services they buy.

Objective 5 ······ ▶
Discuss how companies can react to the marketing environment.

Responding to the Marketing Environment

Someone once observed, "There are three kinds of companies: those who make things happen, those who watch things happen, and those who wonder what's happened." Many companies view the marketing environment as an uncontrollable element to which they must react and adapt. They passively accept the marketing environment and do not try to change it. They analyze environmental forces and design strategies that will help the company avoid the threats and take advantage of the opportunities the environment provides.

Other companies take a *proactive* stance toward the marketing environment. "Instead of letting the environment define their strategy," advises one marketing expert, "craft a strategy that defines your environment."[47] Rather than assuming that strategic options are bounded by the current environment, these firms develop strategies to change the environment. "Business history . . . reveals plenty of cases in which firms' strategies shape industry structure," says the expert, "from Ford's Model T to Nintendo's Wii."

Even more, rather than simply watching and reacting to environmental events, these firms take aggressive actions to affect the publics and forces in their marketing environment. Such companies hire lobbyists to influence legislation affecting their industries and stage media events to gain favorable press coverage. They run "advertorials" (ads expressing editorial points of view) and blogs to shape public opinion. They press lawsuits and file complaints with regulators to keep competitors in line, and they form contractual agreements to better control their distribution channels.

By taking action, companies can often overcome seemingly uncontrollable environmental events. For example, whereas some companies try to hush up negative talk about their products, others proactively counter false information. Taco Bell did this when its brand fell victim to potentially damaging claims about the quality of the beef filling in its tacos.[48]

> When a California woman's class-action suit questioned whether Taco Bell's meat filling could accurately be labeled "beef," the company's reaction was swift and decisive. The suit claimed that Taco Bell's beef filling is 65 percent binders, extenders, preservatives, additives, and other agents. It wanted Taco Bell to stop calling it "beef." But Taco Bell fought back quickly with a major counterattack campaign, in print and on YouTube and Facebook. In full-page ads in the *Wall Street Journal,* the *New York Times,* and *USAToday,* the company boldly thanked those behind the lawsuit for giving it the opportunity to tell the "truth" about its "seasoned beef," which it claimed contains only quality beef with other ingredients added to maintain the product's flavor and quality. Taco Bell further announced that it would take legal action against those making the false statements. The company's proactive counter-campaign quickly squelched the false information in the lawsuit, which was voluntarily withdrawn only a few months later.

Marketing management cannot always control environmental forces. In many cases, it must settle for simply watching and reacting to the environment. For example, a company would have little success trying to influence geographic population shifts, the economic environment, or major cultural values. But whenever possible, smart marketing managers take a *proactive* rather than *reactive* approach to the marketing environment (see Real Marketing 3.2).

Real Marketing 3.2

When the Dialog Gets Nasty:
Turning Negatives into Positives

Marketers have hailed the Internet as the great new relational medium. Companies use the Web to engage customers, gain insights into their needs, and create customer community. In turn, Web-empowered consumers share their brand experiences with companies and with each other. All of this back-and-forth helps both the company and its customers. But sometimes, the dialog can get nasty. Consider the following examples:

- Upon receiving a severely damaged computer monitor via FedEx, YouTube user goobie55 posts footage from his security camera. The video clearly shows a FedEx delivery man hoisting the monitor package over his head and tossing it over goobie55's front gate, without ever attempting to ring the bell, open the gate, or walk the package to the door. The video—with FedEx's familiar purple and orange logo prominently displayed on everything from the driver's shirt to the package and the truck—goes viral with 5 million hits in just five days. TV news and talk shows go crazy discussing the clip.
- Molly Katchpole, a 22-year-old nanny living in Washington, D.C., gets mad when she learns that Bank of America is imposing a $5-a-month fee on debit card users. She starts a petition on Change.org, declaring: "The American people bailed out Bank of America during a financial crisis the banks helped create. How can you justify squeezing another $60 a year from your debit card customers? This is despicable." In less than a month, the petition garners more than 300,000 signatures from similarly enraged consumers.
- When United Airlines rejects musician Dave Carroll's damage claim after its baggage handlers break his guitar, he produces a catchy music video, "United Breaks Guitars," and posts it on YouTube. "I should've flown with someone else or gone by car," he despairs in the video. "'Cause United breaks guitars." The video becomes one of YouTube's greatest hits—nearly 12 million people have now viewed it—and causes an instant media frenzy across major global networks.
- When 8-year-old Harry Winsor sends a crayon drawing of an airplane he's designed to Boeing with a suggestion that they might

want to manufacture it, the company responds with a stern, legal-form letter. "We do not accept unsolicited ideas," the letter states. "We regret to inform you that we have disposed of your message and retain no copies." The embarrassing blunder would probably go unnoticed were it not for the fact that Harry's father—John Winsor, a prominent ad exec—blogs and tweets about the incident, making it instant national news.

Extreme events? Not anymore. The Internet has turned the traditional power relationship between businesses and consumers upside down. In the good old days, disgruntled consumers could do little more than bellow at a company service rep or shout out their complaints from a street corner. Now, armed with only a PC or a smartphone, they can take it public, airing their gripes to millions on blogs, chats, online social networks, or even hate sites devoted exclusively to their least favorite corporations.

"I hate" and "sucks" sites are almost commonplace. These sites target some highly respected companies with some highly disrespectful labels: Walmartblows.com; PayPalSucks .com (aka NoPayPal); IHateStarbucks.com; DeltaREALLYsucks.com; and UnitedPackage Smashers.com (UPS), to name only a few. "Sucks" videos on YouTube and other video sites also abound. For example, a search of "Apple sucks" on YouTube turns up 12,900 videos; a similar search for Microsoft finds 17,900 videos. An "Apple sucks" search on Facebook links to hundreds of groups. If you don't find one you like, try "Apple suks" or "Apple sux" for hundreds more.

Some of these sites, videos, and other online attacks air legitimate complaints that should be addressed. Others, however, are little more than anonymous, vindictive slurs that unfairly ransack brands and corporate reputations. Some of the attacks are only a passing nuisance; others can draw serious attention and create real headaches.

How should companies react to online attacks? The real quandary for targeted

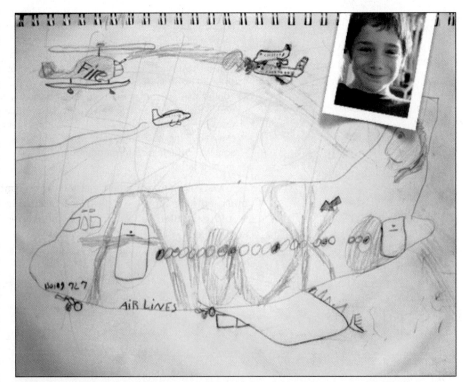

Today's empowered consumers: Boeing's embarrassing blunder over young Harry Winsor's airplane design made instant national news. However, Boeing quickly took responsibility and turned the potential PR disaster into a positive.

John Winsor

companies is figuring out how far they can go to protect their images without fueling the already raging fire. One point on which all experts seem to agree: Don't try to retaliate in kind. "It's rarely a good idea to lob bombs at the fire starters," says one analyst. "Preemption, engagement, and diplomacy are saner tools."

Some companies have tried to silence the critics through lawsuits, but few have succeeded. The courts have tended to regard such criticism as opinion and, therefore, protected speech. In general, attempts to block, counterattack, or shut down consumer attacks may be shortsighted. Such criticisms are often based on real consumer concerns and unresolved anger. Hence, the best strategy might be to proactively monitor these sites and respond to the concerns they express. "The most obvious thing to do is talk to the customer and try to deal with the problem, instead of putting your fingers in your ears," advises one consultant.

For example, Boeing quickly took responsibility for mishandling aspiring Harry Winsor's designs, turning a potential PR disaster into a positive. It called and invited young Harry to visit Boeing's facilities. On its corporate Twitter site, it confessed "We're experts at airplanes but novices in social media. We're learning as we go." Similarly, FedEx drew praise by immediately posting its own YouTube video addressing the monitor-smashing incident. In the video, FedEx Senior Vice President of Operations Matthew Thornton stated that he had personally met with the aggrieved customer, who had accepted the company's apology. "This goes directly against all FedEx values," declared Thornton. The FedEx video struck a responsive chord. Numerous journalists and bloggers responded with stories about FedEx's outstanding package handling and delivering record.

Bank of America and United, however, haven't fared so well. After Bank of America finally backed down and reversed the debit card user fees, an executive eventually called Katchpole to explain. But by then, it had already lost her as a customer. And after Dave Carroll's YouTube video went platinum, United belatedly offered to pay for his ruined guitar. Carroll politely declined but thanked the company for boosting his career. Today Carroll is a professional public speaker and author on the topic of customer service. He also founded Gripevine.com, "the first online social media platform for consumer-complaint resolution." Perhaps United will soon be a client.

Many companies have now created teams of specialists that monitor online conversations and engage unhappy consumers. For example, Dell has set up a 40-member "communities and conversation team," which does outreach on Twitter and Facebook and communicates with bloggers. The social media team at Southwest Airlines includes a chief Twitter officer who tracks Twitter comments and monitors Facebook groups, an online representative who checks facts and interacts with bloggers, and another person who takes charge of the company's presence on sites such as YouTube, Flickr, and LinkedIn. So if someone posts an online complaint, the company can respond in a personal way.

Thus, by listening and proactively responding to seemingly uncontrollable events in the environment, companies can prevent the negatives from spiraling out of control or even turn them into positives. Who knows? With the right responses, Walmart-blows.com might even become Walmart-rules.com. Then again, probably not.

Sources: Quotes, excerpts, and other information from Gregory Karp, "United Breaks Guitars Spawns Complaint Site," *McClatchy-Tribune Business News*, February 3, 2012; Nicholas D. Kristof, "After Recess: Change the World," *New York Times*, February 4, 2012, p. SR11; Vanessa Ko, "FedEx Apologizes after Video of Driver Throwing Fragile Package Goes Viral," *Time*, December 23, 2011, http://newsfeed.time.com/2011/12/23/fedex-apologizes-after-video-of-driver-throwing-fragile-package-goes-viral/; Michelle Conlin, "Web Attack," *BusinessWeek,* April 16, 2007, pp. 54–56; "Boeing's Social Media Lesson," May 3, 2010, http://mediadecoder.blogs.nytimes.com/2010/05/03/boeings-social-media-lesson/; Ben Nuckols, "Part-Time Nanny Helps to End Bank of America Fee," *Herald-Sun (Durham),* November 4, 2011, p. A4; www.youtube.com/watch?v55YGc4zOqozo and www.youtube.com/watch?v5C5ulH0VTg_o, accessed June 2012; and "Corporate Hate Sites," New Media Institute, www.newmedia.org/articles/corporate-hate-sites---nmi-white-paper.html, accessed September 2012.

Reviewing the Concepts

MyMarketingLab™
Go to **mymktlab.com** to complete the problems marked with this icon .

Reviewing Objectives and Key Terms

 Objectives Review

In this chapter and the next three chapters, you'll examine the environments of marketing and how companies analyze these environments to better understand the marketplace and consumers. Companies must constantly watch and manage the *marketing environment* to seek opportunities and ward off threats. The marketing environment consists of all the actors and forces influencing the company's ability to transact business effectively with its target market.

Objective 1 Describe the environmental forces that affect the company's ability to serve its customers. (pp 71–74)

The company's *microenvironment* consists of actors close to the company that combine to form its value delivery network or that affect its ability to serve its customers. It includes the company's *internal environment*—its several departments and management levels—as it influences marketing decision making. *Marketing channel firms*—suppliers, marketing intermediaries, physical distribution firms, marketing services agencies, and financial intermediaries—cooperate to create customer value. *Competitors* vie with the company in an effort to serve customers better. Various *publics* have an actual or potential interest in or impact on the company's ability to meet its objectives. Finally, five types of customer *markets* exist: consumer, business, reseller, government, and international markets.

The *macroenvironment* consists of larger societal forces that affect the entire microenvironment. The six forces making up the company's macroenvironment are demographic, economic, natural, technological, political/social, and cultural forces. These forces shape opportunities and pose threats to the company.

Objective 2 Explain how changes in the demographic and economic environments affect marketing decisions. (pp 74–82)

Demography is the study of the characteristics of human populations. Today's *demographic environment* shows a changing age structure, shifting family profiles, geographic population shifts, a better-educated and more white-collar population, and increasing diversity. The *economic environment* consists of factors that affect buying power and patterns. The economic environment is characterized by more frugal consumers who are seeking greater value—the right combination of good quality and service at a fair price. The distribution of income also is shifting. The rich have grown richer, the middle class has shrunk, and the poor have remained poor, leading to a two-tiered market.

Objective 3 Identify the major trends in the firm's natural and technological environments. (pp 82–84)

The *natural environment* shows three major trends: shortages of certain raw materials, higher pollution levels, and more government intervention in natural resource management. Environmental concerns create marketing opportunities for alert companies. The *technological environment* creates both opportunities and challenges. Companies that fail to keep up with technological change will miss out on new product and marketing opportunities.

Objective 4 Explain the key changes in the political and cultural environments. (pp 85–91)

The *political environment* consists of laws, agencies, and groups that influence or limit marketing actions. The political environment has undergone changes that affect marketing worldwide: increasing legislation regulating business, strong government agency enforcement, and greater emphasis on ethics and socially responsible actions. The *cultural environment* consists of institutions and forces that affect a society's values, perceptions, preferences, and behaviors. The environment shows trends toward "mass mingling," a lessening trust of institutions, increasing patriotism, greater appreciation for nature, a changing spiritualism, and the search for more meaningful and enduring values.

Objective 5 Discuss how companies can react to the marketing environment. (pp 91–93)

Companies can passively accept the marketing environment as an uncontrollable element to which they must adapt, avoiding threats and taking advantage of opportunities as they arise. Or they can take a *proactive* stance, working to change the environment rather than simply reacting to it. Whenever possible, companies should try to be proactive rather than reactive.

 Key Terms

Objective 1

Marketing environment (p 70)
Microenvironment (p 71)
Macroenvironment (p 71)
Marketing intermediaries (p 72)
Public (p 73)

Objective 2

Demography (p 74)
Baby boomers (p 74)
Generation X (p 77)
Millennials (Generation Y) (p 78)
Economic environment (p 81)

Objective 3

Natural environment (p 82)
Environmental sustainability (p 83)
Technological environment (p 84)

Objective 4

Political environment (p 85)
Cultural environment (p 88)

Discussion and Critical Thinking

 Discussion Questions

1. Compare and contrast a company's microenvironment with a company's macroenvironment. (AACSB: Communication)

2. Describe the five types of customer markets. (AACSB: Communication)

3. Compare and contrast core beliefs/values and secondary beliefs/values. Provide an example of each and discuss the potential impact marketers have on each. (AACSB: Communication; Reflective Thinking)

4. How should marketers respond to the changing environment? (AACSB: Communication)

 ## Critical Thinking Exercises

1. The Wall Street Reform and Consumer Protection Act of 2010 created the Consumer Financial Protection Bureau (CFPB). Learn about this act and the responsibilities of the CFPB, then write a brief report about how the act impacts businesses and consumers. (AACSB: Communication; Use of IT)

 2. Cause-related marketing has grown considerably over the past 10 years. Visit www.causemarketingforum.com to learn about companies that have won Halo Awards for outstanding cause-related marketing programs. Present an award-winning case study to your class. (AACSB: Communication; Use of IT)

3. Various federal agencies impact marketing activities. Research each of the following agencies, discuss the elements of marketing that are impacted by each agency, and present a recent marketing case or issue on which each agency has focused. (AACSB: Communication; Reflective Thinking)
a. Federal Trade Commission (www.ftc.gov)
b. Food and Drug Administration (www.fda.gov)
c. Consumer Product Safety Commission (www.cpsc.gov)

Applications and Cases

 ## Marketing Technology Crowdfunding

If you have a great product idea but no money, never fear, there's Kickstarter, an online crowdfunding site. Founded in 2008, Kickstarter enables companies to raise money from multiple individuals and has helped launch more than 60,000 projects. Pebble Technology Corporation created a "smart" wristwatch called Pebble, which works with iPhones or Android phones, but didn't have the funding to produce and market the device. So young CEO Eric Migicovsky turned to Kickstarter for crowdfunding. His modest goal was to raise $100,000, but the company raised $1 million in only one day and a total of $10.27 million in just over one month! Nearly 70,000 people preordered the $115 watch, and Pebble now has to deliver on the promise. Kickstarter takes a 5 percent fee on the total funds raised and Amazon Payments handles the processing of the funds. Kickstarter charges pledgers' credit cards and the project

creator receives the funds within only a few weeks. The JOBS Act legislation signed into law in 2012 provides a legal framework for this type of financing, which is expected to grow even faster as a result. However, Kickstarter and similar sites don't guarantee that the projects will be delivered as promised, and some people are concerned that crowd*funding* will beget crowd*frauding*.

1. Find another crowdfunding site and describe two projects featured on that site. (AACSB: Communication; Use of IT; Reflective Thinking)

2. Learn more about the JOBS Act and how it impacts crowdfunding for start-up businesses. What protections are in place for investors with regard to crowdfrauding? (AACSB: Communication; Use of IT; Reflective Thinking)

 ## Marketing Ethics Targeting Children Online

The almost 24 percent of the U.S. population under 18 years old wields billions of dollars in purchasing power. Companies such as eBay and Facebook want to capitalize on those dollars—legitimately, that is. EBay is exploring ways to allow consumers under 18 years old to set up legitimate accounts to buy and sell goods. Children already trade on the site, either through their parents' accounts or through accounts set up after they lie about their ages. Similarly, even though children under 13 are not allowed to set up Facebook accounts, about 7.5 million of them have accounts, and nearly 5 million account holders are under 10 years old. That translates to almost 20 percent of U.S. 10-year-olds and 70 percent of 13-year-olds active on Facebook.

Many of these accounts were set up with parental knowledge and assistance. Both eBay and Facebook say that protections will be put in place on children's account and that parents will be able to monitor to their children's accounts.

 1. Debate the pros and cons of allowing these companies to target children. Are these efforts socially responsible behavior? (AACSB: Communication; Reflective Thinking; Ethical Reasoning)

2. Review the Children's Online Privacy Protection Act at www.coppa.org/. Explain how eBay and Facebook can target this market and still comply with this act. (AACSB: Communication; Use of IT; Reflective Thinking)

Marketing by the Numbers Demographic Trends

Do you know Danica from the Philippines, Peter from London, Nargis from India, Marina from Russia, Chieko from Japan, or Miran from the United States? These are some of the babies whose parents claimed they were the 7th billion human born into the world. The world population continues to grow, even though women are having fewer children than before. Markets are made up of people, and to stay competitive, marketers must know where populations are located and where they are going. The fertility rate in the United States is declining and the population is aging, creating opportunities as well as threats for marketers. That is why tracking and predicting demographic trends are so important in marketing. Marketers must plan to capitalize on opportunities and deal with the threats before it is too late.

1. Develop a presentation on a specific demographic trend in the United States. Explain the reasons behind this trend and discuss the implications for marketers. (AACSB: Communication; Analytical Reasoning)

2. Discuss global demographic trends. What are the implications of those trends and how should marketers respond to them? (AACSB: Communication; Reflective Thinking)

Video Case Ecoist

At least one company has taken the old phrase "One man's trash is another man's treasure" and turned it into a business model. Ecoist is a company that uses discarded packaging materials from multinational brands like Coca-Cola, Frito-Lay, Disney, and Mars to craft high-end handbags that would thrill even the most discriminating fashionistas.

When the company first started in 2004, consumer perceptions of goods made from recycled materials weren't very positive. This video describes how Ecoist found opportunity in a growing wave of environmentalism. Not only does Ecoist capitalize on low-cost materials and the brand images of some of the world's major brands, it comes out smelling like a rose as it saves tons of trash from landfills.

After viewing the video featuring Ecoist, answer the following questions:

1. How engaged was Ecoist in analyzing the marketing environment before it launched its first company?

2. What trends in the marketing environment have contributed to the success of Ecoist?

3. Is Ecoist's strategy more about recycling or about creating value for customers? Explain.

Company Case Xerox: Adapting to the Turbulent Marketing Environment

Xerox introduced the first plain-paper office copier more than 50 years ago. In the decades that followed, the company that invented photocopying flat-out dominated the industry it had created. The name Xerox became almost generic for copying (as in "I'll Xerox this for you"). Through the years, Xerox fought off round after round of rivals to stay atop the fiercely competitive copier industry. Through the late 1990s, Xerox's profits and stock price were soaring.

Then things went terribly wrong for Xerox. The legendary company's stock and fortunes took a stomach-churning dive. In only 18 months, Xerox lost some $38 billion in market value. By mid-2001, its stock price had plunged from almost $70 in 1999 to under $5. The once-dominant market leader found itself on the brink of bankruptcy. What happened? Blame it on change or—rather—on Xerox's failure to adapt to its rapidly changing marketing environment. The world was quickly going digital, but Xerox hadn't kept up.

In the new digital environment, Xerox customers no longer relied on the company's flagship products—standalone copiers—to share information and documents. Rather than pumping out and distributing stacks of black-and-white copies, they created digital documents and shared them electronically. Or they printed out multiple copies on their nearby networked printer. On a broader level, while Xerox was busy perfecting copy machines, customers were looking for more sophisticated "document management solutions." They wanted systems that would let them scan documents in Frankfurt; weave them into colorful, customized showpieces in San Francisco; and print them on demand in London—even altering for American spelling.

This left Xerox on the edge of financial disaster. "We didn't have any cash and few prospects for making any," says current Xerox CEO Ursula Burns. "The one thing you wanted was good and strong leaders that were aligned and could get us through things and we didn't have that." Burns didn't realize it at the time, but she would one day lead the company where she had been groomed for over 20 years. In fact, she was on the verge of leaving the company when her colleague and friend, Anne Mulcahy, became CEO and convinced Burns to stay. Burns was then given charge to start cleaning house.

The Turnaround Begins

Task number one: outsource Xerox's manufacturing. An often criticized and unpopular move, outsourcing was critical to Xerox's cost-saving efforts. Burns oversaw the process in a way that preserved quality while achieving the desired cost benefits. And she did so with the blessing of Xerox's employee union after convincing the union that it was either lose some jobs or have no jobs at all. With the restructuring of manufacturing, Xerox's workforce dropped from 100,000 employees to 55,000 in just four years. Although this and other efforts returned Xerox to profitability within a few years, the bigger question still remained: What business is Xerox really in?

To answer this question, Xerox renewed its focus on the customer. Xerox had always focused on copier hardware. But "we were being dragged by our customers into managing large, complex business processes for them," says Burns. Before developing new products, Xerox researchers held seemingly endless customer focus groups. Sophie Vandebroek, Xerox's chief technology officer, called this "dreaming with the customer." The goal, she argued, was "involving [Xerox] experts who know the technology with customers who know the pain points. . . .Ultimately innovation is about delighting the customer." Xerox was discovering that understanding customers is just as important as understanding technology.

What Xerox learned is that customers didn't want just copiers; they wanted easier, faster, and less costly ways to share documents and information. As a result, the company had to rethink, redefine, and reinvent itself. Xerox underwent a remarkable transformation. It stopped defining itself as a "copier company." In fact, it even stopped making standalone copiers. Instead, Xerox began billing itself as the world's leading document management technology and services enterprise. The company's newly minted mission was to help companies "be smarter about their documents."

This shift in emphasis created new customer relationships, as well as new competitors. Instead of selling copiers to equipment purchasing managers, Xerox found itself developing and selling document management systems to high-level information technology (IT) managers. Instead of competing head-on with copy machine competitors like Sharp, Canon, and Ricoh, Xerox was now squaring off against IT companies like HP and IBM. Although it encountered many potholes along the way, the company once known as the iconic "copier company" became increasingly comfortable with its new identity as a document management company.

Building New Strengths

Xerox's revenue, profits, and stock price began to show signs of recovery. But before it could declare its troubles over, yet another challenging environmental force arose—the Great Recession. The recession severely depressed Xerox's core printing and copying equipment and services business, and the company's sales and stock price tumbled once again. So in a major move to maintain its transition momentum, Xerox acquired Affiliated Computer Services (ACS), a $6.4-billion IT services powerhouse with a foot in the door of seemingly every back office in the world. The expertise, capabilities, and established channels of ACS were just what Xerox needed to take its new business plan to fruition.

The synergy between Xerox, ACS, and other acquired companies has resulted in a broad portfolio of customer-focused products, software, and services that help the company's customers manage documents and information. In fact, Xerox has introduced more than 130 innovative new products in the past four years alone. It now offers digital products and systems ranging from network printers and multifunction devices to color printing and publishing systems, digital presses, and "book factories." It also offers an impressive array of print management consulting and outsourcing services that help businesses develop online document archives, operate in-house print shops or mailrooms, analyze how employees can most efficiently share documents and knowledge, and build Internet-based processes for personalizing direct mail, invoices, and brochures.

These new products have allowed Xerox to supply solutions to clients, not just hardware. For example, it has a new device for insurance company customers—a compact computer with scanning, printing, and Internet capabilities. Instead of relying on the U.S. Postal Service to transport hard copies of claims, these and related documents are scanned on-site, sorted, routed, and put immediately into a workflow system. This isn't just a fancy new gadget for the insurance companies. They are seeing real benefits. Error rates have plummeted along with processing time, and that means increases in revenues and customer satisfaction.

Dreaming Beyond Its Boundaries

With the combination of Xerox's former strengths and its new acquisitions, Burns and the rest of the Xerox team now have a utopian image of what lies ahead. They believe the tools and services they offer clients are getting smarter. "It's not just processing Medicaid payments," says Stephen Hoover, director of Xerox's research facilities. "It's using our social cognition research to add wellness support that helps people better manage conditions like diabetes." Hoover adds that the future may see a new generation of Xerox devices, such as those that can analyze real-time parking and traffic data for municipal customers, allowing them to help citizens locate parking spots or automatically ticket them when they are going too fast. Already, Xerox is market testing parking meters that are capable of calling 911 or taking photos when a button is pushed. Not all products such as these will hit the market, but Xerox now has a model that allows it to dream beyond its known boundaries.

Throughout this corporate metamorphosis, Xerox isn't focused on trying to make better copiers. Rather, it is focused on improving any process that a business or government needs to perform and perform it more efficiently. Xerox's new-era machines have learned to read and understand the documents they scan, reducing complex tasks that once took weeks down to minutes or even seconds. From now on, Xerox wants to be a leading global document management and business-process technology and services provider.

With all the dazzling technologies emerging today, Burns acknowledges that the business services industry in which Xerox is developing its new core competencies is decidedly unsexy. But, she also points out, "These are processes that a company needs to run their business. They do it as a sideline; it's not their main thing." Her point is, running these business processes is now Xerox's main thing. In other words, Xerox provides document and IT services to customers so that the customers can focus on what matters most—their real businesses.

Xerox's transition is still a work in progress. Over the last three years, the company's revenues and profits have been growing modestly while its stock price has fluctuated. Just as e-mail and desktop software killed photocopying, smartphones and tablets are killing inkjet and photo printers. Even with the recent diversification strategy, Xerox still relies to some extent on these copier and printer product categories. But it depends much less on such products than competitors Hewlett-Packard and Lexmark International do. Thus, experts predict, Xerox will rebound much more quickly than its rivals in the coming years. Burns and crew are also confident that as Xerox continues its transition to a solutions provider, the seeds it has planted over the past few years will soon bear fruit.

Xerox knows that change and renewal are ongoing and never-ending. "The one thing that's predictable about business is that it's fundamentally unpredictable," says the company's annual report. "Macroforces such as globalization, emerging technologies, and, most recently, depressed financial markets bring new challenges every day to businesses of all sizes." The message is clear. Even the most dominant companies can be vulnerable to the often turbulent and changing marketing environment. Companies that understand and adapt well to their environments can thrive. Those that don't risk their very survival.

Questions for Discussion

1. What microenvironmental factors have affected Xerox's performance since the late 1990s?

2. What macroenvironmental factors have affected Xerox's performance during that same period?

3. By focusing on the business services industry, has Xerox pursued the best strategy? Why or why not?

4. What alternative strategy might Xerox have followed in responding to the first signs of declining revenues and profits?

5. Given Xerox's current situation, what recommendations would you make to Burns for the future of Xerox?

Sources: Quotes and other information from or adapted from Ellen McGirt, "Fresh Copy: How Ursula Burns Reinvented Xerox," *Fast Company*, November 29, 2011, www.fastcompany.com/magazine/161/ursula-burns-xerox; "Xerox Expands Electronic Discovery Services Offerings with Acquisition of Lateral Data," *Business Wire*, July 2, 2012, www.bloomberg.com/article/2012-07-02/aNQNfEipo9Lk.html; Scott Gamm, "Xerox Works to Duplicate Copier Glory in Digital Services Model," *Forbes*, July 19, 2012, www.forbes.com/sites/scottgamm/2012/07/19/xerox-works-to-duplicate-copier-glory-in-digital-services-model/; Richard Waters, "Xerox Chief Sets Out the Big Picture," *Financial Times*, May 6, 2010, p. 16; Geoff Colvin, "Ursula Burns Launches Xerox into the Future," Fortune, May 3, 2010, p. 5; and annual reports and other information at www.xerox.com, accessed July 2012.

MyMarketingLab

Go to **mymktlab.com** for Auto-graded writing questions as well as the following Assisted-graded writing questions:

3-1. Discuss current trends in the economic environment of which marketers must be aware and provide examples of companies' responses to each trend. (AACSB: Communication; Reflective Thinking)

3-2. Discuss trends in the natural environment of which marketers must be aware and provide examples of companies' responses to them. (AACSB: Communication)

3-3. Mymktlab Only – comprehensive writing assignment for this chapter.

References

1. Based on information from Emily Glazer, 'Who Is RayWJ? YouTube's Top Star," *Wall Street Journal*, February 2, 2012, p. B1; Rob Waugh, "YouTube Takes Aim at Living Room with Relaunch of Google TV App," *Daily Mail*, February 13, 2012; Michael Humphrey, "YouTube Channels: The Delicate Shift from Social to Mass Media," *Forbes*, October 31, 2011, www.forbes.com/sites/michaelhumphrey/2011/10/31/youtube-channels-the-delicate-shift-from-social-to-mass-media/; Danielle Sacks, "How YouTube's Global Platform Is Redefining the Entertainment Business," *Fast Company,* February 2011, p. 58; Jessica E. Vascellaro, Amir Efrati, and Ethan Smith, "You-Tube Recasts for New Viewers," *Wall Street Journal,* April 7, 2011, p. B1; and www.youtube.com/t/press, www.youtube.com/shows, www.youtube.com/partners, and www.realwomenofphiladelphia.com/, accessed November 2012.

2. Information from www.ikea.com, accessed September 2012.

3. Information from Robert J. Benes, Abbie Jarman, and Ashley Williams, "2007 NRA Sets Records," at www.chefmagazine.com, accessed September 2007; and www.thecoca-colacompany.com/dynamic/press_center/ and www.cokesolutions.com, accessed November 2012.

4. See www.lifeisgood.com/#!/playmakers/, accessed September 2012.

5. World POPClock, U.S. Census Bureau, at www.census.gov/main/www/popclock.html, accessed July 2012. This Web site provides continuously updated projections of the U.S. and world populations.

6. U.S. Census Bureau projections and POPClock Projection, at www.census.gov/main/www/popclock.html, accessed July 2012.

7. See Rick Ferguson and Bill Brohaugh, "The Aging of Core Areas," *Journal of Consumer Marketing*, Vol. 27, No. 1, 2010, p. 76; Suzanne Wilson, "Baby Boomers Thrown a Curve Ball," *Daily Hampshire Gazette,* February 14, 2011, p. D1; Piet Levy, "Segmentation by Generation," *Marketing News*, May 15, 2011, pp. 20–23; and Ben Steveman, "Twelve Financial Nightmares for Baby Boomers," *Bloomberg Businessweek,* http://money.msn.com/baby-boomers/12-financial-nightmares-for-baby-boomers, accessed May 16, 2012.

8. See "Keeping Up with the Baby Boomers," *MarketWatch,* March 20, 2012, www.marketwatch.com/story/keeping-up-with-the-baby-boomers-2012-03-20.

9. See www.eldertreks.com/, accessed November 2012.

10. For more discussion, see Bernadette Turner, "Generation X. . . . Let's GO!" *New Pittsburgh Courier*, March 2–March 8, 2011, p. A11; Piet Levy, "Segmentation by Generation," *Marketing News*, May 15, 2011, pp. 20–23; and Leonard Klie, "Gen X: Stuck in the Middle," *Customer Relationship Management,* February 2012, pp. 24–29.

11. Julie Jargon, "DQ Dips into Humor," *Wall Street Journal,* May 26, 2011, p. B6; "Dairy Queen Ad Strikes Gold with Mary Lou Retton," *QSRweb.com,* July 4, 2011, www.qsrweb.com/article/182364/Dairy-Queen-ad-strikes-gold-with-Mary-Lou-Retton; and "Dairy Queen and Subway Top Lists of Most Effective QSR Advertising," *Quick Serve Leader*, http://quickserveleader.com/article/dairy-queen-and-subway-top-lists-most-effective-qsr-advertising, accessed March 2012.

12. Piet Levy, "Segmentation by Generation," p. 22; and Jon Lafayette, "Marketers Targeting Generation of Millennial's," *Broadcasting Cable*, April 11, 2011, p. 28.

13. Piet Levy, "Segmentation by Generation," p. 23. Also see Sarah Mahoney, "Struggling, Gen Y Redefines Wants, Needs," *Marketing Daily,* March 5, 2012, http://www.mediapost.com/publications/article/169424/struggling-gen-y-redefines-wants-needs.html?print.

14. Tanzina Vega, "A Campaign to Introduce Keds to a New Generation," *New York Times*, February 22, 2011, www.nytimes.com/2011/02/23/business/media/23adco.html; and http://hdyd.keds.com/, accessed September 2012.

15. See U.S. Census Bureau, "Families and Living Arrangements: 2011," at www.census.gov/population/www/socdemo/hh-fam.html, accessed August 2012.

16. U.S. Census Bureau, "Facts for Features," March 2011, accessed at www.census.gov/newsroom/releases/archives/facts_for_features_special_editions/cb12-ff05.html; and U.S. Census Bureau, "America's

Families and Living Arrangements: 2011," Table FG1, www.census .gov/population/www/socdemo/hh-fam/cps2011.html, accessed April 2012.

17. See Marissa Miley and Ann Mack, "The New Female Consumer: The Rise of the Real Mom," *Advertising Age,* November 16, 2009, p. A1; and Christine Birkner, "Mom's the Word," *Marketing News,* May 15, 2011, p. 8.

18. U.S. Census Bureau, "Geographical Mobility/Migration," at www .census.gov/population/www/socdemo/migrate.html, accessed September 2012.

19. See U.S. Census Bureau, "Metropolitan and Micropolitan Statistical Areas," www.census.gov/population/metro/, accessed June 2012; and "Population of 576 U.S. Micropolitan Areas—2010 Census," *The Business Journals*, April 5, 2011, www.bizjournals .com/bizjournals/on-numbers/scott-thomas/2011/04/population-of-micro-areas.html.

20. "Work at Home and in the Workplace, 2010," *TED: The Editor's Desk*, Bureau of Labor Statistics, June 24, 2011, www .bls.gov/opub/ted/2011/ted_20110624.htm; and Kaomi Goetz, "For Freelancers, Landing a Workspace Gets Harder," *NPR,* April 10, 2012, http://www.npr.org/2012/04/10/150286116/for-freelancers-landing-a-workspace-gets-harder?sc=fb&cc=fp.

21. See "About WebEx," at www.webex.com/about-webex/index .html, accessed November 2012; and www.regus.com and http://grindspaces.com/, accessed November 2012.

22. U.S. Census Bureau, "Educational Attainment," at www.census.gov/ population/www/socdemo/educ-attn.html, accessed June 2012.

23. *See* U.S. Census Bureau, *The 2012 Statistical Abstract: Education*, Tables 229, 276, accessed at www.census.gov/compendia/statab/cats/ education.html; and U.S. Department of Labor, "Employment Projections: 2010-2020 Summary," February 1, 2012, www.bls.gov/ooh/.

24. See U.S. Census Bureau, "U.S. Population Projections," www .census.gov/population/www/projections/summarytables.html, accessed August 2012; and "Characteristics of the Foreign-Born Population by Nativity and US Citizenship Status," www.census .gov/population/www/socdemo/foreign/cps2008.html.

25. See www.harlistasfilm.com/ and www.harley-davidson.com/en_US/ Content/Pages/harlistas/harlista.html, accessed November 2012.

26. "America's LGBT 2012 Buying Power Projected at $790 Billion," *Echelon Magazine*, March 27, 2012, www.echelonmagazine.com/ index.php?id=2597&title=America%60s_LGBT_2012_Buying_ Power_Projected_at_$790_Billion.

27. See Brandon Miller, "And the Winner Is . . ." *Out Traveler*, Winter 2008, pp. 64–65; Bradley Johnson, "Why (and How) You Should Go after the Gay Dollar," *Advertising Age,* October 11, 2010, p. 22; Tanya Irwin, "American Airlines, GayCities Partner for Promo," *Marketing Daily,* January 15, 2012, www.mediapost.com/publications/ article/165789/american-airlines-gaycities-partner-for-promo.html; and www.aa.com/rainbow, accessed November 2012.

28. Witeck-Combs Communications, "America's Disability Market at a Glance," Andrew Adam Newman, "Web Marketing to a Segment Too Big to Be a Niche," *New York Times*, October 30, 2007, p. 9; Kenneth Hein, "The Invisible Demographic," *Brandweek*, March 3, 2008, p. 20; Tanya Mohn, "Smoothing the Way," *New York Times*, April 26, 2010, www.nytimes.com; and www.disability-marketing .com/facts/, accessed May 2011.

29. See Alex Taylor III, "Tata Takes on the World: Building an Auto Empire in India," *Fortune*, May 2, 2011, pp. 87–92; and http://tatanano .inservices.tatamotors.com/tatamotors/, accessed November 2012.

30. See U.S. Census Bureau, "Income, Poverty, and Health Insurance Coverage in the United States: 2010," Table 3, September 2011, www.census.gov/prod/2011pubs/p60-239.pdf; and "The Growing Wealth Gap," *Fortune*, November 7, 2011, p. 28.

31. See "Warm Weather Puts Chill on Brands' Winters," *Advertising Age,* February 19, 2012, http://adage.com/print/232824; and Alex Taylor III, "Toyota's Comeback Kid," *Fortune,* February 27, 2012, pp. 72–79.

32. The 2030 Water Resources Group, "Charting Our Water Future: Executive Summary," 2009, www.mckinsey.com/clientservice/water/ charting_our_water_future.aspx; and "The World's Water," *Pacific Institute,* www.worldwater.org/data.htm, accessed June 2012.

33. Information from www.timberland.com and http://earthkeepers .timberland.com/?camp=S:G:SPC:timberland_earthkeepers:TBL#/ howweact, accessed November 2012.

34. Maid Napolitano, "RFID Surges Ahead," *Materials Handling,* April 2012, pp. S48–S50.

35. See Tamara Schweitzer, "The Way I Work," *Inc.*, June 2010, pp. 112–116; Christina Binkley, "Style—On Style: Charity Gives Shoe Brand Extra Shine," *Wall Street Journal*, April 1, 2010, p. D7; and www.toms.com, accessed November 2012.

36. Emily Steel, "Cause-Tied Marketing Requires Care," *Wall Street Journal*, March 21, 2011, p. B4.

37. See "The Growth of Cause Marketing," at www.causemarketingforum .com/site/c.bkLUKcOTLkK4E/b.6452355/apps/s/content.asp? ct=8965443, accessed June 2012.

38. See "10 Crucial Consumer Trends for 2010," Trendwatching.com, http://trendwatching.com/trends/pdf/trendwatching%202009-12%2010trends.pdf; and "The F-Factor," Trendingwatching .com, May 2011, http://trendwatching.com/trends/pdf/trendwatching %202009-12%2010trends.pdf.

39. "The F-Factor," Trendingwatching.com, p. 1.

40. Laura Feldmann, "After 9/11 Highs, America's Back to Good Ol' Patriotism," *Christian Science Monitor*, July 5, 2006, p. 1; Leon F. Dube and Gregory S. Black, "Impact of National Traumatic Events on Consumer Purchasing," *International Journal of Consumer Studies*, May 2010, p. 333; and "Lifestyle Statistics: Very Proud of Their Nationality," at www.nationmaster.com, accessed June 2012.

41. See Stuart Elliott, "This Column Was 100% Made in America," *New York Times,* February 15, 2012; and Jeff Bennett and Suzanne Vranica, "Chrysler Dealers Defend 'Halftime in America' Ad," *Wall Street Journal,* February 9, 2012, http://online.wsj.com/article/ SB10001424052970204136404577211391719237160.html.

42. "Impact Investors to Gather in Boulder at the 2011 LOHAS Forum," *CSRwire,* May 25, 2011; and www.lohas.com, accessed June 2012.

43. See www.tomsofmaine.com/home, accessed November 2012.

44. "Organic Farming Grows to $29-Billion Industry," *Western Farm Press*, April 26, 2011; and "Research and Markets: Global Organic Food," *Reuters,* January 5, 2012.

45. The Pew Forum on Religion & Public Life, "U.S. Religious Landscape Survey," http://religions.pewforum.org/reports, accessed August 2012.

46. For more discussion, see Diana Butler Bass, "The End of Church," *Huffington Post*, February 18, 2012, http://www.huffingtonpost.com/ diana-butler-bass/the-end-of-church_b_1284954.html.

47. W. Chan Kim and Renée Mauborgne, "How Strategy Shaped Structure," *Harvard Business Review*, September 2009, pp. 73–80.

48. Paula Forbes, "Taco Bell Ad: Thank You for Suing Us," January 28, 2011, *Eater,* http://eater.com/archives/2011/01/28/taco-bell-ad-thanks-firm-for-law-suit.php; "Law Firm Voluntarily Withdraws Class-Action Lawsuit Against Taco Bell," April 19, 2011, http:// money.msn.com/business-news/article.aspx?feed=BW&date= 20110419&id=13327023; and Bruce Horovitz, "Taco Bell Comes Out of Its Shell to Ring in New Menu," *USA Today,* February 20, 2012, www.usatoday.com/money/industries/food/story/2012-02-20/ taco-bell/53157494/1.

Part 1: Defining Marketing and the Marketing Process (Chapters 1–2)
Part 2: Understanding the Marketplace and Consumers (Chapters 3–6)
Part 3: Designing a Customer-Driven Strategy and Mix (Chapters 7–17)
Part 4: Extending Marketing (Chapters 18–20)

Managing **Marketing Information** to Gain Customer Insights

4

Chapter Preview In this chapter, we continue our exploration of how marketers gain insights into consumers and the marketplace. We look at how companies develop and manage information about important marketplace elements: customers, competitors, products, and marketing programs. To succeed in today's marketplace, companies must know how to turn mountains of marketing information into fresh customer insights that will help them deliver greater value to customers.

Let's start with a story about marketing research and customer insights in action. Good marketing research can involve a rich variety of sophisticated data collection and analysis techniques. But sometimes research is as simple as just talking with customers directly, listening openly to what they have to say, and using those insights to develop better products and marketing. That's how Domino's Pizza turned a five-year revenue slide into a fresh, hot turnaround.

Domino's Pizza: Listening to Consumers and Letting Them Know You Heard Them

After five years of stagnant or declining revenues, Domino's Pizza did something practically unheard of in the business world. "First," says an industry observer, "it asked customers for honest feedback. Second, it actually listened to the painful truth [punctuated by words like "cardboard crust" and "totally devoid of flavor"]. Finally—and here's the most shocking part—the company reinvented its product 'from the crust up.'" What follows is the full story behind Domino's impressive "Pizza Turnaround" campaign.

The turnaround began with marketing research to understand what customers thought and wanted. Industry research showed that although Domino's was tops in service, convenience, and value for the money, it trailed far behind competitors in taste. One taste preference survey placed Domino's dead last, tied with—of all possibilities—Chuck E. Cheese, a competitor not known for culinary excellence.

To gain deeper insights into what consumers really thought about its pizzas, Domino's turned to research using social media channels and focus groups. It monitored consumer online

chatter and solicited thousands of direct consumer feedback messages via Facebook, Twitter, and other social media. Then, based on insights it gained online, Domino's launched a wave of good old-fashioned, tried-and-true focus groups to engage customers directly in face-to-face conversations.

The online feedback and focus group results were as difficult to digest as a cold Domino's pizza. The most common complaint: Domino's pizza crust "tasted like cardboard." But that was just the beginning. One after another, pizza lovers panned Domino's pies with biting comments such as "Totally devoid of flavor." "The sauce tastes like ketchup." "Worst excuse for pizza I've ever had." "Processed cheese!!"

When consumer research turned up painful truths about its pizza ("cardboard crust," "totally devoid of flavor"), Domino's completely reformulated its product and launched its startlingly honest, highly successful Pizza Turnaround campaign. Thanks to the research insights, says the CEO, "We're a new Domino's."

"Mass-produced, boring, bland pizza." and "Microwave pizza is far superior." One focus group participant concluded: "It doesn't feel like there's much love in Domino's pizza." "They weren't poisoning people," chuckles an analyst, "but taste was [certainly a big] glitch on the radar."

Rather than hiding from these stinging results or waving them off, Domino's executives fessed up to the problems and faced them head on. "We had a focus group webcast to our team," says a Domino's marketing executive. "When somebody's saying something terrible about your pizza, you never get used to it, but for the first time all our executives were face to face with it. They couldn't believe it. We all said: 'we can't just go to the next meeting. We have to do something.'"

Domino's began by completely reinventing its pizzas. It didn't just make improvements to the old product; it threw out the recipe and started over. According to Domino's chief marketing officer, Russell Weiner, "We weren't going to call it 'new and improved' and expect that to break through. We had to blow up the bridge."

Domino's chefs started from scratch with new crusts, sauces, cheese, and other ingredients. The result was an entirely new pizza that Domino's boasts has a "garlic seasoned crust with parsley, baked to a golden brown." The new sauce is "bright, spicy, and robust" with a "little bit of red pepper just to tingle on your tongue." And the new cheese is to die for—mozzarella, shredded not diced, flavored with just a hint of provolone. "We changed everything," says a Domino's product development chef. "Now it tastes better." Customers seem to agree. Two months after the new pizza was introduced, some 1,800 random pizza consumers from eight U.S. markets did a blind taste test. In head-to-head comparisons, consumers picked Domino's pizzas as tasting better than both Papa John's and Pizza Hut by a wide margin.

To announce the changes and to turn around customer opinions, Domino's launched a daring $75 million "Pizza Turnaround" promotion campaign. In the campaign, the research itself was the message. Self-depreciating TV commercials showed real focus groups describing, in vivid detail, how dreadful the pizza was. In the ads, Domino's CEO Patrick Doyle admits that he's heard what customers had to say and has taken it to heart. "There comes a time," he acknowledges, "when you know you've got to make a change."

The startlingly honest campaign was fully integrated into the brand's Facebook and Twitter pages, where the company posted all the bad along with the good and asked for continuing feedback. An online pizza tracker, allowing customers to follow their order, added another layer of transparency. The entire turnaround saga—from biting focus group footage to the shocked reactions of Domino's executives and efforts to reformulate the product—was documented for all to see in a forthright four-and-a-half minute behind-the-scenes documentary on the Web site www .pizzaturnaround.com. The company even posted a stream of customer comments—good, bad, or indifferent—on a 4,630-square-foot billboard in New York City's Times Square area.

When online and focus group research showed that pizza lovers thought Domino's pizza "tasted like cardboard" (and worse), the company threw out the recipe and reinvented its pizza from the ground up. "Oh Yes We Did."
Dominoes Pizza, LLC

The campaign was risky. When Domino's admitted in its ads that its pizza was gross, some analysts predicted that the approach would be brand suicide. CEO Doyle admits that he had knots in his stomach when the chain launched the campaign. But Domino's wanted to shout out loud and clear: We've heard you! Our pizza was lousy but we fixed the recipe. "We had to be open, honest, and transparent," says CMO Weiner.

As it turns out, the upfront approach worked. The transparent ads and message grabbed consumer attention and changed opinions. "The advertising itself scored off the charts," says Weiner. Since the Pizza Turnaround campaign began, Domino's has seen revenues increase by 21 percent and profits increase by 31 percent, even as the pizza-delivery industry and restaurants in general have struggled. The campaign earned Domino's "marketer of the year" honors from two major marketing publications, *Advertising Age* and *Brandweek*, while also landing Doyle at number 9 on Forbes' "most buzzed about CEOs" list.

Domino's continues to ask customers for feedback and uses the insights to improve marketing decisions. It even set up a Web site where diners can upload pictures of Domino's food, breaking one of the ultimate rules of fast-food advertising by displaying real, untouched photos. And the brand remains utterly serious about keeping customers satisfied. At the bottom of its Web page, Domino's also offers the following guarantee: "If you are not completely satisfied with your Domino's Pizza experience, we will make it right or refund your money."

The lesson for marketers is that talking to customers, hearing what they have to say, and acting on the resulting insights can pay big dividends. Marketing research and really listening to customers, says Doyle, "dramatically changed our momentum, and we can build on this going forward. We feel very good now about our understanding of the brand. We're a new Domino's."[1]

Objective Outline

MyMarketingLab™

⭐ **Improve Your Grade!**

Over 10 million students improved their results using the Pearson MyLabs. Visit **mymktlab.com** for simulations, tutorials, and end-of-chapter problems.

As the Domino's story highlights, good products and marketing programs begin with good customer information. Companies also need an abundance of information on competitors, resellers, and other actors and marketplace forces. But more than just gathering information, marketers must *use* the information to gain powerful *customer and market insights*.

Marketing Information and Customer Insights

To create value for customers and build meaningful relationships with them, marketers must first gain fresh, deep insights into what customers need and want. Such customer insights come from good marketing information. Companies use these customer insights to develop a competitive advantage.

For example, Apple wasn't the first company to develop a digital music player. However, Apple's research uncovered two key insights: people wanted personal music players that let them take all of their music with them, and they wanted to be able to listen to it unobtrusively. Based on these insights, Apple applied its design and usability magic to create the phenomenally successful iPod. ● The iPod now captures a 78 percent share of the global MP3 player market. Apple sold more than 45 million iPods last year alone, half of them purchased by first-time buyers. "To put that in context," says Apple CEO Tim Cook, "it took Sony 30 years to sell just 230,000 Walkman cassette players."[2]

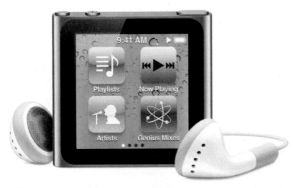

● **Key customer insights, plus a dash of Apple's design and usability magic, have made the iPod a blockbuster. It now captures a more than 78 percent market share and has spawned other Apple blockbusters such as the iPhone and iPad.**

Newscom

Customer insights

Fresh understandings of customers and the marketplace derived from marketing information that become the basis for creating customer value and relationships.

Marketing information system (MIS)

People and procedures dedicated to assessing information needs, developing the needed information, and helping decision makers to use the information to generate and validate actionable customer and market insights.

Although customer and market insights are important for building customer value and relationships, these insights can be very difficult to obtain. Customer needs and buying motives are often anything but obvious—consumers themselves usually can't tell you exactly what they need and why they buy. To gain good customer insights, marketers must effectively manage marketing information from a wide range of sources.

With the recent explosion of information technologies, companies can now generate marketing information in great quantities. Moreover, consumers themselves are now generating tons of marketing information. Through e-mail, text messaging, blogging, Facebook, Twitter, and other grassroots digital channels, consumers are now volunteering a tidal wave of bottom-up information to companies and to each other. Companies that tap into such information can gain rich, timely customer insights at lower cost.

Far from lacking information, most marketing managers are overloaded with data and often overwhelmed by it. For example, when a company such as Pepsi monitors online discussions about its brands by searching key words in tweets, blogs, posts, and other sources, its servers take in a stunning 6 million public conversations a day, more than 2 billion a year.[3] That's far more information than any manager can digest. Thus, marketers don't need *more* information; they need *better* information. And they need to make better *use* of the information they already have.

The real value of marketing research and marketing information lies in how it is used—in the **customer insights** that it provides. Based on such thinking, many companies are now restructuring their marketing research and information functions. They are creating *customer insights teams*, headed by a vice president of customer insights and composed of representatives from all of the firm's functional areas. For example, Coca-Cola's marketing research group is headed by a vice president of marketing strategy and insights. And at Unilever, marketing research is done by the Consumer and Market Insight division, which helps brand teams harness information and turn it into customer insights.

Customer insights groups collect customer and market information from a wide variety of sources, ranging from traditional marketing research studies to mingling with and observing consumers to monitoring consumer online conversations about the company and its products. Then they *use* this information to develop important customer insights from which the company can create more value for its customers.

Thus, companies must design effective marketing information systems that give managers the right information, in the right form, at the right time and help them to use this information to create customer value and stronger customer relationships. A **marketing information system (MIS)** consists of people and procedures dedicated to assessing information needs, developing the needed information, and helping decision makers use the information to generate and validate actionable customer and market insights.

● **Figure 4.1** shows that the MIS begins and ends with information users—marketing managers, internal and external partners, and others who need marketing information. First, it interacts with these information users to *assess information needs*. Next, it interacts with the marketing environment to *develop needed information* through internal company databases, marketing intelligence activities, and marketing research. Finally, the MIS helps users to *analyze and use* the information to develop customer insights, make marketing decisions, and manage customer relationships.

Objective 2 ┄┄➤
Define the marketing information system and discuss its parts.

Assessing Marketing Information Needs

The marketing information system primarily serves the company's marketing and other managers. However, it may also provide information to external partners, such as suppliers, resellers, or marketing services agencies. For example, Walmart's Retail Link system gives key suppliers access to information on everything from customers' buying patterns and store inventory levels to how many items they've sold in which stores in the past 24 hours.[4]

A good MIS balances the information users would *like* to have against what they really *need* and what is *feasible* to offer. Some managers will ask for whatever information they can get without thinking carefully about what they really need. Too much information can be as harmful as too little. Other managers may omit things they ought to know, or they may not

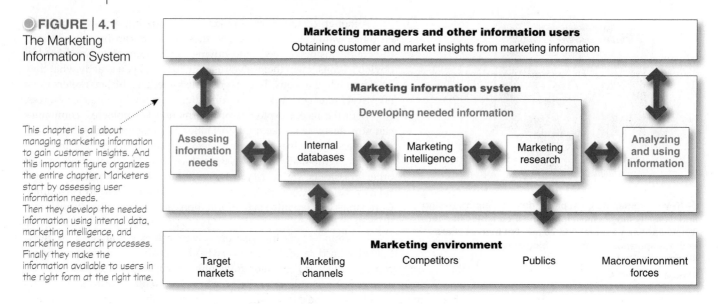

● **FIGURE** | 4.1
The Marketing
Information System

This chapter is all about managing marketing information to gain customer insights. And this important figure organizes the entire chapter. Marketers start by assessing user information needs.
Then they develop the needed information using internal data, marketing intelligence, and marketing research processes. Finally they make the information available to users in the right form at the right time.

know to ask for some types of information they should have. For example, managers might need to know about surges in favorable or unfavorable consumer discussions about their brands on blogs or online social networks. Because they do not know about these discussions, they do not think to ask about them. The MIS must monitor the marketing environment to provide decision makers with information they should have to better understand customers and make key marketing decisions.

Finally, the costs of obtaining, analyzing, storing, and delivering information can quickly mount. The company must decide whether the value of insights gained from additional information is worth the costs of providing it, and both value and cost are often hard to assess.

Developing Marketing Information

Marketers can obtain the needed information from *internal data*, *marketing intelligence*, and *marketing research*.

Internal Data

Internal databases
Electronic collections of consumer and market information obtained from data sources within the company network.

Many companies build extensive **internal databases**, electronic collections of consumer and market information obtained from data sources within the company's network. Information in the database can come from many sources. The marketing department furnishes information on customer characteristics, sales transactions, and Web site visits. The customer service department keeps records of customer satisfaction or service problems. The accounting department provides detailed records of sales, costs, and cash flows. Operations reports on production, shipments, and inventories. The sales force reports on reseller reactions and competitor activities, and marketing channel partners provide data on point-of-sale transactions. Harnessing such information can provide powerful customer insights and competitive advantage.

For example, ● financial services provider USAA uses its internal database to create an incredibly loyal customer base: [5]

USAA provides financial services to U.S. military personnel and their families, largely through direct marketing via the telephone and Internet. It maintains a huge customer database built from customer purchasing histories and information collected directly through customer surveys, transaction data, and browsing

● **Internal data: Financial services provider USAA uses its extensive database to tailor its services to the specific needs of individual customers, creating incredible loyalty.**

Courtney Young

behavior at its online site. USAA uses the database to tailor direct marketing offers to the needs of individual customers. For example, for customers looking toward retirement, it sends information on estate planning. If the family has college-age children, USAA sends those children information on how to manage their credit cards.

One delighted reporter, a USAA customer, recounts how USAA even helped him teach his 16-year-old daughter to drive. Just before her birthday, but before she received her driver's license, USAA sent a "package of materials, backed by research, to help me teach my daughter how to drive, help her practice, and help us find ways to agree on what constitutes safe driving later on, when she gets her license." What's more, marvels the reporter, "USAA didn't try to sell me a thing. My take-away: that USAA is investing in me for the long term." Through such skillful use of its database, USAA serves each customer uniquely, resulting in high customer satisfaction and loyalty. USAA regularly pops up among the leaders in almost every publication's list of "Customer Service Champs," highlighting its legendary customer service. More important, the $19 billion company retains 98 percent of its customers.

Internal databases usually can be accessed more quickly and cheaply than other information sources, but they also present some problems. Because internal information is often collected for other purposes, it may be incomplete or in the wrong form for making marketing decisions. Data also ages quickly; keeping the database current requires a major effort. Finally, managing the mountains of information that a large company produces requires highly sophisticated equipment and techniques.

Competitive Marketing Intelligence

Competitive marketing intelligence

The systematic collection and analysis of publicly available information about consumers, competitors, and developments in the marketing environment.

Competitive marketing intelligence is the systematic collection and analysis of publicly available information about consumers, competitors, and developments in the marketplace. The goal of competitive marketing intelligence is to improve strategic decision making by understanding the consumer environment, assessing and tracking competitors' actions, and providing early warnings of opportunities and threats. Marketing intelligence techniques range from observing consumers firsthand to quizzing the company's own employees, benchmarking competitors' products, researching the Internet, and monitoring Internet buzz.

Good marketing intelligence can help marketers gain insights into how consumers talk about and connect with their brands. Many companies send out teams of trained observers to mix and mingle personally with customers as they use and talk about the company's products. Other companies routinely monitor consumers' online chatter. ● For example, PepsiCo's Gatorade brand has created an extensive control center to monitor brand-related social media activity.[6]

● **Mission control: PepsiCo's Gatorade brand has created an extensive control center to monitor real-time brand-related social media activity.**

The Gatorade Company

The Gatorade Mission Control Center, deep within the company's Chicago headquarters, serves as a nerve center in which Gatorade's four-member Mission Control team monitors the brand in real-time across social media. Whenever someone mentions anything related to Gatorade (including competitors, Gatorade athletes, and sports-nutrition-related topics) on Twitter, Facebook, a blog, or in other social media, it pops up in various visualizations and dashboards on one of six big screens in Mission Control. Staffers also monitor online ad and Web site traffic, producing a consolidated picture of the brand's Internet image.

Gatorade uses what it sees and learns at Mission Control to improve its products, marketing, and interactions with customers. For example, while monitoring its "Gatorade Has Evolved" campaign, the team quickly saw that a commercial featuring a song by rap artist David Banner was being heavily discussed in social media. Within 24 hours, they had worked with Banner to put out a full-length version of the song and distribute it to Gatorade followers and fans on Twitter and Facebook. In another case, the brand knew to bulk up on production of its recovery drinks because of complaints they were selling out. Beyond just monitoring social media conversations, the Mission Control team sometimes joins them, as when staffers recently jumped into a Facebook conversation to answer a poster's questions about where to buy products.

Many companies have even appointed *chief listening officers*, who are charged with sifting through online customer conversations and passing along key insights to marketing decision makers. Dell created a position called *Listening Czar* two years ago. "Our chief listener is critical to making sure that the right people in the organization are aware of what the conversations on the Web are saying about us, so the relevant people in the business can connect with customers," says a Dell marketing executive.[7]

Companies also need to actively monitor competitors' activities. Firms use competitive marketing intelligence to gain early warnings of competitor moves and strategies, new product launches, new or changing markets, and potential competitive strengths and weaknesses. Much competitor intelligence can be collected from people inside the company—executives, engineers and scientists, purchasing agents, and the sales force. The company can also obtain important intelligence information from suppliers, resellers, and key customers. It can monitor competitors' Web sites and use the Internet to search specific competitor names, events, or trends and see what turns up. And tracking consumer conversations about competing brands is often as revealing as tracking conversations about the company's own brands.

Intelligence seekers can also pour through any of thousands of online databases. Some are free. For example, the U.S. Security and Exchange Commission's database provides a huge stockpile of financial information on public competitors, and the U.S. Patent Office and Trademark database reveals patents that competitors have filed. For a fee, companies can also subscribe to any of the more than 3,000 online databases and information search services, such as Hoover's, LexisNexis, and Dun & Bradstreet. Today's marketers have an almost overwhelming amount of competitor information only a few keystrokes away.

The intelligence game goes both ways. Facing determined competitive marketing intelligence efforts by competitors, most companies are now taking steps to protect their own information. For example, Apple is obsessed with secrecy, and it passes that obsession along to its employees. "At Apple everything is a secret," says an insider. "Apple wants new products to remain in stealth mode until their release dates." Information leaks about new products before they are introduced gives competition time to respond, raises customer expectations, and can steal thunder and sales from current products. So Apple employees are taught a "loose-lips-sink-ships" mentality: A T-shirt for sale in the company store reads, "I visited the Apple campus, but that's all I'm allowed to say."[8]

The growing use of marketing intelligence also raises ethical issues. Some intelligence gathering techniques may involve questionable ethics. Clearly, companies should take advantage of publicly available information. However, they should not stoop to snoop. With all the legitimate intelligence sources now available, a company does not need to break the law or accepted codes of ethics to get good intelligence.

Objective 3 ⤳ ➤
Outline the steps in the marketing research process.

Marketing Research

In addition to marketing intelligence information about general consumer, competitor, and marketplace happenings, marketers often need formal studies that provide customer and market insights for specific marketing situations and decisions. For example, Budweiser wants to know what appeals will be most effective in its Super Bowl advertising. Yahoo! wants to know how Web searchers will react to a proposed redesign of its site. Or Samsung wants to know how many and what kinds of people will buy its next-generation, ultrathin televisions. In such situations, managers will need marketing research.

Marketing research
The systematic design, collection, analysis, and reporting of data relevant to a specific marketing situation facing an organization.

Marketing research is the systematic design, collection, analysis, and reporting of data relevant to a specific marketing situation facing an organization. Companies use marketing research in a wide variety of situations. For example, marketing research gives marketers insights into customer motivations, purchase behavior, and satisfaction. It can help them to assess market potential and market share or measure the effectiveness of pricing, product, distribution, and promotion activities.

Some large companies have their own research departments that work with marketing managers on marketing research projects. In addition, these companies—like

●FIGURE | 4.2
The Marketing Research
Process

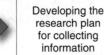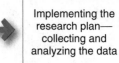

| Defining the problem and research objectives | → | Developing the research plan for collecting information | → | Implementing the research plan— collecting and analyzing the data | → | Interpreting and reporting the findings |

This first step is probably the most difficult but also the most important one. It guides the entire research process. It's frustrating to reach the end of an expensive research project only to learn that you've addressed the wrong problem!

their smaller counterparts—frequently hire outside research specialists to consult with management on specific marketing problems and to conduct marketing research studies. Sometimes firms simply purchase data collected by outside firms to aid in their decision making.

The marketing research process has four steps (see ● **Figure 4.2**): defining the problem and research objectives, developing the research plan, implementing the research plan, and interpreting and reporting the findings.

Defining the Problem and Research Objectives

Marketing managers and researchers must work closely together to define the problem and agree on research objectives. The manager best understands the decision for which information is needed, whereas the researcher best understands marketing research and how to obtain the information. Defining the problem and research objectives is often the hardest step in the research process. The manager may know that something is wrong, without knowing the specific causes.

After the problem has been defined carefully, the manager and the researcher must set the research objectives. A marketing research project might have one of three types of objectives. The objective of **exploratory research** is to gather preliminary information that will help define the problem and suggest hypotheses. The objective of **descriptive research** is to describe things, such as the market potential for a product or the demographics and attitudes of consumers who buy the product. The objective of **causal research** is to test hypotheses about cause-and-effect relationships. For example, would a 10 percent decrease in tuition at a private college result in an enrollment increase sufficient to offset the reduced tuition? Managers often start with exploratory research and later follow with descriptive or causal research.

The statement of the problem and research objectives guides the entire research process. The manager and the researcher should put the statement in writing to be certain that they agree on the purpose and expected results of the research.

Exploratory research
Marketing research to gather preliminary information that will help define problems and suggest hypotheses.

Descriptive research
Marketing research to better describe marketing problems, situations, or markets, such as the market potential for a product or the demographics and attitudes of consumers.

Causal research
Marketing research to test hypotheses about cause-and-effect relationships.

Developing the Research Plan

Once researchers have defined the research problem and objectives, they must determine the exact information needed, develop a plan for gathering it efficiently, and present the plan to management. The research plan outlines sources of existing data and spells out the specific research approaches, contact methods, sampling plans, and instruments that researchers will use to gather new data.

Research objectives must be translated into specific information needs. ● For example, suppose that Red Bull wants to conduct research on how consumers would react to a proposed new vitamin-enhanced water drink that would be available in several flavors and sold under the Red Bull name. Red Bull currently dominates the worldwide energy drink market with a more than 40 percent market share worldwide—it sold more than 4.6 billion cans last year alone. And the brand recently introduced Red Bull Total Zero, an energy drink for calorie-averse consumers.[9] A new line of enhanced waters—akin to Glacéau's vitaminwater—might help Red Bull leverage its strong brand position even further. The proposed research might call for the following specific information:

- The demographic, economic, and lifestyle characteristics of current Red Bull customers. (Do current customers also consume enhanced-water products? Are such products consistent with their lifestyles? Or would Red Bull need to target a new segment of consumers?)
- The characteristics and usage patterns of the broader population of enhanced-water users: What do they need and expect from such products, where do they buy them,

● A decision by Red Bull to add a line of enhanced waters to its already successful mix of energy drinks would call for marketing research that provides lots of specific information.

Jarrod Weaton/Weaton Digital, Inc.

when and how do they use them, and what existing brands and price points are most popular? (The new Red Bull product would need strong, relevant positioning in the crowded enhanced-water market.)

- Retailer reactions to the proposed new product line: Would they stock and support it? Where would they display it? (Failure to get retailer support would hurt sales of the new drink.)
- Forecasts of sales of both the new and current Red Bull products. (Will the new enhanced waters create new sales or simply take sales away from current Red Bull products? Will the new product increase Red Bull's overall profits?)

Red Bull's marketers will need these and many other types of information to decide whether or not to introduce the new product and, if so, the best way to do it.

The research plan should be presented in a *written proposal*. A written proposal is especially important when the research project is large and complex or when an outside firm carries it out. The proposal should cover the management problems addressed, the research objectives, the information to be obtained, and how the results will help management's decision making. The proposal also should include estimated research costs.

To meet the manager's information needs, the research plan can call for gathering secondary data, primary data, or both. **Secondary data** consist of information that already exists somewhere, having been collected for another purpose. **Primary data** consist of information collected for the specific purpose at hand.

Secondary data

Information that already exists somewhere, having been collected for another purpose.

Primary data

Information collected for the specific purpose at hand.

Gathering Secondary Data

Researchers usually start by gathering secondary data. The company's internal database provides a good starting point. However, the company can also tap into a wide assortment of external information sources.

Companies can buy secondary data from outside suppliers. For example, Nielsen sells shopper insight data from a consumer panel of more than 250,000 households in 25 countries worldwide, with measures of trial and repeat purchasing, brand loyalty, and buyer demographics. ● Experian Simmons carries out a full spectrum of consumer studies that provide a comprehensive view of the American consumer. The US MONITOR service by The Futures Company sells information on important social and lifestyle trends. These and other firms supply high-quality data to suit a wide variety of marketing information needs.[10]

Using *commercial online databases*, marketing researchers can conduct their own searches of secondary data sources. General database services such as Dialog, ProQuest, and Lexis-Nexis put an incredible wealth of information at the keyboards of marketing decision makers. Beyond commercial Web sites offering information for a fee, almost every industry association, government agency, business publication, and news medium offers free information to those tenacious enough to find their Web sites.

Internet search engines can also be a big help in locating relevant secondary information sources. However, they can also be very frustrating and inefficient. For example, a Red Bull marketer Googling "enhanced water products" would come up with more than 50,000 hits. Still, well-structured, well-designed online searches can be a good starting point to any marketing research project.

Secondary data can usually be obtained more quickly and at a lower cost than primary data. Also, secondary sources can sometimes provide data an individual company cannot

■ Understand
■ Communicate
■ Measure

For over 50 years, marketing professionals have relied on Experian℠ Simmons℠ as the reliable source of marketing information. Experian Simmons provides the most comprehensive view of the American consumer. Our full spectrum of consumer studies includes:

Simmons National Consumer Study
■ First syndicated national study launched in the U.S.
■ Provides over 60,000 data variables to choose from, and usage behavior for all major media, 450+ product categories and 8,000+ brands on 25,000 U.S. adults
■ Media Ratings Council accredited

Simmons National Hispanic Consumer Study
■ First syndicated national study for U.S. Hispanic adults
■ Surveys over 8,000 Hispanic adults annually providing Hispanic-only information on media, acculturation, language usage and preference, nativity, and country of origin as well as culturally-relevant measures on psychographics, lifestyles, attitudes and opinions
■ Media Ratings Council accredited

Simmons Teens Study
■ Surveys approximately 2,300 teens between the ages 12 and 17
■ Bi-annual release with measures of major media usage, product consumption, demographics, lifestyle/psychographic characteristics as well as information on ownership, purchase, and usage of brands, products and services in the financial, entertainment and consumer package good sectors

Simmons Kids Study
■ Surveys approximately 2,200 kids
■ Provides insight into the brands and products they prefer and how much of each they consume plus in-depth media information

SimmonsLOCAL℠
the power of Simmons at the local level.
■ Reports the unique nuances of all of America's 209 media markets
■ Study is integrated into various platforms (i.e. Nielsen Station Index® and Microsoft MapPoint®) which enables users additional ways to analyze data

Simmons Multi-Media Engagement Study
■ Provides ratings on the cognitive, behavioral and emotional involvement consumers have with media vehicles
■ The only syndicated, cross-channel engagement measurement tool available

Experian™
Simmons

600 Third Avenue | New York, NY 10016
212.471.2850 | www.ExperianSimmons.com

● **Consumer database services such as Experian Simmons sell an incredible wealth of information on everything from the products consumers buy and the brands they prefer to their lifestyles, attitudes, and media preferences. Experian Simmons "provides the most comprehensive view of the American consumer."**
Experian Simmons

Observational research
Gathering primary data by observing relevant people, actions, and situations.

collect on its own—information that either is not directly available or would be too expensive to collect. For example, it would be too expensive for Red Bull's marketers to conduct a continuing retail store audit to find out about the market shares, prices, and displays of competitors' brands. But those marketers can buy the InfoScan service from SymphonyIRI Group, which provides this information based on scanner and other data from 34,000 retail stores in markets around the nation.[11]

Secondary data can also present problems. Researchers can rarely obtain all the data they need from secondary sources. For example, Red Bull will not find existing information regarding consumer reactions about a new enhanced-water line that it has not yet placed on the market. Even when data can be found, the information might not be very usable. The researcher must evaluate secondary information carefully to make certain it is *relevant* (fits the research project's needs), *accurate* (reliably collected and reported), *current* (up-to-date enough for current decisions), and *impartial* (objectively collected and reported).

Primary Data Collection

Secondary data provide a good starting point for research and often help to define research problems and objectives. In most cases, however, the company must also collect primary data. ● **Table 4.1** shows that designing a plan for primary data collection calls for a number of decisions on *research approaches, contact methods,* the *sampling plan,* and *research instruments.*

Research Approaches

Research approaches for gathering primary data include observations, surveys, and experiments. We discuss each one in turn.

Observational Research. **Observational research** involves gathering primary data by observing relevant people, actions, and situations. For example, Trader Joe's might evaluate possible new store locations by checking traffic patterns, neighborhood conditions, and the locations of competing Whole Foods, Fresh Market, and other retail chains.

Researchers often observe consumer behavior to glean customer insights they can't obtain by simply asking customers questions. For instance, Fisher-Price has established an observation lab in which it can observe the reactions little tots have to new toys. The Fisher-Price Play Lab is a sunny, toy-strewn space where lucky kids get to test Fisher-Price prototypes, under the watchful eyes of designers who hope to learn what will get them worked up into a new-toy frenzy.

● **Table 4.1** | **Planning Primary Data Collection**

Research Approaches	Contact Methods	Sampling Plan	Research Instruments
Observation	Mail	Sampling unit	Questionnaire
Survey	Telephone	Sample size	Mechanical instruments
Experiment	Personal	Sampling procedure	
	Online		

Marketers not only observe what consumers do but also observe what consumers are saying. As discussed earlier, marketers now routinely listen in on consumer conversations on blogs, social networks, and Web sites. Observing such naturally occurring feedback can provide inputs that simply can't be gained through more structured and formal research approaches.

A wide range of companies now use **ethnographic research**. Ethnographic research involves sending observers to watch and interact with consumers in their "natural environments." The observers might be trained anthropologists and psychologists or company researchers and managers. For example, P&G uses extensive ethnographic research to gain deep insights into serving the world's poor. Three years ago, P&G launched the "$2-a-Day Project," named for the average income of the people it targets worldwide. The project sends ethnographic researchers trekking through the jungles of Brazil, the slums of India, and farming villages in rural China seeking insights into the needs of very-low-income consumers. ● As an example, P&G researchers recently spent time with poor Chinese potato farmer Wei Xiao Yan, observing in detail as she washed her long black hair using only three cups of water. Her family's water supply is a precious commodity—it comes from storing rainwater. P&G must find affordable and practical solutions that both work in Wei's harsh environment and also support her needs to feel attractive.[12]

Ethnographic research
A form of observational research that involves sending trained observers to watch and interact with consumers in their "natural environments."

Insights from P&G's $2-a-Day Program have already produced some successful new products for emerging markets—such as a skin-sensitive detergent for women who wash clothing by hand. In the works is a body cleanser formulated to clean without much water—it generates foam, which can be easily wiped away, instead of lather. Another product is a leave-in hair conditioner that requires no water at all. For underserved customers like Wei Xiao Yan, P&G has learned, it must develop products that are not just effective and affordable but are also aspirational.

Beyond conducting ethnographic research in physical consumer environments, many companies now routinely conduct *Netnography* research—observing consumers in a natural context on the Internet. Observing people as they interact on and move about the Internet can provide useful insights into both online and offline buying motives and behavior.[13]

● **Ethnographic research: To better understand the needs of the world's poor, P&G sends researchers trekking through the jungles of Brazil, the slums of India, and farming villages in rural China to observe consumers in their "natural environments." Here, they watch Chinese potato farmer Wei Xiao Yan wash her long black hair with great care using only three cups of water.**
Benjamin Lowy/Getty Images

Observational and ethnographic research often yield the kinds of details that just don't emerge from traditional research questionnaires or focus groups. Whereas traditional quantitative research approaches seek to test known hypotheses and obtain answers to well-defined product or strategy questions, observational research can generate fresh customer and market insights that people are unwilling or unable to provide. It provides a window into customers' unconscious actions and unexpressed needs and feelings.

In contrast, however, some things simply cannot be observed, such as attitudes, motives, or private behavior. Long-term or infrequent behavior is also difficult to observe. Finally, observations can be very difficult to interpret. Because of these limitations, researchers often use observation along with other data collection methods.

Survey research
Gathering primary data by asking people questions about their knowledge, attitudes, preferences, and buying behavior.

Survey Research. **Survey research**, the most widely used method for primary data collection, is the approach best suited for gathering descriptive information. A company that wants to know about people's knowledge, attitudes, preferences, or buying behavior can often find out by asking them directly.

The major advantage of survey research is its flexibility; it can be used to obtain many different kinds of information in many different situations. Surveys addressing almost any marketing question or decision can be conducted by phone or mail, in person, or online.

However, survey research also presents some problems. Sometimes people are unable to answer survey questions because they cannot remember or have never thought about what they do and why they do it. People may be unwilling to respond to unknown interviewers or about things they consider private. Respondents may answer survey questions even when they do not know the answer just to appear smarter or more informed. Or they may try to help the interviewer by giving pleasing answers. Finally, busy people may not take the time, or they might resent the intrusion into their privacy.

Experimental research

Gathering primary data by selecting matched groups of subjects, giving them different treatments, controlling related factors, and checking for differences in group responses.

Experimental Research. Whereas observation is best suited for exploratory research and surveys for descriptive research, **experimental research** is best suited for gathering causal information. Experiments involve selecting matched groups of subjects, giving them different treatments, controlling unrelated factors, and checking for differences in group responses. Thus, experimental research tries to explain cause-and-effect relationships.

For example, before adding a new sandwich to its menu, McDonald's might use experiments to test the effects on sales of two different prices it might charge. It could introduce the new sandwich at one price in one city and at another price in another city. If the cities are similar, and if all other marketing efforts for the sandwich are the same, then differences in sales in the two cities could be related to the price charged.

Contact Methods

Information can be collected by mail, telephone, personal interview, or online. ● **Table 4.2** shows the strengths and weaknesses of each contact method.

Mail, Telephone, and Personal Interviewing. *Mail questionnaires* can be used to collect large amounts of information at a low cost per respondent. Respondents may give more honest answers to more personal questions on a mail questionnaire than to an unknown interviewer in person or over the phone. Also, no interviewer is involved to bias respondents' answers.

● **Table 4.2** | **Strengths and Weaknesses of Contact Methods**

	Mail	Telephone	Personal	Online
Flexibility	Poor	Good	Excellent	Good
Quantity of data that can be collected	Good	Fair	Excellent	Good
Control of interviewer effects	Excellent	Fair	Poor	Fair
Control of sample	Fair	Excellent	Good	Excellent
Speed of data collection	Poor	Excellent	Good	Excellent
Response rate	Poor	Poor	Good	Good
Cost	Good	Fair	Poor	Excellent

Source: Based on Donald S. Tull and Del I. Hawkins, *Marketing Research: Measurement and Method,* 7th ed. (New York: Macmillan Publishing Company, 1993). Adapted with permission of the authors.

However, mail questionnaires are not very flexible; all respondents answer the same questions in a fixed order. Mail surveys usually take longer to complete, and the response rate—the number of people returning completed questionnaires—is often very low. Finally, the researcher often has little control over the mail questionnaire sample. Even with a good mailing list, it is hard to control *who* at a particular address fills out the questionnaire. As a result of the shortcomings, more and more marketers are now shifting to faster, more flexible, and lower-cost e-mail and online surveys.

Telephone interviewing is one of the best methods for gathering information quickly, and it provides greater flexibility than mail questionnaires. Interviewers can explain difficult questions and, depending on the answers they receive, skip some questions or probe on others. Response rates tend to be higher than with mail questionnaires, and interviewers can ask to speak to respondents with the desired characteristics or even by name.

However, with telephone interviewing, the cost per respondent is higher than with mail or online questionnaires. Also, people may not want to discuss personal questions with an interviewer. The method introduces interviewer bias—the way interviewers talk, how they ask questions, and other differences that may affect respondents' answers. Finally, in this age of do-not-call lists and promotion-harassed consumers, potential survey respondents are increasingly hanging up on telephone interviewers rather than talking with them.

Personal interviewing takes two forms: individual interviewing and group interviewing. *Individual interviewing* involves talking with people in their homes or offices, on the street, or in shopping malls. Such interviewing is flexible. Trained interviewers can guide interviews, explain difficult questions, and explore issues as the situation requires. They can show subjects actual products, advertisements, or packages and observe reactions and behavior. However, individual personal interviews may cost three to four times as much as telephone interviews.

Group interviewing consists of inviting 6 to 10 people to meet with a trained moderator to talk about a product, service, or organization. Participants normally are paid a small sum for attending. A moderator encourages free and easy discussion, hoping that group interactions will bring out actual feelings and thoughts. At the same time, the moderator "focuses" the discussion—hence the name **focus group interviewing**.

In traditional focus groups, researchers and marketers watch the focus group discussions from behind a one-way mirror and record comments in writing or on video for later study. Focus group researchers often use videoconferencing and Internet technology to connect marketers in distant locations with live focus group action. Using cameras and two-way sound systems, marketing executives in a far-off boardroom can look in and listen, using remote controls to zoom in on faces and pan the focus group at will.

Along with observational research, focus group interviewing has become one of the major qualitative marketing research tools for gaining fresh insights into consumer thoughts and feelings. In focus group settings, researchers not only hear consumer ideas and opinions, they can also observe facial expressions, body movements, group interplay, and conversational flows. However, focus group studies present some challenges. They usually employ small samples to keep time and costs down, and it may be hard to generalize from the results. Moreover, consumers in focus groups are not always open and honest about their real feelings, behavior, and intentions in front of other people.

To overcome these problems, many researchers are tinkering with the focus group design. Some companies use *immersion groups*—small groups of consumers who interact directly and informally with product designers without a focus group moderator present. Other researchers are changing the environments in which they conduct focus groups to help consumers relax and elicit more authentic responses. ● For example, Lexus recently hosted a series of "An Evening with Lexus" dinners with groups of customers in customers' homes:[14]

> According to Lexus group vice president and general manager Mark Templin, the best way to find out why luxury car buyers did or didn't become Lexus owners is to dine with them—up close and personal in their homes. At the first dinner, 16 owners of Lexus, Mercedes, BMW, Audi, Land Rover, and other high-end cars traded their perceptions of the Lexus brand over a

Focus group interviewing
Personal interviewing that involves inviting 6 to 10 people to gather for a few hours with a trained interviewer to talk about a product, service, or organization. The interviewer "focuses" the group discussion on important issues.

● New focus group environments: Lexus USA general manager Mark Templin hosts "An Evening with Lexus" dinners with luxury car buyers to figure out why they did or didn't become Lexus owners.

Courtesy of Lexus

sumptuous meal prepared by a famous chef at a home in Beverly Hills. Templin gained many actionable insights. For example, some owners viewed Lexus vehicles as unexciting. "Everyone had driven a Lexus at some point and had a great experience," he says. "But the Lexus they [had] wasn't as fun to drive as the car they have now. It's our challenge to show that Lexus is more fun to drive today than it was 15 years ago." Templin was also surprised to learn the extent to which the grown children of luxury car buyers influence what car they purchase. Now, Templin says, future Lexus marketing will also target young adults who may not buy luxury cars but who influence their parents' decisions.

Individual and focus group interviews can add a personal touch as opposed to more numbers-oriented research. "We get lots of research, and it tells us what we need to run our business, but I get more out of talking one-on-one," says Lexus's Templin. "It really comes to life when I hear people say it."

Online marketing research

Collecting primary data online through Internet surveys, online focus groups, Web-based experiments, or tracking consumers' online behavior.

Online Marketing Research. The growth of the Internet has had a dramatic impact on how marketing research is conducted. Increasingly, researchers are collecting primary data through **online marketing research**: Internet surveys, online panels, experiments, and online focus groups and brand communities.

Online research can take many forms. A company can use the Internet as a survey medium: It can include a questionnaire on its Web site or use e-mail to invite people to answer questions, create online panels that provide regular feedback, or conduct live discussions or online focus groups. Researchers can also conduct online experiments. They can experiment with different prices, headlines, or product features on different Web or mobile sites or at different times to learn the relative effectiveness of their offers. They can set up virtual shopping environments and use them to test new products and marketing programs. Or a company can learn about the behavior of online customers by following their click streams as they visit the online site and move to other sites.

The Internet is especially well suited to *quantitative* research—for example, conducting marketing surveys and collecting data. More than three-quarters of all Americans now have access to the Internet, making it a fertile channel for reaching a broad cross-section of consumers.[15] As response rates for traditional survey approaches decline and costs increase, the Internet is quickly replacing mail and the telephone as the dominant data collection methodology.

Internet-based survey research offers many advantages over traditional phone, mail, and personal interviewing approaches. The most obvious advantages are speed and low costs. By going online, researchers can quickly and easily distribute Internet surveys to thousands of respondents simultaneously via e-mail or by posting them on selected online sites. Responses can be almost instantaneous, and because respondents themselves enter the information, researchers can tabulate, review, and share research data as the information arrives.

Online research also usually costs much less than research conducted through mail, phone, or personal interviews. Using the Internet eliminates most of the postage, phone, interviewer, and data-handling costs associated with the other approaches. Moreover, sample size has little impact on costs. Once the questionnaire is set up, there's little difference in cost between 10 respondents and 10,000 respondents on the Internet.

Its low cost puts online research well within the reach of almost any business, large or small. In fact, with the Internet, what was once the domain of research experts is now available to almost any would-be researcher. ● Even smaller, less sophisticated researchers can use online survey services such as Snap Surveys (www.snapsurveys.com) and

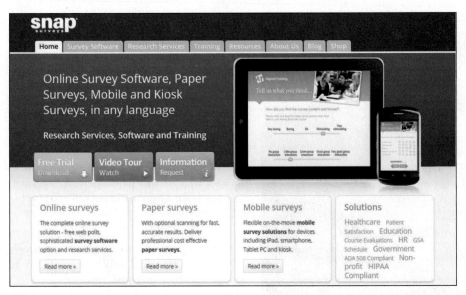

● Online research: Thanks to survey services such as Snap Surveys, almost any business, large or small, can create, publish, and distribute its own custom online or mobile surveys in minutes.

Snap Surveys

Online focus groups
Gathering a small group of people online with a trained moderator to chat about a product, service, or organization and gain qualitative insights about consumer attitudes and behavior.

SurveyMonkey (www.surveymonkey.com) to create, publish, and distribute their own custom surveys in minutes.

Internet-based surveys also tend to be more interactive and engaging, easier to complete, and less intrusive than traditional phone or mail surveys. As a result, they usually garner higher response rates. The Internet is an excellent medium for reaching the hard-to-reach consumer—for example, the often-elusive teen, single, affluent, and well-educated audiences. It's also good for reaching working mothers and other people who lead busy lives. Such people are well represented online, and they can respond in their own space and at their own convenience.

Just as marketing researchers have rushed to use the Internet for quantitative surveys and data collection, they are now also adopting *qualitative* Internet-based research approaches, such as online focus groups, blogs, and social networks. The Internet can provide a fast, low-cost way to gain qualitative customer insights.

A primary qualitative Internet-based research approach is **online focus groups**. For example, online research firm FocusVision offer its InterVu service, which harnesses the power of Web conferencing to conduct focus groups with participants at remote locations, anywhere in the world at any time. ● Using their own Webcams, InterVu participants can log on to focus sessions from their homes or offices and see, hear, and react to each other in real-time, face-to-face discussions.[16] Such focus groups can be conducted in any language and viewed with simultaneous translation. They work well for bringing together people from different parts of the country or world at low cost. Researchers can view the sessions in real-time from just about anywhere, eliminating travel, lodging, and facility costs. Finally, although online focus groups require some advance scheduling, results are almost immediate.

Although growing rapidly, both quantitative and qualitative Internet-based research have some drawbacks. One major problem is controlling who's in the online sample. Without seeing respondents, it's difficult to know who they really are. To overcome such sample and context problems, many online research firms use opt-in communities and respondent panels. Alternatively, many companies are now developing their own custom social networks and using them to gain customer inputs and insights. For example, in addition to picking customers' brains in face-to-face events such as "An Evening with Lexus" dinners in customers' homes, Lexus has built an extensive online research community called the Lexus Advisory Board, which consists of 20,000 invitation-only Lexus owners representing a wide

● Online focus groups: FocusVision's InterVu service lets focus group participants at remote locations see, hear, and react to each other in real-time, face-to-face discussions.

FocusVision Worldwide, Inc.

range of demographics, psychographics, and model ownership. Lexus regularly surveys the group to obtain input on everything from perceptions of the brand to customer relationships with dealers.[17]

Thus, in recent years, the Internet has become an important tool for conducting research and developing customer insights. But today's marketing researchers are going even further—well beyond structured online surveys, focus groups, and Internet communities. Increasingly, they are listening to and watching consumers by actively mining the rich veins of unsolicited, unstructured, "bottom-up" customer information already coursing around the Internet.

This might be as simple as scanning customer reviews and comments on the company's brand site or on shopping sites such as Amazon.com or BestBuy.com. Or it might mean using sophisticated online-analysis tools to deeply analyze mountains of consumer comments and messages found in blogs or on social networking sites, such as Facebook or Twitter. Listening to and watching consumers online can provide valuable insights into what consumers are saying or feeling about brands. As one information expert puts it, "The Web knows what you want."[18] (See Real Marketing 4.1.)

Sampling Plan

Sample

A segment of the population selected for marketing research to represent the population as a whole.

Marketing researchers usually draw conclusions about large groups of consumers by studying a small sample of the total consumer population. A **sample** is a segment of the population selected for marketing research to represent the population as a whole. Ideally, the sample should be representative so that the researcher can make accurate estimates of the thoughts and behaviors of the larger population.

Designing the sample requires three decisions. First, *who* is to be studied (what *sampling unit*)? The answer to this question is not always obvious. For example, to learn about the decision-making process for a family automobile purchase, should the subject be the husband, the wife, other family members, dealership salespeople, or all of these? Second, *how many* people should be included (what *sample size*)? Large samples give more reliable results than small samples. However, larger samples usually cost more, and it is not necessary to sample the entire target market or even a large portion to get reliable results.

Finally, *how* should the people in the sample be *chosen* (what *sampling procedure*)?
● **Table 4.3** describes different kinds of samples. Using *probability samples*, each population member has a known chance of being included in the sample, and researchers can calculate confidence limits for sampling error. But when probability sampling costs too much or takes too much time, marketing researchers often take *nonprobability*

● **Table 4.3** | **Types of Samples**

Probability Sample

Simple random sample	Every member of the population has a known and equal chance of selection.
Stratified random sample	The population is divided into mutually exclusive groups (such as age groups), and random samples are drawn from each group.
Cluster (area) sample	The population is divided into mutually exclusive groups (such as blocks), and the researcher draws a sample of the groups to interview.

Nonprobability Sample

Convenience sample	The researcher selects the easiest population members from which to obtain information.
Judgment sample	The researcher uses his or her judgment to select population members who are good prospects for accurate information.
Quota sample	The researcher finds and interviews a prescribed number of people in each of several categories.

Real Marketing 4.1

Listening Online: Sophisticated Web Research or Just a Little Bit Creepy?

Thanks to the burgeoning world of blogs, social networks, and other Internet forums, marketers now have near-real-time access to a flood of online consumer information. It's all there for the digging—praise, criticism, recommendations, actions—revealed in what consumers are saying and doing as they ply the Internet. Forward-looking marketers are now mining valuable customer insights from this rich new vein of unprompted, "bottom-up" information.

Whereas traditional marketing research provides more logical consumer responses to structured and intrusive research questions, online listening provides the passion and spontaneity of unsolicited consumer opinions.

Listening online might involve something as simple as scanning customer reviews on the company's brand site or on popular shopping sites such as Amazon.com or BestBuy.com. Such reviews are plentiful, address specific products, and provide unvarnished customer reactions. If customers in the market for a company's brands are reading and reacting to such reviews, so should the company's marketers.

At a deeper level, marketers now employ sophisticated Web-analysis tools to listen in on and mine nuggets from the churning mass of consumer comments and conversations in blogs, news articles, online forums, and social networking sites such as Facebook or Twitter. But beyond monitoring what customers are saying about them online, companies are also watching what customers are *doing* online. Marketers scrutinize consumer Web-browsing behavior in precise detail and use the resulting insights to personalize shopping experiences.

For example, based on her current and past browsing behavior, a customer checking out shoes at a favorite online apparel site might also receive unsolicited "just for you" suggestions for matching accessories tailored to her specific needs and tastes. Her online shopping experience might also depend on other browsing behaviors. For instance, more leisurely browsers—say, those

shopping from home and spending lots of time on each screen—might see more videos, features, and product descriptions. Those whose browsing behavior suggests that they might be in a hurry—say, shopping from work and clicking rapidly from screen to screen—might see simpler pages and more direct paths to checkout.

More broadly, information about what consumers do while trolling the vast expanse of the Internet—what searches they make, the sites they visit, what music and programming they consume, how they shop, and what they buy—is pure gold to marketers. And today's marketers are busy mining that gold.

On the Internet today, everybody knows who you are. In fact, legions of Internet companies know your gender, your age, the neighborhood you live in, what you are saying on Facebook and Twitter, that you like pickup trucks, and that you spent, say, three hours and 43 seconds on a Web site for pet lovers on a rainy day in January. All that data streams through myriad computer networks, where it's sorted, cataloged, analyzed, and then used to deliver ads aimed squarely at you, potentially anywhere you travel on the Internet. It's called behavioral targeting—tracking consumers' online behavior and using it to target ads to them. So, for example, if you place a mobile phone in your Amazon.com shopping cart but don't buy it, you might expect to see some ads for that very type of phone the next time you visit your favorite ESPN site to catch up on the latest sports scores.

All this is amazing enough, but the newest wave of Web analytics and targeting takes online eavesdropping even further—from *behavioral* targeting to *social* targeting. Whereas behavioral targeting tracks

consumer movements across online sites, social targeting also mines individual online social connections and conversations. Research shows that consumers shop a lot like their friends and are five times more likely to respond to ads from brands friends use. Social targeting links customer data to social interaction data from social networking sites.

So, instead of just having a Zappos.com ad for running shoes pop up because you've recently searched for running shoes (behavioral targeting), an ad for a specific pair of running shoes pops up because a friend that you're connected to via Twitter just bought those shoes from Zappos.com last week (social targeting). Social targeting can even capture the dynamics of real-time conversations. For example, more than just targeting 24- to 26-year-old males who are both sports fans and car enthusiasts, Chevrolet made its ad message more relevant by targeting those consumers while they are talking about football on a mobile Twitter app during the Super Bowl. When they checked the app, targeted consumers saw an ad that prompted them to check out Chevy's Super Bowl video on YouTube.

Online listening. Behavioral targeting. Social targeting. All of these are great for marketers as they work to mine customer insights from the massive amounts of consumer information swirling around the Internet. The biggest question? You've probably

Marketers watch what consumers say and do online, then use the resulting insights to personalize online shopping experiences. Is it sophisticated Web research or "just a little creepy"?

Andresr/Shutterstock.com

already guessed it. As marketers get more adept at trolling blogs, social networks, and other Internet domains, what happens to consumer privacy? Yup, that's the downside. At what point does sophisticated online research cross the line into consumer stalking?

Proponents claim that behavioral and social targeting benefit more than abuse consumers by feeding back ads and products that are more relevant to their interests. But to many consumers and public advocates, following consumers online and stalking them with ads feels more than just a little creepy. Regulators and others are stepping in. The FTC has recommended the creation of a "Do Not Track" system (the Internet equivalent to the "Do Not Call"

registry)—which would let people opt out of having their actions monitored online—while some Internet browsers have heeded the concerns by adding "Do Not Track" features.

Despite such concerns, however, online listening will continue to grow and to get smarter. And, with appropriate safeguards, it promises benefits for both companies and

customers. Tapping into online conversations and behavior lets companies hear the unprompted voice of customers, providing valuable insights into real consumer feelings, values, and brand perceptions. Companies that can figure out how to tap online consumer conversations in a meaningful way will gain a substantial advantage over competitors who turn a deaf ear.

Sources: Adapted excerpts, quotes, and other information from Amit Avner, "How Social Targeting Can Lead to Discovery," *Adotas,* February 7, 2012, www.adotas.com/2012/02/how-social-targeting-can-lead-to-discovery/; Stephen Baker, "The Web Knows What You Want," *BusinessWeek,* July 27, 2009, p. 48; Brian Morrissey, "Connect the Thoughts," *Adweek,* June 29, 2009, pp. 10–11; Paul Sloan, "The Quest for the Perfect Online Ad," *Business 2.0,* March 2007, p. 88; Elizabeth A. Sullivan, "10 Minutes with Kristin Bush," *Marketing News,* September 30, 2009, pp. 26–28; and Edward Wyatt and Tanzina Vega, "Conflict over How Open 'Do Not Track' Talks Will Be," *New York Times,* March 30, 2012, p. B3.

samples, even though their sampling error cannot be measured. These varied ways of drawing samples have different costs and time limitations as well as different accuracy and statistical properties. Which method is best depends on the needs of the research project.

Research Instruments

In collecting primary data, marketing researchers have a choice of two main research instruments: *questionnaires* and *mechanical devices*.

Questionnaires. The questionnaire is by far the most common instrument, whether administered in person, by phone, by e-mail, or online. Questionnaires are very flexible—there are many ways to ask questions. Closed-end questions include all the possible answers, and subjects make choices among them. Examples include multiple-choice questions and scale questions. Open-end questions allow respondents to answer in their own words. In a survey of airline users, Southwest Airlines might simply ask, "What is your opinion of Southwest Airlines?" Or it might ask people to complete a sentence: "When I choose an airline, the most important consideration is. . . ." These and other kinds of open-end questions often reveal more than closed-end questions because they do not limit respondents' answers.

Open-end questions are especially useful in exploratory research, when the researcher is trying to find out *what* people think but is not measuring *how many* people think in a certain way. Closed-end questions, on the other hand, provide answers that are easier to interpret and tabulate.

Researchers should also use care in the *wording* and *ordering* of questions. They should use simple, direct, and unbiased wording. Questions should be arranged in a logical order. The first question should create interest if possible, and difficult or personal questions should be asked last so that respondents do not become defensive.

Mechanical Instruments. Although questionnaires are the most common research instrument, researchers also use mechanical instruments to monitor consumer behavior. Nielsen Media Research attaches people meters to television sets, cable boxes, and satellite systems in selected homes to record who watches which programs. Retailers likewise use checkout scanners to record shoppers' purchases. Other mechanical devices measure subjects' physical responses to marketing offerings. ● Consider this example:[19]

Time Warner's new Medialab at its New York headquarters looks more like a chic consumer electronics store than a research lab. But the lab employs a nifty collection of high-tech observation techniques to capture the changing ways that today's viewers are using and reacting to television and Web content. The MediaLab uses biometric measures to analyze every show subjects watch, every site they visit, and every commercial they skip. Meanwhile, mechanical devices assess viewer engagement via physiological measures of skin temperature, heart rate, and facial and eye movements. Observers behind two-way mirrors or using cameras that peer over each subject's shoulder make real-time assessments of Web browsing behavior. In all, the deep consumer insights gained from MediaLab observations are helping Time Warner prepare for marketing in today's rapidly changing digital media landscape.

●**Time Warner's Medialab uses high-tech observation to capture the changing ways that today's viewers are using and reacting to television and Web content.**

© Time Warner 2012, photograph by Henrik Olund.

Still other researchers are applying *neuromarketing*, measuring brain activity to learn how consumers feel and respond. Marketing scientists using MRI scans and EEG devices have learned that tracking brain electrical activity and blood flow can provide companies with insights into what turns consumers on and off regarding their brands and marketing. "Companies have always aimed for the customer's heart, but the head may make a better target," suggests one neuromarketer. "Neuromarketing is reaching consumers where the action is: the brain."[20]

Companies ranging from PepsiCo and Disney to Google and Microsoft now hire neuromarketing research companies such as Sands Research, NeuroFocus, and EmSense to help figure out what people are really thinking. For example, PepsiCo's Frito-Lay worked with NeuroFocus to assess consumer motivations underlying the success of its Cheetos snack brand. After scanning the brains of carefully chosen consumers, NeuroFocus learned that part of what makes Cheetos a junk-food staple is the messy orange cheese dust—that's right, the neon stuff that gloms onto your fingers and then smears on your shirt or the couch cushions. As it turns out, the icky coating triggers a powerful brain response: a sense of "giddy subversion" that make the messiness more than worth the trouble it causes. Using this finding, Frito-Lay successfully framed an entire advertising campaign around the mess Cheetos makes. For its part, NeuroFocus won an award for outstanding advertising research.[21]

Although neuromarketing techniques can measure consumer involvement and emotional responses second by second, such brain responses can be difficult to interpret. Thus, neuromarketing is usually used in combination with other research approaches to gain a more complete picture of what goes on inside consumers' heads.

Implementing the Research Plan

The researcher next puts the marketing research plan into action. This involves collecting, processing, and analyzing the information. Data collection can be carried out by the company's marketing research staff or outside firms. Researchers should watch closely to make sure that the plan is implemented correctly. They must guard against problems of interacting with respondents, with the quality of participants' responses, and with interviewers who make mistakes or take shortcuts.

Researchers must also process and analyze the collected data to isolate important information and insight. They need to check data for accuracy and completeness and code it for analysis. The researchers then tabulate the results and compute statistical measures.

Interpreting and Reporting the Findings

The market researcher must now interpret the findings, draw conclusions, and report them to management. The researcher should not try to overwhelm managers with numbers and fancy statistical techniques. Rather, the researcher should present important findings and insights that are useful in the major decisions faced by management.

However, interpretation should not be left only to researchers. Although they are often experts in research design and statistics, the marketing manager knows more about the problem and the decisions that must be made. The best research means little if the manager blindly accepts faulty interpretations from the researcher. Similarly, managers may be biased. They might tend to accept research results that show what they expected and reject those that they did not expect or hope for. In many cases, findings can be interpreted in different ways, and discussions between researchers and managers will help point to the best interpretations. Thus, managers and researchers must work together closely when interpreting research results, and both must share responsibility for the research process and resulting decisions.

Objective 4 ┈┈▶
Explain how companies analyze and use marketing information.

Analyzing and Using Marketing Information

Information gathered in internal databases and through competitive marketing intelligence and marketing research usually requires additional analysis. Managers may need help applying the information to gain customer and market insights that will improve their marketing decisions. This help may include advanced statistical analysis to learn more about the relationships within a set of data. Information analysis might also involve the application of analytical models that will help marketers make better decisions.

Once the information has been processed and analyzed, it must be made available to the right decision makers at the right time. In the following sections, we look deeper into analyzing and using marketing information.

Customer Relationship Management

The question of how best to analyze and use individual customer data presents special problems. Most companies are awash in information about their customers. In fact, smart companies capture information at every possible customer *touch point*. These touch points include customer purchases, sales force contacts, service and support calls, online site visits, satisfaction surveys, credit and payment interactions, market research studies—every contact between a customer and a company.

Unfortunately, this information is usually scattered widely across the organization. It is buried deep in the separate databases and records of different company departments. To overcome such problems, many companies are now turning to **customer relationship management (CRM)** to manage detailed information about individual customers and carefully manage customer touch points to maximize customer loyalty.

Customer relationship management (CRM)

Managing detailed information about individual customers and carefully managing customer touch points to maximize customer loyalty.

CRM consists of sophisticated software and analytical tools from companies such as Oracle, Microsoft, Salesforce.com, and SAS that integrate customer information from all sources, analyze it in depth, and apply the results to build stronger customer relationships. CRM integrates everything that a company's sales, service, and marketing teams know about individual customers, providing a 360-degree view of the customer relationship.

CRM analysts develop *data warehouses* and use sophisticated *data mining* techniques to unearth the riches hidden in customer data. A data warehouse is a company-wide electronic database of finely detailed customer information that needs to be sifted through for gems. The purpose of a data warehouse is not only to gather information but also to pull it together into a central, accessible location. Then, once the data warehouse brings the data together, the company uses high-powered data mining techniques to sift through the mounds of data and dig out interesting findings about customers.

These findings often lead to marketing opportunities. For example, Macy's digs deeply into customer data and uses the insights gained to personalize its customers' shopping experiences:

Seventy percent of Americans visit a Macy's store or its Web site at least once a year. "We don't need more customers—we need the customers we have to spend more time with us," says Macy's chief marketing officer. To that end, Macy's has assembled a huge database of 30 million households, containing reams of data on individual households, including in-store and online purchases, style preferences and personal motivations, and even browsing patterns at Macy's Web sites. ● As part of its MyMacy's program, the retailer deeply analyzes the data and uses the resulting insights to hyper-personalize each customer's experience. "With a business this size, the data they have on their customers is mind-boggling," says an analyst. "They're [the ultimate in] one-to-one marketing."

For example, Macy's now sends out up to 500,000 unique versions of a single direct mail catalogue. "My book might look very different from [someone else's]," says the Macy's CMO. "I'm not such a great homemaker, but I am a cosmetic, shoe, and jewelry person, so what you might see in my book would be all of those categories." Similarly, in the digital space, under its "Intelligent Display" initiative, Macy's can track what customers browse on the company Web site, then have a relevant display ad appear as they are browsing on another site. Future MyMacy's actions will include e-mail, mobile, and Web site customizations. The ultimate goal of the massive database effort, says the CMO, is to "put the customer at the center of all decisions."[22]

● **Through its MyMacy's program, Macy's digs deeply into its huge customer database and uses the resulting insights to hyper-personalize its customers' shopping experiences. "Happy Birthday, Keri!"**

Photo courtesy of Gary Armstrong

By using CRM to understand customers better, companies can provide higher levels of customer service and develop deeper customer relationships. They can use CRM to pinpoint high-value customers, target them more effectively, cross-sell the company's products, and create offers tailored to specific customer requirements. For example, Caesars Entertainment, the world's largest casino operator, maintains a vast customer database and uses its CRM system to manage day-to-day relationships with important customers at its 52 casino properties around the world (see Real Marketing 4.2).

CRM benefits don't come without costs or risk, either in collecting the original customer data or in maintaining and mining it. The most common CRM mistake is to view CRM as a technology and software solution only. Yet technology alone cannot build profitable customer relationships. Companies can't improve customer relationships by simply installing some new software. Instead, marketers should start with the fundamentals of managing customer relationships and *then* employ high-tech solutions. They should focus first on the R—it's the *relationship* that CRM is all about.

Distributing and Using Marketing Information

Marketing information has no value until it is used to gain customer insights and make better marketing decisions. Thus, the marketing information system must make the information readily available to managers and others who need it. In some cases, this means providing managers with regular performance reports, intelligence updates, and reports on the results of research studies.

But marketing managers may also need nonroutine information for special situations and on-the-spot decisions. For example, a sales manager having trouble with a large customer may want a summary of the account's sales and profitability over the past year. Or a brand manager may want to get a sense of the amount of online buzz surrounding the launch of a recent advertising campaign. These days, therefore, information distribution involves entering information into databases and making it available in a timely, user-friendly way.

Many firms use company *intranet* and internal CRM systems to facilitate this process. These systems provide ready access to research and intelligence information, customer contact information, reports, shared work documents, and more. For example, the CRM system at phone and online gift retailer 1-800-Flowers gives customer-facing employees real-time access to customer information. When a repeat customer calls, the system immediately pulls up data on previous transactions and other contacts, helping reps make the customer's experience easier and more relevant. For instance, "If a customer usually buys tulips for his

Real Marketing 4.2

Caesars Entertainment:
Hitting the CRM Jackpot

Caesars Entertainment consists of a huge network of 52 casino resorts in seven countries, operating under well-known brands such as Caesars, Harrah's, Bally's, Paris, Flamingo, and Horseshoe. Each resort is a complex mix of gaming casinos, hotels, restaurants, shops, theaters, and other entertainment venues. "Our business has grown to encapsulate so much more than gaming," says Caesars Entertainment chairman and CEO Gary Loveman. "Every single one of our . . . resorts across the country provides a 360-degree entertainment experience."

What is it that holds this massive conglomeration of resorts together? Anyone at Caesars will tell you that it's all about managing customer relationships. When you get right down to it, in physical terms, most casinos are pretty much alike. Most customers can't distinguish one company's slot machines, game tables, restaurants, shows, and hotel rooms from another's. What sets Caesars apart is the way it relates to its customers and creates customer loyalty. During the past decade and a half, Caesars has become *the* model for CRM excellence.

At the heart of Caesars' CRM strategy is its pioneering card-based Total Rewards program, the gaming industry's first and by far most successful loyalty program. Total Rewards members receive points based on the amount they spend at Caesars facilities, whether through gaming, dining, a hotel stay, or any other type of entertainment spending. They can then redeem the points for a variety of perks, such as free play, food, merchandise, rooms, spa sessions, golfing, and show tickets. Total Rewards forms the basis for a two-part CRM process. First, the company uses the program to collect information about the types and amounts of activities that customers choose most often. Then, it mines this information to identify the best offerings for each customer's specific preferences, with an emphasis on the VIP guests who contribute most to the business.

Caesars maintains a vast database—more than 45 million members in all. Every time a member swipes a Total Rewards card to buy a meal, see a show, check into a hotel, or play at one of Caesars' 55,000 slot machines or 2,500 game tables, the data zips off into Caesars' bulging database. Once gathered, Caesars mines this information deeply to gain important customer insights into the characteristics and behavior of individual customers—who they are, how often they visit, how long they stay, and what forms of entertainment they enjoy most.

From its Total Rewards data, Caesars has learned that its best customers aren't always the "high rollers" that have long been the focus of the industry. Rather, they are often ordinary folks from all walks of life—middle-aged and retired teachers, bankers, and doctors who have discretionary income and time. More often than not, these customers visit casinos for an evening, rather than staying overnight at the hotel, and they are more likely to play at the slots than at tables. What motivates them? For many, it's the intense anticipation and excitement of gambling itself. For others, it's another form of entertainment, whether dining or shopping or golf or shows.

Using such insights, Caesars focuses its marketing and service development strategies on the needs of its best customers. For example, the company's advertising reflects the feeling of exuberance that target customers seek. The data insights also help Caesars do a better job of managing day-to-day customer relationships. After a day's gaming, by the next morning, it knows which customers should be rewarded with free show tickets, dinner vouchers, or room upgrades.

In fact, the sophisticated Total Rewards system now analyzes customer information in real time, from the moment customers swipe their rewards cards, creating the ideal link between data and the customer experience. Based on up-to-the-minute customer information, the clerk at a Caesars hotel can see a customer's history and determine whether that customer should get a room upgrade, based on hotel booking levels at that time and on the customer's past level of play. Or casino staff might walk up to regular customers as they are playing and offer them a free meal, $25 to play more slots, or maybe just wish them a happy birthday.

But Caesars doesn't just wait for customers to walk through its doors. It uses the insights gained from the Total Rewards system to craft personalized offers and promotions. For example, a good customer might receive as many as 150 pieces of direct mail from Caesars in a given year. That might sound like a junk-mail nightmare, but most Total Rewards members actually like it. Each personalized mailing delivers relevant information and rewards.

Caesars Entertainment maintains a vast customer database and uses its Total Rewards CRM program to manage day-to-day relationships with important customers at its casino properties around the world.

Courtesy of Caesars Entertainment Corporation. Used with permission.

Taking its successful loyalty program a step further, Caesars recently expanded the Total Rewards network to include more than 500 online retailers such as Apple, Target, Best Buy, and Banana Republic, as well as travel partners such as Norwegian Cruise Lines and Hawaiian Airlines. Members who opt in can now earn Total Rewards points through these partner companies and redeem points there as well. And every time Total Rewards members do business with one of the partner companies, the Caesars database gets to know them even better.

Caesars' CRM efforts have paid off like a royal flush. The company has found that happy customers are much more loyal, and Caesars' Total Rewards customers appear to be a happier bunch today than ever before. Customer satisfaction scores reached an all-time high last year. Compared with nonmembers, Total Rewards members visit the company's casinos more frequently, stay longer, and spend a greater share of gaming and entertainment dollars in Caesars than in rival casinos. In fact, nearly two-thirds of Total Rewards members report that Total Rewards is their preferred loyalty program in the industry. Since setting up Total Rewards almost fifteen years ago, Caesars has seen its share of customers' average annual casino entertainment budgets rise 20 percent.

Caesars refers to Total Rewards as "the vertebrae of our business," claiming that 85 percent of its revenue is generated in some way by the program. CEO Loveman says that Caesars' CRM efforts are "constantly bringing us closer to our customers so we better understand their preferences, and from that understanding we are able to improve the entertainment experiences we offer." Another Caesars executive puts it even more simply: "It's no different from what a good retailer or grocery store does. We're trying to figure out which products sell, and we're trying to increase our customer loyalty." During a time when a weak economy and reduced consumer spending have wreaked havoc on Caesars and the gaming industry as a whole, the Total Rewards CRM program has emerged as Caesars' ace in the hole. Through smart CRM investments, Caesars has hit the customer-loyalty jackpot.

Sources: Howard Stutz, "Caesars Expands Total Rewards Program," *Las Vegas Review-Journal*, March 1, 2012; "Caesars Entertainment's 'Escape To Total Rewards' Concludes Its Multi-Million Dollar Campaign with Blowout Grand Finale Weekend," *PRNewswire*, May 18, 2012; and www.caesars.com, and www.totalrewards.com, accessed September 2012.

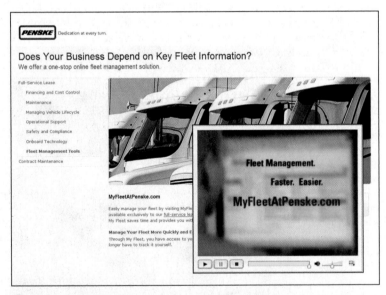

● **Extranets: Penske Truck Leasing's extranet site, MyFleetAtPenske.com, lets Penske customers access all of the data about their fleets in one spot and provides tools to help fleet managers manage their Penske accounts and maximize efficiency.**

Penske Truck Leasing

wife, we [talk about] our newest and best tulip selections," says the company's vice president of customer knowledge management. "No one else in the business is able to connect customer information with real-time transaction data the way we can."[23]

In addition, companies are increasingly allowing key customers and value-network members to access account, product, and other data on demand through *extranets.* Suppliers, customers, resellers, and select other network members may access a company's extranet to update their accounts, arrange purchases, and check orders against inventories to improve customer service. ● For example, Penske Truck Leasing's extranet site, MyFleetAtPenske.com, lets Penske business customers access all the data about their fleets in one spot and provides an array of tools and applications designed to help fleet managers manage their Penske accounts and maximize efficiency.[24]

Thanks to modern technology, today's marketing managers can gain direct access to a company's information system at any time and from virtually anywhere. They can tap into the system from a home office, hotel room, or the local Starbucks—anyplace they can connect on a laptop or smartphone. Such systems allow managers to get the information they need directly and quickly and tailor it to their own needs.

Objective 5 ┈┈▶
Discuss the special issues some marketing researchers face, including public policy and ethics issues.

Other Marketing Information Considerations

This section discusses marketing information in two special contexts: marketing research in small businesses and nonprofit organizations and international marketing research. Then, we look at public policy and ethics issues in marketing research.

Marketing Research in Small Businesses and Nonprofit Organizations

Just like larger firms, small organizations need market information and the customer insights that it can provide. Managers of small businesses and nonprofit organizations often think that marketing research can be done only by experts in large companies with big research budgets. True, large-scale research studies are beyond the budgets of most small businesses. However, many of the marketing research techniques discussed in this chapter also can be used by smaller organizations in a less formal manner and at little or no expense. ● Consider how one small-business owner conducted market research on a shoestring before even opening his doors:[25]

● Before opening Bibbentuckers dry cleaner, owner Robert Byerly conducted research to gain insights into what customers wanted. First on the list: quality.
Bibbentuckers

After a string of bad experiences with his local dry cleaner, Robert Byerley decided to open his own dry-cleaning business. But before jumping in, he conducted plenty of market research. He needed a key customer insight: How would he make his business stand out from the others? To start, Byerley spent an entire week in the library and online, researching the dry-cleaning industry. To get input from potential customers, using a marketing firm, Byerley held focus groups on the store's name, look, and brochure. He also took clothes to the 15 best competing cleaners in town and had focus group members critique their work. Based on his research, he made a list of features for his new business. First on his list: quality. His business would stand behind everything it did. Not on the list: cheap prices. Creating the perfect dry-cleaning establishment simply didn't fit with a discount operation.

With his research complete, Byerley opened Bibbentuckers, a high-end dry cleaner positioned on high-quality service and convenience. It featured a banklike drive-through area with curbside delivery. A computerized bar code system read customer cleaning preferences and tracked clothes all the way through the cleaning process. Byerley added other differentiators, such as decorative awnings, TV screens, and refreshments (even "candy for the kids and a doggy treat for your best friend"). "I wanted a place . . . that paired five-star service and quality with an establishment that didn't look like a dry cleaner," he says. The market research yielded results. Today, Bibbentuckers is a thriving six-store operation.

Thus, small businesses and not-for-profit organizations can obtain good marketing insights through observation or informal surveys using small convenience samples. Also, many associations, local media, and government agencies provide special help to small organizations. For example, the U.S. Small Business Administration offers dozens of free publications and a Web site (www.sba.gov) that give advice on topics ranging from starting, financing, and expanding a small business to ordering business cards. Other excellent resources for small businesses include the U.S. Census Bureau (www.census.gov) and the Bureau of Economic Analysis (www.bea.gov). Finally, small businesses can collect a considerable amount of information at very little cost online. They can scour competitor and customer Web sites and use Internet search engines to research specific companies and issues.

In summary, secondary data collection, observation, surveys, and experiments can all be used effectively by small organizations with small budgets. However, although these informal research methods are less complex and less costly, they still must be conducted with care. Managers must think carefully about the objectives of the research, formulate questions in advance, recognize the biases introduced by smaller samples and less skilled researchers, and conduct the research systematically.[26]

International Marketing Research

International marketing research has grown tremendously over the past decade. International researchers follow the same steps as domestic researchers, from defining the research problem and developing a research plan to interpreting and reporting the results. However, these researchers often face more and different problems. Whereas domestic researchers deal with fairly homogeneous markets within a single country, international researchers deal with diverse markets in many different countries. These markets often vary greatly in their levels of economic development, cultures and customs, and buying patterns.

In many foreign markets, the international researcher may have a difficult time finding good secondary data. Whereas U.S. marketing researchers can obtain reliable secondary data from dozens of domestic research services, many countries have almost no research services at all. Some of the largest international research services operate in many countries. ● For example, The Nielsen Company (the world's largest marketing research company) has offices in more than 100 countries, from Schaumburg, Illinois, to Hong Kong to Nicosia, Cyprus. However, most research firms operate in only a relative handful of countries.[27] Thus, even when secondary information is available, it usually must be obtained from many different sources on a country-by-country basis, making the information difficult to combine or compare.

Because of the scarcity of good secondary data, international researchers often must collect their own primary data. However, obtaining primary data may be no easy task. For example, it can be difficult simply to develop good samples. U.S. researchers can use current telephone directories, e-mail lists, census tract data, and any of several sources of socioeconomic data to construct samples. However, such information is largely lacking in many countries.

Once the sample is drawn, the U.S. researcher usually can reach most respondents easily by telephone, by mail, online, or in person. However, reaching respondents is often not so easy in other parts of the world. Researchers in Mexico cannot rely on telephone, Internet, and mail data collection—most data collection is door-to-door and concentrated in three or four of the largest cities. In some countries, few people have computers, let alone Internet access. For example, whereas there are 79 Internet users per 100 people in the United States, there are only 31 Internet users per 100 people in Mexico. In Libya, the number drops to 6 Internet users per 100 people. In some countries, the postal system is notoriously unreliable. In Brazil, for instance, an estimated 30 percent of the mail is never delivered; in Russia, mail delivery can take several weeks. In many developing countries, poor roads and transportation systems make certain areas hard to reach, making personal interviews difficult and expensive.[28]

Cultural differences from country to country cause additional problems for international researchers. Language is the most obvious obstacle. For example, questionnaires must be prepared in one language and then translated into the languages of each country researched. Responses then must be translated back into the original language for analysis and interpretation. This adds to research costs and increases the risks of error. Even within a given country, language can be a problem. For example, in India, English is the language of business, but consumers may use any of 14 "first languages" with many additional dialects.

Translating a questionnaire from one language to another is anything but easy. Many idioms, phrases, and statements mean different things in different cultures. For example, a Danish executive noted, "Check this out by having a different translator put back into English what you've translated from English. You'll get the shock of your life. I remember [an example in which] 'out of sight, out of mind' had become 'invisible things are insane.'"[29]

Consumers in different countries also vary in their attitudes toward marketing research. People in one country may be very willing to respond; in other countries, nonresponse can be a major problem. Customs in some countries may prohibit people from talking with strangers. In certain cultures, research questions often are considered too personal. For example, in many Muslim countries, mixed-gender focus groups are taboo, as is videotaping female-only focus groups. Even when respondents are *willing* to respond, they may not be *able* to because of high functional illiteracy rates.

● **Some of the largest research services firms have large international organizations. Nielsen has offices in more than 100 countries.**

Copyrighted information of The Nielsen Company, licensed for use herein.

Despite these problems, as global marketing grows, global companies have little choice but to conduct these types of international marketing research. Although the costs and problems associated with international research may be high, the costs of not doing it—in terms of missed opportunities and mistakes—might be even higher. Once recognized, many of the problems associated with international marketing research can be overcome or avoided.

Public Policy and Ethics in Marketing Research

Most marketing research benefits both the sponsoring company and its consumers. Through marketing research, companies gain insights into consumers' needs, resulting in more satisfying products and services and stronger customer relationships. However, the misuse of marketing research can also harm or annoy consumers. Two major public policy and ethics issues in marketing research are intrusions on consumer privacy and the misuse of research findings.

Intrusions on Consumer Privacy

Many consumers feel positive about marketing research and believe that it serves a useful purpose. Some actually enjoy being interviewed and giving their opinions. However, others strongly resent or even mistrust marketing research. They don't like being interrupted by researchers. They worry that marketers are building huge databases full of personal information about customers. Or they fear that researchers might use sophisticated techniques to probe our deepest feelings, peek over our shoulders as we shop, or track us as we browse and interact on the Internet and then use this knowledge to manipulate our buying.

There are no easy answers when it comes to marketing research and privacy. For example, is it a good or bad thing that marketers track and analyze consumers' online clicks and target ads to individuals based on their browsing and social networking behavior? Similarly, should we applaud or resent companies that monitor consumer discussions on You-Tube, Facebook, Twitter, or other public social networks in an effort to be more responsive?

For example, Dunkin' Donuts regularly eavesdrops on consumer online conversations as an important input to its customer relationship-building efforts. Take the case of customer Jeff Lerner, who tweeted last summer about a loose lid that popped off his Dunkin' Donuts drive-through coffee and soaked his white shirt and new car. Within minutes, Dunkin' picked up Lerner's tweet, sent him a direct message asking for his phone number, called him to apologize, and sent him a $10 gift card. Lerner found Dunkin's actions laudable. "*This* is social media. This is listening. This is engagement," he stated in a later blog post. However, some disconcerted consumers might see Dunkin's Twitter monitoring as an invasion of their privacy.[30]

Increasing consumer privacy concerns have become a major problem for the marketing research industry. Companies face the challenge of unearthing valuable but potentially sensitive consumer data while also maintaining consumer trust. At the same time, consumers wrestle with the trade-offs between personalization and privacy. "The debate over online [privacy] stems from a marketing paradox," says a privacy expert. "Internet shoppers want to receive personalized, timely offers based on their wants and needs but they resent that companies track their online purchase and browsing histories." The key question: "Where is the line between questionable and acceptable customer data gathering activities?"[31] Failure to address such privacy issues could result in angry, less cooperative consumers and increased government intervention.

The marketing research industry is considering several options for responding to intrusion and privacy issues. One example is the Marketing Research Association's "Your Opinion Counts" and "Respondent Bill of Rights" initiatives to educate consumers about the benefits of marketing research and distinguish it from telephone selling and database building. The industry also has considered adopting broad standards, perhaps based on the International Chamber of Commerce's International Code of Marketing and Social Research Practice. This code outlines researchers' responsibilities to respondents and the general public. For example, it urges that researchers make their names and addresses available to participants and be open about the data they are collecting.[32]

Most major companies—including Facebook, Microsoft, IBM, Citigroup, American Express, and even the U.S. government—have now appointed a chief privacy officer (CPO), whose job is to safeguard the privacy of consumers who do business with the company. In the end, if researchers provide value in exchange for information, customers will gladly provide it. For example, Amazon.com's customers do not mind if the firm builds a database of products they buy as a way to provide future product recommendations. This saves time and provides value. The best approach is for researchers to ask only for the information they need, use it responsibly to provide customer value, and avoid sharing information without the customer's permission.

Misuse of Research Findings

Research studies can be powerful persuasion tools; companies often use study results as claims in their advertising and promotion. Today, however, many research studies appear to be little more than vehicles for pitching the sponsor's products. In fact, in some cases, research surveys appear to have been designed just to produce the intended effect. Few advertisers openly rig their research designs or blatantly misrepresent the findings—most abuses tend to be more subtle "stretches." Consider the following example:[33]

> Based on a scientific study, the Kellogg Company proclaimed in ads and on packaging for Frosted Mini-Wheats that the cereal was "clinically shown to improve kids' attentiveness by nearly 20%." When challenged by the Federal Trade Commission, however, the claims turned out to be a substantial stretch of the study results. Fine print at the bottom of the box revealed the following: "Based upon independent clinical research, kids who ate Kellogg's Frosted Mini-Wheats cereal for breakfast had up to 18 percent better attentiveness three hours after breakfast than kids who ate no breakfast." That is, as one critic noted, "Frosted Mini-Wheats are (up to) 18 percent better than starving." Moreover, according to the FTC complaint, the clinical study referred to by Kellogg actually showed that children who ate the cereal for breakfast *averaged* just under 11 percent better in attentiveness than children who ate no breakfast, and that only about one in nine improved by 20 percent or more. Kellogg settled with the FTC, agreeing to refrain from making unsubstantiated health claims about Frosted Mini-Wheats or other products and from misrepresenting the results of scientific tests.

Recognizing that surveys can be abused, several associations—including the American Marketing Association, the Marketing Research Association, and the Council of American Survey Research Organizations (CASRO)—have developed codes of research ethics and standards of conduct. For example, the CASRO Code of Standards and Ethics for Survey Research outlines researcher responsibilities to respondents, including confidentiality, privacy, and avoidance of harassment. It also outlines major responsibilities in reporting results to clients and the public.[34]

In the end, however, unethical or inappropriate actions cannot simply be regulated away. Each company must accept responsibility for policing the conduct and reporting of its own marketing research to protect consumers' best interests and its own.

 Misuse of research findings: The Federal Trade Commission recently challenged research-based advertising and packaging claims that Kellogg's Frosted Mini-Wheats were "clinically shown to improve kids' attentiveness by nearly 20%."

Eric Meyerson/Rangelife

Reviewing the Concepts

MyMarketingLab™

Go to **mymktlab.com** to complete the problems marked with this icon ⭐.

Reviewing Objectives and Key Terms

◗ Objectives Review

To create value for customers and build meaningful relationships with them, marketers must first gain fresh, deep insights into what customers need and want. Such insights come from good marketing information. As a result of the recent explosion of marketing technology, companies can now obtain great quantities of information, sometimes even too much. The challenge is to transform today's vast volume of consumer information into actionable customer and market insights.

Objective 1 **Explain the importance of information in gaining insights about the marketplace and customers.** (pp 102–103)

The marketing process starts with a complete understanding of the marketplace and consumer needs and wants. Thus, the company needs sound information to produce superior value and satisfaction for its customers. The company also requires information on competitors, resellers, and other actors and forces in the marketplace. Increasingly, marketers are viewing information not only as an input for making better decisions but also as an important strategic asset and marketing tool.

Objective 2 **Define the marketing information system and discuss its parts.** (pp 103–106)

The *marketing information system* (*MIS*) consists of people and procedures for assessing information needs, developing the needed information, and helping decision makers use the information to generate and validate actionable customer and market insights. A well-designed information system begins and ends with users.

The MIS first *assesses information needs.* The MIS primarily serves the company's marketing and other managers, but it may also provide information to external partners. Then the MIS *develops information* from internal databases, marketing intelligence activities, and marketing research. *Internal databases* provide information on the company's own operations and departments. Such data can be obtained quickly and cheaply but often need to be adapted for marketing decisions. *Marketing intelligence* activities supply everyday information about developments in the external marketing environment. *Market research* consists of collecting information relevant to a specific marketing problem faced by the company. Last, the MIS helps users analyze and use the information to develop customer insights, make marketing decisions, and manage customer relationships.

Objective 3 **Outline the steps in the marketing research process.**
(pp 106–119)

The first step in the marketing research process involves *defining the problem and setting the research objectives*, which may be exploratory, descriptive, or causal research. The second step consists of *developing a research plan* for collecting data from primary and secondary sources. The third step calls for *implementing the marketing research plan* by gathering, processing, and analyzing the information. The fourth step consists of *interpreting and reporting the findings.* Additional information analysis helps marketing managers apply the information and provides

them with sophisticated statistical procedures and models from which to develop more rigorous findings.

Both *internal* and *external* secondary data sources often provide information more quickly and at a lower cost than primary data sources, and they can sometimes yield information that a company cannot collect by itself. However, needed information might not exist in secondary sources. Researchers must also evaluate secondary information to ensure that it is *relevant*, *accurate*, *current*, and *impartial*.

Primary research must also be evaluated for these features. Each primary data collection method—*observational*, *survey*, and *experimental*—has its own advantages and disadvantages. Similarly, each of the various research contact methods—mail, telephone, personal interview, and online—has its own advantages and drawbacks.

Objective 4 **Explain how companies analyze and use marketing information.** (pp 119–122)

Information gathered in internal databases and through marketing intelligence and marketing research usually requires more analysis. To analyze individual customer data, many companies have now acquired or developed special software and analysis techniques—called *customer relationship management* (*CRM*)—that integrate, analyze, and apply the mountains of individual customer data contained in their databases.

Marketing information has no value until it is used to make better marketing decisions. Thus, the MIS must make the information available to managers and others who make marketing decisions or deal with customers. In some cases, this means providing regular reports and updates; in other cases, it means making nonroutine information available for special situations and on-the-spot decisions. Many firms use company intranets and extranets to facilitate this process. Thanks to modern technology, today's marketing managers can gain direct access to marketing information at any time and from virtually any location.

Objective 5 **Discuss the special issues some marketing researchers face, including public policy and ethics issues.**
(pp 122–126)

Some marketers face special marketing research situations, such as those conducting research in small business, not-for-profit, or international situations. Marketing research can be conducted effectively by small businesses and nonprofit organizations with limited budgets. International marketing researchers follow the same steps as domestic researchers but often face more and different problems. All organizations need to act responsibly concerning major public policy and ethical issues surrounding marketing research, including issues of intrusions on consumer privacy and misuse of research findings.

 # Key Terms

Objective 1

Customer insights (p 103)
Marketing information system
 (MIS) (p 103)

Objective 2

Internal databases (p 104)
Competitive marketing intelligence (p 105)

Objective 3

Marketing research (p 106)
Exploratory research (p 107)

Discussion and Critical Thinking

Discussion Questions

⭐ **1.** What is a marketing information system, and how is it used to create customer insights? (AACSB: Communication)

2. Explain how marketing intelligence differs from marketing research. (AACSB: Communication)

3. Explain the role of secondary data in gaining customer insights. Where do marketers obtain secondary data, and what are the potential problems in using it? (AACSB: Communication)

⭐ **4.** What are the advantages of Internet-based survey research over traditional survey research? (AACSB: Communication)

5. What is neuromarketing, and how is it useful in marketing research? Why is this research approach usually used with other approaches? (AACSB: Communication)

Critical Thinking Exercises

1. In a small group, identify a problem faced by a local business or charitable organization and propose a research project addressing that problem. Develop a research proposal that implements each step of the marketing research process. Discuss how the research results will help the business or organization. (AACSB: Communication; Reflective Thinking)

2. Want to earn a little extra cash? Businesses that use focus groups and surveys to make better marketing decisions might

pay for your participation. Visit www.FindFocusGroups.com and review the opportunities available for research participation. Find two more Web sites that recruit research participants. Write a brief report of what you found and discuss the pros and cons to companies of recruiting research participants this way. (AACSB: Communication; Use of IT; Reflective Thinking)

Applications and Cases

Marketing Technology EWA Bespoke Communications

In 1996, Marks & Spencer (M&S), the venerable British retailer, launched "lunchtogo"—an online corporate catering service (see www.lunchtogo-e.com/). But M&S found it difficult to develop long-term relationships with corporate customers due to high personnel turnover within customer organizations, so it turned to EWA Bespoke Communications, a company that uses data mining to "tell you more about your customers." EWA used "propensity modeling" to develop a "critical lag" formula that identified customers whose last order fell outside of their expected

behavior. EWA then developed an automated system to send communications to customers who did not reorder within the maximum allowed order lag determined by the formula. Whereas most customers received e-mails, the system flagged M&S's best corporate catering customers who should receive more personalized phone calls because of their value and importance. EWA also implemented information systems to improve the company's service. Knowing more about its customers paid off—within a short period of time, the EWA system generated more than £1 million, tripling the operation's revenues, and delivered an almost perfect order-accuracy rate.

1. Visit EWA Bespoke Communications at www.ewa.ltd.uk/ to learn more about its Customer Insight services and the types of analyses performed by this company. What is propensity modeling? Review other case studies from this Web site and write a brief report of how data-mining technology was used to gain customer insights. (AACSB: Communication; Use of IT)

2. Describe how other organizations can benefit from these types of data-mining analyses. Find examples of other companies that can offer such analysis to businesses. (AACSB: Communication; Reflective Thinking)

 # Marketing Ethics Reading You

E-book sales have now surpassed print book sales, resulting in lower margins for all companies in the publishing industry value chain. However, there is a silver lining to this trend—e-books can read the readers. Publishers and e-book retailers are gathering billions of bits of information from e-book readers. The publishing industry has been notorious for not conducting research, leaving authors to lament that they didn't know who their readers were or what they wanted. The only way to know if readers liked a book was from sales data after the fact. Not anymore. Now companies know how many hours readers spend reading a book and how far they get when they open it. Some publishers are even testing e-book manuscripts, revising them based on feedback, and then publishing the print version. Scholastic Inc. has set up online message boards and interactive games to learn what storylines and characters are connecting with readers. Coliloquy digital books let readers choose their own stories, which the company

then aggregates and sends to the authors to shape future books. Amazon Kindle users sign an agreement giving the company permission to store their reading behavior data, and the company then highlights some of the data on its Web site. For example, the most highlighted passage in *Catching Fire*, the second book of the popular *Hunger Games* series, is "Because sometimes things happen to people and they're not equipped to deal with them."

1. Most e-book readers do not know that their reading behavior can be tracked. What ethical concerns might readers have? Are there any protections in place for consumers who may not want their reading behavior tracked? (AACSB: Communication; Ethical Reasoning)

2. What would your textbook reading behavior data reveal to publishers? How would the marketing of textbooks change based on your behavior? (AACSB: Communication; Reflective Thinking)

 # Marketing by the Numbers Sample Size

Have you ever been disappointed because a television network cancelled one of your favorite television shows because of "low ratings"? The network didn't ask your opinion, did it? It probably didn't ask any of your friends, either. That's because estimates of television audience sizes are based on research done by The Nielsen Company, which uses a sample of only 9,000 households out of the more than 113 million households in the United States to determine national ratings for television programs. That doesn't seem like enough, does it? As it turns out, statistically, it's many more than enough.

1. Go to www.surveysystem.com/sscalc.htm to determine the appropriate sample size for a population of 113 million households.

Assuming a confidence interval of 5, how large should the sample of households be if desiring a 95 percent confidence level? How large for a 99 percent confidence level? Briefly explain what is meant by *confidence interval* and *confidence level*. (AACSB: Communication; Use of IT; Analytical Reasoning)

2. What sample sizes are necessary at population sizes of 1 billion, 10,000, and 100 with a confidence interval of 5 and a 95 percent confidence level? Explain the effect population size has on sample size. (AACSB: Communication; Use of IT; Analytical Reasoning)

 # Video Case Domino's

As a delivery company, no one delivers better than Domino's. Its reputation for hot pizza in 30 minutes or less is ingrained in customers' minds. But not long ago, Domino's began hearing its customers talking about how its pizza was horrible. As a company that has long focused on solid marketing intelligence to make decisions, Domino's went to work on how it could change consumer perceptions about its pizza.

Through marketing research techniques, Domino's soon realized that it had to take a very risky step and completely re-create the pizza that it had been selling for over 40 years. This video illustrates how research not only enabled Domino's to come up with a winning recipe, but led to a successful promotional campaign

that has made fans of Domino's pizza in addition to its delivery service.

After viewing the video featuring Domino's, answer the following questions:

1. Explain the role that marketing research played in the creation and launch of Domino's new pizza.

2. Are there more effective ways that Domino's could have gone about its research process?

3. Why did it take so long for Domino's to realize that customers didn't like its pizza? Was it an accident that it made this realization?

Company Case

Meredith: Thanks to Good Marketing Information, Meredith *Knows* Women

You may not recognize the name Meredith Corporation, but you have certainly heard of the magazines it publishes. *Better Homes and Gardens*, *Ladies' Home Journal,* and *Family Circle* are some of its oldest and best-known titles. Meredith has been publishing magazines for more than 100 years and maintains many top-10 titles, both by category and overall. With a total of 21 subscription magazines, Meredith is also the creator of *American Baby, Parents, Fitness, Midwest Living, Every Day with Rachael Ray*, and *MORE*. This powerhouse publisher also produces 150 special interest publications—the kind that are available only at retail outlets. Meredith's magazines have a combined circulation of 30 million—*Better Homes and Gardens* alone reaches over 7.5 million paid readers each month.

If Meredith's magazines sound like something your mom would read, that's intentional. Meredith caters to women. In fact, Meredith has become the undisputed leading media and marketing company focused on women. It has earned this reputation by developing an expertise in managing deep relationships with female customers. With core categories of home, health, family, and personal development, Meredith's goal is to touch every lifestage of women, from young adults and new parents to established families and empty nesters.

Print media is hardly a growth industry—in fact, it's been declining in recent years. But building an empire on magazines doesn't mean that Meredith has painted itself into a corner. In fact, Meredith no longer describes itself as a magazine publisher. It claims to be a creator of "content," delivered to women "whenever, wherever, and however [they want] it." Long before print media began its decline, Meredith expanded into television stations, cable programming, and Internet sites.

Today, Meredith has a strong foundation on the Internet and is investing heavily in its future. For example, digital versions of most of its magazines are now available on Google Play. It recently paid $175 million to acquire Allrecipes.com, the largest online food site in the country. With that one acquisition, Meredith doubled the reach of its network of more than 50 online sites to an average of 40 million unique visitors each month. Its Internet empire also includes BHG.com, Parents.com, DivineCaroline.com, and FitnessMagazine.com to name just a few. This network allows Meredith to do more than just distribute content; the company has also become proficient in social networking. With so many brands available through print, television, online, mobile, and video, Meredith plans to continue to touch women's lives in meaningful ways for a long, long time.

Whether through print, broadcast, or digital media, how has Meredith been able to achieve success as the leading expert on women? In short, Meredith *knows* women. The company knows women through a continual strategic effort to manage marketing information about them. In fact, Meredith's marketing information system is its core competency. That system produces customer insights that allow the company to understand women's needs and desires and maintain strong relationships with them.

It Starts with Data

Although there are lots of different ways that companies gather and manage marketing information, Meredith's core strength lies in its massive database. Meredith's database is the largest collection of customer information of any U.S. media company. With more than 85 million unduplicated names, it contains information on 80 percent of U.S. home-owning households as well as a good portion of non-home-owning households. Beyond its breadth, Meredith's database also has unsurpassed depth. On average, each name in the database has more than 700 data points attached to it. If that doesn't impress you, think about how many pieces of information you could think of about your family members, best friends, or even yourself. Those 700 data points allow Meredith to truly know each person on an intimate level.

The basic information in Meredith's database comes from typical internal company sources. Information gathered through sales transactions alone is huge. This includes not only descriptive and demographic information, but also information on which magazines customers buy, to which magazines they subscribe, what kinds of incentive offers they like, and how they have responded to particular creative executions. The database also incorporates additional internal information from product shipments, customer satisfaction surveys, and online site visits for each specific customer. Most companies have no idea how to process and handle all that information. But Meredith effectively puts it all into one place so that managers throughout the company can access it.

Beyond gathering information from internal sources, Meredith also conducts marketing research. Online and traditional surveys allow Meredith to dig deeper into attitudinal information. One of the focal points is questions about customers' life events. "Are you having a baby, are your kids about to go to school, are your oldest kids about to graduate, are you thinking about retiring?" explains Cheryl Dahlquist, director of database marketing services at Meredith. "As much as we can, we'd like to know that information because we feel like those are the things that influence really what's happening with someone." Knowing a single life event can tell a lot about a person's needs and wants. But possessing updated information on dozens of life events for a given person becomes very powerful.

All the information in the world means little unless you can make sense of it. Meredith is as skilled at analyzing and using database information as it is at collecting it. Through complex statistical analysis, Meredith learns about each customer's interests and how those interests evolve throughout the customer's life. Through a concept Meredith calls "passion points," the company computes scores for numerous different interest areas, such as cooking, fitness, and gardening. It then segments each interest area into specifics, such that fitness becomes running, yoga, and hiking, to name just a few. Multiple data points feed into each score.

In this manner, Meredith not only knows what your primary interests are, it also knows how your interest levels compare to those of everyone else in the database. "We've developed through our statistical group the ability to say when somebody reaches a certain score, that's when they're really hot to trot in [say] cooking, and they're ready to respond to just about all the offers that come their way around the cooking category." Meredith employs 20 predictive analytical models, each designed to rank the order of a person's interests. All 20 models are scored and ranked each week. That's how Meredith gets to know women.

Putting Customer Insights to Use

Based on the valuable insights that it extracts from its database, Meredith manages relationships with its customers through various means. For starters, customer insights not only drive the content of its media products, they drive the development of new products. For example, over the years, *Better Homes and Gardens* has spawned spin-offs such as *Country Home* and *Traditional Home*, not to mention BHG.com and the cable program *Better*.

But the insights that come from Meredith's marketing information system also tell the company which products are the most relevant to a given individual. And with its large and holistic portfolio of products, there is something for almost everyone. David Ball, vice president of consumer marketing for Meredith, explains how this works: "We had *American Baby* at the very early stages of a women going into the homeowning and child rearing years. We filled in with *Parents* and *Family Circle*. *American Baby* is prenatal, *Parents* is postnatal, *Family Circle* is teens and tweens. And so now we're able to take someone who subscribes to *American Baby* and really graduate them into our other products."

The fruits of managing customer information don't stop at matching the right product to the customer. Rich customer insights allow Meredith to meet customer needs when it comes to promotion and pricing as well. Because Meredith has so many media products, almost all of its promotional efforts are either through direct mail and e-mail or cross-promoting across titles. Based on what it knows about specific customers, Meredith customizes the types of offers and messages contained in promotions, often in real time. This makes promotional efforts much more effective and must less costly. "I don't want to be sending out a million pieces of direct mail if I could send out a hundred thousand pieces of direct mail only to the people who really want it," says Ball. If you think about it, this is marketing at its finest. When customers and potential customers aren't bothered by irrelevant messages and products, but are approached only with offers that actually interest them, everyone wins.

Meredith's ability to manage marketing information has opened other doors for the company. Given its vast database and its skill at managing information, Meredith can sell marketing research to other companies that need insights on women. Its strength in managing marketing information has also resulted in numerous partnerships with leading companies such as Home Depot, DirectTV, Chrysler, and Carnival Cruise Lines. And Meredith's database and research efforts have resulted in something else

that may be a first: The Meredith Engagement Dividend, a program that guarantees Meredith advertisers an increase in sales. Meredith can make such a guarantee because its database has revealed that its advertisers are able to increase their product sales by an average of 10 percent over a one-year period.

As a whole, magazine advertising has been decreasing for years, and the decline is projected to continue. Meredith's flat revenues over the past 5 years suggest that, as a company, it is still heavily tied to print media for distributing its content. But with a consistent profit margin of 8 to 10 percent of sales, Meredith is holding its own. More important, Meredith's core competency of managing customer information is not exclusive to print. It is something that will fuel the company's expansion into other, faster-growing media. As Meredith maintains its marketing information system strategy, it will continue to develop the right products, price, distribution methods, and promotions for each and every woman in its database.

Questions for Discussion

1. Analyze Meredith's marketing information system. What are its strengths and weaknesses?

2. Can impersonal data points really result in meaningful relationships? Explain.

3. Does Meredith's marketing information expertise transfer into other media and products?

4. As a company still heavily rooted in print, what does Meredith's future hold?

5. What recommendations would you make to Meredith's executives?

Sources: Officials at Meredith Corporation contributed to and supported the development of this case. Additional information comes from Erik Sass, "Meredith Corp. Buys Allrecipes.com," *Media Daily News,* January 24, 2012, www.mediapost.com/publications/article/166420/meredith-corp-buys-allrecipescom.html; and www.meredith.com, accessed August 2012.

MyMarketingLab

Go to **mymktlab.com** for Auto-graded writing questions as well as the following Assisted-graded writing questions:

4-1. What are the similarities and differences when conducting research in another country versus the domestic market? (AACSB: Communication)

4-2. Search "social media monitoring" on a search engine to find companies that specialize in monitoring social media. Discuss two of these companies. Next, find two more sites that allow free monitoring and describe how marketers can use these to monitor their brands. Write a brief report on your findings. (AACSB: Communication; Use of IT; Reflective Thinking)

4-3. Mymktlab Only – comprehensive writing assignment for this chapter.

References

1. Excerpts, quotes, and other information from Anna-Louise Jackson and Anthony Feld, "Domino's 'Brutally Honest' Ads Offset Slow Consumer Spending," *Bloomberg Businessweek*, October 17, 2011, www.businessweek.com/news/2011-10-17/domino-s-brutally-honest-ads-offset-slow-consumer-spending.html; Susan Adams, "Steve Jobs Tops List of 2011's Most Buzzed about CEOs," *Forbes*, November 30, 2011, www.forbes.com/sites/susanadams/2011/11/30/ceos-with-the-best-and-worst-online-buzz/; Mark Brandau, "Domino's Do-Over," *Nation's Restaurant News*, March 8, 2010, p. 44; T. L. Stanley, "Easy As Pie: How Russell Weiner Turned Sabotage into Satisfaction," *Adweek*, September 13, 2010, p. 40; "Domino's Puts Customer Feedback on Times Square Billboard," *Detroit News*, July 26, 2011; "Domino's Announces 2011 Financial Results," *PRNewswire*, February 28, 2012; and annual reports and other information from www.dominosbiz.com and www.pizzaturnaround.com, accessed November 2012.

2. Sheilynn McCale, "Apple Has Sold 300M iPods, Currently Holds 78 Percent of the Music Player Market," *The New Web*, October 4, 2011, http://thenextweb.com/apple/2011/10/04/apple-has-sold-300m-ipods-currently-holds-78-of-the-music-player-market/; and "Apple Crushes Profit Estimates and iPhone, iPod, and iPad Sales Soar," *CNBC*, January 24, 2012, www.cnbc.com/id/46103211/Apple_Crushes_Profit_Estimates_as_iPhone_iPod_Sales_Soar.

3. Carey Toane, "Listening: The New Metric," *Strategy*, September 2009, p. 45.

4. See www.walmartstores.com/Suppliers/248.aspx and http://retaillinkblog.com/what-is-walmarts-retail-link-system/3, accessed November 2012.

5. See James Aldridge, "USAA Posts $2 Billion in Net Income in 2011," *San Antonio Business Journal*, March 12, 2012; Scott Horstein, "Use Care with That Database," *Sales & Marketing Management*, May 2006, p. 22; Jean McGregor, "Customer Service Champs: USAA's Battle Plan," *Bloomberg BusinessWeek*, March 1, 2010, pp. 40–43; Katherine Burger, "The Service Economy," *Insurance & Technology*, May 2012, p. 2; and www.usaa.com, accessed November 2012.

6. Based on information from Adam Ostrow, "Inside the Gatorade's Social Media Command Center," June 6, 2010, accessed at http://mashable.com/2010/06/15/gatorade-sical-media-mission-control/; Valery Bauerlein, "Gatorade's 'Mission': Using Social Media to Boost Sales," *Wall Street Journal Asia*, September 15, 2010, p. 8; and Natalie Zmuda, "Gatorade: We're Necessary Performance Gear," *Advertising Age*, January 2, 2012.

7. Irena Slutsky, "'Chief Listeners Use Technology to Track, Sort Company Mentioned," *Advertising Age*, August 30, 2010, accessed at http://adage.com/digital/article?article_id=145618.; Also see Tina Sharkey, "Who Is Your Chief Listening Officer?" *Forbes*, March 3, 2012, www.forbes.com/sites/tinasharkey/2012/03/13/who-is-your-chief-listening-officer/.

8. Adam Lashinsky, "The Secrets Apple Keeps," *Fortune*, February 6, 2012, pp. 85–94.

9. See http://biz.yahoo.com/ic/101/101316.html, accessed September 2012; and Ray Latif, "Red Bull to Launch Total Zero in April," BevNet, February 27, 2012, www.bevnet.com/news/2012/red-bull-to-launch-total-zero-in-april.

10. For more on research firms that supply marketing information, see Jack Honomichl, "2011 Honomichl Top 50," special section, *Marketing News*, June 15, 2011. Other information from www.nielsen.com/us/en/measurement/retail-measurement.html and www.thefuturescompany.com/, accessed September 2012.

11. See www.symphonyiri.com/default.aspx?TabId=159&productid=84, accessed November 2012.

12. See Jennifer Reingold, "Can P&G Make Money in Places Where People Earn $2 a Day?" *Fortune*, January 17, 2011, pp. 86–91; and C.K. Prahalad, "Bottom of the Pyramid as a Source of Breakthrough Innovations," *Journal of Product Innovation Management*, January, 2012, pp. 6–12.

13. For more discussion of online ethnography, see Pradeep K. Tyagi, "Webnography: A New Tool to Conduct Marketing Research," *Journal of American Academy of Business*, March 2010, pp. 262–268; Robert V. Kozinets, "Netnography: The Marketer's Secret Weapon," March 2010, accessed at http://info.netbase.com/rs/netbase/images/Netnography_WP; and http://en.wikipedia.org/wiki/Online_ethnography, accessed December 2012.

14. Example adapted from information found in "My Dinner with Lexus," *Automotive News*, November 29, 2010, accessed at www.autonews.com/apps/pbcs.dll/article?AID=/20101129/RETAIL03/311299949/1292; and "An Evening with Lexus," YouTube video, www.youtube.com/watch?v=LweS8EScADY, accessed December 2012.

15. See www.internetworldstats.com/stats14.htm, accessed July 2012.

16. For more information, see www.focusvision.com and www.youtube.com/watch?v=PG8RZl2dvNY, accessed November 2012.

17. Derek Kreindler, "Lexus Soliciting Customer Feedback with Lexus Advisory Board," August 24, 2010, accessed at www.autoguide.com/auto-news/2010/08/lexus-soliciting-customer-feedback-with-lexus-advisory-board.html; "20,000 Customers Sign up for the Lexus Advisory Board," August 30, 2010, accessed at www.4wheelsnews.com/20000-customers-signed-up-for-the-lexus-advisory-board/; and www.lexusadvisoryboard.com, accessed November 2012.

18. See Stephen Baker, "The Web Knows What You Want," *BusinessWeek*, July 27, 2009, p. 48; Elizabeth A. Sullivan, "Keep Your Ear to the Ground," *Marketing News*, November 30, 2012, pp. 22–31; and Amit Avner, "How Social Targeting Can Lead to Discovery," *Adotas*, February 7, 2012, www.adotas.com/2012/02/how-social-targeting-can-lead-to-discovery/.

19. Based on information from "Time Warner Opens NYC Neuromarketing Lab," *Neuromarketing*, January 26, 2012, www.neurosciencemarketing.com/blog/articles/new-labs.htm; and Amy Chozick, "These Lab Specimens Watch 3-D Television," *New York Times*, January 25, 2012, p. B3.

20. Jessica Tsai, "Are You Smarter Than a Neuromarketer?" *Customer Relationship Management*, January 2010, pp. 19–20.

21. See Adam L. Penenberg, "NeuroFocus Uses Neuromarketing to Hack Your Brain," *Fast Company*, August 8, 2011, www.fastcompany.com/magazine/158/neuromarketing-intel-paypal.

22. Allison Schiff, "Macy's CMO Shares Loyalty Insights at NRF Big Show," *Direct Marketing News*, January 16, 2012, www.dmnews.com/macys-cmo-shares-loyalty-insights-at-nrf-big-show/article/223344/; and Alex Palmer, "Macy's Transformation," *Direct Marketing News*, April 1, 2012, www.dmnews.com/macys-transformation/article/233631/3/.

23. "SAS helps 1-800-Flowers.com Grow Deep Roots with Customers," www.sas.com/success/1800flowers.html, accessed September 2012.

24. See www.pensketruckleasing.com/leasing/precision/precision_features.html, accessed November 2012.

25. Based on information in Ann Zimmerman, "Small Business; Do the Research," *Wall Street Journal*, May 9, 2005, p. R3; with information from John Tozzi, "Market Research on the Cheap," *BusinessWeek*, January 9, 2008, www.businessweek.com/smallbiz/content/jan2008/sb2008019_352779.htm; and www.bibbentuckers.com, accessed September 2012.

26. For some good advice on conducting market research in a small business, see "Conducting Market Research," www.sba.gov/content/conducting-market-research, accessed November 2012; and "Researching Your Market," *Entrepreneur*, www.entrepreneur.com/article/43024-1, accessed November 2012.

27. See "Top 25 Global Market Research Organizations," *Marketing News*, August 30, 2011, p. 16; and www.nielsen.com/us/en/about-us.html, accessed November 2012.

28. For these and other examples, see "From Tactical to Personal: Synovate's Tips for Conducting Marketing Research in Emerging Markets," *Marketing News*, April 30, 2011, pp. 20–22. Internet stats

are from http://data.worldbank.org/indicator/IT.NET.USER.P2, accessed July 2012.

29. Subhash C. Jain, *International Marketing Management*, 3rd ed. (Boston: PWS-Kent, 1990), p. 338. For more discussion on international marketing research issues and solutions, see Warren J. Keegan and Mark C. Green, *Global Marketing*, 6th ed. (Upper Saddle River, NJ: Prentice Hall, 2011), pp. 170–201.

30. Tina Sharkey, "Who Is Your Chief Listening Officer?" *Forbes,* March 13, 2012, www.forbes.com/sites/tinasharkey/2012/03/13/who-is-your-chief-listening-officer/.

31. For these quotes and discussions of online privacy, see Juan Martinez, "Marketing Marauders or Consumer Counselors?" *CRM Magazine,* January 2011, accessed at www.destinationcrm.com; Lauren McKay, "Eye on Customers: Are Consumers Comfortable with or Creeped out by Online Data Collection Tactics?" *CRM Magazine,* January 2011, accessed at www.destinationcrm.com; and Ki Mae Heussner, "Whose Life Is It, Anyway?" *Adweek,* January 16, 2012, pp. 22–26.

32. "ICC/ESOMAR International Code of Marketing and Social Research Practice," www.esomar.org/index.php/codes-guidelines.html, accessed July 2012. Also see "Respondent Bill of Rights," www.mra-net.org/ga/billofrights.cfm, accessed December 2012.

33. Federal Trade Commission, "Kellogg Settles FTC Charges That Ads for Frosted Mini-Wheats Were False," April 20, 2009, www.ftc.gov/opa/2009/04/kellogg.shtm; "Kellogg's Frosted Mini-Wheats Neuroscience: The FTC Reckoning," http://rangelife.typepad.com/rangelife/2009/04/kelloggs-frosted-miniwheats-neuroscience-the-ftc-reckoning.html, April 21, 2009; Todd Wasserman, "New FTC Asserts Itself," *Brandweek*, April 27, 2009, p. 8; and "FTC Investigation of Ad Claims That Rice Krispies Benefits Children's Immunity Leads to Stronger Order Against Kellogg," *US Fed News Service*, June 4, 2010.

34. Information at www.casro.org/codeofstandards.cfm#intro, accessed December 2012.

Consumer Markets and Consumer Buyer Behavior

Chapter Preview You've studied how marketers obtain, analyze, and use information to develop customer insights and assess marketing programs. In this chapter, we take a closer look at the most important element of the marketplace—customers. The aim of marketing is to affect how customers think and act. To affect the *whats*, *whens*, and *hows* of buyer behavior, marketers must first understand the *whys*. In this chapter, we look at *final consumer* buying influences and processes. In the next chapter, we'll study the buyer behavior of *business customers*. You'll see that understanding buyer behavior is an essential but very difficult task.

To get a better sense of the importance of understanding consumer behavior, we begin by looking at GoPro. You may never have heard of GoPro, the small but fast-growing company that makes tiny, wearable HD video cameras. Yet few brands can match the avid enthusiasm and intense loyalty that GoPro has created in the hearts and minds of its customers. GoPro knows that, deep down, it offers customers much more than just durable little video cameras. More than that, it gives them a way to share action-charged moments and emotions with friends.

GoPro: Be a HERO!

A growing army of GoPro customers—many of them extreme sports enthusiasts—are now strapping amazing little GoPro cameras to their bodies, or mounting them on anything from the front bumpers of race cars to the heels of skydiving boots, in order to capture the extreme moments of their lives and lifestyles. Then, they can't wait to share those emotion-packed GoPro moments with friends. In fact, the chances are good that you've seen a GoPro-created video on YouTube or Facebook, or even on TV.

Maybe it's the one shot by the skier who sets off an avalanche in the Swiss Alps and escapes by parachuting off a cliff—that amateur video received 2.6 million YouTube views in nine months. Or maybe you saw the one where a seagull picks up a tourist's camera and makes off with it, capturing a bird's-eye view of a castle in Cannes, France (3 million views in seven months). Or what about the video of the mountain biker in Africa who is ambushed by a full-grown gazelle (more than 13 million views in four months)?

GoPro's avid customers have become evangelists for the brand. On average, they upload a new video to YouTube every two minutes. In turn, the videos

inspire new GoPro customers and even more video sharing. As a result, GoPro is growing explosively. Last year, the young company sold 800,000 cameras, generating revenues of $250 million—a 300 percent increase over the previous year—and an estimated 90 percent share of the wearable camera market.

What makes GoPro so successful? Part of the formula is the cameras themselves: GoPro cameras are marvels of modern technology, especially given their affordable starting price of less than $200. Only about 2 inches wide, a GoPro HD video camera looks like little more than a small gray box. But the lightweight, wearable or mountable GoPro is extremely versatile, and it packs amazing power for capturing stunning HD-quality video. A removable housing makes GoPro cameras waterproof

> GoPro's runaway success comes from a deep-down understanding of what makes its customers tick. More than just selling tiny, wearable HD video cameras, GoPro "helps people capture and share their lives' most meaningful experiences with others—to celebrate them together."

to depths of 180 feet. And GoPro cameras are drop-proof from 3,000 feet (so claims one skydiver).

But GoPro knows that consumer behavior is driven by much more than just high-quality products with innovative features. The brand is all about what its cameras let customers *do*. GoPro users don't just want to take videos. More than that, they want to tell the stories and share the adrenalin-pumped emotions of the extreme moments in their lifestyles. "Enabling you to share your life through incredible photos and video is what we do," says GoPro. We "help people capture and share their lives' most meaningful experiences with others—to celebrate them together."

When people view a stunning GoPro video clip—like the one of New Zealand's Jed Mildon landing the first-ever BMX triple back flip captured by his helmet camera—to some degree, they experience what the subject experiences. They feel the passion and adrenaline. And when that happens, GoPro creates an emotional connection between the GoPro storyteller and the audience.

Thus, making good cameras is only the start of GoPro's success. GoPro founder Nick Woodman, himself an extreme sports junkie, talks about helping customers through four essential steps in their storytelling and emotion-sharing journeys: capture, creation, broadcast, and recognition. *Capture* is what the cameras do—shooting pictures and videos. *Creation* is the editing and production process that turns raw footage into compelling videos. *Broadcast* involves distributing the video content to an audience. *Recognition* is the payoff for the content creator. Recognition might come in the form of YouTube views or LIKES and SHARES on Facebook. More probably, it's the enthusiastic oohs and ahs that their videos evoke from friends and family. The company's slogan sums up pretty well the consumer's deeper motivations: GoPro—Be a HERO.

So far, GoPro has focused primarily on the capture step of the overall customer storytelling experience. GoPro bills itself as the "World's Most Versatile Camera. Wear It. Mount It. Love It." It offers a seemingly endless supply of rigs, mounts, harnesses, straps, and other accessories that make GoPro cameras wearable or mountable just about anywhere. Users can strap the little cameras to their wrists or mount them on helmets. They can attach them to the tip of a snow ski, the bottom of a skateboard, or the underside of an RC helicopter. The handy little GoPro lets even the rankest video amateur capture some pretty incredible footage.

But Woodman knows that to keep growing, GoPro must broaden its offer to address the full range of customer needs and motivations—not just capture, but also creation, broadcast, and recognition. For example, on the creation side, GoPro recently acquired a digital-video software company, CineForm, and now provides free software for creating 3D videos from footage shot by GoPro cameras rigged side-by-side and calibrated to shoot simultaneously. On the broadcast side, GoPro is working with YouTube to create a GoPro YouTube network and will soon offer a Wi-Fi plug-in that lets GoPro customers upload video directly from their cameras or using a mobile app. As for recognition, GoPro now airs TV commercials created from the best videos submitted by customers at its Web site. GoPro's future lies in enabling and integrating the full user experience, from capturing video to sharing stories and life's emotions with others.

GoPro's rich understanding of what makes its customers tick is serving the young company well. Its enthusiastic customers are

GoPro's amazing little cameras let even the rankest video amateurs take stunning videos, giving them a way to celebrate the action-charged moments and emotions of their lives with others.
GoPro

among the most loyal and engaged of any brand. For example, GoPro's Facebook fan base is more than 1.7 million and growing fast. To put that in perspective, much larger Canon has only 619,000 Facebook followers; Panasonic has 146,000. Beyond uploading nearly half a million videos a year, GoPro fans interact heavily across a broad range of social media. "I think we have the most socially engaged online audience of any consumer brand in the world," claims Woodman.

All that customer engagement and enthusiasm has made GoPro the fastest-growing camera company in the world. Today GoPro cameras are available in more than 10,000 stores, from small sports-enthusiast shops to REI, Best Buy, and Amazon.com. GoPro's remarkable little cameras have also spread beyond amateurs. They have become standard equipment for many professional filmmakers—whether it's the Discovery Channel or a news show team filming rescues, wildlife, and storms or the production crew of hit reality-TV shows such as *Deadliest Catch* taking pictures of underwater crab pots or the sides of ships in heavy seas. The use of GoPro equipment by professionals lends credibility that fuels even greater consumer demand.

The moral of this story: Success begins with understanding customer needs and motivations. GoPro knows that it doesn't just make cameras. More than that, it enables customers to share important moments and emotions. According to one industry expert, "some of the most amazing companies of the coming few years will be businesses that understand how to wrap technology beautifully around human needs so that it matters to people." That's exactly what GoPro does.

Says Woodman: "We spent a lot of time recently thinking about, What are we really doing here? We know that our cameras are arguably the most socially networked consumer devices of our time, so it's clear we're not just building hardware. At a certain point, the services that you build around the hardware become more important than the hardware itself. You think about the implications of that and where it can go. . . . This is our DNA. This is how we grow."[1]

Objective Outline

Objective 1	**Define the consumer market and construct a simple model of consumer buyer behavior.** **Model of Consumer Behavior** (pp 136–137)
Objective 2	**Name the four major factors that influence consumer buyer behavior.** **Characteristics Affecting Consumer Behavior** (pp 137–152)
Objective 3	**List and define the major types of buying decision behavior and the stages in the buyer decision process.** **Types of Buying Decision Behavior** (pp 152–154) **The Buyer Decision Process** (pp 154–156)
Objective 4	**Describe the adoption and diffusion process for new products.** **The Buyer Decision Process for New Products** (pp 156–158)

MyMarketingLab™

⚙ Improve Your Grade!

Over 10 million students improved their results using the Pearson MyLabs.
Visit **mymktlab.com** for simulations, tutorials, and end-of-chapter problems.

The GoPro example shows that factors at many levels affect consumer buying behavior. Buying behavior is never simple, yet understanding it is an essential task of marketing management. **Consumer buyer behavior** refers to the buying behavior of final consumers—individuals and households that buy goods and services for personal consumption. All of these final consumers combine to make up the **consumer market**. The American consumer market consists of more than 313 million people who consume more than $14 trillion worth of goods and services each year, making it one of the most attractive consumer markets in the world.[2]

Consumers around the world vary tremendously in age, income, education level, and tastes. They also buy an incredible variety of goods and services. How these diverse consumers relate with each other and with other elements of the world around them impacts their choices among various products, services, and companies. Here we examine the fascinating array of factors that affect consumer behavior.

Consumer buyer behavior
The buying behavior of final consumers—individuals and households that buy goods and services for personal consumption.

Consumer market
All the individuals and households that buy or acquire goods and services for personal consumption.

Objective 1 ┈┈►
Define the consumer market and construct a simple model of consumer buyer behavior.

Model of Consumer Behavior

Consumers make many buying decisions every day, and the buying decision is the focal point of the marketer's effort. Most large companies research consumer buying decisions in great detail to answer questions about what consumers buy, where they buy, how and how much they buy, when they buy, and why they buy. Marketers can study actual consumer purchases to find out what they buy, where, and how much. But learning about the *whys* of consumer buying behavior is not so easy—the answers are often locked deep within the consumer's mind. Often, consumers themselves don't know exactly what influences their purchases.

● **FIGURE** | 5.1
The Model of Buyer Behavior

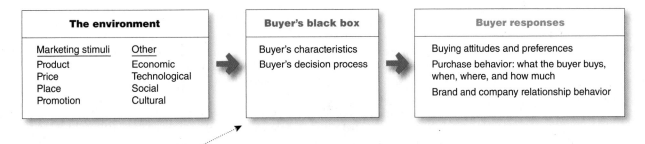

We can measure the whats, wheres, and whens of consumer buying behavior. But it's very difficult to "see" inside the consumer's head and figure out the whys of buying behavior (that's why it's called the black box). Marketers spend a lot of time and dollars trying to figure out what makes customers tick.

The central question for marketers is this: How do consumers respond to various marketing efforts the company might use? The starting point is the stimulus-response model of buyer behavior shown in ● **Figure 5.1**. This figure shows that marketing and other stimuli enter the consumer's "black box" and produce certain responses. Marketers must figure out what is in the buyer's black box.

Marketing stimuli consist of the four Ps: product, price, place, and promotion. Other stimuli include major forces and events in the buyer's environment: economic, technological, social, and cultural. All these inputs enter the buyer's black box, where they are turned into a set of buyer responses—the buyer's brand and company relationship behavior and what he or she buys, when, where, and how much.

Marketers want to understand how the stimuli are changed into responses inside the consumer's black box, which has two parts. First, the buyer's characteristics influence how he or she perceives and reacts to the stimuli. Second, the buyer's decision process itself affects his or her behavior. We look first at buyer characteristics as they affect buyer behavior and then discuss the buyer decision process.

Objective 2 ┄┄►
Name the four major factors that influence consumer buyer behavior.

Characteristics Affecting Consumer Behavior

Consumer purchases are influenced strongly by cultural, social, personal, and psychological characteristics, as shown in ● **Figure 5.2**. For the most part, marketers cannot control such factors, but they must take them into account.

Cultural Factors

Cultural factors exert a broad and deep influence on consumer behavior. Marketers need to understand the role played by the buyer's *culture*, *subculture*, and *social class*.

● **FIGURE** | 5.2
Factors Influencing
Consumer Behavior

Many brands now target specific subcultures—such as Hispanic American, African American, and Asian American consumers—with marketing programs tailored to their specific needs and preferences.

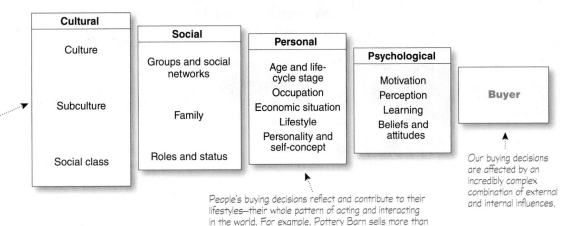

People's buying decisions reflect and contribute to their lifestyles—their whole pattern of acting and interacting in the world. For example, Pottery Barn sells more than just home furnishings. It sells an upscale yet casual, family- and friend-focused lifestyle.

Our buying decisions are affected by an incredibly complex combination of external and internal influences.

Culture

Culture is the most basic cause of a person's wants and behavior. Human behavior is largely learned. Growing up in a society, a child learns basic values, perceptions, wants, and behaviors from his or her family and other important institutions. A child in the United States normally learns or is exposed to the following values: achievement and success, individualism, freedom, hard work, activity and involvement, efficiency and practicality, material comfort, youthfulness, and fitness and health. Every group or society has a culture, and cultural influences on buying behavior may vary greatly from both county to county and country to country.

Marketers are always trying to spot *cultural shifts* so as to discover new products that might be wanted. For example, the cultural shift toward greater concern about health and fitness has created a huge industry for health-and-fitness services, exercise equipment and clothing, organic foods, and a variety of diets.

Culture
The set of basic values, perceptions, wants, and behaviors learned by a member of society from family and other important institutions.

Subculture

Each culture contains smaller **subcultures**, or groups of people with shared value systems based on common life experiences and situations. Subcultures include nationalities, religions, racial groups, and geographic regions. Many subcultures make up important market segments, and marketers often design products and marketing programs tailored to their needs. Examples of three such important subculture groups are Hispanic American, African American, and Asian American consumers.

Subculture
A group of people with shared value systems based on common life experiences and situations.

Hispanic American Consumers. Hispanics represent a large, fast-growing market. The nation's more than 50 million Hispanic consumers will have total annual buying power of $1.5 trillion by 2015, accounting for 11 percent of the nation's total buying power. The U.S. Hispanic population will surge to more than 132 million by 2050, close to 30 percent of the total U.S. population.[3]

Although Hispanic consumers share many characteristics and behaviors with the mainstream buying public, there are also distinct differences. They tend to be deeply family oriented and make shopping a family affair—children have a big say in what brands they buy. Older, first-generation Hispanic consumers tend to be very brand loyal and to favor brands and sellers who show special interest in them. Younger Hispanics, however, have shown increasing price sensitivity in recent years and a willingness to switch to store brands.

Within the Hispanic market, there exist many distinct subsegments based on nationality, age, income, and other factors. A company's product or message may be more relevant to one nationality over another, such as Mexicans, Costa Ricans, Argentineans, or Cubans. Companies must also vary their pitches across different Hispanic economic segments.

Companies such as Nestlé, McDonald's, Walmart, State Farm, Toyota, Verizon, Google, and many others have developed special targeting efforts for this fast-growing consumer segment. For example, Google learned that 78 percent of U.S. Hispanics use the Internet as their primary information source and that Hispanics are 58 percent more likely than the general population to click on search ads, making the online Hispanic market too big to ignore. Hispanics are also more active on social networks than other segments. In response, Google created a "specialist team" that focuses on helping advertisers across all industries reach Hispanic consumers through online and mobile search and display advertising platforms.[4]

Similarly, Hispanic consumers shop for groceries three times more often than the general U.S. shopper, so Nestlé, General Mills, and other food companies

● Targeting Hispanic consumers: Nestlé's Construye el Mejor Nido campaign focuses heavily on how Nestlé and its brands help to build family togetherness and well-being.

NESTLÉ, NEST DEVICE, GOOD FOOD, GOOD LIFE, NIDO, and DIGIORNO are registered trademarks of Societé des Produits Nestlé S.A., Vevey, Switzerland

compete heavily to get their brands into Hispanic shoppers' grocery carts. ● For example, Nestlé targets Hispanic family buyers with its extensive Construye el Mejor Nido (Create the Best Nest) marketing campaign, which connects Nestlé's products with family nutrition and wellness resources. The multipronged campaign includes a bilingual Web site (www.elmejornido.com), a Facebook page, Spanish-language television ads, sampling, and in-store marketing. No matter what the medium, the Construye el Mejor Nido campaign focuses heavily on how Nestlé and its brands help to build family togetherness and well-being. For example, four Hispanic mothers blog on the Web site, offering tips on parenting and healthy eating.[5]

African American Consumers. The U.S. African American population is growing in affluence and sophistication. By 2013, the nation's more than 40 million African American consumers will have a buying power of $1.2 trillion. Although more price conscious than other segments, blacks are also strongly motivated by quality and selection. Brands are important.[6]

In recent years, many companies have developed special products, appeals, and marketing programs for African American consumers. For example, Procter & Gamble has long been the leader in African American advertising, spending nearly twice as much as the second-place spender. P&G also tailors products to the specific needs of black consumers. For example, its CoverGirl Queen Collection is specially formulated "to celebrate the beauty of women of color."

In addition to traditional product marketing efforts, P&G also supports a broader "My Black Is Beautiful" movement.[7]

Created by a group of African American women at P&G, the movement aims "to ignite and support a sustained national conversation by, for, and about black women" and how they are reflected in popular culture. P&G discovered that black women spend three times more than the general market on beauty products yet feel they're portrayed worse than other women in media and advertising. Supported by brands such as Crest, Pantene, the CoverGirl Queen Collection, and Olay Definity, the My Black Is Beautiful movement's goal is to empower African American women to embrace their beauty, health, and wellness and, of course, to forge a closer relationship between P&G brands and African American consumers in the process. ● *My Black Is Beautiful* includes a rich Web site, and Facebook page, national media presence, and presence at key events that allow women to interact with brands and the *My Black is Beautiful* movement in trusted and relevant environments.

● **Procter & Gamble's roots run deep in targeting African American consumers. For example, it's My Black Is Beautiful movement aims to make black women feel beautiful while also forging a closer relationship between P&G brands and African American consumers.**

The Procter & Gamble Company. Photo by Keith Major.

Asian American Consumers. Asian Americans are the most affluent U.S. demographic segment. They now number more than 16 million, with annual buying power approaching $775 billion by 2015. Asian Americans are the second-fastest-growing subsegment after Hispanic Americans. And like Hispanic Americans, they are a diverse group. Chinese Americans constitute the largest group, followed by Filipinos, Asian Indians, Vietnamese, Korean Americans, and Japanese Americans. Yet, unlike Hispanics who all speak various dialects of Spanish, Asians speak many different languages. For example, ads for the 2010 U.S. Census ran in languages ranging from Japanese, Cantonese, Khmer, Korean, and Vietnamese to Thai, Cambodian, Hmong, Hinglish, and Taglish.[8]

As a group, Asian consumers shop frequently and are the most brand conscious of all the ethnic groups. They can be fiercely brand loyal. As a result, many firms now target the Asian American market. For example, Subaru of America actively targets these consumers.[9] Last year it fielded a comprehensive Asian American marketing campaign for its Subaru Legacy model. Called "Sweet Tomorrow," the campaign reinforced the brand's strong connection with Asian Americans, specifically people of Chinese American descent, who make up roughly 23 percent of the U.S. Asian American market. In addition to a billboard in San Francisco's Chinatown, the integrated campaign included Chinese print ads and Cantonese and Mandarin TV ads that also ran on Subaru's Chinese-language Web site and YouTube channel. The Sweet Tomorrow campaign targeted 30-something couples—mostly young parents who are car shopping with their children in mind. For example, one successful TV ad showed an expectant couple trying to balance Chinese tradition with their Chinese American lifestyle (see the ad at www.youtube.com/watch?v=D6BwBpIt8BQ). In the process, the couple chooses Subaru as the car of choice for their impending parenthood.

In a separate effort, Subaru introduced its sporty Subaru WRX model to the Asian American youth market (18–21) via a clever four-minute YouTube video about Brandon, a young Asian American who always does everything very fast—sometimes too fast. Although it never screams "commercial," the humorous video continually showcases a sporty blue WRX and its throaty sound. The highly successful video made it onto YouTube's most-watched page in the first week and netted 1.3 million YouTube views in its first month, earning 20,000 voluntary LIKES to only 230 DISLIKES.

Cross-Cultural Marketing. Beyond targeting segments such as Hispanics, African Americans, and Asian Americans with specially tailored efforts, many marketers now embrace *cross-cultural marketing*—the practice of including ethnic themes and cross-cultural perspectives within their mainstream marketing. Cross-cultural marketing appeals to consumer similarities across subcultures rather than differences. Many marketers are finding that insights gleaned from ethnic consumers can influence their broader markets.

For example, today's youth-oriented lifestyle is influenced heavily by Hispanic and African American entertainers. So it follows that consumers expect to see many different cultures and ethnicities represented in the advertising and products they consume. For instance, McDonald's takes cues from African Americans, Hispanics, and Asians to develop menus and advertising in hopes of encouraging mainstream consumers to buy smoothies, mocha drinks, and snack wraps as avidly as they consume hip-hop and rock 'n' roll. "The ethnic consumer tends to set trends," says McDonald's chief marketing officer. "So they help set the tone for how we enter the marketplace." Thus, McDonald's might take an ad primarily geared toward African Americans and run it in general-market media. "The reality is that the new mainstream is multicultural," concludes one cross-cultural marketing expert.[10]

Social Class

Social class

Relatively permanent and ordered divisions in a society whose members share similar values, interests, and behaviors.

Almost every society has some form of social class structure. **Social classes** are society's relatively permanent and ordered divisions whose members share similar values, interests, and behaviors. Social scientists have identified the seven American social classes shown in ● **Figure 5.3**.

Social class is not determined by a single factor, such as income, but is measured as a combination of occupation, income, education, wealth, and other variables. In some social systems, members of different classes are reared for certain roles and cannot change their social positions. In the United States, however, the lines between social classes are not fixed and rigid; people can move to a higher social class or drop into a lower one.

Marketers are interested in social class because people within a given social class tend to exhibit similar buying behavior. Social classes show distinct product and brand preferences in areas such as clothing, home furnishings, travel and leisure activity, financial services, and automobiles.

Social Factors

A consumer's behavior also is influenced by social factors, such as the consumer's *small groups*, *family*, and *social roles* and *status*.

Groups and Social Networks

Group

Two or more people who interact to accomplish individual or mutual goals.

Many small **groups** influence a person's behavior. Groups that have a direct influence and to which a person belongs are called membership groups. In contrast, reference groups serve as direct (face-to-face) or indirect points of comparison or reference in forming a person's attitudes or behavior. People often are influenced by reference groups to which they do not belong. For example, an aspirational group is one to which the individual wishes to belong, as when a young basketball player hopes to someday emulate basketball star LeBron James and play in the NBA.

●FIGURE | 5.3

The Major American
Social Classes

Wealth

Education

America's social classes show distinct
brand preferences. Social class is not
determined by a single factor but by a ······▶
combination of all of these factors.

Occupation

Income

Upper Class
Upper Uppers (1 percent): The social elite who live on inherited wealth. They give large sums to charity, own more than one home, and send their children to the finest schools.

Lower Uppers (2 percent): Americans who have earned high income or wealth through exceptional ability. They are active in social and civic affairs and buy expensive homes, educations, and cars.

Middle Class
Upper Middles (12 percent): Professionals, independent businesspersons, and corporate managers who possess neither family status nor unusual wealth. They believe in education, are joiners and highly civic minded, and want the "better things in life."

Middle Class (32 percent): Average-pay white- and blue-collar workers who live on "the better side of town." They buy popular products to keep up with trends. Better living means owning a nice home in a nice neighborhood with good schools.

Working Class
Working Class (38 percent): Those who lead a "working-class lifestyle," whatever their income, school background, or job. They depend heavily on relatives for economic and emotional support, advice on purchases, and assistance in times of trouble.

Lower Class
Upper Lowers (9 percent): The working poor. Although their living standard is just above poverty, they strive toward a higher class. However, they often lack education and are poorly paid for unskilled work.

Lower Lowers (7 percent): Visibly poor, often poorly educated unskilled laborers. They are often out of work, and some depend on public assistance. They tend to live a day-to-day existence.

Marketers try to identify the reference groups of their target markets. Reference groups expose a person to new behaviors and lifestyles, influence the person's attitudes and self-concept, and create pressures to conform that may affect the person's product and brand choices. The importance of group influence varies across products and brands. It tends to be strongest when the product is visible to others whom the buyer respects.

Word-of-Mouth Influence and Buzz Marketing. **Word-of-mouth influence** can have a powerful impact on consumer buying behavior. The personal words and recommendations of trusted friends, associates, and other consumers tend to be more credible than those coming from commercial sources, such as advertisements or salespeople. Most word-of-mouth influence happens naturally: Consumers start chatting about a brand they use or feel strongly about one way or the other. Often, however, rather than leaving it to chance, marketers can help to create positive conversations about their brands.

Marketers of brands subjected to strong group influence must figure out how to reach **opinion leaders**—people within a reference group who, because of special skills, knowledge, personality, or other characteristics, exert social influence on others. Some experts call this group *the influentials* or *leading adopters*. When these influentials talk, consumers listen. Marketers try to identify opinion leaders for their products and direct marketing efforts toward them.

Buzz marketing involves enlisting or even creating opinion leaders to serve as "brand ambassadors" who spread the word about a company's products. Many companies are now turning everyday customers into brand evangelists. For example, online shoe-of-the-month club ShoeDazzle has no shortage of big names to tout the company, including its co-founder and chief fashion stylist, reality star Kim Kardashian. But the company has learned that its best spokesperson might be, literally, the girl next door:[11]

Word-of-mouth influence
The impact of the personal words and recommendations of trusted friends, associates, and other consumers on buying behavior.

Opinion leader
A person within a reference group who, because of special skills, knowledge, personality, or other characteristics, exerts social influence on others.

● **Buzz marketing: ShoeDazzle has learned that its best spokesperson might be, literally, the girl next door.**

Jarrod Weaton/Weaton Digital, Inc.

One of ShoeDazzle's most persuasive spokespeople is an anonymous teenage girl whose online video testimonial, posted on the ShoeDazzle Web site, has been viewed more than 37,000 times. ● In it, she explains how she is "obsessed with shoes" and gushes over the service's low prices. "The prices are, like, perfect," she says. At the site, other satisfied customers talk about how they like the price, the selection, the fast shipping, and even the pink shoeboxes their shoes come in. ("The packaging is great," says one happy client. "They come in a cute little pink box. You can even regift it.")

Kim Kardashian's name created lots of buzz when the ShoeDazzle first launched—in less than a year, the company had a million Facebook fans. But to help put a more down-to-earth face on the service, ShoeDazzle began soliciting short Webcam videos in which real customers explained what surprised them most about the company. It then distributed the videos to YouTube, blogs, Twitter, Facebook, and the ShoeDazzle site, letting would-be customers see and hear the inside scoop from like-minded individuals. The persuasive video testimonials have now become a mainstay for ShoeDazzle. One of the top ShoeDazzle testimonials, for instance, has been viewed more than 48,000 times. In it, an enthusiastic woman fawns over a studded blue high-heeled shoe. "What surprised me most was the quality," she says. "I love the detail. I love the pretty pink and cute bag that you sent." No spokesmodel could have said it better.

Online social networks

Online social communities—blogs, social networking Web sites, and other online communities—where people socialize or exchange information and opinions.

Online Social Networks. More broadly, over the past few years, a new type of social interaction has exploded onto the scene—online social networking. **Online social networks** are online communities where people socialize or exchange information and opinions. Social networking media range from blogs (Gizmodo, Zenhabits) and message boards (Craigslist) to social networking Web sites (Facebook, Twitter, and Foursquare) and virtual worlds (Second Life). This new form of consumer-to-consumer and business-to-consumer dialog has big implications for marketers.

Marketers are working to harness the power of these new social networks and other "word-of-Web" opportunities to promote their products and build closer customer relationships. Instead of throwing more one-way commercial messages at consumers, they hope to use the Internet and social networks to *interact* with consumers and become a part of their conversations and lives (see Real Marketing 5.1).

For example, Red Bull has an astounding 8.4 million friends on Facebook; Twitter and Facebook are the primary ways it communicates with college students. JetBlue listens in on customers on Twitter and often responds; one consumer recently tweeted "I'm getting on a JetBlue flight" and JetBlue tweeted back "You should try the smoked almonds [on board]." Southwest Airlines employees share stories with each other and customers on the company's "Nuts about Southwest" blog.

Coca-Cola recently launched Edition 206, which dispatched three "Happiness Ambassadors"—chosen in an online vote—on a 365-day journey across 206 countries where Coca-Cola products are sold. Their mission was to document "what makes people happy" around the world and share their experiences with consumers worldwide through blogs, tweets, videos, and pictures posted on Facebook, Twitter, YouTube, Flickr, and an official Expedition 206 Web site. The idea was to create brand-related conversations, not immediate sales. The ambassadors created lots of online buzz and interaction, all within the context of Coca-Cola's broader "Open Happiness" marketing campaign.[12]

Most brands have built a comprehensive social media presence. ● Eco-conscious outdoor shoe and gear maker Timberland has created an online community (http://community .timberland.com) that connects like-minded "Earthkeepers" with each other and the brand through a network that includes several Web sites, a Facebook page, a YouTube channel, a Bootmakers Blog, an e-mail newsletter, and several Twitter feeds.

But marketers must be careful when tapping into online social networks. Results are difficult to measure and control. Ultimately, the users control the content, so social network marketing attempts can easily backfire. For example, when Skittles designed its Web site

Real Marketing 5.1

Harnessing the Power of Online Social Influence

People love talking with others about things that make them happy—including their favorite products and brands. Say you really like JetBlue Airways—the company flies with flair and gets you there at an affordable price. Or you just plain love your new little GoPro HD HERO2 video camera—it's too cool to keep to yourself. In the old days, you'd have chatted up these brands with a few friends and family members. But these days, thanks to Internet and mobile technology, anyone can share brand experiences with thousands, even millions, of other consumers online.

In response, marketers are now feverishly working to harness today's newfound technologies and get people interacting with their brands online. Whether it's creating online brand ambassadors, tapping into existing online influentials and social networks, or developing conversation-provoking events and videos, the Internet is awash with marketer attempts to create online brand conversations and involvement.

A company can start by creating its own online brand evangelists. That's what Ford did when it launched its Fiesta subcompact model in the United States, targeted heavily toward Web-savvy Millennials.

One study found that 77 percent of Millennials use a social networking site like Facebook or Twitter daily and 28 percent of them have a personal blog. So Ford created the Fiesta Movement campaign, in which it handed Fiestas to 100 influential 20-something Millennials selected from 4,000 applicants. The Fiesta ambassadors lived with the cars for six months, completed monthly "missions" with different themes, and shared their experiences via blogs, tweets, Facebook updates, and YouTube and Flickr posts. Ford didn't tell the ambassadors what to say, nor did it edit their content. "We told them to be completely honest," says Ford's social media manager. The successful Fiesta Movement campaign generated 58 percent pre-launch awareness among Fiesta's under-30 target consumers. In only six months, the consumers posted 60,000 items, generating 4.3 million YouTube views, 50,000 sales leads, and 35,000 test drives.

Beyond creating their own brand ambassadors, companies looking to harness the Web's social power can work with the army of self-made influencers already plying today's Internet—independent bloggers. Believe it or not, there are now almost as many people making a living as bloggers as there are lawyers. No matter what the interest area, there are probably hundreds of bloggers covering it. Moreover, research shows that 90 percent of bloggers post about their favorite and least favorite brands.

As a result, most companies try to form relationships with influential bloggers and online personalities. The key is to find bloggers who have strong networks of relevant readers, a credible voice, and a good fit with the brand. For example, companies ranging from P&G and Johnson & Johnson to Walmart work closely with influential "mommy bloggers." And you'll no doubt cross paths with the likes of climbers blogging for North Face, bikers blogging for Harley-Davidson, and shoppers blogging for Whole Foods Market or Trader Joe's.

Other companies have found that simply joining existing online conversations can pay big dividends. Take Shelly Davis, owner of Kinky-Curly Hair Products. A few years ago, she began scouring YouTube's video blogs on hair care products for African American women. She jumped into the comments sections, offering advice and answering questions about Kinky-Curly products, being careful to maintain a key element of promoting through blogs—authenticity. Within two years, video bloggers had posted more than 5,100 different video clips on YouTube demonstrating and commenting on Kinky-Curly products. All that buzz increased revenues by 40 percent and landed Kinky-Curly products on the shelves of Target and Whole Foods Market.

Perhaps the best way to generate online brand conversations and social involvement is simply to do something conversation worthy—to actually involve people with the brand online. For the past several years, Pepsi's Mountain Dew brand has run "DEWmocracy" campaigns that invite avid Mountain Dew customers to participate at all levels in launching a new Mountain Dew flavor, from choosing and naming the flavor to designing the can

A company can start by creating its own online brand evangelists. That's what Ford did when it launched its Fiesta subcompact model in the United States, targeted heavily toward Web-savvy Millennials.
Ford Motor Company

to submitting and selecting TV commercials and even picking an ad agency and media. Presented through a dedicated Web site, as well as Facebook, Twitter, Flickr, and other public network pages, DEWmocracy has been a perfect forum for getting youthful, socially savvy Dew drinkers talking with each other and the company about the brand. For example, Mountain Dew's Facebook fan page grew fivefold at the launch of the latest DEWmocracy campaign.

Ironically, one of the simplest means of capturing social influence online is one of the oldest—produce a good ad that gets people talking. But in this day and age, both the ads and the conversation media have changed. Almost every brand, large and small, is now creating innovative ads and brand-sponsored videos, posting them online, and hoping they'll go viral. Just ask Volkswagen. Its 2011 Super Bowl ad—featuring a pint-size Darth Vader using the force to start a VW Passat—went way viral, capturing 18 million online views

before it ever aired on TV. The clever commercial went on to become that year's most-watched YouTube video, with more than 50 million views. The next year, a VW-prepared Passat teaser video called "The Bark Side," in which a canine chorus performs "The Imperial March" from *Star Wars*, was viewed by more than 7 million fans before the big game began. The video also directed viewers to the Volkswagen Web site, where they could invite friends to Super Bowl parties with customized versions of the video's opening titles. Such ads and videos create lots of online talk and attention for the brand.

So, whether through online ambassadors, bloggers, social networks, or talked-about videos and events, companies are finding innovative ways to tap social influence online. It's growing fast as *the* place to be—for both consumers and marketers. Last year, the time consumers spent on social networking sites nearly tripled; marketer spending at those sites nearly kept pace. "Social [media] is one of the key trends driving business," says a social marketing executive. "It's more than pure marketing. It's about fast connections with customers and building an ongoing relationship."

Sources: Elisabeth A. Sullivan, "Blog Savvy," *Marketing News*, November 15, 2009, p. 8; Keith Barry, "Ford Bets the Fiesta on Social Marketing," *Wired*, April 17, 2009, www.wired.com/autopia/2009/04/how-the-fiesta; Dennis Nishi, "How to Sell on YouTube Without Showing a Video," *Wall Street Journal*, November 15, 2010; Alan Mitchell, "Word-of-Mouth Is Over-Hyped," *Marketing*, October 6, 2011, accessed at www.marketingmagazine.co.uk; Steven Williams, "Digital, Social Media Take Center Stage," *Advertising Age*, January 12, 2012, accessed at http://adage.com/article/digital/digital-social-media-center-stage-auto-show/232068/; Stuart Elliott, "The Pregame Show (of Commercials) Begins," *New York Times*, January 24, 2012; and information from www.dewmocracy.com, accessed March 2012.

● **Using social networks: Timberland has created an extensive online community that connects like-minded "Earthkeepers" with each other and the brand through several Web sites, a Facebook page, a YouTube channel, a Bootmakers Blog, an e-mail newsletter, and several Twitter feeds.**
Courtesy of Timberland

to include a live Twitter feed for Skittles-related tweets, pranksters laced Skittles tweets with profanities so they would end up on the candy's Web site. Skittles was forced to abandon the campaign. We will dig deeper into online social networks as a marketing tool in Chapter 17.

Family

Family members can strongly influence buyer behavior. The family is the most important consumer buying organization in society, and it has been researched extensively. Marketers are interested in the roles and influence of the husband, wife, and children on the purchase of different products and services.

Husband-wife involvement varies widely by product category and by stage in the buying process. Buying roles change with evolving consumer lifestyles. For example, in the United States, the wife traditionally has been considered the main purchasing agent for the family in the areas of food, household products, and clothing. But with more women working outside the home and the willingness of husbands to do more of the family's purchasing, all this is changing. A recent survey of men ages 18 to 64 found that 51 percent identify themselves as primary grocery shoppers in their households and 39 percent handle most of their household's laundry. At the same time, today women account for 50 percent of all technology purchases and influence two-thirds of all new car purchases.[13]

Such shifting roles signal a new marketing reality. Marketers in industries that have traditionally sold their products to only women or only men—from groceries and personal care products to cars and consumer electronics—are now carefully targeting the opposite sex. For example, most grocery products marketers have now added pitches to dads:

The Jif peanut butter slogan is now "Choosey moms, *and dads*, choose Jif." P&G brands such as Gain, Febreze, and Swiffer have become prominent advertisers on sections of Yahoo.com, such as sports, which are frequented heavily by men. And Kellogg's Frosted Flakes spokesman Tony the Tiger's longtime purpose in life—to sell Frosted Flakes to kids and grocery-buying moms—has changed to include Dads. The brand recently reached out to fathers with an ad showing a dad, son, and Tony tossing a football in the backyard. The trio then heads to the kitchen for some post-game Flakes, as the voiceover intones, "share what you love with who you love." The Frosted Flakes ad, which features ESPN sports anchor and dad Rece Davis, aired during adult programming on male-oriented networks such as ESPN and on an ESPN .com microsite.

To help women who *do* the shopping cope with significant others who hate to come along, furniture retailer IKEA came up with a unique solution. In its Australian stores, it created an in-store area called Män-land, a kind of daycare area where retail-phobic husbands and boyfriends can hang out while the women shop. ● The area was actually modeled after the retailer's toddler-care area, but instead of arts and crafts, the men play pinball and video games, watch sports, and eat free hot dogs. The women are even given a buzzer to remind them to collect their significant others after 30 minutes of shopping.[14]

● Family buying influences: To help women shoppers to cope with significant others who hate to shop, in its Australian stores, IKEA created an in-store daycare area called Mänland for retail-phobic husbands and boyfriends.

Newspix/Getty Images

Children may also have a strong influence on family buying decisions. The nation's 36 million children ages 9 to 12 wield an estimated $43 billion in disposable income. They also influence an additional $150 billion that their families spend on them in areas such as food, clothing, entertainment, and personal care items. One study found that kids significantly influence family decisions about everything from what cars they buy to where they eat out and take vacations.[15]

Roles and Status

A person belongs to many groups—family, clubs, organizations, online communities. The person's position in each group can be defined in terms of both role and status. A role consists of the activities people are expected to perform according to the people around them. Each role carries a status reflecting the general esteem given to it by society.

People usually choose products appropriate to their roles and status. Consider the various roles a working mother plays. In her company, she may play the role of a brand manager; in her family, she plays the role of wife and mother; at her favorite sporting events, she plays the role of avid fan. As a brand manager, she will buy the kind of clothing that reflects her role and status in her company. At the game, she may wear clothing supporting her favorite team.

Personal Factors

A buyer's decisions also are influenced by personal characteristics such as the buyer's *age and life-cycle stage*, *occupation*, *economic situation*, *lifestyle*, and *personality and self-concept*.

Age and Life-Cycle Stage

People change the goods and services they buy over their lifetimes. Tastes in food, clothes, furniture, and recreation are often age related. Buying is also shaped by the stage of the family life cycle—the stages through which families might pass as they mature over time. Life-stage changes usually result from demographics and life-changing events—marriage, having children, purchasing a home, divorce, children going to college, changes in personal income, moving out of the house, and retirement. Marketers often define their target markets in terms of life-cycle stage and develop appropriate products and marketing plans for each stage.

For example, consumer information giant Acxiom's Personicx life-stage segmentation system places U.S. households into one of 70 consumer segments and 21 life-stage groups, based on specific consumer behavior and demographic characteristics. ● Personicx includes life-stage groups with names such as *Beginnings*, *Taking Hold*, *Cash & Careers*, *Jumbo Families*, *Transition Time*, *Our Turn*, *Golden Years*, and *Active Elders*. The *Taking Hold* group consists of young, energetic, well-funded couples and young families who are busy with their careers, social lives, and interests, especially fitness and active recreation. *Transition Time* are blue-collar, less-educated, mid-income consumers who are transitioning to stable lives and talking about marriage and children.

"Consumers experience many life-stage changes during their lifetimes," says Acxiom. "As their life stages change, so do their behaviors and purchasing preferences." Armed with data about the timing and makeup of life-stage changes, marketers can create targeted, personalized campaigns.[16]

In line with recent tougher economic times, Acxiom has also developed a set of economic life-stage segments, including groups such as *Squeaking By*, *Eye on Essentials*, *Tight with a Purpose*, *It's My Life*, *Full Speed Ahead*, and *Potential Rebounders*. The *Potential Rebounders* are those more likely to loosen up on spending sooner. This group appears more likely than other segments to use online research before purchasing electronics, appliances, home decor, and jewelry. Thus, home improvement retailers appealing to this segment should have a strong online presence, providing pricing, features and benefits, and product availability.

PERSONICX

HOUSEHOLD SEGMENTATION
REACHES A NEW LEVEL OF ACCURACY

People aren't just a parent or only a doctor or simply a scuba diver. They can be all of these things – and more. Acxiom's 70 segments and 21 Life Stage groupings will let you know your customers and target them with unmatched precision. And Personicx® is the only household-level segmentation product that uses our industry-leading InfoBase® data. You'll now see your prospects as they really are.

www.acxiom.com • 1.888.3ACXIOM   **ACXIOM**

● **Life-stage segmentation: Personicx 21 life-stage groupings let marketers see customers as they really are and target them precisely. "People aren't just a parent or only a doctor or simply a scuba diver. They are all of these things."**

Acxiom Corporation

Occupation

A person's occupation affects the goods and services bought. Blue-collar workers tend to buy more rugged work clothes, whereas executives buy more business suits. Marketers try to identify the occupational groups that have an above-average interest in their products and services. A company can even specialize in making products needed by a given occupational group.

For example, Carhartt makes rugged, durable, no-nonsense work clothes—what it calls "original equipment for the American worker. From coats to jackets, bibs to overalls . . . if the apparel carries the name Carhartt, the performance will be legendary." Its Web site carries real-life testimonials of hard-working Carhartt customers. One electrician, battling the cold in Canada's arctic region, reports wearing Carhartt's lined Arctic bib overalls, Arctic jacket, and other clothing for more than two years without a single "popped button, ripped pocket seam, or stuck zipper." And a railroadman in northern New York, who's spent years walking rough railroad beds, climbing around trains, and switching cars in conditions ranging from extreme heat to frigid cold, calls his trusty brown Carhartt jacket part of his "survival gear—like a bulletproof vest is to a policeman."[17]

Economic Situation

A person's economic situation will affect his or her store and product choices. Marketers watch trends in personal income, savings, and interest rates. In the more frugal times following the Great Recession, most companies have taken steps to redesign, reposition, and reprice their products and services. For example, upscale discounter Target has replaced some of its "chic" with "cheap." It is putting more emphasis on the "Pay less" side of its "Expect more. Pay less." positioning promise.

Similarly, to become more competitive with discount competitors such as Target and Kohl's in the tighter economy, JCPenney recently announced sweeping changes in its marketing, including an everyday-low-price strategy featuring simpler pricing and an end to seemingly endless deals and sales. "Enough. Is. Enough." says the retailer's new commercials, which depict shoppers screaming in frustration at having to clip coupons, rush to take advantage of sales, and stand in line for blowout promotions.[18]

Lifestyle

Lifestyle

A person's pattern of living as expressed in his or her activities, interests, and opinions.

People coming from the same subculture, social class, and occupation may have quite different lifestyles. **Lifestyle** is a person's pattern of living as expressed in his or her psychographics. It involves measuring consumers' major AIO dimensions—activities (work, hobbies, shopping, sports, social events), interests (food, fashion, family, recreation), and opinions (about themselves, social issues, business, products). Lifestyle captures something more than the person's social class or personality. It profiles a person's whole pattern of acting and interacting in the world.

When used carefully, the lifestyle concept can help marketers understand changing consumer values and how they affect buyer behavior. Consumers don't just buy products; they buy the values and lifestyles those products represent. For example, outdoor outfitter REI sells a lot more than just outdoor gear and clothing. It sells an entire outdoor lifestyle for active people who "love to get outside and play":[19]

> At REI, says the company "we inspire, educate, and outfit for a lifetime of outdoor adventure and stewardship." One REI ad shows a woman biking in the wide-open spaces, proclaiming "REI prefer hitting the trails over the snooze button, whatever that is." Another ad features a man hiking in the great outdoors: "REI know what a treadmill looks like," he says, "but I've never actually seen one in person." At the REI Web site, outdoor enthusiasts can swap outdoors stories, enroll in REI Outdoor School classes at local locations, or even sign up for any of dozens of REI-sponsored outdoor travel adventures around the world.

Marketers look for lifestyle segments with needs that can be served through special products or marketing approaches. Such segments might be defined by anything from family characteristics or outdoor interests to pet ownership. In fact, today's involved pet ownership lifestyles have created a huge market for everything from basic pet supplies to exotic pet services marketed to indulgent "pet parents." (See Real Marketing 5.2.)

Personality and Self-Concept

Personality

The unique psychological characteristics that distinguish a person or group.

Each person's distinct personality influences his or her buying behavior. **Personality** refers to the unique psychological characteristics that distinguish a person or group. Personality is usually described in terms of traits such as self-confidence, dominance, sociability, autonomy, defensiveness, adaptability, and aggressiveness. Personality can be useful in analyzing consumer behavior for certain product or brand choices.

The idea is that brands also have personalities, and consumers are likely to choose brands with personalities that match their own. A *brand personality* is the specific mix of human traits that may be attributed to a particular brand. One researcher identified five brand personality traits: *sincerity* (down-to-earth, honest, wholesome, and cheerful); *excitement* (daring, spirited, imaginative, and up-to-date); *competence* (reliable, intelligent, and successful); *sophistication* (upper class and charming); and *ruggedness* (outdoorsy and tough). "Your personality determines what you consume, what TV shows you watch, what products you buy, and [most] other decisions you make," says one consumer behavior expert.[20]

Most well-known brands are strongly associated with one particular trait: the Ford F150 with "ruggedness," Apple with "excitement," the *Washington Post* with "competence," Method with "sincerity," and ● Gucci with "class" and "sophistication." Hence, these brands will attract persons who are high on the same personality traits.

Many marketers use a concept related to personality—a person's *self-concept* (also called *self-image*). The idea is that people's possessions contribute to and reflect their identities—that is, "we are what we consume." Thus, to understand consumer behavior, marketers must first understand the relationship between consumer self-concept and possessions.

Real Marketing 5.2

Pet Owner Lifestyles—and Marketing to Them

In the old days, it seems, owning a pet didn't require a lot. But today, the lives of many pet owners seem to revolve around their furry (or feathery) friends. Many people treat their pets—whether it's a dog, cat, parakeet, or hedgehog—as important family members. Some 42 percent of dogs now sleep in the same beds as their owners. One-third of pet owners even think of themselves as "pet parents." For such people, pet ownership doesn't just mean having a cute little critter around—it defines an entire lifestyle.

The pet owner lifestyle segment constitutes a huge market. Sixty-two percent of all U.S. households own at least one pet. Collectively, Americans own some 75 million dogs, 88 million cats, 142 million freshwater fish, 10 million saltwater fish, 16 million birds, 24 million small animals, 13 million reptiles, and 14 million horses. They spend more than $50 billion a year on their pets, more than the gross domestic product of all but 72 countries in the world.

For many devoted pet parents, having a pet affects just about every decision they make, from what car they buy or what vacations they take to even what TV channels they watch. As a result, marketers across a broad range of industries are targeting the special needs of this large and growing lifestyle segment, offering everything from basics such as pet food, beds, toys, gates, and other pet gadgets to critter daycare, travel and lodging, pet insurance, and even a cable TV channel.

The U.S. travel industry, for one, has upped the options it offers to indulgent pet owners. For example, many major hotel chains offer "pet friendly" rooms and services for owners who can't stand leaving their pets behind. Some hotels, however, take "pet friendly" to a whole new level. For example, The Benjamin Hotel in New York City features a "Dream Dog" program, which offers "everything a pampered pet needs to enjoy travel in tail-wagging style." The program provides dog beds in a variety of styles (including an orthopedic option), plush doggie bathrobes, canine room service, and DVDs for dogs, as well as access to pet spa treatments and a pet psychic. "We understand that your pet is a special addition to your family," says the hotel. "We will ensure your furry friend never has to lift a paw."

Similarly, most airlines have policies for transporting the 76 million pets that fly each year, either in the cabin or the cargo hold. For some pet owners, however, that's just not good enough. Alysa and Dan Binder had so many problems flying with their dog Zoe that they started the first-ever airline designed specifically for pets, especially dogs and cats. Pet Airways now serves nine U.S. cities with 20 aircraft. Cabins are climate controlled and contain no seats, only pet cages. Pet Airways checks its "Pawsengers" into a pet lounge, gives them pre-boarding walks and bathroom breaks, and checks on them at least every 15 minutes during a flight. Pet parents can track their pets via the company Web site.

As any pet lover will tell you, pet ownership doesn't come cheap. Just the everyday costs of acquiring and maintaining pets can be high. But it's the unexpected costs that can really boost the bills. Health care is often the biggest culprit. Pet health care has improved dramatically in recent years, as innovations on the human side of health care have made their way to the pet side, including CAT scans, MRIs, chemotherapy and radiation, and even plastic surgery. But the costs have soared accordingly. In only the past decade, average annual vet expenses were up 47 percent for dogs and 73 percent for cats.

These increased vet expenses haven't deterred pet owners. One study found that nearly 75 percent of pet owners are willing to go into debt to pay for veterinary care for their furry companions. And for many pet medical procedures, they'd have to! If not diagnosed quickly, even a mundane ear infection in a dog can result in $1,000 worth of medical treatment. Ten days of dialysis treatment can reach $12,000 and cancer treatment as much as $40,000. All of this adds up to a lot of potential growth for pet health insurers. In response, companies such as Petplan USA and Veterinary Pet Insurance (VPI), a subsidiary of Nationwide Insurance, offer pet insurance plans. VPI covers mostly dogs and cats, but also a menagerie of other exotic critters, from birds, rabbits, ferrets, rats, and guinea pigs to snakes, iguanas, turtles, potbellied pigs, and even hedgehogs.

Some owners see the logic in paying as much as $50 a month to defray the costs of major medical bills. For the Bongard family in Wisconsin, for example, pet insurance meant the difference between saving their pet hedgehog, Harriet, or letting her go. Harriet recently had surgery to remove a cancerous tumor, ripped open her sutures, had a second surgery to repair the damage, and ended up on anti-psychotics. Without the insurance, Harriet would have been a goner. Even with the insurance, the Bongards shelled out $1,900 to keep Harriet alive. That kind of expense sounds crazy for a hedgehog, but it all comes back to the pet owner lifestyle and the bond between owners and their pets. As Kristen Bongard puts it, she just melts when Harriet rolls up into a little ball. "It's adorable. All of a sudden you see a nose pop out, and two eyes, and maybe the front two paws, and then some ears. It's a very cute thing to watch."

One of the more unusual businesses targeting pet owner lifestyles is DogTV, a recently launched cable network that aims to reduce

Catering to pet owner lifestyles: The Benjamin Hotel's Dream Dog program "offers everything a pampered pooch needs to enjoy traveling in tail-wagging style, from grooming services to a lush bathrobe to a consultation with a pet psychic."

The Benjamin Hotel

the separation anxiety felt by working owners and their stay-at-home dogs:

> The idea is to keep dogs relaxed and entertained while their owners are at work. Many people already leave their TVs on while away to keep their dogs company, so DogTV appears to have a ready-made market. Although the pet owners pay the $4.99 monthly subscription fee, the network's programming is 100 percent for dogs. The programming is based on research by dog psychologists into what dogs like to see and hear. It's not car chases, sirens, or other fast action—those can cause pet stress. Instead, dogs like shows with other dogs in them, ground-level shots of dogs chasing balls, and—of all things— "SpongeBob SquarePants," a real favorite on the channel. You won't find any advertising on DogTV. "Advertising is difficult for us," says DogTV's CEO. "Our viewers aren't able to speak out or purchase products." It's still too early to tell how successful the show will be, but so far dogs appear to like what they see. "It helps if you put the television near the floor," notes a DogTV spokesperson.

The list of things that pet owners will do (and buy) for their pet goes on and on. For overweight dogs (40 percent of them are), there's the PetZen doggie treadmill ($500 to $900). For those who don't want their male pets to suffer the blow to their self-esteem that comes from being neutered, there are Neuticles, patented testicular implants for pets. Some 425,000 dogs, cats, monkeys, rats, and even a water buffalo sport a pair. And for a growing number of people who find it just too hard to part with their deceased pets, you can have them freeze-dried, stuffed, and preserved in a natural pose so that they'll always be around. Now that's the pet owner lifestyle.

Sources: Quotes, adapted examples, and other information from Marty Graham, "TV Network Aims for New Viewing Audience: Dogs," *Reuters*, February 15, 2012, www.reuters.com/article/2012/02/15/us-dogtv-idUSTRE81E26220120215; Gwendolyn Bounds, "The Dog Maxed Out My Credit Card," *Wall Street Journal*, November 2, 2011, http://online.wsj.com/article/SB10001424052970204394804577011824160591082.html; David Kestenbaum, "Health Insurance: Now for Your Dog, or Hedgehog," *Morning Edition*, October 21, 2009, www.npr.org/templates/story/story.php?storyId=113972847; Morieka Johnson, "My Dog Eats Rocks, and Other Strange Things," *CNN*, January 20, 2012, www.cnn.com/2012/01/20/living/unusual-dog-stories-mnn/index.html; and www.thebenjamin.com/DreamDog.aspx and www.petairways.com, accessed March 2012.

● **Brand personality: Consumers are likely to choose brands with personalities that match their own. The Gucci brand is associated with "class" and "sophistication."**

Associated Press

Motive (drive)
A need that is sufficiently pressing to direct the person to seek satisfaction of the need.

For example, Unilever's Axe men's personal care products brand projects a young, confident, manly, and mischievous personality. The brand's racy and sometimes controversial Axe ads around the world depict "The Axe Effect," how women are insanely attracted to the scent of Axe Body Spray. In one ad, a guy wearing Axe gets stripped down by two blonde TSA agents at the airport. In another, a guy wearing Axe is chased by hundreds of bikini-clad women on a remote island. Including body sprays, such personality positioning has made Axe the largest men's deodorant brand in the United States.[21]

Psychological Factors

A person's buying choices are further influenced by four major psychological factors: *motivation, perception, learning,* and *beliefs and attitudes.*

Motivation

A person has many needs at any given time. Some are biological, arising from states of tension such as hunger, thirst, or discomfort. Others are psychological, arising from the need for recognition, esteem, or belonging. A need becomes a motive when it is aroused to a sufficient level of intensity. A **motive** (or **drive**) is a need that is sufficiently pressing to direct the person to seek satisfaction. Psychologists have developed theories of human motivation. Two of the most popular—the theories of Sigmund Freud and Abraham Maslow—carry quite different meanings for consumer analysis and marketing.

Sigmund Freud assumed that people are largely unconscious about the real psychological forces shaping their behavior. His theory suggests that a person's buying decisions are affected by subconscious motives that even the buyer may not fully understand. Thus, an aging baby boomer who buys a sporty BMW convertible might explain that he simply likes the feel of the wind in his thinning hair. At a deeper level, he may be trying to impress others with his success. At a still deeper level, he may be buying the car to feel young and independent again.

The term *motivation research* refers to qualitative research designed to probe consumers' hidden, subconscious motivations. Consumers often don't know or can't describe why they act as they do. Thus, motivation researchers use a variety of probing techniques to uncover underlying emotions and attitudes toward brands and buying situations.

Many companies employ teams of psychologists, anthropologists, and other social scientists to carry out motivation research. One ad agency routinely conducts one-on-one, therapy-like interviews to delve into the inner workings of consumers. Another company asks consumers to describe their favorite brands as animals or cars (say, a Mercedes versus a Chevy) to assess the prestige associated with various brands. Still others rely on hypnosis, dream therapy, or soft lights and mood music to plumb the murky depths of consumer psyches.

Such projective techniques seem pretty goofy, and some marketers dismiss such motivation research as mumbo jumbo. But many marketers use such touchy-feely approaches, now sometimes called *interpretive consumer research*, to dig deeper into consumer psyches and develop better marketing strategies.

Abraham Maslow sought to explain why people are driven by particular needs at particular times. Why does one person spend a lot of time and energy on personal safety and another on gaining the esteem of others? Maslow's answer is that human needs are arranged in a hierarchy, as shown in ● **Figure 5.4**, from the most pressing at the bottom to the least pressing at the top.[22] They include *physiological* needs, *safety* needs, *social* needs, *esteem* needs, and *self-actualization* needs.

A person tries to satisfy the most important need first. When that need is satisfied, it will stop being a motivator, and the person will then try to satisfy the next most important need. For example, starving people (physiological need) will not take an interest in the latest happenings in the art world (self-actualization needs) nor in how they are seen or esteemed by others (social or esteem needs) nor even in whether they are breathing clean air (safety needs). But as each important need is satisfied, the next most important need will come into play.

Perception

Perception
The process by which people select, organize, and interpret information to form a meaningful picture of the world.

A motivated person is ready to act. How the person acts is influenced by his or her own perception of the situation. All of us learn by the flow of information through our five senses: sight, hearing, smell, touch, and taste. However, each of us receives, organizes, and interprets this sensory information in an individual way. **Perception** is the process by which people select, organize, and interpret information to form a meaningful picture of the world.

People can form different perceptions of the same stimulus because of three perceptual processes: selective attention, selective distortion, and selective retention. People are exposed to a great amount of stimuli every day. For example, people are exposed to an estimated 3,000 to 5,000 ad messages every day.[23] It is impossible for a person to pay attention

● **FIGURE | 5.4**
Maslow's Hierarchy of Needs

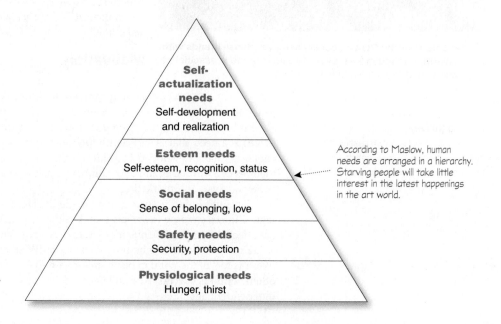

According to Maslow, human needs are arranged in a hierarchy. Starving people will take little interest in the latest happenings in the art world.

to all these stimuli. *Selective attention*—the tendency for people to screen out most of the information to which they are exposed—means that marketers must work especially hard to attract the consumer's attention.

Even noticed stimuli do not always come across in the intended way. Each person fits incoming information into an existing mind-set. *Selective distortion* describes the tendency of people to interpret information in a way that will support what they already believe. People also will forget much of what they learn. They tend to retain information that supports their attitudes and beliefs. *Selective retention* means that consumers are likely to remember good points made about a brand they favor and forget good points made about competing brands. Because of selective attention, distortion, and retention, marketers must work hard to get their messages through.

Learning

Changes in an individual's behavior arising from experience.

Interestingly, although most marketers worry about whether their offers will be perceived at all, some consumers worry that they will be affected by marketing messages without even knowing it—through *subliminal advertising*. More than 50 years ago, a researcher announced that he had flashed the phrases "Eat popcorn" and "Drink Coca-Cola" on a screen in a New Jersey movie theater every five seconds for 1/300th of a second. He reported that although viewers did not consciously recognize these messages, they absorbed them subconsciously and bought 58 percent more popcorn and 18 percent more Coke. Suddenly advertisers and consumer-protection groups became intensely interested in subliminal perception. Although the researcher later admitted to making up the data, the issue has not died. Some consumers still fear that they are being manipulated by subliminal messages.

Numerous studies by psychologists and consumer researchers have found little or no link between subliminal messages and consumer behavior. Recent brain wave studies have found that in certain circumstances, our brains may register subliminal messages. However, it appears that subliminal advertising simply doesn't have the power attributed to it by its critics. ● One classic ad from the American Marketing Association pokes fun at subliminal advertising. "So-called 'subliminal advertising' simply doesn't exist," says the ad. "Overactive imaginations, however, most certainly do."[24]

● **This classic ad from the American Association of Advertising Agencies pokes fun at subliminal advertising. "So-called 'subliminal advertising' simply doesn't exist," says the ad. "Overactive imaginations, however, most certainly do."**

American Association of Advertising Agencies

Learning

When people act, they learn. **Learning** describes changes in an individual's behavior arising from experience. Learning theorists say that most human behavior is learned. Learning occurs through the interplay of drives, stimuli, cues, responses, and reinforcement.

A *drive* is a strong internal stimulus that calls for action. A drive becomes a motive when it is directed toward a particular *stimulus object*. For example, a person's drive for self-actualization might motivate him or her to look into buying a camera. The consumer's response to the idea of buying a camera is conditioned by the surrounding cues. *Cues* are minor stimuli that determine when, where, and how the person responds. For example, the person might spot several camera brands in a shop window, hear of a special sale price, or discuss cameras with a friend. These are all cues that might influence a consumer's *response* to his or her interest in buying the product.

Suppose the consumer buys a Nikon camera. If the experience is rewarding, the consumer will probably use the camera more and more, and his or her response will be *reinforced*. Then the next time he or she shops for a camera, or for binoculars or some similar product, the probability is greater that he or she will buy a Nikon product. The practical significance of learning theory for marketers is that they can build up demand for a product by associating it with strong drives, using motivating cues, and providing positive reinforcement.

Belief

A descriptive thought that a person holds about something.

Beliefs and Attitudes

Through doing and learning, people acquire beliefs and attitudes. These, in turn, influence their buying behavior. A **belief** is a descriptive thought that a person has about something.

Attitude
A person's consistently favorable or unfavorable evaluations, feelings, and tendencies toward an object or idea.

● **Attitudes and beliefs are difficult to change: The Vidalia Onion Committee's award-winning Ogres and Onions campaign made children believers and delighted their parents. Sales of bagged Vidalia onions shot up 30 percent.**

Vidalia® is a registered certification mark of Georgia Department of Agriculture

Objective 3 ⸺▶

List and define the major types of buying decision behavior and the stages in the buyer decision process.

Complex buying behavior
Consumer buying behavior in situations characterized by high consumer involvement in a purchase and significant perceived differences among brands.

Beliefs may be based on real knowledge, opinion, or faith and may or may not carry an emotional charge. Marketers are interested in the beliefs that people formulate about specific products and services because these beliefs make up product and brand images that affect buying behavior. If some of the beliefs are wrong and prevent purchase, the marketer will want to launch a campaign to correct them.

People have attitudes regarding religion, politics, clothes, music, food, and almost everything else. **Attitude** describes a person's relatively consistent evaluations, feelings, and tendencies toward an object or idea. Attitudes put people into a frame of mind of liking or disliking things, of moving toward or away from them. Our camera buyer may hold attitudes such as "Buy the best," "The Japanese make the best electronics products in the world," and "Creativity and self-expression are among the most important things in life." If so, the Nikon camera would fit well into the consumer's existing attitudes.

Attitudes are difficult to change. A person's attitudes fit into a pattern; changing one attitude may require difficult adjustments in many others. Thus, a company should usually try to fit its products into existing attitudes rather than attempt to change attitudes. Of course, there are exceptions. For example, trying to convince parents that their children would actually like onions—that's right, onions—seems like an uphill battle against prevailing attitudes. Convincing the children themselves seems like an even bigger challenge. However, The Vidalia Onion Committee (VOC), formed to promote one of Georgia's most important agricultural products, managed to do just that:[25]

> It can be hard selling children on the idea of eating onions. Onions have a strong smell, they can make you cry, and many kids simply refuse to eat them. So to help change these attitudes, the VOC developed a unique plan. ● It employed Shrek, the famous ogre from the hugely popular animated films. The inspiration came from a scene in the first Shrek film, in which Shrek explains ogres to his friend, Donkey. "Onions have layers, ogres have layers," says Shrek. "Ogres are like onions. End of story."
>
> The result was a national "Ogres and Onions" marketing campaign, launched to coincide with both the onion harvest and the premier of the latest Shrek film. The campaign featured giant Shrek placards in grocery store aisles alongside bags of Vidalia onions on which Shrek asked, "What do ogres and onions have in common?" At the Vidalia Onion Web site, Shrek offered kid-friendly Vidalia onion recipes. The award-winning campaign soon had kids clamoring for onions, and surprised and delighted parents responded. Sales of bagged Vidalia onions increased almost 30 percent for the season.

We can now appreciate the many forces acting on consumer behavior. The consumer's choice results from the complex interplay of cultural, social, personal, and psychological factors.

Types of Buying Decision Behavior

Buying behavior differs greatly for a tube of toothpaste, a smartphone, financial services, and a new car. More complex decisions usually involve more buying participants and more buyer deliberation. ● **Figure 5.5** shows the types of consumer buying behavior based on the degree of buyer involvement and the degree of differences among brands.

Complex Buying Behavior

Consumers undertake **complex buying behavior** when they are highly involved in a purchase and perceive significant differences among brands. Consumers may be highly involved when the product is expensive, risky, purchased infrequently, and highly self-expressive. Typically, the consumer has much to learn about the product category. For example, a PC buyer may not know what attributes to consider. Many product features carry no real meaning: a "2nd Generation Intel Core i7-2670QM processor," "NVIDIA GeForce GT 525M 2GB" video card, or "6GB shared dual-channel DDR3 memory."

This buyer will pass through a learning process, first developing beliefs about the product, then attitudes, and then making a thoughtful purchase choice. Marketers of high-involvement products must understand the information-gathering and evaluation behavior of high-involvement consumers. They need to help buyers learn about product-class attributes and their relative importance. They need to differentiate their brand's features, perhaps by describing the brand's benefits using print media with long copy. They must motivate store salespeople and the buyer's acquaintances to influence the final brand choice.

● **FIGURE | 5.5**
Four Types of Buying Behavior

Source: Adapted from Henry Assael, *Consumer Behavior and Marketing Action* (Boston: Kent Publishing Company, 1987), p. 87. Used with permission of the author.

Buying behavior varies greatly for different types of products. For example, someone buying an expensive new PC might undertake a full information-gathering and brand evaluation process.

	High involvement	Low involvement
Significant differences between brands	Complex buying behavior	Variety-seeking buying behavior
Few differences between brands	Dissonance-reducing buying behavior	Habitual buying behavior

At the other extreme, for low-involvement products, consumers may simply select a familiar brand out of habit. For example, what brand of salt do you buy and why?

Dissonance-reducing buying behavior
Consumer buying behavior in situations characterized by high involvement but few perceived differences among brands.

Habitual buying behavior
Consumer buying behavior in situations characterized by low consumer involvement and few significant perceived brand differences.

Variety-seeking buying behavior
Consumer buying behavior in situations characterized by low consumer involvement but significant perceived brand differences.

Dissonance-Reducing Buying Behavior

Dissonance-reducing buying behavior occurs when consumers are highly involved with an expensive, infrequent, or risky purchase but see little difference among brands. For example, consumers buying carpeting may face a high-involvement decision because carpeting is expensive and self-expressive. Yet buyers may consider most carpet brands in a given price range to be the same. In this case, because perceived brand differences are not large, buyers may shop around to learn what is available but buy relatively quickly. They may respond primarily to a good price or purchase convenience.

After the purchase, consumers might experience *postpurchase dissonance* (after-sale discomfort) when they notice certain disadvantages of the purchased carpet brand or hear favorable things about brands not purchased. To counter such dissonance, the marketer's after-sale communications should provide evidence and support to help consumers feel good about their brand choices.

Habitual Buying Behavior

Habitual buying behavior occurs under conditions of low-consumer involvement and little significant brand difference. For example, take table salt. Consumers have little involvement in this product category—they simply go to the store and reach for a brand. If they keep reaching for the same brand, it is out of habit rather than strong brand loyalty. Consumers appear to have low involvement with most low-cost, frequently purchased products.

In such cases, consumer behavior does not pass through the usual belief-attitude-behavior sequence. Consumers do not search extensively for information about the brands, evaluate brand characteristics, and make weighty decisions about which brands to buy. Because they are not highly involved with the product, consumers may not evaluate the choice, even after purchase. Thus, the buying process involves brand beliefs formed by passive learning, followed by purchase behavior, which may or may not be followed by evaluation.

Because buyers are not highly committed to any brands, marketers of low-involvement products with few brand differences often use price and sales promotions to promote buying. Alternatively, they can add product features or enhancements to differentiate their brands from the rest of the pack and raise involvement. ● For example, to set its brand apart, P&G's Charmin toilet tissue offers Ultrastrong, Ultrasoft, Sensitive, Basic, and Freshmate (wet wipe) versions, so that there's sure to be one that's right for any family's "bottom line." Charmin also raises brand involvement by sponsoring a "Sit or Squat" Web site and mobile app that helps travelers who "Gotta go on the go!" find and rate clean public restrooms wherever they travel.

Variety-Seeking Buying Behavior

Consumers undertake **variety-seeking buying behavior** in situations characterized by low consumer involvement but significant perceived brand differences. In such cases, consumers often do a lot of brand switching. For example, when buying cookies, a consumer may hold some beliefs, choose a cookie brand without much evaluation, and then evaluate that brand during consumption.

● **Creating product involvement: Charmin offers enhancements that boost involvement and set it apart from other brands, including sponsoring a "Sit or Squat" online site and mobile app that helps travelers who "Gotta go on the go!" find and rate clean public restrooms anywhere they travel.**

Jarrod Weaton/Weaton Digital, Inc.

FIGURE | 5.6
Buyer Decision
Process

| Need recognition | → | Information search | → | Evaluation of alternatives | → | Purchase decision | → | Postpurchase behavior |

The buying process starts long before the actual purchase and continues long after. In fact, it might result in a decision not to buy. Therefore, marketers must focus on the entire buying process, not just the purchase decision.

But the next time, the consumer might pick another brand out of boredom or simply to try something different. Brand switching occurs for the sake of variety rather than because of dissatisfaction.

In such product categories, the marketing strategy may differ for the market leader and minor brands. The market leader will try to encourage habitual buying behavior by dominating shelf space, keeping shelves fully stocked, and running frequent reminder advertising. Challenger firms will encourage variety seeking by offering lower prices, special deals, coupons, free samples, and advertising that presents reasons for trying something new.

The Buyer Decision Process

Now that we have looked at the influences that affect buyers, we are ready to look at how consumers make buying decisions. **Figure 5.6** shows that the buyer decision process consists of five stages: *need recognition, information search, evaluation of alternatives, purchase decision,* and *postpurchase behavior.* Clearly, the buying process starts long before the actual purchase and continues long after. Marketers need to focus on the entire buying process rather than on the purchase decision only.

Figure 5.6 suggests that consumers pass through all five stages with every purchase in a considered way. But buyers may pass quickly or slowly through the buying decision process. And in more routine purchases, consumers often skip or reverse some of the stages. Much depends on the nature of the buyer, the product, and the buying situation. A woman buying her regular brand of toothpaste would recognize the need and go right to the purchase decision, skipping information search and evaluation. However, we use the model in Figure 5.6 because it shows all the considerations that arise when a consumer faces a new and complex purchase situation.

Need Recognition

Need recognition
The first stage of the buyer decision process, in which the consumer recognizes a problem or need.

The buying process starts with **need recognition**—the buyer recognizes a problem or need. The need can be triggered by *internal stimuli* when one of the person's normal needs—for example, hunger or thirst—rises to a level high enough to become a drive. A need can also be triggered by *external stimuli.* ● For example, an advertisement or a discussion with a friend might get you thinking about buying a new car. At this stage, the marketer should research consumers to find out what kinds of needs or problems arise, what brought them about, and how they led the consumer to this particular product.

Information Search

Information search
The stage of the buyer decision process in which the consumer is motivated to search for more information.

An interested consumer may or may not search for more information. If the consumer's drive is strong and a satisfying product is near at hand, he or she is likely to buy it then. If not, the consumer may store the need in memory or undertake an **information search** related to the need. For example, once you've decided you need a new car, at the least, you will probably pay more attention to car ads, cars owned by friends, and car conversations. Or you may actively search the Web, talk with friends, and gather information in other ways.

Consumers can obtain information from any of several sources. These include *personal sources* (family, friends, neighbors, acquaintances), *commercial sources* (advertising, salespeople, dealer Web sites, packaging, displays), *public sources* (mass media, consumer rating organizations, online searches and peer reviews), and *experiential sources* (handling, examining, using the product). The relative influence of these information sources varies with the product and the buyer.

Traditionally, consumers have received the most information about a product from commercial sources—those controlled by the marketer. The most effective sources, however, tend to be personal. Commercial sources normally *inform* the buyer, but personal

● Need recognition can be triggered by advertising: Time for a snack?

SNICKERS® and SQUARED & Design® are registered trademarks of Mars, Incorporated. These trademarks are used with permission. Mars, Incorporated is not associated with Pearson. The images of the SNICKERS® and SQUARED & Design® marks, and the SNICKERS® and SNICKERS® Peanut Butter Squared bars are printed with permission of Mars, Incorporated.

Alternative evaluation
The stage of the buyer decision process in which the consumer uses information to evaluate alternative brands in the choice set.

Purchase decision
The buyer's decision about which brand to purchase.

sources *legitimize* or *evaluate* products for the buyer. As one marketer states, "It's rare that an advertising campaign can be as effective as a neighbor leaning over the fence and saying, 'This is a wonderful product.'"[26]

Increasingly, that "neighbor's fence" is a digital one. Today, buyers can find an abundance of user-generated reviews alongside the products they are considering at sites ranging from Amazon.com or BestBuy.com to TripAdvisor, Epinions, and Epicurious. Although individual user reviews vary widely in quality, an entire body of reviews often provides a reliable product assessment—straight from the fingertips of people like you who've actually purchased and experienced the product.

As more information is obtained, the consumer's awareness and knowledge of the available brands and features increase. In your car information search, you may learn about several brands that are available. The information might also help you to drop certain brands from consideration. A company must design its marketing mix to make prospects aware of and knowledgeable about its brand. It should carefully identify consumers' sources of information and the importance of each source.

Evaluation of Alternatives

We have seen how consumers use information to arrive at a set of final brand choices. Next, marketers need to know about **alternative evaluation**, that is, how consumers process information to choose among alternative brands. Unfortunately, consumers do not use a simple and single evaluation process in all buying situations. Instead, several evaluation processes are at work.

How consumers go about evaluating purchase alternatives depends on the individual consumer and the specific buying situation. In some cases, consumers use careful calculations and logical thinking. At other times, the same consumers do little or no evaluating. Instead they buy on impulse and rely on intuition. Sometimes consumers make buying decisions on their own; sometimes they turn to friends, online reviews, or salespeople for buying advice.

Suppose you've narrowed your car choices to three brands. And suppose that you are primarily interested in four attributes—price, style, operating economy, and warranty. By this time, you've probably formed beliefs about how each brand rates on each attribute. Clearly, if one car rated best on all the attributes, the marketer could predict that you would choose it. However, the brands will no doubt vary in appeal. You might base your buying decision mostly on one attribute, and your choice would be easy to predict. If you wanted style above everything else, you would buy the car that you think has the most style. But most buyers consider several attributes, each with different importance. By knowing the importance that you assigned to each attribute, the marketer could predict your car choice more reliably.

Marketers should study buyers to find out how they actually evaluate brand alternatives. If marketers know what evaluative processes go on, they can take steps to influence the buyer's decision.

Purchase Decision

In the evaluation stage, the consumer ranks brands and forms purchase intentions. Generally, the consumer's **purchase decision** will be to buy the most preferred brand, but two factors can come between the purchase *intention* and the purchase *decision*. The first factor is the *attitudes of others*. If someone important to you thinks that you should buy the lowest-priced car, then the chances of you buying a more expensive car are reduced.

The second factor is *unexpected situational factors*. The consumer may form a purchase intention based on factors such as expected income, expected price, and expected product benefits. However, unexpected events may change the purchase intention. For example, the economy might take a turn for the worse, a close competitor might drop its price, or a friend might report being disappointed in your preferred car. Thus, preferences and even purchase intentions do not always result in an actual purchase choice.

Postpurchase Behavior

Postpurchase behavior

The stage of the buyer decision process in which consumers take further action after purchase, based on their satisfaction or dissatisfaction.

The marketer's job does not end when the product is bought. After purchasing the product, the consumer will either be satisfied or dissatisfied and will engage in **postpurchase behavior** of interest to the marketer. What determines whether the buyer is satisfied or dissatisfied with a purchase? The answer lies in the relationship between the *consumer's expectations* and the product's *perceived performance*. If the product falls short of expectations, the consumer is disappointed; if it meets expectations, the consumer is satisfied; if it exceeds expectations, the consumer is delighted. The larger the gap between expectations and performance, the greater the consumer's dissatisfaction. This suggests that sellers should promise only what their brands can deliver so that buyers are satisfied.

Almost all major purchases, however, result in **cognitive dissonance**, or discomfort caused by postpurchase conflict. After the purchase, consumers are satisfied with the benefits of the chosen brand and are glad to avoid the drawbacks of the brands not bought. However, every purchase involves compromise. So consumers feel uneasy about acquiring the drawbacks of the chosen brand and about losing the benefits of the brands not purchased. ● Thus, consumers feel at least some postpurchase dissonance for every purchase.[27]

● Postpurchase cognitive dissonance: No matter what choice they make, consumers feel at least some postpurchase dissonance for every decision.

Stephane Bidouze/Shutterstock.com

Why is it so important to satisfy the customer? Customer satisfaction is a key to building profitable relationships with consumers—to keeping and growing consumers and reaping their customer lifetime value. Satisfied customers buy a product again, talk favorably to others about the product, pay less attention to competing brands and advertising, and buy other products from the company. Many marketers go beyond merely *meeting* the expectations of customers—they aim to *delight* customers.

Cognitive dissonance

Buyer discomfort caused by postpurchase conflict.

A dissatisfied consumer responds differently. Bad word of mouth often travels farther and faster than good word of mouth. It can quickly damage consumer attitudes about a company and its products. But companies cannot simply wait for dissatisfied customers to volunteer their complaints. Most unhappy customers never tell the company about their problems. Therefore, a company should measure customer satisfaction regularly. It should set up systems that *encourage* customers to complain. In this way, the company can learn how well it is doing and how it can improve.

By studying the overall buyer decision process, marketers may be able to find ways to help consumers move through it. For example, if consumers are not buying a new product because they do not perceive a need for it, marketing might launch advertising messages that trigger the need and show how the product solves customers' problems. If customers know about the product but are not buying because they hold unfavorable attitudes toward it, marketers must find ways to change either the product or consumer perceptions.

New product

A good, service, or idea that is perceived by some potential customers as new.

Objective 4 ·······➤

Describe the adoption and diffusion process for new products.

Adoption process

The mental process through which an individual passes from first hearing about an innovation to final adoption.

The Buyer Decision Process for New Products

We now look at how buyers approach the purchase of new products. A **new product** is a good, service, or idea that is perceived by some potential customers as new. It may have been around for a while, but our interest is in how consumers learn about products for the first time and make decisions on whether to adopt them. We define the **adoption process** as the mental process through which an individual passes from first learning about an innovation to final adoption. *Adoption* is the decision by an individual to become a regular user of the product.[28]

Stages in the Adoption Process

Consumers go through five stages in the process of adopting a new product:

Awareness: The consumer becomes aware of the new product but lacks information about it.

Interest: The consumer seeks information about the new product.

Evaluation: The consumer considers whether trying the new product makes sense.

Trial: The consumer tries the new product on a small scale to improve his or her estimate of its value.

Adoption: The consumer decides to make full and regular use of the new product.

This model suggests that new-product marketers should think about how to help consumers move through these stages. For example, Best Buy recently developed a unique way to help concerned customers get past a hurdle in the buying process and make a positive buying decision for new televisions:[29]

● **The adoption process: To help potential customers overcome obsolescence concerns that were keeping them from buying TVs, Best Buy began offering a Future-Proof Buy Back Program.**

Kenneth K. Lam/MCT/Newscom

Prior to a recent holiday shopping season, to convince buyers to upgrade to new models, television manufacturers offered a flurry of new technologies and loaded their marketing pitches with techie jargon such as ultrathin, Wi-Fi-capable, widget-equipped, and Internet-ready. However, rather than spurring new purchases, the pitches created a barrier to buying—fear among buyers that whatever they bought might soon be obsolete. In one study, 40 percent of consumers said that concerns about technology becoming outdated were preventing them from buying electronic products such as TVs, mobile phones, and computers. That left electronics retailers like Best Buy with aisles stacked high with unsold electronics.

To help customers past this buying hurdle, ● Best Buy began offering a Future-Proof Buy Back Program. For an up-front fee of 7 to 20 percent of the price, Best Buy promises customers that, when they're ready for something new, it will redeem purchases in good working order for up to 50 percent of the purchase price, depending on how many months pass before they upgrade. "There is a fair number of consumers on the bubble, not quite willing to make a purchase because they fear some other new thing will come down very quickly," says a Best Buy executive. "We want them to go ahead and make that purchase with confidence." Competitors such as Radio Shack, Office Depot, and Walmart quickly followed with their own buy back plans.

Individual Differences in Innovativeness

People differ greatly in their readiness to try new products. In each product area, there are "consumption pioneers" and early adopters. Other individuals adopt new products much later. People can be classified into the adopter categories shown in ● **Figure 5.7.**[30] As shown by the curve, after a slow start, an increasing number of people adopt the new product. As successive groups of consumers adopt the innovation, it eventually reaches its cumulative saturation level. Innovators are defined as the first 2.5 percent of buyers to adopt a new idea (those beyond two standard deviations from mean adoption time); the early adopters are the next 13.5 percent (between one and two standard deviations); and then come early mainstream, late mainstream, and lagging adopters.

The five adopter groups have differing values. *Innovators* are venturesome—they try new ideas at some risk. *Early adopters* are guided by respect—they are opinion leaders in their communities and adopt new ideas early but carefully. The *early mainstream* is deliberate—although they rarely are leaders, they adopt new ideas before the average person. The *late mainstream* is skeptical—they adopt an innovation only after a majority of people have tried it. Finally, *lagging adopters* are tradition bound—they are suspicious of changes and adopt the innovation only when it has become something of a tradition itself.

This adopter classification suggests that an innovating firm should research the characteristics of innovators and early adopters in their product categories and direct initial marketing efforts toward them.

FIGURE | 5.7
Adopter Categories Based
on Relative Time of Adoption
of Innovations

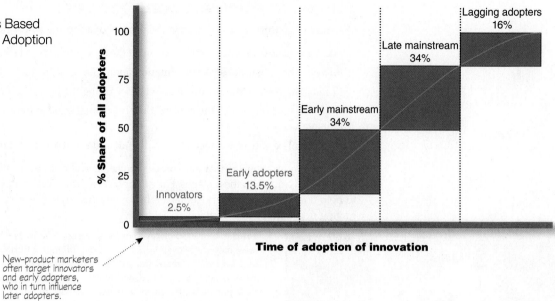

New-product marketers
often target innovators
and early adopters,
who in turn influence
later adopters.

Influence of Product Characteristics on Rate of Adoption

The characteristics of the new product affect its rate of adoption. Some products catch on almost overnight. For example, Apple's iPod, iPhone, and iPad flew off retailers' shelves at an astounding rate from the day they were first introduced. Others take a longer time to gain acceptance. For example, the first HDTVs were introduced in the United States in the 1990s, but the percentage of U.S. households owning a high-definition set stood at only 12 percent by 2007. HDTV penetration reached 66 percent by 2012.[31]

Five characteristics are especially important in influencing an innovation's rate of adoption. For example, consider the characteristics of HDTV in relation to the rate of adoption:

Relative advantage: The degree to which the innovation appears superior to existing products. HDTV offers substantially improved picture quality. This accelerated its rate of adoption.

Compatibility: The degree to which the innovation fits the values and experiences of potential consumers. HDTV, for example, is highly compatible with the lifestyles of the TV-watching public. However, in the early years, HDTV was not yet compatible with programming and broadcasting systems, which slowed adoption. Now, as high-definition programs and channels have become the norm, the rate of HDTV adoption has increased rapidly.

Complexity: The degree to which the innovation is difficult to understand or use. HDTVs are not very complex. Therefore, as more programming has become available and prices have fallen, the rate of HDTV adoption has increased faster than that of more complex innovations.

Divisibility: The degree to which the innovation may be tried on a limited basis. Early HDTVs and HD cable and satellite systems were very expensive, which slowed the rate of adoption. As prices have fallen, adoption rates have increased.

Communicability: The degree to which the results of using the innovation can be observed or described to others. Because HDTV lends itself to demonstration and description, its use will spread faster among consumers.

Other characteristics influence the rate of adoption, such as initial and ongoing costs, risk and uncertainty, and social approval. The new-product marketer must research all these factors when developing the new product and its marketing program.

Reviewing the Concepts

MyMarketingLab™

Go to **mymktlab.com** to complete the problems marked with this icon .

Reviewing Objectives and Key Terms

 ## Objectives Review

The American consumer market consists of more than 313 million people who consume over $14 trillion worth of goods and services each year, making it one of the most attractive consumer markets in the world. Consumers vary greatly in terms of cultural, social, personal, and psychological makeup. Understanding how these differences affect *consumer buying behavior* is one of the biggest challenges marketers face.

Objective 1 **Define the consumer market and construct a simple model of consumer buyer behavior. (pp 136–137)**

The *consumer market* consists of all the individuals and households that buy or acquire goods and services for personal consumption. The simplest model of consumer buyer behavior is the stimulus-response model. According to this model, marketing stimuli (the four Ps) and other major forces (economic, technological, political, cultural) enter the consumer's "black box" and produce certain responses. Once in the black box, these inputs produce observable buyer responses, such as product choice, brand choice, purchase timing, and purchase amount.

Objective 2 **Name the four major factors that influence consumer buyer behavior. (pp 137–152)**

Consumer buyer behavior is influenced by four key sets of buyer characteristics: cultural, social, personal, and psychological. Although many of these factors cannot be influenced by the marketer, they can be useful in identifying interested buyers and shaping products and appeals to serve consumer needs better. *Culture* is the most basic determinant of a person's wants and behavior. *Subcultures* are "cultures within cultures" that have distinct values and lifestyles and can be based on anything from age to ethnicity. Many companies focus their marketing programs on the special needs of certain cultural and subcultural segments.

Social factors also influence a buyer's behavior. A person's *reference groups*—family, friends, social networks, professional associations—strongly affect product and brand choices. The buyer's age, life-cycle stage, occupation, economic circumstances, personality, and other *personal characteristics* influence his or her buying decisions. Consumer *lifestyles*—the whole pattern of acting and interacting in the world—are also an important influence on purchase decisions. Finally, consumer buying behavior is influenced by four major *psychological factors*: motivation,

perception, learning, and beliefs and attitudes. Each of these factors provides a different perspective for understanding the workings of the buyer's black box.

Objective 3 **List and define the major types of buying decision behavior and the stages in the buyer decision process. (pp 152–156)**

Buying behavior may vary greatly across different types of products and buying decisions. Consumers undertake *complex buying behavior* when they are highly involved in a purchase and perceive significant differences among brands. *Dissonance-reducing behavior* occurs when consumers are highly involved but see little difference among brands. *Habitual buying behavior* occurs under conditions of low involvement and little significant brand difference. In situations characterized by low involvement but significant perceived brand differences, consumers engage in *variety-seeking buying behavior*.

When making a purchase, the buyer goes through a decision process consisting of *need recognition*, *information search*, *evaluation of alternatives*, *purchase decision*, and *postpurchase behavior*. The marketer's job is to understand the buyer's behavior at each stage and the influences that are operating. During *need recognition*, the consumer recognizes a problem or need that could be satisfied by a product or service in the market. Once the need is recognized, the consumer is aroused to seek more information and moves into the *information search* stage. With information in hand, the consumer proceeds to *alternative evaluation*, during which the information is used to evaluate brands in the choice set. From there, the consumer makes a *purchase decision* and actually buys the product. In the final stage of the buyer decision process, *postpurchase behavior*, the consumer takes action based on satisfaction or dissatisfaction.

Objective 4 **Describe the adoption and diffusion process for new products. (pp 156–158)**

The product *adoption process* is made up of five stages: awareness, interest, evaluation, trial, and adoption. New-product marketers must think about how to help consumers move through these stages. With regard to the *diffusion process* for new products, consumers respond at different rates, depending on consumer and product characteristics. Consumers may be innovators, early adopters, early majority, late majority, or laggards.

Each group may require different marketing approaches. Marketers often try to bring their new products to the attention of potential early adopters, especially those who are opinion leaders.

Finally, several characteristics influence the rate of adoption: relative advantage, compatibility, complexity, divisibility, and communicability.

 Key Terms

Objective 1

Consumer buyer behavior (p 136)
Consumer market (p 136)

Objective 2

Culture (p 138)
Subculture (p 138)
Social class (p 140)
Group (p 140)
Word-of-mouth influence (p 141)
Opinion leader (p 141)
Online social networks (p 142)

Lifestyle (p 147)
Personality (p 147)
Motive (drive) (p 149)
Perception (p 150)
Learning (p 151)
Belief (p 151)
Attitude (p 152)

Objective 3

Complex buying behavior (p 152)
Dissonance-reducing buying behavior
  (p 153)

Habitual buying behavior (p 153)
Variety-seeking buying behavior (p 153)
Need recognition (p 154)
Information search (p 154)
Alternative evaluation (p 155)
Purchase decision (p 155)
Postpurchase behavior (p 156)
Cognitive dissonance (p 156)

Objective 4

New product (p 156)
Adoption process (p 156)

Discussion and Critical Thinking

 Discussion Questions

1. Review the "black box" model of buyer behavior. Which buyer characteristics that affect buyer behavior influence you most when selecting a restaurant? Are those the same characteristics that would influence you when making a smartphone purchase? Explain. (AACSB: Communication; Reflective Thinking)

2. What is an opinion leader? Describe how marketers attempt to use opinion leaders to help sell their products. (AACSB: Communication; Reflective Thinking)

✪ **3.** Name and describe the types of buying decision behavior and describe a personal example for each. (AACSB: Communication; Reflective Thinking)

✪ **4.** What is a "new product," and how do consumers go about deciding whether to adopt a new product? (AACSB: Communication)

 Critical Thinking Exercises

1. Form a small group of four or five students. Have each group member interview 10 consumers about if and when they purchased their first smartphone. Research when smartphones were first introduced, and based on each respondent's answer, identify which adopter category best describes that consumer. Create a chart similar to Figure 5.7 to present your results for all group members' interviews. How far along are smartphones in their adoption cycle? (AACSB: Communication; Diversity; Reflective Thinking)

2. Go to the Strategic Business Insights (SBI) Web site and complete the VALS survey at www.strategicbusinessinsights.com/vals/presurvey.shtml. What does VALS measure and what is your VALS type? Does it adequately describe you? On what dimensions are the VALS types based, and how can marketers use this tool to better understand consumers? (AACSB: Communication; Use of IT; Reflective Thinking)

Applications and Cases

 ## Marketing Technology Mourning 2.0

Every culture has rituals for mourning the dead, but technology is now changing many of our long-held cultural norms. The conservative funeral industry is slowly embracing new technologies, resulting in new mourning behaviors. High-definition video screens play a video homage to the deceased, live-streamed funerals reach all corners of the globe, digital guest books remain permanently active, e-mails remind the bereaved of the anniversary of a loved-one's death, and digital candles remain perpetually "lit" on memorial pages. The deceased can now live on in cyberspace and friends can visit them on Facebook long after they have passed on. Quick-response code chips ("QR codes") affixed to tombstones can bring a person "back to life" virtually on a smartphone. With nearly half of all Americans owning smartphones, 20 percent owning tablets, 80 percent on the Internet, and almost 70 percent visiting social media sites, the time is now right for the funeral industry to capitalize on these digital trends.

And with the still-sluggish economy and new competitors (for example, Walmart and Costco now sell caskets online) squeezing profit margins, the funeral industry is more open than ever to ways to satisfy consumers' mourning needs digitally.

1. Research mourning customs of other cultures. What role do products and services play in making the experience meaningful for mourners? Is technology changing customs outside of the United States? (AACSB: Communication; Diversity; Reflective Thinking)

2. Describe the characteristics of a new product that affect its rate of adoption. Which characteristics will impact how quickly the new services described for the funeral industry will be accepted by mourners in the United States? (AACSB: Communication; Reflective Thinking)

 ## Marketing Ethics "Vanity Sizing"

What does an "8" mean to you? Well, if you are a female, then it means a lot, especially if you really are a "12"—size, that is. Marketers know that, too, and the trend is for larger sizes to be labeled with smaller numbers. Sizing was standardized in the 1940s and 1950s when women started purchasing mass-produced clothing. But sizes fluctuated in the following decades and the Department of Commerce abandoned sizing standardization in 1983. Now, the size number can mean anything the marketer wants it to mean. Marketers know that a size-12 woman who finds out she can fit into an 8 will get a self-esteem boost and likely purchase more. This practice, known as "vanity sizing," has the potential to pay off big for clothing manufacturers. With 34 percent of adults in the United States overweight and another 40 percent obese, that adds up to a sizable market potential. Plus-sized clothing designer Torrid caters to the full-sized woman with sizes ranging

from 0–5, where a size 4 is actually a size 26. If a large number on the size label really bothers you, stick to the more expensive brands—they tend to be the ones using vanity sizing most.

1. Which factors are clothing marketers using to influence consumers? Ask five female and five male friends how much the size labeled on clothing influences their behavior. Write a brief report of your findings. (AACSB: Communication; Reflective Thinking)

2. Should manufacturers be allowed to pick whatever measurements they want and attach any size number they want to them? Should the government or business set standardized sizes? (AACSB: Communication; Ethical Reasoning)

 ## Marketing by the Numbers Evaluating Alternatives

One way consumers can evaluate alternatives is to identify important attributes and assess how purchase alternatives perform on those attributes. Consider the purchase of an automobile. Each attribute, such as gas mileage, is given a weight to reflect its level of importance to that consumer. Then the consumer evaluates each alternative on each attribute. For example, in the table, gas mileage (weighted at 0.5) is the most important attribute for this consumer. The consumer believes that Brand C performs best on gas mileage, rating it 7 (higher ratings indicate higher performance). Brand B is perceived as performing the worst on this attribute (rating of 3). Styling and price are the consumer's next most important attributes. Warrant is least important.

A score can be calculated for each brand by multiplying the importance weight for each attribute by the brand's score on that

Attributes	Importance Weight (e)	Alternative Brands		
		A	**B**	**C**
Styling	0.2	4	6	2
Gas mileage	0.5	6	3	7
Warranty	0.1	5	5	4
Price	0.2	4	6	7

attribute. These weighted scores are then summed to determine the score for that brand. For example, Score$_{Brand\ A}$ = (0.2 × 4) + (0.5 × 6) + (0.1 × 5) + (0.2 × 4) = 0.8 + 3.0 + 0.5 + 0.8 = 5.1. This consumer will select the brand with the highest score.

1. Calculate the scores for Brands B and C. Which brand would this consumer likely choose? (AACSB: Communication; Analytic Reasoning)

2. Which brand is this consumer least likely to purchase? Discuss two ways the marketer of this brand can enhance consumer attitudes toward purchasing its brand. (AACSB: Communication; Reflective Thinking; Analytic Reasoning)

 # Video Case   Goodwill Industries

Since 1902, Goodwill Industries has funded job training and placement programs through its chain of thrift stores. Although selling used clothing, furniture, and other items may not seem like big business, for Goodwill it amounts to more than $3 billion in annual sales. You might think of thrift stores as musty, low-class operations. But Goodwill is putting an end to such perceptions by focusing on consumer behavior concepts.

Like any good marketing company, Goodwill recognizes that not all customers are the same. This video demonstrates how Goodwill caters to different types of customers by recognizing the cultural, social, personal, and psychological factors that affect how customers make buying decisions. In this way, Goodwill

maximizes customer value by offering the right mix of goods at unbeatable bargains.

After viewing the video featuring Goodwill, answer the following questions:

1. Describe different types of Goodwill customers.

2. Which of the four sets of factors affecting consumer behavior most strongly affects consumers' purchase decisions when shopping at Goodwill?

3. How does Goodwill's recognition of consumer behavior principles affect its marketing mix?

 # Company Case   Porsche: Guarding the Old While Bringing in the New

Porsche (pronounced *Porsh*-uh) is a unique company. It has always been a niche brand that makes cars for a small and distinctive segment of automobile buyers. Last year, Porsche sold only 29,023 cars in the five models it sells in the United States. Honda sold about five times that many Accords alone. But Porsche owners are as rare as their vehicles. For that reason, top managers at Porsche spend a great deal of time thinking about customers. They want to know who their customers are, what they think, and how they feel. They want to know why they buy a Porsche rather than a Jaguar, or a Ferrari, or a big Mercedes coupe. These are challenging questions—even Porsche owners themselves don't know exactly what motivates their buying. But given Porsche's low volume and the increasingly fragmented auto market, it is imperative that management understand its customers and what gets their motors running.

Profile of a Porsche Owner

Porsche was founded in 1931 by Ferdinand Porsche, the man credited with designing the original Volkswagen Beetle, Adolf Hitler's "people's car" and one of the most successful car designs of all time. For most of the first two decades, the company built Volkswagen Beetles for German citizens and tanks and Beetles for the military. As Porsche AG began to sell cars under its own nameplate in the 1950s and 1960s, a few constants developed. The company sold very few models, creating an image of exclusivity. Those early models had a rounded, bubble shape that had its roots in the original Beetle, but design evolved into something more Porsche-like with the world famous 356 and 911 models. Finally, Porsche's automobiles featured air-cooled four- and six-cylinder "boxer" motors (cylinders in an opposed configuration) in the rear of the car. This gave the cars a unique and often dangerous characteristic—a tendency for the rear-end to swing out when cornering hard. That's one of the reasons that Porsche owners were drawn to them. They were challenging to drive and that kept most people away, making the car even more exclusive.

Since its early days, Porsche has appealed to a very narrow segment of financially successful people. These are achievers who see themselves as entrepreneurial, even if they work for a corporation. They set very high goals for themselves and then work doggedly to meet them. And they expect no less from the clothes they wear, the restaurants they go to, or the cars they drive. These individuals see themselves not as a part of the regular world, but as exceptions to it. They buy Porsches because the car mirrors their self-image—it stands for the things owners like to see in themselves and in their lives.

Most of us buy what Porsche executives call utility vehicles. That is, we buy cars to go to work, to deliver the kids, and to run errands. Because we have to use our cars to accomplish these daily tasks, we base buying decisions on features such as price, size, fuel economy, and other practical considerations. But a Porsche is more than a utility car. Its owners see it as a car to be enjoyed, not just used. Most Porsche buyers are not moved by information, but by feelings. A Porsche is like a piece of clothing, something the owner "wears" and is seen in. They develop a personal relationship with their cars, one that has more to do with the way the car sounds, vibrates, and feels than with how many cup holders it has or how much cargo it can tote. They admire their Porsches as machines that perform without being flashy or phony.

People buy Porsches because they enjoy driving. If all they needed was something to get them from point A to point B, they could find something much less expensive. And whereas many Porsche owners are car enthusiasts, some of them are not. One successful businesswoman and owner of a high-end Porsche said, "When I drive this car to the high school to pick up my daughter, I end up with five youngsters in the car. If I drive any other car, I can't even find her; she doesn't want to come home."

From Niche to Numerous

For the first few decades, Porsche AG lived by the philosophy of Ferry Porsche, Ferdinand's son. Ferry created the Porsche 356 because no one else made a car like the one he wanted. "We did not do market research, we had no sales forecasts, no return-on-investment calculations. None of that. I very simply built my dream car and figured that there would be other people who share that dream." So really, Porsche AG from the beginning was very much like its customers: an achiever that set out to make the very best.

But as the years rolled on, Porsche management became concerned with a significant issue: Were there enough Porsche buyers to keep the company afloat? Granted, the company never had illusions of churning out the numbers of Chevrolet or Toyota. But to fund innovation, even a niche manufacturer has to grow a little. And Porsche began to worry that the quirky nature of the people who buy Porsches might just run out on them.

This led Porsche to extend its brand outside the box. In the early 1970s, Porsche introduced the 914, a square-ish, mid-engine two-seater that was much cheaper than the 911. This meant that a different class of people could afford a Porsche. It was no surprise that the 914 became Porsche's top-selling model. By the late 1970s, Porsche replaced the 914 with a hatchback coupe that had something no other regular Porsche model had ever had: an engine in the front. At less than $20,000, more than $10,000 less than the 911, the 924 and later 944 models were once again Porsche's pitch to affordability. At one point, Porsche increased its sales goal by nearly 50 percent to 60,000 cars a year.

Although these cars were in many respects sales successes, the Porsche faithful cried foul. They considered these entry-level models to be cheap and underperforming. Most loyalists never really accepted these models as "real" Porsches. In fact, they were not at all happy that they had to share their brand with a customer who didn't fit the Porsche-owner profile. They were turned off by what they saw as a corporate strategy that had focused on *mass* over *class* marketing. This tarnished image was compounded by the fact that Nissan, Toyota, BMW, and other car makers had ramped up high-end sports car offerings, creating some fierce competition. In fact, both the Datsun 280-ZX and the Toyota Supra were not only cheaper than Porsche's 944, they were faster. A struggling economy threw more sand in Porsche's tank. By 1990, Porsche sales had plummeted and the company flirted with bankruptcy.

Return to Its Roots?

But Porsche wasn't going down without a fight. It quickly recognized the error of its ways and halted production of the entry-level models. It rebuilt its damaged image by revamping its higher-end model lines with more race-bred technology. In an effort to regain rapport with customers, Porsche once again targeted the high end of the market in both price and performance. It set modest sales goals and decided that moderate growth with higher margins would be more profitable in the long term. The company set out to make one less Porsche than the public demanded. According to one executive, "We're not looking for volume, we're searching for exclusivity."

Porsche's efforts had the desired effect. By the late 1990s, the brand was once again favored by the same types of achievers who had so deeply loved the car for decades. The cars were once again exclusive. And the company was once again profitable. But by the early 2000s, Porsche management was asking itself a familiar question: To have a sustainable future, could Porsche rely on only the Porsche faithful? According to then CEO Wendelin Wiedeking, "For Porsche to remain independent, it can't be dependent on the most fickle segment in the market.

We don't want to become just a marketing department of some giant. We have to make sure we're profitable enough to pay for future development ourselves."

So in 2002, Porsche did the unthinkable. It became one of the last car companies to jump into the insatiable SUV market. At roughly 5,000 pounds, the Porsche Cayenne was heavier than anything that Porsche had ever made with the exception of some prototype military tanks it made during WWII. Once again, the new model featured an engine up front. And it was the first Porsche to ever be equipped with seat belts for five. As news spread about the car's development, howls of distress could be heard from Porsche's customer base.

But this time, Porsche did not seem too concerned that the loyalists would be put off. Could it be that the company had already forgotten what happened the last time it deviated from the mold? Apparently not. After driving one of the first Cayennes off the assembly line, one journalist stated, "A day at the wheel of the 444 horsepower Cayenne Turbo leaves two overwhelming impressions. First, the Cayenne doesn't behave or feel like an SUV, and second, it drives like a Porsche." This was no entry-level car. Porsche had created a two-and-a-half ton beast that could accelerate to 60 miles per hour in just over five seconds, corner like it was on rails, and hit 165 miles per hour, all while coddling five adults in sumptuous leather seats with almost no wind noise from the outside world. On top of that, it could keep up with a Land Rover when the pavement ended. Indeed, Porsche had created the Porsche of SUVs.

Recently, Porsche upped the ante one more time. It unveiled another large vehicle. But this time, it was a low-slung, five-door luxury sedan. The Porsche faithful and the automotive press again gasped in disbelief. But by the time the Panamera hit the pavement, Porsche had proven once again that Porsche customers could have their cake and eat it too. The Panamera is almost as big as the Cayenne but can move four adults down the road at speeds of up to 190 miles per hour, accelerate from a standstill to 60 miles per hour in 3.6 seconds, and still wring 23 miles out of a gallon of gasoline.

Although some Porsche traditionalists would never be caught dead driving a front-engine Porsche that has more than two doors, Porsche insists that two trends will sustain these new models. First, a category of Porsche buyers has moved into life stages that have them facing inescapable needs—they need to haul more people and stuff. This not only applies to certain regular Porsche buyers, but Porsche is again seeing buyers enter its dealerships who otherwise wouldn't have. Only this time, the price points of the new vehicles are drawing only the well heeled, allowing Porsche to maintain its exclusivity. These buyers also seem to fit the achiever profile of regular Porsche buyers.

The second trend is the growth of emerging economies. Whereas the United States has long been the world's biggest consumer of Porsches, the company expects China to become its biggest customer before long. Twenty years ago, the United States accounted for about 50 percent of Porsche's worldwide sales. Now, it accounts for less than 25 percent. In China, many people who can afford to buy a car as expensive as a Porsche also hire a chauffer. The Cayenne and the Panamera are perfect for those who want to be driven around in style but who may also want to make a quick getaway if necessary.

The most recent economic downturn brought down the sales of just about every maker of premium automobiles. When times are tough, buying a car like a Porsche is the ultimate postponable purchase. But as this downturn turns back up, Porsche is better positioned than ever to meet the needs of its customer base. In fact, its global unit sales are up by 21 percent to a company record 118,867 vehicles. Porsche is also in better shape than ever to maintain its brand image with the Porsche faithful, and with others as well. Understanding Porsche buyers is still a difficult task. But one former chief executive of Porsche summed it up this way: "If you really want to understand our customers, you have to understand the phrase, 'If I were going to be a car, I'd be a Porsche.'"

Questions for Discussion

1. Analyze the buyer decision process of a traditional Porsche customer.

2. Contrast the traditional Porsche customer decision process to the decision process for a Cayenne or Panamera customer.

3. Which concepts from the chapter explain why Porsche sold so many lower-priced models in the 1970s and 1980s?

4. Explain how both positive and negative attitudes toward a brand like Porsche develop. How might Porsche change consumer attitudes toward the brand?

5. What role does the Porsche brand play in the self-concept of its buyers?

Sources: Andre Tutu, "Porsche Announces 2011 Sales Increase," *Autoevolution*, January 3, 2012, www.autoevolution.com/news/porsche-announces-2011-us-sales-increase-41571.html; David Gumpert, "Porsche on Nichemanship," *Harvard Business Review*, March/April 1986, pp. 98–106; Peter Robinson, "Porsche Cayenne—Driving Impression," *Car and Driver*, January, 2003, www.caranddriver.com/reviews/porsche-cayenne-first-drive-review; Jens Meiners, "2010 Porsche Panamera S/4S/Turbo–First Drive Review," *Car and Driver*, June, 2009, www.caranddriver.com/reviews/2010-porsche-panamera-s-4s-turbo-first-drive-review; and information from www.porsche.com/usa/aboutporsche/pressreleases/, accessed July 2012.

MyMarketingLab

Go to **mymktlab.com** for Auto-graded writing questions as well as the following Assisted-graded writing questions:

5-1. Explain the stages of the consumer buyer decision process and describe how you or your family went through this process to make a recent purchase. (AACSB: Communication; Reflective Thinking)

5-2. Malcolm Gladwell published a book entitled The Tipping Point. He describes the Law of the Few, Stickiness, and the Law of Context. Research these concepts and describe how understanding them helps marketers better understand and target consumers. (AACSB: Communication; Reflective Thinking)

5-3. Mymktlab Only – comprehensive writing assignment for this chapter.

References

1. Portions adapted from information found in Tom Foster, "The Go-Pro Army," *Inc.*, January 26, 2012, accessed at www.inc.com/magazine/201202/the-gopro-army.html; Tom Foster, "How GoPro Measures Social Engagement," *Inc.*, January 26, 2012, accessed at www.inc.com/magazine/201202/the-bare-truth-gopro-social-engagement.html; Peter Burrows, "GoPro's Incredible Small, Durable Camcorder," *Bloomberg Businessweek*, June 30, 2011, accessed at www.businessweek.com/magazine/gopros-incredible-small-durable-camcorder-07012011.html; Casey Newton, "GoPro Positioned to Grab Big Slice of Global Market," *San Francisco Chronicle*, May 6, 2011, p. D1; and www.GoPro.com and http://gopro.com/about-us/, accessed September 2012.

2. Consumer expenditure figures from https://www.cia.gov/library/publications/the-world-factbook/geos/us.html. Population figures from the World POPClock, U.S. Census Bureau, www.census.gov/main/www/popclock.html, accessed March 2012. This Web site provides continuously updated projections of U.S. and world populations.

3. For these and other statistics, see Terry Mangano, "As Hispanic Population Grows, So Too Do Challenges for Marketers—5 Insights," *Promo*, January 23, 2012, http://promomagazine.com/retail/hispanic_shoppers_insights_0123_peo9/; Sam Fahmy, "Despite Recession, Hispanic and Asian Buying Power Expected to Surge in U.S.," November 4, 2010, accessed at www.terry.uga.edu/news/releases/2010/minority-buying-power-report.html; Claudia Goffan, "Hispanic Market Trends Forecast," *Target Latino*, accessed at www.targetlatino.com/hispanicmarketingtrendforecast.html, February 2012; and U.S. Census Bureau, "U.S. Population Projections,"

www.census.gov/population/www/projections/summarytables.html, accessed August 2012.

4. Laurie Sullivan, "Google Puts Resources Behind U.S. Hispanic Market," *Online Media Daily*, January 27, 2012, accessed at www.mediapost.com/publications/article/143763/; and "Hispanics More Active on Social Media Than Other Ethnicities," *eMarketer*, March 2, 2012, www.emarketer.com/Articles/Print.aspx?R=1008877.

5. "Nestlé's New Construye El Mejor Nido ('Create the Best Nest') Program Supports Hispanic Heritage Month," *PRNewswire*, September 29, 2011; Elena del Valle, "Nestlé Targets U.S. Spanish Speakers with New Efforts," *Hispanic Marketing and Public Relations*, November 9, 2011, www.hispanicmpr.com/2011/11/09/nestle-targets-u-s-spanish-speakers-with-new-efforts/; and http://www.elmejornido.com/, accessed September 2012.

6. See "Many Cultures, Many Numbers," *Brandweek*, September 27, 2010, p. 16; Sam Fahmy, "Despite Recession, Hispanic and Asian Buying Power Expected to Surge in U.S.," accessed at www.terry.uga.edu/news/releases/2010/minority-buying-power-report.html; and U.S. Census Bureau reports, www.census.gov, accessed March 2012.

7. "Procter & Gamble; P&G's My Black Is Beautiful TV Series Celebrates Another Successful Season on BET Networks," *Marketing Weekly News*, January 1, 2011, p. 76; "Procter & Gamble's My Black Is Beautiful Honored with City of Cincinnati Proclamation," *PR Newswire*, May 21, 2010; and information from www.myblackisbeautiful.com, accessed September 2012. Also see www.covergirl.com/queen, accessed September 2012.

8. See "Many Cultures, Many Numbers," p. 16; Sam Fahmy, "Despite Recession, Hispanic and Asian Buying Power Expected to Surge in U.S."; Neda Ulaby, "Corporate America Takes on Multilingual PR," NPR, May 5, 2011, www.npr.org/2011/05/05/135985502/corporate-america-take-on-multilingual-pr; and U.S. Census Bureau reports, www.census.gov, accessed March 2012.

9. For more on these and other Subaru Asian American marketing efforts, see "Subaru Launches Ads for Chinese-American Market," *MarketingDaily,* May 19, 2011, accessed at www.mediapost.com; Tim Peterson, "Subaru Campaign Targets Chinese-American Consumers," *Direct Marketing News,* May 20, 2011, accessed at www.dmnews.com; "2011 Subaru WRX Case Study," accessed at http://asianamericanadnetwork.com/#/Video/, March 2012; and www.youtube.com/watch?v=D6BwBpIt8BQ, accessed March 2012.

10. Eleftheria Parpis, "Goodbye Color Codes," *Adweek,* September 27, 2010, pp. 24–25; "Ethnic Marketing: McDonald's Is Lovin' It," *Bloomberg BusinessWeek,* July 18, 2010, pp. 22–23; Stuart Elliott, "Mosaic Marketing Takes a Fresh Look at Changing Society," *New York Times,* July 18, 2011, p. B3; and "Business: One Message, or Many?; Ethnic Advertising," *The Economist*, December 31, 2011.

11. Adapted from information found in Jennifer Alsever, "Video Testimonials Turn Customers into Spokespeople," *Inc.,* December 2011/January 2012, pp. 116–118.

12. Victoria Taylor, "The Best-Ever Social Media Campaign," *Forbes*, August 17, 2010, accessed at www.forbes.com; Bruce Horovitz, "Marketers: Inside Job on College Campuses," *USA Today,* October 4, 2010, p. B1; Alan Mitchell, "Word-of-Mouth Is Over-Hyped," *Marketing,* October 6, 2011, accessed at www.marketingmagazine.co.uk; and Steven Williams, "Digital, Social Media Take Center Stage," *Advertising Age,* January 12, 2012, accessed at http://adage.com/article/digital/digital-social-media-center-stage-auto-show/232068/.

13. Jack Neff, "Time to Rethink Your Message: Now the Cart Belongs to Daddy," *Advertising Age,* January 17, 2011, http://adage.com/article/news/men-main-grocery-shoppers-complain-ads/148252/; George Anderson, "Study: Men Go Grocery Shopping," *Retail Wire,* January 18, 2011, www.retailwire.com/discussion/15007/study-men-go-grocery-shopping; and Emily Bryson York, "Retailers Adjust Marketing as More Men Take over Grocery Shopping," *Los Angeles Times,* December 29, 2011.

14. See Tim Nudd, "IKEA Debuts Mänland, a Daycare for Men while Women Shop," *Adweek,* September 20, 2011, accessed at www.adweek.com.

15. Laura A. Flurry, "Children's Influence in Family Decision Making: Examining the Impact of the Changing American Family," *Journal of Business Research,* April 2007, pp. 322–330; and "Tween Years Prove to Be Rewarding for Toymakers," *USA Today,* December 22, 2010, p. 1B.

16. Information on Acxiom's Personicx segmentation system accessed at www.acxiom.com/Ideas-and-Innovation/Self-Assessment-Tools/, November 2012.

17. For these and other examples and quotes, see www.carhartt.com, accessed September 2012.

18. See Stuart Elliott, "Penney's New Approach Takes Target-Like Tack," *New York Times,* January 25, 2012.

19. Quotes and other information from www.rei.com/aboutrei/about_rei.html and other pages at the www.rei.com site, accessed March 2012.

20. See Jennifer Aaker, "Dimensions of Measuring Brand Personality," *Journal of Marketing Research*, August 1997, pp. 347–356; and Kevin Lane Keller, *Strategic Brand Management*, 3rd ed. (Upper Saddle River, New Jersey, 2008), pp. 66–67. For more on brand personality, see Lucia Malär, Harley Kromer, Wayne D. Hoyer, and Bettina Nyffenegger, "Emotional Brand Attachment and Brand Personality: The Relative Importance of the Actual and the Ideal Self," *Journal of Marketing,* July 2011, pp. 35–52; and Jack Neff, "Just How Well-Defined Is Your Brand's Ideal?" *Advertising Age,* January 16, 2012, p. 4.

21. See Chiara Atik, "Will Women Give Axe Fragrance the Ax?" *The Look on Today,* January 23, 2012, http://thelook.today.msnbc.msn.com/_news/2012/01/23/10216466-will-women-give-axe-fragrance-the-ax; "AXE Unleashes Anarchy with First-Ever Fragrance for Girls," *PR Newswire,* January 12, 2012; and www.unilever.com/brands/personalcarebrands/axe/index.aspx, accessed September 2012.

22. See Abraham H. Maslow, "A Theory of Human Motivation," *Psychological Review*, 50 (1943), pp. 370–396. Also see Maslow, *Motivation and Personality*, 3rd ed. (New York: HarperCollins Publishers, 1987); and Michael R. Solomon, *Consumer Behavior,* 9th ed. (Upper Saddle River, NJ: Prentice Hall, 2011), pp. 135–136.

23. Ellen Moore, "Letter to My Colleague: We Can Do Better," *Adweek,* December 22, 2010, www.adweek.com/news/advertising-branding/letter-my-colleagues-we-can-do-better-104084.

24. For more reading, see Lawrence R. Samuel, *Freud on Madison Avenue: Motivation Research and Subliminal Advertising in America* (Philadelphia: University of Pennsylvania Press, 2010); Charles R. Acland, *Swift Viewing: The Popular Life of Subliminal Influence* (Duke University Press, 2011); and Christopher Shea, "The History of Subliminal Ads," *Wall Street Journal*, February 15, 2012, http://blogs.wsj.com/ideas-market/2012/02/15/the-history-of-subliminal-ads/.

25. Example adapted from information found in John Berman, "Shrek Boosts Vidalia Onion Sales," June 29, 2010, http://abcnews.go.com/WN/shrek-boosts-vidalia-onion-sales/story?id=11047273; and "Vidalia Onion Committee Cinches Triple Crown of National Marketing Awards," October 20, 2011, www.vidaliaonion.org/news/vidalia_onion_committee_cinches_triple_crown_of_national_marketing_awards. Vidalia® is a registered certification mark of Georgia Department of Agriculture.

26. Quotes and information from Yubo Chen and Jinhong Xie, "Online Consumer Review: Word-of-Mouth as a New Element of Marketing Communication Mix," *Management Science*, March 2008, pp. 477–491; "Leo J. Shapiro & Associates: User-Generated Content Three Times More Influential Than TV Advertising on Consumer Purchase Decisions," *Marketing Business Weekly*, December 28, 2008, p. 34; and *The 2011 Digital Marketer: Benchmark and Trend Report,* Experian Marketing Services, accessed at www.experian.com/marketing-services/register-2011-digital-marketer.html.

27. See Leon Festinger, *A Theory of Cognitive Dissonance* (Stanford, CA: Stanford University Press, 1957); Cynthia Crossen, "'Cognitive Dissonance' Became a Milestone in the 1950s Psychology," *Wall Street Journal*, December 12, 2006, p. B1; and Anupam Bawa and Purva Kansal, "Cognitive Dissonance and the Marketing of Services: Some Issues," *Journal of Services Research*, October 2008–March 2009, p. 31.

28. The following discussion draws from the work of Everett M. Rogers. See his *Diffusion of Innovations*, 5th ed. (New York: Free Press, 2003).

29. Jackie Crosbie, "Best Buy Launches Gadget Buyback," *Star Tribune* (Minneapolis–St. Paul), January 10, 2011; Olga Kharif, "Buyback Insurance on an iPad Is $50 and Pays Out Half the Cost of the Device If You Return It Within Six Weeks. Sound Like a Deal?" *Bloomberg Businessweek,* August 1–August 7, 2011, pp. 35–36; and www.bestbuy.com/site/Misc/Buy-Back-Program/pcmcat230000050010.c?id=pcmcat230000050010&DCMP=rdr2161, accessed November 2012.

30. Based on Everett M. Rogers, *Diffusion of Innovation*, 5th ed. (New York: Simon & Schuster, 2003), p. 281. For more discussion, see http://en.wikipedia.org/Everett_Rogers, accessed November 2012.

31. "HDTV Households Now Dominate U.S. Viewing Landscape, According to LRG Study," *Broadcast Engineering,* December 30, 2010, http://broadcastengineering.com/hdtv/hdtv-households-dominate-viewing-landscape-according-to-lrg-study-20110104/; and George Winslow, "Two-Thirds of U.S. Households Have HDTV," *TVNewsCheck,* January 12, 2012, www.tvnewscheck.com/tag/hdtv-penetration.

Part 1: Defining Marketing and the Marketing Process (Chapters 1–2)
Part 2: Understanding the Marketplace and Consumers (Chapters 3–6)
Part 3: Designing a Customer-Driven Strategy and Mix (Chapters 7–17)
Part 4: Extending Marketing (Chapters 18–20)

Business Markets and Business Buyer Behavior

Chapter Preview

In the previous chapter, you studied *final consumer* buying behavior and factors that influence it. In this chapter, we'll do the same for *business customers*—those that buy goods and services for use in producing their own products and services or for resale to others. As when selling to final buyers, firms marketing to business customers must build profitable relationships with business customers by creating superior customer value.

To start, let's look at an American icon—GE. Most of us grew up surrounded by GE consumer products in our homes. But did you know that most of GE's business comes not from consumer products sold to you and me, but from a diverse portfolio of commercial and industrial products sold to large business customers? To succeed in these business-to-business markets, GE must do more than just design and distribute good products. It must work closely and deeply with its business customers to become a strategic, problem-solving partner.

GE: Partnering Strategically with Business Customers

Few brands are more familiar than GE. For more than 130 years, we've packed our homes with GE products—from good ol' GE light bulbs to refrigerators, ranges, clothes washers and dryers, microwave ovens, coffee makers, and hundreds of other products bearing the familiar script GE logo. The company's consumer finance unit—GE Money—helps finance these and other purchases through credit cards, loans, mortgages, and other financial services. In all, GE offers a huge assortment of consumer products and services.

But here's a fact that might startle you. GE's consumer products contribute only about one-third of the company's total $147 billion in annual sales. Surprisingly, most of GE's business comes not from final consumers but from commercial and industrial customers across a wide range of industries. Beyond light bulbs and appliances, GE sells everything from medical imaging technologies, water processing systems, and security solutions to power generation equipment, aircraft engines, and diesel locomotives.

At a general level, marketing medical imaging technology or diesel locomotives to business customers is like selling refrigerators to final buyers. It requires a deep understanding of customer needs and customer-driven marketing strategies that create superior customer value. But that's about where the similarities end. In its business markets, rather than selling to large numbers of small buyers, GE sells to a relative few very large buyers. Losing a single sale to a large business customer can mean the loss of hundreds of millions of dollars in revenues. Also, with GE's business customers, buying decisions are much more complex. Buying a

> To succeed in its business-to-business markets, GE must do more than just design good products and make them available to customers. It must work closely and deeply with its business customers to become a strategic, problem-solving partner.

batch of jet engines, for example, involves a tortuously long buying process, dozens or even hundreds of decision makers, and layer upon layer of subtle and not-so-subtle buying influences.

To get an idea of the complexities involved in selling one of GE's industrial products, let's dig deeper into the company's GE Transportation division and one of its bread-and-butter products, diesel locomotives. GE locomotives might not seem glamorous to you, but they are beautiful brutes to those who buy and use them. It's not difficult to identify potential buyers for a 207-ton, 4,400-horsepower GE locomotive with an average list price of $2.2 million. The real challenge is to win buyers' business by building day-in, day-out, year-in, year-out partnerships with them based on superior products and close collaboration.

In the locomotive buyer's buying decision, performance plays an important role. In such big-ticket purchases, buyers carefully scrutinize factors such as cost, fuel efficiency, and reliability. By most measures, GE's locomotives outperform competing engines on most of these dimensions. The company's innovative Evolution Series locomotives—part of a broader GE "Ecomagination" initiative to develop technologies that help customers meet pressing environmental challenges—are now the most technically advanced, fuel-efficient, and eco-friendly diesel-powered locomotives in history. If a railroad replaced 1,000 average North American locomotives in its existing fleet with new GE Evolution Series Tier 3 locomotives, it would save more than 27 million gallons of diesel fuel annually and reduce carbon emissions by nearly 275,000 metric tons. That's a greenhouse gas impact equivalent to removing more than 53,000 automobiles from the road or planting more than 74,000 acres of trees. Add to all this that GE's clean, efficient haulers have longer maintenance and overhaul cycles, and the total savings for the railroad adds up to hundreds of millions of dollars annually.

But locomotive performance is only part of the buying equation. GE wins contracts by partnering with business customers to help them translate that performance into moving their passengers and freight more efficiently and reliably. CSX Transportation (CSXT), one of GE Transportation's largest customers, has purchased hundreds of GE Evolution locomotives in recent years. According to a CSXT purchasing executive, the company "evaluates many cost factors before awarding . . . a locomotive contract. Environmental impact, fuel consumption, reliability, serviceability [are] all key elements in this decision." But as important is "the value of our ongoing partnership with GE."

A recent high-stakes international deal involving hundreds of GE locomotives demonstrates the potential importance, scope, and complexity of some business-to-business decisions:

> GE Transportation recently landed a huge $650 million contract to supply 310 Evolution locomotives to the Kazakhstan National Railway (KTZ)—the largest-ever order for locomotives delivered outside North America. The deal also included a whopping 15-year, $500 million service contract. Befitting its importance to not just the companies, but to their countries as well, the contracts were inked at the Kazakhstan Embassy in Washington, DC. The

signing was attended by high-level executives from both organizations, including the CEO of GE Transportation and the president of KTZ.

The buying decision was based on a host of factors. KTZ wanted the very best performance technology available, and GE's Evolution locomotives fit the bill nicely. But the deal also hinged on many factors that had little to do with the engine performance. For example, important matters of international economics and politics came into play as well. Whereas the first 10 locomotives were built at GE's U.S. plant, most of the remaining 300 locomotives are being assembled at a newly built, state-owned plant in Pavlodar, Kazakhstan. Thus, the GE/KTZ deal is helping to modernize the country's entire rail infrastructure, diversify its economy, and strengthen its manufacturing industry.

Finally, the latest contract was anything but an impulsive, one-and-done deal. Rather, it represented the culmination of years of smaller steps between the two organizations—the latest episode in a long-running relationship between GE and KTZ that dates back to the mid-1990s. The relationship accelerated in 2003 when GE won the first of several contracts for modernization kits that updated older KTZ locomotives. "I am proud that KTZ and GE are extending our relationship," said the CEO of GE Transportation, "one that has proven to be very beneficial to both organizations over several years."

> **GE locomotives might not seem glamorous to you, but they are beautiful brutes to those who buy and use them. In this market, GE's challenge is to win buyers' business by building day-in, day-out, year-in, year-out partnerships with them.**
> GE Transportation

Thanks to stories like this one, GE Transportation captures a lion's share of the worldwide rail locomotive market. More broadly, people throughout the entire GE organization know that success in business-to-business markets involves more than just developing and selling superior products and technologies. Business customer buying decisions are made within the framework of a strategic, problem-solving partnership. "Customer partnerships are at the center of GE and Ecomagination," confirms GE chairman and CEO Jeffrey Immelt in a letter to shareholders. "We are viewed as a technical partner by customers around the world."[1]

Objective Outline

MyMarketingLab™

⭐ **Improve Your Grade!**

Over 10 million students improved their results using the Pearson MyLabs.
Visit **mymktlab.com** for simulations, tutorials, and end-of-chapter problems.

Like GE, in one way or another, most large companies sell to other organizations. Companies such as Boeing, DuPont, IBM, Caterpillar, and countless other firms sell *most* of their products to other businesses. Even large consumer-products companies, which make products used by final consumers, must first sell their products to other businesses. For example, General Mills makes many familiar consumer brands—Big G cereals (Cheerios, Wheaties, Trix, Chex, Total, Fiber One), baking products (Pillsbury, Betty Crocker, Bisquick, Gold Medal flour), snacks (Nature Valley, Bugles, Chex Mix), Yoplait yogurt, Häagen-Dazs ice cream, and many others. But to sell these products to consumers, General Mills must first sell them to its wholesaler and retailer customers, who in turn serve the consumer market.

Business buyer behavior refers to the buying behavior of the organizations that buy goods and services for use in the production of other products and services that are sold, rented, or supplied to others. It also includes the behavior of retailing and wholesaling firms that acquire goods to resell or rent them to others at a profit. In the **business buying process**, business buyers determine which products and services their organizations need to purchase and then find, evaluate, and choose among alternative suppliers and brands. *Business-to-business (B-to-B) marketers* must do their best to understand business markets and business buyer behavior. Then, like businesses that sell to final buyers, they must build profitable relationships with business customers by creating superior customer value.

Business buyer behavior
The buying behavior of organizations that buy goods and services for use in the production of other products and services that are sold, rented, or supplied to others.

Business buying process
The decision process by which business buyers determine which products and services their organizations need to purchase and then find, evaluate, and choose among alternative suppliers and brands.

Objective 1 ┈┈▶
Define the business market and explain how business markets differ from consumer markets.

Business Markets

The business market is *huge*. In fact, business markets involve far more dollars and items than do consumer markets. For example, think about the large number of business transactions involved in the production and sale of a single set of Goodyear tires. Various suppliers sell Goodyear the rubber, steel, equipment, and other goods that it needs to produce tires. Goodyear then sells the finished tires to retailers, which in turn sell them to consumers.

Derived demand
Business demand that ultimately comes from (derives from) the demand for consumer goods.

Thus, many sets of *business* purchases were made for only one set of *consumer* purchases. In addition, Goodyear sells tires as original equipment to manufacturers that install them on new vehicles and as replacement tires to companies that maintain their own fleets of company cars, trucks, or other vehicles.

In some ways, business markets are similar to consumer markets. Both involve people who assume buying roles and make purchase decisions to satisfy needs. However, business markets differ in many ways from consumer markets. The main differences are in *market structure and demand*, the *nature of the buying unit*, and the *types of decisions and the decision process* involved.

Market Structure and Demand

The business marketer normally deals with *far fewer but far larger buyers* than the consumer marketer does. Even in large business markets, a few buyers often account for most of the purchasing. For example, when Goodyear sells replacement tires to final consumers, its potential market includes millions of car owners around the world. But its fate in business markets depends on getting orders from only a handful of large automakers.

Further, business demand is **derived demand**—it ultimately derives from the demand for consumer goods. For example, W. L. Gore & Associates sells its Gore-Tex brand to manufacturers who make and sell outdoor apparel brands made from Gore-Tex fabrics. If demand for these brands increases, so does demand for Gore-Tex fabrics. ● So to boost demand for Gore-Tex, Gore advertises to final consumers to educate them on the benefits of Gore-Tex fabrics in the brands they buy. It also directly markets brands containing Gore-Tex—from Arc'teryx, Marmot, and The North Face to Burton and L.L. Bean—on its own Web site (www.gore-tex.com).

To deepen its direct relationship with outdoor enthusiasts further, Gore even sponsors an "Experience More" online community in which members can share experiences and videos, connect with outdoor experts, and catch exclusive gear offers from partner brands. As a result, consumers around the world have learned to look for the familiar Gore-Tex brand label, and both Gore and its partner brands win. No matter what brand of apparel or footwear you buy, says the label, if it's made with Gore-Tex fabric, it's "guaranteed to keep you dry."

Finally, many business markets have *inelastic and more fluctuating demand*. The total demand for many business products is not much affected by price changes, especially in the short run. A drop in the price of leather will not cause shoe manufacturers to buy much more leather unless it results in lower shoe prices that, in turn, increase consumer demand for shoes. And the demand for many business goods and services tends to change more—and more quickly—than does the demand for consumer goods and services. A small percentage increase in consumer demand can cause large increases in business demand.

YOU STAY DRY, PROTECTED AND FOCUSED OUTSIDE

WITH GORE-TEX® PRO SHELL INSIDE.

● **Derived demand: You can't buy anything directly from Gore, but to increase demand for Gore-Tex fabrics, the company markets directly to the buyers of outdoor apparel and other brands made from its fabrics. Both Gore and its partner brands—here, The North Face—win.**
Courtesy of W. L. Gore & Associates, Inc.

Nature of the Buying Unit

Compared with consumer purchases, a business purchase usually involves *more decision participants* and a *more professional purchasing effort*. Often, business buying is done by trained purchasing agents who spend their working lives learning how to buy better. The more complex the purchase, the more likely it is that several people will participate in the decision-making process. Buying committees composed of technical experts and top management are common in the buying of major goods. Beyond this, B-to-B marketers now face a new breed of higher-level, better-trained supply managers. Therefore, companies must have well-trained marketers and salespeople to deal with these well-trained buyers.

Types of Decisions and the Decision Process

Business buyers usually face *more complex* buying decisions than do consumer buyers. Business purchases often involve large sums of money, complex technical and economic considerations, and interactions among people at many levels of the buyer's organization.

The business buying process also tends to be *longer* and *more formalized*. Large business purchases usually call for detailed product specifications, written purchase orders, careful supplier searches, and formal approval.

Finally, in the business buying process, the buyer and seller are often much *more dependent* on each other. B-to-B marketers may roll up their sleeves and work closely with their customers during all stages of the buying process—from helping customers define problems, to finding solutions, to supporting after-sale operation. They often customize their offerings to individual customer needs. In the short run, sales go to suppliers who meet buyers' immediate product and service needs. In the long run, however, business-to-business marketers keep customers by meeting current needs *and* by partnering with them to help solve their problems. For example, Dow Performance Plastics doesn't just sell commodity plastics *to* its industrial customers—it works *with* these customers to help them succeed in their own markets:[2]

Dow Performance Plastics

Think of Dow as the team...
　　　behind your team.

● **Dow Performance Plastics isn't just selling commodity plastics—it's helping the businesses that buy its plastics to be heroes with their own customers. "We believe in a simple concept . . . if you win, we win."**

The Dow Chemical Company

At Dow Performance Plastics, thinking about how plastics can make our lives better is at the very core of its business strategy. What makes that noteworthy, however, is that Dow doesn't sell its products to you and me. Instead, it sells mountains of raw materials to its business customers, who in turn sell parts to the companies who sell their products to final users. So Dow understands that it isn't just selling commodity plastics; it's helping the businesses that buy its plastics materials to be heroes with their own customers. Dow Performance Plastics considers itself a partner, not just a supplier. "Whether they're using Dow's plastics to make bags for Safeway or for complex [automotive] applications, we have to help them succeed in their markets," says a Dow spokesperson.

● "Think of Dow as the team behind your team," says Dow at its Web site. "We believe in a simple concept . . . if you win, we win."

As in Dow's case, in recent years, relationships between most customers and suppliers have been changing from downright adversarial to close and chummy. In fact, many customer companies are now practicing **supplier development**, systematically developing networks of supplier-partners to ensure a dependable supply of products and materials that they use in making their own products or reselling to others. For example, Walmart doesn't have a "Purchasing Department"; it has a "Supplier Development Department." The giant retailer knows that it can't just rely on spot suppliers who might be available when needed. Instead, Walmart manages a robust network of supplier-partners that help provide the hundreds of billions of dollars of goods that it sells to its customers each year.

Supplier development

Systematic development of networks of supplier-partners to ensure an appropriate and dependable supply of products and materials for use in making products or reselling them to others.

● **FIGURE** │ **6.1**
A Model of Business Buyer Behavior

In some ways, business markets are similar to consumer markets —this model looks a lot like the model of consumer buyer behavior presented in Figure 5.1. But there are some major differences, especially in the nature of the buying unit, the types of decisions made, and the decision process.

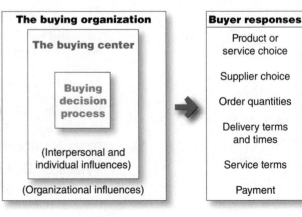

The environment		The buying organization	Buyer responses
Marketing stimuli	**Other stimuli**	**The buying center**	Product or service choice
Product	Economic	**Buying decision process**	Supplier choice
Price	Technological		Order quantities
Place	Political		Delivery terms and times
Promotion	Cultural	(Interpersonal and individual influences)	Service terms
	Competitive	(Organizational influences)	Payment

Objective 2 ⋯⋯▶
Identify the major factors that influence business buyer behavior.

Business Buyer Behavior

At the most basic level, marketers want to know how business buyers will respond to various marketing stimuli. ⬤ **Figure 6.1** shows a model of business buyer behavior. In this model, marketing and other stimuli affect the buying organization and produce certain buyer responses. To design good marketing strategies, marketers must understand what happens within the organization to turn stimuli into purchase responses.

Within the organization, buying activity consists of two major parts: the buying center, composed of all the people involved in the buying decision, and the buying decision process. The model shows that the buying center and the buying decision process are influenced by internal organizational, interpersonal, and individual factors as well as external environmental factors.

The model in Figure 6.1 suggests four questions about business buyer behavior: What buying decisions do business buyers make? Who participates in the business buying process? What are the major influences on buyers? How do business buyers make their buying decisions?

Major Types of Buying Situations

There are three major types of buying situations.[3] In a **straight rebuy**, the buyer reorders something without any modifications. It is usually handled on a routine basis by the purchasing department. To keep the business, "in" suppliers try to maintain product and service quality. "Out" suppliers try to find new ways to add value or exploit dissatisfaction so that the buyer will consider them.

In a **modified rebuy**, the buyer wants to modify product specifications, prices, terms, or suppliers. The "in" suppliers may become nervous and feel pressured to put their best foot forward to protect an account. "Out" suppliers may see the modified rebuy situation as an opportunity to make a better offer and gain new business.

A company buying a product or service for the first time faces a **new task** situation. In such cases, the greater the cost or risk, the larger the number of decision participants and the greater the company's efforts to collect information. The new task situation is the marketer's greatest opportunity and challenge. The marketer not only tries to reach as many key buying influences as possible but also provides help and information. The buyer makes the fewest decisions in the straight rebuy and the most in the new task decision.

Many business buyers prefer to buy a complete solution to a problem from a single seller rather than buying separate products and services from several suppliers and putting them together. The sale often goes to the firm that provides the most complete *system* for meeting the customer's needs and solving its problems. Such **systems selling** (or **solutions selling**) is often a key business marketing strategy for winning and holding accounts. Consider IBM and its customer Six Flags Entertainment Corporation:[4]

Straight rebuy
A business buying situation in which the buyer routinely reorders something without any modifications.

Modified rebuy
A business buying situation in which the buyer wants to modify product specifications, prices, terms, or suppliers.

New task
A business buying situation in which the buyer purchases a product or service for the first time.

Systems selling (or **solutions selling**)
Buying a packaged solution to a problem from a single seller, thus avoiding all the separate decisions involved in a complex buying situation.

Six Flags operates 19 regional theme parks across the United States, Mexico, and Canada, featuring exciting rides and water attractions, world-class roller coasters, and special shows and concerts. ⬤ To deliver a fun and safe experience for guests, Six Flags much carefully and effectively manage thousands of park assets—from rides and equipment to buildings and other facilities. Six Flags needed a tool for managing all those assets efficiently and effectively across its far-flung collection of parks. So it turned to IBM, which has software—called Maximo Asset Management software—that handles that very problem well.

But IBM didn't just hand the software over to Six Flags with best wishes for a happy implementation. Instead, IBM's Maximo Professional Services group is combining the software with an entire set of services designed to get and keep the software up and running. IBM is working hand-in-hand with Six Flags to customize the application and strategically implement it across Six Flags's far-flung facilities, along with on-site immersion training and planning workshops. "We've implemented the solution at five parks to date, and as the implementation team completes each deployment, they move to the next property," says Six Flags's director of corporate project management. "We have one implementation team to

⬤ Solutions selling: Delivering a fun and safe experience for Six Flags guests requires careful and effective management of thousands of park assets across its 19 regional theme parks. IBM works hand-in-hand with Six Flags to provide not just software, but a complete solution.

Bloomberg via Getty Images

make sure that all the deployments across our parks are consistent." IBM will work with Six Flags throughout the process. Thus, IBM isn't just selling the software, it's selling a complete solution to Six Flags's complex asset management problem.

Participants in the Business Buying Process

Buying center

All the individuals and units that play a role in the purchase decision-making process.

Users

Members of the buying organization who will actually use the purchased product or service.

Influencers

People in an organization's buying center who affect the buying decision; they often help define specifications and also provide information for evaluating alternatives.

Buyers

People in an organization's buying center who make an actual purchase.

Deciders

People in an organization's buying center who have formal or informal power to select or approve the final suppliers.

Gatekeepers

People in an organization's buying center who control the flow of information to others.

Who does the buying of the trillions of dollars' worth of goods and services needed by business organizations? The decision-making unit of a buying organization is called its **buying center**. It consists of all the individuals and units that play a role in the business purchase decision-making process. This group includes the actual users of the product or service, those who make the buying decision, those who influence the buying decision, those who do the actual buying, and those who control buying information.

The buying center includes all members of the organization who play any of five roles in the purchase decision process:[5]

- **Users** are members of the organization who will use the product or service. In many cases, users initiate the buying proposal and help define product specifications.
- **Influencers** often help define specifications and also provide information for evaluating alternatives. Technical personnel are particularly important influencers.
- **Buyers** have formal authority to select the supplier and arrange terms of purchase. Buyers may help shape product specifications, but their major role is in selecting vendors and negotiating. In more complex purchases, buyers might include high-level officers participating in the negotiations.
- **Deciders** have formal or informal power to select or approve the final suppliers. In routine buying, the buyers are often the deciders, or at least the approvers.
- **Gatekeepers** control the flow of information to others. For example, purchasing agents often have authority to prevent salespersons from seeing users or deciders. Other gatekeepers include technical personnel and even personal secretaries.

The buying center is not a fixed and formally identified unit within the buying organization. It is a set of buying roles assumed by different people for different purchases. Within the organization, the size and makeup of the buying center will vary for different products and for different buying situations. For some routine purchases, one person—say, a purchasing agent—may assume all the buying center roles and serve as the only person involved in the buying decision. For more complex purchases, the buying center may include 20 or 30 people from different levels and departments in the organization.

The buying center concept presents a major marketing challenge. The business marketer must learn who participates in the decision, each participant's relative influence, and what evaluation criteria each decision participant uses. This can be difficult.

The buying center usually includes some obvious participants who are involved formally in the buying decision. For example, the decision to buy a corporate jet will probably involve the company's CEO, the chief pilot, a purchasing agent, some legal staff, a member of top management, and others formally charged with the buying decision. It may also involve less obvious, informal participants, some of whom may actually make or strongly affect the buying decision. Sometimes, even the people in the buying center are not aware of all the buying participants. For example, the decision about which corporate jet to buy may actually be made by a corporate board member who has an interest in flying and who knows a lot about airplanes. This board member may work behind the scenes to sway the decision. Many business buying decisions result from the complex interactions of ever-changing buying center participants.

Major Influences on Business Buyers

Business buyers are subject to many influences when they make their buying decisions. Some marketers assume that the major influences are economic. They think buyers will favor the supplier who offers the lowest price or the best product or the most service. They concentrate on offering strong economic benefits to buyers. Such economic factors are very important to most buyers, especially in a tough economy. However, business buyers actually respond to both economic and personal factors. Far from being cold, calculating, and impersonal, business buyers are human and social as well. They react to both reason and emotion.

Today, most B-to-B marketers recognize that emotion plays an important role in business buying decisions. Consider this example:[6]

Citrix creates better ways for people, IT, and business to work, using virtual meetings, desktops, and datacenters. Citrix combines virtualization, networking, and cloud computing technologies

The power to consolidate servers through virtual computing.

SIMPLICITY IS POWER

Crush cost and complexity like a can. Through virtual computing

and Citrix® XenServer,® you can eliminate unnecessary

servers and the costs associated

with them. instantly.

And best of all, for free.

Makes you think

twice about complex,

expensive, proprietary

virtualization alternatives. XenServer

puts more control in your

hands than you've ever had before.

Feel the power of virtual computing.

Simplicity is power. Citrix.

CITRIX®

Citrix.com/SimplicityIsPower

● **Emotions play an important role in business buying: The emotion-charged images in this B-to-B ad get across the message that Citrix's virtual computing solutions can put computing power back in the hands of companies and their IT departments.**

© 2011 Citrix Systems, Inc. All rights reserved. Simplicity is Power and its stylized treatment are trademarks and XenServer is a registered trademark of Citrix Systems, Inc.

into products that let people work and play from anywhere on any device. The company helps businesses consolidate server hardware and centrally manage applications and desktops from the datacenter rather than installing them on individual employee computers. With a tech-savvy audience, you might expect Citrix's B-to-B ads to focus entirely on technical features and benefits such as simplicity, productivity, and cost-efficiency. Citrix does promote these benefits, but the ads also pack a decidedly more emotional wallop. Working off the notion that our technology has begun to control us, the Simplicity Is Power campaign from Citrix uses dramatic imagery showing a human hand in complete control of technology. ● For example, one ad shows a hand crushing servers; another shows laptops and applications dangling from fingers like puppets on springs. These emotionally-charged images convey the message that Citrix virtual computing solutions put unprecedented computing power back into the hands of organizations and their IT departments.

● **Figure 6.2** lists various groups of influences on business buyers—environmental, organizational, interpersonal, and individual. Business buyers are heavily influenced by factors in the current and expected *economic environment*, such as the level of primary demand, the economic outlook, and the cost of money. Another environmental factor is the *supply* of key materials. Many companies now are more willing to buy and hold larger inventories of scarce materials to ensure adequate supply. Business buyers also are affected by technological, political, and competitive developments in the environment. Finally, *culture and customs* can strongly influence business buyer reactions to the marketer's behavior and strategies, especially in the international marketing environment (see Real Marketing 6.1). The business buyer must watch these factors, determine how they will affect the buyer, and try to turn these challenges into opportunities.

Organizational factors are also important. Each buying organization has its own objectives, strategies, structure, systems, and procedures, and the business marketer must understand these factors well. Questions such as these arise: How many people are involved in the buying decision? Who are they? What are their evaluative criteria? What are the company's policies and limits on its buyers?

The buying center usually includes many participants who influence each other, so *interpersonal factors* also influence the business buying process. However, it is often difficult to assess such interpersonal factors and group dynamics. Buying center participants do not wear tags that label them as "key decision maker" or "not influential." Nor do buying center participants with the highest rank always have the most influence. Participants may influence the buying decision because they control rewards and punishments, are well liked, have special expertise, or have a special relationship with other important participants. Interpersonal factors are often very subtle. Whenever possible, business marketers must try to understand these factors and design strategies that take them into account.

● **FIGURE | 6.2**
Major Influences on Business
Buyer Behavior

Like consumer buying decisions in Figure 5.2, business buying decisions are affected by an incredibly complex combination of environmental, interpersonal, and individual influences, but with an extra layer of organizational factors thrown into the mix.

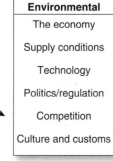
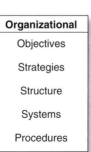

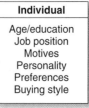

Environmental	Organizational	Interpersonal	Individual	
The economy	Objectives	Influence	Age/education	
Supply conditions	Strategies	Expertise	Job position	
Technology	Structure	Authority	Motives	
Politics/regulation	Systems	Dynamics	Personality	**Buyers**
Competition	Procedures		Preferences	
Culture and customs			Buying style	

Real Marketing 6.1

International Marketing Manners

Picture this: Consolidated Amalgamation, Inc., thinks it's time that the rest of the world enjoyed the same fine products it has offered American consumers for two generations. It dispatches Vice President Harry E. Slicksmile to Europe, Asia, and Africa to explore the territory. Mr. Slicksmile stops first in London, where he makes short work of some bankers—he rings them up on the phone. He handles Parisians with similar ease: After securing a table at La Tour d'Argent, he greets his luncheon guest, the director of an industrial engineering firm, with the words, "Just call me Harry, Jacques." In Germany, Mr. Slicksmile is a powerhouse. Whisking through a flashy multimedia presentation with an ultra-compact projector, he shows 'em that this Georgia boy knows how to make a buck.

Mr. Slicksmile next swings through Saudi Arabia, where he coolly presents a potential client with a multimillion-dollar proposal in a classy pigskin binder. Heading on to Moscow, Harry strikes up a conversation with the Japanese businessman sitting next to him on the plane. Harry complements the man's cufflinks several times, recognizing him as a man of importance. As the two say good-bye, the man gifts his cufflinks to Harry, presents his business card with both hands, and bows at the waist. Harry places his hand firmly on the man's back to express sincere thanks, then slips his own business card into the man's shirt pocket.

Harry takes Russia by storm as he meets with the CEO of a startup tech firm. Feeling very at ease with the Russia executive, Harry sheds his suit coat, leans back, crosses one foot over the other knee, and slips his hands into his pockets. At his next stop in Beijing, China, Harry talks business over lunch with a group of Chinese executives. After completing the meal, he drops his chopsticks into his bowl of rice and presents each guest with a gift as a gesture of his desire to do business with them—an elegant Tiffany clock.

A great tour, sure to generate a pile of orders, right? Wrong. Six months later, Consolidated Amalgamation has nothing to show for the extended trip but a stack of bills. Abroad, they weren't wild about Harry.

This hypothetical case has been exaggerated for emphasis. Americans are seldom such dolts. But experts say success in international business has a lot to do with knowing the territory and its people. By learning English and extending themselves in other ways, the world's business leaders have met Americans more than halfway. In contrast, Americans too often do little except assume that others will march to their music. "We want things to be 'American' when we travel. Fast. Convenient. Easy. So we become 'ugly Americans' by demanding that others change," says one American world trade expert. "I think more business would be done if we tried harder."

Poor Harry tried, all right, but in all the wrong ways. The British do not, as a rule, make deals over the phone as much as Americans do. It's not so much a "cultural" difference as a difference in approach. A proper Frenchman neither likes instant familiarity nor refers to strangers by their first names. "That poor fellow, Jacques, probably wouldn't show anything, but he'd not be pleased," explains an expert on French business practices.

Harry's flashy presentation would likely have been a flop with the Germans, who dislike overstatement and showiness. And to the Saudi Arabians, the pigskin binder would have been considered vile. An American salesperson who actually presented such a binder was unceremoniously tossed out of the country, and his company was blacklisted from working with Saudi businesses.

Harry also committed numerous faux pas with his new Japanese acquaintance. Because the Japanese strive to please others, especially when someone admires their possessions, the executive likely felt obligated rather than pleased to give up his cufflinks. Harry's "hand on the back" probably labeled him as disrespectful and presumptuous. Japan, like many Asian countries, is a "no-contact culture" in which even shaking hands is a strange experience. Harry made matters worse with his casual treatment of the business cards. Japanese people revere the business card as an extension of self and as an indicator of rank. They do not hand it to people; they present it—with both hands.

Things didn't go well in Russia, either. Russian business people maintain a conservative, professional appearance, with dark suits and dress shoes. Taking one's coat off during negotiations of any kind is taken as a sign of weakness. Placing hands in one's pockets is considered rude, and showing the bottoms of one's shoes is a dirty and disgusting gesture. Similarly, in China, Harry casually dropping his chopsticks could have been misinterpreted as an act of aggression. Stabbing chopsticks into a bowl of rice and

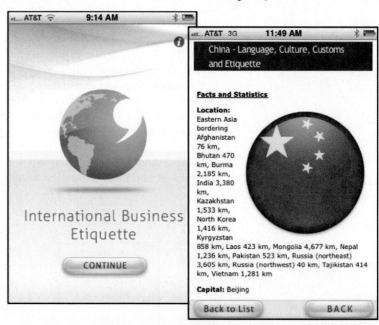

International marketing manners: Several companies now offer smartphone apps—such as this one from Kwintessential—that provide tips to international travelers and help prevent them from making embarrassing mistakes while abroad.
Kwintessential Ltd.

leaving them signifies death to the Chinese. The clocks Harry offered as gifts might have confirmed such dark intentions. To "give a clock" in Chinese sounds the same as "seeing someone off to his end."

Thus, to compete successfully in global markets, or even to deal effectively with international firms in their home markets, companies must help their managers to understand the needs, customs, and cultures of international business buyers. Several companies now offer smartphone apps that provide tips to international travelers and help prevent them from making embarrassing mistakes while abroad. Cultures around the world differ greatly, and marketers must dig deeply to make certain they adapt to these differences.

"When doing business in a foreign country and a foreign culture...take nothing for granted," advises an international business specialist. "Turn every stone. Ask every question. Dig into every detail."

Sources: Portions adapted from Susan Harte, "When in Rome, You Should Learn to Do What the Romans Do," *The Atlanta Journal-Constitution,* January 22, 1990, pp. D1, D6. Additional information and examples can be found in Gary Stroller, "Doing Business Abroad? Simple Faux Pas Can Sink You," *USA Today,* August 24, 2007, p. 1B; Janette S. Martin and Lillian H. Cheney, *Global Business Etiquette* (Santa Barbara, CA: Praeger Publishers, 2013); "Learn Tips to Do Business in China," *The News-Sentinel,* February 9, 2012, accessed at www.news-sentinel.com; and www.cyborlink.com, accessed November 2012.

Problem recognition
The stage of the business buying process in which the company recognizes a problem or need that can be met by acquiring a good or a service.

Each participant in the business buying decision process brings in personal motives, perceptions, and preferences. These *individual factors* are affected by personal characteristics such as age, income, education, professional identification, personality, and attitudes toward risk. Also, buyers have different buying styles. Some may be technical types who make in-depth analyses of competitive proposals before choosing a supplier. Other buyers may be intuitive negotiators who are adept at pitting the sellers against one another for the best deal.

Objective 3 ──────▶
List and define the steps in the business buying decision process.

The Business Buying Process

Figure 6.3 lists the eight stages of the business buying process.[7] Buyers who face a new task buying situation usually go through all stages of the buying process. Buyers making modified or straight rebuys, in contrast, may skip some of the stages. We will examine these steps for the typical new task buying situation.

Problem Recognition

The buying process begins when someone in the company recognizes a problem or need that can be met by acquiring a specific product or service. **Problem recognition** can result from internal or external stimuli. Internally, the company may decide to launch a new product that requires new production equipment and materials. Or a machine may break down and need new parts. Perhaps a purchasing manager is unhappy with a current supplier's product quality, service, or prices. Externally, the buyer may get some new ideas at a trade show, see an ad, or receive a call from a salesperson who offers a better product or a lower price.

In fact, in their advertising, business marketers often alert customers to potential problems and then show how their products and services provide solutions. For example, an award-winning ad from *Quill.com,* an online office products supplier that strives for strong customer service, highlights an important customer problem: what to do when your printer runs out of toner. The visual in the ad—which shows the headline fading then reappearing—effectively suggests both the problem and the solution. "If you run out of toner," says the ad, "we will replace it this quickly. At *Quill.com,* we are here whenever you need us."

Problem recognition: Quill.com uses this award-winning ad to alert customers to both an important problem and the solution. "At Quill.com, we're here whenever you need us."

Quill.com agency—Euro RSCG Chicago, Creative Director, Blake Ebel

General Needs Description

Having recognized a need, the buyer next prepares a **general need description** that describes the characteristics and quantity of the needed item. For standard items, this process presents few problems. For complex items, however, the buyer may need to work with others—engineers, users, consultants—to define the item. The team may want to rank the

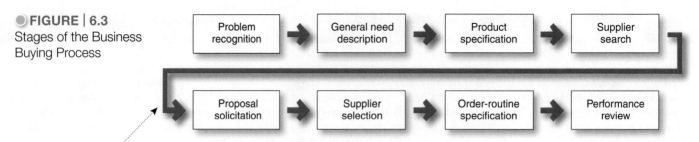

●FIGURE | 6.3
Stages of the Business
Buying Process

Buyers facing new, complex buying
decisions usually go through all of
these stages. Those making rebuys
often skip some of the stages.
Either way, the business buying
process is usually much more
complicated than this simple flow
diagram suggests.

General need description
The stage in the business buying
process in which a buyer describes the
general characteristics and quantity of a
needed item.

Product specification
The stage of the business buying process
in which the buying organization decides
on and specifies the best technical
product characteristics for a needed item.

Supplier search
The stage of the business buying process
in which the buyer tries to find the best
vendors.

Proposal solicitation
The stage of the business buying process
in which the buyer invites qualified
suppliers to submit proposals.

Supplier selection
The stage of the business buying process
in which the buyer reviews proposals and
selects a supplier or suppliers.

importance of reliability, durability, price, and other attributes desired in the item. In this phase, the alert business marketer can help the buyers define their needs and provide information about the value of different product characteristics.

Product Specification

The buying organization next develops the item's technical **product specifications**, often with the help of a value analysis engineering team. *Product value analysis* is an approach to cost reduction in which components are studied carefully to determine if they can be redesigned, standardized, or made by less costly methods of production. The team decides on the best product characteristics and specifies them accordingly. Sellers, too, can use value analysis as a tool to help secure a new account. By showing buyers a better way to make an object, outside sellers can turn straight rebuy situations into new task situations that give them a chance to obtain new business.

Supplier Search

The buyer now conducts a **supplier search** to find the best vendors. The buyer can compile a small list of qualified suppliers by reviewing trade directories, doing computer searches, or contacting other companies for recommendations. Today, more and more companies are turning to the Internet to find suppliers. For marketers, this has leveled the playing field—the Internet gives smaller suppliers many of the same advantages as larger competitors.

The newer the buying task, and the more complex and costly the item, the greater the amount of time the buyer will spend searching for suppliers. The supplier's task is to get listed in major directories and build a good reputation in the marketplace. Salespeople should watch for companies in the process of searching for suppliers and make certain that their firm is considered.

Proposal Solicitation

In the **proposal solicitation** stage of the business buying process, the buyer invites qualified suppliers to submit proposals. In response, some suppliers will refer the buyer to their Web sites or promotional materials or send a salesperson to call on the prospect. However, when the item is complex or expensive, the buyer will usually require detailed written proposals or formal presentations from each potential supplier.

Business marketers must be skilled in researching, writing, and presenting proposals in response to buyer proposal solicitations. Proposals should be marketing documents, not just technical documents. Presentations should inspire confidence and should make the marketer's company stand out from the competition.

Supplier Selection

The members of the buying center now review the proposals and select a supplier or suppliers. During **supplier selection**, the buying center often will draw up a list of the desired supplier attributes and their relative importance. Such attributes include product and service quality, reputation, on-time delivery, ethical corporate behavior, honest communication, and competitive prices. The members of the buying center will rate suppliers against these attributes and identify the best suppliers.

Buyers may attempt to negotiate with preferred suppliers for better prices and terms before making the final selections. In the end, they may select a single supplier or a few suppliers. Many buyers prefer multiple sources of supplies to avoid being totally dependent on one supplier and to allow comparisons of prices and performance of several suppliers over time. Today's supplier development managers want to develop a full network of supplier-partners that can help the company bring more value to its customers.

Order-Routine Specification

Order-routine specification
The stage of the business buying process in which the buyer writes the final order with the chosen supplier(s), listing the technical specifications, quantity needed, expected time of delivery, return policies, and warranties.

The buyer now prepares an **order-routine specification**. It includes the final order with the chosen supplier or suppliers and lists items such as technical specifications, quantity needed, expected delivery time, return policies, and warranties. In the case of maintenance, repair, and operating items, buyers may use blanket contracts rather than periodic purchase orders. A blanket contract creates a long-term relationship in which the supplier promises to resupply the buyer as needed at agreed prices for a set time period.

Many large buyers now practice *vendor-managed inventory*, in which they turn over ordering and inventory responsibilities to their suppliers. Under such systems, buyers share sales and inventory information directly with key suppliers. The suppliers then monitor inventories and replenish stock automatically as needed. For example, most major suppliers to large retailers such as Walmart, Target, Home Depot, and Lowe's assume vendor-managed inventory responsibilities.

Performance Review

Performance review
The stage of the business buying process in which the buyer assesses the performance of the supplier and decides to continue, modify, or drop the arrangement.

In this stage, the buyer reviews supplier performance. The buyer may contact users and ask them to rate their satisfaction. The **performance review** may lead the buyer to continue, modify, or drop the arrangement. The seller's job is to monitor the same factors used by the buyer to make sure that the seller is giving the expected satisfaction.

In all, the eight-stage buying-process model shown in Figure 6.3 provides a simple view of the business buying as it might occur in a new task buying situation. However, the actual process is usually much more complex. In the modified rebuy or straight rebuy situation, some of these stages would be compressed or bypassed. Each organization buys in its own way, and each buying situation has unique requirements.

Different buying center participants may be involved at different stages of the process. Although certain buying-process steps usually do occur, buyers do not always follow them in the same order, and they may add other steps. Often, buyers will repeat certain stages of the process. Finally, a customer relationship might involve many different types of purchases ongoing at a given time, all in different stages of the buying process. The seller must manage the total *customer relationship*, not just individual purchases.

E-Procurement: Buying on the Internet

E-procurement
Purchasing through electronic connections between buyers and sellers—usually online.

Advances in information technology have changed the face of the B-to-B marketing process. Online purchasing, often called **e-procurement**, has grown rapidly in recent years. Virtually unknown a decade and a half ago, online purchasing is standard procedure for most companies today. E-procurement gives buyers access to new suppliers, lowers purchasing costs, and hastens order processing and delivery. In turn, business marketers can connect with customers online to share marketing information, sell products and services, provide customer support services, and maintain ongoing customer relationships.

Companies can do e-procurement in any of several ways. They can conduct *reverse auctions*, in which they put their purchasing requests online and invite suppliers to bid for the business. Or they can engage in online *trading exchanges*, through which companies work collectively to facilitate the trading process. Companies also can conduct e-procurement by setting up their own *company buying sites*. For example, GE operates a company trading site on which it posts its buying needs and invites bids, negotiates terms, and places orders. Or companies can create *extranet links* with key suppliers. For instance, they can create direct procurement accounts with suppliers such as Dell or Staples, through which company buyers can purchase equipment, materials, and supplies directly. Staples operates a business-to-business procurement division called Staples Advantage, which serves the office supplies and services buying needs of businesses of any size, from 20 employees to the Fortune 1000.

B-to-B marketers can help customers online and build stronger customer relationships by creating well-designed, easy-to-use Web sites. For example, *BtoB* magazine recently rated the site of Shaw Floors—a market leader in flooring products—as one of its "10 great B-to-B Web sites." The site helps Shaw build strong links with its business and trade customers.[8]

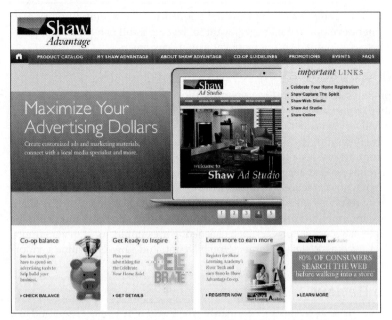

● B-to-B Web sites: This Shaw Floors site builds strong links with Shaw's retailers. It provides marketing ideas and tools that make retailers more effective in selling Shaw's products to final customers.

Shaw Industries, Inc.

At one time, flooring manufacturer Shaw Floors' Web site was nothing more than "brochureware." ● Today, however, the site is a true interactive experience. At the site, design and construction professionals as well as customers can "see"—virtually—the company's many product lines. At the popular "Try on a Floor" area, designers or retailers can even work with final buyers to upload digital images of an actual floor and put any of the company's many carpets on it to see how they look. They can select various lines and colors immediately without digging through samples. And the extremely detailed images can be rotated and manipulated so a designer, for example, can show a client what the pile of the carpet looks like and how deep it is.

The Shaw Floors site also provides a rich set of easy-to-navigate resources for Shaw retailers. The "For Retailers" area lets retail-partners search the company's products, make inventory checks, track order status, or order brochures for their stores. At the Shaw AdSource area, retailers can find resources to create their own ads. The Shaw Web Studio lets retailers—many of which are mom-and-pop stores—download the photography, catalog engines, and other tools they need to build their own Web sites. "So many retailers don't have the time or money to build their own online presence," says Shaw's interactive marketing manager, "so this really helps them."

More generally, today's business-to-business marketers are using a wide range of digital and social marketing approaches—from Web sites, blogs, and smartphone apps to mainstream social networks such as Facebook, LinkedIn, YouTube, and Twitter to reach business customers and manage customer relationships anywhere, anytime. Digital and social marketing has rapidly become *the* new space for engaging business customers (see Real Marketing 6.2).

Business-to-business e-procurement yields many benefits. First, it shaves transaction costs and results in more efficient purchasing for both buyers and suppliers. E-procurement reduces the time between order and delivery. And a Web-powered purchasing program eliminates the paperwork associated with traditional requisition and ordering procedures and helps an organization keep better track of all purchases. Finally, beyond the cost and time savings, e-procurement frees purchasing people from a lot of drudgery and paperwork. In turn, it frees them to focus on more-strategic issues, such as finding better supply sources and working with suppliers to reduce costs and develop new products.

The rapidly expanding use of e-procurement, however, also presents some problems. For example, at the same time that the Internet makes it possible for suppliers and customers to share business data and even collaborate on product design, it can also erode decades-old customer-supplier relationships. Many buyers now use the power of the Internet to pit suppliers against one another and search out better deals, products, and turnaround times on a purchase-by-purchase basis.

E-procurement can also create potential security concerns. Although home shopping transactions can be protected through basic encryption, the secure environment that businesses need to carry out confidential interactions is sometimes still lacking. Companies are spending millions for research on defensive strategies to keep hackers at bay. Cisco Systems, for example, specifies the types of routers, firewalls, and security procedures that its partners must use to safeguard extranet connections. In fact, the company goes even further; it sends its own security engineers to examine a partner's defenses and holds the partner liable for any security breach that originates from its computers.

Objective 4 ┈┈➤

Compare the institutional and government markets and explain how institutional and government buyers make their buying decisions.

Institutional and Government Markets

So far, our discussion of organizational buying has focused largely on the buying behavior of business buyers. Much of this discussion also applies to the buying practices of institutional

Real Marketing 6.2

B-to-B Social Marketing: The Space to Engage Business Customers

There's a hot new video on YouTube these days, featured at the Makino Machine Tools YouTube channel. It shows Makino's D500 five-axis vertical machining center in action, with metal chips flying as the machinery mills a new industrial part. Sound exciting? Probably not to you. But to the right industrial customer, the video is downright spellbinding. "Wow," says one viewer, "that's a new concept to have the saddle ride in Y rather than X. Is that a rigidity enhancement?" In all, the video has been viewed more than 29,000 times, mostly by current or prospective Makino customers. For B-to-B marketer Makino, that's great exposure.

When you think of digital and social marketing, you most likely think of marketing to final consumers. But today, most business-to-business marketers, like Makino, have also upped their use of these new approaches to reach and engage business customers. The use of digital and social marketing channels in business marketing isn't just growing, it's exploding. Even as most major B-to-B marketers are cutting back on traditional media and event marketing, they are ramping up their use of everything from Web sites, blogs, apps, and proprietary online networks to mainstream social networks such as Facebook, LinkedIn, YouTube, and Twitter. Research shows that 79 percent of B-to-B companies now post articles online, 74 percent use existing social media, 65 percent blog, 63 percent send out e-newsletters, 52 percent post videos online, and 46 percent conduct webinars.

Digital and social media have become *the* space in which to engage B-to-B customers and strengthen customer relationships. Again, consider Makino, a leading manufacturer of metal cutting and machining technology:

Makino employs a wide variety of social media initiatives that inform customers and enhance customer relationships. For example, it hosts an ongoing series of industry-specific webinars that position the company as an industry thought leader. Makino produces about three webinars each month and offers a library of more than 100 on topics ranging from optimizing machine tool performance to discovering new metal-cutting processes. Webinar content is tailored to specific industries, such as aerospace or medical, and is promoted through carefully targeted banner ads and e-mails. The webinars help to build Makino's customer database, generate leads, build customer relationships, and prepare the way for salespeople by providing relevant information and educating customers online.

Makino even uses Twitter, Facebook, and YouTube to inform customers and prospects about the latest Makino innovations and events and to vividly demonstrate the company's machines in action. The results have been gratifying. "We've shifted dramatically into the electronic marketing area," says Makino's marketing manager. "It speeds up the sales cycle and makes it more efficient—for both the company and the customer. The results have been outstanding."

Compared with traditional media and sales approaches, digital and social marketing approaches can create greater customer engagement and interaction. B-to-B marketers know that they aren't really targeting *businesses,* they are targeting *individuals* in those businesses who affect buying decisions. "We are selling business-to-people," notes one B-to-B marketer. And today's business buyers are always connected. They have their digital devices—whether PCs, iPads, or smartphones—hardwired to their brains. As one B-to-B marketer puts it, "Being at work is no longer a place; it is a state of mind."

Digital and social media can play an important role in engaging today's always-connected business buyers in a way that personal selling alone cannot. Instead of the old model of sales reps calling on business customers at work or maybe meeting up with them at trade shows, the new digital approaches facilitate anytime, anywhere connections between a wide range of people in the selling and customer organizations. It gives both sellers and buyers more control of and access to important information. B-to-B marketing has always been social network marketing, but today's digital environment offers an exciting array of new networking tools and applications.

No company seems to grasp the new digital and social media opportunities more fully than one of the oldest companies around—IBM. At 114 years old and with 400,000 employees in 170 countries, Big Blue is as fresh and relevant—and profitable—as ever when it comes to social media. It uses a decentralized approach to social media. "We represent our brand online the way it always has been," says an IBM social media executive. "Our brand is largely shaped by the interactions that [IBMers] have with customers."

B-to-B social media: Machining tool manufacturer Makino engages its business customers through extensive digital and social marketing—everything from proprietary online communities and webinars to Facebook, YouTube, and Twitter.

Courtesy of Makino, Inc. Facebook is a trademark of Facebook, Inc.

From that perspective, IBM encourages employees to talk publically in the social media—to each other and to customers—and lets them go about it with no invention or oversight. And go about it they do. Thousands of IBMers are the voice of the company. There are 100,000 IBMers using 17,000 internal blogs and 53,000 members on SocialBlue (IBM's own internal Facebook-like network). "Run an online search for 'IBM blog' and you'll find countless IBMers posting publically on everything from service-oriented architecture to sales to parenthood," says one analyst. "If you want to blog at IBM, you simply start." IBM employees by the tens of thousands or even hundreds of thousands are also actively involved on Twitter, LinkedIn, Facebook, YouTube, and many other public social networks.

All this IBMer-led social networking drives an incredible amount of interaction among IBM employees, customers, and suppliers. For example, an IBM "innovation jam" can include a diverse group of as many as 500,000

people inside and outside the company. Such online interactions helped spawn what is now a major IBM movement, Smarter Planet—an initiative that puts the collective minds and tools at IBM and outside the company toward solving issues ranging from rush-hour traffic to natural disaster response.

Whether it's IBM's decentralized approach to digital and social media or Makino's more focused and deliberate one, B-to-B marketers are discovering just how effective these new networking channels can be for engaging and interacting with business customers. Digital and social marketing aren't passing B-to-B fads; they signal a new way of doing business. Gone are the days when B-to-B marketers can just push out information about their products and services in a sales call or at a marketing event. Instead, marketers need to engage customers in meaningful and relevant ways, whenever and wherever customers demand it, 24 hours a day, 7 days a week. As one B-to-B social media director states, "Customer expectations have changed. Customers want, on demand, to have a say in how they interact with you as a company. We need to change and adapt our thinking and acknowledge this shift."

Sources: Kate Maddox, "Online Marketing Summit Focuses on Social, Search, Content," *btobonline.com*, February 13, 2012; Elizabeth Sullivan, "One to One," *Marketing News*, May 15, 2009, pp. 10–13; Sean Callahan, "Is B2B Marketing Really Obsolete?" *btobonline.com*, January 17, 2011; Casey Hibbard, "How IBM Uses Social Media to Spur Employee Innovation," *Socialmediaexaminer.com*, February 2, 2010; Joe Pulizzi, "2012 B2B Content Marketing Benchmarks, Budgets, and Trends," *contentmarketinginstitute.com*, December 5, 2011; "Analytics, Content, and Apps Are Hot Topics at 'BtoB's' SF NetMarketing Breakfast," *BtoB*, February 17, 2012, www.btobonline.com/article/20120217/EVENT02/302179995/analytics-content-and-apps-are-hot-topics-at-btobs-sf-netmarketing; and www.youtube.com/user/MakinoMachineTools, accessed September 2012.

and government organizations. However, these two nonbusiness markets have additional characteristics and needs. In this final section, we address the special features of institutional and government markets.

Institutional Markets

Institutional market

Schools, hospitals, nursing homes, prisons, and other institutions that provide goods and services to people in their care.

The **institutional market** consists of schools, hospitals, nursing homes, prisons, and other institutions that provide goods and services to people in their care. Institutions differ from one another in their sponsors and their objectives. For example, Tenet Healthcare runs 50 for-profit hospitals in 11 states, generating $9.2 billion in annual revenues. By contrast, the Shriners Hospitals for Children is a nonprofit organization with 22 hospitals that provide free specialized health care for children, whereas the government-run Veterans Affairs Medical Centers located across the country provide special services to veterans.[9] Each institution has different buying needs and resources.

Institutional markets can be huge. Consider the massive and expanding U.S. prisons economy:

Some 7.4 million Americans, more than the individual populations of 38 of the 50 states, are in prison, on parole, or on probation. Criminal correction spending is outpacing budget growth in education, transportation, and public assistance. For instance, during the last two decades, state and federal spending on prisons grew by 127 percent, six times the growth rate of spending on higher education. U.S. prisons, which hold 2.3 million adults, spend about $74 billion annually to keep those facilities running—on average almost more than $32,000 per year per prisoner. "One year in prison costs more than one year at Princeton," remarks one analyst. The ultimate captive market, it translates into plenty of work for companies looking to break into the prison market. "Our core business touches so many things—security, medicine, education, food service, maintenance, technology—that it presents a unique opportunity for any number of vendors to do business with us," says an executive at Corrections Corporation of America, the largest private prison operator in the country.[10]

Many institutional markets are characterized by low budgets and captive patrons. For example, hospital patients have little choice but to eat whatever food the hospital supplies.

A hospital purchasing agent has to decide on the quality of food to buy for patients. Because the food is provided as a part of a total service package, the buying objective is not profit. Nor is strict cost minimization the goal—patients receiving poor-quality food will complain to others and damage the hospital's reputation. Thus, the hospital purchasing agent must search for institutional-food vendors whose quality meets or exceeds a certain minimum standard and whose prices are low.

● **Institutional markets: The Procter & Gamble Professional Division markets professional cleaning and laundry formulations and systems to educational, health-care, and other institutional and commercial customers.**

The Procter & Gamble Company

Government market

Governmental units—federal, state, and local—that purchase or rent goods and services for carrying out the main functions of government.

Many marketers set up separate divisions to meet the special characteristics and needs of institutional buyers. For example, the General Mills Foodservice unit produces, packages, prices, and markets its broad assortment of cereals, cookies, snacks, and other products to better serve the specific food service requirements of hospitals, schools, hotels, and other institutional markets. ● Similarly, the Procter & Gamble Professional Division markets professional cleaning and laundry formulations and systems to educational, health-care, and other institutional and commercial customers.[11]

Government Markets

The **government market** offers large opportunities for many companies, both big and small. In most countries, government organizations are major buyers of goods and services. In the United States alone, federal, state, and local governments contain more than 88,000 buying units that purchase more than $1 trillion in goods and services each year.[12] Government buying and business buying are similar in many ways. But there are also differences that must be understood by companies that wish to sell products and services to governments. To succeed in the government market, sellers must locate key decision makers, identify the factors that affect buyer behavior, and understand the buying decision process.

Government organizations typically require suppliers to submit bids, and normally they award the contract to the lowest bidder. In some cases, a governmental unit will make allowances for the supplier's superior quality or reputation for completing contracts on time. Governments will also buy on a negotiated contract basis, primarily in the case of complex projects involving major research and development (R&D) costs and risks, and in cases where there is little competition.

Government organizations tend to favor domestic suppliers over foreign suppliers. A major complaint of multinationals operating in Europe is that each country shows favoritism toward its nationals in spite of superior offers that are made by foreign firms. The European Economic Commission is gradually removing this bias.

Like consumer and business buyers, government buyers are affected by environmental, organizational, interpersonal, and individual factors. One unique thing about government buying is that it is carefully watched by outside publics, ranging from Congress to a variety of private groups interested in how the government spends taxpayers' money. Because their spending decisions are subject to public review, government organizations require considerable paperwork from suppliers, who often complain about excessive paperwork, bureaucracy, regulations, decision-making delays, and frequent shifts in procurement personnel.

Given all the red tape, why would any firm want to do business with the U.S. government? The reasons are quite simple: The U.S. government is the world's largest buyer of products and services—more than $461 billion worth each year—and its checks don't bounce. The government buys everything from socks to stealth bombers. For example, this year, the federal government will spend a whopping $80.9 billion on information technology, $20 billion of which is earmarked for transitioning to cloud computing systems.[13]

Most governments provide would-be suppliers with detailed guides describing how to sell to the government. For example, the U.S. Small Business Administration provides on its Web site detailed advice for small businesses seeking government contracting opportunities (www.sba.gov/category/navigation-structure/contracting/contracting-opportunities). And the U.S. Commerce Department's Web site is loaded with information and advice on international trade opportunities (www.commerce.gov/about-commerce/grants-contracting-trade-opportunities).

In several major cities, the General Services Administration operates *Business Service Centers* with staffs to provide a complete education on the way government agencies buy, the steps that suppliers should follow, and the procurement opportunities available. Various trade magazines and associations provide information on how to reach schools, hospitals, highway departments, and other government agencies. And almost all of these government organizations and associations maintain Internet sites offering up-to-date information and advice.

Still, suppliers have to master the system and find ways to cut through the red tape, especially for large government purchases. Consider Envisage Technologies, a small software development company that specializes in Internet-based training applications and human resource management platforms. All of its contracts fall in the government sector; 65 percent are with the federal government. Envisage uses the General Services Administration's Web site to gain access to smaller procurements, often receiving responses within 14 days. However, it puts the most sweat into seeking large, highly coveted contracts. A comprehensive bid proposal for one of these contracts can easily run from 600 to 700 pages because of federal paperwork requirements. And the company's president estimates that to prepare a single bid proposal, the firm has spent as many as 5,000 labor-hours over the course of a few years.[14]

Noneconomic criteria also play a growing role in government buying. Government buyers are asked to favor depressed business firms and areas; small business firms; minority-owned firms; and business firms that avoid race, gender, and age discrimination. Sellers need to keep these factors in mind when seeking government business.

Many companies that sell to the government have not been very marketing oriented for a number of reasons. Total government spending is determined by elected officials rather than by any marketing effort to develop this market. Government buying has emphasized price, making suppliers invest their effort in technology to bring costs down. When the product's characteristics are specified carefully, product differentiation is not a marketing factor. Nor do advertising or personal selling matter much in winning bids on an open-bid basis.

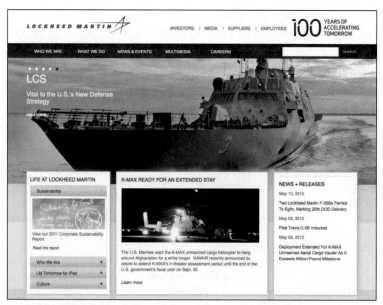

● **Government markets: Some companies sell primarily to government buyers, such as Lockheed Martin, which makes 84 percent of its sales to the U.S. government.**

Courtesy Lockheed Martin Corporation

Several companies, however, have established separate government marketing departments, including GE, Boeing, and Goodyear. ● Other companies sell primarily to government buyers, such as Lockheed Martin, which makes 84 percent of its sales from the U.S. government, either as a prime contractor or a subcontractor. These companies anticipate government needs and projects, participate in the product specification phase, gather competitive intelligence, prepare bids carefully, and produce stronger communications to describe and enhance their companies' reputations.

Other companies have established customized marketing programs for government buyers. For example, Dell has specific business units tailored to meet the needs of federal as well as state and local government buyers. Dell offers its customers tailor-made Premier Dell.com Web pages that include special pricing, online purchasing, and service and support for each city, state, and federal government entity.

During the past decade, a great deal of the government's buying has gone online. The Federal Business Opportunities Web site (FedBizOpps.com at www.fbo.gov) provides a single point of entry through which commercial vendors and government buyers can post, search, monitor, and retrieve opportunities solicited by the entire federal contracting community. The three federal agencies that act as purchasing agents for the rest of government have also launched Web sites supporting online government purchasing activity. The General Services Administration, which influences more than one-quarter of the federal government's total procurement dollars, has set up a GSA Advantage! Web site (www.gsaadvantage.gov). The Defense Logistics Agency offers an Internet Bid Board System (www.dibbs.bsm.dla.mil) for purchases by America's military services. And the Department of Veterans Affairs facilitates e-procurement through its VA Advantage! Web site (https://VAadvantage.gsa.gov).

Such sites allow authorized defense and civilian agencies to buy everything from office supplies, food, and information technology equipment to construction services through online purchasing. The General Services Administration, the Defense Logistics Agency, and Department of Veterans Affairs not only sell stocked merchandise through their Web sites but also create direct links between government buyers and contract suppliers. For example, the branch of the Defense Logistics Agency that sells 160,000 types of medical supplies to military forces transmits orders directly to vendors such as Bristol-Myers Squibb. Such Internet systems promise to eliminate much of the hassle sometimes found in dealing with government purchasing.[15]

Reviewing the Concepts

MyMarketingLab™

Go to **mymktlab.com** to complete the problems marked with this icon .

Reviewing Objectives and Key Terms

 ## Objectives Review

Business markets and consumer markets are alike in some key ways. For example, both include people in buying roles who make purchase decisions to satisfy needs. But business markets also differ in many ways from consumer markets. For one thing, the business market is *huge*, far larger than the consumer market. Within the United States alone, the business market includes organizations that annually purchase trillions of dollars' worth of goods and services.

Objective 1 | **Define the business market and explain how business markets differ from consumer markets.** (pp 168–170)

The *business market* comprises all organizations that buy goods and services for use in the production of other products and services or for the purpose of reselling or renting them to others at a profit. As compared to consumer markets, business markets usually have fewer but larger buyers. Business demand is derived demand, which tends to be more inelastic and fluctuating than consumer demand. The business buying decision usually involves more, and more professional, buyers. Business buyers usually face more complex buying decisions, and the buying process tends to be more

formalized. Finally, business buyers and sellers are often more dependent on each other.

Objective 2 | **Identify the major factors that influence business buyer behavior.** (pp 171–175)

Business buyers make decisions that vary with the three types of *buying situations*: straight rebuys, modified rebuys, and new tasks. The decision-making unit of a buying organization—the *buying center*—can consist of many different persons playing many different roles. The business marketer needs to know the following: Who are the major buying center participants? In what decisions do they exercise influence and to what degree? What evaluation criteria does each decision participant use? The business marketer also needs to understand the major environmental, organizational, interpersonal, and individual influences on the buying process.

Objective 3 | **List and define the steps in the business buying decision process.** (pp 175–180)

The *business buying decision process* itself can be quite involved, with eight basic stages: problem recognition, general need description, product specification, supplier search, proposal solicitation, supplier selection, order-routine specification, and performance review. Buyers who face a new task buying situation usually go through all stages of the buying process. Buyers making modified or straight rebuys may skip some of the stages. Companies must manage the overall customer relationship, which often includes many different buying decisions in various stages of the buying decision process.

Advances in information technology have given birth to "e-procurement," by which business buyers are purchasing all kinds of products and services online. The Internet gives business buyers access to new suppliers, lowers purchasing costs, and hastens order processing and delivery. However, e-procurement can also erode customer-supplier relationships and create potential security problems. Still, business marketers are increasingly connecting with customers online to share marketing information, sell products and services, provide customer support services, and maintain ongoing customer relationships.

| Objective 4 | **Compare the institutional and government markets and explain how institutional and government buyers make their buying decisions. (pp 180–183)** |

The *institutional market* consists of schools, hospitals, prisons, and other institutions that provide goods and services to people in their care. These markets are characterized by low budgets and captive patrons. The *government market*, which is vast, consists of government units—federal, state, and local—that purchase or rent goods and services for carrying out the main functions of government.

Government buyers purchase products and services for defense, education, public welfare, and other public needs. Government buying practices are highly specialized and specified, with open bidding or negotiated contracts characterizing most of the buying. Government buyers operate under the watchful eye of the U.S. Congress and many private watchdog groups. Hence, they tend to require more forms and signatures and respond more slowly and deliberately when placing orders.

 # Key Terms

Objective 1

Business buyer behavior (p 168)
Business buying process (p 168)
Derived demand (p 169)
Supplier development (p 170)

Objective 2

Straight rebuy (p 171)
Modified rebuy (p 171)
New task (p 171)
Systems selling (or solutions selling) (p 171)

Buying center (p 172)
Users (p 172)
Influencers (p 172)
Buyers (p 172)
Deciders (p 172)
Gatekeepers (p 172)

Objective 3

Problem recognition (p 175)
General need description (p 176)
Product specification (p 176)
Supplier search (p 176)

Proposal solicitation (p 176)
Supplier selection (p 176)
Order-routine specification (p 177)
Performance review (p 177)
E-procurement (p 177)

Objective 4

Institutional market (p 180)
Government market (p 181)

Discussion and Critical Thinking

 ## Discussion Questions

1. Explain how the market structure and demand differ for business markets compared to consumer markets. (AACSB: Communication; Reflective Thinking)

⊗ **2.** Name and describe the three types of business buying situations. (AACSB: Communication)

3. Name and describe the roles played by buying center participants in the business buying process. (AACSB: Communication; Reflective Thinking)

⊗ **4.** Explain what is meant by *systems selling* and discuss why it is a preferred approach to buying for many organizations. (AACSB: Communication; Reflective Thinking)

5. Compare the institutional and government markets and explain how institutional and government buyers make their buying decisions. (AACSB: Communication)

Critical Thinking Exercises

1. Business buying occurs worldwide, so marketers need to be aware of cultural factors influencing business customers. In a small group, select a country and develop a multimedia presentation on proper business etiquette and manners, including appropriate appearance, behavior, and communication. Include a map showing the location of the country as well as a description of the country in terms of its demographics, culture, and economic history. (AACSB: Communication; Multicultural and Diversity)

2. The U.S. government is the world's largest purchaser of goods and services, spending more than $425 billion per year. By law, 23 percent of all government buying must be targeted to small firms. Visit http://archive.sba.gov/contractingopportunities/index.html to learn how small businesses can take advantage of government contracting opportunities. Develop a brochure explaining the process to small business owners. (AACSB: Communication; Reflective Thinking; Use of IT)

Applications and Cases

Marketing Technology Apple's Supply Chain

How many parts go into Apple's iPhone? Of course there are the case, screen, camera, processor, and battery, but have you ever considered all the other parts, such as screws and switches? There are 40 to 50 screws alone in an iPhone, and each of the parts—including the screws—must be sourced from suppliers. Apple's list of primary contractors includes more than 20 companies scattered around the globe. Apple's current CEO, Tim Cook, was brought on by Apple co-founder, the late Steve Jobs, to streamline Apple's supply chain. Cook cut component suppliers from 100 to 24 and shut down 19 Apple warehouses, resulting in a reduction of parts inventory from one month to just six days. Most of this is possible through technology, and as a result, Apple's

supply chain has been ranked number one in the world three years in a row by Gartner's and Apple is achieving record-setting profits.

1. Go to www.gartner.com/DisplayDocument?doc_cd=234062, select another company on Gartner's Supply Chain Top 25, and describe that company's supply chain. Discuss the role technology plays in that company's purchasing. (AACSB: Communication; Reflective Thinking; Use of IT)

2. Discuss possible negative consequences of using technology to gain competitive advantage through purchasing and vendor relationship activities. (AACSB: Communication; Reflective Thinking)

Marketing Ethics Pink Slime

In the early 1990s, Eldon Roth figured out a way to profit from slaughterhouse meat trimmings, by-products that were once used only in pet food and cooking oil. This cheap and safe beef product is called "lean, finely textured beef" (LFTB). The fatty bits of beef are heated and treated with a puff of ammonium hydroxide gas to kill bacteria. You've probably eaten many hamburgers that included LFTB prepared by fast-feeders, at school cafeterias, or even in your own kitchen. LFTB makes ground beef leaner and cheaper. Shortly after it was developed, a health safety inspector dubbed LFTB "pink slime," but the name didn't become public until the major "pink slime" media brouhaha erupted in 2012. Consumers were repulsed to learn that they were eating unappealing beef parts that were "soaked in ammonia." Sales of ground beef fell 11 percent in one month. Ground beef producer AFA Foods sought bankruptcy protection and Cargill lost 80 percent of its customers. The industry's leading LFTB manufacturer, Beef Products, Inc., shuttered 75 percent

of its processing plants and laid off 650 workers. McDonald's and other fast-feeders, supermarkets, and institutional buyers such as schools and hospitals discontinued using beef products containing LFTB, even though the safe and inexpensive product has been around for many years.

1. Was the uproar over LFTB warranted, given the fact that it is a product deemed safe for consumption by the U.S. Food and Drug Administration? Research other types of products that are included in consumer products that could face a similar fate if consumers were aware of them. (AACSB: Communication; Reflective Thinking; Ethical Reasoning)

2. Explain the type of buying situation faced by the companies that dropped the use of LFTB. Describe the buying decision process they likely went through to find a replacement product. (AACSB: Communication; Reflective Thinking)

Marketing by the Numbers **fMRI Market Potential**

Functional magnetic resonance imaging technology (fMRI) is making its way into the marketing research field, opening up a new market for this high-tech medical equipment. Using functional MRI technology, or fMRI, marketing researchers can literally see a brain in action when consumers view an advertisement or sample a product. A study in 2004 revealed that different parts of consumers' brains were activated when sampling a product with or without knowing the brand. When consumers tasted a soft drink without knowing the brand, their brains showed activity related to taste and they preferred Brand A. However, when subjects were shown the brands, a different area of the brain was activated and more consumers preferred Brand B, suggesting that advertising and marketing can activate different areas of consumers' brains and cause them to prefer specific brands. Several large marketing research firms

such as Nielsen now offer neuroscience marketing research services.

1. Research the marketing research industry to identify research companies that would be in the target market for fMRI equipment. How many companies make up this market? (AACSB: Communication; Reflective Reasoning)

2. Refer to Appendix 2, Marketing by the Numbers, and use the chain-ratio method to estimate the market potential for fMRI machines among marketing research firms. What factors would you consider when determining the potential number of buyers (that is, research firms) that are willing and able to purchase fMRI machines? Assume a firm purchases one machine at an average price of $1 million in your market potential estimation. (AACSB: Communication; Analytical Reasoning)

Video Case **Eaton**

With approximately 70,000 employees in more than 150 countries and annual revenues of nearly $12 billion, Eaton is one of the world's largest suppliers of diversified industrial goods. Eaton has been known for products that make cars peppier and 18-wheelers safer to drive. But a recent restructuring has made Eaton a powerhouse in the growing field of power management. In short, Eaton is making electrical, hydraulic, and mechanical power systems more accessible to and more efficient for its global customers. But Eaton isn't successful only because of the products and services that it sells. It is successful because it works closely with its business customers to help them solve their problems and create

better products and services of their own. Eaton is known for high-quality, dependable customer service and product support. In this manner, Eaton builds strong relationships with its clients.

After viewing the video featuring Eaton, answer the following questions:

1. What is Eaton's value proposition?

2. Who are Eaton's customers? Describe Eaton's customer relationships.

3. Discuss the different ways that Eaton provides value beyond that which customers can provide for themselves

Company Case **Cisco Systems: Solving Business Problems Through Collaboration**

Perhaps you've heard of Cisco. It's the company known for those catchy "Human Network" ads. It produces the familiar Linksys wireless Internet routers and owns Pure Digital Technologies, the company that makes the trendy Flip video cameras. But most of what Cisco Systems sells is not for regular consumers like you. Cisco is a tried-and-true business-to-business company. In fact, it earned honors as *BtoB* magazine's 2011 "marketer of the year." Three-quarters of Cisco's sales are in routers, switches, and advanced network technologies—the things that keep the data moving around cyberspace 24/7. But ever since the dot-com bust, Cisco has been pioneering the next generation of networking tools, from cybersecurity to set-top boxes to videoconferencing.

This story is about much more than just a tech giant that makes the equipment companies need to run their Internet and intranet activities. It's about a forward-thinking firm that has transitioned from a hardware company to a leadership consultancy. In the process, there is one concept that seems to be the main driver of Cisco's business with other organizations: customer collaboration. Cisco is all about collaborating with its business customers to help them better collaborate internally with employees as well as externally with suppliers, partners, and their customers.

Collaboration Within and Without

John Chambers became the CEO of Cisco way back in 1995, when annual revenues were a mere $1.2 billion. He successfully directed the growth of Cisco as a hardware provider. But following the dot-com bust in the early 2000s, he knew the world had become a different place. In response, he engineered a massive, radical, and often bumpy reorganization of the company. Chambers turned Cisco inside out and created a culture of 71,000 employees that truly thrives on collaboration. As such, Cisco is the perfect laboratory where new products are developed, used, and then sold to external clients. Cisco not only manufactures hardware and software that makes all the sharing activity possible, but is also the expert on how to use it. All this collaboration has helped Cisco's business explode, hitting $43 billion last year.

Perhaps Cisco's advertising campaign, "Human Network Effect," best illustrates the company's philosophy. The campaign highlights the benefits that come to an organization when it utilizes its network of people more effectively. According to Cisco, the pragmatic approach of the campaign helps customers understand how Cisco's technologies can save them money, bring products to market faster, and even have an impact on the environment. This campaign has helped Cisco become the 13th most valuable brand in the world at the same time it has communicated why companies need Cisco's products and services.

Chambers tells the story of how Cisco began its transition from hardware into services. "Our customers literally pulled us kicking and screaming into providing consultancy," says Chambers. Some years ago, the CEO of financial services company USAA asked Chambers to help the company figure out what to do with the Internet. Chambers replied that Cisco wasn't in the Internet consulting business. But when USAA committed to giving all its networking business to Cisco if it would take the job, Chambers proclaimed "We are in that business!" Now, Cisco has both the products and the knowledge to help other companies succeed on the Internet.

A turning point for Chambers in further understanding the impact that Cisco can have on clients was the major earthquake in China in 2008.

> Tae Yoo, a 19-year Cisco veteran, supervises the company's social responsibility efforts and sits on the China strategy board and the emerging-countries council. "I had always been a believer in collaboration," she says, but after the earthquake, "I saw it really happen. Our local team immediately mobilized, checking in with employees, customers, NGO partners. The council got people on the phone, on [video conference], to give us a complete assessment of what was happening locally. We connected West China Hospital to a specialized trauma center in Maryland via the network." High-level medical centers from the other side of the world were able to weigh in on diagnostics remotely. Cisco employees were on the ground helping rural areas recover and rebuild homes and schools. Within 14 days, Yoo continues, "I walked over to the China board with a complete plan and $45 million to fund it." That number ultimately grew to more than $100 million. "Our business is growing 30 percent year over year there," Chambers says, adding that Cisco has committed to investing $16 billion in public-private partnerships in China. "No one has the reach and trust that we do. No one could offer the help that we could."

Collaboration Benefits

Cisco management knows that number one on most CEO's lists is to break down the communication barriers between a company and its customers, suppliers, and partners. According to Jim Grubb, Chambers's longtime product-demo sidekick, "If we can accelerate the productivity of scientists who are working on the next solar technology because we're hooking them together, we're doing a great thing for the world." Doing a great thing for the world, while selling a ton of routers and switches.

But while routers and switches still account for most of Cisco's business, the really interesting things are far more cutting edge. Consider Cisco's involvement in what it calls the Smart+ Connected Communities initiative. Perhaps the best example of a smart and connected community is New Songdo City in South Korea, a city the size of downtown Boston being built from scratch on a man-made island in the Yellow Sea. Cisco was hired as the technology partner for this venture and is teaming up with the construction company, architects, 3M, and United Technologies as partners in the instant-city business.

Cisco's involvement goes way beyond installing routers, switches, and citywide Wi-Fi. The networking giant is wiring every square inch of the city with electronic synapses. Through trunk lines under the streets, filaments will branch out through every wall and fixture like a nervous system. Cisco is intent on having this city run on information, with its control room playing the part of New Songdo's brain stem.

Not content to simply sell the plumbing, Cisco will sell and operate services layered on top of its hardware. Imagine a city where every home and office is wired to Cisco's TelePresence videoconferencing screens. Engineers will listen, learn, and release new Cisco-branded services for modest monthly fees. Cisco intends to bundle urban necessities—water, power, traffic, communications, and entertainment—into a single, Internet-enabled utility. This isn't just Big Brother stuff. This Cisco system will allow New Songdo to reach new heights in environmental sustainability and efficiency. Because of these efficiencies, the cost for such services to residents will be cheaper as well.

Cisco believes that the smart cities business is an emerging industry with a $30-billion potential. Gale International, the construction company behind New Songdo, believes that China alone could use 500 such cities, each with a capacity for 1 million residents. It already has established the goal to build 20 of them.

Smart cities make one of Cisco's other businesses all the more relevant. Studies show that telecommuting produces enormous benefits for companies, communities, and employees. For example, telecommuters have higher job satisfaction. For that reason, they are more productive, giving back as much as 60 percent of their commuting time to the company. There is even evidence that people like working from home so much that they would be willing to work for less pay. An overwhelming majority of telecommuters produce work in a more timely manner with better quality. Their ability to communicate with coworkers is at least as good and in many cases better than when they work in the office. With products like Cisco Virtual Office and the expertise that Cisco offers to go with it, Sun Microsystems saved $68 million. It also reduced carbon emissions by 29,000 metric tons.

Cisco has also recently unveiled a set of Internet-based communication products to enhance organizations' collaborative activities. Cisco says this is all about making business more people-centric than document-centric. Along with a cloud-based mail system, WebEx Mail, Cisco Show and Share "helps organizations create and manage highly secure video communities to share ideas and expertise, optimize global video collaboration, and personalize the connection between customers, employees, and students with user-generated content," according to a PR blurb. Also on its way is what Cisco calls the Enterprise Collaboration Platform, a cross between a corporate directory and Facebook. These products allow the free flow of information to increase exponentially over existing products because they exist behind an organization's firewall with no filters, lawyers, or security issues to get in the way.

A Bright Future

This year, thanks to the still-sluggish economy, Cisco's financial performance is down. But Chambers thinks that's only a blip in the grand scheme of things. He points out that Cisco has emerged from every economic downturn of the past two decades stronger and more flexible. During the most recent downturn, Cisco moved quickly, seizing every opportunity to snatch up businesses and develop new products. During the decade of the 2000s, Cisco acquired 48 venture-backed companies. But last year alone, the company announced an astounding 61 new technologies, all focused on collaboration. With these resources—and $44 billion in cash that it has stowed away—Cisco is now expanding into 30 different markets, each with the potential to produce $1 billion a year in revenue. Moving forward, the company has committed to adding 20 percent more new-market businesses annually. And because Cisco enters a new market only when it's confident that it can gain a 40 percent share, the chance of failure is far below normal.

The collaboration market is estimated at $35 billion, a figure that will grow substantially in years to come. Because Cisco is the leader in this emerging industry, analysts have no problem accepting John Chambers's long-term goal of 12 to 17 percent revenue growth per year. Cisco has demonstrated that it has the product portfolio and the leadership structure necessary to pull it off. One thing is for sure. Cisco is no longer just a plumber, providing the gizmos and gadgets necessary to make the Internet go around. It is a networking leader, a core competency that will certainly make it a force to be reckoned with for years to come.

Questions for Discussion

1. Discuss the nature of the market structure and demand for Cisco's products.

2. Given the industries in which Cisco competes, what are the implications for the major types of buying situations?

3. What specific customer benefits likely result from the Cisco products mentioned in the case?

4. Discuss the customer buying process for one of Cisco's products. In what ways does this process differ from the buying process an end user might go through in buying a broadband router for home use?

5. Is the relationship between Cisco's collaborative culture and the products and services it sells something that could work for all companies? Consider this issue for a consumer-products company such as P&G.

Sources: "Cisco Reports Fourth Quarter and Fiscal Year 2011 Earnings," *Market Wire*, August 10, 2011, http://investor.cisco.com/releasedetail .cfm?ReleaseID=598440; Ellen McGirt, "How Cisco's CEO John Chambers Is Turning the Tech Giant Socialist," *Fast Company*, November 25, 2008, www.fastcompany.com/magazine/131/revolution-in-san-jose .html; Greg Lindsay, "Cisco's Big Bet on New Songdo," *Fast Company*, February 1, 2010, www.fastcompany.com/magazine/142/the-new-new-urbanism.html; "Christie Blair, Cisco Systems," *BtoB*, October 3, 2011, www.btobonline.com/apps/pbcs.dll/article?AID=/20111003/ FREE/310039953/0/SEARCH; and information from www.cisco.com/ web/about/index.html, accessed July 2012.

MyMarketingLab

Go to **mymktlab.com** for Auto-graded writing questions as well as the following Assisted-graded writing questions:

6-1. Describe how online purchasing has changed the business-to-business marketing process and discuss the advantages and disadvantages of electronic purchasing. (AACSB: Communication)

6-2. Compare the similarities and differences between a buyer at a Veteran's Administration Hospital and a buyer at a for-profit hospital like Humana. Compare the buyers on the following four factors environmental, organizational, interpersonal, and individual. (AACSB: Communication; Reflective Thinking)

6-3. Mymktlab Only – comprehensive writing assignment for this chapter.

References

1. Quotes and other information from "Kazakhstan to Start Exports of Locomotives," *Kazakhstan Today*, November 4, 2011; "General Electric Signs Contract to Supply 310 Evolution Series Locomotives to Kazakhstan," *Business Wire*, September 28, 2006; Jim Martin, "GE to Seal $650 Million Deal," *Knight Ridder Tribune Business News*, September 28, 2006, p.1; "GE Demonstrates Technology Leadership at Railway Interchange," *Business Wire*, September 18, 2011; and various pages at www.ge.com and www.getransportation.com, accessed November 2012.

2. Quotes and other information from www.omnexus.com/sf/ dow/?id=plastics, accessed March 2010; and http://plastics.dow .com/, accessed March 2012.

3. This classic categorization was first introduced in Patrick J. Robinson, Charles W. Faris, and Yoram Wind, *Industrial Buying Behavior and Creative Marketing* (Boston: Allyn & Bacon, 1967). Also see James C. Anderson, James A. Narus, and Das Narayandas, *Business Market Management*, 3rd ed. (Upper Saddle River, NJ: Prentice Hall, 2009), Chapter 3; and Philip Kotler and Kevin Lane Keller, *Marketing Management*, 14th ed. (Upper Saddle River, NJ: Prentice Hall, 2012), Chapter 7.

4. Based on information from "Six Flags Entertainment Corporation: Improving Business Efficiency with Enterprise Asset Management,"

July 12, 2012, www-01.ibm.com/software/success/cssdb.nsf/cs/ LWIS-8W5Q84?OpenDocument&Site=gicss67mdia&cty=en_us; and www-01.ibm.com/software/tivoli/products/maximo-asset-mgmt/, accessed November 2012.

5. See Frederick E. Webster Jr. and Yoram Wind, *Organizational Buying Behavior* (Upper Saddle River, NJ: Prentice Hall, 1972), pp. 78–80. Also see Jorg Brinkman and Markus Voeth, "An Analysis of Buying Center Decisions Through the Sales Force," *Industrial Marketing Management*, October 2007, p. 998; and Philip Kotler and Kevin Lane Keller, *Marketing Management*, 14th ed. (Upper Saddle River, NJ: Prentice Hall, 2012), pp. 188–191.

6. Based on "Citrix Systems: Integrated Campaign—Honorable Mention," *BtoB*, August 2009, accessed at www.btobonline.com/apps/ pbcs.dll/article?AID=/20101011/FREE/101019997; information provided by Citrix, July 2011; and information from www.citrix.com, accessed November 2012.

7. Robinson, Faris, and Wind, *Industrial Buying Behavior*, p. 14. Also see Kotler and Keller, *Marketing Management*, pp. 197–203.

8. For this and other examples, see "10 Great Web Sites," *BtoB Online*, September 13, 2010. Other information from www.shawfloors.com/ About-Shaw/Retailer-Support, accessed November 2012.

9. Information from www.shrinershospitalsforchildren.org/Hospitals .aspx and www.tenethealth.com/about/pages/default.aspx, accessed November 2012.

10. Michael Myser, "The Hard Sell," *Business 2.0*, December 2006, pp. 62–65; "U.S. Prison Population Tops 2.4 Million," *PressTV*, August 9, 2011, http://presstv.com/usdetail/193137.html; Brian Resnick, "Chart: One Year of Prison Costs More Than One Year at Princeton," *The Atlantic*, November 1, 2011, www.theatlantic.com/ national/archive/2011/11/chart-one-year-of-prison-costs-more-than-one-year-at-princeton/247629/; and Alan Bluestein, "Marketing: Prison Bound," *Inc.*, February 2012, pp. 96–97.

11. See www.gmifs.com and www.pgpro.com, accessed April 2012.

12. Henry Canaday, "Government Contracts," *Selling Power*, June 2008, pp. 59–62; and "State & Local Government Finances & Employment: Government Units," www.census.gov/compendia/statab/ cats/state_local_govt_finances_employment/governmental_units .html, accessed January 2012.

13. "Federal IT Spending Requests Top 2011 Levels, immixGroup Budget Briefings Reveals," *MarketWatch*, October 21, 2011, www.marketwatch.com/story/federal-it-spending-requests-top-2011-levels-immixgroup-budget-briefing-reveals-2011-10-21; and David Mielach, "Small Businesses Spend More to Do Business with the Government," *BusinessNewsDaily*, December 27, 2011, www .businessnewsdaily.com/1836-government-contracts-2011.html.

14. Based on communications with Ari Vidali, CEO of Envisage Technologies, July 2006 and January 2012.

15. See "GSA Organization Overview," www.gsa.gov/portal/content/ 104438, accessed November 2012; "Defense Logistics Agency: Medical Supply Chain," www.dscp.dla.mil/sbo/medical.asp, accessed November 2012; and Department of Veterans Affairs Office of Acquisition & Material Management, www1.va.gov/oamm, accessed November 2012.

Customer-Driven
Marketing **Strategy** Creating Value for Target Customers

Chapter Preview

So far, you've learned what marketfing is and about the importance of understanding consumers and the marketplace environment. With that as a background, you're now ready to delve deeper into marketing strategy and tactics. This chapter looks further into key customer-driven marketing strategy decisions—dividing up markets into meaningful customer groups (*segmentation*), choosing which customer groups to serve (*targeting*), creating market offerings that best serve targeted customers (*differentiation*), and positioning the offerings in the minds of consumers (*positioning*). The chapters that follow explore the tactical marketing tools—the four Ps—by which marketers bring these strategies to life.

To open our discussion of segmentation, targeting, differentiation, and positioning, let's look at Dunkin' Donuts. Dunkin' is rapidly expanding into a national powerhouse, on par with Starbucks. But Dunkin' is no Starbucks. In fact, it doesn't want to be. It targets a very different kind of customer with a very different value proposition. Grab yourself a cup of coffee and read on.

Dunkin' Donuts: Targeting the Average Joe

A few years ago, Dunkin' Donuts paid dozens of faithful customers in Phoenix, Chicago, and Charlotte, North Carolina, $100 a week to buy coffee at Starbucks instead. At the same time, the no-frills coffee chain paid Starbucks customers to make the opposite switch. When it later debriefed the two groups, Dunkin' says it found them so polarized that company researchers dubbed them "tribes," each of whom loathed the very things that made the other tribe loyal to their coffee shop. Dunkin' fans viewed Starbucks as pretentious and trendy, whereas Starbucks loyalists saw Dunkin' as plain and unoriginal. "I don't get it," one Dunkin' regular told researchers after visiting Starbucks. "If I want to sit on a couch, I stay at home."

Dunkin' Donuts is rapidly expanding into a national coffee powerhouse, on par with Starbucks, the nation's largest coffee chain. But the research confirmed a simple fact: Dunkin' is not Starbucks. In fact, it doesn't want to be. To succeed, Dunkin' must have its own clear vision of just which customers it wants to serve (what segments and targeting strategy) and how (what positioning or value proposition). Dunkin' and Starbucks target very different customers, who want very different things from their favorite coffee shops. Starbucks is strongly positioned as a sort of high-brow "third place"—outside the home and office—featuring couches, eclectic music, wireless Internet access, and art-splashed walls. Dunkin' has a decidedly more low-brow, "everyman" kind of positioning.

Dunkin' Donuts built itself on serving simple fare at a reasonable price to working-class customers. But recently, to broaden its appeal and fuel expansion, the chain has been moving upscale—a bit, but not too far. It's spiffing up its stores and adding new menu items, such as lattes and non-breakfast sandwiches. Dunkin' has made dozens of store redesign decisions, big and small, ranging from where to put the espresso machines to how much of its signature pink and orange color scheme to

> Dunkin' Donuts has a very clear vision of just which customers it wants to serve and how. It targets the "Dunkin' tribe"—everyday Joes who just don't get what Starbucks is all about.

retain and where to display its fresh baked goods.

However, as it inches upscale, Dunkin' Donuts is being careful not to alienate its traditional customer base. There are no couches in the remodeled stores. Dunkin' even renamed a new hot sandwich a "stuffed melt" after customers complained that calling it a "panini" was too fancy; it then dropped it altogether when faithful customers thought it was too messy. "We're walking [a fine] line," says the chain's vice president of consumer insights. "The thing about the Dunkin' tribe is, they see through the hype."

Dunkin' Donuts' research showed that although loyal customers want nicer stores, they were bewildered and turned off by the atmosphere at Starbucks. They groused that crowds of laptop users made it difficult to find a seat. They didn't like Starbucks' "tall," "grande," and "venti" lingo for small, medium, and large coffees. And they couldn't understand why anyone would pay so much for a cup of coffee. "It was almost as though they were a group of Martians talking about a group of Earthlings," says an executive from Dunkin's advertising agency. The Starbucks customers that Dunkin' paid to switch were equally uneasy in Dunkin' shops. "The Starbucks people couldn't bear that they weren't special anymore," says the ad executive.

Such opposing opinions aren't surprising, given the differences in the two stores' customers. Dunkin's customers include more middle-income blue- and white-collar workers across all age, race, and income demographics. By contrast, Starbucks targets a higher-income, more professional group. But Dunkin' researchers concluded that it was more the ideal, rather than income, that set the two tribes apart: Dunkin's tribe members want to be part of a crowd, whereas members of the Starbucks tribe want to stand out as individuals. "You could open a Dunkin' Donuts right next to Starbucks and get two completely different types of consumers," says one retailing expert.

Over the past several years, both Dunkin' Donuts and Starbucks have grown rapidly, each targeting its own tribe of customers and riding the wave of America's growing thirst for coffee. However, the direction of future U.S. growth for each brand highlights the differences in the positioning strategies. With more than 11,000 stores in all 50 U.S. states, Starbucks has penetrated the domestic market more deeply, capturing 33 percent of the $26.5 billion coffee and snack shop market. Rather than relying on new store openings for growth, Starbucks is now looking for ways to get existing customers to spend more time in current stores, especially in the evening. Its latest plan is to sell beer and wine along with complementary items such as fruit-and-cheese plates and focaccia with olive oil. Although this may seem like a dramatic shift for the king of coffee, Starbucks is confident that this new fare is right on target for the somewhat snooty Starbuck's foodie.

By comparison, Dunkin' Donuts operates 7,000 U.S. shops in 36 states, grabbing about 16 percent of the market. Having started as a New England chain in the 1950s, it still has only 75 locations west of the Mississippi River. This means that there

are plenty of folks out there who fit the Dunkin' Donuts tribe profile who aren't yet getting their fix. So Dunkin' can expand by simply moving westward with what it's been doing so well in the East—serving up quality coffee and snacks in a no-frills atmosphere. Dunkin' plans to more than double its number of U.S. locations to 15,000 by 2020. To boost growth even further, Dunkin' has continued to expand its menu beyond breakfast items, adding basic fare ranging from sandwiches served on croissants and French rolls to signature Coolattas and gourmet cookies. Beer, wine, and focaccia? Not anytime soon.

In refreshing its positioning, Dunkin' Donuts has stayed true to the needs and preferences of the Dunkin' tribe. Dunkin' is "not going after the Starbucks coffee snob," says one analyst, it's "going after the average Joe." So far so good. For six years running, Dunkin' Donuts has ranked number one in the coffee category in a leading customer loyalty survey, ahead of number two Starbucks. According to the survey, Dunkin' Donuts was the top brand for consistently meeting or exceeding customer expectations with respect to taste, quality, and customer service. This feat is even more notable considering that Dunkin' only recently launched its first real loyalty program.

Dunkin' Donuts' positioning and value proposition are pretty well summed up in its popular ad slogan "America Runs on Dunkin'." The latest ads show actual customers picked as part of a nationwide casting call, responding to the simple question: "What are you drinkin'?" The answer: "I'm drinkin' Dunkin'." The campaign focuses on real Dunkin' Donuts customers and their love affair with Dunkin' coffee. "We remain committed to keeping America running with our great coffee, baked goods, and snacks served in a friendly environment at a great value," says Dunkin's Chief Global Marketing Officer. Nothing too fancy—just meeting the everyday needs of the Dunkin' tribe.[1]

> Starbucks is strongly positioned as a sort of high-brow "third place"; Dunkin' has a decidedly more low-brow, "everyman" kind of positioning. Dunkin's "not going after the Starbucks coffee snob," it's "going after the average Joe."
> © Bumper DeJesus/Star Ledger/Corbis

Objective Outline

Objective 1	**Define the major steps in designing a customer-driven marketing strategy: market segmentation, targeting, differentiation, and positioning.** **Customer-Driven Marketing Strategy** (pp 192–193)
Objective 2	**List and discuss the major bases for segmenting consumer and business markets.** **Market Segmentation** (pp 193–202)
Objective 3	**Explain how companies identify attractive market segments and choose a market-targeting strategy.** **Market Targeting** (pp 202–210)
Objective 4	**Discuss how companies differentiate and position their products for maximum competitive advantage.** **Differentiation and Positioning** (pp 210–216)

MyMarketingLab™

✪ Improve Your Grade!

Over 10 million students improved their results using the Pearson MyLabs. Visit **mymktlab.com** for simulations, tutorials, and end-of-chapter problems.

Objective 1 ┈┈➤

Define the major steps in designing a customer-driven marketing strategy.

Market segmentation
Dividing a market into smaller segments of buyers with distinct needs, characteristics, or behaviors that might require separate marketing strategies or mixes.

Market targeting (targeting)
Evaluating each market segment's attractiveness and selecting one or more segments to enter.

Differentiation
Differentiating the market offering to create superior customer value.

Positioning
Arranging for a market offering to occupy a clear, distinctive, and desirable place relative to competing products in the minds of target consumers.

Companies today recognize that they cannot appeal to all buyers in the marketplace—or at least not to all buyers in the same way. Buyers are too numerous, widely scattered, and varied in their needs and buying practices. Moreover, companies themselves vary widely in their abilities to serve different market segments. Instead, like Dunkin' Donuts, companies must identify the parts of the market they can serve best and most profitably. They must design customer-driven marketing strategies that build the right relationships with the right customers.

Thus, most companies have moved away from mass marketing and toward *target marketing*: identifying market segments, selecting one or more of them, and developing products and marketing programs tailored to each. Instead of scattering their marketing efforts (the "shotgun" approach), firms are focusing on the buyers who have greater interest in the values they create best (the "rifle" approach).

● **Figure 7.1** shows the four major steps in designing a customer-driven marketing strategy. In the first two steps, the company selects the customers that it will serve. **Market segmentation** involves dividing a market into smaller segments of buyers with distinct needs, characteristics, or behaviors that might require separate marketing strategies or mixes. The company identifies different ways to segment the market and develops profiles of the resulting market segments. **Market targeting** (or **targeting**) consists of evaluating each market segment's attractiveness and selecting one or more market segments to enter.

In the final two steps, the company decides on a value proposition—how it will create value for target customers. **Differentiation** involves actually differentiating the firm's market offering to create superior customer value. **Positioning** consists of arranging for a market offering to occupy a clear, distinctive, and desirable place relative to competing products in the minds of target consumers. We discuss each of these steps in turn.

● FIGURE | 7.1
Designing a Customer-Driven Marketing Strategy

In concept, marketing boils
down to two questions:
(1) Which customers will we
serve? and (2) How will we
serve them? Of course, the
tough part is coming up with
good answers to these simple-
sounding yet difficult questions.
The goal is to create more
value for the customers we
serve than competitors do.

Select customers to serve

Segmentation
Divide the total market into
smaller segments

Targeting
Select the segment or
segments to enter

**Create value
for targeted
customers**

Decide on a value proposition

Differentiation
Differentiate the market offering
to create superior customer value

Positioning
Position the market offering in
the minds of target customers

Objective 2 ·····▶
**List and discuss the major bases
for segmenting consumer and
business markets.**

Market Segmentation

Buyers in any market differ in their wants, resources, locations, buying attitudes, and
buying practices. Through market segmentation, companies divide large, heterogeneous
markets into smaller segments that can be reached more efficiently and effectively with
products and services that match their unique needs. In this section, we discuss four important segmentation topics: segmenting consumer markets, segmenting business markets,
segmenting international markets, and the requirements for effective segmentation.

Segmenting Consumer Markets

There is no single way to segment a market. A marketer has to try different segmenta-
tion variables, alone and in combination, to find the best way to view market structure.
● **Table 7.1** outlines variables that might be used in segmenting consumer markets.
Here we look at the major *geographic, demographic, psychographic,* and *behavioral* variables.

Geographic Segmentation

Geographic segmentation
Dividing a market into different
geographical units, such as nations,
states, regions, counties, cities, or even
neighborhoods.

Geographic segmentation calls for dividing the market into different geographical
units, such as nations, regions, states, counties, cities, or even neighborhoods. A company
may decide to operate in one or a few geographical areas or operate in all areas but pay attention to geographical differences in needs and wants.

Many companies today are localizing their products, advertising, promotion, and
sales efforts to fit the needs of individual regions, cities, and neighborhoods. For example, Domino's Pizza is the nation's largest pizza delivery chain. But a customer ordering a
pizza in Poughkeepsie, New York, doesn't care much about what's happening pizza-wise in
Anaheim, California. So Domino's keeps its marketing and customer focus decidedly local.
● Hungry customers anywhere in the nation can use the pizza peddler's online platform
or smartphone app to track down local coupon offers, locate the nearest store with a GPS

● **Table 7.1** | **Major Segmentation Variables
for Consumer Markets**

Segmentation Variable	Examples
Geographic	Nations, regions, states, counties, cities, neighborhoods, population density (urban, suburban, rural), climate
Demographic	Age, life-cycle stage, gender, income, occupation, education, religion, ethnicity, generation
Psychographic	Social class, lifestyle, personality
Behavioral	Occasions, benefits, user status, usage rate, loyalty status

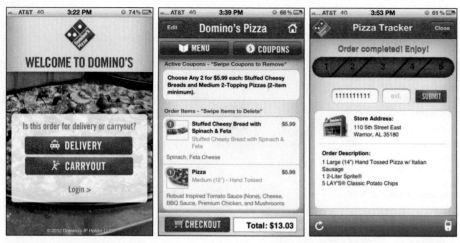

Geographic segmentation: Domino's keeps its marketing and customer focus decidedly local. Hungry customers anywhere can use the pizza peddler's smartphone app to locate the nearest store, order a pizza locally, and even track their pies store to door.

Dominos Pizza LLC

store locator, and quickly receive a freshly made pizza. They can even use Domino's Pizza Tracker to follow their pies locally from store to door.[2]

Similarly, Macy's, the nation's second-largest department-store chain, has rolled out a localization program called MyMacy's in which merchandise is customized under 69 different districts. At stores around the country, Macy's sales clerks record local shopper requests and pass them along to district managers. In turn, blending the customer requests with store transaction data, the district managers customize the mix of merchandise in their stores. So, for example, Macy's stores in Michigan stock more locally made Sanders chocolate candies. In Orlando, Macy's carries more swimsuits in stores near waterparks, and more twin bedding in stores near condominium rentals. The chain stocks extra coffee percolators in its Long Island stores, where it sells more of the 1960s must-haves than anywhere else in the country. In all, the "MyMacy's" strategy is to meet the needs of local markets, making the giant retailer seem smaller and more in touch.[3]

Demographic Segmentation

Demographic segmentation
Dividing the market into segments based on variables such as age, life-cycle stage, gender, income, occupation, education, religion, ethnicity, and generation.

Demographic segmentation divides the market into segments based on variables such as age, life-cycle stage, gender, income, occupation, education, religion, ethnicity, and generation. Demographic factors are the most popular bases for segmenting customer groups. One reason is that consumer needs, wants, and usage rates often vary closely with demographic variables. Another is that demographic variables are easier to measure than most other types of variables. Even when marketers first define segments using other bases, such as benefits sought or behavior, they must know a segment's demographic characteristics to assess the size of the target market and reach it efficiently.

Age and life-cycle segmentation
Dividing a market into different age and life-cycle groups.

Age and Life-Cycle Stage. Consumer needs and wants change with age. Some companies use **age and life-cycle segmentation**, offering different products or using different marketing approaches for different age and life-cycle groups. For example, Kraft promotes JELL-O to children as a fun snack, one that "taught the world to wiggle." For adults, it's a tasty, guilt-free indulgence—"the most sweet-tooth satisfaction 10 calories can hold."

Other companies offer brands that target specific age or life-stage groups. For example, the Kia Soul targets young Millennial consumers. It's an entry-level vehicle with a price to match. Kia Soul "Hamstar" ads have a distinctly youthful appeal, featuring a trio of hamsters cruising through an apocalyptic landscape accompanied by an infectious soundtrack, such as LMFAO's "Party Rock Anthem." In contrast, the Toyota Venza targets older empty nesters. Venza commercials feature clueless, self-absorbed 20-somethings who don't quite get that their Venza-owning parents—who are out leading their own active lives—don't really miss them.[4]

Life-cycle segmentation: The youthful Kia Soul "Hamstar" ads target Millennials, offering an entry-level vehicle with a price to match.

KIA Motors America

Marketers must be careful to guard against stereotypes when using age and life-cycle segmentation. Although some 80-year-olds fit the doddering stereotypes, others ski and play tennis. Similarly, whereas some 40-year-old couples are sending their children off to college, others are just beginning new families. Thus, age is often a poor predictor of a person's life cycle, health, work or family status, needs, and buying power.

Gender segmentation

Dividing a market into different segments based on gender.

Gender. **Gender segmentation** has long been used in clothing, cosmetics, toiletries, and magazines. For example, P&G was among the first to use gender segmentation with Secret, a brand specially formulated for a woman's chemistry, packaged and advertised to reinforce the female image. More recently, the men's cosmetics industry has exploded, and many cosmetics makers that previously catered primarily to women now successfully market men's lines. Just don't call them "cosmetics."[5]

L'Oréal's Men's Expert line includes a host of products with decidedly unmanly names such as Men's Expert Vita Lift SPF 15 Anti-Wrinkle & Firming Moisturizer and Men's Expert Hydra-Energetic Ice Cold Eye Roller (for diminishing under-eye dark circles). Other brands, however, try to craft more masculine positions. For example, Mënaji promises "Skincare for the Confident Man." Manly men such as Tim McGraw and Kid Rock use it. ● Mënaji products come in discreet packaging such as old cigar boxes, and the line's "undetectable" foundation and concealer (or rather "Camo") come in easy-to-apply Chap Stick-style containers. Mënaji founder Michele Probst doesn't call any of it makeup. "The M word is cancer to us," she says. "We are skin care that looks good." Whatever you call it, Mënaji sales have grown 70 percent in each of the past 4 years.

Similarly, Unilever's testosterone-heavy male body spray brand, Axe, is now waking up to new gender segments. It recently released a new scent, Anarchy, marketed in different versions to both men and women. Nearly one-quarter of Axe's 2.6 million Facebook and Twitter fans are women, and Unilever's research suggested that these women have been wanting an Axe scent of their very own. Past Axe commercials have featured young men spraying the brand on themselves to gain an edge in the mating game. "Now women also have something to spray on themselves," notes an Axe marketer, creating "more of an equilibrium between the sexes."[6]

Income segmentation

Dividing a market into different income segments.

Income. The marketers of products and services such as automobiles, clothing, cosmetics, financial services, and travel have long used **income segmentation**. Many companies target affluent consumers with luxury goods and convenience services. Other marketers use high-touch marketing programs to court the well-to-do:[7]

Seadream Yacht Club, a small-ship luxury cruise line, calls select guests after every cruise and offers to have the CEO fly out to their home and host, at Seadream's expense, a brunch or reception for a dozen of the couple's best friends. The cruisers tell the story of their cruise. Seadream offers a great rate to their guests and sells several cruises at $1,000 per person per night to the friends (and even friends of friends). Such highly personal marketing creates a community of "brand evangelists" who tell the story to prospective affluent buyers and friends—precisely the right target group. This has been so successful for Seadream that it has abandoned most traditional advertising.

● Gender segmentation: Many cosmetics makers now successfully market men's lines. Mënaji tells men to "Put your best face forward."

Mënaji Skincare LLC

However, not all companies that use income segmentation target the affluent. For example, many retailers—such as the Dollar General, Family Dollar, and Dollar Tree store chains—successfully target low- and middle-income groups. The core market for such stores is represented by families with incomes under $30,000. When Family Dollar real estate experts scout locations for new stores, they look for lower-middle-class neighborhoods where people wear less-expensive shoes and drive old cars that drip a lot of oil. With their low-income strategies, dollar stores are now the fastest-growing retailers in the nation.

Psychographic Segmentation

Psychographic segmentation

Dividing a market into different segments based on social class, lifestyle, or personality characteristics.

Psychographic segmentation divides buyers into different segments based on social class, lifestyle, or personality characteristics. People in the same demographic group can have very different psychographic characteristics.

In Chapter 5, we discussed how the products people buy reflect their *lifestyles*. As a result, marketers often segment their markets by consumer lifestyles and base their marketing strategies on lifestyle appeals. For example, retailer Anthropologie, with its whimsical, French flea market store atmosphere, sells a Bohemian-chic lifestyle to which its young women customers aspire. And although W Hotels books out hotel rooms by the night, just like any other hotel chain, it doesn't see itself as a hotel company. Instead, it positions itself as "an iconic lifestyle brand," inviting guests to "step inside the worlds of design, music, and fashion." (See Real Marketing 7.1.)

● VF Corporation offers a closet full of more than 30 premium lifestyle brands that "fit the lives of consumers the world over, from commuters to cowboys, surfers to soccer moms, sports fans to rock bands."[8]

● **Differentiated marketing: VF Corporation offers a closet full of over 30 premium lifestyle brands, each of which "taps into consumer aspirations to fashion, status, and well-being" in a well-defined segment.**
VF Corporation

VF is the nation's number-one jeans maker, with brands such as Lee, Riders, Rustler, and Wrangler. But jeans are not the only focus for VF. The company's brands are carefully separated into five major lifestyle segments—Jeanswear, Imagewear (workwear), Outdoor and Action Sports, Sportswear, and Contemporary. The North Face and Timberland brands, both part of the Outdoor unit, offer top-of-the-line gear and apparel for outdoor enthusiasts. From the Sportswear unit, Nautica focuses on people who enjoy high-end casual apparel inspired by sailing and the sea. Vans began as a skate shoemaker, and Reef features surf-inspired footwear and apparel. In the Contemporary unit, Lucy features upscale active-wear, whereas 7 for All Mankind supplies premium denim and accessories sold in boutiques and high-end department stores such as Saks and Nordstrom. At the other end of the spectrum, Sentinel, part of the Imagewear unit, markets uniforms for security officers. No matter who you are, says the company, "We fit your life."

Marketers also use *personality* variables to segment markets. For example, different soft drinks target different personalities. On the one hand, Mountain Dew projects a youthful, rebellious, adventurous, go-your-own-way personality. Its ads remind customers that "It's different on the Mountain." By contrast, Coca-Cola Zero appears to target more mature, practical, and cerebral but good-humored personality types. Its subtly humorous ads promise "Real Coca-Cola taste and zero calories."

Real Marketing 7.1

W Hotels: Not Just a Room— It's a Trendsetter Lifestyle

You approach the glitzy, contemporary building in London, a 10-story structure encased in a translucent glass veil. Cameras mounted on the roof capture the surrounding skyline and project it onto the building's surface, creating a seamless blend of the building with its setting. Inside, you're greeted by thumping hip-hop music, large mirrored glitter balls, open fires, and a huge Chesterfield sofa that snakes around the lounge bar. You're in a nightclub perhaps, or the latest trendy restaurant. No, you're in the W London, a hotel that offers much more than just rooms for the night.

Starwood Hotels and Resorts operates nine different hotel chains, something for everyone you might say. But its W Hotels brand stands out from all the rest. In fact, W Hotels doesn't really think of itself as just a hotel chain. Instead, it positions itself as "an iconic lifestyle brand." More than just rooms, W Hotels prides itself on "offering guests unprecedented insider access to a world of 'Wow' through contemporary cool design, fashion, music, nightlife, and entertainment." W Hotels exudes a youthful, outgoing, jet-setting life style that fits its ultrahip, trendsetter clientele—mostly from the media, music, fashion, entertainment, and consulting industries. For these patrons, W provides an unmatched sense of belonging.

W Hotels' lifestyle positioning starts with unique design. Whereas most hotel chains churn out cookie-cutter locations in search of a consistent brand image, W Hotels's 54 properties worldwide look nothing alike. W's patrons view themselves as unique, so they demand the same from the hotels they choose. Every W Hotel projects a common "energetic, vibrant, forward-thinking attitude," and an appreciation for fashion, art, and music befitting its lifestyle image. But in terms of design, each W Hotel is "uniquely inspired by its destination, mixing cutting-edge design with local influences."

For example, the W Taipei in Taiwan, located in the Xinyi district near Taipei 101, the city's tallest skyscraper, is designed around the theme of "nature electrified," blending soft-wooden walls; geometric, box-shaped shelves; and lighting inspired by Chinese lanterns. The W Koh Samui (in Thailand), an all-villa beach resort, treats guests to the concept of "day and night"—relaxing by the pool by day and partying by night—with modern interiors accented by bright flashes of red, off-white terrazzo floors, and wooden decks for private guest pools. The W Bali features an "inside and outside" theme, with grass-like green pillows that bring a bit of outdoors into the rooms and bed headboards made from the skin of stingrays.

With each unique design, however, W maintains a consistent ambiance that leaves no question in guests' minds that they are living the W lifestyle. The W Paris, for example, blends the facade of its historic and elegant 1870s building with the theme of Paris as the "City of Light," all wrapped in W's signature contemporary energy:

> The hotel design revolves around an oversized backlit digital undulating wall that defines the central core of the building and weaves through the public and private spaces. "Our design feeds off the elegance, richness, and radiance of Paris . . . and W's DNA for infusing a sense of energy" says the head of the hotel's design group. In true W fashion, it brings the historic building to life with a glowing vibrancy.

But unique design is only part of W Hotels' lifestyle formula. The brand also bridges connections with the worlds of fashion, music, and art. For example, the chain acquired a fashion director, Jenné Lombardo, who has been hosting cutting-edge fashion events in New York for years. Lombardo heads up W's ongoing *Fashion Next* program, which forges relationships with up-and-coming designers. W sponsors the young design talent by paying for fees and space at major runway events, supplying a W DJ to help with music, and providing hair and makeup, catering, and other services. In return, the designers participate in shows, art exhibitions, luncheons, and other events that attract fashion-conscious guests at W hotels around the world. Such events provide "insider access" for W's patrons, contributing further to the hotel's lifestyle appeal.

W Hotels works with music in the same way that it works with fashion. Under the direction of a global music director, W's long-running *Symmetry Live* concert series offers guests access to exclusive performances by some of the world's hottest, just-discovered acts, such as Cee Lo Green, Janelle Monae, Ellie Goulding, and Theophilus London. This year, W is sponsoring an exclusive traveling exhibition, called *ROCKED*, shot and curated by legendary music photographer Mick Rock. The exhibit features behind-the-scenes portraits and the on-stage theatrics of emerging artists who have performed as part of the Symmetry Live series, alongside Rock's iconic photographs of David Bowie, Debbie Harry, Queen, and Iggy Pop and never-before-exhibited images of such super talents as Bono, Madonna, Freddie Mercury, and Lady Gaga. "If music is in your DNA, like it is in ours," says a W Hotels brand manager, "this show is not to be missed."

Lifestyle segmentation: W Hotels positions itself as "an iconic lifestyle brand," inviting guests to "step inside the worlds of design, music, and fashion."

©VIEW Pictures Ltd/Alamy

Beyond its passion for art, fashion, and entertainment, as you might expect, another constant at W Hotels is first-class service— what W calls "Whatever-Whenever" service. "We aim to provide whatever, whenever, as long as it is legal—something that is very much consistent throughout the W brand," explains one W Hotel manager. W Hotels don't have concierges; instead, they have "W Insiders." The Insiders go a step beyond. Rather than waiting to be asked for advice, they proactively seek out things they can do to enhance the stay of each guest. In keeping with the brand's lifestyle positioning, insiders stay in tune with special need-to-know happenings and advise guests on all the latest places to see and be seen.

Adding even more luster to W's lifestyle allure, the chain's hotels attract a star-studded list of celebrities. The W South Beach in Miami, for example, in addition to its modern art collection, is known for guests like Sean Penn and Leonardo DiCaprio. The hotel has a basketball court where NBA players are often seen shooting hoops. LeBron James held a party there after announcing that he was taking his "talents to South Beach," and Dwyane Wade celebrates birthdays there. New York Knicks forward Amar'e Stoudemire and Italian soccer sensation Alessandro Nesta paid millions to become residents of the elite W South Beach property.

Staying at a W Hotel isn't cheap. The basic W room runs about $450 a night, with top suites running up to five figures. But a W Hotel isn't just a place where you rent a room and get a good night's sleep. It's the design of the place, the contemporary ambiance, what's hanging on the walls, the music that's playing, the other guests who stay there—all of these things contribute mightily to the W's lifestyle positioning and allure to its young, hip, upscale W clientele. It's not just a room, it's part of an entire trendsetter lifestyle.

Sources: Janet Harmer, "W London—A Hotel That Dares to Be Different," *Caterer & Hotelkeeper*, March 4–10, 2011, pp. 26–28; Nancy Keates, "The Home Front: His Hotel, His Hangout," *Wall Street Journal*, June 3, 2011, p. D6; Christina Binkley, "Putting the Hot Back in Hotel," *Wall Street Journal*, August 18, 2011, accessed at http://online.wsj.com/article/SB10001424053111903596904576514293384502896.html; "W Hotels Unveils Innovative Design Concept of the Soon-to-Open W Paris-Opéra by Acclaimed Rockwell Group Europe," Starwood press release, December 14, 2011, http://development.starwoodhotels.com/news/7/336-w_hotels_unveils_innovative_design_concept_of_the_soon-to-open_w_paris-opera_by_acclaimed_rockwell_group_europe; and information and press releases from www.starwoodhotels.com/whotels/about/index.html, accessed September, 2012.

Behavioral Segmentation

Behavioral segmentation

Dividing a market into segments based on consumer knowledge, attitudes, uses, or responses to a product.

Behavioral segmentation divides buyers into segments based on their knowledge, attitudes, uses, or responses concerning a product. Many marketers believe that behavior variables are the best starting point for building market segments.

Occasions. Buyers can be grouped according to occasions when they get the idea to buy, actually make their purchase, or use the purchased item. **Occasion segmentation** can help firms build up product usage. Campbell's advertises its soups more heavily in the cold winter months, and Home Depot runs special springtime promotions for lawn and garden products. Other marketers prepare special offers and ads for holiday occasions. For example, M&M's runs ads throughout the year but prepares special ads and packaging for holidays and events such as Christmas, Easter, and the Super Bowl.

Occasion segmentation

Dividing the market into segments according to occasions when buyers get the idea to buy, actually make their purchase, or use the purchased item.

Still other companies try to boost consumption by promoting usage during nontraditional occasions. For example, most consumers drink orange juice in the morning, but orange growers have promoted drinking orange juice as a cool, healthful refresher at other times of the day. And Chick-fil-A's "Chikin 4 Brekfust" campaign attempts to increase business by promoting its biscuits and other sandwiches as a great way to start the day.

Benefits Sought. A powerful form of segmentation is grouping buyers according to the different *benefits* that they seek from a product. **Benefit segmentation** requires finding the major benefits people look for in a product class, the kinds of people who look for each benefit, and the major brands that deliver each benefit.

Benefit segmentation

Dividing the market into segments according to the different benefits that consumers seek from the product.

For example, Gillette research revealed four distinct benefit segments of women shavers—perfect shave seekers (seeking a close shave with no missed hairs), EZ seekers (fast and convenient shaves), skin pamperers (easy on the skin), and pragmatic functionalists (basic shaves at an affordable price). So Gillette designed Venus razors for each segment. The Venus Embrace targets perfect shave seekers with five curve-hugging, spring-mounted blades that "hug every curve to get virtually every hair." By contrast, the Venus Breeze is made for EZ seekers—its built-in shave gel bars lather and shave in one step, so there's no need for separate shave gel. The Venus Divine gives skin pamperers "intensive moisture strips for divinely smooth skin"; the Venus & Olay gives them "moisture bars that release skin conditioners to help lock in moisture." And the Simply Venus, a three-bladed disposable razor, provides pragmatic functionalists with "a close shave at an affordable price."[9]

User Status. Markets can be segmented into nonusers, ex-users, potential users, first-time users, and regular users of a product. Marketers want to reinforce and retain regular users, attract targeted nonusers, and reinvigorate relationships with ex-users. Included in the potential users group are consumers facing life-stage changes—such as new parents and newlyweds—who can be turned into heavy users. For example, to get new parents off to the right start, P&G makes certain its Pampers Swaddlers are the diaper provided for newborns at most U.S. hospitals. And to capture newly engaged couples who will soon be equipping their new kitchens, upscale kitchen and cookware retailer Williams-Sonoma takes the usual bridal registry a step further. Through a program called "The Store Is Yours," it opens its stores after hours, by appointment, exclusively for individual couples to visit and make their wish lists. About half the people who register are new to the Williams-Sonoma brand.

Usage Rate. Markets can also be segmented into light, medium, and heavy product users. Heavy users are often a small percentage of the market but account for a high percentage of total consumption. For instance, a recent study showed that heavy seafood consumers in the United States are a small but hungry bunch. Less than 5 percent of all shoppers buy nearly 64 percent of unbreaded seafood consumed in the United States. Only 2.6 percent of shoppers—mostly mothers buying breaded fish sticks and filets for their families—account for more than 54 percent of breaded seafood sales. Not surprisingly, breaded seafood marketers such as Gortons and Van de Kamps target these heavy users with marketing pitches emphasizing kid appeal, family nutrition, and family meal planning tips and recipes.[10]

Loyalty Status. A market can also be segmented by consumer loyalty. Consumers can be loyal to brands (Tide), stores (Target), and companies (Apple). Buyers can be divided into groups according to their degree of loyalty. Some consumers are completely loyal—they buy one brand all the time and can't wait to tell others about it. For example, whether they own a Mac computer, an iPhone, or an iPad, Apple devotees are granite-like in their devotion to the brand. At one end are the quietly satisfied Mac users, folks who own a Mac and use it for e-mail, browsing, and social networking. ● At the other extreme, however, are the Mac zealots—the so-called MacHeads or Macolytes—who can't wait to tell anyone within earshot of their latest Apple gadget. Such loyal Apple devotees helped keep Apple afloat during the lean years, and they are now at the forefront of Apple's burgeoning iPod, iTunes, and iPad empire.[11]

Other consumers are somewhat loyal—they are loyal to two or three brands of a given product or favor one brand while sometimes buying others. Still other buyers show no loyalty to any brand—they either want something different each time they buy, or they buy whatever's on sale.

A company can learn a lot by analyzing loyalty patterns in its market. It should start by studying its own loyal customers. A recent study of highly loyal customers showed that "their passion is contagious," says an analyst. "They promote the brand via blogs, fan Web sites, YouTube videos, and word of mouth." Some companies actually put loyalists to work for the brand. For example, Patagonia relies on its most tried-and-true customers to test products in harsh environments.[12] In contrast, by studying its less-loyal buyers, a company can detect which brands are most competitive with its own. By looking at customers who are shifting away from its brand, the company can learn about its marketing weaknesses and take actions to correct them.

● **Consumer loyalty: "Mac Fanatics"—fanatically loyal Apple users—helped keep Apple afloat during the lean years, and they are now at the forefront of Apple's burgeoning iPod, iTunes, and iPad empire.**

Doug Hardman

Using Multiple Segmentation Bases

Marketers rarely limit their segmentation analysis to only one or a few variables. Rather, they often use multiple segmentation bases in an effort to identify smaller, better-defined target groups. Several business information services—such as Nielsen, Acxiom, and Experian—provide multivariable segmentation systems that merge geographic, demographic, lifestyle, and behavioral data to help companies segment their markets down to zip codes, neighborhoods, and even households.

One of the leading segmentation systems is the Nielsen PRIZM system operated by The Nielsen Company. ● PRIZM classifies every American household based on a host of demographic factors—such as age, educational level, income, occupation, family composition, ethnicity, and housing—and behavioral and lifestyle factors—such as purchases, free-time activities, and media preferences. PRIZM classifies U.S. households into 66 demographically and behaviorally distinct segments, organized into 14 different social groups. PRIZM segments carry such exotic names as "Kids & Cul-de-Sacs," "Gray Power," "Mayberry-ville," "Shotguns & Pickups," "Old Glories," "Multi-Culti Mosaic," "Big City Blues," and "Brite Lites L'il City." The colorful names help to bring the segments to life.[13]

● Using Nielsen's PRIZM system, marketers can paint a surprisingly precise picture of who you are and what you might buy. PRIZM segments carry such exotic names as "Brite Lites, L'il City," "Kids & Cul-de-Sacs," "Gray Power," and "Big City Blues."

PRIZM is a trademark or registered trademark of Nielsen Holdings (US), LLC.

PRIZM and other such systems can help marketers segment people and locations into marketable groups of like-minded consumers. Each segment has its own pattern of likes, dislikes, lifestyles, and purchase behaviors. For example, *Winner's Circle* neighborhoods, part of the Elite Suburbs social group, are suburban areas populated by well-off couples, between the ages of 35 and 54, with large families in new-money neighborhoods. People in this segment are more likely to own a Mercedes GL Class, go jogging, shop at Neiman Marcus, and read the *Wall Street Journal*. In contrast, the *Bedrock America* segment, part of the Rustic Living social group, is populated by young, economically challenged families in small, isolated towns located throughout the nation's heartland. People in this segment are more likely to order from Avon, buy toy cars, and read *Parents Magazine*.

Such segmentation provides a powerful tool for marketers of all kinds. It can help companies identify and better understand key customer segments, reach them more efficiently, and tailor market offerings and messages to their specific needs.

Segmenting Business Markets

Consumer and business marketers use many of the same variables to segment their markets. Business buyers can be segmented geographically, demographically (industry, company size), or by benefits sought, user status, usage rate, and loyalty status. Yet, business marketers also use some additional variables, such as customer *operating characteristics*, *purchasing approaches*, *situational factors*, and *personal characteristics*.

Almost every company serves at least some business markets. For example, Starbucks has developed distinct marketing programs for each of its two business segments: the office coffee and food service segments. In the office coffee and vending segment, Starbucks Office Coffee Solutions markets a variety of workplace coffee services to businesses of any size, helping them to make Starbucks coffee and related products available to their employees in their workplaces. Starbucks helps these business customers design the best office solutions involving its coffees (the Starbucks or Seattle's Best brands), teas (Tazo), syrups, and branded paper products and methods of serving them—portion packs, single cups, or vending. The Starbucks Foodservice division teams up with businesses and other organizations—ranging from airlines, restaurants, colleges, and hospitals to baseball stadiums—to help them serve the well-known Starbucks brand to their own customers. Starbucks provides not only the coffee, tea, and paper products to its food service partners, but also equipment, training, and marketing and merchandising support.[14]

Many companies establish separate systems for dealing with larger or multiple-location customers. For example, Steelcase, a major producer of office furniture, first divides customers into seven segments: biosciences, higher education, U.S. and Canadian governments, state and local governments, health care, professional services, and retail banking. Next, company salespeople work with independent Steelcase dealers to handle smaller, local, or regional Steelcase customers in each segment. But many national, multiple-location customers, such as ExxonMobil or IBM, have special needs that may reach beyond the scope of individual dealers. Therefore, Steelcase uses national account managers to help its dealer networks handle national accounts.

Segmenting International Markets

Few companies have either the resources or the will to operate in all, or even most, of the countries that dot the globe. Although some large companies, such as Coca-Cola or Sony, sell products in more than 200 countries, most international firms focus on a smaller set. Operating in many countries presents new challenges. Different countries, even those that are close together, can vary greatly in their economic, cultural, and political makeup. Thus, just as they do within their domestic markets, international firms need to group their world markets into segments with distinct buying needs and behaviors.

Companies can segment international markets using one or a combination of several variables. They can segment by *geographic location*, grouping countries by regions such as Western Europe, the Pacific Rim, the Middle East, or Africa. Geographic segmentation assumes that nations close to one another will have many common traits and behaviors. Although this is often the case, there are many exceptions. For example, some U.S. marketers lump all Central and South American countries together. However, the Dominican Republic is no more like Brazil than Italy is like Sweden. Many Central and South Americans don't even speak Spanish, including more than 200 million Portuguese-speaking Brazilians and the millions in other countries who speak a variety of Indian dialects.

World markets can also be segmented based on *economic factors*. Countries might be grouped by population income levels or by their overall level of economic development. A country's economic structure shapes its population's product and service needs and, therefore, the marketing opportunities it offers. For example, many companies are now targeting the BRIC countries—Brazil, Russia, India, and China—which are fast-growing developing economies with rapidly increasing buying power.

Countries can also be segmented by *political and legal factors* such as the type and stability of government, receptivity to foreign firms, monetary regulations, and amount of bureaucracy. *Cultural factors* can also be used, grouping markets according to common languages, religions, values and attitudes, customs, and behavioral patterns.

Segmenting international markets based on geographic, economic, political, cultural, and other factors presumes that segments should consist of clusters of countries. However, as new communications technologies, such as satellite TV and the Internet, connect consumers around the world, marketers can define and reach segments of like-minded consumers no matter where in the world they are. Using **intermarket segmentation** (also called **cross-market segmentation**), they form segments of consumers who have similar needs and buying behaviors even though they are located in different countries.

Intermarket (cross-market) segmentation

Forming segments of consumers who have similar needs and buying behaviors even though they are located in different countries.

For example, Lexus targets the world's well-to-do—the "global elite" segment—regardless of their country. ● Retailer H&M targets fashion-conscious but frugal shoppers in 43 countries with its low-priced, trendy apparel and accessories. And Coca-Cola creates special programs to target teens, core consumers of its soft drinks the world over. By 2020, one-third of the world's population—some 2.5 billion people—will be under 18 years of age. To reach this important global segment, Coca-Cola recently launched the Coca-Cola Music campaign in more than 100 markets.

Intermarket segmentation: Retailer H&M targets fashion-conscious but frugal shoppers in 43 countries with its low-priced, trendy apparel and accessories.

REUTERS/Toru Hanai

The campaign opened with "24hr Session," in which singing group Maroon 5 holed up in a London studio for 24 hours to create a new original song. Young consumers worldwide attended the studio session virtually, sharing their ideas for lyrics and rhythms. Coca-Cola extended these efforts to engage the world's teens with a "Move to the Beat" campaign centered on the London 2012 Olympics, inspired by the sounds, spirit, and culture of the host city. "The number one passion point for teens is music," says a Coca-Cola global marketing executive. Says Coca-Cola's CEO: "Our success . . . today depends on our ability to grow and connect with teens, the generation of tomorrow."[15]

Requirements for Effective Segmentation

Clearly, there are many ways to segment a market, but not all segmentations are effective. For example, buyers of table salt could be divided into blonde and brunette customers. But hair color obviously does not affect the purchase of salt. Furthermore, if all salt buyers bought the same amount of salt each month, believed that all salt is the same, and wanted to pay the same price, the company would not benefit from segmenting this market.

To be useful, market segments must be

- *Measurable:* The size, purchasing power, and profiles of the segments can be measured.
- *Accessible:* The market segments can be effectively reached and served.
- *Substantial:* The market segments are large or profitable enough to serve. A segment should be the largest possible homogeneous group worth pursuing with a tailored marketing program. It would not pay, for example, for an automobile manufacturer to develop cars especially for people whose height is greater than seven feet.
- *Differentiable:* The segments are conceptually distinguishable and respond differently to different marketing mix elements and programs. If men and women respond similarly to marketing efforts for soft drinks, they do not constitute separate segments.
- *Actionable:* Effective programs can be designed for attracting and serving the segments. For example, although one small airline identified seven market segments, its staff was too small to develop separate marketing programs for each segment.

Objective 3 ⋯⋯➤

Explain how companies identify attractive market segments and choose a market-targeting strategy.

Market Targeting

Market segmentation reveals the firm's market segment opportunities. The firm now has to evaluate the various segments and decide how many and which segments it can serve best. We now look at how companies evaluate and select target segments.

Evaluating Market Segments

In evaluating different market segments, a firm must look at three factors: segment size and growth, segment structural attractiveness, and company objectives and resources. First, a company wants to select segments that have the right size and growth characteristics. But "right size and growth" is a relative matter. The largest, fastest-growing segments are not always the most attractive ones for every company. Smaller companies may lack the skills and resources needed to serve larger segments. Or they may find these segments too competitive. Such companies may target segments that are smaller and less attractive, in an absolute sense, but that are potentially more profitable for them.

The company also needs to examine major structural factors that affect long-run segment attractiveness.[16] For example, a segment is less attractive if it already contains many strong and aggressive *competitors* or if it is easy for *new entrants* to come into the segment. The existence of many actual or potential *substitute products* may limit prices and the profits that can be earned in a segment. The relative *power of buyers* also affects segment attractiveness. Buyers with strong bargaining power relative to sellers will try to force prices down, demand more services, and set competitors against one another—all at the expense of seller profitability. Finally, a segment may be less attractive if it contains *powerful suppliers* that can control prices or reduce the quality or quantity of ordered goods and services.

Even if a segment has the right size and growth and is structurally attractive, the company must consider its own objectives and resources. Some attractive segments can be dismissed quickly because they do not mesh with the company's long-run objectives. Or the company may lack the skills and resources needed to succeed in an attractive segment. For example, the economy segment of the automobile market is large and growing. But given its objectives and resources, it would make little sense for luxury-performance carmaker BMW to enter this segment. A company should only enter segments in which it can create superior customer value and gain advantages over its competitors.

Selecting Target Market Segments

Target market

A set of buyers sharing common needs or characteristics that the company decides to serve.

After evaluating different segments, the company must decide which and how many segments it will target. A **target market** consists of a set of buyers who share common needs or characteristics that the company decides to serve. Market targeting can be carried out at several different levels. ● **Figure 7.2** shows that companies can target very broadly (*undifferentiated marketing*), very narrowly (*micromarketing*), or somewhere in between (*differentiated or concentrated marketing*).

Undifferentiated Marketing

Undifferentiated (mass) marketing

A market-coverage strategy in which a firm decides to ignore market segment differences and go after the whole market with one offer.

Using an **undifferentiated marketing** (or **mass marketing**) strategy, a firm might decide to ignore market segment differences and target the whole market with one offer. Such a strategy focuses on what is *common* in the needs of consumers rather than on what is *different*. The company designs a product and a marketing program that will appeal to the largest number of buyers.

As noted earlier in the chapter, most modern marketers have strong doubts about this strategy. Difficulties arise in developing a product or brand that will satisfy all consumers. Moreover, mass marketers often have trouble competing with more-focused firms that do a better job of satisfying the needs of specific segments and niches.

Differentiated Marketing

Differentiated (segmented) marketing

A market-coverage strategy in which a firm decides to target several market segments and designs separate offers for each.

Using a **differentiated marketing** (or **segmented marketing**) strategy, a firm decides to target several market segments and designs separate offers for each. P&G markets six different laundry detergent brands in the United States (Bold, Cheer, Dash, Dreft, Gain, and Tide), which compete with each other on supermarket shelves. Then, P&G further segments each brand to serve even narrower niches. For example, you can buy any of a dozen or more versions of Tide—from Tide with Bleach, Tide Coldwater, or Tide HE (high efficiency) to Tide plus Febreze or Tide plus Downey.

Perhaps no brand practices differentiated marketing like Hallmark Cards.[17]

● **FIGURE** | **7.2**
Market Targeting Strategies

This figure covers a broad range of targeting strategies, from mass marketing (virtually no targeting) to individual marketing (customizing products and programs to individual customers). An example of individual marketing: At mymms.com you can order a batch of M&M's with your face and personal message printed on each little candy.

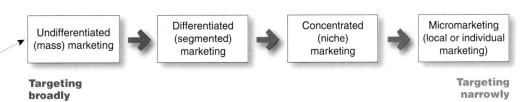

Undifferentiated (mass) marketing → Differentiated (segmented) marketing → Concentrated (niche) marketing → Micromarketing (local or individual marketing)

Targeting broadly

Targeting narrowly

● **Differentiated marketing: In addition to its broad Hallmark card line, Hallmark has introduced lines targeting a dozen or more specific segments, including its Mahogany, Tree of Life, and Sinceramente Hallmark lines shown here.**

Photo courtesy of Gary Armstrong

Hallmark vigorously segments the greeting card market. In addition to its broad Hallmark card line and popular sub-branded lines such as the humorous Shoebox Greetings, Hallmark has introduced lines targeting a dozen or more specific segments. Fresh Ink targets 18- to 39-year-old women. Hallmark Warm Wishes offers hundreds of affordable 99-cent cards. Hallmark's three ethnic lines—Mahogany, Sinceramente Hallmark, and Tree of Life—target African-American, Hispanic, and Jewish consumers, respectively. Hallmark's newer Journeys line of encouragement cards focuses on such challenges as fighting cancer, coming out, and battling depression. Specific greeting cards also benefit charities such as (PRODUCT) RED, UNICEF, and the Susan G. Komen Race for the Cure. Hallmark has also embraced technology. Musical greeting cards incorporate sound clips from popular movies, TV shows, and songs. Recordable storybooks let people record each page of a book and have it played back as the recipient turns the pages. Online, Hallmark offers e-cards as well as personalized printed greeting cards that it mails for consumers. For business needs, Hallmark Business Expressions offers personalized corporate holiday cards and greeting cards for all occasions and events.

By offering product and marketing variations to segments, companies hope for higher sales and a stronger position within each market segment. Developing a stronger position within several segments creates more total sales than undifferentiated marketing across all segments. Thanks to its differentiated approach, Hallmark's brands account for almost one of every two greeting cards purchased in the United States. Similarly, P&G's multiple detergent brands capture four times the market share of its nearest rival.

But differentiated marketing also increases the costs of doing business. A firm usually finds it more expensive to develop and produce, say, 10 units of 10 different products than 100 units of a single product. Developing separate marketing plans for separate segments requires extra marketing research, forecasting, sales analysis, promotion planning, and channel management. And trying to reach different market segments with different advertising campaigns increases promotion costs. Thus, the company must weigh increased sales against increased costs when deciding on a differentiated marketing strategy.

Concentrated Marketing

Concentrated (niche) marketing
A market-coverage strategy in which a firm goes after a large share of one or a few segments or niches.

When using a **concentrated marketing** (or **niche marketing**) strategy, instead of going after a small share of a large market, a firm goes after a large share of one or a few smaller segments or niches. For example, Whole Foods Market has more than 300 stores and over $10 billion in sales, compared with goliaths such as Kroger (more than 3,600 stores and sales of $82 billion) and Walmart (close to 9,000 stores and sales of $421 billion).[18] Yet, over the past five years, the smaller, more upscale retailer has grown faster and more profitably than either of its giant rivals. Whole Foods thrives by catering to affluent customers who the Walmarts of the world can't serve well, offering them "organic, natural, and gourmet foods, all swaddled in Earth Day politics." In fact, a typical Whole Foods customer is more likely to boycott the local Walmart than to shop at it.

Through concentrated marketing, the firm achieves a strong market position because of its greater knowledge of consumer needs in the niches it serves and the special reputation it acquires. It can market more *effectively* by fine-tuning its products, prices, and programs to the needs of carefully defined segments. It can also market more *efficiently*, targeting its products or services, channels, and communications programs toward only consumers that it can serve best and most profitably.

Niching lets smaller companies focus their limited resources on serving niches that may be unimportant to or overlooked by larger competitors. Many companies start as nichers to get a foothold against larger, more resourceful competitors and then grow into broader competitors. For example, Southwest Airlines began by serving intrastate, no-frills commuters in Texas but is now one of the nation's largest airlines. And Enterprise Rent-A-Car began by building a network of neighborhood offices rather than competing with Hertz and Avis in airport locations. Enterprise is now the nation's largest car rental company.

Today, the low cost of setting up shop on the Internet makes it even more profitable to serve seemingly miniscule niches. Small businesses, in particular, are realizing riches from serving small niches on the Web. ● Consider online women's clothing nicher Modcloth.com:[19]

> While her high-school classmates were out partying with friends or shopping at the mall, Susan Gregg Koger was squirreled away in her bedroom, sorting through vintage clothing she'd found at local thrift shops and dreaming up her own online business. At the tender age of 17, she and her boyfriend, now husband, Eric Koger, launched ModCloth.com out of their Carnegie Mellon dorm rooms. Despite these modest beginnings, thanks to the power of the Internet, the fledgling company soared. Today, only a decade later, ModCloth.com boasts more than 275 employees, 700 independent designers, and a closet full of one-of-a-kind finds. ModCloth.com's unique selection of indie clothing, engaging promotions on The ModCloth blog and various social networks, and Web interactivity—such as letting customers play a big role in selecting featured apparel and even its design direction—have attracted a devoted following. ModCloth's revenues have grown to more than $15 million a year and the site draws more than 2 million visitors per month.

● **Concentrated marketing: Thanks to the reach and power of online marketing, online women's clothing ModCloth.com has attracted a devoted following.**

Modcloth Inc.

Concentrated marketing can be highly profitable. At the same time, it involves higher-than-normal risks. Companies that rely on one or a few segments for all of their business will suffer greatly if the segment turns sour. Or larger competitors may decide to enter the same segment with greater resources. For these reasons, many companies prefer to diversify in several market segments.

Micromarketing

Differentiated and concentrated marketers tailor their offers and marketing programs to meet the needs of various market segments and niches. At the same time, however, they do not customize their offers to each individual customer. **Micromarketing** is the practice of tailoring products and marketing programs to suit the tastes of specific individuals and locations. Rather than seeing a customer in every individual, micromarketers see the individual in every customer. Micromarketing includes *local marketing* and *individual marketing*.

Micromarketing

Tailoring products and marketing programs to the needs and wants of specific individuals and local customer segments; it includes *local marketing* and *individual marketing*.

Local marketing

Tailoring brands and marketing to the needs and wants of local customer segments—cities, neighborhoods, and even specific stores.

Local Marketing. **Local marketing** involves tailoring brands and promotions to the needs and wants of local customer groups—cities, neighborhoods, and even specific stores. For example, Walgreens-owned New York City drugstore chain Duane Reade adapts its merchandise assortments to individual neighborhoods. In Manhattan, around Penn Station and the Port Authority, it sells sandwiches and quick lunches to the area's many office workers and commuters. On Wall Street, the Duane Reade features a sushi station, organic fresh foods, a shoeshine area, and a nail salon, all catering to an upscale market. In the Williamsburg neighborhood of Brooklyn—an area short on bars and beer-buying locations—Duane Reade stores sell an abundance of growlers and six-packs of microbrew beer.[20]

Advances in communications technology have given rise to new high-tech versions of location-based marketing. Using location-based social networks such as Foursquare or Shopkick and local-marketing deal-of-the-day services such as Groupon or LivingSocial, retailers can engage consumers with local online or mobile phone deals (see Real Marketing 7.2). Increasingly, location-based marketing is going mobile, reaching on-the-go consumers as they come and go in key local market areas.[21]

Real Marketing 7.2

Location-Based Micromarketing Equals Macro Opportunities

Marketers use a host of factors to target customers—from demographics and psychographics to detailed purchase histories. However, today's marketers are increasingly adding an important new targeting variable: location—where you are, right now. Thanks to the explosion in net-connected smartphones with GPS capabilities and location-based social networks, companies can now track your whereabouts closely and gear their offers accordingly.

Today's high-tech location-based marketing takes two major forms. One is mobile "check-in" services—such as Foursquare, Shopkick, and Loopt—where people check in on their smartphones to reveal their locations and obtain special retail offers. The other is "deal-of-the-day" Web marketers—such as Groupon and LivingSocial—that partner with local businesses to offer local shopping deals to subscribers based on where they live and what they like.

The location-based check-in services bridge the gap between the digital world and the real brick-and-mortar world. For example, Foursquare's location-based mobile app lets its more than 15 million users visit participating retail locations such as Starbucks or their favorite local pizza place, check in by pushing buttons on their mobile phones, and reap special rewards. That typically means discount e-coupons. But most check-in services add additional incentives with an addictive game-like twist. For example, Foursquare members compete to become the "mayor" of a given retail location by having the highest number of check-ins there, earn badges by checking in to specific locations, or gain status designations by making helpful contributions to the Foursquare community. And Scvngr designs smartphone-enabled scavenger hunts, granting discounts for completing certain tasks, such as taking in-store pictures.

But more than just passing out e-coupons and other rewards, Foursquare and the other check-in services are becoming full-fledged, location-based lifestyle networks. The aim is to enrich people's lives by helping them to learn the whereabouts of friends, share location-related experiences, and discover new places

all while linking them to sponsoring locations that match their interests.

Foursquare co-founder Dennis Crowley envisions a futuristic scenario in which your phone checks the calendars and locations of friends on a late Friday afternoon, learns whose available that evening, and suggests a nearby restaurant that everyone has wanted to try. It even notes what tables are available and the restaurant's dinner specials. Foursquare is getting closer and closer to making this scenario a reality. At its Web site, it already promises: "Foursquare makes the real world easier to use. Our app helps you keep up with friends, discover what's nearby, save money, and unlock deals."

Similarly, check-in service Loopt promises to add to both your social life and your shopping life. For starters, it provides a Friends Map that shows where your Loopt and Facebook friends are at any given time. It pairs your text messages with your location, making it really easy to meet up with others. Loopt can even send you a "Friend Alert" when an acquaintance is nearby, creating chance meetings that would otherwise go missed. Loopt can also alert you to nearby retail deals, helping you to

save money or get free stuff. Such check-in networks provide attractive targeting opportunities to retailers, letting them market to people on the go, when they're nearby and ready to eat, shop, and spend.

Such check-in networks provide attractive targeting opportunities to retailers, letting them market to people on the go, when they're nearby and ready to eat, shop, and spend.

The second major form of location-based marketing—"deal-of-the-day" Web sites—has become one of the hottest-ever Internet crazes. Among the thousands of deal-of-the-day services that have copied its model, market leader Groupon dominates with more than 150 million subscribers in hundreds of cities worldwide. Groupon partners with retailers in each city to craft attractive offers promoting their goods and services to area customers. Most of Groupon's local partners are small businesses, but global giants such as Starbucks, Best Buy, Barnes & Noble, Gap, and PepsiCo have also gotten into the Groupon act.

Groupon offers subscribers at least one deal each day in their city—such as paying $40 for an $80 voucher at a local restaurant. But the coupon deals kick in only if enough people sign up, encouraging subscribers to spread word of the deal to friends and neighbors and via social media such as Twitter and Facebook. Hence, the name Groupon—group plus coupon. When a deal "tips," Groupon shares the revenue roughly 50–50 with the retailer. Nearly all of Groupon's deals tip.

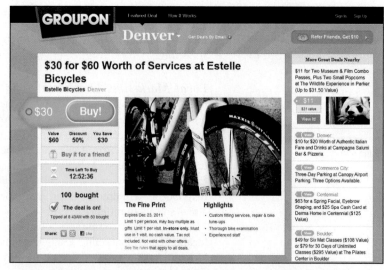

Location-based marketing: "Deal-of-the-day" Web marketers—such as Groupon—partner with local businesses to offer shopping deals to subscribers based on where they live and what they like.
Groupon Inc.

To further personalize its deals, the location-based marketer is now starting to incorporate factors such as gender, age, neighborhood, and a host of interests and preferences members can select in order to narrow the types of deals they receive. Groupon has also expanded its "deal-of-the-day" model to include Groupon Getaways (travel bargains), Groupon Goods (product deals from national brands), and Groupon Now (a mobile app that targets deals based on user location).

Working with Groupon can transform a local business in as little as 24 hours. For example, when the Joffrey Ballet in Chicago offered highly discounted season subscriptions through Groupon, 2,334 people signed up, doubling the performing group's subscription base in a single day. Sometimes, Groupon's deals can work too well. Retailer Gap's server crashed when 445,000 people bought $50 merchandise cards for only $25. Groupon works to minimize such cases by coaching businesses through the deal process and recommending appropriate deal caps.

Groupon may have entered Internet stardom faster than any other dot.com. Its average subscriber is a target marketer's dream: female, between the ages of 18 and 34, single, and making more than $70,000 a year. And Groupon is adding well over a million new members every week. Before Groupon was even two years old, *Forbes* crowned it "the fastest growing company ever." Its revenues have shot up from $14 million in 2009 to $1.6 billion last year, making it the youngest company of any kind to hit $1 billion in total revenue.

More generally, the growth of location-based services has been nothing short of astounding. Whereas no such companies even existed just five years ago, today there are more than 6,000 location-based iPhone apps alone. Perhaps the best indicator of the potential of location-based marketing is the arrival of the Web giants, each trying to capture a piece of the burgeoning location-based marketing action. Google and Facebook are actively experimenting with their own check-in and deal-of-the-day services, and Amazon .com owns a significant chunk of deal-of-the-day service LivingSocial.

With so much competition, the industry is currently working its way through growing pains, and a shake-out seems likely. But one thing is clear. When the dust settles, there will be macro potential for location-based micromarketing.

Sources: Based on quotes, extracts, and other information from Todd Wasserman, "Only 5% of Adults Use Location-Based Check-In Apps," *Mashable*, December 6, 2011, http://mashable.com/2011/12/06/adults-use-location-based-apps/; Diane Brady, "Social Media's New Mantra: Location, Location, Location," *Bloomberg Businessweek*, May 10–May 16, 2010, pp. 34–36; Bari Weiss, "Groupon's $6 Billion Gambler," *Wall Street Journal*, December 20, 2010, p. 12; Joseph Galante, "Groupon Coupons: The Small Biz Challenge," *Bloomberg Businessweek*, June 14, 2010, p. 1; Shayndi Raice, "Groupon and Its 'Weird' CEO," *Wall Street Journal*, January 31, 2012, http://online.wsj.com/video/groupon-and-its-weird-ceo/9AA5073E-89A2-4AD2-B4C9-44584709EF12.html; and http://investor.groupon.com/annuals.cfm, www.groupon.com, www.foursquare.com, and www.loopt.com, accessed November 2012.

With the rise of smartphones and tablets that integrate geo-location technology such as GPS, marketers are now tapping into what experts call the Social Local Mobile (SoLoMo) search revolution. SoLoMo refers to the ability of on-the-go consumers to get local information fast, wherever they may be. Services such as Foursquare, Loopt, and Groupon, and retailers ranging from REI to Starbucks, have jumped onto the SoLoMo bandwagon, primarily in the form of smartphone and tablet apps.

Mobile app Shopkick excels at SoLoMo. It sends special offers and rewards to shoppers simply for checking into client stores such as Target, American Eagle, Best Buy, or Crate&Barrel. ● When shoppers are near a participating store, the Shopkick app on their phone picks up a signal from the store and spits out store coupons, deal alerts, and product information. Similarly, shopping center operator DDR Corporation, which operates 27 open-air malls across 16 markets, uses technology that detects nearby shoppers and sends real-time text messages about various store sales and promotions to customers who have opted in. Such geo-targeting benefits both marketers and consumers. It helps merchants get out their messages while at the same time personalizing the customer's shopping experience.

Local marketing has some drawbacks, however. It can drive up manufacturing and marketing costs by reducing the economies of scale. It can also create logistics problems as companies try to meet the varied requirements of different regional and local markets. Still, as companies face increasingly fragmented

● Increasingly, local marketing is going mobile. Mobile app Shopkick excels at SoLoMo (Social Local Mobile) by sending rewards and special offers to shoppers for simply walking into client stores such as Target, American Eagle, Best Buy, or Crate&Barrel.

Shopkick

markets, and as new supporting technologies develop, the advantages of local marketing often outweigh the drawbacks.

Individual marketing

Tailoring products and marketing programs to the needs and preferences of individual customers.

Individual Marketing. In the extreme, micromarketing becomes **individual marketing**—tailoring products and marketing programs to the needs and preferences of individual customers. Individual marketing has also been labeled *one-to-one marketing, mass customization,* and *markets-of-one marketing.*

The widespread use of mass marketing has obscured the fact that for centuries consumers were served as individuals: The tailor custom-made a suit, the cobbler designed shoes for an individual, and the cabinetmaker made furniture to order. Today, new technologies are permitting many companies to return to customized marketing. More detailed databases, robotic production and flexible manufacturing, and interactive media such as mobile phones and the Internet have combined to foster mass customization. *Mass customization* is the process by which firms interact one-to-one with masses of customers to design products and services tailor-made to individual needs.

Individual marketing has made relationships with customers more important than ever. Just as mass production was the marketing principle of the twentieth century, interactive marketing is becoming a marketing principle for the twenty-first century. The world appears to be coming full circle—from the good old days when customers were treated as individuals to mass marketing when nobody knew your name and then back again.

Companies these days are hypercustomizing everything from food to artwork, earphones, sneakers, and motorcycles.[22]

● Individual marketing: Nike's NikeID program lets users choose shoe materials, personalize colors, imprint text on the heels, and even size the left and right shoes differently.
Getty Images for Nike

At mymms.com, candylovers can buy M&Ms embossed with images of their kids or pets. JH Audio in Orlando makes music earphones based on molds of customers' ears to provide optimized fit and better and safer sound. The company even laser prints designs on the tiny ear buds—some people request a kid for each ear; others prefer a dog. ● Nike's NikeID program lets users choose materials for shoes' tread (say, for trail or street) and upper (Gore-Tex, mesh, or other), pick the color of the swoosh and stitching, and even imprint text on the heels. Different-sized right and left feet? That, too, can be retooled. On a much larger scale, Harley-Davidson's H-D1 factory customization program lets customers go online, design their own Harley, and get it in as little as four weeks. It invites customers to explore some 8,000 ways to create their own masterpiece. "You dream it. We build it," says the company.

Business-to-business marketers are also finding new ways to customize their offerings. For example, John Deere manufactures seeding equipment that can be configured in more than 2 million versions to individual customer specifications. The seeders are produced one at a time, in any sequence, on a single production line. Mass customization provides a way to stand out against competitors.

Choosing a Targeting Strategy

Companies need to consider many factors when choosing a market-targeting strategy. Which strategy is best depends on the company's resources. When the firm's resources are limited, concentrated marketing makes the most sense. The best strategy also depends on the degree of product variability. Undifferentiated marketing is more suited for uniform products, such as grapefruit or steel. Products that can vary in design, such as cameras and cars, are more suited to differentiation or concentration. The product's life-cycle stage also must be considered.

When a firm introduces a new product, it may be practical to launch one version only, as undifferentiated marketing or concentrated marketing may make the most sense. In the mature stage of the product life cycle, however, differentiated marketing often makes more sense.

Another factor is *market variability*. If most buyers have the same tastes, buy the same amounts, and react the same way to marketing efforts, undifferentiated marketing is appropriate. Finally, *competitors' marketing strategies* are important. When competitors use differentiated or concentrated marketing, undifferentiated marketing can be suicidal. Conversely, when competitors use undifferentiated marketing, a firm can gain an advantage by using differentiated or concentrated marketing, focusing on the needs of buyers in specific segments.

Socially Responsible Target Marketing

Smart targeting helps companies become more efficient and effective by focusing on the segments that they can satisfy best and most profitably. Targeting also benefits consumers—companies serve specific groups of consumers with offers carefully tailored to their needs. However, target marketing sometimes generates controversy and concern. The biggest issues usually involve the targeting of vulnerable or disadvantaged consumers with controversial or potentially harmful products.

For example, over the years marketers in a wide range of industries—from cereal, soft drinks, and fast food to toys and fashion—have been heavily criticized for their marketing efforts directed toward children. Critics worry that premium offers and high-powered advertising appeals presented through the mouths of lovable animated characters will overwhelm children's defenses. In recent years, for instance, McDonald's has been criticized by various health advocates and parents groups who are concerned that its popular Happy Meals offers—featuring trinkets and other items tied in with children's movies such as *Toy Story*—create a too-powerful connection between children and the often fat- and calorie-laden meals. Some critics have even asked McDonald's to retire its iconic Ronald McDonald character. McDonald's has responded by putting the Happy Meal on a diet, cutting the overall calorie count by 20 percent and adding fruit to every meal.[23]

Other problems arise when the marketing of adult products spills over into the children's segment—intentionally or unintentionally. For example, Victoria's Secret targets its highly successful Pink line of young, hip, and sexy clothing to young women from 18 to 30 years old. However, critics charge that Pink is now all the rage among girls as young as 11 years old. Responding to Victoria's Secret's designs and marketing messages, tweens are flocking into stores and buying Pink, with or without their mothers. More broadly, critics worry that marketers of everything from Barbie dolls to lingerie are directly or indirectly targeting young girls with provocative products, promoting a premature focus on sex and appearance. ● For example, Barbie now comes in a "bling-bling" style, replete with halter top and go-go boots. And Abercrombie & Fitch recently marketed a padded "push-up" bikini top for girls as young as 8. "The sexualization of teens is bad enough and now it's trickling down to our babies," laments one reporter.[24]

To encourage responsible advertising, the Children's Advertising Review Unit, the advertising industry's self-regulatory agency, has published extensive children's advertising guidelines that recognize the special needs of child audiences. Still, critics feel that more should been done. Some have even called for a complete ban on advertising to children.

Cigarette, beer, and fast-food marketers have also generated controversy in recent years by their attempts to target inner-city minority consumers. For example, fast-food chains have drawn criticism for pitching their high-fat, salt-laden fare to low-income, urban residents who are much more likely than suburbanites to be heavy consumers. Similarly, big banks and mortgage

● **Socially responsible marketing: Critics worry that marketers of everything from lingerie and cosmetics to Barbie dolls are targeting young girls with provocative products.**

Jarrod Weaton/Weaton Digital, Inc.

lenders have been criticized for targeting consumers in poor urban areas with attractive adjustable rate home mortgages that they can't really afford.

The growth of the Internet and other carefully targeted direct media has raised fresh concerns about potential targeting abuses. The Internet allows more precise targeting, letting the makers of questionable products or deceptive advertisers zero in on the most vulnerable audiences. Unscrupulous marketers can now send tailor-made, deceptive messages by e-mail directly to millions of unsuspecting consumers. For example, the FBI's Internet Crime Complaint Center Web site alone received more than 310,000 complaints last year.[25]

Not all attempts to target children, minorities, or other special segments draw such criticism. In fact, most provide benefits to targeted consumers. For example, Pantene markets Relaxed and Natural hair products to women of color. Samsung markets the Jitterbug, an easy-to-use phone, directly to seniors who need a simpler mobile phone with bigger buttons, large screen text, and a louder speaker. And Colgate makes a large selection of toothbrush shapes and toothpaste flavors for children—from Colgate SpongeBob SquarePants Mild Bubble Fruit toothpaste to Colgate Dora the Explorer character toothbrushes. Such products help make tooth brushing more fun and get children to brush longer and more often.

Thus, in target marketing, the issue is not really *who* is targeted but rather *how* and for *what*. Controversies arise when marketers attempt to profit at the expense of targeted segments—when they unfairly target vulnerable segments or target them with questionable products or tactics. Socially responsible marketing calls for segmentation and targeting that serve not just the interests of the company but also the interests of those targeted.

Product position

The way a product is defined by consumers on important attributes— the place the product occupies in consumers' minds relative to competing products.

Objective 4 ······►

Discuss how companies differentiate and position their products for maximum competitive advantage.

Differentiation and Positioning

Beyond deciding which segments of the market it will target, the company must decide on a *value proposition*—how it will create differentiated value for targeted segments and what positions it wants to occupy in those segments. A **product position** is the way a product is *defined by consumers* on important attributes—the place the product occupies in consumers' minds relative to competing products. Products are made in factories, but brands happen in the minds of consumers.

Method laundry detergent is positioned as a smarter, easier, and greener detergent; Dreft is positioned as the gentle detergent for baby clothes. At IHOP, you "Come hungry. Leave happy."; at Olive Garden, "When You're Here, You're Family." In the automobile market, the Nissan Versa and Honda Fit are positioned on economy, Mercedes and Cadillac on luxury, and Porsche and BMW on performance. Folger's Coffee is "The best part of wakin' up"; ● Honest Tea says "Nature got it right. We put it in a bottle."

Consumers are overloaded with information about products and services. They cannot reevaluate products every time they make a buying decision. To simplify the buying process, consumers organize products, services, and companies into categories and "position" them in their minds. A product's position is the complex set of perceptions, impressions, and feelings that consumers have for the product compared with competing products.

Consumers position products with or without the help of marketers. But marketers do not want to leave their products' positions to chance. They must *plan* positions that will give their products the greatest advantage in selected target markets, and they must design marketing mixes to create these planned positions.

Positioning Maps

In planning their differentiation and positioning strategies, marketers often prepare *perceptual positioning maps* that show consumer perceptions of their brands versus competing products on important buying dimensions. ● **Figure 7.3** shows a positioning map for the U.S. large luxury sport utility vehicle (SUV) market.[26] The position of each circle on the map indicates the brand's perceived positioning on two dimensions: price and orientation (luxury versus performance). The size of each circle indicates the brand's relative market share.

Thus, customers view the market-leading Cadillac Escalade as a moderately priced, large, luxury SUV with a balance of luxury and performance. The Escalade is positioned on urban luxury, and, in its case, "performance" probably means

● Positioning: Honest Tea is positioned on "Honest ingredients. No more, no less. Nature got it right. We put it in a bottle."

Coca-Cola Company

FIGURE | 7.3
Positioning Map:
Large Luxury SUVs
Source: Based on data provided by
WardsAuto.com and Edmunds.com, 2012.

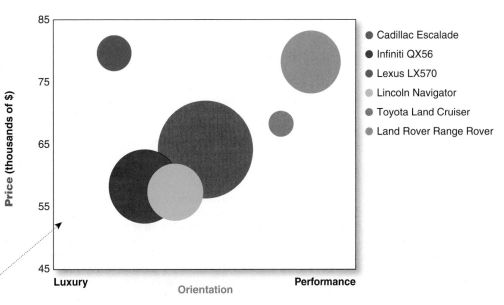

The location of each circle shows where consumers position a brand on two dimensions: price and luxury-performance orientation. The size of each circle indicates the brand's relative market share in the segment. Thus, Toyota's Land Cruiser is a niche brand that is perceived to be relatively affordable and more performance oriented.

power and safety performance. You'll find no mention of off-road adventuring in an Escalade ad.

By contrast, the Range Rover and the Land Cruiser are positioned on luxury with nuances of off-road performance. For example, the Toyota Land Cruiser began in 1951 as a four-wheel-drive, Jeep-like vehicle designed to conquer the world's most grueling terrains and climates. In recent years, the Land Cruiser has retained this adventure and performance positioning but with luxury added. Its Web site brags of "legendary off-road capability," with off-road technologies such as downhill assist control and kinetic dynamic suspension systems. "In some parts of the world, it's an essential." Despite its ruggedness, however, the company notes that "its available Bluetooth hands-free technology, DVD entertainment, and a sumptuous interior have softened its edges."

Choosing a Differentiation and Positioning Strategy

Some firms find it easy to choose a differentiation and positioning strategy. For example, a firm well known for quality in certain segments will go after this position in a new segment if there are enough buyers seeking quality. But in many cases, two or more firms will go after the same position. Then each will have to find other ways to set itself apart. Each firm must differentiate its offer by building a unique bundle of benefits that appeals to a substantial group within the segment.

Above all else, a brand's positioning must serve the needs and preferences of well-defined target markets. For example, as noted in the chapter-opening story, although both Dunkin' Donuts and Starbucks are coffee shops, they offer very different product assortments and store atmospheres. Yet each succeeds because it creates just the right value proposition for its unique mix of customers.

The differentiation and positioning task consists of three steps: identifying a set of differentiating competitive advantages on which to build a position, choosing the right competitive advantages, and selecting an overall positioning strategy. The company must then effectively communicate and deliver the chosen position to the market.

Identifying Possible Value Differences and Competitive Advantages

To build profitable relationships with target customers, marketers must understand customer needs and deliver more customer value better than competitors do. To the extent that a company can differentiate and position itself as providing superior customer value, it gains **competitive advantage**.

But solid positions cannot be built on empty promises. If a company positions its product as *offering* the best quality and service, it must actually differentiate the product so that it *delivers* the promised quality and service. Companies must do much more than simply shout out their

Competitive advantage
An advantage over competitors gained by offering greater customer value, either by having lower prices or providing more benefits that justify higher prices.

positions with slogans and taglines. They must first *live* the slogan. For example, when Staples' research revealed that it should differentiate itself on the basis of "an easier shopping experience," the office supply retailer held back its "Staples: That was easy" marketing campaign for more than a year. First, it remade its stores to actually deliver the promised positioning.[27]

> Only a few years ago, things weren't so easy for Staples—or for its customers. The ratio of customer complaints to compliments was running a dreadful eight to one at Staples stores. Weeks of focus groups produced an answer: Customers wanted an easier shopping experience. That simple revelation has resulted in one of the most successful marketing campaigns in recent history, built around the now-familiar "Staples: That was easy" tagline. But Staples' positioning turnaround took a lot more than simply bombarding customers with a new slogan. Before it could promise customers a simplified shopping experience, Staples had to actually deliver one. First, it had to *live* the slogan.
>
> So, for more than a year, Staples worked to revamp the customer experience. It remodeled its stores, streamlined its inventory, retrained employees, and even simplified customer communications. Only when all of the customer-experience pieces were in place did Staples begin communicating its new positioning to customers. The "Staples: That was easy" repositioning campaign has met with striking success, helping to make Staples the runaway leader in office retail. No doubt about it, clever marketing helped. But marketing promises count for little if they are not backed by the reality of the customer experience.

To find points of differentiation, marketers must think through the customer's entire experience with the company's product or service. An alert company can find ways to differentiate itself at every customer contact point. In what specific ways can a company differentiate itself or its market offer? It can differentiate along the lines of *product, services, channels, people,* or *image.*

Through *product differentiation*, brands can be differentiated on features, performance, or style and design. Thus, Bose positions its speakers on their striking design and sound characteristics. By gaining the approval of the American Heart Association as an approach to a healthy lifestyle, Subway differentiates itself as the healthy fast-food choice. And Seventh Generation, a maker of household cleaning and laundry supplies, paper products, diapers, and wipes, differentiates itself not so much by how its products perform but by the fact that its products are greener. Seventh Generation's mission: "Healthy Products. Healthy Environment. Healthy Communities. Healthy Company."

Beyond differentiating its physical product, a firm can also differentiate the services that accompany the product. Some companies gain *services differentiation* through speedy, convenient, or careful delivery. For example, First Convenience Bank of Texas offers "Real Hours for Real People"; it is open seven days a week, including evenings. Others differentiate their service based on high-quality customer care. In an age where customer satisfaction with airline service is in constant decline, Singapore Airlines sets itself apart through extraordinary customer care and the grace of its flight attendants.  "Everyone expects excellence from us," says the international airline. "[So even] in the smallest details of flight, we rise to each occasion and deliver the Singapore Airlines experience."[28]

● **Service differentiation: Singapore Airlines sets itself apart through extraordinary customer care and the grace of its flight attendants.**
Gilles ROLLE/REA/Redux

Firms that practice *channel differentiation* gain competitive advantage through the way they design their channel's coverage, expertise, and performance. Amazon.com and GEICO, for example, set themselves apart with their smooth-functioning direct channels. Companies can also gain a strong competitive advantage through *people differentiation*—hiring and training better people than their competitors do. People differentiation requires that a company select its customer-contact people carefully and train them well. For example, Disney World people are known to be friendly and upbeat. Disney trains its theme park people thoroughly to ensure that they are competent, courteous, and friendly—from the hotel check-in agents, to the monorail drivers, to the ride attendants, to the people who sweep Main Street USA. Each employee is carefully trained to understand customers and to "make people happy."

Even when competing offers look the same, buyers may perceive a difference based on company or brand *image differentiation*. A company or brand image should convey a product's distinctive benefits and positioning. Developing a strong and distinctive image calls for creativity and hard work. A company cannot develop an image in the public's mind overnight by using only a few ads. If Ritz-Carlton means quality, this image must be supported by everything the company says and does.

Symbols, such as the McDonald's golden arches, the colorful Google logo, the Nike swoosh, or Apple's "bite mark" logo, can provide strong company or brand recognition and image differentiation. The company might build a brand around a famous person, as Nike did with its Michael Jordan, Kobe Bryant, and LeBron James basketball shoe and apparel collections. Some companies even become associated with colors, such as Coca-Cola (red), IBM (blue), or UPS (brown). The chosen symbols, characters, and other image elements must be communicated through advertising that conveys the company's or brand's personality.

Choosing the Right Competitive Advantages

Suppose a company is fortunate enough to discover several potential differentiations that provide competitive advantages. It now must choose the ones on which it will build its positioning strategy. It must decide how many differences to promote and which ones.

How Many Differences to Promote. Many marketers think that companies should aggressively promote only one benefit to the target market. Advertising executive Rosser Reeves, for example, said a company should develop a *unique selling proposition (USP)* for each brand and stick to it. Each brand should pick an attribute and tout itself as "number one" on that attribute. Buyers tend to remember number one better, especially in this overcommunicated society. Thus, Walmart promotes its unbeatable low prices, and Burger King promotes personal choice— "have it your way."

Other marketers think that companies should position themselves on more than one differentiator. This may be necessary if two or more firms are claiming to be best on the same attribute. Today, in a time when the mass market is fragmenting into many small segments, companies and brands are trying to broaden their positioning strategies to appeal to more segments.  For example, whereas Gatorade originally offered a sports drink positioned only on performance hydration, the brand now offers an entire G Series of sports drinks that provide at least three primary benefits. G Series "fuels your body before, during, and after practice, training, or competition." Gatorade Prime 01 is positioned as "pre-game fuel" that provides energy *before* exercise. Gatorade Thirst Quencher is for use "in the moment of activity" *during* exercise. Finally, Gatorade Recover 03 is positioned as a post-game recovering beverage that provides protein for recovery *after* exercise. Clearly, many buyers want these multiple benefits. The challenge is to convince them that one brand can do it all.

● **Positioning on multiple competitive advantages: The Gatorade G Series "fuels your body before, during, and after" exercise.**

Pepsi-Cola North America, Inc.

Which Differences to Promote. Not all brand differences are meaningful or worthwhile, and each difference has the potential to create company costs as well as customer benefits. A difference is worth establishing to the extent that it satisfies the following criteria:

- *Important:* The difference delivers a highly valued benefit to target buyers.
- *Distinctive:* Competitors do not offer the difference, or the company can offer it in a more distinctive way.
- *Superior:* The difference is superior to other ways that customers might obtain the same benefit.
- *Communicable:* The difference is communicable and visible to buyers.
- *Preemptive:* Competitors cannot easily copy the difference.

- *Affordable:* Buyers can afford to pay for the difference.
- *Profitable:* The company can introduce the difference profitably.

Many companies have introduced differentiations that failed one or more of these tests. When the Westin Stamford Hotel in Singapore once advertised that it is the world's tallest hotel, it was a distinction that was not important to most tourists; in fact, it turned many off. Polaroid's Polarvision, which produced instantly developed home movies, bombed too. Although Polarvision was distinctive and even preemptive, it was inferior to another way of capturing motion—namely, camcorders.

Thus, choosing competitive advantages on which to position a product or service can be difficult, yet such choices may be crucial to success. Choosing the right differentiators can help a brand stand out from the pack of competitors. For example, when carmaker Nissan introduced its novel little Cube, it didn't position the car only on attributes shared with competing models, such as affordability and customization. It positioned it as a "mobile device" that fits today's digital lifestyles.

Selecting an Overall Positioning Strategy

Value proposition

The full positioning of a brand—the full mix of benefits on which it is positioned.

The full positioning of a brand is called the brand's **value proposition**—the full mix of benefits on which a brand is differentiated and positioned. It is the answer to the customer's question "Why should I buy your brand?" BMW's "ultimate driving machine" value proposition hinges on performance but also includes luxury and styling, all for a price that is higher than average but seems fair for this mix of benefits.

● **Figure 7.4** shows possible value propositions on which a company might position its products. In the figure, the five green cells represent winning value propositions— differentiation and positioning that give the company a competitive advantage. The red cells, however, represent losing value propositions. The center yellow cell represents at best a marginal proposition. In the following sections, we discuss the five winning value propositions: more for more, more for the same, the same for less, less for much less, and more for less.

More for More. *More-for-more* positioning involves providing the most upscale product or service and charging a higher price to cover the higher costs. A more-for-more market offering not only offers higher quality, it also gives prestige to the buyer. It symbolizes status and a loftier lifestyle. Four Seasons hotels, Rolex watches, Mercedes automobiles, SubZero appliances—each claims superior quality, craftsmanship, durability, performance, or style and, therefore, charges a higher price. When Apple premiered its iPhone, it offered higher-quality features than a traditional mobile phone with a hefty price tag to match.

Similarly, the marketers of Hearts On Fire diamonds have created a more-for-more niche as "The World's Most Perfectly Cut Diamond." Hearts On Fire diamonds have a unique "hearts and arrow" design. When viewed under magnification from the bottom, a perfect ring of eight hearts appears; from the top comes a perfectly formed Fireburst of light. ● Hearts On Fire diamonds aren't for everyone, says the company. "Hearts On Fire is for those who expect more and give more in return." The brand commands a 15 to 20 percent price premium over comparable competing diamonds.[29]

Although more-for-more can be profitable, this strategy can also be vulnerable. It often invites imitators who claim the same quality but at a lower price. For example, more-for-more brand Starbucks now faces "gourmet" coffee competitors ranging from Dunkin' Donuts to McDonald's. Also, luxury goods that sell well during good times may be at risk during economic downturns when buyers become more cautious in their spending. The recent gloomy economy hit premium brands, such as Starbucks, the hardest.

More for the Same. Companies can attack a competitor's more-for-more positioning by introducing a brand offering comparable quality at a lower price. For example, Toyota introduced its Lexus line with a *more-for-the-same* value proposition versus Mercedes and BMW. Its first headline read: "Perhaps the first time in history that trading a $72,000 car for a $36,000 car could be considered trading up." It communicated the high quality of its new Lexus through rave reviews in car magazines and a widely

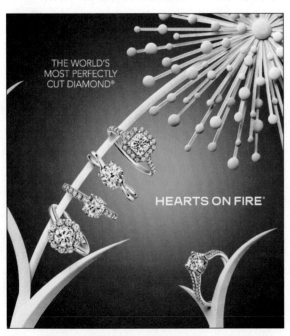

● More-for-more positioning: Hearts On Fire diamonds have created a more-for-more niche as "The World's Most Perfectly Cut Diamond—for those who expect more and give more in return."

Used with permission of Hearts On Fire Company, LLC

FIGURE | 7.4
Possible Value Propositions

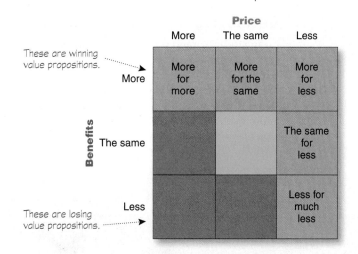

FIGURE | 7.4
Possible Value Propositions

distributed video showing side-by-side comparisons of Lexus and Mercedes automobiles. It published surveys showing that Lexus dealers were providing customers with better sales and service experiences than were Mercedes dealerships. Many Mercedes owners switched to Lexus, and the Lexus repurchase rate has been 60 percent, twice the industry average.

The Same for Less. Offering *the same for less* can be a powerful value proposition—everyone likes a good deal. Discount stores such as Walmart and "category killers" such as Best Buy, PetSmart, David's Bridal, and DSW Shoes use this positioning. They don't claim to offer different or better products. Instead, they offer many of the same brands as department stores and specialty stores but at deep discounts based on superior purchasing power and lower-cost operations. Other companies develop imitative but lower-priced brands in an effort to lure customers away from the market leader. For example, Amazon.com offers the Kindle Fire tablet computer, which sells for less than 40 percent of the price of the Apple iPad or Samsung Galaxy.

Less for Much Less. A market almost always exists for products that offer less and therefore cost less. Few people need, want, or can afford "the very best" in everything they buy. In many cases, consumers will gladly settle for less than optimal performance or give up some of the bells and whistles in exchange for a lower price. For example, many travelers seeking lodgings prefer not to pay for what they consider unnecessary extras, such as a pool, an attached restaurant, or mints on the pillow. Hotel chains such as Ramada Limited, Holiday Inn Express, and Motel 6 suspend some of these amenities and charge less accordingly.

Less-for-much-less positioning involves meeting consumers' lower performance or quality requirements at a much lower price. For example, Family Dollar and Dollar General stores offer more affordable goods at very low prices. Costco warehouse stores offer less merchandise selection and consistency and much lower levels of service; as a result, they charge rock-bottom prices.

More for Less. Of course, the winning value proposition would be to offer *more for less*. Many companies claim to do this. And, in the short run, some companies can actually achieve such lofty positions. For example, when it first opened for business, Home Depot had arguably the best product selection, the best service, *and* the lowest prices compared to local hardware stores and other home improvement chains.

Yet in the long run, companies will find it very difficult to sustain such best-of-both positioning. Offering more usually costs more, making it difficult to deliver on the "for-less" promise. Companies that try to deliver both may lose out to more focused competitors. For example, facing determined competition from Lowe's stores, Home Depot must now decide whether it wants to compete primarily on superior service or on lower prices.

All said, each brand must adopt a positioning strategy designed to serve the needs and wants of its target markets. *More for more* will draw one target market, *less for much less* will draw another, and so on. Thus, in any market, there is usually room for many different companies, each successfully occupying different positions. The important thing is that each company must develop its own winning positioning strategy, one that makes the company special to its target consumers.

Developing a Positioning Statement

Positioning statement

A statement that summarizes company or brand positioning using this form: To (target segment and need) our (brand) is (concept) that (point of difference).

Company and brand positioning should be summed up in a **positioning statement**. The statement should follow the form: To (target segment and need) our (brand) is (concept) that (point of difference).[30] ● Here is an example using the popular digital information management application Evernote: "To busy multitaskers who need help remembering things, Evernote is digital content management application that makes it easy to capture and remember moments and ideas from your everyday life using your computer, phone, tablet, and the Web."

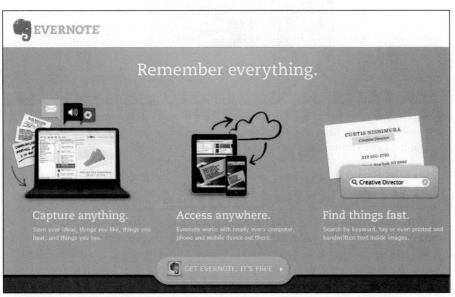

Note that the positioning statement first states the product's membership in a category (digital content management application) and then shows its point of difference from other members of the category (easily capture moments and ideas and remember them later). Evernote helps you "remember everything" by letting you take notes, capture photos, create to-do lists, and record voice reminders, and then makes them easy to find and access using just about any device, anywhere—at home, at work, or on the go.

Placing a brand in a specific category suggests similarities that it might share with other products in the category. But the case for the brand's superiority is made on its points of difference. For example, the U.S. Postal Service ships packages just like UPS and FedEx, but it differentiates its Priority Mail from competitors with convenient, low-price, flat-rate shipping boxes and envelopes. "If it fits, it ships," promises the Post Office.

● **Positioning statement: Evernote is positioned as a digital content management application that helps busy people to capture and remember moments and ideas and find them fast later.**

Evernote Corporation

Communicating and Delivering the Chosen Position

Once it has chosen a position, the company must take strong steps to deliver and communicate the desired position to its target consumers. All the company's marketing mix efforts must support the positioning strategy.

Positioning the company calls for concrete action, not just talk. If the company decides to build a position on better quality and service, it must first *deliver* that position. Designing the marketing mix—product, price, place, and promotion—involves working out the tactical details of the positioning strategy. Thus, a firm that seizes on a more-for-more position knows that it must produce high-quality products, charge a high price, distribute through high-quality dealers, and advertise in high-quality media. It must hire and train more service people, find retailers that have a good reputation for service, and develop sales and advertising messages that broadcast its superior service. This is the only way to build a consistent and believable more-for-more position.

Companies often find it easier to come up with a good positioning strategy than to implement it. Establishing a position or changing one usually takes a long time. In contrast, positions that have taken years to build can quickly be lost. Once a company has built the desired position, it must take care to maintain the position through consistent performance and communication. It must closely monitor and adapt the position over time to match changes in consumer needs and competitors' strategies. However, the company should avoid abrupt changes that might confuse consumers. Instead, a product's position should evolve gradually as it adapts to the ever-changing marketing environment.

Reviewing the Concepts

MyMarketingLab™

Go to **mymktlab.com** to complete the problems marked with this icon .

Reviewing Objectives and Key Terms

 ## Objectives Review

In this chapter, you learned about the major elements of a customer-driven marketing strategy: segmentation, targeting, differentiation, and positioning. Marketers know that they cannot appeal to all buyers in their markets, or at least not to all buyers in the same way. Therefore, most companies today practice *target marketing*—identifying market segments, selecting one or more of them, and developing products and marketing mixes tailored to each.

Objective 1 | Define the major steps in designing a customer-driven marketing strategy: market segmentation, targeting, differentiation, and positioning. (pp 192–193)

A customer-driven marketing strategy begins with selecting which customers to serve and determining a value proposition that best serves the targeted customers. It consists of four steps. *Market segmentation* is the act of dividing a market into distinct segments of buyers with different needs, characteristics, or behaviors who might require separate products or marketing mixes. Once the groups have been identified, *market targeting* evaluates each market segment's attractiveness and selects one or more segments to serve. *Differentiation* involves actually differentiating the market offering to create superior customer value. *Positioning* consists of positioning the market offering in the minds of target customers. A customer-driven marketing strategy seeks to build the *right relationships* with the *right customers*.

Objective 2 | List and discuss the major bases for segmenting consumer and business markets. (pp 193–202)

There is no single way to segment a market. Therefore, the marketer tries different variables to see which give the best segmentation opportunities. For consumer marketing, the major segmentation variables are geographic, demographic, psychographic, and behavioral. In *geographic segmentation*, the market is divided into different geographical units, such as nations, regions, states, counties, cities, or even neighborhoods. In *demographic segmentation*, the market is divided into groups based on demographic variables, including age, life-cycle stage, gender, income, occupation, education, religion, ethnicity, and generation. In *psychographic segmentation*, the market is divided into different groups based on social class, lifestyle, or personality characteristics. In *behavioral segmentation*, the market is divided into groups based on consumers' knowledge, attitudes, uses, or responses concerning a product.

Business marketers use many of the same variables to segment their markets. But business markets also can be segmented by business *demographics* (industry, company size), *operating characteristics*, *purchasing approaches*, *situational factors*, and *personal characteristics*. The effectiveness of the segmentation analysis depends on finding segments that are *measurable*, *accessible*, *substantial*, *differentiable*, and *actionable*.

Objective 3 | Explain how companies identify attractive market segments and choose a market-targeting strategy. (pp 202–210)

To target the best market segments, the company first evaluates each segment's size and growth characteristics, structural attractiveness, and compatibility with company objectives and resources. It then chooses one of four market-targeting strategies—ranging from very broad to very narrow targeting. The seller can ignore segment differences and target broadly using *undifferentiated* (or *mass*) *marketing*. This involves mass producing, mass distributing, and mass promoting about the same product in about the same way to all consumers. Or the seller can adopt *differentiated marketing*—developing different market offers for several segments. *Concentrated marketing* (or *niche marketing*) involves focusing on one or a few market segments only. Finally, *micromarketing* is the practice of tailoring products and marketing programs to suit the tastes of specific individuals and locations. Micromarketing includes *local marketing* and *individual marketing*. Which targeting strategy is best depends on company resources, product variability, the product life-cycle stage, market variability, and competitive marketing strategies.

Objective 4 | Discuss how companies differentiate and position their products for maximum competitive advantage. (pp 210–216)

Once a company has decided which segments to enter, it must decide on its *differentiation and positioning strategy*. The differentiation and positioning task consists of three steps: identifying a set of possible differentiations that create competitive advantage, choosing advantages on which to build a position, and selecting an overall positioning strategy.

The brand's full positioning is called its *value proposition*—the full mix of benefits on which the brand is positioned. In general, companies can choose from one of five winning value propositions on which to position their products: more for more, more for the same, the same for less, less for much less, or more for less.

Company and brand positioning are summarized in positioning statements that state the target segment and need, the positioning concept, and specific points of difference. The company must then effectively communicate and deliver the chosen position to the market.

 Key Terms

Objective 1

Market segmentation (p 192)
Market targeting (targeting) (p 192)
Differentiation (p 192)
Positioning (p 192)

Objective 2

Geographic segmentation (p 193)
Demographic segmentation (p 194)
Age and life-cycle segmentation (p 194)
Gender segmentation (p 195)
Income segmentation (p 195)

Psychographic segmentation (p 196)
Behavioral segmentation (p 198)
Occasion segmentation (p 198)
Benefit segmentation (p 198)
Intermarket (cross-market)
    segmentation (p 201)

Objective 3

Target market (p 203)
Undifferentiated (mass) marketing (p 203)
Differentiated (segmented) marketing
    (p 203)

Concentrated (niche) marketing (p 204)
Micromarketing (p 205)
Local marketing (p 205)
Individual marketing (p 208)

Objective 4

Product position (p 210)
Competitive advantage (p 211)
Value proposition (p 214)
Positioning statement (p 216)

Discussion and Critical Thinking

 Discussion Questions

1. How does market segmentation differ from market targeting? (AACSB: Communication)

2. Name and describe the four major sets of variables that might be used in segmenting consumer markets. Which segmenting variables does Starbucks use? (AACSB: Communication; Reflective Thinking)

3. Name and describe the levels at which market targeting can be carried out. Give an example of a company using each. (AACSB: Communication; Reflective Thinking)

4. Explain how companies segment international markets. (AACSB: Communication)

5. Explain how a company differentiates its products from competitors' products. (AACSB: Communication)

6. In the context of marketing, what is a product's "position"? How do marketers know what it is? (AACSB: Communication)

 Critical Thinking Exercises

1. Advertisers use market segmentation when promoting products to consumers. For each major consumer segmention variable, find an example of a print ad that appears to be based on that variable. For each ad, identify the target market and explain why you think the advertiser is using the segmentation variable you identified for that ad. (AACSB: Communication; Reflective Thinking)

2. When Nissan introduced its large Titan pickup truck in the United States and Toyota introduced the Tundra, each thought it would sell around 200,000 vehicles per year and had planned capacity for hundreds of thousands more because of the huge

U.S. market potential. After all, the "big three" American manufacturers averaged sales in this market of almost 2 million trucks per year. But the two Japanese brands missed their sales goals by a wide margin. In a small group, discuss possible reasons for the dismal sales of the Titan and the Tundra in the U.S. market. (AACSB: Communication; Reflective Thinking)

3. Form a small group and create an idea for a new business. Using the steps described in the chapter, develop a customer-driven marketing strategy. Describe your strategy and conclude with a positioning statement for your business. (AACSB: Communication; Reflective Thinking)

Applications and Cases

Marketing Technology Google's Glasses

Consumers enjoy having Google's search power at their fingertips, but if things go as planned, we'll have that Google power right before our very eyes, no fingers necessary. "Augmented reality"—the ability to project information in front of our eyes—is now being used in commercial and military operations. For example, the U.S. Air Force uses it to display weapons information in fighter pilot helmets. However, it has yet to take off in the consumer market. That's because the required headgear has been uncomfortable, unattractive, and expensive. But Google is peering into the future and has tentative plans to sell its Google Glasses device to consumers in 2013. The sleek wraparound glasses place a single lens above a person's right eye that displays digital information that can be voice- and gesture-controlled. Connecting the device to a smartphone opens up a world of possibilities. The only product close to Google's glasses currently on the consumer market is a GPS device that skiers and snowboarders insert into goggles that displays speed information.

1. How would you market the Google Glasses device in a 30-second commercial to consumers based on one of the segmenting variables you identified in the previous question? (AACSB: Communication; Reflective Thinking)

Marketing Ethics Targeting Young Consumers

You would never know that consumers are more frugal these days if you look at the new children's lines from fashion houses such as Fendi, Versace, and Gucci. Toddler high fashion is not new, but designers are taking it to new levels and extending it beyond special-occasion clothing to everyday wear. In the past, some of the little girls marching down fashion runways carried dolls with matching outfits. But now, many of the little children's fashions are geared around matching mom and dad clothing. Jennifer Lopez and her little ones helped Gucci launch a line for babies and children aged 2 to 8 years old. A Gucci children's outfit with a t-shirt, skinny jeans, a belt with the trademark double-G, a raincoat, and boots will set mom and dad back about $1,000. A Burberry children's double-breasted trench coat for a baby runs $335, a bargain compared to mom's matching $1,195 trench coat. The CEO of the Young Versace brand sees growth in this market and anticipates this brand making up 10 percent of the company's global sales in only a few years.

1. What segmentation variables are marketers using in this example? (AACSB: Communication; Reflective Thinking)

Marketing by the Numbers Kaplan University Recruits Veterans

For-profit universities, such as Kaplan University, DeVry University, and the University of Phoenix, actively target military veterans. In fact, the University of Phoenix has more veterans enrolled than any other college. These schools rely heavily on students receiving federal financial aid, and federal law limits the proportion of for-profit university revenue that can be derived from federal aid to 90 percent. But enrolling veterans helps them stay below this threshold because the law does not count GI benefits as government assistance. With federal spending on veterans' education more than doubling to almost $10 billion between 2009 and 2010, this market is even more attractive. Kaplan University is one of the most aggressive, with a team of 300 representatives focused solely on recruiting military veterans, increasing its enrollment of veterans by almost 30 percent in just one year.

1. Discuss the factors used to evaluate the usefulness of the military veteran segment. (AACSB: Communication; Reflective Thinking)

2. Using the chain ratio method described in Appendix 2: Marketing by the Numbers, estimate the market potential for undergraduate education in the veteran market. Be sure to state any assumptions. (AACSB: Communication; Use of IT; Analytical Reasoning)

Video Case Boston Harbor Cruises

Since 1926, Boston Harbor Cruises has been providing customers with memorable experiences on ocean-going vessels in and around the Boston area. But these days, the term "cruise" has different meanings for the four-generation family business. To thrive in good economic times and in bad, Boston Harbor Cruises has progressively targeted various types of customers with its different boats and different services. Sight-seeing trips around Boston Harbor, whale-watching tours, fast ferry service to Cape Cod, dinner and wedding cruises, and a high-speed thrill ride are among Boston Harbor Cruises offerings. It even offers commuter services and off-shore construction support. Targeting this diverse customer base has become even more challenging as Boston Harbor Cruises has further differentiated the market into local customers, domestic vacationers, and international travelers.

After viewing the video featuring Boston Harbor Cruises, answer the following questions:

1. On what main variables has Boston Harbor Cruises focused in segmenting its markets?

2. Which target marketing strategy best describes the efforts of Boston Harbor Cruises? Support your choice.

3. How does Boston Harbor Cruises use the concepts of differentiation and positioning to build relationships with the right customers?

 Company Case Darden Restaurants: Balancing Standardization and Differentiation

Perhaps you've never heard of Darden Restaurants, but you've probably eaten one of the more than 400 million meals the company serves up every year in its more than 2,000 restaurants. Darden's restaurants include niche brands such as The Capital Grille, Bahama Breeze, and Seasons 52. But you're probably more familiar with Olive Garden, Red Lobster, or LongHorn Steakhouse. Together, these chains account for $8 billion a year in revenues, making Darden Restaurants the largest full-service restaurant operation in the world. Darden isn't just big, however. It is also a pioneer of what is now known as "casual dining," a category that has become so popular that it accounts for 39 percent of all sit-down restaurant meals.

Darden has become a dominant industry force through a strategy of standardization and collaboration. Tearing a page from the Walmart playbook, Darden employs leading-edge technology across multiple brands to make the notoriously unpredictable restaurant business more efficient. At the $100 million state-of-the-art Darden corporate headquarters in Orlando, Florida, executives and support staff for all Darden brands work under the same roof. Test kitchens for each brand operate side by side. Darden encourages and expects employees from each chain to share information and best practices.

At the operating level, each individual Darden restaurant is a just-in-time manufacturing plant, using standardized preparation and service methods. This allows each restaurant to create a wide range of products in minutes that are selected, consumed, and judged by customers who show up unannounced. An order-processing program called "Meal Pacing" helps restaurant personnel turn tables around faster. That has not only generated higher revenues but also higher chain-wide guest-satisfaction scores. Darden's forecasting software is also the best in the business. Each restaurant, no matter what the brand, can pull up a forecast for any hour of any day that is within 1 to 4 percent of actual turnout. This has enabled Darden to reduce unplanned workforce hours by 40 percent and trim excess food costs by 10 percent.

In addition to these standardized practices, Darden chains also share a seafood-sourcing network that contracts directly with fish farms in dozens of countries. This system, put into place by founder Bill Darden, gives Darden an advantage in setting prices and ensuring supply. Darden Restaurants also benefit from corporate initiatives that protect and enhance sea-life ecosystems. This isn't just an effort to save the world. Each of its chains would suffer without a steady flow of affordable seafood.

Thus, standardized practices have played a key role in Darden's rise to dominance. But perhaps the biggest secret to Darden's success doesn't lie in its ability to standardize its operations. Rather, it lies in the company's ability to make brands with similar underlying operations distinct from one another. Darden has spent decades segmenting and targeting dining patrons. Much like P&G, Darden's brands are so well differentiated and positioned—with its corporate name so low profile—that the vast majority of patrons have no idea that the chains have a common owner. According to CEO Clarence Otis, that's because Darden doesn't leave anything to chance. "You hear people in the restaurant industry say, 'I have a feel for the business.'" But Otis is not one of those people. Instead, as his predecessors did before him, Otis guides the Darden brands by making use of marketing intelligence and analytics. "The direction of our business is based on understanding customers." That understanding contributes to the distinct positioning of each of the company's major chains.

Olive Garden: "When You're Here, You're Family"

With its heaping bowls of pasta and all-you-can-eat breadsticks, Olive Garden contributes approximately half of Darden's revenues. Olive Garden was launched in the early 1980s as an affordable Italian restaurant—a safe choice but nothing particularly notable. By the 1990s, it had hundreds of locations, a stale menu, and declining sales. But it didn't take long for Darden to turn Olive Garden into a hot concept. According to Drew Madsen, chief operating officer for the nation's biggest Italian restaurant chain, the key customer insight gleaned from Olive Garden's research was that people go to a restaurant for emotional as well as physical nourishment. In fact, emotional nourishment is most important; it stays with people much longer after they walk out the door.

Today, Olive Garden builds its strategy around the concept of a mythical Italian family. No doubt, you've seen some of Olive Garden's "When you're here, you're family" commercials, showing Italian family members enjoying a meal together. Olive Garden locations are designed to suggest an Italian farmhouse with a large family-style table. And the menu at Olive Garden has been cultivated through a partnership with real Italians at Olive Garden's Culinary Institute of Tuscany, Italy. That's where corporate and restaurant chefs are exposed to authentic Italian recipes and cooking techniques.

All this has led to an authentic Italian eating experience that is rare for a large chain. Hardcore foodies might scoff at the suggestion that Olive Garden is authentic Italian. But the chain has made staples of Chianti-braised short ribs, portabella mushrooms, and risotto. A decade ago, most of middle America had never heard of such culinary ingredients. And when compared to former Olive Garden menu items like Italian nachos, the current fare demonstrates the improved and authentic focus of today's Olive Garden.

Red Lobster: "The Taste of Wood-Grilled Seafood"

The second-biggest brand in Darden's portfolio is also the oldest. Founder Bill Darden opened the first Red Lobster in Lakeland, Florida, in 1968 after 30 years in the restaurant business. He saw a gap in the market between the still-young fast-food concept and upscale white-tablecloth restaurants. His new seafood restaurant filled the niche. And while Bill Darden had seen success as a restaurateur, Red Lobster was the breakthrough concept for expanding to a regional, then national level. In fact, the company is credited with introducing middle America to the wonders of fried shrimp.

But after more than 35 years of expansion and growth, Red Lobster's sales began to flounder. In 2004, quarterly same-store sales dropped for the first time in five years. Darden had taken its eye off the fish market, sticking to the way it had always done things even as consumer trends shifted. At that point, Darden's research indicated that consumers regarded Red Lobster as an out-of-date fried-fish shack.

To turn things around, even at the risk of alienating its core customers, management made substantial changes to Red Lobster's positioning, changes even more extensive than those made to turn Olive Garden around. At the center of these changes was a concept called "stealth health." The chain developed a new menu around wood-fired grilling, which required extensive investments in equipment and training. Classic Red Lobster fans needn't have worried too much—they can still get fried scallops and popcorn shrimp. But grilled items now make up one-third of the offerings. Red Lobster's new pitch is "The taste of wood-grilled seafood." And each restaurant prints a new fresh-fish menu twice a day. Combined with an extensive remodeling plan, the strategic changes will cost Red Lobster more than $350 million. But as an indication that its new healthy strategy is more than just talk, the chain was dubbed "best sit-down chain in America" by *Men's Health* magazine.

LongHorn Steakhouse: "The Flavor of the West"

With about $1 billion in annual revenues, LongHorn Steakhouse is Darden's third-largest and newest brand, acquired as part of a 2007 purchase. The chain is still being "Dardenized." But Otis and LongHorn Steakhouse president Dave George see it as the concept with the most potential. They expect that sales could double not many years into the future. Steak is the second-biggest casual dining sector. LongHorn Steakhouse already has just over 350 restaurants, making it the perfect challenger to the market leader, Outback Steakhouse. Moreover, until just recently, all LongHorn Steakhouse restaurants were in the eastern half of the United States, giving it plenty of room for westward expansion.

Darden has infused LongHorn Steakhouse with the same authenticity and hospitality that have served its other brands so well. Proclaiming itself as "The Flavor of the West," it welcomes "guests into a warm, relaxing atmosphere reminiscent of a Western rancher's home, where friendly, attentive servers help them unwind and savor a great steakhouse meal." Darden has added a touch of class to the old LongHorn Steakhouse. It serves only fresh steaks, chicken, and fish, and the menu has been dressed up with variations on common steakhouse themes, such as steak stuffed with fontina cheese and wild mushrooms. The burgers have been stripped of unwieldy garnishes. And changes to the dining room include replacing musty old deer heads with cowboy sculptures by Frederic Remington. As a result, LongHorn Steakhouse customer traffic is sizzling, even more than at Olive Garden or Red Lobster.

Achieving the Perfect Balance

Although the performance of Darden's big three chains has been historically strong, like most restaurants today, it faces new challenges. The economic environment of the past few years has tightened consumer dining-out budgets. That adds fuel to the fire as sit-down dining has been on the decline for some 18 years. Today, the average American eats 16 percent fewer sit-down meals. At the same time, the number of casual-dining restaurants has grown twice as fast as the U.S. population. And although the restaurant industry as a whole is showing signs of recovery, projected growth is expected to be much more moderate than the rapid growth during the 1990s.

All this means that Darden's future growth will have to come primarily through taking market share from competitors, a trend that is on the company's side. Throughout the tough economic times since 2009, over 7,000 independent restaurants have closed while chains have added more than 4,500 new locations. That bodes well for the biggest company in the business. Indeed, Darden outperformed the rest of the industry throughout the recent Great Recession. But it remains a tough environment as consumers continue to exhibit more frugality when it comes to things like dining out. Last year, Darden's overall revenues increased by 6.6 percent. However, same-store sales at Olive Garden and Red Lobster dropped a few percentage points. Darden recently announced a five-year goal to increase revenue by as much as 50 percent, a growth rate that is considerably higher than that of its previous five years.

Achieving this goal will not be easy. It will need strong performance from each of its brands, especially from its biggest contributor, Olive Garden. The gap between Darden's and competitors' sales is narrowing, an indication that other big chains are stepping up their games. Darden also faces rising food and energy costs, an issue that will have to be carefully balanced with price increases so as not to frighten off customers.

Still, Darden Restaurants hold a competitive advantage based on scale, standardization across brands, and expertise in market segmentation and targeting. Darden is constantly tweaking its formula to achieve the best mix of independence and collaboration among its brands. Darden's different chains may use the same technologies to pace cooking and predict dinner traffic, and they may all serve salmon from the same Norwegian fish farms. But COO Madsen knows that each brand must retain its distinctive positioning. "It's all about balance. There's an art and science to this." For Darden, that means that whatever collaboration takes place across its brands, no one is messing with Olive Garden's breadsticks or Red Lobster's cheese biscuits.

Questions for Discussion

1. Using the full spectrum of segmentation variables, describe how Darden segments and targets the sit-down dining market.

2. Has Darden differentiated and positioned its brands effectively? Explain.

3. Although Darden's efforts to standardize across brands have contributed to its success, how might such practices backfire?

4. Given current conditions, will Darden Restaurants continue to dominate the market? Why or why not?

5. What recommendations would you make that will help Darden's future growth?

Sources: Bob Krummert, "Darden Wants Even More Market Share from You," *Restaurant Hospitality*, March 5, 2012, http://restaurant-hospitality.com/trends/darden-wants-even-more-market-share-you; Annie Gasparro and Victoria Stilwell, "Darden Posts Higher Earnings Despite Soft Sales," *Wall Street Journal*, June 22, 2012, http://professional .wsj.com/article/SB100014240527023047653045774823224388962 12.html?mg[equals]reno64-wsj; Chuck Salter, "Why America Is Addicted to Olive Garden," *Fast Company*, July 1, 2009, p. 102; and quotes and other information are from www.darden.com, accessed November 2012.

MyMarketingLab

Go to **mymktlab.com** for Auto-graded writing questions as well as the following Assisted-graded writing questions:

7-1. Research "augmented reality" on the Internet. Discuss the most appropriate variables for segmenting the consumer market for products based on this technology. Explain why those variables are appropriate. (AACSB: Communication; Reflective Thinking)

7-2. Is it appropriate that marketers focus on such a young market with high-priced clothing? (AACSB: Communication; Reflective Thinking; Ethical Reasoning)

7-3. Mymktlab Only – comprehensive writing assignment for this chapter.

References

1. Quotes and other information from Leslie Patton, "Starbucks Turns to Happy Hour to Bring in More Traffic," *Bloomberg Businessweek,* February 1, 2012, www.businessweek.com/news/2012-02-01/ starbucks-turns-to-happy-hour-to-bring-to-more-traffic-retail.html; Janet Adamy, "Battle Brewing: Dunkin' Donuts Tries to Go Upscale, But Not Too Far," *Wall Street Journal*, April 8, 2006, p. A1; "Dunkin Donuts Launches New Advertising Campaign to Celebrate the Passion of Real Fans: 'I'm Drinkin' Dunkin'!'" *Entertainment Business Newsweekly*, January 23, 2011, p. 33; Leslie Patton and Lee Spears, "Dunkin' Jumps 47% in First Day after $422.8 Million IPO," *Business Week*, July 27, 2011, www.businessweek.com/news/2011-07-27/dunkin-jumps-47-in-first-day-after-422-8-million-ipo.html; "Dunkin' Donuts Is Number One in Coffee Customer Loyalty for Sixth Straight Year," February 7, 2012, news.dunkindonuts.com; and www .starbucks.com, www.dunkindonuts.com, and www.dunkinbrands .com, accessed November 2012.

2. See "Domino's Pizza Continues Bringing Mobile Ordering to the Masses with New Android App and Free Smartphone Offer," *Sacramento Bee,* February 27, 2012.

3. See Cotton Timberlake, "With Stores Nationwide, Macy's Goes Local," *Bloomberg BusinessWeek*, October 4, 2010–October 10, 2010, pp. 21–22; Robert Klara, "For the New Macy's, All Marketing Is Local," *Adweek*, June 7, 2010, pp. 25–26; and "Remarks by Terry J. Lundgren, Chairman, President, and Chief Executive Officer," www.macysinc.com/investors/annualmeeting/, accessed May 20, 2011. For other localization examples, see Philip Kotler and Kevin Lane Keller, *Marketing Management*, 14th ed. (Upper Saddle River, NJ: Prentice Hall, 2012), pp. 234–235.

4. "Kia Motors America; Kia Motors America's Music-Loving Hamsters Shuffle to LMFAO's Smash Hit 'Party Rock Anthem' in New Advertising Campaign for Funky Soul Urban Passenger Vehicle," *Energy Weekly News*, September 9, 2011, p. 67; David Kiefaber, "Millennials Are Clueless Narcissists in Toyota's Empty Nester Ads," *Adweek,*

July 7, 2011, www.adweek.com/adfreak/millennials-are-clueless-narcissists-toyotas-empty-nester-ads-133217; and www.youtube .com/watch?v=4zJWA3Vo6TU, accessed November 2012.

5. Joel Stein, "The Men's 'Skin Care' Product Boom," *Time,* October 30, 2010, www.time.com/time/magazine/article/0,9171,2025576,00 .html; Joyce V. Harrison, "Men Invade Female Turf of Cosmetics," Associated Content from Yahoo!, November 2, 2010, www .associatedcontent.com/article/5922774/men_invade_female_turf_ of_cosmetics_pg2.html?cat[equals]69; Ryan Doran, "Skin Is In," *Fairfield County Business Journal,* October 10, 2011, p. 1; and www .menaji.com, accessed November 2012.

6. Noreen O'Leary, "Talk to Her," *Adweek,* February 27, 2012, www .adweek.com/news/advertising-branding/talk-her-138529; Andrew Adam Newman, "Axe Adds Fragrance for Women to Its Lineup," *New York Times*, January 8, 2012; and www.harley-davidson.com/wcm/ Content/Pages/women_riders/landing.jsp, accessed August 2012.

7. Example from Richard Baker, "Retail Trends—Luxury Marketing: The End of a Mega-Trend," *Retail*, June/July 2009, pp. 8–12.

8. See www.vfc.com/brands, accessed October 2012.

9. See Philip Kotler and Kevin Lane Keller, *Marketing Management*, 14th ed. (Upper Saddle River, NJ: Prentice Hall, 2012), p. 98; and Venus product descriptions from www.gillettevenus.com/en_US/ products/index.jsp, accessed November 2012.

10. See Carolyn Chapin, "Seafood Nets Loyal Consumers," *Refrigerated & Frozen Foods,* June 2009, p. 42; and "Tracking Consumer Attitudes Toward Seafood Safety Resulting from the Gulf of Oil Spill," December 2010, accessed at http://louisianaseafood.com/pdf/ LSPMBSeafoodPhase1-FinalVersion.pdf.

11. See this and other examples in Andreas B. Eisenerich and others, "Behold the Extreme Consumers . . .," *Harvard Business Review*, April 2010, pp. 30–31.

12. For more on the PRIZM Lifestyle Segmentation System, see www .MyBestSegments.com, accessed August 2012.

13. See www.starbucksfs.com and http://starbucksocs.com/, accessed November 2012.

14. "Coca-Cola Launches Global Music Effort to Connect with Teens," *Advertising Age*, March 3, 2011, accessed at http://adage.com/print/149204; and "Coca-Cola's London 2012 Game Plan: Woo Teens Through Music, Parents Through Sustainability," *Brand-Channel*, September 29, 2011, http://brandchannel.com/home/post/2011/09/29/Coca-Cola-London-2012-Move-to-the-Beat.aspx; and "Coca-Cola Launches Global Ads for London 2012 Olympic Games Starring Mark Ronson," *Business Wire*, February 15, 2012.

15. See Michael Porter, *Competitive Advantage* (New York: Free Press, 1985), pp. 4–8, 234–236. For more recent discussions, see Kenneth Sawka and Bill Fiora, "The Four Analytical Techniques Every Analyst Must Know: 2. Porter's Five Forces Analysis," *Competitive Intelligence Magazine*, May–June 2003, p. 57; and Philip Kotler and Kevin Lane Keller, *Marketing Management*, 14th ed. (Upper Saddle River, NJ: Prentice Hall, 2012), p. 232.

16. Example adapted from Philip Kotler and Kevin Lane Keller, *Marketing Management*, 14th ed., p. 235. Also see Brad van Auken, "Leveraging the Brand: Hallmark Case Study," January 11, 2008, www.brandstrategyinsider.com; "Hallmark Breaks Out of Special-Occasion Mold," *Advertising Age,* July 6, 2011, www.adage.com/print/228558; and www.hallmark.com, accessed September 2012.

17. Store information found at www.walmartstores.com, www.wholefoodsmarket.com, and www.kroger.com, accessed September 2012.

18. "America's Fastest-Growing Retailer," *Inc.*, September 1, 2010; David Moin, "Modcloth's M.O.," *Women's Wear Daily*, June 15, 2011; Jordan Speer, "Get Feedback. It Closes the Loop," *Apparel,* November 2011, p. 2; and www.modcloth.com, accessed August 2012.

19. Stephanie Clifford, "Drug Chain's Beer Bar Serves a Neighborhood," *New York Times*, January 14, 2011, p. B. 1; "Duane Reade to Debut New Flagship Store at Iconic 40 Wall Street Building," *Marketing Business Weekly*, July 24, 2011, p. 23; and Robert Klara, "New York's Duane Reade Adds In-Store Yogurt Kiosks," *Adweek*, February 6–February 12, 2012, p. 16.

20. Based on information found in Samantha Murphy, "SoLoMo Revolution Picks Up Where Hyperlocal Search Left Off," *Mashable*, January 12, 2012, http://mashable.com/2012/01/12/solomo-hyperlocal-search/; and "Localeze/15miles Fifth Annual comScore Local Search Usage Study Reveals SoLoMo Revolution Has Taken Over," *Business Wire,* February 29, 2012.

21. Based on information found in Gwendolyn Bounds, "The Rise of Holiday Me-tailers," *Wall Street Journal*, December 8, 2010, p. D1; Abbey Klaassen, "Harley-Davidson Breaks Consumer-Created Work from Victors & Spoils," *Advertising Age,* February 14, 2012, http://adage.com/print?article_id=148873; and www.harley-davidson.com/en_US/Content/Pages/H-D1_Customization/h-d1_customization.html, accessed August 2012.

22. Julie Jargon, "McDonald's under Pressure to Fire Ronald," *Wall Street Journal*, May 18, 2011; Stephanie Strom, "McDonald's Trims *Its* Happy Meal," *New York Times,* July 26, 2011; and "McDonald's Introduces New Automatic Offerings of Fruit in Every Happy Meal," *PRNewswire,* January 20, 2012.

23. For these and other examples, see Stacy Weiner, "Goodbye to Girlhood," *Washington Post*, February 20, 2007, p. HE01; India Knight, "Relax: Girls Will Be Girls," *Sunday Times* (London), February 21, 2010, p. 4; and "Abercrombie & Fitch Removes 'Push-Up' from Girls' Bikini Description Following Outcry," *Fox News,* March 30, 2011, accessed at www.foxnews.com.

24. See "IC3 2011 Internet Crime Report Released," May 10, 2012, www.ic3.gov/media/default.aspx.

25. SUV sales data furnished by www.WardsAuto.com, accessed March 2012. Price data from www.edmunds.com, accessed March 2012.

26. Based on information found in Michael Myser, "Marketing Made Easy," *Business 2.0*, June 2006, pp. 43–44; Sandra Ward, "Nope, That Wasn't Easy," *Barron's,* December 5, 2011, p. 21; and www.staples.com, accessed August 2012.

27. Quote from "Singapore Airlines: Company Information," www.singaporeair.com, accessed November 2012.

28. Based on information from Philip Kotler and Kevin Lane Keller, *Marketing Management,* 14th ed., p. 336; and www.heartsonfire.com/Learn-About-Our-Diamonds.aspx, accessed November 2012.

29. See Bobby J. Calder and Steven J. Reagan, "Brand Design," in Dawn Iacobucci, ed., *Kellogg on Marketing* (New York: John Wiley & Sons, 2001), p. 61. For more discussion, see Kotler and Keller, *Marketing Management*, 14th ed., Chapter 10.

Part 1: Defining Marketing and the Marketing Process (Chapters 1–2)
Part 2: Understanding the Marketplace and Consumers (Chapters 3–6)
Part 3: Designing a Customer-Driven Strategy and Mix (Chapters 7–17)
Part 4: Extending Marketing (Chapters 18–20)

8

Products, Services, and Brands
Building Customer Value

Chapter Preview

After examining customer-driven marketing strategy, we now take a deeper look at the marketing mix: the tactical tools that marketers use to implement their strategies and deliver superior customer value. In this and the next chapter, we study how companies develop and manage products and brands. Then, in the chapters that follow, we look at pricing, distribution, and marketing communication tools. The product and brand are usually the first and most basic marketing consideration. We start with a seemingly simple question: What *is* a product? As it turns out, the answer is not so simple.

Before starting into the chapter, let's look at a good brand story. Marketing is all about creating brands that connect with customers, and few marketers have done that as well as Nike. During the past several decades, Nike has built the Nike swoosh into one of the world's best-known brand symbols. Nike's outstanding success results from much more than just making and selling good sports gear. It's based on a deep-down connection between the iconic Nike brand and its customers.

Nike: Building Deep-Down Brand-Customer Relationships

The Nike "swoosh"—it's everywhere! Just for fun, try counting the swooshes whenever you pick up the sports pages or watch a pickup basketball game or tune into a televised soccer match. Through innovative marketing, Nike has built the ever-present swoosh into one of the best-known brand symbols on the planet.

During the 1980s, Nike revolutionized sports marketing. To build its brand image and market share, Nike lavishly outspent its competitors on big-name endorsements, splashy promotional events, and big-budget, in-your-face "Just Do It" ads. Nike gave customers much more than just good athletic gear. Whereas competitors stressed technical performance, Nike built relationships between the brand and its customers. Beyond shoes, apparel, and equipment, Nike marketed a way of life, a genuine passion for sports, a just-do-it attitude. Customers didn't just wear their Nikes, they experienced them. As the company stated on its Web page, "Nike has always known the truth— it's not so much the shoes but where they take you."

Nike powered its way through the early 1990s, aggressively adding products in a dozen new sports, including baseball, golf, skateboarding, wall climbing, bicycling, and hiking. The then brash young company slapped its familiar brand and swoosh logo on everything from sunglasses and soccer balls to batting gloves and golf clubs. It seemed that things couldn't be going any better.

In the late 1990s, however, Nike stumbled and its sales slipped. As the company grew larger, its creative juices seemed to run a bit dry and buyers seeking a new look switched to competing brands. Looking back, Nike's biggest obstacle may have been its own incredible success. As sales grew, the swoosh may have become too common to be cool. Instead of being *anti* establishment, Nike *was* the establishment, and its hip, once-hot relationship with customers cooled. Nike needed to rekindle the brand's meaning to consumers.

> Nike's outstanding success results from much more than just good sports gear. It's based on a deep-down connection between the iconic Nike brand and its customers. Nike is quietly engineering a new brand marketing revolution.

To turn things around, Nike returned to its roots: new-product innovation and a focus on customer relationships. But it set out to forge a new kind of brand–customer connection—an even deeper, more involving one. This time around, rather than simply outspending competitors on big media ads and celebrity endorsers that talk *at* customers, Nike shifted toward cutting-edge digital and social marketing tools to interact *with* customers to build brand experiences and community. According to one industry analyst, "the legendary brand blew up its single-slogan approach and drafted a whole new playbook for the digital era." Nike is now "quietly engineering a [new] revolution in marketing."

Nike still invests heavily in creative advertising. But its spending on big-budget TV and print media has dropped dramatically, now accounting for only about 20 percent of the brand's $1 billion U.S. promotion budget. Instead, Nike spends the lion's share of its marketing budget on nontraditional media. Using community-oriented, digitally-led social networking tools, Nike is now building communities of customers who talk not just with the company about the brand, but with each other as well.

Nike has mastered social networking, both online and off. Whether customers come to know Nike through ads, in-person events at a Niketown store, Nike's Facebook page or YouTube channel, or one of the company's many community Web sites, more and more people are bonding closely with the Nike brand experience. Consider this example:

At a typical Niketown store, like-minded people meet twice a week for an after-hours run. After the run, Nike running club members swap stories over refreshments in the store. Nike staff keeps track of member performances, applauding individual accomplishments. The event is a classic example of up-close-and-personal relationship building with core customers.

But Nike has taken this personal touch much further. It augments such events with an online social network aimed at striking up meaningful long-term interactions with even more runners. The Nike+ running Web site lets customers with iPod-linked Nike shoes monitor their performances—the distance, pace, time, and calories burned during their runs. Runners can upload and track their own performances over time, compare them with those of other runners, and even participate in local or worldwide challenges.

Talk about brand involvement. Nike+ can be the next best thing to your own personal trainer or jogging buddy. Nike+ offers a "Nike Coach" that provides advice and training routines to help you prepare for competitive races. When running, at the end of every mile a friendly voice tells you how far you've gone and then counts down the final meters. If you hit the wall while running, the push of a button brings up a personally selected "power song" that gives you an extra boost and gets you going again. Back home again, after a quick upload of your running data, Nike+ charts, maps, and helps you analyze your run.

Some 5 million Nike+ members now log on to Nike to check their performance. The long-term goal is to have 15 percent of the world's 100 million runners using the system. The

Nike's deep connections with customers give it a powerful competitive advantage. Nike blurs the line between brand and experience.
Image of Sport Photos/Newscom

huge success of Nike+ has helped Nike to capture a stunning 61 percent the U.S. running market. It has also spawned an entire new Nike division—Nike Digital Sport—that aims to develop digital technologies and devices to help users to track their performance in any sport. For example, it recently introduced the FuelBand, a wristband that tracks energy output in any exercise activity.

Thanks to efforts like Nike+, along with a host of other new digital and social media approaches, Nike has built a new kinship and sense of community with and between the brand and its customers. Rather than relying on big, top-down campaigns, Nike has developed a repertoire of interactive approaches that connect the brand directly with customers, whether it's a performance-tracking wristband, a 30-story billboard that posts fan headlines from Twitter, or a major new commercial that debuts on Facebook rather than on primetime television. More than just something to buy, the Nike brand has once again become a part of customers' lives and times. As a result, Nike remains the world's largest sports apparel company, a full 30 percent bigger than closest rival Adidas. Over the past five years, even as the faltering economy left most sports apparel and footwear competitors gasping for breath, Nike's global sales and income raced ahead.

As in sports competition, the strongest and best-prepared brand has the best chance of winning. With deep brand-customer relationships comes powerful competitive advantage. And Nike is once again very close to its customers—maybe as close as it was in its early days when Phil Knight sold track shoes to customers personally out of the trunk of his car. As one writer notes, "Nike is blurring the line between brand and experience." Says Nike CEO Mark Parker, "Connecting used to be, 'Here's some product, and here's some advertising. We hope you like it.' Connecting today is a dialogue."[1]

Objective Outline

MyMarketingLab™

⭐ **Improve Your Grade!**

Over 10 million students improved their results using the Pearson MyLabs.
Visit **mymktlab.com** for simulations, tutorials, and end-of-chapter problems.

As the Nike example shows, in their quest to create customer relationships, marketers must build and manage products and brands that connect with customers. This chapter begins with a deceptively simple question: *What is a product?* After addressing this question, we look at ways to classify products in consumer and business markets. Then we discuss the important decisions that marketers make regarding individual products, product lines, and product mixes. Next, we examine the characteristics and marketing requirements of a special form of product—services. Finally, we look into the critically important issue of how marketers build and manage product and service brands.

Objective 1 ┈┈┈▶

Define *product* and the major classifications of products and services.

Product
Anything that can be offered to a market for attention, acquisition, use, or consumption that might satisfy a want or need.

Service
An activity, benefit, or satisfaction offered for sale that is essentially intangible and does not result in the ownership of anything.

What Is a Product?

We define a **product** as anything that can be offered to a market for attention, acquisition, use, or consumption that might satisfy a want or need. Products include more than just tangible objects, such as cars, computers, or mobile phones. Broadly defined, *products* also include services, events, persons, places, organizations, ideas, or a mixture of these. Throughout this text, we use the term *product* broadly to include any or all of these entities. Thus, an Apple iPhone, a Toyota Camry, and a Caffè Mocha at Starbucks are products. But so are a trip to Las Vegas, Schwab online investment services, your Facebook page, and advice from your family doctor.

Because of their importance in the world economy, we give special attention to services. **Services** are a form of product that consists of activities, benefits, or satisfactions offered for sale that are essentially intangible and do not result in the ownership of anything. Examples include banking, hotel, airline travel, retail, wireless communication, and home-repair services. We will look at services more closely later in this chapter.

Products, Services, and Experiences

Products are a key element in the overall *market offering*. Marketing mix planning begins with building an offering that brings value to target customers. This offering becomes the basis on which the company builds profitable customer relationships.

A company's market offering often includes both tangible goods and services. At one extreme, the market offer may consist of a *pure tangible good*, such as soap, toothpaste, or salt; no services accompany the product. At the other extreme are *pure services*, for which the market offer consists primarily of a service. Examples include a doctor's exam and financial services. Between these two extremes, however, many goods-and-services combinations are possible.

Today, as products and services become more commoditized, many companies are moving to a new level in creating value for their customers. To differentiate their offers, beyond simply making products and delivering services, they are creating and managing customer *experiences* with their brands or company.

Experiences have always been an important part of marketing for some companies. Disney has long manufactured dreams and memories through its movies and theme parks. And Nike has long declared, "It's not so much the shoes but where they take you." Today, however, all kinds of firms are recasting their traditional goods and services to create experiences. ● For example, Starbucks services up more than just a hot cup of coffee:[2]

Three decades ago, Howard Schultz hit on the idea of bringing a European-style coffeehouse to America. He believed that people needed to slow down, to "smell the coffee" and enjoy life a little more. The result was Starbucks. This coffeehouse doesn't sell just coffee, it sells The Starbucks Experience—one that enriches customers' lives. The smells, the hissing steam, the comfy chairs—all contribute to the Starbucks ambience. Starbucks gives customers what it calls a "third place"—away from home and away from work—a place for conversation and a sense of community. As a result, Starbucks has transformed coffee from a commodity to a $4 splurge and the company's sales and profits have risen like steam off a mug of hot java.

Companies that market experiences realize that customers are really buying much more than just products and services. They are buying what those offers will *do* for them. A recent BMW ad puts it this way: "We realized a long time ago that what you make people feel is just as important as what you make."

● Creating customer experiences: Starbucks doesn't sell just coffee, it sells The Starbucks Experience—what it calls a "third place"—away from home and away from work, a place for conversation and a sense of community.

© Daily Mail/Rex/Alamy

Levels of Product and Services

Product planners need to think about products and services on three levels (see ● **Figure 8.1**). Each level adds more customer value. The most basic level is the *core customer value*, which addresses the question: *What is the buyer really buying?* When designing products, marketers must first define the core, problem-solving benefits or services that consumers seek. A woman buying lipstick buys more than lip color. Charles Revson of Revlon saw this early: "In the factory, we make cosmetics; in the store, we sell hope." ● And people who buy an Apple iPad are buying much more than just a tablet computer. They are buying entertainment, self-expression, productivity, and connectivity with friends and family—a mobile and personal window to the world.

At the second level, product planners must turn the core benefit into an *actual product*. They need to develop product and service features, a design, a quality level, a brand name, and packaging. For example, the iPad is an actual product. Its name, parts, styling,

● **Core, actual, and augmented product: People who buy an iPad are buying much more than a tablet computer. They are buying entertainment, self-expression, productivity, and connectivity—a mobile and personal window to the world.**

Betsie Van der Meer/Getty Images

features, packaging, and other attributes have all been carefully combined to deliver the core customer value of staying connected.

Finally, product planners must build an *augmented product* around the core benefit and actual product by offering additional consumer services and benefits. The iPad is more than just a digital device. It provides consumers with a complete connectivity solution. Thus, when consumers buy an iPad, Apple and its resellers also might give buyers a warranty on parts and workmanship, instructions on how to use the device, quick repair services when needed, and a Web site to use if they have problems or questions. Apple also provides access to a huge assortment of apps and accessories.

Consumers see products as complex bundles of benefits that satisfy their needs. When developing products, marketers first must identify the *core customer value* that consumers seek from the product. They must then design the *actual* product and find ways to *augment* it to create this customer value and the most satisfying brand experience.

Product and Service Classifications

Products and services fall into two broad classes based on the types of consumers that use them: *consumer products* and *industrial products*. Broadly defined, products also include other marketable entities such as experiences, organizations, persons, places, and ideas.

Consumer Products

Consumer product

A product bought by final consumers for personal consumption.

Consumer products are products and services bought by final consumers for personal consumption. Marketers usually classify these products and services further based on how consumers go about buying them. Consumer products include *convenience products*, *shopping products*, *specialty products*, and *unsought products*. These products differ in the ways consumers buy them and, therefore, in how they are marketed (see ● **Table 8.1**).

●**FIGURE | 8.1**
Three Levels of Product

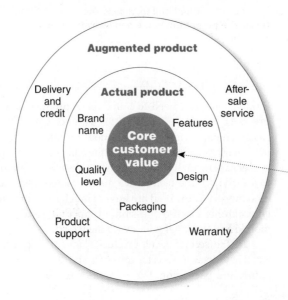

At the most basic level, the company asks, "What is the customer really buying? For example, people who buy an Apple iPad are buying more than just a tablet computer. They are buying entertainment, self-expression, productivity, and connectivity—a mobile and personal window to the world.

● Table 8.1 | Marketing Considerations for Consumer Products

Marketing Considerations	Type of Consumer Product			
	Convenience	Shopping	Specialty	Unsought
Customer buying behavior	Frequent purchase; little planning, little comparison or shopping effort; low customer involvement	Less frequent purchase; much planning and shopping effort; comparison of brands on price, quality, and style	Strong brand preference and loyalty; special purchase effort; little comparison of brands; low price sensitivity	Little product awareness or knowledge (or, if aware, little or even negative interest)
Price	Low price	Higher price	High price	Varies
Distribution	Widespread distribution; convenient locations	Selective distribution in fewer outlets	Exclusive distribution in only one or a few outlets per market area	Varies
Promotion	Mass promotion by the producer	Advertising and personal selling by both the producer and resellers	More carefully targeted promotion by both the producer and resellers	Aggressive advertising and personal selling by the producer and resellers
Examples	Toothpaste, magazines, and laundry detergent	Major appliances, televisions, furniture, and clothing	Luxury goods, such as Rolex watches or fine crystal	Life insurance and Red Cross blood donations

Convenience product
A consumer product that customers usually buy frequently, immediately, and with minimal comparison and buying effort.

Shopping product
A consumer product that the customer, in the process of selecting and purchasing, usually compares on such attributes as suitability, quality, price, and style.

Specialty product
A consumer product with unique characteristics or brand identification for which a significant group of buyers is willing to make a special purchase effort.

Unsought product
A consumer product that the consumer either does not know about or knows about but does not normally consider buying.

Industrial product
A product bought by individuals and organizations for further processing or for use in conducting a business.

Convenience products are consumer products and services that customers usually buy frequently, immediately, and with minimal comparison and buying effort. Examples include laundry detergent, candy, magazines, and fast food. Convenience products are usually low priced, and marketers place them in many locations to make them readily available when customers need or want them.

Shopping products are less frequently purchased consumer products and services that customers compare carefully on suitability, quality, price, and style. When buying shopping products and services, consumers spend much time and effort in gathering information and making comparisons. Examples include furniture, clothing, used cars, major appliances, and hotel and airline services. Shopping product marketers usually distribute their products through fewer outlets but provide deeper sales support to help customers in their comparison efforts.

Specialty products are consumer products and services with unique characteristics or brand identification for which a significant group of buyers is willing to make a special purchase effort. Examples include specific brands of cars, high-priced photography equipment, designer clothes, gourmet foods, and the services of medical or legal specialists. A Lamborghini automobile, for example, is a specialty product because buyers are usually willing to travel great distances to buy one. Buyers normally do not compare specialty products. They invest only the time needed to reach dealers carrying the wanted products.

Unsought products are consumer products that the consumer either does not know about or knows about but does not normally consider buying. Most major new innovations are unsought until the consumer becomes aware of them through advertising. Classic examples of known but unsought products and services are life insurance, preplanned funeral services, and blood donations to the Red Cross. By their very nature, unsought products require a lot of advertising, personal selling, and other marketing efforts.

Industrial Products

Industrial products are those products purchased for further processing or for use in conducting a business. Thus, the distinction between a consumer product and an industrial product is based on the *purpose* for which the product is purchased. If a consumer buys a lawn mower for use around home, the lawn mower is a consumer product. If the same consumer buys the same lawn mower for use in a landscaping business, the lawn mower is an industrial product.

The three groups of industrial products and services are materials and parts, capital items, and supplies and services. *Materials and parts* include raw materials as well as manufactured materials and parts. Raw materials consist of farm products (wheat, cotton, livestock, fruits, vegetables) and natural products (fish, lumber, crude petroleum, iron ore). Manufactured materials and parts consist of component materials (iron, yarn, cement, wires) and component parts (small motors, tires, castings). Most manufactured materials and parts are sold directly to industrial users. Price and service are the major marketing factors; branding and advertising tend to be less important.

Capital items are industrial products that aid in the buyer's production or operations, including installations and accessory equipment. Installations consist of major purchases such as buildings (factories, offices) and fixed equipment (generators, drill presses, large computer systems, elevators). Accessory equipment includes portable factory equipment and tools (hand tools, lift trucks) and office equipment (computers, fax machines, desks). They have a shorter life than installations and simply aid in the production process.

The final group of industrial products is *supplies and services*. Supplies include operating supplies (lubricants, coal, paper, pencils) and repair and maintenance items (paint, nails, brooms). Supplies are the convenience products of the industrial field because they are usually purchased with a minimum of effort or comparison. Business services include maintenance and repair services (window cleaning, computer repair) and business advisory services (legal, management consulting, advertising). Such services are usually supplied under contract.

Organizations, Persons, Places, and Ideas

In addition to tangible products and services, marketers have broadened the concept of a product to include other market offerings: organizations, persons, places, and ideas.

Organizations often carry out activities to "sell" the organization itself. *Organization marketing* consists of activities undertaken to create, maintain, or change the attitudes and behavior of target consumers toward an organization. Both profit and not-for-profit organizations practice organization marketing. Business firms sponsor public relations or *corporate image marketing* campaigns to market themselves and polish their images. IBM's Smarter Planet campaign, for example, markets IBM as a company that provides innovative solutions that improve the world's IQ. IBM smart solutions span an incredible breadth of industries and processes—from commerce and digital communications to health care, education, and sustainability.  For example, one Smarter Planet ad tells how IBM is helping to "track food from farm to fork" in an effort to reduce the 25 percent of the world's food currently lost to spoilage. At the other extreme, ads tell how IBM analytics helped New York City's NYPD cut crime by 35 percent and New York State save $889 million by catching tax dodgers.

People can also be thought of as products. *Person marketing* consists of activities undertaken to create, maintain, or change attitudes or behavior toward particular people. People ranging from presidents, entertainers, and sports figures to professionals such as doctors, lawyers, and architects use person marketing to build their reputations. And businesses, charities, and other organizations use well-known personalities to help sell their products or causes. For example, Nike is represented by well-known athletes such as Kobe Bryant, Serena Williams, and hundreds of others around the globe in sports ranging from tennis and basketball to ice hockey and cricket.

The skillful use of marketing can turn a person's name into a powerhouse brand. Consider the chefs on the Food Network, who now approximate rock stars to their many ardent fans. These days it's hard to shop for kitchen products without bumping into goods endorsed by these culinary all-stars. For example, celebrity chef Rachael Ray is a one-woman marketing phenomenon. Beyond her Food Network shows, she landed her own daytime talk show; endorses a litany of orange-colored cookware, bakeware, and cutlery; has her own brand of dog food called Nutrish; and brands her own EVOO (extra virgin olive oil, for those not familiar with Rayisms). Target even has a Rachael Ray online brand shop, featuring its Rachel Ray collection of "cool tools for your kitchen," along with "ideas for cooking and entertaining that you can use every day."[3]

Place marketing involves activities undertaken to create, maintain, or change attitudes or behavior toward particular places. Cities, states, regions, and even entire nations compete to attract tourists, new residents, conventions,

Food is now followed from farm to fork.

In Manitoba, smarter supply chains help reduce Canada's 13 million food poisoning cases.

ibm.com/smarterplanet

IBM

● **Organization marketing: IBM's Smarter Planet campaign markets IBM as a company that helps improve the world's IQ. This ad tells how IBM technologies are helping to create safer food supply chains.**

Courtesy of International Business Machines Corporation, © International Business Machines Corporation.

and company offices and factories. New York State advertises "I ❤ NY." And Michigan invites you to experience unspoiled nature, lakes that feel like oceans, miles of cherry orchards, glorious sunsets, and nighttime skies scattered with stars in Pure Michigan.

Brand USA, a public-private marketing partnership created by recent act of Congress, promotes the United States as a tourist destination to international travelers. Supported by a $200 million budget, Brand USA's mission is to "represent the true greatness of America—from sea to shining sea." Competition for international tourism is fierce from other countries marketing their attractions, led by Mexico, which spends about $175 annually advertising the country. Great Britain spends $160 million; Australia, $107 million; and Turkey, $99 million. One expert estimates that, without effective marketing, the United States has lost a potential 78 million visitors over the past 10 years, representing an estimated $606 billion in spending. The Brand USA marketing campaign includes country-by-country ads and promotions, as well as a comprehensive DiscoverAmerica.com Web site, which provides featured destinations, U.S. travel information and tips, and travel planning tools.[4]

Ideas can also be marketed. In one sense, all marketing is the marketing of an idea, whether it is the general idea of brushing your teeth or the specific idea that Crest toothpastes create "healthy, beautiful smiles for life." Here, however, we narrow our focus to the marketing of *social ideas*. This area has been called **social marketing**, defined by the Social Marketing Institute (SMI) as the use of commercial marketing concepts and tools in programs designed to influence individuals' behavior to improve their well-being and that of society.[5]

Social marketing programs cover a wide range of issues. The Ad Council of America (*www.adcouncil.org*), for example, has developed dozens of social advertising campaigns involving issues ranging from health care, education, and environmental sustainability to human rights and personal safety. But social marketing involves much more than just advertising—the SMI encourages the use of a broad range of marketing tools. "Social marketing goes well beyond the promotional '*P*' of the marketing mix to include every other element to achieve its social change objectives," says the SMI's executive director.[6]

Social marketing

The use of commercial marketing concepts and tools in programs designed to influence individuals' behavior to improve their well-being and that of society.

Product and Service Decisions

Marketers make product and service decisions at three levels: individual product decisions, product line decisions, and product mix decisions. We discuss each in turn.

Individual Product and Service Decisions

Objective 2 ⤑
Describe the decisions companies make regarding their individual products and services, product lines, and product mixes.

● **Figure 8.2** shows the important decisions in the development and marketing of individual products and services. We will focus on decisions about *product attributes, branding, packaging, labeling,* and *product support services.*

Product and Service Attributes

Developing a product or service involves defining the benefits that it will offer. These benefits are communicated and delivered by product attributes such as *quality, features,* and *style and design.*

Product Quality. **Product quality** is one of the marketer's major positioning tools. Quality affects product or service performance; thus, it is closely linked to customer value and satisfaction. In the narrowest sense, quality can be defined as "freedom from defects." But most marketers go beyond this narrow definition. Instead, they define quality in terms of creating customer value and satisfaction. The American Society for Quality defines *quality* as the characteristics of a product or service that bear on its ability to satisfy stated or implied customer needs. Similarly, Siemens defines quality this way: "Quality is when our customers come back and our products don't."[7]

Total quality management (TQM) is an approach in which all of the company's people are involved in constantly improving the quality of products, services, and business processes.

Product quality

The characteristics of a product or service that bear on its ability to satisfy stated or implied customer needs.

● **FIGURE | 8.2**
Individual Product Decisions

Don't forget Figure 8.1. The focus of all of these decisions is to create core customer value.

For most top companies, customer-driven quality has become a way of doing business. Today, companies are taking a *return on quality* approach, viewing quality as an investment and holding quality efforts accountable for bottom-line results.

Product quality has two dimensions: level and consistency. In developing a product, the marketer must first choose a *quality level* that will support the product's positioning. Here, product quality means *performance quality*—the product's ability to perform its functions. For example, a Rolls-Royce provides higher performance quality than a Chevrolet: It has a smoother ride, provides more luxury and "creature comforts," and lasts longer. Companies rarely try to offer the highest possible performance quality level; few customers want or can afford the high levels of quality offered in products such as a Rolls-Royce automobile, a Viking range, or a Rolex watch. Instead, companies choose a quality level that matches target market needs and the quality levels of competing products.

Beyond quality level, high quality also can mean high levels of quality consistency. Here, product quality means *conformance quality*—freedom from defects and *consistency* in delivering a targeted level of performance. All companies should strive for high levels of conformance quality. In this sense, a Chevrolet can have just as much quality as a Rolls-Royce. Although a Chevy doesn't perform at the same level as a Rolls-Royce, it can just as consistently deliver the quality that customers pay for and expect.

Product Features. A product can be offered with varying features. A stripped-down model, one without any extras, is the starting point. The company can then create higher-level models by adding more features. Features are a competitive tool for differentiating the company's product from competitors' products. Being the first producer to introduce a valued new feature is one of the most effective ways to compete.

How can a company identify new features and decide which ones to add to its product? It should periodically survey buyers who have used the product and ask these questions: How do you like the product? Which specific features of the product do you like most? Which features could we add to improve the product? The answers to these questions provide the company with a rich list of feature ideas. The company can then assess each feature's *value* to customers versus its *cost* to the company. Features that customers value highly in relation to costs should be added.

Product Style and Design. Another way to add customer value is through distinctive *product style and design*. Design is a larger concept than style. *Style* simply describes the appearance of a product. Styles can be eye catching or yawn producing. A sensational style may grab attention and produce pleasing aesthetics, but it does not necessarily make the product *perform* better. Unlike style, *design* is more than skin deep—it goes to the very heart of a product. Good design contributes to a product's usefulness as well as to its looks.

Good design doesn't start with brainstorming new ideas and making prototypes. Design begins with observing customers, deeply understanding their needs, and shaping their product-use experience. Product designers should think less about technical product specifications and more about how customers will use and benefit from the product. ● Consider OXO's outstanding design philosophy and process:[8]

> OXO's uniquely designed kitchen and gardening gadgets look pretty cool. But to OXO, good design means a lot more than good looks. It means that OXO tools work—*really* work—for anyone and everyone. For OXO, design means a salad spinner that can be used with one hand; tools with pressure-absorbing, nonslip handles that make them more efficient; or a watering can with a spout that rotates back toward the body, allowing for easier filling and storing. Ever since it came out with its supereffective Good Grips vegetable peeler in 1990, OXO has been known for clever designs that make everyday living easier. Its eye-catching, super useful

We've remodeled the most important parts of your kitchen.

We've remodeled the peeler. We've remodeled the garlic press, the can opener and the wooden spoon. And we didn't stop there. Any kitchen tools that weren't comfortable or easy to use were fair game. The idea isn't to make the old tools obsolete, it's to make them better. If we can't make them better, we don't make them at all. Pick up OXO Good Grips and you'll feel what we mean. They're easy to hold, easy to use and easy to love. In fact, they might just change the way you feel about your kitchen.

⊂OXO⊃ GOOD GRIPS

For information call 1-800-545-4411

● **Product design: OXO focuses on the desired end-user experience, and then translates its pie-cutter-in-the-sky notions into eminently usable gadgets.**

OXO International Inc.

houseware designs have even been featured in museum exhibitions, and OXO has now extended its design touch to office supplies, medical devices, and baby products.

Much of OXO's design inspiration comes directly from users. "Every product that we make starts with . . . watching how people use things," says Alex Lee, OXO's president. "Those are the gems—when you pull out a latent problem." For example, after watching people struggle with the traditional Pyrex measuring cup, OXO discovered a critical flaw: You can't tell how full it is without lifting it up to eye level. The resulting OXO measuring cups have markings down the *inside* that can be read from above, big enough to read without glasses. Thus, OXO begins with a desired end-user experience and then translates pie-cutter-in-the-sky notions into eminently usable gadgets.

Branding

Brand

A name, term, sign, symbol, or design, or a combination of these, that identifies the products or services of one seller or group of sellers and differentiates them from those of competitors.

Perhaps the most distinctive skill of professional marketers is their ability to build and manage brands. A **brand** is a name, term, sign, symbol, or design, or a combination of these, that identifies the maker or seller of a product or service. Consumers view a brand as an important part of a product, and branding can add value to a consumer's purchase. Customers attach meanings to brands and develop brand relationships. As a result, brands have meaning well beyond a product's physical attributes. For example, consider Coca-Cola:[9]

> In an interesting taste test of Coca-Cola versus Pepsi, 67 subjects were connected to brain-wave-monitoring machines while they consumed both products. When the soft drinks were unmarked, consumer preferences were split down the middle. But when the brands were identified, subjects chose Coke over Pepsi by a margin of 75 percent to 25 percent. When drinking the identified Coke brand, the brain areas that lit up most were those associated with cognitive control and memory—a place where culture concepts are stored. That didn't happen as much when drinking Pepsi. Why? According to one brand strategist, it's because of Coca-Cola's long-established brand imagery—the almost 100-year-old contour bottle, the bright red cans, the cursive font, and its association with iconic images ranging from the Polar Bears to Santa Claus. Pepsi's imagery isn't quite as deeply rooted. People apparently don't link Pepsi to the strong and emotional American icons associated with Coke. The conclusion? Plain and simple: Consumer preference isn't based on taste alone. Coke's iconic brand name appears to make a difference.

Branding has become so strong that today hardly anything goes unbranded. Salt is packaged in branded containers, common nuts and bolts are packaged with a distributor's label, and automobile parts—spark plugs, tires, filters—bear brand names that differ from those of the automakers. Even fruits, vegetables, dairy products, and poultry are branded—Sunkist oranges, Dole Classic iceberg salads, Horizon Organic milk, Perdue chickens, and Eggland's Best eggs.

Branding helps buyers in many ways. Brand names help consumers identify products that might benefit them. Brands also say something about product quality and consistency—buyers who always buy the same brand know that they will get the same features, benefits, and quality each time they buy. Branding also gives the seller several advantages. The seller's brand name and trademark provide legal protection for unique product features that otherwise might be copied by competitors. Branding helps the seller to segment markets. For example, rather than offering just one general product to all consumers, Toyota can offer the different Lexus, Toyota, and Scion brands, each with numerous sub-brands—such as Camry, Corolla, Prius, Matrix, Yaris, Tundra, and Land Cruiser. Finally, a brand name becomes the basis on which a whole story can be built about a product's special qualities. For example, Eggland's Best sets itself apart from ordinary eggs by promising: "Better Taste. Better Nutrition. Better Eggs."

Building and managing brands are perhaps the marketer's most important tasks. We will discuss branding strategy in more detail later in the chapter.

Packaging

Packaging

The activities of designing and producing the container or wrapper for a product.

Packaging involves designing and producing the container or wrapper for a product. Traditionally, the primary function of the package was to hold and protect the product. In recent times, however, packaging has become an important marketing tool as well. Increased competition and clutter on retail store shelves means that packages must now perform many sales tasks—from attracting buyers, to communicating brand positioning, to closing the sale. As one packaging expert notes, "Not every consumer sees a brand's advertising or is exposed to the exciting social media that your brand is doing. But all of the consumers who buy your product do interact with your humble package."[10]

Companies are realizing the power of good packaging to create immediate consumer recognition of a brand. For example, an average supermarket stocks about 38,700 items; the average Walmart supercenter carries 142,000 items. The typical shopper makes 70 percent of all purchase decisions in stores and passes by some 300 items per minute. In this highly competitive environment, the package may be the seller's last and best chance to influence buyers. Thus, for many companies, the package itself has become an important promotional medium.[11]

Poorly designed packages can cause headaches for consumers and lost sales for the company. Think about all those hard-to-open packages, such as DVD cases sealed with impossibly sticky labels, packaging with finger-splitting wire twist-ties, or sealed plastic clamshell containers that cause "wrap rage" and send about 6,000 people to the hospital each year with lacerations and puncture wounds. Another packaging issue is overpackaging—as when a tiny USB flash drive in an oversized cardboard and plastic display package is delivered in a giant corrugated shipping carton. Overpackaging creates an incredible amount of waste, frustrating those who care about the environment.[12]

By contrast, innovative packaging can give a company an advantage over competitors and boost sales. ● For example, Puma recently replace the traditional shoebox with an attractive and functional yet environmentally friendly alternative—the Clever Little Bag:[13]

● Innovative packaging: Puma's next-generation shoe packaging—The Clever Little Box—is more than just friendly to the environment, it's also very friendly to consumers' sensibilities and the company's bottom line. Pretty clever, huh?

PUMA

In their search for the next generation of shoe packaging, Puma's designers spent 21 months road testing 40 shoebox prototypes, checking on their potential environmental impact from production and transport through use and future re-use. They came up with what Puma calls the Clever Little Bag with a big impact. The new container—which consists of a light cardboard insert that slides seamlessly into a colorful, reusable red bag—uses 65 percent less paper to make and reduces water, energy, and fuel consumption during manufacturing by more than 60 percent a year. Because it takes up less space and weighs, the new container also reduces carbon emissions during shipping by 10,000 tons a year. What's more, everything is 100 percent recyclable. In all, Puma's Clever Little Bag is more than just friendly to the environment, it's also very friendly to consumers" likes and the company's bottom line. Pretty clever, huh?

In recent years, product safety has also become a major packaging concern. We have all learned to deal with hard-to-open "childproof" packaging. Due to the rash of product tampering scares in the 1980s, most drug producers and food makers now put their products in tamper-resistant packages. In making packaging decisions, the company also must heed growing environmental concerns. Fortunately, like Puma, many companies have gone "green" by reducing their packaging and using environmentally responsible packaging materials.

Labeling

Labels range from simple tags attached to products to complex graphics that are part of the packaging. They perform several functions. At the very least, the label *identifies* the product or brand, such as the name Sunkist stamped on oranges. The label might also *describe* several things about the product—who made it, where it was made, when it was made, its contents, how it is to be used, and how to use it safely. Finally, the label might help to *promote* the brand, support its positioning, and connect with customers. For many companies, labels have become an important element in broader marketing campaigns.

Labels and brand logos can support the brand's positioning and add personality to the brand. For example, although similar to the familiar red, white, and blue logo that customers would have seen 60 years ago, Pepsi's recently introduced a new, more uplifting smiling logo. "It feels like the same Pepsi we know and love," says a brand expert, "but it's more adventurous, more youthful, with a bit more personality to it." It presents a "spirit of optimism and youth," says a Pepsi marketer.[14]

● Brand labels and logos: When Gap tried to modernize its familiar old logo, customers went ballistic, highlighting the powerful connection people have to the visual representations of their beloved brands.

Jean Francois FREY/PHOTOPQR/L'ALSACE/Newscom

In fact, brand labels and logos can become a crucial element in the brand-customer connection. ● For example, when Gap recently introduced a more contemporary redesign of its familiar old logo—the well-known white text on a blue square—customers went ballistic and imposed intense online pressure. Gap reinstated the old logo after only one week. Such examples "highlight a powerful connection people have to the visual representations of their beloved brands," says an analyst.[15]

Along with the positives, there has been a long history of legal concerns about packaging and labels. The Federal Trade Commission Act of 1914 held that false, misleading, or deceptive labels or packages constitute unfair competition. Labels can mislead customers, fail to describe important ingredients, or fail to include needed safety warnings. As a result, several federal and state laws regulate labeling. The most prominent is the Fair Packaging and Labeling Act of 1966, which set mandatory labeling requirements, encouraged voluntary industry packaging standards, and allowed federal agencies to set packaging regulations in specific industries.

Labeling has been affected in recent times by *unit pricing* (stating the price per unit of a standard measure), *open dating* (stating the expected shelf life of the product), and *nutritional labeling* (stating the nutritional values in the product). The Nutritional Labeling and Educational Act of 1990 requires sellers to provide detailed nutritional information on food products, and recent sweeping actions by the Food and Drug Administration (FDA) regulate the use of health-related terms such as *low fat*, *light*, and *high fiber*. Sellers must ensure that their labels contain all the required information.

Product Support Services

Customer service is another element of product strategy. A company's offer usually includes some support services, which can be a minor part or a major part of the total offering. Later in this chapter, we will discuss services as products in themselves. Here, we discuss services that augment actual products.

Support services are an important part of the customer's overall brand experience. ● For example, upscale department store retailer Nordstrom knows that good marketing doesn't stop with making the sale. Keeping customers happy *after* the sale is the key to building lasting relationships. Nordstrom's motto: "Take care of customers, no matter what it takes," before, during, and after the sale.[16]

Nordstrom thrives on stories about its after-sale service heroics, such as employees dropping off orders at customers' homes or warming up cars while customers spend a little more time shopping. In one case, a sales clerk reportedly gave a customer a refund on a tire—Nordstrom doesn't carry tires, but the store prides itself on a no-questions-asked return policy. In another case, a Nordstrom sales clerk stopped a customer in the store and asked if the shoes she was wearing had been bought there. When a customer said yes, the clerk insisted on replacing them on the spot, saying that they hadn't worn as well as they should. There's even a story about a man whose wife, a loyal Nordstrom customer, died with her Nordstrom

● Customer service: Nordstrom knows that keeping customers happy *after* the sale is the key to building lasting relationships. Nordstrom's motto: "Take care of customers, no matter what it takes."

AP Photo

account $1,000 in arrears. Not only did Nordstrom settle the account, but it also sent flowers to the funeral. Such service heroics keep Nordstrom customers coming back again and again.

The first step in designing support services is to survey customers periodically to assess the value of current services and obtain ideas for new ones. Once the company has assessed the quality of various support services to customers, it can take steps to fix problems and add new services that will both delight customers and yield profits to the company.

Many companies now use a sophisticated mix of phone, e-mail, Internet, and interactive voice and data technologies to provide support services that were not possible before. For example, AT&T offers a complete set of after-sale services for all of its products, from wireless to digital TV. Customers can access 24/7 tech support via an AT&T Live Agent, either by phone or online. In addition, its online support pages offer troubleshooting, virtual tours, and Ask Charlie, AT&T's virtual expert feature.[17]

Product Line Decisions

Product line

A group of products that are closely related because they function in a similar manner, are sold to the same customer groups, are marketed through the same types of outlets, or fall within given price ranges.

Beyond decisions about individual products and services, product strategy also calls for building a product line. A **product line** is a group of products that are closely related because they function in a similar manner, are sold to the same customer groups, are marketed through the same types of outlets, or fall within given price ranges. For example, Nike produces several lines of athletic shoes and apparel, and Marriott offers several lines of hotels.

The major product line decision involves *product line length*—the number of items in the product line. The line is too short if the manager can increase profits by adding items; the line is too long if the manager can increase profits by dropping items. Managers need to analyze their product lines periodically to assess each item's sales and profits and understand how each item contributes to the line's overall performance.

A company can expand its product line in two ways: by *line filling* or *line stretching*. *Product line filling* involves adding more items within the present range of the line. There are several reasons for product line filling: reaching for extra profits, satisfying dealers, using excess capacity, being the leading full-line company, and plugging holes to keep out competitors. However, line filling is overdone if it results in cannibalization and customer confusion. The company should ensure that new items are noticeably different from existing ones.

Product line stretching occurs when a company lengthens its product line beyond its current range. The company can stretch its line downward, upward, or both ways. Companies located at the upper end of the market can stretch their lines *downward*. A company may stretch downward to plug a market hole that otherwise would attract a new competitor or respond to a competitor's attack on the upper end. Or it may add low-end products because it finds faster growth taking place in the low-end segments. Companies can also stretch their product lines *upward*. Sometimes, companies stretch upward to add prestige to their current products. Or they may be attracted by a faster growth rate or higher margins at the higher end.

To broaden its market appeal and boost growth, BMW has in recent years stretched its line in *both directions* while at the same time filling the gaps in between.[18]

Over the past decade, BMW has morphed from a one-brand, five-model carmaker into a powerhouse with three brands, 14 "Series," and more than 30 distinct models. Not only has the carmaker stretched its product line downward, with MINI Cooper and its compact 1-Series models, but it has also stretched it upward with the addition of Rolls-Royce. The company has filled the gaps in between with Z4 roadsters, 6-Series coupe, X-Series crossovers and sports activity vehicles; and M-Series high-performance models. Next up: a growing selection of hybrids and all-electric cars. As a result, BMW has boosted its appeal to the rich, the super-rich, and the wannabe-rich, all without departing from its pure premium positioning.

Product Mix Decisions

Product mix (or product portfolio)

The set of all product lines and items that a particular seller offers for sale.

An organization with several product lines has a product mix. A **product mix** (or **product portfolio**) consists of all the product lines and items that a particular seller offers for sale. Campbell Soup Company's product mix consists of three major product lines: healthy beverages, baked snacks, and simple meals.[19] Each product line consists of several sublines. For example, the simple meals line consists of soups, sauces, and pastas. Each line and subline has many individual items. Altogether, Campbell's product mix includes hundreds of items.

A Winning Combination

At Campbell, we are focused on three large and growing categories: Healthy Beverages, Baked Snacks and Simple Meals. Our brands are market leaders in their principal geographies. We have world-class product technologies, an experienced, talented team and the financial strength to invest in growth. It all adds up to a focused food company with a winning portfolio for nourishing people's lives everywhere, every day.

● The product mix: Campbell Soup Company has a nicely contained product line consistent with its mission of "nourishing people's lives everywhere, every day."

Campbell Soup Company

A company's product mix has four important dimensions: width, length, depth, and consistency. Product mix *width* refers to the number of different product lines the company carries. ● For example, Campbell Soup Company has a fairly contained product mix that fits its mission of "nourishing people's lives everywhere, every day." By contrast, GE manufactures as many as 250,000 items across a broad range of categories, from light bulbs to medical equipment, jet engines, and diesel locomotives.

Product mix *length* refers to the total number of items a company carries within its product lines. Campbell Soup carries several brands within each line. For example, its simple meals line includes Campbell's soups, Wolfgang Puck soups and broths, Prego tomato sauce, Pace salsas, and Swanson broths, plus other international brands.

Product mix *depth* refers to the number of versions offered for each product in the line. Campbell's soups come in seven varieties, ranging from Campbell's Condensed soups and Campbell's Chunky soups to Campbell's Select Harvest soups and Campbell's Healthy Request soups. Each variety offers a number of forms and formulations. For example, you can buy Campbell's Chunky Hearty Beef Noodle soup, Chunky Chicken & Dumplings soup, and Chunky Steak & Potato soup, in either cans or microwavable containers.

Finally, the *consistency* of the product mix refers to how closely related the various product lines are in end use, production requirements, distribution channels, or some other way. Campbell Soup Company's product lines are consistent insofar as they are consumer products and go through the same distribution channels. The lines are less consistent insofar as they perform different functions for buyers.

These product mix dimensions provide the handles for defining the company's product strategy. The company can increase its business in four ways. It can add new product lines, widening its product mix. In this way, its new lines build on the company's reputation in its other lines. The company can lengthen its existing product lines to become a more full-line company. It can add more versions of each product and thus deepen its product mix. Finally, the company can pursue more product line consistency—or less—depending on whether it wants to have a strong reputation in a single field or in several fields.

From time to time, a company may also have to streamline its product mix to pare out marginally performing lines and models and to regain its focus. For example, as a central part of its recent turnaround, Ford gave its product mix a major pruning:[20]

> Ford culled its herd of nameplates from 97 to fewer than 20. It dropped the Mercury line altogether and sold off the Volvo line. Pruning the company's brands especially thrilled Ford CEO Alan Mulally, who still comes unhinged thinking about how unfocused, how uncool, the Ford brand had become. "I mean, we had 97 of these, for [goodness] sake!" he says, pointing to the list of old models. "How you gonna make 'em all cool? You gonna come in at 8 a.m. and say 'from 8 until noon I'm gonna make No. 64 cool? And then I'll make No. 17 cool after lunch?' It was ridiculous.

Objective 3 ⸻▶
Identify the four characteristics that affect the marketing of services and the additional marketing considerations that services require.

Services Marketing

Services have grown dramatically in recent years. Services now account for close to 65 percent of the U.S. gross domestic product (GDP). And the service industry is growing. By 2014, it is estimated that more than four out of five jobs in the United States will be in service industries. Services are growing even faster in the world economy, making up 64 percent of the gross world product.[21]

Service industries vary greatly. *Governments* offer services through courts, employment services, hospitals, military services, police and fire departments, the postal service, and schools. *Private not-for-profit organizations* offer services through museums, charities, churches, colleges, foundations, and hospitals. In addition, a large number of *business organizations* offer services—airlines, banks, hotels, insurance companies, consulting firms, medical and legal practices, entertainment and telecommunications companies, real estate firms, retailers, and others.

The Nature and Characteristics of a Service

A company must consider four special service characteristics when designing marketing programs: intangibility, inseparability, variability, and perishability (see ● **Figure 8.3**).

Service intangibility means that services cannot be seen, tasted, felt, heard, or smelled before they are bought. For example, people undergoing cosmetic surgery cannot see the result before the purchase. Airline passengers have nothing but a ticket and a promise that they and their luggage will arrive safely at the intended destination, hopefully at the same time. To reduce uncertainty, buyers look for *signals* of service quality. They draw conclusions about quality from the place, people, price, equipment, and communications that they can see.

Therefore, the service provider's task is to make the service tangible in one or more ways and send the right signals about quality. ● The Mayo Clinic does this well:[22]

> When it comes to hospitals, most patients can't really judge "product quality." It's a very complex product that's hard to understand, and you can't try it out before buying it. So when considering a hospital, most people unconsciously search for evidence that the facility is caring, competent, and trustworthy. The Mayo Clinic doesn't leave these things to chance. Rather, it offers patients organized and honest evidence of its dedication to "providing the best care to every patient every day."
>
> Inside, staff is trained to act in a way that clearly signals Mayo Clinic's concern for patient wellbeing. For example, doctors regularly follow up with patients at home to see how they are doing, and they work with patients to smooth out scheduling problems. The clinic's physical facilities also send the right signals. They've been carefully designed to offer a place of refuge, show caring and respect, and signal competence. Looking for external confirmation? Go online and hear directly from those who've been to the clinic or work there. The Mayo Clinic now uses social networking—everything from blogs to Facebook and YouTube—to enhance the patient experience. For example, on the Sharing Mayo Clinic blog (http://sharing.mayoclinic.org), patients and their families retell their Mayo experiences, and Mayo employees offer behind-the-scenes views. The result? Highly loyal customers who willingly spread the good word to others, building one of the most powerful brands in health care.

Physical goods are produced, then stored, then later sold, and then still later consumed. In contrast, services are first sold and then produced and consumed at the same time. **Service inseparability** means that services cannot be separated from their providers, whether the providers are people or machines. If a service employee provides the service, then the employee becomes a part of the service. And customers don't just buy and use a service, they play an active role in its delivery. Customer co-production makes *provider-customer interaction* a special feature of services marketing. Both the provider and the customer affect the service outcome.

Service variability means that the quality of services depends on who provides them as well as when, where, and how they are provided. For example, some hotels—say, Marriott—have reputations for providing better service than others. Still, within a given Marriott hotel, one registration-counter employee may be cheerful and efficient, whereas another standing just a few feet away may be grumpy and slow. Even the quality of a single Marriott employee's service varies according to his or her energy and frame of mind at the time of each customer encounter.

Service intangibility
Services cannot be seen, tasted, felt, heard, or smelled before they are bought.

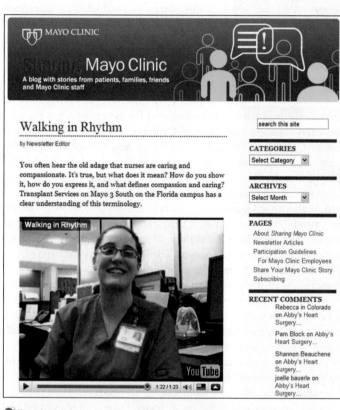

● By providing customers with organized, honest evidence of its capabilities, the Mayo Clinic has built one of the most powerful brands in health care. Its Sharing Mayo Clinic blog lets you hear directly from those who have been to the clinic or who work there.
Mayo Clinic

Service inseparability
Services are produced and consumed at the same time and cannot be separated from their providers.

Service variability
The quality of services may vary greatly depending on who provides them and when, where, and how they are provided.

● FIGURE | 8.3
Four Service Characteristics

Intangibility

Services cannot be seen, tasted, felt, heard, or smelled before purchase

Inseparability

Services cannot be separated from their providers

Services

Although services are "products" in a general sense, they have special characteristics and marketing needs. The biggest differences come from the fact that services are essentially intangible and that they are created through direct interactions with customers. Think about your experiences with an airline versus Nike or Apple.

Variability

Quality of services depends on who provides them and when, where, and how

Perishability

Services cannot be stored for later sale or use

Service perishability
Services cannot be stored for later sale or use.

Service perishability means that services cannot be stored for later sale or use. Some doctors charge patients for missed appointments because the service value existed only at that point and disappeared when the patient did not show up. The perishability of services is not a problem when demand is steady. However, when demand fluctuates, service firms often have difficult problems. For example, because of rush-hour demand, public transportation companies have to own much more equipment than they would if demand were even throughout the day. Thus, service firms often design strategies for producing a better match between demand and supply. Hotels and resorts charge lower prices in the off-season to attract more guests. And restaurants hire part-time employees to serve during peak periods.

Marketing Strategies for Service Firms

Just like manufacturing businesses, good service firms use marketing to position themselves strongly in chosen target markets. FedEx promises to take your packages "faster, farther"; Angie's List offers "Reviews you can trust." At Hampton, "We love having you here." And St. Jude Children's Hospital is "Finding cures. Saving children." These and other service firms establish their positions through traditional marketing mix activities. However, because services differ from tangible products, they often require additional marketing approaches.

The Service Profit Chain

Service profit chain
The chain that links service firm profits with employee and customer satisfaction.

In a service business, the customer and the front-line service employee *interact* to co-create the service. Effective interaction, in turn, depends on the skills of front-line service employees and on the support processes backing these employees. Thus, successful service companies focus their attention on *both* their customers and their employees. They understand the **service profit chain**, which links service firm profits with employee and customer satisfaction. This chain consists of five links:[23]

- *Internal service quality:* superior employee selection and training, a quality work environment, and strong support for those dealing with customers, which results in . . .
- *Satisfied and productive service employees:* more satisfied, loyal, and hardworking employees, which results in . . .
- *Greater service value:* more effective and efficient customer value creation and service delivery, which results in . . .
- *Satisfied and loyal customers:* satisfied customers who remain loyal, make repeat purchases, and refer other customers, which results in . . .
- *Healthy service profits and growth:* superior service firm performance.

As Whole Foods Market co-founder and CEO John Mackey puts it: "Happy team members result in happy customers. Happy customers do more business with you. They become advocates for your enterprise, which results in happy investors."[24] Therefore, all outstanding service companies begin with taking care of those who take care of customers. For example, customer service all-star Zappos.com—the online shoe, clothing, and accessories retailer—knows that happy customers begin with happy, dedicated, and energetic employees (see Real Marketing 8.1).

Real Marketing 8.1

Zappos.com: Taking Care of Those Who Take Care of Customers

Imagine a retailer with service so good its customers wish it would take over the Internal Revenue Service or start up an airline. It might sound like a marketing fantasy, but this scenario is a reality for customer service all-star Zappos.com. At Zappos, the customer experience really does come first—it's a daily obsession. Says Zappos' understated CEO, Tony Hsieh (pronounced shay), "Our whole goal at Zappos is for the Zappos brand to be about the very best customer service and customer experience." Zappos is "Powered by Service."

From the start, the scrappy Web retailer of shoes, clothing, handbags, and accessories made customer service a cornerstone of its marketing. As a result, Zappos has grown astronomically. It now serves more than 10 million customers annually and gross merchandise sales top $1.2 billion each year. In fact, Zappos' online success and passion for customers made it an ideal match for another highly successful, customer-obsessed online retailer, Amazon.com, which purchased Zappos a few years ago and has allowed it to operate as an independent division.

At Zappos, customer care starts with a deep-down, customer-focused culture. How does Zappos turn this culture into a customer reality? It all starts with the company's customer service reps—what the company calls its Customer Loyalty Team. Most of Zappos. com's business is driven by word-of-mouth and customer interactions with company employees. And Zappos knows that happy customers begin with happy, dedicated, and energetic employees. So the company starts by hiring the right people, training them thoroughly in customer service basics, and inspiring them to new heights in taking care of customers.

"Getting customers excited about the service they had at Zappos has to come naturally," says one Zappos marketing executive. "You can't teach it; you have to hire for it." Hiring the right people starts with the application process. The invitation to apply on the Zappos Web site suggests the kind of people Zappos seeks:

Please check out the Zappos Family's 10 Core Values before applying! They are the heart and soul of our culture and central to how we do business. If you are "fun and a little weird"—and think the other 9 Core Values fit you too—please take a look at our openings! "PS: At the Zappos Family of Companies, over-sized egos are not welcome. Over-sized Eggos, however, are most welcome and appreciated!"

Once hired, to make sure Zappos' customer obsession permeates the entire organization, each new employee—everyone from the CEO and chief financial officer to the children's footwear buyer—is required to go through four weeks of customer-loyalty training. In fact, in an effort to weed out the half-hearted, Zappos actually bribes people to quit. During the four weeks of customer service training, it offers employees a whopping $4,000 in cash, plus payment for the time worked, if they leave the company. The theory goes that those willing to take the money and run aren't right for Zappos' culture anyway.

Once in place, Zappos treats employees as well as it treats customers. The Zappos family culture emphasizes "a satisfying and fulfilling job . . . and a career you can be proud of. Work hard. Play hard. All the time!" Zappos wants employees to be engaged—to have fun and feel good about the company. It creates a relaxed, fun-loving, and close-knit family atmosphere, complete with free meals, a nap room, Nerf gun wars, and Oreo-eating contests, not to mention full benefits, profit sharing, and even a full-time life coach—all of which make it a great place to work. In fact, Zappos ranked number 11 on *Fortune* magazine's most recent "100 Best Companies to Work For" list.

The result is what one observer calls "1,550 perpetually chipper employees." Every year, the company publishes a "culture book," filled with unedited, often gushy testimonials from Zapponians about what it's like to work there. "Oh my gosh," says one employee, "this is my home away from home. . . . It's changed my life. . . . Our culture is the best reason to work here." Says another, "The most surprising thing about coming to work here is that there are no limits. So pretty much anything you are passionate about is possible." And what are the things about which Zapponians are most passionate? The Zappos family's No. 1 core value: "Deliver WOW through service."

Such enthusiastic employees, in turn, make outstanding brand ambassadors. Whereas many Web sites bury contact

"A woman just called and asked if we sold dresses. I told her we had hundreds of dresses from the biggest designers. Know what she said? She said, 'I love you.' Actually, she said, 'Thank you,' but I read between the lines."

Zappos knows that happy customers begin with happy, dedicated, and energetic employees. Zappos "is happy to help, 24/7."

© 2013 Zappos.com, Inc. or its affiliates

information several links deep because they don't really want to hear from customers, Zappos puts the number at the top of every single Web page and staffs its call center 24/7. Hsieh sees each customer contact as an opportunity: "We actually want to talk to our customers," he says. "If we handle the call well, we have an opportunity to create an emotional impact and lasting memory."

Hsieh insists that reps be helpful with anything that customers might call about—and he really means it. One customer called in search of a pizza joint open after midnight in Santa Monica, California. Two minutes later, the Zappos rep found him one. And Zappos doesn't hold its reps accountable for call times. Its longest phone call, from a customer who wanted the rep's help while she looked at what seemed like thousands of pairs of shoes, lasted almost six hours.

At Zappos, each employee is like a little marketing department. Relationships—inside and outside the company—mean everything at Zappos. Hsieh and many other employees stay in direct touch with customers, with each other, and with just about anyone else

interested in the company. They use social networking tools such as Facebook, Twitter, and blogs to share information, both good and bad. Such openness might worry some retailers, but Zappos embraces it.

Zappos even features employees in its marketing. For example, it uses associates in short videos to describe and explain its products. In one recent year, it turned out 58,000 such videos of staff—not professional models—showing off shoes, bags, and clothing. Zappos found that when the product includes a personal video explanation, purchases rise and returns decrease. And those Zappos ads you see on television showing

puppet customers talking with puppet service reps are based on actual customer service encounters, with actual Zappos employees doing the voices.

The moral: Just as the service profit chain suggests, taking good care of customers begins with taking good care of those who take care of customers. Zappos' enthusiasm and culture are infectious. Put Zappos customers and reps together and good things will result. "We've actually had customers ask us if we would please start an airline or run the IRS," Hsieh says, adding, "30 years from now I wouldn't rule out a Zappos airline that's all about the very best service."

Sources: Portions adapted from Natalie Zmuda, "Zappos: Customer Service First—and a Daily Obsession," *Advertising Age,* October 20, 2008, p. 36; and http://about.Zappos.com/jobs, accessed April 2012; with additional information and quotes from Tony Hsieh, "Zappos's CEO on Going to Extremes for Customers," *Harvard Business Review,* July–August 2010, pp. 41–44; Sarah Nassauer, "A New Sales Model: Employees," *Wall Street Journal,* March 17, 2011, p. D3; Brian Solis, "Zappos' Tony Hsieh Delivers Happiness through Service and Innovation," April 11, 2011, www.briansolis.com/2011/04/zappos-tony-hsieh-happiness/; Robert Passikoff, "The Zapposification of Brands," *Forbes,* June 23, 2011, www.forbes.com/sites/marketshare/2011/06/23/the-zapposification-of-brands/; "100 Best Companies to Work For," *Fortune,* February 6, 2012, p. 117; and www.youtube.com/users/zappos and www.zappos.com, accessed November 2012.

Internal marketing

Orienting and motivating customer-contact employees and supporting service employees to work as a team to provide customer satisfaction.

Interactive marketing

Training service employees in the fine art of interacting with customers to satisfy their needs.

Service marketing requires more than just traditional external marketing using the four Ps. ● **Figure 8.4** shows that service marketing also requires *internal marketing* and *interactive marketing*. **Internal marketing** means that the service firm must orient and motivate its customer-contact employees and supporting service people to work as a *team* to provide customer satisfaction. Marketers must get everyone in the organization to be customer centered. In fact, internal marketing must *precede* external marketing. For example, Zappos starts by hiring the right people and carefully orienting and inspiring them to give unparalleled customer service.

Interactive marketing means that service quality depends heavily on the quality of the buyer-seller interaction during the service encounter. In product marketing, product quality often depends little on how the product is obtained. But in services marketing, service quality depends on both the service deliverer and the quality of delivery. Service marketers, therefore, have to master interactive marketing skills. Thus, Zappos selects only people with an innate "passion to serve" and instructs them carefully in the fine art of interacting with customers to satisfy their every need. All new hires—at all levels of the company—complete a four-week customer-loyalty training regimen.

● **FIGURE | 8.4**
Three Types of Service Marketing

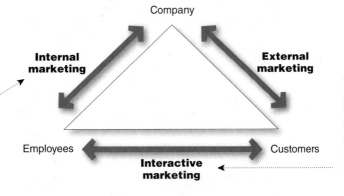

Service firms must sell the importance of delighting customers to customer-contact employees. At Zappos.com, the No.1 core value is "Deliver WOW through service."

Then service firms must help employees master the art of interacting with customers. Every employee at Zappos.com, from the CEO down, goes through four weeks of customer-loyalty training.

Today, as competition and costs increase, and as productivity and quality decrease, more service marketing sophistication is needed. Service companies face three major marketing tasks: They want to increase their *service differentiation*, *service quality*, and *service productivity*.

Managing Service Differentiation

In these days of intense price competition, service marketers often complain about the difficulty of differentiating their services from those of competitors. To the extent that customers view the services of different providers as similar, they care less about the provider than the price. The solution to price competition is to develop a differentiated offer, delivery, and image.

The *offer* can include innovative features that set one company's offer apart from competitors' offers. For example, some retailers differentiate themselves by offerings that take you well beyond the products they stock. Dick's Sporting Goods has grown from a single bait-and-tackle store in Binghamton, New York, into a 450-store, $4.8 billion sporting goods megaretailer in 42 states by offering interactive services that set it apart from ordinary sporting goods stores. Customers can sample shoes on Dick's indoor footwear track, test golf clubs with an on-site golf swing analyzer and putting green, shoot bows in its archery range, and receive personalized fitness product guidance from an in-store team of fitness trainers. Such differentiated services help make Dick's "the ultimate sporting goods destination store for core athletes and outdoor enthusiasts."[25]

Service companies can differentiate their service *delivery* by having more able and reliable customer-contact people, developing a superior physical environment in which the service product is delivered, or designing a superior delivery process. For example, many grocery chains now offer online shopping and home delivery as a better way to shop than having to drive, park, wait in line, and tote groceries home. And most banks allow you to access your account information from almost anywhere—from the ATM to your mobile device.

Finally, service companies also can work on differentiating their *images* through symbols and branding. ● Aflac adopted the duck as its advertising symbol. Today, the duck is immortalized through stuffed animals, golf club covers, and free ring tones and screensavers. The well-known Aflac Duck helped make the big but previously unknown insurance company memorable and approachable. Other well-known service characters and symbols include the GEICO gecko, Progressive Insurance's Flo, McDonald's golden arches, Allstate's "good hands," and the Travelers red umbrella.

● Service differentiation: Service companies can differentiate their images using unique characters or symbols, such as the Aflac Duck.
Aflac

Managing Service Quality

A service firm can differentiate itself by delivering consistently higher quality than its competitors provide. Like manufacturers before them, most service industries have now joined the customer-driven quality movement. And like product marketers, service providers need to identify what target customers expect in regard to service quality.

Unfortunately, service quality is harder to define and judge than product quality. For instance, it is harder to agree on the quality of a haircut than on the quality of a hair dryer. Customer retention is perhaps the best measure of quality; a service firm's ability to hang onto its customers depends on how consistently it delivers value to them.

Top service companies set high service-quality standards. They watch service performance closely, both their own and that of competitors. They do not settle for merely good service—they strive for 100 percent defect-free service. A 98 percent performance standard may sound good, but using this standard, the U.S. Postal Service would lose or misdirect 391,000 pieces of mail each hour, and U.S. pharmacists would misfill more than 1.4 million prescriptions each week.[26]

Unlike product manufacturers who can adjust their machinery and inputs until everything is perfect, service quality will always vary, depending on the interactions between employees and customers. As hard as they may try, even the best companies will have an occasional late delivery, burned steak, or grumpy employee. However, good *service recovery* can turn angry customers into loyal ones. In fact, good recovery can win more customer purchasing and loyalty than if things had gone well in the first place. For example, Southwest Airlines has a proactive customer communications team whose job is to find the situations in which something went wrong—a mechanical delay, bad weather, a medical emergency, or a berserk passenger—then remedy the bad experience quickly, within 24 hours, if possible. The team's communications to passengers, usually e-mails these days, have three basic components: a sincere apology, a brief explanation of what happened, and a gift to make it up, usually a voucher in dollars that can be used on their next Southwest flight. Surveys show that when Southwest handles a delay situation well, customers score it 14 to 16 points higher than on regular on-time flights.

These days, social media such as Facebook and Twitter can help companies to root out and remedy customer dissatisfaction with service. Consider Marriott International:[27]

> John Wolf, Marriott Hotel's director of public relations, heads a team of Marriott people who work full-time monitoring the company's Twitter feed and other social media. The team seeks out people who are complaining about problems they've had at Marriott. "We'd rather know that there's an issue than not know it, and we'd rather be given the opportunity to solve the problem," Wolf says. This strategy helps Marriott to solve customer problems as they arise and to recover previously dissatisfied customers. For example, when the team discovered an unhappy Marriott regular tweeting and blogging about an experience at a Marriott hotel that resulted in a ruined pair of shoes and big dry cleaning bill, they contacted him directly via Twitter, asking for his contact information. The next day, the disgruntled customer received a personal call from Marriott offering an explanation, a sincere apology, and a generous amount of reward points added to his account to be applied to future stays at Marriott. The result: a once-again happy and loyal customer who now blogged and tweeted to others about his positive experience.

Managing Service Productivity

With their costs rising rapidly, service firms are under great pressure to increase service productivity. They do so in several ways. They can train current employees better or hire new ones who will work harder or more skillfully. Or they can increase the quantity of their service by giving up some quality. Finally, a service provider can harness the power of technology. Although we often think of technology's power to save time and costs in manufacturing companies, it also has great—and often untapped—potential to make service workers more productive.

However, companies must avoid pushing productivity so hard that doing so reduces quality. Attempts to streamline a service or cut costs can make a service company more efficient in the short run. But that can also reduce its longer-run ability to innovate, maintain service quality, or respond to consumer needs and desires. ● For example, some airlines have learned this lesson the hard way as they attempt to economize in the face of rising costs. Passengers on many airlines now encounter "time-saving" check-in kiosks rather than personal counter service. And most airlines have stopped offering even the little things for free—such as in-flight snacks—and now charge extra for everything from luggage to aisle seats. The result is a plane full of resentful customers. In their attempts to improve productivity, these airlines have mangled customer service.

Thus, in attempting to improve service productivity, companies must be mindful of how they create and deliver customer value. They should be careful not to take *service* out of the service. In fact, a company may purposely lower service productivity in order to improve service quality, in turn allowing it to maintain higher prices and profit margins.[28]

● **Managing service productivity: Companies should be careful not to take things too far. For example, in their attempts to improve productivity, some airlines have mangled customer service.**

AP Photo/Rick Bowmer

Objective 4 ·······▶

Discuss branding strategy—the decisions companies make in building and managing their brands.

Branding Strategy: Building Strong Brands

Some analysts see brands as *the* major enduring asset of a company, outlasting the company's specific products and facilities. John Stewart, former CEO of Quaker Oats, once said, "If this business were split up, I would give you the land and bricks and mortar, and I would keep the brands and trademarks, and I would fare better than you." A former CEO of McDonald's declared, "If every asset we own, every building, and every piece of equipment were destroyed in a terrible natural disaster, we would be able to borrow all the money to replace it very quickly because of the value of our brand. . . . The brand is more valuable than the totality of all these assets."[29]

Thus, brands are powerful assets that must be carefully developed and managed. In this section, we examine the key strategies for building and managing product and service brands.

Brand Equity

Brands are more than just names and symbols. They are a key element in the company's relationships with consumers. Brands represent consumers' perceptions and feelings about a product and its performance—everything that the product or the service *means* to consumers. In the final analysis, brands exist in the heads of consumers. As one well-respected marketer once said, "Products are created in the factory, but brands are created in the mind." Adds Jason Kilar, CEO of the online video service Hulu, "A brand is what people say about you when you're not in the room."[30]

Brand equity

The differential effect that knowing the brand name has on customer response to the product or its marketing.

A powerful brand has high *brand equity*. **Brand equity** is the differential effect that knowing the brand name has on customer response to the product and its marketing. It's a measure of the brand's ability to capture consumer preference and loyalty. A brand has positive brand equity when consumers react more favorably to it than to a generic or unbranded version of the same product. It has negative brand equity if consumers react less favorably than to an unbranded version.

Brands vary in the amount of power and value they hold in the marketplace. Some brands—such as Coca-Cola, Nike, Disney, GE, McDonald's, Harley-Davidson, and others—become larger-than-life icons that maintain their power in the market for years, even generations. Other brands—such as Google, YouTube, Apple, Facebook, ESPN, and Wikipedia—create fresh consumer excitement and loyalty. These brands win in the marketplace not simply because they deliver unique benefits or reliable service. Rather, they succeed because they forge deep connections with customers. For example, to a devoted Dunkin' Donuts fan, that cup of coffee from Dunkin' isn't just coffee, it's a deeply satisfying experience that no other brand can deliver as well. Dunkin' Donuts regularly beats out Starbucks in customer loyalty ratings.

Ad agency Young & Rubicam's BrandAsset Valuator measures brand strength along four consumer perception dimensions: *differentiation* (what makes the brand stand out), *relevance* (how consumers feel it meets their needs), *knowledge* (how much consumers know about the brand), and *esteem* (how highly consumers regard and respect the brand). Brands with strong brand equity rate high on all four dimensions. The brand must be distinct, or consumers will have no reason to choose it over other brands. However, the fact that a brand is highly differentiated doesn't necessarily mean that consumers will buy it. The brand must stand out in ways that are relevant to

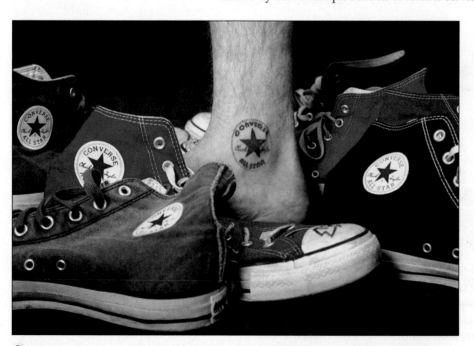

● **Consumers sometimes bond very closely with specific brands. Perhaps the ultimate expression of brand devotion: tattooing the brand on your body.**

Kristoffer Tripplaar/Alamy

consumers' needs. Even a differentiated, relevant brand is far from a shoe-in. Before consumers will respond to the brand, they must first know about and understand it. And that familiarity must lead to a strong, positive consumer-brand connection.[31]

Thus, positive brand equity derives from consumer feelings about and connections with a brand. Consumers sometimes bond *very* closely with specific brands. ● As perhaps the ultimate expression of brand devotion, a surprising number of people—and not just Harley-Davidson fans—have their favorite brand tattooed on their bodies. Whether its contemporary new brand such as Facebook or Amazon or old classics like Harley or Reese's, strong brands are built around an ideal of improving consumers' lives in some relevant way (see Real Marketing 8.2).

A brand with high brand equity is a very valuable asset. *Brand valuation* is the process of estimating the total financial value of a brand. Measuring such value is difficult. However, according to one estimate, the brand value of Apple is a whopping $153 billion, with Google at $112 billion, IBM at $100 billion, McDonald's at $81 billion, Microsoft at $78 billion, and Coca-Cola at $73 billion. Other brands rating among the world's most valuable include AT&T, China Mobile, GE, Walmart, and Amazon.com.[32]

High brand equity provides a company with many competitive advantages. A powerful brand enjoys a high level of consumer brand awareness and loyalty. Because consumers expect stores to carry the particular brand, the company has more leverage in bargaining with resellers. Because a brand name carries high credibility, the company can more easily launch line and brand extensions. A powerful brand also offers the company some defense against fierce price competition.

Above all, however, a powerful brand forms the basis for building strong and profitable customer relationships. The fundamental asset underlying brand equity is *customer equity*—the value of customer relationships that the brand creates. A powerful brand is important, but what it really represents is a profitable set of loyal customers. The proper focus of marketing is building customer equity, with brand management serving as a major marketing tool. Companies need to think of themselves not as portfolios of brands but as portfolios of customers.

Building Strong Brands

Branding poses challenging decisions to the marketer. ● **Figure 8.5** shows that the major brand strategy decisions involve *brand positioning*, *brand name selection*, *brand sponsorship*, and *brand development*.

Brand Positioning

Marketers need to position their brands clearly in target customers' minds. They can position brands at any of three levels.[33] At the lowest level, they can position the brand on *product attributes*. For example, P&G invented the disposable diaper category with its Pampers brand. Early Pampers marketing focused on attributes such as fluid absorption, fit, and disposability. In general, however, attributes are the least desirable level for brand positioning. Competitors can easily copy attributes. More importantly, customers are not interested in attributes as such—they are interested in what the attributes will do for them.

A brand can be better positioned by associating its name with a desirable *benefit*. Thus, Pampers can go beyond technical product attributes and talk about the resulting containment and skin-health benefits from dryness. Some successful brands positioned on benefits are FedEx (guaranteed on-time delivery), Nike (performance), Lexus (quality), and Walmart (low prices).

The strongest brands go beyond attribute or benefit positioning. They are positioned on strong *beliefs and values*, engaging customers on a deep, emotional level. For example, to

Brands are powerful assets that must be carefully developed and managed. As this figure suggests, building strong brands involves many challenging decisions.

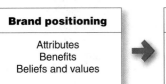

Brand positioning
Attributes
Benefits
Beliefs and values

Brand name selection
Selection
Protection

Brand sponsorship
Manufacturer's brand
Private brand
Licensing
Co-branding

Brand development
Line extensions
Brand extensions
Multibrands
New brands

● **FIGURE | 8.5**
Major Brand Strategy Decisions

Real Marketing 8.2

Breakaway Brands: Connecting with Consumers in a Meaningful Way

What does Facebook—the contemporary, digital social networking powerhouse— have in common with Reese's—the classic, decades-old chocolate-and-peanut-butter candy? Seemingly, not very much. Yet both brands landed in brand consultancy Landor Associates' most recent annual Top Ten Breakaway Brands list, a listing of elite brands based on a comprehensive survey that measures brand strength.

Each year, the Breakaway Brands survey identifies the 10 brands with the greatest percentage gains in brand health and business value as a result of superb brand strategy and execution over the previous three-year period. The survey taps Young & Rubicam's Brand Asset Valuator—a database of responses from 15,000 consumers evaluating 2,500 brands measured across 48 metrics—which looks at consumer brand measures such as differentiation, relevance, esteem, and knowledge. The survey also taps a second set of measures, "Economic Value Added" by BrandEconomics, which assesses the financial performance of each brand. Combined, the BrandAsset Valuator and Economic Value Added models provide a comprehensive brand valuation based on both consumer and financial measures.

Ideas about what constitutes brand strength, that elusive blend of consumer and financial performance, have changed in the past decade. The most recent Breakaway Brands list is dominated by contemporary Internet and high-tech brands—such as Facebook, YouTube, Skype, and Amazon— which have shattered and redefined their categories or built new categories altogether. However, mixed in with these contemporary brands are some old classics, such as Reese's and, of all things, the U.S. military's National Guard, which stand out in the list like a couple of old geezers in a glass-and-chrome Apple store.

Top Ten Breakaway Brands

1. Facebook	6. Samsung
2. YouTube	7. Amazon
3. Apple	8. Reese's
4. Skype	9. iTunes
5. Netflix	10. National Guard

Source: Reprinted with permission of BrandAsset Consulting.

Missing altogether are some brand titans such as Coca-Cola, McDonald's, and Disney—huge brands that grace many "top brands" lists but aren't growing nearly fast enough to be crowned Breakaway Brands.

So just what do these diverse Breakaway Brands have in common? Landor found that each brand, regardless of age, embraces both contemporary and classic values, and that each excels at the basic branding principles of remaining relevant and differentiated. The current Breakaway Brands survey measured brand performance across the worst years of the recent severe economic downturn. It's no surprise, then, that the two most dominant brand values to emerge from the study were comfort and nostalgia, both providing security during tough times. These days, "communicating comfort can help brands really connect with consumers," says one brand consultant. "When times are tough, people are looking for brands they know and the comforts they can bring, not only functionally but also emotionally."

For a brand like Reese's, communicating comfort is a natural. Reese's products are an easy indulgence, reminding people of happier times. But the same is true for dozens of other candy and snack brands. Reese's won because it recognized that the industry practice of trying to please picky palates with a constant stream of new line extensions can actually complicate a brand and dilute its image. Instead, Reese's pared down its product line, refocused its strategy, and simplified its promotional materials. Fans were reminded that Reese's is all about the simple combination of peanut butter wrapped in milk chocolate and sealed in a bright orange wrapper. By simplifying and going retro, Reese's not only gave comfort, it also met the consumer's need for nostalgia at just the right moment.

Breakaway brands: Whether it's a contemporary new brand like Facebook or an old classic like Reese's, strong brands are built around connecting with consumers and improving their lives in some relevant way.

© The Hershey Company

Whereas it's easy to see the comfort in eating salty-sweet peanut-butter-filled chocolate cups, you might wonder how Internet brands like Facebook can strike the same emotional chord. But as it turns out, Facebook also provides comfort, just in a different way. "Just as you might eat Reese's as a comfort activity, you log on to Facebook as part of your daily routine," says a Landor Associates director. "It's comforting to be connected." People find that same kind of connection and comfort when consuming media via YouTube or Netflix or video chatting via Skype.

Then there's Amazon: The world's biggest Internet retailer sells anything and everything at the simple click of a button. But just as important, Amazon connects people to a huge online shopping community, filled with personalized recommendations and crowdsourced reviews and ratings. There's a lot of comfort in community, and connecting with Amazon gives customers assurances that they are making the right buying choices.

Adding to comfort-based consumer connections, two other common themes emerged from the Breakaway Brands survey—simplicity and authenticity. "If there's one [thing all these brands] have in common, they are authentically what they present themselves to be," says the Landor executive. "I can immediately picture what Facebook stands for, what Netflix stands for, what Apple stands for." That may sound easy, but authenticity requires that business strategy be carefully intertwined with brand values.

Still, it seems strange that so many contemporary new brands in the list beat out veteran brands on attributes such as comfort, simplicity, and authenticity. According to the Landor executive, however, it makes good sense. "What's interesting about this apparent paradox of old and new is that in some ways the new brands have become landmarks, comfort brands in and of themselves. Facebook is no longer a newbie; it's a leader in its category." The same holds true for the other contemporary brands. Consumers young and old have a hard time

remembering life without Facebook, YouTube, or Skype, even though each is less than a decade old.

Now, back to that original question: What do these seemingly diverse Breakaway Brands have in common? It all boils down to the brands making meaningful connections with consumers. All strong brands—whether it's Facebook or Reese's—are built around an ideal of improving consumers' lives in some relevant way. The younger Breakaway Brands are mainly trendy digital upstarts that are now maturing and becoming essential to consumers' modern

lives. However, the old familiar favorites on the list still contribute meaningfully. According to Landor, "While the world spins faster, brighter, and bolder around us, we all still yearn for familiar comforts." Compared with the high-tech brands on the list, "the other Breakaway Brands are decidedly old-school classics—tangible, tried and true, comforting and familiar. But most important, they are authentic, and they are still relevant and distinctive even alongside the shiny and new." Thus, whether old or new, it's the meaningful customer value they add that makes them all Breakaway Brands.

Sources: Quotes, extracts, and other information from Mich Bergesen and Josey Duncan Lee, "Facebook, Apple, Netflix Top 2011 Breakaway Brands List," *Forbes*, September 8, 2011, www.forbes.com/sites/onmarketing/2011/09/08/facebook-apple-netflix-top-2011-breakaway-brands-list/; Christine Birkner, "2011 Breakaway Brands Are Classic, Contemporary, Authentic," *Marketing News*, November 15, 2011, p. 11; "Breakaway Brands of 2011," Landor Associates, September 8, 2011, http://landor.com/#!/talk/articles-publications/articles/breakaway-brands-of-2011/; and Jack Neff, "Just How Well-Defined Is Your Brand's Ideal?" *Advertising Age,* January 16, 2012, p. 4.

parents, Pampers mean much more than just containment and dryness. The "Pampers village" Web site (www.pampers.com) positions Pampers as a "where we grow together" brand that's concerned about happy babies, parent-child relationships, and total baby care. Says a former P&G executive, "Our baby care business didn't start growing aggressively until we changed Pampers from being about dryness to helping mom with her baby's development."[34]

Successful brands engage customers on a deep, emotional level. Advertising agency Saatchi & Saatchi suggests that brands should strive to become *lovemarks*, products or services that "inspire loyalty beyond reason." Brands ranging from Apple, Google, Disney, and Coca-Cola to Nike, Trader Joe's, Facebook, Wrangler, In-N-Out Burger, and even WD-40 have achieved this status with many of their customers. Lovemark brands pack an emotional wallop. Customers don't just like these brands, they have strong emotional connections with them and love them unconditionally.[35]

When positioning a brand, the marketer should establish a mission for the brand and a vision of what the brand must be and do. A brand is the company's promise to deliver a specific set of features, benefits, services, and experiences consistently to buyers. The brand promise must be simple and honest. Motel 6, for example, offers clean rooms, low prices, and good service but does not promise expensive furnishings or large bathrooms. In contrast, The Ritz-Carlton offers luxurious rooms and a truly memorable experience but does not promise low prices.

Brand Name Selection

A good name can add greatly to a product's success. However, finding the best brand name is a difficult task. It begins with a careful review of the product and its benefits, the target market, and proposed marketing strategies. After that, naming a brand becomes part science, part art, and a measure of instinct.

Desirable qualities for a brand name include the following: (1) It should suggest something about the product's benefits and qualities. Examples: Beautyrest, Lean Cuisine, Mop & Glo. (2) It should be easy to pronounce, recognize, and remember: iPad, Tide, Jelly Belly, Facebook, JetBlue. (3) The brand name should be distinctive: Panera, Flickr, Swiffer, Zappos. (4) It should be extendable—Amazon.com began as an online bookseller but chose a name that would allow expansion into other categories. (5) The name should translate easily into foreign languages. Before changing its name to Exxon, Standard Oil of New Jersey rejected the name Enco, which it learned meant a stalled engine when pronounced in Japanese. (6) It should be capable of registration and legal protection. A brand name cannot be registered if it infringes on existing brand names.

Choosing a new brand name is hard work. After a decade of choosing quirky names (Yahoo!, Google) or trademark-proof made-up names (Novartis, Aventis, Accenture), today's style is to build brands around names that have real meaning. For example, names like Silk (soy milk), Method (home products), Smartwater (beverages), and Blackboard (school software) are simple and make intuitive sense. But with trademark applications soaring, *available* new names can be hard to find. Try it yourself. Pick a product and see if you can come up with a better name for it. How about Moonshot? Tickle? Vanilla? Treehugger? Simplicity? Google them and you'll find that they're already taken.

Once chosen, the brand name must be protected. Many firms try to build a brand name that will eventually become identified with the product category. Brand names such as Kleenex, Levi's, JELL-O, BAND-AID, Scotch Tape, Formica, and Ziploc have succeeded in this way. However, their very success may threaten the company's rights to the name. Many originally protected brand names—such as cellophane, aspirin, nylon, kerosene, linoleum, yo-yo, trampoline, escalator, thermos, and shredded wheat—are now generic names that any seller can use.

To protect their brands, marketers present them carefully using the word *brand* and the registered trademark symbol, as in "BAND-AID® Brand Adhesive Bandages." Even the long-standing "I am stuck on BAND-AID 'cause BAND-AID's stuck on me" jingle has now become "I am stuck on BAND-AID *brand* 'cause BAND-AID's stuck on me." ● Similarly, a recent Xerox advertisement notes that a brand name can be lost if people misuse it. The ad asks people to use the Xerox name only as an adjective to identify its products and services (such as "Xerox copiers"), not as a verb ("to Xerox" something) or a noun ("I'll make a Xerox").

● **Protecting a brand name: This ad asks people to use the Xerox name only as an adjective to identify its products and services (such as "Xerox copiers"), not as a verb ("to Xerox" something) or a noun ("I'll make a Xerox").**

Associated Press

Brand Sponsorship

A manufacturer has four sponsorship options. The product may be launched as a *national brand* (or *manufacturer's brand*), as when Samsung and Kellogg sell their output under their own brand names (the Samsung Galaxy tablet or Kellogg's Frosted Flakes). Or the manufacturer may sell to resellers who give the product a *private brand* (also called a *store brand* or *distributor brand*). Although most manufacturers create their own brand names, others market *licensed brands*. Finally, two companies can join forces and *co-brand* a product. We discuss each of these options in turn.

National Brands versus Store Brands. National brands (or manufacturers' brands) have long dominated the retail scene. In recent times, however, an increasing number of retailers and wholesalers have created their own **store brands** (or **private brands**). Store brands have been gaining strength for more than two decades, but recent tighter economic times have created a store-brand boom. Studies show that consumers are now buying even more private brands, which on average yield a 29 percent savings. "[Thrifty] times are good times for private labels," says a brand expert. "As consumers become more price-conscious, they also become less brand-conscious."[36]

In fact, store brands are growing much faster than national brands. For example, five years ago, private labels accounted for about 20 percent of U.S. food and beverage purchases. Since the Great Recession of 2008, however, unit sales of private-label goods have grown at more than twice the rate of national brands. Private labels now account

Store brand (or private brand)
A brand created and owned by a reseller of a product or service.

for 29 percent of supermarket sales. Similarly, for apparel sales, private-label brands—such as Hollister, The Limited, Arizona Jean Company (JCPenney), and Xhilaration (Target)—now capture a 50 percent share of all U.S. apparel sales, up from 25 percent a decade ago.[37] Even upscale retailer Saks Fifth Avenue carries its own clothing line, which features $98 men's ties, $200 halter tops, and $250 cotton dress shirts.

● **The popularity of store brands has soared recently. Walmart's store brands account for a whopping 40 percent of its sales, and its Great Value brand is the nation's largest single food brand.**

Photo courtesy of Gary Armstrong

Many large retailers skillfully market a deep assortment of store-brand merchandise. ● For example, Walmart's private brands account for a whopping 40 percent of its sales: brands such as Great Value food products; Sam's Choice beverages; Equate pharmacy, health, and beauty products; White Cloud brand toilet tissue and diapers; Simple Elegance laundry products; and Canopy outdoor home products. Its private-label brands alone generate nearly twice the sales of all P&G brands combined, and Walmart's Great Value is the nation's largest single food brand. At the other end of the grocery spectrum, upscale Whole Foods Market offers an array of store brand products under its 365 Everyday Value brand, from organic Canadian maple syrup and frozen chicken Caesar pizza to chewy children's multivitamins and organic whole wheat pasta.[38]

Once known as "generic" or "no-name" brands, today's store brands are shedding their image as cheap knockoffs of national brands. Store brands now offer much greater selection, and they are rapidly achieving name-brand quality. In fact, retailers such as Target and Trader Joe's are out-innovating many of their national-brand competitors. As a result, consumers are becoming loyal to store brands for reasons besides price. In some cases, consumers are even willing to pay more for store brands that have been positioned as gourmet or premium items.

In the so-called *battle of the brands* between national and private brands, retailers have many advantages. They control what products they stock, where they go on the shelf, what prices they charge, and which ones they will feature in local promotions. Retailers often price their store brands lower than comparable national brands and feature the price differences in side-by-side comparisons on store shelves. Although store brands can be hard to establish and costly to stock and promote, they also yield higher profit margins for the reseller. And they give resellers exclusive products that cannot be bought from competitors, resulting in greater store traffic and loyalty. Fast-growing retailer Trader Joe's, which carries 80 percent store brands, largely controls its own brand destiny, rather than relying on producers to make and manage the brands it needs to serve its customers best.

To compete with store brands, national brands must sharpen their value propositions, especially when appealing to today's more frugal consumers. Many national brands are fighting back by rolling out more discounts and coupons to defend their market share. In the long run, however, leading brand marketers must compete by investing in new brands, new features, and quality improvements that set them apart. They must design strong advertising programs to maintain high awareness and preference. And they must find ways to partner with major distributors to find distribution economies and improve joint performance.

For example, in response to the recent surge in private-label sales, consumer product giant Procter & Gamble has redoubled its efforts to develop and promote new and better products, particularly at lower price points. "We invest $2 billion a year in research and development, $400 million on consumer knowledge, and about 10 percent of sales on advertising," says P&G's CEO, Bob McDonald. "Store brands don't have that capacity."[39]

Licensing. Most manufacturers take years and spend millions to create their own brand names. However, some companies license names or symbols previously created by other manufacturers, names of well-known celebrities, or characters from popular movies and books. For a fee, any of these can provide an instant and proven brand name.

Apparel and accessories sellers pay large royalties to adorn their products—from blouses to ties and linens to luggage—with the names or initials of well-known fashion innovators such as Calvin Klein, Tommy Hilfiger, Gucci, or Armani. Sellers of children's products attach an almost endless list of character names to clothing, toys, school supplies, linens, dolls, lunch boxes, cereals, and other items. Licensed character names range from classics such as Sesame Street, Disney, Barbie, Star Wars, Scooby Doo, Hello Kitty, and Dr. Seuss characters to the more recent Dora the Explorer; Go, Diego, Go!; Little Einsteins; and Hannah Montana. And currently a number of top-selling retail toys are products based on television shows and movies.

Name and character licensing has grown rapidly in recent years. Annual retail sales of licensed products worldwide have grown from only $4 billion in 1977 to $55 billion in 1987 and more than $182 billion today. Licensing can be a highly profitable business for many companies. For example, Disney, the world's biggest licensor, reported nearly $28 billion in worldwide merchandise sales last year and plans to double that figure in the next five to seven years. And Nickelodeon has developed a stable full of hugely popular characters, such as Dora the Explorer; Go, Diego, Go!; iCarly; Team Umizoomi; and SpongeBob SquarePants. SpongeBob alone has generated more than $8 billion in sales and licensing fees over the past decade.[40]

Co-branding

The practice of using the established brand names of two different companies on the same product.

Co-branding. **Co-branding** occurs when two established brand names of different companies are used on the same product. Co-branding offers many advantages. Because each brand dominates in a different category, the combined brands create broader consumer appeal and greater brand equity. For example, PepsiCo's Lay's brand joined KC Masterpiece to create Lay's KC Masterpiece Barbeque chips. Pillsbury and Cinnabon joined forces to create Pillsbury Cinnabon cinnamon rolls. ● And Dairy Queen and the Girl Scouts teamed up to create Girl Scout limited edition cookie-filled Blizzards. The Thin Mint Blizzard is the most popular DQ limited edition to date, selling more than 10 million in one month.

Co-branding can take advantage of the complementary strengths of two brands. For example, the Tim Hortons coffee chain has established co-branded Tim Hortons–Cold Stone Creamery shops. Tim Hortons is strong in the morning and midday periods, with coffee and baked goods, soups, and sandwiches. By contrast, Cold Stone Creamery's ice cream snacks are strongest in the afternoon and evening, which are Tim Hortons's nonpeak periods. The co-branded locations offer customers a reason to visit morning, noon, and night.[41]

Co-branding also allows a company to expand its existing brand into a category it might otherwise have difficulty entering alone. For example, Nike and Apple co-branded the Nike+iPod Sport Kit, which lets runners link their Nike shoes with their iPods to track and enhance running performance in real time. "Your iPod Nano [or iPod Touch] becomes your coach. Your personal trainer. Your favorite workout companion." The Nike+iPod arrangement gives Apple a presence in the sports and fitness market. At the same time, it helps Nike bring new value to its customers.[42]

● Co-branding: Dairy Queen and the Girl Scouts teamed up to create the Girl Scout cookie–filled Thin Mint Blizzard, which sold more than 10 million in one month.
American Dairy Queen Corporation

Co-branding can also have limitations. Such relationships usually involve complex legal contracts and licenses. Co-branding partners must carefully coordinate their advertising, sales promotion, and other marketing efforts. Finally, when co-branding, each partner must trust that the other will take good care of its brand. If something damages the reputation of one brand, it can tarnish the co-brand as well.

Brand Development

A company has four choices when it comes to developing brands (see ● **Figure 8.6**). It can introduce *line extensions*, *brand extensions*, *multibrands*, or *new brands*.

Line extension

Extending an existing brand name to new forms, colors, sizes, ingredients, or flavors of an existing product category.

Line Extensions. **Line extensions** occur when a company extends existing brand names to new forms, colors, sizes, ingredients, or flavors of an existing product category. Thus, the Cheerios line of cereals includes Honey Nut, Frosted, Yogurt Burst, MultiGrain, Banana Nut, and several other variations.

A company might introduce line extensions as a low-cost, low-risk way to introduce new products. Or it might want to meet consumer desires for variety, use excess capacity, or simply command more shelf space from resellers. However, line extensions involve some

● FIGURE | 8.6
Brand Development Strategies

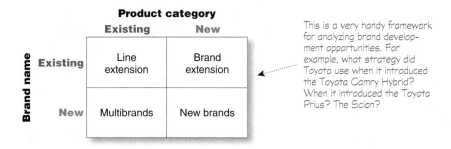

Product category

	Existing	New
Brand name Existing	Line extension	Brand extension
Brand name New	Multibrands	New brands

This is a very handy framework for analyzing brand development opportunities. For example, what strategy did Toyota use when it introduced the Toyota Camry Hybrid? When it introduced the Toyota Prius? The Scion?

risks. An overextended brand name might cause consumer confusion or lose some of its specific meaning. For example, the original Doritos Tortilla Chips have morphed into a U.S. roster of 22 different types of flavors and chips, plus dozens more in foreign markets. Flavors include everything from Nacho Cheese and Pizza Supreme to Blazin' Buffalo & Ranch, Fiery Fusion, and Salsa Verde. Or how about duck-flavored Gold Peking Duck Chips or wasabi-flavored Mr. Dragon's Fire Chips (Japan)? Although the line seems to be doing well with global sales of nearly $5 billion, the original Doritos chips seem like just another flavor.[43] And how much would adding yet another flavor steal from Doritos' own sales versus competitors? A line extension works best when it takes sales away from competing brands, not when it "cannibalizes" the company's other items.

Brand Extensions. A **brand extension** extends a current brand name to new or modified products in a new category. For example, Kellogg's has extended its Special K cereal brand into a full line of cereals plus lines of crackers, fruit crisps, snack and nutrition bars, breakfast shakes, protein waters, and other health and nutrition products. Victorinox extended its venerable Swiss Army brand from multitool knives to products ranging from cutlery and ballpoint pens to watches, luggage, and apparel. And P&G has leveraged the strength of its Mr. Clean household cleaner brand to launch several new lines: cleaning pads (Magic Eraser), bathroom cleaning tools (Magic Reach), and home auto cleaning kits (Mr. Clean AutoDry). ● It even launched Mr. Clean–branded car washes.

Brand extension

Extending an existing brand name to new product categories.

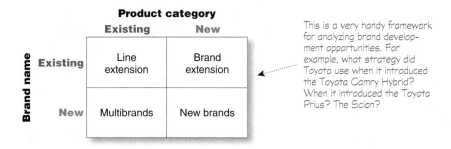

● Brand extensions: P&G has leveraged the strength of its Mr. Clean brand to launch new lines, including Mr. Clean–branded car washes.
The Procter & Gamble Company

A brand extension gives a new product instant recognition and faster acceptance. It also saves the high advertising costs usually required to build a new brand name. At the same time, a brand extension strategy involves some risk. The extension may confuse the image of the main brand. Brand extensions such as Cheetos lip balm, Heinz pet food, and Life Savers gum met early deaths. And if a brand extension fails, it may harm consumer attitudes toward other products carrying the same brand name. Furthermore, a brand name may not be appropriate to a particular new product, even if it is well made and satisfying—would you consider flying on Hooters Air or wearing an Evian water-filled padded bra (both failed)? Thus, before transferring a brand name to a new product, marketers must research how well the product fits the brand's associations.

Multibrands. Companies often market many different brands in a given product category. For example, in the United States, PepsiCo markets at least five brands of soft drinks (Pepsi, Sierra Mist, Slice, Mountain Dew, and Mug root beer), four brands of sports and energy drinks (Gatorade, No Fear, Propel, and AMP Energy), five brands of bottled teas and coffees (Lipton, SoBe, Seattle's Best, Starbucks, and Tazo), two brands of bottled waters (Aquafina and SoBe), and two brands of fruit drinks (Tropicana and Ocean Spray). Each brand includes a long list of sub-brands. For instance, SoBe consists of SoBe Teas & Elixers, SoBe Lifewater, SoBe Lean, and SoBe Lifewater with Purevia. Aquafina includes regular Aquafina, Aquafina Flavorsplash, and Aquafina Sparkling.

Multibranding offers a way to establish different features that appeal to different customer segments, lock up more reseller shelf space, and capture a larger market share. For example, although PepsiCo's many brands of beverages compete with one another on supermarket shelves, the combined brands reap a much greater overall market share than any single brand ever could. Similarly, by positioning multiple brands in multiple segments, Pepsi's five soft drink brands combine to capture much more market share than any single brand could capture by itself.

A major drawback of multibranding is that each brand might obtain only a small market share, and none may be very profitable. The company may end up spreading its resources over many brands instead of building a few brands to a highly profitable level. These companies should reduce the number of brands they sell in a given category and set up tighter screening procedures for new brands. This happened to GM, which in recent years has cut numerous brands from its portfolio, including Saturn, Oldsmobile, Pontiac, Hummer, and Saab.

New Brands. A company might believe that the power of its existing brand name is waning, so a new brand name is needed. Or it may create a new brand name when it enters a new product category for which none of its current brand names are appropriate. For example, Toyota created the separate Lexus brand aimed at luxury car consumers and the Scion brand, targeted toward Millennial consumers.

As with multibranding, offering too many new brands can result in a company spreading its resources too thin. And in some industries, such as consumer packaged goods, consumers and retailers have become concerned that there are already too many brands, with too few differences between them. Thus, P&G, PepsiCo, Kraft, and other large consumer-product marketers are now pursuing *megabrand* strategies—weeding out weaker or slower-growing brands and focusing their marketing dollars on brands that can achieve the number one or number two market share positions with good growth prospects in their categories.

Managing Brands

Companies must manage their brands carefully. First, the brand's positioning must be continuously communicated to consumers. Major brand marketers often spend huge amounts on advertising to create brand awareness and build preference and loyalty. For example, AT&T spends more than $2 billion annually to advertise its brand. McDonald's and Ford spend close to $1 billion. Globally, P&G spends an astounding $11 billion to advertise its many consumer brands.[44]

Such advertising campaigns can help create name recognition, brand knowledge, and perhaps even some brand preference. However, the fact is that brands are not maintained by advertising but by customers' *brand experiences*. Today, customers come to know a brand through a wide range of contacts and touchpoints. These include advertising but also personal experience with the brand, word of mouth and social networks, company Web pages and mobile apps, and many others. The company must put as much care into managing these touchpoints as it does into producing its ads. "Managing each customer's experience is perhaps the most important ingredient in building [brand] loyalty," states one branding expert. "Every memorable interaction . . . must be completed with excellence and . . . must reinforce your brand essence." ● A former Disney top executive agrees: "A brand is a living entity, and it is enriched or undermined cumulatively over time, the product of a thousand small gestures."[45]

The brand's positioning will not take hold fully unless everyone in the company lives the brand. Therefore, the company needs to train its people to be customer centered. Even better, the company should carry on internal brand building to help employees understand and be enthusiastic about the brand promise. Many companies go even further by training and encouraging their distributors and dealers to serve their customers well.

Finally, companies need to periodically audit their brands' strengths and weaknesses. They should ask: Does our brand excel at delivering benefits that consumers truly

● Managing brands requires managing "touchpoints." Says a former Disney executive: "A brand is a living entity, and it is enriched or undermined cumulatively over time, the product of a thousand small gestures."

Joe Raedle/Getty Images

value? Is the brand properly positioned? Do all of our consumer touchpoints support the brand's positioning? Do the brand's managers understand what the brand means to consumers? Does the brand receive proper, sustained support? The brand audit may turn up brands that need more support, brands that need to be dropped, or brands that must be rebranded or repositioned because of changing customer preferences or new competitors.

Reviewing the Concepts

MyMarketingLab™

Go to **mymktlab.com** to complete the problems marked with this icon .

Reviewing Objectives and Key Terms

 ## Objectives Review

A product is more than a simple set of tangible features. Each product or service offered to customers can be viewed on three levels. The *core customer value* consists of the core problem-solving benefits that consumers seek when they buy a product. The *actual product* exists around the core and includes the quality level, features, design, brand name, and packaging. The *augmented product* is the actual product plus the various services and benefits offered with it, such as a warranty, free delivery, installation, and maintenance.

Objective 1 **Define *product* and the major classifications of products and services.** (pp 226–231)

Broadly defined, a *product* is anything that can be offered to a market for attention, acquisition, use, or consumption that might satisfy a want or need. Products include physical objects but also services, events, persons, places, organizations, ideas, or mixtures of these entities. *Services* are products that consist of activities, benefits, or satisfactions offered for sale that are essentially intangible, such as banking, hotel, tax preparation, and home-repair services.

Products and services fall into two broad classes based on the types of consumers that use them. *Consumer products*—those bought by final consumers—are usually classified according to consumer shopping habits (convenience products, shopping products, specialty products, and unsought products). *Industrial products*—purchased for further processing or for use in conducting a business—include materials and parts, capital items, and supplies and services. Other marketable entities—such as organizations, persons, places, and ideas—can also be thought of as products.

Objective 2 **Describe the decisions companies make regarding their individual products and services, product lines, and product mixes.** (pp 231–237)

Individual product decisions involve product attributes, branding, packaging, labeling, and product support services. *Product*

attribute decisions involve product quality, features, and style and design. *Branding* decisions include selecting a brand name and developing a brand strategy. *Packaging* provides many key benefits, such as protection, economy, convenience, and promotion. Package decisions often include designing *labels*, which identify, describe, and possibly promote the product. Companies also develop *product support services* that enhance customer service and satisfaction and safeguard against competitors.

Most companies produce a product line rather than a single product. A *product line* is a group of products that are related in function, customer-purchase needs, or distribution channels. All product lines and items offered to customers by a particular seller make up the *product mix*. The mix can be described by four dimensions: width, length, depth, and consistency. These dimensions are the tools for developing the company's product strategy.

Objective 3 **Identify the four characteristics that affect the marketing of services and the additional marketing considerations that services require.** (pp 237–243)

Services are characterized by four key characteristics: they are *intangible, inseparable, variable,* and *perishable*. Each characteristic poses problems and marketing requirements. Marketers work to find ways to make the service more tangible, increase the productivity of providers who are inseparable from their products, standardize quality in the face of variability, and improve demand movements and supply capacities in the face of service perishability.

Good service companies focus attention on *both* customers and employees. They understand the *service profit chain*, which links service firm profits with employee and customer satisfaction. Services marketing strategy calls not only for external marketing but also for *internal marketing* to motivate employees and *interactive marketing* to create service delivery skills among service providers. To succeed, service marketers must create *competitive differentiation*, offer high *service quality*, and find ways to increase *service productivity*.

| Objective 4 | **Discuss branding strategy—the decisions companies make in building and managing their brands.** (pp 244–253) |

Some analysts see brands as *the* major enduring asset of a company. Brands are more than just names and symbols; they embody everything that the product or the service *means* to consumers. *Brand equity* is the positive differential effect that knowing the brand name has on customer response to the product or the service. A brand with strong brand equity is a very valuable asset.

In building brands, companies need to make decisions about brand positioning, brand name selection, brand sponsorship, and brand development. The most powerful *brand positioning* builds around strong consumer beliefs and values. *Brand name selection* involves finding the best brand name based on a careful review of

product benefits, the target market, and proposed marketing strategies. A manufacturer has four *brand sponsorship* options: it can launch a *national brand* (or manufacturer's brand), sell to resellers who use a *private brand*, market *licensed brands*, or join forces with another company to *co-brand* a product. A company also has four choices when it comes to developing brands. It can introduce *line extensions*, *brand extensions*, *multibrands*, or *new brands*.

Companies must build and manage their brands carefully. The brand's positioning must be continuously communicated to consumers. Advertising can help. However, brands are not maintained by advertising but by customers' *brand experiences*. Customers come to know a brand through a wide range of contacts and interactions. The company must put as much care into managing these touchpoints as it does into producing its ads. Companies must periodically audit their brands' strengths and weaknesses.

 # Key Terms

Objective 1

Product (p 226)
Service (p 226)
Consumer product (p 228)
Convenience product (p 229)
Shopping product (p 229)
Specialty product (p 229)
Unsought product (p 229)
Industrial product (p 229)
Social marketing (p 231)

Objective 2

Product quality (p 231)
Brand (p 233)
Packaging (p 233)
Product line (p 236)
Product mix (product portfolio) (p 236)

Objective 3

Service intangibility (p 238)
Service inseparability (p 238)
Service variability (p 238)

Service perishability (p 239)
Service profit chain (p 239)
Internal marketing (p 241)
Interactive marketing (p 241)

Objective 4

Brand equity (p 244)
Store brand (private brand) (p 248)
Co-branding (p 250)
Line extension (p 251)
Brand extension (p 251)

Discussion and Critical Thinking

 ## Discussion Questions

1. Name and describe the types of consumer products and give an example of each. How does the marketing differ for each product type? (AACSB: Communication; Reflective Thinking)

2. Compare and contrast industrial products and consumer products. (AACSB: Communication; Reflective Thinking)

3. Explain the importance of product quality and discuss how marketers use quality to create customer value. (AACSB: Communication)

✪ **4.** What is a brand? How does branding help both buyers and sellers? (AACSB: Communication)

✪ **5.** What is a product line? Discuss the various product line decisions marketers make and how a company can expand its product line. (AACSB: Communication)

✪ **6.** Describe the four characteristics of services that marketers must consider when designing marketing programs. How do the services offered by a doctor's office differ from those offered by a bank? (AACSB: Communication, Reflective Thinking)

 ## Critical Thinking Exercise

1. Find five examples of service-provider attempts to reduce service intangibility. (AACSB: Communication; Reflective Thinking)

Applications and Cases

Marketing Technology Mobile Hotspot

You've heard of mobile Wi-Fi hotspots, but one is truly mobile—your car. Automobile manufacturers Audi, Ford, Nissan, and General Motors are equipping cars with 10-inch screens and Internet access. Cadillac's new XTS includes an iPad-like touch screen and voice commands so you can keep in touch with your friends on Facebook. The government is concerned that Web access will cause a spike in accidents due to increased driver distraction and wants the devices to only work when the car is in park. Such guidelines are only suggestions, however, leaving car manufacturers to include whatever they think customers want in their vehicles. The industry's argument is that these new gadgets are safer than the handheld ones drivers are already using in their cars. Automakers claim that there will be even fewer buttons than currently found in cars, possibly resulting in greater safety for drivers and passengers.

1. Describe the core, actual, and augmented levels of product associated with an automobile. What level does the mobile Wi-Fi system represent? Explain. (AACSB: Communication; Reflective Thinking)

2. Debate the pros and cons of including Wi-Fi Internet access in automobiles. Should the Internet access feature be included in automobiles? (AACSB: Communication; Reflective Thinking)

Marketing Ethics Outsourced Instructors

Have you taken an online course in high school or college? Many students have, but some traditional brick-and-mortar universities are venturing into uncharted territory by outsourcing the teaching function to online providers. Missouri State University is offering its introductory journalism class through Florida-based Poynter Institute, a non-profit journalism training group. Instructional outsourcing is popping up on campuses throughout the country, and most are serviced by for-profit companies such as Academic Partnerships, StraighterLine, and Smarthinking. These partnerships translate into bigger profit margins for both the university and the instructional partner.

1. What is the product offered by a university? Discuss the levels of product offered and how these might change in the next 10 to 20 years as result of changing technology. (AACSB: Communication; Reflective Thinking)

2. From the point of view of both the school and the students, discuss the pros and cons of outsourcing instructors for courses or even entire degrees. Should technology be used in this way to deliver this type of product? (AACSB: Communication; Reflective Thinking; Ethical Reasoning)

Marketing by the Numbers What's a Brand Worth?

What is a brand worth? It's not just about dollars and cents. Interbrand, a leading brand valuation company, ranks the top 100 global brands annually and considers brand strength in addition to financial performance. The top global brand for years has been Coca-Cola, valued at almost $72 billion in 2011, followed by IBM, Microsoft, Google, GE, McDonald's, Intel, Apple, and Disney. In addition to financial data, Interbrand measures the role the brand plays in that financial outcome by comparing demand to that of an unbranded product in the same category. Nonfinancial factors are examined to assess a brand's strength. Internal brand strength factors include clarity, commitment, protection, and market responsiveness of the company regarding the brand. External factors include authenticity, relevance, differentiation, consistency, presence, and understanding of the brand among consumers in the marketplace.

1. Access the most recent ranking of the Top 100 Brands at www.interbrand.com. Create a chart representing the number of brands from the countries listed. Which country has the most brands in the top 100 ranking? What is the second leading country? (AACSB: Communication; Analytical Reasoning)

2. Click on the "Best Global Brands" dropdown menu at the Interbrand Web site (www.interbrand.com) and select "Interactive Charts." Click on an industry sector on the chart labeled "Brands by Sector." What are the top brands in that sector? Click on one of the brands and examine the change in its brand value over time. What percentage change in value did that brand experience in the last year for which data are available? Research that brand and write a report explaining why that brand's value changed over time. (AACSB: Communication; Reflective Thinking; Use of IT)

Video Case Life Is Good

You're probably familiar with Life Is Good. The company's cheerful logo is prominently featured on everything from t-shirts to dog collars and seems to exude a positive vibe. Although this company has found considerable success in selling its wares based on a happy brand image, consumers aren't getting the complete image that Life Is Good founders intended. This video illustrates the challenges a company faces in balancing the role of the customer and the role of the company in determining the meaning of a brand.

After viewing the video featuring Life Is Good, answer the following questions:

1. What are people buying when they purchase a Life Is Good product?

2. What factors have contributed to the Life Is Good brand image?

3. What recommendations would you make to Life Is Good regarding brand development strategies?

Company Case

Zipcar: "It's Not about Cars— It's about Urban Life"

Imagine a world in which no one owns a car. Cars would still exist, but rather than owning cars, people would just share them. Sounds crazy, right? But Scott Griffith, CEO of Zipcar, the world's largest car-share company, paints a picture of just such an imaginary world. And he has 700,000 passionate customers—or Zipsters, as they are called—who will back him up.

Zipcar specializes in renting out cars by the hour or day. Although this may sound like a minor variation on the established rental car agency business, car sharing—a concept pioneered by Zipcar—is an entirely different concept. As Griffith took the driver's seat of the young start-up company, he knew that if the company was going to achieve cruising speed, it needed to be far more than just another car service. Zipcar needed to be a well-positioned brand that appealed to a customer base with unfulfilled needs.

A Car Rental Company That Isn't about Cars

As Griffith considered what Zipcar had to offer, it was apparent that it couldn't be all things to all people. But the concept seemed particularly well suited to people who live or work in densely populated neighborhoods in cities such as New York City, Boston, Atlanta, San Francisco, and London. For these customers, owning a car (or a second or third car) is difficult, costly, and environmentally irresponsible. Interestingly, Zipcar doesn't see itself as a car-rental company. Instead, it's selling a lifestyle. "It's not about cars," says CEO Griffith, "it's about urban life. We're creating a lifestyle brand that happens to have a lot of cars."

Initially, the Zipcar brand was positioned exclusively round a value system. As an urban lifestyle brand, Zipcar focused on traits that city dwellers have in common. For starters, the lifestyle is rooted in environmental consciousness. At first, Zipcar focused on green-minded customers with promotional pitches such as "We ♥ Earth" and "Imagine a world with a million fewer cars on the road." Zipcar's vibrant green logo reflects this save-the-Earth philosophy. And Zipcar really does deliver on its environmental promises. Studies show that every shared Zipcar takes up to 20 cars off the road and cuts carbon emissions by up to 50 percent per user. On average, Zipsters travel 44 percent fewer miles than when they owned a car.

But it wasn't long before Griffith realized that if Zipcar was going to grow, it needed to move beyond just being green. So the brand has broadened its positioning to include other urban lifestyle benefits—benefits that Zipcar appeals to on its site in response to the question, "Who exactly is the car-sharing type?" Zipcar provides the most common reasons for car-sharing:

- I don't want the hassle of owning a car.
- I want to save money.
- I take public transit, but need a car sometimes.
- Once in a while I need a second car.
- I need a big car for a big job.
- I want a cute car to match my new shoes.
- I want to impress my boss.

One of most important benefits Zipcar provides is convenience. Owning a car in a densely populated urban area can be a real hassle. Zipcar lets customers focus on driving, not on the complexities of car ownership. It gives them "Wheels when you want them," in four easy steps: "Join. Reserve. Unlock. Drive."

Fulfilling Consumer Needs

To join, you pay around $60 for an annual membership and receive your personal Zipcard, which unlocks any of the thousands of cars located in urban areas around the world. Then, when you need a car, reserve one—minutes or months in advance—online, by phone, or using a smartphone app. You can choose the car you want, when and where you want it, and drive it for as little as $7.50 an hour, including gas, insurance, and free miles. When you're ready, walk to the car, hold your Zipcard to the windshield to unlock the doors, and you're good to go. When you're done, you drop the car off at the same parking spot—Zipcar worries about the maintenance and cleaning.

Zipcar not only eliminates the hassle of urban car ownership, it also saves money. By living with less, the average Zipster saves $600 a month on car payments, insurance, gas, maintenance, and other car ownership expenses.

Zipcar's operating system is carefully aligned with its urban lifestyle positioning. For starters, Zipcar "pods" (a dozen or so vehicles located in a given neighborhood) are stocked from a portfolio of over 50 different models that trendy urbanites love. The vehicles are both hip and fuel efficient: Toyota Priuses, Honda CRVs, MINIs, Volvo S60s, BMW 328s, Toyota Tacomas, Toyota Siennas, Subaru Outbacks, and others. And Zipcar is now testing plug-in hybrids and full electric vehicles, as well as full-size vans for big jobs. Each car has its own personality—a name and profile created by a Zipster. For example, Prius Ping "jogs in the morning; doesn't say much," whereas Civic Carlos "teaches yoga; loves to kayak." Such personal touches make it feel like you're borrowing the car from a friend, rather than being assigned whatever piece of metal happens to be available.

To further eliminate hassles and make Zipcar as convenient as possible, company promotional tactics are designed to appeal to city dwellers. The company's goal is for Zipsters to not have to walk more than 10 minutes to get to one of its car pods—no easy task. "Even with today's highly targeted Web, it's hard to target at that hyper-local level," says Griffith. "So our street teams do it block by block, zip code by zip code." Thus, in addition to local ads and transit advertising, Zipcar reps are beating the streets in true guerilla fashion.

For example, in San Francisco, passersby got to swing a sledgehammer at an SUV, while on Harvard's campus, students tried to guess how many frozen IKEA meatballs were stuffed inside a MINI. In Washington, D.C., Zipcar street teams planted a couch on a busy sidewalk with the sign "You need a Zipcar to move this." And the company has launched several local "Low-Car Diet" events, in which it asks urban residents to give up their cars and blog about it. Zipcar gave a free bike to a lucky dieter in each of the cities where it operates. Surveyed dieters reported saving 67 percent on vehicle costs compared to operating their own cars. Nearly half of them also said that they lost weight.

Fostering Brand Community

Zipcar's orientation around the urban, environmentally conscious lifestyle fosters a tight-knit sense of customer community. Zipsters are as fanatically loyal as the hardcore fans of Harley-Davidson or Apple, brands that have been nurturing customer relationships for decades. Loyal Zipsters serve as neighborhood brand ambassadors; 30 percent of new members join up at the recommendation of existing customers. "When I meet another Zipcar member at a party or something, I feel like we have something in common," says one Brooklyn Zipster. "It's like we're both making intelligent choices about our lives." And just like Harley owners get together on weekends to ride, the Internet is littered with announcements for Zipster parties at bars, restaurants, and comedy clubs, among other places.

As Zipcar has taken off, it has broadened the appeal of its brand to include a different type of urban dweller—businesses and other organizations. Companies such as Google now encourage employees to be environmentally conscious by commuting via a company shuttle and then using Zipcars for both business and personal use during the day. Other companies are using Zipcar as an alternative to black sedans, long taxi rides, and congested parking lots. Government agencies are getting into the game as well. The city of Chicago recently partnered with Zipcar to provide a more efficient and sustainable transportation alternative for city agencies. And Washington, D.C., now saves more than $1 million a year using Zipcar. Fleet manager Ralph Burns says that he has departments lining up. "Agencies putting their budgets together for next year are calling me up and saying, 'Ralph, I've got 25 cars I want to get rid of!'"

How is Zipcar's strategy of positioning itself as an urban lifestyle brand working? By all accounts, the young car-sharing nicher has the pedal to the metal and its tires are smoking. In just the past eight years, Zipcar's annual revenues have rocketed 68-fold, from $2 million to more than $136 million, and it's looking double that number in one year's time. Zipcar has also reached the milestone of being profitable. With 10 million people now within a 10-minute walk of a Zipcar, there's plenty of room to grow. And as more cars are added, Zipcar's reach will only increase.

Zipcar's rapid growth has sounded alarms at the traditional car-rental giants. Enterprise, Hertz, Avis, Thrifty, and even U-Haul now have their own car-sharing operations. But Zipcar has a 10-year head start, cozy relationships in targeted neighborhoods, and an urban hipster cred that corporate giants like Hertz will have trouble matching. To Zipsters, Hertz rents cars, but Zipcar is a part of their hectic urban lives.

Questions for Discussion

1. Evaluate Zipcar based on benefit-oriented positioning.

2. Describe the beliefs and values associated with Zipcar's brand image.

3. Compare positioning based on benefits to positioning based on beliefs and values. Which is stronger?

4. Based on what you know about the Zipcar brand, how will the company perform in the future relative to bigger, more experienced competitors?

Sources: Jerry Hirsch, "Zipcar CEO Talks about Car Sharing as Lifestyle Choice," *Seattle Times*, May 13, 2012, http://seattletimes.nwsource.com/html/businesstechnology/2018197748_inpersonzipcar14.html; "Zipcar Rolling into Profits, Stock Headed to $22," *Forbes*, February 23, 2012, www.forbes.com/sites/greatspeculations/2012/02/23/zipcar-rolling-into-profitability-stock-headed-to-22/; Kunur Patel, "Zipcar: An America's Hottest Brands Case Study," *Advertising Age*, November 16, 2009, p. 16; Paul Keegan, "Zipcar: The Best New Idea in Business," *Fortune*, August 27, 2009, accessed at www.fortune.com; Stephanie Clifford, "How Fast Can This Thing Go, Anyway?" *Inc.*, March 1, 2008, www.inc.com/magazine/20080301/how-fast-can-this-thing-go-anyway.html;andwww.zipcar.com, accessed October 2012.

MyMarketingLab

Go to **mymktlab.com** for Auto-graded writing questions as well as the following Assisted-graded writing questions:

8-1. List the names of the store brands found in the following stores: Walmart, Best Buy, and Whole Foods. Identify the private label brands of another retailer of your choice and compare the price and quality of one of the products to a comparable national brand. (AACSB: Communication; Reflective Thinking)

8-2. A product's package is often referred to as a "silent salesperson" and is the last marketing effort consumers see before they make a selection in the store. One model used to evaluate a product's package is the VIEW model: visibility, *infor-mation*, emotion, and *workability*. *Visibility* refers to the package's ability to stand out among competing products on the store shelf. *Information* is the type and amount of information included on the package. Some packages try to simulate *emotion* to influence buyers. Finally, all product packages perform the basic function of workability—protecting and dispensing the product. Select two competing brands in a product category and evaluate each brand's packaging on these dimensions. Which brand has superior packaging? Suggest ways to improve the other brand's packaging. (AACSB: Communication; Reflective Thinking)

8-3. Mymktlab Only – comprehensive writing assignment for this chapter.

References

1. Quotes and other information from Scott Cendrowski, "Nike's New Marketing Mojo," *Fortune*, February 27, 2012, pp. 81–88; Barbara Lippert, "Game Changers," *Adweek*, November 17–24, 2008, p. 20; Mark Borden, "Nike," *Fast Company*, March 2008, p. 93; Jonathon Birchall, "Nike Seeks 'Opportunities' in Turmoil," *Financial Times*, March 16, 2009, p. 20; Brian Morrissey, "Nike Plus Starts to Open up to Web," *Adweek*, July 20–July 27, 2009, p. 8; and annual reports and other sources at www.nikebiz.com, accessed September 2012.

2. Based on information found at www.starbucks.com/about-us/our-heritage, accessed November 2012.

3. See www.target.com/c/brand-shop-Rachael-Ray/-/N-5o5g6, accessed November 2012.

4. Information from Richard N. Velotta, "Brand USA Campaign Revealed," *VegasINC*, November 7, 2011, www.vegasinc.com/news/2011/nov/07/brand-usa-campaign-unveiled/; Harriet Edleson, "Selling America Abroad," *New York Times*, April 2, 2012; p. B7; and www.discoveramerica.com/ca/home.html and www.thebrandusa.com, accessed October 2012.

5. Information from www.social-marketing.org/aboutus.html, accessed November 2012.

6. For more on social marketing, see Alan R. Andreasen, *Social Marketing in the 21st Century* (Thousand Oaks, CA: Sage Publications, 2006); Philip Kotler and Nancy Lee, *Social Marketing: Influencing Behaviors for Good*, 3rd ed. (Thousand Oaks, CA: Sage Publications, 2008); and www.adcouncil.com and www.social-marketing.org, accessed September 2012.

7. Quotes and definitions from Philip Kotler, *Kotler on Marketing* (New York: Free Press, 1999), p. 17; and www.asq.org/glossary/q.html, accessed November 2012.

8. Quotes and other information from Regina Schrambling, "Tool Department; The Sharpest Knives in the Drawer," *Los Angeles Times*, March 8, 2006, p. F1; "Alex Lee at Gel 2008," video and commentary at http://vimeo.com/3200945, accessed June 2009; Reena Jana and Helen Walters, "OXO Gets a Grip on New Markets," *BusinessWeek*, October 5, 2009, p. 71; and www.oxo.com/about.jsp, accessed November 2012.

9. Andy Goldsmith, "Coke vs. Pepsi: The Taste They Don't Want You to Know About," *The 60-Second Marketer*, www.60secondmarketer.com/60SecondArticles/Branding/cokevs.pepsitast.html, accessed September 2011.

10. James Black, "What Is Your Product Saying to Consumers? *Advertising Age*, January 18, 2011, http://adage.com/print?article_id=148283.

11. See Christine Birkner, "Packaging: Thinking Outside of the Box," *Marketing News*, March 30, 2011, pp. 12–15; "FMI—Supermarket Facts," www.fmi.org/facts_figs/?fuseaction=superfact, accessed May 2012; and "Walmart Facts," www.walmartfacts com/StateByState/?id=2, accessed August 2012.

12. See Collin Dunn, "Packaging Design at Its Worst," Treehugger.com, July 6, 2009, www.treehugger.com/galleries/2009/07/packaging-design-at-its-worst.php; and "The Sustainable and Green Packaging Market: 2011–2021," *PR Newswire*, December 1, 2011.

13. Based on information from "PUMA Clever Little Bag," www.idsa.org/puma-clever-little-bag, accessed March 2012; and www.puma.com/cleverlittlebag, accessed August 2012.

14. Natalie Zmuda, "What Went into the Updated Pepsi Logo," *Advertising Age*, October 27, 2008, p. 6; "New Pepsi Logo Kicks off Campaign," *McClatchy-Tribune Business News*, January 15, 2010; and "Pepsi Logo—Design and History," February 4, 2011, www.logodesignsense.com/blog/pepsi-logo-design/.

15. "Leggo Your Logo," *Adweek*, December 6, 2010, p. 12; "New Gap Logo a Neural Failure," October 10, 2010, www.newscientist.com/blogs/shortsharpscience/2010/10/-normal-0-false-false-2.html; and "Marketer in the News," *Marketing*, February 9, 2011, p. 8.

16. For these and other stories, see Bob Janet, "Customers Never Tire of Great Service," *Dealerscope*, July 2008, p. 40; Greta Schulz, "Nordstrom Makes Customer Service Look Easy," December 11,

2009, http://amazingserviceguy.com/2370/2370/; and "Amazon Tops in Customer Service; Nordstrom No. 10," *Business Journal*," January 18, 2012, http://www.bizjournals.com/seattle/morning_call/2012/01/amazon-tops-in-customer-service.html.

17. See the AT&T Support Web site, www.att.com/esupport/, accessed November 2012.

18. Based on an example from Philip Kotler and Kevin Lane Keller, *Marketing Management*, 14th ed. (Upper Saddle River, NJ: Prentice Hall, 2012), p. 343, with additional information from http://en.wikipedia.org/wiki/BMW and www.bmwusa.com/standard/content/byo/default.aspx, accessed September 2012.

19. Information on Campbell Soup Company's product mix from http://investor.campbellsoupcompany.com/phoenix.zhtml?c=88650&p=irol-reportsannual, accessed September 2012.

20. Paul Hochman, "Ford's Big Reveal," *Fast Company*, April 2010, pp. 90–95.

21. See "Table 1.2.5 Gross Domestic Product by Major Type of Product," U.S. Bureau of Economic Analysis, January 27, 2012, www.bea.gov/national/nipaweb/TableView.asp?SelectedTable=19&Freq=Qtr&FirstYear=2009&LastYear=2011; and information from the Bureau of Labor Statistics, www.bls.gov, accessed May 2011.

22. Based on information from Leonard Berry and Neeli Bendapudi, "Clueing in Customers," *Harvard Business Review*, February 2003, pp. 100–106; Jeff Hansel, "Mayo Hits the Blogosphere," *McClatchy-Tribune Business News*, January 22, 2009; "Mayo Clinic Model of Care," www.mayo.edu/pmts/mc4200-mc4299/mc4270.pdf, accessed August 2012; and www.mayoclinic.org, accessed September 2012.

23. See James L. Heskett, W. Earl Sasser, Jr., and Leonard A. Schlesinger, *The Service Profit Chain: How Leading Companies Link Profit and Growth to Loyalty, Satisfaction, and Value* (New York: Free Press, 1997); Heskett, Sasser, and Schlesinger, *The Value Profit Chain: Treat Employees Like Customers and Customers Like Employees* (New York: Free Press, 2003); and Rachael W. Y. Yee and others, "The Service-Profit Chain: An Empirical Analysis in High-Contact Service Industries," *International Journal of Production Economics*, April 2011, p. 36.

24. Justin Fox, "What Is It That Only I Can Do?" *Harvard Business Review*, January–February 2011, pp. 119–123.

25. See annual reports and information accessed at http://phx.corporate-ir.net/phoenix.zhtml?c=132215&p=irol-irhome, August 2012.

26. See "United States: Prescription Drugs," www.statehealthfacts.org/profileind.jsp?sub=66&rgn=1&cat=5, accessed April 2012; and "Postal Facts," http://about.usps.com/who-we-are/postal-facts/welcome.htm, accessed August 2012.

27. Adapted from Sarah Kessler, "The Future of the Hotel Industry and Social Media," *Mashable!*, October 19 2010, http://mashable.com/2010/10/18/hotel-industry-social-media/; and Jeff Williams, "Marriott's SM Team Gets It," *HD Leader*, September 14, 2010, http://hdleader.com/2010/09/14/marriotts-sm-team-gets-it/. Also see https://twitter.com/#!/marriottintl, accessed August 2012.

28. For more discussion on the trade-offs between service productivity and service quality, see Roland T. Rust and Ming-Hui Huang, "Optimizing Service Productivity," *Journal of Marketing*, March 2012, pp. 47–66.

29. See "McAtlas Shrugged," *Foreign Policy*, May–June 2001, pp. 26–37; and Philip Kotler and Kevin Lane Keller, *Marketing Management*, 14th ed. (Upper Saddle River, NJ: Prentice Hall, 2012), p. 256.

30. Quotes from Jack Trout, "'Branding' Simplified," *Forbes*, April 19, 2007, www.forbes.com; and a presentation by Jason Kilar at the Kenan-Flagler Business School, University of North Carolina at Chapel Hill, Fall 2009.

31. For more on Young & Rubicam's BrandAsset Valuator, see W. Ronald Lane, Karen Whitehill King, and Tom Reichert, *Kleppner's Advertising Procedure*, 18th ed. (Upper Saddle River, NJ: Pearson Prentice Hall, 2011), pp. 83–84; "Brand Asset Valuator," ValueBasedManagement.net, www.valuebasedmanagement.net/methods_brand_asset_valuator

.html, accessed May 2012; and www.brandassetconsulting.com, accessed November 2012.

32. See MillwardBrown Optimor, "BrandZ Top 100 Most Valuable Global Brands 2011," www.millwardbrown.com/brandz/.

33. See Scott Davis, *Brand Asset Management*, 2nd ed. (San Francisco: Jossey-Bass, 2002). For more on brand positioning, see Kotler and Keller, *Marketing Management*, 14th ed., Chapter 10.

34. See "For P&G, Success Lies in More Than Merely a Dryer Diaper," *Advertising Age*, October 15, 2007, p. 20; Jack Neff, "Stengel Discusses Transition at P&G," *Advertising Age*, July 21, 2008, p. 17; and Jack Neff, "Just How Well-Defined Is Your Brand's Ideal?" *Advertising Age*, January 16, 2012, p. 4.

35. See www.saatchi.com/the_lovemarks_company and www.lovemarks .com, accessed September 2012; and Aaron Ahuvia Rajeev and Richard P. Bagozzi, "Brand Love," *Journal of Marketing*, March 2012, pp. 1–16.

36. Susan Wong, "Foods OK, But Some Can't Stomach More Ad Increases," *Brandweek*, January 5, 2009, p. 7. Also see "Brand Names Need to Reward Consumers to Keep Them According to Study," *PR Newswire*, October 23, 2009; "IDDBA Study Shows Store Brands Spiking," *Dairy Foods*, January 2010, p. 38; "Consumers Praise Store Brands," *Adweek*, April 8, 2010, www .adweek.com; and ""Hannah Karp, "Store Brands Step up Their Game, and Prices," *Wall Street Journal (Online)*, January 31, 2012, www.wsj.com.

37. See Todd Hale, "Store Brands Flex Muscle in Weak Economy," *Nielsen-Wire*, May 3, 2010, http://blog.nielsen.com/nielsenwire/consumer/ store-brands-flex-muscle-in-weak-economy/; Trefis, "Private Label Surge Threatens Polo Ralph Lauren," *The Street*, July 8, 2010, www.thestreet.com/story/10801997/private-label-surge-threatens-polo-ralph-lauren.html; Hannah Karp, "Store Brands Step up Their Game, and Prices," *Wall Street Journal (Online)*, January 31, 2012, www.wsj.com; and Lien Lamey, et al., "The Effect of Business-Cycle Fluctuations on Private-Label Share: What Has Marketing Conduct to Do with It?" *Journal of Marketing,* January 2012, pp. 1–19.

38. See information from Ely Portillo, "In Weak Economy, Store Brands Prosper," *McClatchy-Tribune News Service,* March 18, 2011; http:// walmartstores.com/Video/?id=1305 and http://walmartstores.com/ pressroom/Photos/Gallery.aspx?id=605, accessed April 2012; and www.wholefoodsmarket.com/products/365-everyday-value.php, accessed April 2012.

39. Daniel Frankel, "Report: Disney Raked in $26.9B from Licensed Merchandise in 2010," *Wrap* Media, May 18, 2011, www.thewrap .com/media/article/report-disney-made-286b-2010-licensed-merchandise-27526; Adam Bluestein, "Unleash the Merch-inator," *Fast Company,* November 2010, pp. 44–48; "Nickelodeon and Partners Unveil New Products at Toy Fair," The Licensing Book Online, February 17, 2012, http://licensingbook.com/nickelodeon-and-partners-unveil-new-products-at-toy-fair; and www.licensingexpo .com, accessed August 2012.

40. For this and other examples, see "Tim Hortons and Cold Stone: Co-Branding Strategies," *Business Week*, July 10, 2009, www .businessweek.com/smallbiz/content/jul2009/sb20090710_574574 .htm; Dan Beem, "The Case for Co-Branding," *Forbes*, March 16, 2010, accessed at www.forbes.com; and www.timhortons.com/ca/ en/about/investing.html, accessed November 2012.

41. Quote from www.apple.com/ipod/nike/, accessed June 2012.

42. See "The Brand That Launched 1000 Ships," *Bloomberg Businessweek,* October 3–October 9, 2011, p. 30; and www.fritolay.com/ our-snacks/doritos.html, accessed November 2012.

43. "Advertising Spending," *Advertising Age*, December 19, 2011, p. 4.

44. Quotes from Stephen Cole, "Value of the Brand," *CA Magazine*, May 2005, pp. 39–40; and Lawrence A. Crosby and Sheree L. Johnson, "Experience Required," *Marketing Management*, July/August 2007, pp. 21–27.

9

New-Product Development
and Product Life-Cycle Strategies

Chapter Preview In previous chapters, you've learned how marketers manage and develop products and brands. In this chapter, we examine two additional product topics: developing new products and managing products through their life cycles. New products are the lifeblood of an organization. However, new-product development is risky, and many new products fail. So, the first part of this chapter lays out a process for finding and growing successful new products. Once introduced, marketers then want their products to enjoy long and happy lives. In the second part of this chapter, you'll see that every product passes through several life-cycle stages, and each stage poses new challenges requiring different marketing strategies and tactics. Finally, we wrap up our product discussion by looking at two additional considerations: social responsibility in product decisions and international product and services marketing.

For openers, consider Samsung, the world's leading consumer electronics maker and one of the world's most innovative companies. Over the past two decades, Samsung has transformed itself by creating a culture of customer-focused innovation and a seemingly endless flow of inspired new products that feature stunning design, innovative technology, life-enriching features, and a big dose of "Wow!"

Samsung: Enriching Customers' Lives Through New-Product Innovation

You're probably familiar with the Samsung brand. Maybe you own one of Samsung's hot new Galaxy smartphones or a Samsung Series 7 Chronos notebook, or maybe you've seen one of those dazzling new Samsung slim bezel Smart TVs. You might even be reading this story on a smart new Samsung Galaxy tablet. Samsung, the world's largest consumer electronics manufacturer, produces "gotta-have" electronics in just about every category, from TVs and Blu-ray players, tablets and mobile phones, and laptops and laser printers to digital camcorders and even a full range of home appliances. Chances are good that you or someone you know owns a Samsung product.

But less than 20 years ago, Samsung was little known, and it was anything but cutting-edge. Back then, Samsung was a Korean copycat brand that you bought off a shipping pallet at Costco if you couldn't afford a Sony, then the world's most coveted consumer electronics brand. However, in 1993 Samsung made an inspired decision. It turned its back on cheap knock-offs and set out to overtake rival Sony. To dethrone the consumer electronics giant, however, Samsung first had to change its entire culture, from copycat to leading-edge. To out *sell* Sony, Samsung decided, it first had to out-*innovate* Sony.

Samsung's dramatic shift began with a top-down mandate for reform. Samsung set out to become a premier brand and a trailblazing product leader. The company hired a crop of fresh, young designers and managers, who unleashed a torrent of new products—not humdrum, me-too products, but sleek, bold, and beautiful products targeted to high-end users. Samsung called them "lifestyle works of art." Every new product had to pass the "Wow!" test: If it didn't get a "Wow!" reaction during market testing, it went straight back to the design studio.

> Samsung has become the world's leading consumer electronics company through customer-focused innovation and new products that enrich customers' lives. At Samsung, every new product has to pass the consumer "Wow!" test.

Beyond cutting-edge technology and stylish designs, Samsung put the customer at the core of its innovation movement. Its primary innovation goal was to improve the customer experience and bring genuine change to people's lives in everything it did.

With its fresh customer-centered new-product focus, Samsung overtook Sony in less than 10 years. Today, Samsung's annual revenues of $138 billion are more than one and one-half times Sony's revenues. And over the past three years, whereas Sony's sales have stagnated and losses have mounted in a difficult economy, Samsung's sales and profits have seen double-digit growth. According to brand tracker Interbrand, Samsung is now the world's 17th most valuable brand—ahead of megabrands such as Pepsi, Nike, and Honda—and one of the fastest-growing brands in the world.

But more than just being biggest, Samsung has now achieved the new-product Wow! factor it sought. For example, Samsung was a dominant force at the most recent International Design Excellence Awards (IDEA)—the Academy Awards of the design world—which judges new products based on appearance, functionality, and inspirational thinking. Samsung tied with Microsoft as the top corporate winner, claiming seven awards, more than twice as many as the next runner-up. Samsung's award-winning products were deemed both stylish and functional, such as a pocket projector that plugs into a USB port, an HD camcorder with a SwitchGrip design for both lefties and righties, and a compact, silicone-rubber-covered external hard drive that protects user's data from impact.

Despite its success, Samsung isn't resting on its innovation laurels. Whatever's next in consumer electronics, Samsung wants to be the first company that finds and develops it. To that end, last year Samsung made an incredible $41 billion technology investment for research and development (R&D), capital expenditures, and new plants and equipment—more than two and one-half times the combined investments of rivals Sony, Toshiba, Hitachi, and Sharp. Further, Samsung's market intelligence and product innovation teams around the globe continually research product usage, purchase behavior, and lifestyle trends, looking for consumer insights and innovative new ways to meet consumer needs.

These days, as consumer technologies become more connected and mobile, Samsung competes less with the Sonys of the world and more with innovation pacesetters like Apple. And against Apple, Samsung is more than holding its own. In mobile devices, for example, Samsung has surged to the top of the market. Just a few years ago, Samsung's goal was to double its market share of smartphones from 5 percent to 10 percent. But the success of its Galaxy line catapulted Samsung's global share to 20 percent, just ahead of Apple's.

In its favor, Samsung holds a piece of the technology puzzle that Apple doesn't—big screens. In fact, Samsung has been the global leader in television sales for six straight years.

Beyond cutting-edge technology and stylish design, Samsung puts the customer at the core of its innovation movement. Its new products "bring genuine change to people's lives."

Sean Gallup/Getty Images

Its new Smart TVs not only offer gesture control, voice control, and face recognition, but also provide seamless Web connectivity that has TV users Facebooking, Skyping, streaming online content, and using their favorite apps with a wave of the hand. Such features are attractive not just to consumers but also to advertisers wanting to reach them. Samsung hopes to take in lots of advertising dollars from companies eager to pitch their products on screens up to 25 times the size of an iPhone's or iPad's. If successful, Samsung will threaten not just Apple but also cable and satellite companies.

Beyond TVs and mobile devices, Samsung is applying its new-product Wow! to categories ranging from household appliances to digital imaging and notebook PCs. Hot off the assembly lines are washing machines with Eco Bubble technology that reduces energy consumption by up to 70 percent; digital cameras with multi-view/multi-angle technology, making it easier for users to capture life's important moments; and Samsung's Series 7 Chronos laptops that start faster, perform faster, and stay charged longer. "All of these are examples of new products that are enriching our customers' lives with innovative technology," says Samsung CMO Shim.

Twenty years ago, few would have predicted that Samsung could have transformed itself so quickly and completely from a low-cost copycat manufacturer into a world-leading innovator of stylish, high-performing, premium products. But through a dedication to customer-focused new-product innovation, that's exactly what Samsung has done. "[We] win by giving consumers what they want," says Samsung Electronics America's president of consumer electronics. "Maybe even . . . features they didn't know they wanted." Whatever gets that "Wow!"[1]

Objective Outline

Objective 1	**Explain how companies find and develop new-product ideas.** New-Product Development Strategy (pp 262–263)
Objective 2	**List and define the steps in the new-product development process and the major considerations in managing this process.** The New-Product Development Process (pp 263–271) Managing New-Product Development (pp 271–273)
Objective 3	**Describe the stages of the product life cycle and how marketing strategies change during a product's life cycle.** Product Life-Cycle Strategies (pp 273–279)
Objective 4	**Discuss two additional product issues: socially responsible product decisions and international product and services marketing.** Additional Product and Service Considerations (pp 279–282)

MyMarketingLab™

⭐ **Improve Your Grade!**

Over 10 million students improved their results using the Pearson MyLabs.
Visit **mymktlab.com** for simulations, tutorials, and end-of-chapter problems.

As the Samsung story suggests, companies that excel at developing and managing new products reap big rewards. Every product seems to go through a life cycle: It is born, goes through several phases, and eventually dies as newer products come along that create new or greater value for customers.

This product life cycle presents two major challenges: First, because all products eventually decline, a firm must be good at developing new products to replace aging ones (the challenge of *new-product development*). Second, a firm must be good at adapting its marketing strategies in the face of changing tastes, technologies, and competition as products pass through stages (the challenge of *product life-cycle strategies*). We first look at the problem of finding and developing new products and then at the problem of managing them successfully over their life cycles.

Objective 1 ⋯⋯▶

Explain how companies find and develop new-product ideas.

New-product development
The development of original products, product improvements, product modifications, and new brands through the firm's own product development efforts.

New-Product Development Strategy

A firm can obtain new products in two ways. One is through *acquisition*—by buying a whole company, a patent, or a license to produce someone else's product. The other is through the firm's own **new-product development** efforts. By *new products* we mean original products, product improvements, product modifications, and new brands that the firm develops through its own R&D efforts. In this chapter, we concentrate on new-product development.

New products are important to both customers and the marketers who serve them: They bring new solutions and variety to customers' lives, and they are a key source of growth for companies. In today's fast-changing environment, many companies rely on new products for the majority of their growth. For example, new products have almost completely transformed Apple in recent years. Sales of the iPhone and iPad—neither of which was available just six years ago—now bring in 72 percent of the company's total revenues.[2]

Yet innovation can be very expensive and very risky. New products face tough odds. By one estimate, 67 percent of all new products introduced by established companies fail. For new companies, the failure rate soars to 90 percent. Each year, U.S. companies lose an estimated $260 billion on failed new products.[3]

Why do so many new products fail? There are several reasons. Although an idea may be good, the company may overestimate market size. The actual product may be poorly designed. Or it might be incorrectly positioned, launched at the wrong time, priced too high, or poorly advertised. A high-level executive might push a favorite idea despite poor marketing research findings. Sometimes the costs of product development are higher than expected, and sometimes competitors fight back harder than expected.

So, companies face a problem: They must develop new products, but the odds weigh heavily against success. To create successful new products, a company must understand its consumers, markets, and competitors and develop products that deliver superior value to customers.

The New-Product Development Process

Objective 2 ──▶

List and define the steps in the new-product development process and the major considerations in managing this process.

Rather than leaving new products to chance, a company must carry out strong new-product planning and set up a systematic, customer-driven *new-product development process* for finding and growing new products. ● **Figure 9.1** shows the eight major steps in this process.

Idea Generation

Idea generation

The systematic search for new-product ideas.

New-product development starts with **idea generation**—the systematic search for new-product ideas. A company typically generates hundreds—even thousands—of ideas to find a few good ones. Major sources of new-product ideas include internal sources and external sources such as customers, competitors, distributors and suppliers, and others.

Internal Idea Sources

Using *internal sources*, the company can find new ideas through formal R&D. However, in a recent study, only 33 percent of companies surveyed rated traditional R&D as a leading source of innovation ideas. In contrast, 41 percent of companies identified customers as a key source, followed by heads of company business units (35 percent), employees (33 percent), and the sales force (17 percent).[4]

Thus, beyond its internal R&D process, a company can pick the brains of its own people—from executives to salespeople to scientists, engineers, and manufacturing staff. Many companies have developed successful internal social networks and *intrapreneurial* programs that encourage employees to develop new-product ideas. ● For example, Twitter hosts an annual "Hack Week: Let's Hack Together" event, which actively promotes internal innovation through experimentation around the company.[5]

> During Hack Week, a wide range of Twitter folks take time away from their day-to-day work to collaborate and see what crazy cool new things they can develop. Says one employee, "No meetings for a week. No releases for a week. And almost no rules. Go Hack Week!" During the most recent Hack Week, some 100 teams worked on wide-ranging projects, from developing

New-product development starts with good new-product ideas—lots of them. For example, Cisco's I-Prize crowdsourcing challenge attracted 824 ideas from 2,900 innovators representing more than 156 countries.

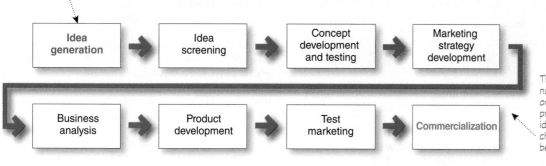

The remaining steps reduce the number of ideas and develop only the best ones into profitable products. Of the 824 ideas from Cisco's I-Prize challenge, only a handful are being developed.

● **FIGURE | 9.1**
Major Stages in New-Product Development

 Internal product ideas: Twitter hosts an annual "Hack Week: Let's Hack Together" event, which actively promotes internal innovation through experimentation around the company.

© The New York Times

new Twitter products and features to improving the Twitter user experience. "Some projects were technical and strategic; some were simply fun and off the wall, giving people a chance to stretch their creative muscles," says Twitter. Some of the ideas developed during Hack Week will become blockbuster additions; others will fall quietly by the wayside. It's still too soon to tell. "We can't wait to find out," says Twitter. But "one thing we do know: We'll have a bunch of awesome new products, features, and ideas."

External Idea Sources

Companies can also obtain good new-product ideas from any of a number of external sources. For example, *distributors and suppliers* can contribute ideas. Distributors are close to the market and can pass along information about consumer problems and new-product possibilities. Suppliers can tell the company about new concepts, techniques, and materials that can be used to develop new products.

Competitors are another important source. Companies watch competitors' ads to get clues about their new products. They buy competing new products, take them apart to see how they work, analyze their sales, and decide whether they should bring out a new product of their own. Other idea sources include trade magazines, shows, Web sites, and seminars; government agencies; advertising agencies; marketing research firms; university and commercial laboratories; and inventors.

Perhaps the most important sources of new-product ideas are *customers* themselves. The company can analyze customer questions and complaints to find new products that better solve consumer problems. Or it can invite customers to share suggestions and ideas. For example, the Danish-based LEGO Group, maker of the classic LEGO plastic bricks that have been fixtures in homes around the world for more than 60 years, systematically taps users for new-product ideas and input:[6]

 New-product ideas from customers: LEGO's CUUSOO Web site invites users to submit and vote on product ideas. LEGO Minecraft Micro World racked up the required 10,000 votes in less than 48 hours.

LEGO and the LEGO logo are trademarks of the LEGO Group of Companies, used here by permission. © 2012 The LEGO Group, CUUSOO System, and Mojang AB. All rights reserved.

At the LEGO CUUSOO Web site, LEGO invites users to submit ideas for new LEGO products and to vote for other users' ideas. Ideas supported by 10,000 votes are reviewed internally with chance of being put into production. Consumers who have their ideas chosen will earn 1 percent of the total net sales of the product. So far, the CUUSOO effort has produced dozens of major product ideas and three new products. The most recent release is LEGO Minecraft Micro World, which lets users of Mojang's popular videogame, Minecraft, recreate the Minecraft experience in LEGO bricks. With support from Minecraft's more than 20 million registered users, the new idea pulled in the required 10,000 votes on CUUSOO in less than 48 hours.

On a broader level, in developing new product ideas, LEGO actively taps into the AFOL (adult fans of LEGO) community. It has created a roster of customer ambassadors who provide regular input, and it even invites customers to participate directly in the idea-development process. For example, it invited 250 LEGO train-set enthusiasts to visit its New York office to assess new designs. The result was the LEGO Santa Fe Super Chief set, which sold out the first 10,000 units in less than two weeks with virtually no additional marketing. Thus, listening to consumers makes good business sense. "If our fans can tell us there's demand for [something], then why wouldn't we consider it?" asks a LEGO senior product-development executive. "And if we can take something like that and turn it into a runaway success for the business, then that will show the value of listening to our consumers."

Crowdsourcing

Crowdsourcing

Inviting broad communities of people—customers, employees, independent scientists and researchers, and even the public at large—into the new-product innovation process.

More broadly, many companies are now developing *crowdsourcing* or *open-innovation* new-product idea programs. **Crowdsourcing** throws the innovation doors wide open, inviting broad communities of people—customers, employees, independent scientists and researchers, and even the public at large—into the new-product innovation process. Tapping into a breadth of sources—both inside and outside the company—can produce unexpected and powerful new ideas. For example, rather than relying only on its own R&D labs to produce all of the new-product innovations needed to support growth, Procter & Gamble developed its Connect + Develop crowdsourcing process. Through Connect + Develop, the company uncovers promising innovations from entrepreneurs, scientists, engineers, and other researchers—even consumers themselves—that will help it meet its goal of improving consumers' lives (see Real Marketing 9.1).

Rather than creating and managing their own crowdsourcing platforms, companies can use third-party crowdsourcing networks, such as InnoCentive, TopCoder, Hypios, and Jovoto. For example, organizations ranging from Facebook and PayPal to ESPN, NASA, and the Salk Institute tap into TopCoder's network of nearly 400,000 mathematicians, engineers, software developers, and designers for ideas and solutions, offering prizes of $100 to $100,000. PayPal recently posted a challenge to the TopCoder community seeking the development of an innovative Android or iPhone app that would successfully and securely run its check-out process, awarding the winners $5,000 each. After only four weeks of competition and two weeks of review, PayPal had its solutions. The Android app came from a programmer in the United States; the iPhone app from a programmer in Colombia.[7]

Crowdsourcing can produce a flood of innovative ideas. In fact, opening the floodgates to anyone and everyone can overwhelm the company with ideas—some good and some bad. For example, when Cisco Systems sponsored an open-innovation effort called I-Prize, soliciting ideas from external sources, it received more than 820 distinct ideas from more than 2,900 innovators from 156 countries. "The evaluation process was far more labor-intensive than we'd anticipated," says Cisco's chief technology officer. It required "significant investments of time, energy, patience, and imagination . . . to discern the gems hidden within rough stones." In the end, a team of six Cisco people worked full-time for three months to carve out 32 semifinalist ideas, as well as nine teams representing 14 countries in six continents for the final phase of the competition.[8]

Truly innovative companies don't rely only on one source or another for new-product ideas. Instead, they develop extensive innovation networks that capture ideas and inspiration from every possible source, from employees and customers to outside innovators and multiple points beyond.

Idea Screening

Idea screening

Screening new-product ideas to spot good ideas and drop poor ones as soon as possible.

The purpose of idea generation is to create a large number of ideas. The purpose of the succeeding stages is to *reduce* that number. The first idea-reducing stage is **idea screening**, which helps spot good ideas and drop poor ones as soon as possible. Product development costs rise greatly in later stages, so the company wants to go ahead only with those product ideas that will turn into profitable products.

Many companies require their executives to write up new-product ideas in a standard format that can be reviewed by a new-product committee. The write-up describes the product or the service, the proposed customer value proposition, the target market, and the competition. It makes some rough estimates of market size, product price, development time and costs, manufacturing costs, and rate of return. The committee then evaluates the idea against a set of general criteria.

One marketing expert proposes an R-W-W ("real, win, worth doing") new-product screening framework that asks three questions. First, *Is it real?* Is there a real need and desire for the product and will customers buy it? Is there a clear product concept and will such a product satisfy the market? Second, *Can we win?* Does the product offer a sustainable competitive advantage? Does the company have the resources to make such a product a

Real Marketing 9.1

Crowdsourcing: P&G's Connect + Develop

Procter & Gamble markets about 300 mega-brands worldwide, reaping nearly $84 billion in annual revenues. By its own estimates, P&G brands touch the lives of 4.4 billion people around the world every day. Since its founding 175 years ago, P&G has set the gold standard for breakthrough innovation and new-product development in its industry. P&G's Tide detergent, introduced in the late 1940s, was the first synthetic laundry detergent for automatic washing machines. Its Pampers was the first successful disposable diaper. Crest was the first toothpaste with fluoride that actually prevented cavities, and Crest White-strips revolutionized at-home teeth whitening. Febreze was the first product to actually eliminate odors rather than simply covering them up. P&G's Olay ProX reduces the appearance of wrinkles as effectively as much more-expensive prescription anti-aging products. Such breakthrough innovations have been a pivotal element in P&G's incredible growth and success.

Until recently, most of the company's innovations came from within P&G's own R&D labs. P&G invests $2 billion a year in R&D, 50 percent more than its largest competitor and more than most of its other competitors combined. The consumer products giant employs more than 8,000 R&D researchers in 26 facilities around the globe, some of the best research talent in the world. But even with this hefty investment, P&G's own research labs simply can't provide the quantity of innovation required to meet all the growth needs of the $84 billion company.

So about 10 years ago, P&G shook up its research process. It transitioned from an internal R&D model that relied on P&G's own labs to produce needed innovation to an open-innovation model that invites outside partners to help develop new products and technologies that will delight customers.

P&G doesn't want to replace its 8,000 researchers; it wants to leverage them better. The company realized that much of today's important innovation is happening at entrepreneurial companies, universities, and government labs all around the world. For every researcher working at P&G, there are hundreds of scientists and engineers working elsewhere—millions in all. Moreover, thanks to the Internet, the world's talent markets are increasingly linked. P&G needed to change from its old "not-invented here" culture to one that embraced ideas found elsewhere. "We needed to change how we defined, and perceived, our R&D organization--from [8,000 people inside to 8,000 plus millions outside], with a permeable boundary between them," says P&G's vice president for innovation and knowledge.

With this objective in mind, P&G launched Connect + Develop, a major crowdsourcing program for uncovering promising innovation ideas from outside sources anywhere in the world. The Connect + Develop Web site invites entrepreneurs, scientists, engineers, and other researchers—even consumers themselves—to submit ideas for new technologies, product design, packaging, marketing models, research methods, engineering, or promotion—anything that has the potential to create better products and services that will help P&G meet its goal of "improving more consumers' lives, in more parts of the world, more completely." At the site, P&G also provides a list of already-identified innovation needs for which it is seeking solutions. "We have a lot to offer you as a business partner," says P&G at the Connect + Develop site, "and believe that, together, we can create more value than we ever could alone."

Launched in 2001 with a goal of delivering 50 percent of P&G's innovation through external collaboration, Connect + Develop has far surpassed that objective. Today, P&G collaborates with a truly global innovation network—more than 50 percent of its innovations involve some kind of external partner. So far, Connect + Develop has resulted in more than 1,000 active agreements. The long list of successful new products brought to market through Connect + Develop includes, among many others, Olay Regenerist, Swiffer Dusters, Tide Total Care, Clairol Perfect 10, the Oral B Pulsonic toothbrush, CoverGirl eyewear, Febreze Candles, and Mr. Clean Magic Eraser.

P&G's highly successful Connect + Develop crowdsourcing program invites outside innovation partners to help develop new technologies and products that will delight customers.

The Procter & Gamble Company

Under Connect + Develop, innovative ideas and technologies roll in from a wide diversity of sources, saving P&G both time and money. For example, the new peptide for P&G's blockbuster Olay Regenerist, a $2 billion brand, came from a small French company. The Oral B Pulsonic sonic toothbrush came from a partnership with a Japanese firm—it was in the market less than a year after the first meeting.

Connect + Develop was the source of the idea behind Febreze Candles, which give off a warm glow and pleasing scent as they neutralize pet odors, cooking smells, or other unwanted household odors. P&G provided the Febreze odor-care technology but worked with an external candle company to develop the candles. In turn, Febreze Candles led to the development of the entire Febreze Home Collection—a line of decorative candles, scented reed diffusers, and flameless scented luminaries—that has helped make Febreze one of P&G's newest billion-dollar brands.

Similarly, P&G's popular Mr. Clean Magic Eraser—the self-cleaning pads that act like an eraser to lift away tough dirt, including difficult scuff and crayon marks—got its start when an independent technology entrepreneur discovered a stain-removing sponge already on the market in Osaka, Japan, and alerted P&G via Connect + Develop. The product's magic ingredient was a packing foam made by Germany chemical company BASF, which happened already to be a major P&G supplier. P&G introduced the new product within a year, and it quickly became yet another blockbuster P&G brand.

The Connect + Develop crowdsourcing program has produced big benefits for P&G. Connect + Develop "opened our minds and doors to external collaboration," says Bruce Brown, P&G's chief technology officer. "It changed our culture from 'invented here' to 'partnering for greater value.'" As a result of the program, P&G's R&D productivity has increased 60 percent, and its innovation success rate has more than doubled, even as the cost of innovation has fallen. "Connect + Develop has created a culture of open innovation that has already generated sustainable growth," says P&G CEO Bob McDonald, "but we know we can do more. We want the best minds in the world to work with us to create big ideas that can touch and improve the lives of more consumers, in more parts of the world, more completely."

Sources: Based on quotes and other information in "P&G Adapts R&D Model," *warc,* January 31, 2012, www.warc.com/LatestNews/News/PG_adapts_RD_model.news?ID=29389; Larry Huston and Nabil Sakkab, "Connect and Develop: Inside Procter & Gamble's New Model for Innovation," *Harvard Business Review,* March 2006, pp. 2–9; Bruce Brown, "Why Technology Matters," *Technology Management,* November–December 2010, pp. 18–23; "P&G Sets Two New Goals for Open Innovation Partnerships," *PR Newswire,* October 28, 2010; Ellen Byron, "Febreze Joins P&G's $1 Billion Club," *Wall Street Journal,* March 9, 2011, http://online.wsj.com/article/SB10001424052748704076804576180683371307932.html; and the P&G Connect + Develop Web site at https://secure3.verticali.net/pg-connection-portal/ctx/noauth/0_0_1_4_83_4_3.do, accessed November 2012.

success? Finally, *Is it worth doing?* Does the product fit the company's overall growth strategy? Does it offer sufficient profit potential? The company should be able to answer yes to all three R-W-W questions before developing the new-product idea further.[9]

Concept Development and Testing

Product concept

A detailed version of the new-product idea stated in meaningful consumer terms.

An attractive idea must then be developed into a **product concept**. It is important to distinguish between a product idea, a product concept, and a product image. A *product idea* is an idea for a possible product that the company can see itself offering to the market. A *product concept* is a detailed version of the idea stated in meaningful consumer terms. A *product image* is the way consumers perceive an actual or potential product.

Concept Development

Suppose a car manufacturer has developed a practical battery-powered, all-electric car. ● Its initial prototype is a sleek, sporty roadster convertible that sells for more than $100,000.[10] However, in the near future it plans to introduce more-affordable, mass-market versions that will compete with recently introduced hybrid-electric or all-electric cars such as the Chevy Volt and Nissan Leaf. This 100 percent electric car will accelerate from 0 to 60 miles per hour in 5.6 seconds, travel up to 300 miles on a single charge, recharge in 45 minutes from a normal 120-volt electrical outlet, and cost about one penny per mile to power.

Looking ahead, the marketer's task is to develop this new product into alternative product concepts,

● This is Tesla's initial all-electric roadster. Later, more-affordable mass-market models will travel more than 300 miles on a single charge, recharge in 45 minutes from a normal 120-volt electrical outlet, and cost about one penny per mile to power.

AP Photo/Rick Bowmer

find out how attractive each concept is to customers, and choose the best one. It might create the following product concepts for this electric car:

- *Concept 1:* An affordably priced midsize car designed as a second family car to be used around town for running errands and visiting friends.
- *Concept 2:* A mid-priced sporty compact appealing to young singles and couples.
- *Concept 3:* A "green" car appealing to environmentally conscious people who want practical, no-polluting transportation.
- *Concept 4:* A high-end midsize utility vehicle appealing to those who love the space SUVs provide but lament the poor gas mileage.

Concept Testing

Concept testing

Testing new-product concepts with a group of target consumers to find out if the concepts have strong consumer appeal.

Concept testing calls for testing new-product concepts with groups of target consumers. The concepts may be presented to consumers symbolically or physically. Here, in more detail, is concept 3:

> An efficient, fun-to-drive, battery-powered compact car that seats four. This 100 percent electric wonder provides practical and reliable transportation with no pollution. It goes 300 miles on a single charge and costs pennies per mile to operate. It's a sensible, responsible alternative to today's pollution-producing gas-guzzlers. Its fully equipped price is $25,000.

Many firms routinely test new-product concepts with consumers before attempting to turn them into actual new products. For some concept tests, a word or picture description might be sufficient. However, a more concrete and physical presentation of the concept will increase the reliability of the concept test. After being exposed to the concept, consumers then may be asked to react to it by answering questions similar to those in ● **Table 9.1**.

The answers to such questions will help the company decide which concept has the strongest appeal. For example, the last question asks about the consumer's intention to buy. Suppose 2 percent of consumers say they "definitely" would buy, and another 5 percent say "probably." The company could project these figures to the full population in this target group to estimate sales volume. Even then, however, the estimate is uncertain because people do not always carry out their stated intentions.

Marketing Strategy Development

Marketing strategy development

Designing an initial marketing strategy for a new product based on the product concept.

Suppose the carmaker finds that concept 3 for the electric car tests best. The next step is **marketing strategy development**, designing an initial marketing strategy for introducing this car to the market.

The *marketing strategy statement* consists of three parts. The first part describes the target market; the planned value proposition; and the sales, market share, and profit goals for the first few years. Thus:

> The target market is younger, well-educated, moderate- to high-income individuals, couples, or small families seeking practical, environmentally responsible transportation. The car will

● **Table 9.1** | **Questions for the All-Electric Car Concept Test**

1. Do you understand the concept of a battery-powered electric car?
2. Do you believe the claims about the car's performance?
3. What are the major benefits of an all-electric car compared with a conventional car?
4. What are its advantages compared with a gas-electric hybrid car?
5. What improvements in the car's features would you suggest?
6. For what uses would you prefer an all-electric car to a conventional car?
7. What would be a reasonable price to charge for the car?
8. Who would be involved in your decision to buy such a car? Who would drive it?
9. Would you buy such a car (definitely, probably, probably not, definitely not)?

be positioned as more fun to drive and less polluting than today's internal combustion engine or hybrid cars. The company will aim to sell 50,000 cars in the first year, at a loss of not more than $15 million. In the second year, the company will aim for sales of 90,000 cars and a profit of $25 million.

The second part of the marketing strategy statement outlines the product's planned price, distribution, and marketing budget for the first year:

The battery-powered all-electric car will be offered in three colors—red, white, and blue—and will have a full set of accessories as standard features. It will sell at a retail price of $25,000, with 15 percent off the list price to dealers. Dealers who sell more than 10 cars per month will get an additional discount of 5 percent on each car sold that month. A marketing budget of $50 million will be split 50–50 between a national media campaign and local event marketing. Advertising, the Web site, and various digital content will emphasize the car's fun spirit and low emissions. During the first year, $100,000 will be spent on marketing research to find out who is buying the car and what their satisfaction levels are.

The third part of the marketing strategy statement describes the planned long-run sales, profit goals, and marketing mix strategy:

We intend to capture a 3 percent long-run share of the total auto market and realize an after-tax return on investment of 15 percent. To achieve this, product quality will start high and be improved over time. Price will be raised in the second and third years if competition and the economy permit. The total marketing budget will be raised each year by about 10 percent. Marketing research will be reduced to $60,000 per year after the first year.

Business Analysis

Business analysis

A review of the sales, costs, and profit projections for a new product to find out whether these factors satisfy the company's objectives.

Product development

Developing the product concept into a physical product to ensure that the product idea can be turned into a workable market offering.

Once management has decided on its product concept and marketing strategy, it can evaluate the business attractiveness of the proposal. **Business analysis** involves a review of the sales, costs, and profit projections for a new product to find out whether they satisfy the company's objectives. If they do, the product can move to the product development stage.

To estimate sales, the company might look at the sales history of similar products and conduct market surveys. It can then estimate minimum and maximum sales to assess the range of risk. After preparing the sales forecast, management can estimate the expected costs and profits for the product, including marketing, R&D, operations, accounting, and finance costs. The company then uses the sales and costs figures to analyze the new product's financial attractiveness.

Product Development

For many new-product concepts, a product may exist only as a word description, a drawing, or perhaps a crude mock-up. If the product concept passes the business test, it moves into **product development**. Here, R&D or engineering develops the product concept into a physical product. The product development step, however, now calls for a huge jump in investment. It will show whether the product idea can be turned into a workable product.

The R&D department will develop and test one or more physical versions of the product concept. R&D hopes to design a prototype that will satisfy and excite consumers and that can be produced quickly and at budgeted costs. Developing a successful prototype can take days, weeks, months, or even years depending on the product and prototype methods.

Often, products undergo rigorous tests to make sure that they perform safely and effectively, or that consumers will find value in them. Companies can do their own product testing or outsource testing to other firms that specialize in testing.

Marketers often involve actual customers in product testing. For example, New Balance's Weartest Program engages consumers throughout the product development process to field test new shoe designs under real-life conditions. Consumer testers attend The New Balance Tester School to learn how to analyze the fit, function, and durability of their assigned test shoes. As they test shoes over an

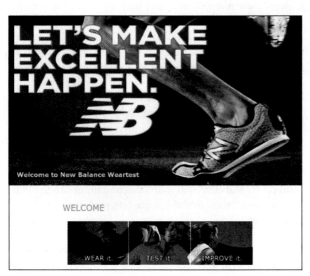

● **Product testing: New Balance's Weartest Program engages consumers to field test new designs under real world conditions.**

New Balance Athletic Shoe, Inc.

eight-week period, they log on to their Wear Test account and complete online surveys and feedback forms documenting their experiences with the test product. Says New Balance, "We believe that subjecting our product line to rigorous field testing ensures that all of our products perform at their peak—so you can too."[11]

A new product must have the required functional features and also convey the intended psychological characteristics. The all-electric car, for example, should strike consumers as being well built, comfortable, and safe. Management must learn what makes consumers decide that a car is well built. To some consumers, this means that the car has "solid-sounding" doors. To others, it means that the car is able to withstand a heavy impact in crash tests. Consumer tests are conducted in which consumers test-drive the car and rate its attributes.

Test Marketing

Test marketing

The stage of new-product development in which the product and its proposed marketing program are tested in realistic market settings.

If the product passes both the concept test and the product test, the next step is **test marketing**, the stage at which the product and its proposed marketing program are introduced into realistic market settings. Test marketing gives the marketer experience with marketing a product before going to the great expense of full introduction. It lets the company test the product and its entire marketing program—targeting and positioning strategy, advertising, distribution, pricing, branding and packaging, and budget levels.

The amount of test marketing needed varies with each new product. Test marketing costs can be high, and it takes time that may allow competitors to gain advantages. When the costs of developing and introducing the product are low, or when management is already confident about the new product, the company may do little or no test marketing. In fact, test marketing by consumer-goods firms has been declining in recent years. Companies often do not test-market simple line extensions or copies of competitors' successful products.

However, when introducing a new product requires a big investment, when the risks are high, or when management is not sure of the product or its marketing program, a company may do a lot of test marketing. ● For instance, Starbucks VIA instant coffee was one of the company's biggest, most risky product rollouts ever. The company spent 20 years developing the coffee and several months testing the product in Starbucks shops in Chicago and Seattle before releasing the product nationally. In the spring and summer of 2009, Starbucks patrons in the two test markets were offered recession-friendly $1.00 cups of coffee as well as coupons and free samples of VIA to take home with them. In addition, a Taste Challenge was created in Chicago to help drum up interest and induce trial. Performance of VIA exceeded expectations in all three cities and the promotional efforts were applied to the national rollout as well. Last year, the new brand generated more than $250 million in sales and Starbucks hopes to build it into a billion-dollar brand. Said CEO Howard Schultz, "We took a lot of time with it because we knew it could undermine the company if we didn't do it right."[12]

● Starbucks tested its VIA instant coffee extensively before launching the new product nationally. "We knew it could undermine the company if we didn't do it right."

Mark Lennihan/ASSOCIATED PRESS

As an alternative to extensive and costly standard test markets, companies can use controlled test markets or simulated test markets. In *controlled test markets*, such as Symphony-IRI's BehaviorScan, new products and tactics are tested among controlled panels of shoppers and stores.[13] By combining information on each test consumer's purchases with consumer demographic and TV viewing information, BehaviorScan can provide store-by-store, week-by-week reports on the sales of tested products and the impact of in-store and in-home marketing efforts. Using *simulated test markets*, researchers measure consumer responses to new products and marketing tactics in laboratory stores or simulated online shopping environments. Both controlled test markets and simulated test markets reduce the costs of test marketing and speed up the process.

Commercialization

Commercialization

Introducing a new product into the market.

Test marketing gives management the information needed to make a final decision about whether to launch the new product. If the company goes ahead with **commercialization**—introducing the new product into the market—it will face high costs. For example, the company may need to build or rent a manufacturing facility. And, in the case of a major new consumer product, it may spend hundreds of millions of dollars for advertising, sales promotion, and other marketing efforts in the first year. For instance, to introduce its McCafé coffee in the United States, McDonald's spent $100 million on an advertising blitz that spanned TV, print, radio, outdoor, the Internet, events, public relations, and sampling. Similarly, Nokia spent $100 million on a campaign to launch its Ace smartphone in the highly competitive U.S. mobile market.[14]

A company launching a new product must first decide on introduction *timing*. If the new product will eat into the sales of other company products, the introduction may be delayed. If the product can be improved further, or if the economy is down, the company may wait until the following year to launch it. However, if competitors are ready to introduce their own competing products, the company may push to introduce its new product sooner.

Next, the company must decide *where* to launch the new product—in a single location, a region, the national market, or the international market. Some companies may quickly introduce new models into the full national market. Companies with international distribution systems may introduce new products through swift global rollouts. General Motors did this with its global car, the new Malibu, which will be sold in 100 countries on six continents. The global Malibu launch was backed by live, high-definition video run on Facebook and various mobile media, timed to coincide with major auto shows in both Shanghai and New York. The car's designers and marketers were available in a live Web session to field consumer questions posted on Twitter or Chevrolet's Facebook page.[15]

Managing New-Product Development

The new-product development process shown in Figure 9.1 highlights the important activities needed to find, develop, and introduce new products. However, new-product development involves more than just going through a set of steps. Companies must take a holistic approach to managing this process. Successful new-product development requires a customer-centered, team-based, and systematic effort.

Customer-Centered New-Product Development

Customer-centered new-product development

New-product development that focuses on finding new ways to solve customer problems and create more customer-satisfying experiences.

Above all else, new-product development must be customer centered. When looking for and developing new products, companies often rely too heavily on technical research in their R&D laboratories. But like everything else in marketing, successful new-product development begins with a thorough understanding of what consumers need and value. **Customer-centered new-product development** focuses on finding new ways to solve customer problems and create more customer-satisfying experiences.

One study found that the most successful new products are ones that are differentiated, solve major customer problems, and offer a compelling customer value proposition. Another study showed that companies that directly engage their customers in the new-product innovation process had twice the return on assets and triple the growth in operating income of firms that did not. Thus, customer involvement has a positive effect on the new-product development process and product success.[16]

For example, whereas the consumer package goods industry's new-product success rate is only about 15 to 20 percent, P&G's success rate is over 50 percent. According to former P&G CEO A. G. Lafley, the most important factor in this success is understanding what consumers want. In the past, says Lafley, P&G tried to push new products down to consumers rather than first understanding their needs. But now, P&G employs an immersion process it calls "Living It," in which researchers go so far as to live with shoppers for several days at a time to envision product ideas based directly on consumer needs. P&Gers also hang out in stores for similar insights, a process they call "Working It." No other company in the world has invested more in consumer research than P&G. Each year, the company interacts with more than 5 million customers in 100 countries. It conducts more than

20,000 research studies every year and invests more than $400 million annually in what it calls "consumer understanding." "We figured out how to keep the consumer at the center of all our decisions," concludes Lafley. "As a result, we don't go far wrong."[17]

Thus, today's innovative companies get out of the research lab and connect with customers in search of fresh ways to meet customer needs. Customer-centered new-product development begins and ends with understanding customers and involving them in the process.

Team-Based New-Product Development

Good new-product development also requires a total-company, cross-functional effort. Some companies organize their new-product development process into the orderly sequence of steps shown in Figure 9.1, starting with idea generation and ending with commercialization. Under this *sequential product development* approach, one company department works individually to complete its stage of the process before passing the new product along to the next department and stage. This orderly, step-by-step process can help bring control to complex and risky projects. But it can also be dangerously slow. In fast-changing, highly competitive markets, such slow-but-sure product development can result in product failures, lost sales and profits, and crumbling market positions.

Team-based new-product development

New-product development in which various company departments work closely together, overlapping the steps in the product development process to save time and increase effectiveness.

To get their new products to market more quickly, many companies use a **team-based new-product development** approach. Under this approach, company departments work closely together in cross-functional teams, overlapping the steps in the product development process to save time and increase effectiveness. Instead of passing the new product from department to department, the company assembles a team of people from various departments that stays with the new product from start to finish. Such teams usually include people from the marketing, finance, design, manufacturing, and legal departments and even supplier and customer companies. In the sequential process, a bottleneck at one phase can seriously slow an entire project. In the team-based approach, however, if one area hits snags, it works to resolve them while the team moves on.

The team-based approach does have some limitations, however. For example, it sometimes creates more organizational tension and confusion than the more orderly sequential approach. However, in rapidly changing industries facing increasingly shorter product life cycles, the rewards of fast and flexible product development far exceed the risks. Companies that combine a customer-centered approach with team-based new-product development gain a big competitive edge by getting the right new products to market faster.

Systematic New-Product Development

Finally, the new-product development process should be holistic and systematic rather than compartmentalized and haphazard. Otherwise, few new ideas will surface, and many good ideas will sputter and die. To avoid these problems, a company can install an *innovation management system* to collect, review, evaluate, and manage new-product ideas.

The company can appoint a respected senior person to be its innovation manager. It can set up Web-based idea management software and encourage all company stakeholders—employees, suppliers, distributors, dealers—to become involved in finding and developing new products. It can assign a cross-functional innovation management committee to evaluate proposed new-product ideas and help bring good ideas to market. It can also create recognition programs to reward those who contribute the best ideas.

The innovation management system approach yields two favorable outcomes. First, it helps create an innovation-oriented company culture. It shows that top management supports, encourages, and rewards innovation. Second, it will yield a larger number of new-product ideas, among which will be found some especially good ones. The good new ideas will be more systematically developed, producing more new-product successes. No longer will good ideas wither for the lack of a sounding board or a senior product advocate.

Thus, new-product success requires more than simply thinking up a few good ideas, turning them into products, and finding customers for them. It requires a holistic approach for finding new ways to create valued customer experiences, from generating and screening new-product ideas to creating and rolling out want-satisfying products to customers.

More than this, successful new-product development requires a whole-company commitment. At companies known for their new-product prowess, such as Google, Apple,

3M, P&G, and GE, the entire culture encourages, supports, and rewards innovation. Consider Google:

> Google is wildly innovative. At many companies, new-product development is a cautious, step-by-step affair. In contrast, Google's new-product development moves at the speed of light. Its famously chaotic innovation process has unleashed a seemingly unending flurry of diverse products, ranging from an e-mail service (Gmail), a blog search engine (Google Blog Search), and a photo sharing service (Google Picasa) to a universal platform for mobile-phone applications (Google Android), a cloud-friendly Web browser (Chrome), projects for mapping and exploring the world (Google Maps and Google Earth), and even an early warning system for flu outbreaks (FluTrends). What ties it all together is the company's passion for helping people find and use information.
>
> Innovation is the responsibility of every Google employee. Google engineers are encouraged to spend 20 percent of their time developing their own "cool and wacky" new-product ideas. The company often asks potential employees how they'd change the world if they worked for Google. Google really wants to know—that's how the company operates. "Thinking—and building—on that scale is what Google does" observes one analyst. "This, after all, is the company that wants to make available online every page of every book ever published. Smaller-gauge ideas die of disinterest." In the end, at Google, innovation is more than a process—it's part of the company's DNA. "It's in the air," says the analyst, "in the spirit of the place."[18]

● **Google is spectacularly successful and wildly innovative. At Google, innovation is more than just a process—"it's in the air, in the spirit of the place."**

Eric Carr/Alamy

New-Product Development in Turbulent Times

When tough economic times hit, or when a company faces financial difficulties, management may be tempted to reduce spending on new-product development. However, such thinking is usually shortsighted. By cutting back on new products, the company may make itself less competitive during or after the downturn. In fact, tough times might call for even greater new-product development, as the company struggles to better align its market offerings with changing consumer needs and tastes. In difficult times, innovation more often helps than hurts in making the company more competitive and positioning it better for the future.

Companies such as Apple, Google, Samsung, and Amazon keep the innovations flowing during down economic times. For example, Apple created its blockbuster iPod, iPhone, and iTunes innovations in the midst of some very difficult times it faced a decade ago. Those innovations not only saved the company, they propelled in into the innovative powerhouse it is today.[19] Thus, rain or shine, good times or bad, a company must continue to innovate and develop new products if it wants to grow and prosper.

Objective 3 ······▶

Describe the stages of the product life cycle and how marketing strategies change during a product's life cycle.

Product life cycle (PLC)
The course of a product's sales and profits over its lifetime.

Product Life-Cycle Strategies

After launching the new product, management wants that product to enjoy a long and happy life. Although it does not expect that product to sell forever, the company wants to earn a decent profit to cover all the effort and risk that went into launching it. Management is aware that each product will have a life cycle, although its exact shape and length is not known in advance.

● **Figure 9.2** shows a typical **product life cycle (PLC)**, the course that a product's sales and profits take over its lifetime. The PLC has five distinct stages:

1. *Product development* begins when the company finds and develops a new-product idea. During product development, sales are zero, and the company's investment costs mount.
2. *Introduction* is a period of slow sales growth as the product is introduced in the market. Profits are nonexistent in this stage because of the heavy expenses of product introduction.

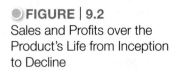

FIGURE | 9.2

Sales and Profits over the Product's Life from Inception to Decline

Some products die quickly; others stay in the mature stage for a long, long time. For example, TABASCO sauce has been around for more than 140 years. Even then, to keep the product young, the company has added a full line of flavors (such as Sweet & Spicy and Chipotle) and a kitchen cabinet full of new TABASCO products (such as spicy beans, a chili mix, and jalapeno nacho slices).

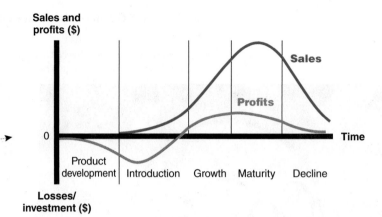

3. *Growth* is a period of rapid market acceptance and increasing profits.
4. *Maturity* is a period of slowdown in sales growth because the product has achieved acceptance by most potential buyers. Profits level off or decline because of increased marketing outlays to defend the product against competition.
5. *Decline* is the period when sales fall off and profits drop.

Not all products follow all five stages of the product life cycle (PLC). Some products are introduced and die quickly; others stay in the mature stage for a long, long time. Some enter the decline stage and are then cycled back into the growth stage through strong promotion or repositioning. It seems that a well-managed brand could live forever. Venerable brands like Coca-Cola, Gillette, Budweiser, Guinness, American Express, Wells Fargo, Kikkoman, Frye, and TABASCO sauce, for instance, are still going strong after more than 100 years. Guinness beer has been around for more than 250 years, ● Life Savers mints recently celebrated "100 years of keeping your mouth fresh," and TABASCO sauce brags that it's "over 140 years old and still able to totally whup your butt!"

● **Product life cycle:** Some brands stay in the mature stage for a long, long time. Life Savers mints recently celebrated "100 years of keeping your mouth fresh."

The Wrigley Company

The PLC concept can describe a *product class* (gasoline-powered automobiles), a *product form* (SUVs), or a *brand* (the Ford Escape). The PLC concept applies differently in each case. Product classes have the longest life cycles; the sales of many product classes stay in the mature stage for a long time. Product forms, in contrast, tend to have the standard PLC shape. Product forms such as "dial telephones" and "VHS tapes" passed through a regular history of introduction, rapid growth, maturity, and decline.

A specific brand's life cycle can change quickly because of changing competitive attacks and responses. For example, although laundry soaps (product class) and powdered detergents (product form) have enjoyed fairly long life cycles, the life cycles of specific brands have tended to be much shorter. Today's leading brands of powdered laundry soap are Tide and Cheer; the leading brands almost 100 years ago were Fels-Naptha, Octagon, and Kirkman.

The PLC concept also can be applied to what are known as styles, fashions, and fads. Their special life cycles are shown in ● **Figure 9.3**. A **style** is a basic and distinctive mode of expression. For example, styles appear in homes (colonial, ranch, transitional), clothing (formal, casual), and art (realist, surrealist, abstract). Once a style is invented, it may last for generations, passing in and out of vogue. A style has a cycle showing several periods of renewed interest.

A **fashion** is a currently accepted or popular style in a given field. For example, the more formal "business attire" look of corporate dress of the 1980s and 1990s gave way to the "business casual" look of the 2000s. Fashions tend to grow slowly, remain popular for a while, and then decline slowly.

Fads are temporary periods of unusually high sales driven by consumer enthusiasm and immediate product or brand popularity.[20] A fad may be part of an otherwise normal life cycle, as in the case of recent surges in the sales of poker chips and accessories. Or the fad may comprise a brand's or product's

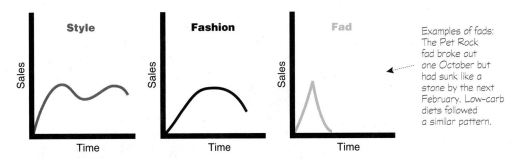

FIGURE | 9.3
Styles, Fashions, and Fads

Examples of fads: The Pet Rock fad broke out one October but had sunk like a stone by the next February. Low-carb diets followed a similar pattern.

Style
A basic and distinctive mode of expression.

Fashion
A currently accepted or popular style in a given field.

Fad
A temporary period of unusually high sales driven by consumer enthusiasm and immediate product or brand popularity.

entire life cycle. Pet Rocks are a classic example. Upon hearing his friends complain about how expensive it was to care for their dogs, advertising copywriter Gary Dahl joked about his pet rock. He soon wrote a spoof of a dog-training manual for it, titled "The Care and Training of Your Pet Rock." Soon Dahl was selling some 1.5 million ordinary beach pebbles at $4 a pop. Yet the fad, which broke one October, had sunk like a stone by the next February. Dahl's advice to those who want to succeed with a fad: "Enjoy it while it lasts." Other examples of fads include Silly Bandz, Crocs, and Pogs.[21]

Marketers can apply the product life-cycle concept as a useful framework for describing how products and markets work. And when used carefully, the PLC concept can help in developing good marketing strategies for its different stages. However, using the PLC concept for forecasting product performance or developing marketing strategies presents some practical problems. For example, in practice, it is difficult to forecast the sales level at each PLC stage, the length of each stage, and the shape of the PLC curve. Using the PLC concept to develop marketing strategy also can be difficult because strategy is both a cause and a result of the PLC. The product's current PLC position suggests the best marketing strategies, and the resulting marketing strategies affect product performance in later stages.

Moreover, marketers should not blindly push products through the traditional product life-cycle stages. Instead, marketers often defy the "rules" of the life cycle and position or reposition their products in unexpected ways. By doing this, they can rescue mature or declining products and return them to the growth phase of the life cycle. Or they can leapfrog obstacles to slow consumer acceptance and propel new products forward into the growth phase.

The moral of the product life cycle is that companies must continually innovate; otherwise, they risk extinction. No matter how successful its current product lineup, a company must skillfully manage the life cycles of existing products for future success. And to grow, the company must develop a steady stream of new products that bring new value to customers.

We looked at the product-development stage of the PLC in the first part of this chapter. We now look at strategies for each of the other life-cycle stages.

Introduction Stage

Introduction stage
The PLC stage in which a new product is first distributed and made available for purchase.

The **introduction stage** starts when a new product is first launched. Introduction takes time, and sales growth is apt to be slow. Well-known products such as frozen foods and HDTVs lingered for many years before they entered a stage of more rapid growth.

In this stage, as compared to other stages, profits are negative or low because of the low sales and high distribution and promotion expenses. Much money is needed to attract distributors and build their inventories. Promotion spending is relatively high to inform consumers of the new product and get them to try it. Because the market is not generally ready for product refinements at this stage, the company and its few competitors produce basic versions of the product. These firms focus their selling on those buyers who are the most ready to buy.

A company, especially the *market pioneer*, must choose a launch strategy that is consistent with the intended product positioning. It should realize that the initial strategy is just the first step in a grander marketing plan for the product's entire life cycle. If the pioneer chooses its launch strategy to make a "killing," it may be sacrificing long-run revenue for the sake of short-run gain. The pioneer has the best chance of building and retaining market leadership if it plays its cards correctly from the start.

Growth Stage

Growth stage
The PLC stage in which a product's sales start climbing quickly.

If the new product satisfies the market, it will enter a **growth stage**, in which sales will start climbing quickly. The early adopters will continue to buy, and later buyers will start following their lead, especially if they hear favorable word of mouth. Attracted by the opportunities for profit, new competitors will enter the market. They will introduce new-product features, and the market will expand. The increase in competitors leads to an increase in the number of distribution outlets, and sales jump just to build reseller inventories. Prices remain where they are or decrease only slightly. Companies keep their promotion spending at the same or a slightly higher level. Educating the market remains a goal, but now the company must also meet the competition.

Profits increase during the growth stage as promotion costs are spread over a large volume and as unit manufacturing costs decrease. The firm uses several strategies to sustain rapid market growth as long as possible. It improves product quality and adds new product features and models. It enters new market segments and new distribution channels. It shifts some advertising from building product awareness to building product conviction and purchase, and it lowers prices at the right time to attract more buyers.

In the growth stage, the firm faces a trade-off between high market share and high current profit. By spending a lot of money on product improvement, promotion, and distribution, the company can capture a dominant position. In doing so, however, it gives up maximum current profit, which it hopes to make up in the next stage.

Maturity Stage

Maturity stage
The PLC stage in which a product's sales growth slows or levels off.

At some point, a product's sales growth will slow down, and it will enter the **maturity stage**. This maturity stage normally lasts longer than the previous stages, and it poses strong challenges to marketing management. Most products are in the maturity stage of the life cycle, and therefore most of marketing management deals with the mature product.

The slowdown in sales growth results in many producers with many products to sell. In turn, this overcapacity leads to greater competition. Competitors begin marking down prices, increasing their advertising and sales promotions, and upping their product development budgets to find better versions of the product. These steps lead to a drop in profit. Some of the weaker competitors start dropping out, and the industry eventually contains only well-established competitors.

Although many products in the mature stage appear to remain unchanged for long periods, most successful ones are actually evolving to meet changing consumer needs. Product managers should do more than simply ride along with or defend their mature products—a good offense is the best defense. They should consider modifying the market, product offering, and marketing mix.

In *modifying the market*, the company tries to increase consumption by finding new users and new market segments for its brands. For example, brands such as Harley-Davidson and Axe fragrances, which have typically targeted male buyers, are introducing products and marketing programs aimed at women. P&G's Swiffer household cleaning brand has developed special promotions for pet owners.

The company may also look for ways to increase usage among present customers. For example, the Glad Products Company helps customers find new uses for its Press'n Seal wrap, the handy plastic wrap that creates a Tupperware-like seal. As more and more customers contacted the company about alternative uses for the product, Glad set up a special "1000s of Uses. What's Yours?" Web site (www.1000uses.com) at which customers can swap usage tips. Suggested uses for Press'n Seal range from protecting a computer keyboard from dirt and spills and keeping garden seeds fresh, to use by soccer moms sitting on damp benches while watching their tykes play. "We just roll out the Glad Press'n Seal over the long benches," says the mom who shared the tip, "and everyone's bottom stays nice and dry."[22]

The company might also try *modifying the product*—changing characteristics such as quality, features, style, packaging, or technology platforms to retain current users or attract new ones. Thus, to freshen up their products for today's technology-obsessed children, many classic toy and game makers are creating new digital versions or add-ons for old favorites. More than a third of children eight years old and younger now use devices such as iPads and smartphones. So toy makers are souping up their products to meet the tastes of the new generation. "Monopoly money can now be counted on a

● **Reinvigorating mature brands: To freshen up their products for today's technology-obsessed children, many classic toy and game makers are creating new digital versions of old favorites. Hot Wheels cars now zoom across iPad screens.**

APPTIVITY and associated trademarks and trade dress are owned by and used with permission from Mattel, Inc.
© 2012 Mattel, Inc. All Rights Reserved.

computer," says one observer. ● "Hot Wheels cars can zoom across iPad screens. And Barbie? She's become a digital camera." "We know the kids are going to play with technology," says a Mattel executive. "If you can't fix it, feature it."[23]

Finally, the company can try *modifying the marketing mix*—improving sales by changing one or more marketing mix elements. The company can offer new or improved services to buyers. It can cut prices to attract new users and competitors' customers. It can launch a better advertising campaign or use aggressive sales promotions—trade deals, cents-off, premiums, and contests. In addition to pricing and promotion, the company can also move into new marketing channels to help serve new users.

Kellogg used all of these approaches to keep its 50+-year-old Special K brand from sinking into decline. Introduced in 1957 as a healthful, high-protein cereal, Special K had matured by the 1990s—sales were flat and the brand had lost its luster. To reinvigorate the brand, Kellogg first extended the cereal line to include a variety of cereal flavors, such as Red Berries, Vanilla Almond, and Chocolatey Delight.

Then, it stretched Special K beyond cereals, turning it into a healthful, slimming lifestyle brand. The expanded line now includes meal and snack bars, protein waters and shakes, crackers and chips, and fruit crisps. To attract new users and more usage, Kellogg promotes the Special K Challenge, a weight management plan built around Special K products. "Whether your goal is to finally slip into those skinny jeans or you're just looking to become a little more fit and fabulous, the Special K Challenge is a great way to kick-start a better you!" The Special K brand-rejuvenation efforts paid off. The Special K line has grown steadily over the past decade and now accounts for more than $2 billion in annual sales.[24]

Decline Stage

The sales of most product forms and brands eventually dip. The decline may be slow, as in the cases of stamps and oatmeal cereal, or rapid, as in the cases of VHS tapes. Sales may plunge to zero, or they may drop to a low level where they continue for many years. This is the **decline stage**.

Decline stage

The PLC stage in which a product's sales fade away.

Sales decline for many reasons, including technological advances, shifts in consumer tastes, and increased competition. As sales and profits decline, some firms withdraw from the market. Those remaining may prune their product offerings. In addition, they may drop smaller market segments and marginal trade channels, or they may cut the promotion budget and reduce their prices further.

Carrying a weak product can be very costly to a firm, and not just in profit terms. There are many hidden costs. A weak product may take up too much of management's time. It often requires frequent price and inventory adjustments. It requires advertising and sales-force attention that might be better used to make "healthy" products more profitable. A product's failing reputation can cause customer concerns about the company and its other products. The biggest cost may well lie in the future. Keeping weak products delays the search for replacements, creates a lopsided product mix, hurts current profits, and weakens the company's foothold on the future.

For these reasons, companies must identify products in the decline stage and decide whether to maintain, harvest, or drop them. Management may decide to *maintain* its brand, repositioning or reinvigorating it in hopes of moving it back into the growth stage of the product life cycle. P&G has done this with several brands, including Mr. Clean and Old Spice. And Converse found fresh strategies for breathing new life into the venerable old Converse All Stars brand (see Real Marketing 9.2.)

Management may decide to *harvest* the product, which means reducing various costs (plant and equipment, maintenance, R&D, advertising, sales force), hoping that sales hold

Real Marketing 9.2

Converse: An Old Brand Story with a New Beginning

The Converse brand has had a long, eventful product life cycle. The company invented basketball shoes, and in 1923 it introduced the first pair of Chuck Taylor All Stars—known around the world as Cons, Connies, Convics, Verses, or just plain Chucks. Throughout the '30s, '40s, '50s, and '60s, Chucks were *the* shoes to have. The first Olympic basketball team wore them, and they dominated basketball courts—amateur and professional—for more than 50 years. By the mid-1970s, 70 to 80 percent of basketball players still wore Converse.

However, every story has a beginning, a middle, and an end, and that holds true for most brand stories as well. For Converse, the story almost came to an end a little more than a decade ago. As the sneaker market exploded in the 1980s and 1990s, Converse failed to keep up with the times. Aggressive new competitors like Nike, Adidas, and Reebok took the market by storm with new high-performance shoes and even higher-performing marketing schemes. By 2001, Converse's market share had dwindled to only 1 percent and the once-dominant brand declared Chapter 11 bankruptcy.

The Converse story would likely have ended right there if not for the foresight of an unlikely suitor. In 2003, market leader Nike stepped in and quietly bought Converse on the cheap. Nike still saw promise in the venerable though depleted old brand. However, it faced a perplexing product life-cycle question: How does a megabrand like Nike bring a fading icon like Converse back to life? To find answers, Nike assigned a new management team to Converse, gave it a fresh infusion of cash, and left the brand alone to shape its own strategy outside the shadow of the swoosh.

The new team discovered that, despite its dwindling market share, the Converse brand had acquired a small but fiercely loyal following. During the 1990s, street kids had begun wearing affordable Converse shoes as an expression of individuality. Soon to follow were emerging artists, designers, and musicians, who wore Chucks because of their simplicity and classic looks. Converse became a favorite of the anti-establishment,

anti-corporate crowd, those tired of trendy fashions. Individualistic Converse fans would take a pair of cheap but comfy All Stars, trash them, scribble on them, and customize them as a canvas for personal expression.

This small but loyal following provided a lifeline for rejuvenating the aging brand. Building on that niche, in the years that followed, Converse would transform the classic yesteryear brand into a fresh, expressive lifestyle brand befitting current times. Today's young consumers don't want a brand that's neatly packaged and handed to them; they want to experience a brand and help shape it. So rather than forcing a new brand story onto the market, Converse decided to turn the brand over to consumers themselves and let them write the next chapter.

To be sure, Converse has been very strategic in its "stand-back" approach. For example, it has taken the original Chuck Taylor All Star shoe and branched out with new designs and new channels. The One Star variant is a low-priced line available at Target. Thousands of higher-priced versions of All Stars, created by fashion designers, are now sold through upscale retailers like Saks and Bloomingdales. And the brand has been extended to offer everything from kids' shoes, work shoes, sandals, and boots to Converse-branded eyewear and watches.

But Converse sees its role simply as making great products that customers want to wear. Beyond that, it participates in the brand story rather than dictating it. At the heart of the rekindled Converse brand is the philosophy that customers control brands, not companies. In the eyes of consumers, Converse today is less about the shoes and more about self-expression and the Converse experience. According to Converse Chief Marketing Officer Geoff Cottrill, largely on their own, consumers have come to define the Converse brand around five ideas: "American, sneaker, youthful, rebellious, and a blank canvas."

Accordingly, the Converse Web site is all about designing your own shoes and using Chucks as your own personal canvas. Also, in recent years, Converse has focused its brand identity on one of the ultimate forms

of youthful self-expression—rock n' roll music. For example, the company has released several popular lines of All Stars designed by legendary rock artists. It has even built its own music studio—Converse Rubber Tracks—where undiscovered artists can have free access to high-end equipment and lay down tracks that might land them record deals elsewhere. Converse's focus on self-expression and music has helped it create real and relevant brand conversations with and among people who might wear its sneakers.

Converse has also embraced social media, an ideal forum for engaging young consumers and letting them help to define the brand. Converse now spends more than 90 percent of its marketing dollars on emerging media. Consider this: Converse has become the most popular sneaker brand on Facebook, with more than 42 million fans on its two Facebook pages, more than four times the number for parent company and market leader Nike, and eight times as many as number two Adidas. Converse also has 50,000 Twitter followers. That's amazing for a niche brand that still captures only 3 percent of the market.

In using social media, however, Converse is careful to stand back and let customers

Product life cycle: The venerable old Converse brand has begun a new life as a small but thriving lifestyle brand. Consumers themselves are helping to write the new Converse story.

Blend Images/Moxie Productions

give voice to the brand. Its approach is to create positive brand experiences and interactions, and then step aside and let customers themselves talk about the brand and share their understanding of the brand with friends. As a result, Converse has now become one of the most democratic brands of all time—a brand of the people, by the people, and for the people. "This brand is a unique brand in that consumers really do own it, and really do direct it, and really do take it into interesting places," says Cottrill. "It's been inspiring to see this brand go into all the places it has gone simply because the consumers have taken us there."

In all, Converse appears now to have begun a new life cycle as a small but thriving lifestyle brand. In the decade or so since

being acquired by Nike, Converse's revenues have more than quadrupled to $1.1 billion. At its Web site, Converse provides a fitting summary of its product life-cycle story, the end of which has yet to be written

> Everyone has a history—an account of the things they've done during the time they've been around. We think of ours as a bunch of cool stories that have led us to where we are and will show us where we'll go. The brand

enters its second century by honoring its heritage of seeing things a little differently, . . . basically celebrating the spirit of rebellion and originality in basketball, Rock & Roll, and anywhere else you find it. The best stories are the ones that don't end—the ones you just keep adding to and adding to—all the while marveling at the creative, disruptive, optimistic, courageous ways things evolve from being what they were, to what they are, to what they will become.

Sources: Quotes, extracts, and other material from Jeffrey Summers, "Why Converse Has 42 Million Facebook Fans," *Forbes* video interview, February 22, 2012, accessed at www.youtube.com/watch?v=BV1ilkKoy1o; Todd Wasserman, "How Converse Became the Biggest Little Sneaker Brand on Facebook," *Mashable*, May 4, 2011; Doug Schumacher, "TopTen: On Converse's Facebook Page, the Fans Do the Selling," *iMedia Connection*, March 13, 2012, http://blogs.imediaconnection.com/blog/2012/03/13/topten-on-converses-facebook-page-the-fans-do-the-selling/; and www.converse.com and www.converse.com/About/, accessed October 2012.

up. If successful, harvesting will increase the company's profits in the short run. Finally, management may decide to *drop* the product from its line. The company can sell the product to another firm or simply liquidate it at salvage value. In recent years, P&G has sold off several lesser or declining brands, such as Folgers coffee, Crisco oil, Comet cleanser, Sure deodorant, Duncan Hines cake mixes, and Jif peanut butter. If the company plans to find a buyer, it will not want to run down the product through harvesting.

● **Table 9.2** summarizes the key characteristics of each stage of the PLC. The table also lists the marketing objectives and strategies for each stage.[25]

Objective 4 ·······►

Discuss two additional product issues: socially responsible product decisions and international product and services marketing.

Additional Product and Service Considerations

We wrap up our discussion of products and services with two additional considerations: social responsibility in product decisions and issues of international product and services marketing.

Product Decisions and Social Responsibility

Marketers should carefully consider public policy issues and regulations regarding acquiring or dropping products, patent protection, product quality and safety, and product warranties.

Regarding new products, the government may prevent companies from adding products through acquisitions if the effect threatens to lessen competition. Companies dropping products must be aware that they have legal obligations, written or implied, to their suppliers, dealers, and customers who have a stake in the dropped product. Companies must also obey U.S. patent laws when developing new products. A company cannot make its product illegally similar to another company's established product.

Manufacturers must comply with specific laws regarding product quality and safety. The Federal Food, Drug, and Cosmetic Act protects consumers from unsafe and adulterated food, drugs, and cosmetics. Various acts provide for the inspection of sanitary conditions in the meat- and poultry-processing industries. Safety legislation has been passed to regulate fabrics, chemical substances, automobiles, toys, and drugs and poisons. The Consumer Product Safety Act of 1972 established the Consumer Product Safety Commission, which

● **Table 9.2** | **Summary of Product Life-Cycle Characteristics, Objectives, and Strategies**

	Introduction	**Growth**	**Maturity**	**Decline**
Characteristics				
Sales	Low sales	Rapidly rising sales	Peak sales	Declining sales
Costs	High cost per customer	Average cost per customer	Low cost per customer	Low cost per customer
Profits	Negative	Rising profits	High profits	Declining profits
Customers	Innovators	Early adopters	Middle majority	Laggards
Competitors	Few	Growing number	Stable number beginning to decline	Declining number
Marketing objectives	Create product awareness and trial	Maximize market share	Maximize profit while defending market share	Reduce expenditure and milk the brand
Strategies				
Product	Offer a basic product	Offer product extensions, service, and warranty	Diversify brand and models	Phase out weak items
Price	Use cost-plus	Price to penetrate market	Price to match or beat competitors	Cut price
Distribution	Build selective distribution	Build intensive distribution	Build more intensive distribution	Go selective: phase out unprofitable outlets
Advertising	Build product awareness among early adopters and dealers	Build awareness and interest in the mass market	Stress brand differences and benefits	Reduce to level needed to retain hard-core loyals
Sales Promotion	Use heavy sales promotion to entice trial	Reduce to take advantage of heavy consumer demand	Increase to encourage brand switching	Reduce to minimal level

Source: Philip Kotler and Kevin Lane Keller, *Marketing Management,* 14th ed. (Upper Saddle River, NJ: Prentice Hall, 2012), p. 317. © 2012. Printed and Electronically reproduced by permission of Pearson Education, Inc., Upper Saddle River, New Jersey.

has the authority to ban or seize potentially harmful products and set severe penalties for violation of the law.

If consumers have been injured by a product with a defective design, they can sue manufacturers or dealers. A recent survey of manufacturing companies found that product liability was the second-largest litigation concern, behind only labor and employment matters. Product liability suits are now occurring in U.S. district courts at the rate of over 60,000 per year, up from 19,500 in 1990. Although manufacturers are found to be at fault in only 6 percent of all product liability cases, when they are found guilty, the median jury award is $1.5 million, and individual awards can run into the tens or even hundreds of millions of dollars. Class-action suits can run into the billions. For example, after it recalled some 7 million vehicles for acceleration-pedal-related issues, Toyota will face more than 100 class-action and individual lawsuits beginning in 2013 that could end up costing the company $3 billion or more.[26]

This litigation phenomenon has resulted in huge increases in product liability insurance premiums, causing big problems in some industries. Some companies pass these higher rates along to consumers by raising prices. Others are forced to discontinue high-risk product lines. Some companies are now appointing *product stewards*, whose job is to protect consumers from harm and the company from liability by proactively ferreting out potential product problems.

International Product and Services Marketing

International product and services marketers face special challenges. First they must figure out what products and services to introduce and in which countries. Then they must decide how much to standardize or adapt their products and services for world markets.

On the one hand, companies would like to standardize their offerings. Standardization helps a company develop a consistent worldwide image. It also lowers the product design, manufacturing, and marketing costs of offering a large variety of products. On the other hand, markets and consumers around the world differ widely. Companies must usually respond to these differences by adapting their product offerings. For example, by carefully adapting its menu and operations to local tastes and eating styles, YUM! Brands—parent company of quintessential fast-food restaurants KFC, Pizza Hut, and Taco Bell—has become the largest restaurant company in mainland China. Consider KFC:[27]

● **Global product adaptation: By adapting to local tastes and eating styles, KFC has achieved finger-lickin' good success in China.**

Gan jun—Imaginechina

A typical Kentucky Fried Chicken meal in the United States features original, extra crispy, and a Pepsi. What do you get at a KFC in China? Of course, you can get some good old Kentucky fried, but more popular items include chicken with Sichuan spicy sauce and rice, egg soup, or a "dragon twister" (KFC's version of a traditional Beijing duck wrap), all washed down with some soybean milk. Also the menu: egg tarts, fried dough sticks, wraps with local sauces, fish and shrimp burgers on fresh buns, and congee, a popular rice porridge that is KFC's number one seller at breakfast. The Chinese menu also offers a large selection—some 50 items compared with 29 in the United States—meant to appeal to the Chinese style of eating, in which groups of people share several dishes. ● And whereas KFC outlets in the United States are designed primarily for takeout and eating at home, outlets in China are about twice the size of their U.S. counterparts, providing more space for eat-in diners, who like to linger with friends and family. Through such adaptation, KFC and YUM!'s other brands in China have positioned themselves not as a foreign presence but as a part of the local community. The result: YUM! Brands has achieved finger lickin' good success in China. Its 3,900 restaurants in China earned more revenue last year than all 19,000 of its restaurants in the United States combined, including KFC, Pizza Hut and Taco Bell.

Service marketers also face special challenges when going global. Some service industries have a long history of international operations. For example, the commercial banking industry was one of the first to grow internationally. Banks had to provide global services to meet the foreign exchange and credit needs of their home country clients who wanted to sell overseas. In recent years, many banks have become truly global. Germany's Deutsche Bank, for example, serves more than 19 million customers through 3,083 branches in 72 countries. For its clients around the world who wish to grow globally, Deutsche Bank can raise money not only in Frankfurt but also in Zurich, London, Paris, Tokyo, and Moscow.[28]

Professional and business services industries, such as accounting, management consulting, and advertising, have also globalized. The international growth of these firms followed the globalization of the client companies they serve. For example, as more clients employ worldwide marketing and advertising strategies, advertising agencies have responded by globalizing their own operations. McCann Worldgroup, a large U.S.-based advertising and marketing services agency, operates in more than 130 countries. It serves international clients such as Coca-Cola, GM, ExxonMobil, Microsoft, MasterCard, Johnson & Johnson, and Unilever in markets ranging from the United States and Canada to Korea and Kazakhstan. Moreover, McCann Worldgroup is one company in the Interpublic Group of Companies, an immense, worldwide network of advertising and marketing services companies.[29]

Retailers are among the latest service businesses to go global. As their home markets become saturated, American retailers such as Walmart, Office Depot, and Saks Fifth Avenue are expanding into faster-growing markets abroad. For example, since 1991, Walmart has entered 27 countries outside the United States; its international division's sales accounts for 26 percent of total sales. Foreign retailers are making similar moves. Asian shoppers can now buy American products in French-owned Carrefour stores. Carrefour, the world's second-largest retailer behind Walmart, now operates more than 15,500 stores in more than 35 countries. It is the leading retailer in Europe, Brazil, and Argentina and the largest foreign retailer in China.[30]

The trend toward growth of global service companies will continue, especially in banking, airlines, telecommunications, and professional services. Today, service firms are no longer simply following their manufacturing customers. Instead, they are taking the lead in international expansion.

Reviewing the Concepts

MyMarketingLab™

Go to **mymktlab.com** to complete the problems marked with this icon .

Reviewing Objectives and Key Terms

 ## Objectives Review

A company's current products face limited life spans and must be replaced by newer products. But new products can fail—the risks of innovation are as great as the rewards. The key to successful innovation lies in a customer-focused, total-company effort; strong planning; and a systematic new-product development process.

Objective 1 │ Explain how companies find and develop new-product ideas.

(pp 262–263)

Companies find and develop new-product ideas from a variety of sources. Many new-product ideas stem from *internal sources*. Companies conduct formal R&D, or they pick the brains of their employees, urging them to think up and develop new-product ideas. Other ideas come from *external sources*. Companies track *competitors'* offerings and obtain ideas from *distributors and suppliers* who are close to the market and can pass along information about consumer problems and new-product possibilities.

Perhaps the most important sources of new-product ideas are customers themselves. Companies observe customers, invite them to submit their ideas and suggestions, or even involve customers in the new-product development process. Many companies are now developing *crowdsourcing* or *open-innovation* new-product idea programs, which invite broad communities of people—customers, employees, independent scientists and researchers, and even the general public—into the new-product innovation process. Truly innovative companies do not rely only on one source or another for new-product ideas.

Objective 2 │ List and define the steps in the new-product development process and the major considerations in managing this process. **(pp 263–273)**

The new-product development process consists of eight sequential stages. The process starts with *idea generation*. Next comes *idea screening*, which reduces the number of ideas based on the company's own criteria. Ideas that pass the screening stage continue through *product concept development*, in which a detailed version of the new-product idea is stated in meaningful consumer terms. This stage includes *concept testing*, in which new-product concepts are tested with a group of target consumers to determine whether the concepts have strong consumer appeal. Strong concepts proceed to *marketing strategy development*, in which an initial marketing strategy for the new product is developed from the product concept. In the *business-analysis* stage, a review of the sales, costs, and profit projections for a new product is conducted to determine whether the new product is likely to satisfy the company's objectives. With positive results here, the ideas become more concrete through *product development* and *test marketing* and finally are launched during *commercialization*.

New-product development involves more than just going through a set of steps. Companies must take a systematic, holistic approach to managing this process. Successful new-product development requires a customer-centered, team-based, systematic effort.

Objective 3 Describe the stages of the product life cycle and how marketing strategies change during a product's life cycle. (pp 273–279)

Each product has a *life cycle* marked by a changing set of problems and opportunities. The sales of the typical product follow an S-shaped curve made up of five stages. The cycle begins with the *product development* stage in which the company finds and develops a new-product idea. *The introduction stage* is marked by slow growth and low profits as the product is distributed to the market. If successful, the product enters a *growth stage*, which offers rapid sales growth and increasing profits. Next comes a *maturity stage* in which the product's sales growth slows down and profits stabilize. Finally, the product enters a *decline stage* in which sales and profits dwindle. The company's task during this stage is to recognize the decline and decide whether it should maintain, harvest, or drop the product. The different stages of the PLC require different marketing strategies and tactics.

Objective 4 Discuss two additional product issues: socially responsible product decisions and international product and services marketing. (pp 279–282)

Marketers must consider two additional product issues. The first is *social responsibility*. This includes public policy issues and regulations involving acquiring or dropping products, patent protection, product quality and safety, and product warranties. The second involves the special challenges facing international product and services marketers. International marketers must decide how much to standardize or adapt their offerings for world markets.

 # Key Terms

Objective 1

New-product development (p 262)

Objective 2

Idea generation (p 263)
Crowdsourcing (p 265)
Idea screening (p 265)
Product concept (p 267)
Concept testing (p 268)

Marketing strategy development (p 268)
Business analysis (p 269)
Product development (p 269)
Test marketing (p 270)
Commercialization (p 271)
Customer-centered new-product
 development (p 271)
Team-based new-product development
 (p 272)

Objective 3

Product life cycle (PLC) (p 273)
Style (p 274)
Fashion (p 274)
Fad (p 274)
Introduction stage (p 275)
Growth stage (p 276)
Maturity stage (p 276)
Decline stage (p 277)

Discussion and Critical Thinking

 ## Discussion Questions

1. Name and describe the major steps in the new-product development process. (AACSB: Communication)

2. What is test marketing? Explain why companies may or may not test market products and discuss alternatives to full test markets. (AACSB: Communication)

3. What are the benefits of an *innovation management system* and how can a company install such a system? (AACSB: Communication)

4. Discuss the three strategies available for products in the mature stage of the product life cycle. For each strategy, describe an example other than the ones in the chapter of a company using that strategy. (AACSB: Communication; Reflective Thinking)

 ## Critical Thinking Exercises

1. Visit http://creatingminds.org/tools/tools_ideation.htm to learn about idea generation techniques. Form a small group and apply one or more of the techniques to generate at least four new-product ideas for a company of your choice. Apply the R-W-W screening framework to assess the idea for that company. (AACSB: Communication; Use of IT; Reflective Thinking)

⊛ 2. Find an example of a company that launched a new consumer product within the last five years. Develop a presentation showing how the company implemented the 4 Ps in launching the product and report on the product's success since the launch. (AACSB: Communication; Reflective Thinking)

3. Visit the Product Development and Management Association's Web site (www.pdma.org) to learn about this organization. Click on "OCI Award" in the "About PDMA" dropdown menu. Describe this award and the criteria used when granting this award and discuss one company receiving the award. (AACSB: Communication; Use of IT)

Applications and Cases

 ## Marketing Technology Fiat Mio

Companies use crowdsourcing to solve problems, generate new-product ideas, and develop promotional campaigns. In August 2009, Brazil's largest carmaker, Fiat, launched Project Mio to develop the world's first fully crowdsourced concept car. The project Web site asked the question, "In the future we're building, what should a car have that makes it mine, while still working for others?" The Web site's 300,000 unique visitors from more than 160 countries generated over 10,000 suggestions. The site had 17,000 people officially registered as potential collaborators. Thousands of comments were posted on Facebook and Twitter. Fiat's staff mulled over the suggestions and the concept car was presented at the 2010 Sao Paulo auto show. Fiat was transparent during the entire process and the car's final specifications are open to anyone—even other car companies. Though the new-product development process has not progressed to the commercialization stage—and perhaps never will—Fiat and other carmakers can use these ideas in future car models.

1. Form a small group and research the Fiat Mio. What are some of the suggestions offered by consumers that influenced the design of the car? Ask your friends and family the same question Fiat asked consumers and compile the responses from your group members. Would the car developed from these responses be similar to Fiat's Mio? Explain. (AACSB: Communication; Reflective Thinking; Use of IT)

2. Several crowdsourcing activities were described in the chapter. Describe an example of a different company using crowdsourcing to develop or modify products. (AACSB: Communication; Reflective Thinking; Use of IT)

 ## Marketing Ethics I Can Find Out Who You Are

Facial recognition technology is not new, but the way it is being used is. If you have a criminal record, police can find that out just by looking at you—through their iPhones, that is. Using a device known as Moris, which stands for Mobile Offender Recognition and Information System, a police officer can snap a picture of a person's face or scan a person's iris and obtain immediate information if there is a match in a criminal database. No more going down to the station and getting inky fingertips—the gadget can collect fingerprints right on the spot. Whereas an iris scan must be conducted with the person's knowledge because of the close-range necessary, a picture can be snapped from several feet away without the person knowing it. Facebook uses facial recognition to allow users to identify friends in pictures, and several mobile phone apps allow users to identify Facebook friends with a mere snap of a picture. Google considered a project that would enable mobile phone users to snap a picture of someone and then conduct an image search but rejected the idea because of ethical concerns.

1. Discuss other commercial applications of facial recognition technology. Come up with two new-product concepts that employ this technology. (AACSB: Communication; Reflective Thinking)

2. Discuss the ethics of incorporating facial recognition technology in products. (AACSB: Communication; Ethical Reasoning)

 ## Marketing by the Numbers Beauty Balm Cannibalization

The newest product in the cosmetic beauty market is BB cream, which combines multiple skin-care benefits into one product. BB stands for "beauty balm," and it is heralded as a "world-wide phenomenon" and a "multitasking miracle" by companies in the industry. But rather than creating new demand, this all-in-one product could cannibalize sales of existing products such as moisturizers, sunscreens, anti-aging creams, primers, and foundations offered by cosmetic manufacturers. With BB cream sales reaching $9 million in the United States in less than a year and promising to go much higher, skin-care and cosmetic products maker Clinique does not want to miss out on this opportunity. It is introducing a new BB cream product under the Clinique brand name. Although the new BB cream will garner a higher price for the manufacturer ($10.00 per ounce for the BB cream versus $8.00 per ounce for the moisturizer product), it also comes with higher variable costs ($6.00 per ounce for the BB cream versus $3.00 per ounce for the moisturizer product).

1. What brand development strategy is Clinique undertaking? (AACSB: Communication; Reflective Thinking)

2. Assume Clinique expects to sell 3 million ounces of BB cream within the first year after introduction but expects that half of those sales will come from buyers who would otherwise purchase Clinique's moisturizer (that is, cannibalized sales). Assuming that Clinique normally sells 10 million ounces of moisturizer per year and that the company will incur an increase in fixed costs of $2 million during the first year of production for the BB cream, will the new product be profitable for the company? Refer to the discussion of cannibalization in Appendix 2: Marketing by the Numbers for an explanation of how to conduct this analysis. (AACSB: Communication; Analytical Reasoning)

Video Case Subaru

When a company has a winning product, it has it made. Or does it? Subaru is a winning company (one of the few automotive companies to sustain growth and profits in hard economic times) with various winning products, including the Impreza, Legacy, Forester, and Outback. But what happens when any one product starts to decline in popularity? This video demonstrates how Subaru constantly engages in new-product development as part of its efforts to manage the product life cycle for each of its models. Subaru is focused on both developing the next version of each existing model and developing possible new models to boost its product portfolio.

After viewing the video featuring Subaru, answer the following questions:

1. Discuss the product life cycle in relation to one Subaru product.
2. How do shifting consumer trends affect Subaru's products?
3. Has Subaru remained customer oriented in its new-product efforts? Explain.

 # Company Case
Google: New-Product Innovation at the Speed of Light

Google is wildly innovative. It recently topped *Fast Company* magazine's list of the world's most innovative companies, and it regularly ranks among everyone else's top two or three most-innovative. Google is also spectacularly successful. Despite formidable competition from giants such as Microsoft and Yahoo!, Google's share in its core business—online search—stands at a decisive 84 percent, more than five times the combined market shares of all other competitors combined. The company also dominates when it comes to paid search advertising, with 80 percent of that online ad segment. And that doesn't include paid search on mobile devices, where Google has close to a monopoly with a 98 percent share.

But Google has grown to become much more than just an Internet search and advertising company. Google's mission is "to organize the world's information and make it universally accessible and useful." In Google's view, information is a kind of natural resource—one to be mined, refined, and universally distributed. That idea unifies what would otherwise appear to be a widely diverse set of Google projects, such as mapping the world, searching the Internet on a smartphone screen, or even providing for the early detection of flu epidemics. If it has to do with harnessing and using information, Google's got it covered in some innovative way.

An Innovative Approach to Innovating

Perhaps more than anything else, Google knows how to innovate. At many companies, new-product development is a cautious, step-by-step affair that might take a year or two to unfold. In contrast, Google's freewheeling new-product development process moves at the speed of light. The nimble innovator implements major new services in less time than it takes competitors to refine and approve an initial idea. For example, a Google senior project manager describes the lightning-quick development of iGoogle, Google's customizable home page:

> It was clear to Google that there were two groups [of Google users]: people who loved the site's clean, classic look and people who wanted tons of information there—e-mail, news, local weather. [For those who wanted a fuller home page,] iGoogle started out with me and three engineers. I was 22, and I thought, "This is awesome." Six weeks later, we launched the first version. The happiness metrics were good, there was healthy growth, and [a few months later], we had [iGoogle fully operational with] a link on Google.com.

Such fast-paced innovation would boggle the minds of product developers at most other companies, but at Google it is standard operating procedure. "That's what we do," says Google's vice president for search products and user experience. "The hardest part about indoctrinating people into our culture is when engineers show me a prototype and I'm like, 'Great, let's go!' They'll say, 'Oh, no, it's not ready.' I tell them, 'The Googly thing is to launch it early on Google Labs [a site where users can try out experimental Google applications] and then to iterate, learning what the market wants—and making it great.'" Adds a Google engineering manager, "We set an operational tempo: When in doubt, do something. If you have two paths and you're not sure which is right, take the fastest path."

When it comes to new-product development at Google, there are no two-year plans. The company's new-product planning looks ahead only four to five months. Google would rather see projects fail quickly than see a carefully planned, long, drawn-out project fail.

Google's famously chaotic innovation process has unleashed a seemingly unending flurry of diverse products, most of which are market leaders in their categories. These include everything from an e-mail service (Gmail), a blog search engine (Google Blog Search), an online payment service (Google Checkout), and a photo-sharing service (Google Picasa) to a universal platform for mobile-phone applications (Google Android), a cloud-friendly Internet browser (Chrome), projects for mapping and exploring the world (Google Maps and Google Earth), and even an early warning system for flu outbreaks in your area (FluTrends). Google claims that FluTrends has identified outbreaks two weeks before the U.S. Centers for Disease Control and Prevention.

Competing Through Innovation

Not only is Google innovative, but it uses this core competency as a primary competitive weapon. Take two of its biggest product introductions to date, both of which have been launched in the last year. First, there's Google Play. Even though it created the number one smartphone operating system in the world—Android—Google still could not capture the purchases and activities of all those Android users when it came to apps and entertainment media. Nor could it come close to matching its operating-systems penetration in the tablet market. So Google combined and redesigned everything it had in that department and launched Google Play, an iTunes-esque marketplace for apps, music, movies, and games. Although one reviewer points out that this launch "lacks the polish of Apple," he goes on to say that "there should be little doubt . . . about Google's determination to change that."

Google's second recent major product introduction is Google+, an all-purpose social network. With Google+, the search leader fired a shot right over the bow of Facebook. In response, Facebook founder and CEO Mark Zuckerberg put all Facebook employees on "lockdown" alert, working around the clock to copy the best features of Google+ and accelerate development of other Facebook features already being developed. In only a year's time, Google+ has acquired 250 million registered members, more than one-quarter of those who now share their lives on Facebook. Like Google Play, Google+ is a cutting-edge product. Such new products put Google in the dash for riches in completely new competitive arenas. In addition, they give Google a new edge against its toughest digital competitors—the likes of Amazon, Facebook, Apple, and Microsoft—in what Nokia's CEO refers to as the "war of Internet ecosystems."

Innovation Without Borders

Google is open to new-product ideas from just about any source. What ties it all together is the company's passion for helping people find and use information. Innovation is the responsibility of every Google employee. Google engineers are encouraged to spend 20 percent of their time developing their own "cool and wacky" new-product ideas. And all new Google ideas are quickly tested in beta form by the ultimate judges—those who will use them. According to one observer, "Anytime you cram some 20,000 of the world's smartest people into one company, you can expect to grow a garden of unrelated ideas. Especially when you give some of those geniuses one workday a week—Google's famous '20 percent time'—to work on whatever projects fan their passions."

Such thinking sends Google beyond its own corporate boundaries in search of the next wave of big ideas. Recently, Google hosted what it called the "Solve For X" conference. The company invited about 50 of the smartest people in the world to tackle some of the world's biggest problems. The emphasis was on "radical." Just how radical were some of the ideas that emerged? How about turning contact lenses into computer monitors with heads-up displays, packed full of data. Or how about solving the world's clean water problems through existing desalinization technologies? If that doesn't go far enough for you, how about using MRI technology to put images from the human mind onto a computer screen?

Just the fact that Google organized Solve For X indicates the type of innovator Google is. For Google, innovation is more than a process—it's part of the company's DNA. "Where does innovation happen at Google? It happens everywhere," says a Google research scientist.

If you talk to Googlers at various levels and departments, one powerful theme emerges: Whether they're designing search engines for the blind or preparing meals for their colleagues, these people feel that their work can change the world. The marvel of Google is its ability to continue to instill a sense of creative fearlessness and ambition in its employees. Prospective hires are often asked, "If you could change the world using Google's resources, what would you build?" But here, this isn't a goofy or even theoretical question: Google wants to know because thinking—and building—on that scale is what Google does. This, after all, is the company that wants to make available online every page of every book ever published. Smaller-gauge ideas die of disinterest. When it comes to innovation, Google is different. But the difference isn't tangible. It's in the air—in the spirit of the place.

Questions for Discussion

1. Based on information in this chapter, identify major similarities and differences between the new-product development process at Google versus that found at most other companies.

2. Is Google's product-development process customer centered? Team based? Systematic?

3. Considering the product life cycle, what challenges does Google face in managing its product portfolio?

4. Is there a limit to how big Google's product portfolio can grow? Explain.

5. Will Google be successful in markets where it does not dominate, such as social networks and app/entertainment stores? Why or why not?

Sources: Matt Lynley, "Here Are the 17 Radical Ideas from Google's Top Genius Conference That Could Change the World," *Business Insider*, February 11, 2012, www.businessinsider.com/here-are-the-17-radical-ideas-from-googles-top-genius-conference-that-could-change-the-world-2012-2?op=1#ixzz21TPojmMs; Matt Warman, "Google Play Review," *The Telegraph*, March 8, 2012, www.telegraph.co.uk/technology/mobile-app-reviews/9130663/Google-Play-review.html; Chuck Salter, "Google: The Faces and Voices of the World's Most Innovative Company," *Fast Company*, March 2008, pp. 74–88; David Pogue, "Geniuses at Play, on the Job," *New York Times*, February 26, 2009, p. B1; "World's Most Admired Companies," *Fortune*, March 2012, http://money.cnn.com/magazines/fortune/most-admired/2012/snapshots/11207.html; "World's 50 Most Innovative Companies," *Fast Company*, March 2012, www.fastcompany.com/most-innovative-companies/2012/full-list; and www.google.com, accessed August 2012.

MyMarketingLab

Go to **mymktlab.com** for Auto-graded writing questions as well as the following Assisted-graded writing questions:

9-1. Compare and contrast a fad and a fashion. Are hipster glasses an example of a fad or are they a fashion? (AACSB: Communication; Reflective Thinking)

9-2. Discuss the special challenges facing international product and service marketers. (AACSB: Communication)

9-3. Mymktlab Only – comprehensive writing assignment for this chapter.

References

1. Miyoung Kim, "Samsung Group Plans Record $41 Billion Investment in 2012," *Reuters*, January 17, 2012, www.reuters.com/article/2012/01/17/us-samsung-investment-idUSTRE80G00W20120117; Shinhye Kang, "Samsung Aims to Double Its Smartphone Market Share," *Bloomberg Businessweek*, June 21, 2010, www.businessweek.com; Laurie Burkitt, "Samsung Courts Consumers, Marketers," *Forbes*, June 7, 2010, p. 27; "Best Global Brands 2011: Samsung," Interbrand, October 4, 2011, www.interbrand.com/en/best-global-brands/Best-Global-Brands-2011/Samsung-SueShim.aspx; Levent Ozler, "Winners of the 2011 International Design Excellence Awards," *Dexigner*, July 1, 2011, www.dexigner.com/news/23309; "Gartner Says Worldwide Smartphone Sales Soared in Fourth Quarter of 2011 with 47 Percent Growth," February 15, 2012, www.gartner.com/it/page.jsp?id=1924314; and information from www.samsung.com and www.sony.com, accessed November 2012.

2. Nick Wingfield, "Apple, Aided by an iPhone Frenzy, Doubles Its Quarterly Profit," *New York Times,* January 25, 2012, p. B1.

3. Rob Adams, "Market Validation: Why Ready, Aim, Fire Beats Ready, Fire, Fire, Fire, Aim," *Inc.,* April 27, 2010, accessed at www.inc.com/rob-adams/market-validation-new-book.html. Also see Joan Schneider and Julie Hall, "Why Most Product Launches Fail," *Harvard Business Review,* April 20, 2011, pp. 21–24; and "Product Failures: The Underlying Whys," January 20, 2012, www.crossinnovation.net/ci/blog/comments/product-failures-the-underlying-whys/.

4. See "Customers and In-house R&D Teams Are the Leading Sources of Innovation Say U.S. Businesses," October 21, 2009, www.grantthornton.com; and Paul Sloane, "Source of Innovative Ideas," *Yahoo! Voices*, June 16, 2010, http://voices.yahoo.com/sources-innovative-ideas-6185898.html.

5. Based on information from "Hack Week @ Twitter," January 25, 2012, blog.twitter.com/2012/01/hack-week-twitter.html; "Twitter's 'Hack Week,' 7 Days for New Ideas," *Mashable,* January 26, 2012, http://mashable.com/2012/01/26/twitter-hack-week/; and "Twitter's 'Hack Week,' 7 Days for New Ideas," *Mashable* video, www.youtube.com/watch?v=8dZZqDOu80o, accessed November 2012.

6. Based on information from Matthew Kronsberg, "How Lego's Great Adventure in Geek-Sourcing Snapped into Place and Boosted the Brand," *Fast Company,* February 2, 2012, www.fastcompany.com/1812959/lego-cuusoo-minecraft-lord-of-rings-hayabusa; "LEGO Minecraft Micro World Details Unveiled, Available for Pre-Order," February 16, 2012, http://aboutus.lego.com/en-us/newsroom/2012/february/lego-minecraft-micro-world/; and http://lego.cuusoo.com/, accessed November 2012.

7. See Andrew Abbott, "Announcing the PayPal Mobile App Challenge Winners!" February 8, 2011, http://topcoder.com/home/x/2011/02/08/announcing-the-paypal-mobile-app-challenges-winners/; and www.topcoder.com and https://www.x.com, accessed August 2012.

8. Guido Jouret, "Inside Cisco's Search for the Next Big Idea," *Harvard Business Review*, September 2009, pp. 43–45; Geoff Livingston, "Real Challenges to Crowdsourcing for Social Good," *Mashable*, October 12, 2010, http://mashable.com/2010/10/12/social-good-crowdsourcing; and www.cisco.com/web/solutions/iprize/index.html, accessed August 2012.

9. See George S. Day, "Is It Real? Can We Win? Is It Worth Doing?" *Harvard Business Review*, December 2007, pp. 110–120.

10. This example is based on Tesla Motors and information obtained from www.teslamotors.com, accessed June 2012. Also see, Jim Motavalli, "Why the Tesla Model X Is a Home Run," *Forbes,* February 13, 2012, www.forbes.com/sites/eco-nomics/2012/02/13/why-the-tesla-model-x-is-a-home-run/.

11. Information from http://weartest.newbalance.com, accessed May 2012.

12. Susan Berfield, "Baristas, Patrons Steaming over Starbucks VIA," *Bloomberg BusinessWeek,* November 13, 2009; and Jodi Westbury, "Starbucks VIA—A Success to Build On," www.jodiwestbury.com/2011/01/28/starbucks-via-a-success-to-build-on/, accessed January 28, 2011; and "Starbucks Exceeds Goals with More Than 100 Million Starbucks K-Pacs Packs Shipped," *Business Wire,* January 27, 2012.

13. For information on BehaviorScan Rx, see www.symphonyiri.com/SolutionsandServices/Detail.aspx?ProductID=186, accessed May 2012.

14. See Emily Bryson York, "McD's Serves up $100M McCafé Ad Blitz," *Crain's Chicago Business*, May 4, 2009, www.chicagobusiness.com; and "Nokia Bets Big on Ace," Mobiledia, January 4, 2012, www.mobiledia.com/news/122642.html.

15. Karl Greenberg, "Brands Take to the Web for Global Reveals," *MediaPost News,* April 15, 2011, www.mediapost.com/publications/article/148705/.

16. See Robert G. Cooper, "Formula for Success," *Marketing Management*, March–April 2006, pp. 19–23; Christoph Fuchs and Martin Schreier, "Customer Empowerment in New Product Development," *Product Innovation Management*, January 2011, pp. 17–32; and Robert Safien, "The Lessons of Innovation," *Fast Company,* March 2012, p. 18.

17. Robert Berner, "How P&G Pampers New Thinking," *BusinessWeek*, April 14, 2008, pp. 73–74; "How P&G Plans to Clean Up," *BusinessWeek*, April 13, 2009, pp. 44–45; "Procter & Gamble Company," www.wikinvest.com/stock/Procter_&_Gamble_Company_(PG), accessed April 2012; and "P&G: Core Strengths," www.pg.com/en_US/company/core_strengths.shtml, accessed September 2012.

18. Based on information from or adapted from Peter Burrows, "Google's Bid to Be Everything to Everyone," *Bloomberg Businessweek,* February 20–February 26, 2012, pp. 37–38; Chuck Salter, "Google: The Faces and Voices of the World's Most Innovative Company," *Fast Company,* March 2008, pp. 74–88; David Pogue, "Geniuses at Play, On the Job," *New York Times,* February 26, 2009, p. B1; "World's 50 Most Innovative Companies," *Fast Company,* March 2012, p. 70; and www.google.com and www.googlelabs.com, accessed September 2012.

19. For more see Darrell K. Rigby, Karen Gruver, and James Allen, "Innovation in Turbulent Times," *Harvard Business Review*, June 2009, pp. 79–86. Also see John Hayes, "In a Tough Economy, Innovation Is King," *Marketing News*, April 15, 2009, pp. 14–17.

20. This definition is based on one found in Bryan Lilly and Tammy R. Nelson, "Fads: Segmenting the Fad-Buyer Market," *Journal of Consumer Marketing*, Vol. 20, No. 3, 2003, pp. 252–265.

21. See Katya Kazakina and Robert Johnson, "A Fad's Father Seeks a Sequel," *New York Times,* May 30, 2004, www.nytimes.com; John Schwartz, "The Joy of Silly," *New York Times,* January 20, 2008, p. 5; and www.crazyfads.com, accessed November 2012.

22. See www.1000uses.com, accessed November 2011.

23. Stephanie Clifford, "Go Digitally, Directly to Jail? Classic Toys Learn New Clicks," *New York Times,* February 25, 2012.

24. Elaine Wong, "Kellogg Makes Special K a Way of Life," *Adweek,* June 7, 2010, p. 18; and www.kellogg.com and www.specialk.com, accessed November 2012.

25. For a more comprehensive discussion of marketing strategies over the course of the PLC, see Philip Kotler and Kevin Lane Keller, *Marketing Management*, 14th ed. (Upper Saddle River, NJ: Prentice Hall, 2012), pp. 310–317.

26. See "Year-by-Year Analysis Reveals an Overall Compensatory Award of $1,500,000 for Products Liability Cases," *Personal Injury Verdict Reviews*, July 3, 2006; Christy Tierney, "Toyota Recalls 2.2M More Vehicles," *Detroit News*, February 25, 2011, A10; United States Courts, "Judicial Facts and Figures 2010," Table 4.5, www.uscourts.gov/Statistics/JudicialFactsAndFigures.aspx, accessed April 2012.

27. Based on information found in Celia Hatton, "KFC's Finger-Lickin' Success in China," CBS News, March 6, 2011, www.cbsnews.com/2100-3445_162-20039783.html; Maggie Starvish, "KFC's Explosive Growth in China, *HBS Working Knowledge*, June 17, 2011, http://hbswk.hbs.edu/cgi-bin/print/6704.html; and David E. Bell and Mary L. Shelman, "KFC's Radical Approach to China, *Harvard Business Review,* November 2011, pp. 137–142.

28. Information from www.db.com, accessed November 2012.

29. Information from www.interpublic.com and www.mccann.com, accessed November 2012.

30. See "Global Powers of Retailing 2011," www.deloitte.com; "Walmart Corporate International," http://walmartstores.com/AboutUs/246.aspx, accessed October 2012; and information from www.carrefour.com, accessed October 2012.

Part 1: Defining Marketing and the Marketing Process (Chapters 1–2)
Part 2: Understanding the Marketplace and Consumers (Chapters 3–6)
Part 3: Designing a Customer-Driven Strategy and Mix (Chapters 7–17)
Part 4: Extending Marketing (Chapters 18–20)

Pricing
Understanding and **Capturing Customer Value**

Chapter Preview We now look at the second major marketing mix tool—pricing. If effective product development, promotion, and distribution sow the seeds of business success, effective pricing is the harvest. Firms successful at creating customer value with the other marketing mix activities must still capture some of this value in the prices they earn. In this chapter, we discuss the importance of pricing, dig into three major pricing strategies, and look at internal and external considerations that affect pricing decisions.

In the next chapter, we examine some additional pricing considerations and approaches.

For openers, let's examine an interesting strategic pricing story. Over the past two decades, JCPenney has steadily lost ground to department store rivals and specialty retail chains. To turn things around, Penney's new CEO has set out to radically reinvent the 110-year-old retailer's operations and marketing. At the core of the transformation is a sweeping new pricing strategy—called "Fair and Square" pricing—that aims to put the "value" back into Penney's price-value equation.

JCPenney: Radical New "Fair and Square" Pricing—No Games, No Gimmicks

JCPenney recently ran ads showing shoppers screaming in frustration after missing out on limited-time sales events, arduously clipping coupons, or standing in long lines at night to be one of the few lucky customers to get "blowout" prices. "Enough. Is. Enough." concluded each ad in stark red letters. At Penney's Facebook page, consumers were greeted with more messages spoofing promotion-crazy retailers with pitches to "enjoy our biggest and best-ever crazy and exhausting and totally confusing sale." The site urged shoppers: "Crazy sales? Endless coupons? Confusing deals? Scream NO into the NO! meter."

The "Enough. Is. Enough." ad campaign announced that things would now be different at JCPenney. The chain has put an end to today's retail pricing insanity. "All retailers [have been] making customers jump through hoops to decide when was the best time to buy," said one JCPenney store manager. "We're ending that madness." With what it calls "Fair and Square" pricing, Penney's halted coupons, doorbuster deals, and nonstop markdowns on artificially inflated prices. In their place, the chain launched a simplified everyday low pricing scheme with only occasional special promotions. Not only will the new pricing make life easier

for promotion-weary customers, Penney's hopes, it will also put much-needed money into the company's till.

Over the past 20 years, JCPenney has been steadily losing ground to department store rivals such as Macy's and Kohl's, on the one hand, and to nimbler specialty store retailers on the other. Desperate for a turnaround, the 110-year-old retailer hired a new CEO, Ron Johnson, who first cut his retailing teeth at Target and then worked wonders for a decade as head of retail operations at Apple. Johnson soon announced that JCPenney would undergo a radical $1 billion, four-year transformation, one of the most sweeping retail makeovers in history.

"We want to become America's favorite store," says Johnson. But "if we're going to be touching the hearts and minds of American customers, we've got to [radically] reinvent the

> Desperate for a turnaround, JCPenney is setting set out to radically reinvent itself. At the core of its transformation is new "Fair and Square" pricing that aims to put the "value" back into Penney's price-value equation.

experience in the store." To make that happen, JCPenney is making seismic changes across almost every aspect of its operations and marketing.

For starters, Johnson is putting the "department" back in department stores. By 2015, each JCPenney store will be reorganized into a collection of 80 to 100 stores-within-a-store—a kind of "Main Street" of in-store brand shops spread along wider, less-cluttered aisles. Like Apple stores, Johnson wants Penney's to be a place where shoppers come to hang out. So each Penney's store will have a "Town Square" at its center, a large area featuring changing services and attractions, such as expert advice plus, say, free haircuts during back-to-school days or free hotdogs and ice cream in July.

Such operational changes are pretty revolutionary for JCPenney. But the lynchpin of Penney's revitalization is the new "Fair and Square" pricing strategy. As Penney's fell behind rivals in recent years, it came to rely on deep and frequent discounts to drive sales. From his first day on the job, Johnson found his e-mail box filling up with seemingly endless sales alerts from his own company—sometimes two a day. The retailer held some 590 separate sales that year alone. Worse, such sales weren't effective. The average JCPenney customer was making only four purchases a year, suggesting that customers were ignoring 99 percent of the retailer's promotional pitches. However, all those sales events were crushing margins and profits. Almost 75 percent of JCPenney's merchandise was being sold at discounts of 50 percent or more, and less than 1 percent was sold at full price. "This is desperation," thought Johnson at the time.

JCPenney's new pricing ditches deep discounts and endless rounds of sales and coupons in favor of lower everyday prices. For starters, in an effort to put the "value" back into its price–value equation—to the benefit of both customers and the company—JCPenney cut its regular retail prices by about 40 percent across the board. It then installed a simpler, steadier three-tiered pricing scheme: "Everyday" prices (red sales tags) featured regular lower prices on most merchandise throughout the store. "Month-long value" prices (white tags) applied to limited monthly themed sales events, such as "back-to-school" pricing in August. "Best prices" (blue tags) offered clearance prices on the first and third Fridays of every month.

All three sets of prices employed simplified tags and signage, with prices ending in "0," rather than ".99" or ".50," to suggest good value. And tags listed only one price, rather than making "previously priced at" comparisons. JCPenney made it clear that its "Fair and Square" pricing wasn't Walmart-like everyday low pricing. Penney's everyday prices were not as low as the biggest discounts it once offered. Instead, the goal was to offer fair, predictable prices for the value received. The message Penney's wanted customers to understand is this: Why play the "wait for the rock-bottom price" game when you can get "pretty good" prices every day on what you want, when you want it? "The customer knows the right price," Johnson says. "She's only going to pay the right price. She's an expert." So why waste her time and ours when we can get to that price from the start?

It remains to be seen how well JCPenney's radical remake will work. Changing store layouts, merchandise, and in-store shopper experiences will take time. In fact, the new

JCPenney's "Fair and Square" pricing strategy and its sweeping new look aim to put an end to today's retail pricing insanity.
Associated Press

pricing strategy got off to a very shaky start. In the quarter following implementation of Fair and Square pricing, deal-prone core customers still looking for deep discounts reacted badly and Penny's sales plunged 20 percent. Still, CEO Johnson remains optimistic, recognizing that it will take a long time to change the thinking and behavior of Penney's customers. The reinvention strategy breaks new ground not just within Penney's but across the entire retail industry as well. "We're not here improve," says the retail veteran. "We're here to transform." Moreover, there has been good news amidst the bad. For example, Levi-Strauss—one of the first major brands to open a store within a store—saw its JCPenney sales increase 25 percent over the previous year.

Thus, although JCPenney has made a few adjustments in its new pricing strategy (such as removing the "month-long specials," which it claims were confusing customers), the company says that it will not waver in its Fair and Square pricing policies. That leaves retail analysts divided—some believe that the strategy is fatally flawed; others see future glory for the reinvented retailer. But Johnson is confident that the venerable old retail chain is back on track. JCPenney's new pricing—and the entire transformation plan—is risky. Yet it's apparent from phrases Johnson throws around that he understands how to create value for customers: phrases like respect the customer, enrich people's lives, and treat them "fair and square."

For now, Johnson is betting the future on the new pricing approach. Ultimately, he believes, customers know when the price is right. Rather than first pricing high in order to mark prices down later, JCPenney is "just going to price things right from the start" says Johnson. "We'll set the table for the customer. We'll bring in the merchandise. We'll set their value. And they can come on their terms rather than ours. And we think it will be really lovely."[1]

Objective Outline

Objective 1	**Answer the question "What is a price?" and discuss the importance of pricing in today's fast-changing environment.** **What Is a Price?** (pp 290–291)
Objective 2	**Identify the three major pricing strategies and discuss the importance of understanding customer-value perceptions, company costs, and competitor strategies when setting prices.** **Major Pricing Strategies** (pp 291–299)
Objective 3	**Identify and define the other important external and internal factors affecting a firm's pricing decisions.** **Other Internal and External Considerations Affecting Price Decisions** (pp 299–306)

MyMarketingLab™

⭐ Improve Your Grade!

Over 10 million students improved their results using the Pearson MyLabs.
Visit **mymktlab.com** for simulations, tutorials, and end-of-chapter problems.

Objective 1 ┄┄►

Answer the question "What is a price?" and discuss the importance of pricing in today's fast-changing environment.

● **Pricing: No matter what the state of the economy, companies should sell value, not price.**
magicoven/Shutterstock.com

Companies today face a fierce and fast-changing pricing environment. Value-seeking customers have put increased pricing pressure on many companies. Thanks to economic woes in recent years, the pricing power of the Internet, and value-driven retailers such as Walmart, today's more frugal consumers are pursuing spend-less strategies. In response, it seems that almost every company has been looking for ways to cut prices.

Yet, cutting prices is often not the best answer. Reducing prices unnecessarily can lead to lost profits and damaging price wars. It can cheapen a brand by signaling to customers that price is more important than the customer value a brand delivers. ● Instead, in both good economic times and bad, companies should sell value, not price. In some cases, that means selling lesser products at rock-bottom prices. But in most cases, it means persuading customers that paying a higher price for the company's brand is justified by the greater value they gain.

What is a Price?

In the narrowest sense, **price** is the amount of money charged for a product or a service. More broadly, price is the sum of all the values that customers give up to gain the benefits of having or using a product or service. Historically, price has been the major factor affecting buyer choice. In recent decades, however, nonprice factors have gained increasing importance. Even so, price remains one of the most important elements that determines a firm's market share and profitability.

Price is the only element in the marketing mix that produces revenue; all other elements represent costs. Price is also one of the most flexible marketing mix elements. Unlike product features and channel commitments, prices can be changed quickly. At the same time, pricing is the number one problem facing many marketing executives, and many companies do not handle pricing well. Some managers view pricing as a big headache, preferring instead to focus on other marketing mix elements. However, smart managers

Price

The amount of money charged for a product or service, or the sum of the values that customers exchange for the benefits of having or using the product or service.

treat pricing as a key strategic tool for creating and capturing customer value. Prices have a direct impact on a firm's bottom line. A small percentage improvement in price can generate a large percentage increase in profitability. More important, as part of a company's overall value proposition, price plays a key role in creating customer value and building customer relationships. "Instead of running away from pricing," says an expert, "savvy marketers are embracing it."[2]

Major Pricing Strategies

Objective 2 ⤳➤

Identify the three major pricing strategies and discuss the importance of understanding customer-value perceptions, company costs, and competitor strategies when setting prices.

The price the company charges will fall somewhere between one that is too low to produce a profit and one that is too high to produce any demand. ● **Figure 10.1** summarizes the major considerations in setting price. Customer perceptions of the product's value set the ceiling for prices. If customers perceive that the product's price is greater than its value, they will not buy the product. Likewise, product costs set the floor for prices. If the company prices the product below its costs, the company's profits will suffer. In setting its price between these two extremes, the company must consider several external and internal factors, including competitors' strategies and prices, the overall marketing strategy and mix, and the nature of the market and demand.

Figure 10.1 suggests three major pricing strategies: customer value-based pricing, cost-based pricing, and competition-based pricing.

Customer Value-Based Pricing

In the end, the customer will decide whether a product's price is right. Pricing decisions, like other marketing mix decisions, must start with customer value. When customers buy a product, they exchange something of value (the price) to get something of value (the benefits of having or using the product). Effective, customer-oriented pricing involves understanding how much value consumers place on the benefits they receive from the product and setting a price that captures that value.

Customer value-based pricing

Setting price based on buyers' perceptions of value rather than on the seller's cost.

Customer value-based pricing uses buyers' perceptions of value as the key to pricing. Value-based pricing means that the marketer cannot design a product and marketing program and then set the price. Price is considered along with all other marketing mix variables *before* the marketing program is set.

● **Figure 10.2** compares value-based pricing with cost-based pricing. Although costs are an important consideration in setting prices, cost-based pricing is often product driven. The company designs what it considers to be a good product, adds up the costs of making the product, and sets a price that covers costs plus a target profit. Marketing must then convince buyers that the product's value at that price justifies its purchase. If the price turns out to be too high, the company must settle for lower markups or lower sales, both resulting in disappointing profits.

Value-based pricing reverses this process. The company first assesses customer needs and value perceptions. It then sets its target price based on customer perceptions of value. The targeted value and price drive decisions about what costs can be incurred and the resulting product design. As a result, pricing begins with analyzing consumer needs and value perceptions, and the price is set to match perceived value.

● **FIGURE | 10.1**
Considerations in Setting Price

If customers perceive that a product's price is greater than its value, they won't buy it. If the company prices the product below its costs, profits will suffer. Between the two extremes, the "right" pricing strategy is one that delivers both value to the customer and profits to the company.

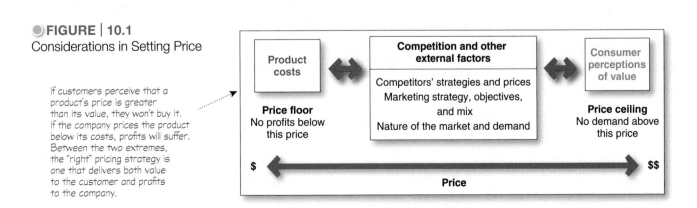

● **FIGURE** │ **10.2**
Value-Based Pricing vs.
Cost-Based Pricing

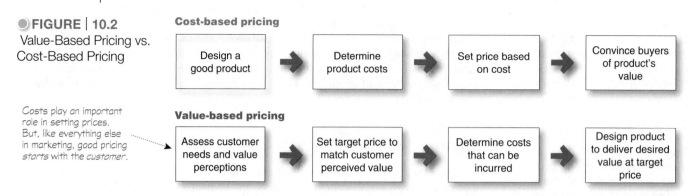

Cost-based pricing

| Design a good product | → | Determine product costs | → | Set price based on cost | → | Convince buyers of product's value |

Costs play an important role in setting prices. But, like everything else in marketing, good pricing starts with the customer.

Value-based pricing

| Assess customer needs and value perceptions | → | Set target price to match customer perceived value | → | Determine costs that can be incurred | → | Design product to deliver desired value at target price |

It's important to remember that "good value" is not the same as "low price." For example, a Steinway piano—any Steinway piano—costs a lot. But to those who own one, a Steinway is a great value:[3]

● **Perceived value: A Steinway piano—any Steinway piano—costs a lot. But to those who own one, price is nothing; the Steinway experience is everything.**
ROBERT CAPLIN/The New York Times

A Steinway grand piano typically runs anywhere from $55,000 to as high as several hundred thousand dollars. The most popular model sells for around $87,000. But ask anyone who owns a Steinway grand piano, and they'll tell you that, when it comes to Steinway, price is nothing; the Steinway experience is everything. Steinway makes very high quality pianos— handcrafting each Steinway requires up to one full year. But, more importantly, owners get the Steinway mystique. The Steinway name evokes images of classical concert stages and the celebrities and performers who've owned and played Steinway pianos across more than 160 years.

But Steinways aren't just for world-class pianists and the wealthy. Ninety-nine percent of all Steinway buyers are amateurs who perform only in their dens. ● To such customers, whatever a Steinway costs, it's a small price to pay for the value of owning one. "A Steinway takes you places you've never been," says an ad. As one Steinway owner puts it, "My friendship with the Steinway piano is one of the most important and beautiful things in my life." Who can put a price on such feelings?

A company will often find it hard to measure the value customers attach to its product. For example, calculating the cost of ingredients in a meal at a fancy restaurant is relatively easy. But assigning value to other satisfactions such as taste, environment, relaxation, conversation, and status is very hard. Such value is subjective; it varies both for different consumers and different situations.

Still, consumers will use these perceived values to evaluate a product's price, so the company must work to measure them. Sometimes, companies ask consumers how much they would pay for a basic product and for each benefit added to the offer. Or a company might conduct experiments to test the perceived value of different product offers. According to an old Russian proverb, there are two fools in every market—one who asks too much and one who asks too little. If the seller charges more than the buyers' perceived value, the company's sales will suffer. If the seller charges less, its products sell very well, but they produce less revenue than they would if they were priced at the level of perceived value.

We now examine two types of value-based pricing: *good-value pricing* and *value-added pricing*.

Good-Value Pricing

Good-value pricing
Offering just the right combination of quality and good service at a fair price.

The Great Recession of 2008 to 2009 caused a fundamental and lasting shift in consumer attitudes toward price and quality. In response, many companies have changed their pricing approaches to bring them in line with changing economic conditions and consumer price perceptions. More and more, marketers have adopted **good-value pricing** strategies— offering the right combination of quality and good service at a fair price.

In many cases, this has involved introducing less-expensive versions of established, brand-name products. For example, fast-food restaurants such as Taco Bell and McDonald's offer value menu and dollar menu items. Every car company now offers small, inexpensive models better suited to tighter consumer budgets and thriftier spending habits. P&G has introduced "Basic" versions of its Bounty and Charmin brands that sell for less and recently launched bargain-priced Gain dish soap, its first new dish soap in almost 40 years. The company has also reduced the size of some Tide laundry detergent packages from 100 ounces to 75 ounces and sells the smaller-size packages for 20 percent less at Walmart and other discount stores. "Today, when you ask the consumer, 'What is value?' the No. 1 answer is 'brand names for less,'" says a pricing expert.[4]

In other cases, good-value pricing has involved redesigning existing brands to offer more quality for a given price or the same quality for less. Some companies even succeed by offering less value but at very low prices. For example, passengers flying low-cost European airline Ryanair won't get much in the way of free amenities, but they'll like the airline's unbelievably low prices (see Real Marketing 10.1). ● Similarly, no-frills Snap Fitness is well positioned to take advantage of either good or bad economic conditions:

● **Good-value pricing: With its no-frills positioning and low prices, Snap Fitness is well positioned to take advantage of either good or bad economic conditions.**
Snap Fitness

Although some gym chains struggled during the recent recession—Bally's Total Fitness filed for bankruptcy twice—24-hour Snap Fitness actually expanded the number of its clubs and its revenues doubled. The franchise chain did all this despite charging members only $35 per month with easy cancellation fees. Its secret? A no-frills approach reinforced by the motto, "Fast, Convenient, Affordable." The small gyms—only 2,500 square feet—typically have five treadmills, two stationary bikes, five elliptical machines, and weight equipment. What's important is what they *don't* have—no classes, spa rooms, on-site childcare, or juice bars. Few clubs have showers and most are staffed only 25 to 40 hours a week. The sweet spot of their target market is married 35- to 55-year-olds with kids who live nearby and are busy enough that they cannot afford more than an hour a day to go to the gym.[5]

An important type of good-value pricing at the retail level is *everyday low pricing* (*EDLP*). EDLP involves charging a constant, everyday low price with few or no temporary price discounts. Retailers such as Costco and Lumber Liquidators practice EDLP. However, the king of EDLP is Walmart, which practically defined the concept. Except for a few sale items every month, Walmart promises everyday low prices on everything it sells. In contrast, *high-low pricing* involves charging higher prices on an everyday basis but running frequent promotions to lower prices temporarily on selected items. Department stores such as Kohl's and Macy's practice high-low pricing by having frequent sale days, early-bird savings, and bonus earnings for store credit-card holders.

Value-Added Pricing

Value-added pricing
Attaching value-added features and services to differentiate a company's offers and charging higher prices.

Value-based pricing doesn't mean simply charging what customers want to pay or setting low prices to meet competition. Instead, many companies adopt **value-added pricing** strategies. Rather than cutting prices to match competitors, they attach value-added features and services to differentiate their offers and thus support their higher prices. For example, even as recession-era consumer spending habits linger, some movie theater chains are *adding* amenities and charging *more* rather than cutting services to maintain lower admission prices.

Some theater chains are turning their multiplexes into smaller, roomier luxury outposts. The new premium theaters offer value-added features such as online reserved seating, high-backed leather executive or rocking chairs with armrests and footrests, the latest in digital sound and super-wide screens, dine-in restaurants serving fine food and drinks, and even valet parking. ● For example, AMC Theatres (the second-largest American theater chain) operates more than 50 theaters with some kind of enhanced food and beverage amenities, including Fork & Screen

Real Marketing 10.1

Ryanair: *Really* Good-Value Pricing— Fly for Free!

The major airlines are struggling with difficult pricing strategy decisions in these tough air-travel times. Pricing strategies vary widely. One airline, however, appears to have found a radical new pricing solution, one that customers are sure to love: Make flying *free*! That's right. Michael O'Leary, CEO of Dublin-based Ryanair, has a dream that someday all Ryanair passengers will fly for free. And with a current average price of $42 per ticket (compared to $87 for closest competitor easyJet and a whopping $130 for "discount airline" Southwest), Ryanair is getting closer.

Even without completely free flights, Ryanair has become Europe's most popular carrier. Last year Ryanair flew 76.8 million passengers to more than 155 European destinations in 26 countries. The budget airline is also Europe's most profitable one. Over the past decade, even as the global airline industry collectively lost nearly $50 billion, Ryanair has turned healthy net profits in 9 out of 10 years. Given the prospects of rising fuel costs, collapsing European economies, and other troubled times ahead for the airline industry, Ryanair seems well positioned to weather the turbulence.

What's the secret? Ryanair's frugal cost structure makes even cost-conscious Southwest look like a reckless spender. In addition, the Irish airline makes money on everything *but* the ticket, from charging for baggage check-in to revenues from seat-back advertising space. Ryanair's low-cost strategy is modeled after Southwest's. Twenty years ago, when Ryanair was just another struggling European carrier, Ryanair's O'Leary went to Dallas to meet with Southwest executives and see what he could learn. The result was a wholesale revamping of the Irish carrier's business model. Following Southwest's lead, to economize, Ryanair began employing only a single type of aircraft— the good-old Boeing 737. Also like Southwest, it began focusing on smaller, secondary airports and offering unassigned passenger seating.

But Ryanair has since taken Southwest's low-cost pricing model even further. When it comes to keeping costs down, O'Leary—who

wears jeans, sneakers, and off-the-rack short-sleeved shirts—is an absolute fanatic. He wants Ryanair to be known as the Walmart of flying. Like the giant retailer, Ryanair is constantly on the lookout for new ways to cut costs—for example, hard plastic seats with no seat-back pockets reduce both weight and cleaning expense. Ryanair flight crews even buy their own uniforms and headquarters staff supply their own pens.

O'Leary equates every cost reduction with the benefit to customers in terms of lower ticket prices. Removing all but one toilet from each plane would cut 5 percent off the average ticket price. Replacing the last 10 rows with a standing cabin—another 20 to 25 percent off. O'Leary's sometimes nutty proposals for cost-cutting—deliberately provocative so that they're sure to gain free publicity—have even included flying planes with only one pilot ("Let's take out the second pilot. Let the bloody computer fly it.") and having customers place their own bags in the belly of Ryanair planes ("You take your own bag with you. You bring it down. You put it on."). It all sounds crazy, but think again about those zero-dollar ticket prices.

O'Leary's dream of customers flying free rests on the eventuality that, someday, all of Ryanair's revenues will come from "ancillary" fees. The penny-pinching airline currently takes in only 20 percent of its revenue from such nonticket charges. But Ryanair is the industry leader in charging passengers for virtually every optional amenity they consume. The brash airline brags about being the first to charge for checked bags and in-flight refreshments. Such tactics, once shunned by the industry, are now standard procedure and bring in billions in airline revenues. But Ryanair takes it

much further. It now charges customers for printing boarding passes, paying with a debit or credit card, or using wheelchairs. It has even proposed charging for overweight customers, or charging a fee for using that one remaining toilet.

In addition to charging customers for every aspect of the flight, Ryanair also envisions big revenues from selling products for other companies. The interiors of Ryanair planes are almost as littered with advertising as Time Square. Once in the air, flight attendants hawk everything from scratch-card games to digital cameras to their captive audience. They peddle croissants and cappuccino; digital gadgets and perfumes; raffle tickets for the airline's sponsored charity; and even smokeless cigarettes for €6 a pack.

Upon arrival at a usually out-of-the-way airport, Ryanair will sell passengers bus or train tickets into town. The company also gets commissions from rental cars, hotel rooms, ski packages, and travel insurance. Every chance it gets, Ryanair tries to squeeze just a little more out of its passengers.

Ryanair makes no excuses for both the additional charges and the absence of creature comforts. In fact, it sees its "less-for-less" value-pricing approach as long overdue in the airline industry. "In many ways, travel is

Good-value pricing: Ryanair's sometimes outrageous CEO, Michael O'Leary, hopes one day to "make flying free."

Maciej Kulczynski/EPA/Newscom

pleasant and enriching," O'Leary states. But "the physical process of getting from point A to point B shouldn't be pleasant, nor enriching. It should be quick, efficient, affordable, and safe." As Ryanair's success suggests, customers seem to agree. Passengers are getting exactly what they want—outrageously low prices. And the additional purchases are discretionary.

Despite the lack of amenities, most passengers seem to appreciate rather than resent Ryanair's open and straight-forward approach to pricing. Compared with the so-called "sophisticated" approaches of other airlines, proclaims one passenger, "I prefer [Ryanair's] crude ways, with its often dirt-cheap tickets and shameless [but plain-speaking] efforts to get its hand in my purse."

And commenting on what some analysts have referred to as Ryanaire's "cattle-car" approach to passengers, another good-humored flier observes, "Only O'Leary will call you a cow, lick his chops, and explain how he plans to carve you up for dinner."

O'Leary's philosophy that commercial air passengers don't need to be coddled to make them loyal appears to fly in the face of modern marketing's focus on providing an exceptional customer experience. But Ryanair is proving that companies can provide customer value in more ways than one. When you look at Ryanair's falling prices and rising profits, O'Leary's dream of flying for free doesn't seem so far-fetched after all. With Ryanair's knack for good-value pricing, not even the sky's the limit.

Sources: Quotes and other information from Cecilia Rodriguez, "Airlines Look to Raise Revenue the Ryanair Way," *Forbes*, March 5, 2012, www.forbes.com/sites/ceciliarodriguez/2012/03/05/105/; Jane Leung, "Ryanair's Five 'Cheapest' Money-Saving Schemes," *CNNTravel*, October 17, 2011, www.cnn.com/2011/10/17/travel/ryanair-money-saving-schemes/index.htm; Felix Gillette, "Ryanair's O'Leary: The Duke of Discomfort," *Businessweek*, September 2, 2010, www.businessweek.com/magazine/content/10_37/b4194058006755.htm; and Steve Rothwell, "Ryanair Lifts Profit Goal as Winter Capacity Cuts Buoy Fares," *Bloomberg Businessweek*, January 30, 2012, www.bloomberg.com/news/2012-01-30/ryanair-lifts-profit-goal-on-winter-capacity.html.

● **Value-added pricing: Rather than cutting services to maintain lower admission prices, premium theaters such as AMC's Cinema Suites are adding amenities and charging more. "Once people experience it, . . . they don't want to go anywhere else."**

Courtesy of AMC Theaters

(upgraded leather seating, seat-side service, extensive menu including dinner offerings, beer, wine, and cocktails) and Cinema Suites (additional upscale food offerings in addition to premium cocktails and an extensive wine list, seat-side service, red leather reclining chairs, and eight to nine feet of spacing between rows).

So at the Cinema Suites at the AMC Easton 30 with IMAX in Columbus, Ohio, bring on the mango margaritas! For $9 to $15 a ticket (depending on the time and day), moviegoers are treated to reserved seating, a strict 21-and-over-only policy, reclining leather seats, and the opportunity to pay even more to have dinner and drinks brought to their seats. Such theaters are so successful that AMC plans to add more. "Once people experience it," says a company spokesperson, "more often than not they don't want to go anywhere else."[6]

Cost-Based Pricing

Whereas customer-value perceptions set the price ceiling, costs set the floor for the price that the company can charge. **Cost-based pricing** involves setting prices based on the costs of producing, distributing, and selling the product plus a fair rate of return for its effort and risk. A company's costs may be an important element in its pricing strategy.

Some companies, such as Walmart or Southwest Airlines, work to become the *low-cost producers* in their industries. Companies with lower costs can set lower prices that result in smaller margins but greater sales and profits. However, other companies—such as Apple, BMW, and Steinway—intentionally pay higher costs so that they can add value and claim higher prices and margins. For example, it costs more to make a "handcrafted" Steinway piano than a Yamaha production model. But the higher costs result in higher quality, justifying that eye-popping $72,000 price. The key is to manage the spread between costs and prices—how much the company makes for the customer value it delivers.

Cost-based pricing

Setting prices based on the costs of producing, distributing, and selling the product plus a fair rate of return for effort and risk.

Types of Costs

Fixed costs (overhead)
Costs that do not vary with production or sales level.

A company's costs take two forms: fixed and variable. **Fixed costs** (also known as **overhead**) are costs that do not vary with production or sales level. For example, a company must pay each month's bills for rent, heat, interest, and executive salaries regardless of the company's level of output. **Variable costs** vary directly with the level of production. Each PC produced by HP involves a cost of computer chips, wires, plastic, packaging, and other inputs. Although these costs tend to be the same for each unit produced, they are called variable costs because the total varies with the number of units produced. **Total costs** are the sum of the fixed and variable costs for any given level of production. Management wants to charge a price that will at least cover the total production costs at a given level of production.

Variable costs
Costs that vary directly with the level of production.

Total costs
The sum of the fixed and variable costs for any given level of production.

The company must watch its costs carefully. If it costs the company more than its competitors to produce and sell a similar product, the company will need to charge a higher price or make less profit, putting it at a competitive disadvantage.

Costs at Different Levels of Production

To price wisely, management needs to know how its costs vary with different levels of production. For example, suppose Texas Instruments (TI) built a plant to produce 1,000 calculators per day. ● **Figure 10.3A** shows the typical short-run average cost curve (SRAC). It shows that the cost per calculator is high if TI's factory produces only a few per day. But as production moves up to 1,000 calculators per day, the average cost per unit decreases. This is because fixed costs are spread over more units, with each one bearing a smaller share of the fixed cost. TI can try to produce more than 1,000 calculators per day, but average costs will increase because the plant becomes inefficient. Workers have to wait for machines, the machines break down more often, and workers get in each other's way.

If TI believed it could sell 2,000 calculators a day, it should consider building a larger plant. The plant would use more efficient machinery and work arrangements. Also, the unit cost of producing 2,000 calculators per day would be lower than the unit cost of producing 1,000 units per day, as shown in the long-run average cost (LRAC) curve (● **Figure 10.3B**). In fact, a 3,000-capacity plant would be even more efficient, according to Figure 10.3B. But a 4,000-daily production plant would be less efficient because of increasing diseconomies of scale—too many workers to manage, paperwork slowing things down, and so on. Figure 10.3B shows that a 3,000-daily production plant is the best size to build if demand is strong enough to support this level of production.

Costs as a Function of Production Experience

Suppose TI runs a plant that produces 3,000 calculators per day. As TI gains experience in producing calculators, it learns how to do it better. Workers learn shortcuts and become more familiar with their equipment. With practice, the work becomes better organized, and TI finds better equipment and production processes. With higher volume, TI becomes more efficient and gains economies of scale. As a result, the average cost tends to decrease with accumulated production experience. This is shown in ● **Figure 10.4**.[7] Thus, the average cost of producing the first 100,000 calculators is $10 per calculator. When the company has produced the first 200,000 calculators, the average cost has fallen to $8.50. After its

● **FIGURE | 10.3**
Cost per Unit at Different Levels of Production per Period

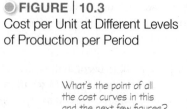
What's the point of all the cost curves in this and the next few figures? Costs are an important factor in setting price, and companies must understand them well!

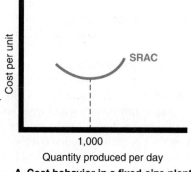
A. Cost behavior in a fixed-size plant

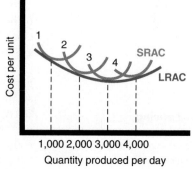
B. Cost behavior over different-size plants

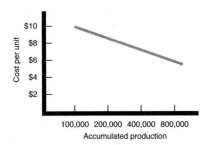

FIGURE | 10.4
Cost per Unit as a Function
of Accumulated Production:
The Experience Curve

accumulated production experience doubles again to 400,000, the average cost is $7. This drop in the average cost with accumulated production experience is called the **experience curve** (or the **learning curve**).

If a downward-sloping experience curve exists, this is highly significant for the company. Not only will the company's unit production cost fall, but it will fall faster if the company makes and sells more during a given time period. But the market has to stand ready to buy the higher output. And to take advantage of the experience curve, TI must get a large market share early in the product's life cycle. This suggests the following pricing strategy: TI should price its calculators low; its sales will then increase, and its costs will decrease through gaining more experience, and then it can lower its prices further.

Some companies have built successful strategies around the experience curve. However, a single-minded focus on reducing costs and exploiting the experience curve will not always work. Experience-curve pricing carries some major risks. The aggressive pricing might give the product a cheap image. The strategy also assumes that competitors are weak and not willing to fight it out by meeting the company's price cuts. Finally, while the company is building volume under one technology, a competitor may find a lower-cost technology that lets it start at prices lower than those of the market leader, which still operates on the old experience curve.

Cost-Plus Pricing

The simplest pricing method is **cost-plus pricing** (or **markup pricing**)—adding a standard markup to the cost of the product. Construction companies, for example, submit job bids by estimating the total project cost and adding a standard markup for profit. Lawyers, accountants, and other professionals typically price by adding a standard markup to their costs. Some sellers tell their customers they will charge cost plus a specified markup; for example, aerospace companies often price this way to the government.

To illustrate markup pricing, suppose a toaster manufacturer had the following costs and expected sales:

Variable cost	$10
Fixed costs	$300,000
Expected unit sales	50,000

Then the manufacturer's cost per toaster is given by the following:

$$\text{unit cost} = \text{variable Cost} + \frac{\text{fixed costs}}{\text{unit sales}} = \$10 + \frac{\$300,000}{50,000} = \$16$$

Now suppose the manufacturer wants to earn a 20 percent markup on sales. The manufacturer's markup price is given by the following:[8]

$$\text{markup price} = \frac{\text{unit cost}}{(1 - \text{desired return on sales})} = \frac{\$16}{1 - 0.2} = \$20$$

The manufacturer would charge dealers $20 per toaster and make a profit of $4 per unit. The dealers, in turn, will mark up the toaster. If dealers want to earn 50 percent on the sales price, they will mark up the toaster to $40 ($20 + 50% of $40). This number is equivalent to a *markup on cost* of 100 percent ($20/$20).

Does using standard markups to set prices make sense? Generally, no. Any pricing method that ignores demand and competitor prices is not likely to lead to the best price. Still, markup pricing remains popular for many reasons. First, sellers are more certain about costs than about demand. By tying the price to cost, sellers simplify pricing; they do not need to make frequent adjustments as demand changes. Second, when all firms in the industry use this pricing method, prices tend to be similar, so price competition is minimized. Third, many people feel that cost-plus pricing is fairer to both buyers and sellers. Sellers earn a fair return on their investment but do not take advantage of buyers when buyers' demand becomes great.

Break-Even Analysis and Target Profit Pricing

Another cost-oriented pricing approach is **break-even pricing** (or a variation called **target return pricing**). The firm tries to determine the price at which it will break even or make the target return it is seeking.

Experience curve (learning curve)
The drop in the average per-unit production cost that comes with accumulated production experience.

Cost-plus pricing (markup pricing)
Adding a standard markup to the cost of the product.

Break-even pricing (target return pricing)
Setting price to break even on the costs of making and marketing a product, or setting price to make a target return.

● **FIGURE | 10.5**

Break-Even Chart for
Determining Target-Return
Price and Break-Even
Volume

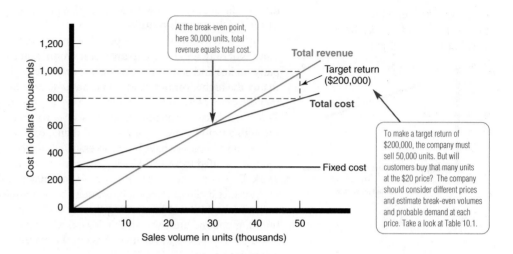

Target return pricing uses the concept of a *break-even chart*, which shows the total cost and total revenue expected at different sales volume levels. ● **Figure 10.5** shows a break-even chart for the toaster manufacturer discussed here. Fixed costs are $300,000 regardless of sales volume. Variable costs are added to fixed costs to form total costs, which rise with volume. The total revenue curve starts at zero and rises with each unit sold. The slope of the total revenue curve reflects the price of $20 per unit.

The total revenue and total cost curves cross at 30,000 units. This is the *break-even volume*. At $20, the company must sell at least 30,000 units to break even, that is, for total revenue to cover total cost. Break-even volume can be calculated using the following formula:

$$\text{break-even volume} = \frac{\text{fixed cost}}{\text{price} - \text{variable cost}} = \frac{\$300,000}{\$20 - \$10} = 30,000$$

If the company wants to make a profit, it must sell more than 30,000 units at $20 each. Suppose the toaster manufacturer has invested $1,000,000 in the business and wants to set a price to earn a 20 percent return, or $200,000. In that case, it must sell at least 50,000 units at $20 each. If the company charges a higher price, it will not need to sell as many toasters to achieve its target return. But the market may not buy even this lower volume at the higher price. Much depends on price elasticity and competitors' prices.

The manufacturer should consider different prices and estimate break-even volumes, probable demand, and profits for each. This is done in ● **Table 10.1**. The table shows that as price increases, the break-even volume drops (column 2). But as price increases, the demand for toasters also decreases (column 3). At the $14 price, because the manufacturer clears only $4 per toaster ($14 less $10 in variable costs), it must sell a very high volume to break even. Even though the low price attracts many buyers, demand still falls below the high break-even

● **Table 10.1** | **Break-Even Volume and Profits at Different Prices**

Price	Unit Demand Needed to Break Even	Expected Unit Demand at Given Price	Total Revenue (1) × (3)	Total Costs*	Profit (4) − (5)
$14	75,000	71,000	$994,000	$1,010,000	−$16,000
16	50,000	67,000	1,072,000	970,000	102,000
18	37,500	60,000	1,080,000	900,000	180,000
20	30,000	42,000	840,000	720,000	120,000
22	25,000	23,000	506,000	530,000	−$24,000

*Assumes fixed costs of $300,000 and constant unit variable costs of $10.

point, and the manufacturer loses money. At the other extreme, with a $22 price, the manufacturer clears $12 per toaster and must sell only 25,000 units to break even. But at this high price, consumers buy too few toasters, and profits are negative. The table shows that a price of $18 yields the highest profits. Note that none of the prices produce the manufacturer's target return of $200,000. To achieve this return, the manufacturer will have to search for ways to lower the fixed or variable costs, thus lowering the break-even volume.

Competition-Based Pricing

Competition-based pricing

Setting prices based on competitors' strategies, prices, costs, and market offerings.

Competition-based pricing involves setting prices based on competitors' strategies, costs, prices, and market offerings. Consumers will base their judgments of a product's value on the prices that competitors charge for similar products.

In assessing competitors' pricing strategies, the company should ask several questions. First, how does the company's market offering compare with competitors' offerings in terms of customer value? If consumers perceive that the company's product or service provides greater value, the company can charge a higher price. If consumers perceive less value relative to competing products, the company must either charge a lower price or change customer perceptions to justify a higher price.

Next, how strong are current competitors and what are their current pricing strategies? If the company faces a host of smaller competitors charging high prices relative to the value they deliver, it might charge lower prices to drive weaker competitors from the market. If the market is dominated by larger, lower-price competitors, the company may decide to target unserved market niches with value-added products at higher prices. ● For example, consider Hot Mama, the fast-growing clothing boutique for moms—and their kids:[9]

With 30 locations and growing, Hot Mama isn't likely to win a price war against giants Macy's or Kohl's. Instead, the boutique, which sells high-end brands such as Joes Jeans and Free People, relies on its personal approach, mom- and kid-friendly atmosphere, and knowledgeable staff to turn harried moms into loyal patrons, even if they have to pay a little more. To give busy mothers freedom to shop, Hot Mama stores entertain their little ones with centrally-located toys, coloring books, video games, and other attractions. Extra-wide aisles leave plenty of room for strollers, and store employees lend a hand as babysitters. Hot Mama emphasizes service, not prices. Sales employees (the store calls them "stylists") complete three demanding certification programs: denim, body type, and maternity. "Our stylists can outfit any woman, aged 25 to 65, based on her body the minute she walks through the door," says Hot Mama president Kimberly Ritzer. However, it's the personal relationships that stylists build with customers that make shopping at Hot Mama really special. "It's like shopping with a girlfriend."

● **Pricing against larger, lower-price competitors: Fast-growing clothing boutique Hot Mama isn't likely to win a price war against giants Macy's or Kohl's. Instead, it relies on personal service, a mom- and kid-friendly atmosphere, and its knowledgeable staff to turn harried moms into loyal patrons. "It's like shopping with a girlfriend."**
Hot Mama

What principle should guide decisions about what price to charge relative to those of competitors? The answer is simple in concept but often difficult in practice: No matter what price you charge—high, low, or in-between—be certain to give customers superior value for that price.

Other Internal and External Considerations Affecting Price Decisions

Objective 3 ┈┈➤

Identify and define the other important external and internal factors affecting a firm's pricing decisions.

Beyond customer value perceptions, costs, and competitor strategies, the company must consider several additional internal and external factors. Internal factors affecting pricing include the company's overall marketing strategy, objectives, and marketing mix, as well as other organizational considerations. External factors include the nature of the market and demand and other environmental factors.

Overall Marketing Strategy, Objectives, and Mix

Price is only one element of the company's broader marketing strategy. So, before setting price, the company must decide on its overall marketing strategy for the product or service.

Sometimes, a company's overall strategy is built around its price and value story. For example, grocery retailer Trader Joe's unique price-value positioning has made it one of the nation's fastest-growing, most popular food stores. Trader Joe's understands that success comes not just from what products you offer customers or from the prices you charge. It comes from offering the combination of products, prices, and store operations that produces the greatest customer *value*—what customers get for the prices they pay (see Real Marketing 10.2).

If the company has selected its target market and positioning carefully, then its marketing mix strategy, including price, will be fairly straightforward. For example, Kohler's Kallista subsidiary offers a line of bath and kitchen fixtures is positioned for the luxury market. It "combines passion with a profound sense of aesthetic and functional efficiency," with designer collections that invite you to "discover" Kallista. Each Kallista product features "exquisite details—from surfaces finished by hand to cultured stone—carefully articulated to express a simple, singular elegance." The Kallista line's luxury positioning requires charging a higher price. In contrast, Kohler's Sterling subsidiary offers more affordable fixtures that are "inspired by the realities of life." Sterling fixtures are positioned on simplicity, convenience, comfort, and economical design for budget-conscious homeowners. Sterling's mid-market positioning calls for charging lower prices.[10] Thus, pricing strategy is largely determined by decisions on market positioning.

Pricing may play an important role in helping to accomplish company objectives at many levels. A firm can set prices to attract new customers or profitably retain existing ones. It can set prices low to prevent competition from entering the market or set prices at competitors' levels to stabilize the market. It can price to keep the loyalty and support of resellers or avoid government intervention. Prices can be reduced temporarily to create excitement for a brand. Or one product may be priced to help the sales of other products in the company's line.

Price decisions must be coordinated with product design, distribution, and promotion decisions to form a consistent and effective integrated marketing mix program. Decisions made for other marketing mix variables may affect pricing decisions. For example, a decision to position the product on high-performance quality will mean that the seller must charge a higher price to cover higher costs. And producers whose resellers are expected to support and promote their products may have to build larger reseller margins into their prices.

Companies often position their products on price and then tailor other marketing mix decisions to the prices they want to charge. Here, price is a crucial product-positioning factor that defines the product's market, competition, and design. Many firms support such price-positioning strategies with a technique called **target costing**. Target costing reverses the usual process of first designing a new product, determining its cost, and then asking, "Can we sell it for that?" Instead, it starts with an ideal selling price based on customer-value considerations and then targets costs that will ensure that the price is met. For example, when Honda initially designed the Fit, it began with a $13,950 starting price point and highway mileage of 33 miles per gallon firmly in mind. It then designed a stylish, peppy little car with costs that allowed it to give target customers those values.

Target costing
Pricing that starts with an ideal selling price, then targets costs that will ensure that the price is met.

● Positioning on high price: Titus features its lofty prices in its advertising— "suggested retail price: $7,750.00."

Titus Bicycles

Other companies deemphasize price and use other marketing mix tools to create *nonprice* positions. Often, the best strategy is not to charge the lowest price but rather differentiate the marketing offer to make it worth a higher price. For example, Bang & Olufsen (B&O)—known for its cutting-edge consumer electronics—builds high value into its products and charges sky-high prices. A B&O 50-inch BeoVision HDTV will cost you $7,500; a 55-inch model runs $18,700, and a 103-inch model goes for almost $100,000. A complete B&O entertainment system? Well, you don't really want to know the price. But target customers recognize B&O's very high quality and are willing to pay more to get it.

Some marketers even position their products on *high* prices, featuring high prices as part of their product's allure. For example, Grand Marnier offers a $225 bottle of Cuvée du Cent Cinquantenaire cognac that's marketed with the tagline "Hard to find, impossible to pronounce, and prohibitively expensive." ● And Titus Cycles, a premium bicycle manufacturer, features its

Real Marketing 10.2

Trader Joe's Unique Price-Value Positioning: "Cheap Gourmet"

On an early July morning in Manhattan's Chelsea neighborhood, a large and enthusiastic crowd has already gathered. The occasion: Trader Joe's is opening a new store, and waiting shoppers are sharing their joy over the arrival of the trendy retailer in their neighborhood. Trader Joe's is more than a grocery store, it's a cultural experience. Its shelves are packed with goods that are at the same time both exotic luxuries and affordable. Whether it's organic creamy Valencia peanut butter or cage-free eggs, Thai lime-and-chili cashews or Belgian butter waffle cookies, you'll find them only at Trader Joe's. Within moments of the new store's opening, the deluge of customers makes it almost impossible to navigate the aisles. They line up 10 deep at checkouts with carts full of Trader Joe's exclusive $2.99 Charles Shaw wine—aka "Two-Buck Chuck"—and an assortment of other exclusive gourmet products at impossibly low prices. All of this has made Trader Joe's one hot retailer.

Trader Joe's isn't really a gourmet food store. Then again, it's not a discount food store either. It's actually a bit of both. Trader Joe's has put its own special twist on the food price-value equation—call it "cheap gourmet." It offers gourmet-caliber, one-of-a-kind products at bargain prices, all served up in a festive, vacation-like atmosphere that makes shopping fun. However you define it, Trader Joe's inventive price-value positioning has earned it an almost cult-like following of devoted customers who love what they get from Trader Joe's for the prices they pay.

Trader Joe's describes itself as an "island paradise" where "value, adventure, and tasty treasures are discovered, every day." Shoppers bustle and buzz amid cedar-plank-lined walls and fake palm trees as a ship's bell rings out occasionally at checkout, alerting them to special announcements. Unfailingly helpful and cheery associates in aloha shirts chat with customers about everything from the weather to menu suggestions for dinner parties. At the Chelsea store opening, workers greeted customers with high-fives and free cookies. Customers don't just shop at Trader Joe's; they experience it.

Shelves bristle with an eclectic assortment of gourmet-quality grocery items. Trader Joe's stocks only a limited assortment of about 4,000 products (compared with the 50,000 items found in a typical grocery store). However, the assortment is uniquely Trader Joe's, including special concoctions of gourmet packaged foods and sauces, ready-to-eat soups, fresh and frozen entrees, snacks, and desserts—all free of artificial colors, flavors, and preservatives. Trader Joe's is a gourmet foodie's delight, featuring everything from kettle corn cookies, organic strawberry lemonade, creamy Valencia peanut butter, and fair trade coffees to kimchi fried rice and triple-ginger gingersnaps.

Another thing that makes Trader Joe's products so special is that you just can't get most of them elsewhere. For example, try finding Ginger Cats cookies or quinoa and black bean tortilla chips at some other store. More than 80 percent of the store's brands are private-label goods, sold exclusively by Trader Joe's. If asked, almost any customer can tick off a ready list of Trader Joe's favorites that they just can't live without—a list that quickly grows. People come in intending to buy a few favorites and quickly fill a cart. "They just seem to turn their customers on," says one food industry analyst.

A special store atmosphere, exclusive gourmet products, helpful and attentive associates—this all sounds like a recipe for high prices. Not so at Trader Joe's. Whereas upscale competitors such as Whole Foods Market charge upscale prices to match their wares ("Whole Foods, Whole Paycheck"), Trader Joe's amazes customers with its relatively frugal prices. The prices aren't all that low in absolute terms, but they're a real bargain compared with what you'd pay for the same quality and coolness elsewhere. "At Trader Joe's, we're as much about value as we are about great food," says the company. "So you can afford to be adventurous without breaking the bank."

How does Trader Joe's keep its gourmet prices so low? It carefully shapes nonprice elements to support its overall price-value strategy. For starters, Trader Joe's has lean operations and a near-fanatical focus on saving money. To keep costs down, Trader Joe's typically locates its stores in low-rent, out-of-the-way locations, such as suburban strip malls. Its small store size with small back rooms and limited product assortment result in reduced facilities and inventory costs. Trader Joe's stores save money by eliminating large produce sections and expensive on-site bakery, butcher, deli, and seafood shops. And for its private-label brands, Trader Joe's buys directly from suppliers and negotiates hard on price.

Trader Joe's unique price-value strategy has earned it an almost cultlike following of devoted customers who love what they get for the prices they pay.
Michael Nagle/Getty Images USA, Inc.

Finally, the frugal retailer saves money by spending almost nothing on advertising, and it offers no coupons, discount cards, or special promotions of any kind. Trader Joe's unique combination of quirky products and low prices produces so much word-of-mouth promotion and buying urgency that the company doesn't really need to advertise or price promote. The closest thing to an official promotion is the company's Web site or *The Fearless Flyer,* a newsletter mailed out monthly to people who opt in to receive it. Trader Joe's most potent promotional weapon is its army of faithful followers. Trader Joe's customers have even started their own fan Web site, www.traderjoesfan .com, where they discuss new products and stores, trade recipes, and swap their favorite Trader Joe's stories.

Thus, building the right price-value formula has made Trader Joe's one of the nation's fastest-growing and most popular food stores. Its more than 375 stores in 32 states now reap annual sales of an estimated $10 billion, more than double its sales five years ago. Trader Joe's stores pull in an amazing $1,750 per square foot, more than twice the supermarket industry average. *Consumer Reports* recently ranked Trader Joe's, along with Wegmans, as the best supermarket chain in the nation.

It's all about value and price—what you get for what you pay. Just ask Trader Joe's regular Chrissi Wright, found early one morning browsing her local Trader Joe's in Bend, Oregon.

Chrissi expects she'll leave Trader Joe's with eight bottles of the popular Charles Shaw wine priced at $2.99 each tucked under her arms. "I love Trader Joe's because they let me eat like a yuppie without taking all my money," says Wright. "Their products are gourmet, often environmentally conscientious and beautiful . . . and, of course, there's Two-Buck Chuck— possibly the greatest innovation of our time."

Sources: Quotes, extracts, and other information from Glenn Llopis, "Why Trader Joe's Stands Out from All the Rest in the Grocery Business," *Forbes,* September 5, 2011, http://www.forbes.com/sites/glennllopis/2011/09/05/why-trader-joes-stands-out-from-all-the-rest-in-the-grocery-business/; Shan Li, "Trader Joe's Tries to Keep Quirky Vibe as It Expands Quickly," *Los Angeles Times,* October 26, 2011; Alicia Wallace, "Crowded Boulder Grocery Field Awaits Trader Joe's," *McClatchy-Tribune Business News,* January 30, 2012; Anna Sowa, "Trader Joe's: Why the Hype?" *McClatchy-Tribune Business News,* March 27, 2008; Beth Kowitt, "Inside the Secret World of Trader Joe's," *Fortune,* August 23, 2010, pp. 86–96; "SN's Top 75 Retailers & Wholesalers 2012," *Supermarket News,* http://supermarket-news.com/top-75-retailers-wholesalers-2012; and www.traderjoes.com, accessed September 2012.

---

high prices in its advertising. One ad humorously shows a man giving his girlfriend a "cubic zirconia" engagement ring so that he can purchase a Titus Vuelo for himself. Suggested retail price: $7,750.00.

Thus, marketers must consider the total marketing strategy and mix when setting prices. But again, even when featuring price, marketers need to remember that customers rarely buy on price alone. Instead, they seek products that give them the best value in terms of benefits received for the prices paid.

Organizational Considerations

Management must decide who within the organization should set prices. Companies handle pricing in a variety of ways. In small companies, prices are often set by top management rather than by the marketing or sales departments. In large companies, pricing is typically handled by divisional or product managers. In industrial markets, salespeople may be allowed to negotiate with customers within certain price ranges. Even so, top management sets the pricing objectives and policies, and it often approves the prices proposed by lower-level management or salespeople.

In industries in which pricing is a key factor (airlines, aerospace, steel, railroads, oil companies), companies often have pricing departments to set the best prices or help others set them. These departments report to the marketing department or top management. Others who have an influence on pricing include sales managers, production managers, finance managers, and accountants.

The Market and Demand

As noted earlier, good pricing starts with an understanding of how customers' perceptions of value affect the prices they are willing to pay. Both consumer and industrial buyers balance the price of a product or service against the benefits of owning it. Thus, before setting prices, the marketer must understand the relationship between price and demand for the company's product. In this section, we take a deeper look at the price-demand relationship and how it varies for different types of markets. We then discuss methods for analyzing the price-demand relationship.

Pricing in Different Types of Markets

The seller's pricing freedom varies with different types of markets. Economists recognize four types of markets, each presenting a different pricing challenge.

Under *pure competition*, the market consists of many buyers and sellers trading in a uniform commodity, such as wheat, copper, or financial securities. No single buyer or seller has much effect on the going market price. In a purely competitive market, marketing research, product development, pricing, advertising, and sales promotion play little or no role. Thus, sellers in these markets do not spend much time on marketing strategy.

Under *monopolistic competition*, the market consists of many buyers and sellers who trade over a range of prices rather than a single market price. A range of prices occurs be-

cause sellers can differentiate their offers to buyers. Because there are many competitors, each firm is less affected by competitors' pricing strategies than in oligopolistic markets. Sellers try to develop differentiated offers for different customer segments and, in addition to price, freely use branding, advertising, and personal selling to set their offers apart. ● Thus, Honda sets its Odyssey minivan apart through strong branding and advertising, reducing the impact of price. Its tongue-in-cheek "Van of Your Dreams" advertisements tell parents "the new Odyssey has everything one would dream about in a van, if one had dreams about vans." Beyond the standard utility features you'd expect in a van, Honda tells them, you'll also find yourself surrounded by a dazzling array of technology, a marvel of ingenuity. "Hook up your MP3 player and summon music like a rock god. Call out a song name and it plays through an audio system that can split the heavens!"

● **Pricing in monopolistic competition: Honda sets its Odyssey minivan apart through strong branding and advertising, reducing the impact of price. Its tongue-in-cheek "Van of Your Dreams" ads tell parents "the new Odyssey has everything one would dream about in a van, if one had dreams about vans."**

Print advertisement provided courtesy of American Honda Motor Co., Inc.

Under *oligopolistic competition*, the market consists of only a few large sellers. For example, only four companies—Verizon, AT&T, Sprint, and T-Mobile—control more than 80 percent of the U.S. wireless service provider market. Because there are few sellers, each seller is alert and responsive to competitors' pricing strategies and marketing moves. In a *pure monopoly*, the market is dominated by one seller. The seller may be a government monopoly (the U.S. Postal Service), a private regulated monopoly (a power company), or a private unregulated monopoly (De Beers and diamonds). Pricing is handled differently in each case.

Analyzing the Price-Demand Relationship

Demand curve

A curve that shows the number of units the market will buy in a given time period, at different prices that might be charged.

Each price the company might charge will lead to a different level of demand. The relationship between the price charged and the resulting demand level is shown in the **demand curve** in ● **Figure 10.6**. The demand curve shows the number of units the market will buy in a given time period at different prices that might be charged. In the normal case, demand and price are inversely related—that is, the higher the price, the lower the demand. Thus, the company would sell less if it raised its price from P_1 to P_2. In short, consumers with limited budgets probably will buy less of something if its price is too high.

FIGURE | 10.6
Demand Curves

Price and demand are related—no big surprise there. Usually, higher prices result in lower demand. But in the case of some prestige goods, the relationship might be reversed. A higher price signals higher quality and status, resulting in more demand, not less.

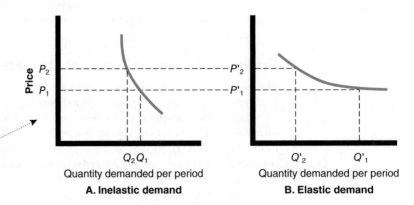

A. Inelastic demand   **B. Elastic demand**

Understanding a brand's price-demand curve is crucial to good pricing decisions. ConAgra Foods learned this lesson when pricing its Banquet frozen dinners.[11]

> When ConAgra recently tried to cover higher commodity costs by raising list price of Banquet dinners from $1 to $1.25, consumers turned up their noses to the higher price. Sales dropped, forcing ConAgra to sell off excess dinners at discount prices. It turns out that "the key component for Banquet dinners—the key attribute—is you've got to be at $1," says ConAgra's CEO Gary Rodkin. "Everything else pales in comparison to that." Banquet dinner prices are now back to a buck a dinner. To make money at that price, ConAgra is doing a better job of managing costs by shrinking portions and substituting less expensive ingredients for costlier ones. Consumers are responding well to the brand's efforts to keep prices down. After all, where else can you find dinner for $1?

Most companies try to measure their demand curves by estimating demand at different prices. The type of market makes a difference. In a monopoly, the demand curve shows the total market demand resulting from different prices. If the company faces competition, its demand at different prices will depend on whether competitors' prices stay constant or change with the company's own prices.

Price Elasticity of Demand

Consider the two demand curves in Figure 10.6. In Figure 10.6A, a price increase from P_1 to P_2 leads to a relatively small drop in demand from Q_1 to Q_2. In Figure 10.6B, however, the same price increase leads to a large drop in demand from Q'_1 to Q'_2. If demand hardly changes with a small change in price, we say the demand is *inelastic*. If demand changes greatly, we say the demand is *elastic*. The **price elasticity** of demand is given by the following formula:

Price elasticity

A measure of the sensitivity of demand to changes in price.

$$\text{price elasticity of demand} = \frac{\% \text{ change in quantity demanded}}{\% \text{ change in price}}$$

Suppose demand falls by 10 percent when a seller raises its price by 2 percent. The price elasticity of demand is therefore –5 (the minus sign confirms the inverse relation between price and demand), and demand is elastic. If demand falls by 2 percent with a 2 percent increase in price, then elasticity is –1. In this case, the seller's total revenue stays the same: The seller sells fewer items but at a higher price that preserves the same total revenue. If demand falls by 1 percent when price is increased by 2 percent, then elasticity is—, and demand is inelastic. The less elastic the demand, the more it pays for the seller to raise the price.

What determines the price elasticity of demand? Buyers are less price sensitive when the product they are buying is unique or when it is high in quality, prestige, or exclusiveness; substitute products are hard to find or when they cannot easily compare the quality of substitutes; and the total expenditure for a product is low relative to their income or when the cost is shared by another party.[12]

If demand is elastic rather than inelastic, sellers will consider lowering their prices. A lower price will produce more total revenue. This practice makes sense as long as the extra costs of producing and selling more do not exceed the extra revenue. At the same time, most firms want to avoid pricing that turns their products into commodities. In recent years, forces such as dips in the economy, deregulation, and the instant price comparisons afforded by the Internet and other technologies have increased consumer price sensitivity, turning products ranging from phones and computers to new automobiles into commodities in some consumers' eyes.

Marketers need to work harder than ever to differentiate their offerings when a dozen competitors are selling virtually the same product at a comparable or lower price. More than ever, companies need to understand the price sensitivity of their customers and the trade-offs people are willing to make between price and product characteristics.

The Economy

Economic conditions can have a strong impact on the firm's pricing strategies. Economic factors such as a boom or recession, inflation, and interest rates affect pricing decisions because they affect consumer spending, consumer perceptions of the product's price and value, and the company's costs of producing and selling a product.

In the aftermath of the recent Great Recession, many consumers have rethought the price-value equation. They have tightened their belts and become more value conscious. Consumers will likely continue their thriftier ways well beyond any economic recovery. As a result, many marketers have increased their emphasis on value-for-the-money pricing strategies.

The most obvious response to the new economic realities is to cut prices and offer discounts. Thousands of companies have done just that. Lower prices make products more affordable and help spur short-term sales. However, such price cuts can have undesirable long-term consequences. Lower prices mean lower margins. Deep discounts may cheapen a brand in consumers' eyes. And once a company cuts prices, it's difficult to raise them again when the economy recovers.

Rather than cutting prices, many companies have instead shifted their marketing focus to more affordable items in their product mixes. For example, whereas its previous promotions emphasized high-end products and pricey concepts such as creating dream kitchens, Home Depot's more recent advertising pushes items like potting soil and hand tools under the tagline: "More saving. More doing. That's the power of Home Depot."

Other companies are holding prices but redefining the "value" in their value propositions. ● Consider upscale grocery retailer Whole Foods Market:

● **When the economy dipped, rather than cutting everyday prices, Whole Foods set out to convince shoppers that it was, in fact, an affordable place to shop. It even assigned workers to serve as "value tour guides," like the one shown here, to escort shoppers around stores pointing out value items.**

© Elise Amendola/AP Wide World

Whole Foods Market grew rapidly by serving up high-quality grocery items to upscale customers who were willing and able to pay more for the extra value they got. Then came the Great Recession of 2008, and even relatively affluent customers began cutting back and spending less. All of a sudden, Whole Foods Market faced a difficult question: Should it hold the line on its premium price positioning, or should it cut prices and reposition itself to fit the leaner times? Whole Foods decided to stick with its core up-market positioning, but it also began to subtly realign its value proposition. Rather than dropping everyday prices across the board, Whole Foods lowered prices on selected basic items and offered significant sales on others. It also started emphasizing its lower-price private-label brand, 365 Everyday Value.

At the same time, however, Whole Foods Market launched a new marketing program that did more than simply promote more affordable merchandise. It convinced shoppers that, for what you get, Whole Foods's regular products and prices offer good value as well. When it comes to quality food, price isn't everything. The upscale retailer even assigned workers to serve as "value tour guides" to escort shoppers around stores and point out the value in both sale and regular items. As one tour guide notes, "Value means getting a good exchange for your money." As a result of subtle shifts in its value strategy, Whole Foods Market is now back on track in the post-recession economy. It is meeting the challenges of more frugal times in a way that preserves all the things that have made it special to customers through the years.[13]

Remember, even in tough economic times, consumers do not buy based on prices alone. They balance the price they pay against the value they receive. For example, according to one survey, despite selling its shoes for as much as $150 a pair, Nike commands the highest consumer loyalty of any brand in the footwear segment.[14] Customers perceive the value of Nike's products and the Nike ownership experience to be well worth the price. Thus, no matter what price they charge—low or high—companies need to offer great *value for the money*.

Other External Factors

Beyond the market and the economy, the company must consider several other factors in its external environment when setting prices. It must know what impact its prices will have on other parties in its environment. How will *resellers* react to various prices? The company should set prices that give resellers a fair profit, encourage their support, and help them to sell the product effectively. The *government* is another important external influence on pricing decisions. Finally, *social concerns* may need to be taken into account. In setting prices, a company's short-term sales, market share, and profit goals may need to be tempered by broader societal considerations. We will examine public policy issues in pricing in Chapter 11.

Reviewing the Concepts

MyMarketingLab™

Go to **mymktlab.com** to complete the problems marked with this icon .

Reviewing Objectives and Key Terms

 ## Objectives Review

Companies today face a fierce and fast-changing pricing environment. Firms successful at creating customer value with the other marketing mix activities must still capture some of this value in the prices they earn. This chapter examines the importance of pricing, general pricing strategies, and the internal and external considerations that affect pricing decisions.

Objective 1 **Answer the question "What is a price?" and discuss the importance of pricing in today's fast-changing environment.** (pp 290–291)

Price can be defined narrowly as the amount of money charged for a product or service. Or it can be defined more broadly as the sum of the values that consumers exchange for the benefits of having and using the product or service. The pricing challenge is to find the price that will let the company make a fair profit by getting paid for the customer value it creates.

Despite the increased role of nonprice factors in the modern marketing process, price remains an important element in the marketing mix. It is the only marketing mix element that produces revenue; all other elements represent costs. More important, as a part of a company's overall value proposition, price plays a key role in creating customer value and building customer relationships. Smart managers treat pricing as a key strategic tool for creating and capturing customer value.

Objective 2 **Identify the three major pricing strategies and discuss the importance of understanding customer-value perceptions, company costs, and competitor strategies when setting prices.** (pp 291–299)

Companies can choose from three major pricing strategies: customer value-based pricing, cost-based pricing, and competition-based pricing. *Customer value-based pricing* uses buyers' perceptions of value as the basis for setting price. Good pricing begins with a complete understanding of the value that a product or service creates for customers and setting a price that captures that value. Customer perceptions of the product's value set the ceiling for prices. If customers perceive that a product's price is greater than its value, they will not buy the product.

Companies can pursue either of two types of value-based pricing. *Good-value pricing* involves offering just the right combination of quality and good service at a fair price. EDLP is an example of this strategy. *Value-added pricing* involves attaching value-added features and services to differentiate the company's offers and support charging higher prices.

Cost-based pricing involves setting prices based on the costs for producing, distributing, and selling products plus a fair rate of return for effort and risk. Company and product costs are an important consideration in setting prices. Whereas customer value perceptions set the price ceiling, costs set the floor for pricing. However, cost-based pricing is product driven rather than customer driven. The company designs what it considers to be a good product and sets a price that covers costs plus a target profit. If the price turns out to be too high, the company must settle for lower markups or lower sales, both resulting in disappointing profits. If the company prices the product below its costs, its profits will also suffer. Cost-based pricing approaches include *cost-plus pricing* and *break-even pricing* (or target profit pricing).

Competition-based pricing involves setting prices based on competitors' strategies, costs, prices, and market offerings. Consumers base their judgments of a product's value on the prices that competitors charge for similar products. If consumers perceive that the company's product or service provides greater value, the company can charge a higher price. If consumers perceive less value relative to competing products, the company must either charge a lower price or change customer perceptions to justify a higher price.

Objective 3	**Identify and define the other important internal and external factors affecting a firm's pricing decisions.**

(pp 299–306)

Other *internal* factors that influence pricing decisions include the company's overall marketing strategy, objectives, and marketing mix, as well as organizational considerations. Price is only one element of the company's broader marketing strategy. If the company has selected its target market and positioning carefully, then its marketing mix strategy, including price, will be fairly straightforward. Some companies position their products on price and then tailor other marketing mix decisions to the prices they want to charge. Other companies deemphasize price and use other marketing mix tools to create *nonprice* positions.

Other *external* pricing considerations include the nature of the market and demand and environmental factors such as the economy, reseller needs, and government actions. The seller's pricing freedom varies with different types of markets. Ultimately, the customer decides whether the company has set the right price. The customer weighs price against the perceived values of using the product: If the price exceeds the sum of the values, consumers will not buy. So the company must understand concepts such as demand curves (the price-demand relationship) and price elasticity (consumer sensitivity to prices).

Economic conditions can also have a major impact on pricing decisions. The Great Recession caused consumers to rethink the price-value equation. Marketers have responded by increasing their emphasis on value-for-the-money pricing strategies. Even in tough economic times, however, consumers do not buy based on prices alone. Thus, no matter what price they charge—low or high—companies need to offer superior value for the money.

 Key Terms

Objective 1

Price (p 290)

Objective 2

Customer value-based pricing (p 291)
Good-value pricing (p 292)
Value-added pricing (p 293)

Objective 3

Cost-based pricing (p 295)
Fixed costs (overhead) (p 296)
Variable costs (p 296)
Total costs (p 296)
Experience curve (learning curve) (p 297)
Cost-plus pricing (markup pricing) (p 297)

Break-even pricing (target return pricing) (p 297)
Competition-based pricing (p 299)
Target costing (p 302)
Demand curve (p 303)
Price elasticity (p 304)

Discussion and Critical Thinking

 Discussion Questions

1. What is price? Discuss factors marketers must consider when setting price. (AACSB: Communication).

⭐ **2.** Compare and contrast *good-value pricing* and *everyday low pricing (EDLP)*. (AACSB: Communication)

⭐ **3.** Name and describe the types of costs marketers must consider when setting prices. Describe the types of cost-based pricing and the methods of implementing each. (AACSB: Communication)

4. What is *target costing* and how is it different from the usual process of setting prices? (AACSB: Communication)

5. Name and describe the four types of markets recognized by economists and discuss the pricing challenges posed by each. (AACSB: Communication)

 Critical Thinking Exercises

1. You can turn your hobby into profits at online sites such as Etsy. In a small group, create ideas for a craft product to sell on Etsy, an online community of buyers and creative businesses. Using the resources available at www.etsy.com as a guide to setting prices, determine the price for your product. Justify why you decided on that price and provide a link to the resources you found most useful on the Etsy site. (AACSB: Communication; Use of IT; Analytical Reasoning)

⭐ **2.** Find estimates of price elasticity for a variety of consumer goods and services. Explain what price elasticities of 0.5 and

2.4 mean (note: these are absolute values, as price elasticity is usually negative). (AACSB: Communication; Reflective Thinking)

⭐ **3.** What is the Consumer Price Index (CPI)? Select one of the reports available at www.bls.gov/cpi/home.htm and create a presentation on price changes over the past two years. Discuss reasons for that change. (AACSB: Communication; Use of IT; Reflective Thinking)

Applications and Cases

 ## Marketing Technology Cheap Gas

It seems a day doesn't go by without some talk about gas prices. Consumers are more keenly aware of the price now that it costs $40 to $100 to fill up the tank. And many consumers are using technology to help find the lowest prices in their area. While there have been Web sites available that map gas prices by zip code, smartphone apps such as GasBuddy, Fuel Finder, and Cheap Gas and in-car navigation systems such as Garmin and Waze put price information at drivers' fingertips while on the road. That's because these systems are based on a driver's actual location based on GPS positioning information. This is an example of crowdsourcing information, because these apps and systems rely on volunteers to update prices.

1. Discuss the pros and cons of gas finder apps from the consumer's viewpoint and the gas retailer's viewpoint. Do you think they have any impact on gas prices? Explain. (AACSB: Communication; Reflective Thinking)

 ## Marketing Ethics You've Been Crammed!

Have you ever tried to figure out what all those charges are on a phone bill? Not all of them are from your phone service provider. A study by a Congressional committee reported that $2 billion a year in "mystery fees" appear on consumers' landline phone bills—a practice called "cramming." It is illegal for a phone company or a third party to tack unauthorized fees onto landline phone bills, but it is still happening. That prompted the Federal Communications Commission to propose new rules requiring companies to disclose charges more clearly so consumers can spot them. The agency would like to see the fees listed in a separate section of customers' bills that will also include the FCC's contact information for filing complaints. The problem is creeping into wireless phone bills as well, and the agency also proposed that companies should provide alerts to wireless customers when they are approaching their monthly voice and data limits. Do you remember what happened the first time you exceeded your texting limit. If you don't, and if your parents paid the bill, they do remember!

1. Look at a phone bill for the same service over several months. How does the service provider price this service? Do you see any suspicious charges, such as any of those listed by the FCC at www.ftc.gov/bcp/edu/pubs/consumer/products/pro18.shtm? Suggest ways to price this service that will make it easier for customers to understand but also allow the company to make a reasonable profit. (AACSB: Communication; Reflective Thinking)

2. How can a third-party vendor place a charge on a phone bill, authorized or unauthorized? Do phone companies benefit from allowing third-party vendor billing? Research this issue and discuss whether or not this should be allowed. (AACSB: Communication; Reflective Thinking; Ethical Reasoning)

 ## Marketing by the Numbers Kei Cars

The U.S. government fuel-economy regulations require carmakers to achieve a fleet average of 54.5 miles per gallon by 2025. Smaller vehicles can help car companies meet those standards. Tiny vehicles in Japan, known as *kei* cars (from "kei-jidosha" or "light automobile"), achieve 55 mpg ratings. Kei cars are not new in Japan. They began as a tax and insurance break to stimulate the Japanese economy after World War II. However, the typical kei buyer in Japan is close to 50 years old, causing concern for Japanese automakers focusing only on the Japanese market. The U.S. regulations provide an opportunity for these automobiles in America. However, profit margins are almost as tiny as the cars themselves, causing carmakers to wonder if they can make an adequate profit when exporting to the United States. Of the big-three Japanese carmakers—Honda, Toyota, and Nissan—Honda is the only one making kei cars. It is considering bringing its new Honda NBox to the United States. Its closest competitor would be Daimler's Smart car, which made a profit of $108.3 million on sales of $10.7 billion in the United States last year. Smart cars sell for around $13,000 but seat only two people. In comparison, Honda's NBox holds four people and would be priced at $16,000, making it an alternative for small-car-minded families. To answer the following questions, refer to Appendix 2, Marketing by the Numbers.

1. What is the profit margin for the Smart car? (AACSB: Communication; Analytical Reasoning)

2. If the unit variable cost for each NBox is $14,000 and the Honda has fixed costs totaling $20 million for this car, how many NBox cars must Honda sell to break even? How many must it sell to realize a profit margin similar to that of the Smart car? (AACSB: Communication; Analytical Reasoning)

Video Case Smashburger

Hamburgers are America's favorite food. Consumers spend more than $100 billion on the beef sandwiches every year. But despite America's infatuation with burgers, there is often considerable dissatisfaction among consumers based on hamburger quality and value. Many customers just aren't happy with what is served up at market-leading fast-food outlets. They want a better burger, and they won't hesitate to pay a higher price to get one. Enter Smashburger. Started just a few years ago in Denver, Colorado, Smashburger is now a rapidly expanding nationwide chain. And all this growth started during a severe economic downturn despite Smashburger's average lunch check of $8. Many customers pay as much as $10 or $12 for a burger, fries, and shake. The

Smashburger video shows how this small startup employed pricing strategy to pull off a seemingly impossible challenge. After viewing the video featuring Smashburger, answer the following questions:

1. Discuss the three major pricing strategies in relation to Smashburger. Which of these three do you think is the company's core strategic strategy?
2. What effect does Smashburger's premium price have on consumer perceptions? How did a restaurant with a premium-priced product and little track record take off during a recession?
3. Is Smashburger's success based on novelty alone or will it continue to succeed?

 # Company Case Burt's Bees: Willfully Overpriced

How much are you willing to pay for a standard-size tube of lip balm? The market leader charges just a bit more than $1. But would you pay $2 for a comparable product? How about $3? When it comes to price, your first thought might be, "The lower the better." Many companies follow this reasoning and try to outdo each other by providing the cheapest option. But such a strategy can lead to razor-thin margins and even losses. And although low price might seem to be the most attractive way to lure customers into purchasing goods and services, when it comes to actually creating value for customers, that's not always the case.

Burt's Bees is one company that understands that sometimes it pays to charge more. Just a decade ago, the popular maker of natural personal-care products was a niche brand, distributed only in boutiques and natural foods stores. But Burt's Bees sales exploded when major supermarket and discount retail chains started carrying the small company's line. And although Walmart and other national chains are known for pressuring manufacturers to cut costs and lower prices, Burt's Bees achieved its distribution victory through a strategy that has been called "willful overpricing." In Burt's Bees' case, that means charging price premiums of 80 percent or more over comparable non-natural brands. Case in point: Burt's Bees lip balm, the brand's best-selling product, sells for $2.99 a tube, whereas market-leading ChapStick can be had for about a third of that price. To understand how Burt's Bees has succeeded with this pricing strategy, let's look at what makes the brand so special.

From Humble Beginnings

Burt's Bees started like many entrepreneurial ventures, with founders that had a good idea but not a penny to their names. In the late 1980s, Burt Shavitz was a beekeeper in northern Maine selling honey out of his pickup truck and living in a modified turkey coop. Roxanne Quimby, a wife and mother looking for a way to supplement the family income, had the idea to buy Burt's surplus beeswax to make and sell candles. Her first venture at a craft fair yielded $200 in sales.

A few years later, Roxanne happened upon a 19th-century book of homemade personal-care recipes and acquired a second-hand industrial mixer from a university cafeteria. That's when the Burt's Bees brand that so many people now know and love began to take shape. The main product line of natural beeswax

candles was slowly replaced by personal-care products, including the brand's famous lip balm made with beeswax, coconut and sunflower oils, and other ingredients that you could just as easily eat as put on your lips.

As Burt's Bees grew, it automated its manufacturing processes one piece of machinery at a time. Yet the products that rolled off those automated lines maintained the quality and feel of natural homemade goods. Burt's Bees developed body lotions featuring natural milk and sugar enzymes, bath products made with sea ingredients, shampoos derived from soy protein and pomegranate extract, and toothpaste infused with spearmint oil and cranberry extract. The company can't claim that all of its products are 100 percent natural. But with more than half its products meeting the 100 percent mark and the rest coming very close, Burt's Bees boasts that its product lines are, on average, 99 percent natural. In fact, the company maintains a commitment to what it calls *The Natural Standard*—a set of guidelines that dictate which ingredients can be considered truly "natural."

With natural ingredients as it main point of differentiation and core values oriented around environmental conservation and social responsibility, Burt's Bees grew very quickly. Once it made the leap to the big regional and national retail chains, company sales grew by an average of 30 percent per year.

Value versus Price

In certain respects, cross-comparing personal-care products is problematic because there is so much variation in both features and price. But consider some popular Burt's Bees products. Its standard shampoos and conditioners run $7.99 for a 12-ounce bottle, whereas you can pick up a same-size bottle with a Pantene label on it for only $3.99. Burt's body lotion runs $9.99 for a 12-ounce bottle, whereas a slightly larger bottle of Nivea body lotion only costs $5.99. Like various brands, Burt's Bees offers a line of anti-aging creams. But at $24.99 for any one of them, the price is almost double that of similar Oil of Olay products at only $12.99.

When making such comparisons, the choice seems obvious. How has Burt's Bees achieved such success with this pricing strategy? You might think that it does so despite higher prices. However, a closer examination suggests that success might actually be the *result* of that pricing. In some cases, higher prices merely serve as an indicator of quality level. But more important to Burt's Bees, higher prices can also pique customer curiosity. When people compare brands, a moderately higher priced option causes them to take notice and look a little deeper to understand why it is more expensive. They may learn that the product contains features that justify the higher price—features they may not have even considered before. Customers then ask themselves, "Do I need this benefit or not?" Some studies show that in such situations, customers recall nearly twice as much product information and can cite more arguments in favor of buying the products. If the price premium charged is too high or too low, however, shoppers ignore the option.

Fortunately for Burt's Bees, its strategy of willful overpricing coincided with a trend of growing consumer preference toward natural products and environmentally friendly goods. Thus, Burt's Bees natural ingredients and company values were enough to justify the brand's higher prices for many. But can a pricing strategy that relies on trends in consumer preferences work forever?

Eco-Brands in Hard Times

Last year on Earth Day, a front page of the *New York Times* featured the headline, "As Consumers Cut Spending, 'Green Products' Lose Allure." The article pointed out that during the Great Recession, the mainstream consumer's love affair with green products faded like a cheap t-shirt. When times are tough, the very features that seem to justify paying a higher price during good times lose their importance as budgets tighten.

But within that economic dynamic, researchers found an interesting exception. "Dark green" consumers—who are more educated, committed, and affluent—don't drop higher-priced green products as quickly as "light green" consumers do. As a result, sales of brands perceived to be less authentic when it comes to eco-friendliness decreased, whereas sales of brands deemed more authentic remained firm. It's a perception of value *and* values. Brands such as Method and Seventh Generation are top on the list of those benefiting from this "authenticity gap," whereas S.C. Johnson's *Nature's Source* and Clorox's *Green Works* are at the bottom.

This phenomenon creates complicated issues for Burt's Bees. The well-known creator of natural products has been a hardcore eco-brand from its beginnings. But while Burt Shavitz's earthy image still adorns the package of many Burt's Bees products, the beekeeper sold his share of the company to Roxanne Quimby more than a decade ago and returned to beekeeping and his turkey coop. Quimby bowed out in 2007 as part of an even bigger shakeup. Clorox purchased Burt's Bees for a whopping $925 million as part of its comprehensive strategy to become more environmentally friendly and to free itself of a chemical-polluting image. Clorox followed in the footsteps of Unilever (which purchased Ben & Jerry's in 2000), Colgate-Palmolive (bought Tom's of Maine in 2006), and PepsiCo (acquired Naked Juice in 2006). Major global players have paid big money for the image and the customer base of good green brands.

After buying Burt's Bees, Clorox immediately ran magazine ads comparing natural ingredients in Burt's Bees to chemical ingredients found in other products. At the same time, Burt's Bees's executives claimed that the brand's quality and standards would only improve. For all intents and purposes, Clorox allows Burt's Bees to operate as an independent division, remaining true to its original mission and values.

Still, many viewed the Burt's Bees acquisition as a big sellout. Fans vented their frustrations online as they created new names for the company like "Burt's Bleach" and "Clorox's Bees." Comments such as "I use lots of Burt's Bees products. I won't be buying them anymore," and "I think I'm going to have to stock up now before Clorox ruins it," indicated the potential fallout of the merger. Burt's Bees risked losing some of its authenticity as an eco-brand, thus becoming more susceptible to the effects of consumer frugality.

Pressing on with Price Premiums

Despite hard economic times and the big changes in Burt's Bees's ownership and management, Burt's Bees seems to be doing very well for Clorox. According to Clorox chief financial officer Dan Heinrich:

> The Burt's Bees business remains a very solid contributor to Clorox's results, with sales growth and profit margins above the company average. Burt's Bees remains the fastest growing business unit in the company, with double-digit fiscal-year-to-date sales growth, and our revised estimates continue to project low double-digit sales growth for this business over the next several years.

If Burt's Bees's Facebook fan base is any indication, Heinrich can be taken at his word. In little more than two years' time, Burt's Bees grew from about 100,000 fans to more than 1.1 million. The corporate buyout and economic trends appear to have had little impact on the brand. In the end, it just may be that Burt's Bees's pricing strategy proves that by leveraging a brand's strengths, a brand can persuade customers to continue to buy on value, not just on price.

Questions for Discussion

1. Does Burt's Bees's pricing strategy truly differentiate it from the competition?

2. Has Burt's Bees executed value-based pricing, cost-based pricing, or competition-based pricing? Explain.

3. Discuss how Burt's Bees has implemented product mix pricing strategies.

4. Could Burt's Bees have been successful as a natural product marketer had it employed a low-price strategy? Explain.

5. Is Burt's Bees's pricing strategy sustainable? Explain.

Sources: Loren Berlin, "Burt's Bees, Tom's of Maine Owned by Fortune 500 Companies," *Huffington Post*, April 20, 2012, www.huffingtonpost.com/2012/04/20/burts-bees-toms-of-maine-green-products_n_1438019.html; Marco Bertini and Luc Wathieu, "How to Stop Customers from Fixating on Price," *Harvard Business Review*, May 2010, pp. 85–91; Mitch Maranowski, "The Triple Value Proposition: Why Inauthentic Green Brands Are Doomed to Fail," *Fast Company*, May 18, 2011, www.fastcompany.com/1754132/the-triple-value-proposition-why-inauthentic-green-brands-are-doomed-to-fail; and quotes and other information from www.burtsbees.com, accessed July 2012.

MyMarketingLab

Go to **mymktlab.com** for Auto-graded writing questions as well as the following Assisted-graded writing questions:

10-1. Discuss the impact of the economy on a company's pricing strategies. (AACSB: Communication)

10-2. Why are consumers so concerned about the price of gas and why are they willing to search out stations with lower prices? (AACSB: Communication; Reflective Thinking)

10-3. Mymktlab Only – comprehensive writing assignment for this chapter.

References

1. Quotes and other information found at Rafi Mohammed, "J.C. Penney's Risky New Pricing Strategy," *Harvard Business Review*, January 30, 2012, http://blogs.hbr.org/cs/2012/01/understanding_jc_penneys_risky.html; Natalie Zmuda, "JCPenney Reinvention Is Bold Bet, But Hardly Fail-Safe," *Advertising Age*, January 30, 2012, pp. 1, 22; Allison Miles, "Change Coming to Victoria's JCPenney Store," *McClatchy-Tribune Business News*, January 28, 2012; Karen Tailey, "Penney CEO Says Profits Won't Suffer," *Wall Street Journal*, January 27, 2012, p. B6; Margret Brennan, "J.C. Penney CEO Johnson on Pricing, Store Overhaul," Bloomberg video, January 25, 2012, www.bloomberg.com/video/84891104/; Dana Mattioli, "J. C. Penney Chief Thinks Different," *Wall Street Journal*, January 26, 2012; http://online.wsj.com; "JCPenney 'Enough Is Enough,'" *International Business Times*, February 1, 2012, www.ibtimes.com; and Andrew Feinberg, "Bullish on J.C. Penney, Despite Doubts," *Kiplinger*, November 2012, www.kiplinger.com/columns/promisedland/archives/bullish-on-jc-penney-despite-doubts.html" www.kiplinger.com/columns/promisedland/archives/bullish-on-jc-penney-despite-doubts.html.

2. For more on the importance of sound pricing strategy, see Thomas T. Nagle, John Hogan, and Joseph Zale, *The Strategy and Tactics of Pricing: A Guide to Growing More Profitably*, 5th ed. (Upper Saddle River, NJ: Prentice Hall, 2011), Chapter 1.

3. Based on information from Anne Marie Chaker, "For a Steinway, I Did It My Way," *Wall Street Journal*, May 22, 2008, www.wsj.com; Brett Arends, "Steinway & Sons: A Grand Investment?" *SmartMoney*, March 20, 2012, www.smartmoney.com/invest/stocks/steinway--sons-a-grand-investment-1332195987741/; and www.steinway.com/steinway and www.steinway.com/steinway/quotes.shtml, accessed November 2012.

4. See Christine Birkner, "Marketing in 2012: The End of the Middle?" *Marketing News*, January 31, 2012, pp. 22–23.

5. See Philip Kotler and Kevin Lane Keller, *Marketing Management*, 14th ed. (Upper Saddle River, NJ: Prentice Hall, 2012), p. 158.

6. Maria Puente, "Theaters Turn Up the Luxury," *USA Today*, March 12, 2010, p. 1A; ""Expansion Ahead for iPic Entertainment: Two New Visionary Movie Theater Escapes Announced for Boca Raton and Hallandale, Florida," *Business Wire*, February 16, 2012; and information from www.amctheatres.com/dinein/cinemasuites/, accessed November 2012.

7. Accumulated production is drawn on a semilog scale so that equal distances represent the same percentage increase in output.

8. The arithmetic of markups and margins is discussed in Appendix 2, Marketing by the Numbers.

9. Stephanie Schomer, "How Retailer Hot Mama Is Rethinking Shopping for Moms," *Fast Company*, February 2011, pp. 40–41; Joyce Smith, "New to Leawood, Hot Mama Offers Designer Clothes for Moms," *Kansas City Star*, March 26, 2012; and www.shopmama.com, accessed November 2012.

10. See www.kohler.com and www.sterlingplumbing.com, accessed November 2012.

11. Adapted from information found in Joseph Weber, "Over a Buck for Dinner? Outrageous," *BusinessWeek*, March 9, 2009, p. 57; and Tom Mulier and Matthew Boyle, "Dollar Dinners from ConAgra's Threatened by Costs," *Bloomberg BusinessWeek*, August 19, 2010, accessed at www.businessweek.com.

12. See Nagle, Hogan, and Zale, *The Strategy and Tactics of Pricing*, Chapter 7.

13. For more information, see Annie Gasparro, "Whole Foods Aims to Alter 'Price Perception' as It Expands," *Wall Street Journal*, February 15, 2012; Ben Fox Rubin, "Whole Foods' Profit Rises 33%," *Wall Street Journal*, February 8, 2012; and www.wholefoodsmarket.com, accessed September 2012.

14. Kenneth Hein, "Study: Value Trumps Price among Shoppers," *Adweek*, July 1, 2010, www.adweek.com/news/advertising-branding/study-value-trumps-price-among-shoppers-94611. See also Erik Seimers, "Nike Sales Up 18% as Demand Trumps Higher Costs," *Portland Business Journal*, December 20, 2011, www.bizjournals.com/portland/news/2011/12/20/nike-boosts-q2-sales-profits-as.html.

Part 1: Defining Marketing and the Marketing Process (Chapters 1–2)
Part 2: Understanding the Marketplace and Consumers (Chapters 3–6)
Part 3: Designing a Customer-Driven Strategy and Mix (Chapters 7–17)
Part 4: Extending Marketing (Chapters 18–20)

Pricing Strategies
Additional Considerations

Chapter Preview In the previous chapter, you learned that price is an important marketing mix tool for both creating and capturing customer value. You explored the three main pricing strategies—customer value-based, cost-based, and competition-based pricing—and the many internal and external factors that affect a firm's pricing decisions. In this chapter, we'll look at some additional pricing considerations: new-product pricing, product mix pricing, price adjustments, and initiating and reacting to price changes. We close the chapter with a discussion of public policy and pricing.

For starters, we look at Panera Bread Company, the fast-casual restaurant chain where value means a lot more than just low prices. At Panera, value means wholesome food and fresh-baked bread, served in a warm and inviting environment, even if you have to pay a little more for it. Adding value and charging accordingly has paid off handsomely for Panera, through bad economic times and good.

Panera Bread Company: Value Isn't Just about Low Prices

In the restaurant business these days, value typically means one thing—cheap. Today's casual restaurants are offering a seemingly endless hodgepodge of value meals, dollar items, budget sandwiches, and rapid-fire promotional deals that scream "value, value, value." But one everyday eatery—Panera Bread—understands that, even when finances are tight, low prices often aren't the best value. Instead, at Panera, value means wholesome food and fresh-baked bread, served in a warm and inviting environment, even if you have to pay a little more for it. Ronald Shaich, founder and executive chairman of Panera, sums up this value-added concept perfectly. "Give people something of value and they'll happily pay for it," he says.

Shaich realized 30 years ago that people wanted something between fast food and casual dining. He perfected the "fast-casual" dining formula—fancier than fast-food but cheaper than sit-down restaurants—and opened Panera (Spanish for "bread basket"). The fast-casual category is the only segment of the restaurant industry that grew during the past five years; the bakery-café concept (which Shaich practically created) has grown fastest. And Panera does bakery-café better than anyone else. In fact, Panera's $1.8 billion in sales more than doubles the combined sales of its next four competitors.

Why is Panera Bread so successful? Unlike many competitors in the post–Great Recession era, Panera isn't about having the lowest prices. Instead, it's about the value you get for what you pay, and what you get is a full-value dining experience.

At Panera, it all starts with the food, which centers around fresh-baked bread. When customers walk through the door, the first thing they see is massive displays of bread, all hand-formed and baked on-site. Bakers pass out warm bread samples to customers throughout the day. All new employees get "dough training," and even employee meetings start with the staff breaking bread together—literally. Bread is so central to Panera's DNA that the company's research and development (R&D) team will scrap new dishes if the bread feels like an afterthought.

Of course, the food at Panera goes well beyond bread. Fresh bagels, pastries, egg soufflés, soups, salads, sandwiches, and

> Panera Bread Company knows that low prices often aren't the best value. Instead, at Panera, value means wholesome food, served in a warm and inviting environment, even if you have to pay a little more for it.

paninis, as well as coffee drinks and smoothies, give customers full meal options at any time of day. Menu items brim with upscale ingredients such as Gorgonzola cheese, fresh basil, tomato aioli, caramelized onions, and applewood-smoked bacon (the kind you'd find at the Four Seasons, not Wendy's). In all, Panera's target audience is more Food Network than fast food. "We hit a chord with people who understand and respond to food," says Scott Davis, chief concept officer. Our profile is "closer to what you'd find in a bistro than a fast-food joint." And to all that good food, Panera adds first-rate customer service. For three years running, Panera has rated among *BusinessWeek*'s top 25 "Customer Service Champs."

But good fast-casual food and outstanding service are only part of Panera's value-added proposition. Perhaps even more important is the Panera experience—one so inviting that people don't want to leave. Comfortable booths, leather sofas and chairs, warm lighting, a fireplace, and free Wi-Fi all beg customers to relax and stay awhile. In fact, the local Panera has become a kind of community gathering spot. At any given moment, you'll find a diverse group of customers hanging out together for a variety of reasons. One recent sample included a bride-to-be chatting with her wedding photographer, two businesspeople with laptops, a teacher grading papers, a church group engaged in Bible study, and a baker's dozen of couples and families just enjoying each others' company. Shaich knows that, although the food's important, what he's really selling is an inviting place to be. "In many ways," he says, "we're renting space to people, and the food is the price of admission."

Even during the Great Recession, rather than cutting back on value and lowering prices in difficult times, Panera boosted quality and value while competitors cut back. Freshness remained a driving force. Shaich improved the freshness of lettuce by cutting the time from field to plate in half and using only the hearts of romaine. Store ovens began producing warm bread throughout the day, rather than just in the wee hours of the morning. And the chain's development labs tested a new grill that churned out paninis in half the time. "This was the time to increase the food experience, when the customer least expected it," Shaich insists. "When everyone else pulled back and we did more, the difference between us and our competitors went up."

Panera's strategy of adding value and charging accordingly has paid off handsomely, through bad economic times and

good. At a time when most chains, including those that slashed their prices, struggled and closed stores, Panera flourished. Over the past five years, its sales have nearly tripled; profits have more than doubled. And according to one restaurant analyst, "There's no end in sight to their growth. They've delivered on consumers' value expectations far more than most fast-food places." This bread company is on a roll and has no plans to let up, boosting its promotional budget by 26 percent for the coming year.

Although everyone wants value, Shaich says, not everyone wants it in the form of a value meal. Anne Skrodzki, a 28-year-old Chicago attorney, agrees. She recently spent $9.72 at Panera on a chicken Caesar salad and frozen lemonade. "I think it's a pretty good value. The portions are generous. The food is high quality. . . . I've also gotten used to coming here for the free Wi-Fi."

So, Panera is a lot more than just a place to buy a fast-casual meal at a low price. It's a bundle of added values that are difficult to quantify. It's the smell of fresh-baked bread and the buzz of warm conversation. It's a morning work routine or a simple lunchtime ritual. It's a place to go with friends—a place to be. In a recent ad campaign, Shaich claims that Panera is "a place with soul." Low prices? Not even on the radar.[1]

Panera Bread understands that low prices often aren't the best value. Says Panera CEO Ronald Shaich, "Give people something of value and they'll happily pay for it."
Associated Press

Objective Outline

MyMarketingLab™

⭐ **Improve Your Grade!**

Over 10 million students improved their results using the Pearson MyLabs. Visit **mymktlab.com** for simulations, tutorials, and end-of-chapter problems.

As we learned in the previous chapter, pricing decisions are subject to a complex array of company, environmental, and competitive forces. To make things even more complex, a company does not set a single price but rather a *pricing structure* that covers different items in its line. This pricing structure changes over time as products move through their life cycles. The company adjusts its prices to reflect changes in costs and demand and to account for variations in buyers and situations. As the competitive environment changes, the company considers when to initiate price changes and when to respond to them.

This chapter examines additional pricing approaches used in special pricing situations and adjusting prices to meet changing situations. We then look at *new-product pricing* for products in the introductory stage of the product life cycle, *product mix pricing* for related products in the product mix, *price adjustment tactics* that account for customer differences and changing situations, and strategies for initiating and responding to *price changes*.[2]

Objective 1 ⸺►

Describe the major strategies for pricing new products.

New-Product Pricing Strategies

Pricing strategies usually change as the product passes through its life cycle. The introductory stage is especially challenging. Companies bringing out a new product face the challenge of setting prices for the first time. They can choose between two broad strategies: *market-skimming pricing* and *market-penetration pricing*.

Market-Skimming Pricing

Market-skimming pricing (price skimming)

Setting a high price for a new product to skim maximum revenues layer by layer from the segments willing to pay the high price; the company makes fewer but more profitable sales.

Many companies that invent new products set high initial prices to *skim* revenues layer by layer from the market. Apple frequently uses this strategy, called **market-skimming pricing** (or **price skimming**). When Apple first introduced the iPhone, its initial price was as much as $599 per phone. The phones were purchased only by customers who really wanted the sleek new gadget and could afford to pay a high price for it. Six months later, Apple dropped the price to $399 for an 8-GB model and $499 for the 16-GB model to attract new buyers. Within a year, it dropped prices again to $199 and $299, respectively, and you can now buy a basic 8-GB model for $49. In this way, Apple has skimmed the maximum amount of revenue from the various segments of the market.

Market skimming makes sense only under certain conditions. First, the product's quality and image must support its higher price, and enough buyers must want the product at that price. Second, the costs of producing a smaller volume cannot be so high that they cancel the advantage of charging more. Finally, competitors should not be able to enter the market easily and undercut the high price.

Market-Penetration Pricing

Market-penetration pricing
Setting a low price for a new product in order to attract a large number of buyers and a large market share.

Rather than setting a high initial price to skim off small but profitable market segments, some companies use **market-penetration pricing**. Companies set a low initial price to *penetrate* the market quickly and deeply—to attract a large number of buyers quickly and win a large market share. The high sales volume results in falling costs, allowing companies to cut their prices even further. For example, the giant Swedish retailer IKEA used penetration pricing to boost its success in the Chinese market:[3]

When IKEA first opened stores in China in 2002, people crowded in but not to buy home furnishings. Instead, they stopped by to lounge around, enjoy the free toilets and air conditioning, or even just take a short snooze on a comfy chair or bed on display. Chinese consumers are famously frugal. When it came time to actually buy, they shopped instead at local stores just down the street that offered knockoffs of IKEA's designs at a much lower price. So to turn finicky Chinese consumers into paying customers, IKEA in China cut costs by boosting the proportion of China-made products on its showroom floors and then slashed its prices. Prices on some merchandise dropped to as low as 70 percent below prices in IKEA stores in other parts of the world. The penetration pricing strategy worked. IKEA now captures a 43 percent market share of China's fast-growing home wares market alone, and the sales at its 10 mammoth Chinese stores surged 20 percent last year. ● One store alone in Beijing draws nearly six million visi-

● Penetration pricing: To lure famously frugal Chinese customers, IKEA slashed its prices. The strategy worked. Weekend crowds in many of IKEA's Chinese stores are so big that employees use megaphones to keep shoppers under control.

© Lou Linwei/Alamy

tors annually. Weekend crowds in many of IKEA's Chinese stores are so big that employees use megaphones to keep shoppers under control.

Several conditions must be met for this low-price strategy to work. First, the market must be highly price sensitive so that a low price produces more market growth. Second, production and distribution costs must decrease as sales volume increases. Finally, the low price must help keep out the competition, and the penetration pricer must maintain its low-price position. Otherwise, the price advantage may be only temporary.

Objective 2 ┈┈┈▶
Explain how companies find a set of prices that maximizes the profits from the total product mix.

Product Mix Pricing Strategies

The strategy for setting a product's price often has to be changed when the product is part of a product mix. In this case, the firm looks for a set of prices that maximizes its profits on the total product mix. Pricing is difficult because the various products have related demand and costs and face different degrees of competition. We now take a closer look at the five product mix pricing situations summarized in ● **Table 11.1**: *product line pricing, optional product pricing, captive product pricing, by-product pricing,* and *product bundle pricing.*

● **Table 11.1** | **Product Mix Pricing**

Pricing Situation	Description
Product line pricing	Setting prices across an entire product line
Optional product pricing	Pricing optional or accessory products sold with the main product
Captive product pricing	Pricing products that must be used with the main product
By-product pricing	Pricing low-value by-products to get rid of or make money on them
Product bundle pricing	Pricing bundles of products sold together

Product line pricing
Setting the price steps between various products in a product line based on cost differences between the products, customer evaluations of different features, and competitors' prices.

Optional-product pricing
The pricing of optional or accessory products along with a main product.

Product Line Pricing

Companies usually develop product lines rather than single products. For example, Rossignol offers seven different collections of alpine skis of all designs and sizes, at prices that range from $150 for its junior skis, such as Fun Girl, to more than $1,100 for a pair from its Radical racing collection. It also offers lines of Nordic and backcountry skis, snowboards, and ski-related apparel. In **product line pricing**, management must determine the price steps to set between the various products in a line.

The price steps should take into account cost differences between products in the line. More importantly, they should account for differences in customer perceptions of the value of different features. ● For example, at a Mr. Clean car wash, you can choose from any of six wash packages, ranging from a basic exterior clean-only "Bronze" wash for $5; to an exterior clean, shine, and protect "Gold" package for $12; to an interior-exterior "Signature Shine" package for $27 that includes the works, from a thorough cleaning inside and out to a tire shine, underbody rust inhibitor, surface protectant, and even air freshener. The car wash's task is to establish perceived value differences that support the price differences.

Optional Product Pricing

Many companies use **optional product pricing**—offering to sell optional or accessory products along with the main product. For example, a car buyer may choose to order a navigation system and premium entertainment system. Refrigerators come with optional ice makers. And when you order a new computer, you can select from a bewildering array of processors, hard drives, docking systems, software options, and service plans. Pricing these options is a sticky problem. Companies must decide which items to include in the base price and which to offer as options.

Captive Product Pricing

Companies that make products that must be used along with a main product are using **captive product pricing**. Examples of captive products are razor blade cartridges, videogames, printer cartridges, and e-books. Producers of the main products (razors, video-game consoles, printers, and tablet computers) often price them low and set high markups on the supplies. For example, Amazon introduced its Kindle Fire tablet for as low as $199, a loss of an estimated $10 per machine. It hoped to more than make up for the loss through sales of digital books, music, and movies to be viewed on the devices.[4]

However, companies that use captive product pricing must be careful. Finding the right balance between the main product and captive product prices can be tricky. Even more, consumers trapped into buying expensive

● **Product line pricing:** Mr. Clean car washes offer a complete line of wash packages priced from $5 for the basic Bronze wash to $27 for the feature-loaded Mr. Clean Signature Shine package.

The Procter & Gamble Company

Captive-product pricing

Setting a price for products that must be used along with a main product, such as blades for a razor and games for a video-game console.

captive products may come to resent the brand that ensnared them. Just ask about any customer how he feels after buying a Gillette Fusion ProGlide razor at a giveaway price only to learn later how expensive the replacements cartridge are. The cartridges are so pricy that they've become a high-value target for professional thieves for black-market resale. Moreover, Gillette's captive pricing strategy has invited direct price challenges from competitors such as Schick and the Dollar Shave Club. Recent Schick ads proclaimed that the Schick Hydro 5 is "Preferred over Fusion ProGlide at a better price." And the direct-response Dollar Shave Club asks, "Do you like spending $20 a month on brand-name razors?" As an alternative, it offers twin-blade razors for $1 a month ($3, including shipping and handling), and four- and six-blade models for $6 to $9, shipping and handling included.[5]

In the case of services, captive product pricing is called *two-part pricing*. The price of the service is broken into a *fixed fee* plus a *variable usage rate*. Thus, at Six Flags and other amusement parks, you pay a daily ticket or season pass charge plus additional fees for food and other in-park features.

By-Product Pricing

By-product pricing

Setting a price for by-products in order to make the main product's price more competitive.

Producing products and services often generates by-products. If the by-products have no value and if getting rid of them is costly, this will affect pricing of the main product. Using **by-product pricing**, the company seeks a market for these by-products to help offset the costs of disposing of them and help make the price of the main product more competitive.

The by-products themselves can even turn out to be profitable—turning trash into cash. ● For example, Seattle's Woodland Park Zoo has learned that one of its major by-products—animal poo—can be an excellent source of extra revenue.[6]

What happens to all that poo at the zoo...

● By-Product Pricing: "There's green and money to be made in animal poop!" exclaims Dan Corum, the Woodland Zoo's enthusiastic Compost and Recycling Coordinator (also known as the Prince of Poo, the Emperor of Excrement, the GM of BM, or just plain Dr. Doo).

Biz Kid$ TV Series. www.bizkids.com

"What happens to all that poo at the zoo?" asks a recent video about the Woodland Park Zoo. Not long ago, the answer was that it had to be hauled away to the landfill at a cost of about $60,000 a year. But now, the zoo carefully collects all that poo, turns it into compost, and sells it under its Zoo Doo and Bedspread brands, pitched as "the most exotic and highly prized compost in the Pacific Northwest, composed of exotic species feces contributed by the zoo's non-primate herbivores." Customers can buy these coveted compost products by the bucket at the zoo's store. The zoo also sponsors annual Fecal Fests, where lucky lottery winners can buy the processed poo by the trash can or truck full. "There's green *and* money to be made in animal poop!" exclaims Dan Corum, the Woodland Zoo's enthusiastic compost and recycling coordinator (also known as the prince of poo, the emperor of excrement, the GM of BM, or just plain Dr. Doo). Selling Zoo Doo keeps it out of the landfill, so it's good for the planet. It's also good for the zoo, saving disposal costs and generating $15,000 to $20,000 in annual sales.

Product Bundle Pricing

Product bundle pricing

Combining several products and offering the bundle at a reduced price.

Using **product bundle pricing**, sellers often combine several products and offer the bundle at a reduced price. For example, fast-food restaurants bundle a burger, fries, and a soft drink at a "combo" price. Bath & Body Works offers "three-fer" deals on its soaps and lotions (such as three antibacterial soaps for $10). And Comcast, Time Warner, Verizon, and other telecommunications companies bundle TV service, phone service, and high-speed Internet connections at a low combined price. Price bundling can promote the sales of products consumers might not otherwise buy, but the combined price must be low enough to get them to buy the bundle.

Objective 3 ⸱⸱⸱⸱▶

Discuss how companies adjust their prices to take into account different types of customers and situations.

Price Adjustment Strategies

Companies usually adjust their basic prices to account for various customer differences and changing situations. Here we examine the seven price adjustment strategies summarized in ● **Table 11.2**: *discount and allowance pricing, segmented pricing, psychological pricing, promotional pricing, geographical pricing, dynamic pricing,* and *international pricing.*

● **Table 11.2** | **Price Adjustments**

Strategy	Description
Discount and allowance pricing	Reducing prices to reward customer responses such as volume purchases, paying early, or promoting the product
Segmented pricing	Adjusting prices to allow for differences in customers, products, or locations
Psychological pricing	Adjusting prices for psychological effect
Promotional pricing	Temporarily reducing prices to spur short-run sales
Geographical pricing	Adjusting prices to account for the geographic location of customers
Dynamic pricing	Adjusting prices continually to meet the characteristics and needs of individual customers and situations
International pricing	Adjusting prices for international markets

Discount and Allowance Pricing

Most companies adjust their basic price to reward customers for certain responses, such as paying bills early, volume purchases, and off-season buying. These price adjustments—called *discounts* and *allowances*—can take many forms.

Discount

A straight reduction in price on purchases during a stated period of time or in larger quantities.

One form of **discount** is a *cash discount*, a price reduction to buyers who pay their bills promptly. A typical example is "2/10, net 30," which means that although payment is due within 30 days, the buyer can deduct 2 percent if the bill is paid within 10 days. A *quantity discount* is a price reduction to buyers who buy large volumes. A seller offers a *functional discount* (also called a *trade discount*) to trade-channel members who perform certain functions, such as selling, storing, and record keeping. A *seasonal discount* is a price reduction to buyers who buy merchandise or services out of season.

Allowance

Promotional money paid by manufacturers to retailers in return for an agreement to feature the manufacturer's products in some way.

Allowances are another type of reduction from the list price. For example, *trade-in allowances* are price reductions given for turning in an old item when buying a new one. Trade-in allowances are most common in the automobile industry but are also given for other durable goods. *Promotional allowances* are payments or price reductions that reward dealers for participating in advertising and sales support programs.

Segmented Pricing

Segmented pricing

Selling a product or service at two or more prices, where the difference in prices is not based on differences in costs.

Companies will often adjust their basic prices to allow for differences in customers, products, and locations. In **segmented pricing**, the company sells a product or service at two or more prices, even though the difference in prices is not based on differences in costs.

Segmented pricing takes several forms. Under *customer-segment* pricing, different customers pay different prices for the same product or service. Museums and movie theaters, for example, may charge a lower admission for students and senior citizens. Under *product-form pricing*, different versions of the product are priced differently but not according to differences in their costs. For instance, a round trip economy seat on a flight from New York to London might cost $1,000, whereas a business class seat on the same flight might cost $4,500 or more. Although business class customers receive roomier, more comfortable seats and higher quality food and service, the differences in costs to the airlines are much less than the additional prices to passengers. ● However, to passengers who can afford it, the additional comfort and services are worth the extra charge.

Using *location-based pricing*, a company charges different prices for different locations, even though the cost of offering each location is the same. For instance, state universities charge higher tuition for out-of-state students, and theaters vary their seat prices because of audience preferences for certain locations. Finally, using *time-based pricing*, a firm varies its price by the season, the month, the day, and even the hour. For example, movie theaters charge matinee pricing during the daytime, and resorts give weekend and seasonal discounts.

● **Product-form pricing: A roomier business class seat on a flight from New York to London is many times the price of an economy seat on the same flight. To customers who can afford it, the extra comfort and service are worth the extra charge.**

© Index Stock Imagery

For segmented pricing to be an effective strategy, certain conditions must exist. The market must be segmentable, and segments must show different degrees of demand. The costs of segmenting and reaching the market cannot exceed the extra revenue obtained from the price difference. Of course, the segmented pricing must also be legal.

Most important, segmented prices should reflect real differences in customers' perceived value. Consumers in higher price tiers must feel that they're getting their extra money's worth for the higher prices paid. By the same token, companies must be careful not to treat customers in lower price tiers as second-class citizens. Otherwise, in the long run, the practice will lead to customer resentment and ill will. For example, in recent years, the airlines have incurred the wrath of frustrated customers at both ends of the airplane. Passengers paying full fare for business or first class seats often feel that they are being gouged. At the same time, passengers in lower-priced coach seats feel that they're being ignored or treated poorly.

Psychological Pricing

Price says something about the product. For example, many consumers use price to judge quality. A $100 bottle of perfume may contain only $3 worth of scent, but some people are willing to pay the $100 because this price indicates something special.

Psychological pricing

Pricing that considers the psychology of prices and not simply the economics; the price is used to say something about the product.

In using **psychological pricing**, sellers consider the psychology of prices, not simply the economics. For example, consumers usually perceive higher-priced products as having higher quality. When they can judge the quality of a product by examining it or by calling on past experience with it, they use price less to judge quality. But when they cannot judge quality because they lack the information or skill, price becomes an important quality signal. For instance, who's the better lawyer, one who charges $50 per hour or one who charges $500 per hour? You'd have to do a lot of digging into the respective lawyers' credentials to answer this question objectively; even then, you might not be able to judge accurately. Most of us would simply assume that the higher-priced lawyer is better.

Reference prices

Prices that buyers carry in their minds and refer to when they look at a given product.

Another aspect of psychological pricing is **reference prices**—prices that buyers carry in their minds and refer to when looking at a given product. The reference price might be formed by noting current prices, remembering past prices, or assessing the buying situation. Sellers can influence or use these consumers' reference prices when setting price. For example, a grocery retailer might place its store brand of bran flakes and raisins cereal priced at $1.89 next to Kellogg's Raisin Bran priced at $3.20. Or a company might offer more expensive models that don't sell very well to make their less expensive but still-high-priced models look more affordable by comparison. For example, Williams-Sonoma once offered a fancy bread maker at the steep price of $279. However, it then added a $429 model. The expensive model flopped but sales of the cheaper model doubled.[7]

For most purchases, consumers don't have all the skill or information they need to figure out whether they are paying a good price. They don't have the time, ability, or inclination to research different brands or stores, compare prices, and get the best deals. Instead, they may rely on certain cues that signal whether a price is high or low. Interestingly, such pricing cues are often provided by sellers, in the form of sales signs, price-matching guarantees, loss-leader pricing, and other helpful hints (see Real Marketing 11.1).

Even small differences in price can signal product differences. For example, in one study, people were asked how likely they were to choose among LASIK eye surgery providers based only on the prices they charged: $299 or $300. The actual price difference was only $1, but the study found that the psychological difference was much greater. Preference

Real Marketing 11.1

Quick, What's a Good Price for...? We'll Give You a Cue

It's Saturday morning and you stop by your local supermarket to pick up a few items for tonight's backyard barbeque. Cruising the aisles, you're bombarded with price signs, all suggesting that you just can't beat this store's deals. A 7-pound bag of Kingsford Match Light Charcoal Briquettes goes for only $5.99 with your frequent shopper card ($7.99 without the card). Cans of Van Camps Pork & Beans are at an "everyday low price" of just 99 cents each. An aisle display hawks bags of Ruffles potato chips at two for $5 for a limited time. And a sign atop a huge pyramid of Coke 12-packs advertises three for $9, down from $4.50 each.

These sure look like good prices, but *are* they? If you're like most shoppers, you don't really know. In a recent article, two pricing researchers conclude, "for most of the items they buy, consumers don't have an accurate sense of what the price should be." In fact, customers often don't even know what prices they're actually paying. In one study, researchers asked supermarket shoppers the price of an item just as they were putting it into their shopping carts. Fewer than half the shoppers gave the right answer.

To know for sure if you're paying the best price, you'd have to compare the marked price to past prices, prices of competing brands, and prices in other stores. For most purchases, consumers just don't bother. Instead, they rely on a most unlikely source. "Remarkably, . . . they rely on the retailer to tell them if they're getting a good price," say the researchers. "In subtle and not-so-subtle ways, retailers send signals [or pricing cues] to customers, telling them whether a given price is relatively high or low." In their article, the researchers outline the following common retailer pricing cues.

- *Sale Signs.* The most straightforward retail pricing cue is a sale sign. It might take any of several familiar forms: "Sale!" "Reduced!" "New low price!" "Price after rebate!" or "Now 2 for only . . .!" Such signs can be very effective in signaling low prices to consumers and increasing sales for the retailer. Studies reveal that using the word "sale" beside a price (even without actually varying the price) can increase demand by more than 50 percent.

Sales signs can be effective, but overuse or misuse can damage both the seller's credibility and its sales. Unfortunately, some retailers don't always use such signs truthfully. Still, consumers trust sale signs. Why? Because they are usually accurate. And when they aren't accurate, customers usually know it. They quickly become suspicious when sale signs are used improperly.

- *Prices Ending in 9.* Just like a sale sign, a 9 or 0.99 at the end of a price often signals a bargain. You see such prices everywhere. For example, browse the Web sites of top discounters such as Target, Best Buy, or Overstock.com, where almost every price ends in 9. Given that the tactic is so commonly used, you'd think it would lose its impact. However, according to the researchers, it's still a powerful pricing cue.

Critics have seriously questioned JCPenney's recent decision to abandoned its use of ".99-ending" prices in favor of prices ending in a whole number (for example, $6, $25, or $200)—a tactic generally used only by high-end retailers. The concern has some merit; the 9-endings provide strong price cues. They've been shown to increase demand, even when prices are raised. In one study involving women's clothing, raising the price of a dress from $34 to $39 actually *increased* demand by a third.

But are prices ending in 9 accurate as pricing cues? According to the researchs, it depends. Some retailers do use 9-ending prices only on discounted items. For example, specialty retailers such as J. Crew and Ralph Lauren tend to use 00-cent endings on regularly priced items and 99-cent endings on discounted merchandise. This practice is also common at major department stores. "But at some stores," note the researchers, "prices that end in 9 are a miscue—they are used on all products regardless of whether the items are discounted."

- *Signpost Pricing (or Loss-Leader Pricing).* Unlike sale signs or 9-ending prices, signpost pricing is used on frequently purchased products about which consumers tend to have accurate price knowledge. For example, you probably know a good price on a 12-pack of Coke when you see one. New parents usually know how much they should expect to pay for disposable diapers and laundry detergent. Research suggests that customers use the prices of such "signpost" items to gauge a store's overall prices. If a store has a good price on Coke or Pampers or Tide, they reason, it probably also has good prices on other items.

Retailers have long known the importance of signpost pricing, often called "loss-leader pricing." They offer selected signpost items at or below cost to pull customers into the store, hoping to make money on the shopper's other purchases. For instance, Walmart often sells merchandise at or below cost, especially during holiday seasons. Last year, on Super Saturday, Walmart put out 42-inch Sanyo LCD TVs for $398, Nook e-book readers for $199, and Rival single-cup coffee makers for $4. Although the retailer lost money on every loss-leader item it sold, the low prices increased store traffic and purchases of higher-margin products made during the same shopping trip.

- *Pricing-Matching Guarantees.* Another widely used retail pricing cue is price matching, whereby stores promise to meet or beat any competitor's price. Best Buy, for example, boasts its "Best Buy Price Match Guarantee," a promise to "match the price if you find a lower price on an identical available product at a local retail competitor's store." This policy holds throughout the 30-day return period.

Evidence suggests that customers perceive that stores offering price-matching

Pricing cues provided by retailers, such as sales signs and prices ending in 9, can provide helpful price hints to consumers, telling them whether a given price is relatively high or low.

Bloomberg via Getty Images

guarantees have overall lower prices than competing stores, especially in markets where they perceive price comparisons to be relatively easy. But are such perceptions accurate? "The evidence is mixed," say the researchers. Consumers can usually be confident that they'll pay the lowest price on eligible items. However, some manufacturers make it hard to take advantage of price-matching policies by introducing "branded variants"—slightly different versions of products with different model numbers for different retailers.

Used properly, pricing cues can help consumers. Careful buyers really can take advantage of signals such as sale signs, 9-endings,

loss-leaders, and price guarantees to locate good deals. Used improperly, however, these pricing cues can mislead consumers, tarnishing a brand and damaging customer relationships.

The researchers conclude that retailers should manage pricing cues in the same way that they manage merchandise quality, facilities, or any other store decision—with an eye

toward building strong long-run customer relationships. "No retailer . . . in [building customer relationships] would purposely offer a defective product. Similarly, no retailer who [values customers] would deceive them with inaccurate pricing cues. By reliably signaling which prices are low, companies can retain customers' trust—and [build better relationships]."

Sources: Quotes and other information from Eric Anderson and Duncan Simester, "Mind Your Pricing Cues," *Harvard Business Review,* September 2003, pp. 96–103; Jessica Dickler, "Wal-Mart to Leak Its Own Black Friday Deals," *CNNMoney,* November 2, 2011, http://money.cnn.com/2011/11/02/pf/walmart_black_friday/index.htm; Qin Zhang, P. B. Seetharaman, and Chakravarthi Narasimhan, "The Indirect Impact of Price Deals on Households' Purchase Decisions through the Formation of Expected Future Prices," *Journal of Retailing*, March, 2012, pp. 88–101; and B. P. S. Murthi and Ram Rao, "Price Awareness and Consumers' Use of Deals in Brand Choice," *Journal of Retailing*, March 2012, pp. 34–46.

ratings for the providers charging $300 were much higher. Subjects perceived the $299 price as significantly less, but the lower price also raised stronger concerns about quality and risk.[8] Some psychologists even argue that each digit has symbolic and visual qualities that should be considered in pricing. Thus, eight (8) is round and even and creates a soothing effect, whereas seven (7) is angular and creates a jarring effect.

Promotional pricing
Temporarily pricing products below the list price, and sometimes even below cost, to increase short-run sales.

Promotional Pricing

With **promotional pricing**, companies will temporarily price their products below list price—and sometimes even below cost—to create buying excitement and urgency. ● Promotional pricing takes several forms. A seller may simply offer *discounts* from normal prices to increase sales and reduce inventories. Sellers also use *special-event pricing* in certain seasons to draw more customers. Thus, TVs and other consumer electronics are promotionally priced in November and December to attract holiday shoppers into the stores. *Limited-time offers,* such as online *flash sales,* can create buying urgency and make buyers feel lucky to have gotten in on the deal.

Manufacturers sometimes offer *cash rebates* to consumers who buy the product from dealers within a specified time; the manufacturer sends the rebate directly to the customer. Rebates have been popular with automakers and producers of mobile phones and small appliances, but they are also used with consumer packaged goods. Some manufacturers offer *low-interest financing, longer warranties,* or *free maintenance* to reduce the consumer's "price." This practice has become another favorite of the auto industry.

● **Promotional pricing: Companies offer promotional prices to create buying excitement and urgency.**

Bloomberg via Getty Images

Promotional pricing, however, can have adverse effects. During most holiday seasons, for example, it's an all-out bargain war. Marketers carpet-bomb consumers with deals, causing buyer wear-out and pricing confusion. Used too frequently, price promotions can create "deal-prone" customers who wait until brands go on sale before buying them. In addition, constantly reduced prices can erode a brand's value in the eyes of customers.

Marketers sometimes become addicted to promotional pricing, especially in difficult economic times. They use price promotions as a quick fix instead of sweating through the difficult process of developing effective longer-term strategies for building their brands. For example, as we learned in the JCPenney story at the beginning of Chapter 10, before announcing its turnaround pricing strategy, Penney's developed an unhealthy reliance on coupons, markdowns, and nonstop sales, which accounted for the vast majority of its revenues. But companies must be careful to balance short-term sales incentives against long-term brand building. Some promotional pricing can be an effective means of generating sales in certain circumstances. But as JCPenney learned, a steady diet of promotional pricing can be destructive to a brand's image and profitability.[9]

Geographical Pricing

A company also must decide how to price its products for customers located in different parts of the United States or the world. Should the company risk losing the business of more-distant customers by charging them higher prices to cover the higher shipping costs? Or should the company charge all customers the same prices regardless of location? We will look at five **geographical pricing** strategies for the following hypothetical situation:

> The Peerless Paper Company is located in Atlanta, Georgia, and sells paper products to customers all over the United States. The cost of freight is high and affects the companies from whom customers buy their paper. Peerless wants to establish a geographical pricing policy. It is trying to determine how to price a $10,000 order to three specific customers: Customer A (Atlanta), Customer B (Bloomington, Indiana), and Customer C (Compton, California).

One option is for Peerless to ask each customer to pay the shipping cost from the Atlanta factory to the customer's location. All three customers would pay the same factory price of $10,000, with Customer A paying, say, $100 for shipping; Customer B, $150; and Customer C, $250. Called **FOB-origin pricing**, this practice means that the goods are placed *free on board* (hence, *FOB*) a carrier. At that point the title and responsibility pass to the customer, who pays the freight from the factory to the destination. Because each customer picks up its own cost, supporters of FOB pricing feel that this is the fairest way to assess freight charges. The disadvantage, however, is that Peerless will be a high-cost firm to distant customers.

Uniform-delivered pricing is the opposite of FOB pricing. Here, the company charges the same price plus freight to all customers, regardless of their location. The freight charge is set at the average freight cost. Suppose this is $150. Uniform-delivered pricing therefore results in a higher charge to the Atlanta customer (who pays $150 freight instead of $100) and a lower charge to the Compton customer (who pays $150 instead of $250). Although the Atlanta customer would prefer to buy paper from another local paper company that uses FOB-origin pricing, Peerless has a better chance of capturing the California customer.

Zone pricing falls between FOB-origin pricing and uniform-delivered pricing. The company sets up two or more zones. All customers within a given zone pay a single total price; the more distant the zone, the higher the price. For example, Peerless might set up an East Zone and charge $100 freight to all customers in this zone, a Midwest Zone in which it charges $150, and a West Zone in which it charges $250. In this way, the customers within a given price zone receive no price advantage from the company. For example, customers in Atlanta and Boston pay the same total price to Peerless. The complaint, however, is that the Atlanta customer is paying part of the Boston customer's freight cost.

Using **basing-point pricing**, the seller selects a given city as a "basing point" and charges all customers the freight cost from that city to the customer location, regardless of the city from which the goods are actually shipped. For example, Peerless might set Chicago as the basing point and charge all customers $10,000 plus the freight from Chicago to their locations. This means that an Atlanta customer pays the freight cost from Chicago to Atlanta, even though the goods may be shipped from Atlanta. If all sellers used the same basing-point city, delivered prices would be the same for all customers, and price competition would be eliminated.

Geographical pricing
Setting prices for customers located in different parts of the country or world.

FOB-origin pricing
A geographical pricing strategy in which goods are placed free on board a carrier; the customer pays the freight from the factory to the destination.

Uniform-delivered pricing
A geographical pricing strategy in which the company charges the same price plus freight to all customers, regardless of their location.

Zone pricing
A geographical pricing strategy in which the company sets up two or more zones. All customers within a zone pay the same total price; the more distant the zone, the higher the price.

Basing-point pricing
A geographical pricing strategy in which the seller designates some city as a basing point and charges all customers the freight cost from that city to the customer.

Freight-absorption pricing

A geographical pricing strategy in which the seller absorbs all or part of the freight charges in order to get the desired business.

Finally, the seller who is anxious to do business with a certain customer or geographical area might use **freight-absorption pricing**. Using this strategy, the seller absorbs all or part of the actual freight charges to get the desired business. The seller might reason that if it can get more business, its average costs will decrease and more than compensate for its extra freight cost. Freight-absorption pricing is used for market penetration and to hold on to increasingly competitive markets.

Dynamic and Internet Pricing

Throughout most of history, prices were set by negotiation between buyers and sellers. *Fixed price* policies—setting one price for all buyers—is a relatively modern idea that arose with the development of large-scale retailing at the end of the nineteenth century. Today, most prices are set this way. However, some companies are now reversing the fixed pricing trend. They are using **dynamic pricing**—adjusting prices continually to meet the characteristics and needs of individual customers and situations.

Dynamic pricing

Adjusting prices continually to meet the characteristics and needs of individual customers and situations.

Dynamic pricing is especially prevalent online, where the Internet seems to be taking us back to a new age of fluid pricing. Such pricing offers many advantages for marketers. For example, Internet sellers such as L.L. Bean, Amazon.com, or Dell can mine their databases to gauge a specific shopper's desires, measure his or her means, instantaneously tailor offers to fit that shopper's behavior, and price products accordingly. Services ranging from airlines and hotels to sports teams change prices on the fly according to changes in demand or costs, adjusting what they charge for specific items on a day-by-day or even hour-by-hour basis. And many direct marketers monitor inventories, costs, and demand at any given moment and adjust prices instantly.

In the extreme, some companies customize their offers and prices based on the specific characteristics and behaviors of individual customers, mined from online browsing and purchasing histories. These days, online offers and prices might well be based on what specific customers search for and buy, how much they pay for other purchases, and whether they might be willing and able to spend more. For example, a consumer who recently went online to purchase a first-class ticket to London or customize a new Mercedes coupe might later get a higher quote on a new Bose Wave Radio. By comparison, a friend with a more modest online search and purchase history might receive an offer of five percent off and free shipping on the same radio.[10]

Although such dynamic pricing practices seem legally questionable, they're not. Dynamic pricing is legal as long as companies do not discriminate based on age, sex, location, or other similar characteristics. Dynamic pricing makes sense in many contexts—it adjusts prices according to market forces and consumer preferences. But marketers need to be careful not to use dynamic pricing to take advantage of certain customer groups, thereby damaging important customer relationships.

The practice of online pricing, however, goes both ways, and consumers often benefit from the online and dynamic pricing. Thanks to the Internet, the centuries-old art of haggling is suddenly back in vogue. For example, consumers can negotiate prices at online auction sites and exchanges. Want to sell that antique pickle jar that's been collecting dust for generations? Post it on eBay or Craigslist. Want to name your own price for a hotel room or rental car? Visit Priceline.com or another reverse auction site. Want to bid on a ticket to a Katy Perry concert? Check out Ticketmaster.com, which offers an online auction service for concert tickets.

Also thanks to the Internet, consumers can get instant product and price comparisons from thousands of vendors at price comparison sites such as Yahoo! Shopping, Epinions.com, PriceGrabber.com, and PriceScan.com, or using ● mobile apps such as TheFind, eBay's RedLaser, Google's Barcode Scanner, or Amazon.com's PriceCheck. For example, the RedLaser mobile app lets customers scan barcodes or QR codes (or search by voice or image) while shopping in stores. It then searches online and at nearby stores to provide thousands of reviews and comparison prices, and even offers buying links for immediate online purchasing. Armed with this information, consumers can often negotiate better in-store prices.

In fact, many retailers are finding that ready online access to comparison prices is giving consumers *too* much of an edge. Store retailers ranging from Target and Best Buy to Brookstone and GNC are now devising strategies to combat the consumer practice of *showrooming*. Increasing, consumers armed with smartphones come to stores to see

RedLaser

Shop Smarter

RedLaser is a free shopping app for iPhone, Windows Phones, and Android that has been downloaded over 18 million times.

Download App!

● **Dynamic and Internet pricing: Using mobile apps such as eBay's RedLaser, consumers can scan barcodes or QR codes while shopping in stores and receive product reviews, availability information, and comparison prices for online and nearby stores.**

These materials have been reproduced with the permission of eBay Inc. © 2012 EBAY INC. ALL RIGHTS RESERVED.

an item, compare prices online while in the store, and then buy the item online at a lower price. Such behavior is called *showrooming* because consumers use store retailers as de facto "showrooms" for online resellers such as Amazon.com. In fact, Amazon.com encourages showrooming: It recently ran a promotion on its PriceCheck shopping app that gave customers discounts on qualifying items if they checked the prices for those items at Amazon.com while browsing at a physical store. To counter showrooming, store retailers must either match online prices or work with manufacturers to develop exclusive or store-branded merchandise on which price comparisons cannot be made.[11]

International Pricing

Companies that market their products internationally must decide what prices to charge in different countries. In some cases, a company can set a uniform worldwide price. For example, Boeing sells its jetliners at about the same price everywhere, whether the buyer is in the United States, Europe, or a third-world country. However, most companies adjust their prices to reflect local market conditions and cost considerations.

The price that a company should charge in a specific country depends on many factors, including economic conditions, competitive situations, laws and regulations, and the nature of the wholesaling and retailing system. Consumer perceptions and preferences also may vary from country to country, calling for different prices. Or the company may have different marketing objectives in various world markets, which require changes in pricing strategy. For example, Nokia might introduce sophisticated, feature-rich mobile phones into carefully segmented mature markets in highly developed countries—this would call for a market-skimming pricing strategy. By contrast, it might enter sizable but less affluent markets in developing countries with more basic phones, supported by a penetration-pricing strategy.

Costs play an important role in setting international prices. Travelers abroad are often surprised to find that goods that are relatively inexpensive at home may carry outrageously higher price tags in other countries. A pair of Levi's selling for $30 in the United States might go for $63 in Tokyo and $88 in Paris. ● A McDonald's Big Mac selling for a modest $3.79 in the United States might cost $6.80 in Switzerland or $5.00 in Russia, and an Oral-B toothbrush selling for $2.49 at home may cost $10 in China. Conversely, a Gucci handbag going for only $140 in Milan, Italy, might fetch $240 in the United States. In some cases, such *price escalation* may result from differences in selling strategies or market conditions. In most instances, however, it is simply a result of the higher costs of selling in another country—the additional costs of operations, product modifications, shipping and insurance, import tariffs and taxes, exchange-rate fluctuations, and physical distribution.

Price has become a key element in the international marketing strategies of companies attempting to enter emerging markets. Typically, entering such markets has meant targeting the exploding middle classes in developing countries such as China, India, Russia, and Brazil, whose economies have been growing by double-digits annually. More recently, however, as the weakened global economy has slowed growth in both domestic and emerging markets, many companies are shifting their sights to include a new

● **Companies that market internationally must decide what prices to charge in different countries.**

Prentice Hall School Division

target—the so-called "bottom of the pyramid," the vast untapped market consisting of the world's poorest consumers. In this market, price is a major consideration. Consider Unilever's pricing strategy for developing countries:[12]

> Not long ago, the preferred way for many Western companies to market their products in developing markets such as India was to paste new labels on them and sell them at premium prices to the privileged few who could afford them. However, when Unilever—the maker of such brands as Dove, Lipton, and Vaseline—realized that such pricing put its products out of the reach of tens of millions of Indian consumers, it forged a different approach. It shrunk its packaging and set low prices that even the world's poorest consumers could afford. By developing single-use packages of its shampoo, laundry detergent, and other products, Unilever can make a profit while selling its brands for just pennies a pack. As a result, today, more than 50 percent of Unilever's revenues come from emerging economies.

Although this strategy has been successful for Unilever, most companies are learning that selling profitably to the bottom of the pyramid requires more than just repackaging or stripping down existing products and selling them at low prices. Just like more well-to-do consumers, low-income consumers want products that are both functional *and* aspirational. Thus, companies today are innovating to create products that not only sell at very low prices but also give bottom-of-the-pyramid consumers more for their money, not less (see Real Marketing 11.2).

International pricing presents many special problems and complexities. We discuss international pricing issues in more detail in Chapter 19.

Objective 4 ┈┈▶

Discuss the key issues related to initiating and responding to price changes.

Price Changes

After developing their pricing structures and strategies, companies often face situations in which they must initiate price changes or respond to price changes by competitors.

Initiating Price Changes

In some cases, the company may find it desirable to initiate either a price cut or a price increase. In both cases, it must anticipate possible buyer and competitor reactions.

Initiating Price Cuts

Several situations may lead a firm to consider cutting its price. One such circumstance is excess capacity. Another is falling demand in the face of strong price competition or a weakened economy. In such cases, the firm may aggressively cut prices to boost sales and market share. But as the airline, fast-food, automobile, and other industries have learned in recent years, cutting prices in an industry loaded with excess capacity may lead to price wars as competitors try to hold onto market share.

A company may also cut prices in a drive to dominate the market through lower costs. Either the company starts with lower costs than its competitors, or it cuts prices in the hope of gaining market share that will further cut costs through larger volume. For example, Lenovo uses an aggressive low-cost, low-price strategy to increase its share of the PC market in developing countries.

Initiating Price Increases

A successful price increase can greatly improve profits. ● For example, if the company's profit margin is 3 percent of sales, a 1 percent price increase will boost profits by 33 percent if sales volume is unaffected. A major factor in price increases is cost inflation. Rising costs squeeze profit margins and lead companies to pass cost increases along to customers. Another factor leading to price increases is overdemand: When a company cannot supply all that its customers need, it may raise its prices, ration products to customers, or both. Consider today's worldwide oil and gas industry.

When raising prices, the company must avoid being perceived as a *price gouger*. For example, when gasoline prices rise rapidly, angry customers often accuse the major

● **Initiating price increases: When gasoline prices rise rapidly, angry consumers often accuse the major oil companies of enriching themselves by gouging customers.**

Louis DeLuca/Dallas Morning News/Corbis

Real Marketing 11.2

International Pricing: Targeting the Bottom of the Pyramid

Many companies are now waking up to a shocking statistic. Of the roughly 7 billion people on this planet, 4 billion of them (that's 57 percent) live in poverty. Known as the "bottom of the pyramid," the world's poor might not seem like a promising market. However, despite their paltry incomes, as a group, these consumers represent an eye-popping $5 trillion in annual purchasing power. Moreover, this vast segment is largely untapped. The world's poor often have little or no access to even the most basic products and services taken for granted by more affluent consumers. As the weakened global economy has flattened domestic markets and slowed the growth of emerging middle-class markets, companies are increasingly looking to the bottom of the pyramid for fresh growth opportunities.

But how can a company sell profitably to consumers with incomes below the poverty level? For starters, the *price* has got to be right. And in this case, says one analyst, "right" means "lower than you can imagine." With this in mind, many companies have made their products more affordable simply by offering smaller package sizes or lower-tech versions of current products. For example, in Nigeria, P&G sells a Gillette razor for 23 cents, a 1-ounce package of Ariel detergent for about 10 cents, and a 10-count pack of one-diaper-a-night Pampers for $2.30. Although there isn't much margin on products selling for pennies apiece, P&G is succeeding through massive volume.

Consider Pampers: In Nigeria alone, 6 million babies are born each year, compared with 4.4 million in the United States, a country with twice the population. Nigeria's astounding birthrate creates a huge, untapped market for Pampers diapers, P&G's top-selling brand. However, the typical Nigerian mother spends only about 5,000 naira a month, about $30, on household purchases. P&G's task is to make Pampers affordable to this mother and to convince her that Pampers are worth some of her scarce spending. To keep costs and prices low in markets like Nigeria, P&G invented an absorbent but fewer-featured diaper. Although much less expensive, the diaper still functions at a high level. When creating such affordable new products, says an R&D manager at P&G, "Delight, don't dilute." That is, the diaper needs to be priced low, but it also has to do what other cheap diapers don't—keep a baby comfortable and dry for 12 hours.

Even with the right diaper at the right price, selling Pampers in Nigeria presents a challenge. In the West, babies typically go through numerous disposable diapers a day. In Nigeria, however, most babies are in cloth diapers. To make Pampers more acceptable and even more affordable for Nigerians, P&G markets the diapers as a one-a-day item. According to company ads, "One Pampers equals one dry night." The campaign tells mothers that keeping babies dry at night helps them to get a good night's sleep, which in turn helps them to grow and achieve. The message taps into a deep sentiment among Nigerians, unearthed by P&G researchers, that their children will have a better life than they do. Thus, thanks to affordable pricing, a product that meets customers' needs, and relevant positioning, Pampers sales are booming. In Nigeria, the name Pampers is now synonymous with diapers.

As P&G has learned, in most cases, selling profitably to the bottom of the pyramid takes much more than just developing single-use packets and pennies-apiece pricing. It requires broad-based innovation that produces not just lower prices but also new products that give people in poverty more for their money, not less. As another example, consider how Indian appliance company Godrej & Boyce used customer-driven innovation to successfully tap the market for low-priced refrigerators in India:

> Because of their high cost to both buy and operate, traditional compressor-driven refrigerators had penetrated only 18 percent of the Indian market. But rather than just produce a cheaper, stripped-down version of its higher-end refrigerators, Godrej assigned a team to study the needs of Indian consumers with poor or no refrigeration. The semi-urban and rural people the team observed typically earned 5,000 to 8,000 rupees (about $125 to $200) a month, lived in single-room dwellings with four or five family members, and changed residences frequently. Unable to

To lower prices in developing countries, Unilever developed smaller, more affordable packages that put the company's premier brands within the reach of cash-strapped customers.

Courtesy Godrej & Boyce Mfg. Co. Ltd.

afford conventional refrigerators, these consumers were making do with communal, usually second-hand ones. But even the shared fridges usually contained only a few items. Their users tended to shop daily and buy only small quantities of vegetables and milk. Moreover, electricity was unreliable, putting even the little food they wanted to keep cool at risk.

Godrej concluded that the low-end segment had little need for a conventional high-end refrigerator; it needed a fundamentally new product. So Godrej invented the Chotu-Kool ("little cool"), a candy red, top-opening, highly-portable, dorm-size unit that has room for the few items users want to keep fresh for a day or two. Rather than a compressor and refrigerant, the miserly little unit uses a chip that cools when current is applied, and its top-opening design keeps cold air inside when the lid is opened. In all, the ChotuKool uses less than half the energy of a conventional refrigerator and can run on a battery during the power outages common in rural villages. The best part: At only $69, "little cool"

does a better job of meeting the needs of low-end consumers at half the price of even the most basic traditional refrigerator.

Thus, the bottom of the pyramid offers huge untapped opportunities to companies that can develop the right products at the right prices. And companies such as P&G are moving aggressively to capture these opportunities. P&G CEO and Chairman Robert McDonald has set a lofty goal of 1 billion new customers by 2015, moving the company's emphasis from the developed West, where it currently gets most of its revenue, to the developing economies of Asia and Africa.

But successfully tapping these new developing markets will require more than just shipping out cheaper versions of existing products. "Our innovation strategy is not just diluting the top-tier product for the lower-end consumer," says McDonald. "You have to discretely innovate for every one of those consumers on that economic curve, and if you don't do that, you'll fail."

Sources: Quotes, extracts, and other information from or based on David Holthaus, "Pampers: P&G's No. 1 Growth Brand," Cincinnati.com, April 17, 2011, http://news.cincinnati.com/article/20110417/BIZ01/104170337/Pampers-P-G-s-No-1-growth-brand; Mya Frazier, "How P&G Brought the Diaper Revolution to China," *CBS News*, January 7, 2010, www.cbsnews.com/8301-505125_162-51379838/how-pg-brought-the-diaper-revolution-to-china/; David Holthaus, "Health Talk First, Then a Sales Pitch," April 17, 2011, Cincinnati.com, http://news.cincinnati.com/apps/pbcs.dll/article?AID=/20110417/BIZ01/104170344/&template=artiphone; Matthew J. Eyring, Mark W. Johnson, and Hari Nair, "New Business Models in Emerging Markets," *Harvard Business Review,* January–February 2011, pp. 89–95; and C. K. Prahalad, "Bottom of the Pyramid as a Source of Breakthrough Innovations," *Journal of Product Innovation Management*, January 2012, pp. 6–12.

oil companies of enriching themselves at the expense of consumers. Customers have long memories, and they will eventually turn away from companies or even whole industries that they perceive as charging excessive prices. In the extreme, claims of price gouging may even bring about increased government regulation.

There are some techniques for avoiding these problems. One is to maintain a sense of fairness surrounding any price increase. Price increases should be supported by company communications telling customers why prices are being raised.

Wherever possible, the company should consider ways to meet higher costs or demand without raising prices. For example, it might consider more cost-effective ways to produce or distribute its products. It can shrink the product or substitute less-expensive ingredients instead of raising the price, as ConAgra did in an effort to hold its Banquet frozen dinner prices at $1. Or it can "unbundle" its market offering, removing features, packaging, or services and separately pricing elements that were formerly part of the offer.

Buyer Reactions to Price Changes

Customers do not always interpret price changes in a straightforward way. A price *increase*, which would normally lower sales, may have some positive meanings for buyers. For example, what would you think if Rolex *raised* the price of its latest watch model? On the one hand, you might think that the watch is even more exclusive or better made. On the other hand, you might think that Rolex is simply being greedy by charging what the traffic will bear.

Similarly, consumers may view a price *cut* in several ways. For example, what would you think if Rolex were to suddenly cut its prices? You might think that you are getting a better deal on an exclusive product. More likely, however, you'd think that quality had been reduced, and the brand's luxury image might be tarnished. A brand's price and image are often closely linked. A price change, especially a drop in price, can adversely affect how consumers view the brand.

Competitor Reactions to Price Changes

A firm considering a price change must worry about the reactions of its competitors as well as those of its customers. Competitors are most likely to react when the number of firms involved is small, when the product is uniform, and when the buyers are well informed about products and prices.

How can the firm anticipate the likely reactions of its competitors? The problem is complex because, like the customer, the competitor can interpret a company price cut in many ways. It might think the company is trying to grab a larger market share or that it's doing poorly and trying to boost its sales. Or it might think that the company wants the whole industry to cut prices to increase total demand.

The company must guess each competitor's likely reaction. If all competitors behave alike, this amounts to analyzing only a typical competitor. In contrast, if the competitors do not behave alike—perhaps because of differences in size, market shares, or policies—then separate analyses are necessary. However, if some competitors will match the price change, there is good reason to expect that the rest will also match it.

Responding to Price Changes

Here we reverse the question and ask how a firm should respond to a price change by a competitor. The firm needs to consider several issues: Why did the competitor change the price? Is the price change temporary or permanent? What will happen to the company's market share and profits if it does not respond? Are other competitors going to respond? Besides these issues, the company must also consider its own situation and strategy and possible customer reactions to price changes.

● **Figure 11.1** shows the ways a company might assess and respond to a competitor's price cut. Suppose the company learns that a competitor has cut its price and decides that this price cut is likely to harm its sales and profits. It might simply decide to hold its current price and profit margin. The company might believe that it will not lose too much market share, or that it would lose too much profit if it reduced its own price. Or it might decide that it should wait and respond when it has more information on the effects of the competitor's price change. However, waiting too long to act might let the competitor get stronger and more confident as its sales increase.

If the company decides that effective action can and should be taken, it might make any of four responses. First, it could *reduce its price* to match the competitor's price. It may decide that the market is price sensitive and that it would lose too much market share to the lower-priced competitor. However, cutting the price will reduce the company's profits in the short run. Some companies might also reduce their product quality, services, and marketing communications to retain profit margins, but this will ultimately hurt long-run market share. The company should try to maintain its quality as it cuts prices.

Alternatively, the company might maintain its price but *raise the perceived value* of its offer. It could improve its communications, stressing the relative value of its product over that of the lower-price competitor. The firm may find it cheaper to maintain price and spend money to improve its perceived value than to cut price and operate at a lower margin. Or, the company might *improve* quality *and increase price*, moving its brand into a higher price-value position. The higher quality creates greater customer value, which justifies the higher

● **FIGURE** │ 11.1

Assessing and Responding to Competitor Price Changes

When a competitor cuts prices, a company's first reaction may be to drop its prices as well. But that is often the wrong response. Instead, the firm may want to emphasize the "value" side of the price-value equation.

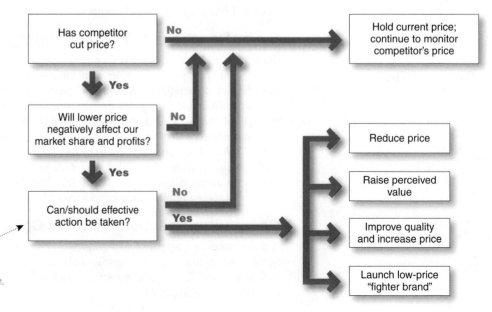

● **Fighter brands: Starbucks has positioned its Seattle's Best Coffee unit to compete more directly with the "mass-premium" brands sold buy Dunkin' Donuts, McDonald's, and other lower-priced competitors.**

AP Images/Eric Risberg

price. In turn, the higher price preserves the company's higher margins.

Finally, the company might *launch a low-price "fighter brand"*—adding a lower-price item to the line or creating a separate lower-price brand. This is necessary if the particular market segment being lost is price sensitive and will not respond to arguments of higher quality. ● Starbucks did this when it acquired Seattle's Best Coffee, a brand positioned with working class, "approachable-premium" appeal compared to the more professional, full-premium appeal of the main Starbucks brand. Seattle's Best coffee is generally cheaper than the parent Starbucks brand. As such, at retail, it competes more directly with Dunkin' Donuts, McDonald's, and other mass-premium brands through its franchise outlets and through partnerships with Subway, Burger King, Delta, AMC theaters, Royal Caribbean cruise lines, and others. On supermarket shelves, it competes with store brands and other mass-premium coffees such as Folgers Gourmet Selections and Millstone.[13]

To counter store brands and other low-price entrants in a tighter economy, P&G turned a number of its brands into fighter brands. Luvs disposable diapers give parents "premium leakage protection for less than pricier brands." And P&G offers popular budget-priced basic versions of several of its major brands. For example, Charmin Basic "holds up at a great everyday price," and Bounty Basic is "more durable than the leading bargain brand." However, companies must use caution when introducing fighter brands, as such brands can tarnish the image of the main brand. In addition, although they may attract budget buyers away from lower-priced rivals, they can also take business away from the firm's higher-margin brands.

Public Policy and Pricing

Objective 5 ┄┄►
Overview the social and legal issues that affect pricing decisions.

Price competition is a core element of our free-market economy. In setting prices, companies usually are not free to charge whatever prices they wish. Many federal, state, and even local laws govern the rules of fair play in pricing. In addition, companies must consider broader societal pricing concerns. In setting their prices, for example, pharmaceutical firms must balance their development costs and profit objectives against the sometimes life-and-death needs of drug consumers.

The most important pieces of legislation affecting pricing are the Sherman Act, the Clayton Act, and the Robinson-Patman Act, initially adopted to curb the formation of monopolies and regulate business practices that might unfairly restrain trade. Because these federal statutes can be applied only to interstate commerce, some states have adopted similar provisions for companies that operate locally.

● **Figure 11.2** shows the major public policy issues in pricing. These include potentially damaging pricing practices within a given level of the channel (price-fixing and

● **FIGURE | 11.2**
Public Policy Issues in Pricing
Source: Based on Dhruv Grewal and Larry D. Compeau, "Pricing and Public Policy: A Research Agenda and Overview of the Special Issues," *Journal of Public Policy and Marketing*, Spring 1999, pp. 3–10.

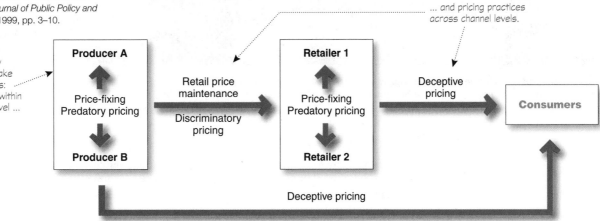

... and pricing practices across channel levels.

Major public policy issues in pricing take place at two levels: Pricing practices within a given channel level ...

| Producer A |
| Price-fixing Predatory pricing |
| Producer B |

Retail price maintenance

Discriminatory pricing

| Retailer 1 |
| Price-fixing Predatory pricing |
| Retailer 2 |

Deceptive pricing

Consumers

Deceptive pricing

predatory pricing) and across levels of the channel (retail price maintenance, discriminatory pricing, and deceptive pricing).[14]

Pricing within Channel Levels

Federal legislation on *price-fixing* states that sellers must set prices without talking to competitors. Otherwise, price collusion is suspected. Price-fixing is illegal per se—that is, the government does not accept any excuses for price-fixing. As such, companies found guilty of these practices can receive heavy fines. Recently, governments at the state and national levels have been aggressively enforcing price-fixing regulations in industries ranging from gasoline, insurance, and concrete to credit cards, CDs, and computer chips. Price-fixing is also prohibited in many international markets. For example, European Union regulators recently fined consumer products giants Unilever and P&G a combined $456 million for fixing laundry detergent prices in eight EU countries. France also fined the two consumer products giants, along with competitors Colgate and Henkel. It claimed that officials from the four companies met regularly at hotels and restaurants in Paris to agree to limits on the size of discounts and on prices differences between their laundry detergent brands.[15]

Sellers are also prohibited from using *predatory pricing*—selling below cost with the intention of punishing a competitor or gaining higher long-run profits by putting competitors out of business. This protects small sellers from larger ones who might sell items below cost temporarily or in a specific locale to drive them out of business. The biggest problem is determining just what constitutes predatory pricing behavior. Selling below cost to unload excess inventory is not considered predatory; selling below cost to drive out competitors is. Thus, a given action may or may not be predatory depending on intent, and intent can be very difficult to determine or prove.

In recent years, several large and powerful companies have been accused of predatory pricing. However, turning an accusation into a lawsuit can be difficult. ● For example, many publishers and booksellers have expressed concerns about Amazon.com's predatory practices, especially book pricing:[16]

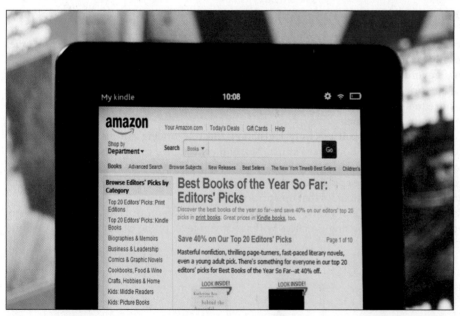

Many booksellers and publishers complain that Amazon.com's book pricing policies are destroying their industry. During past holiday seasons, Amazon has sold top-10 bestselling hardback books as loss leaders at cut-rate prices of less than $10 each. And Amazon now sells e-books at fire-sale prices in order to win customers for its Kindle e-reader. Such very low book prices have caused considerable damage to competing booksellers, many of whom view Amazon's pricing actions as predatory. Says one observer, "The word 'predator' is pretty strong, and I don't use it loosely, but . . . I could have sworn we had laws against predatory pricing. I just don't understand why [Amazon's pricing] is not an issue." Still, no predatory pricing charges have ever been filed against Amazon. It would be extremely difficult to prove that such loss-leader pricing is purposefully predatory as opposed to just plain good competitive marketing.

● **Predatory pricing: Some industry critics have accused Amazon.com of pricing books at fire-sales prices that harm competing booksellers. But is it predatory pricing or just plain good competitive marketing?**

Christopher Schall/Impact Photo

Pricing across Channel Levels

The Robinson-Patman Act seeks to prevent unfair *price discrimination* by ensuring that sellers offer the same price terms to customers at a given level of trade. For example, every retailer is entitled to the same price terms from a given manufacturer, whether the retailer is REI or your local bicycle shop. However, price discrimination is allowed if the seller can prove that its costs are different when selling to different retailers—for example, that it costs less per unit to sell a large volume of bicycles to REI than to sell a few bicycles to the local dealer.

The seller can also discriminate in its pricing if the seller manufactures different qualities of the same product for different retailers. The seller has to prove that these differences are proportional. Price differentials may also be used to "match competition" in "good faith," provided the price discrimination is temporary, localized, and defensive rather than offensive.

Laws also prohibit *retail (or resale) price maintenance*—a manufacturer cannot require dealers to charge a specified retail price for its product. Although the seller can propose a manufacturer's *suggested* retail price to dealers, it cannot refuse to sell to a dealer that takes independent pricing action nor can it punish the dealer by shipping late or denying advertising allowances. For example, the Florida attorney general's office investigated Nike for allegedly fixing the retail price of its shoes and clothing. It was concerned that Nike might be withholding items from retailers who were not selling its most expensive shoes at prices the company considered suitable.

Deceptive pricing occurs when a seller states prices or price savings that mislead consumers or are not actually available to consumers. This might involve bogus reference or comparison prices, as when a retailer sets artificially high "regular" prices and then announces "sale" prices close to its previous everyday prices. For example, Overstock.com recently came under scrutiny for inaccurately listing manufacturer's suggested retail prices, often quoting them higher than the actual price. Such comparison pricing is widespread.

Although comparison pricing claims are legal if they are truthful, the FTC's "Guides against Deceptive Pricing" warn sellers not to advertise (1) a price reduction unless it is a savings from the usual retail price, (2) "factory" or "wholesale" prices unless such prices are what they are claimed to be, and (3) comparable value prices on imperfect goods.[17]

Other deceptive pricing issues include *scanner fraud* and price confusion. The widespread use of scanner-based computer checkouts has led to increasing complaints of retailers overcharging their customers. Most of these overcharges result from poor management, such as a failure to enter current or sale prices into the system. Other cases, however, involve intentional overcharges.

Many federal and state statutes regulate against deceptive pricing practices. For example, the Automobile Information Disclosure Act requires automakers to attach a statement on new vehicle windows stating the manufacturer's suggested retail price, the prices of optional equipment, and the dealer's transportation charges. However, reputable sellers go beyond what is required by law. Treating customers fairly and making certain that they fully understand prices and pricing terms is an important part of building strong and lasting customer relationships.

Reviewing the Concepts

MyMarketingLab™

Go to **mymktlab.com** to complete the problems marked with this icon .

Reviewing Objectives and Key Terms

 ## Objectives Review

In this chapter, we examined some additional pricing considerations— new-product pricing, product mix pricing, price adjustments, initiating and reacting to prices changes, and pricing and public policy. A company sets not a single price but rather a *pricing structure* that covers its entire mix of products. This pricing structure changes over time as products move through their life cycles. The company adjusts product prices to reflect changes in costs and demand and account for variations in buyers and situations. As the competitive environment changes, the company considers when to initiate price changes and when to respond to them.

Objective 1 **Describe the major strategies for pricing new products.**
(pp 314–315)

Pricing is a dynamic process, and pricing strategies usually change as the product passes through its life cycle. The introductory stage—setting prices for the first time—is especially challenging. The company can decide on one of several strategies for pricing innovative new products: It can use *market-skimming pricing* by initially setting high prices to "skim" the maximum amount of revenue from various segments of the market. Or it can use *market-penetrating pricing* by setting a low initial price to penetrate the market deeply and win a large market share. Several conditions must be set for either new-product pricing strategy to work.

Objective 2 **Explain how companies find a set of prices that maximizes the profits from the total product mix.** (pp 315–317)

When the product is part of a product mix, the firm searches for a set of prices that will maximize the profits from the total mix. In *product line pricing*, the company determines the price steps for the entire product line it offers. In addition, the company must set prices for *optional products* (optional or accessory products included with the main product), *captive products* (products that are required for using the main product), *by-products* (waste or residual products produced when making the main product), and *product bundles* (combinations of products at a reduced price).

Objective 3 **Discuss how companies adjust their prices to take into account different types of customers and situations.**
(pp 317–325)

Companies apply a variety of *price adjustment strategies* to account for differences in consumer segments and situations. One is *discount and allowance pricing*, whereby the company establishes cash, quantity, functional, or seasonal discounts, or varying types of allowances. A second strategy is *segmented pricing*, where the company sells a product at two or more prices to accommodate different customers, product forms, locations, or times. Sometimes companies consider more than economics in their pricing decisions, using *psychological pricing* to better communicate a product's intended position. In *promotional*

pricing, a company offers discounts or temporarily sells a product below list price as a special event, sometimes even selling below cost as a loss leader. Another approach is *geographical pricing,* whereby the company decides how to price to distant customers, choosing from such alternatives as FOB-origin pricing, uniform-delivered pricing, zone pricing, basing-point pricing, and freight-absorption pricing. Finally, *international pricing* means that the company adjusts its price to meet different conditions and expectations in different world markets.

Objective 4 **Discuss the key issues related to initiating and responding to price changes.** (pp 325–329)

When a firm considers initiating a *price change*, it must consider customers' and competitors' reactions. There are different implications to *initiating price cuts* and *initiating price increases*. Buyer reactions to price changes are influenced by the meaning customers see in the price change. Competitors' reactions flow from a set reaction policy or a fresh analysis of each situation.

There are also many factors to consider in responding to a competitor's price changes. The company that faces a price change initiated by a competitor must try to understand the competitor's intent as well as the likely duration and impact of the change. If a swift reaction is desirable, the firm should preplan its reactions to different possible price actions by competitors. When facing a competitor's price change, the company might sit tight, reduce its own price, raise perceived quality, improve quality and raise price, or launch a fighter brand.

Objective 5 **Overview the social and legal issues that affect pricing decisions.** (pp 329–331)

Many federal, state, and even local laws govern the rules of fair pricing. Also, companies must consider broader societal pricing concerns. The major public policy issues in pricing include potentially damaging pricing practices *within* a given level of the channel, such as price-fixing and predatory pricing. They also include pricing practices *across* channel levels, such as retail price maintenance, discriminatory pricing, and deceptive pricing. Although many federal and state statutes regulate pricing practices, reputable sellers go beyond what is required by law. Treating customers fairly is an important part of building strong and lasting customer relationships.

 # Key Terms

Objective 1

Market-skimming pricing (price skimming) (p 314)
Market-penetration pricing (p 315)

Objective 2

Product line pricing (p 316)
Optional product pricing (p 316)
Captive product pricing (p 316)

By-product pricing (p 317)
Product bundle pricing (p 317)

Objective 3

Discount (p 318)
Allowance (p 318)
Segmented pricing (p 318)
Psychological pricing (p 319)
Reference prices (p 319)

Promotional pricing (p 321)
Geographical pricing (p 322)
FOB-origin pricing (p 322)
Uniform-delivered pricing (p 322)
Zone pricing (p 322)
Basing-point pricing (p 322)
Freight-absorption pricing (p 323)
Dynamic pricing (p 323)

Discussion and Critical Thinking

Discussion Questions

1. Compare and contrast market-skimming and market-penetration pricing strategies and discuss the conditions under which each is appropriate. For each strategy, give an example of a recently introduced product that used that pricing strategy. (AACSB: Communication; Reflective Thinking)

2. Name and briefly describe the five product mix pricing decisions. (AACSB: Communication)

3. Name and describe the various forms of discounts companies use to reward customers. (AACSB: Communication; Reflective Thinking)

4. Compare and contrast the geographic pricing strategies companies use for customers located in different parts of the country or world. Which strategy is best? (AACSB: Communication; Reflective Thinking)

5. What is dynamic pricing? Why is it especially prevalent online? Is it legal? (AACSB: Communication)

6. Under what circumstances would a company consider cutting its prices? Raising its prices? (AACSB: Communication)

Critical Thinking Exercises

1. What is the price of a Toyota Prius in the United States? Find the price of a Toyota Prius in five countries and convert that price to U.S. dollars (USD). Are the prices the same or different in other countries? Explain why that might be so. (AACSB: Communication; Use of IT; Reflective Thinking)

2. One psychological pricing tactic is "just-below" pricing. It is also called "9-ending" pricing because prices usually end in the number 9 (or 99). In a small group, have each member select five different products and visit a store to learn the price of those items. Is there a variation among the items and stores with regard to 9-ending pricing? Why do marketers use this pricing tactic? (AACSB: Communication; Reflective Thinking)

Applications and Cases

Marketing Technology Talk Less, Pay More

Wireless carriers are trying to get customers to pay more for something they do less and less—making phone calls. It seems consumers are doing everything *but* talking on their mobile phones. Average voice-minute usage has fallen since Apple introduced the iPhone in 2007 and consumers have turned to text and voice-over-Internet calling options such as Skype. But voice billings account for almost 70 percent of what carriers charge mobile phone customers, and they don't want this cash cow to dry up. As a result, carriers are starting to drop plans that allow subscribers to buy only the minutes they need or want and are replacing them with flat rates covering unlimited calling. Carriers say this would be less complicated for consumers, but the real reason is that they do not want customers trading down to cheaper plans when they realize they can save money by scaling back their voice plans. So carriers are eliminating tiered-pricing voice plans altogether.

1. Compare the prices of two mobile phone carriers, such as AT&T and Verizon. What types of pricing strategies are they using? (AACSB: Communication; Reflective Thinking)

2. Visit www.myrateplan.com/wireless_plans/ to compare your mobile phone plan to other carriers' plans. What tactics do carriers use to keep subscribers from switching? Explain. (AACSB: Communication; Use of IT; Reflective Thinking)

Marketing Ethics **The Price of a Song**

Country music stars such as Taylor Swift, Rascal Flatts, and Tim McGraw will be the first artists to be paid every time their songs are played on the radio. In the United States, only songwriters and music publishers receive royalties from radio airplay or when a song is played in a movie, television program, commercial, or even as hold music on telephones. This dates back to a 1917 Supreme Court ruling that composers of copyrighted music are due a royalty every time the music is played or performed through commercial means. But performing artists or recording companies do not receive such royalties. The rationale is that radio play promotes record sales, where the artists earn royalties ranging from 8 to 25 percent of the price of a CD. But thanks to the Internet and music download sites such as iTunes, sales of traditional recorded music have dropped almost 50 percent. In 2011, digital music sales surpassed traditional CD sales. Listeners have also tuned in to Internet sites such as Pandora, Spotify, and Rdio to listen to music. Recording artists did get some relief through the Digital Performance Rights in Sound Recording Act of 1995. The act gave performers their first royalties when their songs are played in a digital format, such as in a Webcast or on satellite radio, where listeners subscribe but cannot select specific songs. Pandora, the online radio company, claims that such royalty payments, equivalent to about 60 percent of revenues, are the reason the company is unprofitable.

1. Research how music royalties work to learn more about the cost and pricing of music. Write a report of what you learned. (AACSB: Communication; Reflective Thinking)

 Marketing by the Numbers **Is Netflix Crazy or Savvy?**

Price increases are always a thorny issue with consumers, and Netflix, the video-streaming and DVD-by-mail giant, set off a firestorm by announcing a 60 percent price increase on its most affordable rental plan. Previously, for $9.99 per month, customers were able to rent one DVD at a time plus enjoy unlimited streaming over the Internet. That same service now costs $15.98 per month, a combination of an existing $7.99-a-month streaming-only plan with a new $7.99-a-month DVD-only plan that allows customers to receive one disc at a time via mail. So customers either had to ante up to continue with the same level of service or step down to one of the more limited services priced at $7.99 per month. Most customers switched to the streaming-only option, which reduced variable costs for Netflix due to postage savings.

Netflix had 23 million subscribers of the $9.99 per month DVD/streaming hybrid plan prior to the price increase.

1. Refer to Appendix 2, Marketing by the Numbers and calculate the monthly contribution Netflix realizes from a subscriber at the price of $9.99 per month and $15.98 per month, respectively. Assume average variable costs per customer are $3.50 per month, which do not change with the price increase. How many disgruntled customers can Netflix lose before profitability is affected negatively? (AACSB: Communications; Analytic Reasoning)

2. Is this a smart move by Netflix? Discuss the pros and cons of such a drastic price increase. (AACSB: Communication; Reflective Thinking)

 Video Case **Hammerpress**

Printing paper goods may not sound like the best business to get into these days. But Hammerpress is a company that is carving out a niche in this old industry. And Hammerpress is doing it by returning to old technology. Today's printing firms use computer-driven graphic design techniques and printing processes. But Hammerpress creates greeting cards, calendars, and business cards that are hand-crafted by professional artists and printed using traditional letterpress technology.

When it comes to competing, this presents both opportunities and challenges. While Hammerpress's products certainly stand out as works of art, the cost for producing such goods is considerably higher than the industry average. This video illustrates how Hammerpress employs dynamic pricing techniques in order to meet the needs of various customer segments and thrive in a competitive environment.

After viewing the video featuring Hammerpress, answer the following questions:

1. How does Hammerpress employ the concept of dynamic pricing?

2. Discuss the three major pricing strategies in relation to Hammerpress. Which of these three do you think is the company's core strategic strategy?

3. Does it make sense for Hammerpress to compete in product categories where the market dictates a price that is not profitable for the company? Explain.

Company Case | **Amazon vs. Walmart: Fighting It Out Online on Price**

Less than a decade ago, no one believed that Amazon posed a credible threat to Walmart. After all, Walmart was the world's biggest retailer, selling everything under the sun. Amazon was just an online upstart, known mostly as a seller of books and CDs. Back then, Walmart's revenues eclipsed Amazon's by more than 120 times.

But what a difference a decade makes. Although Walmart still dominates the physical retail sphere and remains the world's biggest company to boot, Amazon's growth has put it squarely in the sights of the brick-and-mortar giant. These days, it seems, everyone is comparing the two. Ali had Frazier. Coke has Pepsi. The Yankees have the Red Sox. And now these two heavyweight retailers are waging a war online. The weapon of choice? Prices—not surprising, given the two combatants' long-held low-cost positions.

The price war between Walmart and Amazon began three years ago, with skirmishes over online prices for new books and DVDs. It then escalated quickly to video game consoles, mobile phones, and even toys. At stake: not only the fortunes of the two companies but also those of whole industries whose products they sell, both online and in retail stores. Price can be a potent strategic weapon, but it can also be a double-edged sword.

Amazon, it seems, wants to be the "Walmart of the Internet"— our digital general store—and it's well on its way to achieving that goal. Although Walmart's overall sales total was an incredible $444 billion last year—nine times Amazon's $48 billion—Amazon.com's online sales were nearly nine times greater than Walmart.com's online sales. Moreover, Amazon.com attracts more than 100 million unique U.S. visitors to its site monthly, more than double Walmart.com's number. One analyst estimates that more than one-half of all U.S. consumers who look online for retail items start their search at Amazon.com.

Why does this worry Walmart? After all, online sales account for only 7 percent of total U.S. retail sales. Walmart captures most of its business by offering affordable prices to middle Americans in its more than 4,400 brick-and-mortar stores. By comparison, according to one analyst, Amazon has made its name by selling mostly to "affluent urbanites who would rather click with their mouse than push around a cart."

But this battle isn't about now—it's about the future. Although still a small market by Walmart's standards, online sales will soar within the next decade to an estimated 15 percent of total U.S. retail sales. And, increasingly, Amazon.com owns the online space. Last year, Amazon.com's sales climbed 40 percent compared to the prior year. Even more important, Amazon.com's electronics and general merchandise sales, which compete directly with much of the selection found in Walmart stores, are growing even faster than its overall sales.

The Battle Begins

Amazon has shown a relentless ambition to offer more of almost everything on the Internet. It started by selling only books online, but now it sells everything from books, movies, and music to consumer electronics, home and garden products, clothing, jewelry, toys, tools, and even groceries. Acquiring numerous online retailers like Zappos.com and Diapers.com has helped this rapid expansion. The online retailer is even beefing up its private-label selection, adding new lines of Amazon-branded goods. If Amazon.com's expansion continues and online sales grow as predicted, the online seller will eat further and further into Walmart's bread-and-butter store sales. In fact, as lower-income consumers become more tech savvy, Amazon.com is even pulling in Walmart's traditional customer—bargain hunters making less than $50,000 a year.

But Walmart isn't giving up without a fight. Instead, it's taking the battle to Amazon's home territory—the Internet. Through aggressive pricing, it is now fighting for every dollar consumers spend online. Walmart fired the first shot before the 2009 holiday shopping season. It announced that it would take online preorders for 10 soon-to-be-released hardback books—all projected bestsellers by authors such as John Grisham, Stephen King, Barbara Kingsolver, and James Patterson—at an unprecedented low price of just $9.99 each—the same price that Amazon.com was already charging for e-book versions of bestsellers downloaded to its Kindle or other readers. To take it a step further, Walmart.com also cut prices by 50 percent on 200 other bestsellers, undercutting Amazon.com's prices. When Amazon quickly announced that it would match Walmart's price on the 10 bestsellers, the price war was on. Walmart.com dropped its price to $9.00, Amazon.com did likewise, and Walmart.com lowered its prices yet again, to $8.98.

These low book prices represented a 59 to 74 percent reduction off list price, much more than the 30 to 40 percent reduction you might expect in traditional retail bookstores such as Barnes & Noble. In fact, Walmart.com and Amazon.com discounted these bestsellers below costs—as so-called loss leaders—to lure shoppers to their sites in hopes that they would buy other, more profitable items.

Today, the book price war continues. And it's having an impact beyond the two primary combatants, causing collateral damage across the entire book industry. "When your product is treated as a loss leader, it lowers its perceived value," says one publishing executive. In the long run, that's not great for either the companies that publish the books or the retailers who sell them. Price carries messages about customer value, notes another publisher. Companies want to be careful about the messages they send.

The price war is not taking place over just books. If you compare prices at Walmart.com and Amazon.com, you'll find the price battle raging across a broad range of product categories. And although Walmart has a head start on low prices, it is apparent that Amazon can match and even beat Walmart with its own low-cost structure that has no overhead from stores.

Who will win the online battle for the hearts and dollars of online buyers? Certainly, low prices will be an important factor. But given the dramatically changing nature of how consumers shop and buy, price alone may not be enough. Let's look at how each of these retailers is prepared to do battle.

Walmart: More Ways to Buy

When it comes to low prices, Walmart has an advantage in terms of years of experience, scale of operations, and negotiating power with its suppliers. But Walmart is also focused on making dramatic strides in online sales. Whereas Walmart's overall sales growth may be modest, plugging along in single digits, its online sales are growing at a much more rapid pace. The chain's online sales more than doubled last year, and the number of unique visitors to Walmart.com shot up by 26 percent to 42 million, while Amazon.com's monthly traffic remained relatively flat.

Walmart has a few advantages over Amazon. The fact that it has both a huge network of physical stores in convenient locations plus a well-established online presence allows it to offer customers more ways to buy online. Customers can buy online and have purchases shipped to their homes. Or they can buy items online and pick them up at a Walmart store. For items that a local store carries, customers can pick them up the same day. And Walmart recently started its "Pay With Cash" program, aimed at the 20 percent of Walmart shoppers who can't shop online because they don't have a bank account or a credit card.

The "cash" option supports Walmart's new online slogan, "Anytime, Anywhere." Walmart wants its shoppers to know that it can provide the most seamless combination of online and offline shopping, unmatched by any retailer in any space. Walmart envisions a day in the not-too-distant future when consumers will be able to shop for anything that's available online or in stores from their home computers, while out about town on their digital devices, or even from those same devices while browsing the aisles of its stores. Walmart expects that having every one of its stores serve as a pickup center will give it a huge advantage over online-only retailers, especially Amazon. Walmart is even experimenting with drive-through windows, where shoppers can pick up their Internet orders. The pickup centers also double as easy return centers.

Amazon: Covering All the Bases

Amazon also has advantages. For starters, Walmart's online sales may be growing rapidly, but Amazon's momentum may make it impossible for Walmart to ever catch up online. When Walmart doubled its online revenue last year, that meant an increase of only $2 billion to $3 billion. Amazon increased its sales by more than $10 billion. If Amazon keeps growing as expected, it will exceed $100 billion in sales by 2015, achieving that milestone in just 21 years and becoming the fastest company in history to do so (it took Walmart 36 years). At that point, it is possible that Amazon will have pulled off the impossible—becoming the second-largest U.S. retailer with only one more to pass.

Amazon also has diversification in its DNA. It recognizes that online commerce is just one element of a comprehensive strategy. From its beginnings, Amazon has invested heavily in acquiring and developing technologies that are allowing it to branch into online services that form an entire online ecosystem, capturing every aspect of a person's life—from entertainment to social networking to mobile communications—all with links to its online superstore.

In addition to its highly recognizable online brand, Amazon.com sports a larger assortment than Walmart and an unparalleled online customer shopping experience. Its sophisticated distribution network, built specifically for Internet shopping, means shipping is always fast. And with Amazon Prime, it's even faster—and free.

The Double-Edged Sword

For now, price remains a central competitive weapon as Walmart and Amazon battle online. But in the long run, reckless price cutting may do more damage than good to both Walmart and Amazon. Price wars can turn whole product categories into unattractive, low-margin commodities (think DVDs, for example). And buying online is about much more than just getting the best prices, even in today's economy. In the end, winning online consumers will require offering not only the lowest prices but also the best customer value in terms of price and product selection, speed, convenience, and overall shopping experience.

For now, the two retailers, especially Walmart, seem determined to fight it out on price. Amazon's CEO, Jeff Bezos, has long maintained that there's plenty of room for all competitors in the big world of retailing. However, Paul Vazquez, former president and CEO of Walmart.com, says that it's "only a matter of time" before Walmart dominates Internet shopping. Pricing, he thinks, will be key. "Our company is based on low prices," says Vazquez, laying down the challenge. "Even in books, we kept going until we were the low-priced leader. And we will do that in every category we need to. Our company is based on low prices." Still, the question remains, will low price be enough?

Questions for Discussion

1. Can consumers actually determine whether Amazon or Walmart has lower overall prices? Explain.

2. For Amazon and Walmart, is it more important to have lower prices or to have the perception of lower prices?

3. Just how far should either Amazon or Walmart take the tactic of warring on price? Base your answer on Figure 11.1 in the text.

4. In the battle for online dominance, just how important is low price? How important are the other benefits that Amazon and Walmart each deliver?

Sources: "Walmart Vs. Amazon: Can Brick-And-Mortar Stores Hang onto Shoppers?" *The Week*, April 12, 2012, http://theweek.com/article/index/226736/walmart-vs-amazon-can-brick-and-mortar-stores-hang-onto-shoppers; "Wal-Mart Reaches More Shoppers Online by Letting Them Pay with Cash," *Forbes*, June 25, 2012, www.forbes.com/sites/greatspeculations/2012/06/25/wal-marts-reaches-more-shoppers-online-by-letting-them-pay-with-cash/; David Welch, "Wal-Mart Gears Up Online as Customers Defect to Amazon," *Businessweek*, March 20, 2012, www.businessweek.com/news/2012-03-20/wal-mart-gears-up-online-as-customers-defect-to-amazon; Brad Stone and Stephanie Rosenbloom, "The Gloves Come Off at Amazon and Walmart," *New York Times*, November 24, 2009, p. 1; Gayle Feldman, "Behind the US Price War," *Bookseller*, November 13, 2009, p. 16; and Jeffrey A. Trachtenberg and Miguel Bustillo, "Amazon, Walmart Cut Deeper in Book Duel," *Wall Street Journal*, October 19, 2009, p. B1.

MyMarketingLab

Go to **mymktlab.com** for Auto-graded writing questions as well as the following Assisted-graded writing questions:

11-1. Identify three online price-comparison shopping Web sites or apps and shop for a product you are interested in purchasing. Compare the price ranges given at the three sites. Based on your search, determine a "fair" price for the product. (AACSB: Communication; Use of IT; Reflective Thinking)

11-2. Should artists and record labels be paid royalties every time their music is played? What type of cost does this represent for a radio station? (AACSB: Communication; Reflective Thinking)

11-3. Mymktlab Only – comprehensive writing assignment for this chapter.

References

1. Quotes and other information from Annie Gasparro, "Panera Boosts Ad Budget as 'Fast Casual' Heats Up," *Wall Street Journal*, March 8, 2012, p. B7; Mark Brandau, "Bakery-Café Segment Expanding," *Restaurant News*, October 11, 2011, http://nrn.com/article/study-bakery-caf%C3%A9-segment-expanding; Kate Rockwood, "Rising Dough: Why Panera Bread Is on a Roll," *Fast Company*, October 2009, pp. 69–70; "Standouts in Customer Service," *Bloomberg Businessweek*, April 14, 2011, www.businessweek.com/interactive_reports/customer_service_2010.html; Tiffany Hsu, "Fast-Casual Restaurants Gobble Up Market Share," *Los Angeles Times*, December 22, 2011; and www.panerabread.com, accessed November 2012.

2. For comprehensive discussions of pricing strategies, see Thomas T. Nagle, John E. Hogan, and Joseph Zale, *The Strategy and Tactics of Pricing*, 5th ed. (Upper Saddle River, New Jersey: Prentice Hall, 2011).

3. Adapted from information found in Mei Fong, "IKEA Hits Home in China; The Swedish Design Giant, Unlike Other Retailers, Slashes Prices for the Chinese," *Wall Street Journal*, March 3, 2006, p. B1; "Beijing Loves IKEA—But Not for Shopping," *Los Angeles Times*, http://articles.latimes.com/2009/aug/25/business/fi-china- ikea25; "China: Assembling Ideas for IKEAs in China," *Asia News Monitor*, February 17, 2012; and www.ikea.com/ms/en_US/about_ikea/facts_and_figures/index.html, accessed September 2012.

4. Danielle Kucera, "Amazon Profit Plunges after New Products Increase Expenses; Shares Tumble," *Bloomberg*, October 25, 2011, www.bloomberg.com/news/2011-10-25/amazon-profit-plunges-after-new-products-increase-expenses-shares-tumble.html.

5. See Steve Henshaw, "Some Products No Longer a Steal," *McClatchy-Tribune Business News*, March 19, 2012; and "Gillette Shaves Prices as It's Nicked by Rivals Both New and Old," *Advertising Age*, April 2, 2012, http://adage.com/print/234019.

6. Information from "What Happens to All That Poo at the Zoo . . .," www.youtube.com/watch?v=kjfNVEvRI3w&feature=player_embedded#, accessed /June 2012; "Zoo Doo® at Woodland Park Zoo," www.zoo.org/zoo-doo, accessed November 2012.

7. For this and other examples, see Peter Coy, "Why the Price Is Rarely Right," *Bloomberg Businessweek*, February 1 & 8, 2010, pp. 77–78.

8. Anthony Allred, E. K. Valentin, and Goutam Chakraborty, "Pricing Risky Services: Preference and Quality Considerations," *Journal of Product and Brand Management*, Vol. 19, No. 1, 2010, p. 54. Also see Kenneth C. Manning and David E. Sprott, "Price Endings, Left-Digit Effects, and Choice," *Journal of Consumer Research*, August 2009, pp. 328–336; and Carl Bialik, Elizabeth Holmes, and Ray Smith, "Many Discounts, Few Deals," *Wall Street Journal*, December 15, 2010, p. D12.

9. See the Chapter 10 opening story on JCPenney and Rafi Mohammed, "J.C. Penney's Risky New Pricing Strategy," *Harvard Business Review*, January 30, 2012, http://blogs.hbr.org/cs/2012/01/understanding_jc_penneys_risky.html; and Margret Brennan, "J.C. Penney CEO Johnson on Pricing, Store Overhaul," Bloomberg video, January 25, 2012, www.bloomberg.com/video/84891104/.

10. Adapted from Justin D. Martin, "Dynamic Pricing: Internet Retailers Are Treating Us Like Foreign Tourists in Egypt," *Christian Science Monitor*, January 7, 2011. See also Patrick Rishe, "Dynamic Pricing: The Future of Ticket Pricing in Sports," *Forbes*, January 6, 2012, www.forbes.com/sites/prishe/2012/01/06/dynamic-pricing-the-future-of-ticket-pricing-in-sports/; and Mike Southon, "Time to Ensure the Price Is Right," *Financial Times*, January 21, 2012, p. 30.

11. For more on showrooming, see Dana Matioli, "Retailers Try to Thwart Price Apps," *Wall Street Journal*, December 23, 2011; Miguel Bustillo, "Best Buy Forced to Rethink Big-Box," *Wall Street Journal*, March 29, 2012; and Ann Zimmerman, "Can Retailers Halt 'Showrooming'?" *Wall Street Journal*, April 11, p. B1.

12. Based on information found in "The World's Most Influential Companies: Unilever," *BusinessWeek*, December 22, 2008, p. 47; and www.unilever.com/sustainability/, accessed November 2009. Also see Ashish Karamchandani, Mike Kubzansky, and Nishant Lalwani, "Is the Bottom of the Pyramid Really for You?" *Harvard Business Review*, March 2011, pp. 107–112; and C. K. Prahalad, "Bottom of the Pyramid as a Source of Breakthrough Innovations," *Journal of Product Innovation Management*, January, 2012, pp. 6–12.

13. Information from Maureen Morrison, "Seattle's Best Launches First Major Ad Campaign," *Advertising Age*, January 10, 2011, http://adage.com/article/news/seattle-s-coffee-launches-ad-campaign/148118/; "Starbuck's Kid Brother Grows Up Fast," *Bloomberg Businessweek*, April 25–May 1, 2011, pp. 26–27; "Seattle's Best Coffee: Forget the Flowers, Poems, and Chocolate," *Marketing Weekly News*, February 25, 2012, p. 585; and www.starbucks.com, accessed September 2012.

14. For discussions of these issues, see Dhruv Grewel and Larry D. Compeau, "Pricing and Public Policy: A Research Agenda and Overview of the Special Issue," *Journal of Public Policy and Marketing*, Spring 1999, pp. 3–10; Michael V. Marn, Eric V. Roegner, and Craig C. Zawada, *The Price Advantage* (Hoboken, New Jersey: John Wiley & Sons, 2004), Appendix 2; and Thomas T. Nagle, John E. Hogan, and Joseph Zale, *The Strategy and Tactics of Pricing*, 5th ed. (Upper Saddle River, NJ: Prentice Hall, 2011).

15. See Foo Yun Chee, "Unilever, P&G Fined 315 Million Euros for Price Fixing," *Reuters*, April 13, 2011, www.reuters.com/article/2011/04/13/us-eu-cartel-idUSTRE73C1XV20110413; "France Fines P&G and Colgate for Laundry Prices," *Bloomberg Businessweek*, December 8, 2011, www.businessweek.com/ap/financialnews/D9RGGB3O0.htm; and Joseph Vogel, "Laundry Detergent Cartel Members Fined Heavily Following Leniency Procedure," *International Law Office*, February 23, 2012, www.internationallawoffice.com/newsletters/detail.aspx?g=ad5133b6-98a3-4fe9-b344-bef35c531234.

16. Based on information found in Lynn Leary, "Publishers and Booksellers See a 'Predatory' Amazon," *NPR Books*, January 23, 2012, www.npr.org/2012/01/23/145468105/publishers-and-booksellers-see-a-predatory-amazon.

17. "FTC Guides against Deceptive Pricing," www.ftc.gov/bcp/guides/decptprc.htm, accessed November 2012.

Marketing Channels
Delivering Customer Value

Chapter Preview We now arrive at the third marketing mix tool—distribution. Companies rarely work alone in creating value for customers and building profitable customer relationships. Instead, most are only a single link in a larger supply chain and marketing channel. As such, a firm's success depends not only on how well *it* performs but also on how well its *entire marketing channel* competes with competitors' channels. The first part of this chapter explores the nature of marketing channels and the marketer's channel design and management decisions. We then examine physical distribution—or

logistics—an area that is growing dramatically in importance and sophistication. In the next chapter, we'll look more closely at two major channel intermediaries: retailers and wholesalers.

We start by looking at Netflix. Though innovative distribution, Netflix has become the world's largest video subscription service. But as baseball great Yogi Berra, known more for his mangled phrasing than for his baseball prowess, once said, "The future ain't what it used to be." To stay atop the churning video distribution industry, Netflix must continue to innovate at a break-neck pace or risk being pushed aside.

Netflix's Channel Innovation: Finding the Future by Abandoning the Past

Time and again, Netflix has innovated its way to the top in the distribution of video entertainment. In the early 2000s, Netflix's revolutionary DVD-by-mail service put all but the most powerful movie-rental stores out of business. In 2007, Netflix's then ground-breaking move into digital streaming once again revolutionized how people accessed movies and other video content. Now, with Netflix leading the pack, video distribution has become a boiling, roiling pot of emerging technologies and high-tech competitors, one that offers both mind-bending opportunities and stomach-churning risks.

Just ask Blockbuster. Only a few years ago, the giant brick-and-mortar movie-rental chain flat-out owned the industry. Then along came Netflix, the fledgling DVD-by-mail service. First thousands then millions of subscribers were drawn to Netflix's innovative distribution model—no more trips to the video store, no more late fees, and a selection of more than 100,000 titles that dwarfed anything Blockbuster could offer. Even better, Netflix's $5-a-month subscription rate cost little more than renting a single video from Blockbuster. In 2010, as Netflix surged, once-mighty Blockbuster fell into bankruptcy.

The Blockbuster riches-to-rags story underscores the turmoil that typifies today's

video distribution business. In only the past few years, a growing glut of video access options has materialized. At the same time that Netflix ascended and Blockbuster plunged, Coinstar's Redbox came out of nowhere to build a novel national network of $1-a-day DVD-rental kiosks. Then high-tech start-ups such as Hulu—with its high-quality, ad-supported free access to movies and current TV shows—began pushing digital streaming via the Internet.

All along the way, Netflix has acted boldly to stay ahead of the competition. For example, in 2007 rather than sitting on the success of its still-hot DVD-by-mail business, Netflix and its CEO, Reed Hastings, set their sights on a then-revolutionary new video distribution model: Deliver the Netflix service to every Internet-connected screen, from laptops to Internet-ready TVs to mobile phones and other Wi-Fi-enabled devices. Netflix

> Time and again, Netflix has innovated its way to the top in the distribution of video entertainment. But to stay atop its boiling, roiling industry, Netflix must keep the innovation pedal to the metal.

began by launching its Watch Instantly service, which let Netflix members stream movies instantly to their computers as part of their monthly membership fee, even if it came at the expense of Netflix's still-booming DVD business.

Although Netflix didn't pioneer digital streaming, it poured resources into improving the technology and building the largest streaming library. It built a customer base of nearly 25 million subscribers, and sales and profits soared. With its massive physical DVD library and a streaming library of more than 20,000 high-definition movies accessible via 200 different Internet-ready devices, it seemed that nothing could stop Netflix.

But Netflix's stunning success drew a slew of resourceful competitors. In 2010, video giants such as Google's YouTube and Apple's iTunes began renting movie downloads and Hulu introduced subscription-based Hulu Plus. To stay ahead, even to survive, Netflix needed to keep the innovation pedal to the metal. So in the summer of 2011, in an ambitious but risky move, CEO Hastings made an all-in bet on digital streaming. He split off Netflix's still-thriving DVD-by-mail service into a separate business named Qwikster and required separate subscriptions for DVD rentals and streaming (at a startling 60 percent price increase for customers using both). The Netflix name would now stand for nothing but digital streaming, which would be the primary focus of the company's future growth.

Although perhaps visionary, Netflix's abrupt changes didn't sit well with customers. Tens of thousands spoke out angrily on Web sites and social networks, and some 800,000 subscribers dropped the service. Netflix's stock price plummeted by almost two-thirds. To repair the damage, Netflix quickly admitted its blunder and reversed its decision to set up a separate Qwikster operation. "There is a difference between moving quickly—which Netflix has done very well for years—and moving too fast, which is what we did in this case," Hastings confessed. However, despite the setback, Netflix retained its separate, higher pricing for DVDs by mail.

In the aftermath of the Qwikster blunder, Netflix soon replaced almost all of its lost subscribers. What's more, with a 60 percent higher price on roughly the same number of customers, revenues jumped a whopping 47 percent year over year. Given Netflix's fast recovery, now more than ever, Hastings seems bent on speeding up the company's leap from success in DVDs to success in streaming. "I'm moving ahead step by step, despite the foot with the bullet hole," he says. Although customers can still access Netflix's world's-biggest DVD library, the company's promotions and Web site barely mention that option. The focus is now squarely on streaming video.

Despite its continuing success, Netflix knows that it can't rest its innovation machine. Competition continues to move at a blurring rate. For example, Amazon has begun its own streaming-video subscription service, available to Amazon

Netflix's innovative distribution strategy: Netflix and its CEO, Reed Hastings, are bent on speeding up the company's leap from success in DVD rentals to success in digital streaming. What's next?
REUTERS/Mike Cassese

Prime members at no additional cost. Google recently moved beyond its YouTube rental service with Google Play, an all-media entertainment portal for movies, music, e-books, and apps. Comcast has joined forces with Verizon to launch Xfinity Streampix, which offers subscribers streaming access to older movies and television programs via their TVs or mobile devices. Apple and Samsung are creating smoother integration with streaming content via smart TVs. And Hulu is considering the launch of a virtual cable service, which would offer online access to packages of TV channels similar to those from cable operators but at a lower price.

Moving ahead, as the industry settles into streaming as the main delivery model, content—not just delivery—will be a key to distancing Netflix from the rest of pack. Given its head start, Netflix remains well ahead in the content race. Amazon and Hulu Plus currently have only a fraction of Netflix's offerings, and Netflix captures 10 times the total viewing hours of either competitor. But as content-licensing deals with movie and television studios become harder to get, in yet another innovative video distribution twist, Netflix and its competitors are now starting to develop their own original programming. For example, Netflix recently shocked the media industry by committing $100 million for exclusive rights to air *House of Cards*, a brand new series produced by Hollywood bigwigs David Fincher and Kevin Spacey.

Thus, from DVDs by mail, to Watch Instantly, to video streaming on almost any device, to developing original content, Netflix has stayed ahead of the howling pack by doing what it does best—innovate and revolutionize distribution. What's next? No one really knows. But one thing seems certain: Whatever's coming, if Netflix doesn't lead the change, it risks being left behind—and quickly. In this fast-changing business, new tricks grow old in a hurry. To stay ahead, as one headline suggests, Netflix must "find its future by abandoning its past."[1]

Objective Outline

Objective 1	**Explain why companies use marketing channels and discuss the functions these channels perform.**
	## Supply Chains and the Value Delivery Network (pp 340–341)
	## The Nature and Importance of Marketing Channels (pp 341–344)

Objective 2	**Discuss how channel members interact and how they organize to perform the work of the channel.**
	## Channel Behavior and Organization (pp 344–349)

Objective 3	**Identify the major channel alternatives open to a company.**
	## Channel Design Decisions (pp 349–353)

Objective 4	**Explain how companies select, motivate, and evaluate channel members.**
	## Channel Management Decisions (pp 353–354)
	## Public Policy and Distribution Decisions (pp 354–357)

Objective 5	**Discuss the nature and importance of marketing logistics and integrated supply chain management.**
	## Marketing Logistics and Supply Chain Management (pp 357–364)

MyMarketingLab™

⭐ Improve Your Grade!

Over 10 million students improved their results using the Pearson MyLabs.
Visit **mymktlab.com** for simulations, tutorials, and end-of-chapter problems.

As the Netflix story shows, good distribution strategies can contribute strongly to customer value and create competitive advantage for a firm. But firms cannot bring value to customers by themselves. Instead, they must work closely with other firms in a larger value delivery network.

Objective 1 ┈┈▶
Explain why companies use marketing channels and discuss the functions these channels perform.

Supply Chains and the Value Delivery Network

Producing a product or service and making it available to buyers requires building relationships not only with customers but also with key suppliers and resellers in the company's *supply chain*. This supply chain consists of upstream and downstream partners. Upstream from the company is the set of firms that supply the raw materials, components, parts, information, finances, and expertise needed to create a product or service. Marketers, however, have traditionally focused on the downstream side of the supply chain—the *marketing channels* (or *distribution channels*) that look toward the customer. Downstream marketing channel partners, such as wholesalers and retailers, form a vital link between the firm and its customers.

you know who could use a
car like this? everyone.

the INSiGHT. a new hybrid from Honda. Honda and hybrid. AKA. reliability and efficiency, two
things everyone can use. Other useful things: an innovative battery, split fold-down rear seats and
43 hwy mpg: The hybrid designed and priced for us all. The new Insight. from Honda. for everyone.

Insight.honda.com 1-800-33-Honda EX model shown. *Based on 2010 EPA mileage estimates, reflecting new EPA fuel economy methods, beginning with 2008
models. Use for comparison purposes only. Do not compare to models before 2008. Actual mileage will vary. The Eco Assist symbol is a trademark of Honda Motor Co., Ltd.
and may not be used or reproduced without prior written approval. ©2009 American Honda Motor Co., Inc.

● **Value delivery network: In making and marketing just one of its many models—say, the Honda Insight hybrid—Honda manages a huge network of people within Honda plus thousands of suppliers and dealers outside the company who work together to give final customers an innovative car "from Honda. for Everyone."**

Print advertisement provided courtesy of American Honda Motor Co., Inc.

The term *supply chain* may be too limited, as it takes a *make-and-sell* view of the business. It suggests that raw materials, productive inputs, and factory capacity should serve as the starting point for market planning. A better term would be *demand chain* because it suggests a *sense-and-respond* view of the market. Under this view, planning starts by identifying the needs of target customers, to which the company responds by organizing a chain of resources and activities with the goal of creating customer value.

Yet, even a demand chain view of a business may be too limited because it takes a step-by-step, linear view of purchase-production-consumption activities. Instead, most large companies today are engaged in building and managing a complex, continuously evolving value delivery network. As defined in Chapter 2, a **value delivery network** is made up of the company, suppliers, distributors, and, ultimately, customers who "partner" with each other to improve the performance of the entire system. ● For example, in making and marketing just one of its many models for the global market—say, the Honda Insight hybrid—Honda manages a huge network of people within Honda plus thousands of suppliers and dealers outside the company who work together effectively to give final customers an innovative car "from Honda. for Everyone."

This chapter focuses on marketing channels—on the downstream side of the value delivery network. We examine four major questions concerning marketing channels: What is the nature of marketing channels and why are they important? How do channel firms interact and organize to do the work of the channel? What problems do companies face in designing and managing their channels? What role do physical distribution and supply chain management play in attracting and satisfying customers? In the next chapter, we will look at marketing channel issues from the viewpoints of retailers and wholesalers.

Value delivery network
A network composed of the company, suppliers, distributors, and, ultimately, customers who partner with each other to improve the performance of the entire system in delivering customer value.

Marketing channel (or distribution channel)
A set of interdependent organizations that help make a product or service available for use or consumption by the consumer or business user.

The Nature and Importance of Marketing Channels

Few producers sell their goods directly to final users. Instead, most use intermediaries to bring their products to market. They try to forge a **marketing channel** (or **distribution channel**)—a set of interdependent organizations that help make a product or service available for use or consumption by the consumer or business user.

A company's channel decisions directly affect every other marketing decision. Pricing depends on whether the company works with national discount chains, uses high-quality specialty stores, or sells directly to consumers online. The firm's sales force and communications decisions depend on how much persuasion, training, motivation, and support its channel partners need. Whether a company develops or acquires certain new products may depend on how well those products fit the capabilities of its channel members.

Companies often pay too little attention to their distribution channels—sometimes with damaging results. In contrast, many companies have used imaginative distribution systems to gain a competitive advantage. Enterprise Rent-A-Car revolutionized the car-rental business by setting up off-airport rental offices. Apple turned the retail music business on its head by selling music for the iPod via the Internet on iTunes. FedEx's creative and imposing distribution system made it a leader in express package delivery. And Amazon.com forever changed the face of retailing and became the Walmart of the Internet by selling anything and everything without using physical stores.

Distribution channel decisions often involve long-term commitments to other firms. For example, companies such as Ford, McDonald's, or HP can easily change their advertising, pricing, or promotion programs. They can scrap old products and introduce new ones as market tastes demand. But when they set up distribution channels through contracts with franchisees, independent dealers, or large retailers, they cannot readily replace these channels with company-owned stores or Internet sites if the conditions change. Therefore, management must design its channels carefully, with an eye on both today's likely selling environment and tomorrow's as well.

How Channel Members Add Value

Why do producers give some of the selling job to channel partners? After all, doing so means giving up some control over how and to whom they sell their products. Producers use intermediaries because they create greater efficiency in making goods available to target markets. Through their contacts, experience, specialization, and scale of operation, intermediaries usually offer the firm more than it can achieve on its own.

● **Figure 12.1** shows how using intermediaries can provide economies. Figure 12.1A shows three manufacturers, each using direct marketing to reach three customers. This system requires nine different contacts. Figure 12.1B shows the three manufacturers working through one distributor, which contacts the three customers. This system requires only six contacts. In this way, intermediaries reduce the amount of work that must be done by both producers and consumers.

From the economic system's point of view, the role of marketing intermediaries is to transform the assortments of products made by producers into the assortments wanted by consumers. Producers make narrow assortments of products in large quantities, but consumers want broad assortments of products in small quantities. Marketing channel members buy large quantities from many producers and break them down into the smaller quantities and broader assortments desired by consumers.

For example, Unilever makes millions of bars of Lever 2000 hand soap each week. However, you most likely only want to buy a few bars at a time. Therefore, big food, drug, and discount retailers, such as Safeway, Walgreens, and Target, buy Lever 2000 by the truckload and stock it on their stores' shelves. In turn, you can buy a single bar of Lever 2000, along with a shopping cart full of small quantities of toothpaste, shampoo, and other related products, as you need them. Thus, intermediaries play an important role in matching supply and demand.

In making products and services available to consumers, channel members add value by bridging the major time, place, and possession gaps that separate goods and services from those who use them. Members of the marketing channel perform many key functions. Some help to complete transactions:

- *Information:* Gathering and distributing information about consumers, producers, and other actors and forces in the marketing environment needed for planning and aiding exchange.
- *Promotion:* Developing and spreading persuasive communications about an offer.
- *Contact:* Finding and communicating with prospective buyers.

● **FIGURE | 12.1**
How a Distributor
Reduces the Number of
Channel Transactions

Marketing channel intermediaries make buying a lot easier for consumers. Again, think about life without grocery retailers. How would you go about buying that 12-pack of Coke or any of the hundreds of other items that you now routinely drop into your shopping cart?

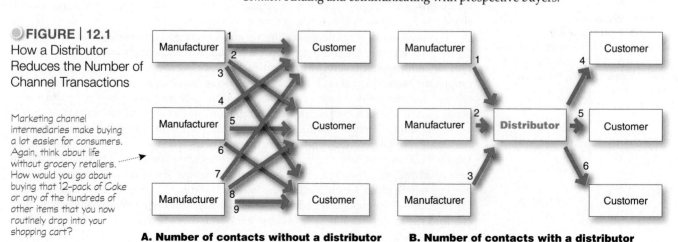

A. Number of contacts without a distributor　　**B. Number of contacts with a distributor**

- *Matching:* Shaping offers to meet the buyer's needs, including activities such as manufacturing, grading, assembling, and packaging.
- *Negotiation:* Reaching an agreement on price and other terms so that ownership or possession can be transferred.

Others help to fulfill the completed transactions:

- *Physical distribution:* Transporting and storing goods.
- *Financing:* Acquiring and using funds to cover the costs of the channel work.
- *Risk taking:* Assuming the risks of carrying out the channel work.

The question is not *whether* these functions need to be performed—they must be—but rather *who* will perform them. To the extent that the manufacturer performs these functions, its costs go up; therefore, its prices must be higher. When some of these functions are shifted to intermediaries, the producer's costs and prices may be lower, but the intermediaries must charge more to cover the costs of their work. In dividing the work of the channel, the various functions should be assigned to the channel members who can add the most value for the cost.

Number of Channel Levels

Channel level
A layer of intermediaries that performs some work in bringing the product and its ownership closer to the final buyer.

Direct marketing channel
A marketing channel that has no intermediary levels.

Indirect marketing channel
A marketing channel containing one or more intermediary levels.

Companies can design their distribution channels to make products and services available to customers in different ways. Each layer of marketing intermediaries that performs some work in bringing the product and its ownership closer to the final buyer is a **channel level**. Because both the producer and the final consumer perform some work, they are part of every channel.

The *number of intermediary levels* indicates the *length* of a channel. ● **Figure 12.2** shows both consumer and business channels of different lengths. Figure 12.2A shows several common consumer distribution channels. Channel 1, called a **direct marketing channel**, has no intermediary levels—the company sells directly to consumers. For example, Mary Kay Cosmetics and Amway sell their products door-to-door, through home and office sales parties, and on the Internet; companies ranging from GEICO insurance to Omaha Steaks sell directly to customers via the Internet and telephone. The remaining channels in Figure 12.2A are **indirect marketing channels**, containing one or more intermediaries.

Figure 12.2B shows some common business distribution channels. The business marketer can use its own sales force to sell directly to business customers. Or it can sell to

●**FIGURE | 12.2**
Consumer and Business
Marketing Channels

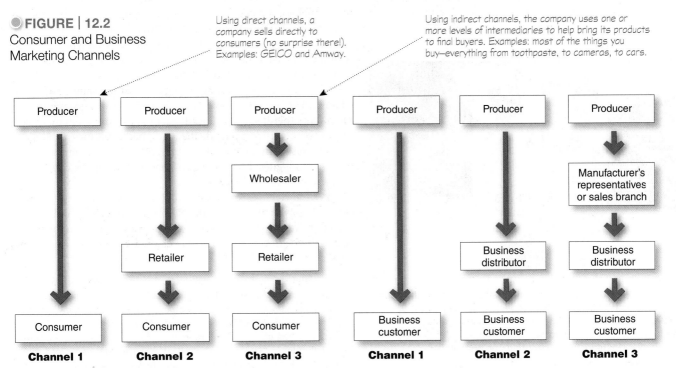

Using direct channels, a company sells directly to consumers (no surprise there!). Examples: GEICO and Amway.

Using indirect channels, the company uses one or more levels of intermediaries to help bring its products to final buyers. Examples: most of the things you buy—everything from toothpaste, to cameras, to cars.

A. Consumer marketing channels

B. Business marketing channels

various types of intermediaries, who in turn sell to these customers. Although consumer and business marketing channels with even more levels can sometimes be found, these are less common. From the producer's point of view, a greater number of levels means less control and greater channel complexity. Moreover, all the institutions in the channel are connected by several types of *flows*. These include the *physical flow* of products, the *flow of ownership*, the *payment flow*, the *information flow*, and the *promotion flow*. These flows can make even channels with only one or a few levels very complex.

Channel Behavior and Organization

Objective 2 ⸻▶
Discuss how channel members interact and how they organize to perform the work of the channel.

Distribution channels are more than simple collections of firms tied together by various flows. They are complex behavioral systems in which people and companies interact to accomplish individual, company, and channel goals. Some channel systems consist of only informal interactions among loosely organized firms. Others consist of formal interactions guided by strong organizational structures. Moreover, channel systems do not stand still—new types of intermediaries emerge and whole new channel systems evolve. Here we look at channel behavior and how members organize to do the work of the channel.

Channel Behavior

A marketing channel consists of firms that have partnered for their common good. Each channel member depends on the others. For example, a Ford dealer depends on Ford to design cars that meet customer needs. In turn, Ford depends on the dealer to attract customers, persuade them to buy Ford cars, and service the cars after the sale. Each Ford dealer also depends on other dealers to provide good sales and service that will uphold the brand's reputation. In fact, the success of individual Ford dealers depends on how well the entire Ford marketing channel competes with the channels of other auto manufacturers.

Each channel member plays a specialized role in the channel. For example, the role of Samsung is to produce electronics products that consumers will like and create demand through national advertising. Best Buy's role is to display these Samsung products in convenient locations, answer buyers' questions, and complete sales. The channel will be most effective when each member assumes the tasks it can do best.

Channel conflict
Disagreements among marketing channel members on goals, roles, and rewards—who should do what and for what rewards.

Ideally, because the success of individual channel members depends on the overall channel's success, all channel firms should work together smoothly. They should understand and accept their roles, coordinate their activities, and cooperate to attain overall channel goals. However, individual channel members rarely take such a broad view. Cooperating to achieve overall channel goals sometimes means giving up individual company goals. Although channel members depend on one another, they often act alone in their own short-run best interests. They often disagree on who should do what and for what rewards. Such disagreements over goals, roles, and rewards generate **channel conflict**.

Horizontal conflict occurs among firms at the same level of the channel. For instance, some Ford dealers in Chicago might complain that other dealers in the city steal sales from them by pricing too low or advertising outside their assigned territories. Or Holiday Inn franchisees might complain about other Holiday Inn operators overcharging guests or giving poor service, hurting the overall Holiday Inn image.

Vertical conflict, conflict between different levels of the same channel, is even more common. ● For example, KFC and its franchisees came into conflict over the company's decision to emphasize grilled chicken and sandwiches over the brand's traditional fried chicken.[2]

● Channel conflict: KFC came into conflict with its franchisees over the brand's "Unthink KFC" repositioning, which emphasized grilled chicken over its traditional Kentucky fried. "We ought to be shooting the competition," says one franchisee. "Instead, we're shooting one another."
Joshua Lutz/Redux

KFC claimed that it must reposition the brand around grilled chicken rather than fried to reach today's increasingly health-conscious, on-the-go consumers. However, a sizable group of the company's more than 4,000 U.S. franchisees have cried "foul" when the chain introduced grilled chicken, supported by a major marketing campaign with the slogan "Unthink KFC." The franchisees were concerned that abandoning the brand's Southern fried chicken legacy would confuse consumers and hurt sales. It "tells our customers not to think of us as a fried chicken chain," complained one franchisee who operates 60 franchises in five states. Soon after the "Unthink" campaign began, the KFC National Council & Advertising Cooperative, which represents all U.S. KFC franchisees, sued KFC to halt it. And the Association of Kentucky Fried Chicken Franchises, which represents two-thirds of U.S. franchisees, developed its own local marketing campaign emphasizing good old Kentucky fried. In the ongoing conflict, franchisees appear to have gained the upper hand. They won their lawsuit and KFC has dropped "Unthink KFC." However, the conflict has left a bad aftertaste in mouths on both sides. "We ought to be walking arm in arm to figure out a way out of [the current] sales decline. We ought to be shooting the competition," says one franchisee. "Instead, we're shooting one another."

Some conflict in the channel takes the form of healthy competition. Such competition can be good for the channel; without it, the channel could become passive and noninnovative. For example, KFC's conflict with its franchisees might represent normal give-and-take over the respective rights of the channel partners. However, severe or prolonged conflict can disrupt channel effectiveness and cause lasting harm to channel relationships. KFC should manage the channel conflict carefully to keep it from getting out of hand.

Vertical Marketing Systems

For the channel as a whole to perform well, each channel member's role must be specified, and channel conflict must be managed. The channel will perform better if it includes a firm, agency, or mechanism that provides leadership and has the power to assign roles and manage conflict.

Conventional distribution channel

A channel consisting of one or more independent producers, wholesalers, and retailers, each a separate business seeking to maximize its own profits, perhaps even at the expense of profits for the system as a whole.

Historically, *conventional distribution channels* have lacked such leadership and power, often resulting in damaging conflict and poor performance. One of the biggest channel developments over the years has been the emergence of *vertical marketing systems* that provide channel leadership. ● **Figure 12.3** contrasts the two types of channel arrangements.

A **conventional distribution channel** consists of one or more independent producers, wholesalers, and retailers. Each is a separate business seeking to maximize its own profits, perhaps even at the expense of the system as a whole. No channel member has much control over the other members, and no formal means exists for assigning roles and resolving channel conflict.

Vertical marketing system (VMS)

A channel structure in which producers, wholesalers, and retailers act as a unified system. One channel member owns the others, has contracts with them, or has so much power that they all cooperate.

In contrast, a **vertical marketing system (VMS)** consists of producers, wholesalers, and retailers acting as a unified system. One channel member owns the others, has contracts with them, or wields so much power that they must all cooperate. The VMS can be dominated by the producer, the wholesaler, or the retailer.

● **FIGURE | 12.3**
Comparison of Conventional Distribution Channel with Vertical Marketing System

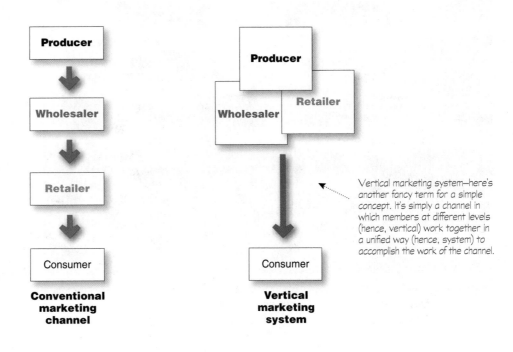

Vertical marketing system—here's another fancy term for a simple concept. It's simply a channel in which members at different levels (hence, vertical) work together in a unified way (hence, system) to accomplish the work of the channel.

Conventional marketing channel

Vertical marketing system

We look now at three major types of VMSs: *corporate*, *contractual*, and *administered*. Each uses a different means for setting up leadership and power in the channel.

Corporate VMS

Corporate VMS
A vertical marketing system that combines successive stages of production and distribution under single ownership—channel leadership is established through common ownership.

A **corporate VMS** integrates successive stages of production and distribution under single ownership. Coordination and conflict management are attained through regular organizational channels. For example, the grocery giant Kroger owns and operates 40 manufacturing plants—18 dairies, 10 deli and bakery plants, 10 grocery product plants, and 2 meat plants—that give it factory-to-store channel control over 40 percent of the more than 11,000 private-label items found on its shelves.[3] And integrating the entire distribution chain—from its own design and manufacturing operations to distribution through its own managed stores—has turned Spanish clothing chain Zara into the world's fastest-growing fashion retailer:[4]

> In recent years, fashion retailer Zara has attracted a near cultlike clientele of shoppers swarming to buy its "cheap chic"—stylish designs that resemble those of big-name fashion houses but at moderate prices. However, Zara's amazing success comes not just from *what* it sells, but from *how fast* its cutting-edge distribution system *delivers* what it sells. Zara delivers fast fashion—*really fast* fashion. Thanks to vertical integration, Zara can take a new fashion concept through design, manufacturing, and store-shelf placement in as little as two weeks, whereas competitors such as Gap, Benetton, or H&M often take six months or more. And the resulting low costs let Zara offer the very latest midmarket chic at downmarket prices.
>
> Speedy design and distribution allows Zara to introduce a copious supply of new fashions—at three times the rate of competitor introductions. Then, Zara's distribution system supplies its stores with small shipments of new merchandise two to three times each week, compared with competing chains' outlets, which get large shipments seasonally, usually just four to six times per year. The combination of a large number of timely new fashions delivered in frequent small batches gives Zara stores a continually updated merchandise mix that brings customers back more often. Fast turnover also results in less outdated and discounted merchandise. "Instead of betting on tomorrow's hot look," says one analyst, "Zara can wait to see what customers are actually buying—and make that."

Contractual VMS

Contractual VMS
A vertical marketing system in which independent firms at different levels of production and distribution join together through contracts.

A **contractual VMS** consists of independent firms at different levels of production and distribution who join together through contracts to obtain more economies or sales impact than each could achieve alone. Channel members coordinate their activities and manage conflict through contractual agreements.

Franchise organization
A contractual vertical marketing system in which a channel member, called a franchisor, links several stages in the production-distribution process.

The **franchise organization** is the most common type of contractual relationship. In this system, a channel member called a *franchisor* links several stages in the production-distribution process. In the United States alone, some 3,000 franchisors and 825,000 franchise outlets account for more than $2.1 trillion of economic output. Industry analysts estimate that a new franchise outlet opens somewhere in the United States every eight minutes and that about one out of every 12 retail business outlets is a franchised business.[5] Almost every kind of business has been franchised—from motels and fast-food restaurants to dental centers and dating services, from wedding consultants and handyman services to fitness centers and funeral homes.

There are three types of franchises. The first type is the *manufacturer-sponsored retailer franchise system*—for example, Ford and its network of independent franchised dealers. The

Franchising systems: Almost every kind of business has been franchised—from motels and fast-food restaurants to dating services and cleaning and handyman companies.

Mr. Handyman International

second type is the *manufacturer-sponsored wholesaler franchise system*—Coca-Cola licenses bottlers (wholesalers) in various world markets who buy Coca-Cola syrup concentrate and then bottle and sell the finished product to retailers locally. The third type is the *service-firm-sponsored retailer franchise system*—for example, Burger King and its nearly 12,300 franchisee-operated restaurants around the world. ● Other examples can be found in everything from auto rentals (Hertz, Avis), apparel retailers (The Athlete's Foot, Plato's Closet), and motels (Holiday Inn, Ramada Inn) to supplemental education (Huntington Learning Center, Kumon) and personal services (Great Clips, Massage Envy, Mr. Handyman).

The fact that most consumers cannot tell the difference between contractual and corporate VMSs shows how successfully the contractual organizations compete with corporate chains. The next chapter presents a fuller discussion of the various contractual VMSs.

Administered VMS

Administered VMS
A vertical marketing system that coordinates successive stages of production and distribution through the size and power of one of the parties.

In an **administered VMS**, leadership is assumed not through common ownership or contractual ties but through the size and power of one or a few dominant channel members. Manufacturers of a top brand can obtain strong trade cooperation and support from resellers. For example, GE, P&G, and Kraft can command unusual cooperation from many resellers regarding displays, shelf space, promotions, and price policies. In turn, large retailers such as Walmart, Home Depot, and Barnes & Noble can exert strong influence on the many manufacturers that supply the products they sell.

For example, with commodity prices increasing, many consumer goods manufacturers want to pass these costs along to Walmart and other retailers in the form of higher prices. However, Walmart wants to hold the line on its own costs and prices in order to maintain its low-price positioning with customers in tighter times. This creates push and pull between Walmart and its suppliers, a tussle in which Walmart—the biggest grocery seller in the United States—usually gets its way. Take Clorox Company, for instance. Although the company's strong consumer brand preference gives it significant negotiating power, Walmart simply holds more cards. Sales to Walmart make up 26 percent of Clorox's sales, so maintaining a strong relationship with the giant retailer is crucial.[6]

Horizontal Marketing Systems

Horizontal marketing system
A channel arrangement in which two or more companies at one level join together to follow a new marketing opportunity.

Another channel development is the **horizontal marketing system**, in which two or more companies at one level join together to follow a new marketing opportunity. By working together, companies can combine their financial, production, or marketing resources to accomplish more than any one company could alone.

Companies might join forces with competitors or noncompetitors. They might work with each other on a temporary or permanent basis, or they may create a separate company. For example, Walmart—famous for squeezing costs out of its supply chain—wants to team with PepsiCo's Frito-Lay unit to buy potatoes jointly for a lower price than either company could get alone. That would help both companies to earn more on the spuds and chips they sell in Walmart's stores. ● Walmart also partners with McDonald's to place "express" versions of McDonald's restaurants in Walmart stores. McDonald's benefits from Walmart's heavy store traffic, and Walmart keeps hungry shoppers from needing to go elsewhere to eat.[7]

Competitors Microsoft and Yahoo! have joined forces to create a horizontal Internet search alliance. Until 2020, Microsoft's Bing will power Yahoo! searches. In turn, Yahoo! will sell premium search advertising services for both companies. The collaboration, dubbed Bingahoo by industry insiders, has proven beneficial. Because one advertising purchase

● **Horizontal marketing channels: McDonald's places "express" versions of its restaurants in Walmart stores. McDonald's benefits from Walmart's heavy store traffic and Walmart keeps hungry shoppers from needing to go elsewhere to eat.**

Photo courtesy of Gary Armstrong

brings results on both Bing and Yahoo!, advertisers have more incentive to use the combined platform. In the first year, total ad spending climbed 44 percent, making the two companies together a stronger challenger to industry leader Google.[8]

Multichannel Distribution Systems

Multichannel distribution system

A distribution system in which a single firm sets up two or more marketing channels to reach one or more customer segments.

In the past, many companies used a single channel to sell to a single market or market segment. Today, with the proliferation of customer segments and channel possibilities, more and more companies have adopted **multichannel distribution systems**. Such multichannel marketing occurs when a single firm sets up two or more marketing channels to reach one or more customer segments.

Figure 12.4 shows a multichannel marketing system. In the figure, the producer sells directly to consumer segment 1 using catalogs, telemarketing, and the Internet and reaches consumer segment 2 through retailers. It sells indirectly to business segment 1 through distributors and dealers and to business segment 2 through its own sales force.

These days, almost every large company and many small ones distribute through multiple channels. For example, John Deere sells its familiar green and yellow lawn and garden tractors, mowers, and outdoor power products to consumers and commercial users through several channels, including John Deere retailers, Lowe's home improvement stores, and online. It sells and services its tractors, combines, planters, and other agricultural equipment through its premium John Deere dealer network. And it sells large construction and forestry equipment through selected large, full-service John Deere dealers and their sales forces.

Multichannel distribution systems offer many advantages to companies facing large and complex markets. With each new channel, the company expands its sales and market coverage and gains opportunities to tailor its products and services to the specific needs of diverse customer segments. But such multichannel systems are harder to control, and they generate conflict as more channels compete for customers and sales. For example, when John Deere began selling selected consumer products through Lowe's home improvement stores, many of its dealers complained loudly. To avoid such conflicts in its Internet marketing channels, the company routes all of its Web site sales to John Deere dealers.

Changing Channel Organization

Disintermediation

The cutting out of marketing channel intermediaries by product or service producers or the displacement of traditional resellers by radical new types of intermediaries.

Changes in technology and the explosive growth of direct and online marketing are having a profound impact on the nature and design of marketing channels. One major trend is toward **disintermediation**—a big term with a clear message and important consequences. Disintermediation occurs when product or service producers cut out intermediaries and go directly to final buyers or when radically new types of channel intermediaries displace traditional ones.

FIGURE | 12.4
Multichannel Distribution System

Most large companies distribute through multiple channels. For example, you could buy a familiar green and yellow John Deere lawn tractor from a neighborhood John Deere dealer or from Lowe's. A large farm or forestry business would buy larger John Deere equipment from a premium full-service John Deere dealer and its sales force.

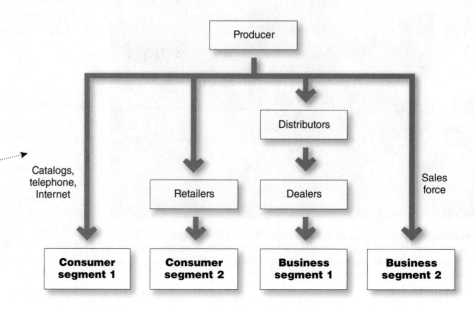

● **Disintermediation: Resellers must innovate or risk being swept aside. For example, Barnes & Noble, the giant that helped put so many independent booksellers out of business, now faces disintermediation at the hands of online booksellers and digital e-book downloads.**

Bloomberg via Getty Images

Thus, in many industries, traditional intermediaries are dropping by the wayside. For example, Southwest, JetBlue, and other airlines sell tickets directly to final buyers, cutting travel agents from their marketing channels altogether. In other cases, new forms of resellers are displacing traditional intermediaries, as is the case with online marketers taking business from traditional brick-and-mortar retailers. For example, online music download services such as iTunes and Amazon MP3 have pretty much put traditional music-store retailers out of business. And Amazon.com almost single-handedly bankrupted the nation's number two bookseller, Borders, in less than 10 years, and it has recently forced highly successful store retailers such as Best Buy to dramatically rethink their entire operating models. In fact, many retailing experts question whether stores like Best Buy can compete in the long run against online rivals.[9]

Disintermediation presents both opportunities and problems for producers and resellers. Channel innovators who find new ways to add value in the channel can displace traditional resellers and reap the rewards. In turn, traditional intermediaries must continue to innovate to avoid being swept aside. For example, superstore booksellers Borders and Barnes & Noble pioneered huge book selections and low prices, sending most small independent bookstores into ruin. Then, along came Amazon.com, which threatened even the largest brick-and-mortar bookstores through online book sales. Now, both offline and online sellers of physical books are being threatened by digital book downloads and e-readers. Rather than being threatened by these digital developments, however, Amazon.com is leading them with its highly successful Kindle e-readers. By contrast, Barnes & Noble—the giant that helped put so many independent bookstores out of business—is a latecomer to e-books with its Nook e-reader and now finds itself locked in a battle for survival.[10]

Like resellers, to remain competitive, product and service producers must develop new channel opportunities, such as the Internet and other direct channels. However, developing these new channels often brings them into direct competition with their established channels, resulting in conflict. To ease this problem, companies often look for ways to make going direct a plus for the entire channel. For example, guitar and amp maker Fender knows that many customers would prefer to buy its guitars, amps, and accessories online. But selling directly through its Web site would create conflicts with retail partners, from large chains such as Guitar Center, Sam Ash, and Best Buy to small shops scattered throughout the world, such as the Musician's Junkyard in Windsor, Vermont, or Freddy for Music in Amman, Jordan. So Fender's Web site provides detailed information about the company's products, but you can't buy a new Fender Stratocaster or Acoustasonic guitar there. Instead, the Fender Web site refers you to its resellers' Web sites and stores. Thus, Fender's direct marketing helps both the company and its channel partners.

Objective 3 ┄┄►

Identify the major channel alternatives open to a company.

Channel Design Decisions

We now look at several channel design decisions manufacturers face. In designing marketing channels, manufacturers struggle between what is ideal and what is practical. A new firm with limited capital usually starts by selling in a limited market area. In this case, deciding on the best channels might not be a problem: The problem might simply be how to convince one or a few good intermediaries to handle the line.

If successful, the new firm can branch out to new markets through existing intermediaries. In smaller markets, the firm might sell directly to retailers; in larger markets, it might sell through distributors. In one part of the country, it might grant exclusive franchises; in another, it might sell through all available outlets. Then it might add an Internet store that sells directly to hard-to-reach customers. In this way, channel systems often evolve to meet market opportunities and conditions.

For maximum effectiveness, however, channel analysis and decision making should be more purposeful. **Marketing channel design** calls for analyzing consumer needs, setting channel objectives, identifying major channel alternatives, and evaluating those alternatives.

Marketing channel design
Designing effective marketing channels by analyzing customer needs, setting channel objectives, identifying major channel alternatives, and evaluating those alternatives.

Analyzing Consumer Needs

As noted previously, marketing channels are part of the overall *customer-value delivery network*. Each channel member and level adds value for the customer. Thus, designing the marketing channel starts with finding out what target consumers want from the channel. Do consumers want to buy from nearby locations or are they willing to travel to more distant and centralized locations? Would customers rather buy in person, by phone, or online? Do they value breadth of assortment or do they prefer specialization? Do consumers want many add-on services (delivery, installation, repairs), or will they obtain these services elsewhere? The faster the delivery, the greater the assortment provided, and the more add-on services supplied, the greater the channel's service level.

Providing the fastest delivery, the greatest assortment, and the most services may not be possible or practical, however. The company and its channel members may not have the resources or skills needed to provide all the desired services. Also, providing higher levels of service results in higher costs for the channel and higher prices for consumers. ● For example, your local independent hardware store probably provides more personalized service, a more convenient location, and less shopping hassle than the nearest huge Home Depot or Lowe's store. But it may also charge higher prices. The company must balance consumer needs not only against the feasibility and costs of meeting these needs but also against customer price preferences. The success of discount retailing shows that consumers will often accept lower service levels in exchange for lower prices.

● **Meeting customers' channel service needs: Your local hardware store probably provides more personalized service, a more convenient location, and less shopping hassle than a huge Home Depot or Lowe's store. But it may also charge higher prices.**

DAVID WALTER BANKS/The New York Times/Redux Pictures

Setting Channel Objectives

Companies should state their marketing channel objectives in terms of targeted levels of customer service. Usually, a company can identify several segments wanting different levels of service. The company should decide which segments to serve and the best channels to use in each case. In each segment, the company wants to minimize the total channel cost of meeting customer service requirements.

The company's channel objectives are also influenced by the nature of the company, its products, its marketing intermediaries, its competitors, and the environment. For example, the company's size and financial situation determine which marketing functions it can handle itself and which it must give to intermediaries. Companies selling perishable products, for example, may require more direct marketing to avoid delays and too much handling.

In some cases, a company may want to compete in or near the same outlets that carry competitors' products. For example, Maytag wants its appliances displayed alongside competing brands to facilitate comparison shopping. In other cases, companies may avoid the channels used by competitors. Mary Kay Cosmetics, for example, sells directly to consumers through its corps of more than two million independent beauty consultants in more than

35 markets worldwide rather than going head-to-head with other cosmetics makers for scarce positions in retail stores.[11] GEICO primarily markets auto and homeowner's insurance directly to consumers via the telephone and the Internet rather than through agents.

Finally, environmental factors such as economic conditions and legal constraints may affect channel objectives and design. For example, in a depressed economy, producers will want to distribute their goods in the most economical way, using shorter channels and dropping unneeded services that add to the final price of the goods.

Identifying Major Alternatives

When the company has defined its channel objectives, it should next identify its major channel alternatives in terms of the *types* of intermediaries, the *number* of intermediaries, and the *responsibilities* of each channel member.

Types of Intermediaries

A firm should identify the types of channel members available to carry out its channel work. Most companies face many channel member choices. For example, until recently, Dell sold directly to final consumers and business buyers only through its sophisticated phone and Internet marketing channel. It also sold directly to large corporate, institutional, and government buyers using its direct sales force. However, to reach more consumers and match competitors such as HP and Apple, Dell now sells indirectly through retailers such as Best Buy, Staples, and Walmart. It also sells indirectly through value-added resellers, independent distributors and dealers who develop computer systems and applications tailored to the special needs of small- and medium-sized business customers.

Using many types of resellers in a channel provides both benefits and drawbacks. For example, by selling through retailers and value-added resellers in addition to its own direct channels, Dell can reach more and different kinds of buyers. However, the new channels will be more difficult to manage and control. In addition, the direct and indirect channels will compete with each other for many of the same customers, causing potential conflict. In fact, Dell often finds itself "stuck in the middle," with its direct sales reps complaining about competition from retail stores, whereas its value-added resellers complain that the direct sales reps are undercutting their business.

Number of Marketing Intermediaries

Companies must also determine the number of channel members to use at each level. Three strategies are available: intensive distribution, exclusive distribution, and selective distribution. Producers of convenience products and common raw materials typically seek **intensive distribution**—a strategy in which they stock their products in as many outlets as possible. These products must be available where and when consumers want them. For example, toothpaste, candy, and other similar items are sold in millions of outlets to provide maximum brand exposure and consumer convenience. Kraft, Coca-Cola, Kimberly-Clark, and other consumer-goods companies distribute their products in this way.

By contrast, some producers purposely limit the number of intermediaries handling their products. The extreme form of this practice is **exclusive distribution**, in which the producer gives only a limited number of dealers the exclusive right to distribute its products in their territories. Exclusive distribution is often found in the distribution of luxury brands. For example, exclusive Bentley automobiles are typically sold by only a handful of authorized dealers in any given market area. However, some shopping goods producers also practice exclusive distribution. ● For instance, outdoor power equipment maker STIHL doesn't sell its chain saws, blowers, hedge trimmers, and other products through mass merchandisers such as Lowe's, Home Depot, or Sears. Instead, it sells through a select corps of independent hardware and lawn and garden dealers. By granting exclusive distribution, STIHL gains stronger dealer selling support. Exclusive distribution also enhances the STIHL brand's image and allows for higher markups resulting from greater value-added dealer service.

Between intensive and exclusive distribution lies **selective distribution**—the use of more than one but fewer than all of the intermediaries who are willing to carry a company's products. Most television, furniture, and home appliance brands are distributed in this manner. For example, Whirlpool and GE sell their major appliances

Intensive distribution
Stocking the product in as many outlets as possible.

Exclusive distribution
Giving a limited number of dealers the exclusive right to distribute the company's products in their territories.

Selective distribution
The use of more than one but fewer than all of the intermediaries who are willing to carry the company's products.

Why is the world's number one selling brand of chain saw not sold at Lowe's or The Home Depot?

We can give you 8,000 reasons, our legion of independent STIHL dealers nationwide. We count on them every day and so can you. To give you a product demonstration, straight talk and genuine advice about STIHL products. To

offer fast and expert on-site service. And to stand behind every product they carry, always fully assembled. You see, we won't sell you a chain saw in a box, not even in a big one. **Are you ready for a STIHL?**

To find a dealer: stihlusa.com or call 1-800 GO STIHL.

The Home Depot and Lowe's are registered trademarks of their respective companies.

STIHL

● **Exclusive distribution: STIHL sells its chain saws, blowers, hedge trimmers, and other products through a select corps of independent hardware and lawn and garden retailers. "We count on them every day and so can you."**

Courtesy of STIHL, Inc.

through dealer networks and selected large retailers. By using selective distribution, they can develop good working relationships with selected channel members and expect a better-than-average selling effort. Selective distribution gives producers good market coverage with more control and less cost than does intensive distribution.

Responsibilities of Channel Members

The producer and the intermediaries need to agree on the terms and responsibilities of each channel member. They should agree on price policies, conditions of sale, territory rights, and the specific services to be performed by each party. The producer should establish a list price and a fair set of discounts for the intermediaries. It must define each channel member's territory, and it should be careful about where it places new resellers.

Mutual services and duties need to be spelled out carefully, especially in franchise and exclusive distribution channels. For example, McDonald's provides franchisees with promotional support, a record-keeping system, training at Hamburger University, and general management assistance. In turn, franchisees must meet company standards for physical facilities and food quality, cooperate with new promotion programs, provide requested information, and buy specified food products.

Evaluating the Major Alternatives

Suppose a company has identified several channel alternatives and wants to select the one that will best satisfy its long-run objectives. Each alternative should be evaluated against economic, control, and adaptability criteria.

Using *economic criteria*, a company compares the likely sales, costs, and profitability of different channel alternatives. What will be the investment required by each channel alternative, and what returns will result? The company must also consider *control issues*. Using intermediaries usually means giving them some control over the marketing of the product, and some intermediaries take more control than others. Other things being equal, the company prefers to keep as much control as possible. Finally, the company must apply *adaptability criteria*. Channels often involve long-term commitments, yet the company wants to keep the channel flexible so that it can adapt to environmental changes. Thus, to be considered, a channel involving long-term commitments should be greatly superior on economic and control grounds.

Designing International Distribution Channels

International marketers face many additional complexities in designing their channels. Each country has its own unique distribution system that has evolved over time and changes very slowly. These channel systems can vary widely from country to country. Thus, global marketers must usually adapt their channel strategies to the existing structures within each country.

In some markets, the distribution system is complex and hard to penetrate, consisting of many layers and large numbers of intermediaries. For example, many Western companies find Japan's distribution system difficult to navigate. It's steeped in tradition and very complex, with many distributors touching the product before it arrives on the store shelf.

At the other extreme, distribution systems in developing countries may be scattered, inefficient, or altogether lacking. For example, China and India are huge markets—each with a population well over one billion people. However, because of inadequate distribution systems, most companies can profitably access only a small portion of the population located in each country's most affluent cities. Rural markets in both countries are highly decentralized, made of many distinct submarkets, each with its own subculture. China's distribution system is so fragmented that logistics costs to wrap, bundle, load, unload, sort, reload, and transport goods amount to more than 17 percent of the nation's GDP, far higher than in most other countries. (U.S. logistics costs account for just under 9 percent of the nation's GDP.) After years of effort, even Walmart executives admit that they have been unable to assemble an efficient supply chain in China.[12]

Sometimes local conditions can greatly influence how a company distributes products in global markets. For example, in low-income neighborhoods in Brazil where consumers have limited access to supermarkets, Nestlé supplements its distribution with thousands of self-employed salespeople who sell Nestlé products door to door. And in crowded cities in Asia and Africa, fast-food restaurants such as McDonald's and KFC offer delivery:[13]

⬤ **The McDonald's delivery guy: In cities like Beijing, Seoul, and Cairo, armies of motorbike delivery drivers outfitted in colorful uniforms and bearing food in specially designed boxes strapped to their backs make their way through bustling traffic to deliver Big Macs.**

Li shengli - Imaginechina

Whereas Americans who want a quick meal delivered to their homes are likely to order in Chinese, people in China and elsewhere around the world are now ordering in from McDonald's or KFC. In big cities such as Beijing, Cairo, and Seoul, South Korea, where crowded streets and high real estate costs make drive-throughs impractical, delivery is becoming an important part of fast-food strategy. In these markets, McDonald's and KFC now dispatch legions of motorbike delivery drivers in colorful uniforms to dispense Big Macs and buckets of chicken to customers who call in. In McDonald's Asia/Pacific, Middle East, and Africa division, 1,500 of its 8,800 restaurants now offer delivery. "We've used the slogan, 'If you can't come to us, we'll come to you,'" says the division's president. More than 30 percent of McDonald's total sales in Egypt and 12 percent of its Singapore sales come from delivery. Similarly, for KFC, delivery accounts for nearly half of all sales in Kuwait and a third of sales in Egypt.

Thus, international marketers face a wide range of channel alternatives. Designing efficient and effective channel systems between and within various country markets poses a difficult challenge. We discuss international distribution decisions further in Chapter 19.

Objective 4 ⤑
Explain how companies select, motivate, and evaluate channel members.

Channel Management Decisions

Once the company has reviewed its channel alternatives and determined the best channel design, it must implement and manage the chosen channel. **Marketing channel management** calls for selecting, managing, and motivating individual channel members and evaluating their performance over time.

Selecting Channel Members

Marketing channel management
Selecting, managing, and motivating individual channel members and evaluating their performance over time.

Producers vary in their ability to attract qualified marketing intermediaries. Some producers have no trouble signing up channel members. For example, when Toyota first introduced its Lexus line in the United States, it had no trouble attracting new dealers. In fact, it had to turn down many would-be resellers.

At the other extreme are producers who have to work hard to line up enough qualified intermediaries. For example, when Timex first tried to sell its inexpensive watches through regular jewelry stores, most jewelry stores refused to carry them. The company then managed to get its watches into mass-merchandise outlets. This turned out to be a wise decision because of the rapid growth of mass merchandising.

Even established brands may have difficulty gaining and keeping their desired distribution, especially when dealing with powerful resellers. For example, you won't find P&G's Pampers diapers in a Costco store. After P&G declined to manufacture Costco's Kirkland store brand diapers a few years ago, Costco gave Pampers the boot and now only carries Huggies and its own Kirkland brand (manufactured by Huggies maker Kimberly-Clark). The removal by Costco, the number two diaper retailer after Walmart, has cost P&G an estimated $150 million to $200 million in annual sales.[14]

When selecting intermediaries, the company should determine what characteristics distinguish the better ones. It will want to evaluate each channel member's years in business, other lines carried, location, growth and profit record, cooperativeness, and reputation.

Managing and Motivating Channel Members

Once selected, channel members must be continuously managed and motivated to do their best. The company must sell not only *through* the intermediaries but also *to* and *with* them. Most companies see their intermediaries as first-line customers and partners. They practice strong *partner relationship management* to forge long-term partnerships with channel members. This creates a value delivery system that meets the needs of both the company *and* its marketing partners.

In managing its channels, a company must convince suppliers and distributors that they can succeed better by working together as a part of a cohesive value delivery system. Thus, P&G works closely with Target to create superior value for final consumers. The two jointly plan merchandising goals and strategies, inventory levels, and advertising and promotion programs. Similarly, Toyota works to create supplier satisfaction, which in turn helps to create greater customer satisfaction. Whether it's heavy-equipment manufacturer Caterpillar partnering with its network of large dealers or cosmetics maker L'Oréal building mutually beneficial relationships with its large network of suppliers, companies must work in close harmony with others in the channel to find better ways to bring value to customers (see Real Marketing 12.1).

Many companies are now installing integrated high-tech partnership relationship management (PRM) systems to coordinate their whole-channel marketing efforts. Just as they use CRM software systems to help manage relationships with important customers, companies can now use PRM and supply chain management (SCM) software to help recruit, train, organize, manage, motivate, and evaluate relationships with channel partners.

Evaluating Channel Members

The company must regularly check channel member performance against standards such as sales quotas, average inventory levels, customer delivery time, treatment of damaged and lost goods, cooperation in company promotion and training programs, and services to the customer. The company should recognize and reward intermediaries who are performing well and adding good value for consumers. Those who are performing poorly should be assisted or, as a last resort, replaced.

Finally, companies need to be sensitive to the needs of their channel partners. Those who treat their partners poorly risk not only losing their support but also causing some legal problems. The next section describes various rights and duties pertaining to companies and other channel members.

Public Policy and Distribution Decisions

For the most part, companies are legally free to develop whatever channel arrangements suit them. In fact, the laws affecting channels seek to prevent the exclusionary tactics of some companies that might keep another company from using a desired channel. Most

Real Marketing 12.1

Working with Channel Partners to Create Value for Customers

Today's successful companies know that they can't go it alone in creating value for customers. Instead they must create effective value delivery systems, consisting of suppliers, producers, and distributors who work together to get the job done. Partnering with suppliers and distributors can yield big competitive advantages. Consider these examples.

Caterpillar

Heavy-equipment manufacturer Caterpillar produces innovative, high-quality industrial equipment products. But ask anyone at Caterpillar and they'll tell you that the most important reason for Caterpillar's dominance is its outstanding distribution network of 191 independent dealers in more than 180 countries. "Our dealers [have] been the source of our Cat brand advantage more than most people really understand," says Caterpillar CEO Doug Oberhelman.

According to Oberhelman, dealers are the ones on the front line. Once the product leaves the factory, the dealers take over. They're the ones that customers see. So rather than selling to or through its dealers, Caterpillar treats dealers as inside partners. When a big piece of Caterpillar equipment breaks down, customers know that they can count on both Caterpillar and its dealer network for support. On a deeper level, dealers play a vital role in almost every aspect of Caterpillar's operations, from product design and delivery to service and support.

Dealers are a key element in what Caterpillar insiders call the "Caterpillar flywheel"—a kind of virtuous circle of success. Big, healthy dealers help Caterpillar sell the most machines. In turn, all those machines in the field bring dealers lots of parts and service revenues, so much that they can survive even in lean years when they don't sell many new machines. That financial stability helps dealers grow bigger, attracting even more customers who buy machines from Caterpillar.

In sum, a strong dealer network makes for a strong Caterpillar and the other way around. So it makes sense that Caterpillar really knows its dealers and cares about their success. In fact, high on Cat's 13-point list of priorities is "dealer health." The company closely monitors each dealership's sales, market position, service capabilities, and financial situation. When it sees a problem, it jumps in to help.

In addition to more formal business ties, Caterpillar also forms close personal ties with dealers in a kind of family relationship. This leads to a deep sense of pride among dealers at what they are accomplishing together—a feeling that they are an important part of an organization that makes, sells, and tends to the machines that make the world work.

As a result of its close partnership with dealers, the big Cat is purring. Caterpillar dominates the world's markets for heavy construction, mining, and logging equipment. Its familiar yellow tractors, crawlers, loaders, bulldozers, and trucks capture well over a third of the worldwide heavy-equipment business, more than twice that of number two Komatsu.

Toyota

Achieving satisfying supplier relationships has been a cornerstone of Toyota's stunning success. Historically, Toyota's U.S. competitors often alienated their suppliers through self-serving, heavy-handed dealings. "The [U. S. automakers] set annual cost-reduction targets [for the parts they buy]," said one supplier. "To realize those targets, they'll do anything. [They've unleashed] a reign of terror, and it gets worse every year." Says another, "[One automaker] seems to send its people to 'hate school' so that they learn how to hate suppliers."

By contrast, Toyota has long known the importance of building close relationships with suppliers. In fact, it even includes the phrase "achieve supplier satisfaction" in its mission statement. Rather than bullying suppliers, Toyota partners with them and helps them to meet its very high expectations. It learns about their businesses, conducts joint improvement activities, helps train supplier employees, gives daily performance feedback, and actively seeks out supplier concerns. It even recognizes top suppliers with annual performance awards.

Caterpillar partners closely with its worldwide network of independent dealers to bring value to customers. When a big piece of Caterpillar equipment breaks down, customers know that they can count on both Caterpillar and its outstanding dealer network for support.
© Horizon International Images Limited/Alamy

In a recent annual survey of auto parts makers—which measured items such as trust, open and honest communication, help given to reduce costs, and opportunities to make a profit—Toyota scored higher than any other automaker. The survey showed that Toyota suppliers consider themselves true partners with the automotive giant.

Such high supplier satisfaction means that Toyota can rely on suppliers to help it improve its own quality, reduce costs, and develop new products quickly. For example, when Toyota recently launched a program to reduce prices by 30 percent on 170 parts that it would buy for its next generation of cars, suppliers didn't complain. Instead, they pitched in, trusting that Toyota would help them achieve the targeted reductions, in turn making them more competitive and profitable in the future. In all, creating satisfied suppliers helps Toyota produce lower-cost, higher-quality cars, which in turn results in more satisfied customers.

L'Oréal

L'Oréal is the world's largest cosmetics maker, with 23 global brands ranging from Maybelline and Kiehl's to Lancôme and Redken. What does a cosmetics maker have in common with down-and-dirty industrial giants like Caterpillar and Toyota? Like both of those companies, L'Oréal's extensive supplier network—which supplies everything from polymers and fats to spray cans and packaging to production equipment and office supplies—is crucial to its success.

As a result, L'Oréal treats suppliers as respected partners. On the one hand, it expects a lot from suppliers in terms of design innovation, quality, and socially responsible actions. The company carefully screens new suppliers and regularly assesses the performance of current suppliers. On the other hand, L'Oréal works closely with suppliers to help them meet its exacting standards. Whereas some companies make unreasonable demands of their suppliers and "squeeze" them for short-term gains, L'Oréal builds long-term supplier relationships based on mutual benefit and growth.

According to the company's supplier Web site, it treats suppliers with "fundamental respect for their business, their culture, their growth, and the individuals who work there." Each relationship is based on "dialogue and joint efforts. L'Oréal seeks not only to help its suppliers meet its expectations but also to contribute to their growth, through opportunities for innovation and competitiveness." As a result, more than 75 percent of L'Oréal's supplier partners have been working with the company for 10 years or more and the majority of them for several decades. Says the company's head of purchasing, "The CEO wants to make L'Oréal a top performer and one of the world's most respected companies. Being respected also means being respected by our suppliers."

Sources: Geoff Colvin, "Caterpillar Is Absolutely Crushing It," *Fortune,* May 12, 2011, pp. 136–144; Jeffery K. Liker and Thomas Y. Choi, "Building Deep Supplier Relationships," *Harvard Business Review,* 2004, pp. 104–113; "What the World Needs: 2011 Year in Review," Caterpillar Annual Report, February 2012, www.caterpillar.com/cda/files/2674611/7/cat_yir_1.pdf, p. 37; Paul Eisensten, "Toyota Tops in Supplier Relations—Just Barely," *The Detroit Bureau,* May 23, 2011, www.thedetroitbureau.com/2011/05/toyota-tops-in-supplier-relations-but-just-barely/; and www.caterpillar.com, www.toyotasupplier.com, and www.loreal.com/_en/_ww/html/suppliers/, accessed November, 2012.

channel law deals with the mutual rights and duties of channel members once they have formed a relationship.

Many producers and wholesalers like to develop exclusive channels for their products. When the seller allows only certain outlets to carry its products, this strategy is called *exclusive distribution*. When the seller requires that these dealers not handle competitors' products, its strategy is called *exclusive dealing*. Both parties can benefit from exclusive arrangements: The seller obtains more loyal and dependable outlets, and the dealers obtain a steady source of supply and stronger seller support. But exclusive arrangements also exclude other producers from selling to these dealers. This situation brings exclusive dealing contracts under the scope of the Clayton Act of 1914. They are legal as long as they do not substantially lessen competition or tend to create a monopoly and as long as both parties enter into the agreement voluntarily.

Exclusive dealing often includes *exclusive territorial agreements*. The producer may agree not to sell to other dealers in a given area, or the buyer may agree to sell only in its own territory. The first practice is normal under franchise systems as a way to increase dealer enthusiasm and commitment. It is also perfectly legal—a seller has no legal obligation to sell through more outlets than it wishes. The second practice, whereby the producer tries to keep a dealer from selling outside its territory, has become a major legal issue.

Producers of a strong brand sometimes sell it to dealers only if the dealers will take some or all of the rest of its line. This is called *full-line forcing*. Such *tying agreements* are not necessarily illegal, but they violate the Clayton Act if they tend to lessen competition substantially. The practice may prevent consumers from freely choosing among competing suppliers of these other brands.

Finally, producers are free to select their dealers, but their right to terminate dealers is somewhat restricted. In general, sellers can drop dealers "for cause." However, they cannot drop dealers if, for example, the dealers refuse to cooperate in a doubtful legal arrangement, such as exclusive dealing or tying agreements.

Marketing Logistics and Supply Chain Management

Objective 5 ┈┈➤
Discuss the nature and importance of marketing logistics and integrated supply chain management.

In today's global marketplace, selling a product is sometimes easier than getting it to customers. Companies must decide on the best way to store, handle, and move their products and services so that they are available to customers in the right assortments, at the right time, and in the right place. Logistics effectiveness has a major impact on both customer satisfaction and company costs. Here we consider the nature and importance of logistics management in the supply chain, the goals of the logistics system, major logistics functions, and the need for integrated supply chain management.

Nature and Importance of Marketing Logistics

Marketing logistics (or physical distribution)

Planning, implementing, and controlling the physical flow of materials, final goods, and related information from points of origin to points of consumption to meet customer requirements at a profit.

To some managers, marketing logistics means only trucks and warehouses. But modern logistics is much more than this. **Marketing logistics**—also called **physical distribution**—involves planning, implementing, and controlling the physical flow of goods, services, and related information from points of origin to points of consumption to meet customer requirements at a profit. In short, it involves getting the right product to the right customer in the right place at the right time.

In the past, physical distribution planners typically started with products at the plant and then tried to find low-cost solutions to get them to customers. However, today's *customer-centered* logistics starts with the marketplace and works backward to the factory or even to sources of supply. Marketing logistics involves not only *outbound logistics* (moving products from the factory to resellers and ultimately to customers) but also *inbound logistics* (moving products and materials from suppliers to the factory) and *reverse logistics* (reusing, recycling, refurbishing, or disposing of broken, unwanted, or excess products returned by consumers or resellers). That is, it involves entire **supply chain management**—managing upstream and downstream value-added flows of materials, final goods, and related information among suppliers, the company, resellers, and final consumers, as shown in ● **Figure 12.5**.

Supply chain management

Managing upstream and downstream value-added flows of materials, final goods, and related information among suppliers, the company, resellers, and final consumers.

The logistics manager's task is to coordinate the activities of suppliers, purchasing agents, marketers, channel members, and customers. These activities include forecasting, information systems, purchasing, production planning, order processing, inventory, warehousing, and transportation planning.

Companies today are placing greater emphasis on logistics for several reasons. First, companies can gain a powerful competitive advantage by using improved logistics to give customers better service or lower prices. Second, improved logistics can yield tremendous cost savings to both a company and its customers. As much as 20 percent of an average product's price is accounted for by shipping and transport alone.

● FIGURE | 12.5
Supply Chain Management

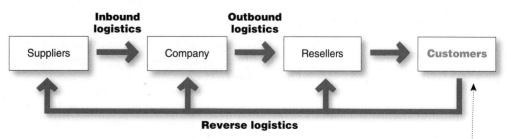

Managing the supply chain calls for *customer-centered* thinking. Remember, it's also called the customer-value delivery network.

Logistics: As this huge stockpile of shipping containers suggests, American companies spent $1.1 trillion last year—7.7 percent of U.S. GDP—to bundle, load, unload, sort, reload, and transport goods.

E.G. Pors/Shutterstock.com

This far exceeds the cost of advertising and many other marketing costs. ● American companies spend $1.1 trillion each year—about 7.7 percent of GDP—to wrap, bundle, load, unload, sort, reload, and transport goods. That's more than the national GDPs of all but 13 countries worldwide.[15]

Shaving off even a small fraction of logistics costs can mean substantial savings. For example, Walmart recently undertook a program of logistics improvements through more efficient sourcing, better inventory management, and greater supply chain productivity that will reduce supply chain costs by 5 to 15 percent over the next five years—that's a whopping $4 billion to $12 billion.[16]

Third, the explosion in product variety has created a need for improved logistics management. For example, in 1916 the typical Piggly Wiggly grocery store carried only 605 items. Today, a Piggly Wiggly carries a bewildering stock of between 20,000 and 35,000 items, depending on store size. A Walmart Supercenter store carries more than 100,000 products, 30,000 of which are grocery products.[17] Ordering, shipping, stocking, and controlling such a variety of products presents a sizable logistics challenge.

Improvements in information technology have also created opportunities for major gains in distribution efficiency. Today's companies are using sophisticated supply chain management software, Internet-based logistics systems, point-of-sale scanners, RFID tags, satellite tracking, and electronic transfer of order and payment data. Such technology lets them quickly and efficiently manage the flow of goods, information, and finances through the supply chain.

Finally, more than almost any other marketing function, logistics affects the environment and a firm's environmental sustainability efforts. Transportation, warehousing, packaging, and other logistics functions are typically the biggest supply chain contributors to the company's environmental footprint. At the same time, they also provide one of the most fertile areas for cost savings. In other words, developing a *green supply chain* is not only environmentally responsible but can also be profitable. Here's a simple example:[18]

> Consumer package goods maker SC Johnson made a seemingly simple but smart—and profitable—change in the way it packs its trucks. Under the old system, a load of its Ziploc products filled a truck trailer before reaching the maximum weight limit. In contrast, a load of Windex glass cleaner hit the maximum weight before the trailer was full. By strategically mixing the two products, SC Johnson found it could send the same amount of products with 2,098 fewer shipments, while burning 168,000 fewer gallons of diesel fuel and eliminating 1,882 tons of greenhouse gasses. Thus, smart supply chain thinking not only helped the environment, it also saved the company money. Says the company's director of environmental issues, "Loading a truck may seem simple, but making sure that a truck is truly full is a science. Consistently hitting a trailer's maximum weight provided a huge opportunity to reduce our energy consumption, cut our greenhouse gas emissions, and save money [in the bargain.]" Green supply chains aren't just something companies have to do, they make good business sense. "Sustainability shouldn't be about Washington jamming green stuff down your throat," concludes one supply chain expert. "This is a lot about money, about reducing costs."

Goals of the Logistics System

Some companies state their logistics objective as providing maximum customer service at the least cost. Unfortunately, as nice as this sounds, no logistics system can *both* maximize customer service *and* minimize distribution costs. Maximum customer service implies rapid delivery, large inventories, flexible assortments, liberal returns policies, and other services—all of which raise distribution costs. In contrast, minimum distribution costs imply slower delivery, smaller inventories, and larger shipping lots—which represent a lower level of overall customer service.

The goal of marketing logistics should be to provide a *targeted* level of customer service at the least cost. A company must first research the importance of various distribution services to customers and then set desired service levels for each segment. The objective is to maximize *profits*, not sales. Therefore, the company must weigh the benefits of providing higher levels of service against the costs. Some companies offer less service than their competitors and charge a lower price. Other companies offer more service and charge higher prices to cover higher costs.

Major Logistics Functions

Given a set of logistics objectives, the company designs a logistics system that will minimize the cost of attaining these objectives. The major logistics functions are *warehousing*, *inventory management*, *transportation*, and *logistics information management*.

Warehousing

Production and consumption cycles rarely match, so most companies must store their goods while they wait to be sold. For example, Snapper, Toro, and other lawn mower manufacturers run their factories all year long and store up products for the heavy spring and summer buying seasons. The storage function overcomes differences in needed quantities and timing, ensuring that products are available when customers are ready to buy them.

A company must decide on *how many* and *what types* of warehouses it needs and *where* they will be located. The company might use either *storage warehouses* or *distribution centers*. Storage warehouses store goods for moderate to long periods. In contrast, **distribution centers** are designed to move goods rather than just store them. They are large and highly automated warehouses designed to receive goods from various plants and suppliers, take orders, fill them efficiently, and deliver goods to customers as quickly as possible.

Distribution center
A large, highly automated warehouse designed to receive goods from various plants and suppliers, take orders, fill them efficiently, and deliver goods to customers as quickly as possible.

For example, Home Depot operates 19 giant Rapid Deployment Centers (RDCs)—huge, highly mechanized distribution centers that supply almost all of the daily needs of Home Depot's 2,250 stores around the country. The RDC in Westfield, Massachusetts, covers 657,000 square feet under a single roof (13 football fields) and serves some 115 Home Depot stores throughout New England. Nothing is stored at the RDCs. Instead, they are "pass-through" centers at which product shipments are received from suppliers, processed, and efficiently redistributed to individual Home Depot stores. The RDCs provide a maximum 72-hour turnaround from the time products reach the center until their delivery to stores, where 80 percent go directly to the sales floor. With such rapid and accurate delivery, individual Home Depot stores can improve merchandise availability to customers while at the same time carrying less in-store stock and reducing inventory costs.[19]

Like almost everything else these days, warehousing has seen dramatic changes in technology in recent years. Outdated materials-handling methods are steadily being replaced by newer, computer-controlled systems requiring few employees. Computers and scanners read orders and direct lift trucks, electric hoists, or robots to gather goods, move them to loading docks, and issue invoices. For example, office supplies retailer Staples now employs teams of day-glo orange robots in its warehouses around the country. The robots work tirelessly 16 hours a day, seven days a week, carrying racks of pens, paper clips, pads of paper, and other items to packing stations, where humans fill and pack customer orders. The super-efficient robots, who never complain about the workload or ask for pay raises, are pretty much maintenance free. "When they run low on power, they head to battery-charging terminals," notes one observer, "or, as warehouse personnel say, 'They get themselves a drink of water.'" At Staples' huge Chambersburg, Pennsylvania, distribution center, some 150 robots have helped improve average daily output by 60 percent.[20]

High-tech distribution centers: Staples employs a team of super-retrievers—in day-glo orange—to keep its warehouse humming.

Brent Humphreys/Redux Pictures

Inventory Management

Inventory management also affects customer satisfaction. Here, managers must maintain the delicate balance between carrying too little inventory and carrying too much. With too little stock, the firm risks not having products when customers want to buy. To remedy this, the firm may need costly emergency shipments or production. Carrying too much inventory results in higher-than-necessary inventory-carrying costs and stock obsolescence. Thus, in managing inventory, firms must balance the costs of carrying larger inventories against resulting sales and profits.

Many companies have greatly reduced their inventories and related costs through *just-in-time* logistics systems. With such systems, producers and retailers carry only small inventories of parts or merchandise, often enough for only a few days of operations. New stock arrives exactly when needed, rather than being stored in inventory until being used. Just-in-time systems require accurate forecasting along with fast, frequent, and flexible delivery so that new supplies will be available when needed. However, these systems result in substantial savings in inventory-carrying and handling costs.

Marketers are always looking for new ways to make inventory management more efficient. In the not-too-distant future, handling inventory might even become fully automated. For example, in Chapter 3 we discussed RFID or "smart tag" technology, by which small transmitter chips are embedded in or placed on products and packaging for everything from flowers and razors to tires. "Smart" products could make the entire supply chain—which accounts for nearly 75 percent of a product's cost—intelligent and automated.

Companies using RFID know, at any time, exactly where a product is located physically within the supply chain. "Smart shelves" would not only tell them when it's time to reorder but also place the order automatically with their suppliers. Such exciting new information technology is revolutionizing distribution as we know it. Many large and resourceful marketing companies, such as Walmart, P&G, Kraft, IBM, and HP are investing heavily to make the full use of RFID technology a reality.[21]

Transportation

The choice of transportation carriers affects the pricing of products, delivery performance, and the condition of goods when they arrive—all of which will affect customer satisfaction. In shipping goods to its warehouses, dealers, and customers, the company can choose among five main transportation modes: truck, rail, water, pipeline, and air, along with an alternative mode for digital products—the Internet.

Trucks have increased their share of transportation steadily and now account for 40 percent of total cargo ton-miles moved in the United States. U.S. trucks travel more than 397 billion miles a year—more than double the distance traveled 25 years ago—carrying 9.2 billion tons of freight. ● According to the American Trucking Association, 80 percent of U.S. communities depend solely on trucks for their goods and commodities. Trucks are highly flexible in their routing and time schedules, and they can usually offer faster service than railroads. They are efficient for short hauls of high-value merchandise. Trucking firms have evolved in recent years to become full-service providers of global transportation services. For example, large trucking firms now offer everything from satellite tracking, Internet-based shipment management, and logistics planning software to cross-border shipping operations.[22]

Railroads account for 40 percent of the total cargo ton-miles moved. They are one of the most cost-effective modes for shipping large amounts of bulk products—coal, sand, minerals, and farm and forest products—over long distances. In recent years, railroads have increased their customer services by designing new equipment to handle special categories of goods, providing flatcars for carrying truck trailers by rail (piggyback), and providing in-transit services such as the diversion of shipped goods to other destinations en route and the processing of goods en route.

Water carriers, which account for less than 5 percent of the cargo ton-miles, transport large amounts of goods by ships and

If you rely on it,

wear it,

consume it,

or depend on it,

Trucks Bring It.

Trucks are essential to deliver everything America needs.
Eighty-two percent of U.S. communities depend solely on truck transport for their goods and commodities.
Simply put, trucks move America safely, efficiently and on time.

Good stuff.

www.TrucksBringIt.com

● Truck transportation: More than 80 percent of American communities depend solely on the trucking industry for the delivery of their goods. "Good stuff. Trucks bring it."

American Trucking Association

barges on U.S. coastal and inland waterways. Although the cost of water transportation is very low for shipping bulky, low-value, nonperishable products such as sand, coal, grain, oil, and metallic ores, water transportation is the slowest mode and may be affected by the weather. *Pipelines*, which account for less than 1 percent of the cargo ton-miles, are a specialized means of shipping petroleum, natural gas, and chemicals from sources to markets. Most pipelines are used by their owners to ship their own products.

Although *air* carriers transport less than 1 percent of the cargo ton-miles of the nation's goods, they are an important transportation mode. Airfreight rates are much higher than rail or truck rates, but airfreight is ideal when speed is needed or distant markets have to be reached. Among the most frequently airfreighted products are perishables (such as fresh fish, cut flowers) and high-value, low-bulk items (technical instruments, jewelry). Companies find that airfreight also reduces inventory levels, packaging costs, and the number of warehouses needed.

The *Internet* carries digital products from producer to customer via satellite, cable, phone wire, or wireless signal. Software firms, the media, music and video companies, and education all make use of the Internet to transport digital products. The Internet holds the potential for lower product distribution costs. Whereas planes, trucks, and trains move freight and packages, digital technology moves information bits.

Intermodal transportation

Combining two or more modes of transportation.

Shippers also use **intermodal transportation**—combining two or more modes of transportation. Twelve percent of the total cargo ton-miles are moved via multiple modes. *Piggyback* describes the use of rail and trucks; *fishyback*, water and trucks; *trainship*, water and rail; and *airtruck*, air and trucks. Combining modes provides advantages that no single mode can deliver. Each combination offers advantages to the shipper. For example, not only is piggyback cheaper than trucking alone, but it also provides flexibility and convenience.

In choosing a transportation mode for a product, shippers must balance many considerations: speed, dependability, availability, capacity, cost, and others. Thus, if a shipper needs speed, air and truck are the prime choices. If the goal is low cost, then water or rail might be best.

Logistics Information Management

Companies manage their supply chains through information. Channel partners often link up to share information and make better joint logistics decisions. From a logistics perspective, flows of information, such as customer transactions, billing, shipment and inventory levels, and even customer data, are closely linked to channel performance. Companies need simple, accessible, fast, and accurate processes for capturing, processing, and sharing channel information.

Information can be shared and managed in many ways, but most sharing takes place through *electronic data interchange* (*EDI*), the digital exchange of data between organizations, which primarily is transmitted via the Internet. Walmart, for example, requires EDI links with its more than 100,000 suppliers through its Retail Link sales data system. If new suppliers don't have EDI capability, Walmart will work with them to find and implement the needed tools.[23]

In some cases, suppliers might actually be asked to generate orders and arrange deliveries for their customers. Many large retailers—such as Walmart and Home Depot—work closely with major suppliers such as P&G or Moen to set up *vendor-managed inventory (VMI)* systems or *continuous inventory replenishment* systems. Using VMI, the customer shares real-time data on sales and current inventory levels with the supplier. The supplier then takes full responsibility for managing inventories and deliveries. Some retailers even go so far as to shift inventory and delivery costs to the supplier. Such systems require close cooperation between the buyer and seller.

Integrated logistics management

The logistics concept that emphasizes teamwork—both inside the company and among all the marketing channel organizations—to maximize the performance of the entire distribution system.

Integrated Logistics Management

Today, more and more companies are adopting the concept of **integrated logistics management**. This concept recognizes that providing better customer service and trimming distribution costs require *teamwork*, both inside the company and among all the marketing channel organizations. Inside, the company's various departments must work closely together to maximize its own logistics performance. Outside, the company must integrate its logistics system with those of its suppliers and customers to maximize the performance of the entire distribution network.

Cross-Functional Teamwork Inside the Company

Most companies assign responsibility for various logistics activities to many different departments—marketing, sales, finance, operations, and purchasing. Too often, each function tries to optimize its own logistics performance without regard for the activities of the other functions. However, transportation, inventory, warehousing, and information management activities interact, often in an inverse way. Lower inventory levels reduce inventory-carrying costs. But they may also reduce customer service and increase costs from stockouts, back orders, special production runs, and costly fast-freight shipments. Because distribution activities involve strong trade-offs, decisions by different functions must be coordinated to achieve better overall logistics performance.

The goal of integrated supply chain management is to harmonize all of the company's logistics decisions. Close working relationships among departments can be achieved in several ways. Some companies have created permanent logistics committees composed of managers responsible for different physical distribution activities. Companies can also create supply chain manager positions that link the logistics activities of functional areas. For example, P&G has created product supply managers who manage all the supply chain activities for each product category. Many companies have a vice president of logistics with cross-functional authority.

Finally, companies can employ sophisticated, system-wide supply chain management software, now available from a wide range of software enterprises large and small, from SAP and Oracle to Infor and Logility. The important thing is that the company must coordinate its logistics and marketing activities to create high market satisfaction at a reasonable cost.

Building Logistics Partnerships

Companies must do more than improve their own logistics. They must also work with other channel partners to improve whole-channel distribution. The members of a marketing channel are linked closely in creating customer value and building customer relationships. One company's distribution system is another company's supply system. The success of each channel member depends on the performance of the entire supply chain. For example,

● **Integrated logistics management: Many companies now employ sophisticated, system-wide supply chain management software, available from companies such as Logility.**
Logility, Inc.

IKEA can create its stylish but affordable furniture and deliver the "IKEA lifestyle" only if its entire supply chain—consisting of thousands of merchandise designers and suppliers, transport companies, warehouses, and service providers—operates at maximum efficiency and customer-focused effectiveness.

Smart companies coordinate their logistics strategies and forge strong partnerships with suppliers and customers to improve customer service and reduce channel costs. Many companies have created *cross-functional, cross-company teams*. For example, Nestlé's Purina pet food unit has a team of dozens of people working in Bentonville, Arkansas, the home base of Walmart. The Purina Walmart team members work jointly with their counterparts at Walmart to find ways to squeeze costs out of their distribution system. Working together benefits not only Purina and Walmart but also their shared, final consumers.

Other companies partner through *shared projects*. For example, many large retailers conduct joint in-store programs with suppliers. Home Depot allows key suppliers to use its stores as a testing ground for new merchandising programs. The suppliers spend time at Home Depot stores watching how their product sells and how customers relate to it. They then create programs specially tailored to Home Depot and its customers. Clearly, both the supplier and the customer benefit from such partnerships. The point is that all supply chain members must work together in the cause of bringing value to final consumers.

Third-Party Logistics

Third-party logistics (3PL) provider

An independent logistics provider that performs any or all of the functions required to get a client's product to market.

Although most big companies love to make and sell their products, many loathe the associated logistics "grunt work." They detest the bundling, loading, unloading, sorting, storing, reloading, transporting, customs clearing, and tracking required to supply their factories and get products to their customers. They hate it so much that a growing number of firms now outsource some or all of their logistics to **third-party logistics (3PL) providers** such as Ryder, Penske Logistics, BAX Global, DHL Logistics, FedEx Logistics, and UPS Business Solutions. Outsourced logistics providers can help companies improve their own logistics systems or even take over and manage part or all of their logistics operations (see Real Marketing 12.2). Here's an example:[24]

Stonyfield Farm, the world's largest yogurt maker, had a distribution problem. As the company grew, inefficiencies had crept into its distribution system. To help fix the problem, Stonyfield turned to 3PL provider Ryder Supply Chain Solutions. Together, Ryder and Stonyfield designed a new transportation system that cut processing and distribution costs and improved service levels, while at the same time dramatically reducing the company's carbon footprint. After evaluating the Stonyfield network, Ryder identified optimal transportation solutions, including the use of fuel-efficient RydeGreen vehicles. It helped Stonyfield set up a small, dedicated truck fleet to make regional deliveries in New England and replaced Stonyfield's national less-than-truckload distribution network with a regional multistop truckload system. As a result, Stonyfield now moves more product in fewer trucks, cutting in half the number of miles traveled. In all, the changes produced a 40 percent reduction in transportation-related carbon dioxide emissions and knocked an eye-popping 13 percent off Stonyfield's transportation costs.

Ryder, UPS, and other 3PL providers help clients tighten up sluggish, overstuffed supply chains; slash inventories; and get products to customers more quickly and reliably. According to a survey of chief logistics executives at *Fortune 500* companies, 82 percent of these companies use 3PL (also called *outsourced logistics* or *contract logistics*) services. In all, North American shippers spend 47 percent of their logistics budget on outsourced logistics.[25]

Companies use third-party logistics providers for several reasons. First, since getting the product to market is their main focus, using these providers makes the most sense, as they can often do it more efficiently and at lower cost. Outsourcing typically results in a 15 to 30 percent cost savings. Second, outsourcing logistics frees a company to focus more intensely on its core business. Finally, integrated logistics companies understand increasingly complex logistics environments.

Real Marketing 12.2

UPS: "We Love Logistics"—Put UPS to Work for You and You'll Love Logistics Too

Mention UPS and most people envision one of those familiar brown trucks with a friendly driver, rumbling around their neighborhood dropping off parcels. For most of us, seeing a brown UPS truck evokes fond memories of past package deliveries. However, most of UPS's revenue comes not from the residential customers who receive the packages, but from the business customers who send them. And for its business customers, UPS does more than just get Grandma's holiday package there on time.

For most businesses, physical package delivery is just part of a much more complex logistics process that involves purchase orders, inventories, order status checks, invoices, payments, returned merchandise, fleets of delivery vehicles, and even cross-border dealings. Companies need timely information about their outbound and inbound packages—what's in them, where they're now located, to whom they are going, when they'll get there, and how much is owed. UPS knows that, for many companies, logistics can be a real nightmare.

That's where UPS can help. Logistics is exactly what UPS does best. Over the years, UPS has grown to become much more than a neighborhood package delivery service. It is now a $65 billion corporate giant providing a broad range of global logistics solutions. Whereas many customers hate dealing with the logistics process, UPS proclaims "We ♥ logistics." To UPS's thinking, the new logistics is today's most powerful force for creating competitive advantage. Today's logistics offers a lot more than just getting products efficiently where they need to be. It contributes broadly to better business practice. Says UPS: "It makes running your business easier. It lets you serve your customers better. And it can help you grow. It's a whole new way of thinking. It's the new logistics."

If it has to do with logistics, anywhere in the world, UPS can probably do it better than any other company. UPS offers customers efficient multi-modal package, mail, and freight distribution services. But it can also help customers streamline sourcing, maintain leaner inventories, manage and fulfill orders, warehouse goods, assemble or even customize products, and manage post-sales warranty repair and returns services. And with

36 percent of its revenues now coming from outside the United States, UPS offers the most extensive global network for handling logistics in an increasingly global environment.

UPS has the resources to handle the logistics needs of just about any size business. It employs nearly 400,000 people, owns almost 100,000 delivery vehicles, runs the world's ninth-largest airline, and maintains 1,860 operating facilities in more than 220 countries. Last year, UPS delivered 4 *billion* packages worldwide. The distribution giant is also the world's largest customs broker. With some 882 international flights per day to or from 323 international destinations, UPS can also help businesses to navigate the complexities of international shipping.

At one level, UPS can simply handle a company's package shipments. On a deeper level, however, UPS can advise businesses on how to improve their own overall logistics operations. It can help clients redesign their logistics systems to better synchronize the flow of goods, funds, and information up and down the entire supply chain. At a still deeper level, companies can let UPS take

over and manage part or all of their logistics operations.

For example, Zappos.com relies on UPS to help run its efficient, customer-friendly returns process. Returns are key to Zappos' customer satisfaction strategy, and outstanding logistics is key to a smooth-running returns process. Customers can order lots of different styles and sizes from Zappos, try them on, and then return the ones they don't want at no charge. In fact, the company encourages it. Zappos has teamed with UPS on logistics from the start, building its distribution center minutes from UPS's Worldport air hub in Louisville, Kentucky. UPS delivers all of Zappos' packages. Then, to return unwanted items, all customers have to do is put them back in the box, call for pickup, and let UPS handle the rest. This seamless, UPS-run returns process is one reason 75 percent of Zappos.com shoppers are repeat customers. Moreover, by using UPS's integrated shipping and tracking tools, Zappos can monitor incoming returns along with inbound goods from vendors to quickly and efficiently plan and replenish stock for resale.

Consumer electronics maker Toshiba lets UPS handle its entire laptop PC repair process—lock, stock, and barrel:

UPS's logistics prowess was the answer to one of Toshiba's biggest challenges—turn-around time on laptop repairs. Toshiba once used UPS only to ship its finished PCs from the factory to customers. But when the two

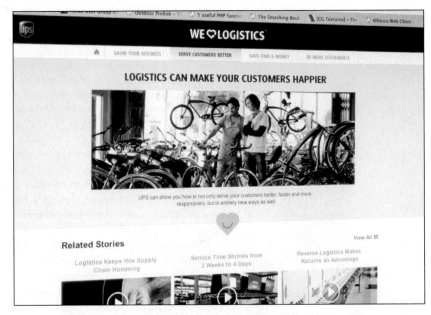

Whereas many customers hate dealing with the logistics process, UPS proclaims "We ♥ logistics." "It makes running your business easier. It helps you create better customer experiences. It's a whole new way of thinking."

Jarrod Weaton/Weaton Digital, Inc.

companies worked together to examine the entire supply chain, including parts management and the PC repair process, they forged a much broader logistics relationship. Now, customers ship laptops needing repair to a special UPS facility near the Worldport air hub in Louisville. There, UPS employees receive the units, run diagnostics to assess the repairs needed, pick the necessary parts, quickly complete the service, and return the laptops to their owners. UPS can now fix and ship a laptop in a single day, shortening a door-to-door repair process that once took two to three weeks down to four or fewer days. Together, UPS and Toshiba greatly improved the customer repair experience.

So, UPS does much more than just deliver packages. It provides a rich range of logistics services that can help businesses to sharpen their logistics strategies, cut costs, and serve customers better. More than just providing shipping services, UPS becomes a strategic logistics partner. "One of the things we've learned with UPS is their willingness to be a partner," says Toshiba America CEO Simon. "They really understand the overall experience we're trying to create for the customers."

Says a UPS operations manager, "We want to understand the complete supply chain for our customers. When there are issues in the field and you resolve those issues—quickly resolve those issues so that you can maintain a high level of customer satisfaction—that's logistics." Letting UPS help with the logistics lets companies focus on what they do best. And it helps take the nightmares out of the logistics process. As one UPS ad concludes: "We love logistics. Put UPS to work for you and you'll love logistics too."

Sources: Quotes, examples, and other information from "How to Level a Playing Field: Why Even the Smallest Companies Should Embrace Logistics," special advertising feature, *Inc.,* June 2011, p. 94; Brian Shactman, "How UPS, FedEx Grow by Tapping 'Adjacent Business,'" *USA Today*, February 5, 2012; http://thenewlogistics.ups.com/swf#/stories?page_1, accessed October 2012; and www.thenewlogistics.com and www.ups.com/content/us/en/about/facts/worldwide.html, accessed November 2012.

Reviewing the Concepts

MyMarketingLab™

Go to **mymktlab.com** to complete the problems marked with this icon .

Reviewing Objectives and Key Terms

 ## Objectives Review

Some companies pay too little attention to their distribution channels; others, however, have used imaginative distribution systems to gain a competitive advantage. A company's channel decisions directly affect every other marketing decision. Management must make channel decisions carefully, incorporating today's needs with tomorrow's likely selling environment.

Objective 1 **Explain why companies use marketing channels and discuss the functions these channels perform.** (pp 340–344)

In creating customer value, a company can't go it alone. It must work within an entire network of partners—a value delivery network—to accomplish this task. Individual companies and brands don't compete, their entire value delivery networks do.

Most producers use intermediaries to bring their products to market. They forge a *marketing channel* (or *distribution channel*)—a set of interdependent organizations involved in the process of making a product or service available for use or consumption by the consumer or business user. Through their contacts, experience, specialization, and scale of operation, intermediaries usually offer the firm more than it can achieve on its own.

Marketing channels perform many key functions. Some help *complete transactions* by gathering and distributing *information* needed for planning and aiding exchange, developing and spreading persuasive *communications* about an offer, performing *contact* work (finding and communicating with prospective buyers), *matching* (shaping and fitting the offer to the buyer's needs), and entering into *negotiation* to reach an agreement on price and other terms of the offer so that ownership can be transferred. Other functions help to *fulfill* the completed transactions by offering *physical distribution* (transporting and storing goods), *financing* (acquiring and using funds to cover the costs of the channel work), and *risk taking* (assuming the risks of carrying out the channel work).

Objective 2 **Discuss how channel members interact and how they organize to perform the work of the channel.** (pp 344–349)

The channel will be most effective when each member assumes the tasks it can do best. Ideally, because the success of individual channel members depends on overall channel success, all channel firms should work together smoothly. They should understand and accept their roles, coordinate their goals and activities, and cooperate to attain overall channel goals. By cooperating, they can more effectively sense, serve, and satisfy the target market.

In a large company, the formal organization structure assigns roles and provides needed leadership. But in a distribution channel composed of independent firms, leadership and power are not formally set. Traditionally, distribution channels have lacked the leadership needed to assign roles and manage conflict. In recent years, however, new types of channel organizations have appeared that provide stronger leadership and improved performance.

Objective 3 — Identify the major channel alternatives open to a company. (pp 349–353)

Channel alternatives vary from direct selling to using one, two, three, or more intermediary *channel levels*. Marketing channels face continuous and sometimes dramatic change. Three of the most important trends are the growth of *vertical*, *horizontal*, and *multichannel marketing systems*. These trends affect channel cooperation, conflict, and competition.

Channel design begins with assessing customer channel service needs and company channel objectives and constraints. The company then identifies the major channel alternatives in terms of the *types* of intermediaries, the *number* of intermediaries, and the *channel responsibilities* of each. Each channel alternative must be evaluated according to economic, control, and adaptive criteria. *Channel management* calls for selecting qualified intermediaries and motivating them. Individual channel members must be evaluated regularly.

Objective 4 — Explain how companies select, motivate, and evaluate channel members. (pp 353–357)

Producers vary in their ability to attract qualified marketing intermediaries. Some producers have no trouble signing up channel members, whereas others have to work hard to line up enough qualified intermediaries. When selecting intermediaries, the company should evaluate each channel member's qualifications and select those that best fit its channel objectives.

Once selected, channel members must be continuously motivated to do their best. The company must sell not only *through* the intermediaries but also *with* them. It should forge strong partnerships with channel members to create a marketing system that meets the needs of both the manufacturer *and* the partners.

Objective 5 — Discuss the nature and importance of marketing logistics and integrated supply chain management. (pp 357–364)

Marketing logistics (or *physical distribution*) is an area of potentially high cost savings and improved customer satisfaction. Marketing logistics addresses not only *outbound logistics* but also *inbound logistics* and *reverse logistics*. That is, it involves the entire *supply chain management*—managing value-added flows between suppliers, the company, resellers, and final users. No logistics system can both maximize customer service and minimize distribution costs. Instead, the goal of logistics management is to provide a *targeted* level of service at the least cost. The major logistics functions are *warehousing*, *inventory management*, *transportation*, and *logistics information management*.

The *integrated supply chain management concept* recognizes that improved logistics requires teamwork in the form of close working relationships across functional areas inside the company and across various organizations in the supply chain. Companies can achieve logistics harmony among functions by creating cross-functional logistics teams, integrative supply manager positions, and senior-level logistics executives with cross-functional authority. Channel partnerships can take the form of cross-company teams, shared projects, and information-sharing systems. Today, some companies are outsourcing their logistics functions to third-party logistics (3PL) providers to save costs, increase efficiency, and gain faster and more effective access to global markets.

 # Key Terms

Objective 1

Value delivery network (p 341)
Marketing channel (or distribution channel) (p 341)
Channel level (p 343)
Direct marketing channel (p 343)
Indirect marketing channel (p 343)

Objective 2

Channel conflict (p 344)
Conventional distribution channel (p 345)
Vertical marketing system (VMS) (p 345)

Corporate VMS (p 346)
Contractual VMS (p 346)
Franchise organization (p 346)
Administered VMS (p 347)
Horizontal marketing system (p 347)
Multichannel distribution system (p 348)
Disintermediation (p 348)

Objective 3

Marketing channel design (p 350)
Intensive distribution (p 351)
Exclusive distribution (p 351)
Selective distribution (p 351)

Objective 4

Marketing channel management (p 353)

Objective 5

Marketing logistics (physical distribution) (p 357)
Supply chain management (p 357)
Distribution center (p 359)
Intermodal transportation (p 361)
Integrated logistics management (p 361)
Third-party logistics (3PL) provider (p 363)

Discussion and Critical Thinking

 ## Discussion Questions

1. Describe the key functions performed by marketing channel members. (AACSB: Communication)

2. Describe multichannel distribution systems and the advantages and disadvantages of using them. (AACSB: Communication; Reflective Thinking)

3. Compare and contrast intensive, selective, and exclusive distribution. Which channel design decision does this involve? (AACSB: Communication; Reflective Thinking)

4. Discuss the complexities international marketers face when designing channels in other countries. (AACSB: Communication)

5. Explain how information is managed in the distribution channel. What types of information are managed? (AACSB: Communication)

6. Describe intermodal transportation and list the different combinations used to distribute products and the benefits of using this mode of transportation. (AACSB: Communication)

 ## Critical Thinking Exercises

1. In a small group, debate whether or not the Internet will result in disintermediation of the following retail stores: (1) video rental stores, (2) music stores, (3) grocery stores, (4) book stores, and (3) clothing stores. (AACSB: Communication; Reflective Thinking)

2. The most common type of contractual vertical marketing system is the franchise organization. Visit the International Franchise Association at www.franchise.org/ and find a franchise that interests you. Write a report describing the franchise.

Identify what type of franchise it represents and research the market opportunities for that product or service. (AACSB: Communication; Use of IT; Reflective Thinking)

3. Visit www.youtube.com/watch?v=eob532iEpqk and watch "The Future Market" video. What impact will radio frequency identification (RFID) tags have on each of the major logistical functions? What are the biggest current obstacles to adopting this technology? (AACSB: Communication; Use of IT; Reflective Thinking)

Applications and Cases

 ## Marketing Technology Omnichannels

A key to satisfying retail customers is to carry products they want. However, Macy's used to find that although an item was out of stock online, it had plenty of stock in the physical stores and ended up marking it down to clear the item out. Not anymore. Macy's is now turning almost 300 of its 800-plus stores into combination retail outlets and online warehouses to combat competitors such as Amazon.com, which has an extensive network of warehouses located near high-population areas. New technology dynamically updates the status of all items in every store, so if an online shopper wants an item, and it exists in any Macy's store, the store will ship the item to the consumer. In-store shoppers can also have an item shipped to them from another store if it's out of stock where they are shopping. Items not selling well in stores are shifted to the online site, where they can be sold at full price rather than marked down. Integrated Internet and physical stores are called "omnichannels." Nordstrom and Toys R Us have used omnichannels for a few years and realize fewer markdowns, improved margins, and faster inventory turnover.

1. What are the disadvantages of also treating retail stores as warehouses? Is this a good solution for competing with Amazon.com? (AACSB: Communication; Reflective Thinking)

Marketing Ethics Slow-Motion Video

Movie and television program distribution technology is changing fast. Consumers can now watch movies and TV shows on demand on TVs, computers, tablets, and smartphones. This has caused a surge in demand for online video-streaming services such as Netflix and Hulu. However, it's causing problems for subscription-TV services such as Comcast Cable, which offer scheduled programming and are facing increased competition from the video-streaming services. Interestingly, however, as one of the country's largest Internet service providers, Comcast is also the distribution channel for competitors such as Netflix and Hulu. The fact that Comcast has control over its competitors' distribution channel causes some uncomfortable conflicts. It has invested billions building its scheduled programming network, and it doesn't want to become a mere conduit as its subscribers drop cable in favor of streamed programming from one of the competing services. And because it controls the Internet channel, it can cause problems for those competitors. For example, the U.S. Justice Department is investigating whether cable companies such as Comcast are attempting to squash competition from video-streaming providers such as Netflix by limiting the amount of data their Internet service subscribers can download. Comcast has also countered with its own online video-streaming app called Xfinity, by which subscribers can stream programming using Xbox game consoles. Video content streamed through Xfinity is not counted against Comcast's data limits the way that videos streamed through other services such as Netflix are.

1. What types of channel conflict are present in this channel of distribution? Explain. (AACSB: Communication; Reflective Thinking)

Marketing by the Numbers Expanding Distribution

Lightco, Inc., manufactures decorative lighting fixtures sold primarily in the eastern United States. Lightco wants to expand to the Midwest and southern United States and intends to hire 10 new sales representatives to secure distribution for its products. Sales reps will acquire new retail accounts and manage those accounts after acquisition. Each sales rep earns a salary of $50,000 plus 2 percent commission. Each retailer generates an average $50,000 in revenue for Lightco. Refer to Appendix 2: Marketing by the Numbers to answer the following questions.

1. If Lightco's contribution margin is 40 percent, what increase in sales will it need to break even on the increase in fixed costs to hire the new sales reps? (AACSB: Communication; Analytical Reasoning)

2. How many new retail accounts must the company acquire to break even on this tactic? What average number of accounts must each new rep acquire? (AACSB: Communication; Analytical Reasoning)

Video Case Gaviña Gourmet Coffee

These days, there seems to be plenty of coffee to go around. So how does a small-time coffee roaster like Gaviña make it in an industry dominated by big players? By carefully crafting a distribution strategy that moves its products into the hands of consumers.

Without a big advertising budget, Gaviña has creatively pursued channel partners in the grocery, restaurant, and hospitality industries. Now, major chains like McDonald's and Publix make Gaviña's coffees available to the public. This video also illustrates the impact of distribution strategy on supply chain and product development issues.

After viewing the video featuring Gaviña, answer the following questions:

1. Apply the concept of the supply chain to Gaviña.

2. Sketch out as many consumer and business channels for Gaviña as you can. How does each of these channels meet distinct customer needs?

3. How has Gaviña's distribution strategy affected its product mix?

Company Case Pandora: Disintermediator or Disintermediated?

For Pandora, one of the biggest players in Internet radio, figuring out the future is both challenging and intimidating. If the regular challenges of growing a new company aren't enough, Pandora also faces a market that is reeling in turmoil. In the new digital world, the way people listen to music continues to change dramatically. It seems likely that Pandora will either lead the changes or fall victim to them.

Pandora was founded just over a decade ago. At that time, a vast majority of music listeners were still getting their groove on in one of two ways: They either popped a CD into their home, car, or personal CD player or they turned on the old AM/FM radio. But the advent of digital formats such as MP3s drove the first nail into the CD's coffin and drew many people away from traditional or "terrestrial" radio. Moreover, like the music business, the radio business has faced major changes of its own. The Telecommunications Act of 1996 reduced limitations on the number of stations that one owner could hold. This led to huge ownership groups that consolidated and standardized listening formats. The result is less diversity on the radio, with shorter playlists and fewer artists represented. From one city to the next, all across the United States, radio stations have become a homogenous lot.

Both of these trends—combined with the explosion of Internet usage and changes in online technologies—have led to a deluge of companies trying to capitalize on the future of music distribution. This includes download services such as iTunes, subscription services such as Rhapsody and eMusic, cloud music players from Google and Amazon, an endless number of Internet radio stations, and even satellite radio network SiriusXM. Today, with an ever-growing list of listening devices and music service models, listening trends continue to evolve. But one thing about the future is certain: The business of listening to music is full of disruption and confusion. Things are changing fast and the winning products and services—indeed, the survivors—are yet to be determined.

The Power of People

Amid the chaos, Pandora has carved out its own niche, setting itself apart as an automated music recommendation service. It isn't a play-on-demand service, where members can simply choose the exact song and artist they want. Rather, listeners enter an artist or song suggestion. The playlist starts with a track by the requested artist and inserts additional songs by that artist every once in a while. But in between, Pandora cues up songs by other artists similar in nature to the requested material. If an unliked or unwanted song plays, the listener can click the "thumbs down" icon or just skip the song and it will be removed from the list. Users can also create stations by browsing artists alphabetically, or they can tune in to pre-made genre stations or to other users' stations. Listeners can create as many stations as they wish, each oriented around the initial input.

Lots of online services employ similar recommendation features (consider Netflix and Amazon). But Pandora has set a precedent by the predictive power of its recommendation software. The Pandora software is amazingly precise in choosing material that fits with what the user wants. According to Tim Westergren, founder and chief strategy officer for Pandora, the secret sauce is the people behind the software. Behind this digitized, automated, software-driven machine, Westergren says, "You need a human ear to discern. It's true that the algorithms mathematically match songs, but the math, all it's doing is translating what a human being is actually measuring."

Each of the approximately 1 million songs in Pandora's library has been analyzed and coded by a professional musician. Each song is rated on as many as 400 different musical attributes or "genes." Each gene corresponds to a music characteristic, such as gender of the lead vocalist, level of distortion on the electric guitar, syncopation, and vocal harmonies, to name just a few. Pandora's music analysts must pass application tests. As junior analysts, they are required to sit in the same room with other analysts so they can regularly peel back their headphones and engage the others about the music they're coding. Senior analysts can take their work on the road—often dissecting songs between gigs as they play on tour. "That is the magic bullet for us," Westergren says of the company's human element. "I can't overstate it. It's been the most important part of Pandora. It defines us in so many ways."

Pandora takes this unmatched competency for coding music and adds features and options that further differentiate its service. For starters, listeners can choose from two subscription plans. On the free plan, listeners hear an advertisement every now and then, but far fewer ads than are heard on terrestrial radio. This plan also sets certain user limits, such as a 40-hour-per-month listening maximum and 12 total skips every 24 hours. For $36 a year, the subscription-based plan provides members with unlimited listening hours, higher-quality audio, a desktop player, and no ads.

Once a user selects a plan, Pandora's brain takes in all the listener's inputs and marks them as unique to that person's musical tastes. With each indication of "likes" and "dislikes," Pandora gets smarter. Listeners can further empower Pandora's guru-like prowess with such responses as "I'm tired of this song," "Why was this song selected?", "Move song to another station," "New station," and "Bookmark." No rewinding or repeating is available (just like terrestrial radio). But further customization occurs when users modify their preference settings for additions such as not allowing explicit lyrics. And blurring the line between radio service and music ownership, a "buy" button is located at the top of each song that takes listeners directly to iTunes or Amazon.com.

From Net Radio to Everywhere Radio

At first, the only way you could listen to Pandora was via Pandora's Web page on a computer. But Pandora's "Anytime, anywhere," mantra has guided its distribution strategy. As music enthusiasts have become more mobile, Pandora has followed. By forging strategic partnerships, Pandora has pushed the music service into a variety of channels, including apps for smartphones and tablets as well as through home entertainment systems such as video game players, DVD players, and Internet radios. Pandora has also pioneered one of the hottest trends—providing alternatives to terrestrial radio in new vehicles. "Half of radio listening happens in cars," Westergren points out. "It's an important place for us to be." Systems in new automobiles allow people to access Pandora on the car's sound system via Internet-connected smartphone apps. Similar integrations with Alpine and Pioneer aftermarket systems make access available in virtually any vehicle.

All this access and the allure of cool features have allowed Pandora to dominate Internet radio. Its 54 million active users (over one in every seven Americans) dwarf SiriusXM's 23 million subscribers. And Pandora's base is growing at a much more rapid rate than that of its satellite competitor, progressively eroding the listenership of terrestrial radio. And Pandora members—especially young ones—listen longer on average than listeners of terrestrial radio or satellite radio. Despite all the competition, its current market share of 69 percent of the digital listening market is expected to continue to climb steadily and could reach 80 percent by next year. Pandora also now claims 6 percent of the total radio market.

Not Out of the Woods

Although a large and growing member base is encouraging, Pandora is far from declaring financial success. True, its revenues of $274 million for 2012 were 99 percent higher than those of the previous year. During the same year, its active user base grew by 51 percent and total listening hours grew by 77 percent. Only one number is not growing for Pandora—profits. To date, Pandora has seen profits during only one quarter, and the company is not expected to be basking in the black any time soon. In fact, Pandora's own projections don't forecast an annual profit. And other substantial threats have some investors worried. To name a few:

- Cost structure—Pandora pays royalties for every song played. Thus, as it increases its membership and listening hours, royalty expenses increase at a linear rate, unlike the decreasing rate for most producers of goods and services. Because Internet radio is new, royalty rates have been volatile as the music industry tries to arrive at a fair value. Only a few short years ago, Pandora was on the verge of collapse because royalties doubled. But Pandora was successful in renegotiating lower royalty rates. Further, any given music label could decide to end its contract with Pandora, thus reducing the volume of content. The future on this matter is uncertain, especially as international options are considered. (Pandora is currently available only in the United States because of royalty issues.)

- Fees for advertising dollars—Pandora derives 86 percent of its revenues from advertising dollars. It must convince advertisers of the benefits of advertising on Pandora or it will not be able to create sustainable profits. This issue is complicated by Pandora's growth on mobile devices, as the value for mobile advertising is even less certain than that of standard Web advertising.

- Dependence on devices—Pandora's ability to grow depends entirely on its ability to establish and maintain relationships with makers of connected devices, especially mobile devices. Such manufacturers may have reasons to contract with other services under exclusive conditions. This also puts a burden on Pandora to make and keep its technologies compatible with the many platforms used in the device field.

In addition to these threats, competition continues to loom. Whereas Pandora continues to grow rapidly despite efforts by others to cause Pandora to blow a sour note, the shifting nature of technology and consumer preference in the music industry makes competitive threats even more dangerous. Just look at all the competitive services noted earlier. Then, consider that changes in the marketing environment could lead to competitive threats not yet considered that could potentially upend the entire market.

Currently, Pandora is most often compared to Spotify, the Swedish-based music service that offers pretty much everything Pandora does with some notable differences. For starters, Spotify's library has 16 times the number of songs available through Pandora. Its tight integration with Facebook makes the social networking aspect of Spotify's listening experience seamless. And in addition to a Pandora-like custom radio station generator, Spotify allows users to choose exactly what they want to hear, including single songs, full albums, and playlists of their own making. Spotify has only a fraction of Pandora's active user base, yet its revenues are more than three times those of Pandora. However, Spotify is losing even more money than Pandora.

The digital world is full of failed dreams. Pets.com shipped a lot of 50-pound bags of dog food before realizing that its business model simply wasn't cost effective. Myspace signed up over 200 million members before crashing to its current membership of less than 20 million, leading News Corp to sell it for pennies on the dollar after just six short years. And a host of other dot-coms have achieved high levels of Internet traffic and huge stock valuations, only to fall because of threats similar to those just noted. Will that be Pandora's fate? Or will the Internet radio giant ultimately declare, "Let the music play?"

Questions for Discussion

1. As completely as possible, sketch the value chain for Pandora from the production of content to the listener.

2. How do horizontal and vertical conflict impact Pandora?

3. How does Pandora add value for customers through its distribution functions?

4. Will Pandora be successful in the long term? Why or why not?

Sources: Matthew Bryan Beck, "Pandora Vs. Spotify: Who Will Win the Battle for Streaming Music?, *Mashable,* February 12, 2012, http://mashable.com/2012/02/07/pandora-spotify/; Tyler Gray, "Pandora Pulls Back the Curtain on Its Magic Music Machine," *Fast Company*, January 21, 2011, www.fastcompany.com; Steven Bertoni, "Spotify Launches Another Torpedo at Pandora," *Forbes*, June 19, 2012, www.forbes.com/sites/stevenbertoni/2012/06/19/spotify-launches-another-torpedo-at-pandora/; and other information from www.pandora.com/about, accessed August 2012.

MyMarketingLab

Go to **mymktlab.com** for Auto-graded writing questions as well as the following Assisted-graded writing questions:

12-1. What functions does Macy's perform in the distribution channel? How is Macy's using technology to add value in the channel? (AACSB: Communication; Reflective Thinking)

12-2. Experts are predicting that cable and satellite television will become obsolete because of the Internet. With respect to the channel of distribution, what trend does this reflect? Is it right for Comcast to use data limits to lessen competition? (AACSB: Communication; Ethical Reasoning)

12-3. Mymktlab Only – comprehensive writing assignment for this chapter.

References

1. Kevin Kelleher, "The Mistake Netflix Is Now Making," *Fortune*, March 14, 2012, http://tech.fortune.cnn.com/2012/03/14/netflix-2/; Cliff Edwards and Ronald Grover, "Companies and Industries: Netflix," *Bloomberg Businessweek,* October 24–October 30, 2011, pp. 21–22; Stu Woo, "Under Fire, Netflix Rewinds DVD Plan," *Wall Street Journal*, October 11, 2011, p. A1; Charlie Rose, "Charlie Rose Talks to Reed Hastings," *Bloomberg Businessweek*, May 9–May 15, 2011, p. 26; "An Explanation and Some Reflections," an e-mail from Reed Hastings to Netflix customers, September 19, 2011; Ronald Grover and Cliff Edwards, "Can Netflix Find Its Future by Abandoning Its Past?" *Bloomberg Businessweek,* September 26–October 2, 2011, pp. 29–30; Stu Woo and Ian Sherr, "Netflix Recovers Subscribers," *Wall Street Journal,* January 26, 2012, p. B1; and www.netflix.com, accessed November 2012.

2. Bert Helm, "At KFC, a Battle among the Chicken-Hearted," *Bloomberg Businessweek,"* August 16–August 29, 2010, p. 19; and Janet Sparks, "KFC Franchisees Win Flap over Ad Control," February 2, 2011, www.bluemaumau.org/9928/kfc_franchisees_win_flap_over_ad_control.

3. "Operations: Manufacturing," www.thekrogerco.com/operations/operations_manufacturing.htm, accessed November 2012.

4. See "Fashion Forward; Inditex," *The Economist,* March 24, 2012, pp. 63–64; and information from the Inditex Press Dossier, www.inditex.com/en/press/information/press_kit, accessed October 2012.

5. Franchising facts from www.azfranchises.com/franchisefacts.htm, accessed May 2012. Also see *2012 Franchise Business Economic Outlook*, January 2012, http://emarket.franchise.org/EconOutlookFactSheetfinal.pdf.

6. Martinne Geller and Jessica Wohl, "Analysis: Walmart's Price Push Tests Manufacturers' Prowess," *Reuters,* March 6, 2012.

7. "To Boost Buying Power, Walmart Woos Partners," *Bloomberg Businessweek*, October 11–October 17, 2010, p. 23.

8. Brent Kendall and Scott Morrison, "Regulators Clear Microsoft-Yahoo Alliance," *Wall Street Journal*, February 19, 2010, p. B5; Loren Baker, "Bing Yahoo 'Bingahoo' Alliance Shows a Payoff," *Search Engine Journal*, February 2, 2011, www.searchenginejournal.com/bing-yahoo-bingahoo-alliance-shows-a-payoff/27606/; and Chris Crum, "Microsoft/Yahoo Search Alliance Expands in UK, Ireland, France," *WebProNews*, February 23, 2012, www.webpronews.com/microsoft-yahoo-search-alliance-expands-in-uk-ireland-france-2012-02.

9. For more discussion, see Larry Downes, "Why Best Buy Is Going Out of Business…Gradually," *Forbes*, January 2, 2012, www.forbes.com; Miguel Bustillo, "Best Buy Forced to Rethink Big Box," *Wall Street Journal,* March 30, 2012, p. B1.

10. Julie Bosman, "The Bookstore's Last Stand," *New York Times,* January 28, 2012.

11. Information from http://www.marykay.com/content/company/aroundtheworld.aspx, accessed November 2012.

12. See Ming-Ling Chuang, et al., "Walmart and Carrefour Experiences in China: Resolving the Structural Paradox," *Cross Cultural Management*, Vol. 18, No. 4, pp. 443–463; and "Heavy Logistics Costs Weigh on China's Economy," *Business China*, February 14, 2012, http://en.21cbh.com/HTML/2012-2-14/yMMjUzXzIxMTcyMg.html.

13. Based on information from Julie Jargon, "Asia Delivers for McDonald's," *Wall Street Journal,* December 13, 2012, http://online.wsj.com/article/SB10001424052970204397704577074982151549316.html.

14. Mark Ritson, "Why Retailers Call the Shots," *Marketing*, February 18, 2009, p. 24; and www.costco.com/Common/Category.aspx?cat=56098&eCat=BC%7C48022%7C56098&lang=en-US&whse=BC, accessed November 2012.

15. See supply chain facts from "Fast Facts on the Global Supply Chain," CSCMP, http://cscmp.org/press/fastfacts.asp, accessed November 2012.

16. William B. Cassidy, "Walmart Squeezes Costs from Supply Chain," *Journal of Commerce*, January 5, 2010; and "Walmart Vows to 'Drive Unnecessary Costs Out of Supply Chain,'" *Procurement Leaders,* January 24, 2011, www.procurementleaders.com/news/latestnews/0401-walmart-drives-supply-chain/.

17. Andy Brack, "Piggly Wiggly Center Offers Info-Packed Field Trip,*"* *Charleston Currents,* January 4, 2010, www.charlestoncurrents.com/issue/10_issues/10.0104.html; and information from http://en.wikipedia.org/wiki/Piggly_wiggly and http://walmartstores.com, accessed November 2012.

18. Bill Mongrelluzzo, "Supply Chain Expert Sees Profits in Sustainability," *Journal of Commerce*, March 11, 2010, www.joc.com/logistics-economy/sustainability-can-lead-profits-says-expert. SC Johnson example from "SC Johnson Reduces Greenhouse Gasses by the Truckload," *CRS Press Release,* www.csrwire.com/press_releases/22882-SC-Johnson-Reduces-Greenhouse-Gases-by-the-Truckload. Also see Leon Kaye, "Environmental Leaders," *Sustainable Industries,* April 4, 2012, http://sustainableindustries.com/articles/2012/04/johnson-controls?page=2.

19. See Ted LaBorde, "Home Depot Opens New Record Limited Distribution Center in Westfield," masslive.com, December 14, 2010, www.masslive.com/news/index.ssf/2010/12/home_depot_opens_new_rapid_dep.html; and "Home Depot Distribution Efficiencies Improve In-Stock Positions," *Retailed Info Systems News,* November 21, 2011, http://risnews.edgl.com/retail-best-practices/Home-Depot-Distribution-Efficiencies-Improve-In-Stock-Positions76905.

20. See Evan West, "These Robots Play Fetch," *Fast Company*, July/August 2007, pp. 49–50; "Rise of the Orange Machines," *Bloomberg Businessweek,* November 15–November 21, 2010, p. 47; Julianne Pepitone, "Amazon Buys Army of Robots," *CNNMoney,* March 20, 2012, http://money.cnn.com/2012/03/20/technology/amazon-kiva-robots/index.htm; and www.kivasystems.com, accessed November 2012.

21. See Maida Napolitano, "RFID Revisited," *Modern Materials Handling*, February 2010, p. 45; Nick Hughes, "Printed RFID: Why the Radio Heads Are Receiving Static," *Printweek*, February 25, 2011, p. 21; and "Research and Markets: Global RFID Market Forecast to 2014," *Business Wire,* April 2012.

22. Michael Margreta, Chester Ford, and M. Adhi Dipo, "U.S. Freight on the Move: Highlights from the 2007 Commodity Flow Survey Preliminary Data," September 30, 2009, www.bts.gov/publications/special_reports_and_issue_briefs/special_report/2009_09_30/html/entire.html; Bureau of Transportation Statistics, "Pocket Guide to Transportation 2012," January 2012, www.bts.gov/publications/pocket_guide_to_transportation/2012; and American Trucking Association, www.truckline.com, accessed November 2012.

23. See Walmart's supplier requirements at http://walmartstores.com/Suppliers/248.aspx, accessed November 2012.

24. "Stonyfield Farm: Ringer Supply Chain Accelerates Profit and Carbon Footprint Reduction," www.ryder.com/supplychain_case-studies_stonyfield.shtml, accessed November 2011.

25. David Biederman, "3PL Slowdown Goes Global," *Journal of Commerce*, February 8, 2010, www.joc.com/logistics-economy/3pl-slowdown-goes-global; Patrick Burnson, "Top 50 3PLs: Getting the Balance Right," *Supply Chain Management Review,* July/August 2011, p. 4; and Evan Armstrong, "2011/2012 Annual Review & Outlook: 3PLs Weathering the Storm," *Journal of Commerce,* January 6, 2012, www.joc.com/logistics-economy/3pls-weathering-storm.

13 Retailing and Wholesaling

Chapter Preview We now look more deeply into the two major intermediary marketing channel functions: retailing and wholesaling. You already know something about retailing—retailers of all shapes and sizes serve you every day. However, you probably know much less about the hoard of wholesalers working behind the scenes. In this chapter, we examine the characteristics of different kinds of retailers and wholesalers, the marketing decisions they make, and trends for the future.

When it comes to retailers, you have to start with Walmart. This megaretailer's phenomenal success has resulted from an unrelenting focus on bringing value to its customers. Day in and day out, Walmart lives up to its promise: "Save money. Live better." That focus on customer value has made Walmart not only the world's largest *retailer* but also the world's largest *company*.

Walmart: The World's Largest *Retailer*—the World's Largest *Company*

Walmart is almost unimaginably big. It's the world's largest retailer—the world's largest company. It rang up an incredible $444 billion in sales last year—1.8 times the sales of competitors Costco, Target, Sears/Kmart, Macy's, JCPenney, and Kohl's combined.

Walmart is the number one seller in several categories of consumer products, including groceries, clothing, toys, DVDs, and pet care products. It sells well over twice as many groceries as Kroger, the leading grocery-only food retailer, and its clothing and shoe sales alone last year exceeded the total revenues of Macy's Inc., parent of both Macy's and Bloomingdale's department stores. Incredibly, Walmart sells 30 percent of the disposable diapers purchased in the United States each year, 30 percent of the hair care products, 30 percent of all health and beauty products, 26 percent of the toothpaste, and 20 percent of the pet food. On average, worldwide, Walmart serves customers more than 200 million times per week in more than 10,000 stores in 27 countries.

It's also hard to fathom Walmart's impact on the U.S. economy. It's the nation's largest employer—one out of every 223 men, women, and children in the United States is a Walmart associate. Its average daily sales of $1.22 billion exceed the GDPs of 29 countries. According to one study, through its own low prices and impact on competitors' prices, Walmart saves the average American household $2,500 each year, equivalent to more than six months' worth of groceries for the average family.

What's behind this spectacular success? First and foremost, Walmart is passionately dedicated to its long-time, low-price value proposition and what its low prices mean to customers: "Save money. Live better." To accomplish this mission, Walmart offers a broad selection of carefully selected goods at "unbeatable low prices." No other retailer has come nearly so close to mastering the concepts of everyday low prices and one-stop shopping. As one analyst put it, "The company gospel . . . is relatively simple: Be an agent for customers—find

Day in and day out, giant Walmart lives up to its promise: "Save money. Live better." Its obsession with customer value has made Walmart not only the world's largest retailer but also the world's largest company.

out what they want and sell it to them for the lowest possible price." Sam Walton himself summed up Walmart's mission best when he said, "If we work together, we'll lower the cost of living for everyone . . . we'll give the world an opportunity to see what it's like to save and have a better life."

How does Walmart make money with such low prices? Walmart is a lean, mean, distribution machine—it has the lowest cost structure in the industry. Low costs let the giant retailer charge lower prices while remaining profitable. Lower prices attract more shoppers, producing more sales, making the company more efficient and enabling it to lower prices even more.

Walmart's low costs result from superior operations management, sophisticated information technology, and good-old "tough buying." Its huge, fully automated distribution centers supply stores efficiently. It employs an information technology system that the U.S. Department of Defense would envy, giving managers around the world instant access to sales and operating information.

Walmart is also known for using its massive scale to wring low prices from suppliers. "Don't expect a greeter and don't expect friendly," said one supplier's sales executive after a visit to Walmart's buying offices. "Once you are ushered into one of the spartan little buyers' rooms, expect a steely eye across the table and be prepared to cut your price. They are very, very focused people, and they use their buying power more forcefully than anyone else in America."

Despite its incredible success over the past five decades, mighty Walmart faces some weighty challenges ahead. Having grown so big, the maturing giant is having difficulty maintaining the rapid growth rates of its youth. Think about this: To grow just 7 percent next year, Walmart will have to add more than $31 billion in new sales. That's a sales *increase* greater than the *total* sales of all but the top 90 companies on the *Fortune* 500, including companies such as American Express, Google, Macy's, McDonald's, Motorola, Xerox, and Nike. The bigger Walmart gets, the harder it is to maintain a high rate of growth.

To keep growing, Walmart has pushed into new, faster-growing product and service lines, including organic foods, store brands, in-store health clinics, and consumer financial services. To combat younger, hipper competitors such as Target, Walmart even gave itself a modest image face-lift. It spruced up its stores with a cleaner, brighter, more open look and less

At Walmart: "Save money. Live better." Says Walmart's CEO, "We're obsessed with delivering value to customers."

Bloomberg via Getty Images

clutter to make them more shopper friendly. In search of broader appeal, it has added new, higher-quality products. Many Walmart stores now carry a selection of higher-end consumer electronics products, from Samsung LED televisions to Dell and Toshiba laptops to Apple iPhones and iPads. The retailer has also dressed up its apparel racks with more-stylish fashion lines.

Despite its massive presence, Walmart still has room to expand geographically. Believe it or not, there are plenty of places in the United States that still don't have a Walmart. And the giant retailer is expanding rapidly in international markets, where sales grew more than 15 percent last year to $126 billion. Walmart also faces substantial growth opportunities—and challenges—in e-commerce. Its online sales of just $4 billion account for less than 1 percent of total sales, making it a distant also-ran online compared to Amazon.com, which this year topped $48 billion in online sales. Walmart is now pouring money into developing its e-commerce capabilities.

As Walmart continues to adapt and grow, however, one thing seems certain. The giant retailer may add new product lines and services. It might go digital and global. It might brush up its look and image. But Walmart has no intention of ever giving up its core low-price value proposition. After all, Walmart is and always will be a discounter. "I don't think Walmart's . . . ever going to be edgy," says a Walmart marketer. "I don't think that fits our brand. Our brand is about saving people money" so that they can live better.[1]

Objective Outline

Objective 1	**Explain the role of retailers in the distribution channel and describe the major types of retailers.** Retailing (pp 374–380)
Objective 2	**Describe the major retailer marketing decisions.** Retailer Marketing Decisions (pp 380–386)
Objective 3	**Discuss the major trends and developments in retailing.** Retailing Trends and Developments (pp 386–392)
Objective 4	**Explain the major types of wholesalers and their marketing decisions.** Wholesaling (pp 392–397)

MyMarketingLab™

✪ Improve Your Grade!

Over 10 million students improved their results using the Pearson MyLabs.
Visit **mymktlab.com** for simulations, tutorials, and end-of-chapter problems.

The Walmart story sets the stage for examining the fast-changing world of today's resellers. This chapter looks at *retailing* and *wholesaling*. In the first section, we look at the nature and importance of retailing, the major types of store and nonstore retailers, the decisions retailers make, and the future of retailing. In the second section, we discuss these same topics as they apply to wholesalers.

Objective 1 ┈┈➤

Explain the role of retailers in the distribution channel and describe the major types of retailers.

Retailing

All the activities involved in selling goods or services directly to final consumers for their personal, nonbusiness use.

Retailer

A business whose sales come *primarily* from retailing.

Shopper marketing

Using in-store promotions and advertising to extend brand equity to "the last mile" and encourage favorable point-of-purchase decisions.

Retailing

What is retailing? We all know that Costco, Home Depot, Macy's, Best Buy, and Target are retailers, but so are Amazon.com, the local Hampton Inn, and a doctor seeing patients. **Retailing** includes all the activities involved in selling products or services directly to final consumers for their personal, nonbusiness use. Many institutions—manufacturers, wholesalers, and retailers—do retailing. But most retailing is done by **retailers**, businesses whose sales come *primarily* from retailing.

Retailing plays a very important role in most marketing channels. Last year, retailers accounted for more than $4.6 trillion of sales to final consumers. They play an important role in connecting brands to consumers in what marketing agency OgilvyAction calls "the last mile"—the final stop in the consumer's path to purchase. It's the "distance a consumer travels between an attitude and an action," explains OgilvyAction's CEO. Some 40 percent of all consumer decisions are made in or near the store. Thus, retailers "reach consumers at key moments of truth, ultimately [influencing] their actions at the point of purchase."[2]

In fact, many marketers are now embracing the concept of **shopper marketing**, using point-of-purchase promotions and advertising to extend brand equity to "the last mile" and encourage favorable point-of-purchase decisions. Shopper marketing involves focusing the entire marketing process—from product and brand development to logistics, promotion, and merchandising—toward turning shoppers into buyers at the point of sale.

Of course, every well-designed marketing effort focuses on customer buying behavior. What differentiates the concept of shopper marketing is the suggestion that these efforts should be coordinated around the shopping process itself. For example, P&G follows a "store back" concept, in which all marketing ideas need to be effective at the store-shelf level and work back from there. The strategy builds around what P&G calls the "First Moment

● Shopper marketing: The dramatic growth of digital shopping has added a new dimension to "point of purchase." Influencing consumers' buying decisions as they shop involves efforts aimed at in-store, online, and mobile shopping.

Inmagine

of Truth"—the critical 3 to 7 seconds that a shopper considers a product on a store shelf. "We are now brand-building from the eyes of the consumer toward us," says a P&G executive.[3]

The dramatic growth of digital shopping, or combined digital and in-store shopping, has added a new dimension to shopper marketing. ● The "last mile" or "first moment of truth" no longer takes place only in stores. Most consumers now make at least some of their purchases online, without even setting foot into a retail store. Alternatively, they may research a purchase on the Internet before—or even during—a store visit. For example, it's not uncommon to see a consumer looking at new TVs in a Best Buy while at the same time using a mobile app to check product reviews and prices at Amazon.com. Thus, shopper marketing isn't just about in-store buying these days. Influencing consumers' buying decisions as they shop involves efforts aimed at in-store, online, and mobile shopping.[4]

Although most retailing is still done in retail stores, in recent years direct and online retailing have been growing much faster than store retailing. We discuss direct and online retailing in detail later in this chapter and in Chapter 17. For now, we will focus on store retailing.

Types of Retailers

Retail stores come in all shapes and sizes—from your local hairstyling salon or family-owned restaurant to national specialty chain retailers such as REI or Williams-Sonoma to megadiscounters such as Costco or Walmart. The most important types of retail stores are described in ● **Table 13.1** and discussed in the following sections. They can be classified in terms of several characteristics, including the *amount of service* they offer, the breadth and depth of their *product lines*, the *relative prices* they charge, and how they are *organized*.

Amount of Service

Different types of customers and products require different amounts of service. To meet these varying service needs, retailers may offer one of three service levels: self-service, limited service, and full service.

Self-service retailers serve customers who are willing to perform their own *locate-compare-select* process to save time or money. Self-service is the basis of all discount operations and is typically used by retailers selling convenience goods (such as supermarkets) and nationally branded, fast-moving shopping goods (such as Target or Kohl's). *Limited-service retailers*, such as Sears or JCPenney, provide more sales assistance because they carry more shopping goods about which customers need information. Their increased operating costs result in higher prices.

Full-service retailers, such as high-end specialty stores (for example, Tiffany or Williams-Sonoma) and first-class department stores (such as Nordstrom or Neiman Marcus) assist customers in every phase of the shopping process. Full-service stores usually carry more specialty goods for which customers need or want assistance or advice. They provide more services, which results in much higher operating costs. These higher costs are passed along to customers as higher prices.

Product Line

Retailers can also be classified by the length and breadth of their product assortments. Some retailers, such as **specialty stores**, carry narrow product lines with deep assortments within those lines. Today, specialty stores are flourishing. The increasing use of market segmentation, market targeting, and product specialization has resulted in a greater need for stores that focus on specific products and segments.

By contrast, **department stores** carry a wide variety of product lines. In recent years, department stores have been squeezed between more focused and flexible specialty stores on the one hand and more efficient, lower-priced discounters on the other. In response, many have added promotional pricing to meet the discount threat. Others have stepped up the use of store brands and single-brand *designer shops* to compete with specialty stores. Still others are trying catalog, telephone, and online selling. Service remains the key differentiating

Specialty store
A retail store that carries a narrow product line with a deep assortment within that line.

Department store
A retail store that carries a wide variety of product lines, each operated as a separate department managed by specialist buyers or merchandisers.

● **Table 13.1** | **Major Store Retailer Types**

Type	Description	Examples
Specialty store	A store that carries a narrow product line with a deep assortment, such as apparel stores, sporting-goods stores, furniture stores, florists, and bookstores.	REI, Radio Shack, Williams-Sonoma
Department store	A store that carries several product lines—typically clothing, home furnishings, and household goods—with each line operated as a separate department managed by specialist buyers or merchandisers.	Macy's, Sears, Neiman Marcus
Supermarket	A relatively large, low-cost, low-margin, high-volume, self-service operation designed to serve the consumer's total needs for grocery and household products.	Kroger, Safeway, SuperValu, Publix
Convenience store	A relatively small store located near residential areas, open long hours seven days a week, and carrying a limited line of high-turnover convenience products at slightly higher prices.	7-Eleven, Stop-N-Go, Circle K, Sheetz
Discount store	A store that carries standard merchandise sold at lower prices with lower margins and higher volumes.	Walmart, Target, Kohl's
Off-price retailer	A store that sells merchandise bought at less-than-regular wholesale prices and sold at less than retail. These include *factory outlets* owned and operated by manufacturers; *independent off-price retailers* owned and run by entrepreneurs or by divisions of larger retail corporations; and *warehouse* (or *wholesale*) *clubs* selling a limited selection of goods at deep discounts to consumers who pay membership fees.	Mikasa (factory outlet); TJ Maxx (independent off-price retailer); Costco, Sam's Club, BJ's (warehouse clubs)
Superstore	A very large store that meets consumers' total needs for routinely purchased food and nonfood items. This includes *supercenters*, combined supermarket and discount stores, and *category killers*, which carry a deep assortment in a particular category.	Walmart Supercenter, SuperTarget, Meijer (discount stores); Best Buy, PetSmart, Staples, Barnes & Noble (category killers)

factor. Retailers such as Nordstrom, Saks, Neiman Marcus, and other high-end department stores are doing well by emphasizing exclusive merchandise and high-quality service.

Supermarkets are the most frequently visited type of retail store. Today, however, they are facing slow sales growth because of slower population growth and an increase in competition from discounters (Walmart, Costco, and Dollar General) on the one hand and specialty food stores (Whole Foods Market, Trader Joe's, Sprouts) on the other. Supermarkets also have been hit hard by the rapid growth of out-of-home eating over the past two decades. In fact, supermarkets' share of the groceries and food market plunged from 66 percent in 2002 to less than 62 percent in 2009. Meanwhile, during the same time period, supercenters boosted their market share from 15.6 percent to 20.6 percent.[5]

In the battle for "share of stomachs," some supermarkets have moved upscale, providing improved store environments and higher-quality food offerings, such as from-scratch bakeries, gourmet deli counters, natural foods, and fresh seafood departments. Others, however, are attempting to compete head-on with food discounters such as Costco and Walmart by cutting costs, establishing more-efficient operations, and lowering prices. ● Publix, the nation's largest employee-owned supermarket chain, has done this successfully:[6]

Despite recent belt-tightening by consumers, while other Southeast grocery chains have struggled, Publix has grown steadily and profitably. The $27 billion chain has opened and acquired more new stores than any other supermarket during the past five years, and it boasts the second-highest annualized sales per square foot in the industry, behind only Whole Foods.

● **Despite recent belt-tightening by consumers, the Publix supermarket chain has succeeded by lowering prices and helping customers get the most out of today's tighter food budgets.**

Lannis Waters/ZUMA Press/Newscom

Supermarket

A large, low-cost, low-margin, high-volume, self-service store that carries a wide variety of grocery and household products.

Publix's success comes from its focus on helping customers get the most out of today's tighter food budgets. Despite its own rapidly rising purchasing and transportation costs, the chain introduced Publix Essentials, a consumer program that reduced its prices for basics such as bread, milk, and laundry detergent by as much as 20 percent. In addition, Publix began a Savings Made Easy program that offers Meal Deal and Thrifty Tips advice to customers trying to stretch their shopping dollars. "In today's economy, Publix is working hard to help," says the chain. "In addition to lowering prices on groceries you need most, we're giving you simple strategies for saving." Says one retail consultant, "Publix is always at its best when the economy is at its worst." Customers seem to agree. According to the American Customer Satisfaction Index (ACSI), for the 18th consecutive year, Publix is the highest-ranking supermarket for customer satisfaction.

Convenience store

A small store, located near a residential area, that is open long hours seven days a week and carries a limited line of high-turnover convenience goods.

Convenience stores are small stores that carry a limited line of high-turnover convenience goods. After several years of stagnant sales, these stores are now experiencing growth. Many convenience store chains have tried to expand beyond their primary market of young, blue-collar men by redesigning their stores to attract female shoppers. They are shedding the image of a "truck stop" where men go to buy gas, beer, cigarettes, or shriveled hotdogs on a roller grill and are instead offering freshly prepared foods and cleaner, safer, more-upscale environments.

For example, consider Sheetz, widely recognized as one of the nation's top convenience store chains. ● Driven by its Total Customer Focus mission and the motto "Feel the Love," Sheetz aims to provide "convenience without compromise while being more than just a convenience store. It's our devotion to your satisfaction that makes the difference."[7]

● Convenience stores: Sheetz positions itself as more than just a convenience store. Driven by its Total Customer Focus mission and the motto—"Feel the Love"—Sheetz aims to provide "convenience without compromise."

Sheetz Inc.

Whether it's for road warriors, construction workers, or soccer moms, Sheetz offers "a mecca for people on the go"—fast, friendly service and quality products in clean and convenient locations. "We really care about our customers," says the company. "If you need to refuel your car or refresh your body, . . . Sheetz has what you need, when you need it. And, we're here 24/7/365." Sheetz certainly isn't your run-of-the-mill convenience store operation. The average Sheetz store is nearly twice the size of the average 7-Eleven. Stores offer up a menu of made-to-order cold and toasted subs, sandwiches, and salads, along with hot fries, onion rings, chicken fingers, and burgers—all ordered through touch-screen terminals. Stores also feature Sheetz Bros. Coffeez, a full-service espresso bar staffed by a trained barista. Frozen fruit smoothies round out the menu.

All stores also offer made-to-go sandwiches, wraps, and parfaits that make it even more convenient for customers on the move to grab a quick bite. This food and a full line of Shweetz bakery items are made fresh daily at the company's own kitchen/bakery, Sheetz Bros. Kitchen. To help make paying easier, Sheetz was the first chain in the nation to install system-wide MasterCard PayPass, allowing customers to quickly tap their credit cards and go. Sheetz also partnered with M&T Bank to offer ATM services at Sheetz locations without a surcharge. Some analysts say that Sheetz aims to become the Walmart of convenience stores, and it just might get there.

Superstore

A store much larger than a regular supermarket that offers a large assortment of routinely purchased food products, nonfood items, and services.

Superstores are much larger than regular supermarkets and offer a large assortment of routinely purchased food products, nonfood items, and services. Walmart, Target, Meijer, and other discount retailers offer *supercenters*, very large combination food and discount stores. Whereas a traditional grocery store brings in about $466,000 a week in sales, a supercenter brings in about $1.5 million a week. Walmart, which opened its first supercenter in 1988, now has more than 3,000 supercenters in North America and is opening new ones at a rate of about 140 per year.[8]

Recent years have also seen the rapid growth of superstores that are actually giant specialty stores, the so-called **category killers** (for example, Best Buy, Home Depot, and PetSmart). They feature stores the size of airplane hangars that carry a very deep assortment of a particular line. Category killers are found in a wide range of categories, including electronics, home-improvement products, books, baby gear, toys, linens and towels, party goods, sporting goods, and even pet supplies.

Category killer

A giant specialty store that carries a very deep assortment of a particular line.

Service retailer

A retailer whose product line is actually a service; examples include hotels, airlines, banks, colleges, and many others.

Finally, for many retailers, the product line is actually a service. **Service retailers** include hotels and motels, banks, airlines, restaurants, colleges, hospitals, movie theaters, tennis clubs, bowling alleys, repair services, hair salons, and dry cleaners. Service retailers in the United States are growing faster than product retailers.

Relative Prices

Retailers can also be classified according to the prices they charge (see Table 13.1). Most retailers charge regular prices and offer normal-quality goods and customer service. Others offer higher-quality goods and service at higher prices. Retailers that feature low prices are discount stores and "off-price" retailers.

Discount Stores. A **discount store** (for example, Target, Kmart, or Walmart) sells standard merchandise at lower prices by accepting lower margins and selling higher volume. The early discount stores cut expenses by offering few services and operating in warehouse-like facilities in low-rent, heavily traveled districts. Today's discounters have improved their store environments and increased their services, while at the same time keeping prices low through lean, efficient operations.

Leading "big-box" discounters, such as Walmart, Costco, and Target, now dominate the retail scene. However, even "small-box" discounters are thriving in the current economic environment. For example, dollar stores are now today's fastest-growing retail format. Back in the day, dollar stores sold mostly odd-lot assortments of novelties, factory overruns, closeouts, and outdated merchandise—most priced at $1. Not anymore. ● Dollar General, the nation's largest small-box discount retailer, makes a powerful value promise for the times: "Save time. Save money. Every day":

Dollar General's slogan isn't just for show. It's a careful statement of the store's value promise. The retailer's goal is to keep things simple by offering only a selected assortment of popular brands at everyday low prices in small and convenient locations. Dollar General's slimmed-down product line and smaller stores (you could fit more than 25 Dollar General stores inside the average Walmart supercenter) add up to a quick trip—the average customer is in and out of the store in less than 10 minutes. And its prices on the popular brand-name products it carries are an estimated 20 to 40 percent lower than grocery store prices. Put it all together, and things are sizzling right now at Dollar General. Moreover, the fast-growing retailer is well positioned for the future. We "see signs of a new consumerism," says Dollar General's CEO, as people shift where they shop, switch to lower-cost brands, and stay generally more frugal." Convenience and low prices, it seems, never go out of style.[9]

Off-Price Retailers. As the major discount stores traded up, a new wave of **off-price retailers** moved in to fill the ultralow-price, high-volume gap. Ordinary discounters buy at regular wholesale prices and accept lower margins to keep prices down. By contrast, off-price retailers buy at less-than-regular wholesale prices and charge consumers less than retail. Off-price retailers can be found in all areas, from food, clothing, and electronics to no-frills banking and discount brokerages.

The three main types of off-price retailers are *independents, factory outlets,* and *warehouse clubs.* **Independent off-price retailers** either are independently owned and run or are divisions of larger retail corporations. Although many off-price operations are run by smaller independents, most large off-price retailer operations are owned by bigger retail chains. Examples include store retailers such as TJ Maxx and Marshalls, which are owned by TJX Companies, and online sellers such as Overstock.com.

Factory outlets—manufacturer-owned and operated stores by firms such as J. Crew, Gap, Levi Strauss, and others—sometimes group together in *factory outlet malls* and *value-retail centers.* At these centers, dozens of outlet stores offer prices as much as 50 percent below retail on a wide range of mostly surplus, discounted, or irregular goods. Whereas outlet malls consist primarily of manufacturers' outlets, value-retail centers combine manufacturers' outlets with off-price retail stores and department store clearance outlets.

The malls in general are now moving upscale—and even dropping *factory* from their descriptions. A growing number of outlet malls now feature luxury brands such as Coach, Polo Ralph Lauren, Dolce&Gabbana, Giorgio Armani, Burberry, and Versace. As consumers become more value-minded, even upper-end retailers are accelerating their factory outlet

---

Discount store

A retail operation that sells standard merchandise at lower prices by accepting lower margins and selling at higher volume.

● Discounter Dollar General, the nation's largest small-box discount retailer, makes a powerful value promise for the times: "Save time. Save money. Every day."

Photo courtesy of Gary Armstrong

Off-price retailer

A retailer that buys at less-than-regular wholesale prices and sells at less than retail.

Independent off-price retailer

An off-price retailer that is either independently owned and run or is a division of a larger retail corporation.

Factory outlet

An off-price retailing operation that is owned and operated by a manufacturer and normally carries the manufacturer's surplus, discontinued, or irregular goods.

strategies, placing more emphasis on outlets such as Nordstrom Rack, Neiman Marcus Last Call, Bloomingdale's Outlets, and Saks Off 5th. Many companies now regard outlets not simply as a way of disposing of problem merchandise but as an additional way of gaining business for fresh merchandise. The combination of highbrow brands and lowbrow prices found at outlets provides powerful shopper appeal, especially in thriftier times.

Warehouse clubs (also known as *wholesale clubs* or *membership warehouses*), such as Costco, Sam's Club, and BJ's, operate in huge, drafty, warehouse-like facilities and offer few frills. However, they offer ultralow prices and surprise deals on selected branded merchandise. Warehouse clubs have grown rapidly in recent years. These retailers appeal not only to low-income consumers seeking bargains on bare-bones products but also to all kinds of customers shopping for a wide range of goods, from necessities to extravagances.

Consider Costco, now the nation's third-largest retailer, behind only Walmart and Kroger. Low price is an important part of Costco's equation, but what really sets Costco apart is the products it carries and the sense of urgency that it builds into the Costco shopper's store experience.[10]

Warehouse clubs: Costco is a retail treasure hunt, where one's shopping cart could contain a $50,000 diamond ring resting on top of a vat of mayonnaise.
Suzanne Dechillo/The New York Times

Warehouse club

An off-price retailer that sells a limited selection of brand-name grocery items, appliances, clothing, and other goods at deep discounts to members who pay annual membership fees.

Costco brings flair to an otherwise dreary setting. Alongside the gallon jars of peanut butter and 2,250-count packs of Q-Tips, Costco offers an ever-changing assortment of high-quality products—even luxuries—all at tantalizingly low margins. As one industry analyst puts it, "Costco is a retail treasure hunt, where one's shopping cart could contain a $50,000 diamond ring resting on top of a vat of mayonnaise." It's the place where high-end products meet deep-discount prices. Last year, Costco sold more than 69 million hot dog and soda combinations (still only $1.50 as they have been for more than 25 years). At the same time, it sold more than 100,000 carats of diamonds at up to $100,000 per item. It is the nation's biggest baster of poultry (more than 70,000 rotisserie chickens a day at $4.99) but also the country's biggest seller of fine wines (including the likes of a Chateau Cheval Blanc Premier Grand Cru Classe at $1,750 a bottle).

Each Costco store is a theater of retail that creates buying urgency and excitement. Mixed in with its regular stock of staples, Costco features a glittering, constantly shifting array of one-time specials, such as discounted Prada bags, Calloway golf clubs, or Kenneth Cole bags—deals you just won't find anywhere else. In fact, of the 4,000 items that Costco carries, 1,000 are designated as "treasure items" (Costco's words). The changing assortment and great prices keep people coming back, wallets in hand. Costco stores average $1,000 of sales per square foot of selling space, compared with Sam's at $586 per square foot and BJs Wholesale at $500. There was a time when only the great, unwashed masses shopped at off-price retailers, but Costco has changed all that. Now, even people who don't have to pinch pennies shop there.

Organizational Approach

Although many retail stores are independently owned, others band together under some form of corporate or contractual organization. ● **Table 13.2** describes four major types of retail organizations—*corporate chains, voluntary chains, retailer cooperatives,* and *franchise organizations.*

Corporate chains are two or more outlets that are commonly owned and controlled. They have many advantages over independents. Their size allows them to buy in large quantities at lower prices and gain promotional economies. They can hire specialists to deal with areas such as pricing, promotion, merchandising, inventory control, and sales forecasting.

The great success of corporate chains caused many independents to band together in one of two forms of contractual associations. One is the *voluntary chain*—a wholesaler-sponsored group of independent retailers that engages in group buying and common merchandising. Examples include the Independent Grocers Alliance (IGA), Western Auto, and Do-It Best hardwares. The other type of contractual association is the *retailer cooperative*—a group of independent retailers that bands together to set up a jointly owned, central wholesale operation and conduct joint merchandising and promotion efforts. Examples are Associated Grocers and Ace Hardware. These organizations give independents the buying and promotion economies they need to meet the prices of corporate chains.

Another form of contractual retail organization is a **franchise**. The main difference between franchise organizations and other contractual systems (voluntary chains and

Corporate chains

Two or more outlets that are commonly owned and controlled.

Franchise

A contractual association between a manufacturer, wholesaler, or service organization (a franchisor) and independent businesspeople (franchisees) who buy the right to own and operate one or more units in the franchise system.

● **Table 13.2** │ **Major Types of Retail Organizations**

Type	Description	Examples
Corporate chain	Two or more outlets that are commonly owned and controlled. Corporate chains appear in all types of retailing but they are strongest in department stores, discount stores, food stores, drugstores, and restaurants.	Sears (department stores), Target (discount stores), Kroger (grocery stores), CVS (drugstores)
Voluntary chain	Wholesaler-sponsored group of independent retailers engaged in group buying and merchandising.	Independent Grocers Alliance (IGA), Do-It Best (hardware), Western Auto, True Value
Retailer cooperative	Group of independent retailers who jointly establish a central buying organization and conduct joint promotion efforts.	Associated Grocers (groceries), Ace Hardware (hardware)
Franchise organization	Contractual association between a franchisor (a manufacturer, wholesaler, or service organization) and franchisees (independent businesspeople who buy the right to own and operate one or more units in the franchise system).	McDonald's, Subway, Pizza Hut, Jiffy Lube, Meineke Mufflers, 7-Eleven

● **Franchising: These days, it's nearly impossible to stroll down a city block or drive on a suburban street without seeing an abundance of franchise businesses.**

© Prisma Bildagentur AG /Alamy

retail cooperatives) is that franchise systems are normally based on some unique product or service; a method of doing business; or the trade name, goodwill, or patent that the franchisor has developed. Franchising has been prominent in fast-food restaurants, motels, health and fitness centers, auto sales and service dealerships, and real estate agencies.

However, franchising covers a lot more than just burger joints and fitness centers. Franchises have sprung up to meet just about any need. For example, Mad Science Group franchisees put on science programs for schools, scout troops, and birthday parties. And Mr. Handyman provides repair services for homeowners while Merry Maids tidies up their houses.

Franchises now command 40 percent of all retail sales in the United States. ● These days, it's nearly impossible to stroll down a city block or drive on a city street without seeing a McDonald's, Subway, Jiffy Lube, or Holiday Inn. One of the best-known and most successful franchisers, McDonald's, now has more than 33,000 stores in 119 countries, including almost 14,000 in the United States. It serves 68 million customers a day and racks up more than $85 billion in annual system-wide sales. More than 80 percent of McDonald's restaurants worldwide are owned and operated by franchisees. Gaining fast is Subway, one of the fastest-growing franchise restaurants, with system-wide sales of $16.2 billion and more than 36,000 shops in 99 countries, including nearly 25,000 in the United States.[11]

Objective 2 ┈┈►

Describe the major retailer marketing decisions.

Retailer Marketing Decisions

Retailers are always searching for new marketing strategies to attract and hold customers. In the past, retailers attracted customers with unique product assortments and more or better services. Today, the assortments and services of various retailers are looking more and more alike. You can find most consumer brands not only in department stores but also in mass-merchandise discount stores, off-price discount stores, and all on the Internet. Thus, it's now more difficult for any one retailer to offer exclusive merchandise.

Service differentiation among retailers has also eroded. Many department stores have trimmed their services, whereas discounters have increased theirs. In addition, customers have become smarter and more price sensitive. They see no reason to pay more for identical brands, especially when service differences are shrinking. For all these reasons, many retailers today are rethinking their marketing strategies.

As shown in ● **Figure 13.1**, retailers face major marketing decisions about *segmentation and targeting*, *store differentiation and positioning*, and the *retail marketing mix*.

FIGURE | 13.1
Retailer Marketing Strategies

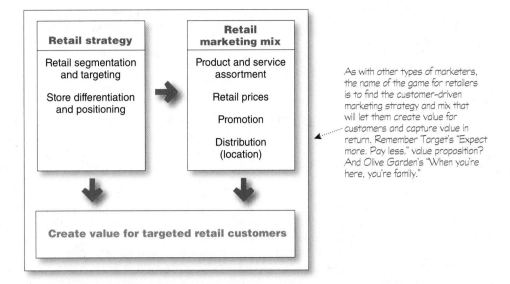

As with other types of marketers, the name of the game for retailers is to find the customer-driven marketing strategy and mix that will let them create value for customers and capture value in return. Remember Target's "Expect more. Pay less." value proposition? And Olive Garden's "When you're here, you're family."

Segmentation, Targeting, Differentiation, and Positioning Decisions

Retailers must first segment and define their target markets and then decide how they will differentiate and position themselves in these markets. Should the store focus on upscale, midscale, or downscale shoppers? Do target shoppers want variety, depth of assortment, convenience, or low prices? Until they define and profile their markets, retailers cannot make consistent decisions about product assortment, services, pricing, advertising, store décor, or any of the other decisions that must support their positions.

Too many retailers, even big ones, fail to clearly define their target markets and positions. For example, what market does Sears target? For what is the department store known? What is its value proposition versus, say, Walmart on one hand and Macy's or Nordstrom on the other? If you're having trouble answering those questions, you're not alone—so is Sears's management (see Real Marketing 13.1).

By contrast, successful retailers define their target markets well and position themselves strongly. For example, Trader Joe's positions itself strongly with its "cheap gourmet" value proposition. Walmart is strongly positioned on low prices and what those always low prices mean to its customers. And highly successful outdoor products retailer Bass Pro Shops positions itself powerfully as being "as close to the Great Outdoors as you can get indoors!"

Retail targeting and positioning: Five Guys Burger and Fries succeeds by positioning itself strongly away from McDonald's and other large fast-food giants. The menu is very limited, but what you can get at Five Guys you simply can't get at McDonald's.

Jerry Huddleston/Flickr

With solid targeting and positioning, a retailer can compete effectively against even the largest and strongest competitors. For example, compare little Five Guys Burger and Fries to giant McDonald's. Five Guys has less than 1,000 stores and $1 billion in sales; McDonald's has more than 33,000 stores worldwide and sales of $85 billion. How does this smaller burger chain compete with Big Mac? It doesn't—at least not directly. Five Guys succeeds by carefully positioning itself *away* from McDonald's:[12]

Five Guys' menu is limited—really limited. Aside from hamburgers, the chain has only hot dogs and grilled cheese or veggie sandwiches (which hardly anyone buys). You won't find salads or breakfasts or Chicken McBites at Five Guys, or even a chocolate milk shake. But what you *can* get at Five Guys you simply *can't* get at McDonald's—such as a mouth-watering Five Guys cheeseburger consisting of two patties and 840 gluttonous calories, piled high with cheese, lettuce, tomatoes, pickles, jalapenos, grilled mushrooms, or any of 11 free toppings, made to order with all-fresh ingredients and buried under an absurdly large serving of just-cooked hand-cut fries. The chain claims that there are more than 250,000 ways to order a Five Guys burger, recently crowned Zagat's "Best Burger." What's more it's all very fresh—there are no freezers in any Five Guys locations, just coolers. The small burger joint's unique offerings and generous portions set it apart, allowing it to charge more than regular fast-food places.

Real Marketing 13.1

Positioning Sears: Why Should You Shop There?

If you're like many Americans, you probably don't shop much at Sears. And when you do shop there, it's probably to catch a sale on appliances or tools, or maybe to browse the selection of Lands' End apparel, a brand owned by Sears since 2002. Even then, the merchandise and brands at your local Sears probably seem a bit stale, and the store itself feels a little old and run down. Shopping at Sears just doesn't provide the modern, feel-good shopping experience that you get at competing retailers such as Macy's or Nordstrom, or even Target or Walmart.

Today's successful retailers position themselves strongly—customers know what the store stands for and how it delivers value. Mention Walmart and people think "Save money. Live better." Bring up Target, and they know to "Expect more. Pay less." Successful discounter Kohl's tells customers to "Expect great things." At Macy's you get "the magic of Macy's," and Nordstrom promises to "take care of customers no matter what it takes." But mention Sears and people are stumped. They are left wondering, "Why should I shop at Sears?"

Founded in 1886, over the next century, Sears grew to become America's iconic retailer. It began as a mail-order catalog company in the 1880s, grew into a national chain of urban department stores during the early- to mid-1900s, and became an important anchor store in the fast-growing suburban malls of the 1960s and 1970s. Through the 1980s, Sears was the nation's largest retail chain—the Walmart of its time. Its then well-known slogan, "Where America Shops," was more than just an advertising tagline—it was a meaningful positioning statement. Almost every American relied on Sears for everything from basic apparel and home goods to appliances and tools.

But during the past two decades, as the retail landscape has shifted, once-mighty Sears has lost its way. Squeezed between lower-priced big-box discount stores on the one hand, and trendier, more targeted up-scale department and specialty stores on the other, Sears has gotten lost in the murky middle. Its old "Where America shops" positioning has little meaning these days for a store with

less than one-tenth the sales of competitor Walmart. And Sears has failed to refresh its positioning to make itself relevant in today's marketplace.

A look at Sears advertising or a visit to the Sears Web site testifies to the retailer's almost complete lack of current positioning. Headlines scream "Buy more, save more on appliances," "50% off your favorite apparel brands," "Lowest prices on Craftsman lawn and garden," and "Big brand sale: great values, top brands." It seems that about the only thing Sears has going for it these days is that everything it sells is always on sale. However, price is not a convincing value proposition for Sears, which has trouble matching the low prices of competitors such as Walmart, Target, or Kohl's.

In 2005, a struggling Sears merged with an even more distressed Kmart to become Sears Holding Corporation. The merger of the two failing retailers left analysts scratching their heads and customers even more confused about the value propositions of the respective chains. Following the merger, the corporation jumped from one questionable tactic to another. For example, Kmart stores began carrying well-known Sears brands such as Craftsman tools, Kenmore appliances, and Diehard batteries, diluting one of Sears's only remaining differentiating assets.

Sears Holding has also tried a variety of store formats. For instance, it converted 400 Kmart stores to Sears Essentials stores, which it later changed to Sears Grand stores—Walmart-like outlets that carry regular Sears merchandise plus everything from health and beauty brands, toys, and baby products to party supplies and groceries. It has also dabbled with a confusing assortment of other formats carrying the Sears name, such as Sears Hometown

stores (a franchised smaller version of full-sized Sears stores), Sears Hardware stores, Sears Home Appliance Showrooms, Sears Outlet stores, and Sears Auto Centers.

Despite all the new store formats, Sears has done little to refresh its positioning. "A lot of traditional department stores have reinvigorated themselves through merchandising. You haven't seen that from Sears," says one analyst. To make matters worse, while most competing retailers have invested heavily to spruce up their stores, Sears has spent less than one-quarter the industry average on store maintenance and renovation, leaving many of its outlets looking old and shabby. "There's no reason to shop at Sears," concludes a retailing expert. "It offers a depressing shopping experience and uncompetitive prices."

Many critics place the blame for Sears's lack of sound marketing and positioning on Sears Holding Company chairman Edward Lampert, a hedge fund manager and the driving force behind the Sears/Kmart merger. Lampert and his funds own about 60 percent of Sears Holding's stock. Critics claim that since the 2005 merger, Lampert has run the company more as a portfolio of financial assets than as a retail chain. Indeed, Lampert has hired four CEOs since the merger, not a single one with any retailing experience. "Being a successful hedge fund manager doesn't make you a good retailer," says one Sears watcher.

Sears's lack of customer and marketing thinking has taken a big toll. Sears Holding Corporation revenues have fallen every year since the Sears/Kmart merger, ending last year down 4.1 percent at $41.6 billion, with loses of $3.1 billion. Sears's stock price has

To once again position Sears as the place "Where America Shops," the retailer must first answer the question, "Why should people shop at Sears?"

TANNEN MAURY/EPA/Newscom

fallen 80 percent since 2007. With no cogent marketing plan and seemingly no way out of its financial tailspin, some analysts even predict that once-dominant Sears will soon disappear entirely. "They are letting . . . Sears die on the vine," says one doubter. "As strong as a brand is, and it has huge familiarity and favorability over the years, you can't continue to have a lack of focus without causing long-term damage."

Sears does have some strengths. One bright spot is online sales, which account for 8.7 percent of Sears's total revenues, compared with only the 1 to 2 percent of sales that Walmart and Target have struggled to achieve online. Another positive is Sears's enduring store brands. Craftsman tools and Kenmore appliances still lead their categories, and the DieHard brand of automotive batteries remains

strong. Sears is opening new Hometown stores to focus on a narrower assortment of merchandise built around these core brands. And the company has announced that it will license its brands to makers of related products. Thus, we might soon see Craftsman work apparel, Kenmore kitchenware, and DieHard flashlights and household batteries.

However, creating more online business and renting out its store brands will not overcome what one industry expert characterizes as "the horror show that is the . . . Sears stores themselves." Restoring Sears's relevance and luster will require nothing short of a complete strategic turnaround that positions Sears and its brands on differentiated customer value. To once again position Sears as the place "Where America Shops," the retailer must first answer the question, "Why should people shop at Sears?"

Sources: Quotes and other information from Lauren Coleman-Lochner and Carol Hymowitz, "A Money Man's Trials in Retailing," *Businessweek*, January 5, 2012, pp. 24–25; "Prediction: These Famous Brands Will Disappear In 2012," *The Business Insider*, January 5, 2012, http://finance.yahoo.com/blogs/daily-ticker/prediction-famous-brands-disappear-2012-010414512.html; Phil Wahba, "Sears Closing More Stores as Holiday Sales Slide," *Reuters*, December 27, 2011, www.reuters.com/article/2011/12/27/us-sears-sales-idUSTRE7BQ0AV20111227; Karen Talley, "Sears to License Names of Kenmore, Craftsman Brands," *Wall Street Journal*, April 5, 2012, http://online.wsj.com/article/SB10001424052702303299604577325643404448050.html; "Largest U.S. Corporations," *Fortune*, May 21, 2012, pp. 63–104; and various pages at www.sears.com, accessed November 2012.

Five Guys can't match McDonald's massive economies of scale, incredible volume purchasing power, ultraefficient logistics, diverse menu, and low prices. But then again, it doesn't even try. By positioning itself away from McDonald's and other large competitors, Five Guys has become one of the nation's fastest-growing fast-casual restaurant chains.

Product Assortment and Services Decision

Retailers must decide on three major product variables: product assortment, services mix, and store atmosphere.

The retailer's product assortment should differentiate it while matching target shoppers' expectations. One strategy is to offer merchandise that no other competitor carries, such as store brands or national brands on which it holds exclusive rights. For example, Saks gets exclusive rights to carry a well-known designer's labels. It also offers its own private-label lines—the Saks Fifth Avenue Signature, Classic, and Sport collections. Alternatively, a retailer can differentiate itself by offering a highly targeted product assortment: Lane Bryant carries plus-size clothing; Brookstone offers an unusual assortment of gadgets and gifts; and BatteryDepot.com offers about every imaginable kind of replacement battery.

The *services mix* can also help set one retailer apart from another. For example, some retailers invite customers to ask questions or consult service representatives in person or via phone or keyboard. Nordstrom promises to "take care of the customer, no matter what it takes." Home Depot offers a diverse mix of services to do-it-yourselfers, from "how-to" classes and "do-it-herself" and kid workshops to a proprietary credit card.

The *store's atmosphere* is another important element in the reseller's product arsenal. Retailers want to create a unique store experience, one that suits the target market and moves customers to buy. Many retailers practice *experiential retailing*. For example, outdoor goods retailer Cabela's stores are as much natural history museums for outdoor enthusiasts as they are retail outlets.[13]

Despite Cabela's often remote locations, customers flock to its 34 superstores to buy hunting, fishing, and outdoor gear. A typical Cabela's store draws 4.4 million customers a year; half of Cabela's customers drive 100 miles or more to get there. What is it that attracts these hordes of shoppers to Cabela's stores? Part of the answer lies in all the stuff the stores sell. Cabela's huge superstores house a vast assortment of quality merchandise at reasonable prices. ● But Cabela's real magic lies in the *experiences* it creates for those who visit. "This is more than a place to go get fishhooks," says a Cabela's spokesperson. "We want to create a sense of wonder" for those who visit.

● Store atmosphere: Cabela's real magic lies in the experiences it creates for those who visit. "This is more than a place to go get fishhooks . . . we wanted to create a sense of wonder."

Getty ImagesED

Mission accomplished! Each Cabela's store creates what amounts to a natural history theme park. Take the store near Fort Worth, Texas, for example. Dominating the center of the store is Conservation Mountain, a two-story mountain replica with two waterfalls and cascading streams. The mountain is divided into four ecosystems and five bioregions: a Texas prairie, an Alaskan habitat, an Arctic icecap, an American woodland, and an Alpine mountaintop. Each bioregion is populated by lifelike, museum-quality taxidermy animals in action poses—everything from prairie dogs, deer, elk, and caribou to brown bears, polar bears, musk oxen, and mountain goats. Getting hungry? Drop by the Mesquite Grill café for an elk, ostrich, or wild boar sandwich—no Big Macs here! The nearby General Store offers old-fashioned candy and snacks. Put it all together and Cabela's is creating total experiences that delight the senses as well as the wallets of its carefully targeted customers.

Today's successful retailers carefully orchestrate virtually every aspect of the consumer store experience. The next time you step into a retail store—whether it sells consumer electronics, hardware, or high fashion—stop and carefully consider your surroundings. Think about the store's layout and displays. Listen to the background sounds. Smell the smells. Chances are good that everything in the store, from the layout and lighting to the music and even the smells, has been carefully orchestrated to help shape the customers' shopping experiences—and open their wallets. For example, most large retailers have developed signature scents that you smell only in their stores:[14]

Luxury shirtmaker Thomas Pink pipes the smell of clean, pressed shirts into its stores—its signature "line-dried linen" scent. Sheraton Hotels employs Welcoming Warmth, a mix of fig, Jasmine, and freesia; whereas Westin Hotel & Resorts disperses White Tea, which attempts to provide the indefinable "Zen-retreat" experience. Bloomingdale's uses different essences in different departments: the soft scent of baby powder in the baby store, coconut in the swimsuit area, lilacs in intimate apparel, and sugar cookies and evergreen scent during the holiday season. At Abercrombie and Fitch, it's a "woody" aroma—a combination of orange, fir resin, and Brazilian rosewood, among others. Theme park operators send popcorn aromas wafting down the midway—they don't pop the corn there, but the aroma puts visitors in a snacking mood. Such scents can increase customer "dwell times" and, in turn, buying. Says the founder of ScentAir, a company that produces such scents, "Developing a signature fragrance is much like [developing] a message in print or radio: What do you want to communicate to consumers and how often?"

Such *experiential retailing* confirms that retail stores are much more than simply assortments of goods. They are environments to be experienced by the people who shop in them. In fact, retail establishments sometimes become small communities in themselves—places where people get together. For example, women's sports and fitness chain Title Nine is part women's active apparel shop and part women's gathering spot. Beyond selling apparel for everything from running to rock climbing, it sponsors local fitness events, in-store get-togethers, and an online community for women on the move—called *timeout with Title Nine*—all announced via each store's individual Facebook page. The Portland, Oregon, Title Nine hosts moonlight snowshoe outings, in-store yoga classes, and a weekend cycling series.[15]

Price Decision

A retailer's price policy must fit its target market and positioning, product and service assortment, the competition, and economic factors. All retailers would like to charge high markups and achieve high volume, but the two seldom go together. Most retailers seek *either* high markups on lower volume (most specialty stores) *or* low markups on higher volume (mass merchandisers and discount stores).

Thus, 110-year-old Bergdorf Goodman caters to the upper crust by selling apparel, shoes, and jewelry created by designers such as Chanel, Prada, and Hermes. ● The upmarket retailer pampers its customers with services such as a personal shopper and in-store showings of the upcoming season's trends with cocktails and hors d'oeuvres. By contrast, TJ Maxx sells brand-name clothing at discount prices aimed at Middle Americans. As it

● A retailer's price policy must fit its targeting and positioning. Bergdorf Goodman caters to the upper crust with prices to match.

Deidre Schoo/The New York Times/Redux

stocks new products each week, the discounter provides a treasure hunt for bargain shoppers.

Retailers must also decide on the extent to which they will use sales and other price promotions. Some retailers use no price promotions at all, competing instead on product and service quality rather than on price. For example, it's difficult to imagine Bergdorf Goodman holding a two-for-the-price-of-one sale on Chanel handbags, even in a tight economy. Other retailers—such as Walmart, Costco, and Family Dollar—practice *everyday low pricing (EDLP)*, charging constant, everyday low prices with few sales or discounts.

Still other retailers practice *high-low pricing*—charging higher prices on an everyday basis, coupled with frequent sales and other price promotions, to increase store traffic, create a low-price image, or attract customers who will buy other goods at full prices. The recent economic downturn caused a rash of high-low pricing, as retailers poured on price cuts and promotions to coax bargain-hunting customers into their stores. Which pricing strategy is best depends on the retailer's overall marketing strategy, the pricing approaches of its competitors, and the economic environment.

Promotion Decision

Retailers use any or all of the five promotion tools—advertising, personal selling, sales promotion, public relations (PR), and direct marketing—to reach consumers. They advertise in newspapers and magazines and on radio, television, and the Internet. Advertising may be supported by newspaper inserts and catalogs. Store salespeople greet customers, meet their needs, and build relationships. Sales promotions may include in-store demonstrations, displays, sales, and loyalty programs. PR activities, such as new-store openings, special events, newsletters and blogs, store magazines, and public service activities, are also available to retailers. Most retailers have also created Web sites and mobile apps that offer customers information and other features while selling merchandise directly.

Place Decision

Retailers often point to three critical factors in retailing success: *location, location,* and *location*! It's very important that retailers select locations that are accessible to the target market in areas that are consistent with the retailer's positioning. For example, Apple locates its stores in high-end malls and trendy shopping districts—such as the "Magnificent Mile" on Chicago's Michigan Avenue or Fifth Avenue in Manhattan—not low-rent strip malls on the edge of town. By contrast, Trader Joe's places its stores in low-rent, out-of-the-way locations to keep costs down and support its "cheap gourmet" positioning. Small retailers may have to settle for whatever locations they can find or afford. Large retailers, however, usually employ specialists who use advanced methods to select store locations.

Most stores today cluster together to increase their customer pulling power and give consumers the convenience of one-stop shopping. *Central business districts* were the main form of retail cluster until the 1950s. Every large city and town had a central business district with department stores, specialty stores, banks, and movie theaters. When people began moving to the suburbs, however, these central business districts, with their traffic, parking, and crime problems, began to lose business. In recent years, many cities have joined with merchants to revive downtown shopping areas, generally with only mixed success.

Shopping center

A group of retail businesses built on a site that is planned, developed, owned, and managed as a unit.

A **shopping center** is a group of retail businesses built on a site that is planned, developed, owned, and managed as a unit. A *regional shopping center*, or *regional shopping mall*, the largest and most dramatic shopping center, has from 50 to more than 100 stores, including two or more full-line department stores. It is like a covered mini-downtown and attracts customers from a wide area. A *community shopping center* contains between 15 and 50 retail stores. It normally contains a branch of a department store or variety store, a supermarket, specialty stores, professional offices, and sometimes a bank. Most shopping centers are *neighborhood shopping centers* or *strip malls* that generally contain between 5 and 15 stores. These centers, which are close and convenient for consumers, usually contain a supermarket, perhaps a discount store, and several service stores—dry cleaner, drugstore, hardware store, local restaurant, or other stores.[16]

A newer form of shopping center is the so-called power center. *Power centers* are huge unenclosed shopping centers consisting of a long strip of retail stores, including large, free-standing anchors such as Walmart, Home Depot, Costco, Best Buy, Michaels, PetSmart, and OfficeMax. Each store has its own entrance with parking directly in front for shoppers who wish to visit only one store.

In contrast, *lifestyle centers* are smaller, open-air malls with upscale stores, convenient locations, and nonretail activities, such as a playground, skating rink, hotel, dining establishments, and a movie theater. "Think of lifestyle centers as part Main Street and part Fifth Avenue," comments an industry observer. In fact, the original power center and lifestyle center concepts are now morphing into hybrid lifestyle-power centers. In fact, the original power center and lifestyle center concepts are now morphing into hybrid lifestyle-power centers that combine the convenience and community feel of a neighborhood center with the brute force of a power center. In all, today's centers are more places to hang out than just places to shop.[17]

The past few years have brought hard times for shopping centers. With more than 100,000 centers in the United States, many experts suggest that the country has been "over-malled." Not surprisingly, the recent Great Recession hit shopping malls hard. Consumer spending cutbacks forced many retailers—small and large—out of business, increasing mall vacancy rates. Power centers were especially hard hit as their big-box retailer tenants suffered during the downturn. Some of the pizzazz has also gone out of lifestyle centers, whose upper-middle-class shoppers suffered most during the recession. Many lifestyle centers are even adding lower-price retailers to replace classier tenants that have folded. "We've learned that lifestyle centers have to adapt to a changing environment to survive," says one mall developer.[18]

Retailing Trends and Developments

Objective 3 ┄┄➤
Discuss the major trends and developments in retailing.

Retailers operate in a harsh and fast-changing environment, which offers threats as well as opportunities. Consumer demographics, lifestyles, and spending patterns are changing rapidly, as are retailing technologies. To be successful, retailers need to choose target segments carefully and position themselves strongly. They need to take the following retailing developments into account as they plan and execute their competitive strategies.

Tighter Consumer Spending

Following many years of good economic times for retailers, the Great Recession turned many retailers' fortunes from boom to bust. Even as the economy has recovered, retailers will feel the effects of changed consumer spending patterns well into the future.

Some retailers actually benefit from a down economy. For example, as consumers cut back and looked for ways to spend less on what they bought, big discounters such as Costco scooped up new business from bargain-hungry shoppers. Similarly, lower-priced fast-food chains, such as McDonald's, took business from their pricier eat-out competitors.

For most retailers, however, tighter consumer spending has meant tough times. During and following the recent recession, several large and familiar retailers declared bankruptcy or closed their doors completely—including household names such as Linens 'n Things, Circuit City, KB Toys, Borders Books, and Sharper Image, to name a few. Other retailers, from Macy's and Home Depot to Starbucks, laid off employees, cut their costs, and offered deep price discounts and promotions aimed at luring cash-strapped customers back into their stores.

Beyond cost-cutting and price promotions, many retailers also added new value pitches to their positioning. ⬤ For example, Home Depot replaced its older "You can do it. We can help." theme with a thriftier one: "More saving. More doing." Similarly, Whole Foods Market kicked up the promotion of its 365 Everyday Value private-label brand with ads sporting headlines such as "Sticker shock, but in a good way" and "No wallets were harmed in the buying of our 365 Everyday Value products." And following significant declines in same-store sales caused by the recession, Target, for the first time in its history, introduced TV ads featuring price messages. "Our [tagline] is 'Expect more. Pay less.'" a Target marketer said. "We're putting more emphasis on the pay less promise." And in the more frugal postrecession economy, Target's marketing

More saving. **More doing.**™

⬤ Value positioning: Facing tighter consumer spending, Home Depot adopted a thriftier theme: "More saving. More doing."

(logo) The Home Depot, (photo) iofoto/Shutterstock.com

continues to feature more practical price and savings appeals. In fact, in its now famous tagline, the "Pay less." part is now often underlined.[19]

When reacting to economic difficulties, retailers must be careful that their short-run actions don't damage their long-run images and positions. For example, drastic price discounting can increase immediate sales but damage brand loyalty. Instead of relying on cost-cutting and price reductions, retailers should focus on building greater customer value within their long-term store positioning strategies. For example, although it makes sense to boost the "Pay less" part of Target's positioning, Target has not abandoned the quality and design that differentiate it from Walmart and other discounters. As the economy has recovered, although it has shifted the balance a bit toward lower prices, Target still asserts its "Target-ness" by continuing to support the "Expect more" side of its value equation as well.

New Retail Forms, Shortening Retail Life Cycles, and Retail Convergence

New retail forms continue to emerge to meet new situations and consumer needs, but the life cycle of new retail forms is getting shorter. Department stores took about 100 years to reach the mature stage of the life cycle; more recent forms, such as warehouse stores, reached maturity in about 10 years. In such an environment, seemingly solid retail positions can crumble quickly. Of the top 10 discount retailers in 1962 (the year that Walmart and Kmart began), not one exists today. Even the most successful retailers can't sit back with a winning formula. To remain successful, they must keep adapting.

Many retailing innovations are partially explained by the **wheel-of-retailing concept**. According to this concept, many new types of retailing forms begin as low-margin, low-price, and low-status operations. They challenge established retailers that have become "fat" by letting their costs and margins increase. The new retailers' success leads them to upgrade their facilities and offer more services. In turn, their costs increase, forcing them to increase their prices. Eventually, the new retailers become like the conventional retailers they replaced. The cycle begins again when still newer types of retailers evolve with lower costs and prices. The wheel-of-retailing concept seems to explain the initial success and later troubles of department stores, supermarkets, and discount stores and the recent success of dollar stores and off-price retailers.

Wheel-of-retailing concept
A concept that suggests new types of retailers usually begin as low-margin, low-price, low-status operations but later evolve into higher-price, higher-service operations, eventually becoming like the conventional retailers they replaced.

New retail forms are always emerging. For example, many retailers are now experimenting with limited-time *pop-up stores* that let them promote their brands to seasonal shoppers and create buzz in busy areas. ● During the last holiday season, for instance, Toys"R"Us set up approximately 150 temporary pop-up toy boutiques, many located in malls that formerly housed recently bankrupt KB Toys stores. Target recently opened pop-up stores to celebrate limited-run collections by Jason Wu in Toronto and Missoni in New York. The online and mobile equivalent is *flash sales* sites such as Sak's FashionFix and Nordstrom's HauteLook, which host time-limited sales events on top fashion and lifestyle brands.[20]

Today's retail forms appear to be converging. Increasingly, different types of retailers now sell the same products at the same prices to the same consumers. For example, you can buy brand-name home appliances at department stores, discount stores, home improvement stores, off-price retailers, electronics superstores, and a slew of online sites that all compete for the same customers. If you can't find the microwave oven you want at Sears, you can step across the street and find one for a better price at Lowe's or Best Buy—or just order one online from Amazon.com or even RitzCamera.com. This merging of consumers, products, prices, and retailers is called *retail convergence*. Such convergence means greater competition for retailers and greater difficulty in differentiating the product assortments of different types of retailers.

● **New retail forms: Many retailers—such as Toys"R"Us—are setting up limited-time "pop-up" stores that let them promote their brands to seasonal shoppers and create buzz in busy areas.**
Courtesy Toys "R" Us, Inc.

The Rise of Megaretailers

The rise of huge mass merchandisers and specialty superstores, the formation of vertical marketing systems, and a rash of retail mergers and acquisitions have created a core of superpower megaretailers. With their size and buying power, these giant retailers can offer better merchandise selections, good service, and strong price savings to consumers. As a result, they grow even larger by squeezing out their smaller, weaker competitors.

The megaretailers have shifted the balance of power between retailers and producers. A small handful of retailers now control access to enormous numbers of consumers, giving them the upper hand in their dealings with manufacturers. For example, you may never have heard of specialty coatings and sealants manufacturer RPM International, but you've probably used one or more of its many familiar do-it-yourself brands—such as Rust-Oleum paints, Plastic Wood and Dap fillers, Mohawk and Watco finishes, and Testors hobby cements and paints—all of which you can buy at your local Home Depot store. Home Depot is a very important customer to RPM, accounting for a significant share of its consumer sales. However, Home Depot's sales of $70 billion are 20 times RPM's sales of $3.3 billion. As a result, the giant retailer can, and often does, use this power to wring concessions from RPM and thousands of other smaller suppliers.[21]

Growth of Direct and Online Retailing

Most consumers still make a majority of their purchases the old-fashioned way: They go to the store, find what they want, wait patiently in line to plunk down their cash or credit cards, and bring home the goods. However, consumers now have a broad array of nonstore alternatives, including direct and online shopping. As we'll discuss in Chapter 17, direct and online marketing are currently the fastest-growing forms of marketing.

Today, thanks to advanced technologies, easier-to-use and enticing online sites and mobile apps, improved online services, and the increasing sophistication of search technologies, online retailing is thriving. In fact, although it currently accounts for only about 8 percent of total U.S. retail sales, online buying is growing at a much brisker pace than retail buying as a whole. Last year's U.S. online retail sales reached an estimated $194.3 billion, up 16 percent over the previous year, and will reach an estimated $279 billion by 2015.[22]

Retailer online sites and mobile apps also influence a large amount of in-store buying. One recent survey revealed that more than 60 percent of shoppers say they look for deals online before at least half of all shopping trips. What's more, to the dismay of store retailers, many shoppers now check out merchandise at brick-and-mortar store showrooms before buying it online—a process called *showrooming*. Today, half of shoppers who buy products online first check them out at a traditional store. Large retailers such as Target, Walmart, and Best Buy have been hardest hit by showrooming and are busy devising strategies designed to thwart such shopping behavior (see Real Marketing 13.2).[23]

Thus, it's no longer a matter of customers deciding whether to shop in the store *or* shop online. Increasingly, customers are merging store, online, and mobile outlets into a single shopping process. The Internet and digital devices have spawned a whole new breed of shopper and way of shopping. Whether shopping for cars, homes, electronics, consumer products, or medical care, many people just can't buy anything unless they first look it up online and get the lowdown. And they've gotten used to buying anywhere, anytime— whether it's in the store, online, or even online while in the store.

All types of retailers now employ direct and online channels. The Web and mobile online sales of large brick-and-mortar retailers, such as Walmart, Target, Staples, and Best Buy, are increasing rapidly. Many large online-only retailers—Amazon.com, Zappos.com, online travel companies such as Travelocity.com and Expedia.com, and others—have made it big on the Internet. At the other extreme, hordes of niche marketers have used the Internet to reach new markets and expand their sales.

Still, much of the anticipated growth in online sales will go to multichannel retailers— the click-and-brick marketers who can successfully merge the virtual and physical worlds. In a recent ranking of the top-20 online retail sites, 70 percent were owned by store-based retail chains.[24] For example, thanks largely to rapid growth in online sales, upscale home products retailer Williams-Sonoma now captures more than 40 percent of its total revenues from its direct-to-consumer channel. Like many retailers, Williams-Sonoma has discovered that many of its best customers visit and shop both online and offline. Beyond just offering online shopping, the retailer engages customers through online communities, social media, mobile apps, a blog, and special online programs. "The Internet has changed the way our customers shop," says Williams-Sonoma CEO Laura Alber, "and the online brand experience has to be inspiring and seamless."[25]

Real Marketing 13.2

Showrooming: Shopping in Stores but Buying Online

At the local Best Buy, a helpful sales associate in the familiar blue shirt patiently assists a customer who's itching to buy a new computer monitor. After 20 minutes, the customer settles on a beautiful new aluminum-framed, 27-inch Samsung 3D LED monitor, priced at $699. Everyone seems happy and it looks like the associate has earned a well-deserved sale.

However, instead of reaching for his credit card, the customer whips out his smartphone. With the salesperson looking on, he uses an app called TheFind to scan the Samsung's barcode. The app spouts out a list of eight online retailers who sell the same model, along with their prices. Amazon.com has the best price—only $617, and with his Amazon Prime membership, says the customer, he can have it delivered to his doorstep in two days, with no shipping fee and no sales tax. Best Buy doesn't price-match online competitors. So with apologies to the helpful sales associate, the customer pushes the Amazon. com "Buy Now" button and walks out of the store empty-handed.

This now-common shopping practice of coming into store showrooms to scope out merchandise but instead buying it from an online-only rival—a practice called *showrooming*—has become the bane of store retailers. According to one recent survey, half of shoppers who buy products online now check them out first in a traditional store. Another survey shows that about 40 percent of shoppers have used an in-store shopping app—such as TheFind, eBay's RedLaser, or Amazon's Price Check—to find better prices online and purchase from an online retailer while still in the store.

Showrooming has wrought damage to store retailers, especially those selling consumer electronics, which are easy to order online and expensive enough to make price comparisons worthwhile. For example, Target's sales during the most recent holiday season fell short of expectations, with the greatest fallout in electronics, movies, books, and music—products experiencing the biggest shift in sales to e-tailers. It's no surprise then that Best Buy—still the largest consumer electronics retailer—has recently been posting losses, closing stores, and laying off workers.

But store retailers in all categories—from electronics retailers such as Best Buy to general discounters such as Target and Walmart to specialty stores such as GNC and Brookstone—are now looking for ways to keep smartphone-wielding shoppers from defecting. Says one store retailing executive, who refers to Amazon.com as "the A-word," comparison shopping in the post-smartphone and iPad era has "amped up to a whole 'nother level."

Price-matching is one way to thwart showrooming, but it's usually not a realistic option. Online sellers have significant cost advantages—they don't bear the expense of running physical store locations and they aren't required to collect sales taxes in most states. One recent study found that, even before the "no-sales-tax" benefit, Amazon. com's average prices were 8 to 14 percent lower than those of major store retailers, including Target, Walmart, and Best Buy. Most major brick-and-mortar retailers aggressively track online competitor pricing and do their best to match it. They've already trimmed costs and are running on paper-thin margins. So, in most cases, store retailers simply can't match online prices and remain profitable.

With so little room to maneuver on price, store retailers are exploring nonprice tactics to combat showrooming. One tactic is to shift toward exclusive products and store-branded merchandise that don't allow direct comparisons. For example, 56 percent of the products offered by health-and-wellness retailer GNC are either exclusives or GNC-branded items. At specialty retailer Brookstone, many recent best sellers, such as a $229 iPhone projector, have been developed internally. Similarly, Target recently sent an urgent letter to suppliers requesting that they create exclusive Target-only lines and models that would shield it from showrooming price comparisons. It

suggested that such exclusives could include all-new products or modifications in packaging and model numbers that would make direct comparisons difficult.

However, rather than just side-stepping the issue of showrooming—or online shopping more generally—many store retailers are trying to ride the trend by boosting their own online and digital options as an alternative or enhancement to shopping in their stores. For example, Target recently upgraded its Web site and quadrupled the number of items it sells online. Walmart has upped its emphasis on in-store pickups for online orders. It tells customers that they can order from its Walmart.com site, sometimes pick up items on the same day, avoid shipping fees, and easily return items to the store if not satisfied. Customers now pick up half of all Walmart. com purchases in stores, often buying additional merchandise during the visit.

Both Walmart and Target are also testing digital apps that pull customers to both their Web sites and stores, let them prepare shopping lists, and, in Target's case, receive personalized daily-alert deals and exclusive discounts sent to their phones. To help keep customers in the store once they arrive, Walmart has adopted a new strategy that it calls the "endless aisle," by which it trains in-store clerks to direct customers to Walmart.com in the store when they can't find a particular item.

Best Buy is looking for additional ways to make in-store buying more attractive. In a strategy that mimics the "Genius Bars" at Apple stores, Best Buy has tested what it calls "Connected Stores," which feature tech support, wireless connections, and a large customer-assistance hub at the center,

Showrooming: The now-common shopping practice of viewing products in stores but buying them online has become the bane of store retailers. But what can they do about it?

ZUMA Press/Newscom

as well as new areas and checkout lanes to speed pickup on items purchased online. The hope is that additional in-store services will make higher shelf prices more palatable.

Despite such tactics to combat showrooming and digital buying, many experts remain skeptical about the future of store retailers such as Best Buy. "The traditional retailers are still doing business the old way while Amazon has reinvented the model," says one retail analyst. In many categories, the skeptics say, the momentum favors online commerce. "You can try and dance around it," says the analyst, "but it's a fact." And when it comes to online commerce, traditional retailers have a lot of catching up to do. Online sales account for only 1 to 2 percent of Target's and Walmart's total sales. And although online sales currently represent only about 8 percent

of total retail buying, they are growing at a breathtaking rate. For example, Amazon.com, with sales of $48 billion, is growing at an average annual rate of 36 percent. It's positioned to top Best Buy as the 10th largest retailer this year, up from 19th only two years ago.

For now, although it's a clear and present danger to Best Buy and certain other specialty retailers, showrooming is little more than a nuisance to the Targets and Walmarts of the world. But showrooming sales have more than doubled in just the past year, from

$3.4 billion to $8 billion. And as more and more shoppers are leaving stores empty-handed, brick-and-mortar retailers are rising to meet the threat. Target laid out the challenge in its recent petition to suppliers: "What we aren't willing to do is let online-only retailers use our brick-and-mortar stores as a showroom for their products and undercut our prices without making investments, as we do, to proudly display your brands." However, the key question for Target is this: "What are you going to do about it?"

Sources: Ann Zimmerman, "Can Retailers Halt 'Showrooming'?" *Wall Street Journal*, April 11, 2012, p. B1; Jennifer Van Grove, "Everyone Except Grandma Is Comparison Shopping Via Mobile, Study Finds," *Venturebeat*, January 30, 2012, http://venturebeat.com/2012/01/30/in-store-mobile-commerce/; Dana Mattioli, "Retailers Try to Thwart Price Apps," *Wall Street Journal*, December 23, 2011, http://online.wsj.com/article/SB10001424052970203686204 577114901480554444.html; Ann Zimmerman, "Showdown over 'Showrooming,'" *Wall Street Journal*, January 23, 2012, p. B1; and Miguel Bustillo, "Best Buy Forced to Rethink Big Box," *Wall Street Journal*, March 29, 2012, p. B1.

Growing Importance of Retail Technology

Retail technologies have become critically important as competitive tools. Progressive retailers are using advanced IT and software systems to produce better forecasts, control inventory costs, interact electronically with suppliers, send information between stores, and even sell to customers within stores. They have adopted sophisticated systems for checkout scanning, RFID inventory tracking, merchandise handling, information sharing, and customer interactions.

Perhaps the most startling advances in retail technology concern the ways in which retailers are connecting with consumers. Today's customers have gotten used to the speed and convenience of buying online and to the control that the Internet gives them over the buying process. The Internet lets consumers shop when they like and where they like, with instant access to gobs of information about competing products and prices. No real-world store can do all that.

Increasingly, however, retailers are attempting to meet these new consumer expectations by bringing online-style technologies into their stores. Many retailers now routinely use technologies ranging from touch-screen kiosks, mobile hand-held shopping assistants, and customer-loyalty apps to interactive dressing-room mirrors and virtual sales associates. ● For example, Eastern Mountain Sports uses an iPad app to assist in outfitting shoppers for their next adventure with items available both in the store and on the company's Web site. "No longer are we constrained by square footage as to what we can sell," says an EMS marketer.[26]

The future of technology in retailing lies in merging the online and offline shopping experiences. It's not a matter of online retailing growing while physical retailing declines. Instead, both will be important, and the two must be integrated. For example, you've probably had many

● Retail technology: The future belongs to retailers who can blend in-store and online technologies into a seamless shopping experience. Here, an Eastern Mountain Sports associate uses an iPad app to help outfit a shopper for his next adventure.

Eastern Mountain Sports

shopping experiences in which you began by browsing a retailer's Internet site or interactive catalog app, then visited the store, interacted with store sales personnel, and tried out the product. While shopping in the store, you might well have used your smartphone to comparison shop other retailers before making a purchase in the store or online later. The future belongs to retailers who can blend various in-store and online technologies into a seamless shopping experience.[27]

This functional scenario is neither as futuristic nor as fanciful as it might seem. All the technology is already available and will soon be found everywhere. The future belongs to retailers who can blend various in-store and online technologies into a seamless shopping experience.

Green Retailing

Today's retailers are increasingly adopting environmentally sustainable practices. They are greening up their stores and operations, promoting more environmentally responsible products, launching programs to help customers be more responsible, and working with channel partners to reduce their environmental impact.

At the most basic level, most large retailers are making their stores more environmentally friendly through sustainable building design, construction, and operations. For example, all new Kohl's stores are constructed with recycled and regionally sourced building materials, water-efficient landscaping and plumbing fixtures, and ENERGY STAR-rated roofs that reduce energy usage. Inside, new stores use occupancy sensor lighting for stockrooms, dressing rooms, and offices; energy management systems to control heating and cooling; and a recycling program for cardboard boxes, packaging, and hangers. "Kohl's cares," says the store. "From large-scale initiatives like constructing environmentally friendly buildings to everyday practices like recycling hangers, we're taking big steps to ensure we leave a smaller footprint."[28]

Retailers are also greening up their product assortments. For example, Safeway offers its own Bright Green line of home care products, featuring cleaning and laundry soaps made with biodegradable and naturally derived ingredients, energy-efficient light bulbs, and paper products made from a minimum of 60 percent recycled content. Such products can both boost sales and lift the retailer's image as a responsible company.

Many retailers have also launched programs that help consumers make more environmentally responsible decisions. Staples' EcoEasy program "makes it easier to make a difference" by helping customers to identify green products sold in its stores and to recycle printer cartridges, mobile phones, computers, and other office technology products. Staples recycles some 30 million printer cartridges and 10 million pounds of old technology each year.[29]

Finally, many large retailers are joining forces with suppliers and distributors to create more sustainable products, packaging, and distribution systems. For example, Amazon.com works closely with the producers of many of the products it sells to reduce and simplify their packaging. And beyond its own substantial sustainability initiatives, Walmart wields its huge buying power to urge its army of suppliers to improve their environmental impact and practices. The retailer has even developed a worldwide Sustainable Product Index, by which it rates suppliers. It plans to translate the index into a simple rating for consumers to help them make more sustainable buying choices.

Green retailing yields both top- and bottom-line benefits. Sustainable practices lift a retailer's top line by attracting consumers looking to support environmentally friendly sellers and products. They also help the bottom line by reducing costs. For example, Amazon.com's reduced-packaging efforts increase customer convenience and eliminate "wrap rage" while at the same time saving packaging costs. And Kohl's earth-friendly environmentally friendly buildings not only appeal to customers and helps save the planet but also cost less to operate.

● **Green retailing: Safeway offers its own Bright Green line of home care products, including cleaning and laundry products made from biodegradable and naturally derived ingredients.**

Safeway Inc.

Global Expansion of Major Retailers

Retailers with unique formats and strong brand positions are increasingly moving into other countries. Many are expanding internationally to escape saturated home markets. Over the

Wholesaling

All the activities involved in selling goods and services to those buying for resale or business use.

Wholesaler

A firm engaged *primarily* in wholesaling activities.

years, some giant U.S. retailers, such as McDonald's, have become globally prominent as a result of their marketing prowess. Others, such as Walmart, are rapidly establishing a global presence. Walmart, which now operates more than 5,600 stores in 26 non-U.S. markets, sees exciting global potential. Its international division alone last year racked up sales of more than $126 billion, 80 percent more than rival Target's *total* sales of $69.8 billion.[30]

However, most U.S. retailers are still significantly behind Europe and Asia when it comes to global expansion. Although nine of the world's top 20 retailers are U.S. companies, only four of these retailers have set up stores outside North America (Walmart, Home Depot, Costco, and Best Buy). Of the 11 non-U.S. retailers in the world's top 20, 8 have stores in at least 10 countries. Foreign retailers that have gone global include France's Carrefour and Auchan chains, Germany's Metro and Aldi chains, Britain's Tesco, and Japan's Seven & I.[31]

International retailing presents challenges as well as opportunities. Retailers can face dramatically different retail environments when crossing countries, continents, and cultures. Simply adapting the operations that work well in the home country is usually not enough to create success abroad. Instead, when going global, retailers must understand and meet the needs of local markets.

Objective 4 ┈┈▶

Explain the major types of wholesalers and their marketing decisions.

Wholesaling

Wholesaling includes all the activities involved in selling goods and services to those buying them for resale or business use. Firms engaged *primarily* in wholesaling activities are called **wholesalers**.

Wholesalers buy mostly from producers and sell mostly to retailers, industrial consumers, and other wholesalers. As a result, many of the nation's largest and most important wholesalers are largely unknown to final consumers. ● For example, you may never have heard of Grainger, even though it's very well known and much valued by its more than 2 million business and institutional customers in 157 countries.[32]

Grainger may be the biggest market leader you've never heard of. It's an $8.1 billion business that offers more than 1 million maintenance, repair, and operating (MRO) products from 3,500 manufacturers in 30 countries to 2 million active customers. Through its branch network, service centers, sales reps, catalog, and online sites, Grainger links customers with the supplies they need to keep their facilities running smoothly—everything from light bulbs, cleaners, and display cases to nuts and bolts, motors, valves, power tools, test equipment, and safety supplies. Grainger's 711 branches, 28 strategically located distribution centers, nearly 21,500 employees, and innovative Web sites handle more than 115,000 transactions a day. Grainger's customers include organizations ranging from factories, garages, and grocers to schools and military bases. Grainger operates on a simple value proposition: to make it easier and less costly for customers to find and buy MRO supplies. It starts by acting as a one-stop shop for products needed to maintain facilities. On a broader level, it builds lasting relationships with customers by helping them find *solutions* to their overall MRO problems. Acting as consultants, Grainger sales reps help buyers with everything from improving their supply chain management to reducing inventories and streamlining warehousing operations. So, how come you've never heard of Grainger? Perhaps it's because the company operates in the not-so-glamorous world of MRO supplies, which are important to every business but not so important to consumers. More likely, it's because Grainger is a wholesaler. And like most wholesalers, it operates behind the scenes, selling mostly to other businesses.

Why are wholesalers important to sellers? For example, why would a producer use wholesalers rather than selling directly to retailers or consumers? Simply put, wholesalers add value by performing one or more of the following channel functions:

● **Wholesaling: Many of the nation's largest and most important wholesalers—like Grainger—are largely unknown to final consumers. But they are very well known and much valued by the business customers they serve.**

W. W. Grainger, Inc.

- *Selling and promoting:* Wholesalers' sales forces help manufacturers reach many small customers at a low cost. The wholesaler has more contacts and is often more trusted by the buyer than the distant manufacturer.
- *Buying and assortment building:* Wholesalers can select items and build assortments needed by their customers, thereby saving much work.

- *Bulk breaking:* Wholesalers save their customers money by buying in carload lots and breaking bulk (breaking large lots into small quantities).
- *Warehousing:* Wholesalers hold inventories, thereby reducing the inventory costs and risks of suppliers and customers.
- *Transportation:* Wholesalers can provide quicker delivery to buyers because they are closer to buyers than are producers.
- *Financing:* Wholesalers finance their customers by giving credit, and they finance their suppliers by ordering early and paying bills on time.
- *Risk bearing:* Wholesalers absorb risk by taking title and bearing the cost of theft, damage, spoilage, and obsolescence.
- *Market information:* Wholesalers give information to suppliers and customers about competitors, new products, and price developments.
- *Management services and advice:* Wholesalers often help retailers train their salesclerks, improve store layouts and displays, and set up accounting and inventory control systems.

Types of Wholesalers

Wholesalers fall into three major groups (see ● **Table 13.3**): *merchant wholesalers, brokers and agents,* and *manufacturers' and retailers' branches and offices.* **Merchant wholesalers** are the largest single group of wholesalers, accounting for roughly 50 percent of all wholesaling. Merchant wholesalers include two broad types: full-service wholesalers and limited-service wholesalers. *Full-service wholesalers* provide a full set of services, whereas the various *limited-service wholesalers* offer fewer services to their suppliers and customers. The different types of limited-service wholesalers perform varied specialized functions in the distribution channel.

Brokers and *agents* differ from merchant wholesalers in two ways: They do not take title to goods, and they perform only a few functions. Like merchant wholesalers, they generally specialize by product line or customer type. A **broker** brings buyers and sellers together and assists in negotiation. **Agents** represent buyers or sellers on a more permanent basis. *Manufacturers' agents* (also called *manufacturers' representatives*) are the most common type of agent wholesaler. The third major type of wholesaling is that done in **manufacturers' sales branches and offices** by sellers or buyers themselves rather than through independent wholesalers.

Wholesaler Marketing Decisions

Wholesalers now face growing competitive pressures, more-demanding customers, new technologies, and more direct-buying programs on the part of large industrial, institutional, and retail buyers. As a result, they have taken a fresh look at their marketing strategies. As with retailers, their marketing decisions include choices of segmentation and targeting, differentiation and positioning, and the marketing mix—product and service assortments, price, promotion, and distribution (see ● **Figure 13.2**).

Merchant wholesaler
An independently owned wholesale business that takes title to the merchandise it handles.

Broker
A wholesaler who does not take title to goods and whose function is to bring buyers and sellers together and assist in negotiation.

Agent
A wholesaler who represents buyers or sellers on a relatively permanent basis, performs only a few functions, and does not take title to goods.

Manufacturers' sales branches and offices
Wholesaling by sellers or buyers themselves rather than through independent wholesalers.

● FIGURE | 13.2
Wholesaler Marketing Strategies

Why does this figure look so much like Figure 11.1? You guessed it. Like retailers, wholesalers must develop customer-driven marketing strategies and mixes that create value for customers and capture value in return. For example, Grainger helps its business customers "save time and money by providing them with the right products to keep their facilities up and running."

● **Table 13.3** | **Major Types of Wholesalers**

Type	Description
Merchant wholesalers	Independently owned businesses that take title to all merchandise handled. There are full-service wholesalers and limited-service wholesalers.
Full-service wholesalers	Provide a full line of services: carrying stock, maintaining a sales force, offering credit, making deliveries, and providing management assistance. Full-service wholesalers include wholesale merchants and industrial distributors.
Wholesale merchants	Sell primarily to retailers and provide a full range of services. General merchandise wholesalers carry several merchandise lines, whereas general line wholesalers carry one or two lines in great depth. Specialty wholesalers specialize in carrying only part of a line.
Industrial distributors	Sell to manufacturers rather than to retailers. Provide several services, such as carrying stock, offering credit, and providing delivery. May carry a broad range of merchandise, a general line, or a specialty line.
Limited-service wholesalers	Offer fewer services than full-service wholesalers. Limited-service wholesalers are of several types:
Cash-and-carry wholesalers	Carry a limited line of fast-moving goods and sell to small retailers for cash. Normally do not deliver.
Truck wholesalers (or truck jobbers)	Perform primarily a selling and delivery function. Carry a limited line of semiperishable merchandise (such as milk, bread, snack foods), which is sold for cash as deliveries are made to supermarkets, small groceries, hospitals, restaurants, factory cafeterias, and hotels.
Drop shippers	Do not carry inventory or handle the product. On receiving an order, drop shippers select a manufacturer, who then ships the merchandise directly to the customer. Drop shippers operate in bulk industries, such as coal, lumber, and heavy equipment.
Rack jobbers	Serve grocery and drug retailers, mostly in nonfood items. Rack jobbers send delivery trucks to stores, where the delivery people set up toys, paperbacks, hardware items, health and beauty aids, or other items. Rack jobbers price the goods, keep them fresh, set up point-of-purchase displays, and keep inventory records.
Producers' cooperatives	Farmer-owned members that assemble farm produce for sale in local markets. Producers' cooperatives often attempt to improve product quality and promote a co-op brand name, such as Sun-Maid raisins, Sunkist oranges, or Diamond nuts.
Mail-order or Web wholesalers	Send catalogs to or maintain Web sites for retail, industrial, and institutional customers featuring jewelry, cosmetics, specialty foods, and other small items. Its primary customers are businesses in small outlying areas.
Brokers and agents	Do not take title to goods. Main function is to facilitate buying and selling, for which they earn a commission on the selling price. Generally specialize by product line or customer type.
Brokers	Bring buyers and sellers together and assist in negotiation. Brokers are paid by the party who hired the broker and do not carry inventory, get involved in financing, or assume risk. Examples include food brokers, real estate brokers, insurance brokers, and security brokers.
Agents	Represent either buyers or sellers on a more permanent basis than brokers do. There are four types:
Manufacturers' agents	Represent two or more manufacturers of complementary lines. Often used in such lines as apparel, furniture, and electrical goods. A manufacturer's agent is hired by small manufacturers who cannot afford their own field sales forces and by large manufacturers who use agents to open new territories or cover territories that cannot support full-time salespeople.

Type	Description
Selling agents	Have contractual authority to sell a manufacturer's entire output. The selling agent serves as a sales department and has significant influence over prices, terms, and conditions of sale. Found in product areas such as textiles, industrial machinery and equipment, coal and coke, chemicals, and metals.
Purchasing agents	Generally have a long-term relationship with buyers and make purchases for them, often receiving, inspecting, warehousing, and shipping the merchandise to buyers. Purchasing agents help clients obtain the best goods and prices available.
Commission merchants	Take physical possession of products and negotiate sales. Used most often in agricultural marketing by farmers who do not want to sell their own output. Take a truckload of commodities to a central market, sell it for the best price, deduct a commission and expenses, and remit the balance to the producers.
Manufacturers' and retailers' branches and offices	Wholesaling operations conducted by sellers or buyers themselves rather than operating through independent wholesalers. Separate branches and offices can be dedicated to either sales or purchasing.
Sales branches and offices	Set up by manufacturers to improve inventory control, selling, and promotion. Sales branches carry inventory and are found in industries such as lumber and automotive equipment and parts. Sales offices do not carry inventory and are most prominent in the dry goods and notions industries.
Purchasing officers	Perform a role similar to that of brokers or agents but are part of the buyer's organization. Many retailers set up purchasing offices in major market centers, such as New York and Chicago.

Segmentation, Targeting, Differentiation, and Positioning Decisions

Like retailers, wholesalers must segment and define their target markets and differentiate and position themselves effectively—they cannot serve everyone. They can choose a target group by size of customer (for example, large retailers only), type of customer (convenience stores only), the need for service (customers who need credit), or other factors. Within the target group, they can identify the more profitable customers, design stronger offers, and build better relationships with them. They can propose automatic reordering systems, establish management-training and advisory systems, or even sponsor a voluntary chain. They can discourage less-profitable customers by requiring larger orders or adding service charges to smaller ones.

Marketing Mix Decisions

Like retailers, wholesalers must decide on product and service assortments, prices, promotion, and place. Wholesalers add customer value though the *products and services* they offer. They are often under great pressure to carry a full line and stock enough for immediate delivery. But this practice can damage profits. Wholesalers today are cutting down on the number of lines they carry, choosing to carry only the more-profitable ones. They are also rethinking which services count most in building strong customer relationships and which should be dropped or paid for by the customer. The key for companies is to find the mix of services most valued by their target customers.

Price is also an important wholesaler decision. Wholesalers usually mark up the cost of goods by a standard percentage—say, 20 percent. Expenses may run 17 percent of the gross margin, leaving a profit margin of 3 percent. In grocery wholesaling, the average profit margin is often less than 2 percent. The recent recession put heavy pressure on wholesalers to cut their costs and prices. As their retail and industrial customers face sales and margin declines, these customers turn to wholesalers looking for lower prices. Wholesalers may, in turn, cut their margins on some lines to keep important customers. They may also ask suppliers for special price breaks in cases when they can turn them into an increase in the supplier's sales.

Although *promotion* can be critical to wholesaler success, most wholesalers are not promotion minded. They use largely scattered and unplanned trade advertising, sales promotion, personal selling, and public relations. Many are behind the times in personal selling; they still see selling as a single salesperson talking to a single customer instead of as a team effort to sell, build, and service major accounts. Wholesalers also need to adopt some of the nonpersonal promotion techniques used by retailers. They need to develop an overall promotion strategy and make greater use of supplier promotion materials and programs.

Finally, *distribution* (location) is important. Wholesalers must choose their locations, facilities, and Web locations carefully. There was a time when wholesalers could locate in low-rent, low-tax areas and invest little money in their buildings, equipment, and systems. Today, however, as technology zooms forward, such behavior results in outdated systems for material handling, order processing, and delivery.

Instead, today's large and progressive wholesalers have reacted to rising costs by investing in automated warehouses and IT systems. Orders are fed from the retailer's information system directly into the wholesaler's, and the items are picked up by mechanical devices and automatically taken to a shipping platform where they are assembled. Most large wholesalers use technology to carry out accounting, billing, inventory control, and forecasting. Modern wholesalers are adapting their services to the needs of target customers and finding cost-reducing methods of doing business. They are also transacting more business online. For example, e-commerce is Grainger's fastest growing sales channel, making Grainger the 15th largest e-tailer in the United States and Canada. Online purchasing now accounts for more than 27 percent of the wholesaler's total sales.

Trends in Wholesaling

Today's wholesalers face considerable challenges. The industry remains vulnerable to one of its most enduring trends—the need for ever-greater efficiency. Recent economic conditions have led to demands for even lower prices and the winnowing out of suppliers who are not adding value based on cost and quality. Progressive wholesalers constantly watch for better ways to meet the changing needs of their suppliers and target customers. They recognize that their only reason for existence comes from adding value, which occurs by increasing the efficiency and effectiveness of the entire marketing channel.

As with other types of marketers, the goal is to build value-adding customer relationships. McKesson provides an example of progressive, value-adding wholesaling. The company is a diversified health care services provider and the nation's leading wholesaler of pharmaceuticals, health and beauty care, home health care, and medical supply and equipment products. To survive, especially in a tight economic environment, McKesson has to be more cost effective than manufacturers' sales branches. Thus, the company has built efficient automated warehouses, established direct computer links with drug manufacturers, and created extensive online supply management and accounts receivable systems for customers. It offers retail pharmacists a wide range of online resources, including supply-management assistance, catalog searches, real-time order tracking, and an account-management system. It has also created solutions such as automated pharmaceutical-dispensing machines that assist pharmacists by reducing costs and improving accuracy. Retailers can even use the McKesson systems to maintain prescription histories and medical profiles on their customers.

McKesson's medical-surgical supply and equipment customers receive a rich assortment of online solutions and supply management tools, including an online order management system and real-time information on products and pricing, inventory availability, and order status. According to McKesson, it adds value in the channel by providing "supply, information, and health care management products and services designed to reduce costs and improve quality across healthcare."[33]

The distinction between large retailers and large wholesalers continues to blur. Many retailers now operate formats such as wholesale clubs and supercenters that perform many wholesale functions. In return, some large wholesalers are setting up their own retailing operations. For example, until recently, SuperValu was classified as a food wholesaler, with a majority of its business derived from supplying grocery products to

● **Pharmaceuticals wholesaler McKesson helps its retail pharmacist customers be more efficient by offering a wide range of online resources. Retail pharmacists can even use the McKesson system to maintain medical profiles on their customers.**

Jose Luis Pelaez/Corbis

independent grocery retailers. However, over the past dozen years, SuperValu has started or acquired several retail food chains of its own—including Albertsons, Jewel-Osco, Save-A-Lot, Cub Foods, Acme, and others—to become the nation's third-largest food retailer (behind Walmart and Kroger). Thus, even though it remains the country's largest food wholesaler, SuperValu is now classified as a retailer because nearly 78 percent of its $40 billion in sales comes from retailing. In fact, SuperValu now bills itself as "America's neighborhood grocer."[34]

Wholesalers will continue to increase the services they provide to retailers—retail pricing, cooperative advertising, marketing and management information services, accounting services, online transactions, and others. However, both the recently tight economy and the demand for increased services have put the squeeze on wholesaler profits. Wholesalers who do not find efficient ways to deliver value to their customers will soon drop by the wayside. Fortunately, the increased use of computerized, automated, and Internet-based systems will help wholesalers contain the costs of ordering, shipping, and inventory holding, thus boosting their productivity.

Reviewing the Concepts

MyMarketingLab™

Go to **mymktlab.com** to complete the problems marked with this icon .

Reviewing Objectives and Key Terms

 Objectives Review

Retailing and wholesaling consist of many organizations bringing goods and services from the point of production to the point of use. In this chapter, we examined the nature and importance of retailing, the major types of retailers, the decisions retailers make, and the future of retailing. We then examined these same topics for wholesalers.

Objective 1 **Explain the role of retailers in the distribution channel and describe the major types of retailers.** (pp 374–380)

Retailing includes all the activities involved in selling goods or services directly to final consumers for their personal, nonbusiness use. Retailers play an important role in connecting brands to consumers in the final phases of the buying process. *Shopper marketing* involves focusing the entire marketing process on turning shoppers into buyers at the point of sale, whether it's in-store, online, or mobile shopping.

Retail stores come in all shapes and sizes, and new retail types keep emerging. Store retailers can be classified by the *amount of service* they provide (self-service, limited service, or full service), *product line sold* (specialty stores, department stores, supermarkets, convenience stores, superstores, and service businesses), and *relative prices* (discount stores and off-price retailers). Today, many retailers are banding together in corporate and contractual *retail organizations* (corporate chains, voluntary chains, retailer cooperatives, and franchise organizations).

Objective 2 **Describe the major retailer marketing decisions.** (pp 380–386)

Retailers are always searching for new marketing strategies to attract and hold customers. They face major marketing decisions about segmentation and targeting, store differentiation and positioning, and the retail marketing mix.

Retailers must first segment and define their target markets and then decide how they will differentiate and position themselves in these markets. Those that try to offer "something for everyone" end up satisfying no market well. By contrast, successful retailers define their target markets well and position themselves strongly.

Guided by strong targeting and positioning, retailers must decide on a retail marketing mix—product and services assortment, price, promotion, and place. Retail stores are much more than simply an assortment of goods. Beyond the products and services they offer, today's successful retailers carefully orchestrate virtually every aspect of the consumer store experience. A retailer's price policy must fit its target market and positioning, products and services assortment, and competition. Retailers use any or all of the five promotion tools—advertising, personal selling, sales promotion, PR, and direct marketing—to reach consumers. Finally, it's very important that retailers select locations that are accessible to the target market in areas that are consistent with the retailer's positioning.

Objective 3

Discuss the major trends and developments in retailing.
(pp 386–392)

Retailers operate in a harsh and fast-changing environment, which offers threats as well as opportunities. Following years of good economic times for retailers, the Great Recession turned many retailers' fortunes from boom to bust. New retail forms continue to emerge. At the same time, however, different types of retailers are increasingly serving similar customers with the same products and prices (retail convergence), making differentiation more difficult. Other trends in retailing include the rise of megaretailers, the rapid growth of direct and online retailing, the growing importance of retail technology, a surge in green retailing, and the global expansion of major retailers.

Objective 4

Explain the major types of wholesalers and their marketing decisions. (pp 392–397)

Wholesaling includes all the activities involved in selling goods or services to those who are buying for the purpose of resale or business use. Wholesalers fall into three groups. First, *merchant wholesalers* take possession of the goods. They include *full-service wholesalers* (wholesale merchants and industrial distributors) and *limited-service wholesalers* (cash-and-carry wholesalers, truck wholesalers, drop shippers, rack jobbers, producers' cooperatives, and mail-order wholesalers). Second, *brokers* and *agents* do not take possession of the goods but are paid a commission for aiding companies in buying and selling. Finally, *manufacturers' sales branches and offices* are wholesaling operations conducted by non-wholesalers to bypass the wholesalers.

Like retailers, wholesalers must target carefully and position themselves strongly. And, like retailers, wholesalers must decide on product and service assortments, prices, promotion, and place. Progressive wholesalers constantly watch for better ways to meet the changing needs of their suppliers and target customers. They recognize that, in the long run, their only reason for existence comes from adding value, which occurs by increasing the efficiency and effectiveness of the entire marketing channel. As with other types of marketers, the goal is to build value-adding customer relationships.

 Key Terms

Objective 1

Retailing (p 374)
Retailer (p 374)
Shopper marketing (p 374)
Specialty store (p 375)
Department store (p 375)
Supermarket (p 376)
Convenience store (p 377)
Superstore (p 377)
Category killer (p 377)
Service retailer (p 377)
Discount store (p 378)

Off-price retailer (p 378)
Independent off-price retailer (p 378)
Factory outlet (p 378)
Warehouse club (p 379)
Corporate chains (p 379)
Franchise (p 379)

Objective 2

Shopping center (p 385)

Objective 3

Wheel-of-retailing concept (p 387)

Objective 4

Wholesaling (p 392)
Wholesaler (p 392)
Merchant wholesaler (p 393)
Broker (p 393)
Agent (p 393)
Manufacturers' sales branches and offices (p 393)

Discussion **and** Critical Thinking

 Discussion Questions

1. Discuss factors used to classify retail establishments and list the types within each classification. (AACSB: Communication)

2. Name and describe the types of corporate or contractual organization of retail stores and the advantages of each. (AACSB: Communication)

3. Develop a concept for a new retail store and explain the marketing decisions that must be made. (AACSB: Communication; Reflective Thinking)

4. What is retail convergence? Has it helped or harmed small retailers? (AACSB: Communication; Reflective Thinking)

Critical Thinking Exercises

1. Visit a local mall and evaluate five stores. What type of retailer is each of these stores? What is the target market for each? How is each store positioned? Do the retail atmospherics of each store enhance this positioning effectively to attract and satisfy the target market? (AACSB: Communication; Reflective Thinking)

2. Retailers that accept credit cards pay a "swipe fee" to credit card issuers such as Visa and Mastercard ranging from 1 to 3 percent of the purchase. The credit card companies prohibited retailers from passing that fee on to consumers, but a recent lawsuit settlement proposal lifted that restriction. Under the settlement, retailers can charge 2.5 to 3 percent on each transaction. Research this issue and develop a report on the pros and cons of retailers adding a surcharge to credit purchases. (AACSB: Communication; Reflective Thinking)

3. As discussed at the start of Chapter 10, in 2012, JCPenney changed its pricing strategy from one in which it charged relatively high prices and aggressively discounted them to one in which it charges lower but constant everyday "fair and square prices." Evaluate the effectiveness of this pricing strategy change. (AACSB: Communication; Reflective Thinking)

Applications and Cases

 Marketing Technology **Tracking Customers**

According to Nielsen, more than 50 percent of mobile phone consumers own smartphones. Many of them use free Wi-Fi when available for faster connections and to reduce data usage charges. But even when they don't log on to the Wi-Fi, the device continues to search, giving information on users' locations. By using the signals emitted by shoppers' smartphones, retailers can keep tabs on shoppers, knowing where they are and what they are searching for on their phones' browsers. Retailers can learn in which aisles shoppers are most likely to check online prices at retailers such as Amazon.com and can send an alert to a sales representative. "Heat mapping" identifies traffic patterns and locations attracting the greatest number of shoppers checking the Internet. This gives retailers an idea of the products most vulnerable to "showrooming"—the practice of shoppers visiting stores to learn about and try products and later purchasing them for less online.

1. What is *shopper marketing,* and how might retailers use Wi-Fi technology to implement it? (AACSB: Communication; Use of IT; Reflective Thinking)

2. What will be the likely response as more shoppers learn that retailers gather information without their knowledge? (AACSB: Communication; Reflective Thinking)

 Marketing Ethics **Roll-Your-Own Shops**

In 2009, federal taxes on a carton of cigarettes increased $6.16 to $10.06. The tax on a pound of loose pipe tobacco increased $1.73, resulting in a total tax per pound of only $2.83. The tax on loose cigarette tobacco increased the most—from $1.09 to $24.78 per pound. Small tobacco shops have purchased machines that allow shoppers to make 20 cigarettes per minute. The loose tobacco is labeled "pipe tobacco," allowing smokers to make their cigarettes for almost half the price of ready-made cigarettes because of the much lower taxes. The U.S. Government Accountability Office claims federal tobacco tax revenue decreased almost $500 million between April 2009 and September 2011 as a result of the booming roll-your-own shops sales. The Alcohol and Tobacco Tax and Trade Bureau declared that retailers using these machines are manufacturers. Makers of the machines got a court injunction, giving temporary reprieve for retailers. However, in 2012 Congress approved an amendment tucked into a highway bill expanding the definition of a manufacturer to include these retailers, which would subject them to federal excise taxes. Lawmakers felt these retailers were taking advantage of an unintended tax loophole.

1. Is it fair that Congress defined retailers operating roll-your-own machines as manufacturers? (AACSB: Communication; Ethical Reasoning; Reflective Thinking)

2. Are the tobacco retailers being ethical by labeling the loose tobacco as pipe tobacco so that smokers can avoid the high tax and by providing roll-your-own machines for consumers? (AACSB: Communication; Ethical Reasoning; Reflective Thinking)

Marketing by the Numbers Mark Up

Consumers typically buy products such as toiletries, food, and clothing from retailers rather than directly from the manufacturer. Likewise, retailers buy from wholesalers. Resellers perform functions for the manufacturer and the consumer and mark up the price to reflect that value. Refer to Appendix 2: Marketing by the Numbers to answer the following questions.

1. If a manufacturer sells its laundry detergent to a wholesaler for $2.50, for how much will the wholesaler sell it to a retailer if the wholesaler wants a 15 percent margin based on the selling price? (AACSB: Communication; Analytical Reasoning)

2. If a retailer wants a 20 percent margin based on the selling price, at what price will the retailer sell the product to the consumers? (AACSB: Communication; Analytical Reasoning)

 # Video Case Home Shopping Network

Shopping on television has been around almost as long as television itself. But the Home Shopping Network (HSN) made it a full-time endeavor in 1982, giving birth to a new retail outlet. Since then, HSN has been a pioneer in products, presentation, and order taking. The company has sold millions of products and has been known for giving an outlet to legitimate products that otherwise would not reach customers.

But what does a company do when the very retail channel that it depends upon starts to fizzle out? This video illustrates how HSN has met the challenges of a changing marketplace to continue its innovative methods for reaching its customer base.

After viewing the video featuring HSN, answer the following questions:

1. How has HSN differentiated itself from other retailers through each element of the retail marketing mix?

2. Discuss the concept of the retail life cycle as it relates to HSN.

3. Do you think HSN has a bright future? Why or why not?

 # Company Case Dollar General: Today's Hottest Retailing Format

"Save time. Save money. Every day." Given today's economics, that sounds like a winning proposition. In fact, it's the slogan of discount retailer Dollar General—and it *is* a winning proposition. Dollar stores and other hard discounters are today's hottest retailing format, and Dollar General is the nation's leading dollar store.

Whereas the Walmarts, Costcos, and Targets of the world are big-box discounters, Dollar General and the other dollar stores are small-box discounters. They remain a relatively small threat to their bigger rivals. For example, the combined annual sales of all dollar stores amount to only about 15 percent of Walmart's annual sales. But they are one of the fastest-growing threats. Throughout the Great Recession, as the big-box discounters struggled, the dollar stores spurted, rapidly adding new stores, customers, and sales. In the post-recession economy, big-box stores have lumbered along at a lukewarm pace while the dollar stores have continued to thrive.

How is Dollar General doing it? A famous ad person once wrote, "A company can become incredibly successful if it can find a way to own a word. Not a complicated word. Not an invented one. The simple words are best, words taken right out of the dictionary." In this case, the word "dollar." Not only have Dollar General and the others seized this critically differentiating word from Walmart and Target, they've also seized it from grocery stores, drug stores, and any other types of retailers that ever laid claim to low prices.

If you haven't been in a dollar store lately, you might be surprised at what you'll find. Back in the day, dollar stores sold mostly odd lot assortments of novelties, factory overruns, close-outs, and outdated merchandise. Not anymore. "Dollar stores have come a long way, baby," says a retail analyst. "The Great Recession accelerated the iconic American chains' transformation from purveyors of kitschy $1 trinkets to discounters in a position to lure shoppers from the likes of supermarkets, drugstores, and Walmart stores." Dollar General now sells a carefully selected assortment of mostly brand-name items. More than two-thirds of its sales come from groceries and household goods.

A Retail Concept Is Born
In the late 1800s, the Woolworth brothers invented the concept of five-and-dime stores. By the mid-1900s, it was apparent to J. L. Turner that although the original concept was a winner, inflation had watered it down to the point that the "five-and-dime" price point was no longer relevant. In 1955, Turner opened the first Dollar General store in Springfield, Kentucky. Following the lead of the Woolworth brothers, he priced no item in the store at more than one dollar. Word spread quickly, and the store was such a huge success that Turner and his son, Cal, quickly converted other stores they owned to Dollar Generals. Within a few years, they were operating 29 Dollar General stores generating $5 million a year in sales.

After his father's death in 1964, Cal Turner Jr. led Dollar General until 2002. By that time, the template was set and the momentum irreversible. Today, there are more than 10,000 Dollar General stores in 40 states. And today more than ever, Dollar General's cash registers are ringing. Last year, the company hit revenues of $14.8 billion. That's an average annual growth rate of 14 percent per year since the company went public in 1968. Even more significant, Dollar General's revenues are three times what they were just five years ago. In the next few years, Dollar General plans to grow to more than 12,000 stores (about the same as the number of McDonald's restaurants nationwide and more than 20 times the number of Target stores).

Saving Customers Money—and Time

Dollar General's "Save time. Save money. Every day." slogan isn't just for show. It's a carefully crafted statement of the store's value promise. In addition to low prices, the company emphasizes convenience and quality brands in its positioning statement: "Our goal is to provide our customers a better life. And we think our customers are best served when we keep it real and keep it simple. Dollar General stands for convenience, quality brands, and low prices. Dollar General's successful prototype makes shopping a truly hassle-free experience. We design small neighborhood stores with carefully edited merchandise assortments to make shopping simpler."

Saving money is clearly at the heart of Dollar General's positioning, demonstrating that the Turners were able to accomplish what the Woolworths could not. As the old five-and-dime format gave way to the dollar positioning, the Turners kept an eye on the marketing environment to ensure that their chain remained relevant. The result is that today's Dollar General is no longer a pure "dollar store" (about a third of its merchandise is priced at a dollar or less). Still, Dollar General has retained its positioning of having the lowest price point in retail.

Dollar General's prices on the brand-name products it carries are an estimated 20 to 40 percent lower than grocery store prices and are roughly in line with those of the big-name discount stores. There are also plenty of savings to be had on dollar items and the increasing selection of Dollar General private-label merchandise. Finally, Dollar General gets a boost from customer perceptions of its dollar-store format. The $1 price point not only draws customers in but also lets them shop a little more freely than they would elsewhere. Almost anything in the store can be had for less than $10.

When it comes to saving customers time, Dollar General's "hassle-free" and "keep it simple" model kicks in. Its carefully edited product assortment includes only about 12,000 core items (compared with 47,000 items in an average supermarket or 142,000 items in a Walmart supercenter), making things easier to find. But that doesn't mean that customers have to do without. As Dollar General points out, "We don't carry every brand and size, just the most popular ones." The focus is on life's simple necessities, such as laundry detergent, toilet paper, soap, shampoo, and food items, with quality brands such as Gain, Clorox, Charmin, Dove, Pantene, Palmolive, Kraft, Betty Crocker, and Coca-Cola. Dollar General has even added brands such as Hanes underwear, L'Oréal cosmetics, and Rexall vitamins and herbal supplements.

Keeping it simple also means smaller stores—more than 25 Dollar General stores could fit inside the average Walmart supercenter. In addition, most stores are located in convenient strip malls, which usually allow customers to park right in front of a store. Once inside, customers encounter fewer aisles to navigate, fewer goods to consider, and smaller crowds to outwrangle than in big-box stores. All that adds up to a quick trip. The average Dollar General customer is in and out of the store in less than 10 minutes. Try that at a Walmart. And although Dollar General is experimenting with larger-format stores that carry produce, meat, and baked goods, those Super Dollar Generals are still much, much smaller and more manageable than a Walmart supercenter.

A Winning Combination

Keeping things simple for consumers also benefits the company's bottom line. Smaller stores are less expensive to operate, and locating them in smaller markets and less glamorous neighborhoods keeps real estate costs down as well. Dollar General's cost per square foot is as low as one-tenth that of supermarkets. By constructing its stores more cheaply, Dollar General is able to build more of them. In fact, Dollar General now has more stores in the United States than any other discounter.

Dollar General's product mix strategy also contributes to its financial performance. Although it carries top brands, it leans toward brands that are not market leaders. For example, customers are more likely to encounter Gain than Tide. Furthermore, stores don't stock products in all sizes, just the ones that sell the best. Finally, Dollar General's merchandise buyers focus on getting the best deals possible at any given time. This opportunistic buying might mean that the chain stocks Heinz ketchup one month and Hunts the next. Such practices contribute to lower costs and higher margins.

The post-recessionary trend toward more sensible consumer spending has given Dollar General and other dollar stores a real boost. Not only is Dollar General attracting more sales from existing customers, it's also attracting new higher-income customers. A recent survey showed that 65 percent of consumers with incomes under $50,000 had shopped at a dollar store in the past three months. However, 47 percent of households with incomes over $100,000 had done so as well. Although its core customers are still those who make less than $40,000 a year, Dollar General's fastest-growth segment is those earning more than $75,000 a year.

Put it all together, and things are sizzling right now at the nation's largest small-box discount retailer. Dollar General has the right value proposition for the times. But what will happen to Dollar General and its fellow dollar stores as economic conditions continue to improve? Will newly acquired customers abandon them and return to their previous shopping haunts?

Dollar General doesn't think so. Dollar stores seem to do as well in good times as in bad. The format had already been growing at a healthy rate before the Great Recession hit. And customers who switched over show no signs of relapsing into their old, free-spending ways. We "see signs of a new consumerism," says Dollar General's CEO, as people shift where they shop, switch to lower-cost brands, and stay generally more frugal. Company research shows that 97 percent of new customers plan to continue shopping at Dollar General even as the economy improves, the same percentage as old customers. Low prices and convenience, it seems, will not soon go out of style.

Questions for Discussion

1. Describe Dollar General according to the different types of retailers discussed in the chapter.

2. As a retail brand, assess the Dollar General strategy with respect to segmentation, targeting, differentiation, and positioning.

3. List all the reasons why Dollar General has been so successful over the past 40 years.

4. In competing against other brick-and-mortar retailers, will Dollar General succeed or fail in the long term? Support your answer.

5. Against online retailers, will Dollar General succeed or fail in the long term? Support your answer.

Sources: Brad Thomas, "Dollar Stores Take on Wal-Mart, and Are Starting to Win," *Forbes*, April 16, 2012, www.forbes.com/sites/investor/2012/04/16/dollar-stores-take-on-wal-mart-and-are-starting-to-win/; "A Discount Retailer Even Walmart Envies," *Wall Street Journal*, January 3, 2012, http://professional.wsj.com/article/SB10001424052702304821304577440722400718232.html?mg=reno64-wsj; Kelly Evans, "Dollar General Flexing Its Discount Muscle," *Wall Street Journal*, March 31, 2010, http://professional.wsj.com/article/SB1000142405270230360150457515419263908154 2.html?mg=reno64-wsj; Suzanne Kapner, "The Mighty Dollar," *Fortune*, April 27, 2009, p. 64; Rebecca Tonn, "Dollar General Expansion in Colorado Will Mean 6,000 Jobs," *Colorado Springs Journal*, January 5, 2011; John Jannarone, "Will Dollar General Be Leading Retailers into Battle?" *Wall Street Journal*, June 6, 2011, p. C10; and information from www.dollargeneral.com, accessed August 2012.

MyMarketingLab

Go to **mymktlab.com** for Auto-graded writing questions as well as the following Assisted-graded writing questions:

13-1. List and briefly discuss the trends impacting the future of retailing. (AACSB: Communication)

13-2. Explain how wholesalers add value in the channel of distribution. (AACSB: Communication)

13-3. Mymktlab Only – comprehensive writing assignment for this chapter.

References

1. Quotes and other information from "Why Walmart Is Worried about Amazon," *Bloomberg Businessweek*, April 2, 2012, pp. 25–26; "The Fortune 500," *Fortune*, May 21, 2012, pp. F1–F51; "Wal-Mart's Makeover," *Fortune*, December 26, 2011, pp. 50–55; Lydia Dishman, "Why Walmart and JCPenney Are Still Struggling," *Forbes*, February 24, 2012, www.forbes.com/sites/lydiadishman/2012/02/24/why-walmart-and-jcpenney-are-still-struggling/; Karen Talley, "Wal-Mart's U.S. Sales Rise," *Wall Street Journal*, November 15, 2011, http://online.wsj.com/article/SB10001424052970204323904577039782083201296.html; John Jannarone, "Walmart Stores' Giant Disadvantage," *Wall Street Journal*, May 18, 2011, p. C20; Miguel Bustillo, "Walmart to Tout Goods Returning to Shelves," *Wall Street Journal*, April 11, 2011, p. B3; and various fact sheets and annual reports found at www.walmartstores.com, accessed November 2012.

2. See "Shopper Decisions Made In-Store by OgilvyAction," \www.wpp.com/wpp/marketing/consumerinsights/shopper-decisions-made-instore.htm, accessed June 2012; Katy Bachman, "Suit Your Shelf," *AdweekMedia*, January 19, 2009, pp. 10–12; and Jack Neff, "Trouble in Store for Shopper Marketing," *Advertising Age*, March 2, 2009, pp. 3–4. Retail sales statistics from "Monthly and Annual Retail Trade," U.S. Census Bureau, www.census.gov/retail/, accessed June 2012.

3. Jack Neff, "P&G Pushes Design in Brand-Building Strategy," April 12, 2010, http://adage.com/print?article_id=143211; and "The Zero Moment of Truth: A New Marketing Strategy," *Google Inside Adwords*, July 6, 2011, http://adwords.blogspot.com/2011/07/zero-moment-of-truth-new-marketing.html.

4. For more on digital aspects of shopper marketing, see Ken Schept, "Digital and Mobile Disrupt Traditional Shopping Path," *Advertising Age*, May 2, 2011, p. 92; Ellen Byron, "In-Store Sales Begin at Home," *Wall Street Journal*, April 25, 2011, www.wsj.com; Gordon Wyner, "Shopper Marketing: How to Engage and Inspire Consumers at Critical Points in the Shopping Cycle," *Marketing Management*, Spring 2011, pp. 44–48; and Ann Zimmerman, "Can Retailers Halt 'Showrooming'?" *Wall Street Journal*, April 11, 2012, p. B1.

5. David Rogers, "Grocery Market Share Trends," *Progressive Grocer*, September 16, 2010, www.progressivegrocer.*com*/top-stories/special-features/industry-intelligence/id30449/grocery-market-share-trends/.

6. Timothy W. Martin, "May I Help You?" *Wall Street Journal*, April 22, 2009, http://online.wsj.com/article/SB124025177889535871.html; "The Top 10 Companies by Revenue," *Inc.*, August 22, 2011, www.inc.com/ss/2011-inc-5000-top-10-companies-revenue; "The American Customer Satisfaction Index," www.theacsi.org/index.php?option=com_content&view=article&id=12&Itemid=110, accessed June 2012; and www.publix.com, accessed November 2012.

7. See Alan J. Liddle, "Sheetz Highlights Value, Convenience to Build Sales," *Nation's Restaurant News*, July 21, 2010, www.nrn.com/article/sheetz-highlights-value-convenience-build-sales; "Sheetz Opens New Store in McGee's Crossroads, North Carolina and Welcomes New Customers with Contests and Prizes," *PR Newswire*, January 25, 2012; and www.sheetz.com/main/about/definition.cfm, accessed November 2012.

8. Statistics based on information from "SN Top 75 2012," http://supermarketnews.com/top-75-retailers-wholesalers-2012, accessed June 2012; "Walmart's 50 Years: From Rogers, Ark., to Global Behemoth," *Supermarket News*, February 20, 2012, http://supermarketnews.com/wal-mart-stores/wal-mart-s-50-years-rogers-ark-global-behemoth;and "Supermarket Facts," www.fmi.org/facts_figs/?fuseaction=superfact, accessed June 2012.

9. See John Jannarone, "Will Dollar General Be Leading Retailers into Battle?" *Wall Street Journal*, June 6, 2011, p. C10; Gary Stern, "Are All Dollar Stores Alike? Not If They Want to Win," *Investor's Business Daily*, September 6, 2011; "Dollar General to Open 625 New Stores and Create More Than 6000 New Jobs in 2012," January 3, 2012, http://newscenter.dollargeneral.com/article_display.cfm?article_id=1787; and information from www.dollargeneral.com, accessed October 2012.

10. Quotes and other information from "Retail Quick Facts: 10 Things about Costco You Probably Don't Know," *RetailSails*, April 27, 2011, http://retailsails.com/2011/04/27/retail-quick-facts-10-things-about-costco-you-probably-dont-know/; Matthew Boyle, "Why Costco Is So Addictive," *Fortune*, October 25, 2006, pp. 126–132; "2011 Top 100 Retailers," NRF Stores, July 2011, www.stores.org/2011/Top-100-Retailers; and www.costco.com and http://shop.costco.com/Membership/Welcome/Amazing-Facts.aspx, accessed October 2012.

11. Company information from http://en.oboulo.com/subway-operations-82799.html, www.aboutmcdonalds.com/mcd, and www.subway.com/subwayroot/About_Us/default.aspx, accessed November 2012.

12. Based on information found in Maureen Morrison, "Fast-Casual Burger Joints Snag a Seat at the Table," *Advertising Age*, September 26, 2011, http://adage.com/article/news/burger-joints-guys-smashburger-drive-growth/230005/; Karen Weise, "Behind Five Guys' Beloved Burgers," *Bloomberg Businessweek*, August 11, 2011, www.businessweek.com/printer/magazine/behind-five-guys-beloved-burgers-08112011.html; and www.aboutmcdonalds.com/mcd and www.fiveguys.com, accessed November 2012.

13. Based on information from "Cabela's Has Lived Up to Its Hype," *McClatchy-Tribune Business News*, March 31, 2010; Jan Falstad, "Outdoor Retailer Adds New Dynamic to Local Marketplace," *McClatchy-Tribune Business News*, May 10, 2009; "Sporting Goods Retail Companies: Cabela's Announces Opening Date for Tulalip, Wash. Store," *Entertainment Weekly*, March 23, 1012, p. 50; and information from www.cabelas.com, accessed November 2012.

14. See Sandy Smith, "Scents and Sellability," *Stores*, July 2009, www.stores.org/stores-magazine-july-2009/scents-and-sellability; Spencer Morgan, "The Sweet Smell of Excess," *Bloomberg Businessweek*, June 21–June 27, 2010, pp. 85–87; Jane Sutton, "Scent Makers Sweeten the Smell of Success," *Reuters*, December 19, 2011, www.reuters.com/article/2011/12/19/us-usa-scented-idUSTRE7BI1PF20111219; and www.scentair.com, accessed November 2012.

15. See www.titlenine.com and https://www.facebook.com/pages/Title-Nine-Portland/62987646947, accessed October 2012.

16. For definitions of these and other types of shopping centers, see "Dictionary," American Marketing Association, www.marketingpower.com/_layouts/Dictionary.aspx, accessed November 2012.

17. Courtenay Edelhart, "Malls Can't Take Customers for Granted as New Outdoor Centers Pop Up," *McClatchy-Tribune Business News*, January 16, 2010; and Eric Schwartzberg, "Lifestyle Centers Draw Retailers, Shoppers," *The Oxford Press*, November 21, 2011, www.oxfordpress.com/news/oxford-news/lifestyle-centers-draw-retailers-shoppers--1287539.html.

18. See H. Lee Murphy, "Life Ebbs Out of Many Lifestyle Centers," *National Real Estate Investor*, May 1, 2011, p. 31; Elaine Misonzhnik, "Borders Bankruptcy Shines Light on Continued Weakness of Power Centers" *Retail Traffic*, February 16, 2011; and Jon Chavez, "Major Retail Expansion Called Unlikely," *McClatchy-Tribune Business News*, March 18, 2012.

19. Kenneth Hein, "Target Tries First Price Point Driven TV Ads," *Brandweek*, January 14, 2009, accessed at www.brandweek.com; Sharon Edelson, "Target Eying $100 Billion in Sales," *WWD*, February 25, 2011, p. 2; and "Target Corporation; Target Reports Fourth Quarter and Fiscal 2011 Earnings," *Investment Weekly News*, March 10, 2012.

20. See David Kaplan, "A Permanent Trend of Pop-Up Shops," *McClatchy-Tribune Business News*, December 21, 2011; Carolyn King, "Target Brings Jason Wu to Canada," *Wall Street Journal*, February 23, 2012; and Judith Lamont, "Tuning in to Customers: Optimizing the Online Experience," *KM World*, February 2012, pp. 8–9.

21. See www.rpminc.com/consumer.asp, accessed October 2012.

22. U.S. Census Bureau News, "Quarterly Retail E-Commerce Sales, 4th Quarter 2011," February 16, 2012, www.census.gov/retail/mrts/www/data/pdf/ec_current.pdf; and Robin Wauters, "Forrester: Online Retail Industry in the US Will Be Worth $279 Billion in 2015," *TechCrunch*, February 28, 2011, http://techcrunch.com/2011/02/28/forrester-online-retail-industry-in-the-us-will-be-worth-279-billion-in-2015/.

23. Ann Zimmerman, "Can Retailers Halt 'Showrooming'?" *Wall Street Journal*, April 11, 2012, p. B1.

24. "Top 500 Guide," *Internet Retailer*, www.internetretailer.com/top500/list/, accessed November 2012.

25. Adam Blair, "Williams-Sonoma Invests $75M in Fast-Growing, Profitable E-Commerce," *RIS*, March 22, 2011, http://risnews.edgl.com/retail-best-practices/Williams-Sonoma-Invests-$75M-in-Fast-Growing,-Profitable-E-Commerce71523; and "Williams-Sonoma, Inc. Announces Fourth Quarter and Fiscal Year 2011 Results and Provides Financial Guidance for Fiscal Year 2012," March 8, 2012, www.williams-sonomainc.com/investors/financial-releases.html.

26. See "Eastern Mountain Sports Blazes New Trails with VeriFone iPad Retailing Solution," January 12, 2012, www.verifone.com/2012/eastern-mountain-sports-blazes-new-trails-with-verifone-ipad-retailing-solution.aspx.

27. The quote is from "Retail Isn't Broken. Stores Are," *Harvard Business Review*, December 2011, pp. 79-82. The futuristic scenario is adapted from information found in Darrell Rigby, "The Future of Shopping," *Harvard Business Review*, December 2011, pp. 65-76.

28. "Kohl's Opens Eight New Stores Creating Approximately 1,000 Jobs," *Business Wire*, March 8, 2012; and www.kohlsgreenscene.com/, accessed November 2012.

29. See www.staples.com/sbd/cre/marketing/ecoeasy/recycling.html, accessed November 2012.

30. See "Walmart Stores, Inc. Data Sheet—Worldwide Unit Details: January 2012," February 22, 2012, www.walmartstores.com/pressroom/news/10821.aspx; and "Walmart Corporate and Financial Facts," accessed at www.walmartstores.com/pressroom/FactSheets/, November 2012.

31. See "Switching Channels: Global Powers of Retailing 2012," *Stores*, January 2012, accessed at www.deloitte.com/view/en_GX/global/f9f6b21f1d464310VgnVCM1000001a56f00aRCRD.htm.

32. Grainger facts and other information are from the *Grainger: Beyond the Box 2012 Fact Book* accessed at http://invest.grainger.com/phoenix.zhtml?c=76754&p=irol-irFactBook and www.grainger.com, accessed October 2012.

33. Information from "About Us," www.mckesson.com; and "Supply Management Online," www.mckesson.com/en_us/McKesson.com/For+Pharmacies/Retail+National+Chains/Ordering+and+Inventory+Management/Supply+Management+Online.html, accessed June 2012.

34. Facts from www.supervalu.com, accessed November 2012.

14

Communicating
Customer Value — Integrated Marketing Communications Strategy

Chapter Preview In this and the next four chapters, we'll examine the last of the marketing mix tools—promotion. Companies must do more than just create customer value; they must also use promotion to clearly and persuasively communicate that value. Promotion is not a single tool but, rather, a mix of several tools. Under the concept of integrated marketing communications, the company must carefully coordinate these promotion tools to deliver a clear, consistent, and compelling message about its organization and its brands.

We begin by introducing the various promotion mix tools. Next, we examine the rapidly changing communications environment and the need for integrated marketing communications. Finally, we discuss the steps in developing marketing communications and the promotion budgeting process. In the next three chapters, we'll present the specific marketing communications tools.

Let's start by looking at a good integrated marketing communications campaign. In an industry characterized by constantly shifting promotional themes, Chick-fil-A's remarkably enduring "Eat Mor Chikin" campaign—featuring an unlikely herd of quirky cows—has successfully engaged customers, communicated the brand's personality and positioning, and made Chick-fil-A one of America's most successful quick-service restaurant chains.

Chick-fil-A: A Remarkably Enduring Integrated Marketing Communications Campaign

Nearly two decades ago, regional fast-food chain Chick-fil-A set out in search of a promotion strategy that would set it apart from its big-three fast-food competitors—burger joints McDonald's, Burger King, and Wendy's. Chick-fil-A's strength had always been its signature fried chicken sandwich—you still won't find anything but chicken on the menu. But somehow, just saying "we make good chicken sandwiches" wasn't enough. Chick-fil-A needed a creative "big idea"—something memorable that would communicate the brand's unique value proposition.

What it came up with—of all things—was an improbable herd of renegade black-and-white cows that couldn't spell. Their message: "Eat Mor Chikin." Their goal: to convince consumers to switch from hamburgers to chicken. Acting in their own self-interest, the fearless cows realized that when people eat chicken, they don't eat beef. So in 1995, the first mischievous cow, paintbrush in mouth, painted "Eat Mor Chikin" on a billboard. From

that first billboard, the effort has now grown to become one of the most consistent and enduring integrated marketing communications campaigns in history, a full multimedia campaign that has forever changed the burger-eating landscape.

The key to the "Eat Mor Chikin" campaign's success lies in its remarkable consistency. As industry publication *Advertising Age* pointed out when it recently crowned Chick-fil-A as its runner-up marketer of the year, "Often, the smartest marketing is the most patient marketing." And few promotion campaigns have been more persistently patient than this one. For more

> Chick-fil-A's remarkably enduring "Eat Mor Chikin" integrated marketing communications campaign is more than just an advertising campaign. The renegade cows have "become part of our passion and our brand."

than 17 years, Chick-fil-A has stuck steadfastly to its simple but potent "Eat Mor Chikin" message, and the brand's racscally cows have now become pop culture icons.

Building on the basic "Eat Mor Chikin" message, Chick-fil-A keeps the campaign fresh with an ever-changing mix of clever message executions and innovative media placements. Today, you find the cows just about anywhere and everywhere—from traditional television, print, and radio ads, to imaginative sales promotions and event sponsorships, to online social networks and smartphone apps, with an occasional water tower still thrown in.

For example, in a TV ad promoting Chick-fil-A's growing breakfast menu, the pesky cows set off car alarm after car alarm, awakening an apartment building full of tenants to the message, "Wake up—itz chikin time." In print ads, the cows promote menu staples with taglines like "Milk shakes—the after chikin dinner drink." Billboards sport quotes such as "Lose that burger belly." During election years, the cows show their nonpartisanship with phrases like "Vote chikin. Itz not right wing or left." The ubiquitous cows even pull zany stunts, such as parachuting into football stadiums with signs reading "Du the wave. Eat the chikin."

Although the "Eat Mor Chikin" campaign has made plentiful use of the traditional media, it is perhaps the nontraditional promotional tactics that have won the cows a special place in the hearts of Chick-fil-A's fiercely loyal customers. Shortly after the start of the campaign, the company began its now-packed promotional merchandise catalogue with an annual cow-themed calendar. Last year's $6 datebook calendar, titled "Trail Grazers: Blazing New Paths That All Lead to Chicken," paid tribute to some of the brand's more famous bovine explorers, such as Amealia Airhoof, the "first heifer in flight who took to the skies to spread the message of chicken," and Corralin' Shepard, the cow who ventured into space to "make one giant leap for cow-kind aboard Apoultry 14." Today, Chick-fil-A loyalists snap up large quantities of cow-themed mugs, T-shirts, stuffed animals, refrigerator magnets, laptop cases, and dozens of other items. These promotional items not only generate revenue, they also help to strengthen the company-customer bond while at the same time spreading the brand's "Eat Mor Chikin" message.

Chick-fil-A further engages customers through an assortment of in-store promotional events. Every July, for example, the company promotes "Cow Appreciation Day," on which customers who show up at any Chick-fil-A store dressed as a cow get a free meal. Last year, 600,000 cow-clad customers cashed in on the event. A few months later, more than 800,000 customers scrawled their names on in-store reservation sheets to receive free entrées in the chain's Breakfast Variety Giveaway. And when a new Chick-fil-A restaurant opens, under the chain's "First 100" promotion, fans who camp out for 24 hours in advance of the opening get a chance to be one of the lucky 100 who win free Chick-fil-A meals for a year. While waiting, they'll likely meet Chick-fil-A CEO Dan Cathy—known for his customer-centered leadership style—who often camps out overnight with customers, signing T-shirts, posing for pictures, and ultimately handing out those vouchers for a free year's worth of Chick-fil-A.

Most recently, Chick-fil-A has taken its "Eat Mor Chikin" message to the social media, including Facebook, YouTube, Pinterest, and Twitter. When the company first plotted its social media strategy a few years back, it discovered that it already had a robust Facebook fan page with some 25,000 fans. The page was created by customer Brandy Bitzer, a true Chick-fil-A brand evangelist. In a genuine gesture of customer appreciation, Chick-fil-A joined forces with Bitzer, who continues to administer the page while the company provides assets to fuel enthusiasm for the brand. The strategy is working. Today, the Chick-fil-A Facebook page boasts more than 5 million fans. It's packed with information, customer-engaging communications, and plenty of cow advice like "Eat chikin or I'll de-friend u."

For nearly two decades, Chick-fil-A has stuck steadfastly to its simple but potent "Eat Mor Chikin" message, and the brand's rascally cows have now become pop culture icons.
Pr Newswire

These days, you never know where the quirky cows will show up next. But no matter where you see them—on TV, in a sports arena, on your smartphone, or in your local Chick-fil-A restaurant—the long-standing brand message remains consistent. Over the years, the "Eat Mor Chikin" campaign has racked up a who's who list of major advertising awards and honors. More important, the campaign has helped to engage customers and communicate Chick-fil-A's personality and positioning, making it one of the nation's most successful quick-service chains.

Chick-fil-A's more than 1,600 restaurants in 39 states rang up more than $4 billion in sales last year. Since the first Chick-fil-A store opened, the company has posted revenue increases for

Objective Outline

Objective 1	**Define the five promotion mix tools for communicating customer value.** **The Promotion Mix** (pp 406–407)
Objective 2	**Discuss the changing communications landscape and the need for integrated marketing communications.** **Integrated Marketing Communications** (pp 407–412)
Objective 3	**Outline the communication process and the steps in developing effective marketing communications.** **A View of the Communication Process** (pp 412–413) **Steps in Developing Effective Marketing Communication** (pp 413–418)
Objective 4	**Explain the methods for setting the promotion budget and factors that affect the design of the promotion mix.** **Setting the Total Promotion Budget and Mix** (pp 418–424) **Socially Responsible Marketing Communication** (pp 424–425)

44 straight years. Since the "Eat Mor Chikin" campaign began, Chick-fil-A sales have increased more than six-fold. The average Chick-fil-A restaurant now pulls in more sales per year—over $3 million—than the average McDonald's, despite being open only six days a week (all Chick-fil-A stores are famously closed on Sundays for both practical and spiritual reasons). Chick-fil-A is now America's number two chicken chain, and it's phenomenal growth has contributed greatly to KFC's plummeting market share in the category.

In all, Chick-fil-A's now-classic but still-contemporary integrated marketing communications campaign "has been more successful than we ever imagined it could be," concludes the company's senior vice president of marketing. "The Cows started as part of our advertising campaign, and now they have become part of our passion and our brand." Who knows what the cows can accomplish in yet another 5 or 10 years. Whatever the future brings, the Chick-fil-A message will still be loud and clear: Eat Mor Chikin![1]

MyMarketingLab™

⊛ **Improve Your Grade!**

Over 10 million students improved their results using the Pearson MyLabs.
Visit **mymktlab.com** for simulations, tutorials, and end-of-chapter problems.

Building good customer relationships calls for more than just developing a good product, pricing it attractively, and making it available to target customers. Companies must also *communicate* their value propositions to customers, and what they communicate should not be left to chance. All communications must be planned and blended into carefully integrated programs. Just as good communication is important in building and maintaining any other kind of relationship, it is a crucial element in a company's efforts to build profitable customer relationships.

Objective 1 ┈┈▶
Define the five promotion mix tools for communicating customer value.

The Promotion Mix

A company's total **promotion mix**—also called its **marketing communications mix**—consists of the specific blend of advertising, public relations, personal selling, sales

Promotion mix (or marketing communications mix)
The specific blend of promotion tools that the company uses to persuasively communicate customer value and build customer relationships.

Advertising
Any paid form of nonpersonal presentation and promotion of ideas, goods, or services by an identified sponsor.

Sales promotion
Short-term incentives to encourage the purchase or sale of a product or service.

Personal selling
Personal presentation by the firm's sales force for the purpose of making sales and building customer relationships.

Public relations (PR)
Building good relations with the company's various publics by obtaining favorable publicity, building up a good corporate image, and handling or heading off unfavorable rumors, stories, and events.

promotion, and direct marketing tools that the company uses to persuasively communicate customer value and build customer relationships. The five major promotion tools are defined as follows:[2]

- **Advertising**: Any paid form of nonpersonal presentation and promotion of ideas, goods, or services by an identified sponsor.
- **Sales promotion**: Short-term incentives to encourage the purchase or sale of a product or service.
- **Personal selling**: Personal presentation by the firm's sales force for the purpose of making sales and building customer relationships.
- **Public relations**: Building good relations with the company's various publics by obtaining favorable publicity, building up a good corporate image, and handling or heading off unfavorable rumors, stories, and events.
- **Direct marketing**: Direct connections with carefully targeted individual consumers to both obtain an immediate response and cultivate lasting customer relationships.

Each category involves specific promotional tools that are used to communicate with customers. For example, *advertising* includes broadcast, print, Internet, mobile, outdoor, and other forms. *Sales promotion* includes discounts, coupons, displays, and demonstrations. *Personal selling* includes sales presentations, trade shows, and incentive programs. *Public relations (PR)* includes press releases, sponsorships, events, and Web pages. And *direct marketing* includes catalogs, direct-response TV, kiosks, the Internet, mobile marketing, and more.

At the same time, marketing communication goes beyond these specific promotion tools. The product's design, its price, the shape and color of its package, and the stores that sell it—*all* communicate something to buyers. Thus, although the promotion mix is the company's primary communications activity, the entire marketing mix—promotion, *as well as* product, price, and place—must be coordinated for greatest impact.

Objective 2 ⤵
Discuss the changing communications landscape and the need for integrated marketing communications.

Direct marketing
Direct connections with carefully targeted individual consumers to both obtain an immediate response and cultivate lasting customer relationships.

Integrated Marketing Communications

In past decades, marketers perfected the art of mass marketing: selling highly standardized products to masses of customers. In the process, they developed effective mass-media communications techniques to support these strategies. Large companies now routinely invest millions or even billions of dollars in television, magazine, or other mass-media advertising, reaching tens of millions of customers with a single ad. Today, however, marketing managers face some new marketing communications realities. Perhaps no other area of marketing is changing so profoundly as marketing communications, creating both exciting and anxious times for marketing communicators.

The New Marketing Communications Model

Several major factors are changing the face of today's marketing communications. First, *consumers* are changing. In this digital, wireless age, they are better informed and more communications empowered. Rather than relying on marketer-supplied information, they can use the Internet and other technologies to find information on their own. They can connect more easily with other consumers to exchange brand-related information or even create their own marketing messages.

Second, *marketing strategies* are changing. As mass markets have fragmented, marketers are shifting away from mass marketing. More and more, they are developing focused marketing programs designed to build closer relationships with customers in more narrowly defined micromarkets.

Finally, sweeping advances in *communications technology* are causing remarkable changes in the ways in which companies and customers communicate with each other. The digital age has spawned a host of new information and communication tools—from smartphones and iPads to satellite and cable television systems to the many faces of the Internet (e-mail, brand Web sites, online social networks, blogs, and so much more). These explosive developments have had a dramatic impact on marketing communications. Just as mass marketing once gave rise to a new generation of mass-media communications, the new digital media have given birth to a new marketing communications model.

Although network television, magazines, newspapers, and other traditional mass media remain very important, their dominance is declining. In their place, advertisers are now adding a broad selection of more-specialized and highly targeted media to reach smaller customer segments with more-personalized, interactive messages. The new media range from specialty cable television channels and made-for-the-Web videos to Internet catalogs, e-mail, blogs, mobile phone content, and online social networks. In all, companies are doing less *broadcasting* and more *narrowcasting*.

Some advertising industry experts even predict that the old mass-media communications model will eventually become obsolete. Mass-media costs are rising, audiences are shrinking, ad clutter is increasing, and viewers are gaining control of message exposure through technologies such as video streaming or DVRs that let them skip disruptive television commercials. As a result, they suggest, marketers are shifting ever-larger portions of their marketing budgets away from old-media mainstays and moving them to digital and other new-age media. In recent years, although TV still dominates as an advertising medium, ad spending on the major TV networks has stagnated as ad spending on the Internet and other digital media has surged. Ad spending in magazines, newspapers, and radio, in contrast, has lost considerable ground.[3]

● **The new marketing communication model: Heinz introduced its new balsamic-vinegar-flavored ketchup using no traditional media, relying instead on its 825,000 Facebook followers to spread the word.**

©H. J. Heinz Co., L. P. 2011. Facebook is a trademark of Facebook, Inc.

In some cases, marketers are skipping traditional media altogether. ● For example, when Heinz introduced its limited-time Heinz Tomato Ketchup with Balsamic Vinegar flavor, customers were able to learn about and buy the product only through the brand's Facebook page, until it appeared on store shelves six weeks later. Heinz used no TV or print advertising for the introduction, instead relying on its 825,000 Facebook followers to spread the word. Customers responded strongly, and six months later Heinz added the product to its standard lineup, the first new flavor from Heinz Ketchup in nearly a decade.[4]

Similarly, eco-friendly household products maker Method recently employed a digital-only promotional campaign themed "Clean happy":[5]

Method is known for offbeat campaigns using slogans like "People against dirty" and "For the love of clean." But the most notable thing about the "Clean happy" campaign is that, unlike previous Method campaigns, it uses zero ads in traditional media like TV or magazines. Instead, the centerpiece of the campaign is a two-minute brand video clip that can be watched only on YouTube and on the Method Facebook page. That video is followed at monthly intervals by four other clips that focus on individual Method products. The campaign also employs online media ads, as well as a major presence in social media that includes, in addition to YouTube and Facebook, the Method Twitter feed and blogs.

The "Clean happy" campaign fits both Method's personality and its budget. "Method is the type of brand that benefits from word-of-mouth—from "the moms in mom groups telling each other about it," says an ad agency executive associated with the campaign. Moreover, "Clean happy" ran a first-year budget of only about $3.5 million, compared with the whopping $150 million or so that rival P&G might spend to bring out a new product, such as its new tablet version of Tide called Tide Pods. "We're embracing this grass-roots movement," says the Method ad executive. "When you don't have $150 million bucks, that's what you have to do."

In the new marketing communications world, rather than using old approaches that interrupt customers and force-feed them mass messages, new media formats let marketers reach smaller groups of consumers in more interactive, engaging ways. For example, think about television viewing these days. Consumers can now watch their favorite programs on just about anything with a screen—on televisions but also laptops, mobile phones, or tablets. And they can choose to watch programs whenever and wherever they wish, often without commercials. Increasingly, some programs, ads, and videos are being produced only for Internet viewing.

Despite the shift toward new digital media, however, traditional mass media still capture a lion's share of the promotion budgets of most major marketing firms, a fact that probably won't change quickly. For example, P&G, a leading proponent of digital media, still spends the majority of its huge advertising budget on mass media. Although P&G's digital outlay more than doubled last year to $169 million, digital still accounts for less than 5 percent of the company's annual global advertising budget.[6]

At a broader level, although some may question the future role of TV advertising, it's still very much in use today. Last year, television captured more than 40 percent of global advertising spending compared to the 21 percent captured by all online advertising media. Still, online advertising remains the fastest growing medium. It is now the second largest medium behind television, well ahead of newspapers and magazines.[7]

Thus, rather than the old-media model rapidly collapsing, most industry insiders see a more gradual blending of new and traditional media. The new marketing communications model will consist of a shifting mix of both traditional mass media and a wide array of exciting, new, more-targeted, and more-personalized but sometimes less-controllable media.

Many advertisers and ad agencies are now grappling with this transition. In the end, however, regardless of the communications channel, the key is to integrate all of these media in a way that best communicates the brand message and enhances the customer's brand experience. As the marketing communications environment shifts, so will the role of marketing communicators. Rather than just creating and placing "TV ads" or "print ads" or "Facebook display ads," many marketers now view themselves more broadly as *brand content managers* who manage brand conversations with and among customers across a fluid mix of channels, both traditional and new, controlled and not controlled (see Real Marketing 14.1).

The Need for *Integrated* Marketing Communications

The shift toward a richer mix of media and communication approaches poses a problem for marketers. Consumers today are bombarded by commercial messages from a broad range of sources. But consumers don't distinguish between message sources the way marketers do. In the consumer's mind, messages from different media and promotional approaches all become part of a single message about the company. Conflicting messages from these different sources can result in confused company images, brand positions, and customer relationships.

All too often, companies fail to integrate their various communications channels. The result is a hodgepodge of communications to consumers. Mass-media advertisements say one thing, whereas an in-store promotion sends a different signal, and the company's Internet site, e-mails, Facebook page, or videos posted on YouTube say something altogether different. The problem is that these communications often come from different parts of the company. Advertising messages are planned and implemented by the advertising department or an ad agency. Other company departments are responsible for PR, sales promotion events, and Internet or social network efforts. However, whereas companies may have separated their communications tools, customers don't. Mixed communications from these sources result in blurred brand perceptions by consumers.

The new world of digital and social marketing, tablet computers, smartphones, and apps presents tremendous opportunities but also big challenges. It can "give companies increased access to their customers, fresh insights into their preferences, and a broader creative palette to work with," says one marketing executive. But "the biggest issue is complexity and fragmentation ... the amount of choice out there," says another. The challenge is to "make it come together in an organized way."[8]

To that end, more companies today are adopting the concept of **integrated marketing communications (IMC)**. Under this concept, as illustrated in ● **Figure 14.1**, the

Integrated marketing communications (IMC)

Carefully integrating and coordinating the company's many communications channels to deliver a clear, consistent, and compelling message about the organization and its products.

●**FIGURE | 14.1**
Integrated Marketing Communications

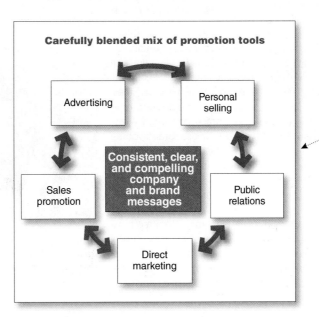

Carefully blended mix of promotion tools

Advertising

Personal selling

Consistent, clear, and compelling company and brand messages

Sales promotion

Public relations

Direct marketing

Today's customers are bombarded by company messages from all directions. For example, think about all the ways you interact with companies such as Nike, Apple, or Coca-Cola. Integrated marketing communications means that companies must carefully coordinate all of these customer touchpoints to ensure clear brand messages.

Real Marketing 14.1

New Communications Thinking:
Paid, Owned, Earned, and Shared

In the good old days, life seemed so simple for advertisers: Come up with a good creative idea, develop a media plan, produce and run a set of TV commercials and magazine ads, and maybe issue a press release to stir up some news. But today's marketing communications landscape seems more complex, characterized by a spate of new digital media and rapidly blurring lines within and between traditional and new channels. The old practice of placing "advertisements" in well-defined "media," within the tidy framework of a carefully managed promotional campaign, doesn't work as well as it once did.

Traditional message and media classifications just don't fit like they did. For example, a TV ad isn't really just a TV ad anymore. Instead, it's "video content" that might be seen anywhere—on a consumer's TV screen but also on a PC, tablet, or phone. Other brand video content looks a lot like TV advertising but was never intended for TV, such as made-for-the-Web videos posted on YouTube, Facebook, or another social network. Video content about the brand may be prepared by consumers and shared with others online.

Similarly, printed brand messages and pictures no longer appear only in carefully crafted ads placed in magazines, newspapers, or direct mail pieces. Instead, such content, created by a variety of sources, pops up in anything from formal advertisements and brand Web pages to consumer posts on online social networks and editorials by independent bloggers. In the hands of today's empowered consumers, the creation and distribution of brand messages can—and often does—take on a life of its own, beyond the design or control of the brand's marketers.

As a result, as the message and media environments are changing, so are the old notions about placing "ads" in well-defined "media." Instead of creating "TV ads" or "print ads" or "PR press releases," many marketers now view themselves more broadly as managing "brand content" and leveraging it across a wealth of integrated communications channels—both traditional and new, controlled and not controlled. This new thinking has led to a

new marketing communications framework. Rather than classifying communications by traditional media breakdowns, the new framework builds on the broader concept of how and by whom brand content is created, controlled, and distributed. The new classification identifies four major types of media: paid, owned, earned, and shared (POES):

Paid media—includes promotional channels paid for by the sponsor, including traditional media (such as TV, radio, print, or outdoor) and online and digital media (paid search ads, display ads, mobile ads, or e-mail marketing).

Owned media—includes promotional channels owned and controlled by the company, including company Web sites, corporate blogs, owned social media pages, proprietary brand communities, sales forces, and events.

Earned media—includes PR media channels, such as television, newspapers, blogs, online video sites, and other media not directly paid for or controlled by the marketer.

Shared media—includes media shared by consumers with other consumers and brands, such as social media, blogs, mobile media, and viral channels, as well as traditional word-of-mouth.

In the past, marketers have focused on traditional paid (broadcast, print) or earned (public relations) media. Now, however, they are rapidly adding the new generation of owned (Web sites, blogs, brand communities) and shared (online social networks, mobile, e-mail) media. Whereas a successful paid ad or PR piece used to be an end in itself, marketers are now asking "What else can I do with this content?" The marketer's goal is to leverage the combined power of

all the POES channels. "The important thing is to be in all streams—paid, owned, earned, and shared—so the message is heard," says one expert.

Careful integration across the POES channels can produce striking communications results. A now-classic example is the highly successful Old Spice "The Man Your Man Could Smell Like" campaign, featuring football player Isaiah Mustafa. The campaign began with TV commercials (paid), which Old Spice then posted to its Web site and its YouTube and Facebook pages (owned). The campaign quickly went viral, as consumers by the millions buzzed about the ads through e-mail, Facebook, and Twitter (shared). In turn, Old Spice received seemingly endless media coverage on everything from network TV to professional blog editorials (earned). In all, the campaign was viewed and discussed hundreds of millions of times across dozens of channels, all voicing the same integrated brand message.

Here's another example of a brand that successfully leveraged its campaign across paid, owned, earned, and shared media:

> Hormel's wholly-owned subsidiary JENNIE-O Turkey Store wanted to find a way to get consumers to appreciate how easy—and tasty—it was to substitute JENNIE-O ground turkey in recipes that called for ground beef. To get things cooking, it staged an imaginative "Make the Switch" marketing event (owned media). For five days, JENNIE-O took over the Bistro Truck, a popular Manhattan food truck, wrapping it with "Make the Switch" banners. Instead of ground beef, the truck's burgers were made from ground turkey. Each day, courtesy of JENNIE-O, the truck gave away

Hormel's JENNIE-O turkey brand successfully leveraged its imaginative "Make the Switch" campaign across paid, owned, earned, and shared media.

© 2012 Jennie-O Turkey Store , LLC.

500 free gourmet turkey burgers at lunch. The truck's location and menu were previewed to local foodies and bloggers (earned media), and posted daily on Facebook, Twitter, and a special microsite (owned media). Then, the social media universe took over (shared media). About 450,000 tweets and retweets mentioned the "Make the Switch" promotion and locations. People lined up for thousands of free JENNIE-O burgers. Within five days the Facebook page had 23,000 "likes," and ground turkey sales rose 7 percent in New York. The "Make the Switch" takeover was so successful it has been extended to other cities and has become the subject of JENNIE-O TV commercials (paid).

Thus, today's shifting and sometimes chaotic marketing communications environment calls for more than simply creating and placing some ads in well-defined and controlled media spaces. Rather, it calls for an integrated effort to create and inspire the right brand content, whatever the sources, and help it catch fire. Today's marketing communicators must be more than just advertising copywriters or media analysts. They must be brand content strategists, creators, connectors, and catalysts who manage brand conversations with and among customers across a fluid mix of message channels. That's a tall order, but with today's new communications thinking, anything is POES–ible!

Source: Extract example and quotes from Julie Liesse, "The Big Idea," *Advertising Age*, November 28, 2011, pp. C4–C6; with additional information from Julie Liesse, "Top Trends For 2012," *Advertising Age*, November 28, 2011, p. C8; Peter Himler, "Paid, Earned & Owned: Revisited," Theflack.blogspot.com, June 21, 2011; and www.hormelfoods.com/brands/jennie0/ and www.switchtoturkey.com, accessed October 2012. JENNIE-O® and "Make the Switch®" are registered trademarks of JENNIE-O Turkey Store, LLC.

company carefully integrates its many communications channels to deliver a clear, consistent, and compelling message about the organization and its brands.

Integrated marketing communications calls for recognizing all touchpoints where the customer may encounter the company and its brands. Each contact with the brand will deliver a message—whether good, bad, or indifferent. The company's goal should be to deliver a consistent and positive message at each contact. Integrated marketing communications ties together all of the company's messages and images. Its television and print ads have the same message, look, and feel as its e-mail and personal selling communications. And its PR materials project the same image as its Web site, online social networks, or mobile marketing efforts. Often, different media play unique roles in attracting, informing, and persuading consumers; these roles must be carefully coordinated under the overall marketing communications plan.

A great example of a well-integrated marketing communications effort comes from premium ice cream maker Häagen-Dazs. To strengthen its emotional connection with consumers, Häagen-Dazs launched the "Häagen-Dazs loves honey bees" campaign, centered on an issue important to both the brand and its customers—a mysterious colony-collapse disorder threatening the U.S. honey bee population. Honey bees pollinate one-third of all the natural products we eat and up to 40 percent of the natural flavors used in Häagen-Dazs ice cream, making the "HD loves HB" message a natural for the brand. ● But perhaps even more important than the "help the honey bees" message itself was the way that Häagen-Dazs communicated that message:[9]

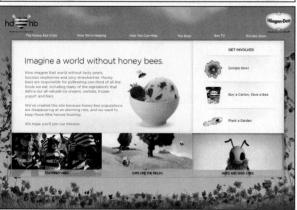

● The "HD loves HB" integrated marketing communications campaign uses a rich, well-coordinated blend of promotion elements to successfully deliver Häagen-Dazs' unique message.

Year 2 site: Design and Production by InTacto.com - Digital Partner. Year 1 site: Design by UNIT9 and Helpful Strangers.

More than just running a few ads, Häagen-Dazs created a full-fledged, beautifully integrated marketing communications campaign, using a wide range of media that worked harmoniously for the cause. It started with broadcast and print ads that drove traffic to the campaign's helpthehoneybees.com Web site, a kind of honey bee central where customers could learn about the problem and how to help. At the site, visitors could tap into a news feed called *The Buzz*, turn on "Bee TV," purchase Bee-Ts with phrases like "Long live the queen" and "Bee a hero," send "Bee-mail" messages to friends, or make donations to support honey bee research. To create even more bee buzz,

Häagen-Dazs handed out samples of Vanilla Honey Bee ice cream and wildflower seeds at local farmers markets across the country and sponsored fund-raisers by local community and school groups. The campaign also incorporated social networks such as Twitter and Facebook. In all, the rich, well-coordinated blend of communications elements successfully delivered Häagen-Dazs' unique message and positioning. It became "a brand with a heart and a soul," says the brand's director. "We not only raised brand awareness," she says, "but made a difference in the world."

In the past, no one person or department was responsible for thinking through the communication roles of the various promotion tools and coordinating the promotion mix. To help implement integrated marketing communications, some companies have appointed a marketing communications director who has overall responsibility for the company's communications efforts. This helps to produce better communications consistency and greater sales impact. It places the responsibility in someone's hands—where none existed before—to unify the company's image as it is shaped by thousands of company activities.

Objective 3 ┈┈┈▶

Outline the communication process and the steps in developing effective marketing communications.

A View of the Communication Process

Integrated marketing communications involves identifying the target audience and shaping a well-coordinated promotional program to obtain the desired audience response. Too often, marketing communications focus on immediate awareness, image, or preference goals in the target market. But this approach to communication is too shortsighted. Today, marketers are moving toward viewing communications as *managing the customer relationship over time.*

Because customers differ, communications programs need to be developed for specific segments, niches, and even individuals. And, given the new interactive communications technologies, companies must ask not only "How can we reach our customers?" but also "How can we let our customers reach us?"

Thus, the communications process should start with an audit of all the potential touchpoints that target customers may have with the company and its brands. For example, someone purchasing a new phone plan may talk to others, see television or magazine ads, visit various Web sites for prices and reviews, and check out plans at Best Buy, Walmart, or a wireless provider's kiosk or store. The marketer needs to assess what influence each communication experience will have at different stages of the buying process. This understanding helps marketers allocate their communication dollars more efficiently and effectively.

To communicate effectively, marketers need to understand how communication works. Communication involves the nine elements shown in ⬤ **Figure 14.2**. Two of these elements are the major parties in a communication—the *sender* and the *receiver*. Another two are the major communication tools—the *message* and the *media*. Four more are major communication functions—*encoding, decoding, response,* and *feedback.* The last element is *noise* in the system. Definitions of these elements follow and are applied to a McDonald's "I'm lovin' it" television commercial.

- *Sender:* The *party sending the message* to another party—here, McDonald's.
- *Encoding:* The process of *putting thought into symbolic form*—for example, McDonald's ad agency assembles words, sounds, and illustrations into a TV advertisement that will convey the intended message.
- *Message:* The *set of symbols* that the sender transmits—the actual McDonald's ad.
- *Media:* The *communication channels* through which the message moves from the sender to the receiver—in this case, television and the specific television programs that McDonald's selects.
- *Decoding:* The process by which the receiver *assigns meaning to the symbols* encoded by the sender—a consumer watches the McDonald's commercial and interprets the words and images it contains.
- *Receiver:* The *party receiving the message* sent by another party—the customer who watches the McDonald's ad.
- *Response:* The *reactions of the receiver* after being exposed to the message—any of hundreds of possible responses, such as the consumer likes McDonald's better, is

● **FIGURE** | **14.2**
Elements in the Communication
Process

There is a lot going on in this figure! For example, apply this model to McDonald's. To create great advertising—such as its long-running "I'm lovin' it" campaign—McDonald's must thoroughly understand its customers and how communication works.

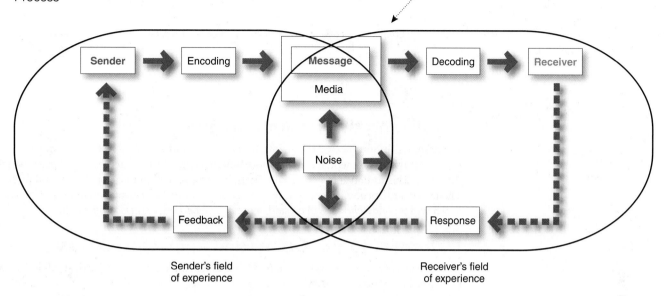

Sender's field
of experience

Receiver's field
of experience

more likely to eat at McDonald's next time, hums the "I'm lovin' it" jingle, or does nothing.

- *Feedback:* The part of the *receiver's response communicated back to the sender*—McDonald's research shows that consumers are either struck by and remember the ad or they write or call McDonald's, praising or criticizing the ad or its products.
- *Noise:* The *unplanned static or distortion* during the communication process, which results in the receiver getting a different message than the one the sender sent—the consumer is distracted while watching the commercial and misses its key points.

For a message to be effective, the sender's encoding process must mesh with the receiver's decoding process. The best messages consist of words and other symbols that are familiar to the receiver. The more the sender's field of experience overlaps with that of the receiver, the more effective the message is likely to be. Marketing communicators may not always *share* the customer's field of experience. For example, an advertising copywriter from one socioeconomic level might create ads for customers from another level—say, wealthy business owners. However, to communicate effectively, the marketing communicator must *understand* the customer's field of experience.

This model points out several key factors in good communication. Senders need to know what audiences they wish to reach and what responses they want. They must be good at encoding messages that take into account how the target audience decodes them. They must send messages through media that reach target audiences, and they must develop feedback channels so that they can assess an audience's response to the message. Also, in today's interactive media environment, companies must be prepared to "flip" the communications process—to become good receivers of and responders to messages sent by consumers.

Steps in Developing Effective Marketing Communication

We now examine the steps in developing an effective integrated communications and promotion program. Marketers must do the following: Identify the target audience, determine the communication objectives, design a message, choose the media through which to send the message, select the message source, and collect feedback.

FIGURE | 14.3
Buyer-Readiness Stages

A goal of marketing in general, and of marketing communications in particular, is to move target customers through the buying process. Once again, it all starts with understanding customer needs and wants.

Identifying the Target Audience

A marketing communicator starts with a clear target audience in mind. The audience may be current users or potential buyers, those who make the buying decision or those who influence it. The audience may be individuals, groups, special publics, or the general public. The target audience will heavily affect the communicator's decisions on *what* will be said, *how* it will be said, *when* it will be said, *where* it will be said, and *who* will say it.

Determining the Communication Objectives

Once the target audience has been defined, marketers must determine the desired response. Of course, in many cases, they will seek a *purchase* response. But purchase may result only after a lengthy consumer decision-making process. The marketing communicator needs to know where the target audience now stands and to what stage it needs to be moved. The target audience may be in any of six **buyer-readiness stages**, the stages consumers normally pass through on their way to making a purchase. These stages are *awareness, knowledge, liking, preference, conviction,* and *purchase* (see ● **Figure 14.3**).

The marketing communicator's target market may be totally unaware of the product, know only its name, or know only a few things about it. Thus, the communicator must first build *awareness* and *knowledge*. ● For example, Procter & Gamble used a massive $150 million marketing campaign to introduce consumers to its innovative new laundry product, Tide Pods, single-use tablets called pods that combine liquid detergent, stain remover, and brightener. The introductory campaign, themed "Pop in. Stand out," showed consumers how simply popping a Tide Pod into the washing machine could clean and freshen clothes while also making colors pop. The extensive introductory campaign used a broad range of traditional, digital, mobile, social, and in-store media to quickly create awareness and knowledge across the entire market.[10]

Buyer-readiness stages
The stages consumers normally pass through on their way to a purchase, including awareness, knowledge, liking, preference, conviction, and, finally, the actual purchase.

● **Moving consumers through the buyer-readiness stages: P&G used an extensive $150 million marketing campaign to create awareness and knowledge for its innovative new laundry product, Tide Pods.**

The Procter & Gamble Company

Assuming that target consumers *know* about a product, how do they *feel* about it? Once potential buyers knew about Tide Pods, marketers wanted to move them through successively stronger stages of feelings toward the new model. These stages include *liking* (feeling favorable about Tide Pods), *preference* (preferring Tide Pods to regular detergents and competing pod products), and *conviction* (believing that Tide Pods are the best laundry product for them).

Tide marketers used a combination of the promotion mix tools to create positive feelings and conviction. The initial commercials helped build anticipation and an emotional brand connection. Video clips on YouTube and the Tide Facebook fan page demonstrated the product's use and features. Press releases and other PR activities helped keep the buzz going about the product. A packed microsite (tidepods.com) provided additional information.

Finally, some members of the target market might be convinced about the product but not quite get around to making the *purchase*. The communicator must lead these consumers to take the final step. To help reluctant consumers over such hurdles, Tide offered buyers special promotional prices, samples, and supporting comments from customers at its Web site, Facebook page, and elsewhere.

Of course, marketing communications alone could not create positive feelings and purchases for the new Tide Pods. The product itself must provide superior value for the customer. In fact, outstanding marketing communications can actually speed the demise of a poor product. The more quickly potential buyers learn about a poor product, the more quickly they become aware of its faults. Thus, good marketing communications call for "good deeds followed by good words."

Designing a Message

Having defined the desired audience response, the communicator then turns to developing an effective message. Ideally, the message should get *attention*, hold *interest*, arouse *desire*, and obtain *action* (a framework known as the *AIDA model*). In practice, few messages take the consumer all the way from awareness to purchase, but the AIDA framework suggests the desirable qualities of a good message.

When putting a message together, the marketing communicator must decide what to say (*message content*) and how to say it (*message structure* and *format*).

Message Content

The marketer has to figure out an appeal or theme that will produce the desired response. There are three types of appeals: rational, emotional, and moral. *Rational appeals* relate to the audience's self-interest. They show that the product will produce the desired benefits. Examples are messages showing a product's quality, economy, value, or performance. Thus, an ad for Aleve makes this matter-of-fact claim: "More pills doesn't mean more pain relief. Aleve has the strength to keep back, body, and arthritis pain away all day with fewer pills than Tylenol." And a Weight Watchers' ad states this simple fact: "The diet secret to end all diet secrets is that there is no diet secret."

Emotional appeals attempt to stir up either negative or positive emotions that can motivate purchase. Communicators may use emotional appeals ranging from love, joy, and humor to fear and guilt. Advocates of emotional messages claim that they attract more attention and create more belief in the sponsor and the brand. The idea is that consumers often feel before they think, and persuasion is emotional in nature. Good storytelling in a commercial often strikes an emotional chord. For example, to promote its Chrome browser, Google ran a heart-warming 90-second "Dear Sophie" commercial that shows a father using Google products to catalog his daughter Sophie's life events, from birth and important birthdays to loss of baby teeth and learning how to ski. He writes her notes using Gmail and posts videos of her on YouTube. The ad closes with "The web is what you make of it." To date, the ad has captured nearly 6 million YouTube views.

These days, it seems as if every company is using humor in its advertising, from consumer product firms such as Anheuser-Busch to old-line insurance companies such as Allstate. For example, 9 of the top 10 most popular ads in *USA Today*'s ad meter consumer rankings of last year's Super Bowl ads used humor. Properly used, humor can capture attention, make people feel good, and give a brand personality. However, advertisers must be careful when using humor. Used poorly, it can detract from comprehension, wear out its welcome fast, overshadow the product, and even irritate consumers.

Moral appeals are directed to an audience's sense of what is "right" and "proper." They are often used to urge people to support social causes, such as a cleaner environment or aid to the disadvantaged. For example, the United Way's Live United campaign urges people to give back to their communities—to "Live United. Make a difference. Help create opportunities for everyone in your community." An EarthShare ad urges environmental involvement by reminding people that "We live in the house we all build. Every decision we make has consequences. . . . We choose the world we live in, so make the right choices. . . ."

Message Structure

Marketers must also decide how to handle three message structure issues. The first is whether to draw a conclusion or leave it to the audience. Research suggests that, in many cases, rather than drawing a conclusion, the advertiser is better off asking questions and letting buyers come to their own conclusions.

● **Message format: To attract attention, advertisers can use novelty and contrast, eye-catching pictures and headlines, or distinctive formats, as in this Snickers ad.**

Snickers® is a registered trademark of Mars, Incorporated. This trademark is used with permission. Mars, Incorporated is not associated with Pearson. The image of the SNICKERS® mark is printed with permission of Mars, Incorporated.

The second message structure issue is whether to present the strongest arguments first or last. Presenting them first gets strong attention but may lead to an anticlimactic ending.

The third message structure issue is whether to present a one-sided argument (mentioning only the product's strengths) or a two-sided argument (touting the product's strengths while also admitting its shortcomings). Usually, a one-sided argument is more effective in sales presentations—except when audiences are highly educated or likely to hear opposing claims or when the communicator has a negative association to overcome. In this spirit, Heinz ran the message "Heinz Ketchup is slow good," and Listerine ran the message "Listerine tastes bad twice a day." In such cases, two-sided messages can enhance an advertiser's credibility and make buyers more resistant to competitor attacks.

Message Format

The marketing communicator also needs a strong *format* for the message. In a print ad, the communicator has to decide on the headline, copy, illustration, and colors. ● To attract attention, advertisers can use novelty and contrast; eye-catching pictures and headlines; distinctive formats; message size and position; and color, shape, and movement. If the message is to be communicated by television or video, the communicator must incorporate motion, pace, and sound. Presenters plan every detail carefully, from start to finish.

If the message is carried on the product or its package, the communicator must watch texture, scent, color, size, and shape. For example, color alone can enhance message recognition for a brand. One study suggests that color increases brand recognition by up to 80 percent—think about Target (red), McDonald's (yellow and red), John Deere (green and yellow), IBM (blue), or UPS (brown). Thus, in designing effective marketing communications, marketers must consider color and other seemingly unimportant details carefully.

Choosing Media

The communicator must now select the *channels of communication*. There are two broad types of communication channels: *personal* and *nonpersonal*.

Personal Communication Channels

In **personal communication channels**, two or more people communicate directly with each other. They might communicate face to face, on the phone, via mail or e-mail, or even through texting or an Internet chat. Personal communication channels are effective because they allow for personal addressing and feedback.

Some personal communication channels are controlled directly by the company. For example, company salespeople contact business buyers. But other personal communications about the product may reach buyers through channels not directly controlled by the company. These channels might include independent experts—consumer advocates, online buying guides, bloggers, and others—making statements to buyers. Or they might be neighbors, friends, family members, associates, or other consumers talking to target buyers. This last channel, **word-of-mouth influence**, has considerable effect in many product areas.

Personal influence carries great weight, especially for products that are expensive, risky, or highly visible. One recent survey found that recommendations from friends and family are far and away the most powerful influence on consumers worldwide: More than 50 percent of consumers said friends and family are the number one influence on their awareness and purchase. Another study found that 90 percent of customers trust recommendations from people they know and 70 percent trust consumer opinions

Personal communication channels

Channels through which two or more people communicate directly with each other, including face to face, on the phone, via mail or e-mail, or even through texting or an Internet chat.

Word-of-mouth influence

Personal communications about a product between target buyers and neighbors, friends, family members, associates, and other consumers.

Buzz marketing
Cultivating opinion leaders and getting them to spread information about a product or a service to others in their communities.

posted online, whereas trust in ads runs from a high of about 62 percent to less than 24 percent, depending on the medium.[11] Is it any wonder, then, that few consumers buy a big-ticket item before checking out what existing users have to say about the product at a site such as Amazon.com? Who hasn't made an Amazon purchase based on another customer's review or the "Customers who bought this also bought . . ." section?

Companies can take steps to put personal communication channels to work for them. For example, as we discussed in Chapter 5, they can create *opinion leaders* for their brands—people whose opinions are sought by others—by supplying influencers with the product on attractive terms or by educating them so that they can inform others. **Buzz marketing** involves cultivating opinion leaders and getting them to spread information about a product or a service to others in their communities.

P&G has created a huge word-of-mouth marketing arm—Vocalpoint—consisting of 500,000 moms. Vocalpoint recruits "connectors"—natural-born buzzers with vast networks of friends and a gift for gab. They create buzz not only for P&G brands but also for those of other client companies as well—half its business comes from non-P&G brands. P&G routinely uses the Vocalpoint network in the launch of new products such as the Bounce Dryer Bar and Tide Pods. P&G doesn't pay the moms or coach them on what to say. It simply educates Vocalpointers about a new product, arms them with free samples and coupons for friends, and then asks them to share their "honest opinions with us and with other real women." In turn, the Vocalpoint moms create hundreds of thousands of personal recommendations for the new products.[12]

Buzz marketing: P&G has created a huge word-of-mouth marketing arm—Vocalpoint—consisting of 500,000 moms who create word-of-mouth for P&G and other brands.

The Procter & Gamble Company

Nonpersonal Communication Channels

Nonpersonal communication channels
Media that carry messages without personal contact or feedback, including major media, atmospheres, and events.

Nonpersonal communication channels are media that carry messages without personal contact or feedback. They include major media, atmospheres, and events. Major *media* include print media (newspapers, magazines, direct mail), broadcast media (television, radio), display media (billboards, signs, posters), and online media (e-mail, company Web sites, and online social and sharing networks). *Atmospheres* are designed environments that create or reinforce the buyer's leanings toward buying a product. Thus, lawyers' offices and banks are designed to communicate confidence and other qualities that might be valued by clients. *Events* are staged occurrences that communicate messages to target audiences. For example, public relations departments arrange grand openings, shows and exhibits, public tours, and other events.

Nonpersonal communication affects buyers directly. In addition, using mass media often affects buyers indirectly by causing more personal communication. For example, communications might first flow from television, magazines, and other mass media to opinion leaders and then from these opinion leaders to others. Thus, opinion leaders step between the mass media and their audiences and carry messages to people who are less exposed to media. Interestingly, marketers often use nonpersonal communications channels to replace or stimulate personal communications by embedding consumer endorsements or word-of-mouth testimonials in their ads and other promotions.

Selecting the Message Source

In either personal or nonpersonal communication, the message's impact also depends on how the target audience views the communicator. Messages delivered by highly credible sources are more persuasive. Thus, many food companies promote to doctors, dentists, and other health-care providers to motivate these professionals to recommend specific food products to their patients. And marketers hire celebrity endorsers—well-known athletes, actors, musicians, and even cartoon characters—to deliver their messages. A host of NBA superstars lend their images to brands such as Nike, McDonald's, and Coca-Cola.

THE SECOND COMING.

● **Celebrity endorsers: LeBron James, Kobe Bryant, and a host of other NBA superstars lend their images to Nike brands.**
Newscom

Colombian actress Sofia Vergara from *Modern Family* endorsees Pepsi and CoverGirl, and celebrities ranging from Vergara, Jay Leno, and Mary J. Blige to David Beckham and Aerosmith's Steven Tyler helped draw attention to Burger King's new menu.[13]

But companies must be careful when selecting celebrities to represent their brands. Picking the wrong spokesperson can result in embarrassment and a tarnished image. For example, more than a dozen big brands—including Nike, Gatorade, Gillette, EA Sports, and Accenture—faced embarrassment when golfer Tiger Woods's personal problems were publically exposed, tarnishing his previously pristine image. "Arranged marriages between brands and celebrities are inherently risky," notes one expert. "Ninety-nine percent of celebrities do a strong job for their brand partners," says another, "and 1 percent goes off the rails."[14] More than ever, it's important to pick the right celebrity for the brand (see Real Marketing 14.2).

Collecting Feedback

After sending the message, the communicator must research its effect on the target audience. This involves asking target audience members whether they remember the message, how many times they saw it, what points they recall, how they felt about the message, and their past and present attitudes toward the product and company. The communicator would also like to measure behavior resulting from the message—how many people bought the product, talked to others about it, or visited the store.

Feedback on marketing communications may suggest changes in the promotion program or in the product offer itself. For example, Macy's uses television and newspaper advertising to inform area consumers about its stores, services, and merchandising events. Suppose feedback research shows that 80 percent of all shoppers in an area recall seeing the store's ads and are aware of its merchandise and sales. Sixty percent of these aware shoppers have visited a Macy's store in the past month, but only 20 percent of those who visited were satisfied with the shopping experience.

These results suggest that although promotion is creating *awareness*, Macy's stores aren't giving consumers the *satisfaction* they expect. Therefore, Macy's needs to improve the shopping experience while staying with the successful communications program. In contrast, suppose research shows that only 40 percent of area consumers are aware of the store's merchandise and events, only 30 percent of those aware have shopped recently, but 80 percent of those who have shopped return soon to shop again. In this case, Macy's needs to strengthen its promotion program to take advantage of its power to create customer satisfaction in the store.

Objective 4 ┈┈▶
Explain the methods for setting the promotion budget and factors that affect the design of the promotion mix.

Setting the Total Promotion Budget and Mix

We have looked at the steps in planning and sending communications to a target audience. But how does the company determine its total *promotion budget* and the division among the major promotional tools to create the *promotion mix*? By what process does it blend the tools to create integrated marketing communications? We now look at these questions.

Setting the Total Promotion Budget

One of the hardest marketing decisions facing a company is how much to spend on promotion. ● John Wanamaker, the department store magnate, once said, "I know that half of my advertising is wasted, but I don't know which half. I spent $2 million for advertising, and I don't know if that is half enough or twice too much." Thus, it is not surprising that industries and companies vary widely in how much they spend on promotion. Promotion spending may be 10–12 percent of sales for consumer packaged goods, 20 percent for cosmetics, and only 1.9 percent for household appliances. Within a given industry, both low and high spenders can be found.[15]

Real Marketing 14.2

Celebrity Endorsers: Finding the Right Celebrity for the Brand

Ever since Red Rock Cola hired baseball legend Babe Ruth to endorse its soft drink in the late 1930s, companies have been paying big bucks to have their products associated with big-name celebrities. Brands seek an endorser's "halo effect"—the positive association that surrounds a product after a popular celebrity has pitched it.

As evidence of the popularity of celebrities in today's marketing, check out recent Super Bowl advertising. Over the past few years, big-budget Super Bowl ads have showcased stars ranging from Jerry Seinfeld and Jay Leno (Acura), Matthew Broderick (Honda), Clint Eastwood (Chrysler), Kim Kardashian (Sketchers), and Betty White (Snickers) to Elton John (Pepsi), Justin Bieber (Best Buy), and even a claymation Eminem (Brisk Iced Tea).

Celebrity endorsements are big business, for both the brands and the endorsers. For example, Nike spends an estimated half-billion dollars a year to pay celebrities to hawk its goods. But the payoff appears to be well worth the price. For example, Nike's Jordan Brand subsidiary (which includes Air Jordans as well as brands endorsed by Dwyane Wade, Carmelo Anthony, and Chris Paul) enjoys annual revenues topping $1 billion and reaps a 71 percent share of the U.S. basketball shoe market. In turn, even though he hasn't played professional basketball in nearly a decade, Michael Jordan earns $60 million annually from endorsement deals with Nike, Gatorade, Hanes, and other big brands.

However, although linking up with the right celebrity can add substantial appeal to a brand, using celebrities doesn't guarantee success. For example, according to one recent study, ads with celebrities are on average 3 percent less effective than ads without them. "During last year's Super Bowl," says an analyst, "ads without celebrities performed 9.2 percent better than those with celebrities." In fact, "ads with animals performed 21 percent better than ads with celebrities." Moreover, celebrity partnerships can create difficulties. When a major celebrity deal turns sour, or when a celebrity falls from grace, it can tarnish rather than enhance a brand's image.

Despite the potential pitfalls, however, celebrity endorsements are bigger today than ever. By one estimate, celebrities now appear in roughly one-fifth of all ads. In fact, the age-old technique is moving into dynamic new areas, in line with the social media revolution. Beyond simply employing celebs as brand icons or ad spokespeople, many marketers are putting them squarely in the middle of consumers' social dialogue. For example, Twitter is now at the center of a new celebrity endorsement revolution. Here are just a few recent examples of celebrities propping brands on Twitter:

> Snoop Dogg: "These homies [Toyota] know the deal. Wonder if this swagger wagon can fit 22's? SPINNIN!"

> Khloe Kardashian: "Want to know how Old Navy makes your butt look scary good? Ask a Kardashian J."

> Terrell Owens: "Free flight, VIP access, $1500 in ur pocket and…football! Comfort Inn is hooking up 3 days of it! Check it out."

These celebs aren't just spontaneously tweeting about their favorite minivans, jeans, and motels. They're being well paid for their plugs. Whereas some celebrity tweets go for as little as $2,000, tweets by Khloe Kardashian run $8,000 each; top stars routinely pull in $10,000 per brand-endorsing tweet.

Having celebrities tweet about a brand can add instant interest to the message. But many marketers question the effectiveness of this latest celebrity endorsement trend. For starters, only 11 percent of U.S. adults even use Twitter, and only a fraction of those follow a given celebrity. And by itself, the brief, "drive-by" nature of the typical Twitter campaign isn't likely to build a long-term celebrity-brand relationship or have much brand-building impact. Still, as with many other promotional efforts today, marketers are working feverishly to make more effective use of celebrities in the social media.

According to Carol Goll, head of global branded entertainment for Hollywood talent agency International Creative Management, the success of celebrity endorsements comes down to matching the right celebrity with the right brand. That's how she has put together major endorsement deals for clients such as Beyoncé (American Express, Vivio, Nintendo, General Mills, Crystal Geyser) and Kim Cattrall (Olay, I Can't Believe It's Not Butter). Goll and her team start by deeply analyzing the characteristics of a celebrity's Twitter followers and Facebook fans, as well as the social media buzz surrounding the celebrity's recent projects. That information helps find the celebrity that best fits a given brand.

Goll notes that it's also important to avoid the "sellout" factor sometimes associated with celebrity endorsements. Too often, endorsement deals come off to consumers as offhand paid commercial pairings of the celebrity and the brand. For example, Snoop Dogg's fans must have been surprised when

Rapper Eminem speaks for Lipton's Brisk Iced Tea brand. The relationship produced one of the decade's most talked-about Super Bowl ads and has extended to YouTube, Facebook, and even Eminem's record label and tour.

© 2011 The Pepsi Lipton Partnership. Used with permission.

his sponsored Twitter link sent them to an ad on YouTube for a Toyota Sienna. And how many Terrell Owens fans think that he actually cares about Comfort Inn?

The best use of celebrities requires authenticity—even a touch of elusiveness. For example, one of Goll's biggest hits was matching rapper Eminem with Lipton's Brisk Iced Tea brand. Eminem—the most-liked musician on Facebook (58.2 million fans vs. Lady Gaga's 51.8 million)—has shied away from commercial deals. "What was important to Eminem was he wanted to be authentic," says Goll. In fact, Eminem wouldn't sign with a company unless he could maintain his artistic integrity by creating his own dialogue. Brisk agreed. The result

was one of the decade's most talked-about Super Bowl ads and an ongoing Brisk-Eminem relationship that has extended to YouTube, Facebook, and even his record label and tour.

Thanks to success stories like this one, although the whos and hows might change to

fit the shifting marketing communications environment, celebrity power will likely remain an important element in the marketing of many brands. "We live in a celebrity-crazed culture," concludes the analyst. "Advertisers will never abandon them."

Sources: Andrew Hampp, "Social-Media Buzz Helps ICM Match Marketers with the Best Celeb Endorsers—Even the Elusive Ones," *Advertising Age,* May 22, 2011, accessed at http://adage.com/article/227662/; Christina Rexrode, "Twitter Celebrity Endorsements Are Big Business for Starts and Companies," *Huffington Post,* November 3, 2011, www.huffingtonpost.com/2011/11/03/celebrity-twitter-endorsements_n_1073577.html; Bruce Horovitz, "Cooking Up a Super Bowl Ad? Just Add Celebrities," *USA Today,* February 2, 2012, www.usatoday.com/money/advertising/story/2012-02-02/super-bowl-ads-celebrities/52939714/1; and www.youtube.com?watch?v-B2n_sqrGrF8, accessed November 2012. Text from Carol Goll used with permission of Carol Goll, International Creative Management, Head of Global Branded Entertainment.

How does a company determine its promotion budget? Here, we look at four common methods used to set the total budget for advertising: the *affordable method,* the *percentage-of-sales method,* the *competitive-parity method,* and the *objective-and-task method.*[16]

Affordable Method

Affordable method
Setting the promotion budget at the level management thinks the company can afford.

Some companies use the **affordable method**: They set the promotion budget at the level they think the company can afford. Small businesses often use this method, reasoning that the company cannot spend more on advertising than it has. They start with total revenues, deduct operating expenses and capital outlays, and then devote some portion of the remaining funds to advertising.

Unfortunately, this method of setting budgets completely ignores the effects of promotion on sales. It tends to place promotion last among spending priorities, even in situations in which advertising is critical to the firm's success. It leads to an uncertain annual promotion budget, which makes long-range market planning difficult. Although the affordable method can result in overspending on advertising, it more often results in underspending.

Percentage-of-sales method
Setting the promotion budget at a certain percentage of current or forecasted sales or as a percentage of the unit sales price.

Percentage-of-Sales Method

Other companies use the **percentage-of-sales method**, setting their promotion budget at a certain percentage of current or forecasted sales. Or they budget a percentage of the unit sales price. The percentage-of-sales method is simple to use and helps management think about the relationships between promotion spending, selling price, and profit per unit.

Despite these claimed advantages, however, the percentage-of-sales method has little to justify it. It wrongly views sales as the *cause* of promotion rather than as the *result.* Although studies have found a positive correlation between promotional spending and brand strength, this relationship often turns out to be effect and cause, not cause and effect. Stronger brands with higher sales can afford the biggest ad budgets.

Thus, the percentage-of-sales budget is based on the availability of funds rather than on opportunities. It may prevent the increased spending sometimes needed to turn around falling sales. Because the budget varies

● Setting the promotion budget is one of the hardest decisions facing a company. Coca-Cola spends hundreds of millions of dollars annually, but is that "half enough or twice too much"?
Associated Press

with year-to-year sales, long-range planning is difficult. Finally, the method does not provide any basis for choosing a *specific* percentage, except what has been done in the past or what competitors are doing.

Competitive-Parity Method

Competitive-parity method
Setting the promotion budget to match competitors' outlays.

Still other companies use the **competitive-parity method**, setting their promotion budgets to match competitors' outlays. They monitor competitors' advertising or get industry promotion spending estimates from publications or trade associations and then set their budgets based on the industry average.

Two arguments support this method. First, competitors' budgets represent the collective wisdom of the industry. Second, spending what competitors spend helps prevent promotion wars. Unfortunately, neither argument is valid. There are no grounds for believing that the competition has a better idea of what a company should be spending on promotion than does the company itself. Companies differ greatly, and each has its own special promotion needs. Finally, there is no evidence that budgets based on competitive parity prevent promotion wars.

Objective-and-Task Method

Objective-and-task method
Developing the promotion budget by (1) defining specific promotion objectives, (2) determining the tasks needed to achieve these objectives, and (3) estimating the costs of performing these tasks. The sum of these costs is the proposed promotion budget.

The most logical budget-setting method is the **objective-and-task method**, whereby the company sets its promotion budget based on what it wants to accomplish with promotion. This budgeting method entails (1) defining specific promotion objectives, (2) determining the tasks needed to achieve these objectives, and (3) estimating the costs of performing these tasks. The sum of these costs is the proposed promotion budget.

The advantage of the objective-and-task method is that it forces management to spell out its assumptions about the relationship between dollars spent and promotion results. But it is also the most difficult method to use. Often, it is hard to figure out which specific tasks will achieve the stated objectives. For example, suppose Samsung wants a 95-percent-awareness level for its latest camcorder model during the six-month introductory period. What specific advertising messages and media schedules should Samsung use to attain this objective? How much would these messages and media schedules cost? Samsung management must consider such questions, even though they are hard to answer.

Shaping the Overall Promotion Mix

The concept of integrated marketing communications suggests that the company must blend the promotion tools carefully into a coordinated *promotion mix*. But how does it determine what mix of promotion tools to use? Companies within the same industry differ greatly in the design of their promotion mixes. For example, cosmetics maker Mary Kay spends most of its promotion funds on personal selling and direct marketing, whereas competitor CoverGirl spends heavily on consumer advertising. We now look at factors that influence the marketer's choice of promotion tools.

The Nature of Each Promotion Tool

Each promotion tool has unique characteristics and costs. Marketers must understand these characteristics in shaping the promotion mix.

Advertising. Advertising can reach masses of geographically dispersed buyers at a low cost per exposure, and it enables the seller to repeat a message many times. For example, television advertising can reach huge audiences. Nearly 111 million Americans watched the most recent Super Bowl, more than 39 million people watched at least part of the last Academy Awards broadcast, and more than 26 million fans tuned in for the kick-off of the 11th season of *American Idol*. And consumers viewing the ads again on YouTube and company Web sites extended their reach by millions more. For companies that want to reach a mass audience, TV is the place to be.[17]

Beyond its reach, large-scale advertising says something positive about the seller's size, popularity, and success. Because of advertising's public nature, consumers tend to view advertised products as more legitimate. Advertising is also very expressive; it allows the company to dramatize its products through the artful use of visuals, print, sound, and color. On the one hand, advertising can be used to build up a long-term image for a product (such

● **With personal selling, the customer feels a greater need to listen and respond, even if the response is a polite "No thank you."**

SelectStock

as Coca-Cola ads). On the other hand, advertising can trigger quick sales (as when Kohl's advertises weekend specials).

Advertising also has some shortcomings. Although it reaches many people quickly, advertising is impersonal and lacks the direct persuasiveness of company salespeople. For the most part, advertising can carry on only a one-way communication with an audience, and the audience does not feel that it has to pay attention or respond. In addition, advertising can be very costly. Although some advertising forms, such as newspaper and radio advertising, can be done on smaller budgets, other forms, such as network TV advertising, require very large budgets.

Personal Selling. Personal selling is the most effective tool at certain stages of the buying process, particularly in building up buyers' preferences, convictions, and actions. It involves personal interaction between two or more people, so each person can observe the other's needs and characteristics and make quick adjustments. Personal selling also allows all kinds of customer relationships to spring up, ranging from matter-of-fact selling relationships to personal friendships. An effective salesperson keeps the customer's interests at heart to build a long-term relationship by solving a customer's problems. ● Finally, with personal selling, the buyer usually feels a greater need to listen and respond, even if the response is a polite "No thank-you."

These unique qualities come at a cost, however. A sales force requires a longer-term commitment than does advertising—although advertising can be turned up or down, the size of a sales force is harder to change. Personal selling is also the company's most expensive promotion tool, costing companies on average $350 or more per sales call, depending on the industry.[18] U.S. firms spend up to three times as much on personal selling as they do on advertising.

Sales Promotion. Sales promotion includes a wide assortment of tools—coupons, contests, discounts, premiums, and others—all of which have many unique qualities. They attract consumer attention, offer strong incentives to purchase, and can be used to dramatize product offers and boost sagging sales. Sales promotions invite and reward quick response. Whereas advertising says, "Buy our product," sales promotion says, "Buy it now." Sales promotion effects are often short lived, however, and often are not as effective as advertising or personal selling in building long-run brand preference and customer relationships.

Public Relations. Public relations is very believable—news stories, features, sponsorships, and events seem more real and believable to readers than ads do. PR can also reach many prospects who avoid salespeople and advertisements—the message gets to buyers as "news" rather than as a sales-directed communication. And, as with advertising, public relations can dramatize a company or product. Marketers tend to underuse public relations or use it as an afterthought. Yet a well-thought-out public relations campaign used with other promotion mix elements can be very effective and economical.

Direct Marketing. Although there are many forms of direct marketing—direct mail and catalogs, online marketing, mobile marketing, and others—they all share four distinctive characteristics. Direct marketing is less public: The message is normally directed to a specific person. Direct marketing is immediate and customized: Messages can be prepared very quickly and can be tailored to appeal to specific consumers. Finally, direct marketing is interactive: It allows a dialogue between the marketing team and the consumer, and messages can be altered depending on the consumer's response. Thus, direct marketing is well suited to highly targeted marketing efforts and building one-to-one customer relationships.

Push strategy

A promotion strategy that calls for using the sales force and trade promotion to push the product through channels. The producer promotes the product to channel members, which in turn promote it to final consumers.

Promotion Mix Strategies

Marketers can choose from two basic promotion mix strategies: *push* promotion or *pull* promotion. ● **Figure 14.4** contrasts the two strategies. The relative emphasis given to the specific promotion tools differs for push and pull strategies. A **push strategy** involves "pushing" the product through marketing channels to final consumers. The producer directs its marketing activities (primarily personal selling and trade promotion) toward

FIGURE | 14.4
Push versus Pull Promotion Strategy

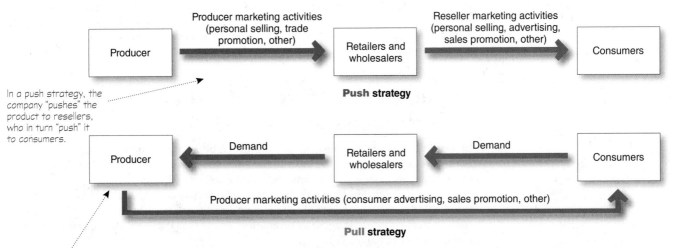

In a push strategy, the company "pushes" the product to resellers, who in turn "push" it to consumers.

Push strategy

In a pull strategy, the company promotes directly to final consumers, creating a demand vacuum that "pulls" the product through the channel. Most companies use some combination of push and pull.

Pull strategy

Pull strategy

A promotion strategy that calls for spending a lot on consumer advertising and promotion to induce final consumers to buy the product, creating a demand vacuum that "pulls" the product through the channel.

channel members to induce them to carry the product and promote it to final consumers. For example, John Deere does very little promoting of its lawn mowers, garden tractors, and other residential consumer products to final consumers. Instead, John Deere's sales force works with Lowe's, Home Depot, independent dealers, and other channel members, who in turn push John Deere products to final consumers.

Using a **pull strategy**, the producer directs its marketing activities (primarily advertising and consumer promotion) toward final consumers to induce them to buy the product. For example, Unilever promotes its Axe grooming products directly to its young male target market using TV and print ads, a brand Web site, its YouTube channel and Facebook page, and other channels. If the pull strategy is effective, consumers will then demand the brand from retailers, such as CVS, Walgreens, or Walmart, which will in turn demand it from Unilever. Thus, under a pull strategy, consumer demand "pulls" the product through the channels.

Some industrial-goods companies use only push strategies; likewise, some direct marketing companies use only pull strategies. However, most large companies use some combination of both. For example, Unilever spends more than $8 billion worldwide each year on consumer marketing and sales promotions to create brand preference and pull customers into stores that carry its products.[19] At the same time, it uses its own and distributors' sales forces and trade promotions to push its brands through the channels, so that they will be available on store shelves when consumers come calling.

Companies consider many factors when designing their promotion mix strategies, including the type of product and market. For example, the importance of different promotion tools varies between consumer and business markets. Business-to-consumer companies usually pull more, putting more of their funds into advertising, followed by sales promotion, personal selling, and then public relations. In contrast, business-to-business marketers tend to push more, putting more of their funds into personal selling, followed by sales promotion, advertising, and public relations.

Now that we've examined the concept of integrated marketing communications and the factors that firms consider when shaping their promotion mixes, let's look more closely at the specific marketing communications tools.

Integrating the Promotion Mix

Having set the promotion budget and mix, the company must now take steps to see that each promotion mix element is smoothly integrated. Guided by the company's overall communications strategy, the various promotion elements should work together to carry the firm's unique brand messages and selling points. Integrating the promotion mix starts with customers. Whether it's advertising, personal selling, sales promotion, public relations, or direct marketing, communications at each customer touchpoint must deliver consistent messages and positioning. An integrated promotion mix ensures that communications efforts occur when, where, and how *customers* need them.

To achieve an integrated promotion mix, all of the firm's functions must cooperate to jointly plan communications efforts. Many companies even include customers, suppliers, and other stakeholders at various stages of communications planning. Scattered or disjointed promotional activities across the company can result in diluted marketing communications impact and confused positioning. By contrast, an integrated promotion mix maximizes the combined effects of all a firm's promotional efforts.

Socially Responsible Marketing Communication

In shaping its promotion mix, a company must be aware of the many legal and ethical issues surrounding marketing communications. Most marketers work hard to communicate openly and honestly with consumers and resellers. Still, abuses may occur, and public policy makers have developed a substantial body of laws and regulations to govern advertising, sales promotion, personal selling, and direct marketing. In this section, we discuss issues regarding advertising, sales promotion, and personal selling. We discuss direct marketing issues in Chapter 17.

Advertising and Sales Promotion

By law, companies must avoid false or deceptive advertising. Advertisers must not make false claims, such as suggesting that a product cures something when it does not. They must avoid ads that have the capacity to deceive, even though no one actually may be deceived. An automobile cannot be advertised as getting 32 miles per gallon unless it does so under typical conditions, and a diet bread cannot be advertised as having fewer calories simply because its slices are thinner.

Sellers must avoid bait-and-switch advertising that attracts buyers under false pretenses. For example, a large retailer advertised a sewing machine at $179. However, when consumers tried to buy the advertised machine, the seller downplayed its features, placed faulty machines on showroom floors, understated the machine's performance, and took other actions in an attempt to switch buyers to a more expensive machine. Such actions are both unethical and illegal.

A company's trade promotion activities also are closely regulated. For example, under the Robinson-Patman Act, sellers cannot favor certain customers through their use of trade promotions. They must make promotional allowances and services available to all resellers on proportionately equal terms.

● Promoting socially responsible programs and actions: To help restore tourism along the Gulf Coast, BP's MyGulf campaign features local spokespeople discussing their state's great beaches, fishing, and seafood and extending an invitation to vacation along the coast.

BP p.l.c.

Beyond simply avoiding legal pitfalls, such as deceptive or bait-and-switch advertising, companies can use advertising and other forms of promotion to encourage and promote socially responsible programs and actions. For example, following the explosion and oil spill at the Deepwater Horizon oil rig in the Gulf of Mexico in 2010, BP has spent billions of dollars on Gulf Coast restoration efforts. The efforts include a 3-year "Voices from the Gulf" promotion campaign designed to help restore tourism along the Gulf Coast. The integrated television, online, and social media campaign features spokespeople from the Gulf Coast states discussing their states' great beaches, fishing, and seafood and extending an invitation to vacation along the coast. ● In addition to the tourism series, BP has also been running an online MyGulf campaign featuring videos of people who live and work in the Gulf. Thanks in part to the BP-sponsored promotion campaigns, despite the still-sluggish economy, tourism in many Gulf Coast areas has now surpassed pre-spill levels.[20]

Personal Selling

A company's salespeople must follow the rules of "fair competition." Most states have enacted deceptive sales acts that spell out what is not allowed. For example, salespeople may not lie to consumers or mislead them about the advantages of buying a particular product. To avoid bait-and-switch practices, salespeople's statements must match advertising claims.

Different rules apply to consumers who are called on at home or who buy at a location that is not the seller's permanent place of business versus those who go to a store in search of a product. Because people who are called on may be taken by surprise and may be especially vulnerable to high-pressure selling techniques, the Federal Trade Commission (FTC) has adopted a *three-day cooling-off rule* to give special protection to customers who are not seeking products. Under this rule, customers who agree in their own homes, workplace, dormitory, or facilities rented by the seller on a temporary basis—such as hotel rooms, convention centers, and restaurants—to buy something costing more than $25 have 72 hours in which to cancel a contract or return merchandise and get their money back—no questions asked.

Much personal selling involves business-to-business trade. In selling to businesses, salespeople may not offer bribes to purchasing agents or others who can influence a sale. They may not obtain or use technical or trade secrets of competitors through bribery or industrial espionage. Finally, salespeople must not disparage competitors or competing products by suggesting things that are not true.

Reviewing the Concepts

MyMarketingLab™
Go to **mymktlab.com** to complete the problems marked with this icon .

Reviewing Objectives and Key Terms

 ## Objectives Review

In this chapter, you learned how companies use integrated marketing communications (IMC) to communicate customer value. Modern marketing calls for more than just creating customer value by developing a good product, pricing it attractively, and making it available to target customers. Companies also must clearly and persuasively *communicate* that value to current and prospective customers. To do this, they must blend five promotion mix tools, guided by a well-designed and implemented IMC strategy.

Objective 1 | Define the five promotion mix tools for communicating customer value. (pp 406–407)

A company's total *promotion mix*—also called its *marketing communications mix*—consists of the specific blend of *advertising, personal selling, sales promotion, public relations,* and *direct marketing* tools that the company uses to persuasively communicate customer value and build customer relationships. *Advertising* includes any paid form of nonpersonal presentation and promotion of ideas, goods, or services by an identified sponsor. In contrast, *public relations* focuses on building good relations with the company's various publics. *Personal selling* is personal presentation by the firm's sales force for the purpose of making sales and building customer relationships. Firms use *sales promotion* to provide short-term incentives to encourage the

purchase or sale of a product or service. Finally, firms seeking immediate response from targeted individual customers use *direct marketing* tools to communicate with customers and cultivate relationships with them.

Objective 2 | Discuss the changing communications landscape and the need for integrated marketing communications. (pp 407–412)

The explosive developments in communications technology and changes in marketer and customer communication strategies have had a dramatic impact on marketing communications. Advertisers are now adding a broad selection of more-specialized and highly targeted media—including digital and online media—to reach smaller customer segments with more-personalized, interactive messages. As they adopt richer but more fragmented media and promotion mixes to reach their diverse markets, they risk creating a communications hodgepodge for consumers. To prevent this, companies are adopting the concept of *integrated marketing communications (IMC)*. Guided by an overall IMC strategy, the company works out the roles that the various promotional tools will play and the extent to which each will be used. It carefully coordinates the promotional activities and the timing of when major campaigns take place.

Objective 3 Outline the communication process and the steps in developing effective marketing communications. (pp 412–418)

The communication process involves nine elements: two major parties (sender, receiver), two communication tools (message, media), four communication functions (encoding, decoding, response, and feedback), and noise. To communicate effectively, marketers must understand how these elements combine to communicate value to target customers.

In preparing marketing communications, the communicator's first task is to *identify the target audience* and its characteristics. Next, the communicator has to determine the *communication objectives* and define the response sought, whether it be *awareness*, *knowledge*, *liking*, *preference*, *conviction*, or *purchase*. Then a *message* should be constructed with an effective content and structure. *Media* must be selected, both for personal and nonpersonal communication. The communicator must find highly credible sources to deliver messages. Finally, the communicator must collect *feedback* by watching how much of the market becomes aware, tries the product, and is satisfied in the process.

Objective 4 Explain the methods for setting the promotion budget and factors that affect the design of the promotion mix. (pp 418–425)

The company must determine how much to spend for promotion. The most popular approaches are to spend what the company can afford, use a percentage of sales, base promotion on competitors' spending, or base it on an analysis and costing of the communication objectives and tasks. The company has to divide the *promotion budget* among the major tools to create the *promotion mix*. Companies can pursue a *push* or a *pull* promotional strategy—or a combination of the two. The best specific blend of promotion tools depends on the type of product/market, the buyer's readiness stage, and the PLC stage. People at all levels of the organization must be aware of the many legal and ethical issues surrounding marketing communications. Companies must work hard and proactively at communicating openly, honestly, and agreeably with their customers and resellers.

 # Key Terms

Objective 1

Promotion mix (marketing communications mix) (p 407)
Advertising (p 407)
Sales promotion (p 407)
Personal selling (p 407)
Public relations (PR) (p 407)
Direct marketing (p 407)

Objective 2

Integrated marketing communications (IMC) (p 409)

Objective 3

Buyer-readiness stages (p 414)
Personal communication channels (p 416)
Word-of-mouth influence (p 416)
Buzz marketing (p 417)
Nonpersonal communication channels (p 417)

Objective 4

Affordable method (p 420)
Percentage-of-sales method (p 420)
Competitive-parity method (p 421)
Objective-and-task method (p 421)
Push strategy (p 422)
Pull strategy (p 423)

Discussion and Critical Thinking

 # Discussion Questions

1. List and briefly describe the five major promotion mix tools. (AACSB: Communication)

✪ 2. Discuss the external factors that impact an organization's marketing communication function. Will traditional mass-media advertising soon be dead, as some have predicted? (AACSB: Communication; Reflective Thinking)

3. Name and briefly describe the nine elements of the communications process. Why do marketers need to understand these elements? (AACSB: Communication; Reflective Thinking)

4. Name and describe the four promotion budgeting methods and discuss the pros and cons of each. Which method is best? (AACSB: Communication; Reflective Thinking)

5. Compare and contrast personal and nonpersonal communication channels. (AACSB: Communication)

◗ Critical Thinking Exercises

1. In a small group, develop an integrated marketing communications plan for a local business or nonprofit organization. Does your plan employ a push or pull promotion strategy? Explain. (AACSB: Communication; Reflective Thinking)

2. Find three examples of advertisements that incorporate socially responsible marketing in the message. Some companies are criticized for exploiting social issues or organizations by promoting them for their own gain. Do the examples you found do that? Explain. (AACSB: Communication; Ethical Reasoning; Reflective Thinking)

Applications **and** Cases

◗ Marketing Technology Online-Advertising Auctions

Have you ever wondered how ads for relevant brands and businesses pop up around Google search results or appear on just about every site you visit on the Internet? Advertisers pay to have these ads placed based on your keyword searches, your Web-surfing behavior, and even what you post on Facebook or write in Gmail messages. While concerns over privacy mount, the online tracking industry just keeps ramping up. Krux Digital reports that the average visit to a Web page generated 56 instances of data collection, representing a five-fold increase from the previous year. A 2010 investigation by the *Wall Street Journal* found that the 50 most popular U.S. Web sites installed more than 3,000 tracking files on the computer used in the study. The total was even higher—4,123 tracking files—for the top 50 sites that are popular with children and teens. Many sites installed more than 100 tracking tools each during the tests. Tracking tools include files placed on users' computers and on Web sites. Marketers use this information to target online advertisements. But this wouldn't be possible without online-ad auctions. When a user visits a Web page, that information is auctioned among computers to the highest bidder. Bids are based on the user's Internet browsing behavior. The bidder in such an auction is a technology broker acting on behalf of the advertiser. Real-time bidding makes up 18 percent of the online display ad market, and bids sell for less than $1 per thousand viewers. Web-tracking provides the user data to sell in the auction, and more than 300 companies are gathering this data. Data collectors often share information with each other, called "piggybacking," so they have more information about a Web site's user than the owner—the ad seller—of a Web site has.

1. Write a report explaining how online-ad auctions work and the impact they have on Internet advertising. (AACSB: Communication; Reflective Thinking)

2. Critics claim that Internet tracking infringes consumer privacy rights and that the industry is out of control. Should marketers have access to such information? Discuss the advantages and disadvantages of this activity for both marketers and consumers. (AACSB Communication; Ethical Reasoning; Reflective Thinking)

◗ Marketing Ethics Advertising Claims

Several well-known companies are making headlines after paying huge fines to settle deceptive advertising complaints with the Federal Trade Commission (FTC). Skechers, the leading toning shoe company, agreed to pay $40 million to settle charges of unsubstantiated claims. Skechers made billions claiming its shoes were more effective in toning posture and buttock muscles compared to regular walking and running shoes. Celebrities such as Kim Kardashian and Joe Montana endorsed the products. The FTC said the study on which the claims were based did not even conclude what was claimed in the ads. Not helping Skechers' case was the fact that the study was conducted by the husband of a Skechers marketing executive. Reebok, after making similar claims, settled with the FTC for $25 million. Other well-known companies recently settling with the FTC over deceptive advertising claims are POM, Dannon, Oreck, and Nivea. Dannon settled for $45 million after featuring Jamie Lee Curtis touting the digestive regularity benefits of Activia yogurt. Oreck and Nivea got off relatively cheap. Oreck had to pay only $750,000 to settle the complaint against its claim that its vacuum's ultraviolet light and filter killed and trapped flu and other germs, and Nivea had to pay only $900,000 to settle the complaint against claims that its My Silhouette! skin cream reduced a user's body size.

1. Research the FTC's deceptive advertising policy and report on another case involving substantiation of specific claims. (AACSB: Communication; Reflective Thinking)

2. The advertising industry has established the National Advertising Division (www.NAD.org), which oversees a self-regulatory process administered by the Council of Better Business Bureaus. Compare and contrast how this body resolves deceptive advertising cases with how the FTC handles cases, and then report on a case handled by this process. (AACSB: Communication; Reflective Thinking)

Marketing by the Numbers Advertising-to-Sales Ratios

Using the percent of sales method, an advertiser sets its budget at a certain percentage of current or forecasted sales. However, determining what percentage to use is not always clear. Many marketers look at industry averages and competitor spending for comparisons, and companies such as Schonfeld & Associates provide annual reports on advertising-to-sales ratios by industry. While this information is published in proprietary reports, many Web sites and trade publications, such as *Advertising Age*, publish summary data regarding industry averages as well as advertising-to-sales ratios for top advertisers.

1. Find advertising-to-sales ratios for four different industries for the past 10 years or more. Try to find as much data as possible for this period, but be sure to find enough data to indicate the trend in advertising-to-sales ratios for each industry. Develop a chart illustrating these trends and offer reasons for the trends. (AACSB: Communication; Use of IT)

2. Explain why there is variation in the percentage of sales spent on advertising among the four industries. (AACSB: Communication; Reflective Thinking)

 # Video Case OXO

For over 20 years, OXO has put its well-known kitchen gadgets into almost every home in the United States through word-of-mouth, product placement, and other forms of nontraditional promotional techniques. But OXO has decided to enter the world of broadcast advertising as it attempts to meet the challenges of a more competitive environment.

This video demonstrates how a successful company can remain on top through modifying its promotional mix. With its Good Grips, SteeL, Candela, Tot, and Staples/OXO brands, OXO has expanded its advertising efforts with a major new campaign and, in the process, is proving that good-old advertising is still a good bet.

After viewing the video featuring OXO, answer the following questions:

1. Why has OXO chosen to change its promotional strategy at this time?

2. Describe OXO's overall advertising strategy.

3. Is OXO abandoning its old promotional methods? How is OXO blending a new advertising strategy with the promotional techniques that have made it a success?

 # Company Case Red Bull: A Different Kind of Integrated Campaign

It's a calm day in the desert town of Roswell, New Mexico. Thirteen miles above the ground, a giant helium balloon ascends with a space capsule tethered beneath it. The capsule door slides open, revealing the Earth as a sphere—the curve of the horizon bending dramatically around the planet, the sky above almost black. A man in a full space suit steps onto a small platform and secures his footing. Then, with a quick salute to the camera, he jumps.

A NASA test? No. It's the latest promotional effort from Red Bull—another extreme stunt designed to evoke reactions of shock and awe while driving home the now famous slogan, "Red Bull Gives You Wings." Today, through a bevy of other such events, Red Bull's message is broadcast far and wide via an army of celebrity endorsers as well as sports, music, and entertainment event sponsorships. Red Bull is not the most conventional marketer. It spreads its brand message across an eclectic mix of promotional efforts while largely shunning traditional media. But the manner in which Red Bull has integrated its diverse messages is a model of success that cuts straight to the heart of building deep emotional connections with customers.

An Unlikely Start
It all started about 30 years ago when Austrian toothpaste salesman Dietrich Mateschitz traveled to Thailand. While there, he tried a "tonic" called Krating Daeng—Thai for "water buffalo." It tasted terrible but instantly cured his jet lag. One thing led to another, and within a few years Mateschitz and a partner had acquired the rights to sell the formula throughout the rest of the world. They named it Red Bull.

From the beginning, nothing about Red Bull was conventional. The slim blue-and-silver can, emblazoned with two muscular red bulls about to smash heads in front of a yellow sun, was unlike anything on the market. At 8.3 ounces, so was its size. With mystical ingredients such as taurine and glucuronolactone, and a sickeningly sweet taste often described as "liquid Sweet Tarts" or "cough medicine in a can," the drink didn't fit any established beverage category. And with a $2 price tag, Red Bull was by far the most expensive carbonated beverage on any shelf. But with that unlikely combination, Red Bull gave birth to the energy drink category.

Mateschitz launched Red Bull in native Austria under the only slogan to ever accompany the brand, "Red Bull Gives You Wings." The moment he heard it, Mateschitz knew that this slogan would be the core of Red Bull's brand image. He didn't care about the product's taste. "It's not just another flavored sugar water differentiated by color or taste or flavor," he says. "It's an efficiency product. I'm talking about improving endurance, concentration, reaction time, speed, vigilance, and emotional status. Taste is of no importance whatsoever." Despite negative initial product reviews, Red Bull's young male target market agreed. Sales in Europe were positively bullish.

An Unlikely Promotional Program

As head of a young company without much of an advertising budget, Mateschitz continued in his unorthodox ways when launching Red Bull in the United States in 1997. He bucked the trend of aggressive and excessive promotional campaigns flaunted by other start-ups in the 1990s. Instead, his young, attractive army of marketers tossed out free cans of Red Bull from a fleet of shiny logo-bearing off-roaders with giant cans attached to the trunk. Word of mouth took care of the rest. In this manner, Mateschitz introduced Red Bull to the masses and built a brand image for next to nothing.

As a product that thrived on grassroots marketing, Red Bull depended on word of mouth. As word about Red Bull spread throughout Europe's all-night-party circuit, so did rumors. Tales circulated that taurine was a derivative of bull testicles or even bull semen. Even worse, there were rumors that young people had died while partying too hard and drinking too much Red Bull. Although none of these rumors was ever substantiated, Mateschitz is convinced that one of the most important promotional techniques the company ever employed was to let the rumors fly and say nothing. "In the beginning, the high-school teachers who were against the product were at least as important as the students who were for it," said Mateschitz. "Newspapers asked, 'Is it a drug? Is it harmless? Is it dangerous?' That ambivalence is so important. The most dangerous thing for a branded product is low interest."

Bit by bit, Red Bull's portfolio of promotional weapons grew. At times, the company dabbled in TV and print advertising. But Red Bull's primary tactics have steered clear of such mainstream techniques. Instead, it was Mateschitz's plan to promote the brand in a way that would go way beyond reach and frequency of coverage. He wanted the brand to hit young people right in the face in a way that they experienced Red Bull to the fullest. He wanted to engage customers through activities so meaningful to them that deep relationships would form quickly.

With that philosophy, Red Bull's promotional mix evolved into what it is today. The following descriptions are just a sample of Red Bull's promotional techniques.

Athletes and Teams. With the claim that Red Bull improves athletic performance at the center of its promotional message, the brand took a page right out of the book used by Nike and Gatorade and began signing up athlete endorsers early on. Today, Red Bull sponsors more than 500 athletes—100 in the United States—in 97 sports, mostly "extreme" sports. And sticking with its unconventional ways, Red Bull brings these athletes into the "family" with nothing more than a verbal agreement to "support" them in achieving their dreams. Today, Red Bull's family includes such top-tier athletes as Shaun White and Travis Pastrana as well as niche athletes such as courier-style bike racer Austin Horse and wind surfer Levi Siver. Whenever these athletes make official public appearances, the Red Bull name or logo is visible somewhere on their person.

But Red Bull's endorsement strategy goes beyond propping individual athletes. Red Bull owns four soccer teams: New York's Red Bulls, Red Bull Salzburg, Red Bull Brazil, and RB Leipzig. The brand also owns a NASCAR team and two Formula 1 racing teams. Many have asserted that team ownership is merely a hobby for Mateschitz, noting that none of these teams makes money. But Mateschitz says that misses the point. "In literal financial terms, our sports teams are not yet profitable, but in value

terms, they are," he says. "The total editorial media value plus the media assets created around the teams are superior to pure advertising expenditures."

Sports Events. As Red Bull built relationships through athletes and teams, it wasn't long before it began sponsoring events. Today, Red Bull has its name on dozens of major annual events, including the Red Bull U.S. Grand Prix (MotoGP), Red Bull Wake Open (wake boarding), Red Bull Rampage (mountain biking), and Red Bull Sharpshooters (basketball). With such event sponsorships, Red Bull has more than once invented an entirely new sport.

Consider Red Bull Crashed Ice, a world tour winter extreme sport. It's similar to ski cross or snowboard cross—only with skates, on ice. In this sport, some of the toughest ice hockey players in the world jockey for position at speeds of up to 40 miles per hour. But the real catch is that the race takes place in a 500-meter ice canal filled with bumps, jumps, berms, and other obstacles. The cameras capture all the action as competitors race past screaming fans and Red Bull banners.

Music and Entertainment. Recognizing that its target customers weren't "all sports all the time," Red Bull extended its strategy for endorsements and events to the world of music and entertainment. With its penchant for sniffing out the unique, Red Bull sponsors artists, teams, and events in dance, music, film, video games, and other creative media. Red Bull Flying Bach is a performance troupe that wraps breakdancing around the music of Bach. The Red Bull Canvas Cooler is a nationwide invitational competition for top artists to redesign the iconic Red Bull cooler. And Red Bull Common Thread is a new concept on the concert circuit—back-to-back performances by bands that shared members at different points in their evolution.

Programming. As the producer of such TV programs as *No Limits* on ESPN and such films as *That's It, That's All*, Red Bull is not new to media production. But in perhaps its most ambitious undertaking yet, Red Bull has created Red Bull Media House— "the centre of the global Red Bull media network" and "your gateway into the World of Red Bull." The network spans TV, print, mobile, digital, and music. With this move, Red Bull has defined itself as a major multimedia content provider.

As just one example of how extensive this network is, consider the music arm of Red Bull Media House. Nothing short of a complete music division, it includes Red Bull Publishing (a hub for all music and audio generated in the Red Bull Media House), Red Bull Records (its own music label), and Red Bull Radio Services (an Internet-based radio network and original shows). Through this music media network, Red Bull puts its brand at the center of a cooperative of companies, brands, and artists, encouraging them to take part in Red Bull's resources.

Multiplying this across the other major media in the Red Bull Media House network, it's clear that Mateschitz sees Red Bull not as a beverage brand, but as a global lifestyle brand with boundaries that have not yet been reached. He calls the recent multimedia assault "our most important line extension so far," with the goal to "communicate and distribute the 'World of Red Bull' in all major media segments." As with all the other promotional ventures, Mateschitz hopes Red Bull Media House will turn a profit. But as with his sport teams, he's willing to be patient and bank on the promotional value of these activities.

Doing It All for Customers

Felix Baumgartner's successful jump from 17 miles up was only a dry run. When he made the real jump later in the year, it was from the stratosphere, 23 miles above sea level. In the process, he broke four world records: the highest manned balloon flight, the highest skydive, the longest freefall, and the first parachutist to break the sound barrier. He also tested the next-generation space suit to be worn by astronauts. And the Red Bull brand was plastered all over the entire event. But more than promotional coverage, this feat served the same purpose that all other Red Bull promotions serve—to forge deep relationships with customers through emotional experiences.

From its unlikely origins, Red Bull has grown into a massive enterprise. Last year, the company sold 4.2 billion cans of the drink with revenues of more than $5 billion, a 16 percent increase over the year before. As Red Bull's growth continues, Mateschitz has no intention of slowing down. In fact, he confesses, he has always been attracted to the idea of creating an independent nation state—the country of Red Bull. "The rules would be simple. Nobody tells you what you have to do—only what you don't have to do."

Questions for Discussion

1. List all the ways that Red Bull's promotional efforts are unique from those of the mainstream.

2. Which promotional mix elements does Red Bull use? What grade would you give Red Bull on integrating these elements into a core marketing communications campaign?

3. Will Red Bull eventually need to embrace more traditional media marketing techniques in order to keep growing? Why or why not?

4. Describe Red Bull's target audience. Are Red Bull's promotional techniques consistent with that audience?

5. At some point, will Red Bull have to branch out beyond its target market? Will it need to alter its promotional strategy in order to do so?

Source: "Felix Baumgartner Prepares for Daredevil Freefall from 17 Miles," *Fox News*, July 24, 2012, www.foxnews.com/scitech/2012/07/24/final-test-jump-from-edge-space-set-for-tuesday/; "Red Bull's Adrenaline Marketing Mastermind Pushes into Media," *Business Week*, May 19, 2011, www.bloomberg.com/news/print/2011-05-19/red-bull-s-adrenaline-marketing-billionaire-mastermind.html; and other information found at www.redbullusa.com and www.redbullmediahouse.com, accessed August 2012.

MyMarketingLab

Go to **mymktlab.com** for Auto-graded writing questions as well as the following Assisted-graded writing questions:

14-1. Discuss the legal and ethical issues regarding advertising, sales promotion, and personal selling. (AACSB: Communication)

14-2. Select an advertisement for a national brand. What type of appeal is the advertiser using? Describe the message structure used. Create an advertisement for the brand that communicates the same information but uses a different type of appeal and message structure. (AACSB: Communication; Reflective Thinking)

14-3. Mymktlab Only – comprehensive writing assignment for this chapter.

References

1. Based on information from "The Cow Campaign: A Brief History," www.chick-fil-a.com/Cows/Campaign-History, accessed July 2012; "Company Fact Sheet," www.chick-fil-a.com/Company/Highlights-Fact-Sheets, accessed July 2012; Thomas Pardee, "Armed with a Beloved Product and a Strong Commitment to Customer Service, Fast Feeder Continues to Grow," *Advertising Age*, October 18, 2010, http://adage.com/article/146491/; Emily Bryson York, "Game of Chicken Against Leader Pays Off for Chick-fil-A, Popeyes," *Advertising Age*, May 3, 2010, http://adage.com/article/143642/; Brian Morrissey, "Chick-fil-A's Strategy: Give Your Fans Something to Do," *AdWeek*, October 3, 2009, www.adweek.com/print/106477; and information from various other pages and press releases at www.chick-fil-a.com and www.chick-fil-a.com/Pressroom/Press-Releases, accessed November, 2012.

2. For other definitions, see www.marketingpower.com/_layouts/Dictionary.aspx, accessed November 2012.

3. See Martin Peers, "Television's Fuzzy Ad Picture," *Wall Street Journal*, May 10, 2011, p. C22; Lisa Waananen, "How Agencies Are Spending OnlineMediaBudgets,"Mashable.com,June9,2011,http://mashable.com/2011/06/09/media-agency-budgets/; and "U.S. Online Ad Spend to Close in on $40 Billion," *eMarketer*, January 19, 2012, www.emarketer.com/Article.aspx?id=1008783&R=1008783.

4. See Andrew Adam Newman, "Ketchup Moves Upmarket, with a Balsamic Tinge," *New York Times*, October 25, 2011, p. B3; and "Heinz Tomato Ketchup Blended with Balsamic Vinegar Satisfies Fan Hunger as Newest Member of Heinz Ketchup's Standard Line Up," *Business Wire*, May 1, 2012.

5. This example is based on information from Stuart Elliott, "Ad for Method Celebrate the Madness," *New York Times*, March 12, 2012, p. B1.

6. "100 Leading National Advertisers," *Advertising Age*, June 20, 2012, p. 10.

7. David Gelles, "Advertisers Rush to Master Fresh Set of Skills," *Financial Times*, March 7, 2012, www.ft.com/intl/cms/s/0/8383bbae-5e20-11e1-b1e9-00144feabdc0.html#axzz1xUrmM3KK; "Online Ad Spend to Overtake TV by 2016," *Forbes*, August 26, 2011, www.forbes.com/sites/roberthof/2011/08/26/online-ad-spend-to-overtake-tv/; and "U.S. Online Ad Spend to Close in on $40 Billion," *eMarketer,* January 19, 2012, www.emarketer.com/Article.aspx?id=1008783&R=1008783.

8. See Jon Lafayette, "4A's Conference: Agencies Urged to Embrace New Technologies," *Broadcasting & Cable,* March 8, 2011, www.broadcastingcable.com/article/464951-4A_s_Conference_Agencies_Urged_To_Embrace_New_Technologies.php; and Gelles, "Advertisers Rush to Master Fresh Set of Skills," *Financial Times,* March 7, 2012, www.ft.com/intl/cms/s/0/8383bbae-5e20-11e1-b1e9-00144feabdc0.html#axzz1xUrmM3KK.

9. See "Integrated Campaigns: Häagen-Dazs," *Communication Arts Advertising Annual 2009,* pp. 158–159; Tiffany Meyers, "Marketing 50: Häagen-Dazs, Katty Pien," *Advertising Age,* November 17, 2008, p. S15; "Häagen-Dazs Loves Honey Bees," April 28, 2010, a summary video accessed at http://limeshot.com/2010/haagen-dazs-loves-honey-bees-titanium-silver-lion-cannes-2009; Alan Bjerga, "U.S. Queen Bees Work Overtime to Save Hives," *Bloomberg Businessweek,* April 3, 2011, pp. 27–28; and information from www.helpthehoneybees.com, accessed October 2012.

10. See Stuart Elliott, "A Product to Add Sparkle and Pop to Laundry Day," *New York Times,* February 15, 2012, p. B3.

11. Jonah Bloom, "The Truth Is: Consumers Trust Fellow Buyers Before Marketers," *Advertising Age,* February 13, 2006, p. 25; and "Jack Morton Publishes New Realities 2012 Research," press release, January 26, 2012, www.jackmorton.com/news/article.aspx?itemID=106.

12. See Jack Neff, "P&G's Buzz-Building Networks Thrive in Age of Social Networks," *Advertising Age,* October 10, 2011, p. 19; and www.vocalpoint.com//index.html and www.tremor.com/Revealing-Case-Studies/Bounce-Dryer-Bar/, accessed November 2012.

13. See Lacey Rose, "The 10 Most Trusted Celebrities," *Forbes,* February 8, 2011, accessed at www.forbes.com/2011/02/07/most-trustworthy-celebrities-business-entertainment.html; and Noreen O'Leary "Ad of the Day: Burger King," *Adweek,* April 3, 2012, www.adweek.com/print/139384.

14. T. L. Stanley, "Dancing with the Stars," *Brandweek,* March 8, 2010, pp. 10–12. Also see Pam Garfield, "The Very Public Risks of Celebrity Endorsements," *Medial Marketing & Media,* March 1, 2012, www.mmm-online.com/the-very-public-risks-of-celebrity-endorsements/article/229009/; and Mo Moumenine, "Using Celebrity Endorsement in Social Media, IncresaseRSS, February 17, 2012, http://increas-erss.com/using-celebrity-endorsement-in-social-media/.

15. For more on advertising spending by company and industry, see "Datacenter: Advertising Sepnding," *Advertising Age,* June 28, 2012, http://adage.com/article/ 106575/.

16. For more on setting promotion budgets, see W. Ronald Lane, Karen Whitehill King, and J. Thomas Russell, *Kleppner's Advertising Procedure,* 18th ed. (Upper Saddle River, NJ: Prentice Hall, 2011), chapter 6.

17. See Christopher S. Stewart, "Super Bowl Viewers Set Record," *Wall Street Journal,* February 6, 2012; Lisa de Moraes, "Oscar 2012 Ratings: About 39 Million Viewers," *Washington Post,* February 27, 2012; and Verne Gray, "American Idol: 21.6 Million Viewers," *Newsday,* January 19, 2012, www.newsday.com/entertainment/tv/tv-zone-1.811968/american-idol-21-6-million-viewers-1.3464121.

18. See discussions at "The Costs of Personal Selling," April 13, 2011, www.seekarticle.com/business-sales/personal-selling.html; and "What Is the Real Cost of a B2B Sales Call?" www.marketing-playbook.com/sales-marketing-strategy/what-is-the-real-cost-of-a-b2b-sales-call, October 2012.

19. Jack Neff, "Unilever Cuts Agency, Production Spending as Ad Costs Rise," *Advertising Age,* February 2, 2012, http://adage.com/article//232485/.

20. See "New Ads Promote Tourism along the Gulf Coast," http://www.bp.com/sectiongenericarticle.do?categoryId=9039335&contentId=7072076; "Restoring the Economy: Promoting Tourism along the Gulf Coast," *Gulf of Mexico Restoration,* p. 7, http://bp.com/gulfofmexico, accessed November 2012.

15

Advertising and Public Relations

Chapter Preview After an analysis of overall IMC planning, we dig more deeply into the specific marketing communications tools. In this chapter, we explore advertising and public relations (PR). Advertising involves communicating the company's or brand's value proposition by using paid media to inform, persuade, and remind consumers. PR involves building good relations with various company publics— from consumers and the general public to the media, investor, donor, and government publics. As with all the promotion mix tools, advertising and PR must be blended into the overall IMC program. In Chapters 16 and 17, we will discuss the remaining promotion mix tools: personal selling, sales promotion, and direct marketing.

Let's start with the question: Does advertising really make a difference? Auto insurance companies certainly must think so. Market leader State Farm spends more than $800 million a year on advertising and number two Allstate spends more than $500 million a year; number three GEICO runs up a whopping $1 billion annual advertising bill. Combined, auto insurers now spend more than $4 billion every year getting their messages out. All that spending—plus ever-more-creative ad campaigns—has created an auto insurance advertising war. To stay in the fight, Allstate has created its own brand of advertising mayhem.

Allstate: Bringing Mayhem to the Auto Insurance Advertising Wars

In its current advertising campaign, Allstate Insurance brings mayhem to life—literally. Played by actor Dean Winters, the creepy Mayhem character portrays all of the unlikely events that can lead to a major auto insurance claim. As a deer, he jumps into the path of a moving car at night, "because that's what we deer do." As a torrential downpour, he loves leaky sunroofs. As a malfunctioning GPS, he sends a driver swerving into another car. As snow, he weighs down the roof of a garage until it collapses, smashing the car within. Each quirky ad ends with the statement and question, "If you have cut-rate insurance, you could be paying for this yourself. Are you in good hands?"

Through clever ads like these, Allstate's creative and award-winning "Mayhem. It's Everywhere." campaign has put a contemporary, attention-grabbing twist on the company's long-standing "You're in good hands with Allstate" slogan, helping to position the brand as a superior alternative to price-oriented competitors. But why was this unconventional campaign necessary? As it turns out, mayhem doesn't just describe the Allstate campaign—it characterizes the entire world of auto insurance advertising over the past decade.

Not long ago, big auto insurance companies spent modestly on sleepy ad campaigns featuring touchy-feely, reassuring messages such as Allstate's "You're in good hands," or State Farm's "like a good neighbor." In an industry characterized by low budgets and even lower-key ads, no brand's marketing stood out. However, the serenity ended with the first appearance of the now-iconic GEICO Gecko in 2000, backed by a big budget and pitching direct sales and low prices. Since then, insurance industry ad spending and creativity have escalated into a full-scale advertising war. In just the past decade, the amount spent on auto insurance advertising has more than doubled. And the once-conservative car insurance ads have now become creative showstoppers, as edgy and creative as those you'd find in any industry. Here are a few highlights:

> When Allstate's competitors boosted both their advertising budgets and creative splash, the company needed its own over-the-top advertising campaign and spokesperson. So it created mayhem—literally.

- *GEICO:* GEICO got the auto insurance advertising wars rolling when it was acquired by billionaire Warren Buffet's Berkshire-Hathaway in 1996 and given a blank check to aggressively increase market share. That led to an onslaught of advertising the likes of which the auto insurance industry had never seen before. A string of creative GEICO campaigns featured everything from civilized cavemen to cash with googly eyes. But it's the GEICO Gecko that's had the biggest impact. With his signature English accent, the Gecko has made GEICO's simple message clear—"15 minutes can save you 15 percent or more on car insurance." More than any other industry spokesperson, the Gecko has positioned auto insurance as a commodity-like product where price rules. Along the way, during the past decade, GEICO's market share has more than doubled to 8.5 percent.

- *Progressive:* Following GEICO's lead, in 2008 Progressive created its own endearing personality—perky sales clerk Flo. The ever-upbeat Flo was created to help convince consumers who are already in the market that they can get a better price deal from Progressive. Flo has helped put Progressive hot on the heels of GEICO at fourth place in the industry. Whereas Flo assists people when they are ready to shop, Progressive's newer character—the Messenger—reminds them that they should shop. Appearing in reality-style TV ads and videos, the mustachioed, leather-jacket-wearing Messenger approaches unsuspecting customers and sells them on Progressive's discounts. Like the GEICO Gecko, both Flo and the Messenger pitch price savings as their primary appeal.

- *State Farm:* As GEICO and Progressive have shaken up the industry with their direct, low-price, high-profile selling models, the conventional agent-based auto insurers have been forced to respond. For example, 90-year-old State Farm, the industry leader with an 18.7 percent market share, has fought back vigorously with a new campaign centered on its enduring "Like a Good Neighbor" jingle. In the company's recent "magic jingle" campaign, State Farm agents magically appear when summoned with the jingle by young drivers in trouble—including the likes of LeBron James. The campaign's goal is to convince consumers that they still need the services of one of State Farm's 18,000 agents. To help make the point more forcefully, State Farm recently doubled its ad budget.

As these and other Allstate competitors boost both their ad spending and their creative splash, "this category has gone from a kind of forgotten category to a category with real sizzle," says Progressive's chief marketing officer. Today, no less than 11 car insurance brands are running TV advertising campaigns. Combined, the auto insurers now spend more than $4 billion each year to get their messages out. That makes things confusing for consumers, who struggle to match the deluge of clever ads with the respective brands.

Amid this surge in competition, Allstate struggled just to hold its own, let alone to grow. Entering 2010, even with the longtime, deep-voiced pitchman Dennis Haysbert asking "Are you in good hands?" Allstate had lost market share for two years

Allstate's award-winning "Mayhem. It's Everywhere." advertising campaign has put a quirky, attention-grabbing twist on the company's long-standing "You're in good hands with Allstate" slogan.
Allstate Insurance Company

running. The brand needed its own over-the-top personality. Enter Mayhem, Allstate's villainous counterpart to Haysbert's soothing hero. The campaign's goal: to convince consumers that there is more to buying car insurance than just price. To put it a little more bluntly, says an ad agency executive involved with the campaign, "We wanted to kick Flo's [behind]."

The Mayhem campaign quickly won many top ad industry awards. But perhaps a bigger indication of the campaign's impact is the extent to which the character has become ingrained in pop culture. Although Mayhem has only about a quarter of Flo's 4-million-plus Facebook fans, he commands an engagement score nearly eight times that of Progressive's cherry-lipped spokeswoman. And when the ad agency executive recently saw a Mayhem-costumed trick-or-treater walking down her street, she called it "a career highlight that gave her chills."

More than just popular, Mayhem is right on message. At the end of many ads, he warns, "If you've got cut-rate insurance, you could be paying for this yourself." Then a reassuring Haysbert provides the solution: "So get an Allstate Agent. Are you in good hands?" he asks. This "worth-paying-a-little-more" message puts Allstate back at the top in terms of customer value.

The attention-getting Mayhem campaign seems to be paying off. Allstate's unaided brand awareness of 74 percent trails State Farm's by only a slight margin, despite State Farm's 60 percent greater ad spending. More important, the Mayhem campaign has been very good for business. All this has prompted Allstate to extend the campaign, including the introduction of Mayhem's Hispanic cousin, Mala Suerte (bad luck), aimed at Hispanic consumers. With the all-out war being waged in auto insurance advertising, Allstate can't back off. Then again, given the success of its Mayhem campaign, it seems that the Good Hands company is moving in the right direction.[1]

Objective Outline

MyMarketingLab™

⭐ **Improve Your Grade!**

Over 10 million students improved their results using the Pearson MyLabs.
Visit **mymktlab.com** for simulations, tutorials, and end-of-chapter problems.

As we discussed in the previous chapter, companies must do more than simply create customer value. They must also clearly and persuasively communicate that value to target customers. In this chapter, we take a closer look at two marketing communications tools: *advertising* and *public relations*.

Objective 1 ┈┈▶
Define the role of advertising in the promotion mix.

Advertising
Any paid form of nonpersonal presentation and promotion of ideas, goods, or services by an identified sponsor.

Advertising

Advertising can be traced back to the very beginnings of recorded history. Archaeologists working in countries around the Mediterranean Sea have dug up signs announcing various events and offers. The Romans painted walls to announce gladiator fights and the Phoenicians painted pictures on large rocks to promote their wares along parade routes. During the golden age in Greece, town criers announced the sale of cattle, crafted items, and even cosmetics. An early "singing commercial" went as follows: "For eyes that are shining, for cheeks like the dawn/For beauty that lasts after girlhood is gone/For prices in reason, the woman who knows/Will buy her cosmetics from Aesclyptos."

Modern advertising, however, is a far cry from these early efforts. U.S. advertisers now run up an estimated annual bill of almost $144 billion on measured advertising media; worldwide ad spending is an estimated $489 billion. P&G, the world's largest advertiser, last year spent $4.6 billion on U.S. advertising and $11.4 billion worldwide.[2]

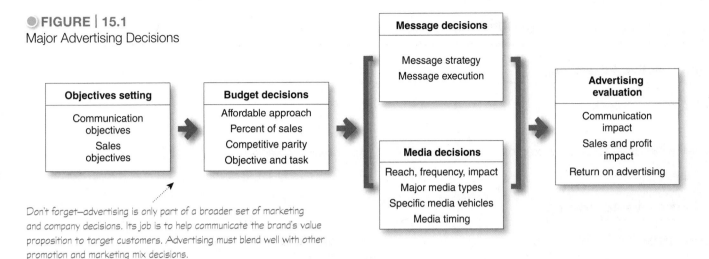

FIGURE | 15.1
Major Advertising Decisions

Don't forget—advertising is only part of a broader set of marketing and company decisions. Its job is to help communicate the brand's value proposition to target customers. Advertising must blend well with other promotion and marketing mix decisions.

Although advertising is used mostly by business firms, a wide range of not-for-profit organizations, professionals, and social agencies also use advertising to promote their causes to various target publics. In fact, the 28th largest advertising spender is a not-for-profit organization—the U.S. government, which advertises in many ways. For example, the federal government recently spent some $300 million on an advertising campaign to motivate Americans to take part in the 2010 Census.[3] Advertising is a good way to inform and persuade, whether the purpose is to sell Coca-Cola worldwide or educate people in developing nations on how to prevent the spread of HIV/AIDS.

Marketing management must make four important decisions when developing an advertising program (see **Figure 15.1**): *setting advertising objectives, setting the advertising budget, developing advertising strategy (message decisions and media decisions), and evaluating advertising campaigns.*

Setting Advertising Objectives

Objective 2 ····▶

Describe the major decisions involved in developing an advertising program.

The first step is to set *advertising objectives*. These objectives should be based on past decisions about the target market, positioning, and the marketing mix, which define the job that advertising must do in the total marketing program. The overall advertising objective is to help build customer relationships by communicating customer value. Here, we discuss specific advertising objectives.

Advertising objective

A specific communication *task* to be accomplished with a specific *target* audience during a specific period of *time*.

An **advertising objective** is a specific communication *task* to be accomplished with a specific *target* audience during a specific period of *time*. Advertising objectives can be classified by their primary purpose—to *inform, persuade,* or *remind.* **Table 15.1** lists examples of each of these specific objectives.

Informative advertising is used heavily when introducing a new-product category. In this case, the objective is to build primary demand. Thus, early producers of HDTVs first had to inform consumers of the image quality and size benefits of the new product. *Persuasive advertising* becomes more important as competition increases. Here, the company's objective is to build selective demand. For example, once HDTVs became established, Samsung began trying to persuade consumers that *its* brand offered the best quality for their money.

Some persuasive advertising has become *comparative advertising* (or *attack advertising*), in which a company directly or indirectly compares its brand with one or more other brands. You see examples of comparative advertising in almost every product category, ranging from sports drinks, coffee, and soup to computers, car rentals, and credit cards. For example, over the past few years, Verizon Wireless and AT&T have attacked each other ruthlessly in comparative ads. When Verizon Wireless began offering the iPhone, it used its "Can you hear me now?" slogan to attack AT&T's rumored spotty service. AT&T retaliated with showing that its customers could talk on the phone and surf the Web at the same time, a feature not yet available via Verizon Wireless.

Advertisers should use comparative advertising with caution. All too often, such ads invite competitor responses, resulting in an advertising war that neither competitor can win. Upset competitors might also take more drastic action, such as filing complaints

● **Table 15.1 | Possible Advertising Objectives**

Informative Advertising

Communicating customer value	Suggesting new uses for a product
Building a brand and company image	Informing the market of a price change
Telling the market about a new product	Describing available services and support
Explaining how a product works	Correcting false impressions

Persuasive Advertising

Building brand preference	Persuading customers to purchase now
Encouraging switching to a brand	Persuading customers to receive a sales call
Changing customer perceptions of product value	Convincing customers to tell others about the brand

Reminder Advertising

Maintaining customer relationships	Reminding consumers where to buy the product
Reminding consumers that the product may be needed in the near future	Keeping the brand in a customer's mind during off-seasons

with the self-regulatory National Advertising Division of the Council of Better Business Bureaus or even filing false-advertising lawsuits. ● For example, Sara Lee's Ball Park brand hot dogs and Kraft's Oscar Mayer brand recently waged a nearly two-year "weiner war." It started when Sara Lee sued Kraft, challenging advertising claims that Oscar Mayer franks had won a national taste test over Ball Park and other brands and that they were "100% beef." Kraft, in turn, filed a countersuit, accusing Sara Lee of making similar advertising misstatements about its own "all-beef" Ball Park hot dogs, along with claims touting Ball Park as "America's best." By the time the lawsuits were settled, about all that the competitors had accomplished was to publicly call into question the taste and contents of both hot dog brands.[4]

● Comparative advertising: Sara Lee's Ball Park brand and Kraft's Oscar Mayer brand recently waged a nearly two-year "wiener war" that left customers wondering about the taste and content of both brands.

Associated Press/Charlie Neibergall

Reminder advertising is important for mature products; it helps to maintain customer relationships and keep consumers thinking about the product. Expensive Coca-Cola television ads primarily build and maintain the Coca-Cola brand relationship rather than inform consumers or persuade them to buy it in the short run.

Advertising's goal is to help move consumers through the buying process. Some advertising is designed to move people to immediate action. For example, a direct-response television ad by Weight Watchers urges consumers to pick up the phone and sign up right away, and a Best Buy newspaper insert for a weekend sale encourages immediate store visits. However, many ads focus on building or strengthening long-term customer relationships. For example, a Nike television ad in which well-known athletes work through extreme challenges in their Nike gear never directly asks for a sale. Instead, the goal is to somehow change the way the customers think or feel about the brand.

Setting the Advertising Budget

Advertising budget
The dollars and other resources allocated to a product or a company advertising program.

After determining its advertising objectives, the company next sets its **advertising budget** for each product. Four commonly used methods for setting promotion budgets are discussed in Chapter 14. Here we discuss some specific factors that should be considered when setting the advertising budget.

A brand's advertising budget often depends on its *stage in the product life cycle.* For example, new products typically need relatively large advertising budgets to build awareness and to gain consumer trial. In contrast, mature brands usually require lower budgets as a ratio to sales. *Market share* also impacts the amount of advertising needed: Because building the market or taking market share from competitors requires larger advertising spending than does simply maintaining current share, low-share brands usually need more advertising spending as a percentage of sales.

Also, brands in a market with many competitors and high advertising clutter must be advertised more heavily to be noticed above the noise in the marketplace. Undifferentiated brands—those that closely resemble other brands in their product class (soft drinks, laundry detergents)—may require heavy advertising to set them apart. When the product differs greatly from those of competitors, advertising can be used to point out the differences to consumers.

No matter what method is used, setting the advertising budget is no easy task. How does a company know if it is spending the right amount? Some critics charge that large consumer packaged-goods firms tend to spend too much on advertising and that business-to-business marketers generally underspend on advertising. They claim that, on the one hand, the large consumer companies use lots of image advertising without really knowing its effects. They overspend as a form of "insurance" against not spending enough. On the other hand, business advertisers tend to rely too heavily on their sales forces to bring in orders. They underestimate the power of company and product image in preselling industrial customers. Thus, they do not spend enough on advertising to build customer awareness and knowledge.

Companies such as Coca-Cola and Kraft have built sophisticated statistical models to determine the relationship between promotional spending and brand sales, and to help determine the "optimal investment" across various media. Still, because so many factors affect advertising effectiveness, some controllable and others not, measuring the results of advertising spending remains an inexact science. In most cases, managers must rely on large doses of judgment along with more quantitative analysis when setting advertising budgets.[5]

As a result of such thinking, advertising is one of the easiest budget items to cut when economic times get tough. Cuts in brand-building advertising appear to do little short-term harm to sales. For example, in the wake of the recent recession, U.S. advertising expenditures plummeted 12 percent over the previous year. In the long run, however, slashing ad spending may cause long-term damage to a brand's image and market share. In fact, companies that can maintain or even increase their advertising spending while competitors are decreasing theirs can gain competitive advantage.

For example, during the recent Great Recession, while competitors were cutting back, car maker Audi actually increased its marketing and advertising spending.  Audi "kept its foot on the pedal while everyone else [was] pulling back," said an Audi ad executive. "Why would we go backwards now when the industry is generally locking the brakes and cutting spending?" As a result, Audi's brand awareness and buyer consideration reached record levels during the recession, outstripping those of BMW, Mercedes, and Lexus, and positioning Audi strongly for the postrecession era. Audi is now one of the hottest auto brands on the market.[6]

●Setting the promotion budget: Promotion spending is one of the easiest items to cut in tough economic times. But Audi has gained competitive advantage by keeping its foot on the promotion pedal as competitors have retrenched.

Used with permission of Audi of America

Developing Advertising Strategy

Advertising strategy consists of two major elements: creating advertising *messages* and selecting advertising *media*. In the past,

Advertising strategy
The strategy by which the company accomplishes its advertising objectives. It consists of two major elements: creating advertising messages and selecting advertising media.

companies often viewed media planning as secondary to the message-creation process. After the creative department created good advertisements, the media department then selected and purchased the best media for carrying those advertisements to the desired target audiences. This often caused friction between creatives and media planners.

Today, however, soaring media costs, more-focused target marketing strategies, and the blizzard of new digital and interactive media have promoted the importance of the media-planning function. The decision about which media to use for an ad campaign—television, newspapers, magazines, a Web site or online social network, mobile phones, or e-mail—is now sometimes more critical than the creative elements of the campaign. As a result, more and more advertisers are orchestrating a closer harmony between their messages and the media that deliver them. As discussed in the previous chapter, the goal is to create and manage brand content across a full range of media, whether they are paid, owned, earned, or shared.

Creating the Advertising Message

No matter how big the budget, advertising can succeed only if it gains attention and communicates well. Good advertising messages and content are especially important in today's costly and cluttered advertising environment. In 1950, the average U.S. household received only three network television channels and a handful of major national magazines. Today, the average household receives about 135 channels, and consumers have more than 20,000 magazines from which to choose.[7] Add in the countless radio stations and a continuous barrage of catalogs, direct mail, e-mail and online ads, out-of-home media, and social networking exposures, and consumers are being bombarded with ads at home, work, and all points in between. As a result, consumers are exposed to as many as 3,000 to 5,000 commercial messages every day.[8]

Breaking Through the Clutter. If all this advertising clutter bothers some consumers, it also causes huge headaches for advertisers. Take the situation facing network television advertisers. They pay an average of $324,000 to produce a single 30-second commercial. Then, each time they show it, they pay an average of $122,000 for 30 seconds of advertising time during a popular primetime program. They pay even more if it's an especially popular program, such as *American Idol* ($502,000), *Sunday Night Football* ($512,000), *Modern Family* ($249,000), or a mega-event such as the Super Bowl ($3.5 million per 30 seconds!).[9]

Then their ads are sandwiched in with a clutter of other commercials, announcements, and network promotions, totaling nearly 20 minutes of nonprogram material per primetime hour, with commercial breaks coming every six minutes on average. Such clutter in television and other ad media has created an increasingly hostile advertising environment. According to one study, more than 70 percent of Americans think there are too many ads on TV, and another study shows that 69 percent of national advertisers themselves agree.[10]

Until recently, television viewers were pretty much a captive audience for advertisers. But today's digital wizardry has given consumers a rich new set of information and entertainment choices. With the growth in cable and satellite TV, the Internet, video streaming, tablets, and smartphones, today's viewers have many more options.

Digital technology has also armed consumers with an arsenal of weapons for choosing what they watch or don't watch. ● Increasingly, thanks to the growth of DVR systems, consumers are choosing *not* to watch ads. Forty-three percent of American TV households now have DVRs, triple the number reached only five years earlier. One ad agency executive calls these DVR systems "electronic weedwhackers" when it comes to viewing commercials. It is estimated that DVR owners view only about 40 percent of the commercials during DVR playback. At the same time, video downloads and streaming are exploding, letting viewers watch entertainment on their own time—with or without commercials.[11]

Thus, advertisers can no longer force-feed the same old cookie-cutter message content to captive consumers through traditional media. Just to gain and hold attention, today's content must be better planned, more imaginative, more entertaining, and more emotionally engaging. Simply interrupting or disrupting consumers no longer works. Unless ads provide information that is interesting, useful, or entertaining, many consumers will simply skip by them.

● **Advertising clutter: Today's consumers, armed with an arsenal of weapons, can choose what they watch and don't watch. Increasingly, they are choosing not to watch ads.**
© Corbis Flirt/Alamy

Madison & Vine

A term that has come to represent the merging of advertising and entertainment in an effort to break through the clutter and create new avenues for reaching customers with more engaging messages.

Merging Advertising and Entertainment. To break through the clutter, many marketers have subscribed to a new merging of advertising and entertainment, dubbed "**Madison & Vine**." You've probably heard of Madison Avenue, the New York City street that houses the headquarters of many of the nation's largest advertising agencies. You may also have heard of Hollywood & Vine, the intersection of Hollywood Avenue and Vine Street in Hollywood, California, long the symbolic heart of the U.S. entertainment industry. Now, Madison Avenue and Hollywood & Vine have come together to form a new intersection—Madison & Vine—that represents the merging of advertising and entertainment in an effort to create new avenues for reaching consumers with more engaging messages.

This merging of advertising and entertainment takes one of two forms: advertainment or branded entertainment. The aim of *advertainment* is to make ads themselves so entertaining, or so useful, that people *want* to watch them. There's no chance that you'd watch ads on purpose, you say? Think again. For example, the Super Bowl has become an annual advertainment showcase. Tens of millions of people tune in to the Super Bowl each year, as much to watch the entertaining ads as to see the game.

In fact, DVR systems can actually *improve* viewership of a really *good* ad. For example, most Super Bowl ads are typically viewed more in DVR households than non-DVR households. Rather than zipping past the ads, many people skip back to re-watch them during halftime and following the game.

These days, it's not unusual to see an entertaining ad or other brand message on YouTube before you see it on TV. And you might well seek it out at a friend's suggestion rather than having it forced on you by the advertiser. Moreover, beyond making their regular ads more entertaining, advertisers are also creating new advertising forms that look less like ads and more like short films or shows. A range of new brand messaging platforms—from Webisodes and blogs to viral videos and apps—now blur the line between ads and entertainment. ● For example, T-Mobile created an entertaining two-minute video ad based on the royal wedding between Prince William and Kate Middleton, using impressive lookalikes of British royal family members dancing down the aisle to a funky pop song. The fun ad was never shown on TV but pulled down more than 26 million views on YouTube.

Branded entertainment (or *brand integrations*) involves making the brand an inseparable part of some other form of entertainment. The most common form of branded entertainment is product placements—embedding brands as props within other programming. It might be a brief glimpse of the latest LG phone on *Grey's Anatomy* or of Starbuck's coffee products on *Morning Joe* on MSNBC. Or the product placement might be scripted into an episode, as when *Big Bang Theory* character Sheldon Cooper uses Purell hand sanitizer after putting a live snake in his friend's desk drawer, spitting out the memorable line, "Oh dear. Oh dear. Purell, Purell, Purell, Purell. . . ." An entire episode of *The Middle* centered on the show's Heck family coveting their neighbor's new VW Passat. Similarly, one memorable episode of *Modern Family* was built around the Dunphy family trying to find the recently released, hard-to-find Apple iPad their father, Phil, coveted as his special birthday present. Other episodes have featured brands ranging from Oreos to Target to Toyota Prius, all carefully integrated with the show's theme.[12]

● Madison & Vine: Marketers are creating new advertising forms that blur the line between ads and entertainment, such as this T Mobile video ad spoofing the royal wedding between Prince William and Kate Middleton. It pulled down 26 million views on YouTube.

T-Mobile Limited

Originally created with TV in mind, branded entertainment has spread quickly into other sectors of the entertainment industry. For example, it is widely used in movies. Last year's top 40 films contained 710 identifiable brand placements—*Transformers: Dark of the Moon* alone had 71 placements. If you look carefully, you'll also see product placements in video games, comic books, Broadway musicals, and even pop music. For example, in *Call of Duty: Modern Warfare 3*, a Jeep Wrangler is prominently featured. Chrysler even sells a Call of Duty: MW3 limited edition Jeep Wrangler.

Many companies are even producing their own branded entertainment. For example, Denny's sponsors an online video series called *Always Open* (in line with its "America's diner is always open" positioning theme), now in its second season. Designed to appeal to 18- to 25-year-olds, the edgy Web series features comedian David Koechner, who engages guest celebrities in unscripted, anything-goes conversations filmed at a working Denny's restaurant. While the show's content is not blatantly commercial, the host and guest eat Denny's food during each three-minute video episode, and Denny's name appears prominently in the credits. Shown on outlets such as CollegeHumor.com and Denny's Facebook page, the first season drew more than 6 million views.[13]

So, Madison & Vine is now the meeting place for the advertising and entertainment industries. The goal is for brand messages to become a part of the entertainment rather than interrupting it. As advertising agency JWT puts it, "We believe advertising needs to stop *interrupting* what people are interested in and *be* what people are interested in." However, advertisers must be careful that the new intersection itself doesn't become too congested. With all the new ad formats and product placements, Madison & Vine threatens to create even more of the very clutter that it was designed to break through. At that point, consumers might decide to take yet a different route.

Message Strategy. The first step in creating effective advertising messages is to plan a *message strategy* —the general message that will be communicated to consumers. The purpose of advertising is to get consumers to think about or react to the product or company in a certain way. People will react only if they believe they will benefit from doing so. Thus, developing an effective message strategy begins with identifying customer *benefits* that can be used as advertising appeals. Ideally, the message strategy will follow directly from the company's broader positioning and customer value creation strategies.

Message strategy statements tend to be plain, straightforward outlines of benefits and positioning points that the advertiser wants to stress. The advertiser must next develop a compelling **creative concept**—or *big idea*—that will bring the message strategy to life in a distinctive and memorable way. At this stage, simple message ideas become great ad campaigns. Usually, a copywriter and an art director will team up to generate many creative concepts, hoping that one of these concepts will turn out to be the big idea. The creative concept may emerge as a visualization, a phrase, or a combination of the two.

The creative concept will guide the choice of specific appeals to be used in an advertising campaign. *Advertising appeals* should have three characteristics. First, they should be *meaningful*, pointing out benefits that make the product more desirable or interesting to consumers. Second, appeals must be *believable*. Consumers must believe that the product or service will deliver the promised benefits.

However, the most meaningful and believable benefits may not be the best ones to feature. Appeals should also be *distinctive*. They should tell how the product is better than competing brands. For example, the most meaningful benefit of owning a wristwatch is that it keeps accurate time, yet few watch ads feature this benefit. Instead, based on the distinctive benefits they offer, watch advertisers might select any of a number of advertising themes. For years, Timex has been the affordable watch that "takes a licking and keeps on ticking." Similarly, Rolex ads never talk about keeping time. Instead, they talk about the brand's "obsession with perfection" and the fact that "Rolex has been the preeminent symbol of performance and prestige for more than a century."

Message Execution. The advertiser now must turn the big idea into an actual ad execution that will capture the target market's attention and interest. The creative team must find the best approach, style, tone, words, and format for executing the message. The message can be presented in various **execution styles**, such as the following:

- *Slice of life:* This style shows one or more "typical" people using the product in a normal setting. For example, a Silk Soymilk "Rise and Shine" ad shows a young professional starting the day with a healthier breakfast and high hopes.
- *Lifestyle:* This style shows how a product fits in with a particular lifestyle. For example, an ad for Athleta active wear shows a woman in a complex yoga pose and states: "If your body is your temple, build it one piece at a time."
- *Fantasy:* This style creates a fantasy around the product or its use. For example, recent IKEA ads show consumers creating fanciful room designs with IKEA furniture, such as "a bedroom for a queen made by Bree and her sister, designed by IKEA."
- *Mood or image:* This style builds a mood or image around the product or service, such as beauty, love, intrigue, or serenity. Few claims are made about the product or service

Creative concept

The compelling "big idea" that will bring an advertising message strategy to life in a distinctive and memorable way.

Execution style

The approach, style, tone, words, and format used for executing an advertising message.

except through suggestion. For example, a Nestlé Toll House ad shows a daughter hugging her mother after surprising her with an unexpected weekend home from college. The mother responds, "So I baked her the cookies she's loved since she was little."

- *Musical:* This style shows people or cartoon characters singing about the product. For example, Chevrolet recently ran a two-minute-long TV commercial featuring most of the cast of the TV show *Glee* in an elaborate production number set to the 1950s brand jingle, "See the U.S.A. in Your Chevrolet."
- *Personality symbol:* This style creates a character that represents the product. The character might be animated (Mr. Clean, the GEICO Gecko, or the Zappos Zappets) or real (perky Progressive Insurance spokeswoman Flo, the E*TRADE babies, Ronald McDonald).
- *Technical expertise:* This style shows the company's expertise in making the product. Thus, natural foods maker Kashi shows its buyers carefully selecting ingredients for its products, and Jim Koch of the Boston Beer Company tells about his many years of experience in brewing Samuel Adams beer.
- *Scientific evidence:* This style presents survey or scientific evidence that the brand is better or better liked than one or more other brands. For years, Crest toothpaste has used scientific evidence to convince buyers that Crest is better than other brands at fighting cavities.
- *Testimonial evidence or endorsement:* This style features a highly believable or likable source endorsing the product. It could be ordinary people saying how much they like a given product. For example, Subway's spokesman Jared is a customer who lost 245 pounds on a diet of Subway sandwiches. Or it might be a celebrity presenting the product. Olympic gold medal swimmer Michael Phelps also speaks for Subway.

The advertiser also must choose a *tone* for the ad. For example, P&G always uses a positive tone: Its ads say something very positive about its products. Other advertisers now use edgy humor to break through the commercial clutter. Bud Light commercials are famous for this.

The advertiser must use memorable and attention-getting *words* in the ad. For example, rather than claiming simply that its laundry detergent is "superconcentrated," Method asks customers, "Are you jug addicted?" The solution: "Our patent-pending formula that's so fricken' concentrated, 50 loads fits in a teeny bottle. . . . With our help, you can get off the jugs and get clean."

Finally, *format* elements make a difference in an ad's impact as well as in its cost. A small change in an ad's design can make a big difference in its effect. In a print ad, the *illustration* is the first thing the reader notices—it must be strong enough to draw attention. Next, the *headline* must effectively entice the right people to read the copy. Finally, the *copy*—the main block of text in the ad—must be simple but strong and convincing. Moreover, these three elements must effectively work *together* to persuasively present customer value. However, novel formats can help an ad stand out from the clutter. For example, striking Benjamin Moore paint ads consist mostly of a single long headline in mixed fonts balanced against a color swatch and background that illustrate the color discussed in the headline.

Consumer-Generated Messages. Taking advantage of today's interactive technologies, many companies are now tapping consumers for message ideas or actual ads. They are searching existing video sites, setting up their own sites, and sponsoring ad-creation contests and other promotions. Sometimes the results are outstanding; sometimes they are forgettable. If done well, however, user-generated content can incorporate the voice of the customer into brand messages and generate greater consumer brand involvement (see Real Marketing 15.1).

Many brands hold contests that invite consumers to submit ad message ideas and videos. For example, for the past several years, PepsiCo's Doritos brand has held its annual "Crash the Super Bowl Challenge" contest that invites consumers to create their own video ads about the tasty triangular corn chips. The consumer-generated Doritos ads have been a smashing success. At the other end of the size spectrum, online crafts marketplace/

● **Novel formats can help an advertisement stand out from the crowd. This Benjamin Moore paint ad consists mostly of a single long headline balanced against a color swatch and background that illustrate the color discussed in the ad.**

Courtesy of Benjamin Moore Paints

Real Marketing 15.1

Consumer-Generated Advertising:
Fresh Consumer Insights and Brand Involvement

Fueled by the likes of YouTube, Facebook, Pinterest, Twitter, and other social networks, user-generated content has become thoroughly ingrained in modern culture. So it's no surprise that consumer-generated advertising has also spread like wildfire in recent years. Today, marketers large and small are inviting consumers to co-create brand messages, gaining fresh customer insights and creating deeper brand involvement. They've learned that customers involved in generating marketing ideas for a brand are likely to be more satisfied and to spread more positive word of mouth.

When it comes to consumer-generated advertising, perhaps no brand has more experience and success than PepsiCo's Doritos brand. For six years running, the Doritos "Crash the Super Bowl" contest has invited consumers to create their own 30-second video ads featuring the market-leading tortilla chip. A jury of ad pros and Doritos brand managers whittle down the thousands of entries submitted and post the finalists online. Then consumers go online to vote for their favorites, creating even more consumer involvement and buzz. The winners receive cash prizes and have their ads run during the Super Bowl.

For last year's Super Bowl, PepsiCo threw prize money around like a rich uncle home for the holidays. Five finalists each claimed $25,000 and an all-expense paid trip for two to the Super Bowl. To put more icing on the cake, Doritos promised to pay a whopping $1 million to any entrant whose ad placed first in either of two *USA Today* AdMeter ratings. Second place was good for $600,000, and third place would take home $400,000. The top winner would also land a gig as a consultant for an additional Doritos commercial. Not surprisingly, the contest attracted more than 6,100 entries.

For the first time ever, Dorito's awarded not one but two grand prizes. "Man's Best Friend"—a consumer-produced ad featuring a murderous Great Dane who bribes a human with Doritos to not tell about the dead cat it's burying in the yard—achieved the top score in *USA Today's* traditional AdMeter ratings, based on second-by-second responses of a panel of 286 adults. That first-place showing gave former Los Angeles special education

teacher Kevin Willson $1 million to pursue his dream of becoming a real film maker, not a bad return for an ad that cost only $24 to make. In addition, this year, *USA Today* teamed with Facebook, allowing viewers to cast their votes in a two-day social media version of its AdMeter ratings, involving millions more viewers in the process. The favorite in online voting was another consumer-generated Doritos ad, "Sling Baby," in which a grandmother slingshots a baby across the yard to nab a bag of chips from a taunting neighbor kid. The ad earned its creator, 31-year-old Jonathan Friedman of Virginia Beach, Virginia, a second $1 million prize.

For Doritos, the "Crash the Super Bowl" consumer-generated advertising effort triggered consumer involvement far beyond simply airing the ads during the big game. The contest was a social media touchdown. During the three months leading up to the big game, hundreds of thousands of consumers voted on the ads and millions viewed the winning ads prior to game time. After the game, the Super Bowl ads generated more sharing and click-throughs than ever before, along with more social media comments than the entire Academy Awards. "It's gone way beyond the water cooler," says Frito-Lay's chief marketing officer.

Doritos isn't the only brand getting into the consumer-generated content act. According to one global report that ranks the world's top creative work, 9 of the top 10 campaigns during a recent year involved some kind of consumer input. "This is a seismic shift in our business," says the former ad agency executive who assembled the report. "We've had 100 years of

Consumer-generated messages: Last year, two Doritos "Crash the Super Bowl" ads took first place in *USA Today's* AdMeter ratings, including this "Sling Baby" ad.

Frito-Lay, Inc.

business-to-consumer advertising, but now the Internet has enabled us to get people actively involved in talking to each other. If the idea is interesting enough, consumers will do the work for you."

That kind of talk makes some ad agencies nervous. However, the idea isn't that companies should fire their ad agencies and have consumers create their ads instead. In fact, most consumer-generated ad campaigns—including the Doritos "Crash the Super Bowl" contest—are coordinated by ad agencies.

One agency—Victors & Spoils of Boulder, Colorado—was recently founded as the first creative agency built entirely on crowdsourcing principles. Harley-Davidson tapped Victors & Spoils to handle the creative work for a consumer-generated ad campaign to promote its HD1 program—an initiative that allows customers to go online and design a fully-customized, factory-made Harley. Consumer-generated advertising seemed like a no-brainer to promote Harley-Davidson's consumer-customized motorcycles program.

Whit Hiler, a "passionate amateur" from Kentucky, came up with the winning ad idea.

The resulting Harley-Davidson ad, entitled "No Cages," shows people going about their everyday, boring lives enclosed in iron cages. When a rider on a cageless Harley speeds by, everyone stares with envy. The ad's tagline, "Build your bike. Build your freedom," encapsulates a message that Harley-Davidson now plans to carry beyond the single ad, and even beyond its HD1 customization program. Harley-Davidson's marketers couldn't be more pleased with the results of involving consumers in creating ads. As the brand extends the "No Cages" campaign into

print, social media, and Web video, Harley's chief marketing officer has anointed "sourcing ideas from customers" as Harley-Davidson's "new creativity model."

Doritos, Harley-Davidson, and dozens of other examples demonstrate that when it is done right, consumer-generated advertising can strengthen a brand's ability to involve and engage consumers, turning them into brand advocates. What could be better than engaging consumers in telling the brand story? As one marketer puts it, "We believe that marketing will be much more participatory in the next few years and we want to be at the leading edge of that."

Sources: Bruce Horovitz, Laura Petrecca, and Gary Strauss, "Super Bowl AdMeter Winner: Score One for the Doritos Baby," *USA Today,* February 7, 2012; Laura Petrecca, "Doritos AdMeter Winners Each Receive a $1 Million Bonus," *USA Today,* February 8, 2012; Andrew McMains, "Unilever Embraces UGC," *Adweek,* April 20, 2010, www.adweek.com/print/107289; Emma Hall, "Most Winning Creative Work Involves Consumer Participation," *Advertising Age,* January 6, 2010, http://adage.com/print/141329; Abbey Klaassen, "Harley-Davidson Breaks Consumer-Created Work from Victors & Spoils," *Advertising Age,* February 14, 2011, http://adage.com/print/148873/; and Riley Gibson, "Crowdsourcing on Facebook Gets You Consumers' Ideas and Their Purchases," *Advertising Age,* April 13, 2012, http://adage.com/print/234086/.

community Etsy.com—"Your best place to buy and sell all things handmade"—ran a contest inviting consumers to tell the Etsy.com story in 30-second videos. The results were what one well-known former advertising critic called "positively remarkable":[14]

> The 10 semifinalists ads are better conceived and developed than any 10 randomly selected commercials that you'll find anywhere in the world, says the critic. The best user-created Etsy ad features a simple, sad, animated robot, consigned to a life of soul-crushing assembly-line production. "See, there's a lot of robots out there," says the voice of the unseen Etsy craftswomen who crafted him. "A lot of these robots are sad because they're stuck making these boring, mass-produced things. Me, I really can believe all that great stuff about how it helps the environment and microeconomics and feeling special about getting something handmade by someone else. But the real reason I make handmade goods is because every time somebody buys something handmade, a robot gets its wings." The user-made ad received rave reviews. It "is simply magnificent," concludes the ad critic, "in a way that the agency business had better take note of."

Not all consumer-generated advertising efforts, however, are so successful. As many big companies have learned, ads made by amateurs can be . . . well, pretty amateurish. If done well, however, consumer-generated advertising efforts can produce new creative ideas and fresh perspectives on the brand from consumers who actually experience it. Such campaigns can boost consumer involvement and get consumers talking and thinking about a brand and its value to them. "For those willing to give up control and trust the wisdom of the crowd," says one analyst, "collaboration on . . . marketing campaigns can bear amazing results."[15]

Selecting Advertising Media

Advertising media

The vehicles through which advertising messages are delivered to their intended audiences.

The major steps in **advertising media** selection are (1) determining *reach*, *frequency*, and *impact*; (2) choosing among major *media types*; (3) selecting specific *media vehicles*; and (4) choosing *media timing*.

Determining Reach, Frequency, and Impact. To select media, the advertiser must determine the reach and frequency needed to achieve the advertising objectives. *Reach* is a measure of the *percentage* of people in the target market who are exposed to the ad campaign during a given period of time. For example, the advertiser might try to reach 70 percent of the target market during the first three months of the campaign. *Frequency* is a measure of how many *times* the average person in the target market is exposed to the message. For example, the advertiser might want an average exposure frequency of three.

But advertisers want to do more than just reach a given number of consumers a specific number of times. The advertiser also must determine the desired *media impact*—the *qualitative value* of message exposure through a given medium. For example, the same message in one magazine (say, *Newsweek*) may be more believable than in another (say, the *National Enquirer*). For products that need to be demonstrated, messages on television or in an online video may have more impact than messages on radio because they use sight, motion, *and* sound. Products for which consumers provide input on design or features might be better promoted at an interactive Web site than in a direct mailing.

More generally, the advertiser wants to choose media that will *engage* consumers rather than simply reach them. In any medium, how relevant ad content is for its audience is often much more important than how many people it reaches. ● For example, in an effort to make every advertising dollar count, Ford has recently been selecting TV programs based on viewer engagement ratings. As an example, it didn't seem to make much sense a few years back when Ford began advertising on the Discovery Channel's Dirty Jobs series, starring Mike Rowe. The program had only a small following. However, as it turns out, the viewers most involved with the series—truck-buying men aged 18 to 49—are a prime buying group for the Ford F-Series pickup. Thus, not only did Ford advertise heavily and successfully on Dirty Jobs, it hired Rowe as its spokesman for Web videos and TV and radio ads.[16]

● **Viewer engagement: Viewers most deeply engaged in the Discovery Channel's *Dirty Jobs* series turned out to be truck-buying men, a ripe demographic for Ford's F-Series pickups.**

Michael Segal Photography. Mike Rowe and mikeroweworks.com.

Although Nielsen is beginning to measure the levels of television *media engagement*, such measures are hard to come by for most media. Current media measures are things such as ratings, readership, listenership, and click-through rates. However, engagement happens inside the consumer. Notes one expert, "Just measuring the number of eyeballs in front of a television set is hard enough without trying to measure the intensity of those eyeballs doing the viewing."[17] Still, marketers need to know how customers connect with an ad and brand idea as a part of the broader brand relationship.

Engaged consumers are more likely to act upon brand messages and even share them with others. Thus, rather than simply tracking *consumer impressions* for a media placement—how many people see, hear, or read an ad—Coca-Cola now also tracks the *consumer expressions* that result, such as a comment, a "like," uploading a photo or video, or passing content onto their networks. Today's empowered consumers often generate more messages about a brand than a company can. Through engagement, "instead of having to always pay for their message to run somewhere, [marketers] can 'earn' media for free, via consumer spreading YouTube clips, Groupons, and tweets," says an advertising consultant.[18]

For example, Coca-Cola estimates that on YouTube there are about 146 million views of content related to Coca-Cola. However, only about 26 million of those are of content that Coca-Cola created. The other 120 million are of content created by engaged consumers. "We can't match the volume of our consumers' output," says Coca-Cola's chief marketing officer, "but we can spark it with the right type [and placement] of content."[19]

Choosing among Major Media Types. As summarized in ● **Table 15.2**, the major media types are television, the Internet, newspapers, direct mail, magazines, radio, and outdoor. Advertisers can also choose from a wide array of new digital media, such as mobile phones and other digital devices, which reach consumers directly. Each medium has its advantages and its limitations.

Media planners want to choose media that will effectively and efficiently present the advertising message to target customers. Thus, they must consider each medium's impact,

● Table 15.2 | Profiles of Major Media Types

Medium	Advantages	Limitations
Television	Good mass-marketing coverage; low cost per exposure; combines sight, sound, and motion; appealing to the senses	High absolute costs; high clutter; fleeting exposure; less audience selectivity
The Internet	High selectivity; low cost; immediacy; interactive capabilities	Potentially low impact; the audience controls exposure
Newspapers	Flexibility; timeliness; good local market coverage; broad acceptability; high believability	Short life; poor reproduction quality; small pass-along audience
Direct mail	High audience selectivity; flexibility; no ad competition within the same medium; allows personalization	Relatively high cost per exposure; "junk mail" image
Magazines	High geographic and demographic selectivity; credibility and prestige; high-quality reproduction; long life and good pass-along readership	Long ad purchase lead time; high cost; no guarantee of position
Radio	Good local acceptance; high geographic and demographic selectivity; low cost	Audio only; fleeting exposure; low attention ("the half-heard" medium); fragmented audiences
Outdoor	Flexibility; high repeat exposure; low cost; low message competition; good positional selectivity	Little audience selectivity; creative limitations

message effectiveness, and cost. As discussed in the previous chapter, it's typically not a question of which one medium to use. Rather, the advertiser selects a mix of media and blends them into a fully integrated marketing communications campaign.

The mix of media must be reexamined regularly. For a long time, television and magazines dominated the media mixes of national advertisers, with other media often neglected. However, as discussed previously, the media mix appears to be shifting. As mass-media costs rise, audiences shrink, and exciting new digital and interactive media emerge, many advertisers are finding new ways to reach consumers. They are supplementing the traditional mass media with more-specialized and highly targeted media that cost less, target more effectively, and engage consumers more fully. Today's marketers want to assemble a full mix of paid, owned, earned, and shared media that create and deliver involving brand content to target consumers.

In addition to the explosion of online and mobile media, cable and satellite television systems are thriving. Such systems allow narrow programming formats, such as all sports, all news, nutrition, arts, home improvement and gardening, cooking, travel, history, finance, and others that target select groups. Time Warner, Comcast, and other cable operators are even testing systems that will let them target specific types of ads to TVs in specific neighborhoods or individually to specific types of customers. For example, ads for a Spanish-language channel would run in only Hispanic neighborhoods, or only pet owners would see ads from pet food companies. Advertisers can take advantage of such *narrowcasting* to "rifle in" on special market segments rather than use the "shotgun" approach offered by network broadcasting.

Finally, in their efforts to find less costly and more highly targeted ways to reach consumers, advertisers have discovered a dazzling collection of *alternative media*. These days, no matter where you go or what you do, you will probably run into some new form of advertising.

Tiny billboards attached to shopping carts urge you to buy JELL-O Pudding Pops or Pampers, while ads roll by on the store's checkout conveyor touting your local Chevy dealer. Step outside and there goes a city trash truck sporting an ad for Glad trash bags or a school bus displaying a Little Caesar's pizza ad. A nearby fire hydrant is emblazoned with advertising for KFC's "fiery" chicken wings. You escape to the ballpark, only to find billboard-size video screens running Budweiser ads while a blimp with an electronic message board circles lazily overhead. ● In mid-winter, you wait in a city bus shelter that looks like an oven—with heat coming from the coils—introducing Caribou Coffee's line-up of hot breakfast sandwiches. How about a quiet trip in the country? Sorry—you find an enterprising farmer using his milk cows as four-legged billboards mounted with ads for Ben & Jerry's ice cream.

Marketers have discovered a dazzling array of alternative media, like this heated Caribou Coffee bus shelter.
Caribou Coffee

These days, you're likely to find ads—well—anywhere. Taxi cabs sport electronic messaging signs tied to GPS location sensors that can pitch local stores and restaurants wherever they roam. Ad space is being sold on DVD cases, parking-lot tickets, airline boarding passes, subway turnstiles, highway toll booth gates, golf scorecards, ATMs, municipal garbage cans, and even police cars, doctors' examining tables, and church bulletins. One agency even leases space on the shaved heads of college students for temporary advertising tattoos ("cranial advertising").

Such alternative media seem a bit far-fetched, and they sometimes irritate consumers who resent it all as "ad nauseam." But for many marketers, these media can save money and provide a way to hit selected consumers where they live, shop, work, and play. Of course, all this may leave you wondering if there are any commercial-free havens remaining for ad-weary consumers. Public elevators, perhaps, or stalls in a public restroom? Forget it! Each has already been invaded by innovative marketers.

Another important trend affecting media selection is the rapid growth in the number of *media multitaskers*, people who absorb more than one medium at a time. For example, it's not uncommon to find someone watching TV with a smartphone in hand, posting on Facebook, texting friends, and chasing down product information on Google. One recent survey found that a whopping 86 percent of U.S. mobile Internet users watch TV with their devices in hand. Another study found that 60 percent of TV viewers go online via their smartphones, tablets, or PCs during their TV viewing time. Still another study found that a majority of these multitaskers focus mostly on the Internet rather than TV, and that their online activities are largely unrelated to what they are watching on TV. Marketers need to take such media interactions into account when selecting the types of media they will use.[20]

Selecting Specific Media Vehicles. Media planners must also choose the best media vehicles—specific media within each general media type. For example, television vehicles include *30 Rock* and *ABC World News Tonight*. Magazine vehicles include *Newsweek*, *Real Simple*, and *ESPN The Magazine*. Online and mobile vehicles include Facebook, Pinterest, and YouTube.

Media planners must compute the cost per 1,000 persons reached by a vehicle. For example, if a full-page, four-color advertisement in the U.S. national edition of *Newsweek* costs $178,400 and *Newsweek's* readership is 1.5 million people, the cost of reaching each group of 1,000 persons is about $119. The same advertisement in *Bloomberg BusinessWeek's* Northeast U.S. regional edition may cost only $46,700 but reach only 155,000 people—at a cost per 1,000 of about $300.[21] The media planner ranks each magazine by cost per 1,000 and favors those magazines with the lower cost per 1,000 for reaching target consumers. In the above case, if a marketer is targeting business managers, *BusinessWeek* might be the more cost-effective buy, even at a higher cost per thousand.

Media planners must also consider the costs of producing ads for different media. Whereas newspaper ads may cost very little to produce, flashy television ads can be very costly. Many online ads cost little to produce, but costs can climb when producing made-for-the-Web videos and ad series.

In selecting specific media vehicles, media planners must balance media costs against several media effectiveness factors. First, the planner should evaluate the media vehicle's audience quality. For a Huggies disposable diapers advertisement, for example, *Parents* magazine would have a high exposure value; *Maxim* would have a low exposure value. Second, the media planner should consider audience engagement. Readers of *Vogue*, for example, typically pay more attention to ads than do *Newsweek* readers. Third, the planner should assess the vehicle's editorial quality. *Time* and the *Wall Street Journal* are more believable and prestigious than *Star* or the *National Enquirer*.

Deciding on Media Timing. An advertiser must also decide how to schedule the advertising over the course of a year. Suppose sales of a product peak in December and drop in March (for winter outdoor gear, for instance). The firm can vary its advertising to follow the seasonal pattern, oppose the seasonal pattern, or be the same all year. Most firms do some seasonal advertising. For example, Mars currently runs M&M's special ads for almost every holiday and "season," from Easter, Fourth of July, and Halloween to the Super Bowl season and the Oscar season. The Picture People, the national chain of portrait studios, advertises more heavily before major holidays, such as Christmas, Easter, Valentine's Day, and Halloween. Some marketers do *only* seasonal advertising: For instance, P&G advertises its Vicks NyQuil only during the cold and flu season.

Finally, the advertiser must choose the pattern of the ads. *Continuity* means scheduling ads evenly within a given period. *Pulsing* means scheduling ads unevenly over a given time period. Thus, 52 ads could either be scheduled at one per week during the year or pulsed in several bursts. The idea behind pulsing is to advertise heavily for a short period to build awareness that carries over to the next advertising period. Those who favor pulsing feel that it can be used to achieve the same impact as a steady schedule but at a much lower cost. However, some media planners believe that although pulsing achieves minimal awareness, it sacrifices depth of advertising communications.

Evaluating Advertising Effectiveness and the Return on Advertising Investment

Return on advertising investment
The net return on advertising investment divided by the costs of the advertising investment.

Measuring advertising effectiveness and the **return on advertising investment** has become a hot issue for most companies, especially in a challenging economic environment. Even in a recovering economy with marketing budgets again on the rise, like consumers, advertisers are still pinching their pennies and spending conservatively.[22] That leaves top management at many companies asking their marketing managers, "How do we know that we're spending the right amount on advertising?" and "What return are we getting on our advertising investment?"

Advertisers should regularly evaluate two types of advertising results: the communication effects and the sales and profit effects. Measuring the *communication effects* of an ad or ad campaign tells whether the ads and media are communicating the ad message well. Individual ads can be tested before or after they are run. Before an ad is placed, the advertiser can show it to consumers, ask how they like it, and measure message recall or attitude changes resulting from it. After an ad is run, the advertiser can measure how the ad affected consumer recall or product awareness, knowledge, and preference. Pre- and postevaluations of communication effects can be made for entire advertising campaigns as well.

Advertisers have gotten pretty good at measuring the communication effects of their ads and ad campaigns. However, *sales and profit* effects of advertising are often much harder to measure. For example, what sales and profits are produced by an ad campaign that increases brand awareness by 20 percent and brand preference by 10 percent? Sales and profits are affected by many factors other than advertising—such as product features, price, and availability.

One way to measure the sales and profit effects of advertising is to compare past sales and profits with past advertising expenditures. Another way is through experiments. For example, to test the effects of different advertising spending levels, Coca-Cola could vary the amount it spends on advertising in different market areas and measure the differences in the resulting sales and profit levels. More complex experiments could be designed to include other variables, such as differences in the ads or media used.

However, because so many factors affect advertising effectiveness, some controllable and others not, measuring the results of advertising spending remains an inexact science. Managers often must rely on large doses of judgment along with quantitative analysis when assessing advertising performance.

Other Advertising Considerations

In developing advertising strategies and programs, the company must address two additional questions. First, how will the company organize its advertising function—who will perform which advertising tasks? Second, how will the company adapt its advertising strategies and programs to the complexities of international markets?

Organizing for Advertising

Different companies organize in different ways to handle advertising. In small companies, advertising might be handled by someone in the sales department. Large companies have advertising departments whose job it is to set the advertising budget, work with the ad agency, and handle other advertising not done by the agency. However, most large companies use outside advertising agencies because they offer several advantages.

Advertising agency

A marketing services firm that assists companies in planning, preparing, implementing, and evaluating all or portions of their advertising programs.

How does an **advertising agency** work? Advertising agencies originated in the mid-to late-1800s by salespeople and brokers who worked for the media and received a commission for selling advertising space to companies. As time passed, the salespeople began to help customers prepare their ads. Eventually, they formed agencies and grew closer to the advertisers than to the media.

Today's agencies employ specialists who can often perform advertising tasks better than the company's own staff can. Agencies also bring an outside point of view to solving the company's problems, along with lots of experience from working with different clients and situations. So, today, even companies with strong advertising departments of their own use advertising agencies.

Some ad agencies are huge; the largest U.S. agency, BBDO Worldwide, has annual gross U.S. revenues of $495 million. In recent years, many agencies have grown by gobbling up other agencies, thus creating huge agency holding companies. The largest of these megagroups, WPP, includes several large advertising, PR, and promotion agencies with combined worldwide revenues of more than $16 billion.[23] Most large advertising agencies have the staff and resources to handle all phases of an advertising campaign for their clients, from creating a marketing plan to developing ad campaigns and preparing, placing, and evaluating ads and other brand content.

International Advertising Decisions

International advertisers face many complexities not encountered by domestic advertisers. The most basic issue concerns the degree to which global advertising should be adapted to the unique characteristics of various country markets.

Some advertisers have attempted to support their global brands with highly standardized worldwide advertising, with campaigns that work as well in Bangkok as they do in Baltimore. For example, McDonald's unifies its creative elements and brand presentation under the familiar "i'm lovin' it" theme in all its 100-plus markets worldwide. Visa coordinates worldwide advertising for its debit and credit cards under the "more people go with Visa" creative platform, which works as well in Korea as it does in the United States or Brazil. ● And ads from Brazilian flip-flops maker Havaianas make the same outrageously colorful splash worldwide, no matter what the country.

In recent years, the increased popularity of online social networks and video sharing has boosted the need for advertising standardization for global brands. Most big marketing and advertising campaigns include a large online presence. Connected consumers can now zip easily across borders via the Internet, making it difficult for advertisers to roll out adapted campaigns in a controlled, orderly fashion. As a result, at the very least, most global consumer brands coordinate their Web sites internationally. For example, check out the McDonald's Web sites from Germany to Jordan to China. You'll find the golden arches logo, the "i'm lovin' it" logo and jingle, a Big Mac equivalent, and maybe even Ronald McDonald himself.

Standardization produces many benefits—lower advertising costs, greater global advertising coordination, and a more consistent worldwide image. But it also has drawbacks. Most important, it ignores the fact that country markets differ greatly in their cultures, demographics, and economic conditions. Thus, most international advertisers "think globally

● Ads from colorful Brazilian flip-flops maker Havaianas make the same outrageously colorful splash worldwide, no matter what the country, here the United States and Brazil.

Estudio Collectivo De Design Ltda; Alpargatas S/A.

but act locally." They develop global advertising *strategies* that make their worldwide efforts more efficient and consistent. Then they adapt their advertising *programs* to make them more responsive to consumer needs and expectations within local markets. For example, although Visa employs its "more people go with Visa" theme globally, ads in specific locales employ local language and inspiring local imagery that make the theme relevant to the local markets in which they appear.

Global advertisers face several special problems. For instance, advertising media costs and availability differ vastly from country to country. Countries also differ in the extent to which they regulate advertising practices. Many countries have extensive systems of laws restricting how much a company can spend on advertising, the media used, the nature of advertising claims, and other aspects of the advertising program. Such restrictions often require advertisers to adapt their campaigns from country to country.

For example, alcohol products cannot be advertised in India or in Muslim countries. In many countries, such as Sweden and Canada, junk food ads are banned from children's television programming. To play it safe, McDonald's advertises itself as a family restaurant in Sweden. Comparative ads, although acceptable and even common in the United States and Canada, are less commonly used in the United Kingdom and are illegal in India and Brazil. China bans sending e-mail for advertising purposes to people without their permission, and all advertising e-mail that is sent must be titled "advertisement."

China also has restrictive censorship rules for TV and radio advertising; for example, the words *the best* are banned, as are ads that "violate social customs" or present women in "improper ways." McDonald's once avoided government sanctions in China by publicly apologizing for an ad that crossed cultural norms by showing a customer begging for a discount. Similarly, Coca-Cola's Indian subsidiary was forced to end a promotion that offered prizes, such as a trip to Hollywood, because it violated India's established trade practices by encouraging customers to "gamble."

Thus, although advertisers may develop global strategies to guide their overall advertising efforts, specific advertising programs must usually be adapted to meet local cultures and customs, media characteristics, and regulations.

Objective 3 ┈┈▶

Define the role of PR in the promotion mix.

Public Relations

Another major mass-promotion tool, public relations, consists of activities designed to build good relations with the company's various publics. PR departments may perform any or all of the following functions:[24]

- *Press relations or press agency:* Creating and placing newsworthy information in the news media to attract attention to a person, product, or service.
- *Product publicity:* Publicizing specific products.
- *Public affairs:* Building and maintaining national or local community relationships.
- *Lobbying:* Building and maintaining relationships with legislators and government officials to influence legislation and regulation.
- *Investor relations:* Maintaining relationships with shareholders and others in the financial community.
- *Development:* Working with donors or members of nonprofit organizations to gain financial or volunteer support.

Public relations (PR)

Building good relations with the company's various publics by obtaining favorable publicity; building up a good corporate image; and handling or heading off unfavorable rumors, stories, and events.

Public relations is used to promote products, people, places, ideas, activities, organizations, and even nations. Companies use PR to build good relations with consumers, investors, the media, and their communities. Trade associations have used PR to rebuild interest in commodities, such as eggs, apples, potatoes, milk, and even onions. For example, the Vidalia Onion Committee built a PR campaign around the DreamWorks character Shrek—complete with Shrek images on packaging and in-store displays with giant inflatable Shreks—that successfully promoted onions to children. Even government organizations use PR to build awareness. For example, the National Heart, Lung, and Blood Institute (NHLBI) of the National Institutes of Health sponsors a long-running PR campaign that builds awareness of heart disease in women:[25]

Heart disease is the number one killer of women; it kills more women each year than all forms of cancer combined. But a 2000 survey by the NHLBI showed that only 34 percent of women knew this, and that most people thought of heart disease as a problem mostly affecting men. So with the help of Ogilvy Public Relations Worldwide, the NHLBI set out to "create a personal and urgent wakeup call to American women." In 2002, it launched a national PR campaign—"The Heart Truth"—to raise awareness of heart disease among women and get women to discuss the issue with their doctors.

● The centerpiece of the campaign is the Red Dress, now the national symbol for women and heart disease awareness. The campaign creates awareness through an interactive Web site, Facebook and Pinterest pages, mass media placements, and campaign materials—everything from brochures, DVDs, and posters to speaker's kits and airport dioramas. It also sponsors several major national events, such as the National Wear Red Day, an annual Red Dress Collection Fashion Show, and The Heart Truth Road Show, featuring heart disease risk factor screenings in major U.S. cities. Finally, the campaign works with more than three-dozen corporate sponsors, such as Diet Coke, St. Joseph aspirin, Tylenol, Cheerios, CVS Pharmacy, Swarovski, and Bobbi Brown Cosmetics. So far, some 2.65 billion product packages have carried the Red Dress symbol.

The results are impressive: Awareness among American women of heart disease as the number one killer of women has increased to 57 percent, and the number of heart disease deaths in women has declined steadily from one in three women to one in four. The American Heart Association has also adopted the Red Dress symbol and introduced its own complementary campaign.

HEART DISEASE *doesn't*

CARE WHAT YOU WEAR

IT'S THE #1 KILLER OF WOMEN

These women know *The Heart Truth®*—no matter how great you look on the outside, heart disease can strike on the inside. And being a woman won't protect you.

Try these risk factors on for size: Do you have high blood pressure? High blood cholesterol? Diabetes? Are you inactive? Are you a smoker? Overweight? If so, this could damage your heart and lead to disability, heart attack, or both.

The Red Dress® is a red alert to take heart disease seriously. Talk to your doctor and get answers that may save your life. *The Heart Truth* is, it's best to know your risks and take action now. **www.hearttruth.gov**

U.S. Department of Health and Human Services
National Institutes of Health

**National Heart
Lung and Blood Institute**
People Science Health

THE *heart* **TRUTH™**

®, ™ *The Heart Truth, its logo, The Red Dress, and Heart Disease Doesn't Care What You Wear—It's the #1 Killer of Women are trademarks of HHS.*

● **Public relations campaigns: NHLBI's "The Heart Truth" campaign has produced impressive results in raising awareness of the risks of heart disease in women.**

Courtesy of the National Heart, Lung, and Blood Institute. The Heart Truth and Red Dress are trademarks of DHHS.

The Role and Impact of PR

Public relations can have a strong impact on public awareness at a much lower cost than advertising can. When using public relations, the company does not pay for the space or time in the media. Rather, it pays for a staff to develop and circulate information and manage events. If the company develops an interesting story or event, it could be picked up by several different media and have the same effect as advertising that would cost millions of dollars. What's more, public relations has the power to engage consumers and make them a part of the brand story and its telling (see Real Marketing 15.2).

PR results can sometimes be spectacular. Consider the launches of Apple's iPad and iPad 2:[26]

> Apple's iPad was one of the most successful new-product launches in history. The funny thing: Whereas most big product launches are accompanied by huge prelaunch advertising campaigns, Apple pulled this one off with no advertising. None at all. Instead, it simply fed the PR fire. It built buzz months in advance by distributing iPads for early reviews, feeding the offline and online press with tempting tidbits, and offering fans an early online peek at thousands of new iPad apps that would be available. At launch time, it fanned the flames with a cameo on the TV sitcom *Modern Family*, a flurry of launch-day appearances on TV talk shows, and other launch-day events. In the process, through PR alone, the iPad launch generated unbounded consumer excitement, a media frenzy, and long lines outside retail stores on launch day. Apple sold more than 300,000 of the sleek gadgets on the first day alone and more than two million in the first two months—even as demand outstripped supply. Apple repeated the feat a year later with the equally successful launch of iPad 2, which sold close to one million devices the weekend of its launch.

Despite its potential strengths, public relations is occasionally described as a marketing stepchild because of its sometimes limited and scattered use. The PR department is often located at corporate headquarters or handled by a third-party agency. Its staff is so busy dealing with various publics—stockholders, employees, legislators, and the press—that PR programs to support product marketing objectives may be ignored. Moreover, marketing managers and PR practitioners do not always speak the same language. Whereas many PR practitioners see their jobs as simply communicating, marketing managers tend to be much more interested in how advertising and PR affect brand building, sales and profits, and customer involvement and relationships.

This situation is changing, however. Although public relations still captures only a small portion of the overall marketing budgets of most firms, PR can be a powerful brand-building tool. And in this digital age, the lines between advertising and PR are becoming more and more blurred. For example, are brand Web sites, blogs, online social networks, and viral brand videos advertising efforts or PR efforts? All are both. The point is that PR should work hand in hand with advertising within an integrated marketing communications program to help build brands and customer relationships.

Objective 4 ┄┄┄ ➤

Explain how companies use PR to communicate with their publics.

Major Public Relations Tools

Public relations uses several tools. One of the major tools is *news*. PR professionals find or create favorable news about the company and its products or people. Sometimes news stories occur naturally; sometimes the PR person can suggest events or activities that would create news. Another common PR tool is *special events*, ranging from news conferences and speeches, press tours, grand openings, and fireworks displays to laser light shows, hot air balloon releases, multimedia presentations, or educational programs designed to reach and interest target publics.

Public relations people also prepare *written materials* to reach and influence their target markets. These materials include annual reports, brochures, articles, and company newsletters and magazines. *Audiovisual materials*, such as DVDs and online videos, are being used increasingly as communication tools. *Corporate identity materials* can also help create a corporate identity that the public immediately recognizes. Logos, stationery, brochures, signs, business forms, business cards, buildings, uniforms, and company cars and trucks all become marketing tools when they are attractive, distinctive, and memorable. Finally, companies can improve public goodwill by contributing money and time to *public service activities*.

As previously discussed, the Web is also an important PR channel. Web sites, blogs, and social networks such as YouTube, Facebook, Pinterest, and Twitter are providing new ways to reach and engage people. "The core strengths of public relations—the ability to tell a story and spark conversation—play well into the nature of such social media," says a PR expert. Consider the recent Wrangler NextBlue PR campaign:[28]

> Wrangler wanted to reach out beyond its core consumers—to a young, metropolitan mindset. But rather than using ads or standard PR approaches, it created NextBlue, an online project giving

Real Marketing 15.2

PR at Coca-Cola: From Impressions to Expressions to Transactions

Coca-Cola aims to do much more with public relations than just create passive "impressions." It's looking to inspire customer "expressions." According to Coca-Cola's chief marketing officer, Joe Tripodi, the PR goal is to develop "strongly sharable pieces of communication information that generate huge numbers of impressions online—and then, crucially, lead to expressions from consumers, who join the story and extend it, and then finally to transactions." That is, Coca-Cola uses PR to start customer conversations that will inspire consumers themselves to extend the brand's theme of open happiness and optimism.

Consider Coca-Cola's recent "Hug Me" campaign, in which the company installed a "happiness" vending machine overnight at a university in Singapore. The machine had a solid red front and trademark wavy white stripe, but it contained no Coca-Cola logo, no coin slot, and no soda selection buttons. Only the words "Hug Me" were visible in large white letters printed in Coca-Cola's famous script. With hidden cameras rolling, Coca-Cola captured the quizzical reactions of passersby as they first scratched their heads, then slowly approached the machine, and, finally, with smiles on their faces, gave it a big hug. Responding to that simple act of happiness, the machine magically dispensed a cold can of Coca-Cola, free of charge.

Coca-Cola's "Hug Me" video shows one person after another hugging the machine, receiving their Coke, and sharing their delight with others. Coca-Cola placed the video online, then stepped back and let the media and consumers carry the story forward. Within only one week's time, the video generated 112 million impressions. Given the low costs of the free Cokes and producing the video, the "Hug Me" campaign resulted in an amazingly low cost per impression. But even more valuable were the extensive customer expressions that followed, such as "liking" the video and forwarding it to others. "The Coca Cola Hug Machine is a simple idea to spread some happiness," says a Coca-Cola marketer.

Our strategy is to deliver doses of happiness in an unexpected, innovative way . . . and happiness is contagious."

The "Hug Me" campaign was only the most recent in a long line of similar conversation-starting PR tactics by Coca-Cola. This past Valentine's Day, the company placed a modified vending machine in the middle of a busy shopping mall that dispensed free Cokes to folks that confirmed their "couple" status with a hug or a kiss. A few years ago, another Coca-Cola Happiness machine placed at a university dispensed everything from free Cokes to popcorn, pizza, flowers, handshakes, and Polaroid photos. Making periodic "jackpot" sounds, the machine dispensed dozens of Cokes and a long plank layered with colorful cupcakes. These unexpected actions not only prompted smiles and cheers, but recipients could hardly wait to share their bounty and the story with anyone and everyone, extending Coke's happiness positioning.

Coca-Cola has fielded many other PR campaigns that employ its "impressions-expressions-transactions" model to inspire brand conversations. In its "Project Connect" campaign, the company printed 150 common first names on Coke bottles, an exploit that had consumers by the hundreds of thousands rifling through Coca-Cola displays in retail stores looking for their names. In its "Move to the Beat" project, Coca-Cola brought music, youth, and sports together for the London 2012 Olympics through an original music track by British music producer Mark Ronson, which wrapped the live sounds of five different Olympic sports around the vocals of Katy B.

Coca-Cola's long-running Arctic Home campaign

employs the power of publicity and shared media to connect the company's brands to a culturally relevant cause. In that campaign, Coca-Cola has partnered with the World Wildlife Fund (WWF) to protect the habitat of polar bears—a cause that fits perfectly with Coke's longstanding use of digitally produced polar bears as spokes-critters in its ads. The Arctic Home campaign goes well beyond clever seasonal ads by integrating PR efforts with virtually every aspect of promotion and marketing. The campaign includes a dedicated Web site, a smartphone app, a pledge of $3 million to the WWF, advertisements and online videos featuring footage from the IMAX film *To the Arctic 3D*, and attention-grabbing white Coke cans highlighting the plight of polar bears. In its first year, Arctic Home produced an astounding 1.3 billion impressions, which in turn inspired untold customer expressions.

Coca-Cola's "BHAG," or "big hairy audacious goal," is not just to hold its market share in the soft drink category, where sales have been flat for years, but to double its business by the end of the decade. Public relations and the social media will play a central role in achieving this goal by making

The power of PR: Coca-Cola's "Hug Me" campaign created 112 million impressions in only one week's time. More important, it created countless customer expressions that extended the brand's theme of happiness and optimism.

© 2012 The Coca-Cola Company. All rights reserved.

customers a part of the brand story and turning them into an army of brand advocates who will carry the Coca-Cola Open Happiness message forward. "It's not just about pushing stuff out as we've historically done," says CMO Tripodi. "We have to create experiences that perhaps are had only by a few but are compelling enough to fuel conversations with many."

Sources: Tim Nudd, "Coca-Cola Joins the Revolution in a World Where the Mob Rules," *Adweek*, June 19, 2012, www.adweek.com/print/141217; Thomas Pardee, "Olympics Campaigns Go Big on the Viral Video Chart," *Advertising Age*, May 17, 2012, http://adage.com/print/234790/; Natalie Zmuda, "Coca-Cola Gets Real with Polar Bears," *Advertising Age*, October 25, 2011, http://adage.com/print/230632/; Emma Hall, "Coca-Cola Launches Global 2012 Olympics Campaign with Mark Ronson," *Advertising Age*, September 29, 2011, http://adage.com/print/230107/; Anthony Wing Kosner, "Hug Me: Coca-Cola Introduces Gesture Based Marketing in Singapore," *Forbes*, April 11, 2012, www.forbes.com/sites/anthonykosner/2012/04/11/hug-me-coca-cola-introduces-gesture-based-marketing-in-singapore/; and "Cannes Lions 2012: Five-Points to a Great Marketing Strategy," afaqs.com, June 20, 2012, www.afaqs.com/news/story/34444.

consumers and fledgling designers a chance to create the next style of Wrangler jeans. Working with its PR agency, Wrangler created a microsite that asked consumers to create videos of themselves and their jeans designs. The campaign was promoted on Wrangler's Web site and Facebook page and in its e-mails to Wrangler subscribers. The brand also used a mix of traditional PR media, along with paid ads on Facebook and social media promotions on YouTube and Twitter, allowing the public to comment and vote on the submitted designs.

The rich integration of a paid, owned, earned, and shared PR media produced the desired results. Within just two weeks, Wrangler received 50 video submissions. The winning entry will be sold on Wrangler.com as the first design in the NextBlue line. But in addition to the new design, Wrangler also signed up 19 young designers to blog for its NextBlue site, garnered 5,000 new subscribers to its e-mail database, and counted more than 80,000 views of the finalist videos. "The heart of the NextBlue [PR] project was a brand collaboration with consumers," says a Wrangler marketing communications executive. "The social media are a natural fit for [that]."

As with the other promotion tools, in considering when and how to use product public relations, management should set PR objectives, choose the PR messages and vehicles, implement the PR plan, and evaluate the results. The firm's PR should be blended smoothly with other promotion activities within the company's overall integrated marketing communications effort.

Reviewing the Concepts

MyMarketingLab™

Go to **mymktlab.com** to complete the problems marked with this icon .

Reviewing Objectives and Key Terms

 ## Objectives Review

Companies must do more than make good products; they have to inform consumers about product benefits and carefully position products in consumers' minds. To do this, they must master *advertising* and *PR*.

Objective 1 — Define the role of advertising in the promotion mix. (pp 434–435)

Advertising—the use of paid media by a seller to inform, persuade, and remind buyers about its products or its organization—is an important promotion tool for communicating the value that marketers create for their customers. American marketers spend more than $163 billion each year on advertising, and worldwide spending exceeds $450 billion. Advertising takes many forms and has many uses. Although advertising is employed mostly by business firms, a wide range of not-for-profit organizations, professionals, and social agencies also employ advertising to promote their causes to various target publics. *PR*—gaining favorable publicity and creating a favorable company image—is the least used of the major promotion tools, although it has great potential for building consumer awareness and preference.

Objective 2 Describe the major decisions involved in developing an advertising program. (pp 435–449)

Advertising decision making involves making decisions about the advertising objectives, budget, message, and media and, finally, culminates with an evaluation of the results. Advertisers should set clear target, task, and timing *objectives*, whether the aim is to inform, persuade, or remind buyers. Advertising's goal is to move consumers through the buyer-readiness stages discussed in Chapter 14. Some advertising is designed to move people to immediate action. However, many of the ads you see today focus on building or strengthening long-term customer relationships. The advertising *budget* depends on many factors. No matter what method is used, setting the advertising budget is no easy task.

Advertising strategy consists of two major elements: creating advertising *messages* and selecting advertising *media*. The *message decision* calls for planning a message strategy and executing it effectively. Good messages are especially important in today's costly and cluttered advertising environment. Just to gain and hold attention, today's messages must be better planned, more imaginative, more entertaining, and more rewarding to consumers. In fact, many marketers are now subscribing to a new merging of advertising and entertainment, dubbed *Madison & Vine*. The *media decision* involves defining reach, frequency, and impact goals; choosing major media types; selecting media vehicles; and choosing media timing. Message and media decisions must be closely coordinated for maximum campaign effectiveness.

Finally, *evaluation* calls for evaluating the communication and sales effects of advertising before, during, and after ads are placed. Advertising accountability has become a hot issue for most companies. Increasingly, top management is asking: "What return are we getting on our advertising investment?" and "How do we know that we're spending the right

amount?" Other important advertising issues involve *organizing* for advertising and dealing with the complexities of international advertising.

Objective 3 Define the role of PR in the promotion mix. (pp 450–451)

PR—gaining favorable publicity and creating a favorable company image—is the least used of the major promotion tools, although it has great potential for building consumer awareness and preference. PR is used to promote products, people, places, ideas, activities, organizations, and even nations. Companies use PR to build good relationships with consumers, investors, the media, and their communities. PR can have a strong impact on public awareness at a much lower cost than advertising can, and PR results can sometimes be spectacular. Although PR still captures only a small portion of the overall marketing budgets of most firms, it is playing an increasingly important brand-building role. In the digital age, the lines between advertising and PR are becoming more and more blurred.

Objective 4 Explain how companies use PR to communicate with their publics. (pp 451–453)

Companies use PR to communicate with their publics by setting PR objectives, choosing PR messages and vehicles, implementing the PR plan, and evaluating PR results. To accomplish these goals, PR professionals use several tools, such as *news*, *speeches*, and *special events*. They also prepare *written*, *audiovisual*, and *corporate identity materials* and contribute money and time to *public service activities*. The Web has also become an increasingly important PR channel, as Web sites, blogs, and social networks are providing interesting new ways to reach more people.

Key Terms

Objective 1

Advertising (p 434)

Objective 2

Advertising objective (p 435)
Advertising budget (p 437)

Advertising strategy (p 437)
Madison & Vine (p 439)
Creative concept (p 440)
Execution style (p 440)
Advertising media (p 443)

Return on advertising investment (p 447)
Advertising agency (p 448)

Objective 3

Public relations (PR) (p 450)

Discussion and Critical Thinking

Discussion Questions

1. Describe the decisions marketing managers must make when developing an advertising program. (AACSB: Communication)

2. Why is it important that the advertising media and creative departments work closely together? (AACSB: Communication)

3. Discuss the characteristics advertising appeals should possess to be effective. (AACSB: Communication)

4. What are the pros and cons of standardization for international advertising? How do most companies approach the complexities of international advertising? (AACSB: Communication)

5. What are the role and functions of public relations within an organization? (AACSB: Communication)

6. Discuss the tools used by public relations professionals. Is public relations free promotion for a company? (AACSB: Communication)

Critical Thinking Exercise

1. The Public Relations Society of America (PRSA) awards the best public relations campaigns with Silver Anvil Awards. Visit www.prsa.org/Awards/Search and review several case reports of previous winners. What does the field of public relations seem to encompass? Write a report on one of the award winners focusing on marketing-related activities. (AACSB: Communication; Use of IT; Reflective Thinking)

Applications and Cases

 ## Marketing Technology Twitter—Media Friend or Foe?

Visit any media outlet's Internet site and you'll see the familiar Facebook and Twitter icons. Traditional news media have migrated to online versions and beyond through social media. But social media have become a major source of news for many people. Sixty percent of respondents in one study indicated Facebook as a source of news, and 20 percent used Twitter to learn what's happening in the world. Twitter might have a growing advantage because of the nature of short tweets and how quickly they spread. Most news outlets have a presence on Twitter, promoting their content and directing audiences to their online sites. But Twitter has found a way to make money through advertising and is hiring editorial personnel to produce and manage content. It appears that Twitter is moving away from being just a media platform to becoming a media entity, which concerns traditional media outlets. Twitter has been a partner with traditional media, but now it appears to be moving in the direction of being a competitor. Twitter's NASCAR and Olympics Hub editorial offerings were just the beginning. Part of Twitter's success is due to the relationships it has fostered with these outlets, but now Twitter is building a digital-media business on content provided by its media partners as well as eye-witness input from people located where the news is happening.

1. Explain how Twitter makes money through advertising. Find examples of companies using Twitter as a promotional tool. (AACSB: Communication; Reflective Thinking)

2. How does social media advertising spending compare to traditional mass-media advertising spending? How likely is it that Twitter can become a media entity rather than just a media platform, and what are the implications for advertisers? (AACSB: Communication; Reflective Thinking)

 ## Marketing Ethics Don't Say That!

If you like a restaurant . . . Yelp about it! If you don't . . . Yelp about it! Yelp is an online guide that posts customers' reviews of local businesses such as restaurants, spas, and even doctors. Businesses are rated based on the reviews posted about them, with 5 stars being the best. Although almost 60 percent are 4- or 5-star reviews, the remaining reviews are less positive. Bad reviews can be the kiss-of-death for a small business. Businesses do not put this information on the Yelp site—others do. This is creating a problem for many businesses. Some customers demand something in return for posting a positive review, or worse, for not posting a negative review. One restaurant owner claimed a customer threatened to post a "scathing" review after allegedly getting food poisoning from eating at the restaurant unless he received a $100 gift card. This is not much different than the unethical customers who put glass shards or a dead cockroach on their plates and demand their meal for free (conveniently when they've almost finished the dish). Most restaurants capitulate to avoid a scene. But a negative Yelp or other online review is more ominous, with "word-of-mouse" having such far-reaching and lasting consequences. Some medical professionals have gone so far as to require new patients to sign anti-defamation contracts called "medical gag-orders" before receiving treatment. These waivers attempt to prevent patients from posting negative reviews online and often include signing over copyrights of any reviews posted in an attempt to gain leverage in removing any negative content from rating sites. Some sites, such as Angie's List, flag physicians requiring such waivers, and one state—Michigan—has introduced a bill deeming such waivers illegal.

1. Visit Yelp and other sites such as Angie's List, RateMDs.com, and Rate My Professor. Are reviewers limited in any way regarding what they can say on such sites? Should they be limited? (AACSB: Communication; Ethical Reasoning; Reflective Thinking)

2. Discuss the arguments for and against doctors' rights to require medical gag-orders. Recommend how doctors should handle this situation. (AACSB: Communication; Ethical Reasoning; Reflective Thinking)

Marketing by the Numbers C3, CPM, and CPP

Nielsen ratings are very important to both advertisers and television programmers because the cost of television advertising time is based on these ratings. A show's *rating* is the number of households in Nielsen's sample that are tuned to that show divided by the number of television-owning households—115 million in the United States. One rating point represents 1 percent of the TV market, so one point equals 1.15 million households. Nielsen's TV ratings are referred to as C3 and measure viewers who watch commercials live or watch recorded commercials up to three days later. A common measure of advertising efficiency is cost per thousand (CPM), which is the ad cost per thousand potential audience contacts. Advertisers also assess the cost per rating point by dividing the ad cost by the rating. These numbers are used to assess the efficiency of a media buy. Use the following average price and rating information, which was used to pre-sell advertising for the 2012–2013 television season, to answer the questions.

Program	Cost per 0:30 spot	C3 Rating
Sunday Night Football	$425,000	11.8
American Idol	$475,000	9.0
Grey's Anatomy	$225,000	5.3
Two and a Half Men	$215,000	6.0
The Vampire Diaries	$ 75,000	1.2

1. How many households are expected to watch each program? (AACSB: Communication; Analytical Reasoning)

2. Calculate the cost per thousand (CPM) and cost per point (CPP) for each program. How should advertisers use these measures when planning a television media buy? (AACSB: Communication; Analytical Reasoning; Reflective Thinking)

 # Video Case E*trade

Super Bowl XXXIV, the first of the new millennium, was known as the Dot-com Bowl because of the glut of Internet companies that plopped down an average of $2.2 million per 30-second spot ad. Today, most of the companies that defined the dot-com glory days are gone. But one darling of the dot-com era, E*trade, remains among the few survivors. Although E*trade has experienced challenges since the turn of the century, it has also turned profits. Advertising on the big game hasn't worked out well for everyone. But for E*trade, Super Bowl ads have been part of a larger advertising effort that played a role in its survival. Although E*trade has altered its marketing mix strategies to adapt to changes in the marketing environment, it has continued to invest in the Super

Bowl as an advertising medium. In this video segment, E*trade reports on its advertising strategy as well as the advantages and disadvantages of Super Bowl advertising.

After viewing the video featuring E*trade, answer the following questions:

1. What has been the role of advertising at E*trade?

2. What factors have played a role in E*trade's decision to advertise on the Super Bowl?

3. Analyze E*trade's most recent Super Bowl ads. Is E*trade still getting its money's worth from Super Bowl advertising? Explain.

 # Company Case The Super Bowl: More Than a Single Advertising Event

Every year around Super Bowl season, a debate heats up among advertising professionals and media pundits. At the core is the big question: Is Super Bowl Advertising worth the cost? Last year, major advertisers plunked down an average of $3.5 million per 30-second spot—that's $117,000 per second! And that's just for the airtime. Throw in ad production costs—which average $2 to $3 million per showcase commercial—and running even a single Super Bowl ad becomes a super-expensive proposition. Among other points, the naysayers assert that with a cost so high there is no reasonable hope for a return on the advertising investment.

But supporters of Super Bowl advertising have plenty of evidence on their side. For starters, the big game is always the most-watched television event of the year. Last year's Super Bowl drew more than 111.3 million viewers, breaking the previous Super Bowl's record for the most-watched program in history. In addition to sheer numbers of viewers, the Super Bowl stands alone as the TV program during which the ads draw as much or more viewership than the program itself. With that consideration, one recent study asserted that for consumer packaged-goods firms, the return on investment (ROI) for one Super Bowl ad is equivalent to that of 250 regular TV ads.

Although there's no easy answer to the question of the Super Bowl's value as an advertising venue, the debates of the past miss a key issue that has evolved in the last few years. These days, the Super Bowl is merely a gateway to something much bigger. Before the game begins and long after it's over, ad critics, media pundits, and consumers are previewing and reviewing, speculating, and rating the commercials. With this perspective, no longer do advertisers create an ad that will run for one 30-second time slot. They create a broader campaign that revolves around the Super Bowl ad with strategies that include before-, during-, and after-game tactics.

Before the Game

For many years, advertisers have recognized the potential for water cooler buzz about ads following the Super Bowl. As Internet video became prevalent, the focus turned to creating an ad with the potential to go viral. But in the last couple of years, social media and mobile communications have changed the game once again. The previous rule of thumb was to build anticipation for ads by keeping them secret and unveiling them during the Super Bowl. Now, however, many advertisers try to generate excitement before the game airs by seeding information about the ad, releasing teaser ads, or even making the ad available for viewing online—essentially starting the water cooler conversation before the game.

Referring to this trend just prior to the 2012 Super Bowl, one media buyer said, "This is the first Super Bowl where social media has been an integral part of marketers' plans," suggesting that this is happening because marketers realize "you can get more bang for your buck." This is no small trend. Almost half of the 55 ads that aired during this year's Super Bowl were viewable online in one form or another prior to the date of the big game. "So many people are launching commercials early to feed the beast," says a media analyst.

While ad previews were available for ads from all different types of companies, this technique was especially popular with car brands looking to stand out amid the clutter of the 11 Super Bowl spots for automotive brands. This year, Chevrolet started months before the Super Bowl in an effort to grab a piece of Doritos' perennial consumer-generated ad buzz. Much like Doritos' annual "Crash the Super Bowl" event, Chevy's "Route 66" contest enticed entrants with a cash prize and a spot for their ad during the Super Bowl. The winning ad for the Chevy Camaro called "Happy Grad" was the first to go online, 17 days before the game aired.

Kia Motors rolled out a preview that was also clearly strategic. First, the company issued a press release describing its 60-second Super Bowl ad called "Drive the Dream." Then, nine days before the game, Kia showed a 15-second teaser ad featuring super model Adriana Lima waving a checkered flag in slow motion and the tag line "See you Sunday" in 18,000 theaters nationwide. Six days later, the full ad was shown in the same theaters, jam-packed with all the over-the-top elements sure to please any Super Bowl viewer: "a woman sprinkled with fairy dust, a man sprinkled with even more fairy dust, a Fabio-like hunk, Mötley Crüe, Adriana Lima, UFC fighter Chuck Liddell, champion bull rider Judd Leffew [on a giant rhino], an 'extreme dream sequence,' thousands of bikini-clad fans, bursts of flames and fireworks, a pair of lumberjacks sawing a massive sandwich, and a Snow White Pearl Optima Limited."

Did such pre-game buzz efforts pay off? Social media analytics company General Sentiment seems to think so. It has created a metric it calls Impact Media Value—basically, a measure of consumer impact and awareness that identifies which Super Bowl advertisers are getting the most bang for their buck prior to the game. According to General Sentiment, numerous advertisers saw a powerful return on their investment in terms of both increased social media mentions and real revenue dollars generated before the game even aired. Top performers included Kia, Volkswagen, Honda, Coca-Cola, Doritos, Samsung, and first-time Super Bowl advertiser Dannon.

During the Game

In addition to pre-game festivities, companies are recognizing the potential to increase the effectiveness of their Super Bowl ads by engaging viewers during the game. The trend of "second-screen viewing"—using a laptop or mobile device while watching TV—is exploding. One recent Nielsen survey revealed that 88 percent of tablet owners and 86 percent of smartphone owners had used their mobile devices while watching television in a 30-day period, numbers supported by Twitter activity during the 2012 Super Bowl. Throughout the game, Twitter activity registered thousands of tweets per second (TPS). The highest moments occurred at the end of the Giants–Patriots game (12,223 TPS) and during Madonna's half-time show (10,245 TPS)—rates that captured the number two and number three spots on Twitter's all-time highest activity list.

In addition to its pre-game efforts, Chevrolet set out to maximize engagement for the five ads it ran during the Super Bowl with a first-of-its-kind app designed to be used during the game. The app allowed viewers to play Super Bowl trivia, interact with each other via Twitter, participate in polls, and possibly win one of 20 Chevrolets or thousands of other prizes from the likes of Bridgestone, Motorola, NFLShop.com, Papa Johns, and Sirius XM Radio. "This is the first time any company has attempted such a large-scale app, which will enhance the game watching experience and help them engage in the online conversation about the Super Bowl," said Joel Ewanick, global chief marketing officer for General Motors. "This app takes that interactivity to a whole new level on one of the biggest days for television viewing." Some 725,000 people had downloaded the app by game time. This was all part of GM's overall goal: 1.5 billion brand impressions before, during, and after the game.

But Chevrolet wasn't the only marketer trying new techniques to turn people's attention toward their brand during the game. Estimating that 60 percent of Super Bowl viewers would have a mobile device during the broadcast, Coca-Cola ran a live, animated simulcast featuring the brand's Polar Bears as hosts of their own Super Bowl party. Dubbed the "Polar Bowl," it featured the bears and their arctic visitors reacting in real time to the game, ads, Tweets, and Facebook messages.

Representatives from Coca-Cola reported that the response dramatically exceeded its expectations. By game time, the number of fans who had RSVP'd to the event on Facebook reached 15 times Coca-Cola's goal. This led the king of cola to ramp up server capacity to accommodate up to 300,000 concurrent viewers, estimating viewers would watch for an average of 2.5 minutes each. As a backup, Coca-Cola had plenty of excess server capacity waiting in the wings.

By the third quarter, the peak number of viewers had hit 600,000. In all, more than 9 million people watched the Polar Bowl for an average of 28 minutes each. On top of this, Coca-Cola saw its number of Twitter followers grow by a whopping 38 percent during the four-hour game period. Referring to the Polar Bowl, Jennifer Healan, director of integrated marketing content for Coca-Cola, said the experiment is redefining marketing at the company. "It's a conversation, not a monologue" that Coca-Cola is striving to have with its consumers.

The After Party

For Super Bowl advertisers, when the game is over, the advertising event is still in full swing. The traditional buzz factor results from the numerous "best and worst" lists generated by journalists and bloggers. And although "winners" and "losers" vary from list to list, it is clear that all ads that air on the Super Bowl achieve post-game buzz from all the online viewing and discussion. A few examples illustrate the tremendous impact such buzz can have.

Chrysler kicked off its "Imported from Detroit" campaign during the 2011 Super Bowl with a two-minute epic featuring rapper Eminem and a resurgent Detroit as the backdrop. For 2012, Chrysler produced the two-minute sequel "It's Half-Time in America," a patriotic tribute to the soul of America starring Clint Eastwood. Both ads came out at the top of the heap in terms of pre-game buzz and post-game ratings, discussion, and views. The ads also served as anchors for a series of ads as part of an ongoing campaign. Sixteen months after the launch of the campaign, Chrysler won the Grand Effie—the top award granted at the advertising industry's Oscars. According to one jury member, "Imported from Detroit was the Grand Effie winner because they sold the product, the category, and the city."

Volkswagen also had a stellar showing during the 2011 Super Bowl with its ad "The Force"—a 60-second spot featuring a pint-sized Darth Vader who surprises himself when he brings a Passat to life. Volkswagen approached the 2012 game with the intention to extend its success. A pre-game online teaser entitled "The Bark Side" featured a chorus of dogs barking out the "Imperial March." Continuing the Star Wars theme, Volkswagen's 2012 Super Bowl ad "The Dog Strikes Back" was a viewer favorite and a top finisher on most lists. But in perhaps the biggest indicator of the post-game value of Super Bowl ads, "The Force" not only finished out 2011 as the most viral auto video with over 63 million views, it was also one of the most buzzed about ads during the 2012 Super Bowl season. For January 2012, Volkswagen reported a 48 percent increase in U.S. sales, its best performance since 1974. Although it's impossible to say just how much the Super Bowl ads have contributed to Volkswagen's success, VW is confident that its Super Bowl investment has more than paid for itself.

The efforts and successes by the most recent Super Bowl sponsors are far too numerous to mention here. And whether every tactic employed by every advertiser worked perfectly is not the point. The point is that now more than ever, advertising during the Super Bowl isn't about gaining huge exposure by running a single ad or group of ads in a television event with a huge audience. This year more than ever before, viewers watched, buzzed, shared, clicked, streamed, and responded to Super Bowl advertisers before, during, and after the game. To get the most out of their investments, marketers must have a comprehensive program that takes advantage of the broad Super Bowl season.

Questions for Discussion

1. What factors have played the biggest role in changing the dynamics of Super Bowl advertising in recent years?

2. Discuss the concepts of reach, frequency, and impact as they relate to Super Bowl advertising. How does consideration and planning for these concepts differ between the Super Bowl and other television events?

3. When assessing return on investment, what objectives must Super Bowl advertisers consider?

4. Choose a brand that has not recently run a Super Bowl ad. Design an effective campaign with before-, during-, and after-game promotional tactics.

Sources: Bruce Horovitz, Laura Petrecca, and Gary Strauss, "Super Bowl Ad Meter Winner: Score One for the Doritos Baby," *USA Today*, February 8, 2012, www.usatoday.com/money/advertising/story/2012-02-07/usa-today-facebook-super-bowl-ad-meter-winner/53004032/1; "Play to Win with Interactive Chevy App for Super Bowl XLVI," January 19, 2012, www.media.gm.com; Todd Cunningham, "Super Bowl Ads: Which Ones Generated the Most Pre-Game Buzz?" Reuters, February 5, 2012, www.reuters.com/article/2012/02/05/idUS138752904220120205; Jonathan Welch, "Volkswagen Super Bowl Sequel: 'Dog Strikes Back,'" *Wall Street Journal*, February 1, 2012, http://blogs.wsj.com/drivers-seat/2012/02/01/volkswagen-super-bowl-sequel-dog-strikes-back-video/; Paul A. Eisenstein, "Chrysler Wins Big for 'Imported from Detroit' Campaign," *Detroit Bureau*, May 25, 2012, www.thedetroitbureau.com/2012/05/chrysler-wins-big-for-imported-from-detroit-campaign/; and Natalie Zmuda, "Coca-Cola Polar Bowl Engaged 9 Million People," *Advertising Age*, May 9, 2012, http://adage.com/print/234645/.

MyMarketingLab

Go to **mymktlab.com** for Auto-graded writing questions as well as the following Assisted-graded writing questions:

15-1. Any message can be presented using different execution styles. Select a brand and target audience and design two advertisements, each using a different execution style to deliver the same message to the target audience but in a different way. Identify the types of execution styles you are using and present your advertisements. (AACSB: Communication; Reflective Thinking)

15-2. Brands are now starring in movies, television shows, video games, and books. Form a small group and monitor primetime television programming across a network or cable channel for one week. Identify the brands shown or mentioned in an episode of a program. What product categories seem to be more prevalent? How were the brands presented? Write a report on what you find. (AACSB: Communication; Reflective Thinking)

15-3. Mymktlab Only – comprehensive writing assignment for this chapter.

References

1. Based on information found in Terry Golesworthy, "You Talkin' to Me?" Customerrespect.com, May 10, 2012, http://customerrespect.com/blog/2012/05/10/you-talkin-to-me-you-talkin-to-me-you-talkin-to-me/; Judann Pollack, "In the Insurance Ad War, Consumers Ask: Who's Who?" *Advertising Age*, February 21, 2011; http://adage.com/print/148994/; E. J. Schultz, "Cheat Sheet: Facts and Figures Behind the Faces in Those Car Insurance Ads," *Advertising Age*, February 21, 2011, http://adage.com/print/148986/; E. J. Schultz, "How the Insurance Industry Got into a $4 Billion Ad Brawl," *Advertising Age*, February 21, 2011, http://adage.com/print/148992/; "GEICO Ad Spending Far Outstrips Its Peers—Study," *Reuters*, June 22, 2012; and advertisements and other information accessed at www.allstate.com/mayhem-is-everywhere.aspx, October 2012. Allstate®, "Good Hands®", "Mayhem®", "You're in good hands with Allstate®", "Are you in good hands?®" are registered trademarks of the Allstate Insurance Company.

2. "Advertising Spending," *Advertising Age*, December 19, 2011, p. 4; Ryan Joe, "North American Advertising Spend to Increase in 2012," *Direct Marketing News*, March 14, 2012, www.dmnews.com/north-american-advertising-spend-to-increase-in-2012/article/232016/; and Ryan Joe, "U.S. Advertising Spend Increases Slightly in 2011," *Direct Marketing News*, March 13, 2012, www.dmnews.com/us-advertising-spend-increases-slightly-in-2011/article/231864/.

3. See http://2010.census.gov/mediacenter/paid-ad-campaign/new-ads/index.php?vn11, accessed June 2010; and "100 Leading National Advertisers," *Advertising Age,* June 20, 2011, p. 10.

4. For this and other examples of comparative advertising, see "Kraft, Sara Lee Call Truce in Weiner War," *Chicago Tribune,* September 8, 2011; "What Marketers Can Learn from the Great Weiner War," *Advertising Age,* August 17, 2011, http://adage.com/article/229299/; and Gabriel Beltrone; "Creatives Discuss How to Be Provocative and Effective," *Adweek,* May 8, 2012, www.adweek.com/print/140140.

5. For more on advertising budgets, see Ronald Lane, Karen King, and Thomas Russell, *Kleppner's Advertising Procedure,* 18th ed. (Upper Saddle River, NJ: Prentice Hall, 2011), Chapter 6.

6. See Jean Halliday, "Thinking Big Takes Audi from Obscure to Awesome," *Advertising Age,* February 2, 2009, accessed at http://adage.com/print ?article_id=134234; Chad Thomas and Andreas Cremer, "Audi Feels a Need for Speed in the U.S.," *Bloomberg BusinessWeek,* November 22, 2010, p. 1; Tito F. Hermoso, "Watch Out for Audi," *BusinessWorld,* June 15, 2011, p. 1; and Christina Rogers, "Audi of America Sees a Year in 2 Halves: Good and Better," *Automotive News,* June 4, 2012, p. 22.

7. "Forget the Bundle, Consumers Have an Appetite for Choice," *Videomind,* December 16, 2011, http://videomind.ooyala.com/blog/forget-bundle-consumers-have-appetite-choice; and "Number of Magazine Titles," www.magazine.org/ASME/EDITORIAL_TRENDS/1093.aspx, accessed July 2012.

8. Caitlin A. Johnson, "Cutting Through the Advertising Clutter," *CBS Sunday Morning,* February 11, 2009, www.cbsnews.com/2100-3445_162-2015684.html.

9. Steve McClellan, "4As: Costs Rose for Spots; Agency Markup Came Down," *MediaDailyNews,* December 24, 2011, www.mediapost.com/publications/article/164727/4as-costs-rose-for-spots-agency-markup-came-down.html; Brian Steinberg "'American Idol,' NFL Duke It Out for Priciest TV Spot," *Advertising Age,* October 24, 2011, p. 4; and "Cost of Average Super Bowl Commercial? $3.5M," *USA Today,* January 3, 2012, www.usatoday.com/sports/football/nfl/story/2012-01-03/super-bowl-ad/52360232/1.

10. "Advertising in the U.S.: Synovate Global Survey Shows Internet, Innovation and Online Privacy a Must," December 3, 2009, accessed at www.synovate.com/news/article/2009/12/advertising-in-the-us-synovate-global-survey-shows-internet-innovation-and-online-privacy-a-must.html; and "Disconnect: Marketers Say TV Ads More Effective in General, Yet Traditional Spots 'Dissatisfy,'" TVexchanger.com, February 16, 2012, www.tvexchanger.com/interactive-tv-news/disconnect-marketers-say-tv-ads-more-effective-in-general-yet-traditional-spots-dissatisfy/.

11. Jared Sternberg, "The DVR Ate My Ad—A Lot More People Fast-Forward Through TV Commercials Than You Think," *The Sternberg Report,* April 5, 2011, http://thestarryeye.typepad.com/sternberg/2011/04/the-dvr-ate-my-ad-a-lot-more-people-fast-forward-through-commercials-than-you-think.html; and Brian Stelter, "On Sundays, the DVR Runneth Over," *New York Times,* April 20, 2012, p. C1.

12. See Brian Steinberg, "Why So Many Brands Want to Be on *Modern Family . . .* and So Few Will," *Advertising Age,* January 23, 2012, pp. 2+.

13. "Denny's; Jessica Biel, Maya Rudolph, and Andy Richter Are Some of the Next to 'Open Up' in Denny's Latest Celebrity Web Series," *Marketing Weekly News,* April 28, 2012, p. 594; and Andrew Adam Newman, "Denny's Uses Web Series to Speak to Young Adults," *New York Times,* April 11, 2012, p. B13.

14. Based on information found in Bob Garfield, "How Etsy Made Us Rethink Consumer-Generated Ads," *Advertising Age,* September 21,

2009, p. 4. Also see Benjamin Lawrence, Susan Fournier, and Frederic Brunel, "Online Word-of-Mouth in the Co-Creation and Dissemination of Consumer-Generated Ads," Boston University School of Management Research Paper Series, May 8, 2012, http://papers.ssrn.com/sol3/papers.cfm?abstract_id=2052661.

15. Michael Bourne, "Sailing the 14 Social C's," Mullen, February 12, 2012, www.mullen.com/sailing-the-14-social-cs.

16. See David Kiley, "Paying for Viewers Who Pay Attention," *BusinessWeek,* May 18, 2009, p. 56.

17. Brian Steinberg, "Viewer-Engagement Rankings Signal Change for TV Industry," *Advertising Age,* May 10, 2010, p. 12.

18. Tavis Coburn, "Mayhem on Madison Avenue," *Fast Company,* January 2011, pp. 110–115.

19. Joe Tripoti, "Coca-Cola Marketing Shifts from Impressions to Expressions," April 27, 2011, http://blogs.hbr.org/cs/2011/04/coca-colas_marketing_shift_fro.html; and Tim Nudd, "Coca-Cola Joins the Revolution in a World Where the Mod Rules," *Adweek,* June 19, 2012, www.adweek.com/print/141217.

20. See Jon Swartz, "Multitasking at Home: Internet and TV Viewing," *USA Today,* July 6, 2010, www.usatoday.com; Dan Zigmond and Horst Stipp, "Vision Statement: Multitaskers May Be Advertisers' Best Audience," *Harvard Business Review,* January–February 2011, http://hbr.org/2011/01/vision-statement-multitaskers-may-be-advertisers-best-audience/ar/1; Kunar Patel, "When's Prime Time in Mobile? Same as TV," *Advertising Age,* July 5, 2011, www.adage.com/print/228536; and Mike Chapman, "Fighting for Attention," *Adweek,* June 6, 2011, p. 14.

21. *Newsweek* and *BusinessWeek* cost and circulation data online at http://bloombergmedia.com/pdfs/bbw_2012_rates.pdf and http://mediakit.newsweekdailybeast.com/pdf/2012_NW_RateCard.pdf, accessed September 2012.

22. See Stuart Elliott, "Marketing Budgets Rise for Some Giants," *New York Times,* February 21, 2012, p. B1; and "ANA 2012 Recession Survey Shows Steadfast, Conservative Outlook," Association of National Advertisers, April 2, 2012, www.ana.net/content/show/id/23198.

23. Information on advertising agency revenues from "Agency Report," *Advertising Age,* April 30, 2012, pp. 14–34.

24. Adapted from Scott Cutlip, Allen Center, and Glen Broom, *Effective Public Relations,* 10th ed. (Upper Saddle River, NJ: Prentice Hall, 2009), Chapter 1.

25. Information from "The Heart Truth: Making Healthy Hearts Fashionable," Ogilvy Public Relations Worldwide, www.ogilvypr.com/en/case-study/heart-truth ?page=0, www.goredforwomen.org/; www.nhlbi.nih.gov/educational/hearttruth/; and www.nhlbi.nih.gov/educational/hearttruth/about/index.htm, accessed November 2012.

26. See Geoffrey Fowler and Ben Worthen, "Buzz Powers iPad Launch," *Wall Street Journal,* April 2, 2010; "Apple iPad Sales Top 2 Million Since Launch," *Tribune-Review* (Pittsburgh), June 2, 2010; "PR Pros Must Be Apple's iPad as a True Game-Changer," *PRweek,* May 2010, p. 23; Yukari Iwatani Kane, "Apple's iPad 2 Chalks up Strong Sales in Weekend Debut," *Wall Street Journal,* March 14, 2011, http://online.wsj.com/article/SB1000142405274870402750457619883266773862.html; and "Apple Launches New iPad," March 7, 2012, www.apple.com/pr/library/2012/03/07Apple-Launches-New-iPad.html.

27. Michael Bush, "P&G's Marc Pritchard Touts Value of PR," *Advertising Age,* October 27, 2010, http://adage.com/article/news/p-g-s-marc-pritchard-touts-pr/146749/.

28. Adapted from information in Julie Liesse, "The Big Idea," *Advertising Age,* November 28, 2011, pp. C4–C6.

Part 1: Defining Marketing and the Marketing Process (Chapters 1–2)
Part 2: Understanding the Marketplace and Consumers (Chapters 3–6)
Part 3: Designing a Customer-Driven Strategy and Mix (Chapters 7–17)
Part 4: Extending Marketing (Chapters 18–20)

Personal **Selling** and Sales **Promotion**

16

Chapter Preview

In the previous two chapters, you learned about communicating customer value through integrated marketing communications (IMC) and two elements of the promotion mix: advertising and public relations. In this chapter, we examine two more IMC elements: personal selling and sales promotion. Personal selling is the interpersonal arm of marketing communications, in which the sales force interacts with customers and prospects to build relationships and make sales. Sales promotion consists of short-term incentives to encourage the purchase or sale of a product or service. As you read, remember that although this chapter presents personal selling and sales promotion as separate tools, they must be carefully integrated with the other elements of the promotion mix.

To start, what is your first reaction when you think of a salesperson or a sales force? Perhaps you think of pushy retail sales clerks, "yell-and-sell" TV pitchmen, or the stereotypical glad-handing "used-car salesman." In reality, such stereotypes simply don't fit most of today's salespeople. Instead, today's sales professionals succeed not by taking advantage of customers but by listening to their needs and helping them to forge solutions. Consider IBM, whose customer-focused sales force has been the model for modern personal selling for nearly a century.

IBM: A Classic Model for Modern Customer-Focused Selling

When Thomas J. Watson Sr. became president of the young Computing Tabulating Recording Corporation—as IBM was known in 1915—sales was considered by many to be a barely reputable profession. Back then, in the minds of most folks, salespeople were slick, fast-talking men who employed hard-sell tactics and fast-and-loose claims to peddle whatever they thought would make them a buck. Watson was a salesman at heart—he'd cut his teeth selling pianos off the back of a horse-drawn wagon to farmers in upstate New York. But he had a different vision for selling. By the time his company was renamed IBM in 1924, he had already put in place a sales force template that would forever change the face of professional sales.

At IBM, Watson hired only top-performing graduates from Ivy League universities, and he insisted that they wear conservative suits and white dress shirts. He demanded the highest ethical standards. IBM provided intensive sales training that focused on developing a deep knowledge of the company and its customers. Above all, Watson stressed, "be a good listener, observe, study through observation." This advice became the foundation of what the company later came to call "solutions selling." By the time Watson handed over the reins of IBM to his son in the 1950s, his forward-looking sales principles were firmly engrained in the company's culture, and IBM had become the model for modern customer-centered selling.

Now a $107 billion company, IBM has survived and prospered for nearly 100 years—something no other *Fortune* top-25 company can claim. During that time, *what* IBM sells has changed dramatically, from cash registers to typewriters to mainframe computers and PCs to its current complex mix of information technology hardware, software, and services. What hasn't changed is *how* IBM sells. IBM salespeople have always been customer relationship developers and solutions providers.

> Over the past 100 years, *what* IBM sells has changed dramatically. What hasn't changed is *how* IBM sells. IBM's customer-focused salespeople have always been customer relationship developers and solutions providers.

Consider Vivek Gupta, who became IBM's top salesperson in its fastest-growing industry (telecommunications) and fastest-growing market (India). When Gupta first joined IBM in 2003, his sales strengths and philosophies were a perfect fit for the company. IBM was a newcomer in India, struggling to gain a foothold in a market where more than 70 percent of corporations are family controlled, where relationships, trust, and family ties trump almost everything else. In addition to his formal IBM training, Gupta launched his own extensive investigative effort, getting to know people, learning about IBM and its customers, and developing a rock-solid knowledge of how the company's products and services fit customer needs.

When Gupta first approached potential customer Vodafone—the dominant firm in India's exploding mobile phone market—the managing director there told him, "I don't do any business with IBM and I don't intend to." But the quietly determined Gupta kept at it, getting to know Vodafone's key decision makers and patiently listening, observing, and identifying how IBM might be able to help Vodafone succeed in its volatile and competitive markets. Gupta came to know more about Vodafone than many people who worked there. It took him nearly four years, but Gupta finally sold Vodafone—the same people who vowed never to do business with IBM—on a gigantic five-year, $600-million turn-key contract to handle everything from Vodafone's customer service to its finances. Gupta became such a well-known figure at Vodafone's offices in Mumbai that many people there were surprised that his badge said "IBM" not "Vodafone."

Gupta thrives on rooting out customer problems to solve. "You have to understand [customers'] pain points," he explains. "And they are not going to spell them out." For example, when another big prospect told him "Thanks, but we don't need anything," Gupta asked for permission to study the potential customer's business anyway, no strings attached. Chatting with the company's engineers, he learned that the microwave radio technology they were using in their mobile phone towers was crashing their network six or seven times each week, a very costly problem that greatly annoyed mobile customers. Returning to make a second sales call on the decision maker who'd snubbed him initially, Gupta explained that he understood the network reliability problem and that IBM had a relatively inexpensive fix. That call resulted in a small contract for new microwave radios—not much to brag about. But within a year, the small foothold had led to additional business worth more than $100 million.

Flush with success, Gupta set his sights on still bigger targets. He realized that many big Indian telecoms were so busy simply hammering out their basic back-office operating systems that they had little money and brainpower left for strategy, branding, and marketing. However, IBM had all the technology and expertise required to build and maintain such systems. What if IBM were to take over managing the system innards, freeing the customer to attend to strategy and marketing? Gupta proposed just such a novel solution to Bharti Airtel, then a relative newcomer to India's wireless industry. The result: IBM now runs the bulk of Bharti Airtel's

back-office operations, while Bharti Airtel focuses on taking care of its own customers. In the first five years, the deal produced an incredible $1 billion for IBM. Bharti Airtel is now India's wireless industry leader and the deal is a staple "how-to" case study in IBM's emerging markets sales training.

IBM's culture has always dictated that its salespeople be "part teacher, part psychologist, and part glad-hander," observes one IBM watcher. But Vivek Gupta's success demonstrates that, to be really good in sales today, they also must be "part diplomat, part entrepreneur, and part inventor"—complete customer problem solvers. Gupta doesn't just sell IBM computer hardware and software, he sells the people and systems that will make the hardware and software come to life. He sells the essential concepts behind the entire system of IBM people and products that will deliver results for the customer. "It's at once radically simple and just plain radical," says the analyst. "He wants to convince you that IBM can run your business—your entire business, save for strategy and marketing—better than you can."

Thus, over the past 100 years, many things have changed as IBM has adapted to the turbulent technological environment. But one thing has remained constant—IBM salespeople are still inspired by Watson's founding principles of selling. Today, IBM still asks aspiring prospective sales candidates, "Can you sell a solution? Can you sell change? Can you create value through industry knowledge?" Vivek Gupta is all about solutions. That's what made him a sales superstar at Big Blue. "I don't remember a single deal in my career which I pursued and I lost," he says. "It's just a question of time. If I play very smart, I can crack the nuts very quickly. If I don't play smart, it might take some time."[1]

Vivek Gupta became IBM's top salesperson in its fastest-growing marketing division (telecommunications) and fastest-growing market (India). He wins business by patiently listening, observing, and identifying how IBM can solve customers' problems.

© anaymann.com. Courtesy Vivek Gupta

Objective Outline

Objective 1	**Discuss the role of a company's salespeople in creating value for customers and building customer relationships.** **Personal Selling** (pp 462–464)
Objective 2	**Identify and explain the six major sales force management steps.** **Managing the Sales Force** (pp 464–475)
Objective 3	**Discuss the personal selling process, distinguishing between transaction-oriented marketing and relationship marketing.** **The Personal Selling Process** (pp 475–479)
Objective 4	**Explain how sales promotion campaigns are developed and implemented.** **Sales Promotion** (pp 479–484)

MyMarketingLab™
★ Improve Your Grade!
Over 10 million students improved their results using the Pearson MyLabs.
Visit **mymktlab.com** for simulations, tutorials, and end-of-chapter problems.

In this chapter, we examine two more promotion mix tools: *personal selling* and *sales promotion*. Personal selling consists of interpersonal interactions with customers and prospects to make sales and maintain customer relationships. Sales promotion involves using short-term incentives to encourage customer purchasing, reseller support, and sales force efforts.

Personal Selling

Objective 1 ┈┈➤
Discuss the role of a company's salespeople in creating value for customers and building customer relationships.

Robert Louis Stevenson once noted, "Everyone lives by selling something." Companies around the world use sales forces to sell products and services to business customers and final consumers. But sales forces are also found in many other kinds of organizations. For example, colleges use recruiters to attract new students, and churches use membership committees to attract new members. Museums and fine arts organizations use fund-raisers to contact donors and raise money. Even governments use sales forces. The U.S. Postal Service, for instance, uses a sales force to sell Express Mail and other services to corporate customers. In the first part of this chapter, we examine personal selling's role in the organization, sales force management decisions, and the personal selling process.

The Nature of Personal Selling

Personal selling
Personal presentations by the firm's sales force for the purpose of making sales and building customer relationships.

Personal selling is one of the oldest professions in the world. The people who do the selling go by many names, including salespeople, sales representatives, agents, district managers, account executives, sales consultants, and sales engineers.

People hold many stereotypes of salespeople—including some unfavorable ones. *Salesman* may bring to mind the image of Dwight Schrute, the opinionated Dunder Mifflin

● Professional selling: It takes more than fast talk and a warm smile to sell expensive airplanes. Boeing's real challenge is to win business by building partnerships—day-in, day-out, year-in, year-out—with its customers.
Boeing

paper salesman from the TV show *The Office*, who lacks both common sense and social skills. Or they may think of the real-life "yell-and-sell" TV pitchmen, who hawk everything from the ShamWow to the Swivel Sweeper and Flex Seal in infomercials. However, the majority of salespeople are a far cry from these unfortunate stereotypes.

As the opening IBM story shows, most salespeople are well-educated and well-trained professionals who add value for customers and maintain long-term customer relationships. They listen to their customers, assess customer needs, and organize the company's efforts to solve customer problems. The best salespeople are the ones who work closely with customers for mutual gain. ● Consider Boeing, the aerospace giant competing in the rough-and-tumble worldwide commercial aircraft market. It takes more than fast talk and a warm smile to sell expensive airplanes:

> Selling high-tech aircraft at $150 million or more a copy is complex and challenging. A single big sale to an airline, air-freight carrier, government, and military customer can easily run into billions of dollars. Boeing salespeople head up an extensive team of company specialists—sales and service technicians, financial analysts, planners, engineers—all dedicated to finding ways to satisfy a large customer's needs. On the customer side, buying a batch of jetliners involves dozens or even hundreds of decision-makers from all levels of the buying organization, and layer upon layer of subtle and not-so-subtle buying influences. The selling process is nerve-rackingly slow—it can take two or three years from the first sales presentation to the day the sale is announced. After getting the order, salespeople then must stay in almost constant touch to keep track of the account's equipment needs and to make certain the customer stays satisfied. The real challenge is to win buyers' business by building day-in, day-out, year-in, year-out partnerships with them based on superior products and close collaboration.

Salesperson

An individual who represents a company to customers by performing one or more of the following activities: prospecting, communicating, selling, servicing, information gathering, and relationship building.

The term **salesperson** covers a wide range of positions. At one extreme, a salesperson might be largely an *order taker*, such as the department store salesperson standing behind the counter. At the other extreme are *order getters*, whose positions demand *creative selling* and *relationship building* for products and services ranging from appliances, industrial equipment, and airplanes to insurance and information technology services. In this chapter, we focus on the more creative types of selling and the process of building and managing an effective sales force.

The Role of the Sales Force

Personal selling is the interpersonal arm of the promotion mix. Advertising consists largely of nonpersonal communication with large groups of consumers. By contrast, personal selling involves interpersonal interactions between salespeople and individual customers—whether face to face, by phone, via e-mail, through video or Internet conferences, or by other means. Personal selling can be more effective than advertising in more complex selling situations. Salespeople can probe customers to learn more about their problems and then adjust the marketing offer and presentation to fit each customer's special needs.

The role of personal selling varies from company to company. Some firms have no salespeople at all—for example, companies that sell only online or through catalogs, or companies that sell through manufacturer's reps, sales agents, or brokers. In most firms, however, the sales force plays a major role. In companies that sell business products and services, such as IBM, DuPont, or Boeing, salespeople work directly with customers. In consumer product companies such as Nestlé or Nike, the sales force plays an important behind-the-scenes role. It works with wholesalers and retailers to gain their support and help them be more effective in selling the company's products to final buyers.

Linking the Company with Its Customers

The sales force serves as a critical link between a company and its customers. ● In many cases, salespeople serve two masters—the seller and the buyer. First, they *represent the company to customers*. They find and develop new customers and communicate information about the company's products and services. They sell products by approaching customers, presenting their offerings, answering objections, negotiating prices and terms, closing sales, and servicing accounts.

At the same time, salespeople *represent customers to the company*, acting inside the firm as "champions" of customers' interests and managing the buyer-seller relationship. Salespeople relay customer concerns about company products and actions back inside to those who can handle them. They learn about customer needs and work with other marketing and nonmarketing people in the company to develop greater customer value.

In fact, to many customers, the salesperson *is* the company—the only tangible manifestation of the company that they see. Hence, customers may become loyal to salespeople as well as to the companies and products they represent. This concept of *salesperson-owned loyalty* lends even more importance to the salesperson's customer-relationship-building abilities. Strong relationships with the salesperson will result in strong relationships with the company and its products. Conversely, poor salesperson relationships will probably result in poor company and product relationships.

Given its role in linking the company with its customers, the sales force must be strongly customer-solutions focused. In fact, such a customer-solutions focus is a must not only for the sales force but also for the entire organization.

● **Salespeople link the company with its customers. To many customers, the salesperson is the company.**

Digital Vision

Coordinating Marketing and Sales

Ideally, the sales force and other marketing functions (marketing planners, brand managers, and researchers) should work together closely to jointly create value for customers. Unfortunately, however, some companies still treat sales and marketing as separate functions. When this happens, the separate sales and marketing groups may not get along well. When things go wrong, marketers blame the sales force for its poor execution of what they see as an otherwise splendid strategy. In turn, the sales team blames the marketers for being out of touch with what's really going on with customers. Neither group fully values the other's contributions. However, if not repaired, such disconnects between marketing and sales can damage customer relationships and company performance.

A company can take several actions to help bring its marketing and sales functions closer together. At the most basic level, it can increase communications between the two groups by arranging joint meetings and spelling out communications channels. It can create opportunities for salespeople and marketers to work together. Brand managers and researchers can tag along on sales calls or sit in on sales planning sessions. In turn, salespeople can sit in on marketing planning sessions and share their firsthand customer knowledge.

A company can also create joint objectives and reward systems for sales and marketing teams or appoint marketing-sales liaisons—people from marketing who "live with the sales force" and help coordinate marketing and sales force programs and efforts. Finally, it can appoint a high-level marketing executive to oversee both marketing and sales. Such a person can help infuse marketing and sales with the common goal of creating value for customers to capture value in return.[2]

Sales force management
Analyzing, planning, implementing, and controlling sales force activities.

Objective 2 ┈┈▶
Identify and explain the six major sales force management steps.

Managing the Sales Force

We define **sales force management** as analyzing, planning, implementing, and controlling sales force activities. It includes designing sales force strategy and structure, as well as

FIGURE | 16.1
Major Steps in Sales Force
Management

The goal of this process? You guessed it! The company wants to build a skilled and motivated sales team that will help to create customer value and build strong customer relationships.

recruiting, selecting, training, compensating, supervising, and evaluating the firm's salespeople. These major sales force management decisions are shown in ● **Figure 16.1** and discussed in the following sections.

Designing the Sales Force Strategy and Structure

Marketing managers face several sales force strategy and design questions. How should salespeople and their tasks be structured? How big should the sales force be? Should salespeople sell alone or work in teams with other people in the company? Should they sell in the field, by phone, or on the Internet? We address these issues next.

The Sales Force Structure

A company can divide sales responsibilities along any of several lines. The structure decision is simple if the company sells only one product line to one industry with customers in many locations. In that case the company would use a *territorial sales force structure*. However, if the company sells many products to many types of customers, it might need a *product sales force structure*, a *customer sales force structure*, or a combination of the two.

Territorial sales force structure
A sales force organization that assigns each salesperson to an exclusive geographic territory in which that salesperson sells the company's full line.

In the **territorial sales force structure**, each salesperson is assigned to an exclusive geographic area and sells the company's full line of products or services to all customers in that territory. This organization clearly defines each salesperson's job and fixes accountability. It also increases the salesperson's desire to build local customer relationships that, in turn, improve selling effectiveness. Finally, because each salesperson travels within a limited geographic area, travel expenses are relatively small. A territorial sales organization is often supported by many levels of sales management positions. For example, individual territory sales reps may report to area managers, who in turn report to regional managers who report to a director of sales.

Product sales force structure
A sales force organization in which salespeople specialize in selling only a portion of the company's products or lines.

If a company has numerous and complex products, it can adopt a **product sales force structure**, in which the sales force specializes along product lines. For example, GE employs different sales forces within different product and service divisions of its major businesses. Within GE Infrastructure, for instance, the company has separate sales forces for aviation, energy, transportation, and water processing products and technologies. No single salesperson can become expert in all of these product categories, so product specialization is required. Similarly, GE Healthcare employs different sales forces for diagnostic imaging, life sciences, and integrated IT products and services. In all, a company as large and complex as GE might have dozens of separate sales forces serving its diverse product and service portfolio.

Customer (or market) sales force structure
A sales force organization in which salespeople specialize in selling only to certain customers or industries.

Using a **customer** (or **market**) **sales force structure**, a company organizes its sales force along customer or industry lines. Separate sales forces may be set up for different industries, serving current customers versus finding new ones, and serving major accounts versus regular accounts. Organizing the sales force around customers can help a company build closer relationships with important customers. Many companies even have special sales forces to handle the needs of individual large customers. ● For example, appliance maker Whirlpool assigns individual teams of salespeople to big retail customers such as Sears, Lowe's, Best Buy, and Home Depot. Each Whirlpool sales team aligns with the large customer's buying team.[3]

When a company sells a wide variety of products to many types of customers over a broad geographic area, it often employs a *complex sales force structure*, which combines several types of organization. Salespeople can be specialized by customer and territory; product and territory; product and customer; or territory, product, and customer. For example, Whirlpool specializes its sales force by customer (with different sales teams for Sears, Lowe's, Best Buy, Home Depot, and smaller independent retailers) *and* by territory

● Sales force structure: Whirlpool specializes its sales force by customer and by territory for each key customer group.

Paul Sancya/Associated Press

for each key customer group (territory representatives, territory managers, regional managers, and so on). No single structure is best for all companies and situations. Each company should select a sales force structure that best serves the needs of its customers and fits its overall marketing strategy.

Sales Force Size

Once the company has set its structure, it is ready to consider *sales force size*. Sales forces may range in size from only a few salespeople to tens of thousands. Some sales forces are huge—for example, PepsiCo employs 36,000 salespeople; American Express, 23,400; GE, 16,400; and Xerox, 15,000.[4] Salespeople constitute one of the company's most productive—and most expensive—assets. Therefore, increasing their numbers will increase both sales and costs.

Many companies use some form of *workload approach* to set sales force size. Using this approach, a company first groups accounts into different classes according to size, account status, or other factors related to the amount of effort required to maintain the account. It then determines the number of salespeople needed to call on each class of accounts the desired number of times.

The company might think as follows: Suppose we have 1,000 A-level accounts and 2,000 B-level accounts. A-level accounts require 36 calls per year, and B-level accounts require 12 calls per year. In this case, the sales force's *workload*—the number of calls it must make per year—is 60,000 calls [(1,000 × 36) + (2,000 × 12) = 36,000 + 24,000 = 60,000]. Suppose our average salesperson can make 1,000 calls a year. Thus, we need 60 salespeople (60,000 ÷ 1,000).

Other Sales Force Strategy and Structure Issues

Sales management must also determine who will be involved in the selling effort and how various sales and sales support people will work together.

Outside sales force (or field sales force)

Salespeople who travel to call on customers in the field.

Inside sales force

Salespeople who conduct business from their offices via telephone, the Internet, or visits from prospective buyers.

Outside and Inside Sales Forces. A company may have an **outside sales force** (or **field sales force**), an **inside sales force**, or both. Outside salespeople travel to call on customers in the field. In contrast, inside salespeople conduct business from their offices via telephone, the Internet, or visits from buyers.

Some inside salespeople provide support for the outside sales force, freeing them to spend more time selling to major accounts and finding new prospects. For example, *technical sales support people* provide technical information and answers to customers' questions. *Sales assistants* provide administrative backup for outside salespeople. They call ahead and confirm appointments, follow up on deliveries, and answer customers' questions when outside salespeople cannot be reached. Using such combinations of inside and outside salespeople can help serve important customers better. The inside rep provides daily access and support, whereas the outside rep provides face-to-face collaboration and relationship building.

Other inside salespeople do more than just provide support. *Telemarketers* and *Internet sellers* use the phone and Internet to find new leads and qualify their prospects or sell and service accounts directly. Telemarketing and Internet selling can be very effective, less costly ways to sell to smaller, harder-to-reach customers. Depending on the complexity of the product and customer, for example, a telemarketer can make from 20 to 33 decision-maker contacts a day, compared to the average of 4 that an outside salesperson can make. In addition, whereas an average business-to-business field sales call can cost $350 or more, a routine industrial telemarketing call costs only about $5; a complex call costs about $20.[5]

Although the federal government's Do Not Call Registry put a dent in telephone sales to consumers, telemarketing remains a vital tool for most B-to-B marketers. For some smaller companies, telephone and Internet selling may be the primary sales approaches.

However, larger companies also use these tactics, either to sell directly to small and midsize customers or help out with larger ones.

In the leaner times following the recent recession, many companies have reduced their in-person customer visits in favor of more telephone, e-mail, and Internet selling. Moreover, in today's digital environment, many buyers are more receptive to phone and Internet selling. "Today's generation of buyer simply does not need the same level of face-to-face contact that it once did," says a telephone selling expert. "They are quite content to use the Internet to gather information and use the telephone to cement the deal." As a result of these trends, according to one study, telephone selling is growing at a rate of 7.5 percent per year compared with field sales at 0.5 percent.[6] The study also notes the emergence of the "hybrid sales rep," a modern cross between a field sales rep and an inside rep, who often works from a remote location. Some 41 percent of outside sales activity is now done over the phone, from either a home office, a company office, or on the go.

● For many types of products and selling situations, phone or Internet selling can be as effective as a personal sales call:[7]

● **For many types of selling situations, phone or Web selling can be as effective as a personal sales call. At Climax Portable Machine Tools, phone reps build surprisingly strong and personal customer relationships.**

Helen King/Corbis Images

Climax Portable Machine Tools, which manufactures portable maintenance tools for the metal cutting industry, has proven that telemarketing can save money and still lavish attention on buyers. Under the old system, Climax sales engineers spent one-third of their time on the road, training distributor salespeople and accompanying them on calls. They could make about four contacts a day. Now, each of five sales engineers on Climax's inside sales team calls about 30 prospects a day, following up on leads generated by ads and e-mails. Because it takes about five calls to close a sale, the sales engineers update a prospect's profile after each contact, noting the degree of commitment, requirements, next call date, and personal comments. "If anyone mentions he's going on a fishing trip, our sales engineer enters that in the sales information system and uses it to personalize the next phone call," says Climax's president, noting that this is one way to build good relations.

Another is that the first contact with a prospect includes the sales engineer's business card with his or her picture on it. Climax's customer information system also gives inside reps instant access to customer information entered by the outside sales force and service people. Armed with all the information, inside reps can build surprisingly strong and personal customer relationships. Of course, it takes more than friendliness to sell $15,000 machine tools over the phone (special orders may run $200,000), but the telemarketing approach works well. When Climax customers were asked, "Do you see the sales engineer often enough?" the response was overwhelmingly positive. Obviously, many people didn't realize that the only contact they had with Climax had been on the phone.

Team selling

Using teams of people from sales, marketing, engineering, finance, technical support, and even upper management to service large, complex accounts.

Team Selling. As products become more complex, and as customers grow larger and more demanding, a single salesperson simply can't handle all of a large customer's needs. Instead, most companies now use **team selling** to service large, complex accounts. Sales teams can unearth problems, solutions, and sales opportunities that no individual salesperson could. Such teams might include experts from any area or level of the selling firm—sales, marketing, technical and support services, research and development (R&D), engineering, operations, finance, and others.

In many cases, the move to team selling mirrors similar changes in customers' buying organizations. Many large customer companies have implemented team-based purchasing, requiring marketers to employ equivalent team-based selling. When dealing with large, complex accounts, one salesperson can't be an expert in everything the customer needs. Instead, selling is done by strategic account teams, quarterbacked by senior account managers or customer business managers.

Some companies, such as IBM, Xerox, and P&G, have used teams for a long time. As we will discuss again later in the chapter, P&G sales reps are organized into Customer Business

Development (CBD) teams. Each CBD team is assigned to a major P&G customer, such as Walmart, Safeway, or CVS Pharmacy. The CBD organization places the focus on serving the complete needs of each major customer. It lets P&G "grow business by working as a 'strategic partner' with our accounts," not just as a supplier.[8]

Team selling does have some pitfalls, however. For example, salespeople are by nature competitive and have often been trained and rewarded for outstanding individual performance. Salespeople who are used to having customers all to themselves may have trouble learning to work with and trust others on a team. In addition, selling teams can confuse or overwhelm customers who are used to working with only one salesperson. Finally, difficulties in evaluating individual contributions to the team selling effort can create some sticky compensation issues.

Recruiting and Selecting Salespeople

At the heart of any successful sales force operation is the recruitment and selection of good salespeople. The performance difference between an average salesperson and a top salesperson can be substantial. In a typical sales force, the top 30 percent of the salespeople might bring in 60 percent of the sales. Thus, careful salesperson selection can greatly increase overall sales force performance. Beyond the differences in sales performance, poor selection results in costly turnover. When a salesperson quits, the costs of finding and training a new salesperson—plus the costs of lost sales—can be very high. Also, a sales force with many new people is less productive, and turnover disrupts important customer relationships.

What sets great salespeople apart from all the rest? In an effort to profile top sales performers, Gallup Consulting, a division of the well-known Gallup polling organization, has interviewed hundreds of thousands of salespeople. ● Its research suggests that the best salespeople possess four key talents: intrinsic motivation, a disciplined work style, the ability to close a sale, and, perhaps most important, the ability to build relationships with customers.[9]

Super salespeople are motivated from within— they have an unrelenting drive to excel. Some salespeople are driven by money, a desire for recognition, or the satisfaction of competing and winning. Others are driven by the desire to provide service and build relationships. The best salespeople possess some of each of these motivations. They also have a disciplined work style. They lay out detailed, organized plans and then follow through in a timely way.

But motivation and discipline mean little unless they result in closing more sales and building better customer relationships. Super salespeople build the skills and knowledge they need to get the job done. Perhaps most important, top salespeople are excellent customer problem solvers and relationship builders. They understand their customers' needs. Talk to sales executives and they'll describe top performers in these terms: good listeners, empathetic, patient, caring, and responsive. Top performers can put themselves on the buyer's side of the desk and see the world through their customers' eyes. They don't want just to be liked; they want to add value for their customers.

● **Great salespeople:** The best salespeople possess intrinsic motivation, disciplined work style, the ability to close a sale, and perhaps most important, the ability to build relationships with customers.
© Rido

That said, there is no one right way to sell. Each successful salesperson uses a different approach, one that best applies his or her unique strengths and talents. For example, some salespeople enjoy the thrill of a harder sell in confronting challenges and winning people over. Others might apply "softer" talents to reach the same goal. "The key is for sales reps to understand and nurture their innate talents so they can develop their own personal approach and win business *their* way," says a selling expert.[10]

When recruiting, a company should analyze the sales job itself and the characteristics of its most successful salespeople to identify the traits needed by a successful salesperson in their industry. Then it must recruit the right salespeople. The human resources department looks for applicants by getting names from current salespeople, using employment agencies, searching the Internet, placing classified ads, and working through college placement services. Another source is to attract top salespeople from other companies. Proven salespeople need less training and can be productive immediately.

Recruiting will attract many applicants from which the company must select the best. The selection procedure can vary from a single informal interview to lengthy testing and interviewing. Many companies give formal tests to sales applicants. Tests typically measure sales aptitude, analytical and organizational skills, personality traits, and other characteristics. But test scores provide only one piece of information in a set that includes personal characteristics, references, past employment history, and interviewer reactions.

Training Salespeople

New salespeople may spend anywhere from a few weeks or months to a year or more in training. After the initial training ends, most companies provide continuing sales training via seminars, sales meetings, and Internet e-learning throughout the salesperson's career. According to one source, North American firms spent more than nearly $2 billion on sales training last year. Although training can be expensive, it can also yield dramatic returns. For instance, one recent study showed that sales training conducted by ADP, an administrative services firm, resulted in an ROI of nearly 338 percent in only 90 days.[11]

Training programs have several goals. First, salespeople need to know about customers and how to build relationships with them. Therefore, the training program must teach them about different types of customers and their needs, buying motives, and buying habits. It must also teach them how to sell effectively and train them in the basics of the selling process. Salespeople also need to know and identify with the company, its products, and its competitors. Therefore, an effective training program teaches them about the company's objectives, organization, products, and the strategies of major competitors.

Today, many companies are adding e-learning to their sales training programs. Online training may range from simple text-based product training and Internet-based sales exercises that build sales skills to sophisticated simulations that re-create the dynamics of real-life sales calls. One of the most basic forms is virtual instructor-led training (VILT). Using this method, a small group of salespeople at remote locations logs on to a Web conferencing site, where a sales instructor leads training sessions using online visual, audio, and interactive learning tools.

Training online instead of on-site can cut travel and other training costs, and it takes up less of a salesperson's selling time. It also makes on-demand training available to salespeople, letting them train as little or as much as needed, whenever and wherever needed. Although most e-learning is Web-based, many companies now offer on-demand training from anywhere via almost any mobile digital device.

Many companies are now using imaginative and sophisticated e-learning techniques to make sales training more efficient—and sometimes even more fun. For example, Bayer HealthCare Pharmaceuticals worked with Concentric Pharma Advertising, a health-care marketing agency, to create a role-playing simulation video game to train its sales force on a new drug marketing program:[12]

● **E-training can make sales training more efficient—and more fun. Bayer HealthCare Pharmaceuticals' role-playing video game—Rep Race—helped improve sales rep effectiveness by 20 percent.**

Concentric Pharma Advertising

> Most people don't usually associate fast-paced rock music and flashy graphics with online sales training tools. ● But Concentric Pharma Advertising's innovative role-playing video game—Rep Race: The Battle for Office Supremacy—has all that and a lot more. Rep Race gives Bayer sales reps far more entertainment than the staid old multiple-choice skills tests it replaces. The game was created to help breathe new life into a mature Bayer product—Betaseron, an 18-year-old multiple sclerosis (MS) therapy treatment. The aim was to find a fresh, more active way to help Bayer sales reps apply the in-depth information they learned about Betaseron to actual selling and objections-handling situations. Bayer also wanted to increase rep engagement through interactive learning and feedback through real-time results. Bayer reps

liked Rep Race from the start. According to Bayer, when the game was first launched, reps played it as many as 30 times. In addition to its educational and motivational value, Rep Race allowed Bayer to measure sales reps' individual and collective performance. In the end, Bayer calculated that the Rep Race simulation helped improve the Betaseron sales team's effectiveness by 20 percent.

Compensating Salespeople

To attract good salespeople, a company must have an appealing compensation plan. Compensation consists of four elements: a fixed amount, a variable amount, expenses, and fringe benefits. The fixed amount, usually a salary, gives the salesperson some stable income. The variable amount, which might be commissions or bonuses based on sales performance, rewards the salesperson for greater effort and success.

Management must determine what *mix* of these compensation elements makes the most sense for each sales job. Different combinations of fixed and variable compensation give rise to four basic types of compensation plans: straight salary, straight commission, salary plus bonus, and salary plus commission. According to one study of sales force compensation, 18 percent of companies pay straight salary, 19 percent pay straight commission, and 63 percent pay a combination of salary plus incentives. A study showed that the average salesperson's pay consists of about 67 percent salary and 33 percent incentive pay.[13]

A sales force compensation plan can both motivate salespeople and direct their activities. Compensation should direct salespeople toward activities that are consistent with the overall sales force and marketing objectives. For example, if the strategy is to acquire new business, grow rapidly, and gain market share, the compensation plan might include a larger commission component, coupled with a new-account bonus to encourage high sales performance and new account development. In contrast, if the goal is to maximize current account profitability, the compensation plan might contain a larger base-salary component with additional incentives for current account sales or customer satisfaction.

In fact, more and more companies are moving away from high-commission plans that may drive salespeople to make short-term grabs for business. They worry that a salesperson who is pushing too hard to close a deal may ruin the customer relationship. Instead, companies are designing compensation plans that reward salespeople for building customer relationships and growing the long-run value of each customer.

When times get tough economically, some companies are tempted to cut costs by reducing sales compensation. However, although some cost-cutting measures make sense when business is sluggish, cutting sales force compensation across the board is usually a "don't-go-there, last-of-the-last-resorts" action, says one sales compensation expert. "Keep in mind that if you burn the salesperson, you might burn the customer relationship." If the company must reduce its compensation expenses, says the expert, a better strategy than across-the-board cuts is to "keep the pay up for top performers and turn the [low performers] loose."[14]

Supervising and Motivating Salespeople

New salespeople need more than a territory, compensation, and training—they need supervision and motivation. The goal of *supervision* is to help salespeople "work smart" by doing the right things in the right ways. The goal of *motivation* is to encourage salespeople to "work hard" and energetically toward sales force goals. If salespeople work smart and work hard, they will realize their full potential—to their own and the company's benefit.

Supervising Salespeople

Companies vary in how closely they supervise their salespeople. Many help salespeople identify target customers and set call objectives. Some may also specify how much time the sales force should spend prospecting for new accounts and set other time management priorities. One tool is the weekly, monthly, or annual *call plan* that shows which customers and prospects to call on and which activities to carry out. Another tool is *time-and-duty analysis*. In addition to time spent selling, the salesperson spends time traveling, waiting, taking breaks, and doing administrative chores.

Figure 16.2 shows how salespeople spend their time. On average, active selling time accounts for only 11 percent of total working time! If selling time could be raised from 11 percent to 33 percent, this would triple the time spent selling.[15] Companies are always looking for ways to save time—simplifying administrative duties, developing better

FIGURE | 16.2

How Salespeople Spend
Their Time

Source: Proudfoot Consulting. Data used with
permission.

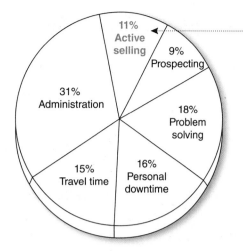

11%
Active
selling

9%
Prospecting

This is far too little. Companies
need to free up salespeople to
spend much more face-to-face
time with customers and prospects.
For example, GE wants its
salespeople to "spend four days
a week in front of the customer
and one day a week for all the
admin stuff."

31%
Administration

18%
Problem
solving

15%
Travel time

16%
Personal
downtime

sales-call and routing plans, supplying more and better customer information, and using phone, e-mail, or Internet conferencing instead of traveling.

Many firms have adopted *sales force automation systems*: computerized, digitized sales force operations that let salespeople work more effectively anytime, anywhere. Companies now routinely equip their salespeople with technologies such as laptops or tablets, smartphones, wireless connections, videoconferencing technologies, and customer-contact and relationship management software. Armed with these technologies, salespeople can more effectively and efficiently profile customers and prospects, analyze and forecast sales, schedule sales calls, make presentations, prepare sales and expense reports, and manage account relationships. The result is better time management, improved customer service, lower sales costs, and higher sales performance. In all, technology has reshaped the ways in which salespeople carry out their duties and engage customers.

Selling and the Internet

Perhaps the fastest-growing sales technology tool is the Internet. The Internet offers explosive potential for conducting sales operations and interacting with and serving customers. Some analysts even predict that the Internet will mean the death of person-to-person selling, as salespeople are ultimately replaced by Web sites, online social networking, mobile apps, and other tools that allow direct customer contact. "Don't believe it," says one sales expert (see Real Marketing 16.1). These technologies will make salespeople more effective rather than replacing them. Sales organizations are now both enhancing their effectiveness and saving time and money by using a host of innovative Internet approaches to train sales reps, hold sales meetings, service accounts, and conduct sales meetings with customers:[16]

> With the Internet as a new business platform, all stakeholders—prospects, customers, salespeople, and marketers—can now connect, learn, plan, analyze, engage, collaborate, and conduct business together in ways that were not even imaginable a few years ago. The Internet supports customer-focused methodologies and productivity-enhancing technologies that transform selling from an art to an interactive science. It has forever changed the process by which people buy and companies sell. Will all this new sales technology reduce the role of face-to-face selling? The good news is that the Internet will not make salespeople obsolete. It will make them a lot more productive and effective.

Internet-based technologies can produce big organizational benefits for sales forces. They help conserve salespeople's valuable time, save travel dollars, and give salespeople a new vehicle for selling and servicing accounts. Over the past decade, customer buying patterns have changed. In today's digital world, customers often know almost as much about a company's products as their salespeople do. This gives customers more control over the sales process than they had in the days when brochures and pricing were only available from a sales rep. New sales force technologies recognize and take advantage of these buying process changes, creating new avenues for connecting with customers in the Internet age.

For example, sales organizations now generate lists of prospective customers from online databases and networking sites, such as Hoovers and LinkedIn. They create dialogs

Real Marketing 16.1

B-to-B Salespeople: Who Needs Them Anymore?

It's hard to imagine a world without salespeople. But according to some analysts, there will be a lot fewer of them a decade from now. With the explosion of the Internet, mobile devices, and other technologies that link customers directly with companies, they reason, who needs face-to-face selling anymore? According to the doubters, salespeople are rapidly being replaced by Web sites, e-mail, blogs, mobile apps, video sharing, virtual trade shows, social networks such as Facebook and LinkedIn, and a host of other new-age interaction tools.

Research firm Gartner predicts that by 2020, 85 percent of all interactions between businesses will be executed without human intervention, requiring fewer salespeople. Of the 18 million salespeople now employed in the United States, the firm says, there will be only about 4 million left. "The world no longer needs salespeople," one doomsayer boldly proclaims. "Sales is a dying profession and soon will be as outmoded as oil lamps and the rotary phone." Says another, "If we don't find and fill a need faster than a computer, we won't be needed."

So, is business-to-business selling really dying? Will the Internet, mobile technologies, and online networks replace the age-old art of selling face to face? To answer these questions, *SellingPower* magazine called together a panel of five sales experts and asked them to weigh in on the future of B-to-B sales. The panel members agreed that technology is radically transforming the selling profession. Today's revolutionary changes in how people communicate are affecting every aspect of business, and selling is no exception.

But is B-to-B selling dead in this Internet age? Don't believe it, says the *SellingPower* panel. Technology and the Internet won't soon be replacing person-to-person buying and selling. Selling has changed, agrees the panel, and the technology can greatly enhance the selling process. But it can't replace many of the functions that salespeople perform. "The Internet can take orders and disseminate content, but what it can't do is discover customer needs," says one panelist. "It can't build relationships, and it can't prospect on its own."

Adds another panelist, "Someone must define the company's value proposition and unique message and communicate it to the market, and that person is the sales rep."

What is dying, however, is what one panelist calls the account-maintenance role—the order taker who stops by the customer's office on Friday and says, "Hey, got anything for me?" Such salespeople are not creating value and can easily be replaced by automation. However, salespeople who excel at new-customer acquisition, relationship management, and account growth with existing customers will always be in high demand.

There's no doubt about it—technology is transforming the profession of selling. Instead of relying on salespeople for basic information and education, customers can now do much of their own prepurchase research via Web sites, Internet searches, online-community contacts, and other venues. Many customers now start the sales process online and do their homework about competing suppliers and products before the first sales meeting ever takes place. They don't need basic information or product education, they need solutions. So today's salespeople need "to move into the discovery and relationship-building phase, uncovering pain points and focusing on the prospect's business," says a panelist.

Rather than replacing salespeople, however, technology is augmenting them. Today's salespeople aren't really doing anything fundamentally new. They've always done customer research and social networking. Today, however, they are "doing it on steroids," using a new kit of high-tech tools and applications.

For example, many companies are moving rapidly into online community-based selling. Case in point: enterprise-software company SAP, which has set up EcoHub, its own online, community-powered marketplace consisting of customers, partners, and almost anyone else who wants to join. The EcoHub community (ecohub.sap.com) has 2 million users in 200 countries and extends across a broad Internet spectrum—a dedicated Web site, Twitter channels, LinkedIn groups, Facebook fan pages, YouTube channels, Flickr groups, mobile apps, and more. It includes 600 "solution storefronts" where visitors can "easily discover, evaluate, and initiate the purchase of software solutions and services from SAP and its partners." EcoHub also lets users rate the solutions and advice they get from other community members.

Online selling tools, such as SAP's EcoHub online community-based marketplace, are coming into their own in helping to build customer awareness and generate consideration, purchase interest, and sales. But rather than replacing salespeople, such efforts extend their reach and effectiveness.

© Copyright 2012 SAP AG. All rights reserved. Facebook is a trademark of Facebook, Inc.

SAP was surprised to learn that what it had originally seen as a place for customers to discuss issues, problems, and solutions has turned into a significant point of sale. The information, give-and-take discussions, and conversations at the site draw in customers, even for big-ticket sales. "Some customers are spending $20 to $30 million due to EcoHub," says the SAP vice president who heads up the community.

However, although EcoHub draws in new potential customers and takes them through many of the initial stages of product discovery and evaluation, it doesn't replace SAP's or its partners' salespeople. Instead, it extends their reach and effectiveness. The real value of EcoHub is the flood of sales leads it creates for the SAP and partner sales forces. Once

prospective customers have discovered, discussed, and evaluated SAP solutions on EcoHub, SAP invites them to "initiate contact, request a proposal, or start the negotiation process." That's where the person-to-person selling begins.

All this suggests that B-to-B selling isn't dying, it's just changing. The tools and techniques may be different as selling leverages and adapts to selling in the digital age. But the panelists agree strongly that B-to-B

marketers will never be able to do without strong sales teams. Salespeople who can discover customer needs, solve customer problems, and build relationships will be needed and successful, regardless of what else changes. Especially for those big-ticket B-to-B sales, "all the new technology may make it easier to sell by building strong ties to customers even before the first sit-down, but when the signature hits the dotted line, there will be a sales rep there."

Sources: Quotes and other information from Robert McGarvey, "All About Us," *SellingPower,* March 7, 2011, p. 48; Lain Chroust Ehmann, "Sales Up!" *SellingPower*, January/February 2011, p. 40; James Ledbetter, "Death of a Salesman. Of Lots of Them, Actually," *Slate*, September 21, 2010, www.slate.com/id/2268122/; Sean Callahan, "Is B-to-B Marketing Really Obsolete?" *BtoB,* January 17, 2011, p. 1; Gerhared Gschwandtner, "How Many Salespeople Will Be Left by 2020?" *SellingPower,* May/June 2011, p. 7; and "Getting Started with SAP EcoHub," http://ecohub.sap.com/getting-started, accessed November 2012.

when prospective customers visit their Web sites through live chats with the sales team. They use Internet conferencing tools such as WebEx, GoToMeeting, or TelePresence to talk live with customers about products and services. They provide informational videos and other information on their YouTube channels and Facebook pages. Other digital tools allow salespeople to monitor Internet interactions between customers about how they would like to buy, how they feel about a vendor, and what it would take to make a sale.

Today's sales forces are also ramping up their use of social networking media. A recent survey of business-to-business marketers found that, although they have recently cut back on traditional media and event spending, 68 percent are investing more in social media, ranging from proprietary online customer communities to webinars and Twitter, Facebook, and YouTube applications. Consider Makino, a leading manufacturer of metal cutting and machining technology:[17]

> Makino complements its sales force efforts through a wide variety of social media initiatives that inform customers and enhance customer relationships. For example, it hosts an ongoing series of industry-specific webinars that position the company as an industry thought leader. Makino produces about three webinars each month and has archived more than 100 on topics

● **Selling and the Internet: Companies use Internet collaboration tools such as Cisco's TelePresence to talk live with customers about products and services.**
Courtesy of Cisco

ranging from how to get the most out of your machine tools to how metal-cutting processes are done. Webinar content is tailored to specific industries, such as aerospace or medical, and is promoted through carefully targeted banner ads and e-mail invitations. The webinars help to build Makino's customer database, generate leads, build customer relationships, and prepare the way for salespeople by serving up relevant information and educating customers online. Makino also uses Twitter, Facebook, and YouTube to inform customers and prospects about the latest Makino innovations and events and dramatically demonstrate the company's machines in action. "We've shifted dramatically into the electronic marketing area," says Makino's marketing manager. "It speeds up the sales cycle and makes it more efficient—for both the company and the customer. The results have been 'outstanding.'"

Ultimately, digital technologies are "delivering instant information that builds relationships and enables sales to be more efficient and cost-effective and more productive," says one sales technology analyst. "Think of it as . . . doing what the best reps always did but doing it better, faster, and cheaper," says another.[18]

However, the technologies also have some drawbacks. For starters, they're not cheap. In addition, such systems can intimidate low-tech salespeople or clients. Even more, there are some things you just can't present or teach via the Internet—things that require personal interactions. For these reasons, some high-tech experts recommend that sales executives use Internet technologies to supplement training, sales meetings, and preliminary client sales presentations but resort to old-fashioned, face-to-face meetings when the time draws near to close the deal.

Motivating Salespeople

Beyond directing salespeople, sales managers must also motivate them. Some salespeople will do their best without any special urging from management. To them, selling may be the most fascinating job in the world. But selling can also be frustrating. Salespeople often work alone, and they must sometimes travel away from home. They may also face aggressive competing salespeople and difficult customers. Therefore, salespeople often need special encouragement to do their best.

Management can boost sales force morale and performance through its organizational climate, sales quotas, and positive incentives. *Organizational climate* describes the feeling that salespeople have about their opportunities, value, and rewards for a good performance. Some companies treat salespeople as if they are not very important, so performance suffers accordingly. Other companies treat their salespeople as valued contributors and allow virtually unlimited opportunity for income and promotion. Not surprisingly, these companies enjoy higher sales force performance and less turnover.

Sales quota

A standard that states the amount a salesperson should sell and how sales should be divided among the company's products.

Many companies motivate their salespeople by setting **sales quotas**—standards stating the amount they should sell and how sales should be divided among the company's products. Compensation is often related to how well salespeople meet their quotas. Companies also use various *positive incentives* to increase the sales force effort. *Sales meetings* provide social occasions, breaks from the routine, chances to meet and talk with "company brass," and opportunities to air feelings and identify with a larger group. Companies also sponsor *sales contests* to spur the sales force to make a selling effort above and beyond what is normally expected. Other incentives include honors, merchandise and cash awards, trips, and profit-sharing plans.

Evaluating Salespeople and Sales Force Performance

We have thus far described how management communicates what salespeople should be doing and how it motivates them to do it. This process requires good feedback, which means getting regular information about salespeople to evaluate their performance.

Management gets information about its salespeople in several ways. The most important source is *sales reports*, including weekly or monthly work plans and longer-term territory marketing plans. Salespeople also write up their completed activities on *call reports* and turn in *expense reports* for which they are partly or wholly reimbursed. The company can also monitor the sales and profit performance data in the salesperson's territory. Additional information comes from personal observation, customer surveys, and talks with other salespeople.

Using various sales force reports and other information, sales management evaluates the members of the sales force. It evaluates salespeople on their ability to "plan their work and work their plan." Formal evaluation forces management to develop and communicate clear standards for judging performance. It also provides salespeople with constructive feedback and motivates them to perform well.

On a broader level, management should evaluate the performance of the sales force as a whole. Is the sales force accomplishing its customer relationship, sales, and profit objectives? Is it working well with other areas of the marketing and company organization? Are sales force costs in line with outcomes? As with other marketing activities, the company wants to measure its *return on sales investment*.

Objective 3 ➤
Discuss the personal selling process, distinguishing between transaction-oriented marketing and relationship marketing.

The Personal Selling Process

We now turn from designing and managing a sales force to the personal selling process. The **selling process** consists of several steps that salespeople must master. These steps focus on the goal of getting new customers and obtaining orders from them. However, most salespeople spend much of their time maintaining existing accounts and building long-term customer *relationships*. We will discuss the relationship aspect of the personal selling process in a later section.

Steps in the Selling Process

Selling process
The steps that salespeople follow when selling, which include prospecting and qualifying, preapproach, approach, presentation and demonstration, handling objections, closing, and follow-up.

As shown in ● **Figure 16.3**, the selling process consists of seven steps: prospecting and qualifying, preapproach, approach, presentation and demonstration, handling objections, closing, and follow-up.

Prospecting and Qualifying

The first step in the selling process is **prospecting**—identifying qualified potential customers. Approaching the right customers is crucial to selling success. Salespeople don't want to call on just any potential customers. They want to call on those who are most likely to appreciate and respond to the company's value proposition—those the company can serve well and profitably.

Prospecting
The sales step in which a salesperson or company identifies qualified potential customers.

A salesperson must often approach many prospects to get only a few sales. Although the company supplies some leads, salespeople need skill in finding their own. The best source is referrals. Salespeople can ask current customers for referrals and cultivate other referral sources, such as suppliers, dealers, noncompeting salespeople, and Web or other social network contacts. They can also search for prospects in directories or on the Internet and track down leads using the telephone and e-mail. Or, as a last resort, they can drop in unannounced on various offices (a practice known as *cold calling*).

Salespeople also need to know how to *qualify* leads—that is, how to identify the good ones and screen out the poor ones. Prospects can be qualified by looking at their financial ability, volume of business, special needs, location, and possibilities for growth.

● **FIGURE | 16.3**
Steps in the Selling Process

As shown here, these steps are transaction-oriented—aimed at closing a specific sale with the customer...

...but remember that in the long run, a single sale is only one element of a long-term customer relationship. So the selling process steps must be understood in the broader context of maintaining profitable customer relationships.

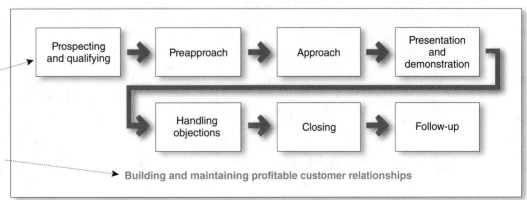

Preapproach

Preapproach
The sales step in which a salesperson learns as much as possible about a prospective customer before making a sales call.

Before calling on a prospect, the salesperson should learn as much as possible about the organization (what it needs, who is involved in the buying) and its buyers (their characteristics and buying styles). This step is known as **preapproach**. A successful sale begins long before the salesperson sets foot into a prospect's office. Preapproach begins with good research and preparation. The salesperson can consult standard industry and online sources, acquaintances, and others to learn about the company. Then the salesperson must apply the research gathered to develop a customer strategy.

The salesperson should set *call objectives*, which may be to qualify the prospect, gather information, or make an immediate sale. Another task is to determine the best approach, which might be a personal visit, a phone call, a letter, or an e-mail. The ideal timing should be considered carefully because many prospects are busiest at certain times of the day or week. Finally, the salesperson should give thought to an overall sales strategy for the account.

Approach

Approach
The sales step in which a salesperson meets the customer for the first time.

During the **approach** step, the salesperson should know how to meet and greet the buyer and get the relationship off to a good start. This step involves the salesperson's appearance, opening lines, and follow-up remarks. The opening lines should be positive to build goodwill from the outset. This opening might be followed by some key questions to learn more about the customer's needs or by showing a display or sample to attract the buyer's attention and curiosity. As in all stages of the selling process, listening to the customer is crucial.

Presentation and Demonstration

Presentation
The sales step in which a salesperson tells the "value story" to the buyer, showing how the company's offer solves the customer's problems.

During the **presentation** step of the selling process, the salesperson tells the "value story" to the buyer, showing how the company's offer solves the customer's problems. The *customer-solution approach* fits better with today's relationship marketing focus than does a hard sell or glad-handing approach. "Stop selling and start helping," advises one sales consultant. "Your goal should be to sell your customers exactly what will benefit them most," says another.[19] Buyers today want solutions, not smiles; results, not razzle-dazzle. Moreover, they don't want just products. More than ever in today's economic climate, buyers want to know how those products will add value to their businesses. They want salespeople who listen to their concerns, understand their needs, and respond with the right products and services.

But before salespeople can *present* customer solutions, they must *develop* solutions to present. The solutions approach calls for good listening and problem-solving skills. The qualities that buyers *dislike most* in salespeople include being pushy, late, deceitful, unprepared, disorganized, or overly talkative. The qualities they *value most* include good listening, empathy, honesty, dependability, thoroughness, and follow-through. ● Great salespeople know how to sell, but more important, they know how to listen and build strong customer relationships. According to an old sales adage, "You have two ears and one mouth. Use them proportionally." A classic ad from office products maker Boise Cascade makes the listening point. It shows a Boise salesperson with huge ears drawn on. "With Boise, you'll notice a difference right away, especially with our sales force," says the ad. "At Boise . . . our account representatives have the unique ability to listen to your needs."

Finally, salespeople must also plan their presentation methods. Good interpersonal communication skills count when it comes to making effective sales presentations. However, the current media-rich and cluttered communications environment presents many new challenges for sales presenters. Today's information-overloaded customers demand richer presentation experiences. For their part, presenters now face multiple distractions during presentations from mobile phones, text messages, and mobile Internet devices. As a result, salespeople must deliver their messages in more engaging and compelling ways.

● **Great salespeople know how to sell, but more important, they know how to listen and build strong customer relationships.**
Tony Garcia/Getty Images

Thus, today's salespeople are employing advanced presentation technologies that allow for full multimedia presentations to only one or a few people. The venerable old sales presentation flip chart has been replaced with sophisticated presentation software, online presentation technologies, interactive whiteboards, digital projectors, and tablet computers.

Handling Objections

Handling objections

The sales step in which a salesperson seeks out, clarifies, and overcomes any customer objections to buying.

Customers almost always have objections during the presentation or when asked to place an order. The objections can be either logical or psychological, and are often unspoken. In **handling objections**, the salesperson should use a positive approach, seek out hidden objections, ask the buyer to clarify any objections, take objections as opportunities to provide more information, and turn the objections into reasons for buying. Every salesperson needs training in the skills of handling objections.

Closing

Closing

The sales step in which a salesperson asks the customer for an order.

After handling the prospect's objections, the salesperson next tries to close the sale. However, some salespeople do not get around to **closing** or handle it well. They may lack confidence, feel guilty about asking for the order, or fail to recognize the right moment to close the sale. Salespeople should know how to recognize closing signals from the buyer, including physical actions, comments, and questions. For example, the customer might sit forward and nod approvingly or ask about prices and credit terms.

Salespeople can use any of several closing techniques. They can ask for the order, review points of agreement, offer to help write up the order, ask whether the buyer wants this model or that one, or note that the buyer will lose out if the order is not placed now. The salesperson may offer the buyer special reasons to close, such as a lower price, an extra quantity at no charge, or additional services.

Follow-Up

Follow-up

The sales step in which a salesperson follows up after the sale to ensure customer satisfaction and repeat business.

The last step in the selling process—**follow-up**—is necessary if the salesperson wants to ensure customer satisfaction and repeat business. Right after closing, the salesperson should complete any details on delivery time, purchase terms, and other matters. The salesperson then should schedule a follow-up call after the buyer receives the initial order to make sure proper installation, instruction, and servicing occur. This visit would reveal any problems, assure the buyer of the salesperson's interest, and reduce any buyer concerns that might have arisen since the sale.

Personal Selling and Managing Customer Relationships

The steps in the just-described selling process are *transaction oriented*—their aim is to help salespeople close a specific sale with a customer. But in most cases, the company is not simply seeking a sale. Rather, it wants to serve the customer over the long haul in a mutually profitable *relationship*. The sales force usually plays an important role in customer relationship building. Thus, as shown in Figure 16.3, the selling process must be understood in the context of building and maintaining profitable customer relationships.

Successful sales organizations recognize that winning and keeping accounts requires more than making good products and directing the sales force to close lots of sales. If the company wishes only to close sales and capture short-term business, it can do this by simply slashing its prices to meet or beat those of competitors. Instead, most companies want their salespeople to practice *value selling*—demonstrating and delivering superior customer value and capturing a return on that value that is fair for both the customer and the company. For example, companies like Procter & Gamble understand that they aren't just selling products to and through their retailer customers. They are partnering with these retail accounts to create more value for final consumers to their mutual benefit. P&G knows that it can succeed only if its retail partners succeed (see Real Marketing 16.2).

Unfortunately, in the heat of closing sales—especially in a tight economy—salespeople too often take the easy way out by cutting prices rather than selling value. Sales management's challenge is to transform salespeople from customer advocates for price cuts into

Real Marketing 16.2

P&G: It's Not Sales, It's Customer Business Development

For decades, Procter & Gamble has been at the top of almost every expert's A-list of outstanding marketing companies. The experts point to P&G's stable of top-selling consumer brands, or to the fact that year in and year out, P&G is the world's largest advertiser. Consumers seem to agree. You'll find at least one of P&G's blockbuster brands in 99 percent of all American households; in many homes, you'll find a dozen or more familiar P&G products. But P&G is also highly respected for something else—its top-notch, customer-focused sales force.

P&G's sales force has long been an American icon for personal selling at its very best. When it comes to selecting, training, and managing salespeople, P&G sets the gold standard. The company employs a massive sales force of more than 5,000 salespeople worldwide. At P&G, however, they rarely call it "sales." Instead, it's "Customer Business Development" (CBD). And P&G sales reps aren't "salespeople"; they're "CBD managers" or "CBD account executives." All this might seem like just so much "corp-speak," but at P&G the distinction goes to the very core of how selling works.

P&G understands that if its customers don't do well, neither will the company. To grow its own business, therefore, P&G must first grow the business of the retailers that sell its brands to final consumers. And at P&G, the primary responsibility for helping customers grow falls to the sales force. In P&G's own words, "CBD is more than mere 'selling'—it's a P&G-specific approach which enables us to grow our business by working as a 'strategic partner' (as opposed to just a supplier) with those who ultimately sell our products to consumers." Says one CBD manager, "We depend on them as much as they depend on us." By partnering with each other, P&G and its customers create "win-win" relationships that help both to prosper.

Most P&G customers are huge and complex businesses—such as Walgreens, Walmart, or Dollar General—with thousands of stores and billions of dollars in revenues. Working with and selling to such customers can be a very complex undertaking, more than

any single salesperson or sales team could accomplish. Instead, P&G assigns a full CBD team to every large customer account. Each CBD team contains not only salespeople but also a full complement of specialists in every aspect of selling P&G's consumer brands at the retail level.

CBD teams vary in size depending on the customer. For example, P&G's largest customer, Walmart, which accounts for an amazing 20 percent of the company's sales, commands a 350-person CBD team. By contrast, the P&G Dollar General team consists of about 30 people. Regardless of size, every CBD team constitutes a complete, multifunctional customer service unit. Each team includes a CBD manager and several CBD account executives (each responsible for a specific P&G product category), supported by specialists in marketing strategy, product development, operations, information systems, logistics, finance, and human resources.

To deal effectively with large accounts, P&G salespeople must be smart, well-trained, and strategically grounded. They deal daily with high-level retail category buyers who may purchase hundreds of millions of dollars'

worth of P&G and competing brands annually. It takes a lot more than a friendly smile and a firm handshake to interact with such buyers. Yet, individual P&G salespeople can't know everything, and thanks to the CBD sales structure, they don't have to. Instead, as members of a full CBD team, P&G salespeople have at hand all the resources they need to resolve even the most challenging customer problems. "I have everything I need right here," says a household care account executive. "If my customer needs help from us with in-store promotions, I can go right down the hall and talk with someone on my team in marketing about doing some kind of promotional deal. It's that simple."

Customer Business Development involves partnering with customers to jointly identify strategies that create shopper value and satisfaction and drive profitable sales at the store level. When it comes to profitably moving Tide, Pampers, Gillette, or other P&G brands off store shelves and into consumers' shopping carts, P&G reps and their teams often know more than the retail buyers they advise. In fact, P&G's retail partners often rely on CBD teams to help them manage not only the P&G brands on their shelves but also entire product categories, including competing brands.

Wait a minute. Does it make sense to let P&G advise on the stocking and placement of competitors' brands as well as its own? Would a P&G CBD rep ever tell a retail buyer to stock fewer P&G products and more of a

P&G Customer Business Development managers know that to grow P&G's business, they must first help their retail partners to sell P&G's brands.

Jin Lee/Getty Images USA, Inc.

competing brand? Believe it or not, it happens all the time. The CBD team's primary goal is to help the customer win in each product category. Sometimes, analysis shows that the best solution for the customer is "more of the other guy's product." For P&G, that's okay. It knows that creating the best situation for the retailer ultimately pulls in more customer traffic, which in turn will likely lead to increased sales for other P&G products in the same category. Because most of P&G's brands are market share leaders, it stands to benefit more from the increased traffic than competitors do. Again, what's good for the customer is good for P&G—it's a win-win situation.

Honest and open dealings also help to build long-term customer relationships. P&G salespeople become trusted advisors to their retailer-partners, a status they work hard to maintain. "It took me four years to build the trust I now have with my buyer," says a veteran CBD account executive. "If I talk her into

buying P&G products that she can't sell or out of stocking competing brands that she should be selling, I could lose that trust in a heartbeat."

Finally, collaboration is usually a two-way street—P&G gives and customers give back in return. "We'll help customers run a set of commercials or do some merchandising events, but there's usually a return-on-investment," explains another CBD manager. "Maybe it's helping us with distribution of a new product or increasing space for fabric care. We're very willing if the effort creates value for us as well as for the customer and the final consumer."

According to P&G, "Customer Business Development is selling and a whole lot

more. It's a P&G-specific approach [that lets us] grow business by working as a 'strategic partner' with our accounts, focusing on mutually beneficial business building opportunities. All customers want to improve their business; it's [our] role to help them identify the biggest opportunities."

Thus, P&G salespeople aren't the stereotypical glad-handers that some people have come to expect when they think of selling. P&G's "salespeople"—its CBD managers—are talented, well-educated, well-trained sales professionals who do all they can to help customers succeed. They know that good selling involves working with customers to solve their problems for mutual gain. They know that if customers succeed, they succeed.

Sources: Based on information from numerous P&G managers; with information from "500 Largest Sales Forces in America," *Selling Power*, September/October 2011, pp. 33–50; and www.experiencepg.com/jobs/customer-business-development-sales.aspx, accessed October 2012.

company advocates for value. Here's how Rockwell Automation sells value and relationships rather than price:[20]

> Under pressure from Walmart to lower its prices, a condiment producer asked several competing supplier representatives—including Rockwell Automation sales rep Jeff Policicchio—to help it find ways to reduce its operating costs. After spending a day in the customer's plant, Policicchio quickly put his finger on the major problem: Production was suffering because of down time due to poorly performing pumps on the customer's 32 large condiment tanks. Quickly gathering cost and usage data, Policicchio used his Rockwell Automation laptop value-assessment tool to develop an effective solution for the customer's pump problem.
>
> The next day, as he and competing reps presented their cost-reduction proposals to plant management, Policicchio offered the following value proposition: "With this Rockwell Automation pump solution, through less downtime, reduced administrative costs in procurement, and lower spending on repair parts, your company will save at least $16,268 per pump—on up to 32 pumps—relative to our best competitor's solution." Compared with competitors' proposals, Policicchio's solution carried a higher initial price. However, no competing rep offered more than fuzzy promises about possible cost savings. Most simply lowered their prices.
>
> Impressed by Policicchio's value proposition—despite its higher initial price—the plant managers opted to buy and try one Rockwell Automation pump. When the pump performed even better than predicted, the customer ordered all of the remaining pumps. By demonstrating tangible value rather than simply selling price, Policicchio not only landed the initial sale but also earned a loyal future customer.

Value selling requires listening to customers, understanding their needs, and carefully coordinating the whole company's efforts to create lasting relationships based on customer value. "If you're not selling value, you're not selling smart," concludes one sales consultant.[21]

Sales Promotion

Personal selling and advertising often work closely with another promotion tool, sales promotion. **Sales promotion** consists of short-term incentives to encourage the purchase or sales of a product or service. Whereas advertising offers reasons to buy a product or service, sales promotion offers reasons to buy *now*.

Sales promotion
Short-term incentives to encourage the purchase or sales of a product or a service.

Objective 4 ▸
Explain how sales promotion campaigns are developed and implemented.

How much do you love saving 20%?

20% OFF
One single item!

BED BATH & BEYOND

Present this coupon.
SAMPLE NOT VALID
IN-STORE OR ONLINE
Coupon Expires XX/XX/XX

**CHOOSE FROM ONE OF
OUR HUNDREDS OF
THOUSANDS OF ITEMS.**

CUT COUPON ALONG DOTTED LINE

**BED BATH &
BEYOND®**

SIGN UP AT bedbathandbeyond.com/TheNest.asp
to keep the savings coming all year long

For locations nearest you visit bedbathandbeyond.com and click on Store Locator or call 1-800 GO BEYOND® (1-800 462-3966)

● **Sales promotions are found everywhere. For example, your favorite magazine is loaded with offers like this one that promote a strong and immediate response.**

Bed Bath & Beyond Inc.

Examples of sales promotions are found everywhere. A free-standing insert in the Sunday newspaper contains a coupon offering $1 off PEDIGREE GoodBites treats for your dog. ● A Bed Bath & Beyond ad in your favorite magazine offers 20 percent off on any single item. The end-of-the-aisle display in the local supermarket tempts impulse buyers with a wall of Coca-Cola cases—four 12-packs for $12. Buy a new HP laptop and get a free memory upgrade. A hardware store chain receives a 10 percent discount on selected Stihl power lawn and garden tools if it agrees to advertise them in local newspapers. Sales promotion includes a wide variety of promotion tools designed to stimulate earlier or stronger market response.

The Rapid Growth of Sales Promotion

Sales promotion tools are used by most organizations, including manufacturers, distributors, retailers, and not-for-profit institutions. They are targeted toward final buyers (*consumer promotions*), retailers and wholesalers (*trade promotions*), business customers (*business promotions*), and members of the sales force (*sales force promotions*). Today, in the average consumer packaged-goods company, sales promotion accounts for 73 percent of all marketing expenditures.[22]

Several factors have contributed to the rapid growth of sales promotion, particularly in consumer markets. First, inside the company, product managers face greater pressures to increase current sales, and they view promotion as an effective short-run sales tool. Second, externally, the company faces more competition, and competing brands are less differentiated. Increasingly, competitors are using sales promotion to help differentiate their offers. Third, advertising efficiency has declined because of rising costs, media clutter, and legal restraints. Finally, consumers have become more deal oriented. In the current economy, consumers are demanding lower prices and better deals. Sales promotions can help attract today's more thrift-oriented consumers.

The growing use of sales promotion has resulted in *promotion clutter*, which is similar to advertising clutter. According to one recent study, 37 percent of all groceries were sold with some sort of promotional support.[23] A given promotion runs the risk of being lost in a sea of other promotions, weakening its ability to trigger an immediate purchase. Manufacturers are now searching for ways to rise above the clutter, such as offering larger coupon values, creating more dramatic point-of-purchase displays, or delivering promotions through new interactive media—such as the Internet or mobile phones.

In developing a sales promotion program, a company must first set sales promotion objectives and then select the best tools for accomplishing these objectives.

Sales Promotion Objectives

Sales promotion objectives vary widely. Sellers may use *consumer promotions* to urge short-term customer buying or boost customer brand involvement. Objectives for *trade promotions* include getting retailers to carry new items and more inventory, buy ahead, or promote the company's products and give them more shelf space. *Business promotions* are used to generate business leads, stimulate purchases, reward customers, and motivate salespeople. For the sales force, objectives include getting more sales force support for current or new products and getting salespeople to sign up new accounts.

Sales promotions are usually used together with advertising, personal selling, direct marketing, or other promotion mix tools. Consumer promotions must usually be advertised and can add excitement and pulling power to ads. Trade and business sales promotions support the firm's personal selling process.

When the economy tightens and sales lag, it's tempting to offer deep promotional discounts to spur consumer spending. In general, however, rather than creating only

● **Customer loyalty programs: Kroger keeps its Plus Card holders coming back by linking food purchases to discounts on gasoline prices.**

Photo courtesy of Gary Armstrong

Consumer promotions
Sales promotion tools used to boost short-term customer buying and involvement or enhance long-term customer relationships.

short-term sales or temporary brand switching, sales promotions should help to reinforce the product's position and build long-term customer relationships. If properly designed, every sales promotion tool has the potential to build both short-term excitement and long-term consumer relationships. Marketers should avoid "quick fix," price-only promotions in favor of promotions that are designed to build brand equity. Examples include the various *frequency marketing programs* and loyalty cards that have mushroomed in popularity in recent years. Most hotels, supermarkets, and airlines offer frequent-guest/buyer/flyer programs that give rewards to regular customers to keep them coming back. All kinds of companies now offer rewards programs. Such promotional programs can build loyalty through added value rather than discounted prices.

For example, Kroger Plus Card holders receive the usual frequent shopper perks—special in-store discounts on selected items, exclusive e-mail offers and coupons, and the ability to create and save their shopping lists online. But the grocery chain also keeps customers coming back by linking cumulative food purchases to discounts on gasoline prices. ● Shoppers who use the company's loyalty card when they shop can accrue 10 cents off each gallon of gas for every $100 spent in the store, up to a $2-per-gallon discount when they fill up their tanks. "We're delighted to offer [customers] more control at the pump," says a Kroger marketing executive. "This is another way we're rewarding our customers for choosing to shop with us."[24]

Major Sales Promotion Tools

Many tools can be used to accomplish sales promotion objectives. Descriptions of the main consumer, trade, and business promotion tools follow.

Consumer Promotions

Consumer promotions include a wide range of tools—from samples, coupons, refunds, premiums, and point-of-purchase displays to contests, sweepstakes, and event sponsorships.

Samples are offers of a trial amount of a product. Sampling is the most effective—but most expensive—way to introduce a new product or create new excitement for an existing one. Some samples are free; for others, the company charges a small amount to offset its cost. The sample might be sent by mail, handed out in a store or at a kiosk, attached to another product, or featured in an ad or an e-mail. Samples are sometimes combined into sample packs, which can then be used to promote other products and services. Sampling can be a powerful promotional tool.

Coupons are certificates that save buyers money when they purchase specified products. Most consumers love coupons. U.S. consumer packaged-goods companies distributed 305 billion coupons with an average face value of $1.55 last year, a 26 percent increase since 2007. Consumers redeemed more than 3.5 billion of them for a total savings of about $4.6 billion, 58.6 percent higher than five years ago.[25] Coupons can promote early trial of a new brand or stimulate sales of a mature brand. However, to combat the increase in coupon clutter, most major consumer-goods companies are issuing fewer coupons and targeting them more carefully.

Marketers are also cultivating new outlets for distributing coupons, such as supermarket shelf dispensers, electronic point-of-sale coupon printers, and online and mobile coupon programs. According to a recent study, digital coupons represent today's fastest-growing coupon segment. Digital coupons now account for 11 percent of all coupons redeemed. More than 25 percent of the U.S. population uses online coupons from sites such as Coupons.com, MyCoupster, Groupon, LivingSocial, and Cellfire.[26] And as mobile phones become appendages that many people can't live without, businesses are increasingly eyeing them as prime real estate for coupons, offers, and other marketing messages. ● For example, drugstore chain Walgreens makes coupons available to its customers through several mobile channels:[27]

Using the Walgreens smartphone app, customers can instantly download coupons ranging in value from 50 cents to $5, good toward anything from health and beauty products to everyday essentials such as diapers. The coupons are conveniently scannable—no clipping or printing required. Customers simply pull up the coupons on the Walgreens app and cashiers scan them straight from the customer's phone. Walgreens also tweets mobile coupons to customers who

Mobile coupons: Drug store chain Walgreens makes coupons available to its customers through several mobile channels, including its own smartphone app and via tweets to customers using mobile check-in services such as Foursquare, Yelp, or Facebook Places.

Walgreens Digital Marketing & Emerging Media Team. Rich Lesperance, Director.

Event marketing (or event sponsorships)

Creating a brand-marketing event or serving as a sole or participating sponsor of events created by others.

check in to any of its 8,000 stores nationwide using check-in apps such as Foursquare, Yelp, or Facebook Places. Walgreens has mobile scanning capabilities available at all of its stores, giving it the nation's largest retail mobile coupon program. "Through our mobile application, no matter where people are, they can find an easy way to save next time they come to Walgreens," says the company's president of e-commerce.

Rebates (or *cash refunds*) are like coupons except that the price reduction occurs after the purchase rather than at the retail outlet. The customer sends proof of purchase to the manufacturer, which then refunds part of the purchase price by mail. For example, Toro ran a clever preseason promotion on some of its snowblower models, offering a rebate if the snowfall in the buyer's market area turned out to be below average. Competitors were not able to match this offer on such short notice, and the promotion was very successful.

Price packs (also called *cents-off deals*) offer consumers savings off the regular price of a product. The producer marks the reduced prices directly on the label or package. Price packs can be single packages sold at a reduced price (such as two for the price of one) or two related products banded together (such as a toothbrush and toothpaste). Price packs are very effective—even more so than coupons—in stimulating short-term sales.

Premiums are goods offered either free or at low cost as an incentive to buy a product, ranging from toys included with kids' products to phone cards and DVDs. A premium may come inside the package (in-pack), outside the package (on-pack), or through the mail. For example, over the years, McDonald's has offered a variety of premiums in its Happy Meals—from *Madagascar* characters to Beanie Babies and *Pokémon* toy figures. Customers can visit www.happymeal.com to play games and watch commercials associated with the current Happy Meal sponsor.[28]

Advertising specialties, also called *promotional products*, are useful articles imprinted with an advertiser's name, logo, or message that are given as gifts to consumers. Typical items include T-shirts and other apparel, pens, coffee mugs, calendars, key rings, mouse pads, tote bags, coolers, golf balls, and caps. U.S. marketers spent nearly $18 billion on advertising specialties last year. Such items can be very effective. The "best of them stick around for months, subtly burning a brand name into a user's brain," notes a promotional products expert.[29]

Point-of-purchase (POP) promotions include displays and demonstrations that take place at the point of sale. Think of your last visit to the local Safeway, Costco, CVS, or Bed Bath & Beyond. Chances are good that you were tripping over aisle displays, promotional signs, "shelf talkers," or demonstrators offering free tastes of featured food products. Unfortunately, many retailers do not like to handle the hundreds of displays, signs, and posters they receive from manufacturers each year. Manufacturers have therefore responded by offering better POP materials, offering to set them up, and tying them in with television, print, or online messages.

Contests, sweepstakes, and *games* give consumers the chance to win something, such as cash, trips, or goods, by luck or through extra effort. A *contest* calls for consumers to submit an entry—a jingle, guess, suggestion—to be judged by a panel that will select the best entries. A *sweepstakes* calls for consumers to submit their names for a drawing. A *game* presents consumers with something—bingo numbers, missing letters—every time they buy, which may or may not help them win a prize.

All kinds of companies use sweepstakes and contests to create brand attention and boost consumer involvement. For example, Outback's Kick Back with the Guys Sweepstakes offers chances to win a dinner for four of "crave-able appetizers and juicy steaks." The O'Reilly Auto Parts Win Free Gas for a Year Giveaway promises to let you "forget about gas prices for a year." Enter the Coleman Great American Family Vacation Sweepstakes and you could win a family trip to Yellowstone and a Coleman camping package. And separate Chevrolet Race to Win sweepstakes recently offered either a new Corvette 427 convertible plus a trip to the 24 Hours of Le Mans, France, or a new Camaro plus a weekend at the Indy500.

Finally, marketers can promote their brands through **event marketing** (or **event sponsorships**). They can create their own brand-marketing events or serve as sole or participating sponsors of events created by others. The events might include anything from mobile brand tours to festivals, reunions, marathons, concerts, or other sponsored gatherings. Event marketing is huge, and it may be the fastest-growing area of promotion. Effective event marketing links events and sponsorships to a brand's value proposition.

All kinds of brands now hold events. One week, it might be the National Football League filling the southern tip of Times Square with NFL players to promote new NFL jersey designs. The next week, it's a mob of Russian models on the 45th street island between Broadway and Seventh Avenue in New York City, using it as a fashion runway for Maybelline. But according to one business reporter, energy drink maker Red Bull is the "mother of all event marketers":[30]

Event pioneer Red Bull holds hundreds of events each year in dozens of sports around the world. Each event features off-the-grid experiences designed to bring the high-octane world of Red Bull to its community of enthusiasts. The brand even hosts a "Holy S**t" tab on its Web site, featuring videos of everything from 27-meter ocean cliff dives at its Cliff Diving Series event in Grimstad, Norway, to dare-devil freeskiing feats at its Red Bull Cold Rush event in the Colorado mountain peaks, to absolutely breathtaking wind suit flights at Red Bull events staged in exotic locations from Monterrey, Mexico, to Hunan Province, China. The Red Bull Final Descent series is a mountain biking challenge that pushes riders to the brink and back, over some of the most technically challenging terrain in North America. Red Bull events draw large crowds and plenty of media coverage. But it's about more than just the events—it's about customer involvement. It's about creating face-to-face experiences in which customers can actually feel the excitement and live the brand. "It's about deepening and enhancing relationships," says one analyst.

● **Event marketing: Red Bull hosts hundreds of events each year in dozens of sports around the world, designed to bring the high-octane world of Red Bull to its community of enthusiasts.**
REUTERS/Max Rossi

Trade Promotions

Trade promotions
Sales promotion tools used to persuade resellers to carry a brand, give it shelf space, promote it in advertising, and push it to consumers.

Manufacturers direct more sales promotion dollars toward retailers and wholesalers (79 percent) than to final consumers (21 percent).[31] **Trade promotions** can persuade resellers to carry a brand, give it shelf space, promote it in advertising, and push it to consumers. Shelf space is so scarce these days that manufacturers often have to offer price-offs, allowances, buy-back guarantees, or free goods to retailers and wholesalers to get products on the shelf and, once there, to keep them on it.

Manufacturers use several trade promotion tools. Many of the tools used for consumer promotions—contests, premiums, displays—can also be used as trade promotions. Or the manufacturer may offer a straight *discount* off the list price on each case purchased during a stated period of time (also called a *price-off, off-invoice,* or *off-list*). Manufacturers also may offer an *allowance* (usually so much off per case) in return for the retailer's agreement to feature the manufacturer's products in some way. For example, an advertising allowance compensates retailers for advertising the product, whereas a display allowance compensates them for using special displays.

Manufacturers may offer *free goods*, which are extra cases of merchandise, to resellers who buy a certain quantity or who feature a certain flavor or size. They may also offer *push money*—cash or gifts to dealers or their sales forces to "push" the manufacturer's goods. Manufacturers may give retailers free *specialty advertising items* that carry the company's name, such as pens, calendars, memo pads, flashlights, and tote bags.

Business Promotions

Business promotions
Sales promotion tools used to generate business leads, stimulate purchases, reward customers, and motivate salespeople.

Companies spend billions of dollars each year on promotion geared toward industrial customers. **Business promotions** are used to generate business leads, stimulate purchases, reward customers, and motivate salespeople. Business promotions include many of the same tools used for consumer or trade promotions. Here, we focus on two additional major business promotion tools: conventions and trade shows and sales contests.

Many companies and trade associations organize *conventions and trade shows* to promote their products. Firms selling to the industry show their products at the trade

 **Some trade shows are huge. At this year's International Consumer Electronics Show, 3,100 exhibitors attracted more than 153,000 professional visitors.**

Consumer Electronics Association (CEA)

show. Vendors at these shows receive many benefits, such as opportunities to find new sales leads, contact customers, introduce new products, meet new customers, sell more to present customers, and educate customers with publications and audiovisual materials. Trade shows also help companies reach many prospects that are not reached through their sales forces.

Some trade shows are huge. ● For example, at this year's International Consumer Electronics Show, 3,100 exhibitors attracted some 153,000 professional visitors. Even more impressive, at the BAUMA mining and construction equipment trade show in Munich, Germany, more than 3,200 exhibitors from 53 countries presented their latest product innovations to over 420,000 attendees from more than 200 countries. Total exhibition space equaled about 5.9 million square feet (more than 124 football fields).[32]

A *sales contest* is a contest for salespeople or dealers to motivate them to increase their sales performance over a given period. Sales contests motivate and recognize good company performers, who may receive trips, cash prizes, or other gifts. Some companies award points for performance, which the receiver can turn in for any of a variety of prizes. Sales contests work best when they are tied to measurable and achievable sales objectives (such as finding new accounts, reviving old accounts, or increasing account profitability).

Developing the Sales Promotion Program

Beyond selecting the types of promotions to use, marketers must make several other decisions in designing the full sales promotion program. First, they must determine the *size of the incentive*. A certain minimum incentive is necessary if the promotion is to succeed; a larger incentive will produce more sales response. The marketer also must set *conditions for participation*. Incentives might be offered to everyone or only to select groups.

Marketers must determine how to *promote and distribute the promotion* program itself. For example, a $2-off coupon could be given out in a package, in an advertisement, at the store, via the Internet, or in a mobile download. Each distribution method involves a different level of reach and cost. Increasingly, marketers are blending several media into a total campaign concept. The *length of the promotion* is also important. If the sales promotion period is too short, many prospects (who may not be buying during that time) will miss it. If the promotion runs too long, the deal will lose some of its "act now" force.

Evaluation is also very important. Marketers should work to measure the returns on their sales promotion investments, just as they should seek to assess the returns on other marketing activities. The most common evaluation method is to compare sales before, during, and after a promotion. Marketers should ask: Did the promotion attract new customers or more purchasing from current customers? Can we hold onto these new customers and purchases? Will the long-run customer relationship and sales gains from the promotion justify its costs?

Clearly, sales promotion plays an important role in the total promotion mix. To use it well, the marketer must define the sales promotion objectives, select the best tools, design the sales promotion program, implement the program, and evaluate the results. Moreover, sales promotion must be coordinated carefully with other promotion mix elements within the overall IMC program.

Reviewing the Concepts

MyMarketingLab™

Go to **mymktlab.com** to complete the problems marked with this icon .

Reviewing Objectives and Key Terms

 ## Objectives Review

This chapter is the third of four chapters covering the final marketing mix element—promotion. The previous two chapters dealt with overall integrated marketing communications and with advertising and public relations. This one investigated personal selling and sales promotion. Personal selling is the interpersonal arm of the communications mix. Sales promotion consists of short-term incentives to encourage the purchase or sale of a product or service.

Objective 1 **Discuss the role of a company's salespeople in creating value for customers and building customer relationships.** (pp 462–464)

Most companies use salespeople, and many companies assign them an important role in the marketing mix. For companies selling business products, the firm's sales force works directly with customers. Often, the sales force is the customer's only direct contact with the company and therefore may be viewed by customers as representing the company itself. In contrast, for consumer-product companies that sell through intermediaries, consumers usually do not meet salespeople or even know about them. The sales force works behind the scenes, dealing with wholesalers and retailers to obtain their support and helping them become more effective in selling the firm's products.

As an element of the promotion mix, the sales force is very effective in achieving certain marketing objectives and carrying out such activities as prospecting, communicating, selling and servicing, and information gathering. But with companies becoming more market oriented, a customer-focused sales force also works to produce both customer satisfaction and company profit. The sales force plays a key role in developing and managing profitable customer relationships.

Objective 2 **Identify and explain the six major sales force management steps.** (pp 464–475)

High sales force costs necessitate an effective sales management process consisting of six steps: designing sales force strategy and structure, recruiting and selecting, training, compensating, supervising, and evaluating salespeople and sales force performance.

In designing a sales force, sales management must address various issues, including what type of sales force structure will work best (territorial, product, customer, or complex structure), sales force size, who will be involved in selling, and how various sales and sales-support people will work together (inside or outside sales forces and team selling).

Salespeople must be recruited and selected carefully. In recruiting salespeople, a company may look to the job duties and the characteristics of its most successful salespeople to suggest the traits it wants in new salespeople. It must then look for applicants through recommendations of current salespeople, ads, and the Internet and other social networks, as well as college recruitment/placement centers. In the selection process, the procedure may vary from a single informal interview to lengthy testing and interviewing. After the selection process is complete, training programs familiarize new salespeople not only with the art of selling but also with the company's history, its products and policies, and the characteristics of its customers and competitors.

The sales force compensation system helps to reward, motivate, and direct salespeople. In addition to compensation, all salespeople need supervision, and many need continuous encouragement because they must make many decisions and face many frustrations. Periodically, the company must evaluate their performance to help them do a better job. In evaluating salespeople, the company relies on information gathered from sales reports, personal observations, customer surveys, and conversations with other salespeople.

Objective 3 **Discuss the personal selling process, distinguishing between transaction-oriented marketing and relationship marketing.** (pp 475–479)

Selling involves a seven-step process: prospecting and qualifying, preapproach, approach, presentation and demonstration, handling objections, closing, and follow-up. These steps help marketers close a specific sale and, as such, are transaction oriented. However, a seller's dealings with customers should be guided by the larger concept of relationship marketing. The company's sales force should help to orchestrate a whole-company effort to develop profitable long-term relationships with key customers based on superior customer value and satisfaction.

Objective 4 | **Explain how sales promotion campaigns are developed and implemented.** (pp 479–484)

Sales promotion campaigns call for setting sales promotions objectives (in general, sales promotions should be *consumer relationship building*); selecting tools; and developing and implementing the sales promotion program by using *consumer promotion tools* (from coupons, refunds, premiums, and point-of-purchase promotions to contests, sweepstakes, and events), *trade promotion tools* (from discounts and allowances to free goods and push money), and *business promotion tools* (conventions, trade shows, and sales contests), as well as determining such things as the size of the incentive, the conditions for participation, how to promote and distribute the promotion package, and the length of the promotion. After this process is completed, the company must evaluate its sales promotion results.

 Key Terms

Objective 1

Personal selling (p 462)
Salesperson (p 463)

Objective 2

Sales force management (p 464)
Territorial sales force structure (p 465)
Product sales force structure (p 465)
Customer (or market) sales force structure (p 465)
Outside sales force (or field sales force) (p 466)

Inside sales force (p 466)
Team selling (p 467)

Objective 3

Sales quota (p 474)
Selling process (p 475)
Prospecting (p 475)
Preapproach (p 476)
Approach (p 476)
Presentation (p 476)
Handling objections (p 477)

Closing (p 477)
Follow-up (p 477)

Objective 4

Sales promotion (p 479)
Consumer promotions (p 481)
Event marketing (or event sponsorships) (p 482)
Trade promotions (p 483)
Business promotions (p 483)

Discussion and Critical Thinking

 Discussion Questions

⚙ **1.** Discuss how the salesperson is a critical link between the company and the customer. (AACSB: Communication; Reflective Thinking)

2. Compare the three sales force structures outlined in the chapter. Which structure is most effective? (AACSB: Communication; Reflective Thinking)

3. Discuss the activities involved in sales force management. (AACSB: Communication)

4. Define *sales promotion* and discuss its objectives. (AACSB: Communication)

5. Name and describe the types of consumer promotions. (AACSB: Communication; Reflective Thinking)

6. Discuss the different types of trade sales promotions and distinguish these types of promotions from business promotions. (AACSB: Communication)

 Critical Thinking Exercise

⚙ **1.** Suppose you are the marketing coordinator responsible for recommending a sales promotion plan for the market launch of a new brand of energy drink to be sold in supermarkets. What promotional tools would you consider for this task, and what decisions must be made? (AACSB: Communications; Reflective Thinking)

Applications and Cases

 ## Marketing Technology Another Day, Another Deal

The humble coupon has gotten a boost from social media. Groupon, the group deal-of-the-day coupon service that started in late 2008, is exceeding even Google's and Facebook's phenomenal early growth rates. It now offers about 1,000 deals every day to more than 70 million subscribers in almost 50 countries. The business model is simple. A business sets up a deal through Groupon, such as offering $50 worth of merchandise for $25, but the deal is only honored if enough people sign up for it. Groupon typically takes a 50 percent cut of all the revenue generated on the deal (that is, $12.50 of the $25 the consumer pays for the groupon). In return, the business gets a lot of store traffic from the deal. Because the business model is so simple and the entry barriers so small, there are now more than 600 of these digital daily-deal online sites.

✪ **1.** Debate the pros and cons of offering coupons through digital deal-of-the-day Internet sites such as Groupon from the perspective of the businesses offering the deals. (AACSB: Communication; Use of IT; Reflective Thinking)

2. Create an idea for a local group-buying promotional service based on Groupon's model as a class project or as a fundraiser for a student organization at your school. Students will be the target market of this digital-deal online site. Develop a sales plan to recruit local businesses to offer deals as well as the promotion plan to attract students to the site. Present your plans to the class. (AACSB: Communication; Reflective Thinking)

 ## Marketing Ethics Off-Label Marketing

Johnson & Johnson agreed to a $2.2-billion settlement over the marketing of its antipsychotic drug Risperdal. Pfizer agreed to a $2.3-billion settlement and Eli Lilly paid $1.4 billion to settle disputes with the U.S. government. Glaxo recently agreed to a $3-million settlement—its fourth settlement with the government over the marketing of its products. By law, pharmaceutical companies are allowed to market their drugs only for uses approved by the Food and Drug Administration (FDA), but doctors may prescribe any approved drug as they see fit. Drug manufacturers have been training their sales forces to educate doctors on nonapproved uses and dosages, called "off-label" marketing. Almost 75 percent of the largest pharmaceutical settlements with the government are for off-label marketing. Glaxo even went so far as to have a questionable article ghost-written by a company and later published in a medical journal under the names of academic authors to convince doctors that Paxil was proven effective in treating depression in children, a use that the FDA has not approved. The reported clinical trial was later criticized by the medical community, but doctors probably are not aware of that because a majority of them rely on pharmaceutical companies for

information on drugs. Most unlawful practices by the pharmaceutical industry come to light only because an insider—someone in management or a sales rep—blows the whistle. Fortunately, the Federal False Claim Act provides protection and even incentive for employees to come forward. Pharmaceutical companies settle these types of investigations because, even if they plead guilty to criminal charges, which J&J and Glaxo did, they don't lose the ability to sell drugs to the government as they would if found guilty after a trial.

1. What would you do if you were a pharmaceutical sales rep and were told to promote a drug for off-label use? What protections and incentives are available under the Federal False Claim Act to encourage employees to report illegal behavior? (AACSB: Communication; Ethical Reasoning; Reflective Thinking)

2. What traits and behaviors should an ethical salesperson possess? What role does the sales manager play in ethical selling behavior? (AACSB: Communication; Ethical Reasoning; Reflective Thinking)

 ## Marketing by the Numbers Sales Force Analysis

Brown, Inc. is a manufacturer of furniture sold through retail furniture outlets in the southeastern United States. The company has two salespeople who do more than just sell the products—they manage relationships with retail customers to enable them to better meet consumers' needs. The company's sales reps visit retail customers several times per year, often for hours at a time. Brown is considering expanding to other regions of the country and would like to have distribution through 1,000 retail customer accounts. To do so, however, the company would have to hire more salespeople. Each salesperson earns $50,000 plus 2 percent commission on all sales. Another alternative is to use the services of sales agents instead of its own sales force. Sales agents would be paid 10 percent of sales.

1. Refer to Appendix 2 to answer this question. Determine the number of salespeople Brown needs if it has 1,000 retail customer accounts that need to be called on five times per year. Each sales call lasts approximately 2.5 hours, and each sales rep has approximately 1,250 hours per year to devote to customers. (AACSB: Communication; Analytical Reasoning)

2. At what level of sales would it be more cost efficient for Brown to use its own sales force as compared to sales agents? To determine this, consider the fixed and variable costs for each alternative. What are the pros and cons of using a company's own sales force over independent sales agents? (AACSB: Communication; Analytical Reasoning; Reflective Thinking)

Video Case MedTronic

Many companies sell products that most customers can literally live without. But the devices that MedTronic sells are a matter of life and death. Patient well-being depends upon the insulin delivery devices, implantable defibrillators, and cardiac pacemakers designed and manufactured by MedTronic. In some markets, seven out of eight medical devices in use are MedTronic devices.

But what happens when you know you have a product that will help a given customer in terms of cost, time, and end-user well-being, but you can't get a foot in the door to communicate that information? This video demonstrates how MedTronic sales representatives maintain a customer-centered approach to the personal selling process as a means for effectively communicating MedTronic's product benefits.

After viewing the video featuring MedTronic, answer the following questions:

1. How is the sales force at MedTronic structured?

2. Identify the selling process for MedTronic. Give an example of each step.

3. Is MedTronic effective at building long-term customer relationships through its sales force? If so, how? If not, what could be improved?

Company Case   Salesforce.com: Helping Companies Super-Charge the Selling Process

As Internet, social, and mobile media have proliferated, the nature of business-to-business (B-to-B) selling has changed. In fact, some have predicted the death of the professional salesperson, claiming that today's interactive technologies make it possible to sell products and services to the business customer with little to no human interaction.

But that perspective overlooks one very important characteristic of successful selling: The objective of making a sale and getting customers to purchase again and again is to build solid, enduring customer relationships. And to do that, salespeople are more important than ever. But these days, for salespeople to be effective at everything from prospecting to staying connected to customers between purchases, they must stay abreast of technologies that facilitate the management of customer relationships.

A New Era for Sales Support

Enter Salesforce.com. Marc Benioff started the online company in 1999 to compete in a crowded marketplace of companies that provide support to sales forces of companies large and small. At first glance, not much differentiated Salesforce.com's system as only one of many that enabled corporate sales representatives to gather and manage information about existing and prospective customers, leading to greater selling productivity.

But Salesforce.com's mission was nothing less than visionary. What made the company different was communicated in the Salesforce.com logo—the word "software" with a red circle around it and a line drawn through it. The company's call-in number was (and still is) "800-NOSOFTWARE." With Salesforce.com, Benioff was declaring the death of expensive packaged customer relationship management (CRM) software—the type peddled by then-industry leaders Siebel and SAP. With its stock symbol, "CRM," Benioff declared early on that Salesforce.com would be *the* force for helping business sales forces manage customer relationships.

Salesforce.com's products were subscription based and accessed through the Web. With nothing to install and no owned software, customers could get up and running quickly and inexpensively. Although that "cloud" model is standard practice for many companies today, it was a radical idea in 1999. But more than just introducing an innovative method for selling software, Benioff was establishing Salesforce.com as an innovative company that would consistently seek new ways to help companies achieve greater sales force efficiency. Since its introduction, Salesforce.com has remained one step ahead of the competition by augmenting its products and services in ways that seem to foreshadow trends in B-to-B selling.

During the last 10 years, the company has expanded from its core sales management services to a complete portfolio of Internet-based services that put every aspect of selling and sales management in the cloud. This includes Data.com (B-to-B sales and marketing account and contact data), Database.com (a cloud database), Site.com (cloud-based Internet content management), Desk.com (a social help desk for small business), and Sales Cloud (the world's number one sales app). A few years ago, Salesforce.com recognized that social media would play a huge role in B-to-B sales. To remain on the cutting edge, Salesforce.com acquired Radian6 (the social media monitoring firm used by more than half of Fortune 500 companies) and launched Chatter (a sort of Facebook for the business world).

The Salesforce.com product portfolio is carefully integrated so that each tool works with every other tool. And whereas each Salesforce.com product has broadened the company's offerings beyond sales force support functions, each also facilitates the sales process. As Salesforce.com puts it, these tools allow companies to "supercharge their sales." Consider how Salesforce.com has helped the following companies achieve better-than-ever customer relationships through selling.

NBCUniversal

NBCUniversal (NBCU) is home to 20 popular media and entertainment brands, including NBC, CNBC, Bravo, Universal, and Telemundo. In the topsy-turvy media world, NBCUniversal has been challenged in recent years by the dramatic changes that have hit the industry, including the growing number of media outlets competing for viewer attention, the increased popularity of online media, and shifts in the nature and type of advertising. Because of NBCU's huge scope, it has perhaps been hit harder by the changes than any media organization.

NBCU's media empire is so vast that it represents a combined total of more than 2 million ads every year. Managing that many ads across various channels for thousands of advertiser-customers was a daunting task. In fact, at one point, NBCU had more than 250 different portals for viewing information and interactions between the company and the advertisers who purchase its ad space. Managing that kind of interaction was fraught with lost opportunities for providing advertisers with the best way to reach the right customers with the right message.

Salesforce.com, however, has helped NBCU integrate its sales force across its customers. In fact, the portal for managing relationships is now simplified to only one view, allowing all sales reps in every NBCU property to see what all advertisers are doing across all properties. "As business moves into the 21st century, you need social collaboration tools to pull everything together," says Eric Johnson, vice president for Sales Force Effectiveness at NBCU. "Salesforce.com helps capture the collaboration that's happening across the company—to mobilize and grow the business." With the Salesforce.com portfolio of products, NBCU is able to distribute the right social information to account executives at the right time, dramatically improving customer relationships with advertisers. As a result, NBCU has seen big increases in cross-selling.

Salesforce.com tools enable sales reps to manage customer relationships better through more open internal collaboration as well. For example, when the NBCU product team comes up with new advertising and product placement opportunities, it uses Salesforce.com social tools to quickly provide the sales team with everything it needs to sell the new inventory. In this manner, sales reps are more connected than ever. And a better-equipped sales force is a happier sales force. "The collaboration with marketing in the first six months was meteoric," says Dan Sztorc, CNBC account executive. With Salesforce.com, he and his colleagues are continuously connected with each other and with the customers. "We're free to venture out and try different things and take some three-point shots."

NBCU gave all its account executives iPads equipped with a Salesforce.com app that allows them to access all of their Salesforce.com tools and other marketing and client information from any place, any time. Just how successful has NBCU been with Salesforce.com's tools? "The first week we launched this application, we had a 300 percent return on investment," says Johnson. "Social collaboration, social networking—it's here to stay."

GE Capital

In the modern, more social world of business, GE Capital was beginning to realize the importance of building connections with its customers. "The power of the social enterprise in the B-to-B space is that you can really connect with your customers and bring them value in ways that everyday interactions don't typically allow," says Sigal Zarmi, chief information officer (CIO) of GE Capital. For this reason, GE Capital tapped into Salesforce.com's portfolio of tools.

One tactic that the company employed was building what it calls Access GE, a new collaborative community based on Salesforce.com's Force.com platform. After only five weeks of development, Access GE was launched, providing a thriving community where mid-market CEOs and CFOs could tap into the expertise of their peers as well as that of GE Capital employees. This allows executives at customer organizations to connect with GE and other customers based on similar needs and shared experiences, participating in discussions on topics of mutual interest.

As Access GE allows customers to receive better information more quickly, the power of Salesforce.com's social technologies is boosting collaboration among GE Capital's employees as well. The company's commercial sales team of more than 3,100 employees also connects on Chatter to share sales strategies, find internal experts, and uncover opportunities to cross-sell.

How does all this help to sell GE Capital's products and services? Access GE accelerates the time it takes for customers to get the answers and information they seek in order to make purchase decisions. "We're connecting customers to GE Capital—and to

each other—quickly, efficiently, and socially, building deeper relationships with important clients," explains Zarmi. "That's the power of the social network." All this has helped GE Capital better fulfill its mission to provide financing and expertise that helps its customers' capital go farther. With Salesforce.com's help, the company is also developing stronger and deeper connections to its customers, encouraging greater employee engagement and collaboration, and achieving growth in ways that it had never before experienced.

Moving Forward with New Products

Based on the success of the customized social tool Access GE, Salesforce.com is expanding its product line. After all, Chatter is a one-to-many communication tool. With Access GE, Salesforce.com recognized the value that its clients could gain by having a many-to-many forum such as that provided by Access GE. For this reason, Salesforce.com has introduced Salesforce.com Communities as a branch of Chatter, providing an organized free-for-all for managers and client organizations to meet and collaborate online with each other as well as with company representatives.

Salesforce.com is quick to note that there are risks associated with giving customers an open forum. In addition to sharing valuable positive information, they can also air complaints and negative comments to thousands of customers at a time. But the innovative Salesforce.com has embraced that kind of risk from the beginning. With every new technology that it unveils, it focuses on the same trump card to convince reluctant users—productivity enhancements. With Chatter, customer users see an average of 12.5 percent gains in productivity over companies that do not use the B-to-B social network. And Salesforce.com expects that there will be similar productivity gains with Communities as well.

Salesforce.com has remained innovative from the start, keeping ahead of the trends and technologies that are shaping modern B-to-B interactions. Its tools are state-of-the-art, providing sales reps with a more accurate and timely infusion of customer information and insight into the sales process than ever before. As Salesforce.com puts it, "With sales for the social enterprise, reps, managers, and execs have everything they need to win deals." Salesforce.com continues to deliver on its promise to supercharge sales.

Questions for Discussion

1. When Salesforce.com launched as an Internet-based service, how did that innovation help sales reps to interact better with customers?

2. Describe the differences that Salesforce.com has made for customers NBCU and GE Capital.

3. Consider the selling process. How might any of the Salesforce.com tools described in this case facilitate each step?

4. Looking forward, what products will Salesforce.com have to develop in order to remain on the cutting edge of supporting sales staffs with information and collaboration?

Sources: Based on information from www.salesforce.com, accessed August 2012. Also see Erika Morphy, "Are Enterprises Really Ready for True Social Collaboration?" *Forbes*, August, 14, 2012, www.forbes.com/sites/erikamorphy/2012/08/14/are-enterprises-really-for-true-social-collaboration-salesforce-coms-betting-they-cant-resist-the-productivity-gains/; and Shel Israel, "Does Salesforce.com Own the Social Enterprise?" *Forbes*, March 20, 2012, www.forbes.com/sites/shelisrael/2012/03/20/does-salesforce-own-the-social-enterprise/.

MyMarketingLab

Go to **mymktlab.com** for Auto-graded writing questions as well as the following
Assisted-graded writing questions:

16-1. Interview a salesperson. Is this salesperson an order taker or an order getter?
How much training did he or she receive to perform the sales job? Write a
report of what you learned. (AACSB: Communication; Reflective Thinking)

16-2. Select a product or service and role-play a sales call—from the approach to
the close—with another student. Have one member of the team act as the
salesperson with the other member acting as the customer, raising at least
three objections. Select another product or service and perform this exercise
again with your roles reversed. (AACSB: Communication; Reflective Thinking)

16-3. Mymktlab Only – comprehensive writing assignment for this chapter.

References

1. Portions adapted from information found in Jesi Hempel, "IBM's All-Star Salesman," *Fortune*, September 26, 2008, http://money.cnn.com/2008/09/23/technology/hempel_IBM.fortune/index.htm; and www-03.ibm.com/employment/jobs/softwaresales/ and www-03.ibm.com/ibm/history/ibm100/us/en/icons/ibmsales/, accessed November 2012.

2. See Philip Kotler, Neil Rackham, and Suj Krishnaswamy, "Ending the War Between Sales and Marketing," *Harvard Business Review*, July–August 2006, pp. 68–78; Elizabeth A. Sullivan, "The Ties That Bind," *Marketing News*, May 15, 2010; Allan Mayer, "Improving the Relationships Between Sales and Marketing," *OneAccord*, May 30, 2012, www.oneaccordpartners.com/blog/bid/132539/; Philip Kotler and Kevin Lane Keller, *Marketing Management,* 14th ed. (Upper Saddle River, NJ: Prentice Hall, 2012), p. 554.

3. See Henry Canaday, "Give It a Whirl," *Selling Power,* May/June 2010, pp. 22–24; and Canaday, "How One Enterprise Sales Force Works with Channel Partners to Maintain and Build Sales," *Selling Power,* June 27, 2012, www.sellingpower.com/enterprise-sales/.

4. "Selling Power 500: The Largest Sales Force in America," *Selling Power,* September/October 2011, pp. 33–49.

5. See discussions at "The Costs of Personal Selling," April 13, 2011, www.seekarticle.com/business-sales/personal-selling.html; and "What Is the Real Cost of a B2B Sales Call?" accessed at www.marketing-playbook.com/sales-marketing-strategy/what-is-the-real-cost-of-a-b2b-sales-call, October 2012.

6. Quote and facts from Jim Domanski, "Special Report: The 2012 B@B Tele-Sales Trend Report," www.salesopedia.com/downloads/2012%20B2B%20Tele-Sales%20Trend%20Special%20Reportl.pdf; accessed July 2012.

7. See "Case Study: Climax Portable Machine Tools," www.selltis.com/selltis-sales/Case-Studies/Climax-Portable-Machine-Tools and www.climaxportable.com, accessed November 2012.

8. "Customer Business Development," www.experiencepg.com/jobs/customer-business-development-sales.aspx, accessed October 2012.

9. For this and more information and discussion, see www.gallupaustralia.com.au/consulting/118729/sales-force-effectiveness.aspx, accessed July 2012; Lynette Ryals and Iain Davies, "Do You Really Know Who Your Best Salespeople Are?" *Harvard Business Review,* December 2010, pp. 34–35; "The 10 Skills of Super' Salespeople," www.businesspartnerships.ca/articles/the_10_skills_of_super_salespeople.phtml, accessed July 2012; and "Salesperson Recruiting Expert Steve Suggs Shows How to Hire the Best Salespeople," *PRNewswire,* April 19, 2012.

10. Barbara Hendricks, "Strengths-Based Selling," February 8, 2011, www.gallup.com/press/146246/Strengths-Based-Selling.aspx.

11. "ADP Case Study," Corporate Visions, Inc., http://win.corporatevisions.com/caseStudy_ADP.html, accessed July 2011; and Henry Canaday, "Higher Expectations," *Selling Power,* November/December 2011, pp. 50–51.

12. Based on information found in Sara Donnelly, "Staying in the Game," *Pharmaceutical Executive,* May 2008, pp. 158–159; "Improving Sales Force Effectiveness: Bayer's Experiment with New Technology," Bayer Healthcare Pharmaceuticals, Inc., 2008, www.icmrindia.org/casestudies/catalogue/Marketing/MKTG200.htm; Tanya Lewis, "Concentric," *Medical Marketing and Media,* July 2008, p. 59; www.hydraframe.com/mobile/project_reprace.htm, accessed July 2012; and Andrew Tolve, "Pharma Sales: How Simulation Can Help Reps Sell," *Eye for Pharma,* March 28, 2012, http://social.eyeforpharma.com/sales/pharma-sales-how-simulation-can-help-reps-sell. For more on e-learning, see Sarah Boehle, "Global Sales Training's Balancing Act," *Training,* January 2010, p. 29; and Henry Canaday, "The Personal Virtual Classroom," *Selling Power,* May/June 2011, p. 55.

13. For this and more discussion, see Joseph Kornak, "07 Compensation Survey: What's It All Worth?" *Sales & Marketing Management,* May 2007, pp. 28–39; William L. Cron and Thomas E. DeCarlo, *Dalrymple's Sales Management,* 10th ed. (New York: John Wiley & Sons Inc., 2009), p. 303; Ken Sundheim, "How Sales Professionals Are Paid," *Salesopedia,* www.salesopedia.com/compensation-compensationdesign, accessed July 2012; and Alexander Group, "2012 Sales Compensation Trends Survey Results," January 6, 2012, www.alexandergroup.com/resources/survey-findings.

14. Susan Greco, "How to Reduce Your Cost of Sales," *Inc.,* March 5, 2010, www.inc.com/guide/reducing-cost-of-sales.html. Also see Robert McGarvey, "Pay for Performance," *Selling Power,* February 2011, p. 54.

15. See Charles Fifield, "Necessary Condition #3 The Right Day-to-Day Operational Focus," December 2010, www.baylor.edu/content/services/document.php/127101.pdf. For another summary, see Gerhard Gschwandtner, "How Much Time Do Your Salespeople Spend Selling?" *Selling Power,* March/April 2011, p. 8.

16. Quote above from Lain Chroust Ehmann, "Sales Up!" *Selling Power,* January/February 2011, p. 40. Extract adapted from information found in Pelin Wood Thorogood, "Sales 2.0: How Soon Will It Improve Your Business?" *Selling Power,* November/December 2008, pp. 58–61; Gerhard Gschwandtner, "What Is Sales 2.0, and Why Should You Care?" *Selling Power,* March/April 2010, p. 9. Also see Michael Brenner, "The State of the Union in B2B Marketing," January 25, 2011, www.b2bmarketinginsider.com/strategy/the-state-of-the-union-in-b2b-marketing.

17. Adapted from information in Elizabeth A. Sullivan, "B-to-B Marketers: One-to-One Marketing," *Marketing News,* May 15, 2009, pp. 11–13. Also see Robert McGarvey, "All about Us: How the Social-Community Phenomenon Has Affected B2B Sales," *Selling Power,* November/December 2010, p. 48; and Kim Wright Wiley,

"The Electronic Click," *Selling Power,* January/February/March 2012, pp. 14–16. For more on Makino's social networking efforts, see www .facebook.com/MakinoMachine, www.youtube.com/user/Makino MachineTools, and http://twitter.com/#!/makinomachine, accessed November 2012.

18. Quotes from David Thompson, "Embracing the Future: A Step by Step Overview of Sales 2.0," *Sales and Marketing Management*, July/August 2008, p. 21; and "Ahead of the Curve: How Sales 2.0 Will Affect Your Sales Process For the Better," *Selling Power*, March/April 2010, pp. 14–17. Also see Robert McGarvey, "All About Us," *Selling Power,* March 7, 2011, p. 48; Lain Chroust Ehmann, "Sales Up!" *Selling Power*, January/February 2011, p. 40; and Kim Wright Wiley, "The Electronic Click," *Selling Power,* January/February/March 2012, pp. 14–16.

19. John Graham, "Salespeople under Siege: The Profession Redefined," *Agency Sales*, January 2010, pp. 20–25; Rick Phillips, "Don't Pressure, Persuade," *Selling Power*, January/February 2010, p. 22; and Bill Farquharson and T. J. Tedesco, "How to Build' a Sales Rep," *Printing Impressions,* April 2011, p. 38.

20. Example based on information from James C. Anderson, Nirmalya Kumar, and James A. Narus, "Become a Value Merchant," *Sales & Marketing Management*, May 6, 2008, pp. 20–23; and "Business Market Value Merchants," *Marketing Management*, March/April 2008, pp. 31+. For more discussion and examples, see Heather Baldwin, "Deeper Value Delivery," *Selling Power*, September/October 2010, p. 16.

21. Thomas P. Reilly, "Value-Added Selling Is Smart," *Selling Power,* June 27, 2012, www.sellingpower.com/content/article.php?a=8917.

22. *Making Connections: Trade Promotion Integration Across the Marketing Spectrum,* Kantar Retail (Wilton, CT: Kantar Retail, July 2010), p. 10.

23. "High Level of Promotions Pushes Down Grocery Spend," *Retail Week*, September 13, 2011.

24. "Kroger Doubles Fuel Discount Opportunities for Summer," May 25, 2012, http://www.csnews.com/top-story-kroger_doubles_fuel_discount_opportunities_for_summer-61195.html; and www.kroger .com/in_store/fuel/Pages/B1.aspx, accessed July 2012.

25. Shannon Bryant, "Consumers Saved $4.6 Billion Dollars in 2011 with Coupons," *Marketing Forecast*, March 2, 2012, www.marketingforecast .com/archives/17156.

26. "Research and Market Adds Report: Mobile Coupons: Market Analysis and Forecasts," *Entertainment Close-Up*, January 23, 2012; and "New Research Reveals Shopping Behavior of Digital Coupon Users," *Business Wire*, April 2, 2012.

27. Based on information from "Walgreens Brings Mobile Couponing and Exclusive Offers to Smartphone Users Beginning Black Friday," November 17, 2011, http://news.walgreens.com/article_display .cfm?article_id=5504; and Kunar Patel, "At Walgreens, a Mobile Check-In Acts Like a Circular," *Advertising Age,* February 8, 2012, http://adage.com/print/232584/.

28. See www.happymeal.com/en_US/, accessed October 2012.

29. See "2011 Estimate of Promotional Products Distributor Sales," www .ppai.org/inside-ppai/research/Documents/2011%20SalesVolume% 20Sheet.pdf, accessed July 2011.

30. Adapted from information found in Patrick Hanlon, "Face Slams: Event Marketing Takes Off," *Forbes,* May 9, 2012, www.forbes.com/sites/ patrickhanlon/2012/05/09/face-slams-event-marketing-takes-off/; and www.redbull.com/cs/Satellite/en_INT/Events/001242745950157 and www.redbull.com/cs/Satellite/en_INT/Red-Bull.com/HolyShit/ 011242745950125, accessed July 2012. The referenced wing suit flying video can be found at http://player.vimeo.com/video/31481531? autoplay=1.

31. *Making Connections: Trade Promotion Integration Across the Marketing Spectrum,* Kantar Retail, p. 10.

32. See "About CES: Attendee Profile," accessed at www.cesweb.org/ aboutces.asp, May 2012; and "Bauma 2010 Closing Report," www .bauma.de/en/Press/Closingreport, accessed October 2012.

17

Direct and Online

Marketing Building Direct Customer Relationships

Chapter Preview In the previous three chapters, you learned about communicating customer value through integrated marketing communication and about four elements of the marketing communications mix: advertising, publicity, personal selling, and sales promotion. In this chapter, we examine direct marketing and its fastest-growing form, online marketing. Actually, direct marketing can be viewed as more than just a communications tool. In many ways it constitutes an overall marketing approach—a blend of communication and distribution channels all rolled into one. As you read this chapter, remember that although direct marketing is presented as a separate tool, it must be carefully integrated with the other elements of the promotion mix.

Let's start by looking at Facebook, a company that exists only online. The giant online social network promises to become one of the world's most powerful and profitable online marketers. Yet, as a marketing company, Facebook is just getting started.

Facebook: "We Are One Percent Done With Our Mission"

The world is rapidly going social and online. And no company is more social or more online than Facebook. The huge online social network has a deep and daily impact on the lives of hundreds of millions of members around the world. Yet Facebook is now grappling with a crucial question: How can it profitably tap the marketing potential of its massive community to make money without driving off its legions of loyal users?

Facebook is humongous. In little more than eight years, it has signed up more than 850 million members—one-eighth of the world's population. Every 60 seconds, Facebook users share 700,000 messages, update 95,000 statuses, write 80,000 wall posts, tag 65,000 photos, share 50,000 links, and write a half-million comments affirming or disparaging all that activity. Facebook's U.S. members alone log a combined equivalent of more than 100,000 person-years on the site every month.

With that many eyeballs glued to one virtual space for that much time, Facebook has tremendous impact and influence, not just as a sharing community but also as an Internet gateway. It is the default home page for many users, and some users have it on their screens 24/7. But Facebook's power comes not just from its size and omnipresence. Rather, it lies in the deep social connections between users. Facebook's mission is "Giving people the power to share." It's a place where friends and family meet, share their stories, display their photos, and chronicle their lives. Hordes of people have made Facebook their digital home.

By wielding all of that influence, Facebook has the potential to become one of the world's most powerful and profitable online marketers. Yet the burgeoning social network is only now beginning to realize that potential. Although Facebook's membership exploded from the very start, CEO Mark Zuckerberg and the network's other idealistic young co-founders gave little thought to making money. They actually opposed running ads or other forms of marketing, worried that marketing might damage Facebook's free (and commercial-free) sharing culture. So instead they focused on simply trying to manage the online revolution they'd begun.

In fact, without any help from Facebook, companies themselves were first to discover the network's commercial value. Most brands—small and large—have now built their own

> Online social network Facebook
> is grappling with a crucial question: How can
> it profitably tap into its massive marketing potential
> to make money without driving off its legions
> of loyal users?

Facebook pages, gaining free and relatively easy access to the gigantic community's word-of-Web potential. Today, people "like" a Facebook brand page 50 million times every day. At one extreme, The Runcible Spoon Bakery in Nyack, New York, has 227 Facebook fans. At other extremes, the Los Angeles Lakers boast nearly one-half million fans while Coca-Cola—the most "liked" brand on Facebook—has 43.4 million.

As the company has matured, however, Facebook has come to realize it must make its own marketing and moneymaking moves. If it doesn't make money, it can't continue to serve its members. So Facebook has changed its philosophy on advertising. Today, companies can place display or video ads on users' home, profile, or photo pages. The ads are carefully targeted based on user profile data. But taking advantage of the core characteristics of its site, Facebook offers "engagement ads" designed to blend in with regular user activities. Users can interact with the ads by leaving comments, making recommendations, clicking the "like" button, or following a link to a brand-sponsored page within Facebook.

One version of engagement advertising is "sponsored stories," by which one member's interactions with a brand appear in the news feeds on their friends' Facebook pages. For example, if you see an item that says "Harry Gold: Second time today at Starbucks with Jenny Novak," followed by a Starbucks logo and link, Starbucks paid a fee for the placement. The organic feel of these sponsored stories increases user involvement by making the ad feel like just another part of the Facebook experience.

Advertising is proving to be a real moneymaker for Facebook. Its ad revenues increased 69 percent last year, helping to boost Facebook's overall revenue by 88 percent to $3.71 billion. Facebook charges companies nothing to create and maintain fan pages, but the fan pages and advertising interact as a part of a brand's integrated Facebook presence. Brands advertise on Facebook to spark consumer conversations and draw attention to the experiences created on the brand's fan pages.

But advertising is only the tip of the marketing iceberg for Facebook. Other moneymaking ventures are growing even faster than advertising. As a global gathering place where people spend time with friends, Facebook is also a natural for selling entertainment. For instance, take social gaming, one of the most popular activities on Facebook. Millions of people log on each month to play games from developers such as Playmonk, Geewa, wooga, and Zynga. Users play the games for free, but the developers make money by selling virtual goods that enhance the playing experience. And Facebook gets 30 percent of every dollar spent. Zynga—which offers the six most popular games on Facebook— by itself contributed 12 percent of Facebook's revenues last year.

Facebook now hopes to duplicate its gaming successes with other forms of entertainment. For example, recognizing that members often exit the Facebook environment to listen to music or watch movies, the social network is now providing more of these services to keep people at the site. For instance, Facebook has partnered with Spotify, the ultra-hot online music service that's giving Pandora a run for its money. Similarly, Facebook has moved into the movie rental business, partnering with content providers such as Warner Bros., Paramount, Universal, and Miramax to make streamed movies available within the Facebook community.

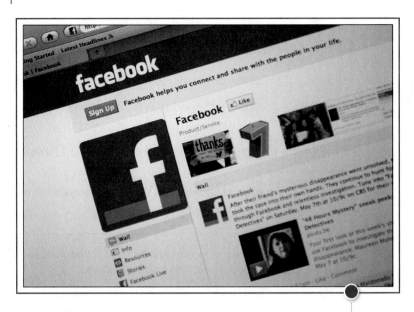

In line with its goal to keep everything within the community, Facebook has even entered the banking business. That's right, banking. Facebook Payments—an official Facebook subsidiary—lets businesses and customers make purchase transactions by exchanging various world currencies for Facebook Credits. Facebook's banking activities over the past few years amount to a declaration of war on payment providers such as PayPal and Google Wallet. In only three years, Facebook Payments revenues have grown to $557 million. That's only a fraction of PayPal's $4.4 billion revenues, but with Facebook's massive membership and growing e-commerce presence, it could quickly pass PayPal as the online payments leader. Perhaps more impressive, Facebook Credits could become a powerful global currency all by itself.

Will increased marketing on Facebook alienate loyal Facebook fans? Not if it's done right. Research shows that online users readily accept—even welcome—well-targeted online advertising and marketing. Tasteful and appropriately targeted offers can enhance rather than detract from the Facebook user experience. "We've found, frankly, that users are getting more value [because of our marketing efforts]," says a Facebook marketing executive, so that companies are "getting value by putting more [marketing] in."

It's too soon to say whether Facebook will eventually challenge the likes of Google in online advertising or whether its ability to sell entertainment to users will ever expand into selling other types of products on a large scale. But its immense, closely knit social network gives Facebook staggering potential. As a marketing company, Facebook is just getting started. Carolyn Everson, Facebook's vice president of global sales, sums up Facebook's growth potential this way: "I'm not sure the marketing community understands our story yet. We evolve so quickly. We have a saying here: 'We are one percent done with our mission.'"[1]

The burgeoning young Facebook online social network is only now beginning to realize its staggering marketing potential. It "helps you connect and share with the people in your life."
Justin Sullivan /Getty Images

Objective Outline

MyMarketingLab™

⭐ **Improve Your Grade!**

Over 10 million students improved their results using the Pearson MyLabs.
Visit **mymktlab.com** for simulations, tutorials, and end-of-chapter problems.

Many of the marketing and promotion tools that we've examined in previous chapters were developed in the context of *mass marketing*: targeting broad markets with standardized messages and offers distributed through intermediaries. Today, however, with the trend toward narrower targeting and the surge in digital technologies, many companies are adopting *direct marketing*, either as a primary marketing approach or as a supplement to other approaches. In this section, we explore the exploding world of direct marketing.

Direct marketing consists of connecting directly with carefully targeted consumers, often on a one-to-one, interactive basis. Using detailed databases, companies tailor their marketing offers and communications to the needs of narrowly defined segments or individual buyers.

Beyond brand and relationship building, direct marketers usually seek a direct, immediate, and measurable consumer response. For example, Amazon.com interacts directly with customers via its Web site or mobile app to help them discover and buy almost anything and everything on the Internet. Similarly, GEICO interacts directly with customers—by telephone, through its Web site or phone app, or on its Facebook, Twitter, and YouTube pages—to build individual brand relationships, give insurance quotes, sell policies, or service customer accounts.

Direct marketing
Connecting directly with carefully targeted segments or individual consumers, often on a one-to-one, interactive basis.

Objective 1 ┈┈►
Define direct marketing and discuss its benefits to customers and companies.

The New Direct Marketing Model

Early direct marketers—catalog companies, direct mailers, and telemarketers—gathered customer names and sold goods mainly by mail and telephone. Today, however, spurred

Save money.

Get GEICO.

Get a free rate quote today.
GEICO
geico.com
1-800-947-AUTO
Obtenga una cotización gratis
en español en migeico.com.

● **The new direct marketing model: Companies such as GEICO have built their entire approach to the marketplace around direct marketing—just visit geico.com or call 1-800-947-auto.**

All text and images are copy written with permission from GEICO

by rapid advances in database technologies and new interactive media—especially the Internet—direct marketing has undergone a dramatic transformation.

In previous chapters, we discussed direct marketing as direct distribution—as marketing channels that contain no intermediaries. We also included direct marketing as one element of the promotion mix—as an approach for communicating directly with consumers. In actuality, direct marketing is both of these things and more.

Most companies still use direct marketing as a supplementary channel or medium. Thus, most department stores, such as Sears or Macy's, sell the majority of their merchandise off their store shelves, but they also sell through direct mail and online catalogs. Lexus markets mostly through mass-media advertising and its high-quality dealer network. However, it also supplements these channels with direct marketing, such as promotional videos and other materials mailed or e-mailed directly to prospective buyers. Its brand Web site provides prospective customers with information about various models, competitive comparisons, financing, and dealer locations. And its Lexus Drivers Web site, YouTube channel, and Facebook page assist and build community among current and future Lexus owners.

However, for many companies today, direct marketing is more than just a supplementary channel or advertising medium—it constitutes a complete model for doing business. Firms employing this *direct model* use it as the *only* approach. ● Companies such as Amazon, eBay, Priceline, Netflix, and GEICO have built their entire approach to the marketplace around direct marketing. Many, like Amazon.com, have employed this model with tremendous success.

Growth and Benefits of Direct Marketing

Direct marketing has become the fastest-growing form of marketing. According to the Direct Marketing Association (DMA), U.S. companies spent almost $163 billion on direct and digital marketing last year. As a result, direct-marketing-driven sales now amount to nearly $2 trillion, accounting for 8.7 percent of the U.S. economy. The DMA estimates that direct marketing sales will grow 4.9 percent annually through 2016, compared with a projected 4.1 percent annual growth for total U.S. sales.[2]

Direct marketing continues to become more Internet-based, and Internet marketing is claiming a fast-growing share of marketing spending and sales. For example, U.S. marketers spent an estimated $31 billion on online advertising last year, a whopping 22 percent increase over the previous year. These efforts generated more than $202 billion in online consumer spending. The DMA predicts that over the next five years, Internet marketing expenditures and Internet-driven sales will grow at a blistering 11 percent a year.[3]

Benefits to Buyers

For buyers, direct marketing is convenient, easy, and private. Direct marketers never close their doors, and customers don't have to trek to and through stores to find products. From almost any location, customers can shop online at any time of the day or night. Likewise, business buyers can learn about products and services without tying up time with salespeople.

Direct marketing gives buyers ready access to a wealth of products. Direct marketers can offer an almost unlimited selection to customers almost anywhere in the world. Just compare the huge selections offered by many online merchants to the more meager assortments of their brick-and-mortar counterparts. For instance, go to Bulbs.com, the Internet's number one light bulb superstore, and you'll have instant access to every imaginable kind of light bulb or lamp—incandescent bulbs, fluorescent bulbs, projection bulbs, surgical bulbs, automotive bulbs—you name it. Similarly, direct retailer Zappos.com stocks millions of shoes, handbags, clothing items, accessories, and housewares from more than 1,000 brands. No physical store could offer handy access to such vast selections.

Direct marketing channels also give buyers access to a wealth of comparative information about companies, products, and competitors. Good catalogs or online sites often provide more information in more useful forms than even the most helpful retail salesperson can provide. For example, Amazon.com offers more information than most of us can digest, ranging from top-10 product lists, extensive product descriptions, and expert and user product reviews to recommendations based on customers' previous purchases.

Finally, direct marketing is immediate and interactive: Buyers can interact with sellers by phone or on the seller's Web site to create exactly the configuration of information, products, or services they desire and then order them on the spot. Moreover, direct marketing gives consumers a greater measure of control. Consumers decide which catalogs they will browse and which online sites they will visit.

Benefits to Sellers

For sellers, direct marketing is a powerful tool for building customer relationships. Today's direct marketers can target small groups or individual customers. Because of the one-to-one nature of direct marketing, companies can interact with customers by phone or online, learn more about their needs, and personalize products and services to specific customer tastes. In turn, customers can ask questions and volunteer feedback.

Direct marketing also offers sellers a low-cost, efficient, speedy alternative for reaching their markets. Direct marketing has grown rapidly in business-to-business (B-to-B) marketing, partly in response to the ever-increasing costs of marketing through the sales force. When personal sales calls cost an average of $350 or more per contact, they should be made only when necessary and to high-potential customers and prospects.[4] Lower-cost-per-contact media—such as B-to-B telemarketing, direct mail, and company Internet sites—often prove more cost effective.

Similarly, online direct marketing results in lower costs, improved efficiencies, and speedier handling of channel and logistics functions, such as order processing, inventory handling, and delivery. Direct marketers such as Amazon.com and Netflix also avoid the expense of maintaining stores and the related costs of rent, insurance, and utilities, passing the savings along to customers. Direct marketing can also offer greater flexibility. It allows marketers to make ongoing adjustments to prices and programs or make immediate, timely, and personal announcements and offers.

Especially in today's digital environment, new direct marketing tools provide rich opportunities for building close, personalized, interactive customer relationships. For example, Southwest Airlines uses a full range of high-tech direct marketing tools—including a desktop widget (DING!), smartphone apps, e-mail, texting, a blog (Nuts About Southwest), and a heavy online social networking presence—to inject itself directly into customers' everyday lives (see Real Marketing 17.1).

Finally, direct marketing gives sellers access to buyers that they could not reach through other channels. Smaller firms can mail catalogs to customers outside their local markets and post toll-free telephone numbers to handle orders and inquiries. Internet marketing is a truly global medium that allows buyers and sellers to click from one country to another in seconds. A Internet user from Paris or Istanbul can access an L.L.Bean online catalog as easily as someone living in Freeport, Maine, the direct retailer's hometown. Even small marketers find that they have ready access to global markets.

● **Internet marketing is a truly global medium. Using L.L.Bean's online catalog, an Internet user from Paris or Istanbul can access an L.L.Bean catalog as easily as someone living in Freeport, Maine, the direct retailer's hometown.**

L.L.Bean Inc.

Customer Databases and Direct Marketing

Customer database
An organized collection of comprehensive data about individual customers or prospects, including geographic, demographic, psychographic, and behavioral data.

Effective direct marketing begins with a good customer database. A **customer database** is an organized collection of comprehensive data about individual customers or prospects. A good customer database can be a potent relationship-building tool. The database gives companies a 360-degree view of their customers and how they behave. A company is no better than what it knows about its customers.

Real Marketing 17.1

Southwest Airlines: Direct Marketing Relationships in a Digital World

For decades, Southwest Airlines has communicated directly with customers through traditional direct marketing approaches. And the company still uses lots of direct mail, sending promotional messages directly to customers through the good old U.S. Postal Service. But in recent years, Southwest has expanded its direct marketing strategy to take advantage of the surging digital opportunities for direct, up-close-and-personal interactions with customers. Today, Southwest's new-age direct marketing capability makes the passenger-centered company the envy of its industry.

When it comes to building direct customer relationships, Southwest Airlines is "the undisputed ruler of the social atmosphere," declares one travel expert. In addition to standard direct marketing tools, such as direct mail and its Web site, Southwest's broad-based direct marketing strategy employs a wide range of cutting-edge digital tools to connect directly with customers. Consider these examples:

- *DING!* Available as a desktop widget or a smartphone app, DING! offers exclusive, limited-time airfare deals. When an enticing new deal becomes available, DING! emits the familiar in-flight seatbelt-light bell-dinging sound. The deep discounts last only 6 to 12 hours and can be accessed only online through the application. DING! lets Southwest Airlines bypass the reservations system and pass bargain fares directly to interested customers. Eventually, DING! may even allow Southwest Airlines to customize fare offers based on each customer's unique characteristics and travel preferences.
- *Smartphone app.* In addition to the DING! app, Southwest's regular smartphone app lets customers book reservations directly, arrange car rentals, check in for flights, check flight status, access their Rapid Rewards accounts, and view flight schedules at any time from any location. "You asked for it," says the company. "The Southwest Airlines app is here to make traveling with Southwest Airlines even more convenient."
- *E-mail.* With their high response rates, Web and mobile e-mail are effective ways to build long-term, one-to-one relationships with carefully targeted customers. Working from

its huge opt-in database, Southwest tailors Web and mobile e-mails—the design, message, offer, and even copy length—to the characteristics and needs of specific customers. Most important, Southwest's e-mails offer real value. For example, recent Southwest mobile ads in smartphone apps such as Pandora and Draw with Friends promised, "Only people who sign up get the e-mails—Click 'N Save." The enticing message worked and customers signed up in droves to start saving money by receiving e-mails from Southwest.

- *Texting.* With more than 3,200 flights every day, some of those flights are bound to be delayed, rescheduled, or canceled because of weather or other unforeseen circumstances. Because most of its customers carry a mobile device when they travel, Southwest now communicates with customers via text messaging to save them time, ensure they get important information, and provide them with peace of mind. "As more passengers adopt mobile devices, [they] are starting to expect information at their fingertips, and waiting in line to speak to customer service agents is not always acceptable,"

says Fred Taylor, senior manager of proactive customer service communications at Southwest. By providing customers with up-to-date information instantly, Southwest has created sky-high customer awareness, satisfaction, and loyalty.

- *Nuts About Southwest blog.* Written by Southwest employees, this creative blog allows for a two-way customer-employee dialogue that gives customers a look inside the company's culture and operations. At the same time, it lets Southwest talk directly with and get feedback from customers.
- *The social networking media.* Finally, of course, Southwest's customers interact directly with the company and with each other at the airline's many Web and mobile-based social media sites, from Facebook, Twitter, and YouTube to Pinterest and Flickr. "Southwest is an incredibly social company," says a social media analyst. "Its Twitter feed, which abounds with 'thank you' tweets and @mentions, has [nearly 1.4 million] followers. Nearly [3 million] people 'like' the airline's comment-packed Facebook page, and its Nuts About Southwest blog is an industry standard." Another analyst agrees: "It's no surprise to find Southwest at the forefront of social media marketing. Southwest…has always been a leader in passenger and public engagement. Social media fits the Southwest culture perfectly, where older airlines seem to be playing catch-up in this powerful modern marketing arena."

Digital direct marketing: Southwest's broad-based direct marketing strategy employs a wide range of cutting-edge digital tools to connect directly with customers.

Southwest Airlines; Facebook is a trademark of Facebook, Inc.

Southwest's creative, energetic, and super-friendly employees have long been an important competitive advantage. You might worry that with all of these new digital direct marketing tools, Southwest might lose some of its human touch. Not at all. First, the digital touchpoints are only one option—customers are still only a phone call away from a human voice, and they still interact face-to-face with Southwest employees during flights. More important, the new digital approaches actually enhance customer contact with Southwest's people rather than substitute for it. In many of its direct marketing efforts, Southwest lets its employees do the talking. For example, at its Nuts About Southwest blog, flight attendants, pilots, mechanics, and other employees armed with Flip cams tell

insider stories. The company also encourages employees to create local Facebook pages to connect with their communities and lets them be creative in their approaches. As a result, Southwest's direct marketing communications are loaded with employee personality. "You should sound like you're talking to a person," says a Southwest direct marketer. "People embrace our quirkiness."

Thus, Southwest's high-tech direct marketing strategy hasn't changed the company's people orientation. In fact, digital direct marketing brings Southwest's people and customers closer together than ever.

Sources: Lauren Johnson, "Southwest Airlines Builds Email Database via Mobile Initiative," *Mobile Marketer*, June 26, 2012, www.mobilemarketer.com/cms/news/email/13177.html; "Southwest Airlines Taps SMS to Streamline Customer Service," *Mobile Marketer*, May 6, 2010, www.mobilemarketer.com/cms/news/database-crm/6174.html; Samantha Hosenkamp, "How Southwest Manages Its Popular Social Media Sites," *Ragan's PR Daily*, February 10, 2012, www.prdaily.com/Main/Articles/How_Southwest_manages_its_popular_social_media_sit_10788.aspx; "Southwest Airlines Rules the Social Atmosphere, Dominating Facebook and Twitter," *PRWeb*, May 23, 2012, www.prweb.com/releases/2012/5/prweb9536405.htm; and information from "Nuts About Southwest," www.blogsouthwest.com; "What Is DING!?" www.southwest.com/ding; and www.southwest.com/iphone/, accessed November 2012.

In consumer marketing, the customer database might contain a customer's geographic data (address, region), demographic data (age, income, family members, birthdays), psychographic data (activities, interests, and opinions), and buying behavior (buying preferences and the recency, frequency, and monetary value [RFM] of past purchases). In B-to-B marketing, the customer profile might contain the products and services the customer has bought, past volumes and prices, key contacts, competing suppliers, the status of current contracts, estimated future spending, and competitive strengths and weaknesses in selling and servicing the account.

Some of these databases are huge. For example, Walmart captures data from more than 1 million customer transactions every hour, resulting in a database containing more than 2.5 petabytes of data—that's equivalent to some 1,200 billion pages of standard printed text. As a more digestible example, retailer Williams-Sonoma maintains a customer database on more than 60 million U.S. households, including transaction data and third-party data such as income, number of children, home value, and many other factors. It uses the database to create different versions of catalogs and e-mails tailored to the needs of individual customers.[5]

Companies use their databases in many ways. They use databases to locate good potential customers and generate sales leads. They also mine their databases to learn about customers in detail and then fine-tune their market offerings and communications to the special preferences and behaviors of target segments or individuals. In all, a company's database can be an important tool for building stronger long-term customer relationships.

For example,  retailer Best Buy mines its huge customer database to glean actionable insights, which it uses to personalize promotional messages and offers:[6]

Best Buy's 15-plus terabyte customer database contains seven years of data on more than 75 million customer households. The retail chain captures every scrap of store and online interaction data—from purchase transactions to phone calls and mouse clicks to delivery and rebate check addresses—and merges it

● **Customer databases: Best Buy mines its huge database to glean actionable insights on customer interests, lifestyles, passions, and likely next purchases. It uses this information to develop personalized, customer-triggered promotional messages and offers.**

© incamerastock/Alamy

with third-party and publicly available data to create multidimensional customer profiles. Then, sophisticated match-and-merge algorithms score individual customers in terms of their interests, lifestyles, and passions, and use this information to identify their likely next purchases. Based on these profiles, Best Buy then develops personalized, customer-triggered promotional messages and offers. So if your previous interactions suggest that you are a young tech enthusiast assembling a home entertainment system, and you recently used Best Buy's smartphone app to look up product details and customer ratings on a specific component, you might soon receive a spot-on mobile coupon offering discounts on that and related products.

Objective 2 ⤑ ➤
Identify and discuss the major forms of direct marketing.

Forms of Direct Marketing

The major forms of direct marketing—as shown in ● **Figure 17.1**—are face-to-face or personal selling, direct-mail marketing, catalog marketing, telemarketing, direct-response television (DRTV) marketing, kiosk marketing, and online marketing. We examined personal selling in depth in Chapter 16. Here, we look into the other forms of direct marketing.

Direct-Mail Marketing

Direct-mail marketing
Marketing that occurs by sending an offer, announcement, reminder, or other item directly to a person at a particular address.

Direct-mail marketing involves sending an offer, announcement, reminder, or other item to a person at a particular address. Using highly selective mailing lists, direct marketers send out millions of mail pieces each year—letters, catalogs, ads, brochures, samples, videos, and other "salespeople with wings." Direct mail is by far the largest direct marketing medium. The DMA reports that U.S. marketers spent more than $50 billion on direct mail last year (including both catalog and noncatalog mail), which accounted for 30 percent of all direct marketing spending and generated 31 percent of all direct marketing sales. According to the DMA, every dollar spent on direct mail generates $12.57 in sales.[7]

Direct mail is well suited to direct, one-to-one communication. It permits high target-market selectivity, can be personalized, is flexible, and allows the easy measurement of results. Although direct mail costs more per thousand people reached than mass media such as television or magazines, the people it reaches are much better prospects. Direct mail has proved successful in promoting all kinds of products, from books, insurance, travel, gift items, gourmet foods, clothing, and other consumer goods to industrial products of all kinds. Charities also use direct mail heavily to raise billions of dollars each year.

● **FIGURE | 17.1**
Forms of Direct Marketing

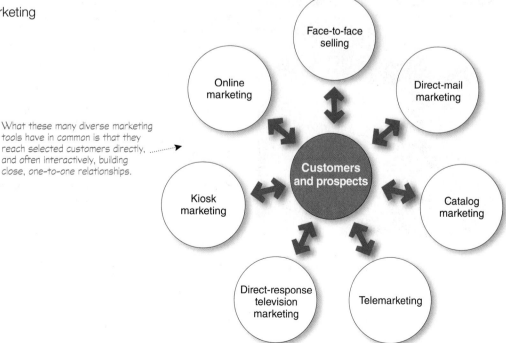

What these many diverse marketing tools have in common is that they reach selected customers directly, ⋯⋯➤ and often interactively, building close, one-to-one relationships.

Some analysts predict a decline in the use of traditional forms of direct mail in coming years, as marketers switch to newer digital forms, such as e-mail and mobile marketing. E-mail, mobile, and other newer forms of direct marketing deliver messages at incredible speeds and lower costs compared to the U.S. Post Office's "snail mail" pace. We will discuss e-mail and mobile marketing in more detail later in the chapter.

However, even though the new digital forms of direct marketing are gaining popularity, traditional direct mail is still by far the most widely used method. Mail marketing offers some distinct advantages over digital forms. It provides something tangible for people to hold and keep and it can be used to send samples. "Mail makes it real," says one analyst. It "creates an emotional connection with customers that digital cannot. They hold it, view it, and engage with it in a manner entirely different from their online experiences." In contrast, e-mail is easily screened or trashed. "[With] spam filters and spam folders to keep our messaging away from consumers' inboxes," says a direct marketer, "sometimes you have to lick a few stamps."[8]

Traditional direct mail can be an effective component of a broader integrated marketing campaign. For example, most large insurance companies rely heavily on TV advertising to establish broad customer awareness and positioning. However, the insurance companies also use lots of good old direct mail to break through the glut of insurance advertising on TV. Whereas TV advertising talks to broad audiences, direct mail communicates in a more direct and personal way. "Mail is a channel that allows all of us to find the consumer with a very targeted, very specific message that you can't do in broadcast," says John Ingersoll, vice president of marketing communications for Farmers Insurance. And "most people are still amenable to getting marketing communications in their mailbox, which is why I think direct mail will grow."[9]

Direct mail may be resented as *junk mail* or *spam* if sent to people who have no interest in it. For this reason, smart marketers are targeting their direct mail carefully so as not to waste their money and recipients' time. They are designing permission-based programs that send direct mail only to those who want to receive it.

Catalog Marketing

Catalog marketing
Direct marketing through print, video, or digital catalogs that are mailed to select customers, made available in stores, or presented online.

Advances in technology, along with the move toward personalized, one-to-one marketing, have resulted in exciting changes in **catalog marketing**. *Catalog Age* magazine used to define a *catalog* as "a printed, bound piece of at least eight pages, selling multiple products, and offering a direct ordering mechanism." Today, this definition is sadly out of date.

● More and more catalogs are going digital: Days before the latest Lands' End catalog arrives in the mail, customers can access it digitally at landsend.com, at Facebook, or via the Lands' End mobile app. With Lands' End Mobile, "You're carrying every item we carry."

Photo courtesy of Gary Armstrong

With the stampede to the Internet, more and more catalogs are going digital. A variety of online-only catalogers have emerged, and most print catalogers have added Web-based catalogs and smartphone catalog shopping apps to their marketing mixes. For example, apps such as Catalog Spree put a mall full of classic catalogs from retailers such as Neiman Marcus, Merrell, Hammacher Schlemmer, Coldwater Creek, or Sephora only a swipe of the finger away on a smartphone or tablet. ● And days before the latest Lands' End catalog arrives in the mail, customers can access it digitally at landsend.com, at social media outlets such as Facebook, or via the Lands' End mobile app. With Lands' End Mobile, says the company, "You're carrying every item we carry."[10]

Digital catalogs eliminate printing and mailing costs. And whereas space is limited in a print catalog, online catalogs can offer an almost unlimited amount of merchandise. They also offer a broader assortment of presentation formats, including search and video. Finally, online catalogs allow real-time merchandising; products and features can be added or removed as needed, and prices can be adjusted instantly to match demand.

However, despite the advantages of digital catalogs, as your overstuffed mailbox may suggest, printed catalogs are still thriving. U.S. direct marketers mailed out some 12.5 billion catalogs last year—more than 100 per American household. Why aren't companies ditching their old-fashioned paper catalogs in this new digital era? For one thing, paper catalogs create emotional connections with customers that digital sales spaces simply can't. "Glossy catalog pages still entice buyers in a way that computer images don't," says an analyst.[11]

In addition, printed catalogs are one of the best ways to drive online sales, making them more important than ever in the digital era. According to a recent study, 70 percent of online purchases are driven by catalogs. Another study found that consumers who received catalogs from the retailer spent 28 percent more on that retailer's Web site than those who didn't get a catalog. Thus, even dedicated online-only retailers, such as Zappos.com, have started producing catalogs with the hopes of driving online sales.[12]

Telemarketing

Telemarketing

Using the telephone to sell directly to customers.

Telemarketing involves using the telephone to sell directly to consumers and business customers. Last year, telemarketing accounted for almost 14.9 percent of all direct-marketing-driven sales. We're all familiar with telephone marketing directed toward consumers, but B-to-B marketers also use telemarketing extensively, accounting for nearly 56 percent of all telephone marketing sales.[13] Marketers use *outbound* telephone marketing to sell directly to consumers and businesses. ● They also use *inbound* toll-free numbers to receive orders from television and print ads, direct mail, or catalogs.

Properly designed and targeted telemarketing provides many benefits, including purchasing convenience and increased product and service information. However, the explosion in unsolicited outbound telephone marketing over the years annoyed many consumers, who objected to the almost daily "junk phone calls." In 2003, U.S. lawmakers responded with the National Do Not Call Registry, which is managed by the Federal Trade Commission (FTC). The legislation bans most telemarketing calls to registered phone numbers (although people can still receive calls from non-profit groups, politicians, and companies with which they have recently done business). Consumers responded enthusiastically. To date, more than 209 million home and mobile phone numbers have been registered at www.donotcall.gov or by calling 888-382-1222. Businesses that break do-not-call laws can be fined up to $16,000 per violation. As a result, reports an FTC spokesperson, the program "has been exceptionally successful."[14]

Do-not-call legislation has hurt parts of the consumer telemarketing industry. However, two major forms of telemarketing—inbound consumer telemarketing and outbound B-to-B telemarketing—remain strong and growing. Telemarketing also remains a major fund-raising tool for nonprofit and political groups. Interestingly, do-not-call regulations appear to be helping some direct marketers more than it's hurting them. Rather than making unwanted calls, many of these marketers are developing "opt-in" calling systems, in which they provide useful information and offers to customers who have invited the company to contact them by phone or e-mail. The opt-in model provides better returns for marketers than the formerly invasive one.

Careful...you might sprain a taste bud.

Don't wait another day! Call now to place an order or request a catalog. Also, go on line at **www.carolinacookie.com** to place an order, request a catalog or view our entire selection of products.

1-800-447-5797

● **Marketers use inbound toll-free 800 numbers to receive orders from television and print ads, direct mail, or catalogs. Here, the Carolina Cookie Company urges, "Don't wait another day. Call now to place an order or request a catalog."**

Carolina Cookie Company

Direct-Response Television Marketing

Direct-response television (DRTV) marketing

Direct marketing via television, including direct-response television advertising (or infomercials) and interactive television (iTV) advertising.

Direct-response television (DRTV) marketing takes one of two major forms: direct-response television advertising and interactive TV (iTV) advertising. Using *direct-response television advertising*, direct marketers air television spots, often 60 or 120 seconds in length, which persuasively describe a product and give customers a toll-free number or a Web site for ordering. It also includes full 30-minute or longer advertising programs, called *infomercials*, for a single product.

Successful direct-response advertising campaigns can ring up big sales. For example, little-known infomercial maker Guthy-Renker has helped propel its Proactiv Solution acne treatment and other "transformational" products into power brands that pull in $1.8 billion in sales annually to 5 million active customers (compare that to only about $150 million in annual drugstore sales of acne products in the United States).[15]

DRTV ads are often associated with somewhat loud or questionable pitches for cleaners, stain removers, kitchen gadgets, and nifty ways to stay in shape without working very hard at it. For example, over the past few years yell-and-sell TV pitchmen like Anthony Sullivan (Swivel Sweeper, Awesome Auger) and Vince Offer (ShamWow, SlapChop) have racked up billions of dollars in sales of "As Seen on TV" products. Brands like OxiClean, ShamWow, and the Snuggie (a blanket with sleeves) have become DRTV cult classics. And infomercial viral sensation PajamaJeans ("Pajamas you live in, Jeans you sleep in") created buzz on everything from YouTube to *The Tonight Show,* selling more than 2 million pairs at $39.95 each, plus $7.95 shipping and handling.[16]

In recent years, however, a number of large companies—from P&G, Disney, Revlon, Apple, and Kodak to Toyota, Coca-Cola, Anheuser-Busch, and even the U.S. Navy—have begun using infomercials to sell their wares, refer customers to retailers, recruit members, or attract buyers to their online sites.

A more recent form of direct-response television marketing is *interactive TV (iTV),* which lets viewers interact with television programming and advertising. Thanks to technologies such as interactive cable systems, Internet-ready smart TVs, and smartphones and tablets, consumers can now use their TV remotes, phones, or other devices to obtain more information or make purchases directly from TV ads. Also, increasingly, as the lines continue to blur between TV screens and other video screens, interactive ads and infomercials are appearing not just on TV, but also on mobile, online, and social media platforms, adding even more TV-like interactive direct marketing venues.

Kiosk Marketing

As consumers become more and more comfortable with digital and touch-screen technologies, many companies are placing information and ordering machines—called *kiosks* (good old-fashioned vending machines but so much more)—in stores, airports, hotels, college campuses, and other locations. Kiosks are everywhere these days, from self-service hotel and airline check-in devices, to unmanned product and information kiosks in malls, to in-store ordering devices that let you order merchandise not carried in the store. "Vending machines, which not long ago had mechanical levers and coin trays, now possess brains," says one analyst. Many modern "smart kiosks" are now wireless-enabled. And some machines can even use facial recognition software that lets them guess gender and age and make product recommendations based on that data.[17]

In-store Kodak, Fuji, and HP kiosks let customers transfer pictures from memory cards, mobile phones, and other digital storage devices; edit them; and make high-quality color prints. Seattle's Best kiosks in grocery, drug, and mass merchandise stores grind and brew fresh coffee beans and serve coffee, mochas, and lattes to on-the-go customers around the clock. Redbox operates more than 30,000 DVD rental kiosks in McDonald's, Walmart, Walgreens, CVS, Family Dollar, and other retail outlets—customers make their selections on a touch screen, then swipe a credit or debit card to rent DVDs at $1 a day.

ZoomSystems creates small, free-standing kiosks called ZoomShops for retailers ranging from Apple, Sephora, and The Body Shop to Macy's and Best Buy. ● For example, 100 Best Buy Express ZoomShop kiosks across the country—conveniently located in airports, busy malls, military bases, and resorts—automatically dispense an assortment of portable media players, digital cameras, gaming consoles, headphones, phone chargers, travel gadgets, and other popular products. According to ZoomSystems, today's automated retailing "offers [consumers] the convenience of online shopping with the immediate gratification of traditional retail."[18]

● Kiosk marketing: ZoomShop kiosks across the country automatically dispense an assortment of popular consumer electronics products. This ZoomShop is located in a Macy's store and features Apple products among others.

ZoomSystems

Online Marketing

As noted earlier, **online marketing** is the fastest-growing form of direct marketing. Widespread use of the Internet is having a dramatic impact on both buyers and the marketers who serve them. In this section, we examine how marketing strategy and practice are changing to take advantage of today's Internet technologies.

Marketing and the Internet

Much of the world's business today is carried out over digital networks that connect people and companies. The **Internet**, a vast public web of computer networks, connects users of all types all around the world to each other and an amazingly large information repository. These days, people connect with the Internet at almost any time and from almost anywhere using their computers, smartphones, tablets, or even TVs and gaming devices. The Internet has fundamentally changed customers' notions of convenience, speed, price, product information, and service. As a result, it has given marketers a whole new way to create value for customers and build relationships with them.

Internet usage and impact continues to grow steadily. More than 80 percent of all U.S. households now use the Internet, and the average U.S. Internet user spends some 32 hours a month online. Moreover, more than 63 million people in the United States access the Internet via their smartphones. Worldwide, more than 2 billion people now have Internet access. And 1 billion people around the globe access the mobile Internet, a number that's expected to double over the next five years as mobile becomes an ever-more popular way to get online.[19]

To reach this burgeoning market, all kinds of companies now market online. **Click-only companies** operate on the Internet only. They include a wide array of firms, from *e-tailers* such as Amazon.com and Expedia.com that sell products and services directly to final buyers via the Internet to *search engines and portals* (such as Yahoo!, Google, and MSN), *transaction sites* (eBay, Craigslist), *content sites* (the *New York Times* on the Web, ESPN.com, and *Encyclopædia Britannica*), and *online social networks* (Facebook, YouTube, Pinterest, Twitter, and Flickr).

The success of the dot-coms has caused existing *brick-and-mortar* manufacturers and retailers to reexamine how they serve their markets. Now, almost all of these traditional companies have created their own online sales and communications channels, becoming **click-and-mortar companies**. It's hard to find a company today that doesn't have a substantial online presence.

In fact, many click-and-mortar companies are now having more online success than their click-only competitors. A recent ranking of the world's 10 largest online retail sites contained only one click-only retailer (Amazon.com, which was ranked number one). All the others were multichannel retailers.[20] ⬤ For example, number two on the list was Staples, the $25 billion office supply retailer. Staples operates more than 2,295 superstores worldwide. But you might be surprised to learn that more than 42 percent of Staples' sales come from its online marketing operations.[21]

> Selling on the Internet lets Staples build deeper, more personalized relationships with customers large and small. A large customer, such as GE or P&G, can create lists of approved office products at discount prices and then let company departments or even individuals do their own online purchasing. This reduces ordering costs, cuts through the red tape, and speeds up the ordering process for customers. At the same time, it encourages companies to use Staples as a sole source for office supplies. Even the smallest companies and individual consumers find 24-hour-a-day online ordering via the Web or Staples mobile app easier and more efficient.
>
> In addition, Staples' online operations complement store sales. The Staples.com site and mobile app build store traffic by offering hot deals and by helping customers find a local store and check stock and prices. In return, the local store promotes online buying through in-store kiosks. If customers don't find what they need on the shelves, they can quickly order it via the kiosk. Thus, Staples backs its "that was easy" positioning by offering a full range of contact points and delivery modes—online, mobile, catalogs, phone, and in the store. No click-only or brick-only seller can match that kind of call, click, or visit convenience and support.

Online marketing

Efforts to market products and services and build customer relationships over the Internet.

Internet

A vast public web of computer networks that connects users of all types around the world to each other and an amazingly large information repository.

Click-only companies

The so-called dot-coms, which operate online only and have no brick-and-mortar market presence.

Click-and-mortar companies

Traditional brick-and-mortar companies that have added online marketing to their operations.

⬤ **Click-and-mortar marketing: Staples backs its "that was easy" positioning by offering a full range of contact points and delivery modes.**

Courtesy of Staples the Office Superstore, LLC & Staples, Inc.

FIGURE | 17.2
Online Marketing Domains

Online marketing can be classified by who initiates it and to whom it is targeted. As consumers, we're most familiar with B-to-C and C-to-C, but B-to-B is also flourishing.

	Targeted to consumers	Targeted to businesses
Initiated by business	B-to-C (business-to-consumer)	B-to-B (business-to-business)
Initiated by consumer	C-to-C (consumer-to-consumer)	C-to-B (consumer-to-business)

Online Marketing Domains

The four major online marketing domains are shown in **Figure 17.2**: business-to-consumer (B-to-C), business-to-business (B-to-B), consumer-to-consumer (C-to-C), and consumer-to-business (C-to-B).

Business-to-Consumer

Business-to-consumer (B-to-C) online marketing
Businesses selling goods and services online to final consumers.

The popular press has paid the most attention to **business-to-consumer (B-to-C) online marketing**—businesses selling goods and services online to final consumers. Today's consumers can buy almost anything online. More than half of all U.S. households now regularly shop online, and online consumer buying continues to grow at a healthy double-digit rate. U.S. online retail sales were an estimated $202 billion last year and are expected to grow 62 percent to $327 billion by 2016 as consumers shift their spending from physical to online stores.[22]

Perhaps even more important, although online shopping currently captures 7 percent of total U.S. retail sales, by one estimate, the Internet influences a staggering 48 percent of total sales—including sales transacted online plus those made in stores but encouraged by online research.[23] And a growing number of consumers armed with smartphones use them while shopping to find better deals and score price-matching offers. Thus, smart marketers are employing integrated multichannel strategies that use the Internet to drive sales to other marketing channels.

Online shopping differs from traditional offline shopping in both consumer approaches to buying and consumer responses to marketing. In the online exchange process, customers initiate and control the contact. Buyers actively select which online sites and shopping apps they will use and what marketing information they will receive about which products. Thus, online marketing requires new marketing approaches.

Business-to-Business

Business-to-business (B-to-B) online marketing
Businesses using online marketing to reach new business customers, serve current customers more effectively, and obtain buying efficiencies and better prices.

Although the popular press has given the most attention to B-to-C online marketing, **business-to-business (B-to-B) online marketing** is also flourishing. B-to-B marketers use Web sites, e-mail, online social networks, mobile apps, and other online resources to reach new business customers, sell to current customers, and serve customers more efficiently and effectively. Beyond simply selling their products and services online, companies can use the Internet to build stronger relationships with important business customers.

Most major B-to-B marketers now offer product information, customer purchasing, and customer-support services online. For example, corporate buyers can visit networking equipment and software maker Cisco Systems' Internet site (www.cisco.com), select detailed descriptions of Cisco's products and service solutions, request sales and service information, attend events and training seminars, view videos on a wide range of topics, have live chats with Cisco staff, and place orders. They can visit Cisco's Facebook page and YouTube channel to hook into the Cisco network, view informational and instructional videos, and much more. Some major companies conduct almost all of their business online. For example, Cisco Systems takes more than 80 percent of its orders over the Internet.

Consumer-to-Consumer

Consumer-to-consumer (C-to-C) online marketing
Online exchanges of goods and information between final consumers.

Considerable **consumer-to-consumer (C-to-C) online marketing** and communication occurs online between interested parties over a wide range of products and subjects. In some cases, the Internet provides an excellent means by which consumers can buy or exchange goods or information directly with one another. For example, eBay, Overstock

.com Auctions, Craigslist.com, and other auction sites offer popular market spaces for displaying and selling almost anything, from art and antiques, coins and stamps, and jewelry to computers and consumer electronics. eBay's C-to-C online trading community of more than 99 million active users worldwide (that's more than the total populations of Great Britain, Egypt, or Turkey) transacted some $60 billion in trades last year—more than $1,900 every second.[24]

In other cases, C-to-C involves interchanges of information through Internet forums that appeal to specific special-interest groups. Such activities may be organized for commercial or noncommercial purposes. Web logs, or **blogs**, are online journals where people post their thoughts, usually on a narrow topic. Blogs can be about anything, from politics or baseball to haiku, car repair, or the latest television series. According to one study, there are now more than 164 million blogs. Many bloggers use social networks such as Twitter and Facebook to promote their blogs, giving them huge reach. Such numbers give blogs—especially those with large and devoted followings—substantial influence.[25]

Many marketers are now tapping into the blogosphere as a medium for reaching carefully targeted consumers. For example, most large companies have set up their own blogs. Sony has a PlayStation Blog, where fans can exchange views and submit and vote on ideas for improving PlayStation products. The Disney Parks Blog is a place to learn about and discuss all things Disney, including a Behind the Scenes area with posts about dance rehearsals, sneak peeks at new construction sites, interviews with employees, and more.

Dell has a dozen or more blogs that facilitate "a direct exchange with Dell customers about the technology that connects us all." The blogs include Direct2Dell (the official Dell corporate blog), Dell TechCenter (IT brought into focus), DellShares (insights for investor relations), Health Care (about health care technology that connects us all), and Education (insights on using technology to enhance teaching, learning, and educational administration). Dell also has a very active and successful YouTube presence that it calls DellVlog, with 1,700 videos and more than 13 million video views. Dell bloggers often embed these YouTube videos into blog posts.[26]

Companies can also advertise on existing blogs or influence content there. They might even encourage "sponsored conversations" by influential bloggers. One recent survey found that 54 percent of marketers had used third-party blogs to help get their messages out.[27] ● For example, McDonald's systematically reaches out to key "mommy bloggers," those who influence the nation's homemakers, who in turn influence their families' eating-out choices:[28]

Blogs

Online journals where people post their thoughts, usually on a narrowly defined topic.

● **Using the blogosphere to reach carefully targeted consumers: McDonald's reaches out to inform key "mommy bloggers," those who in turn influence the nation's homemakers.**

Courtesy of Grace Biskie, www.gabbingwithgrace.com

McDonald's recently hosted 15 bloggers on an all-expenses-paid tour of its headquarters in Oak Brook, Illinois. The bloggers toured the facilities (including the companies test kitchens), met McDonald's USA president Jan Fields, and had their pictures taken with Ronald at a nearby Ronald McDonald House. McDonald's knows how important such influencers can be. "Bloggers, and specifically mom bloggers, talk a lot about McDonald's," says the company's director of social media. "They're customers. They're going to restaurants. And even more important, these women have loyal followings." So McDonald's is turning the bloggers into believers by giving them a behind-the-scenes view.

McDonald's doesn't try to tell the bloggers what to say in their posts about the visit. It simply asks them to write one honest recap of their trip. As you might expect, however, the resulting posts (each acknowledging the blogger's connection with McDonald's) were mostly very positive. Thanks to this and many other such efforts, mommy bloggers around the country are now more informed about and connected with McDonald's. "I know they have smoothies and they have yogurt and they have other things that my kids would want," says one prominent blogger. "I really couldn't tell you what Burger King's doing right now," she adds. "I have no idea."

As a marketing tool, blogs offer some advantages. They can offer a fresh, original, personal, and cheap way to enter into consumer online conversations. However, the blogosphere is cluttered and difficult to control. Blogs remain largely a C-to-C medium. Although companies can sometimes leverage blogs to engage in meaningful customer relationships, consumers remain largely in control.

Whether or not they actively participate in the blogosphere or other C-to-C conversations, companies should monitor and listen to them. C-to-C means that online buyers don't just consume product information—increasingly, they create it. Marketers should use insights from consumer online conversations to improve their marketing programs.

Consumer to Business

Consumer-to-business (C-to-B) online marketing

Online exchanges in which consumers search out sellers, learn about their offers, initiate purchases, and sometimes even drive transaction terms.

The final online marketing domain is **consumer-to-business (C-to-B) online marketing**. Thanks to the Internet, today's consumers are finding it easier to communicate with companies. Most companies now invite prospects and customers to submit suggestions and questions via company Web and mobile sites. Beyond this, rather than waiting for an invitation, consumers can search out sellers online, learn about their offers, initiate purchases, and give feedback. Consumers can even drive online transactions with businesses, rather than the other way around. For example, at Priceline.com, would-be buyers can bid for airline tickets, hotel rooms, rental cars, cruises, and vacation packages, leaving the sellers to decide whether to accept their offers.

Consumers can also use Web sites such as GetSatisfaction.com, Complaints.com, and PlanetFeedback.com to ask questions, offer suggestions, lodge complaints, or deliver compliments to companies. GetSatisfaction.com provides "people-powered customer service" by creating a user-driven customer service community. The site provides forums where customers ask questions, share ideas, give praise, or report problems they're having with the products and services of 65,000 companies—from Microsoft and P&G to Google and Zappos.com—whether the company participates or not. GetSatisfaction.com also provides tools by which companies can adopt GetSatisfaction.com as an official customer service resource.[29]

Objective 4 ┄┄►

Discuss how companies go about conducting online marketing to profitably deliver more value to customers.

Setting Up an Online Marketing Presence

In one way or another, most companies have now moved online. Companies conduct online marketing in any or all of the five ways shown in ⬤ **Figure 17.3**: creating Web sites, placing ads and promotions online, setting up or participating in online social networks, sending e-mail, and using mobile marketing.

Creating Web Sites

Corporate (or brand) Web site

A Web site designed to build customer goodwill, collect customer feedback, and supplement other sales channels rather than sell the company's products directly.

For most companies, the first step in conducting online marketing is to create a Web site. However, beyond simply creating a Web site, marketers must design an attractive site and find ways to get consumers to visit the site, stay around, and come back often.

Web sites vary greatly in purpose and content. The most basic type is a **corporate (or brand) Web site**. This type of site is designed to build customer goodwill, collect customer feedback, and supplement other sales channels rather than to sell the company's products directly. It typically offers a rich variety of information and other features in an effort to

⬤**FIGURE | 17.3**
Setting Up for Online Marketing

It's hard to find a company today that doesn't have a substantial Web presence. The first step is one or more Web sites. But most large companies use all of these approaches. Don't forget, they all need to be integrated—with each other and with the rest of the promotion mix.

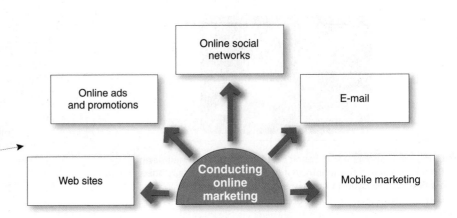

answer customer questions, build closer customer relationships, and generate excitement about the company or brand.

For example, you can't buy anything at Nestlé's colorful Wonka.com site, but you can learn about different Nestlé candy products, enter the latest contest, or hang around a while and doodle with Nerds, "paint your dreams" with the Wonka imaginator, or post Wonka-inspired digital art. Similarly, you can't buy anything at GE's corporate Web site. Instead, the site serves as a global public face for the huge company. It presents a massive amount of product, service, and company information to a diverse audience of customers, investors, journalists, and employees. It's both a B-to-B site and a portal for consumers, whether it's a U.S. consumer researching a microwave, an Indonesian business buyer checking into eco-friendly locomotives, or a German investor looking for shareholder information.

Marketing Web site

A Web site that interacts with consumers to move them closer to a direct purchase or other marketing outcome.

Other companies create a **marketing Web site**. These sites interact with consumers to move them closer to a direct purchase or other marketing outcome.  For example, Samsung operates a marketing Web site at www.samsung.com. Once potential customers click in, the consumer electronics maker wastes no time trying to turn the visit into a sale, and then into a long-term relationship. Whether customers are looking for a TV, camera, computer, mobile device, or other Samsung product, the well-organized site quickly directs them to the specific products and detailed information they need to make a buying decision. The site also offers unedited user product reviews, along with product prices, locations, and links for online and local store retailers in a customer's area. To build and maintain longer-term relationships, the Samsung marketing site offers comprehensive customer support. It also invites customers to join the Samsung Nation, the brand's social loyalty program. Samsung Nation members can earn badges, move up in the ranks, and connect with other Samsung users by visiting Samsung's Web and social media sites, reviewing products, watching videos, and participating in user-generated Q&A sessions.

● Marketing Web sites: Samsung's Web site isn't all that flashy. But once potential customers click in, the site wastes no time turning the visit into a sale, and then into a long-term relationship.

Photo courtesy of Gary Armstrong

Creating a Web site is one thing; getting people to *visit* the site is another. To attract visitors, companies aggressively promote their Web sites in offline print and broadcast advertising and through ads and links on other sites. But today's Web users are quick to abandon any Web site that doesn't measure up. The key is to create enough value and excitement to get consumers who come to the site to stick around and come back again.

At the very least, a Web site should be easy to use, professional looking, and physically attractive. Ultimately, however, Web sites must also be *useful*. When it comes to Web browsing and shopping, most people prefer substance over style and function over flash. For example, Samsung's site isn't all that flashy, but it gets customers quickly and effectively to all the product information they are seeking. Thus, effective Web sites contain deep and useful information, interactive tools that help buyers find and evaluate products of interest, links to other related sites, changing promotional offers, and entertaining features that lend relevant excitement.

Placing Ads and Promotions Online

Online advertising

Advertising that appears while consumers are browsing the Internet, including display ads, search-related ads, online classifieds, and other forms.

As consumers spend more and more time on the Internet, companies are shifting more of their marketing dollars to **online advertising** to build their brands or attract visitors to their Internet, mobile, and social media sites. Online advertising has become a major medium. Total U.S. Internet advertising spending reached $31 billion last year and is expected to surpass print advertising this year, making it the second largest medium behind TV—ahead of even newspapers and magazines.[30]

The major forms of online advertising are search-related ads, display ads, and online classifieds. Online display ads might appear anywhere on an Internet user's screen and are often related to the information being viewed. For instance, while browsing vacation packages on Travelocity.com, you might encounter a display ad offering a free upgrade on a rental car from Enterprise Rent-A-Car. Or while visiting the Yahoo! Finance site, a flashing E*TRADE ad might promise a free Android phone with a two-year wireless plan when you open a new account. Internet display ads have come a long way in recent years in terms of attracting and holding consumer attention. New *rich media* ads now incorporate animation, video, sound, and interactivity.

The largest form of online advertising is *search-related ads* (or *contextual advertising*), which accounted for 46.5 percent of all online advertising spending last year. In search advertising, text-based ads and links appear alongside search engine results on sites such as Google, Yahoo!, and Bing. For example, search Google for "LCD TVs." At the top and side of the resulting search list, you'll see inconspicuous ads for 10 or more advertisers, ranging from Samsung and Dell to Best Buy, Sears, Amazon.com, Walmart.com, and Nextag.com. Nearly all of Google's $37 billion in revenues last year came from ad sales. Search is an always-on kind of medium. And in today's tight economy, the results are easily measured.[31]

A search advertiser buys search terms from the search site and pays only if consumers click through to its site. For instance, type "Coke" or "Coca-Cola" or even just "soft drinks" or "rewards" into your Google, Bing, or Yahoo! search engine and almost without fail "My Coke Rewards" comes up as one of the top options, perhaps along with a display ad and link to Coca-Cola's official Google+ page. This is no coincidence. Coca-Cola supports its popular online loyalty program largely through search buys. The soft drink giant started first with traditional TV and print advertising but quickly learned that search was the most effective way to bring consumers to its www.mycokerewards.com Web site to register. Now, any of dozens of purchased search terms will return MyCokeRewards.com at or near the top of the search list.

Other forms of online promotions include content sponsorships and viral advertising. Using *content sponsorships*, companies gain name exposure on the Internet by sponsoring special content on various Web sites, such as news or financial information or special interest topics. For example, Alamo sponsors the "Vacation and Travel Planner and Guides" on Weather.com. And Marriott sponsors a "Summer to the Rescue!" microsite at Travelocity.com. Sponsorships are best placed in carefully targeted sites where they can offer relevant information or service to the audience.

Finally, online marketers use **viral marketing**, the Internet version of word-of-mouth marketing. Viral marketing involves creating a Web site, video, e-mail, mobile message, advertisement, or other marketing event that is so infectious that customers will seek it out or pass it along to their friends. Because customers find and pass along the message or promotion, viral marketing can be very inexpensive. And when the information comes from a friend, the recipient is much more likely to view or read it.

For example, P&G's Old Spice brand created a now-classic viral sensation with its "Smell like a man, man" campaign featuring Isaiah Mustafa. The campaign consisted of TV ads and made-for-the-Internet videos designed to go viral on YouTube, Facebook, and other social media. The initial campaign garnered tens of millions of viral views. A second campaign, which consisted of nearly 200 videos in which Mustafa responded personally to digital inquiries from users, including Ellen DeGeneres and Alyssa Milano, scored 21 million views in only its first week. It increased the brand's Facebook interaction by 800 percent and OldSpice.com traffic by 300 percent. After the introduction of these videos, Old Spice's YouTube page became the all-time-most-viewed channel on the site.[32]

Sometimes a well-made regular ad can go viral with the help of targeted "seeding." ● For example, Volkswagen's clever "The Force" Super Bowl ad, featuring a pint-sized Darth Vader using The Force to start a VW Passat, turned viral after a team at VW's ad agency seeded it to selected auto, pop culture, and Star Wars sites the week before the sporting event. By the time the ad aired during the Super Bowl, it had received more than 18 million hits online. By the end of the year, "The Force" had received more than 80 million online views. Volkswagen repeated the feat in the

Viral marketing

The Internet version of word-of-mouth marketing: a Web site, video, e-mail message, or other marketing event that is so infectious that customers will seek it out or pass it along to friends.

● Viral marketing: Sometimes a well-made regular ad can go viral. For example, Volkswagen's clever "The Force" Super Bowl ad, featuring a pint-sized Darth Vader, received more than 18 million online hits the week before it aired on TV during the Super Bowl.
Associated Press

following year's Super Bowl with an ad called "Matthew's day off." The ad, which paid homage to the classic 1980s film *Ferris Bueller's Day Off,* drew 18.4 million views by the morning following the big game.[33]

However, marketers usually have little control over where their viral messages end up. They can seed messages online, but that does little good unless the message itself strikes a chord with consumers. For example, why did the seeded VW Darth Vader ad explode virally? Because the sentimental ad appealed to parents—the car's target demographic—who want a responsible suburban family ride. And it appealed to the child inside the parent, who may have once been wowed by *Star Wars* and now wanted a car with a little bit of magic. Says one creative director, "you hope that the creative is at a high enough mark where the seeds grow into mighty oaks. If they don't like it, it ain't gonna move. If they like it, it'll move a little bit; and if they love it, it's gonna move like a fast-burning fire through the Hollywood hills."[34]

Creating or Participating in Online Social Networks

Online social networks

Online communities where people congregate, socialize, and exchange views and information.

As we discussed in Chapters 1 and 5, the popularity of the Internet has resulted in a rash of **online social networks** or online communities. Countless independent and commercial sites have arisen that give consumers online places to congregate, socialize, and exchange views and information. These days, it seems, almost everyone is buddying up on Facebook, checking in with Twitter, tuning into the day's hottest videos at YouTube, pinning interesting things on Pinterest, or checking out photos on Flickr. And, of course, wherever consumers congregate, marketers will surely follow. Most marketers are now riding the huge social networking wave.

Marketers can engage in online communities in two ways: They can participate in existing communities or they can set up their own. Joining existing networks seems the easiest. Thus, most major brands—from Dunkin' Donuts and Harley-Davidson to Nissan and Victoria's Secret—have created YouTube channels. GM and other companies have posted visual content on Flickr and Pinterest. Coca-Cola's Facebook page has more than 43 million fans.

Some of the major social networks are huge. More than 50 percent of Internet users in the United States and Canada use Facebook. That rivals the 55 percent who watch any TV channel and trounces the percentage listening to radio (37 percent) and reading newspapers (22 percent) daily. Facebook now reaches more than 835 million members worldwide, almost 2.5 times the combined populations of the United States and Canada.[35]

Although large online social networks such as Facebook, YouTube, Pinterest, and Twitter have grabbed most of the headlines, a new breed of more focused niche networks has emerged. These networks cater to the needs of smaller communities of like-minded people, making them ideal vehicles for marketers who want to target special interest groups. There's at least one social network for just about every interest or hobby.[36]

Yub.com and Kaboodle.com are for shopaholics, whereas moms advise and commiserate at CafeMom.com. GoFISHn, a community of 4,000 anglers, features maps that pinpoint where fish are biting and a photo gallery where members can show off their catches. ● At Dogster, 700,000 members set up profiles of their four-legged friends, read doggy diaries, or just give a dog a bone. On Ravelry. com, 1.4 million registered knitters, crocheters, designers, spinners, and dyers share information about yarn, patterns, methods, and tools.

Some niche sites cater to the obscure. Passions Network is an "online dating niche social network" with 600,000 members and more than 200 groups for specific interests,

● **Thousands of social networking sites have popped up to cater to specific interests, backgrounds, professions, and age groups. At Dogster, 700,000 members set up profiles of their four-legged friends, read doggy diaries, or just give a dog a bone.**

Dogster.com

including Star Trek fans, truckers, atheists, and people who are shy. FarmersOnly.com provides online dating for down-to-earth "country folks" who enjoy "blue skies, living free and at peace in wide open spaces, raising animals, and appreciating nature"—"because city folks just don't get it." Others niche networks reach more technical communities: More than a million scientists use ResearchGATE to coordinate research in areas such as artificial intelligence and cancer biology. And at myTransponder .com, pilots find work, students locate flight instructors, and trade-specific advertisers—such as aviation software maker ForeFlight—hone in on a hard-to-reach audience of more than 2,000 people who love aviation. The myTransponder community aims to "make aviation more social."

But participating successfully in existing online social networks presents challenges. First, most companies are still experimenting with how to use them effectively, and results are hard to measure. Second, such online networks are largely user controlled. The company's goal is to make the brand a part of consumers' conversations and their lives. However, marketers can't simply muscle their way into consumers' online interactions—they need to earn the right to be there. Rather than intruding, marketers must learn to become a valued part of the online experience.

To avoid the mysteries and challenges of building a presence on existing online social networks, many companies have created their own targeted online communities. For example, on Nike's Nike+ Web site, more than 6 million runners with more than 375 million miles logged in 243 countries join together online to upload, track, and compare their performances. Due to its success, Nike has expanded Nike+ to both basketball and general training, each with its own unique site and corresponding products.[37]

Similarly, *Men's Health* magazine created an online community in conjunction with its Belly Off! program (http://my.menshealth.com/bellyoff/). The magazine's long-running program helps readers develop a solid plan for exercise and diet over a set schedule. The community Web site incorporates user-generated content and offers workout and eating plans, reports on progress, how-to videos, and success stories. In all, the Belly Off! site serves a community of nearly 145,000 members who share similar weight-loss and fitness goals. Since 2001, the program has helped 400,000 people lose nearly 2 million pounds.[38]

Sending E-Mail

E-mail marketing
Sending highly targeted, highly personalized, relationship-building marketing messages via e-mail.

E-mail marketing is an important and growing online marketing tool. E-mail is a much-used communication tool; by one estimate, there are more than 3 billion e-mail accounts worldwide. Not surprisingly, then, a recent study by the DMA found that 78 percent of all direct marketing campaigns employ e-mail. Despite all the e-mail clutter, e-mail marketing still brings one of the highest marketing returns on investment. According to the DMA, marketers get a return of $40 on every $1 they spend on e-mail. U.S. companies spent $1.15 billion on e-mail marketing last year, up from only $243 million 10 years earlier.[39]

When used properly, e-mail can be the ultimate direct marketing medium. Most blue-chip marketers use it regularly and with great success. E-mail lets these marketers send highly targeted, tightly personalized, relationship-building messages. For example, the National Hockey League (NHL) sends hypertargeted e-newsletters to fans based on their team affiliations and locations. It sends 62 versions of the e-newsletter weekly—two for each of the 30 teams, tailored to fans in the United States and Canada, respectively, and two generic league e-newsletters for the two countries. Another NHL e-mail campaign promoting the start of single-game ticket sales had 930 versions.[40]

Spam
Unsolicited, unwanted commercial e-mail messages.

But there's a dark side to the growing use of e-mail marketing. The explosion of **spam**—unsolicited, unwanted commercial e-mail messages that clog up our e-mail boxes—has produced consumer irritation and frustration.

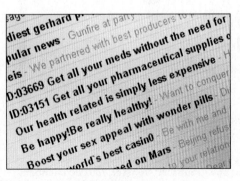

E-mail can be an effective marketing tool. But there's a dark side—spam, unwanted commercial e-mail that clogs up our inboxes and causes frustration.

© Yong Hian Lim/istockphoto; © adimas/Fotolia

According to one research company, spam now accounts for 68 percent of all e-mail sent.[41] E-mail marketers walk a fine line between adding value for consumers and being intrusive.

To address these concerns, most legitimate marketers now practice *permission-based e-mail marketing*, sending e-mail pitches only to customers who "opt in." Many companies use configurable e-mail systems that let customers choose what they want to get. Amazon .com targets opt-in customers with a limited number of helpful "we thought you'd like to know" messages based on their expressed preferences and previous purchases. Few customers object, and many actually welcome such promotional messages. Amazon.com benefits through higher return rates and by avoiding alienating customers with e-mails they don't want.

Given its targeting effectiveness and low costs, e-mail can be an outstanding marketing investment. According to the DMA, e-mail marketing produces the greatest return on investment of all direct marketing media.[42]

Using Mobile Marketing

Mobile marketing

Marketing to on-the-go consumers through mobile phones, smartphones, tablets, and other mobile communication devices.

Mobile marketing features marketing messages and promotions delivered to on-the-go consumers through their mobile devices. Marketers use mobile marketing to reach and interact with customers anywhere, anytime during the buying and relationship-building processes. The widespread adoption of mobile devices and the surge in mobile Web traffic have made mobile marketing a must for most brands.

With the recent proliferation of mobile phones, smartphone devices, and tablets, more than 96 percent of U.S. households own some sort of mobile device. Nearly one-third of U.S. households are currently mobile-only households; this means they have no landline and instead depend on mobile devices to make and receive all calls. Furthermore, nearly 85 million people in the United States own a smartphone device, and about 35 percent of smartphone users use it to access the mobile Internet. They not only browse the mobile Internet but are also avid mobile app users. The mobile apps market has exploded: The Apple App Store offers more than 500,000 iPhone apps plus another 200,000 iPad apps. Android Market offers more than 150,000 apps.[43]

A recent study estimates that mobile advertising spending in the United States will surge from $1.45 billion in 2011 to $2.55 billion by 2014. Almost every major marketer—from Pepsi and Nordstrom to nonprofits such as the ASPCA to the local bank or supermarket—are now integrating mobile platforms into their direct marketing. Forty-two percent of mobile users currently click on a mobile ad at least once a week.[44]

A mobile marketing campaign might involve placing search ads, display ads, or videos on relevant mobile Internet sites and online communities such as Facebook or YouTube. Mobile search ads account for almost half of all mobile ad spending; mobile banner and display ads account for another one-third of spending. Mobile marketing gives brands an opportunity to engage consumers by providing immediate information, incentives, and choices at the moment they are expressing an interest or when they are in a position to make a buying choice. "Mobile ads aim for 'of-the-moment' targeting, anywhere and everywhere," says one expert, whether it's at the time of a mobile search or in a store during the purchase decision.[45]

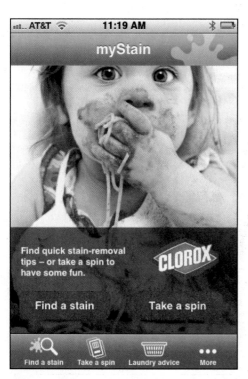

Mobile marketing: Many brands have created mobile apps to engage customers and help them shop. Clorox's myStain app targets young moms with useful on-the-go stain removal solutions.

CLOROX® and myStain® are registered trademarks of The Clorox Company. Used with permission.

Today's rich media mobile ads can create substantial impact and involvement. For example, HBO ran engaging mobile ads for the season premiere of its *True Blood* series. As consumers browsed their Flixter apps looking for good movies or their Variety apps seeking the latest entertainment news, touches on their screens turned into bloody fingerprints. Blood quickly filled their screens, followed by a tap-to-watch trailer invitation. The spine-chilling *True Blood* mobile ad campaign helped draw 5.1 million viewers to the show's season premier and increased viewership 38 percent.[46]

A mobile marketing effort might also involve texting promotions to consumers—anything from retailer announcements of discounts, brand coupons, and gift suggestions to mobile games and contests. Many marketers have also created their own mobile online sites, optimized for specific phones and mobile service providers. Others have created useful or entertaining mobile apps to engage customers with their brands and help them shop (see Real Marketing 17.2). ● For example, Clorox offers a myStain app that targets young moms with useful

Real Marketing 17.2

Mobile Marketing: Customers Come Calling

You're at the local Best Buy checking out portable GPS navigation systems. You've narrowed it down to the latest Garmin nüvi versus a less-expensive competing model, but you're not certain that Best Buy has the best prices. Also, you'd love to know how other consumers rate the two brands. No problem. Just pull out your smartphone and launch your Amazon Mobile app, which lets you browse the brands you're considering, read customer reviews, and compare prices of portable GPS systems sold by Amazon.com and its retail partners. The application even lets you snap a photo or scan a barcode from an item; Amazon.com employees will then search for a similar item available from Amazon. If Amazon.com offers a better deal, you can make the purchase directly from the app.

Welcome to the world of mobile marketing. Today's smartphones and other mobile devices are changing the way we live—including the way we shop. And as they change how we shop, they also change how marketers sell to us. A growing number of consumers are using their mobile phones as a "third screen" for texting, browsing the mobile Internet, watching videos and shows, and checking e-mail. Many experts believe that mobile will soon become the "first screen." According to one expert, "the mobile phone . . . is morphing into a content device, a kind of digital Swiss army knife with the capability of filling its owner's every spare minute with games, music, live and on-demand TV, Internet browsing, and, oh yes, advertising."

For some, that day has already come. For example, for U.S. Facebook members who use both its mobile and Web interfaces, time spent per month on the social network's mobile site and apps (441 minutes) recently surpassed usage of its classic Web site (391 minutes). For Twitter, 55 percent of all traffic is mobile. In fact, U.S. consumers spend an average of 2.7 hours per day socializing on their mobile devices—twice the amount of time they spend eating and one-third the amount of time they spend sleeping.

But beyond socializing, analysts predict that by 2014 total mobile Internet use will overtake desktop Internet use.

Marketers are responding to this massive growth in mobile access and use. Mobile ad spending is doubling every year, and corporate use of mobile Internet sites grew by 210 percent in the last 12 months. Mobile phones, tablets, and other mobile devices have become today's brave new marketing frontier, especially for brands courting younger consumers. Mobile devices are very personal, ever-present, and always on. That makes them an ideal medium for obtaining quick responses to individualized, time-sensitive offers. Mobile marketing reaches consumers with the right message in the right place at the right time.

Marketers large and small are weaving mobile marketing into their direct marketing mixes. And the successful campaigns go beyond just giving people a link to buy. They attract attention by providing helpful services, useful information, and entertainment. For example, Tide's Stain Brain app helps customers find ways to remove stains while out and about. A Sit or Squat app that directs people to nearby public restrooms opens with a splash page for Charmin bathroom tissue. Ace Hardware works with the National Weather Service to provide timely, location-based weather alerts to customers, along with valuable information on how to prepare for the bad weather plus special offers on related merchandise. And REI's The Snow Report app gives ski slope information for locations throughout the United States and Canada, such as snow depth, snow conditions, and the number of open lifts. The app also helps you share resort information with friends via Twitter and Facebook, and it links you to "Shop REI" for times "when you decide you can't live without a new set of K2 skis or a two-man Hoo-Doo tent."

Mobile marketing: Zipcar's iPhone app lets members find and book a Zipcar, honk the horn (so they can find it in a crowd), and even lock and unlock the doors—all from their iPhones.
Zipcar

Beyond helping customers buy, mobile apps provide other helpful services. For example, Target sends out scannable mobile coupons for groceries and other merchandise: Just hold up your mobile phone at the checkout, and the cashier will scan the barcode off the screen. Zipcar's app lets members find and reserve a Zipcar, honk the horn (so they can find it in a crowd), and even lock and unlock the doors—all from their phones. And with MasterCard's PayPass app, cardholders can pay instantly and securely with their phones at any participating retailer.

One of the most effective mobile marketing apps is Kraft's iFood Assistant, which provides easy-to-prepare recipes for food shoppers on the go, how-to videos, a recipe box, and a built-in shopping list. The iFood Assistant app supplies advice on how to prepare thousands of simple but satisfying meals—literally decades worth of recipes. The app will even give you directions to local stores. Of course, most of the meals call for ingredients that just happen to be Kraft brands. The iFood Assistant app cost Kraft less than $100,000 to create but has engaged millions of shoppers, providing great marketing opportunities for Kraft and its brands.

As the Amazon example suggests, consumers are increasingly using their phones as in-store shopping aids, and retailers are responding accordingly. For example, Walgreens has created the mobile equivalent of the local newspaper circular. Using a new technology, Walgreens knows when participating customers check in to one of its 8,000 stores via Foursquare, Yelp, Twitter, Facebook, and a host of other location-based services. The retailer then tweets or texts the customers, sending mobile coupons or directing them to in-store deals with a message such as "Check out the specials on Halls new cough drops in the cold aisle." It's like taking shoppers by the hand and guiding them through the store.

According to one mobile marketing expert, the real advantage to targeting shoppers while they are out and about is the ability to reach consumers when they are closest to buying. "Ask yourself," he says, "are your customers more likely to leave their homes and their pantries . . . to go out and get a sub sandwich . . . or [is it more likely] when they've been out running errands all day, missed lunch, and you sent them a text with an offer for a half-price sub [at a nearby] shop?"

Many consumers are initially skeptical about mobile marketing. But they often change their minds if mobile marketers deliver value in the form of useful brand and shopping information, entertaining content, or discounted prices and coupons for their favorite products and services. Most mobile marketing efforts target only consumers who voluntarily opt in or who download apps. In the increasingly cluttered mobile marketing space, customers just won't do that unless they see real value in it. The challenge for marketers: Develop useful and engaging mobile marketing apps that make customers come calling.

Sources: Josh Constine, "Americans Now Spend More Time on Facebook Mobile Than Its Website," *TechCrunch*, May 11, 2012, http://techcrunch.com/2012/05/11/time-spent-on-facebook-mobile/; "Current Mobile Marketing Trends," *Retail Touch Points*, January 24, 2012, www.retailtouchpoints.com/datapoints-of-the-week/1310-current-mobile-marketing-trends-infographic; Paul Davidson, "Ad Campaigns for Your Tiny Cellphone Screen Get Bigger," *USA Today*, August 9, 2006, www.usatoday.com/money/advertising/2006-08-08-mobile-ads_x.htm; Alice Z. Cuneo, "Scramble for Content Drives Mobile," *Advertising Age* , October 24, 2005, p. S6; Jichél Stewart, "8 Mobile Marketing Trends You Should Track in 2012," *Business 2 Community*, December 18, 2011, www.business2community.com/mobile-apps/8-mobile-marketing-trends-you-should-track-in-2012-0108821; and Kunur Patel, "At Walgreens, a Mobile Check-In Acts Like Circular," *Advertising Age*, February 8, 2012, http://adage.com/print/232584/.

on-the-go stain removal solutions. Schwab offers "Schwab to Go," a mobile app that lets customers get up-to-the-minute investment news, monitor their accounts, and make trades at any time from any location. Starbucks' mobile app lets customers use their phones as a Starbucks card to make fast and easy purchases. And Nike gained unprecedented direct access to runners with a Nike+ GPS mobile app for real-time tracking of runs and bike rides.

As with other forms of direct marketing, however, companies must use mobile marketing responsibly or risk angering already ad-weary consumers. "If you were interrupted every two minutes by advertising, not many people want that," says a mobile marketing expert. "The industry needs to work out smart and clever ways to engage people on mobiles." The key is to provide genuinely useful information and offers that will make consumers want to opt in or call in.

In all, online marketing continues to offer both great promise and many challenges for the future. Its most ardent apostles still envision a time when the Internet and online marketing will replace magazines, newspapers, and even stores as sources for information and buying. Most marketers, however, hold a more realistic view. To be sure, online marketing has become a successful business model for some companies—Internet firms such as Amazon.com, Facebook, and Google, as well as direct marketing companies such as GEICO and Netflix. However, for most companies, online marketing will remain just one important approach to the marketplace that works alongside other approaches in a fully integrated marketing mix.

Objective 5 ⟶ ▶
Overview the public policy and ethical issues presented by direct marketing.

Public Policy Issues in Direct Marketing

Direct marketers and their customers usually enjoy mutually rewarding relationships. Occasionally, however, a darker side emerges. The aggressive and sometimes shady tactics of a few direct marketers can bother or harm consumers, giving the entire industry a black eye. Abuses range from simple excesses that irritate consumers to instances of unfair practices or even outright deception and fraud. The direct marketing industry has also faced growing privacy concerns, and online marketers must deal with Internet security issues.

Irritation, Unfairness, Deception, and Fraud

Direct marketing excesses sometimes annoy or offend consumers. For example, most of us dislike direct-response TV commercials that are too loud, long, and insistent. Our mailboxes fill up with unwanted junk mail, our e-mailboxes bulge with unwanted spam, and our computer screens flash with unwanted display or pop-up ads.

Beyond irritating consumers, some direct marketers have been accused of taking unfair advantage of impulsive or less-sophisticated buyers. Television shopping channels and program-long infomercials targeting television-addicted shoppers seem to be the worst culprits. They feature smooth-talking hosts, elaborately staged demonstrations, claims of drastic price reductions, "while they last" time limitations, and unequaled ease of purchase to inflame buyers who have low sales resistance. Worse yet, so-called heat merchants design mailers and write copy intended to mislead buyers.

Fraudulent schemes, such as investment scams or phony collections for charity, have also multiplied in recent years. *Internet fraud*, including identity theft and financial scams, has become a serious problem. ● Last year alone, the FBI's Internet Crime Complaint Center (IC3) received more than 314,000 complaints related to Internet fraud involving monetary loss.[47]

One common form of Internet fraud is *phishing*, a type of identity theft that uses deceptive e-mails and fraudulent online sites to fool users into divulging their personal data. For example, consumers may receive an e-mail, supposedly from their bank or credit card company, saying that their account's security has been compromised. The sender asks them to log onto a provided Web address and confirm their account number, password, and perhaps even their social security number. If they follow the instructions, users are actually turning this sensitive information over to scam artists. Although many consumers are now aware of such schemes, phishing can be extremely costly to those caught in the net. It also damages the brand identities of legitimate online marketers who have worked to build user confidence in Web and e-mail transactions.

Many consumers also worry about *online security*. They fear that unscrupulous snoopers will eavesdrop on their online transactions, picking up personal information or intercepting credit and debit card numbers. Although online shopping has grown rapidly, one study showed that 59 percent of participants were still concerned about identity theft.[48] Consumers are also concerned about contracting annoying or harmful viruses, spyware, and other malware (malicious software) while shopping on the Internet.

Another Internet marketing concern is that of *access by vulnerable or unauthorized groups*. For example, marketers of adult-oriented materials and sites have found it difficult to restrict access by minors. A survey by *Consumer Reports* found 5 million U.S. children under age 10 on Facebook, which supposedly allows no children under age 13 to have a profile. It found another 2.5 million 11- and 12-year-old Facebook subscribers. And it's not just Facebook. Young users are logging onto social networks such as Formspring, tweeting their location to the Web, and making friends out of strangers on Disney and other games sites. Concerned state and national

● Internet fraud has multiplied in recent years. The FBI's Internet Crime Complaint Center provides consumers with a convenient way to alert authorities to suspected violations.

FBI

lawmakers are currently debating bills that would help better protect children online. Unfortunately, this requires the development of technology solutions, and as Facebook puts it, "That's not so easy."[49]

Consumer Privacy

Invasion of privacy is perhaps the toughest public policy issue now confronting the direct marketing industry. Consumers often benefit from database marketing; they receive more offers that are closely matched to their interests. However, many critics worry that marketers may know *too* much about consumers' lives and that they may use this knowledge to take unfair advantage of consumers. At some point, they claim, the extensive use of databases intrudes on consumer privacy.

These days, it seems that almost every time consumers enter a sweepstakes; apply for a credit card; visit a Web site; or order products by mail, phone, or the Internet, their names are entered into some company's already bulging database. Using sophisticated computer technologies, direct marketers can mine these databases to "microtarget" their selling efforts. Most marketers have become highly skilled at collecting and analyzing detailed consumer information. Even the experts are sometimes surprised by how much marketers can learn. Consider this account by one *Advertising Age* reporter:[50]

> I'm no neophyte when it comes to targeting—not only do I work at *Ad Age*, but I cover direct marketing. Yet even I was taken aback when, as an experiment, we asked the database-marketing company to come up with a demographic and psychographic profile of me. Was it ever spot-on. Using only publicly available information, it concluded my date of birth, home phone number, and political-party affiliation. It gleamed that I was a college graduate, that I was married, and that one of my parents had passed away. It found that I have several bank, credit, and retail cards at "low-end" department stores. It knew not just how long I've lived at my house but how much it costs, how much it was worth, the type of mortgage that's on it, and—within a really close ballpark guess—how much is left to pay on it. It estimated my household income—again nearly perfectly—and determined that I am of British descent.
>
> But that was just the beginning. The company also nailed my psychographic profile. It correctly placed me into various groupings such as: someone who relies more on their own opinions than the recommendations of others when making a purchase; someone who is turned off by loud and aggressive advertising; someone who is family-oriented and has an interest in music, running, sports, computers, and is an avid concert-goer; someone who is never far from an Internet connection, generally used to peruse sports and general news updates; and someone who sees health as a core value. Scary? Certainly.

Some consumers and policy makers worry that the ready availability of information may leave consumers open to abuse. For example, they ask, should online sellers be allowed to plant cookies in the browsers of consumers who visit their sites and use tracking information to target ads and other marketing efforts? Should credit card companies be allowed to make data on their millions of cardholders worldwide available to merchants who accept their cards? Or is it right for states to sell the names and addresses of driver's license holders, along with height, weight, and gender information, allowing apparel retailers to target tall or overweight people with special clothing offers?

A Need for Action

To curb direct marketing excesses, various government agencies are investigating not only do-not-call lists but also do-not-mail lists, do-not-track online lists, and Can Spam legislation. In response to online privacy and security concerns, the federal government has considered numerous legislative actions to regulate how Internet and mobile operators obtain and use consumer information. For example, Congress is drafting legislation that would give consumers more control over how online information is used. In addition, the FTC is taking a more active role in policing online privacy.

All of these concerns call for strong actions by marketers to monitor and prevent privacy abuses before legislators step in to do it for them. For example, to head off increased government regulation, four advertiser groups—the American Association of Advertising Agencies, the Association of National Advertisers, the DMA, and the Interactive Advertising Bureau—recently issued new guidelines for sites. Among other measures, the

● **Consumer privacy: By clicking on the little AdChoices advertising option icon in the upper right of this online ad, consumers can learn why they are seeing the ad and opt out if they wish.**

Reproduced with permission of Yahoo! Inc. © 2012 Yahoo! Inc. YAHOO! and the YAHOO! logo are registered trademarks of Yahoo! Inc.

guidelines call for Web marketers to alert consumers if their activities are being tracked. ● The ad industry has agreed on an *advertising option icon*—a little "i" inside a triangle—that it will add to most behaviorally targeted online ads to tell consumers why they are seeing a particular ad and allowing them to opt out.[51]

Of special concern are the privacy rights of children. In 2000, Congress passed the Children's Online Privacy Protection Act (COPPA), which requires online operators targeting children to post privacy policies on their sites. They must also notify parents about any information they're gathering and obtain parental consent before collecting personal information from children under age 13. With the subsequent advent of online social networks, mobile phones, and other new technologies, privacy groups are now urging the U.S. Senate to extend COPPA to include both the new technologies and teenagers. The main concern is the amount of data mined by third parties from social networks as well as the social networks' own hazy privacy policies.[52]

Many companies have responded to consumer privacy and security concerns with actions of their own. Still others are taking an industry-wide approach. For example, TRUSTe, a nonprofit self-regulatory organization, works with many large corporate sponsors, including Microsoft, Yahoo!, AT&T, Facebook, Disney, and Apple, to audit privacy and security measures and help consumers navigate the Internet safely. According to the company's Web site, "TRUSTe believes that an environment of mutual trust and openness will help make and keep the Internet a free, comfortable, and richly diverse community for everyone." To reassure consumers, the company lends its TRUSTe privacy seal to Web sites, mobile apps, e-mail marketing, and other online channels that meet its privacy and security standards.[53]

The direct marketing industry as a whole is also addressing public policy issues. For example, in an effort to build consumer confidence in shopping direct, the DMA—the largest association for businesses practicing direct, database, and interactive marketing, including nearly half of the Fortune 100 companies—launched a "Privacy Promise to American Consumers." The Privacy Promise requires that all DMA members adhere to a carefully developed set of consumer privacy rules. Members must agree to notify customers when any personal information is rented, sold, or exchanged with others. They must also honor consumer requests to opt out of receiving further solicitations or having their contact information transferred to other marketers. Finally, they must abide by the DMA's Preference Service by removing the names of consumers who do not wish to receive mail, phone, or e-mail offers.[54]

Direct marketers know that, if left untended, such direct marketing abuses will lead to increasingly negative consumer attitudes, lower response rates, and calls for more restrictive state and federal legislation. Most direct marketers want the same things that consumers want: honest and well-designed marketing offers targeted only toward consumers who will appreciate and respond to them. Direct marketing is just too expensive to waste on consumers who don't want it.

Reviewing the Concepts

MyMarketingLab™

Go to **mymktlab.com** to complete the problems marked with this icon .

Reviewing Objectives and Key Terms

 ## Objectives Review

This chapter is the last of four chapters covering the final marketing mix element—promotion. The previous chapters dealt with advertising, public relations, personal selling, and sales promotion. This one investigates the burgeoning field of direct and online marketing.

Objective 1 Define direct marketing and discuss its benefits to customers and companies. (pp 494–499)

Direct marketing consists of direct connections with carefully targeted segments or individual consumers. Beyond brand and relationship building, direct marketers usually seek a direct, immediate, and measurable consumer response. Using detailed databases, direct marketers tailor their offers and communications to the needs of narrowly defined segments or even individual buyers.

For buyers, direct marketing is convenient, easy to use, and private. It gives buyers ready access to a wealth of products and information, at home and around the globe. Direct marketing is also immediate and interactive, allowing buyers to create exactly the configuration of information, products, or services they desire and then order them on the spot. For sellers, direct marketing is a powerful tool for building customer relationships. Using database marketing, today's marketers can target small groups or individual customers, tailor offers to individual needs, and promote these offers through personalized communications. It also offers them a low-cost, efficient alternative for reaching their markets. As a result of these advantages to both buyers and sellers, direct marketing has become the fastest-growing form of marketing.

Objective 2 Identify and discuss the major forms of direct marketing. (pp 499–502)

The main forms of direct marketing are *personal face-to-face selling*, *direct-mail marketing*, *catalog marketing*, *telemarketing*, *DRTV marketing*, *kiosk marketing*, and *online marketing*. We discussed personal selling in the previous chapter.

Direct-mail marketing, the largest form of direct marketing, consists of the company sending an offer, announcement, reminder, or other item to a person at a specific address. Some marketers rely on catalog marketing—selling through catalogs mailed to a select list of customers, made available in stores, or

accessed on the Internet. Telemarketing consists of using the telephone to sell directly to consumers. DRTV marketing has two forms: direct-response advertising (or infomercials) and interactive television (iTV) marketing. Kiosks are information and ordering machines that direct marketers place in stores, airports, hotels, and other locations. Online marketing involves online channels that digitally link sellers with consumers.

Objective 3 Explain how companies have responded to the Internet and other powerful new technologies with online marketing strategies. (pp 503–506)

Online marketing is the fastest-growing form of direct marketing. The *Internet* enables consumers and companies to access and share huge amounts of information through their computers, smartphones, tablets, and other devices. In turn, the Internet has given marketers a whole new way to create value for customers and build customer relationships. It's hard to find a company today that doesn't have a substantial online marketing presence.

Online consumer buying continues to grow at a rapid rate. Most American online users now use the Internet to shop. Perhaps more important, the Internet influences offline shopping as well. Thus, smart marketers are employing integrated multichannel strategies that use the Internet to drive sales to other marketing channels.

Objective 4 Discuss how companies go about conducting online marketing to profitably deliver more value to customers. (pp 506–514)

Companies of all types are now engaged in online marketing. The Internet gave birth to the *click-only companies* that operate online only. In addition, most traditional brick-and-mortar companies have added online marketing operations, transforming themselves into *click-and-mortar companies*. Many click-and-mortar companies are now having more online success than the click-only companies.

Companies can conduct online marketing in any or all of these five ways: creating Web sites, placing ads and promotions online, setting up or participating in online communities and social networks, sending e-mail, or using mobile marketing. The first step typically is to create a Web site. Beyond simply creating a site, however, companies must make their sites engaging, easy to use, and useful to attract visitors, hold them, and bring them back again.

Online marketers can use various forms of online advertising and promotion to build their Internet brands or attract visitors to their sites. Forms of online promotion include online display advertising, search-related advertising, content sponsorships, and viral marketing, the Internet version of word-of-mouth marketing. Online marketers can also participate in online social networks and other online communities, which take advantage of the *C-to-C* properties of the Internet. Finally, e-mail and mobile marketing have become a fast-growing tool for both *B-to-C* and *B-to-B* marketers. Whatever direct marketing tools they use, marketers must work hard to integrate them into a cohesive marketing effort.

| Objective 5 | Overview the public policy and ethical issues presented by direct |

marketing. (pp 514–516)

Direct marketers and their customers usually enjoy mutually rewarding relationships. Sometimes, however, direct marketing presents a darker side. The aggressive and sometimes shady tactics of a few direct marketers can bother or harm consumers, giving the entire industry a black eye. Abuses range from simple excesses that irritate consumers to instances of unfair practices or even outright deception and fraud. The direct marketing industry has also faced growing concerns about invasion-of-privacy and Internet security issues. Such concerns call for strong action by marketers and public policy makers to curb direct marketing abuses. In the end, most direct marketers want the same things that consumers want: honest and well-designed marketing offers targeted only toward consumers who will appreciate and respond to them.

 # Key Terms

Objective 1

Direct marketing (p 494)
Customer database (p 496)

Objective 2

Direct-mail marketing (p 499)
Catalog marketing (p 500)
Telemarketing (p 501)
Direct-response television (DRTV) marketing (p 501)

Objective 3

Online marketing (p 503)
Internet (p 503)
Click-only companies (p 503)
Click-and-mortar companies (p 503)
Business-to-consumer (B-to-C) online marketing (p 504)
Business-to business (B-to-B) online marketing (p 504)
Consumer-to-consumer (C-to-C) online marketing (p 504)
Blogs (p 505)
Consumer-to-business (C-to-B) online marketing (p 506)

Objective 4

Corporate (or brand) Web site (p 506)
Marketing Web site (p 507)
Online advertising (p 507)
Viral marketing (p 508)
Online social networks (p 509)
E-mail marketing (p 510)
Spam (p 510)
Mobile marketing (p 511)

Discussion and Critical Thinking

 ## Discussion Questions

⭐ **1.** Define *direct marketing* and discuss its benefits to customers and companies. (AACSB: Communication)

2. Describe the type of information contained in a company's customer database and how that information is used. (AACSB: Communication)

3. Name and describe the major forms of direct-response television marketing. (AACSB: Communication)

4. Explain the ways in which companies can set up an online marketing presence. (AACSB: Communication)

⭐ **5.** Compare and contrast the different forms of online advertising. What factors should a company consider in deciding among these different forms? (AACSB: Communication)

⭐ **6.** What is *phishing,* and how does it harm consumers and marketers? (AACSB: Communication; Reflective Thinking)

 ## Critical Thinking Exercises

1. In a small group, design and deliver a direct-response television ad (DRTV) for a national brand not normally associated with this type of promotion, such as an athletic shoe, automobile, or food product. (AACSB: Communication; Reflective Thinking)

2. Review the guidelines of the Federal Trade Commission (FTC) on sponsored conversations (www.ftc.gov/os/2009/10/091005revisedendorsementguides.pdf) and visit the Word of Mouth Marketing Association's Web site (womma .org) and IZEA's Web site (IZEA.com). Write a report on how marketers can effectively use sponsored conversations within the FTC's guidelines. (AACSB: Communication; Reflective Thinking)

3. Find news articles about two data security breaches. How did the breaches occur, and who was potentially affected by them? (AACSB: Communication; Reflective Thinking)

Applications and Cases

 ## Marketing Technology Marketing to Those on the Go

Your smartphone might be the only thing you'll need for locking your door, starting a car, paying for purchases, or even just paying your friend the $20 you owe him. Mobile technologies allow users to do almost anything remotely and allow marketers to target services and promotions directly to consumers based on where they are. You may have noticed that some Starbucks customers just wave their phones in front of a scanner—no

wallet, cash, or card required. Those customers may have gotten discount offers that lured them to Starbucks because their phone tipped the marketer off that they were nearby.

 1. What are the barriers to adoption of mobile applications? (AACSB: Communication; Reflective Thinking)

 ## Marketing Ethics Online Tax Battle

Online retailing is experiencing phenomenal growth, but struggling states are not reaping the spoils—in taxes, that is. One study estimates that lost state and local revenue equals upwards of $10 billion a year on nontaxed e-commerce. Amazon is the biggest beneficiary. States are battling back by introducing, and sometimes successfully passing, laws informally dubbed "Amazon laws" that require online retailers to collect state sales taxes. The efforts have the support of rivals such as Walmart and Target. Amazon strategically sought to minimize sales tax collection across the country by using legal loopholes and even limiting employees' activities when traveling to certain states deemed "bad states" because of efforts to enact tax laws to grab a piece of Amazon's profits. Credit Suisse estimated Amazon would lose $653 million in sales if it had to collect sales taxes in all states, but surprisingly, Amazon has done an about-face on this issue and is currently supporting states' initiatives to collect sales taxes. This is because Amazon wants to institute same-day delivery, and to

do that, it must have more distribution centers. Distribution centers constitute a "physical presence" in a state, and therefore the online reseller must collect state sales taxes. Other online resellers such as Overstock.com are opposed to the initiatives, claiming that collection of taxes is based on where customers live and that brick-and-mortar resellers don't ask where customers live to collect the proper sales tax. Given that there are already nearly 10,000 state, local, and municipal tax jurisdictions, the task of collecting and distributing the correct tax is untenable for most online resellers.

1. Research online tax rules. Look specifically at the 1992 Supreme Court ruling in *Quill Corp. v. North Dakota,* on which the current rules are based. Is the rule in the 1992 Supreme Court case still relevant? Are Amazon and other online retailers being ethical by using this rule to their advantage? (AACSB: Communication; Reflective Thinking; Ethical Reasoning)

 ## Marketing by the Numbers The Power of "Like"

Marketers know that Facebook is a force to be reckoned with, but until now they have not been able to measure that force and compare it to traditional media. Whereas traditional media have established ratings and other metrics to measure what marketers are getting for their money, an entirely new set of metrics—such as "click-through rates" and "impressions"—has evolved for online media. Unfortunately, the two metrics are not comparable. ComScore and Nielsen are two companies attempting to rectify that situation by developing a rating system based on "gross rating points" to show the power of Facebook as a marketing tool.

1. Research marketing expenditure trends in social media marketing as well as other forms of online advertising. Compare these trends with traditional advertising media expenditures. Develop a presentation illustrating those trends. (AACSB: Communication; Analytical Reasoning; Reflective Thinking)

2. Visit www.comScore.com and www.Nielsen.com to learn more about the metrics these companies have developed for measuring the marketing exposure of brands on Facebook. How do these metrics differ from those that have been used with regard to measuring online advertising impact? (AACSB: Communication; Use of IT; Reflective Thinking)

Video Case Home Shopping Network

Long ago, television shopping was associated with low-quality commercials broadcast in the wee hours of the morning selling obscure merchandise. But Home Shopping Network (HSN) has played an instrumental role in making television shopping a legitimate outlet. Around-the-clock top-quality programming featuring name-brand merchandise is now the norm.

But just like any retailer, HSN has had it share of challenges. This video illustrates how HSN has focused on the principles of direct marketing in order to overcome challenges and form strong customer relationships. As market conditions continue to shift, HSN explores new ways to form and strengthen direct relationships with customers.

After viewing the video featuring HSN, answer the following questions:

1. Explain the different ways that HSN engages in direct marketing.

2. What advantages does HSN have, specifically over brick-and-mortar retailers?

3. Make recommendations for how HSN could make better use of its role as a direct marketer.

Company Case eBay: Fixing an Online Marketing Pioneer

Pop quiz: Name the high-tech company that got its start in someone's living room, grew from zero revenue to a multibillion-dollar corporation in less than a decade, and pioneered the model for an entire industry to follow. If you're thinking that the list of companies that fit this description is a mile long, you're right. But in this case, we're talking about eBay.

eBay is one of the biggest Internet success stories in the history of, well, the Internet. But sooner or later, every high-growth company hits a speed bump and experiences growing pains. After amazing growth in its first 15 years, eBay hit that speed bump. When John Donahoe took over as CEO in 2008, he faced the difficult challenge of putting eBay back on the superhighway to prosperity. And with a comprehensive strategic plan now years under way, eBay vital signs are once again showing some life.

eBay started in 1995 as an auction house. Unlike most dot-coms, eBay was based on a model that produced profits, not just revenue. Whenever a user posted an item for auction, eBay collected a fee. The more products that went up for auction, the more money eBay made. eBay has tinkered with its fee structure over the years. But the basic idea has remained the same. The online auction formula took off like wildfire and eBay dominated the industry. eBay's revenue, stock price, profits, and number of employees soared. By the year 2000, eBay was the number one e-commerce site in the world by sales revenue.

The Changing Face of a Growing Company

With explosive growth, change is inevitable. As the new century dawned, eBay embraced that change in two ways. First, eBay expanded the scope of its business. Its list of categories and subcategories grew into the hundreds. The e-commerce giant also added international sites for different countries. And it began to launch sub-sites (such as eBay Motors) and to acquire other dot.coms relevant to its business. Such acquisitions ultimately included Half.com, PayPal, StubHub, Shopping.com, and Skype.

But eBay also recognized that the novelty of buying and selling based on its auction format would not last. Trends indicated that people didn't want to wait for an auction to end in order to make a purchase. So eBay added fixed-price selling with its "Buy It Now" option. Two years later, it took that concept much further with the introduction of eBay Stores. With eBay stores, a seller could create an online "storefront" within eBay. The feature allowed sellers to post items more quickly, making it easier for high-volume sellers to do business. It also gave fixed-price options with no bidding whatsoever and virtually eliminated the sales period for an item.

Both of these dynamics continued to fuel eBay's steady, strong growth for years. In 2006, eBay achieved revenue of $5.97 billion with a profit of $1.12 billion—tremendous numbers for a dot.com that had only been doing business for a single decade. But in 2007, eBay began to show signs of slowing down. When Donahoe took over as CEO, he acknowledged that eBay faced issues, including the fact that it had been resting on its laurels and had stopped innovating. Consumer behavior was also shifting. Online shopping using the tried-and-true method of finding the best price on a new piece of merchandise and buying it from a reputable retailer moved Amazon into the top e-commerce position as its growth took off while eBay's stagnated.

Shortly after taking over, Donahoe said at a public event, "We need to redo our playbook, we need to redo it fast, and we need to take bold actions." He unveiled the details of a three-year revival plan for eBay's turnaround. This included stripping out layers of bureaucracy, opening up PayPal to outside developers, investing in new e-commerce technologies, and divesting businesses such as Skype that had little to do with eBay's core marketplace. But Donahoe's strategy also focused on changing the identity of the eBay marketplace by moving further away from auctions. Donahoe specified that the new strategy would focus on building the site's business in the secondary market, the $500-billion-a-year slice of retail that includes out-of-season and overstock items as well as the used and antique items for which eBay had always been known.

Core to Donahoe's strategy, eBay changed its fee structure, search-engine algorithm, and feedback rating system in ways that favored highly rated sellers, fixed-price listings, and sellers offering free shipping. Donahoe claimed that all these tactics helped align eBay's interests with those of its best sellers. But the strategy to focus on gaining new business came at the expense of losing the portion of its customer base that still came to eBay for used goods and auctions.

Traditional eBay sellers cried foul, asserting that the company's new strategy made it harder for them to do business profitably while favoring the high-volume sellers. Donahoe responded that the managers at eBay knew there would be growing pains, but that the transformation was essential. He strongly believed that buyers wanted a fixed price, quick service, and free shipping. Donahoe made the case to investors, vendors, and customers that for eBay to not focus on market demands would ultimately be bad for everyone.

From Bad to Worse

As with many great plans, things sometimes have to get worse before they get better. Instead of immediate evidence of the fruits of the turnaround plan, eBay's financials slid badly. In the final quarter of 2008, typically eBay's strongest period with holiday shopping, eBay experienced its first ever quarterly decline. For its core marketplace, revenue was down 16 percent from the previous year, while net income dropped a whopping 31 percent. It would have been very easy for Donahoe and his team to blame the company's woes on the economic downturn. But even as eBay experienced a drop in traffic, competitors Amazon.com and Walmart enjoyed increases.

Still, Donahoe moved forward with even greater resolve. "The 'buyer beware' experience has run its course," he said. He reiterated eBay's plans to focus on the secondary market. "We're going to focus where we can win," Donahoe said, indicating that the shift away from new merchandise where its biggest competitors dominated would give eBay a strong point of differentiation. "We have begun significant change. The eBay you knew is not the eBay we are, or the eBay we will become." As these changes began to take root, eBay's financials began to stabilize. But with total e-commerce growth in the low double digits and the likes of Amazon growing considerably faster, it was clear the eBay would continue to lag behind for the foreseeable future.

A New Point of Differentiation

As the turnaround strategy moved into its final year, Donahoe began unrolling a new layer. Just as eBay was starting to adapt, market trends were again starting to shift as shoppers began spending more time and money shopping through mobile devices. Determined not to be behind the curve again, Donahoe began expressing his vision of eBay as the innovative pioneer that it was during its first decade. "In the next three to five years, we're about to see more change in how consumers shop and pay than in the last decade," says Donahoe. "So our challenge as a company, our opportunity, is to help shape and be part of that next period."

With that goal in mind, eBay started buying up technology companies that would help it become a leader in the emerging mobile shopping trend. This led to the creation of an eBay shopping app as well as various category apps for eBay Motors and eBay Fashion. The idea is to engage consumers even when they aren't thinking about buying something. For example, the eBay Fashion app emphasizes browsing over buying, featuring a style guide and a shared virtual closet where users can mix, match, and model different outfits with friends. But even though the focus is on browsing, eBay knows that browsers will buy. Users spend an average of 10 minutes browsing on the eBay Fashion app—40 percent longer than they spend on the main eBay app. In the Fashion app's first year, eBay mobile fashion sales tripled.

But if eBay is to return to e-commerce stardom, the strong growth that it seeks will have to break open the boundaries of the core eBay marketplace. Donahoe imagines certain possibilities:

Imagine you meet your girlfriend for brunch, and you are sweating her new taupe Marc Jacobs Kitty Clutch. Then imagine that you snap a picture of her purse with your iPhone, which uses an eBay app to reveal the three boutiques within a 3-mile radius that have the same bag in the same color in stock right this minute, with prices to boot. You decide which store has the best combination of price and location, and order via your phone. After brunch, you swing by and bypass the line because you show the salesperson your digital receipt. Voilà! Your new Marc Jacobs clutch—and all the pleasure of instant gratification.

Not only does Donahoe believe this scenario will become shopping reality, he is confident that eBay will lead the charge. To that end, the once online-only auction house is moving fast to capitalize on the disintegrating boundary between shopping online and shopping offline. As more and more shoppers use their mobile devices for "showrooming"—looking up information, comparing prices, and even purchasing online while in a brick-and-mortar store—eBay expects to be there. Known as "cross-channel retail," purchases blending online and offline shopping accounted for $1 trillion last year—about 33 percent of retail sales—and that number is rising rapidly.

With the acquisition of RedLaser—a scanning tool that recognizes just about any product on a shelf—shoppers can immediately cross-shop through online sources. And although RedLaser can't recognize photo images (yet), it does recognize bar codes, VINs, gift cards, and QR codes. It also suggests nearby stores that have the product in stock. But for Donahoe, there isn't nearly enough store inventory accessible electronically. That's why eBay is working on an initiative to "bring every product on every shelf in every store in the physical world onto the Internet." More acquisitions that can make that data available are bringing eBay closer to Donahoe's vision.

And as eBay's mobile network takes off, every transaction will end with PayPal. From "inventory where you are" to "paying where you are," the shopping experience will be much more seamless. As the market leader in online payments, PayPal is up to the task. PayPal would earn a transaction fee for every item purchased as well as a referral fee for driving store traffic to other retailers. Although many pieces still need to fall into place and Donahoe doesn't expect it to happen overnight, eBay is well on its way. Last year, eBay sold $5 billion worth of goods via smartphones and tablets, more than double its total from the year before. PayPal processed $4 billion worth of mobile payments, up from only $750 million. And although Amazon is still way ahead in terms of total sales and sales growth, eBay now has the jump in mobile commerce. Amazon had only $2 billion in mobile sales in the most recent year, including Kindle e-books.

With the developments in eBay's marketplace, mobile commerce, and online payments, Donahoe's confidence is becoming more credible. "We have gone from turnaround to offensive," the CEO states. "Our purpose is to bring consumers the best experience to find what they want, how they want, and when they want it, whether it's on eBay or otherwise." As e-commerce and mobile shopping continue to evolve at a blistering pace, only time will tell if Donahoe's strategy will pay off.

Questions for Discussion

1. Analyze the marketing environment and the forces shaping eBay's business over the years.

2. How has the change in the nature of eBay sellers affected the creation of value for buyers?

3. Do you agree or disagree with CEO Donahoe that eBay's turnaround strategy is the best way to go?

4. Based on eBay's current developments with PayPal and mobile apps, predict the outcome for the company in five years.

Sources: Danielle Sacks, "How Jack Abraham Is Reinventing EBay," *Fast Company*, July 22, 2011, www.fastcompany.com/magazine/157/jack-abraham-ebay-milo; Kevin Kelleher, "EBay Has Yet to Sell Turnaround to Investors" *Fortune*, January 17, 2012, http://tech.fortune.cnn.com/2012/01/17/ebay-has-yet-to-sell-its-turnaround-to-investors/; Geoffrey Fowler, "Auctions Fade in eBay's Bid for Growth," *Wall Street Journal*, May 26, 2009, p. A1; Peter Burrows, "EBay Outlines Three-Year Revival Plan," *BusinessWeek*, March 12, 2009, www.businessweek.com; and Max Colchester and Ruth Bender, "EBay CEO Continues to Seek Acquisitions," *Wall Street Journal*, May 23, 2011, www.wsj.com.

MyMarketingLab

Go to **mymktlab.com** for Auto-graded writing questions as well as the following Assisted-graded writing questions:

17-1. What mobile applications currently exist and what's on the horizon? How many of these applications do you or someone you know use?

17-2. Debate whether or not online retailers should be required to collect state sales taxes. Suggest an equitable solution to this issue. (AACSB: Communication; Ethical Reasoning)

17-3 Mymktlab Only – comprehensive writing assignment for this chapter.

References

1. Based on information from Cotton Delo, "Facebook Files for IPO," *Advertising Age,* February 1, 2012, http://adage.com/article/digital/facebook-files-ipo-reveals-1-billion-2011-profit/232484/; Tomio Geron, "Zynga Makes Up 12 Percent of Facebook's 2011 Revenue," *Forbes,* February 1, 2012, www.forbes.com/sites/tomiogeron/2012/02/01/zynga-makes-up-12-of-facebooks-2011-revenue/; Leah Fabel, "The Business of Facebook," *Fast Company,* April 1, 2011, www.fastcompany.com/node/1740204/; Venessa Miemis, "The Bank of Facebook: Currency, Identify, Reputation," *Forbes,* April 4, 2011, http://blogs.forbes.com/venessamiemis/2011/04/04/the-bank-of-facebook-currencyidentity-reputation/; "Facebook's Sales Chief: Madison Avenue Doesn't Understand Us Yet," *Advertising Age,* April 29, 2011, http://adage.com/print/227314/; and information from www.facebook.com, accessed November 2012.

2. For these and other direct marketing statistics in this section, see Direct Marketing Association, *The DMA 2012 Statistical Fact Book,* 34th ed., February 2012; Direct Marketing Association, *The Power of Direct Marketing: 2011–2012 Edition,* August 2011; "DMA Releases New 'Power of Direct' Report," October 2, 2011, www.the-dma.org/cgi/dispannouncements?article=1590; and a wealth of other information at www.the-dma.org, accessed November 2012.

3. "U.S. Internet Ad Revenue Hits Record $31 Billion in 2011," *USA Today,* April 18, 2012, www.usatoday.com/tech/news/story/2012-04-18/internet-ad-revenue-record/54386820/1; "U.S. Online Advertising Spending to Surpass Print in 2012," *eMarketer,* January 19, 2012, www.emarketer.com/PressRelease.aspx?R=1008788; Thad Rueter, "E-retail Spending to Increase 62% by 2016," *Internet Retailer,* February 27, 2012, www.internetretailer.com/2012/02/27/e-retail-spending-increase-45-2016; and *The Power of Direct Marketing: 2011–2012 Edition.*

4. See discussions at "The Costs of Personal Selling," April 13, 2011, www.seekarticle.com/business-sales/personal-selling.html; and "What Is the Real Cost of a B2B Sales Call?" www.marketing-playbook.com/sales-marketing-strategy/what-is-the-real-cost-of-a-b2b-sales-call, accessed November 2012.

5. See "Big Security Data to Big Security Intelligence," *Infosec Professional,* April 22, 2012, www.infosecprofessional.com/2012/04/big-security-data-to-big-security.html; and Ian Greenleigh, "Will Consumers Ever Wish Companies Had More of Their Data?" *Bizaarvoice: blog,* June 6, 2012, www.bazaarvoice.com/blog/2012/06/06/5-reasons-to-wish-companies-had-more-of-your-data/.

6. See Philip Kotler and Kevin Lane Keller, *Marketing Management,* 14th ed. (Upper Saddle River, NJ: Prentice Hall, 2012), p. 71.

7. See DMA, *The Power of Direct Marketing, 2011–2012 Edition*; "It's Never Been Easier to Send Direct Mail," *PRNewswire,* June 8, 2011.

8. Julie Liesse, "When Times Are Hard, Mail Works," *Advertising Age,* March 30, 2009, p. 14; and Paul Vogel, "Marketers Are Rediscovering the Value of Mail," *Deliver Magazine,* January 11, 2011, www.delivermagazine.com/2011/01/marketers-are-rediscovering-the-value-of-mail/; and "The Resurrection of Direct Mail in 2012," *PRWeb,* www.prweb.com/releases/Direct-mail/Resurection/prweb9301877.htm, accessed July 2012.

9. Bruce Britt, "Marketing Leaders Discuss the Resurgence of Direct Mail," *Deliver Magazine,* January 18, 2011, www.delivermagazine.com/2011/01/marketing-leaders-discuss-resurgence-of-direct-mail/.

10. See "Catalog Spree Survey Shows 89.8 Percent of Shoppers Prefer Digital Catalogs," April 19, 2012, http://catalogspree.com/catalog-spree-survey-shows-89-8-percent-of-shoppers-prefer-digital-catalogs; and www.landsend.com/mobile/index.html and http://catalogspree.com/, accessed November 2012.

11. Jeffrey Ball, "Power Shift: In Digital Era, Marketers Still Prefer a Paper Trail," *Wall Street Journal,* October 16, 2009, p. A3; Jennifer Valentino-DeVries, "With Catalogs, Opt-Out Policies Vary," *Wall Street Journal,* April 13, 2011, p. B7; and *The DMA 2012 Statistical Fact Book.*

12. Ball, "Power Shift: In Digital Era, Marketers Still Prefer a Paper Trail"; and "Report: Catalogs Increasingly Drive Online Sales," RetailCustomerExperience.com, March 17, 2010, www.retailcustomerexperience.com/article/21521/Report-Catalogs-increasingly-drive-online-sales.

13. DMA, *The Power of Direct Marketing, 2011–2012 Edition.*

14. Melissa Hoffmann, "Report: Telecommunications Advances Affecting Do Not Call Registry," *Direct Marketing News,* December 30, 2011, www.dmnews.com/report-telecommunications-advances-affecting-do-not-call-registry/article/221264/; and www.donotcall.gov, accessed November 2012.

15. See Rachel Brown, "Perry, Fischer, Lavigne Tapped for Proactiv," *WWD,* January 13, 2010, p. 3; Rahul Parikh, "Proactiv's Celebrity Shell Game," Salon.com, February 28, 2011, www.salon.com/2011/02/28/proactiv_celebrity_sham; www.proactiv.com, accessed August 2012.

16. Mercedes Cardona, "Hampton's PajamaJeans Go Viral with DRTV Campaign," *Direct Marketing News,* December 2011, p. 17.

17. Stephanie Rosenbloom, "The New Touch-Face of Vending Machines," *New York Times,* May 25, 2010, accessed at www.nytimes.com/2010/05/26/business/26vending.html; and "Automating Retail Success," www.businessweek.com/adsections/2011/pdf/111114_Verizon3.pdf; accessed July 2012.

18. "Best Buy: Consumer Electronics Retailing on the Go," www.zoomsystems.com/our-partners/partner-portfolio/; and www.zoomsystems.com/about-us/company-overview/; accessed November 2012.

19. See "Household Internet Usage In and Outside the Home," U.S. Census Bureau, www.census.gov/compendia/statab/2012/tables/12s1155.pdf, accessed July 2012; "How People Spend Their Time Online," February 2, 2012, www.go-gulf.com/blog/online-time; "Global Mobile Statistics," *MobiThinking,* June 2011, http://mobithinking.com/stats-corner/global-mobile-statistics-2011-all-quality-mobile-marketing-research-mobile-web-stats-su; and Greg Sterling, "Google: 1 Billion People Will Use Mobile as Primary Internet Access Point in 2012," February 27, 2012, http://searchengineland.com/google-95-percent-of-us-smartphone-owners-use-search-113017.

20. See "Internet Retailer: Top 500 Guide," www.internetretailer.com/top500/list, accessed November 2012.

21. See "How Staples Generates More than $10 Billion in Online Sales," March 7, 2012, http://electronicbankingoptions.com/2012/03/07/how-staples-generates-more-than-10-billion-in-online-sales/; and Staples data from annual reports and other information found at www.staples.com, accessed October 2012.

22. See Thad Rueter, "E-retail Spending to Increase 62% by 2016," *Internet Retailer*, February 27, 2012, www.internetretailer.com/2012/02/27/e-retail-spending-increase-45-2016.

23. Rueter, "E-retail Spending to Increase 62% by 2016"; and Jack Loechner, "Web Influences Trillion Dollar Retail Sales," *Media-Post*, October 27, 2011, www.mediapost.com/publications/article/160988/web-influences-trillion-dollar-retail-sales.html.

24. See facts from eBay annual reports and other information at www.ebayinc.com, accessed August 2012.

25. "State of the Blogosphere 2011," Technorati, November 2011, accessed at http://technorati.com/social-media/feature/state-of-the-blogosphere-2011.

26. See http://en.community.dell.com/dell-blogs/default.aspx and www.youtube.com/user/DellVlog, accessed November 2012.

27. "Marketers Up the Ante on Social Media Sponsorships," *eMarketer*, July 13, 2012, www.emarketer.com/Articles/Print.aspx?R=1009188.

28. Adapted from information found in Keith O'Brien, "How McDonald's Came Back Bigger Than Ever," *New York Times*, May 6, 2012, p. MM44.

29. See David F. Carr, "Get Satisfaction Embeds Customer Feedback on Client Websites," *Informationweek*, May 1, 2012; and www.getsatisfaction.com, accessed November 2012.

30. "U.S. Internet Ad Revenue Hits Record $31 Billion in 2011," *USA Today*, April 18, 2012, www.usatoday.com/tech/news/story/2012-04-18/internet-ad-revenue-record/54386820/1; and "US Online Advertising Spending to Surpass Print in 2012," *eMarketer*, January 19, 2012, www.emarketer.com/PressRelease.aspx?R=1008788.

31. Internet Advertising Bureau, *IAB Internet Advertising Revenue Report*, April 18, 2012; www.iab.net/about_the_iab/recent_press_releases/press_release_archive/press_release/pr-041812; and Google annual reports, http://investor.google.com/proxy.html, accessed August 2012.

32. See "Campaigns Creativity Liked," *Advertising Age*, December 13, 2010, p. 18; Dan Sewell, "Old Spice Teases Its Sexy New Ad Campaign," *USA Today*, January 26, 2011, www.usatoday.com/money/advertising/2011-01-26-old-spice-mustafa-ad_N.htm; and Dave Parrack, "10 of the Best Viral Video Ad Campaigns," February 16, 2012, www.makeuseof.com/tag/10-viral-video-ad-campaigns/.

33. Michael Learmonth, "Fresh Numbers: Honda Won Super Bowl Before It Even Began," *Advertising Age*, February 6, 2012, http://adage.com/print/ 232543/.

34. David Gelles, "The Public Image: Volkswagen's 'The Force' Campaign," *Financial Times*, February 22, 2011, p. 14; and Troy Dreier, "The Force Was Strong with This One," *Streaming Media Magazine*, April/May 2011, pp. 66–68. Also see Thales Teixeira, "The New Science of Viral Ads," *Harvard Business Review*, March 2012, pp. 25–28.

35. Mark Hachman, "Facebook Used by Half of the World's Internet Users, Save Asia," *PC Magazine*, February 2, 2012, www.pcmag.com/article2/0,2817,2399732,00.asp; and List of Countries by Population," http://en.wikipedia.org/wiki/List_of_countries_by_population, accessed October 2012.

36. For these and other examples, see Douglas MacMillan, "With Friends Like This, Who Needs Facebook?" *Bloomberg Businessweek*, September 13–September 19, 2010, pp. 35–37; and www.yub.com, www.kaboodle.com, www.farmersonly.com, www.gofishn.com/, www.ravelry.com, www.dogster.com, www.researchgate.net, www.passionsnetwork.com, and www.cafemom.com, all accessed November 2012.

37. "Happy Birthday to Nike+," *Run247*, May 23, 2011, "Happy Birthday to Nike+," May 23, 2011, www.run247.com/articles/article-1337-happy-birthday-to-nike%2B.html; and "Nike Shows Us How to Adapt to a Digital Era," *AD60*, February 27, 2012, www.ad60.com/2012/02/27/nike-shows-adapt-digital-era/.

38. See http://my.menshealth.com/bellyoff/, accessed October 2012.

39. See "Internet 2011 in Numbers," *Pingdom*, January 17, 2012, http://royal.pingdom.com/2012/01/17/internet-2011-in-numbers; Ken Magill, "Email Remains ROI King; Net Marketing Set to Overtake DM, Says DMA," *The Magill Report*, October 4, 2011, www.magillreport.com/Email-Remains-ROI-King-Net-Marketing-Set-to-Overtake-DM/; and "Marketers Use Growing Number of Tools to Spur Website Engagement," *eMarketer*, May 11, 2012, www.emarketer.com/Article.aspx?R=1009040.

40. Elizabeth A. Sullivan, "Targeting to the Extreme," *Marketing News*, June 15, 2010, pp. 17–19.

41. Symantec, *The State of Spam and Phishing: Home of the Monthly Report—February 2012*, accessed at http://go.symantec.com/spam_report/.

42. Mark Brownlow, "Why Do Email Marketing?" *Email Marketing Reports*, November 2011, www.email-marketing-reports.com/basics/why.htm; and Carroll Trosclair, "Direct Marketing, Advertising and ROI: Commercial E-Mail Delivers Highest DM Return on Investment," *Suite101.com*, April 2, 2010, http://advertising.suite101.com/article.cfm/direct-marketing-advertising-and-roi. For examples of outstanding e-mail marketing campaigns, see "MarketingSherpa Email Awards 2012," *MarketingSherpa*, www.marketingsherpa.com/data/members/special-reports/OPEN-SR-10-Email-Awards-2012.pdf.

43. Facts in this paragraph are from Joe McKendrick, "One-Third of U.S. Households Chuck Landlines; Now Use Mobile Only," *SmartPlanet*, December 21, 2011, www.smartplanet.com/blog/business-brains/one-third-of-us-households-chuck-landlines-now-use-mobile-only/20746; Kunur Patel, "When Placing Advertising, Don't Underrate the Value of Mobile," *Advertising Age*, November 7, 2011, p. 38; and www.apple.com/ipad/from-the-app-store/, www.apple.com/iphone/apps-for-iphone/, and https://play.google.com/store/apps/details?id=com.google.android.finsky&hl=en, accessed October 2012.

44. "New Forecast: US Mobile Ad Spending Soars Past Expectations," January 25, 2012, http://www.emarketer.com/PressRelease.aspx?R=1008798; "Global Mobile Statistics 2012," *mobiThinking*, February 2012, http://mobithinking.com/mobile-marketing-tools/latest-mobile-stats.

45. See "Location, Location, Location," *Adweek*, February 13, 2012, pp. M9–M11.

46. Adapted from Giselle Tsirulnik, "Most Impressive Mobile Advertising Campaigns in 2010," December 29, 2010, www.mobilemarketer.com/cms/news/advertising/8617.html.

47. See Internet Crime Complaint Center, "IC3 2011 Annual Report on Internet Crime Released," May10, 2012, http://www.ic3.gov/media/2012/120511.aspx.

48. See Molly Bernhart Walker, "America's Less Concerned about Internet Security," *FierceGovernmentIT*, May 10, 2012, www.fiercegovernmentit.com/story/americans-less-concerned-about-internet-security/2012-05-10.

49. See Cecilia Kang, "Underage and on Facebook," *Washington Post*, June 13, 2011, www.washingtonpost.com/blogs/post-tech/post/underage-and-on-facebook/2011/06/12/AGHKHySH_blog.html; and Susan Dominus, "Underage on Facebook," *MSN Living*, March 15, 2012; http://living.msn.com/family-parenting/underage-on-facebook-5.

50. Adapted from information in Michael Bush, "My Life, Seen Through the Eyes of Marketers," *Advertising Age*, April 26, 2010, http://adage.com/print/143479.

51. See "Digital Advertising Alliance Announces First 100 Companies Participating in Self-Regulatory Program for Online Behavioral Advertising," June 7, 2011, www.the-dma.org/cgi/dispannouncements?article=1558; and www.aboutads.info/, accessed August 2012.

52. See Wendy Davis, "Rockefeller Urges FTC to Move Faster on COPPA Rules," *Daily Online Examiner*, May 19, 2011, www.mediapost.com/publications/?fa=Articles.showArticle&art_aid=150867; and http://epic.org/privacy/kids/ and http://business.ftc.gov/privacy-and-security/children%E2%80%99s-privacy, accessed October 2012.

53. Information on TRUSTe at www.truste.com, accessed October 2012.

54. Information on the DMA Privacy Promise at www.the-dma.org/cgi/dispissue?article=129 and www.dmaconsumers.org/privacy.html, accessed November 2012.

Creating Competitive Advantage

18

Chapter Preview In previous chapters, you explored the basics of marketing. You learned that the aim of marketing is to create value *for* customers in order to capture value *from* them in return. Good marketing companies win, keep, and grow customers by understanding customer needs, designing customer-driven marketing strategies, constructing value-delivering marketing programs, and building customer and marketing partner relationships. In the final three chapters, we'll extend this concept to three special areas: creating competitive advantage,

global marketing, and social and environmental marketing sustainability.

To start, let's look at the competitive marketing strategy of Four Seasons, a hotel and resort company renown for creating unparalleled customer experiences. To its core, Four Seasons practices a "customer intimacy" strategy—pampering customers to keep them coming back (more on this strategy later in the chapter). The luxury chain enlists *everyone*—from the CEO to the doorman—in its mission to create superior customer value and keep customers coming back.

Four Seasons: Inspiring Everyone to Create Customer Satisfaction and Value

At a Four Seasons hotel, every guest is a somebody. Other exclusive resorts pamper their guests, but Four Seasons has perfected the art of high-touch, carefully crafted service. Guests paying $1,000 or more a night expect to have their minds read, and this luxury hotel doesn't disappoint. Its mission is to perfect the travel experience through the highest standards of hospitality. "From elegant surroundings of the finest quality, to caring, highly personalized 24-hour service," says the company, "Four Seasons embodies a true home away from home for those who know and appreciate the best."

As a result of its "customer intimacy" strategy, Four Seasons has a cult-like customer clientele. As one Four Seasons Maui guest recently told a manager, "If there's a heaven, I hope it's run by Four Seasons." But what's the secret to bringing the Four Seasons customer intimacy strategy to life? It's really no secret. Just ask anyone who works there. From the CEO to the doorman, they'll tell you—it's the quality of the Four Seasons staff. Its people are

"the heart and soul of what makes this company succeed," says Four Seasons founder and CEO Isadore Sharp. "When we say people are our most important asset—it's not just talk." Just as it does for customers, Four Seasons respects and pampers its employees. It knows that happy, satisfied employees make for happy, satisfied customers.

The Four Seasons customer-service legacy is deeply rooted in the company's culture, which in turn is grounded in the Golden Rule. In all of its dealings with both guests and staff, the luxury resort chain seeks to treat others as it wishes to be treated. "How you treat your employees is a reflection of how you expect

> At Four Seasons, competitive marketing strategy isn't something that's just handed down from the top. The company enlists everyone—from the CEO to the doorman—in its mission to create unparalleled customer value.

them to treat customers," says Sharp.

Four Seasons brings this customer service culture to life by hiring the best people, orienting them carefully, instilling in them a sense of pride, and motivating them by recognizing and rewarding outstanding service deeds. It all starts with hiring the right people—those who fit the Four Seasons culture. Every applicant—whether it's a potential receptionist, a hopeful pool manager, or a would-be backroom financial manager—undergoes multiple job interviews. "We look for employees who share that Golden Rule—people who, by nature, believe in treating others as they would have them treat us," says Sharp.

Four Seasons and its employees create unparalleled customer experiences. Says one customer, "If there's a heaven, I hope it's run by Four Seasons."

© Archimage/Alamy

Once on board, all new employees receive three months of training, including improvisation exercises that help them to fully understand customer needs and behavior. At Four Seasons, the training never stops. But even more important is the people themselves and the culture under which they work. The most important cultural guideline: the good old Golden Rule. "That's not a gimmick," Sharp insists. As a result, Four Seasons employees know what good service is and are highly motivated to give it.

Most important, once it has the right people in place, Four Seasons treats them as it would its most important guests. Compared with the competition, Four Seasons salaries are in the 75th to 90th percentile, with generous retirement and profit sharing plans. All employees—from the maids who make up the rooms to the general manager—dine together (free of charge) in the hotel cafeteria. Perhaps best of all, every employee receives free stays at other Four Seasons resorts, starting at three free nights per year after six months with the company, then six free nights or more after one year.

The room stays make employees feel as important and pampered as the guests they serve, and they motivate employees to achieve even higher levels of service in their own jobs.

Kanoe Braun, a pool attendant at the Four Seasons Maui, has visited several other Four Seasons resorts in his ten years with the company. "I've been to the one in Bali. That was by far my favorite," he proclaims. "You walk in, and they say, 'How are you, Mr. Braun?' and you say, `Yeah, I'm somebody!'" Adds another Four Season staffer, "You're never treated like just an employee. You're a guest. You come back from those trips on fire. You want to do so much for the guests."

As a result, the Four Seasons staff loves the hotel just as much as customers do. Although guests can check out anytime they like, employees never want to leave. The annual turnover for full-time employees is only 18 percent, half the industry average. Four Seasons has been included for 15 straight years on *Fortune* magazine's list of 100 Best Companies to Work For. And that's the biggest secret to Four Seasons' success. Creating customer satisfaction and value involves more than just crafting a lofty competitive marketing strategy and handing it down from the top. At Four Season, creating customer value is a whole-company affair.[1]

Competitive advantage
An advantage over competitors gained by offering consumers greater value.

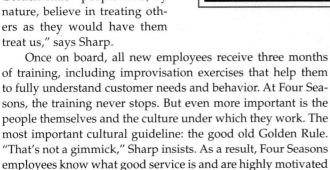Today's companies face their toughest competition ever. In previous chapters, we argued that to succeed in today's fiercely competitive marketplace, companies must move from a product-and-selling philosophy to a customer-and-marketing philosophy.

This chapter spells out in more detail how companies can go about outperforming competitors to win, keep, and grow customers. To win in today's marketplace, companies must become adept not only in managing products but also in managing customer relationships in the face of determined competition and a difficult economic environment. Understanding customers is crucial, but it's not enough. Building profitable customer relationships and gaining **competitive advantage** requires delivering more value and satisfaction to target

Objective Outline

Objective 1	**Discuss the need to understand competitors as well as customers through competitor analysis.**
	Competitor Analysis (pp 526–533)
Objective 2	**Explain the fundamentals of competitive marketing strategies based on creating value for customers.**
	Competitive Strategies (pp 533–543)
Objective 3	**Illustrate the need for balancing customer and competitor orientations in becoming a truly market-centered organization.**
	Balancing Customer and Competitor Orientations (pp 543–544)

MyMarketingLab™

⭐ **Improve Your Grade!**

Over 10 million students improved their results using the Pearson MyLabs.
Visit **mymktlab.com** for simulations, tutorials, and end-of-chapter problems.

customers than competitors do. Customers will see competitive advantages as *customer advantages*, giving the company an edge over its competitors.

In this chapter, we examine competitive marketing strategies—how companies analyze their competitors and develop successful, customer-value-based strategies for building and maintaining profitable customer relationships. The first step is **competitor analysis**, the process of identifying, assessing, and selecting key competitors. The second step is developing **competitive marketing strategies** that strongly position the company against competitors and give it the greatest possible competitive advantage.

Competitive marketing strategies
Strategies that strongly position the company against competitors and give the company the strongest possible strategic advantage.

Objective 1 ┈┈▶
Discuss the need to understand competitors as well as customers through competitor analysis.

Competitor Analysis

To plan effective marketing strategies, a company needs to find out all it can about its competitors. It must constantly compare its marketing strategies, products, prices, channels, and promotions with those of close competitors. In this way, the company can find areas of potential competitive advantage and disadvantage. As shown in ● **Figure 18.1**, competitor analysis involves first identifying and assessing competitors and then selecting which competitors to attack or avoid.

● **FIGURE | 18.1**
Steps in Analyzing Competitors

Identifying competitors isn't as easy as it seems. For example, Kodak saw other camera film makers as its major competitors. But its real competitors turned out to be the makers of digital cameras that used no film at all. Kodak fell behind in digital technologies and ended up declaring bankruptcy.

Identifying the company's competitors	→	**Assessing** competitors' objectives, strategies, strengths and weaknesses, and reaction patterns	→	**Selecting** which competitors to attack or avoid

Competitor analysis
Identifying key competitors; assessing their objectives, strategies, strengths and weaknesses, and reaction patterns; and selecting which competitors to attack or avoid.

Identifying Competitors

Normally, identifying competitors would seem to be a simple task. At the narrowest level, a company can define its competitors as other companies offering similar products and services to the same customers at similar prices. Thus, Abercrombie & Fitch might see the Gap as a major competitor, but not Nordstrom or Target. The Ritz-Carlton might see the Four Seasons hotels as a major competitor, but not Holiday Inn, the Hampton Inn, or any of the thousands of bed-and-breakfasts that dot the nation.

However, companies actually face a much wider range of competitors. The company might define its competitors as all firms with the same product or class of products. Thus, the Ritz-Carlton would see itself as competing against all other hotels. Even more broadly, competitors might include all companies making products that supply the same service. Here the Ritz-Carlton would see itself competing not only against other hotels but also against anyone who supplies rooms for weary travelers. Finally, and still more broadly, competitors might include all companies that compete for the same consumer dollars. Here the Ritz-Carlton would see itself competing with travel and leisure products and services, from cruises and summer homes to vacations abroad.

Companies must avoid "competitor myopia." A company is more likely to be "buried" by its latent competitors than its current ones. For example, it wasn't direct competitors that put an end to Western Union's telegram business after 161 years; it was mobile phones and the Internet. Music superstore Tower Records didn't go bankrupt at the hands of other traditional music stores; it fell victim to unexpected competitors such as discounters Best Buy and Walmart, and iTunes and the host of other digital music download services. Kodak didn't lose out to competing film makers such as Fuji; it fell to the makers of digital cameras that use no film at all (see Real Marketing 18.1). Another classic example of competitor myopia is the U.S. Postal Service (USPS):[2]

The USPS is losing money at a mind-boggling rate—$5.1 billion in losses last year alone. But it's not direct competitors such as FedEx or UPS that are the problem. Instead, it's a competitor that the USPS could hardly have even imagined two decades ago—the soaring use of personal and business e-mail, texting, and online transactions, what the USPS calls "electronic diversion." As Internet usage has surged, personal and business letter mail have plunged. Last year, the USPS delivered an eye-popping 45 billion fewer mail pieces than five years earlier. That's 45 *billion*! The USPS's response: Proposed increases in postage stamp prices, employee layoffs, and a reduction from five-day delivery to three-day delivery, moves that will almost certainly reduce mail volume further. The solution? When I figure it out, I'll e-mail you.

Companies can identify their competitors from an *industry* point of view. They might see themselves as being in the oil industry, the pharmaceutical industry, or the beverage industry. A company must understand the competitive patterns in its industry if it hopes to be an effective player in that industry. Companies can also identify competitors from a *market* point of view. Here they define competitors as companies that are trying to satisfy the same customer need or build relationships with the same customer group.

From an industry point of view, Pepsi might see its competition as Coca-Cola and Dr Pepper Snapple Group (maker of Dr Pepper, 7 Up, A&W, and other brands). From a market point of view, however, the customer really wants "thirst quenching"—a need that can be satisfied by bottled water, energy drinks, fruit juice, iced tea, and many other fluids. ● Similarly, Dole might define competitors for its bananas as other fresh fruit producers. But based on research showing that bananas provide the same energy boost as sports drinks but with more nutrition, no artificial ingredients, and a much lower price, Dole redefined its competitive point of view and began positioning its bananas as "Nature's Original Energy Bar."[3] In general, the market concept of competition opens the company's eyes to a broader set of actual and potential competitors.

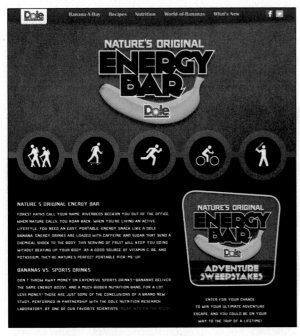

● **Identifying competitors: In its "Nature's Original Energy Bar" campaign, Dole positions its bananas not as a fruit, but as a nutritious, affordable energy booster.**

Dole Fresh Fruit Company

Real Marketing 18.1

Kodak: The Competitor It Didn't See Soon Enough—No Film

Kodak. That venerable brand name has been a household word for generations worldwide. For more than a century, people relied on Kodak for products to help them capture "Kodak moments"—important personal and family events to be shared and recorded for posterity. The Hollywood movie industry evolved around Kodak technology. In 1972, Paul Simon even had a number two hit single called "Kodachrome," a song that put into words the emotional role that Kodak products played in people's lives.

Today, however, Kodak is bankrupt, a company working its way through Chapter 11 reorganization. Once ranked among the bluest of blue chips, Kodak's shares are now penny stocks. The brand that once monopolized its industry, capturing 85 percent of all camera sales and 90 percent of a huge film market, now struggles to compete in any market at all. Once rolling in cash, for the last four years Kodak has been losing $43 million a month. And once employing more than 100,000 people worldwide, the company's mostly U.S. workforce has now dwindled to less than 10,000 workers.

How could such a storied brand fall so far so fast? Kodak fell victim to marketing and competitor myopia—focusing on a narrow set of current products and competitors rather than on underlying customer needs and emerging market dynamics. It wasn't competing film makers that brought Kodak down. It was the competitor Kodak didn't see soon enough—digital photography and cameras that used no film at all. All along, Kodak continued to make the very best film. But in an increasingly digital world, customers no longer needed film. Clinging to its legacy products, Kodak lagged competitors in making the shift to digital.

In 1880, George Eastman founded Kodak based on a method for dry-plate photography. In 1888, he introduced the Kodak camera, which used glass plates for capturing images. Looking to expand the market, Eastman next developed film and the innovative little Kodak Brownie film camera. He sold the camera for only $1 but reaped massive profits from the sale of film, along with the chemicals and paper required to produce photographs. Although Kodak also developed innovative imaging technologies for industries ranging from health care to publishing, throughout the twentieth century, cameras and film remained the company's massive cash cow.

Interestingly, way back in 1975, Kodak engineers invented the first digital camera—a toaster-sized image sensor that captured rough hues of black and white. However, failing to recognize the mass-market potential of digital photography, and fearing that digital technology would cannibalize its precious film business, Kodak shelved the digital project. Company managers simply could not envision a filmless world. So Kodak held fast to film and focused its innovation and competitive energies on making better film and out-innovating other film producers. When the company later realized its mistake, it was too late.

Blinded by its film fixation, Kodak failed to see emerging competitive trends associated with capturing and sharing images. Kodak's culture became bound up in its history and the nostalgia that accompanied it. "They were a company stuck in time," says one analyst. "Their history was so important to them—this rich century-old history when they made a lot of amazing things and a lot of money along the way. [Then,] their history [became] a liability."

By the time Kodak finally introduced a line of pocket-sized digital cameras in the late 1990s, the market was already crowded with digital products from Sony, Canon, and a dozen other camera makers. That was soon followed by a completely new category of competitors, as more and more people began pointing-and-clicking their phones and other mobile devices and sharing photos instantly via texting, e-mail, and online photo-sharing networks. Late to the digital game, Kodak became a relic of the past and an also-ran to a host of new-age digital competitors that hadn't even existed a decade or two earlier.

Somewhere along the way, swelled with success, once-mighty Kodak lost sight of founder George Eastman's visionary knack for defining customer needs and competitor dynamics. According to one biographer, Eastman's legacy was not film; it was innovation. "George Eastman never looked back. He always looked forward to doing something better than what he had done, even if he had the best on the market at the time." If it had retained Eastman's philosophy, Kodak might well have been the market leader in digital technologies. We might all still be capturing "Kodak moments" on Kodak digital cameras and smartphones and sharing them on

Competitor myopia: It wasn't competing film makers that brought Kodak down. It was the competitor Kodak didn't see soon enough—digital photography and cameras that use no film at all.
© Finnbarr Webster/Alamy

Kodak-run online sites and image-sharing social networks.

As Kodak emerges from bankruptcy, given the strength of the Kodak brand name, those things could still happen. But it's not likely. As a part of its bankruptcy plan, Kodak announced that it will stop making digital cameras (it has also discontinued its famous Kodachrome color film). Instead, it plans to license its name to other manufacturers that will make cameras under the Kodak brand. Some three-fourths of the company's revenues will now come from business segments, such as commercial digital printing and entertainment films. So, along with the company's fortunes, it looks as though the famed "Kodak moment" may have now passed into history.

Sources: Sam Gustin, "In Kodak Bankruptcy, Another Casualty of the Digital Revolution," *Time*, January 20, 2012, http://business.time.com/2012/01/20/in-kodak-bankruptcy-another-casualty-of-the-digital-revolution/; Ernest Scheyder, "Focus on Past Glory Kept Kodak from Digital Win," Reuters, January 19, 2012, www.reuters.com/article/2012/01/19/us-kodak-bankruptcy-idUSTRE80I1N020120119; Dawn McCarty and Beth Jink, "Kodak Files for Bankruptcy as Digital Era Spells End to Film," *Bloomberg Businessweek*, January 25, 2012, www.businessweek.com/news/2012-01-25/kodak-files-for-bankruptcy-as-digital-era-spells-end-to-film.html; Michael Hiltzik, "Kodak's Long Fade to Black," *Los Angeles Times*, December 4, 2011; and "Kodak to Stop Making Digital Cameras," *Digital Photography Review*, February 9, 2012, www.dpreview.com/news/2012/02/09/Kodak_exits_camera_business.

Assessing Competitors

Having identified the main competitors, marketing management now asks: What are the competitors' objectives? What does each seek in the marketplace? What is each competitor's strategy? What are various competitors' strengths and weaknesses, and how will each react to actions the company might take?

Strategic group

A group of firms in an industry following the same or a similar strategy.

Determining Competitors' Objectives

Each competitor has a mix of objectives. The company wants to know the relative importance that a competitor places on current profitability, market share growth, cash flow, technological leadership, service leadership, and other goals. Knowing a competitor's mix of objectives reveals whether the competitor is satisfied with its current situation and how it might react to different competitive actions. For example, a company that pursues low-cost leadership will react much more strongly to a competitor's cost-reducing manufacturing breakthrough than to the same competitor's increase in advertising.

A company also must monitor its competitors' objectives for various segments. If the company finds that a competitor has discovered a new segment, this might be an opportunity. If it finds that competitors plan new moves into segments now served by the company, it will be forewarned and, hopefully, forearmed.

Identifying Competitors' Strategies

The more that one firm's strategy resembles another firm's strategy, the more the two firms compete. In most industries, the competitors can be sorted into groups that pursue different strategies. A **strategic group** is a group of firms in an industry following the same or a similar strategy in a given target market. For example, in the major appliance industry, GE and Whirlpool belong to the same strategic group. Each produces a full line of medium-price appliances supported by good service. In contrast, Sub-Zero and Viking belong to a different strategic group. They produce a narrower line of higher-quality appliances, offer a higher level of service, and charge a premium price. "We're as passionate about building Viking products as chefs are about cooking with them," says Viking. "We innovate. We over-engineer. And then we use high-grade, heavy-duty materials to create the most powerful products available. At Viking, it's more than just steel on the line. It's our pride."[4]

Some important insights emerge from identifying strategic groups. For example, if a company enters a strategic group, the

● Strategic groups: Viking belongs to the appliance industry strategic group offering a narrow line of very high quality products. "Every one of us is committed to every Viking that comes off the line," says this ad. At Viking, it's more than just steel on the line. It's our pride."

Viking Range Corporation

members of that group become its key competitors. Thus, if the company enters a group containing GE and Whirlpool, it can succeed only if it develops strategic advantages over these two companies.

Although competition is most intense within a strategic group, there is also rivalry among groups. First, some strategic groups may appeal to overlapping customer segments. For example, no matter what their strategy, all major appliance manufacturers will go after the apartment and homebuilders segment. Second, customers may not see much difference in the offers of different groups; they may see little difference in quality between GE and Whirlpool. Finally, members of one strategic group might expand into new strategy segments. Thus, GE's Monogram and Profile lines of appliances compete in the premium-quality, premium-price line with Viking and Sub-Zero.

The company needs to look at all the dimensions that identify strategic groups within the industry. It must understand how each competitor delivers value to its customers. It needs to know each competitor's product quality, features, and mix; customer services; pricing policy; distribution coverage; sales force strategy; and advertising, sales promotion, and online and social media programs. And it must study the details of each competitor's research and development (R&D), manufacturing, purchasing, financial, and other strategies.

Assessing Competitors' Strengths and Weaknesses

Marketers need to carefully assess each competitor's strengths and weaknesses to answer a critical question: What *can* our competitors do? As a first step, companies can gather data on each competitor's goals, strategies, and performance over the past few years. Admittedly, some of this information will be hard to obtain. For example, business-to-business (B-to-B) marketers find it hard to estimate competitors' market shares because they do not have the same syndicated data services that are available to consumer packaged-goods companies.

Benchmarking
Comparing the company's products and processes to those of competitors or leading firms in other industries to identify best practices and find ways to improve quality and performance.

Companies normally learn about their competitors' strengths and weaknesses through secondary data, personal experience, and word of mouth. They can also conduct primary marketing research with customers, suppliers, and dealers. They can check competitors' online and social networking sites. Or they can **benchmark** themselves against other firms, comparing the company's products and processes to those of competitors or leading firms in other industries to identify best practices and find ways to improve quality and performance. Benchmarking has become a powerful tool for increasing a company's competitiveness.

● Competitor reactions: In some industries, competitors live in relative harmony; in others, they fight constantly. For example, in the U.S. wireless industry, Verizon Wireless and AT&T have attacked each other ruthlessly in comparison ads for years.

(iphone image) © L_amica-Fotolia.com/istockphoto; (Verizon logo) PR Newswire; (AT&T logo) Staff/MCT/Newscom

Estimating Competitors' Reactions

Next, the company wants to know: What *will* our competitors do? A competitor's objectives, strategies, and strengths and weaknesses go a long way toward explaining its likely actions. They also suggest its likely reactions to company moves, such as price cuts, promotion increases, or new-product introductions. In addition, each competitor has a certain philosophy of doing business, a certain internal culture and guiding beliefs. Marketing managers need a deep understanding of a competitor's mentality if they want to anticipate how that competitor will act or react.

Each competitor reacts differently. Some do not react quickly or strongly to a competitor's move. They may feel their customers are loyal, they may be slow in noticing the move, or they may lack the funds to react. Some competitors react only to certain types of moves and not to others. Other competitors react swiftly and strongly to any action. Thus, P&G does not allow a competitor's new product to come easily into the market. Many firms avoid direct competition with P&G and look for easier prey, knowing that P&G will react fiercely if it is challenged.

In some industries, competitors live in relative harmony; in others, they fight constantly. ● For example, competitors in the U.S. wireless industry have been at each other's throats for years. Verizon Wireless and AT&T have attacked each other ruthlessly in comparative ads. When Verizon Wireless began offering the iPhone, it used its "Can you hear me now?" slogan to attack AT&T's rumored spotty service. AT&T retaliated by showing that its customers could talk on the phone and surf the Internet at the same time, a feature not yet available via Verizon Wireless. Most recently, in selling Apple's 4G-enabled iPad, an advertising battle has been raging over which company has the largest 4G coverage.[5] Knowing how major competitors react gives the company clues on how best to attack competitors or how best to defend its current positions.

Selecting Competitors to Attack and Avoid

A company has already largely selected its major competitors through prior decisions on customer targets, positioning, and its marketing mix strategy. Management now must decide which competitors to compete against most vigorously.

Strong or Weak Competitors

A company can focus on one of several classes of competitors. Most companies prefer to compete against weak competitors. This requires fewer resources and less time. But in the process, the firm may gain little. You could argue that a firm also should compete with strong competitors to sharpen its abilities. And sometimes, a company can't avoid its largest competitors, as in the case of Verizon and AT&T. But even strong competitors have some weaknesses, and succeeding against them often provides greater returns.

Customer value analysis

An analysis conducted to determine what benefits target customers value and how they rate the relative value of various competitors' offers.

A useful tool for assessing competitor strengths and weaknesses is **customer value analysis**. The aim of customer value analysis is to determine the benefits that target customers value and how customers rate the relative value of various competitors' offers. In conducting a customer value analysis, the company first identifies the major attributes that customers value and the importance customers place on these attributes. Next, it assesses its performance against competitors on those valued attributes.

The key to gaining competitive advantage is to examine how a company's offer compares to that of its major competitors in each customer segment. The company wants to find the place in the market where it meets customers' needs in a way rivals can't. If the company's offer delivers greater value than the competitor's offer on important attributes, it can charge a higher price and earn higher profits, or it can charge the same price and gain more market share. But if the company is seen as performing at a lower level than its major competitors on some important attributes, it must invest in strengthening those attributes or finding other important attributes where it can build a lead.

Close or Distant Competitors

Most companies will compete with close competitors—those that resemble them most—rather than distant competitors. Thus, Nike competes more against Adidas than against Timberland or Keen. And Target competes against Walmart rather than Neiman Marcus or Nordstrom.

At the same time, the company may want to avoid trying to "destroy" a close competitor. For example, in the late 1970s, then-market leader Bausch & Lomb moved aggressively against other soft contact lens manufacturers with great success. However, this forced weak competitors to sell out to larger firms such as Johnson & Johnson (J&J). As a result, Bausch & Lomb then faced much larger competitors—and it suffered the consequences. J&J acquired Vistakon, a small nicher with only $20 million in annual sales. Backed by J&J's deep pockets, the small but nimble Vistakon developed and introduced its innovative Acuvue disposable lenses. With Vistakon leading the way, J&J is now the dominant U.S. contact lens maker, with a nearly 42 percent market share, while Bausch & Lomb lags in fourth place with about an 11 percent market share. In this case, success in hurting a close rival brought in tougher competitors.[6]

Good or Bad Competitors

A company really needs and benefits from competitors. The existence of competitors results in several strategic benefits. Competitors may share the costs of market and product development and help legitimize new technologies. They may serve less-attractive segments or lead to more product differentiation. Finally, competitors may help increase total demand. For example, you might think that Apple's introduction of the stylish and trendy iPad tablet would have spelled trouble for Amazon's smaller, dowdier Kindle e-reader, which had been on the market for three years prior to the iPad's debut. Many analysts thought that Apple had created the "Kindle killer." ● However, as it turns out, the competing iPad created a stunning surge in tablet demand that benefited both companies. Kindle sales have increased sharply since the iPad introduction. And whereas Apple now enjoys a major share of the high-priced tablet market, Amazon's Kindle leads the market for low-priced tablets. As an added bonus, the surge in iPad usage has increased Amazon's sales of e-books and

● Good or bad competitors: Rather than spelling trouble for Amazon's Kindle e-reader, Apple's introduction of the iPad created a surge in tablet demand that benefited both companies.
Kyodo

other digital content, which can be read on the iPad using a free Kindle for iPad app.[7]

However, a company may not view all its competitors as beneficial. An industry often contains *good competitors* and *bad competitors*. Good competitors play by the rules of the industry. Bad competitors, in contrast, break the rules. They try to buy share rather than earn it, take large risks, and play by their own rules.

For example, the nation's traditional newspapers face a lot of bad competitors these days. Digital services that overlap with traditional newspaper content are bad competitors because they offer for free real-time content that subscription-based newspapers printed once a day can't match. An example is Craigslist, the online community that lets local users post largely free classified ads. Started as a hobby almost 20 years ago by Craig Newmark, Craigslist has never cared all that much about profit margins, and that's about as bad as the competitor can get.

Another example is the *Huffington Post*, the Pulitzer Prize–winning online newspaper started in 2005 by Arianna Huffington as an outlet for liberal commentary. The publication has since expanded and is now owned by AOL. The site offers news, blogs, and original content, and covers politics, business, entertainment, technology, popular media, lifestyle, culture, comedy, healthy living, women's interest, and local news. The ad-supported site is free to users, versus the subscription rates charged by traditional newspapers. Last year the publication attracted 54 million comment posts and 1.2 trillion page views. Such unorthodox digital competitors have helped to drive many traditional newspapers into bankruptcy in recent years.[8]

Finding Uncontested Market Spaces

Rather than competing head to head with established competitors, many companies seek out unoccupied positions in uncontested market spaces. They try to create products and services for which there are no direct competitors. Called a "blue-ocean strategy," the goal is to make competition irrelevant:[9]

> Companies have long engaged in head-to-head competition in search of profitable growth. They have fought for competitive advantage, battled over market share, and struggled for differentiation. Yet in today's overcrowded industries, competing head-on results in nothing but a bloody "red ocean" of rivals fighting over a shrinking profit pool. In their book *Blue Ocean Strategy*, two strategy professors contend that although most companies compete within such red oceans, the strategy isn't likely to create profitable growth in the future. Tomorrow's leading companies will succeed not by battling competitors but by creating "blue oceans" of uncontested market space. Such strategic moves—termed value innovation—create powerful leaps in value for both the firm and its buyers, creating all new demand and rendering rivals obsolete. By creating and capturing blue oceans, companies can largely take rivals out of the picture.

Apple has long practiced this strategy, introducing product firsts such as the iPod, iPhone, and iPad that created whole new categories. ● Another example is Cirque du Soleil, which reinvented the circus as a higher form of modern entertainment. At a time when the circus industry was declining, Cirque du Soleil innovated by eliminating high-cost and controversial elements such as animal acts and instead focused on the theatrical experience. Cirque du Soleil did not compete with then market leader Ringling Bros. and Barnum & Bailey; it was altogether different from anything that preceded it. Instead, it created an uncontested new market space that made existing competitors irrelevant. The results have been spectacular. Thanks to its blue-ocean

● Blue-ocean strategy: Cirque du Soleil reinvented the circus, finding an uncontested new market space that made existing competitors irrelevant.
© ITAR-TASS Photo Agency/Alamy

strategy, in only its first 20 years, Cirque du Soleil achieved more revenues than Ringling Brothers and Barnum & Bailey achieved in its first 100 years.

Designing a Competitive Intelligence System

We have described the main types of information that companies need about their competitors. This information must be collected, interpreted, distributed, and used. Gathering competitive intelligence can cost much money and time, so the company must design a cost-effective competitive intelligence system.

The competitive intelligence system first identifies the vital types of competitive information needed and the best sources of this information. Then, the system continuously collects information from the field (sales force, channels, suppliers, market research firms, Internet sites, online monitoring, and trade associations) and published data (government publications, speeches, and online databases). Next the system checks the information for validity and reliability, interprets it, and organizes it in an appropriate way. Finally, it sends relevant information to decision makers and responds to inquiries from managers about competitors.

With this system, company managers receive timely intelligence about competitors in the form of reports, phone calls, e-mails alerts, bulletins, and newsletters. Managers can also connect with the system when they need to interpret a competitor's sudden move, know a competitor's weaknesses and strengths, or assess how a competitor will respond to a planned company move.

Smaller companies that cannot afford to set up formal competitive intelligence offices can assign specific executives to watch particular competitors. Thus, a manager who used to work for a competitor might follow that competitor closely, becoming the "in-house expert" on that competitor. A manager needing to know the thinking of a given competitor could contact the assigned in-house expert.

Objective 2 ───►
Explain the fundamentals of competitive marketing strategies based on creating value for customers.

Competitive Strategies

Having identified and evaluated its major competitors, a company now must design broad marketing strategies by which it can gain competitive advantage. But what broad competitive marketing strategies might the company use? Which ones are best for a particular company or for the company's different divisions and products?

Approaches to Marketing Strategy

No one strategy is best for all companies. Each company must determine what makes the most sense given its position in the industry and its objectives, opportunities, and resources. Even within a company, different strategies may be required for different businesses or products. Johnson & Johnson uses one marketing strategy for its leading brands in stable consumer markets, such as BAND-AID, Tylenol, Listerine, or J&J's baby products, and a different marketing strategy for its high-tech health-care businesses and products, such as Monocryl surgical sutures or NeuFlex finger joint implants.

Companies also differ in how they approach the strategy-planning process. Many large firms develop formal competitive marketing strategies and implement them religiously. However, other companies develop strategy in a less formal and orderly fashion. Some companies, such as Harley-Davidson, Red Bull, Virgin Atlantic Airways, and BMW's MINI Cooper unit, succeed by breaking many of the rules of marketing strategy. Such companies don't operate large marketing departments, conduct expensive marketing research, spell out elaborate competitive strategies, and spend huge sums on advertising. Instead, they sketch out strategies on the fly, stretch their limited resources, live close to their customers, and create more satisfying solutions to customer needs. They form buyer's clubs, use buzz marketing, and focus on winning customer loyalty. It seems that not all marketing must follow in the footsteps of marketing giants such as Nike and P&G.

In fact, approaches to marketing strategy and practice often pass through three stages—entrepreneurial marketing, formulated marketing, and intrepreneurial marketing:

- *Entrepreneurial marketing:* Most companies are started by individuals who live by their wits. For example, in the beginning, Robert Ehrlich, founder and CEO of Pirate

Brands, a snack food company, didn't believe in formal marketing—or formal anything else. Pirate Brands markets a pantry full of all-baked, all-natural, trans-fat-free, and gluten-free snacks, including favorites such as Pirate's Booty, Potato Flyers, Smart Puffs, and Tings. Over the past 25 years, Ehrlich has built Pirate Brands into a thriving $100-million business that's become a thorn in the paw of snack food lions like Nabisco and Frito-Lay.[10]

But until only a few years ago, Ehrlich did that with virtually no formal marketing. New-product development was whatever popped into his head. Product names and advertising slogans—just whatever came to him at the time. Ehrlich's cartoonist friend from *Mad Magazine* helped him design packaging and labels. Promotion consisted of 20 guys dressed as pirates handing out snack samples at grocery stores around the country. "We do no marketing," Ehrlich announced proudly at the time. "Zero." When it came to marketing, he said, "There's no real thought to it. We're not Exxon Mobil, thank you very much. We don't want to be."

- *Formulated marketing:* As small companies achieve success, they inevitably move toward more-formulated marketing. They develop formal marketing strategies and adhere to them closely. For example, as Pirate Brands has grown, it now takes a more formal approach to product development and its public relations and distributor relations strategies. It has also developed more formal customer outreach efforts, such as a full-feature Web page, a Facebook page, a "Booty Blog," and a Captain's Newsletter, which features product updates, coupons, special offers, and event listings. Although Pirate Brands will no doubt remain less formal in its marketing than the Frito-Lays of the marketing world, as it grows, it will adopt more-developed marketing tools.

- *Intrepreneurial marketing:* Many large and mature companies get stuck in formulated marketing. They pore over the latest Nielsen numbers, scan market research reports, and try to fine-tune their competitive strategies and programs. These companies sometimes lose the marketing creativity and passion they had at the start. They now need to reestablish within their companies the entrepreneurial spirit and actions that made them successful in the first place. They need to encourage more marketing initiative and "intrepreneurship" at the local level.

For example, intrepreneurial thinking has helped the Virgin Group grow into a collection of more 200 companies, from established giants such as Virgin Atlantic Airways and Virgin Mobile to smaller start-ups such as Virgin Games (online and mobile casinos) and Virgin Wines (which sells handcrafted, international wines online). ● Virgin founder Richard Branson attributes the company's success to its intrepreneurial culture. "Virgin could never have grown [so successfully] were it not for a steady stream of intrepreneurs who found and developed new opportunities, often leading efforts that went against the grain," he says.[11] According to Branson, intrepreneurship starts at the top. The key is to give key employees the freedom and support that enables them to pursue their visions and develop new products, services, and systems. The CEO should be a "chief enabling officer" who seeks out people with an intrapreneurial bent, supports them, and then steps back and lets them operate in their own way. Branson did this when Virgin entered the mobile phone industry. "We had no experience, so we looked for our rivals' best managers, hired them away, took off their ties, and gave them the freedom to set up their own ventures within the Virgin Group." The new managers became so immersed in running the new business that they didn't really feel like employees. They felt more like owners in an entrepreneurial venture.

The bottom line is that there are many approaches to developing effective competitive marketing strategies. There will be a constant tension between the formulated side of marketing and the creative side. It is easier to learn the formulated side of marketing, which has occupied most of our attention in this

● **Intrepreneurial marketing: According to founder Richard Branson (above), intrepreneurial thinking has helped the Virgin Group grow successfully into a collection of more 200 companies, from established giants such as Virgin Atlantic Airways and Virgin Mobile to smaller start-ups such as Virgin Wines.**
AP Photo/Bridget Jones

book. But we have also seen how marketing creativity and passion in the strategies of many of the companies studied—whether small or large, new or mature—have helped to build and maintain success in the marketplace. With this in mind, we now look at the broad competitive marketing strategies companies can use.

Basic Competitive Strategies

Three decades ago, Michael Porter suggested four basic competitive positioning strategies that companies can follow—three winning strategies and one losing one.[12] The three winning strategies are as follows:

- *Overall cost leadership:* Here the company works hard to achieve the lowest production and distribution costs. Low costs let it price lower than its competitors and win a large market share. Texas Instruments, Walmart, and JetBlue Airways are leading practitioners of this strategy.
- *Differentiation:* Here the company concentrates on creating a highly differentiated product line and marketing program so that it comes across as the class leader in the industry. Most customers would prefer to own this brand if its price is not too high. Nike and Caterpillar follow this strategy in sports apparel and heavy construction equipment, respectively.
- *Focus:* Here the company focuses its effort on serving a few market segments well rather than going after the whole market. For example, Ritz-Carlton focuses on the top 5 percent of corporate and leisure travelers. Tetra Food supplies 60 percent of pet tropical fish food—it's "the leader in underwater wonder." Similarly, Hohner owns a stunning 85 percent of the harmonica market.

Companies that pursue a clear strategy—one of the above—will likely perform well. The firm that carries out that strategy best will make the most profits. But firms that do not pursue a clear strategy—*middle-of-the-roaders*—do the worst. Sears and Holiday Inn encountered difficult times because they did not stand out as the lowest in cost, highest in perceived value, or best in serving some market segment. Middle-of-the-roaders try to be good on all strategic counts but end up being not very good at anything.

Two marketing consultants, Michael Treacy and Fred Wiersema, offer a more customer-centered classification of competitive marketing strategies.[13] They suggest that companies gain leadership positions by delivering superior value to their customers. Companies can pursue any of three strategies—called *value disciplines*—for delivering superior customer value:

- *Operational excellence:* The company provides superior value by leading its industry in price and convenience. It works to reduce costs and create a lean and efficient value delivery system. It serves customers who want reliable, good-quality products or services but want them cheaply and easily. Examples include Walmart, Costco, and Southwest Airlines.

- *Customer intimacy:* The company provides superior value by precisely segmenting its markets and tailoring its products or services to exactly match the needs of targeted customers. It specializes in satisfying unique customer needs through a close relationship with and intimate knowledge of the customer. It empowers its people to respond quickly to customer needs. Customer-intimate companies serve customers who are willing to pay a premium to get precisely what they want. They will do almost anything to build long-term customer loyalty and to capture customer lifetime value.

For example, consider Ritz-Carlton hotels. ● Year after year, Ritz-Carlton ranks at or near the top of the hospitality industry in terms of customer satisfaction. Its passion for satisfying customers is summed up in the company's credo, which promises that its luxury hotels will deliver a truly memorable experience—one that "enlivens the senses, instills well-being, and fulfills even the unexpressed wishes and needs of our guests."[14]

Check into any Ritz-Carlton hotel around the world, and you'll be amazed by the company's fervent dedication to anticipating and meeting even your slightest need. Without ever asking, they seem to know that you're allergic to peanuts and want a

● **Customer intimacy:** The Ritz-Carlton promises that the company's luxury hotels will deliver a truly memorable experience—one that "enlivens the senses, instills well-being, and fulfills even the unexpressed wishes and needs of our guests."
AFP/Getty Images

king-size bed, a nonallergenic pillow, the blinds open when you arrive, and breakfast with decaffeinated coffee in your room. Each day, hotel staffers—from those at the front desk to those in maintenance and housekeeping—discreetly observe and record even the smallest guest preferences. Then, every morning, each hotel reviews the files of all new arrivals who have previously stayed at a Ritz-Carlton and prepares a list of suggested extra touches that might delight each guest.

Once they identify a special customer need, Ritz-Carlton employees go to legendary extremes to meet it. For example, to serve the needs of a guest with food allergies, a Ritz-Carlton chef in Bali located special eggs and milk in a small grocery store in another country and had them delivered to the hotel. In another case, when the hotel's laundry service failed to remove a stain on a guest's suit before the guest departed, the hotel manager traveled to the guest's house and personally delivered a reimbursement check for the cost of the suit. According to one Ritz-Carlton manager, if the chain gets hold of a picture of a guest's pet, it will make a copy, have it framed, and display it in the guest's room in whatever Ritz-Carlton the guest visits. As a result of such customer service heroics, an amazing 95 percent of departing guests report that their stay has been a truly memorable experience. More than 90 percent of Ritz-Carlton's delighted customers return.

- *Product leadership:* The company provides superior value by offering a continuous stream of leading-edge products or services. It aims to make its own and competing products obsolete. Product leaders are open to new ideas, relentlessly pursue new solutions, and work to get new products to market quickly. They serve customers who want state-of-the-art products and services, regardless of the costs in terms of price or inconvenience. Examples include Samsung and Apple (see Real Marketing 18.2).

Some companies successfully pursue more than one value discipline at the same time. For example, FedEx excels at both operational excellence and customer intimacy. However, such companies are rare; few firms can be the best at more than one of these disciplines. By trying to be *good at all* value disciplines, a company usually ends up being *best at none*.

Thus, most excellent companies focus on and excel at a single value discipline, while meeting industry standards on the other two. Such companies design their entire value delivery network to single-mindedly support the chosen discipline. For example, Walmart knows that customer intimacy and product leadership are important. Compared with other discounters, it offers very good customer service and an excellent product assortment. Still, it purposely offers less customer service and less product depth than does Nordstrom or Williams-Sonoma, which pursue customer intimacy. Instead, Walmart focuses obsessively on operational excellence—on reducing costs and streamlining its order-to-delivery process to make it convenient for customers to buy just the right products at the lowest prices.

By the same token, the Ritz-Carlton wants to be efficient and employ the latest technologies. But what really sets the luxury hotel chain apart is its customer intimacy. The Ritz-Carlton creates custom-designed experiences to coddle its customers.

Classifying competitive strategies as value disciplines is appealing. It defines marketing strategy in terms of the single-minded pursuit of delivering superior value to customers. Each value discipline defines a specific way to build lasting customer relationships.

Competitive Positions

Firms competing in a given target market, at any point in time, differ in their objectives and resources. Some firms are large; others are small. Some have many resources; others are strapped for funds. Some are mature and established; others new and fresh. Some strive for rapid market share growth; others for long-term profits. And these firms occupy different competitive positions in the target market.

FIGURE | 18.2
Competitive Market Positions and Roles

Each market position calls for a different competitive strategy. For example, the market leader wants to expand total demand and protect or expand its share. Market nichers seek market segments that are big enough to be profitable but small enough to be of little interest to major competitors.

Market leader	Market challengers	Market followers	Market nichers
40%	30%	20%	10%

Real Marketing 18.2

Product Leader Apple: The Keeper of All Things Cool

In a now-classic ad shown during Super Bowl XVIII in 1984, Apple introduced the world to a new personal computer called the Macintosh, the first computer ever to feature a graphic user interface and mouse. The innovative Mac changed the computer industry forever. It gained an immediate and enthusiastic throng of fans, and it set in motion a chain of events that would establish Apple as one of the world's most innovative product leaders.

Today, nearly three decades later, few brands engender such intense loyalty as that found in the hearts of core Apple buyers. At one end are the quietly satisfied Mac, iPod, iPhone, and iPad users, folks who own an Apple device and use it for e-mail, texting, browsing, and social networking. At the other extreme, however, are the Mac zealots—the so-called MacHeads or Macolytes. There's at least a little MacHead in every Apple customer. Apple enthusiasts see late Apple founder Steve Jobs as the Walt Disney of technology. Say the word "Apple" in front of hard-core fans and they'll go into rhapsodies about the superiority of the brand. Buy an Apple product and you join a whole community of fervent fellow believers.

What is it that makes Apple buyers so loyal? Why do they buy a MacBook instead of an HP or a Dell, or an iPhone instead of a Samsung, LG, or Motorola? Ask the true believers, and they'll tell you simply that Apple's products work better and are simpler to use. From the beginning, Apple has been a product leader, churning out one cutting-edge product after another. But those products aren't just the creations of engineers and designers sealed off from the world behind the closed doors of Apple laboratories. Apple's product leader prowess results from putting top priority on understanding its customers and what makes them tick, then creating products that put customers at the front of the crowd.

Apple has shown "a marketing and creative genius with a rare ability to get inside the imaginations of consumers and understand what will captivate them," says one analyst. Apple has been "obsessed with the Apple user's experience." Apple's obsession with understanding customers and deepening their Apple experience shows in everything the company does.

Many tech companies make products that just occupy space and do work. By contrast, Apple creates "life-feels-good" experiences.

Making products customers want—usually before consumers themselves even know what they want—has resulted in one Apple-led revolution after another. In the last decade alone, the iPod, iTunes, iPhone, and iPad have all created whole new product categories where none previously existed. In each case, Apple not only pioneered the category but remains the dominant market leader. For example, the iPod still holds more than 78 percent of the MP3 market. And despite an onslaught of competing products and predictions of declining market share for iPad in a maturing market, Apple's share of the tablet market rose to 68 percent last year.

Apple's innovative product leadership extends well beyond its products. Just peek inside an Apple store, where the "life-feels-good" experiences abound. The store design is clean, simple, and just oozing with style—much like an Apple iPad or a featherweight MacBook Air. The bustling stores feel more like community centers than retail outlets. Apple stores encourage a lot of purchasing, to be sure. But they also encourage lingering, with tables full of fully functioning Macs, iPods, iPads, and iPhones sitting out for visitors to try and dozens of laid-back Apple employees close at hand to answer questions and cater to every whim. You don't just visit an Apple store—you experience it. Apple combines product leadership with enough customer intimacy thrown in to create an experience that no other consumer electronics company can match.

According to one industry expert, "some of the most amazing companies of the coming few years will be businesses that understand how to wrap technology beautifully around human needs so that it matters to people." That's an apt description of Apple and its core segment of enthusiastic disciples. *Fast Company* seems to agree. It recently crowned Apple "The world's most innovative company" for the second year in a row. In the consumer electronics industry, Apple has dominated the American Consumer Satisfaction Index for the past eight years, leading this year's field with another record-setting score of 87—a full 9 points above its nearest industry competitor.

Product leadership and the consumer love affair with Apple have produced stunning sales and profit results. In the past five years, despite the worst economic conditions since the Great Depression, Apple sales have more than quadrupled to nearly $110 billion, including a whopping 200 percent increase in the previous two years alone. Profits have skyrocketed sevenfold to $26 billion—an incredible 24 percent net margin. During that time,

Product leadership: Apple churns out one cutting-edge product after another, often creating whole new product categories. Apple's diehard fans have anointed the brand "the keeper of all things cool."

© Michael Nagle/Liaison/Getty Images

Apple's stock price has increased more than 300 percent.

The recent passing of founder and CEO Steve Jobs has cast a small shadow of doubt on the future of the company. Perhaps no large corporation in history has been so strongly tied to the creative genius of its leader. But Jobs left a legacy that many believe will carry on. And for now, product leader Apple continues to soar. "To say Apple is hot just doesn't do the company justice," concludes one Apple watcher.

"Apple is smoking, searing, blisteringly hot, not to mention hip, with a side order of funky. Gadget geeks around the world have crowned Apple the keeper of all things cool." Just ask your Macolyte friends. In fact, don't bother—they've probably already brought it up.

Sources: "For Walking the Talk," *Fast Company*, March, 2012, www.fastcompany.com/most-innovative-companies/2012/apple; Steve Maich, "Nowhere to Go But Down," *Maclean's,* May 9, 2005, p. 32; Jim Joseph, "How Do I Love Thee, Apple? Let Me Count the Ways," *Brandweek*, May 24, 2010, p. 30; Henrik Werdelin, "Three Things Google Can Learn from Apple," *Fast Company,* July 13, 2010, www.fastcompany.com/1669457/3-things-google-can-learn-from-apple; "Apple Crushes Profit Estimates and iPhone, iPod, and iPad Sales Soar," CNBC, January 24, 2012, www.cnbc.com/id/46103211/Apple_Crushes_Profit_Estimates_as_iPhone_iPod_Sales_Soar; and information found at www.fortune.com and www.apple.com, accessed October 2012.

Market leader

The firm in an industry with the largest market share.

Market challenger

A runner-up firm that is fighting hard to increase its market share in an industry.

Market follower

A runner-up firm that wants to hold its share in an industry without rocking the boat.

Market nicher

A firm that serves small segments that the other firms in an industry overlook or ignore.

We now examine competitive strategies based on the roles firms play in the target market—leader, challenger, follower, or nicher. Suppose that an industry contains the firms shown in ● **Figure 18.2**. Forty percent of the market is in the hands of the **market leader**, the firm with the largest market share. Another 30 percent is in the hands of **market challengers**, runner-up firms that are fighting hard to increase their market share. Another 20 percent is in the hands of **market followers**, other runner-up firms that want to hold their share without rocking the boat. The remaining 10 percent is in the hands of **market nichers**, firms that serve small segments not being pursued by other firms.

● **Table 18.1** shows specific marketing strategies that are available to market leaders, challengers, followers, and nichers.[15] Remember, however, that these classifications often do not apply to a whole company but only to its position in a specific industry. Large companies such as GE, Microsoft, P&G, or Disney might be leaders in some markets and nichers in others. For example, P&G leads in many segments, such as laundry detergents and shampoo. But it challenges Unilever in hand soaps and Kimberly-Clark in facial tissues. Such companies often use different strategies for different business units or products, depending on the competitive situations of each.

Market Leader Strategies

Most industries contain an acknowledged market leader. The leader has the largest market share and usually leads the other firms in price changes, new-product introductions, distribution coverage, and promotion spending. The leader may or may not be admired or respected, but other firms concede its dominance. Competitors focus on the leader as a company to challenge, imitate, or avoid. Some of the best-known market leaders are Walmart (retailing), McDonald's (fast food), Verizon (wireless), Coca-Cola (beverages), Caterpillar (earth-moving equipment), Nike (athletic footwear and apparel), Facebook (online social networking), and Google (Internet search services).

● **Table 18.1** │ **Strategies for Market Leaders, Challengers, Followers, and Nichers**

Market Leader Strategies	Market Challenger Strategies	Market Follower Strategies	Market Nicher Strategies
Expand total market	Full frontal attack	Follow closely	By customer, market, quality-price, service
Protect market share	Indirect attack	Follow at a distance	
Expand market share			Multiple niching

A leader's life is not easy. It must maintain a constant watch. Other firms keep challenging its strengths or trying to take advantage of its weaknesses. The market leader can easily miss a turn in the market and plunge into second or third place. A product innovation may come along and hurt the leader (as when Apple developed the iPod and took the market lead from Sony's Walkman portable audio devices). The leader might grow arrogant or complacent and misjudge the competition (as when Sears lost its lead to Walmart). Or the leader might look old-fashioned against new and peppier rivals (as when Gap lost serious ground to stylish niche brands such as 7 for All Mankind and American Apparel and mall brands such as Abercrombie & Fitch, Aeropostale, and J. Crew).

To remain number one, leading firms can take any of three actions. First, they can find ways to expand total demand. Second, they can protect their current market share through good defensive and offensive actions. Third, they can try to expand their market share further, even if market size remains constant.

Expanding Total Demand

The leading firm normally gains the most when the total market expands. If Americans eat more fast food, McDonald's stands to gain the most because it holds more than three times the fast-food market share of nearest competitors Subway and Burger King. If McDonald's can convince more Americans that fast food is the best eating-out choice in these economic times, it will benefit more than its competitors.

Market leaders can expand the market by developing new users, new uses, and more usage of its products. They usually can find *new users* or untapped market segments in many places. For example, Weight Watchers has typically targeted its weight-loss programs toward women. Recently, however, it stepped up its efforts to attract male customers, with the help of its first male spokesperson, former NBA star Charles Barkley. It launched a product online called Weight Watchers for Men, aimed at helping men deal with weight issues. "When you have a role model like Charles Barkley—who's about as manly as anybody can possibly get, who's actually eating fruits and vegetables for the first time in his life—it signals to men everywhere that this is OK to do," says Weight Watchers' David Kirchoff. Weight Watchers is also looking for new users by expanding its online presence, launching mobile apps, and targeting emerging markets such as China.[16]

Marketers can expand markets by discovering and promoting *new uses* for the product. ● For example, the WD-40 Company's real knack for expanding the market by finding new uses has made this popular substance one of the truly essential survival items in most American homes:[17]

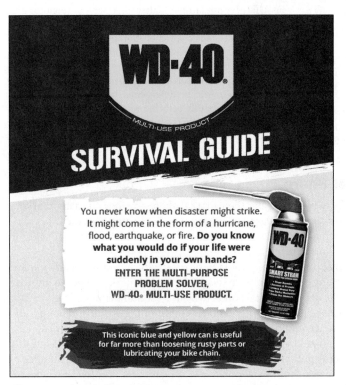

● **Promoting new uses:** The WD-40 Company's knack for finding new uses has made this popular substance one of the truly essential survival items in most American homes.

WD-40 MUP is the sole property of the WD-40 Company

Some years ago, the company launched a search to uncover 2,000 unique uses for WD-40 Multi-Use Product. After receiving 300,000 individual submissions, it narrowed the list to the best 2,000, which are now posted on the company's Web site. Some consumers suggested simple and practical uses, such as cleaning crayon marks from just about anywhere or freeing stuck LEGO bricks. One teacher uses WD-40 to clean old chalkboards in her classroom. "Amazingly, the boards started coming to life again," she reported. "Not only were they restored, but years of masking and Scotch tape residue came off as well." Others, however, reported some pretty unusual applications. One man uses WD-40 to polish his glass eye; another uses it to remove a prosthetic leg. And did you hear about the nude burglary suspect who had wedged himself in a vent at a cafe in Denver? The fire department extracted him with a large dose of WD-40. Or how about the Mississippi naval officer who used WD-40 to repel an angry bear? Then there's the college student who wrote to say that a friend's nightly amorous activities in the next room were causing everyone in his dorm to lose sleep—he solved the problem by treating the squeaky bedsprings with WD-40. "This iconic blue and yellow can is useful for far more than loosening rusty parts or lubricating your bike chain," says the company.

Finally, market leaders can encourage *more usage* by convincing people to use the product more often or use more per occasion. For example, Campbell urges people to eat soup and other Campbell's products more often by running ads containing new recipes. At the Campbell's Kitchen Web site (www.campbellskitchen.com), visitors can search for or exchange recipes, create their own personal recipe box, learn ways to eat healthier, and sign up for a daily or weekly Meal Mail program. At the Campbell's Facebook and Twitter sites, consumers can join in on Campbell's Kitchen Community conversations.

Protecting Market Share

While trying to expand total market size, the leading firm also must protect its current business against competitors' attacks. Walmart must constantly guard against Target and Costco; Caterpillar against Komatsu; and McDonald's against Wendy's and Burger King.

What can the market leader do to protect its position? First, it must prevent or fix weaknesses that provide opportunities for competitors. It must always fulfill its value promise and work tirelessly to keep strong relationships with valued customers. Its prices must remain consistent with the value that customers see in the brand. The leader should "plug holes" so that competitors do not jump in.

But the best defense is a good offense, and the best response is *continuous innovation*. The market leader refuses to be content with the way things are and leads the industry in new products, customer services, distribution effectiveness, promotion, and cost cutting. It keeps increasing its competitive effectiveness and value to customers. And when attacked by challengers, the market leader reacts decisively. For example, in the laundry products category, market leader P&G has been relentless in its offense against challengers such as Unilever.

In one of the classic marketing battles of the past century, an aggressive P&G simply overpowered challenger Unilever in the U.S. laundry market. A decade ago, despite its already dominating 50 percent U.S. laundry detergent market share, P&G continued to hammer Unilever and other competitors with a barrage of new-product introductions backed by heavy marketing spending. By 2007, P&G was outgunning Unilever on annual spending in the category by a whopping $218 million to $25 million. By 2008, its aggressive marketing plus new products such as Tide with Downy, Tide Coldwater, and Tide Simple Pleasures had boosted P&G to an incredible 62.5 percent laundry-detergent market share, versus Unilever's relatively paltry 12.9 percent (including Unilever's All, Wisk, and Surf brands). P&G also dominated the U.S. fabric softener market with a 66 percent share versus Unilever's 8.4 percent (Unilever's Snuggle brand). ⬤ In the face of P&G's relentless assault, in mid-2008, Unilever finally threw in the towel and sold its North American detergents business. Although Unilever successfully sells laundry brands such as Surf, Omo, Comfort, and Cif globally, it has yet to return to the P&G-dominated U.S. market.[18]

⬤ **Protecting market share: In the face of market leader P&G's relentless assault in the laundry war, Unilever threw in the towel by putting its U.S. detergents business up for sale.**

Amanda Kamen

Expanding Market Share

Market leaders also can grow by increasing their market shares further. In many markets, small market share increases mean very large sales increases. For example, in the U.S. shampoo market, a 1 percent increase in market share is worth $14 million in annual sales; in carbonated soft drinks, $757 million![19]

Studies have shown that, on average, profitability rises with increasing market share. Because of these findings, many companies have sought expanded market shares to improve profitability. GE, for example, declared that it wants to be at least number one or two in each of its markets or else get out. GE shed its computer, air-conditioning, small appliances, and television businesses because it could not achieve top-dog position in those industries.

However, some studies have found that many industries contain one or a few highly profitable large firms, several profitable and more focused firms, and a large number of medium-sized firms with poorer profit performance. It appears that profitability increases as a business gains share relative to competitors in its *served market*. For example, Lexus holds only a small share of the total car market, but it earns a high profit because it is the leading brand in the luxury-performance car segment. And it has achieved this high share in its served market because it does other things right, such as producing high-quality products, creating outstanding service experiences, and building close customer relationships.

Companies must not think, however, that gaining increased market share will automatically improve profitability. Much depends on their strategy for gaining increased share. There are many high-share companies with low profitability and many low-share companies with high profitability. The cost of buying higher market share may far exceed the returns. Higher shares tend to produce higher profits only when unit costs fall with increased market share or when the company offers a superior-quality product and charges a premium price that more than covers the cost of offering higher quality.

Market Challenger Strategies

Firms that are second, third, or lower in an industry are sometimes quite large, such as PepsiCo, Ford, Lowe's, Hertz, and AT&T. These runner-up firms can adopt one of two competitive strategies: They can challenge the market leader and other competitors in an aggressive bid for more market share (market challengers), or they can play along with competitors and not rock the boat (market followers).

A market challenger must first define which competitors to challenge and its strategic objective. The challenger can attack the market leader, a high-risk but potentially high-gain strategy. Its goal might be to take over market leadership. Or the challenger's objective may simply be to wrest more market share.

Although it might seem that the market leader has the most going for it, challengers often have what some strategists call a "second-mover advantage." The challenger observes what has made the market leader successful and improves on it. For example, Home Depot invented the home-improvement superstore. However, after observing Home Depot's success, number two Lowe's, with its brighter stores, wider aisles, and arguably more helpful salespeople, has positioned itself as the friendly alternative to Big Bad Orange. Over the past decade, follower Lowe's has consistently grown faster and more profitably than Home Depot.

In fact, challengers often become market leaders by imitating and improving on the ideas of pioneering processors. For example, Chrysler invented the modern minivan and led in that market for more than a decade. However, then-followers Honda and Toyota improved on the concept and now dominate the minivan market. Similarly, McDonald's first imitated and then mastered the fast-food system first pioneered by White Castle. And founder Sam Walton admitted that Walmart borrowed most of its practices from discount pioneer Sol Price's FedMart and Price Club chains and then perfected them to become today's dominant retailer.[20]

Alternatively, the challenger can avoid the leader and instead challenge firms its own size or smaller local and regional firms. These smaller firms may be underfinanced and not serving their customers well. Several of the major beer companies grew to their present size not by challenging large competitors but by gobbling up small local or regional competitors. For example, SABMiller became the world's number two brewer by acquiring brands such as Miller, Molson, Coors, and dozens of others. If the challenger goes after a small local company, its objective may be to put that company out of business. The important point remains: The challenger must choose its opponents carefully and have a clearly defined and attainable objective.

How can the market challenger best attack the chosen competitor and achieve its strategic objectives? It may launch a full *frontal attack*, matching the competitor's product, advertising, price, and distribution efforts. It attacks the competitor's strengths rather than its weaknesses. The outcome depends on who has the greater strength and endurance. PepsiCo challenges Coca-Cola in this way.

If the market challenger has fewer resources than the competitor, however, a frontal attack makes little sense. Thus, many new market entrants avoid frontal attacks, knowing that market leaders can head them off with ad blitzes, price wars, and other retaliations. Rather than challenging head-on, the challenger can make an *indirect attack* on the competitor's weaknesses or on gaps in the competitor's market coverage. It can carve out toeholds using tactics that established leaders have trouble responding to or choose to ignore.

For example, consider how European challenger Red Bull entered the U.S. soft drink market in the late 1990s against market leaders Coca-Cola and PepsiCo.[21] ● Red Bull tackled the leaders indirectly by selling a high-priced niche product in nontraditional distribution points. "It started by selling Red Bull through unconventional outlets not dominated by the market leaders, such as bars and nightclubs, where twenty-somethings gulped down the caffeine-rich drink so they could dance all night," observes one analyst. Once it had

When it entered the U.S. market, rather than attacking market leaders Coca-Cola and Pepsi directly, Red Bull used indirect, unconventional marketing approaches.

© Clive Sawyer/Alamy

built a core customer base, the brand expanded into more traditional outlets. "Red Bull used the pull of high margins to elbow its way into the corner store, where it now sits in refrigerated bins within arm's length of Coke and Pepsi," says the analyst. Despite rapidly intensifying competition in the United States, Red Bull captures a 44 percent share of the energy drink market.

Market Follower Strategies

Not all runner-up companies want to challenge the market leader. The leader never takes challenges lightly. If the challenger's lure is lower prices, improved service, or additional product features, the market leader can quickly match these to defuse the attack. The leader probably has more staying power in an all-out battle for customers. For example, a few years ago, when Kmart launched its renewed low-price "bluelight special" campaign, directly challenging Walmart's everyday low prices, it started a price war that it couldn't win. Walmart had little trouble fending off Kmart's challenge, leaving Kmart worse off for the attempt. Thus, many firms prefer to follow rather than challenge the market leader.

A follower can gain many advantages. The market leader often bears the huge expenses of developing new products and markets, expanding distribution, and educating the market. By contrast, as with challengers, the market follower can learn from the market leader's experience. It can copy or improve on the leader's products and programs, usually with much less investment. Although the follower will probably not overtake the leader, it often can be as profitable.

Following is not the same as being passive or a carbon copy of the market leader. A follower must know how to hold current customers and win a fair share of new ones. It must find the right balance between following closely enough to win customers from the market leader and following at enough of a distance to avoid retaliation. Each follower tries to bring distinctive advantages to its target market—location, services, financing. A follower is often a major target of attack by challengers. Therefore, the market follower must keep its manufacturing costs and prices low or its product quality and services high. It must also enter new markets as they open up.

Market Nicher Strategies

Almost every industry includes firms that specialize in serving market niches. Instead of pursuing the whole market or even large segments, these firms target subsegments. Nichers are often smaller firms with limited resources. But smaller divisions of larger firms also may pursue niching strategies. Firms with low shares of the total market can be highly successful and profitable through smart niching.

Why is niching profitable? The main reason is that the market nicher ends up knowing the target customer group so well that it meets their needs better than other firms that casually sell to that niche. As a result, the nicher can charge a substantial markup over costs because of the added value. Whereas the mass marketer achieves high volume, the nicher achieves high margins.

Nichers try to find one or more market niches that are safe and profitable. An ideal market niche is big enough to be profitable and has growth potential. It is one that the firm can serve effectively. Perhaps most important, the niche is of little interest to major competitors. And the firm can build the skills and customer goodwill to defend itself against a major competitor as the niche grows and becomes more attractive. For example, car-sharing nicher Zipcar has carved out its own small profitable corner of the huge car-rental market:

Zipcar specializes in renting out cars by the hour or the day. The service isn't for everyone—it doesn't try to be. Instead, it zeros in on narrowly defined lifestyle segments, people who live or work in densely populated neighborhoods in New York City, Boston, Atlanta, San Francisco, London, or one of the more than 18 major metropolitan areas in which Zipcar operates (or on more than 250 college campuses across North America). Owning a car (or a second or third car) in a densely populated urban area is difficult and costly. ● Zipcar lets urban customers focus on driving, not on the complexities of car ownership. It gives them "Wheels when you want them" without the hassle. It also saves money—by living with less, the average Zipster saves $600 a month on car payments, insurance, gas, maintenance, and other car ownership expenses.

By all accounts, the young car-sharing nicher has the pedal to the metal and its tires are smoking. In just the past four years, Zipcar's annual revenues have rocketed more than four-fold to $242 million. Although that's only a small fraction of market leader Enterprise's $14 billion a

Market nichers: Car-sharing nicher Zipcar has carved out its own profitable corner of the huge car-rental market. It gives urban customers "wheels when you want them" without the costs and hassles of car ownership.

Zipcar

year in sales, little Zipcar's rapid growth has caught the eye of the traditional car-rental giants. Enterprise, Hertz, Avis, Thrifty, and even U-Haul now have their own car-sharing operations. But Zipcar has a 10-year head start, cozy relationships in targeted neighborhoods, and a fanatically loyal fan base that the corporate giants will have trouble matching. To Zipsters, Enterprise rents cars, but Zipcar is part of their hectic urban lives.[22]

The key idea in niching is specialization. A market nicher can specialize along any of several market, customer, product, or marketing mix lines. For example, it can specialize in serving one type of *end user*, as when a law firm specializes in the criminal, civil, or business law markets. The nicher can specialize in serving a given *customer-size* group. Many nichers specialize in serving small and midsize customers who are neglected by the majors.

Some nichers focus on one or a few *specific customers*, selling their entire output to a single company, such as Walmart or GM. Still other nichers specialize by *geographic market*, selling only in a certain locality, region, or area of the world. *Quality-price* nichers operate at the low or high end of the market. For example, HP specializes in the high-quality, high-price end of the hand-calculator market. Finally, *service nichers* offer services not available from other firms. For example, LendingTree provides online lending and realty services, connecting homebuyers and sellers with national networks of mortgage lenders and realtors who compete for the customer's business. "When lenders compete," it proclaims, "you win."

Niching carries some major risks. For example, the market niche may dry up, or it might grow to the point that it attracts larger competitors. That is why many companies practice *multiple niching*. By developing two or more niches, a company increases its chances for survival. Even some large firms prefer a multiple niche strategy to serving the total market. For example, as discussed in Chapter 7, apparel maker VF Corporation markets more than 30 lifestyle brands in niche markets ranging from jeanswear, sportswear, and contemporary styles to outdoor gear and imagewear (workwear). For example, VF's Vans unit creates footwear, apparel, and accessories for skate-, surf-, and snowboarders. Its 7 for All Mankind brand offers premium denim and accessories sold in boutiques and high-end department stores. In contrast, the company's Red Kap, Bulwark, and Chef Designs workwear brands provide an array of uniforms and protective apparel for businesses and public agencies, whether it's outfitting a police force or a chef's crew. Together, these separate niche brands combine to make VF a $9.5-billion apparel powerhouse.[23]

Objective 3 ⟶
Illustrate the need for balancing customer and competitor orientations in becoming a truly market-centered organization.

Competitor-centered company
A company whose moves are mainly based on competitors' actions and reactions.

Customer-centered company
A company that focuses on customer developments in designing its marketing strategies and delivering superior value to its target customers.

Balancing Customer and Competitor Orientations

Whether a company is the market leader, challenger, follower, or nicher, it must watch its competitors closely and find the competitive marketing strategy that positions it most effectively. And it must continually adapt its strategies to the fast-changing competitive environment. This question now arises: Can the company spend *too* much time and energy tracking competitors, damaging its customer orientation? The answer is yes. A company can become so competitor centered that it loses its even more important focus on maintaining profitable customer relationships.

A **competitor-centered company** is one that spends most of its time tracking competitors' moves and market shares and trying to find strategies to counter them. This approach has some pluses and minuses. On the positive side, the company develops a fighter orientation, watches for weaknesses in its own position, and searches out competitors' weaknesses. On the negative side, the company becomes too reactive. Rather than carrying out its own customer relationship strategy, it bases its own moves on competitors' moves. As a result, it may end up simply matching or extending industry practices rather than seeking innovative new ways to create more value for customers.

A **customer-centered company**, by contrast, focuses more on customer developments in designing its strategies. Clearly, the customer-centered company is in a better position to identify

FIGURE | 18.3
Evolving Company
Orientations

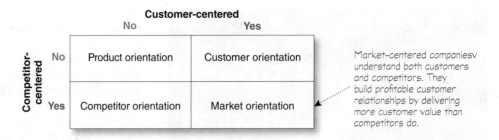

Customer-centered

		No	**Yes**
Competitor-centered	**No**	Product orientation	Customer orientation
	Yes	Competitor orientation	Market orientation

Market-centered companiesv understand both customers and competitors. They build profitable customer relationships by delivering more customer value than competitors do.

new opportunities and set long-run strategies that make sense. By watching customer needs evolve, it can decide what customer groups and what emerging needs are the most important to serve. Then it can concentrate its resources on delivering superior value to target customers.

In practice, today's companies must be **market-centered companies**, watching both their customers and their competitors. But they must not let competitor watching blind them to customer focusing.

 Figure 18.3 shows that companies might have any of four orientations. First, they might be product oriented, paying little attention to either customers or competitors. Next, they might be customer oriented, paying attention to customers. In the third orientation, when a company starts to pay attention to competitors, it becomes competitor oriented. Today, however, companies need to be market oriented, paying balanced attention to both customers and competitors. Rather than simply watching competitors and trying to beat them on current ways of doing business, they need to watch customers and find innovative ways to build profitable customer relationships by delivering more customer value than competitors do.

Market-centered company
A company that pays balanced attention to both customers and competitors in designing its marketing strategies.

Reviewing the Concepts

MyMarketingLab™

Go to **mymktlab.com** to complete the problems marked with this icon ⭐.

Reviewing Objectives and Key Terms

▶ Objectives Review

Today's companies face their toughest competition ever. Understanding customers is an important first step in developing strong customer relationships, but it's not enough. To gain competitive advantage, companies must use this understanding to design market offers that deliver more value than the offers of *competitors* seeking to win over the same customers. This chapter examines how firms analyze their competitors and design effective competitive marketing strategies.

Objective 1 | Discuss the need to understand competitors as well as customers through competitor analysis. (pp 526–533)

To prepare an effective marketing strategy, a company must consider its competitors as well as its customers. Building profitable customer relationships requires satisfying target consumer needs *better than competitors do*. A company must continuously analyze competitors and develop *competitive marketing strategies* that position it effectively against competitors and give it the strongest possible *competitive advantage*.

Competitor analysis first involves identifying the company's major competitors, using both an industry-based and a market-based analysis. The company then gathers information on competitors' objectives, strategies, strengths and weaknesses, and reaction patterns. With this information in hand, it can select competitors to attack or avoid. Competitive intelligence must be collected, interpreted, and distributed continuously. Company marketing managers should be able to obtain full and reliable information about any competitor affecting their decisions.

Objective 2 | Explain the fundamentals of competitive marketing strategies based on creating value for customers. (pp 533–543)

Which competitive marketing strategy makes the most sense depends on the company's industry and on whether it is the market leader, challenger, follower, or nicher. The *market leader* has to mount strategies to expand the total market, protect market share, and expand market share. A *market challenger* is a firm that tries aggressively to expand its market share by attacking the leader, other runner-up companies, or smaller firms in the industry. The challenger can select from a variety of direct or indirect attack strategies.

A *market follower* is a runner-up firm that chooses not to rock the boat, usually from fear that it stands to lose more than it might gain. But the follower is not without a strategy and seeks to use its particular skills to gain market growth. Some followers enjoy a higher rate of return than the leaders in their industry. A *market nicher* is a smaller firm that is unlikely to attract the attention of larger firms. Market nichers often become specialists in some end use, customer size category, specific customer group, geographic area, or service.

<table>
<tr><td>Objective 3</td><td>**Illustrate the need for balancing customer and competitor**</td></tr>
</table>

orientations in becoming a truly market-centered organization. (pp 543–544)

A competitive orientation is important in today's markets, but companies should not overdo their focus on competitors. Companies are more likely to be hurt by emerging consumer needs and new competitors than by existing competitors. *Market-centered companies* that balance customer and competitor considerations are practicing a true market orientation.

Key Terms

Objective 1

Competitive advantage (p 526)
Competitor analysis (p 526)
Competitive marketing strategies (p 526)
Strategic group (p 529)
Benchmarking (p 530)
Customer value analysis (p 531)

Objective 2

Market leader (p 538)
Market challenger (p 538)
Market follower (p 538)
Market nicher (p 538)

Objective 3

Competitor-centered company (p 543)
Customer-centered company (p 543)
Market-centered company (p 544)

Discussion and Critical Thinking

Discussion Questions

✪ 1. Which point of view is best for identifying competitors—industry or market? (AACSB: Communication)

✪ 2. Explain the difference between a good and a bad competitor. (AACSB: Communication; Reflective Thinking)

3. Name and describe the three stages that marketing strategy and practice often pass through. (AACSB: Communication)

4. Describe the three value disciplines for delivering superior customer value and explain why classifying competitive strategies in this way is appealing. (AACSB: Communication)

5. Describe market leaders and the actions they can take to maintain that position. (AACSB: Communication)

✪ 6. Compare and contrast competitor-centered, customer-centered, and market-centered companies. Which orientation is best? (AACSB: Communication; Reflective Thinking)

Critical Thinking Exercises

1. Form a small group and discuss the differences between increasing market share and increasing share of customer. What factors should a company consider when deciding upon which one to focus? (AACSB: Communication; Reflective Thinking)

2. Form a small group and conduct a customer value analysis for five local restaurants. Who are the strong and weak competitors? For the strong competitors, what are their vulnerabilities? (AACSB: Communication; Reflective Thinking)

3. One source of competitive information is product teardowns. Information such as a bill of materials (BOM)—a listing of all the elements of a product and their costs—can be very useful. Find an example of a product teardown with cost information, and discuss the value of that information for competitors. (AACSB: Communication; Reflective Thinking)

Applications and Cases

 ## Marketing Technology Gene Patents

Can a company patent a human gene? According to a federal appeals court, it can. In fact, 80 percent of our genes are patented and "owned" by companies. The latest battle has been with biotechnology company Myriad Genetics. Myriad has been fighting for several years over its patents for two genes—BRCA1 and BRCA2—that the company has isolated and found to signal a woman's risk of developing breast and ovarian cancers. The process of isolating genes is complex and very costly, and patenting the isolated genes allows Myriad exclusivity in providing genetic screenings for these diseases. The American Civil Liberties Union filed a lawsuit claiming that Myriad is trying to patent "products of nature," and that many women will not be able to afford potentially life-saving screening.

Legal experts predicted that a loss for Myriad in this case would have severely threatened DNA-related research in the agricultural, biopharmaceutical, and cosmetics industries. Dissenters argue that patents limit genetic research because only the patent owners are allowed to conduct research on those genes.

✪ 1. Debate the pros and cons of allowing companies to patent genes. (AACSB: Communication; Ethical Reasoning; Reflective Thinking)

2. The U.S. Patent and Trademark Office has granted several patents for DNA sequences in the past. Discuss one example and explain how a patent gives a company a competitive advantage. (AACSB: Communication; Reflective Thinking)

 ## Marketing Ethics Right to Repair

Automobiles have become so complicated that mechanics need computers to diagnose problems. Independent car mechanics may have the computers, but they don't have the codes or tools necessary to diagnose and fix problems on newer-model cars. Those are reserved for car makers' dealerships. Some critics claim that creates an unfair advantage for auto dealerships over independent mechanics and auto-parts retailers and keeps repair prices higher for consumers. The Massachusetts Right to Repair Coalition put a stop to that by first getting a right-to-repair initiative on the November 2012 ballot, but it then got the state's legislature and governor to sign it into law before the vote even took place. In that state, car makers must make the diagnostic information available. On a national level, the Motor Vehicle Owner's Right

to Repair Act was introduced in the House of Representatives in 2011. Of course, automakers and dealerships oppose these initiatives. Opponents claim that right-to-repair initiatives will allow auto-parts makers access to manufacturers' proprietary information as well as endanger the safety of consumers due to possibly faulty repairs. Supporters of the initiatives say manufacturers are just looking to keep their unfair advantage and protect their repair businesses.

1. What is the status of the Motor Vehicle Owner's Right to Repair Act? If it has not become law, explain why. If it has, what are the implications of the law? (AACSB: Communication; Reflective Thinking)

 ## Marketing by the Numbers Market Share

Consumers will always need to purchase groceries, making this a $700 billion industry. But where they shop for groceries has changed with the entry of big-box discounters such as Walmart and Target. Almost 25 years ago, executives at Walmart made a strategic decision to expand into the grocery industry. Now more than half of Walmart's sales are from this category. Walmart has more than 3,000 Supercenters with full grocery stores and another 200 smaller "Neighborhood Markets" that offer primarily groceries. Walmart captures more than $145 billion of the $700 billion U.S. consumers spend on groceries annually. Walmart's Sam's Club grabs another $30 billion of annual

grocery sales. As a result, the share of grocery sales captured by traditional supermarkets fell to 51 percent in 2011, a 23 percent drop from 2000.

1. Calculate Walmart's market share in the grocery industry. How much sales revenue is each share point worth in this industry? (AACSB: Communication; Analytical Reasoning)

2. How have traditional supermarkets responded to the threat posed by Walmart's entry into this industry? Suggest strategies to help stem the loss of market share to superstores such as Walmart and Target. (AACSB: Communication; Reflective Thinking)

 ## Video Case Umpqua Bank

The retail banking industry has become very competitive. And with a few powerhouses that dominate the market, how is a small bank to thrive? By differentiating itself through a competitive advantage that the big guys can't touch.

That's exactly what Umpqua has done. One step inside a branch of this Oregon-based community bank and it is immediately

apparent that this is not your typical Christmas club savings account/free toaster bank. Umpqua has created a business model that has transformed banking from retail drudgery to a holistic experience. Umpqua has created an environment where people just love to hang out. It not only has its own music download service featuring local artists, it even has its own blend of coffee.

But under all these bells and whistles lies the core of what makes Umpqua so different: a rigorous service culture where every branch and each employee gets measured on how well they serve customers. That's why every customer feels like they get the help and attention they need from employees.

After viewing the video featuring Umpqua Bank, answer the following questions about creating competitive advantage:

1. With what companies does Umpqua compete?

2. What is Umpqua's competitive advantage?

3. Do you think that Umpqua will be able to maintain this advantage in the long run? Why or why not?

Company Case Ford: Resurrecting an Iconic Company

The old phrase, "The bigger they are, the harder they fall," describes perfectly what happened to the U.S. auto industry during the first 10 years of this century. Consider Ford. In 1998, the iconic company accounted for 25 percent of all cars and trucks sold. Its F-series pickup was the best-selling vehicle on the planet, with more than 800,000 units rolling off assembly lines. The Ford Explorer held the top slot in the hot SUV market. And the Ford Taurus had been a perennial contender for the top-selling sedan. Ford was #2 on the Fortune 500 (GM was #1), with $153 billion in revenues. A strong stock price gave Ford a market value of $73 billion. According to Interbrand, the Ford brand alone was the sixth most valuable brand in the world, worth $36 billion.

But in only 10 years, Ford's position at the top crumbled. In 2008, Ford's market share sat at just 14 percent. Revenues had dropped to $146 billion and the company lost $14.7 billion, the biggest loss in its history. Its stock price had plummeted to only $2 a share, erasing 93 percent of Ford's market value. And Ford was no longer a top-10 brand. It had dropped to the 49th position on the Interbrand top-100 list, worth only $7 billion. Ford was on the verge of collapse.

Ford could have blamed its misfortunes on the fact that the entire auto industry was reeling by 2008. High gas prices and the weakest global economy in over 70 years had made a mess of automobile sales. But that wouldn't explain Ford's drastic drop in market share or the magnitude of its losses relative to the rest of the industry. Ford was in far worse shape than most car companies.

Looking back, it's clear that Ford had taken its eye off the market. It had become too dependent on gas-guzzling trucks and SUVs and could not shift quickly enough to more fuel-efficient vehicles. Its vehicle quality had suffered and its operations were bloated with excessive costs. In a quest to serve every customer segment—acquiring Land Rover, Volvo, Aston Martin, and Jaguar—Ford had lost touch with the needs of any specific customer segment. All those luxury brands were sapping valuable company resources as well. Finally, the company's innovation was at an all-time low. Mark Fields, Ford's president for the Americas, adds, "We used to have a saying in the company that we were a fast follower. Which meant we were slow."

A New Direction

Even as Ford's financials looked their worst in years, a strategy was already under way to resurrect the company. In 2006, Ford had brought in an industry outsider—Alan Mulally—to perform CPR on the ailing giant. As he took the reins as Ford's new CEO, a cheerful and fresh-faced Mulally exuded optimism. "I am here to save an American and global icon," he declared.

Mulally got to work right away. He cut labor costs by almost 22 percent, bringing the company more in line with new industry leader Toyota. He shuttered unprofitable factories and cut out as much operational fat as possible. In 2008, as GM and Chrysler held out their hats for a government bailout, Ford managed to raise cash the old-fashioned way—by borrowing from a bank to the tune of $23.5 billion. By remaining financially independent, Ford avoided giving Uncle Sam a say in how the company was run. It also avoided bankruptcy, a fate that befell its two Detroit siblings.

But the move that put Ford back on the highway was the crafting of a good-old-fashioned mission statement. Mulally ordered up small plastic cards that Ford's 200,000 employees could carry in their wallets featuring what he called "Expected Behaviors." Those expectations were really four goals that Mulally fully believed would make the company competitive again. To Mulally, this was sacred text. "This is me," he said. "I wrote it. It's what I believe in. You can't make this [stuff] up."

Focus on the Ford Brand. According to Mulally, "Nobody buys a house of brands." It was the Ford name and the legacy of the Ford family that had propelled the company to greatness. Mulally considered the conglomeration of automotive companies a failed experiment and immediately set out to divest the company of Jaguar, Volvo, Aston Martin, and Land Rover. He even went one step further. Ford's storied Mercury division had always had the mission of providing Ford with a mid-priced car that fit between inexpensive Ford models and its more luxurious Lincolns. But Mercury was a dying brand, so Mulally gave it the axe.

Compete in Every Market Segment with Carefully Defined Products. Even with only the Ford and Lincoln divisions left, Mulally was convinced that Ford could compete in all major industry segments: cars, SUVs, and small, medium, and large trucks. Mulally loves to tell the story of how he started revamping Ford's product line:

> I arrive here, and the first day I say, "Let's go look at the product lineup." And they lay it out, and I said, "Where's the Taurus?" They said, "Well, we killed it." I said, "What do you mean, you killed it?" "Well, we made a couple that looked like a football. They didn't sell very well, so we stopped it." "You stopped the Taurus?" I said. "How many billions of dollars does it cost to build brand loyalty around a name?" "Well, we thought it was so damaged that we named it the Five Hundred." I said, "Well, you've got until tomorrow to find a vehicle to put the Taurus name on because that's why I'm here. Then you have two years to make the coolest vehicle that you can possibly make."

Mulally had good reason to insist on the Taurus. It was the fourth-best-selling vehicle in the history of the company, behind the Model T, F-Series, and Mustang. But Mulally's biggest news in the product department was a shift to small "world cars" that could be sold in every country with little change. Ford had tried the world car idea various times in the past and failed. But that was largely because the regional divisions of the company couldn't agree on what kinds of cars to build. Mulally has now reorganized the company around the world car concept. If it works, the benefits of reduced costs based on economies of scale are obvious.

The "small" part of Mulally's product strategy is a bit foreign to Ford's truck-heavy culture. "Everybody says you can't make money off small cars," he says. "Well, you'd better damn well figure out how to make money, because that's where the world is going." Mulally's plan isn't just to make more small cars, but to make nicer small cars. The current Fiesta and Focus models were designed in Europe and are the first vehicles that are part of Mulally's "One Ford" program. More fuel-efficient vehicles (including electrics) will also help position Ford to meet stricter government fuel-economy standards.

Market Fewer Nameplates. According to Mulally, the "more-is-better" rule is not a good branding strategy. When he arrived at Ford, the company sold 97 nameplates around the world. To him, that was just an indication of how unfocused and uncool the Ford brand had become. "I mean, we had 97 of these, for God's sake! How you gonna make 'em all cool? You gonna come in at 8 a.m. and say, 'From 8 until noon, I'm gonna make No. 64 cool? And then I'll make No. 17 cool after lunch?' It was ridiculous!" Mulally's goal was to bring the number of nameplates down to 40 by 2013. Instead, Ford now has just 20. This thrills Mulally.

Become Best in Class in Quality, Fuel Efficiency, Safety, and Value. The smaller cars are certainly achieving the fuel-efficiency goal. But Mulally has the Ford culture once again thinking along the lines of its old slogan, "Quality Is Job One." This focus has paid off. Ford's ratings in *Consumer Reports* are higher than they've ever been, rivaling those of Toyota and other Asian brands in the magazine's reliability survey. "Our product lineup is stronger than ever, and our leadership in quality, fuel, safety, smart design, and value is resonating with consumers," Mulally says, as if reciting his own mission statement.

A New Competitive Advantage

In his quest to redefine Ford's image, thrill young customers, and even revolutionize the car itself, Mulally may very well have stumbled upon a competitive advantage that will carry Ford into the future. He wants to connect his autos to the Internet and to the souls of the people who surf it. "Look, it's cool to connect. But it's past cool. It's a reason to buy. Tech is why people are going to buy Ford! We're going to be the coolest, most useful app you've ever had, seamlessly keeping you connected."

Mulally is talking about Ford's Sync option. In short, a Sync-equipped vehicle connects the driver to the smartphone in her pocket through the vehicle's systems. Unlike GM's OnStar and other similar systems, Sync is an interface, not a system that is hardwired to the car. Other systems are obsolete by the time they hit the showroom and they are not upgradable. With Sync, the connection is to whatever technology drivers carry with them.

But Sync takes existing technologies and makes them even better. With two LCD panels on either side of the speedometer, the user interface is bigger, in the driver's field of vision, and customizable. If you don't need to know about the car's climate but you're lost, the climate-control readout can be replaced with navigation. If you're on a long stretch of highway and don't need navigation help, the display can connect the driver to phone controls or music (including satellite radio and even Pandora). Drivers can even watch video on these screens, but only when the car is in park.

The latest Sync system also brings voice recognition to the cockpit, transforming the car into *2001: A Space Odyssey*'s HAL 9000 (only without the evil desire to take over the universe). All the driver has to do is speak normally to the car instead of fumbling with buttons or navigating through screen-based menus. Simple commands like "I'm hungry" produce spoken restaurant advice matched to the GPS location. If the driver is in the mood for some Dave Brubeck, "I'd like to hear some jazz," brings up every piece

of jazz attached to the car, whether it's on a smartphone, tablet, or iPod.

All this is not only cool, "it makes you a better driver," claims Mulally. His first commandment is, "We won't do it unless it lets you keep your eyes on the road and your hands on the wheel." This will actually make people less likely to fumble with their tech gadgets or even look down to adjust the radio.

Sync was already in development when Mulally took over. But he surprised everyone when he announced that Sync would be the future of the company. And he insisted that it be available in all Ford vehicles, not just the high-end luxury products. In this respect, Mulally sees Sync as a way to do what Henry Ford did in the beginning. "Democratize a brand new technology. Make it available to the masses."

Signs of Life

Today, Ford's sales and market share are back on the rise. In fact, Ford has picked up unit sales and at least one point of market share for each of the last three years in a row—a feat it has not achieved since 1970. Ford's mid-sized Fusion had a record sales year and topped off a four-year streak up 66 percent—a feat even more amazing considering sales for Toyota's Camry and Honda's Accord fell 31 percent and 28 percent, respectively, for the same period. But perhaps most thrilling for Mulally, Ford's small car sales shot up by 25 percent last year alone, supporting his strategy to sell more in that segment. On top of big unit sales numbers, customers are paying more for Fords without the huge discount incentives that the company ran for many years. And all of this means net income is back in black. Ford has turned a profit in each of the last three years, the most recent hitting $20 billion.

Ford is back on track but far from out of the woods. Because it didn't take the government's bailout, it has a long way to go before paying off its heavy debt burden. GM and Chrysler are emerging from bankruptcy with clean balance sheets and are on the warpath. Yet while Mulally worries about this and about global economic conditions, he is relentlessly optimistic. "To serve is to live and I am so honored to serve Ford customers, employees, dealers, investors, suppliers, and communities," he said recently in an interview. "We have the very best cars and trucks in the world: quality, fuel-efficient, safe, smart, fun, and a great value!"

Questions for Discussion

1. Where would you put Ford in terms of its competitive position? Why?

2. Is Ford a market-centered company? How can it improve in this area?

3. How does Ford's Sync contribute to its competitive advantage? Is this a sustainable advantage?

4. Can Mulally succeed with small world cars?

5. What other recommendations would you make for Mulally and Ford?

Sources: Carmine Gallo, "Alan Mulally, Optimism, and the Power of Vision," *Forbes*, April 25, 2012, www.forbes.com/sites/carminegallo/2012/04/25/alan-mulully-optimism-and-the-power-of-vision/; Doron Levin, "Alan Mulally: Worth Every Penny," *Fortune*, March 9, 2012, http://features.blogs.fortune.cnn.com/2012/03/09/alan-mulally-worth-every-penny/; Paul Hochman, "Ford's Big Reveal," *Fast Company*, April 2010, pp. 90–97; Alex Taylor, "Fixing Up Ford," *Fortune*, May 25, 2009, p. 44; Joann Muller, "Ford's Rebound Is for Real," *Forbes*, April 27, 2010, www.forbes.com/2010/04/27/ford-alan-mulally-business-autos-ford.html; and "2011 Ford Brand Sales Up 17 Percent for the Year in U.S.," http://media.ford.com/article_display.cfm?article_id=35785.

MyMarketingLab

Go to **mymktlab.com** for Auto-graded writing questions as well as the following Assisted-graded writing questions:

18-1. Discuss the differences between increasing market share and increasing share of customer. What factors should a company consider when deciding upon which one to focus? (AACSB: Communication; Reflective Thinking)

18-2. Are automobile manufacturers and their dealerships creating an unfair competitive advantage by not sharing information and special tools with independent mechanics? Write an argument supporting the automakers' actions. (AACSB: Communication; Ethical Reasoning; Reflective Thinking)

18-3. Mymktlab Only – comprehensive writing assignment for this chapter.

References

1. Extract adapted from Jeffrey M. O'Brien, "A Perfect Season," *Fortune*, January 22, 2008, pp. 62–66. Other quotes and information from Michael B. Baker, "Four Seasons Tops Ritz-Carlton in Deluxe Photo-Finish," *Business Travel News*, March 23, 2009, p. 10; Sean Drakes, "Keeping the Brand Sacred," *Black Enterprise*, April 2009, p. 47; "100 Best Companies to Work For," *Fortune*, February 6, 2012, p. 117; and http://jobs.fourseasons.com/Pages/Home.aspx and www.fourseasons.com/about_us/, accessed October 2012.

2. Example based on information found in Frank James, "Postal Service Quarterly Losses Surge; Internet Gets Blamed," August 5, 2009, www.npr.org/blogs/thetwo-way/2009/08/postal_service_quarterly_losse.html; "Post Office Makeover," *Fortune*, December 12, 2011, p. 17; and "Postal Facts 2012" and other information from www.usps.com, accessed October 2012.

3. "Dole Positions Banana as 'Nature's Original Energy Bar,'" *Progressive Grocer*, July 9, 2012, www.progressivegrocer.com.

4. See www.vikingrange.com/consumer/category/products/3-year-signature-warranty, accessed October 2012.

5. Garett Sloane, "War of 4G Networks Pits Verizon vs. AT&T," *New York Post*, March 12, 2012.

6. See "Contact Lenses 2011," Contact Lens Spectrum, January 1, 2012, www.clspectrum.com/articleviewer.aspx?articleid=106550; and "Bausch & Lomb," www.wikinvest.com/wiki/Bausch_&_Lomb, accessed August 2012.

7. See John P. Falcone, "Kindle vs. Nook vs. iPad: Which E-Book Reader Should You Buy?" cnet News, May 5, 2012, www.digitaltrends.com/mobile/is-the-amazon-kindle-in-trouble/; Geoff Duncan, "Amazon Says Kindle Sales Tripled During Holidays," Digital Trends, February 1, 2012, www.digitaltrends.com/mobile/amazon-says-kindle-sales-tripled-during-holidays/; and Geoff Duncan, "Is Amazon Kindle in Trouble?" Digital Trends, May 4, 2012, www.digitaltrends.com/mobile/is-the-amazon-kindle-in-trouble/.

8. Arianna Huffington, "HuffPost + AOL: The First Year in Numbers," HuffPost Media, February 2, 2012, www.huffingtonpost.com/arianna-huffington/huffington-post-aol-first-year_b_1249497.html.

9. Adapted from information found in W. Chan Kim and Renée Mauborgne, "Blue Ocean Strategy: How to Create Uncontested Market Space and Make Competition Irrelevant," www.blueoceanstrategy.com/pre/downloads/BlueOceanStrategySummary.pdf, accessed September 2012. Also see Kim and Mauborgne, *Blue Ocean Strategy: How to Create Uncontested Market Space and Make Competition Irrelevant* (Boston: Harvard Business Press, 2005). For other discussion, see "Blue Ocean Strategy," www.blueoceanstrategy.com/, accessed October 2012.

10. Adapted from information found in Robert Klara, "Puff Daddy," *Brandweek*, May 19, 2008, pp. 25–27; Eric Slack, "Pirate Brands: Healthy Treasure," *Retail Merchandisers*, March/April 2010, pp. 125–127, "Call Him Coach," *Success*, www.success.com/articles/1268-call-him-coach, accessed August 2012; and http://piratebrands.com/, accessed October 2012.

11. Richard Branson, "Richard Branson on Intrepreneurs," *Entrepreneur*, January 31, 2011, www.entrepreneur.com/article/218011.

12. Michael E. Porter, *Competitive Strategy: Techniques for Analyzing Industries and Competitors* (New York: Free Press, 1980), chapter 2; and Porter, "What Is Strategy?" *Harvard Business Review*, November– December 1996, pp. 61–78. Also see Stefan Stern, "May the Force Be with You and Your Plans for 2008," *Financial Times*, January 8, 2008, p. 14; and "Porter's Generic Strategies," www.quickmba.com/strategy/generic.shtml, accessed October 2012.

13. See Michael Treacy and Fred Wiersema, "Customer Intimacy and Other Value Disciplines," *Harvard Business Review*, January–February 1993, pp. 84–93; Treacy and Wiersema, *The Discipline of Market Leaders: Choose Your Customers, Narrow Your Focus, Dominate Your Market* (New York: Perseus Press, 1997); and Wiersema, *Double-Digit Growth: How Great Companies Achieve It—No Matter What* (New York: Portfolio, 2003). Also see Elaine Cascio, "Fast, Cheap, or Good—Pick Two," *Inter@ction Solutions*, January/February 2012, p. 8; and Jürgen Kai-Uwe Brock and Josephine Yu Zhou, "Customer Intimacy," *Journal of Business and Industrial Marketing*, 2012, pp. 370–383.

14. Based on information from Michael Bush, "Why You Should Be Putting on the Ritz," *Advertising Age*, June 21, 2010, p. 1; Julie Barker, "Power to the People," *Incentive*, February 2008, p. 34; and Carmine Gallo, "Employee Motivation the Ritz-Carlton Way," *BusinessWeek*, February 29, 2008, accessed at www.businessweek.com/smallbiz/content/feb2008/sb20080229_347490.htm; Stuart Elliott, "Luxury Hotels Market the Memories They Can Make," *New York Times*, September 14, 2012, p. B3; and Philip Kotler and Kevin Lane Keller, *Marketing Management*, 14th ed. (Upper Saddle River, NJ: Prentice Hall, 2012), p. 381. Also see http://corporate.ritzcarlton.com/en/About/Awards.htm#Hotel, accessed October 2012.

15. For more discussion, see Philip Kotler and Kevin Lane Keller, *Marketing Management*, 14th ed. (Upper Saddle River, NJ: Prentice Hall, 2012), chapter 11.

16. Leslie Kwoh, "Weight Watchers Chief Looks to Men, China for Growth," *Wall Street Journal*, January 9, 2012, http://online.wsj.com/article/SB10001424052970204331304577144613938815858.html.

17. See "2000+ Uses," www.wd40.com/uses-tips/, accessed October 2012.

18. Adapted from information found in Jack Neff, "Why Unilever Lost the Laundry War," *Advertising Age*, August 6, 2007, pp. 1, 25; "Bidders Eye Unilever's US Detergent Arm," *Financial Times*, April 9, 2008, p. 24; "Unilever Sells North American Detergents Unit," July 28, 2008, accessed at www.msnbc.msn.com/id/25884712; and www.unilever.com/brands/homecarebrands/ and www.unileverusa.com/brands/personalcarebrands/, accessed October 2012.

19. See "U.S. Sales of Shampoo via Different Sales Channels in 2010/2011," *Statista*, accessed at www.statista.com/statistics/193102/us-shampoo-sales-via-different-sales-channels-in-2010-and-2011/; and Martinne Geller, "Update 2-U.S. Soda Consumption Fell Faster in 2011," Reuters, March 20, 2012, www.reuters.com/article/2012/03/20/drinks-idUSL1E8EK1P620120320.

20. See Oded Shenkar, "Defend Your Research: Imitation Is More Valuable Than Innovation," *Harvard Business Review*, April 2010, pp. 28–29.

21. Example based on information from David J. Bryce and Jeffrey H. Dyer, "Strategies to Crack Well-Guarded Markets," *Harvard Business Review*, May 2007, pp. 84–91; with information from Teressa Iezzi, "For Showing What It Really Means to Transform Yourself into a Media Brand," *Fast Company*, www.fastcompany.com/most-innovative-companies/2012/red-bull-media-house, accessed August 2012.

22. "Zipcar Expands Service to Austin, Texas," April 27, 2012, http://ir.zipcar.com/releasedetail.cfm?ReleaseID=668036; and annual reports and other information from www.zipcar.com and www.enterpriseholding.com, accessed October 2012.

23. Information from www.vfc.com, accessed October 2012.

The Global Marketplace

Chapter Preview You've now learned the fundamentals of how companies develop competitive marketing strategies to create customer value and build lasting customer relationships. In this chapter, we extend these fundamentals to global marketing. Although we discussed global topics in each previous chapter—it's difficult to find an area of marketing that doesn't contain at least some international elements—here we'll focus on special considerations that companies face when they market their brands globally. Advances in communication, transportation, and other technologies have made the world a much smaller place. Today, almost every firm, large or small, faces international marketing issues. In this chapter, we will examine six major decisions marketers make in going global.

To start our exploration of global marketing, let's look at Coca-Cola, a truly global operation. You'll find a Coca-Cola product within arm's length of almost anyone, anywhere in the world. "We sell moments of happiness, for cents at a time, more than 1.7 billion times a day in more than 200 countries," says the company in its annual report. Like many companies, Coca-Cola's greatest growth opportunities lie in international markets. Here, we examine the company's odyssey into Africa.

Coca-Cola in Africa: "Everything Is Right There to Have It Happen."

Coca-Cola is one of the world's truly iconic brands—a $46-billion global powerhouse. It puts Coke products within "an arm's length" of 98 percent of the world's population. Already the world's number one soft drink maker, Coca-Cola plans to double its global system revenues between 2008 and 2020. But achieving such growth won't be easy. The major problem: Soft drink-sales growth has lost its fizz in North America and Europe, two of Coca-Cola's largest and most profitable markets. In fact, the U.S. soft drink market has shrunk for five straight years. With sales stagnating in its mature markets, Coca-Cola must look elsewhere to meet its ambitious growth goals.

In recent years, Coca-Cola has sought growth primarily in developing global markets such as China and India, which boast large emerging middle classes but relatively low per capita consumption of Coke. However, both China and India are now crowded with competitors and notoriously difficult for outsiders to navigate. So while Coca-Cola will continue to compete heavily in those countries, it has set its sights on an even more promising long-term growth opportunity—Africa.

Many Western companies view Africa as an untamed final frontier—a kind of no man's land plagued by poverty, political corruption and instability, unreliable transportation, and shortages of fresh water and other essential resources. But Coca-Cola sees plenty of opportunity in Africa to justify the risks. Africa has a growing population of more than 1 billion people and a just-emerging middle class. The number of African households earning at least $5,000—the income level where families begin to spend at least half their income on non-food items—is expected to exceed 106 million by 2014, almost double the number in 2000. "You've got an incredibly young population, a dynamic population," says Coca-Cola CEO Muhtar Kent, "[and] huge

With its home markets losing their fizz, Coca-Cola is looking for growth in emerging markets such as Africa. But in Africa, "Coke is, in a sense, sticking its hand into a bees' nest to get some honey."

disposable income. I mean $1.6 trillion of GDP, which is bigger than Russia, bigger than India."

Coca-Cola is no stranger to Africa. It has operated there since 1929, and it's the only multinational that offers its products in every African country. The company has a dominant 29 percent market share in Africa and the Middle East, as compared with Pepsi's 15 percent share. Africa and the Middle East now contribute 6 percent of Coca-Cola's global revenues.

But there's still plenty of room for Coca-Cola to grow in Africa. For example, annual per capita consumption of Coke in Kenya is just 40 servings, compared with more developed countries like Mexico, where consumption runs at an eye-popping 728 servings per year. So the stage is set for Coca-Cola on the African continent, not just for its flagship Coke brand but also for its large stable of other soft drinks, waters, and juices. Whereas the beverage giant invested $6 billion in the African market over the past decade, it plans to invest twice that amount during the next 10 years—an effort that includes bottling plants, distribution networks, retailer support, and an Africa-wide promotional campaign called "One Billion Reasons to Believe in Africa."

Marketing in Africa is a very different proposition from marketing in more developed regions. "Africa . . . is not Atlanta," observes one analyst, "and Coke is, in a sense, sticking its hand into a bees' nest to get some honey." To grow its sales in Africa, beyond just marketing through traditional channels in larger African cities, Coca-Cola is now invading smaller communities with more grassroots tactics. "[Just] being in a country is very easy; you can go and set up a depot in every capital city," says CEO Kent. But in Africa, "that's not what we're about. There's nowhere in Africa that we don't go. We go to every town, every village, every community, every township." In Africa, every small shop in every back alley has become important, as Coca-Cola launches what another analyst describes as "a street-by-street campaign to win drinkers . . . not yet used to guzzling Coke by the gallon."

For example, take the Mamakamau Shop in Uthiru, a poor community outside Nairobi, Kenya. Piles of trash burn outside the shop and sewage trickles by in an open trench. Besides Coca-Cola products, the shop—known as a duka —also carries everything from mattresses to plastic buckets, all in a room about the size of a small bedroom. Still, proprietor Mamakamau Kingori has earned Coca-Cola's "Gold" vendor status, its highest level, for selling about 72 cola products a day, priced at 30 Kenyan shillings (37 U.S. cents) for a 500-milliliter bottle. Most customers drink the soda in the store while sitting on overturned red crates—they can't afford to pay the bottle deposit. Coca-Cola's Kenyan bottler will reuse the glass bottles up to 70 times.

To earn her "Gold" status, Kingori follows carefully prescribed selling techniques. She uses a red, Coke-provided, refrigerated cooler by the front entrance, protected by a blue cage. Like other mom-and-pop stores in her area, she keeps the cooler fully stocked with Coke on top, Fanta in the middle, and large bottles on the bottom. Inside the store, she posts red menu signs provided by Coca-Cola that push combo meals, such as a 300-milliliter Coke and a ndazi, a type of local donut, for 25 Kenyan shillings.

In Kabira, another poor Nairobi neighborhood, the crowded streets are lined with shops painted Coke red. The local bottler hires an artist to paint the shops with logos and Swahili phrases like "Burudika na Coke Baridi," meaning "enjoy Coke cold." In countless communities across Africa, whether it's the dukas in Nairobi or tuck shops in Johannesburg, South Africa, small stores play a big role in helping Coca-Cola grow.

With sales stagnating in its mature markets, Coca-Cola is looking to emerging markets—such as Africa— to meet its ambitious growth goals. Its African distribution network is rudimentary but effective.
Marco Di Lauro/Getty Images

Such shops are supplied by a rudimentary but effective network of Coca-Cola distributors. For example, in downtown Nairobi, men in red lab coats load hand-pulled trolleys with 22 to 40 crates of Coke and other soft drinks from Rosinje Distributors, one of 2,800 Micro Distribution Centers (MDCs) that Coca-Cola operates in Africa. These centers are the spine of Coca-Cola's African distribution network. For example, the Nairobi plant ships Coke, Fanta, Stoney Ginger Beer, and other Coca-Cola brands to 367 area MDCs. From there, crews hustle the products—sometimes a case at a time carried on their heads—to local shops and beverage kiosks. Because of the poor roads crowded with traffic, moving drinks by hand is often the best method. The MDCs help Coca-Cola to get its products into remote areas, making them available as people develop a taste for soft drinks and have the income to buy them.

Despite their elemental nature, Coca-Cola's marketing approaches in Africa are proving effective. The company's first rule is to get its products "cold and close." "If they don't have roads to move products long distances on trucks, we will use boats, canoes, or trolleys," says the president of Coca-Cola South Africa. For example, in Nigeria's Makako district—a maze of stilt houses on the Lagos lagoon—women criss-cross the waterways selling Coca-Cola directly from canoes to residents.

There's little doubt that Coca-Cola's increased commitment to Africa will be key to its achieving its global goals. As CEO Muhtar Kent concludes: "Africa is the untold story and could be the big story of the next decade, like India and China were this past decade. . . . Everything is right there to have it happen."[1]

Objective Outline

MyMarketingLab™

⭐ **Improve Your Grade!**

Over 10 million students improved their results using the Pearson MyLabs.
Visit **mymktlab.com** for simulations, tutorials, and end-of-chapter problems.

In the past, U.S. companies paid little attention to international trade. If they could pick up some extra sales via exports, that was fine. But the big market was at home, and it teemed with opportunities. The home market was also much safer. Managers did not need to learn other languages, deal with strange and changing currencies, face political and legal uncertainties, or adapt their products to different customer needs and expectations. Today, however, the situation is much different. Organizations of all kinds, from Coca-Cola and HP to Google, MTV, and even the NBA, have gone global.

Objective 1 ┈┈▶
Discuss how the international trade system and the economic, political-legal, and cultural environments affect a company's international marketing decisions.

Global Marketing Today

The world is shrinking rapidly with the advent of faster communication, transportation, and financial flows. Products developed in one country—Samsung electronics, McDonald's hamburgers, Zara fashions, Caterpillar construction equipment, German BMWs, Facebook social networking—have found enthusiastic acceptance in other countries. It would not be surprising to hear about a German businessman wearing an Italian suit meeting an English friend at a Japanese restaurant who later returns home to drink Russian vodka and watch *American Idol* on TV.

International trade has boomed over the past three decades. Since 1990, the number of multinational corporations in the world has more than doubled to more than 63,000. Some of these multinationals are true giants. In fact, of the largest 150 economies in the world, only 83 are countries. The remaining 67 are multinational corporations. Exxon Mobil, the world's largest company (based on a weighted average of sales, profits, assets, and market value), has annual revenues greater than the gross domestic product (GDP) of all but the world's 25 largest countries.[2]

● Many American companies have now made the world their market, as this Niketown storefront in China featuring NBA star Kobe Bryant suggests. Quintessentially American Nike draws 65 percent of its sales from non-U.S. markets.

Dorothea Schmid/Redux Pictures

Between 2005 and 2011, total value of world trade merchandise and commercial services grew 10 and 9 percent, respectively. Despite a dip in world trade caused by the recent worldwide recession, the world trade of products and services last year was valued at more than $22.3 trillion, about 28 percent of GDP worldwide.[3]

● Many U.S. companies have long been successful at international marketing: Coca-Cola, McDonald's, Starbucks, Nike, GE, IBM, Apple, Colgate, Caterpillar, Boeing, and dozens of other American firms have made the world their market. In the United States, names such as Toyota, Nestlé, IKEA, Canon, Adidas, and Samsung have become household words. Other products and services that appear to be American are, in fact, produced or owned by foreign companies, such as Ben & Jerry's ice cream, Budweiser beer, 7-Eleven, GE and RCA televisions, Carnation milk, Universal Studios, and Motel 6. Michelin, the oh-so-French tire manufacturer, now does 33 percent of its business in North America; J&J, the maker of quintessentially all-American products such as BAND-AIDs and Johnson's Baby Shampoo, does nearly 56 percent of its business abroad. And America's own Caterpillar belongs more to the wider world, with almost 70 percent of its sales coming from outside the United States.[4]

But as global trade grows, global competition is also intensifying. Foreign firms are expanding aggressively into new international markets, and home markets are no longer as rich in opportunity. Few industries are currently safe from foreign competition. If companies delay taking steps toward internationalizing, they risk being shut out of growing markets in Western and Eastern Europe, China and the Pacific Rim, Russia, India, Brazil, and elsewhere. Firms that stay at home to play it safe might not only lose their chances to enter other markets but also risk losing their home markets. Domestic companies that never thought about foreign competitors suddenly find these competitors in their own backyards.

Ironically, although the need for companies to go abroad is greater today than in the past, so are the risks. Companies that go global may face highly unstable governments and currencies, restrictive government policies and regulations, and high trade barriers. The recently dampened global economic environment has also created big global challenges. In addition, corruption is an increasing problem; officials in several countries often award business not to the best bidder but to the highest briber.

Global firm

A firm that, by operating in more than one country, gains R&D, production, marketing, and financial advantages in its costs and reputation that are not available to purely domestic competitors.

A **global firm** is one that, by operating in more than one country, gains marketing, production, research and development (R&D), and financial advantages that are not available to purely domestic competitors. Since the global company sees the world as one market, it minimizes the importance of national boundaries and develops global brands. The global company raises capital, obtains materials and components, and manufactures and markets its goods wherever it can do the best job.

For example, U.S.-based Otis Elevator, the world's largest elevator maker, is headquartered in Farmington, Connecticut. However, it offers products in more than 200 countries and achieves more than 83 percent of its sales from outside the United States. It gets elevator door systems from France, small geared parts from Spain, electronics from Germany, and special motor drives from Japan. It operates manufacturing facilities in the Americas, Europe, and Asia, and engineering and test centers in the United States, Austria, Brazil, China, Czech Republic, France, Germany, India, Italy, Japan, Korea, and Spain. In turn, Otis Elevator is a wholly owned subsidiary of global commercial and aerospace giant United Technologies Corporation.[5] Many of today's global corporations—both large and small—have become truly borderless.

This does not mean, however, that every firm must operate in a dozen countries to succeed. Smaller firms can practice global niching. But the world is becoming smaller, and every company operating in a global industry—whether large or small—must assess and establish its place in world markets.

The rapid move toward globalization means that all companies will have to answer some basic questions: What market position should we try to establish in our country, in our economic region, and globally? Who will our global competitors be and what are their strategies and resources? Where should we produce or source our products? What strategic alliances should we form with other firms around the world?

| Looking at the global marketing environment | → | Deciding whether to go global | → | Deciding which markets to enter | → | Deciding how to enter the market | → | Deciding on the global marketing program | → | Deciding on the global marketing organization |

It's a big and beautiful but threatening world out there for marketers! Most large American firms have made the world their market. For example, once all-American McDonald's now captures 66 percent of its sales from outside the United States.

● **FIGURE | 19.1**
Major International Marketing Decisions

As shown in ● **Figure 19.1**, a company faces six major decisions in international marketing. We discuss each decision in detail in this chapter.

Looking at the Global Marketing Environment

Before deciding whether to operate internationally, a company must understand the international marketing environment. That environment has changed a great deal in recent decades, creating both new opportunities and new problems.

The International Trade System

U.S. companies looking abroad must start by understanding the international *trade system*. When selling to another country, a firm may face restrictions on trade between nations.

● **Nontariff trade barriers:** Walmart and other foreign businesses in China appear to receive unusually close scrutiny and harsh treatment from Chinese authorities, aimed at boosting the fortunes of local Chinese competitors.

REUTERS/Jason Lee

Governments may charge *tariffs*, taxes on certain imported products designed to raise revenue or protect domestic firms. Tariffs are often used to force favorable trade behaviors from other nations. For example, Chinese solar cell and panel manufacturers were recently found to be charging under-market prices in the United States, putting America producers out of business. In retaliation, to help level the highly competitive playing field, the U.S. government placed a 31 percent tariff on solar cells and panels imported from China. New Chinese companies importing solar cells and panels into the United States could face a tariff up to 250 percent.[6]

Countries may set *quotas*, limits on the amount of foreign imports that they will accept in certain product categories. The purpose of a quota is to conserve on foreign exchange and protect local industry and employment. Firms may also encounter *exchange controls*, which limit the amount of foreign exchange and the exchange rate against other currencies.

A company also may face *nontariff trade barriers*, such as biases against its bids, restrictive product standards, or excessive host-country regulations or enforcement. For example, foreign businesses in China appear to receive unusually close scrutiny and harsh treatment from Chinese authorities, aimed at boosting the fortunes of local competitors. Last year, for instance, national and local Chinese regulators lunched what appeared to be a new wave of protectionism, with the goal of shielding Chinese brands from their Western rivals in a slowing economy. The harshest treatment was reserved for Western retailers such as Walmart. The retailer was first fined for misleading pricing in several of its stores. Next, it paid fines for allegedly selling expired products in the city of Changsha. Then, Chinese regulators in Chongqing accused Walmart of selling regular pork improperly labeled as organic, forcing the chain to temporarily close 13 stores and pay a $573,000 fine. The motives behind these protectionist moves appeared to be more to hinder Walmart's operations in China than to improve the operations of local retailers. As one analyst puts it, "Why go to the effort of getting your own guys to raise their game when you can tear down a foreign guy instead?"[7]

At the same time, certain other forces can *help* trade between nations. Examples include the World Trade Organization (WTO) and various regional free trade agreements.

The World Trade Organization

The General Agreement on Tariffs and Trade (GATT), established in 1947 and modified in 1994, was designed to promote world trade by reducing tariffs and other international trade barriers. ● It established the World Trade Organization (WTO), which replaced GATT in 1995 and now oversees the original GATT provisions. WTO and GATT member nations (currently numbering 153) have met in eight rounds of negotiations to reassess trade barriers and establish new rules for international trade. The WTO also imposes international trade sanctions and mediates global trade disputes. Its actions have been productive. The first seven rounds of negotiations reduced the average worldwide tariffs on manufactured goods from 45 percent to just 5 percent.[8]

The most recently completed negotiations, dubbed the Uruguay Round, dragged on for seven long years before concluding in 1994. The benefits of the Uruguay Round will be felt for many years, as the accord promoted long-term global trade growth, reduced the world's remaining merchandise tariffs by 30 percent, extended the WTO to cover trade in agriculture and a wide range of services, and toughened the international protection of copyrights, patents, trademarks, and other intellectual property. A new round of global WTO trade talks, the Doha Round, began in Doha, Qatar, in late 2001 and was set to conclude in 2005; however, the discussions still continued through 2012.[9]

● **The WTO promotes trade by reducing tariffs and other international trade barriers. It also imposes international trade sanctions and mediates global trade disputes.**

(left) Corbis Images; (right) Donald Stampfli/Associated Press

Regional Free Trade Zones

Economic community

A group of nations organized to work toward common goals in the regulation of international trade.

Certain countries have formed *free trade zones* or **economic communities**. These are groups of nations organized to work toward common goals in the regulation of international trade. One such community is the *European Union (EU)*. Formed in 1957, the EU set out to create a single European market by reducing barriers to the free flow of products, services, finances, and labor among member countries and developing policies on trade with nonmember nations. Today, the EU represents one of the world's largest single markets. ● Currently, it has 27 member countries containing more than half a billion consumers and accounting for almost 20 percent of the world's exports.[10]

The EU offers tremendous trade opportunities for U.S. and other non-European firms. However, it also poses threats. As a result of increased unification, European companies have grown bigger and more competitive. Perhaps an even greater concern, however, is that lower barriers *inside* Europe will create only thicker *outside* walls. Some observers envision a "Fortress Europe" that heaps favors on firms from EU countries but hinders outsiders by imposing obstacles.

Progress toward European unification has been slow. Over the past decade, however, 17 member nations have taken a significant step toward unification by adopting the euro as a common currency. Widespread adoption of the euro has decreased much of the currency risk associated with doing business in Europe, making member countries with previously weak currencies more attractive markets. However, the adoption of a common currency has also caused problems as European economic powers such as Germany and France have had to step in recently to prop up weaker economies such as those of Greece and Portugal.[11]

Even with the adoption of the euro, it is unlikely that the EU will ever go against 2,000 years of tradition and become the "United States of Europe." A community with more than two-dozen different languages and cultures will always have difficulty coming together and acting as a single entity. Still, with a combined annual GDP of more than $17 trillion, the EU has become a potent economic force.[12]

In 1994, the *North American Free Trade Agreement (NAFTA)* established a free trade zone among the United States, Mexico, and Canada. The agreement created a single market of

● **Economic communities: The European Union represents one of the world's single largest markets. Its current member countries contain more than half a billion consumers and account for 20 percent of the world's exports.**

© European Community

463 million people who produce and consume over $18 trillion worth of goods and services annually. Over the past 18 years, NAFTA has eliminated trade barriers and investment restrictions among the three countries. Total trade among the NAFTA countries nearly tripled from $288 billion in 1993 to $1 trillion in 2011.[13]

Following the apparent success of NAFTA, in 2005 the Central American Free Trade Agreement (CAFTA-DR) established a free trade zone between the United States and Costa Rica, the Dominican Republic, El Salvador, Guatemala, Honduras, and Nicaragua. Other free trade areas have formed in Latin America and South America. For example, the Union of South American Nations (UNASUR), modeled after the EU, was formed in 2004 and formalized by a constitutional treaty in 2008. Consisting of 12 countries, UNASUR makes up the largest trading bloc after NAFTA and the EU, with a population of 361 million, a combined economy of more than $973 billion, and exports worth $182 billion. Similar to NAFTA and the EU, UNASUR aims to eliminate all tariffs between nations by 2019.[14]

Each nation has unique features that must be understood. A nation's readiness for different products and services and its attractiveness as a market to foreign firms depend on its economic, political-legal, and cultural environments.

Economic Environment

The international marketer must study each country's economy. Two economic factors reflect the country's attractiveness as a market: its industrial structure and its income distribution.

The country's *industrial structure* shapes its product and service needs, income levels, and employment levels. The four types of industrial structures are as follows:

- *Subsistence economies:* In a subsistence economy, the vast majority of people engage in simple agriculture. They consume most of their output and barter the rest for simple goods and services. These economies offer few market opportunities. Many African countries fall into this category.
- *Raw material exporting economies:* These economies are rich in one or more natural resources but poor in other ways. Much of their revenue comes from exporting these resources. Some examples are Chile (tin and copper) and the Democratic Republic of the Congo (copper, cobalt, and coffee). These countries are good markets for large equipment, tools and supplies, and trucks. If there are many foreign residents and a wealthy upper class, they are also a market for luxury goods.
- *Emerging economies (industrializing economies):* In an emerging economy, fast growth in manufacturing results in rapid overall economic growth. Examples include the BRIC countries—Brazil, Russia, India, and China. As manufacturing increases, the country needs more imports of raw textile materials, steel, and heavy machinery, and fewer imports of finished textiles, paper products, and automobiles. Industrialization typically creates a new rich class and a growing middle class, both demanding new types of imported goods. As more developed markets stagnate and become increasingly competitive, many marketers are now targeting growth opportunities in emerging markets (see Real Marketing 19.1)
- *Industrial economies:* Industrial economies are major exporters of manufactured goods, services, and investment funds. They trade goods among themselves and also export them to other types of economies for raw materials and semifinished goods. The varied manufacturing activities of these industrial nations and their large middle class make them rich markets for all sorts of goods. Examples include the United States, Japan, and Norway.

Real Marketing 19.1

Brazil: An Emerging Market or Already Emerged?

When it comes to talk of the world's emerging economies, China and India seem to ink most of the headlines. But ask Brazilians what they think of their country and they'll likely respond that it's "O pais maior do mundo"—"The greatest country in the world." And based on the strength of Brazil's growing consumer markets, many global marketers would agree.

South America's largest country, Brazil also boasts the world's sixth-largest economy; it's expected to pass France to take the number five spot within the next decade. And although both India and China each have more than six times Brazil's population of 200 million, Brazil bests both countries by a wide margin in per capita purchasing power. In fact, Brazil's GDP is 200 percent larger than India's.

Thanks to historically low unemployment, rising wages, and an influx of foreign direct investment, Brazil's consumer markets are soaring. And the world's marketers are beginning to covet Brazil's rapidly exploding middle class—a group that has grown by 40 million in just the past five years. The growing prosperity and aspirations of this segment have resulted in rapidly growing demand for higher-value brands in categories ranging from soft drinks to mobile phones to imported luxury goods.

The world's largest retailers are now setting up shop in Brazil. They are finding success through innovative formats that target mixed segments of the middle-class consumers, small businesses, and wealthier shoppers. France's Carrefour is a market leader with its Costco-like Atacadao warehouse stores. Like Costco, Atacadao stores offer premium brands in large quantities in a modern warehouse-like store environment combined with enticing promotions and low prices. Walmart is also experiencing big growth in Brazil with 532 stores, including Walmart Supercenters, Sam's Clubs, and its fast-growing chain TodoDia—low-price supermarkets featuring the assortment of national brands and private labels that Walmart is known for around the world, but served up in a way that appeals to Brazilians.

One product category showing strong growth among Brazil's increasingly affluent middle class is child's play—literally. With Brazilian disposable income on the rise, spending on traditional toys and games has grown by more than 25 percent annually in recent years. Mattel leads the market with a substantial 30 percent share, followed by Hasbro. Brazil's toy market looks a lot like the U.S. toy market, with Brazilian tots and preteens clamoring not only for Hot Wheels and Barbies but also for other North American favorites ranging from Disney's princesses, Shrek, and Toy Story characters to Nickelodeon's "Dora la Exploradora."

Just as it offers opportunities, Brazil also presents challenges. Although its market infrastructure is light years ahead of what it was even a decade ago, the country's still-fragmented social classes and regional variances create difficulties for multinational marketers. For example, southern and southeastern Brazil contain some of the country's wealthiest, most-populated, and easiest-to-reach areas, such as Sao Paulo, Brazil's richest state. In contrast, the northeast region is Brazil's poorest, and many residents there lack access to basics such as roads and running water. This region historically prefers local markets over supermarkets and regional brands over global brands. With more mouths to feed in every household, northeastern Brazilian consumers are also sticklers for low prices.

But as it happens, northeast Brazil is also the region with the greatest growth in household income. So as Brazil's more affluent regions become increasingly competitive, marketers are finding innovative ways to meet the distribution challenges in regions like the northeast to capture the growing potential there. For example, Nestlé developed its "Ate Voce" ("Reaching You") program, by which its reps go door-to-door with push carts—a method residents find very appealing—selling "kits" full of dairy products, cookies, yogurt, and desserts. More than just selling products, these Nestlé vendors are trained to serve as nutrition consultants, helping customers to develop healthier diets.

To serve consumers in northeast Brazil's Amazon River basin, which lacks a solid network of roads and highways, Nestlé has even launched a floating supermarket that takes goods directly to consumers. Setting sail from Belem, Brazil's biggest city along the Amazon, the boat serves 1.5 million consumers in 27 riverside towns with 300 different Nestlé products. It spends one day at each stop. Customers can check the floating store's schedule at nestleatevoce.com.br, call a toll-free number, or text for more information and plan their

Marketing in Brazil presents both opportunities and challenges. Nestlé's "Ate Voce" ("Reaching You") program includes innovative distribution approaches, such as this floating supermarket that serves customers in northeast Brazil's Amazon River basin.

Bloomberg via Getty Images

shopping accordingly. This and other innovative Ate Voce marketing initiatives are paying off for Nestlé. "Demand for our products has more than doubled in the north and northeast compared to other Brazilian regions," says Nestlé's marketing manager in Brazil.

Many companies are adapting their products to meet local northeastern Brazilian tastes. For example, Nestlé makes a cookie based on a popular local sweet-corn dish that it sells only in northeast Brazil. Huge multinational agribusiness firm Bunge has developed a best-selling Brazilian version of its Primor margarine—a firmer, saltier version that doesn't melt in northeast Brazil's searing heat. Even Nike scored a hit with the launch of a regional sneaker—the Lanceiro—a shoe designed to appeal to northeastern Brazilians by evoking images of a state flag.

Keeping up with local brands can be challenging, even for the biggest global brands. For example, Coca-Cola has long been the number one soft drink brand in Brazil. However, a local beverage brand—Guaraná Jesus—runs a close second. Named for the druggist who formulated it from extracts of Brazil's guarana plant in 1920, the local favorite was giving Coca-Cola a real run for its money. The solution: Coca-Cola bought the brand. Now, in Brazil, the company makes and sells both the world's favorite global soft drink brand (Coca-Cola) and the country's favorite local brand (Guaraná Jesus). In the words of Coca-Cola's marketing slogan, that's "Open Happiness."

As Brazil's poverty fades and its middle class continues to burst its boundaries, more and more global marketers will find fertile ground for growing their brands there. As Brazil prepares to host the 2014 Football World Cup and the 2016 Olympics, foreign investment and business activity in Brazil are booming. Global marketers that can tap into the unique tastes of Brazil's growing middle class will reap the benefits. Many global marketers are now asking: Does Brazil still belong among the ranks of the world's emerging economies? Or has it already emerged?

Sources: Claudia Penteado, "Brazil's Northeast Goes from 'Land of Laziness' to Next China," *Advertising Age*, June 13, 2011, http://adage.com/print/228070/; Richard Wallace, "Middle-Classes on the Up: Why Brazil Is Growing," IGD, September 15, 2011, www.igd.com/index.asp?id=1&fid=1&sid=7&tid=10&cid=2128; "Brazil Fact Sheet," www.walmartstores.com/AboutUs/259.aspx, accessed September 2012; and Giedrius Daujotas, "Brazil's Emerging Middle-Class Offers Opportunities for Toymakers," *Euromonitor*, February 27, 2012, http://blog.euromonitor.com/2012/02/brazils-emerging-middle-class-offers-opportunities-for-toymakers.html.

The second economic factor is the country's *income distribution*. Industrialized nations may have low-, medium-, and high-income households. In contrast, countries with subsistence economies consist mostly of households with very low family incomes. Still other countries may have households with either very low or very high incomes. Even poor or emerging economies may be attractive markets for all kinds of goods. These days, companies in a wide range of industries—from cars to computers to candy—are increasingly targeting even low- and middle-income consumers in emerging economies.

For example, in India, Ford recently introduced a new model targeted to consumers who are only now able to afford their first car. In an effort to boost its presence in Asia's third-largest auto market behind Japan and China, Ford introduced the Figo, a successful new $6,900 hatchback designed for a hypothetical twenty-something Indian consumer named Sandeep. Sandeep is a young professional who currently drives a motorcycle. But given his improving means and pending family, he now wants something bigger. "There are huge numbers of people wanting to move off their motorbikes," says Ford's India general manager. As a result, demand is booming in India for cars in the Figo's size and price range. After just two years, the diminutive Figo has become Ford's best-selling car in India and is now also selling well in 50 other emerging markets across Asia and Africa.[15]

● **Economic environment: In India, Ford's $6,900 Figo targets low- to middle-income consumers who are only now able to afford their first car**

Namas Bhojani/Namas Bhojani Photography

Political-Legal Environment

Nations differ greatly in their political-legal environments. In considering whether to do business in a given country, a company should consider factors such as the country's attitudes toward international buying, government bureaucracy, political stability, and monetary regulations.

Some nations are very receptive to foreign firms; others are less accommodating. For example, India has tended to bother foreign businesses with import quotas, currency restrictions, and other limitations that make operating there a challenge. In contrast, neighboring Asian countries, such as Singapore and Thailand, court foreign investors and shower them with incentives and favorable operating conditions. Political and regulatory stability is another issue. For example, Venezuela's government is notoriously volatile—because of economic factors such as inflation and steep public spending—which increases the risk of doing business there. Although most international marketers still find the Venezuelan market attractive, the unstable political and regulatory situation will affect how they handle business and financial matters.[16]

Companies must also consider a country's monetary regulations. Sellers want to take their profits in a currency of value to them. Ideally, the buyer can pay in the seller's currency or in other world currencies. Short of this, sellers might accept a blocked currency—one whose removal from the country is restricted by the buyer's government—if they can buy other goods in that country that they need or can sell elsewhere for a needed currency. In addition to currency limits, a changing exchange rate also creates high risks for the seller.

Most international trade involves cash transactions. Yet many nations have too little hard currency to pay for their purchases from other countries. They may want to pay with other items instead of cash. *Barter* involves the direct exchange of goods or services. For example, China agreed to help the Democratic Republic of Congo develop $6 billion of desperately needed infrastructure—2,400 miles of roads, 2,000 miles of railways, 32 hospitals, 145 health centers, and two universities—in exchange for natural resources needed to feed China's booming industries—10 million tons of copper and 400,000 tons of cobalt.[17]

Cultural Environment

Each country has its own folkways, norms, and taboos. When designing global marketing strategies, companies must understand how culture affects consumer reactions in each of its world markets. In turn, they must also understand how their strategies affect local cultures.

The Impact of Culture on Marketing Strategy

Sellers must understand the ways that consumers in different countries think about and use certain products before planning a marketing program. There are often surprises. For example, the average French man uses almost twice as many cosmetics and grooming aids as his wife. The Germans and the French eat more packaged, branded spaghetti than Italians do. Some 49 percent of Chinese eat on the way to work. Most American women let down their hair and take off makeup at bedtime, whereas 15 percent of Chinese women style their hair at bedtime and 11 percent put *on* makeup.[18]

Companies that ignore cultural norms and differences can make some very expensive and embarrassing mistakes. Here are two examples:

> Nike inadvertently offended Chinese officials when it ran an ad featuring LeBron James crushing a number of culturally revered Chinese figures in a kung fu–themed television ad. The Chinese government found that the ad violated regulations to uphold national dignity and respect the "motherland's culture" and yanked the multimillion-dollar campaign. With egg on its face, Nike released a formal apology. Burger King made a similar mistake when it created in-store ads in Spain showing Hindu goddess Lakshmi atop a ham sandwich with the caption "a snack that is sacred." Cultural and religious groups worldwide objected strenuously—Hindus are vegetarian. Burger King apologized and pulled the ads.[19]

Business norms and behaviors also vary from country to country. For example, American executives like to get right down to business and engage in fast and tough face-to-face bargaining. However, Japanese and other Asian businesspeople often find this behavior offensive. They prefer to start with polite conversation, and they rarely say no in face-to-face conversations. As another example, firm handshakes are a common and expected greeting in most Western countries; in some Middle Eastern countries, however, handshakes might be refused if offered. In some countries, when being entertained at a meal, not finishing all the food implies that it was somehow substandard. In other countries, in contrast, wolfing down every last bite might be taken as a mild insult, suggesting that the host didn't supply enough quantity.[20] American business executives need to understand these kinds of cultural nuances before conducting business in another country.

By the same token, companies that understand cultural nuances can use them to their advantage in the global markets. For example, furniture retailer IKEA's stores are a big draw for up-and-coming Chinese consumers. But IKEA has learned that customers in China want a lot more from its stores then just affordable Scandinavian-designed furniture:[21]

> In China, IKEA stores have become popular destinations--a respite from the hustle and smog and a place to grab a reliable lunch. "Customers come on family outings, hop into display

> beds and nap, pose for snapshots with the décor, and hang out for hours to enjoy the air conditioning and free soda refills," notes one observer. ● On a typical Saturday afternoon, for example, display beds and other furniture in a huge Chinese IKEA store are occupied, with customers of all ages lounging or even fast asleep. IKEA managers encourage such behavior, figuring that familiarity with the store will result in later purchasing when shoppers' incomes eventually rise to match their aspirations. "Maybe if you've been visiting IKEA, eating meatballs, hot dogs, or ice cream for 10 years, then maybe you will consider IKEA when you get yourself a sofa," says the company's Asia-Pacific president. Thanks to such cultural understandings, IKEA already captures about 7 percent of the surging Chinese home-furnishings market, and its sales in China increased 20 percent last year.

Thus, understanding cultural traditions, preferences, and behaviors can help companies not only avoid embarrassing mistakes but also take advantage of cross-cultural opportunities.

● The impact of culture on marketing strategy: IKEA customers in China want a lot more from its stores than just affordable Scandinavian-designed furniture.

Lou Linwei/Alamy

The Impact of Marketing Strategy on Cultures

Whereas marketers worry about the impact of global cultures on their marketing strategies, others may worry about the impact of marketing strategies on global cultures. For example, social critics contend that large American multinationals, such as McDonald's, Coca-Cola, Starbucks, Nike, Google, Disney, and Facebook, aren't just globalizing their brands; they are Americanizing the world's cultures. Other elements of American culture have become pervasive worldwide.[22] For instance, more people now study English in China than speak it in the United States. Of the 10 most watched TV shows in the world, 7 are American. If you assemble businesspeople from Brazil, Germany, and China, they'll likely transact in English. And the thing that binds the world's teens together in a kind of global community, notes one observer, "is American culture—the music, the Hollywood fare, the electronic games, Google, Facebook, American consumer brands. The . . . rest of the world is becoming [evermore] like us—in ways good and bad."

"Today, globalization often wears Mickey Mouse ears, eats Big Macs, drinks Coke or Pepsi, and does its computing with Windows," says Thomas Friedman in his book *The Lexus and the Olive Tree: Understanding Globalization.* "Some Chinese kids' first English word [is] Mickey," notes another writer.[23]

Critics worry that, under such "McDomination," countries around the globe are losing their individual cultural identities. Teens in Turkey watch MTV, connect with others globally through Facebook, and ask their parents for more Westernized clothes and other symbols of American pop culture and values. Grandmothers in small European villas no longer spend each morning visiting local meat, bread, and produce markets to gather the ingredients for dinner. Instead, they now shop at Walmart Supercenters. Women in Saudi Arabia see American films, question their societal roles, and shop at any of the country's growing number of Victoria's Secret boutiques. In China, most people never drank coffee before Starbucks entered the market. Now Chinese consumers rush to Starbucks stores "because it's a symbol of a new kind of lifestyle." ● Similarly, in China,

● The impact of marketing strategy on culture: Nearly half of all children in China identify McDonald's as a domestic brand.

Tomoko Kunihiro

where McDonald's operates more than 80 restaurants in Beijing alone, nearly half of all children identify the chain as a domestic brand.

Such concerns have sometimes led to a backlash against American globalization. Well-known U.S. brands have become the targets of boycotts and protests in some international markets. As symbols of American capitalism, companies such as Coca-Cola, McDonald's, Nike, and KFC have been singled out by antiglobalization protestors in hot spots around the world, especially when anti-American sentiment peaks.

Despite such problems, defenders of globalization argue that concerns of Americanization and the potential damage to American brands are overblown. U.S. brands are doing very well internationally. In the most recent Millward Brown Optimor brand value survey of global consumer brands, 16 of the top 20 brands were American owned, including megabrands such as Apple, IBM, Google, McDonald's, Microsoft, Coca-Cola, GE, Amazon.com, and Walmart.[24] Many iconic American brands are soaring globally. For example, Chinese consumers appear to have an insatiable appetite for Apple iPhones and iPads. When Apple introduced its latest iPhone model in China last year, demand was so heavy that the company had to abandon sales in some Beijing stores to avert the threat of rioting by mobs of eager consumers. China is now Apple's second biggest market behind the United States. "It's mind-boggling that we can do this well," says Apple CEO Tim Cook.[25]

More fundamentally, the cultural exchange goes both ways: America gets as well as gives cultural influence. True, Hollywood dominates the global movie market, but British TV originated the programming that was Americanized into such hits as *The Office*, *American Idol*, and *Dancing with the Stars*. Although Chinese and Russian youth are donning NBA superstar jerseys, the increasing popularity of American soccer has deep international roots.

Even American childhood has been increasingly influenced by European and Asian cultural imports. Most kids know all about imports such as Hello Kitty, the Bakugan Battle Brawler, or any of a host of Nintendo or Sega game characters. And J. K. Rowling's so-very-British Harry Potter books have shaped the thinking of a generation of American youngsters, not to mention the millions of American oldsters who've fallen under their spell as well. For the moment, English remains the dominant language of the Internet, and having Web access often means that third-world youth have greater exposure to American popular culture. Yet these same technologies let Eastern European students studying in the United States hear Webcast news and music from Poland, Romania, or Belarus.

Thus, globalization is a two-way street. If globalization has Mickey Mouse ears, it is also talking on an LG mobile phone, buying furniture at IKEA, driving a Toyota Camry, and watching a British-inspired show on a Samsung plasma TV.

Deciding Whether to Go Global

Not all companies need to venture into international markets to survive. For example, most local businesses need to market well only in their local marketplaces. Operating domestically is easier and safer. Managers don't need to learn another country's language and laws. They don't have to deal with unstable currencies, face political and legal uncertainties, or redesign their products to suit different customer expectations. However, companies that operate in global industries, where their strategic positions in specific markets are affected strongly by their overall global positions, must compete on a regional or worldwide basis to succeed.

Any of several factors might draw a company into the international arena. For example, global competitors might attack the company's home market by offering better products or lower prices. The company might want to counterattack these competitors in their home markets to tie up their resources. The company's customers might be expanding abroad and require international servicing. Or, most likely, international markets might simply provide better opportunities for growth. For example, as we discovered in the story at the start of the chapter, Coca-Cola has emphasized international growth in recent years to offset stagnant or declining U.S. soft drink sales. Today, nearly 80 percent of Coca-Cola's sales come from outside the United States, and the company is making major pushes into 90 emerging markets, such as China, India, and the entire African continent.[26]

Before going abroad, the company must weigh several risks and answer many questions about its ability to operate globally. Can the company learn to understand the preferences and buyer behavior of consumers in other countries? Can it offer competitively attractive products? Will it be able to adapt to other countries' business cultures and deal effectively with foreign nationals? Do the company's managers have the necessary international experience? Has management considered the impact of regulations and the political environments of other countries?

Deciding Which Markets to Enter

Before going abroad, the company should try to define its international *marketing objectives and policies*. It should decide what *volume* of foreign sales it wants. Most companies start small when they go abroad. Some plan to stay small, seeing international sales as a small part of their business. Other companies have bigger plans, however, seeing international business as equal to or even more important than their domestic business.

The company also needs to choose in *how many* countries it wants to market. Companies must be careful not to spread themselves too thin or expand beyond their capabilities by operating in too many countries too soon. Next, the company needs to decide on the *types* of countries to enter. A country's attractiveness depends on the product, geographical factors, income and population, political climate, and other considerations. In recent years, many major new markets have emerged, offering both substantial opportunities and daunting challenges.

After listing possible international markets, the company must carefully evaluate each one. It must consider many factors. For example, Walmart's decision to enter Africa seems like a no-brainer: Taken as a whole, the African market is three times the size of China and is home to more than 1 billion people and 6 of the world's 10 fastest-growing economies. In fact, Walmart recently gained a toehold in Africa by acquiring a majority stake in South African retailer Massmart, which operates its Makro, Game, and other discount and warehouse stores mostly in South Africa but also in 13 other African countries.

However, as Walmart considers expanding into African markets, it must ask some important questions. Can it compete effectively on a country-by-country basis with hundreds of local competitors? Will the various African governments be stable and supportive? Does Africa provide for the needed logistics technologies? Can Walmart master the varied and vastly different cultural and buying differences of African consumers?

Walmart's expansion in Africa will likely be a slow process, as it confronts many unfamiliar cultural, political, and logistical challenges. Along with the huge opportunities, many African countries rank among the world's most difficult places to do business. "You see a market like Nigeria [with a population of more than 150 million] and it feels like a big opportunity," says the chief executive of Walmart International. "But we've learned [that] we really need to think about it a city at a time as opposed to a country at a time."[27]

Possible global markets should be ranked on several factors, including market size, market growth, the cost of doing business, competitive advantage, and risk level. The goal is to determine the potential of each market, using indicators such as those shown in ● **Table 19.1**. Then the marketer must decide which markets offer the greatest long-run return on investment.

Table 19.1 | Indicators of Market Potential

Demographic Characteristics	Sociocultural Factors
Education	Consumer lifestyles, beliefs, and values
Population size and growth	Business norms and approaches
Population age composition	Cultural and social norms
	Languages
Geographic Characteristics	**Political and Legal Factors**
Climate	National priorities
Country size	Political stability
Population density—urban, rural	Government attitudes toward global trade
Transportation structure and market accessibility	Government bureaucracy
	Monetary and trade regulations
Economic Factors	
GDP size and growth	
Income distribution	
Industrial infrastructure	
Natural resources	
Financial and human resources	

Objective 2 ⸺▶
Describe three key approaches to entering international markets.

Deciding How to Enter the Market

Once a company has decided to sell in a foreign country, it must determine the best mode of entry. Its choices are *exporting*, *joint venturing*, and *direct investment*. ● **Figure 19.2** shows three market entry strategies, along with the options each one offers. As the figure shows, each succeeding strategy involves more commitment and risk but also more control and potential profits.

Exporting

Exporting
Entering foreign markets by selling goods produced in the company's home country, often with little modification.

The simplest way to enter a foreign market is through **exporting**. The company may passively export its surpluses from time to time, or it may make an active commitment to expand exports to a particular market. In either case, the company produces all its goods in its home country. It may or may not modify them for the export market.

● **FIGURE | 19.2**
Market Entry Strategies

Exporting is the simplest way to enter a foreign market, but it usually offers less control and profit potential.

Exporting	Joint venturing	Direct investment
Indirect Direct	Licensing Contract manufacturing Management contracting Joint ownership	Assembly facilities Manufacturing facilities

Amount of commitment, risk, control, and profit potential

Direct investment—owning your own foreign-based operation—affords greater control and profit potential, but it's often riskier.

Joint venturing

Entering foreign markets by joining with foreign companies to produce or market a product or service.

Licensing

Entering foreign markets through developing an agreement with a licensee in the foreign market.

Contract manufacturing

A joint venture in which a company contracts with manufacturers in a foreign market to produce its product or provide its service.

Management contracting

A joint venture in which the domestic firm supplies the management know-how to a foreign company that supplies the capital; the domestic firm exports management services rather than products.

Exporting involves the least change in the company's product lines, organization, investments, or mission.

Companies typically start with *indirect exporting*, working through independent international marketing intermediaries. Indirect exporting involves less investment because the firm does not require an overseas marketing organization or network. It also involves less risk. International marketing intermediaries bring know-how and services to the relationship, so the seller normally makes fewer mistakes. Sellers may eventually move into *direct exporting*, whereby they handle their own exports. The investment and risk are somewhat greater in this strategy, but so is the potential return.

Joint Venturing

A second method of entering a foreign market is by **joint venturing**—joining with foreign companies to produce or market products or services. Joint venturing differs from exporting in that the company joins with a host country partner to sell or market abroad. It differs from direct investment in that an association is formed with someone in the foreign country. There are four types of joint ventures: licensing, contract manufacturing, management contracting, and joint ownership.

Licensing

Licensing is a simple way for a manufacturer to enter international marketing. The company enters into an agreement with a licensee in the foreign market. For a fee or royalty payments, the licensee buys the right to use the company's manufacturing process, trademark, patent, trade secret, or other item of value. The company thus gains entry into a foreign market at little risk; at the same time, the licensee gains production expertise or a well-known product or name without having to start from scratch.

In Japan, Budweiser beer flows from Kirin breweries, and Moringa Milk Company produces Sunkist fruit juice, drinks, and dessert items. Coca-Cola markets internationally by licensing bottlers around the world and supplying them with the syrup needed to produce the product. Its global bottling partners range from the Coca-Cola Bottling Company of Saudi Arabia to Europe-based Coca-Cola Hellenic, which bottles and markets 90 Coca-Cola brands to 560 million people in 30 countries, from Italy and Greece to Nigeria and Russia.

Licensing has potential disadvantages, however. The firm has less control over the licensee than it would over its own operations. Furthermore, if the licensee is very successful, the firm has given up these profits, and if and when the contract ends, it may find it has created a competitor.

● **Licensing: In Japan, Sunkist fruit juices, drinks, and dessert items are produced by Moringa Milk Company.**

Reprinted with permission of Sunkist Growers, Inc. All rights reserved.

Contract Manufacturing

Another option is **contract manufacturing**, in which the company makes agreements with manufacturers in the foreign market to produce its product or provide its service. Sears used this method in opening up department stores in Mexico and Spain, where it found qualified local manufacturers to produce many of the products it sells. The drawbacks of contract manufacturing are decreased control over the manufacturing process and loss of potential profits on manufacturing. The benefits are the chance to start faster, with less risk, and the later opportunity either to form a partnership with or buy out the local manufacturer.

Management Contracting

Under **management contracting**, the domestic firm provides the management know-how to a foreign company that supplies the capital. In other words, the domestic firm exports management services rather than products. Hilton uses this arrangement in managing hotels around the world. For example, the hotel chain operates DoubleTree by Hilton hotels in countries ranging from the UK and Italy to Peru and Costa Rica, to China, Russia, and Tanzania. The properties are locally owned, but Hilton manages the hotels with its world-renowned hospitality expertise.[28]

Management contracting is a low-risk method of getting into a foreign market, and it yields income from the beginning. The arrangement is even more attractive if the contracting firm has an option to buy some share in the managed company later on. The arrangement is not sensible, however, if the company can put its scarce management talent to better uses or if it can make greater profits by undertaking the whole venture. Management contracting also prevents the company from setting up its own operations for a period of time.

Joint Ownership

Joint ownership

A cooperative venture in which a company creates a local business with investors in a foreign market, who share ownership and control.

Joint ownership ventures consist of one company joining forces with foreign investors to create a local business in which they share possession and control. A company may buy an interest in a local firm, or the two parties may form a new business venture. Joint ownership may be needed for economic or political reasons. For example, the firm may lack the financial, physical, or managerial resources to undertake the venture alone. Alternatively, a foreign government may require joint ownership as a condition for entry.

Often, companies form joint ownership ventures to merge their complementary strengths in developing a global marketing opportunity. ● For example, Campbell Soup Company recently formed a 60/40 joint venture with Hong Kong-based Swire Pacific—called Campbell Swire—to help better distribute the company's soups in China.[29]

China represents a tremendous opportunity for Campbell: The Chinese population consumes about 355 billion servings of soup annually. However, Chinese consumers currently prefer the homemade variety, leaving plenty of room for growth of commercial soups. Campbell Swire will manufacture and market Campbell's soups in China. Each company brings unique strengths to the partnership. Campbell knows how to make and market soup; Swire Pacific has long experience in food distribution in China and a deep understanding of the Chinese market. Together, each can accomplish more than either could alone. "This partnership will help unlock the potential of the soup market in China by pairing Campbell's brands, recipes, and consumer insights with Swire's sales force, logistics capabilities, and overall market knowledge," says the president of Campbell International.

Joint ownership has certain drawbacks, however. The partners may disagree over investment, marketing, or other policies. Whereas many U.S. firms like to reinvest earnings for growth, local firms often prefer to take out these earnings; whereas U.S. firms emphasize the role of marketing, local investors may rely on selling.

● Direct investment: Ford has made major direct investments in several countries, such as India, China, and Thailand, to help satisfy Ford's burgeoning demand in Asian markets.
AFP/Getty Images

Direct Investment

Direct investment

Entering a foreign market by developing foreign-based assembly or manufacturing facilities.

The biggest involvement in a foreign market comes through **direct investment**—the development of foreign-based assembly or manufacturing facilities. For example, Ford has made direct investments in several Asian countries, including India, China, and Thailand. It recently began building its second facility in India, a $1 billion state-of-the-art manufacturing and engineering plant that will produce 240,000 cars a year, helping to satisfy Ford's burgeoning demand in India and other Asian markets. Similarly, Honda and Toyota have made substantial direct manufacturing investments in North America. For example, more than 87 percent of the Honda and Acura models sold in the United States are made in North America. "Our fundamental philosophy is to produce where we sell," says a Honda executive.[30]

If a company has gained experience in exporting and if the foreign market is large enough, foreign production facilities offer many advantages. The firm may have lower costs in the form of cheaper labor or raw materials, foreign government investment incentives, and freight savings. The firm may also improve its image in the host country because it creates jobs. Generally, a firm develops a deeper relationship with the government, customers, local suppliers, and distributors, allowing it to adapt its products to the local market better. Finally, the firm keeps full control over the investment and therefore can develop manufacturing and marketing policies that serve its long-term international objectives.

The main disadvantage of direct investment is that the firm faces many risks, such as restricted or devalued currencies, falling markets, or government changes. In some cases, a firm has no choice but to accept these risks if it wants to operate in the host country.

Deciding on the Global Marketing Program

Objective 3 ┄┄┄►

Explain how companies adapt their marketing strategies and mixes for international markets.

Standardized global marketing
An international marketing strategy that basically uses the same marketing strategy and mix in all of the company's international markets.

Adapted global marketing
An international marketing approach that adjusts the marketing strategy and mix elements to each international target market, which creates more costs but hopefully produces a larger market share and return.

Companies that operate in one or more foreign markets must decide how much, if at all, to adapt their marketing strategies and programs to local conditions. At one extreme are global companies that use **standardized global marketing**, essentially using the same marketing strategy approaches and marketing mix worldwide. At the other extreme is **adapted global marketing**. In this case, the producer adjusts the marketing strategy and mix elements to each target market, resulting in more costs but hopefully producing a larger market share and return.

The question of whether to adapt or standardize the marketing strategy and program has been much debated over the years. On the one hand, some global marketers believe that technology is making the world a smaller place, and consumer needs around the world are becoming more similar. This paves the way for global brands and standardized global marketing. Global branding and standardization, in turn, result in greater brand power and reduced costs from economies of scale.

On the other hand, the marketing concept holds that marketing programs will be more effective if tailored to the unique needs of each targeted customer group. If this concept applies within a country, it should apply even more across international markets. Despite global convergence, consumers in different countries still have widely varied cultural backgrounds. They still differ significantly in their needs and wants, spending power, product preferences, and shopping patterns. Because these differences are hard to change, most marketers today adapt their products, prices, channels, and promotions to fit consumer desires in each country.

However, global standardization is not an all-or-nothing proposition. It's a matter of degree. Most international marketers suggest that companies should "think globally but act locally"—that they should seek a balance between standardization and adaptation. Starbucks has found this balance internationally, leveraging its substantial global brand recognition but adapting its marketing and operations to specific markets. The company's overall brand strategy provides global strategic direction. Then regional or local units focus on adapting the strategy and brand to specific local markets such as India and China (see Real Marketing 19.2). "The best brand organizations drive a single-minded brand purpose and then challenge and empower local marketers to develop the best activation mix to bring that to fruition in every market," says a global branding expert.[31]

Collectively, local brands still account for the overwhelming majority of consumers' purchases. "The vast majority of people still lead very local lives," says a global analyst. "By all means go global, but the first thing you have to do is win on the ground. You have to go local." Another analyst agrees: "You need to respect local culture and become part of it." A global brand must "engage with consumers in a way that feels local to them." Simon Clift, former chief marketing officer at global consumer-goods giant Unilever, put it this way: "We're trying to strike a balance between being mindlessly global and hopelessly local."[32]

McDonald's operates this way: It uses the same basic fast-food look, layout, and operating model in its restaurants around the world but adapts its menu and design to local tastes. For example, McDonald's France uses the power of its global brand and operating model but has redefined itself as a French company that adapts to the needs and preferences of French consumers:[33]

"France—the land of haute cuisine, fine wine, and cheese—would be the last place you would expect to find a thriving [McDonald's]," opines one observer. Yet the fast-food giant has turned France into its

Real Marketing 19.2

Starbucks in India: A Global Brand in a Local Market

Starbucks is now opening for business in India, with 50 stores planned by the end of 2012 and a bunch more to follow quickly. Given India's rapidly emerging economy and its huge population of well over 1.2 billion people, entering the Indian market seems like a no brainer for the global brand.

Opportunities abound for Starbucks in India. Long a country of tea drinkers, India is now in the midst of a coffee café explosion, fueled by the nation's growing middle class and large youth population. India—especially the young adult segment—is ready for Starbucks. In a country that still largely disapproves of young adults, especially young women, socializing in bars or pubs, coffee shops provide ideal hangouts. "When you don't want to drink, when you just want to chill, you come here," says a 22-year-old female week-night patron at a Coffee Bean & Tea Leaf outlet in New Delhi. It's worth paying 150 rupees (about $3) for a cup of coffee and time away from home with her friends.

If the coffee market is heating up in India, so is the Starbucks brand. Even though it's just now setting up shop there, thanks to Starbucks' global prowess, many Indians are already familiar with the brand. In fact, according to Bhandari, the growth of India's coffee market in the first place resulted in part from Starbucks' global success. "The growth didn't only come because [of local coffee shops. It] came because of the lifestyle that Starbucks started in the United States and other places." So, because of its global brand power, the café tables are already set for Starbucks as it enters India.

However, global brand power won't automatically translate into local brand success for Starbucks. India is very different from the United States, Canada, or Europe. To succeed in India's complex market environment, Starbucks must carefully adapt to the tastes of Indian consumers and the complexities of India's political, business, and social environments.

For example, doing business in India heavily favors insiders. By market capitalization, more than 70 percent of Indian business is family-controlled. Developing commercial relationships in India takes time and patience,

and even then family ties can dominate. To make things even more challenging for outside firms, the Indian government is notoriously slow when it comes to making foreign investment decisions. For instance, in response to protests from local businesses, the Indian government recently put off a long-awaited decision to let foreign retailers own a 51 percent or greater stake in Indian retail operations. In such an uncertain political environment, foreign investment in India has declined in recent years and economic growth has slowed.

But Starbucks—the world's largest coffee chain with nearly 17,500 stores in 59 countries—is no stranger to the difficulties of entering new global markets. The company has studied India for years, learning all it can and patiently honing its entry strategy. To smooth the way, Starbucks forged a 50-50 joint venture with Tata Global Beverages, a division of India's largest business group. The Tata alliance eases the financial risks and gives Starbucks insider business and political status. It also helps the coffee-house giant to understand the needs of Indian consumers. According to John Culver, president of Starbucks China and Asia Pacific, even without government restrictions on foreign ownership, Starbucks would never have considered trying to go it alone in India. "We never considered 51 percent," he says. "When we looked at the opportunity to enter India, understanding the complexities of the market and the uniqueness that is India, we wanted to find a local business partner."

In entering India, Starbucks also faces a market that's percolating with well-established competitors. One local competitor—Café Coffee Day—dominates with 1,200 stores and a planned 2,000 stores by the end of 2014. Self-described as "India's favorite coffee shop,

where the young and young at heart unwind," Café Coffee Day promises a world-class coffee experience at affordable prices. Several foreign coffee chains have also invaded India, such as Italy's Lavazza and California-based Coffee Bean & Tea Leaf. Most competitors feature low prices, with small cappuccinos commonly selling for $1 or less.

But despite the growing competition, Starbucks has been welcomed in India, even by the leading local competitor. Given the huge size and rapid growth of the Indian coffee market, there appears to be plenty of room for all players. "There are a lot of foreign brands already available in India, and still it hasn't made any difference from a competition point of view," says Café Coffee Day's chief operating officer. And "when companies like Starbucks come in," he says, "the awareness levels go up tremendously [and] the overall market size grows." Adds another Café Coffee Day executive, "We will hopefully learn a few things from them." According to one analyst, at some point India can easily

Starbucks' global brand power won't automatically translate into local success in India. The brand must adapt to the tastes of Indian consumers and the complexities of India's political and business environments.
© Michele Falzone/Alamy

support 5,000 Starbucks, enough stores in India alone to increase Starbucks' worldwide count by nearly 30 percent.

Starbucks' strategy in India for adapting to local consumer preferences is still emerging, but many analysts expect that the company will apply the lessons it learned in China. When Starbucks entered China in 1998, given the strong Chinese tea-drinking culture, few observers expected success. But Starbucks quickly proved the doubters wrong; China will soon be Starbucks' largest market outside of the United States.

Starbucks' success in China results from adapting its global brand strategy to the unique characteristics of Chinese consumers. Rather than forcing U.S. products on the Chinese, Starbucks developed new flavors—such as green-tea-flavored coffee drinks—that appeal to local tastes. Rather than pushing take-out orders, which account for most of its U.S. revenues, Starbucks promoted dine-in services—making its stores the perfect meeting place for Chinese professionals and their friends. And rather than just charging U.S.-style premium prices in China, Starbucks boosted prices even higher, positioning the brand as a status symbol for the rapidly growing Chinese middle and upper classes. Under this adapted strategy, Starbucks China is thriving.

For now, Indian consumers may not know which Starbucks size is bigger, grande or venti. And they might not know the exact difference between a Frappuccino and a Caffè Mocha. But all that will likely change soon as the Starbucks brand grows and prospers. Success will depend on how well Starbucks applies its global brand muscle to the unique tastes of Indian customers. According to Starbucks' president Culver, it's full steam ahead. "We're going to move as fast as possible in opening as many stores as we can, so long as we are successful and so long as we are embraced by the Indian consumers."

Sources: Vikas Bajaj, "After a Year of Delays, the First Starbucks Is to Open in Tea-Loving India This Fall," *New York Times*, January 31, 2012, p. B2; Erika Kinetz, "Starbucks India: Coffee Chain to Open First India Outpost with Tata Global Beverages," *Huffington Post*, January 30, 2012, www.huffingtonpost.com/2012/01/30/starbucks-india_n_1241553.html; Elliot Hannon, "Will Global Coffee Giant Starbucks Conquer India?" *Time*, January 31, 2012, http://world.time.com/2012/01/31/will-global-coffee-giant-starbucks-conquer-india/; and Shaun Rein, "Why Starbucks Succeeds in China and Others Haven't," *USA Today*, February 12, 2012, www.usatoday.com/money/industries/food/story/2012-02-12/cnbc-starbucks-secrets-of-china-success/53040820/1.

● **Think globally, act locally: By leveraging the power of its global brand but constantly adapting to the needs and preferences of French consumers and their culture, McDonald's has turned France into its second-most-profitable world market.**

ERIC PIERMONT/AFP/Getty Images/Newscom

second-most profitable world market. Although a McDonald's in Paris might at first seem a lot like one in Chicago, McDonald's has carefully adapted its French operations to the preferences of local customers. At the most basic level, although a majority of revenues still come from burgers and fries, McDonald's France has changed its menu to please the French palate. For example, it offers up burgers with French cheeses such as chevre, cantel, and bleu, topped off with whole-grain French mustard sauce. ● French consumers love baguettes, so McDonald's bakes them fresh in its restaurants and sells them in oh-so-French McBaguette sandwiches. And in response to the growing French trend for healthy eating, the menu in France includes reduced-salt french fries, fresh fruit, and "le Big Mac"—the McDonald's classic but with a whole-wheat-bun option.

But perhaps the biggest difference isn't in the food, but in the design of the restaurants themselves, which have been adapted to suit French lifestyles. For example, French meal times tend to be longer, with more food consumed per sitting. So McDonald's has refined its restaurant interiors to create a comfortable, welcoming environment where customers want to linger and perhaps order an additional coffee or dessert. McDonald's even provides table-side service. As a result, the average French McDonald's customer spends about four times what an American customer spends per visit.

Product

Five strategies are used for adapting product and marketing communication strategies to a global market (see ● **Figure 19.3**).[34] We first discuss the three product strategies and then turn to the two communication strategies.

Straight product extension means marketing a product in a foreign market without making any changes to the product. Top management tells its marketing people, "Take

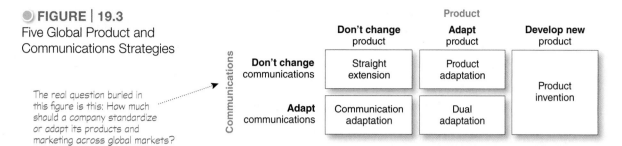

FIGURE | 19.3

Five Global Product and
Communications Strategies

The real question buried in
this figure is this: How much
should a company standardize
or adapt its products and
marketing across global markets?

Straight product extension

Marketing a product in a foreign market
without making any changes to the
product.

the product as is and find customers for it." The first step, however, should be to find out
whether foreign consumers use that product and what form they prefer.

Straight extension has been successful in some cases and disastrous in others. Apple iPads, Gillette razors, Black & Decker tools, and even 7–11 Slurpees are all sold
successfully in about the same form around the world. But when General Foods introduced its standard powdered JELL-O in the British market, it discovered that British
consumers prefer a solid wafer or cake form. Likewise, Philips began to make a profit
in Japan only after it reduced the size of its coffeemakers to fit into smaller Japanese
kitchens and its shavers to fit smaller Japanese hands. Straight extension is tempting
because it involves no additional product development costs, manufacturing changes,
or new promotion. But it can be costly in the long run if products fail to satisfy consumers in specific global markets.

Product adaptation

Adapting a product to meet local
conditions or wants in foreign markets.

Product adaptation involves changing the product to meet local requirements, conditions, or wants. For example, Kraft has adapted its popular Oreo cookie to the unique
tastes of consumers all around the world, whether it's mango-and-orange flavored Oreos
in the Asia Pacific region, green tea Oreos in China, a chocolate and peanut variety in Indonesia, or banana and dulce de leche in Argentina. Chinese Oreos are less sweet than the
American standard; Oreos in India are less bitter.[35]

As another example, although the U.S. and European versions of the feisty little Fiat
500 might look a lot alike, Fiat has made stem-to-stern adaptations in the U.S. model to
meet U.S. safety standards and American buyer expectations. To name just a few modifications, the U.S. Fiat 500 has a redesigned engine that offers the power demanded by U.S.
consumers while simultaneously providing the better gas mileage and lower emissions
required by the country's regulations. The gas tank is 40 percent larger to accommodate
the longer driving distances that are typical in the United States, and there's lots more insulation in the U.S. car to keep it quiet enough for Americans. Another big difference—the
cupholders:[36]

> A silly matter to Europeans, but vital to Americans, the U.S. Fiat 500 has an enlarged pod of holders up front to fit U.S.-size drinks, instead of the small European holders, plus two additional
> holders at the rear of the floor console. The in-car beverage concept is so foreign to Europeans that
> the 500 design team didn't understand the need for more and bigger holders—until one engineer
> drew a cartoon of an American wearing one of those gimmick hats that hold two beer cans and
> have long tubes at straws. Then everybody said, "Ah, yes."

Product invention

Creating new products or services for
foreign markets.

Product invention consists of creating something new to meet the needs of consumers in a given country. As markets have gone global, companies ranging from appliance manufacturers and carmakers to candy and soft drink producers have developed
products that meet the special purchasing needs of low-income consumers in developing economies. For example, Ford developed the economical, low-priced Figo model
especially for entry-level consumers in India; GM created the inexpensive Baojun for
China (the name means "treasured horse"). Chinese appliance producer Haier developed sturdier washing machines for rural users in emerging markets, where it found that
lighter-duty machines often became clogged with mud when farmers used them to clean
vegetables as well as clothes.[37]

Similarly, Finnish mobile phone maker Nokia has created full-featured but rugged
and low-cost phones especially designed for the harsher living conditions faced by
less-affluent consumers in large developing countries such as India, China, and Kenya.
For instance, it developed dustproof keypads, which are crucial in dry, hot countries
with many unpaved roads. Some phones have built-in radio antennas for areas where
radio is the main source of entertainment. And after learning that poor people often

share their phones, the company developed handsets with multiple address books. Thanks to such innovation, Nokia is the market leader in Africa, the Middle East, Eastern Europe, and Asia.[38]

Promotion

Companies can either adopt the same communication strategy they use in the home market or change it for each local market. Consider advertising messages. Some global companies use a standardized advertising theme around the world. For example, Apple sold millions of iPods with a single global campaign featuring silhouetted figures dancing against a colorful background. And other than for language, the Apple Web site looks about the same for any of the more than 70 countries in which Apple markets its products, from Australia to Senegal to the Czech Republic.

Of course, even in highly standardized communications campaigns, some adjustments might be required for language and cultural differences. For example, in Western markets, fast-casual clothing retailer H&M runs fashion ads with models showing liberal amounts of bare skin. But in the Middle East, where attitudes toward public nudity are more conservative, the retailer runs the same ads digitally adapted to better cover its models.

Global companies often have difficulty crossing the language barrier, with results ranging from mild embarrassment to outright failure. Seemingly innocuous brand names and advertising phrases can take on unintended or hidden meanings when translated into other languages. For example, Interbrand of London, the firm that created household names such as Prozac and Acura, recently developed a brand name "hall of shame" list, which contained these and other foreign brand names you're never likely to see inside the local Kroger supermarket: Krapp toilet paper (Denmark), Plopp chocolate (Scandinavia), Crapsy Fruit cereal (France), Poo curry powder (Argentina), and Pschitt lemonade (France). Similarly, advertising themes often lose—or gain—something in the translation. In Chinese, the KFC slogan "finger-lickin' good" came out as "eat your fingers off." And Motorola's Hellomoto ringtone sounds like "Hello, Fatty" in India. Marketers must be watchful to avoid such mistakes.

Other companies follow a strategy of **communication adaptation**, fully adapting their advertising messages to local markets. Consumer-products marketer Unilever does this for many of its brands. ● For example, whereas ads for Unilever toothpaste brands in Western markets might emphasize anything from whiter teeth or fresher breath to greater sex appeal, ads in Africa take a more basic educational approach, emphasizing the importance of brushing twice a day. And Unilever adapts the positioning, formulation, and appeals for its Sunsilk Lively Clean & Fresh shampoo to serve the varying needs of consumers in different markets. Whereas its standard Western shampoo ads tend to show young women flirtatiously tossing their freshly-washed locks over their shoulders, Sunsilk's Lively Clean & Fresh ads in Malaysia show no hair at all. Instead, they feature modern young women wearing tudungs—traditional Muslim headscarves that completely cover the hair. To tap the large and growing Malaysian Islamic market, Unilever positions Lively Clean & Fresh directly to the "lifestyle of the tudung wearer," as a remedy for the problem of excess hair and scalp oil that wearing a tudung can cause.[39]

Media also need to be adapted internationally because media availability and regulations vary from country to country. TV advertising time is very limited in Europe, for instance, ranging from four hours a day in France to none in Scandinavian countries. Advertisers must buy time months in advance, and they have little

Communication adaptation
A global communication strategy of fully adapting advertising messages to local markets.

● **Adapting advertising messages:** Whereas Western ads for Unilever toothpaste brands might emphasize whiter teeth, fresher breath, or greater sex appeal, its ads in Africa take a more educational approach emphasizing healthy teeth.

Unilever plc

Whole-channel view

Designing international channels that take into account the entire global supply chain and marketing channel, forging an effective global value delivery network.

control over airtimes. However, mobile phone ads are much more widely accepted in Europe and Asia than in the United States. Magazines also vary in effectiveness. For example, magazines are a major medium in Italy but a minor one in Austria. Newspapers are national in the United Kingdom but only local in Spain.[40]

Price

Companies also face many considerations in setting their international prices. For example, how might Makita price its tools globally? It could set a uniform price globally, but this amount would be too high of a price in poor countries and not high enough in rich ones. It could charge what consumers in each country would bear, but this strategy ignores differences in the actual costs from country to country. Finally, the company could use a standard markup of its costs everywhere, but this approach might price Makita out of the market in some countries where costs are high.

Regardless of how companies go about pricing their products, their foreign prices probably will be higher than their domestic prices for comparable products. An Apple iPad 3 that sells for $499 in the United States goes for $624 in the United Kingdom. Why? Apple faces a *price escalation* problem. It must add the cost of transportation, tariffs, importer margin, wholesaler margin, and retailer margin to its factory price. Depending on these added costs, a product may have to sell for two to five times as much in another country to make the same profit.

To overcome this problem when selling to less-affluent consumers in developing countries, many companies make simpler or smaller versions of their products that can be sold at lower prices. Others have introduced new, more affordable brands in emerging markets. ● For example, Levi recently launched the Denizen brand, created for teens and young adults in emerging markets such as China, India, and Brazil who cannot afford Levi's-branded jeans. The name combines the first four letters of *denim* with *zen*, a word with Japanese and Chinese roots that means "meditative state" or "escape from the hustle and bustle of everyday life."[41]

● International pricing: Levi Strauss recently launched the Denizen brand, created for teens and young adults in emerging markets such as China, India, and Brazil who cannot afford Levi's-branded jeans.

Nelson Ching/Getty Images USA, Inc.

Recent economic and technological forces have had an impact on global pricing. For example, the Internet is making global price differences more obvious. When firms sell their wares over the Internet, customers can see how much products sell for in different countries. They can even order a given product directly from the company location or dealer offering the lowest price. This is forcing companies toward more standardized international pricing.

Distribution Channels

An international company must take a **whole-channel view** of the problem of distributing products to final consumers. ● **Figure 19.4** shows the two major links between the seller and the final buyer. The first link, *channels between nations*, moves company products from points of production to the borders of countries within which they are sold. The second link, *channels within nations*, moves products from their market entry points to the final consumers. The whole-channel view takes into account the entire global supply chain and marketing channel. It recognizes that to compete well internationally, the company must effectively design and manage an entire *global value delivery network*.

● **FIGURE | 19.4**

Whole-Channel Concept for International Marketing

Distribution channels can vary dramatically around the world. For example, in the U.S., Nokia distributes phones through a network of sophisticated retailers. In rural India, it maintains a fleet of Nokia-branded vans that prowl the rutted country roads.

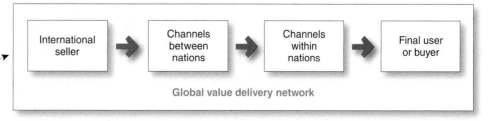

International seller → Channels between nations → Channels within nations → Final user or buyer

Global value delivery network

Channels of distribution within countries vary greatly from nation to nation. There are large differences in the numbers and types of intermediaries serving each country market and in the transportation infrastructure serving these intermediaries. For example, whereas large-scale retail chains dominate the U.S. scene, most of the retailing in other countries is done by small, independent retailers. In India, millions of retailers operate tiny shops or sell in open markets. Thus, in its efforts to sell those rugged, affordable phones discussed earlier to Indian consumers, Nokia has had to forge its own distribution structure:[42]

In India, Nokia has a presence in almost 90 percent of retail outlets selling mobile phones. It estimates there are 90,000 points-of-sale for its phones, ranging from modern stores to makeshift kiosks. That makes it difficult to control how products are displayed and pitched to consumers. "You have to understand where people live, what the shopping patterns are," says a Nokia executive. "You have to work with local means to reach people—even bicycles or rickshaws." ● To reach rural India, Nokia has outfitted its own fleet of distinctive blue Nokia-branded vans that prowl the rutted country roads. Staffers park these advertisements-on-wheels in villages, often on market or festival days. There, with crowds clustering around, Nokia reps explain the basics of how the phones work and how to buy them. Nokia has extended the concept to minivans, which can reach even more remote places. Thanks to smart product development and innovative channels, Nokia now owns an impressive 30 percent share of India's mobile device market.

● **Distribution channels vary greatly from nation to nation. In its efforts to sell rugged, affordable phones to Indian consumers, Nokia forged its own distribution structure, including a fleet of distinctive blue Nokia-branded vans that prowl rutted country roads to visit remote villages.**

Atul Loke/Panos Pictures

Similarly, as we learned in the story about its ventures in Africa, Coca-Cola adapts its distribution methods to meet local challenges in global markets. For example, in Montevideo, Uruguay, where larger vehicles are challenged by traffic, parking, and pollution difficulties, Coca-Cola purchased 30 small, efficient, three-wheeled ZAP alternative transportation trucks. The little trucks average about one-fifth the fuel consumption and scoot around congested city streets with greater ease. In rural areas, Coca-Cola uses a manual delivery process. In China, an army of more than 10,000 Coca-Cola sales reps makes regular visits to small retailers, often on foot or bicycle. To reach the most isolated spots, the company even relies on teams of delivery donkeys. In Tanzania, 93 percent of Coca-Cola's products are manually delivered via pushcarts and bicycles.[43]

Objective 4 ┈┈┈▶

Identify the three major forms of international marketing organization.

Deciding on the Global Marketing Organization

Companies manage their international marketing activities in at least three different ways: Most companies first organize an export department, then create an international division, and finally become a global organization.

A firm normally gets into international marketing by simply shipping out its goods. If its international sales expand, the company will establish an *export department* with a sales manager and a few assistants. As sales increase, the export department can expand to include various marketing services so that it can actively go after business. If the firm moves into joint ventures or direct investment, the export department will no longer be adequate.

Many companies get involved in several international markets and ventures. A company may export to one country, license to another, have a joint ownership venture in a third, and own a subsidiary in a fourth. Sooner or later it will create *international divisions* or subsidiaries to handle all its international activity.

International divisions are organized in a variety of ways. An international division's corporate staff consists of marketing, manufacturing, research, finance, planning, and personnel specialists. It plans for and provides services to various operating units, which can be organized in one of three ways. They can be *geographical organizations*, with country managers who are responsible for salespeople, sales branches, distributors, and licensees in their respective countries. Or the operating units can be *world product groups*, each responsible for worldwide sales of different product groups. Finally, operating units can be *international subsidiaries*, each responsible for their own sales and profits.

Many firms have passed beyond the international division stage and are truly *global organizations*. For example, consider Reckitt Benckiser (RB), a $15-billion European producer of household, health, and personal care products and consumer goods with a stable full of familiar brands (Air Wick, Lysol, Woolite, Calgon, Mucinex, Clearasil, French's, and many others—see www.rb.com):[44]

 European household, health, and consumer-goods producer Reckitt Benckiser has a truly global organization. "Most of our top managers . . . view themselves as global citizens rather than as citizens of any given nation."

Reckitt Benckiser plc.

RB operates in more than 60 countries. Its top 400 managers represent 53 different nationalities. The company is headquartered in the United Kingdom, but its German business is run by an American, its Chinese business by an Indian, its UK business by an Italian, and its Middle East North African business by a Brit. Its U.S. business is run by a Dutchman, its Russian business by a Frenchman, its Brazilian business by a Belgian, its Japanese business by an Argentine, and its South African business by a Czech. "Most of our top managers . . . view themselves as global citizens rather than as citizens of any given nation," says RB's chief executive officer.

RB recently relocated several of its operations to put key marketers in key countries within their regions. For example, it recently moved its Latin American headquarters from Miami to Sao Paulo, Brazil. The company has spent the past decade building a culture of global mobility because it thinks that's one of the best ways to generate new ideas and create global entrepreneurs. And it has paid off. Products launched in the past three years—all the result of global cross-fertilization—account for 35–40 percent of net revenue. Over the past few years, even during the economic downturn, the company has outperformed its rivals—P&G, Unilever, and Colgate—in growth.

Global organizations don't think of themselves as national marketers who sell abroad but as global marketers. The top corporate management and staff plan worldwide manufacturing facilities, marketing policies, financial flows, and logistical systems. The global operating units report directly to the chief executive or the executive committee of the organization, not to the head of an international division. Executives are trained in worldwide operations, not just domestic *or* international operations. Global companies recruit management from many countries, buy components and supplies where they cost the least, and invest where the expected returns are greatest.

Today, major companies must become more global if they hope to compete. As foreign companies successfully invade their domestic markets, companies must move more aggressively into foreign markets. They will have to change from companies that treat their international operations as secondary to companies that view the entire world as a single borderless market.

Reviewing the Concepts

MyMarketingLab™
Go to **mymktlab.com** to complete the problems marked with this icon ⭐.

Reviewing Objectives and Key Terms

Objectives Review

Companies today can no longer afford to pay attention only to their domestic market, regardless of its size. Many industries are global industries, and firms that operate globally achieve lower costs and higher brand awareness. At the same time, global marketing is risky because of variable exchange rates, unstable governments, tariffs and trade barriers, and several other factors. Given the potential gains and risks of international marketing, companies need a systematic way to make their global marketing decisions.

Objective 1 **Discuss how the international trade system and the economic, political-legal, and cultural environments affect a company's international marketing decisions.** (pp 552–563)

A company must understand the *global marketing environment*, especially the international trade system. It should assess each foreign market's *economic*, *political-legal*, and *cultural characteristics*. The company can then decide whether it wants to go abroad and consider the potential risks and benefits. It must decide on the volume of international sales it wants, how many countries it wants to market in, and which specific markets it wants to enter. These decisions call for weighing the probable returns against the level of risk.

Objective 2 **Describe three key approaches to entering international markets.** (pp 563–566)

The company must decide how to enter each chosen market—whether through *exporting*, *joint venturing*, or *direct investment*. Many companies start as exporters, move to joint ventures, and finally make a direct investment in foreign markets. In *exporting*, the company enters a foreign market by sending and selling products through international marketing intermediaries (indirect exporting) or the company's own department, branch, or sales representatives or agents (direct exporting). When establishing a *joint venture*, a company enters foreign markets by joining with foreign companies to produce or market a product or service. In *licensing*, the company

enters a foreign market by contracting with a licensee in the foreign market and offering the right to use a manufacturing process, trademark, patent, trade secret, or other item of value for a fee or royalty.

Objective 3 **Explain how companies adapt their marketing strategies and mixes for international markets.** (pp 566–572)

Companies must also decide how much their marketing strategies and their products, promotion, price, and channels should be adapted for each foreign market. At one extreme, global companies use *standardized global marketing* worldwide. Others use *adapted global marketing*, in which they adjust the marketing strategy and mix to each target market, bearing more costs but hoping for a larger market share and return. However, global standardization is not an all-or-nothing proposition. It's a matter of degree. Most international marketers suggest that companies should "think globally but act locally"—that they should seek a balance between globally standardized strategies and locally adapted marketing mix tactics.

Objective 4 **Identify the three major forms of international marketing organization.** (pp 572–573)

The company must develop an effective organization for international marketing. Most firms start with an *export department* and graduate to an *international division*. A few become *global organizations*, with worldwide marketing planned and managed by the top officers of the company. Global organizations view the entire world as a single, borderless market.

 Key Terms

Objective 1

Global firm (p 553)
Economic community (p 555)

Objective 2

Exporting (p 563)
Joint venturing (p 564)
Licensing (p 564)

Contract manufacturing (p 564)
Management contracting (p 564)
Joint ownership (p 565)
Direct investment (p 565)

Objective 3

Standardized global marketing (p 566)
Adapted global marketing (p 566)

Straight product extension (p 568)
Product adaptation (p 569)
Product invention (p 569)
Communication adaptation (p 570)
Whole-channel view (p 571)

Discussion and Critical Thinking

 Discussion Questions

1. Explain what is meant by the term *global firm,* and list the six major decisions involved in international marketing. (AACSB: Communication)

2. Compare and contrast a *tariff* and a *quota*. (AACSB: Communication)

3. Name and define the four types of country industrial structures. (AACSB: Communication)

4. Discuss the strategies used for adapting products to a global market. Which strategy is best? (AACSB: Communication)

5. Discuss how global distribution channels differ from domestic channels. (AACSB: Communication)

Critical Thinking Exercises

1. Visit www.transparency.org and click on "corruption perception index" (CPI). What is the most recent CPI for the following countries: Denmark, Jamaica, Malaysia, Myanmar, New Zealand, Somali, and the United States? What are the implications of this index for U.S.-based companies doing business in these countries? (AACSB: Communication; Use of IT; Reflective Thinking)

2. Selling a product in a foreign country is difficult, and many companies make mistakes. Find and report on two examples of companies making marketing mistakes when entering a foreign country. (AACSB: Communication; Reflective Thinking)

3. One way to analyze the cultural differences among countries is to conduct a Hofestede analysis. Visit http://geert-hofstede .com/ to learn what this analysis considers. Develop a presentation explaining how three countries of your choice differ from the United States when analyzed using this method. (AACSB: Communication; Use of IT; Reflective Thinking)

Applications and Cases

 ## Marketing Technology Pixels Instead of Pine

Swedish company IKEA releases a 300-plus-page catalog each year featuring its furniture in fashionably modern room settings. The 2013 catalog comes in 62 different versions for 43 countries. IKEA's photo shoots for the catalog take place in one of Europe's largest studios—94,000 square feet—which employs almost 300 photographers, interior designers, carpenters, and others involved in making each scene just perfect. The process is very labor-intensive and wasteful because rooms are built up and torn down and often thrown into a dumpster after the photo shoot. The catalog typically consumes 70 percent of the company's marketing budget each year. However, all that is being reduced thanks to technology. IKEA's catalog is going digital. Instead of a couch or bed or table or entire room, many items depicted in the catalogs are now merely pixels instead of pine. This year, 12 percent of the content online, in catalogs, and in brochures is not even real, and that proportion will increase to 25 percent next year. Using 3-D graphics to create the scenes, IKEA can cut costs and more easily manipulate imagery from one country to the next. Whereas Americans might prefer darker woods, a given living room can be shown with lighter woods for Japanese consumers. Don't expect to find any fake people or pets, however, because 3-D figures tend to look like ghosts.

1. Visit www.ikea.com and compare a catalog from one country to that of another. What differences do you notice? Can you discern that some photos are 3-D mockups instead of real rooms with furniture? (AACSB: Communication; Use of IT; Reflective Thinking)

2. Note the prices of some of the products. Convert some of the foreign prices to U.S. dollars and compare them to the prices in the U.S. catalog. Are the prices equivalent? Are they consistently higher or lower? (AACSB: Communication; Reflective Thinking)

 ## Marketing Ethics Trade Incentives

The U.S. apparel industry is fiercely competitive, and marketers often need to keep prices low to survive. Many apparel manufacturers have shuttered their U.S. factories in favor of cheaper labor across the globe, and our government is encouraging this behavior. For example, the African Growth and Opportunity Act (AGOA) was signed into law in 2000 to foster economic growth in sub-Saharan Africa countries. Consequently, several clothing manufacturers have located in Africa to take advantage of the cheap labor and liberal U.S. market access to these countries. The AGAO allows poorly developed African countries to export to the United States duty-free. There has been an unintended consequence, however, as more-developed African countries such as South Africa, which must pay regular duties to export to the United States, are seeing their textile industries suffer. One factor is rising labor costs—65 cents per hour in South Africa but only 19 cents in neighboring African countries such as Lesotho, Swaziland, and Mozambique. Another significant factor is the ability of these countries to export to the United States duty-free as allowed by the AGAO. As a result, the South African textile industry saw 52 factories closed in the first half of 2011 alone, 8,000 jobs lost, and a reduction of $1.5 billion in direct investment. Although regulations enacted in the United States are not completely responsible for this decline, critics argue that the AGOA plays a major role.

1. Find another example of a U.S. law or trade agreement that encourages or discourages trade with foreign countries. Discuss the positive and negative consequences of the law. (AACSB: Communication; Reflective Thinking)

 ## Marketing by the Numbers Balance of Trade

The United States exported more than $2 trillion worth of goods and services in 2011 yet realized a trade deficit of more than $500 million, meaning it imported more than it exported. The U.S. balance of trade has been negative for decades, although the

2011 deficit was lower than it was in 2004 through 2008. Some Americans believe trade deficits harm the country.

1. Visit www.bea.gov and find the U.S. balance of trade in goods and services. Create a line chart showing the balance of trade

from 1992 to present. (AACSB: Communication; Use of IT; Reflective Thinking)

2. Debate the pros and cons of the United States having trade deficits consistently year after year. (AACSB: Communication; Reflective Thinking)

 # Video Case The U.S. Film Industry

If you like movies, you've no doubt seen a foreign film at some point. But did you know that American films are some of the biggest and most anticipated foreign films in the world? In fact, foreign box office and DVD sales account for nearly 70 percent of all revenues for the U.S. film industry. With that much financial impact, foreign markets are playing a bigger and bigger role not only in the pricing, distribution, and promotion of U.S. films, but in the product itself.

This video illustrates the challenges faced by the U.S. film industry stemming from differences in the marketing environment throughout different international markets. The result is that this industry is now like any other export industry: The marketing mix must be adapted at an optimum level in order to meet

the needs of global markets while still maintaining the benefits of standardization.

After viewing this video, answer the following questions about the U.S. film industry and the global marketplace:

1. Which part of the marketing environment seems to be having the greatest impact on U.S. films abroad?

2. Which of the five strategies for adapting products and promotion for the global market is most relevant to the U.S. film industry?

3. Is the U.S. film industry now dependent upon foreign markets for success? Compare the export of U.S. films to other U.S. exports.

 # Company Case Buick: Number One Import Brand

There's an old joke that goes something like this: A certain Buick dealer went broke as the popularity of imported cars finally took its toll and forced him out of business. One day he found a bottle from which a genie emerged, offering to grant him one wish. He wished for a successful foreign car dealership in a major city. Instantly, he found himself smack dab in the showroom of his old Buick dealership—but in Tokyo!

Most Americans perceive Buick as a brand that sells only in the United States. But there has always been one big exception to that—China. In fact, if the dealer in the genie tale had found his dealership in Shanghai or Beijing, he truly would have gotten his wish. You see, Buick sells more premium vehicles in China than any other brand—even BMW or Mercedes-Benz. Moreover, Buick is the number five auto brand in China, luxury or otherwise.

Buick's success in China makes an interesting story. But perhaps more important than how the brand got there is what General Motors is doing now to take advantage of it. GM is not only embracing the Chinese market for Buick (and for some of its other brands), it's using the Chinese market as a key driver for Buick products in the United States and other countries. Globalization for Buick no longer means exporting the domestic product. Rather, GM is looking to China for key customer insights into creating a truly global product.

A Car for Royalty

Folks in the United States might think that American products in China today are a relatively recent phenomenon. However, Buick's place at the top of the Chinese market has a history almost as old as the brand itself. Buick first hung out its shingle in 1899, making it the oldest American automotive brand still in existence. Soon after, Chinese government officials began showing an interest in introducing the vehicle to China. The first Buicks arrived on the streets of Shanghai in 1912.

Buick immediately became associated with Chinese political leaders. Pu Yi, China's last emperor, owned a Buick in the 1920s,

while provincial presidents were also known for choosing Buicks over brands such as Rolls-Royce and Mercedes-Benz. That led Buick to open a sales office in Shanghai in 1929 and start advertising there. Some early examples of advertising copy include, "One out of every six cars [in China] is a Buick," and "Buick owners are mostly the leading men in China."

Over the years, Buick's image as the vehicle of choice for China's elite burned itself into the minds of the Chinese people. As China's market economy began to take off in the late 1900s, its exploding middle class fueled the demand for cars. Buick was poised to ride the trend to the top. In 1997, GM formed a joint venture with Shanghai Automotive Industry Corporation—Shanghai GM—to build GM cars in China. The first Chinese-made Buick rolled off the assembly line in 1998. Shanghai GM would go on to become the first Chinese auto manufacturer to sell more than 1 million vehicles in a single year. Around that time, Buick enjoyed a brand familiarity rating of more than 85 percent in China.

An Evolving Global Strategy

For decades, GM's international marketing strategy was largely characterized by exporting products made for the U.S. market. In GM's thinking, what worked in America would work globally. This included selling left-hand drive cars in right-hand drive countries like Japan and Great Britain. The strategy made sense at a time when the United States was far and away the biggest car market in the world and GM was selling far more cars in the United States than anywhere else.

But U.S. automotive sales matured years ago at a time when growth in other markets took off. China is now the world's largest passenger car market, and with over 1.3 billion people, it has a way to go before the market is saturated. Fortunately for GM, Buick had rubber on the road in China before that market started accelerating. When the Chinese market took off, GM put things into overdrive. As a result, GM sold 2.55 million cars in China in 2011—a car every 12 seconds! That marks the seventh consecutive year for GM as

China's number one automaker. It's also the second time that GM sold more cars outside the United States than it did at home.

As GM's overall growth dynamics shifted, Buick was ahead of the curve. The year 2000 was one of Buick's best years ever in the United States, with sales of more than 400,000 vehicles. But that began a steady and steep decline for the brand. As GM worked its way through the recession, bankruptcy, and a government bailout, it considered eliminating Buick entirely. But in China, Buick sales were rising as fast as they were sinking in the United States. In 2009, the same year that Buick's U.S. sales hit an all-time low of just 102,000 units, the brand sold 450,000 cars in China. No doubt about it, China saved Buick from the fate that befell discontinued GM brands Oldsmobile, Pontiac, and Saturn.

As Buick's sales have shifted, so has its Chinese portfolio of models. Currently at the bottom of Buick's Chinese line is the Excelle. It may be a Korean Daewoo dressed up to look like a Buick, but it's also the number one selling passenger car in China. That car is not to be confused with the top-trim Excelle GT, based on an entirely different vehicle, the German-designed Opel Astra. China's Regal and LaCrosse models are assembled at Shanghai GM, but share their designs with the same models assembled at other GM plants. The Enclave SUV is built in Lansing, Michigan. And the top-of-the line Park Avenue is built on a platform from GM's Australian division, Holden. Buick China also sells a minivan—a vehicle class that still enjoys popularity in the Land of the Rising Sun.

China Takes the Lead

Buick's Chinese lineup seems like a better international product strategy than the old approach of selling only domestic U.S. models. But in many respects, it's a hodgepodge of cars from GM's world operations that have little in common other than the trademark three-shield emblem. What isn't apparent from the description of these models alone is the extent to which the Chinese market is influencing the design not only of future Buick vehicles for China, but also for the rest of world. Enter car designer Joe Qiu.

> Joe Qiu doesn't own a car. He doesn't even have a driver's license. His favorite vehicle, actually, is a go-kart with a top speed of 75 miles per hour. His distressed leather bomber jacket, which he rarely takes off, betrays his fascination with airplanes and all things military. His jeans, the hems unfashionably turned up, and a brushlike crewcut, are pure 21st-century China. His TAG Heuer watch: a nod to the international uniform of designers. At 31, Qiu still lives with his parents. But he spends much of his time drinking in the vibes at the expensive high-end clubs, over-the-top shopping malls, and elegant, luxurious hotels where Shanghai's burgeoning middle class gathers. "I'm just a piece of white paper," he says, collecting insights into China's sky-rocketing consumer culture. He has an uncanny knack for divining Chinese tastes and whims, what it is they'll buy.

Joe Qiu is also a designer for Shanghai GM's Pan Asia Technical Automotive Center (PATAC). A few years ago, Qiu and a team of PATAC designers won a competition with other GM design centers throughout the world to take charge of designing what is now the current-model Buick LaCrosse. As one of the smallest and least-known GM design houses, this was akin to a high school basketball team competing in the NBA playoffs and winning the finals. As Qiu and his colleagues considered the rounded-exterior and plain-vanilla interior of the original LaCrosse, they knew that Chinese consumers would sneer at such frumpy wheels meant to appeal to Buick's aging U.S. consumers. Buick's Chinese customers were in their mid-30s, successful, entrepreneurial, fashionable, and much more discerning—a demographic profile that made the bosses back in Michigan drool.

The PATAC team rethought and reshaped every piece of sheet metal on the LaCrosse. What came out was a glamorous, elegant sedan, with enough bling to turn the heads of status-conscious young Shanghai buyers. Qui was in charge of the interior. With Shanghai's trendy clubs in mind, Qui states, "I looked at where people lived, where they hung out, and then I tried to create that same feeling inside the car." The result feels more like a beautifully designed living room than the stoic interiors common to other Buicks. Soft, buttery-colored ambient light glows from the instrument panel as well as from hidden lights in the rear. The front and back seats are well padded and feature power massage.

PATAC's LaCrosse sold more than 110,000 units in China during its second year of production. That's more cars than all the Buicks sold in the United States during that same year. The LaCrosse was instrumental in pushing Buick's 2011 total Chinese sales to 645,000 units. "Our LaCrosse pushed the expectations," says Raymond Bierzynski, president of PATAC. "Our Buick is what the brand wants to be everywhere in the world." The move to incorporate PATAC's designs into a vehicle that would sell in all of Buick's markets signals that GM is recognizing that the world is bigger than North America. PATAC is taking the lead on creative strategy. "We aren't the little voice at the end of the phone anymore," Bierzynski says. "China commands 8 million units a year. We're GM's [biggest] market. We are the experts."

The big question is this: How will Chinese-influenced designs be received in the United States and other markets? While the LaCrosse is never expected to be as successful here as it is in China, 2011 was Buick's best year in the United States in more than a decade. Total sales of over 177,000 cars may be a far cry from its U.S. peak, but it's a whopping 73.5 percent increase over what Buick sold just two years prior.

Perhaps more important are changes in consumer perceptions of the brand that indicate potential for future growth. Last year, public opinion of Buick improved by 125 percent while purchase consideration went up 65 percent. That's not all because of the LaCrosse, mind you. But it is worth noting that automotive journalists gave PATAC's redesign rave reviews. In fact, the LaCrosse was one of *Car and Driver* magazine's three finalists for "Car of the Year." The magazine proclaimed it, "Easily the best Buick sedan in a long time." The outcome of PATAC's LaCrosse has earned the design studio other projects that will sell in multiple world markets.

Buick will be introducing 12 new models to China in the near future as GM has its sights set on big targets. Its goal is to double its Chinese sales by 2015, putting its tally at nearly 5 million vehicles, with Buick accounting for more than 1 million of that. Ford barely broke the 500,000 mark in China for the first time in 2011, and Chrysler isn't even on the radar. But some financial analysts aren't so optimistic, estimating that GM will grow to only 3.3 million units in China by 2015 and will actually lose market share in the rapidly growing Chinese market. Whatever the outcome, it's clear that Buick is a global brand with momentum in the right place.

Questions for Discussion

1. Does Buick have a truly global strategy, or just a series of regional strategies? Explain.

2. Do GM's global manufacturing facilities, such as Shanghai GM, solidify a global strategy? Why or why not?

3. Discuss Buick's global strategy in terms of the five global product and communications strategies.

4. Can competitors easily replicate Buick's strategy in China? Why or why not?

5. Based on Buick's goals as discussed in the case, what do you predict for Buick in the coming years in China? In the United States?

Sources: Jessica Caldwell, "Drive by the Numbers—Buick Excelling in China," Edmunds, May 8, 2012, www.edmunds.com/industry-center/analysis/drive-by-numbers-buick-excelling-in-china.html; Steve Shannon, "Buick Is Popular in China?," http://fastlane.gmblogs.com/archives/2006/12/buick_is_popula_1.html; Jeremy Cato, "Buick Making a Comeback in North America," *The Globe and Mail*, July 17, 2012, www.theglobeandmail.com/globe-drive/new-cars/auto-news/buick-making-a-comeback-in-north-america/article4423994/; Fara Warner, "Made in China," *Fast Company*, December 2007, www.fastcompany.com/magazine/114/open_features-made-in-china.html; and "General Motors Sets Sales Record in China in 2011," http://media.gm.com/media/us/en/gm/news.detail.html/content/Pages/news/us/en/2012/Jan/0109_Sales_China.html.

MyMarketingLab

Go to **mymktlab.com** for Auto-graded writing questions as well as the following Assisted-graded writing questions:

19-1. Name and describe the advantages and disadvantages of the different types of joint venturing when entering a foreign market. (AACSB: Communication; Reflective Thinking)

19-2. Should the U.S. government make laws that favor some countries and impact the United States and other countries so dramatically? (AACSB: Communication; Ethical Reasoning)

19-3. Mymktlab Only – comprehensive writing assignment for this chapter.

References

1. Based on information from Monica Mark, "Coca-Cola and Nestlé Target New Markets in Africa," *The Guardian*, May 4, 2012, www.guardian.co.uk/world/2012/may/04/coca-cola-nestle-markets-africa; Duane Stanford, "Africa: Coke's Last Frontier," *Bloomberg Businessweek*, November 1, 2010, pp. 54–61; Annaleigh Vallie, "Coke Turns 125 and Has Much Life Ahead," *Business Day*, May 16, 2011, www.businessday.co.za/articles/Content.aspx?id_142848; "Coca-Cola Makes Big Bets on Africa's Future," *Trefis*, May 25, 2012, www.trefis.com/stock/ko/articles/123022/coca-cola-makes-big-bets-on-africas-future/2012-05-25; and Coca-Cola annual reports and other information from www.thecoca-colacompany.com, accessed November 2012.

2. Data from "Fortune 500," *Fortune*, May 21, 2012, p. F1; Christopher Stolarski, "The FDI Effect," Marquette University Research and Scholarship 2011, www.marquette.edu/research/documents/discover-2011-FDI-effect.pdf; and "List of Countries by GDP: List by the CIA World Factbook," Wikipedia, http://en.wikipedia.org/wiki/List_of_countries_by_GDP_ (nominal), accessed November 2012.

3. "Trade Growth to Slow in 2012 after Strong Deceleration in 2011," WTO Press Release, April 12, 2012, www.wto.org/english/news_e/pres12_e/pr658_e.htm.

4. Information from www.michelin.com/corporate, www.jnj.com, and www.caterpillar.com, accessed October 2012.

5. See www.otisworldwide.com/d1-about.html, accessed November 2012.

6. Don Lee, "U.S. Orders Tariffs on Chinese Solar Panels," *Los Angeles Times*, May 18, 2012, http://articles.latimes.com/2012/may/18/business/la-fi-china-solar-dumping-20120518.

7. See Dexter Roberts and Michael Wei, "China's New Protectionism" *Bloomberg Businessweek*, October 27, 2011, www.businessweek.com/magazine/chinas-new-protectionism-10272011.html; and Arun Sudhaman, "Walmart Brings in PR Counsel in China," *The Holmes Report*, April 24, 2012, www.holmesreport.com/news-info/11755/WalMart-Brings-In-PR-Counsel-In-China.aspx.

8. "What Is the WTO?" www.wto.org/english/thewto_e/whatis_e/whatis_e.htm, accessed November 2012.

9. Cai U. Ordinario, "Developed Countries Still Committed to Complete Doha Round," *Business Mirror*, January 29, 2012, www.businessmirror.com.ph/home/top-news/22586-developed-countries-still-committed-to-complete-doha-round; *WTO Annual Report 2012*, www.wto.org/english/res_e/publications_e/anrep12_e.htm, accessed October 2012; and World Trade Organization, "10 Benefits of the WTO Trading System," www.wto.org/english/thewto_e/whatis_e/10ben_e/10b00_e.htm, accessed October 2012.

10. "The EU at a Glance," http://europa.eu/about-eu/index_en.htm; and "EU Statistics and Opinion Polls," http://europa.eu/documentation/statistics-polls/index_en.htm; accessed September 2012.

11. "Economic and Monetary Affairs," http://europa.eu/pol/emu/index_en.htm, accessed November 2012.

12. CIA, *The World Factbook*, https://www.cia.gov/library/publications/the-world-factbook, accessed August 2012.

13. Statistics and other information from CIA, *The World Factbook*, https://www.cia.gov/library/publications/the-world-factbook/, accessed August 2012; and Office of the United States Trade Representative, "Joint Statement from 2012 NAFTA Commission Meeting," April 2012, www.ustr.gov/about-us/press-office/press-releases/2012/april/joint-statement-2012-nafta-commission-meeting.

14. See www.comunidadandina.org/ingles/sudamerican.htm, accessed August 2012.

15. Example based on information found in Bruce Einhorn, "Alan Mulally's Asian Sales Call," *Bloomberg BusinessWeek*, April 12, 2010, pp. 41–43; "Ford, Volkswagen Eye Up North India to Set Up New Facilities," *Businessline*, December 8, 2010, p. 1; and "Ford to Tag New Figo 2012 Less by INR 16,000," *Crazy About Cars*, March 9, 2012, www.carzy.co.in/blog/car-news/ford-tag-figo-2012-inr-16000.html/.

16. See "2012 Investment Climate Statement—Venezuela," U.S. Bureau of Economic and Business Affairs, June 2012, www.state.gov/e/eb/rls/othr/ics/2012/191262.htm; and "Welcome to the U.S. Commercial Service Venezuela," http://export.gov/venezuela/, accessed October 2012.

17. See "$9 Billion Barter Deal," BarterNews.com, April 19, 2008, www.barternews.com/9_billion_dollar_barter_deal.htm; David Pilling, "Africa Builds as Beijing Scrambles to Invest," *Financial Times*, December 10, 2009, p. 11; and International Reciprocal Trade Association, www.irta.com/modern-trade-a-barter.html, accessed November 2012.

18. For these and other examples, see Emma Hall, "Do You Know Your Rites? BBDO Does," *Advertising Age*, May 21, 2007, p. 22.

19. Jamie Bryan, "The Mintz Dynasty," *Fast Company*, April 2006, pp. 56–61; Viji Sundaram, "Offensive Durga Display Dropped," *India-West*, February 2006, p. A1; and Emily Bryson York and Rupal Parekh, "Burger King's MO: Offend, Earn Media, Apologize, Repeat," *Advertising Age*, July 8, 2009, accessed at http://adage.com/print?article_id=137801.

20. For these and other examples, see "Managing Quality Across the (Global) Organization, Its Stakeholders, Suppliers, and Customers," Chartered Quality Institute, www.thecqi.org/Knowledge-Hub/Knowledge-portal/Corporate-strategy/Managing-quality-globally, accessed October 2012.

21. Quotes and other information found in David Pierson, "Beijing Loves IKEA—but Not for Shopping," *Los Angeles Times,* August 25, 2009, http://articles.latimes.com/2009/aug/25/business/fi-china-ikea25; Michael Wei, "In IKEA's China Stores, Loitering Is Encouraged," *Bloomberg Businessweek,* November 1, 2010, pp. 22–23; and Jens Hansegard, "Ikea Taking China by Storm," *Wall Street Journal,* March 2012, http://online.wsj.com/article/SB10001424052702304 63640457729308348182153.html.

22. Andres Martinez, "The Next American Century," *Time,* March 22, 2010, p. 1.

23. Thomas L. Friedman, *The Lexus and the Olive Tree: Understanding Globalization* (New York: Anchor Books, 2000); and Michael Wei and Margaret Conley, "Global Brands: Some Chinese Kids' First Word: Mickey," *Bloomberg Businessweek,* June 19, 2011, pp. 24–25.

24. "BrandZ Top Global Brands 2012," Millward Brown Optimor, www.millwardbrown.com/BrandZ/Top_100_Global_Brands.aspx, accessed August 2012.

25. See Kim-Mai Cutler, "Apple's Chinese iPhone Sales 'Mind-Boggling,' Bring China Revenues to $7.9 Billion," *Tech Crunch,* April 24, 2012, http://techcrunch.com/2012/04/24/apples-iphone-sales-in-china-are-up-by-fivefold-from-a-year-ago/; and Nick Wingfield, "Apple Profit Rises on Higher iPhone and iPad Sales," *New York Times,* April 24, 2012, p. B1.

26. Duane Stanford, "Can Coke Surpass Its Record High of $88 a Share?" *Bloomberg Businessweek,* June 2, 2011, p. 1; William J. Holstein, "How Coca-Cola Manages 90 Emerging Markets," *Strategy+Business,* November 7, 2011, www.strategy-business.com/article/00093?gko=f3ca6; and Monica Mark, "Coca-Cola and Nestlé Target New Markets in Africa," *The Guardian,* May 4, 2012, www.guardian.co.uk/world/2012/may/04/coca-cola-nestle-markets-africa.

27. Barney Jopson and Andrew England, "Walmart to Apply 'Sweat and Muscle' to Africa," *Financial Times,* June 5, 2011, p. 18; Emma Hall, "Marketers, Agencies Eye Booming Africa for Expansion," *Advertising Age,* June 13, 2011, p. 28; and Addis Ababa, "Walmart Focused on Existing Africa Markets," *Reuters,* May 10, 2012, www.reuters.com/article/idUSBRE8490L120120510.

28. See http://en.wikipedia.org/wiki/Doubletree, accessed October 2012.

29. Example based on information from "Campbell Soup Company and Swire Pacific Form Joint Venture in China," *BusinessWire,* January 12, 2011, www.businesswire.com/news/home/20110112005834/en/Campbell-Soup-Company-Swire-Pacific-Form-Joint.

30. "Ford India Lays Foundation Store for Sanand Plant," March 22, 2012, www.drivingford.in/tag/ford-india-plant/; and Alan Ohnsman, "Major Auto Production at Toyota, Honda Boosts U.S. Economy," July 17, 2012, www.autonews.com.

31. Marc de Swaan Arons, "There Is Absolutely a Need for One Single Global Vision," *Marketing News,* September 30, 2011, p. 30.

32. Quotes from Andrew McMains, "To Compete Globally, Brands Must Adapt," *Adweek,* September 25, 2008, www.adweek.com; Pankaj Ghemawat, "Regional Strategies for Global Leadership," *Harvard Business Review,* December 2005, pp. 97–108; Eric Pfanner, "The Myth of the Global Brand," *New York Times,* January 11, 2009, www.nytimes.com; and Marc de Swaan Arons, "There Is Absolutely a Need for One Single Global Vision," *Marketing News,* September 30, 2011, p. 30. Also see Pankej Ghemawat, "Finding Your Strategy in the New Landscape," *Harvard Business Review,* March 2010, pp. 54–60.

33. Based on information from Lucy Fancourt, Bredesen Lewis, and Nicholas Majka, "Born in the USA, Made in France: How McDonald's Succeeds in the Land of Michelin Stars," Knowledge@ Wharton, January 3, 2012, http://knowledge.wharton.upenn.edu/article.cfm?articleid=2906.

34. See Warren J. Keegan and Mark C. Green, *Global Marketing,* 6th ed. (Upper Saddle River, NJ: Prentice Hall, 2011), pp. 314–321.

35. For these and other examples, see Bruce Einhorn, "There's More to Oreo Than Black and White," *Bloomberg Businessweek,* May 3, 2012, www.businessweek.com/articles/2012-05-03/theres-more-to-oreo-than-black-and-white.

36. James R. Healey, "Fiat 500: Little Car Shoulders Huge Responsibility in U.S.; Retro Cutie Had to Be Redone from Inside Out for Sale Here," *USA Today,* June 1, 2011, p. B1; and "New 2012 Fiat 500 Named 'Best Car' in Travel + Leisure Annual Design Awards Issue," *PRNewswire,* February 15, 2012.

37. See "Easier Said Than Done," *The Economist,* April 15, 2010, www.economist.com/node/15879299; and Normandy Madden, "In China, Multinationals Forgo Adaptation for New-Brand Creation," *Advertising Age,* January 17, 2011, p. 10.

38. "Nokia Still Dominant in Africa in Market Share," Celebrating Progress Africa, June 12, 2011, www.cp-africa.com/2011/06/12/nokia-still-dominant-in-africa-in-market-share-ad-impressions; and "Nokia Still a Hot Brand among Indian Consumers: Survey," The Press Trust of India, July 10, 2011.

39. Emma Hall, "Marketers, Agencies Eye Booming Africa for Expansion," *Advertising Age,* June 13, 2011, p. 28; and Liz Gooch, "The Biggest Thing Since China: Global Companies Awake to the Muslim Consumer, and Marketers Follow Suit," *International Herald Tribune,* August 12, 2010, p. 1.

40. See George E. Belch and Michael A. Belch, *Advertising and Promotion: An Integrated Marketing Communications Perspective,* 7th ed. (New York: McGraw Hill, 2007), Chapter 20; Shintero Okazaki and Charles R. Taylor, "What Is SMS Advertising and Why Do Multinationals Adopt It?" *Journal of Business Research,* January 2008, pp. 4–12; and Warren J. Keegan and Mark C. Green, *Global Marketing,* 6th ed. (Upper Saddle River, NJ: Prentice Hall, 2011), pp. 413–415.

41. For these and other examples, see Normandy Madden, "In China, Multinationals Forgo Adaptation for New-Brand Creation," *Advertising Age,* January 17, 2011, p. 10; Cristina Drafta, "Levi Strauss Targets Asia with Denizen," *EverythingPR,* May 16, 2011, www.pamil-visions.net/denizen/228239/; and www.levistrauss.com/brands/denizen/, accessed October 2012.

42. Adapted from Jack Ewing, "First Mover in Mobile: How It's Selling Cell Phones to the Developing World," *BusinessWeek,* May 14, 2007, p. 60; with information from "Nokia's Market Share Troubles to Hit Profits," Reuters, January 19, 2011, www.reuters.com/article/2011/01/19/us-nokia-idUSTRE70I25P20110119.

43. See "Coca-Cola Rolls Out New Distribution Model with ZAP," ZAP, January 23, 2008, www.zapworld.com/zap-coca-cola-truck; Jane Nelson, Eriko Ishikawa, and Alexis Geaneotes, "Developing Inclusive Business Models: A Review of Coca-Cola's Manual Distribution Centers in Ethiopia and Tanzania," Harvard Kennedy School, 2009, www.hks.harvard.edu/ m-rcbg/CSRI/publications/other_10_MDC_report.pdf; and "How Coca-Cola's Distribution System Works," *Colalife,* December 19, 2010, www.colalife.org/2010/12/19/how-coca-colas-distribution-system-works/. For some interesting photos of Coca-Cola distribution methods in third-world and emerging markets, see www.flickr.com/photos/73509998@N00/sets/72157594299144032/, accessed November 2012.

44. Adapted from information found in Bart Becht, "Building a Company Without Borders," *Harvard Business Review,* April 2010, pp. 103–106; "From Cincy to Singapore: Why P&G, Others Are Moving Key HQs," *Advertising Age,* June 10, 2012, http://adage.com/print/235288; and www.rb.com/Investors-media/Investor-information, accessed November 2012.

Part 1: Defining Marketing and the Marketing Process (Chapters 1–2)
Part 2: Understanding the Marketplace and Consumers (Chapters 3–6)
Part 3: Designing a Customer-Driven Strategy and Mix (Chapters 7–17)
Part 4: Extending Marketing (Chapters 18–20)

Sustainable Marketing

Social Responsibility and Ethics

Chapter Preview In this final chapter, we'll examine the concepts of sustainable marketing, meeting the needs of consumers, businesses, and society—now and in the future—through socially and environmentally responsible marketing actions. We'll start by defining sustainable marketing and then look at some common criticisms of marketing as it impacts individual consumers, as well as public actions that promote sustainable marketing. Finally, we'll see how companies themselves can benefit from proactively pursuing sustainable marketing practices that bring value to not only individual customers but also society as a whole. Sustainable marketing actions are more than just the right thing to do; they're also good for business.

First, let's look at an example of sustainable marketing in action at Unilever, the world's third-largest consumer products company. For 13 years running, Unilever has been named sustainability leader in the food and beverage industry by the Dow Jones Sustainability Indexes. The company recently launched its Sustainable Living Plan, by which it intends to double its size by 2020 while at the same time reducing its impact on the planet and increasing the social benefits arising from its activities. That's an ambitious goal.

Sustainability at Unilever: Creating a Better Future Every Day

When Paul Polman took over as CEO of Unilever in 2009, the foods, home and personal care products company was a slumbering giant. Despite its stable of star-studded brands—including the likes of Dove, Axe, Noxema, Sunsilk, OMO, Hellmann's, Knorr, Lipton, and Ben & Jerry's—Unilever had experienced a decade of stagnant sales and profits. The company needed renewed energy and purpose. "To drag the world back to sanity, we need to know why we are here," said Polman.

To answer the "why are we here" question and find a more energizing mission, Polman looked beyond the usual corporate goals of growing sales, profits, and shareholder value. Instead, he asserted, growth results from accomplishing a broader social and environmental mission. Unilever exists "for consumers, not shareholders," he said. "If we are in sync with consumer needs and the environment in which we operate, and take responsibility for our [societal impact], then the shareholder will also be rewarded."

Evaluating and working on societal and environmental impact is nothing new at Unilever. Prior to Polman taking the reins, the company already had multiple programs in place to manage the impact of its products and operations. But the existing programs and results— while good—simply didn't go far enough for Polman. So in late 2010 Unilever launched its

Sustainable Living Plan—an aggressive long-term plan that takes capitalism to the next level. Under the plan, the company has set out to "create a better future every day for people around the world: the people who work for us, those we do business with, the billions of people who use our products, and future generations whose quality of life depends on the way we protect the environment today." According to Polman, Unilever's long-run *commercial* success depends on how well it manages the *social* and *environmental* impact of its actions.

The Sustainable Living Plan sets out three major social and environmental objectives to be accomplished by 2020: "(1) To help more than one billion people take action to improve their health and well-being; (2) to halve the environmental footprint of the making and use of our products; and (3) to source 100 percent of our agricultural raw materials sustainably."

> Under Unilever's Sustainable Living Plan, the consumer goods giant has set out to "create a better future every day for people around the world." Unilever's long-run *commercial* success depends on how well it manages the *social* and *environmental* impact of its actions.

The Sustainable Living Plan pulls together all of the work Unilever had already been doing and sets ambitious new sustainability goals. These goals span the entire value chain, from how the company sources raw materials to how consumers use and dispose of its products. "Our aim is to make our activities more sustainable and also encourage our customers, suppliers, and others to do the same," says the company.

On the "upstream supply side," more than half of Unilever's raw materials come from agriculture, so the company is helping suppliers develop sustainable farming practices that meet its own high expectations for environmental and social impact. Unilever assesses suppliers against two sets of standards. The first is the Unilever Supplier Code, which calls for socially responsible actions regarding human rights, labor practices, product safety, and care for the environment. Second, specifically for agricultural suppliers, the Unilever Sustainable Agriculture Code details Unilever's expectations for sustainable agriculture practices, so that it and its suppliers "can commit to the sustainability journey together."

But Unilever's Sustainable Living Plan goes far beyond simply creating more responsible supply and distribution chains. Approximately 68 percent of the total greenhouse gas footprint of Unilever's products, and 50 percent of the water footprint, occur during consumer use. So Unilever is also working with its consumers to improve the social and environmental impact of its products in use. Around two billion people in 190 markets worldwide use a Unilever product on any given day. Therefore, small everyday consumer actions can add up to a big difference. Unilever sums it up with this equation: "Unilever brands × small everyday actions × billions of consumers = big difference."

For example, almost one-third of households worldwide use Unilever laundry products to do their washing—approximately 125 billion washes every year. Therefore, under its Sustainable Living Plan, Unilever is both creating more eco-friendly laundry products and motivating consumers to improve their laundry habits.

Around the world, for instance, Unilever is encouraging consumers to wash clothes at lower temperatures and use the correct dosage of detergent. Unilever products such as OMO and Persil Small & Mighty concentrated laundry detergents use less packaging, making them cheaper and less polluting to transport. More important, they wash efficiently at lower temperatures and use less energy. Another Unilever product, Comfort One Rinse fabric conditioner, was created for hand washing clothes in developing and emerging markets where water is often in short supply. The innovative product requires only one bucket of water for rinsing rather than three, saving consumers time, effort, and 30 liters of water per wash.

Such energy and water savings don't show up on Unilever's income statement, but they will be extremely important to the people and the planet. Similarly, small changes in product nutrition and customer eating habits can have a surprisingly big impact on human health. "Ultimately," says the company, "we will only succeed if we inspire people around the world to take small, everyday actions that can add up to a big difference for the world." To meet this objective, Unilever has identified "Five Levers for Change"—things that its marketers can do to inspire people to adopt specific sustainable behaviors. The model helps marketers identify the barriers and triggers for change. The levers for change include: make it understood, make it easy, make it desirable, make it rewarding, and make it a habit.

Will Unilever's Sustainable Living Plan produce results for the company? So far, so good. Unilever's revenues in 2011 grew

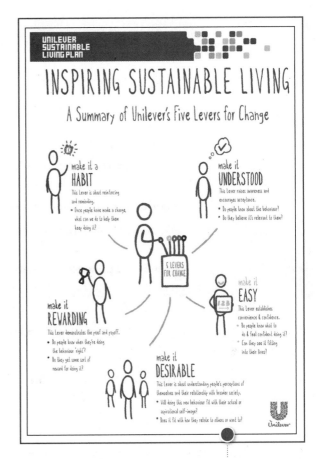

6.5 percent, a modest figure, but one that exceeded market growth rates where the company does business. Perhaps more important, at the same time that it improves its top-line performance, Unilever is progressing toward its aggressive Sustainable Living Plan goals. The company is right on target with 50 of its 58 specific targets involving improved health and well-being, reducing its environmental footprint, and sustainably sourcing raw materials; and it's making good progress on the other seven.

The sustainability plan is not just the right thing to do for people and the environment, claims Polman, it's also right for Unilever. The quest for sustainability saves money by reducing energy use and minimizing waste. It fuels innovation, resulting in new products and new consumer benefits. And it creates new market opportunities: More than half of Unilever's sales are from developing countries, the very places that face the greatest sustainability challenges.

In all, Polman predicts, the sustainability plan will help Unilever double in size, while also creating a better future for billions of people without increasing the environmental footprint. "We do not believe there is a conflict between sustainability and profitable growth," he concludes. "The daily act of making and selling consumer goods drives economic and social progress. There are billions of people around the world who deserve the better quality of life that everyday products like soap, shampoo, and tea can provide. Sustainable living is not a pipedream. It can be done, and there is very little downside."[1]

Under its Sustainable Living Plan, Unilever has identified "Five Levers for Change"—things it can do to inspire its more than 2 billion consumers around the world to adopt sustainable behaviors.

Reproduced with kind permission of Unilever PLC and group companies

Objective Outline

MyMarketingLab™

⭐ **Improve Your Grade!**

Over 10 million students improved their results using the Pearson MyLabs. Visit **mymktlab.com** for simulations, tutorials, and end-of-chapter problems.

Responsible marketers discover what consumers want and respond with market offerings that create value for buyers and capture value in return. The *marketing concept* is a philosophy of customer value and mutual gain. Its practice leads the economy by an invisible hand to satisfy the many and changing needs of millions of consumers.

Not all marketers follow the marketing concept, however. In fact, some companies use questionable marketing practices that serve their own rather than consumers' interests. Moreover, even well-intentioned marketing actions that meet the current needs of some consumers may cause immediate or future harm to other consumers or the larger society. Responsible marketers must consider whether their actions are sustainable in the longer run.

This chapter examines sustainable marketing and the social and environmental effects of private marketing practices. First, we address the question: What is sustainable marketing and why is it important?

Sustainable marketing

Socially and environmentally responsible marketing that meets the present needs of consumers and businesses while also preserving or enhancing the ability of future generations to meet their needs.

Objective 1 ········▶

Define sustainable marketing and discuss its importance.

Sustainable Marketing

Sustainable marketing calls for socially and environmentally responsible actions that meet the present needs of consumers and businesses while also preserving or enhancing the ability of future generations to meet their needs. ● **Figure 20.1** compares the sustainable marketing concept with marketing concepts we studied in earlier chapters.[2]

The *marketing concept* recognizes that organizations thrive from day to day by determining the current needs and wants of target customers and fulfilling those needs and

● FIGURE | 20.1
Sustainable Marketing

The marketing concept means meeting the current needs of both customers and the company. But that can sometimes mean compromising the future of both.

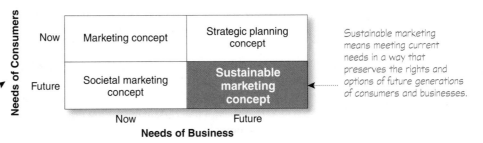

Sustainable marketing means meeting current needs in a way that preserves the rights and options of future generations of consumers and businesses.

wants more effectively and efficiently than competitors do. It focuses on meeting the company's short-term sales, growth, and profit needs by giving customers what they want now. However, satisfying consumers' immediate needs and desires doesn't always serve the future best interests of either customers or the business.

For example, McDonald's early decisions to market tasty but fat- and salt-laden fast foods created immediate satisfaction for customers, as well as sales and profits for the company. However, critics assert that McDonald's and other fast-food chains contributed to a longer-term national obesity epidemic, damaging consumer health and burdening the national health system. In turn, many consumers began looking for healthier eating options, causing a slump in the sales and profits of the fast-food industry. Beyond issues of ethical behavior and social welfare, McDonald's was also criticized for the sizable environmental footprint of its vast global operations, everything from wasteful packaging and solid waste creation to inefficient energy use in its stores. Thus, McDonald's strategy was not sustainable in terms of either consumer or company benefit.

Whereas the *societal marketing concept* identified in Figure 20.1 considers the future welfare of consumers and the *strategic planning concept* considers future company needs, the *sustainable marketing concept* considers both. Sustainable marketing calls for socially and environmentally responsible actions that meet both the immediate and future needs of customers and the company.

For example, as we discussed in Chapter 2, McDonald's has responded to these challenges in recent years with a more sustainable "Plan to Win" strategy of diversifying into salads, fruits, grilled chicken, low-fat milk, and other healthy fare. Also, after a seven-year search for healthier cooking oil, McDonald's phased out traditional artery-clogging trans fats without compromising the taste of its french fries. The company also launched a major multifaceted education campaign—called "it's what i eat and what i do . . . i'm lovin' it"—to help consumers better understand the keys to living balanced, active lifestyles. And recently, McDonald's began a "favorites under 400 calories" campaign in which 400-and-fewer-calorie items are featured in its advertising and on menu boards in its restaurant. The chain points out that 80 percent of its national menu is under 400 calories and that it wants to help customers feel better about the items they are choosing.[3]

● The McDonald's "Plan to Win" strategy also addresses environmental issues. For example, it calls for food-supply sustainability, reduced and environmentally sustainable packaging, reuse and recycling, and more responsible store designs. McDonald's has even developed an environmental scorecard that rates its suppliers' performance in areas such as water use, energy use, and solid waste management.

McDonald's more sustainable strategy is benefiting the company as well as its customers. Since announcing its "Plan to Win" strategy, McDonald's sales have increased by almost 60 percent, and profits have more than tripled. Thus, McDonald's is well positioned for a sustainably profitable future.[4]

Truly sustainable marketing requires a smooth-functioning marketing system in which consumers, companies, public policy makers, and others work together to ensure socially and environmentally responsible marketing actions. Unfortunately, however, the marketing system doesn't always work smoothly. The following sections examine several sustainability questions: What are the most frequent social criticisms of marketing? What steps have private citizens taken to curb marketing ills? What steps have legislators and government agencies taken to promote sustainable marketing? What steps have enlightened companies taken to

● Sustainable marketing: McDonald's "Plan to Win" strategy has both created sustainable value for customers and positioned the company for a profitable future.

Alexandre Gelebart/REA/Redux

carry out socially responsible and ethical marketing that creates sustainable value for both individual customers and society as a whole?

Social Criticisms of Marketing

Marketing receives much criticism. Some of this criticism is justified; much is not. Social critics claim that certain marketing practices hurt individual consumers, society as a whole, and other business firms.

Marketing's Impact on Individual Consumers

Consumers have many concerns about how well the American marketing system serves their interests. Surveys usually show that consumers hold mixed or even slightly unfavorable attitudes toward marketing practices. Consumer advocates, government agencies, and other critics have accused marketing of harming consumers through high prices, deceptive practices, high-pressure selling, shoddy or unsafe products, planned obsolescence, and poor service to disadvantaged consumers. Such questionable marketing practices are not sustainable in terms of long-term consumer or business welfare.

High Prices

Many critics charge that the American marketing system causes prices to be higher than they would be under more "sensible" systems. Such high prices are hard to swallow, especially when the economy takes a downturn. Critics point to three factors—*high costs of distribution*, *high advertising and promotion costs*, and *excessive markups*.

High Costs of Distribution. A long-standing charge is that greedy marketing channel members mark up prices beyond the value of their services. Critics charge that there are too many intermediaries, that intermediaries are inefficient, or that they provide unnecessary or duplicate services. As a result, distribution costs too much, and consumers pay for these excessive costs in the form of higher prices.

How do resellers answer these charges? They argue that intermediaries do work that would otherwise have to be done by manufacturers or consumers. Markups reflect services that consumers themselves want—more convenience, larger stores and assortments, more service, longer store hours, return privileges, and others. In fact, they argue, retail competition is so intense that margins are actually quite low. If some resellers try to charge too much relative to the value they add, other resellers will step in with lower prices. Low-price stores such as Walmart, Costco, and other discounters pressure their competitors to operate efficiently and keep their prices down. In fact, in the wake of the recent recession, only the most efficient retailers have survived profitably.

● A heavily promoted national brand sells for much more than a virtually identical nonbranded or store-branded product. Critics charge that promotion adds only psychological value to the product rather than functional value.

Photo courtesy of Gary Armstrong

High Advertising and Promotion Costs. Modern marketing is also accused of pushing up prices to finance heavy advertising and sales promotion. ● For example, a heavily promoted national brand sells for much more than a virtually identical non-branded or store-branded product. Differentiated products—cosmetics, detergents, toiletries—include promotion and packaging costs that can amount to 40 percent or more of the manufacturer's price to the retailer. Critics charge that much of this packaging and promotion adds only psychological, not functional, value to the product.

Marketers respond that although advertising adds to product costs, it also adds value by informing potential buyers of the availability and merits of a brand. Brand name products may cost more, but branding gives buyers assurances of consistent quality.

Moreover, although consumers can usually buy functional versions of products at lower prices, they *want* and are willing to pay more for products that also provide psychological benefits—that make them feel wealthy, attractive, or special. In addition, heavy advertising and promotion may be necessary for a firm to match competitors' efforts; the business would lose "share of mind" if it did not match competitive spending.

At the same time, companies are cost conscious about promotion and try to spend their funds wisely. Today's more frugal consumers are demanding genuine value for the prices they pay. The continuing shift toward buying store brands and generics suggests that when it comes to value, consumers want action, not just talk.

Excessive Markups. Critics also charge that some companies mark up goods excessively. They point to the drug industry, where a pill costing five cents to make may cost the consumer $2 to buy. They point to the pricing tactics of funeral homes that prey on the confused emotions of bereaved relatives, and the high charges for auto repairs and other services.

Marketers respond that most businesses try to deal fairly with consumers because they want to build customer relationships and repeat business, and that most consumer abuses are unintentional. When shady marketers take advantage of consumers, they should be reported to Better Business Bureaus and state and federal agencies. Marketers also respond that consumers often don't understand the reasons for high markups. For example, pharmaceutical markups must cover the costs of purchasing, promoting, and distributing existing medicines plus the high R&D costs of formulating and testing new medicines. As pharmaceuticals company GlaxoSmithKline has stated in its ads, "Today's medicines finance tomorrow's miracles."

Deceptive Practices

Marketers are sometimes accused of deceptive practices that lead consumers to believe they will get more value than they actually do. Deceptive practices fall into three groups: pricing, promotion, and packaging. *Deceptive pricing* includes practices such as falsely advertising "factory" or "wholesale" prices or a large price reduction from a phony high retail list price. *Deceptive promotion* includes practices such as misrepresenting the product's features or performance or luring customers to the store for a bargain that is out of stock. *Deceptive packaging* includes exaggerating package contents through subtle design, using misleading labeling, or describing size in misleading terms.

Deceptive practices have led to legislation and other consumer protection actions. For example, in 1938 Congress enacted the Wheeler-Lea Act, which gave the Federal Trade Commission (FTC) power to regulate "unfair or deceptive acts or practices." The FTC has since published several guidelines listing deceptive practices. Despite regulations, however, some critics argue that deceptive claims are still common, even for well-known brands. For example, Skechers recently paid $50 million to resolve allegations by the FTC and attorneys general in 44 states that it made false advertising claims that its rocker-bottom Shape-ups and other toning shoes would help customers tone muscles and lose weight.[5] And several consumer groups recently complained that Coca-Cola's vitaminwater brand made deceptive and unsubstantiated—even "outlandish"— health claims for its products.[6]

● **Deceptive practices: Critics argue that deceptive claims are still common, even for well-known brands. Coca-Cola's vitaminwater brand recently faced allegations of deceptive and unsubstantiated—even "outlandish"— health claims for its products.**

Photo courtesy of Gary Armstrong

Coca-Cola has marketed vitaminwater as a healthy alternative to regular water. However, the National Consumers League (NCL) and other consumer groups strongly disagree. The NCL, for example, recently filed complaints with the FTC and lawsuits alleging that the brand made "dangerously misleading" claims. The NCL objected to language on the vitaminwater label suggesting, "vitamins + water = all you need." It also cited claims in vitaminwater print and TV ads that implied that the beverage served as a substitute for seasonal flu shots or helped boost the immune system and fend off ordinary ailments. For instance, one TV ad depicted a woman who had so many unused sick days at work that she could take them to stay home and watch movies with her boyfriend. The ad stated: "One of my secrets? vitaminwater power-c. It's got vitamin C and zinc to help support a healthy immune system. So I can stay home with my boyfriend—who's also playing hooky."

Such claims are both misleading and dangerous to public health, claims the NCL. Although vitaminwater suggests that it contains only vitamins and water, it also contains 125 calories per bottle. "Two-thirds of Americans are overweight or obese; the last thing people need is sugar water with vitamins you could get from eating a healthy diet, or by taking a vitamin pill," says the NCL. Britain's Advertising Standards Authority appears to agree. It recently banned as deceptive a vitaminwater ad claiming that the drink is "nutritious," ruling that consumers would not expect a nutritious drink to have the equivalent of up to five teaspoons of added sugar.

The toughest problem is defining what is "deceptive." For instance, an advertiser's claim that its chewing gum will "rock your world" isn't intended to be taken literally. Instead, the advertiser might claim, it is "puffery"—innocent exaggeration for effect. However, others claim that puffery and alluring imagery can harm consumers in subtle ways. Think about the popular and long-running MasterCard Priceless commercials that painted pictures of consumers fulfilling their priceless dreams despite the costs. The ads suggested that your credit card can make it happen. But critics charge that such imagery by credit card companies encouraged a spend-now-pay-later attitude that caused many consumers to *over*use their cards, contributing heavily to the nation's recent financial crisis.

Marketers argue that most companies avoid deceptive practices. Because such practices harm a company's business in the long run, they simply aren't sustainable. Profitable customer relationships are built on a foundation of value and trust. If consumers do not get what they expect, they will switch to more reliable products. In addition, consumers usually protect themselves from deception. Most consumers recognize a marketer's selling intent and are careful when they buy, sometimes even to the point of not believing completely true product claims.

High-Pressure Selling

Salespeople are sometimes accused of high-pressure selling that persuades people to buy goods they had no thought of buying. It is often said that insurance, real estate, and used cars are *sold*, not *bought*. Salespeople are trained to deliver smooth, canned talks to entice purchases. They sell hard because sales contests promise big prizes to those who sell the most. Similarly, TV infomercial pitchmen use "yell and sell" presentations that create a sense of consumer urgency that only those with the strongest willpower can resist.

But in most cases, marketers have little to gain from high-pressure selling. Although such tactics may work in one-time selling situations for short-term gain, most selling involves building long-term relationships with valued customers. High-pressure or deceptive selling can seriously damage such relationships. For example, imagine a P&G account manager trying to pressure a Walmart buyer or an IBM salesperson trying to browbeat an information technology manager at GE. It simply wouldn't work.

Shoddy, Harmful, or Unsafe Products

Another criticism concerns poor product quality or function. One complaint is that, too often, products and services are not made well or do not perform well. A second complaint concerns product safety. Product safety has been a problem for several reasons, including company indifference, increased product complexity, and poor quality control. A third complaint is that many products deliver little benefit, or may even be harmful.

For example, think about the soft drink industry. Many critics blame the plentiful supply of sugar-laden, high-calorie soft drinks for the nation's rapidly growing obesity epidemic. Studies show that more than two-thirds of American adults are either obese or overweight. In addition, one-third of American children are obese. This national weight issue continues despite repeated medical studies showing that excess weight brings increased risks for heart disease, diabetes, and other maladies, even cancer.[7] ● The critics are quick to fault what they see as greedy beverage marketers who are cashing in on vulnerable consumers, turning us into a nation of Big Gulpers. New York City's mayor even proposed a ban on soft drinks 16 ounces and larger.

Is the soft drink industry being socially irresponsible by aggressively promoting overindulgence to ill-informed or unwary consumers? Or is it simply serving the wants of customers by offering products that ping consumer taste buds while letting consumers make their own consumption choices? Is it the industry's job to police public tastes? As in many matters of social responsibility, what's right and wrong may be a matter of opinion. Whereas some analysts criticize the industry, others suggest that responsibility lies with

1 CAN
10 SPOONS OF SUGAR

DRAW THE LINE ON GAINING WEIGHT

You wouldn't eat it, so why drink it? A 375ml can of regular non-diet soft drink contains around 10 teaspoons of sugar. Grab a water instead. Act now to draw the line on gaining weight. For more information visit our website.

www.drawthelinewa.com.au/drinks

Supported by

Department of Health   wa   Cancer Council Western Australia   Heart Foundation

● **Harmful products: Is the soft drink industry being irresponsible by promoting overindulgence, or is it simply serving the wants of customers by offering products that ping consumer taste buds while letting consumers make their own consumption choices?**

Department of Health Western Australia

consumers. "Soft drinks have unfairly become the whipping boy of most anti-obesity campaigns," suggests one business reporter. "Maybe friends shouldn't give friends Big Gulps, but to my knowledge, no one's ever been forced to buy and drink one. There's an element of personal responsibility and control that [needs to be addressed.]"[8]

Most manufacturers *want* to produce quality goods. After all, the way a company deals with product quality and safety problems can damage or help its reputation. Companies selling poor-quality or unsafe products risk damaging conflicts with consumer groups and regulators. Unsafe products can result in product liability suits and large awards for damages. More fundamentally, consumers who are unhappy with a firm's products may avoid future purchases and talk other consumers into doing the same. Thus, quality missteps are not consistent with sustainable marketing. Today's marketers know that good quality results in customer value and satisfaction, which in turn creates sustainable customer relationships.

Planned Obsolescence

Critics also have charged that some companies practice *planned obsolescence*, causing their products to become obsolete before they actually should need replacement. They accuse some producers of using materials and components that will break, wear, rust, or rot sooner than they should. And if the products themselves don't wear out fast enough, other companies are charged with *perceived obsolescence*—continually changing consumer concepts of acceptable styles to encourage more and earlier buying.[9] An obvious example is constantly changing clothing fashions.

Still others are accused of introducing planned streams of new products that make older models obsolete, turning consumers into "serial replacers." Critics claim that this occurs in the consumer electronics industries. If you're like most people, you probably have a drawer full of yesterday's hottest technological gadgets—from mobile phones and cameras to iPods and flash drives—now reduced to the status of fossils. It seems that anything more than a year or two old is hopelessly out of date.

Marketers respond that consumers *like* style changes; they get tired of the old goods and want a new look in fashion. Or they *want* the latest high-tech innovations, even if older models still work. No one has to buy a new product, and if too few people like it, it will simply fail. Finally, most companies do not design their products to break down earlier because they do not want to lose customers to other brands. Instead, they seek constant improvement to ensure that products will consistently meet or exceed customer expectations.

Much of the so-called planned obsolescence is the working of the competitive and technological forces in a free society—forces that lead to ever-improving goods and services. For example, if Apple produced a new iPhone or iPad that would last 10 years, few consumers would want it. Instead, buyers want the latest technological innovations. "Obsolescence isn't something companies are forcing on us," confirms one analyst. "It's progress, and it's something we pretty much demand. As usual, the market gives us exactly what we want."[10]

Poor Service to Disadvantaged Consumers

Finally, the American marketing system has been accused of poorly serving disadvantaged consumers. For example, critics claim that the urban poor often have to shop in smaller stores that carry inferior goods and charge higher prices. The presence of large national chain stores in low-income neighborhoods would help to keep prices down. However, the critics accuse major chain retailers of *redlining*, drawing a red line around disadvantaged neighborhoods and avoiding placing stores there.

● Underserved consumers: Because of the lack of supermarkets in low-income areas, many disadvantaged consumers find themselves in "food deserts," with little or no access to healthy, affordable fresh foods.

© dbimages/Alamy

For example, the nation's poor areas have 30 percent fewer supermarkets than affluent areas do. ● As a result, many low-income consumers find themselves in *food deserts*, which are awash with small markets offering frozen pizzas, Cheetos, Moon Pies, and Cokes, but where fruits and vegetables or fresh fish and chicken are out of reach. Currently, some 23.5 million Americans—including 6.5 million children—live in low-income areas that lack stores selling affordable and nutritious foods. What's more, 2.3 million households have no access to a car but live more than a mile from a supermarket, forcing them to shop at convenience stores where expensive processed food is the only dietary choice. In turn, the lack of access to healthy, affordable fresh foods has a negative impact on the health of underserved consumers in these areas. Many national chains, such as Walmart, Walgreens, and SuperValu, have recently agreed to open or expand more stores that bring nutritious and fresh foods to underserved communities.[11]

Clearly, better marketing systems must be built to service disadvantaged consumers. In fact, many marketers profitably target such consumers with legitimate goods and services that create real value. In cases in which marketers do not step in to fill the void, the government likely will. For example, the FTC has taken action against sellers who advertise false values, wrongfully deny services, or charge disadvantaged customers too much.

Marketing's Impact on Society as a Whole

The American marketing system has been accused of adding to several "evils" in American society at large, such as creating too much materialism, too few social goods, and a glut of cultural pollution.

False Wants and Too Much Materialism

Critics have charged that the marketing system urges too much interest in material possessions, and that America's love affair with worldly possessions is not sustainable. Too often, people are judged by what they *own* rather than by who they *are*. The critics do not view this interest in material things as a natural state of mind but rather as a matter of false wants created by marketing. Marketers, they claim, stimulate people's desires for goods and create materialistic models of the good life. Thus, marketers have created an endless cycle of mass consumption based on a distorted interpretation of the "American Dream."

In this view, marketing's purpose is to promote consumption, and the inevitable outcome of successful marketing is unsustainable *over*consumption. Says one critic: "For most of us, our basic material needs are satisfied, so we seek in ever-growing consumption the satisfaction of wants, which consumption cannot possibly deliver. More is not always better; it is often worse."[12] Some critics have taken their concerns straight to the public. ● For example, consumer activist Annie Leonard founded *The Story of Stuff* project with a 20-minute online video about the social and environmental consequences of America's love affair with stuff—"How our obsession with stuff is trashing the planet, our communities, and our health." The video has been viewed more than 9.2 million times online and in thousands of schools and community centers around the world.[13]

Marketers respond that such criticisms overstate the power of business to create needs. They claim people have strong defenses against advertising and other marketing tools. Marketers are most effective when they appeal to existing wants rather than when they attempt to create new ones. Furthermore, people seek information when making important purchases and often do not rely on single sources. Even minor purchases that may be affected by advertising messages lead to repeat purchases only if the product delivers the promised customer value. Finally, the high failure rate of new products shows that companies are not able to control demand.

● Materialism: Consumer activist Annie Leonard's "The Story of Stuff" video about the social and environmental consequences of America's love affair with stuff has been viewed more than 1.2 million times online and in thousands of schools and community centers around the world.

Handout/MCT/Newscom

On a deeper level, our wants and values are influenced not only by marketers but also by family, peer groups, religion, cultural background, and education. If Americans are highly materialistic, these values arose out of basic socialization processes that go much deeper than business and mass media could produce alone.

Moreover, consumption patterns and attitudes are also subject to larger forces, such as the economy. As discussed in Chapter 1, the recent Great Recession put a damper on materialism and conspicuous spending. Many observers predict a new age of more sensible consumption. "The [materialistic] American dream is on pause," says one analyst. Says another, shoppers "now are taking pride in their newfound financial discipline." As a result, far from encouraging today's more sensible consumers to overspend their means, marketers are working to help them find greater value with less.[14]

Too Few Social Goods

Business has been accused of overselling private goods at the expense of public goods. As private goods increase, they require more public services that are usually not forthcoming. For example, an increase in automobile ownership (private good) requires more highways, traffic control, parking spaces, and police services (public goods). The overselling of private goods results in social costs. For cars, some of the social costs include traffic congestion, gasoline shortages, and air pollution. For example, American travelers lose, on average, 34 hours a year in traffic jams, costing the United States more than $100 billion a year—$750 per commuter. In the process, they waste 1.9 billion gallons of fuel and emit millions of tons of greenhouse gases.[15]

A way must be found to restore a balance between private and public goods. One option is to make producers bear the full social costs of their operations. For example, the government is requiring automobile manufacturers to build cars with more efficient engines and better pollution-control systems. Automakers will then raise their prices to cover the extra costs. If buyers find the price of some car models too high, however, these models will disappear. Demand will then move to those producers that can support the sum of the private and social costs.

A second option is to make consumers pay the social costs. For example, many cities around the world are now charging congestion tolls in an effort to reduce traffic congestion. ● To reduce rush hour traffic on the Bay Bridge between Oakland and San Francisco, California, the Metropolitan Transportation Commission charges a $6 toll during peak commute hours versus $4 at other times. The charge reduced the flow of drivers during peak hours, cutting the average 32-minute wait time some bridges approach in half.[16]

● **Balancing private and public goods: Raising the peak-load toll on the Bay Bridge between Oakland and San Francisco reduced traffic flow and cut the average wait time in half.**

© Jim Goldstein/Alamy

Cultural Pollution

Critics charge the marketing system with creating *cultural pollution*. They feel our senses are being constantly assaulted by marketing and advertising. Commercials interrupt serious programs; pages of ads obscure magazines; billboards mar beautiful scenery; spam fills our e-mailboxes. What's more, the critics claim, these interruptions continually pollute people's minds with messages of materialism, sex, power, or status. Some critics call for sweeping changes.

Marketers answer the charges of commercial noise with these arguments: First, they hope that their ads primarily reach the target audience. But because of mass-communication channels, some ads are bound to reach people who have no interest in the product and are therefore bored or annoyed. People who buy magazines they like or who opt in to e-mail or mobile marketing programs rarely complain about the ads because they involve products and services of interest.

Second, because of ads, many television, radio, and online sites are free to users. Ads also help keep down the costs of magazines and newspapers. Many people think viewing ads is a small price to pay for these benefits. In addition, consumers find many television commercials entertaining and seek them out; for example, ad viewership during the Super Bowl usually equals or exceeds game viewership. Finally, today's consumers have alternatives. For example, they can zip or zap TV commercials on recorded programs or avoid them altogether on many paid cable, satellite, and online channels. Thus, to hold consumer attention, advertisers are making their ads more entertaining and informative.

Marketing's Impact on Other Businesses

Critics also charge that a company's marketing practices can harm other companies and reduce competition. They identify three problems: acquisitions of competitors, marketing practices that create barriers to entry, and unfair competitive marketing practices.

Critics claim that firms are harmed and competition is reduced when companies expand by acquiring competitors rather than by developing their own new products. The large number of acquisitions and the rapid pace of industry consolidation over the past several decades have caused concern that vigorous young competitors will be absorbed, thereby reducing competition. In virtually every major industry—retailing, entertainment, financial services, utilities, transportation, automobiles, telecommunications, health care—the number of major competitors is shrinking.

Acquisition is a complex subject. In some cases, acquisitions can be good for society. The acquiring company may gain economies of scale that lead to lower costs and lower prices. In addition, a well-managed company may take over a poorly managed company and improve its efficiency. An industry that was not very competitive might become more competitive after the acquisition. But acquisitions can also be harmful, and therefore are closely regulated by the government.

Critics have also charged that marketing practices bar new companies from entering an industry. Large marketing companies can use patents and heavy promotion spending or tie up suppliers or dealers to keep out or drive out competitors. Those concerned with antitrust regulation recognize that some barriers are the natural result of the economic advantages of doing business on a large scale. Existing and new laws can challenge other barriers. For example, some critics have proposed a progressive tax on advertising spending to reduce the role of selling costs as a major barrier to entry.

Finally, some firms have, in fact, used unfair competitive marketing practices with the intention of hurting or destroying other firms. They may set their prices below costs, threaten to cut off business with suppliers, or discourage the buying of a competitor's products. Although various laws work to prevent such predatory competition, it is often difficult to prove that the intent or action was really predatory.

In recent years, Walmart has been accused of using predatory pricing in selected market areas to drive smaller, mom-and-pop retailers out of business. Walmart has become a lightning rod for protests by citizens in dozens of towns who worry that the megaretailer's unfair practices will choke out local businesses. However, whereas critics charge that Walmart's actions are predatory, others assert that its actions are just the healthy competition of a more-efficient company against less-efficient ones.

For instance, ● when Walmart began a program to sell generic drugs at $4 a prescription, local pharmacists complained of predatory pricing. They charged that at those low prices, Walmart must be selling under cost to drive them out of business. But Walmart claimed that, given its substantial buying power and efficient operations, it could make a profit at those prices. The $4 pricing program, the retailer claimed, was not aimed at putting competitors out of business. Rather, it was simply a good competitive move that served customers better and brought more of them in the door. Moreover, Walmart's program drove down prescription prices at the pharmacies of other supermarkets and discount stores, such as Kroger and Target. Currently more than 300 prescription drugs are

● **Walmart prescription pricing: Is it predatory pricing or is it just good business?**

Associated Press

available for $4 at the various chains, and Walmart claims that the program has saved its customers more than $3 billion.[17]

Objective 3 ┈┈▶
Define consumerism and environmentalism and explain how they affect marketing strategies.

Consumer Actions to Promote Sustainable Marketing

Sustainable marketing calls for more responsible actions by both businesses and consumers. Because some people view businesses as the cause of many economic and social ills, grassroots movements have arisen from time to time to keep businesses in line. Two major movements have been *consumerism* and *environmentalism*.

Consumerism

Consumerism

An organized movement of citizens and government agencies designed to improve the rights and power of buyers in relation to sellers.

Consumerism is an organized movement of citizens and government agencies to improve the rights and power of buyers in relation to sellers. Traditional *sellers' rights* include the following:

- The right to introduce any product in any size and style, provided it is not hazardous to personal health or safety, or, if it is, to include proper warnings and controls
- The right to charge any price for the product, provided no discrimination exists among similar kinds of buyers
- The right to spend any amount to promote the product, provided it is not defined as unfair competition
- The right to use any product message, provided it is not misleading or dishonest in content or execution
- The right to use buying incentive programs, provided they are not unfair or misleading

  Traditional *buyers' rights* include the following:

- The right not to buy a product that is offered for sale
- The right to expect the product to be safe
- The right to expect the product to perform as claimed

Comparing these rights, many believe that the balance of power lies on the seller's side. True, the buyer can refuse to buy. But critics feel that the buyer has too little information, education, and protection to make wise decisions when facing sophisticated sellers. Consumer advocates call for the following additional consumer rights:

- The right to be well informed about important aspects of the product
- The right to be protected against questionable products and marketing practices
- The right to influence products and marketing practices in ways that will improve "quality of life"
- The right to consume now in a way that will preserve the world for future generations of consumers

Each proposed right has led to more specific proposals by consumerists and consumer protection actions by the government. ● The right to be informed includes the right to know the true interest on a loan (truth in lending), the true cost per unit of a brand (unit pricing), the ingredients in a product (ingredient labeling), the nutritional value of foods (nutritional labeling), product freshness (open dating), and the true benefits of a product (truth in advertising). Proposals related to consumer protection include strengthening consumer rights in cases of business fraud and financial protection, requiring greater product safety, ensuring information privacy, and giving more power to government agencies. Proposals relating to quality of life include controlling the ingredients that go into

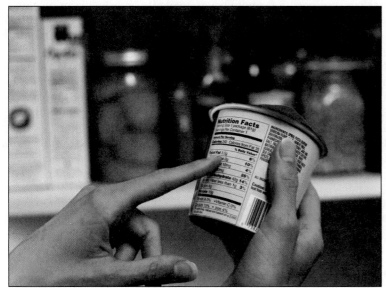

● Consumer desire for more information led to packing labels with useful facts, from ingredients and nutrition facts to recycling and country of origin information.
Ryan McVay

certain products and packaging and reducing the level of advertising "noise." Proposals for preserving the world for future consumption include promoting the use of sustainable ingredients, recycling and reducing solid wastes, and managing energy consumption.

Sustainable marketing applies not only to businesses and governments but also to consumers. Consumers have not only the *right* but also the *responsibility* to protect themselves instead of leaving this function to the government or someone else. Consumers who believe they got a bad deal have several remedies available, including contacting the company or the media; contacting federal, state, or local agencies; and going to small-claims courts. Consumers should also make good consumption choices, rewarding companies that act responsibly while punishing those that don't. Ultimately, the move from irresponsible consumption to sustainable consumption is in the hands of consumers.

Environmentalism

Environmentalism

An organized movement of concerned citizens, businesses, and government agencies designed to protect and improve people's current and future living environment.

Whereas consumerists consider whether the marketing system is efficiently serving consumer wants, environmentalists are concerned with marketing's effects on the environment and the environmental costs of serving consumer needs and wants. **Environmentalism** is an organized movement of concerned citizens, businesses, and government agencies designed to protect and improve people's current and future living environment.

Environmentalists are not against marketing and consumption; they simply want people and organizations to operate with more care for the environment. "The road to well-being doesn't go via reduced consumption," says sustainability advocate and Unilever CEO Paul Polman. "It has to be done via more responsible consumption."[18] However, the marketing system's goal, environmentalists assert, should not be to maximize consumption, consumer choice, or consumer satisfaction but rather to maximize life quality. Life quality means not only the quantity and quality of consumer goods and services but also the quality of the environment, now and for future generations.

Environmentalism is concerned with damage to the ecosystem caused by global warming, resource depletion, toxic and solid wastes, litter, the availability of fresh water, and other problems. Other issues include the loss of recreational areas and the increase in health problems caused by bad air, polluted water, and chemically treated food.

Over the past several decades, such concerns have resulted in federal and state laws and regulations governing industrial commercial practices impacting the environment. Some companies have strongly resented and resisted such environmental regulations, claiming that they are too costly and have made their industries less competitive. These companies responded to consumer environmental concerns by doing only what was required to avert new regulations or keep environmentalists quiet.

Environmental sustainability

A management approach that involves developing strategies that both sustain the environment and produce profits for the company.

In recent years, however, most companies have accepted responsibility for doing no harm to the environment. They are shifting from protest to prevention and from regulation to responsibility. More and more companies are now adopting policies of **environmental sustainability**. Simply put, environmental sustainability is about generating profits while helping to save the planet. Today's enlightened companies are taking action not because someone is forcing them to or to reap short-run profits but because it's the right thing to do—because it's for their customers' well-being, the company's well-being, and the planet's environmental future. For example, fast-food chain Chipotle has successfully built its core mission around environmental sustainability (see Real Marketing 20.1).

Figure 20.2 shows a grid that companies can use to gauge their progress toward environmental sustainability. It includes both internal and external *greening* activities that will pay off for the firm and environment in the short run, and *beyond greening*

FIGURE | 20.2
The Environmental
Sustainability Portfolio

Source: Stuart L. Hart, "Innovation, Creative Destruction, and Sustainability," *Research Technology Management,* September–October 2005, pp. 21–27.

	Today: Greening	Tomorrow: Beyond Greening
Internal	**Pollution prevention** Eliminating or reducing waste before it is created	**New clean technology** Developing new sets of environmental skills and capabilities
External	**Product stewardship** Minimizing environmental impact throughout the entire product life cycle	**Sustainability vision** Creating a strategic framework for future sustainability

How does "environmental sustainability" relate to "marketing sustainability"? Environmental sustainability involves preserving the natural environment, whereas marketing sustainability is a broader concept that involves both the natural and social environments—pretty much everything in this chapter.

Real Marketing 20.1

Chipotle's Environmental Sustainability Mission:
Food With Integrity

Envision this. You're sitting in a restaurant where the people—from the CEO on down to the kitchen crew—obsess over using only the finest ingredients. They come to work each morning inspired by all the "fresh produce and meats they have to marinate, rice they have to cook, and fresh herbs they have to chop," says the CEO. The restaurant prefers to use sustainable, naturally raised ingredients sourced from local family farms. This restaurant is on a mission not just to serve its customers good food but to change the way its entire industry produces food. This sounds like one of those high-falutin', gourmet specialty restaurants, right? Wrong. It's your neighborhood Chipotle Mexican Grill. That's right, it's a fast-food restaurant.

In an age when many fast-feeders seem to be finding ever-cheaper ingredients and centralizing much of their food preparation to cut costs and keep prices low, Chipotle is doing just the opposite. The chain's core sustainable mission is to serve "Food With Integrity." What does that mean? The company explains it this way:

> Chipotle is committed to finding the very best ingredients raised with respect for animals, the environment, and farmers. It means serving the very best sustainably raised food possible with an eye to great taste, great nutrition, and great value. It means that we support and sustain family farmers who respect the land and the animals in their care. It means that whenever possible we use meat from animals raised without the use of antibiotics or added hormones. And it means that we source organic and local produce when practical, and that we use dairy from cows raised without the use of synthetic hormones. In other words, "integrity" is kind of a funny word for "good."

When founder and CEO Steve Ells opened the first Chipotle in Denver in 1993, his primary goal was to make the best gourmet burrito around. However, as the chain grew, Ells found that he didn't like the way the ingredients Chipotle used were raised and processed. So in 2000, Chipotle began developing a supply chain with the goal of producing and using naturally raised, organic, hormone-free, non-genetically-modified ingredients. Pursuing this healthy-food mission was no easy task. As the fast-food industry

increasingly moved toward low-cost, efficient food processing, factory farms were booming, whereas independent farms producing naturally raised and organic foods were in decline.

To obtain the ingredients it needed, Chipotle had to develop many new sources. To help that cause, the company founded the Chipotle Cultivate Foundation, which supports family farming and encourages sustainable farming methods. Such efforts have paid off. For example, when Chipotle first started serving naturally raised pork in 2000, there were only 60 to 70 farms producing meat for the Niman Ranch pork cooperative, an important Chipotle supplier. Now, there are 600 to 700.

Sourcing such natural and organic ingredients not only serves Chipotle's sustainability mission, it results in one of the most nutritious, best-tasting fast-food burritos on the market—something the company can brag about to customers. "Typically, fast-food marketing is a game of trying to obscure the truth," says Chipotle's chief marketing officer. "The more people know about most fast-food companies, the less likely they'd want to be a customer." But Chipotle doesn't play that game. Instead, it commits fast-food heresy: Proudly telling customers what's really inside its burritos.

Chipotle chose the "Food With Integrity" slogan because it sends the right message in an appetizing way. "Saying that we don't buy

dairy from cows that are given the hormone rBGH is not an appetizing message," says Ells. So the company is building its marketing campaign around the more positive message that food production should be healthier and more ethical. Chipotle communicates this positioning via an integrated mix of traditional and digital promotion venues, ranging from its Farm Team invitation-only loyalty program—by which customers earn rewards based not on frequent buying but on knowledge about food and how it is produced—to its Pasture Pandemonium smartphone app, where players try to get their pig across a pasture without getting trapped in pens or pricked by antibiotic needles.

Last year, Chipotle made a big splash during the broadcast for the Grammy Awards with its first-ever national television ad—a two-and-a-half-minute stop-motion animation film showing a family hog farm converting to an efficient, industrialized farm. Then, when the farmer realizes that it's not the right thing to do, he tears down his factory farm and reverts to raising hogs sustainably in open pastures. Willie Nelson provides the soundtrack with a cover of Coldplay's "The Scientist," giving the ad its name, "Back to the Start." Before it ever aired as a TV ad, the video played in 10,000 movie theaters and online, where it became a viral hit on YouTube. Viewers were urged to download the Willie Nelson tune via iTunes, with the proceeds going to the Chipotle Cultivate Foundation.

Companies with a socially responsible business model often struggle to grow and make profits. But Chipotle is proving that a company can do both. Last year, its 30,000 employees chopped, sliced, diced, and grilled their way to $2.3 billion in revenues and $215 million in profits at Chipotle's 1,230 restaurants in 41 states. And the chain is growing fast, opening a new restaurant almost every two days. In the past

Fast-food chain Chipotle has successfully built its core mission around an environmental sustainability theme: "Food With Integrity."

© Chipotle Mexican Grill, Inc.

three years, Chipotle's stock price has tripled, suggesting that the company's investors are as pleased as its fast-growing corps of customers.

Founder and CEO Ells wants Chipotle to grow and make money. But ultimately, on a larger stage, he wants to change the way fast food is produced and sold—not just by Chipotle but by the entire industry. "We think the more people understand where their food comes from and the impact that has on independent family farmers [and] animal welfare, the more they're going to ask for better ingredients," says Ells. Whether customers stop by Chipotle's restaurants to support the cause, gobble down the tasty food, or both, it all suits Ells just fine. Chipotle's sustainability mission isn't an add-on, created just to position the company as "socially responsible." Doing good "is the company's ethos and ingrained in everything we do," says Chipotle's director of communications. "Chipotle is a very different kind of company where the deeper you dig into what's happening, the more there is to like and feel good about."

Sources: Based on information and quotes from Danielle Sacks, "Chipotle: For Exploding All the Rules of Fast Food," *Fast Company*, March 2012, pp. 125–126; John Trybus, "Chipotle's Chris Arnold and the Food With Integrity Approach to Corporate Social Responsibility," *The Social Strategist*, March 22, 2012, https://blogs.commons.georgetown.edu/socialimpact/2012/03/22/the-social-strategist-part-xvi-chipotle's-chris-arnold-and-the-food-with-integrity-approach-to-corporate-social-responsibility/; Emily Bryson York, "Chipotle Ups the Ante on Its Marketing," *Chicago Tribune*, September 30, 2011; Elizabeth Olson, "An Animated Ad with a Plot Line and a Moral," *New York Times*, February 10, 2012, p. B2; and information from www.chipotle.com and www.chipotle.com/en-US/fwi/fwi.aspx, accessed October 2012.

activities that will pay off in the longer term. At the most basic level, a company can practice *pollution prevention*. This involves more than pollution control—cleaning up waste after it has been created. Pollution prevention means eliminating or minimizing waste *before* it is created. Companies emphasizing prevention have responded with internal green marketing programs—designing and developing ecologically safer products, recyclable and biodegradable packaging, better pollution controls, and more energy-efficient operations.

For example, Nike makes shoes out of "environmentally preferred materials," recycles old sneakers, and educates young people about conservation, reuse, and recycling. SC Johnson—maker of familiar household brands ranging from Windex, Pledge, Shout, and Scrubbing Bubbles to Ziploc, Off, and Raid—sells concentrated versions of all of its household cleaners in recyclable bottles, helping eliminate empty trigger bottles from entering landfills. The company currently obtains 40 percent of its electricity from renewable sources. And by rating the environmental impact of product ingredients, it has cut nearly 48 million pounds of volatile organic compounds (VOCs) from its products in the last five years. SC Johnson boasts that since 1886, it has been "committed to working every day to do what's right for people, the planet, and generations to come."[19]

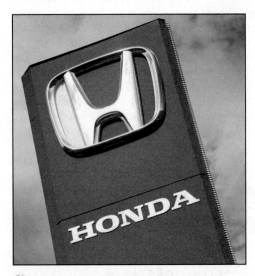

● Honda of America boasts that its huge manufacturing plants now send almost no waste to landfills. For years, the auto giant has been on a search-and-destroy mission to eliminate waste. A majority of its North American plants now send no waste at all to landfills; the remaining few dump only small amounts of plastic and paper trash from their cafeterias. To ferret out sources of waste, Honda even sends teams of employees to comb through plant dumpsters and refuse piles. Such teams have initiated hundreds of waste-reduction and recycling efforts. Whether it's by reducing metal scrap in manufacturing processes or replacing cafeteria paper and plastic with washable dishware, during the past 10 years, Honda's garbage-picking employees have eliminated 4.4 billion pounds of potential landfill waste. Whereas the company sent 62.8 pounds of waste per car to landfills in 2001, it now sends only 1.8 pounds per car.[20]

● **Pollution prevention: The total amount of industrial waste that Honda of America sends to landfills has dwindled from 62.8 pounds per vehicle produced in 2001 to an estimated 1.8 pounds per vehicle now. Incredibly, most of its North American plants send no waste at all to landfills.**

© Errol Rait/Alamy

At the next level, companies can practice *product stewardship*—minimizing not only pollution from production and product design but also all environmental impacts throughout the full product life cycle, while at the same time reducing costs. Many companies are adopting *design for environment (DFE)* and *cradle-to-cradle* practices. This involves thinking ahead to design products that are easier to recover, reuse, recycle, or safely return to nature after usage, thus becoming part of the ecological cycle. DFE and cradle-to-cradle practices not only help to sustain the environment, but they can also be highly profitable for the company.

For example, more than a decade ago, IBM started a business—IBM Global Asset Recovery Services—designed to reuse and recycle parts from returned mainframe computers and other equipment. Last year, IBM processed more than 36,600 metric tons of end-of-life products and product waste worldwide, stripping down old equipment to recover chips and valuable metals. The cumulative weight processed by IBM's remanufacturing and de-manufacturing operations would fill 4,480 rail cars stretching 49 miles. IBM Global Asset Recovery Services finds uses for more than 99 percent of what it takes in, sending less than 1 percent to landfills and incineration facilities. What started out as an environmental effort has now grown into a multibillion-dollar IBM business that profitably recycles electronic equipment at 22 sites worldwide.[21]

Today's *greening* activities focus on improving what companies already do to protect the environment. The *beyond greening* activities identified in Figure 20.2 look to the future. First, internally, companies can plan for *new clean technology*. Many organizations that have made good sustainability headway are still limited by existing technologies. To create fully sustainable strategies, they will need to develop innovative new technologies.

For example, by 2020, Coca-Cola has committed to reclaiming and recycling the equivalent of all the packaging it uses around the world. It has also pledged to dramatically reduce its overall environmental footprint. To accomplish these goals, the company invests heavily in new clean technologies that address a host of environmental issues, such as recycling, resource usage, distribution, and even outdoor advertising:[22]

> First, to attack the solid waste problem caused by its plastic bottles, Coca-Cola invested heavily to build the world's largest state-of-the-art plastic-bottle-to-bottle recycling plant. As a more permanent solution, Coke is researching and testing new bottles made from aluminum, corn, or bioplastics. This year it's piloting its PlantBottle line, which incorporates 30 percent plant-based materials. The company is also designing more eco-friendly distribution alternatives. Currently, some 10 million vending machines and refrigerated coolers gobble up energy and use potent greenhouse gases called hydrofluorocarbons (HFCs) to keep Cokes cold. To eliminate them, the company invested $40 million in research and recently began installing sleek new HFC-free coolers that use 30 to 40 percent less energy. Coca-Cola also aims to become "water neutral" by researching ways to help its bottlers add back all the fresh water they extract during the production of Coca-Cola beverages.

Finally, companies can develop a *sustainability vision*, which serves as a guide to the future. It shows how the company's products and services, processes, and policies must evolve and what new technologies must be developed to get there. This vision of sustainability provides a framework for pollution control, product stewardship, and new environmental technology for the company and others to follow.

Most companies today focus on the upper-left quadrant of the grid in Figure 20.2, investing most heavily in pollution prevention. Some forward-looking companies practice product stewardship and are developing new environmental technologies. However, emphasizing only one or two quadrants in the environmental sustainability grid can be shortsighted. Investing only in the left half of the grid puts a company in a good position today but leaves it vulnerable in the future. In contrast, a heavy emphasis on the right half suggests that a company has good environmental vision but lacks the skills needed to implement it. Thus, companies should work at developing all four dimensions of environmental sustainability.

Walmart, for example, is doing just that. ● Through its own environmental sustainability actions and its impact on the actions of suppliers, Walmart has emerged in recent years as the world's super "eco-nanny":[23]

When it comes to sustainability, perhaps no company in the world is doing more good these days than Walmart. That's right—big, bad Walmart. The giant retailer is now one of the world's biggest crusaders for the cause of saving

● **For Walmart, sustainability is about more than just doing the right thing. Above all, it's makes good business sense—"driving out hidden costs, conserving our natural resources for future generations, and providing sustainable and affordable products for our customers so they can save money and live better."**

AP Images/PRNewsFoto/Walmart; Bebay/iStockphoto

the world for future generations. For starters, Walmart is rolling out new high-efficiency stores, each one saving more energy than the last. These stores use wind turbines to generate energy, high-output linear fluorescent lighting to reduce what energy stores do use, and native landscaping to cut down on watering and fertilizer. Store heating systems burn recovered cooking oil from the deli fryers and motor oil from the Tire and Lube Express centers. All organic waste, including produce, meats, and paper, is hauled off to a company that turns it into mulch for the garden.

Walmart is not only greening up its own operations but also laying down the eco-law to its vast networks of 100,000 suppliers to get them to do the same. It recently announced plans to cut some 20 million metric tons of greenhouse gas emissions from its supply chain by the end of 2015—equivalent to removing more than 3.8 million cars from the road for a year. To get this done, Walmart is asking its huge corps of suppliers to examine the carbon life cycles of their products and rethink how they source, manufacture, package, and transport these goods. With its immense buying power, Walmart can humble even the mightiest supplier. When imposing its environmental demands on suppliers, Walmart has even more clout than government regulators. Whereas the EPA can only level nominal fines, Walmart can threaten a substantial chunk of a supplier's business.

For Walmart, leading the eco-charge is about more than just doing the right thing. Above all, it also makes good business sense. More efficient operations and less wasteful products are not only good for the environment but also save Walmart money. Lower costs, in turn, let Walmart do more of what it has always done best—save customers money.

Public Actions to Regulate Marketing

Citizen concerns about marketing practices will usually lead to public attention and legislative proposals. Many of the laws that affect marketing were identified in Chapter 3. The task is to translate these laws into a language that marketing executives understand as they make decisions about competitive relations, products, price, promotion, and distribution channels. ● **Figure 20.3** illustrates the major legal issues facing marketing management.

Business Actions Toward Sustainable Marketing

Objective 4 ┈┈┈▶

Describe the principles of sustainable marketing.

At first, many companies opposed consumerism, environmentalism, and other elements of sustainable marketing. They thought the criticisms were either unfair or unimportant. But by now, most companies have grown to embrace sustainability principles as a way to create both immediate and future customer value and strengthen customer relationships.

Sustainable Marketing Principles

Under the sustainable marketing concept, a company's marketing should support the best long-run performance of the marketing system. It should be guided by five sustainable marketing principles: *consumer-oriented marketing, customer-value marketing, innovative marketing, sense-of-mission marketing,* and *societal marketing.*

Consumer-Oriented Marketing

Consumer-oriented marketing
A principle of sustainable marketing that holds a company should view and organize its marketing activities from the consumer's point of view.

Consumer-oriented marketing means that the company should view and organize its marketing activities from the consumer's point of view. It should work hard to sense, serve, and satisfy the needs of a defined group of customers—both now and in the future. The good marketing companies that we've discussed throughout this text have had this in common: an all-consuming passion for delivering superior value to carefully chosen customers. Only by seeing the world through its customers' eyes can the company build sustainable and profitable customer relationships.

Customer-Value Marketing

Customer-value marketing
A principle of sustainable marketing holding that a company should put most of its resources into customer-value-building marketing investments.

According to the principle of **customer-value marketing**, the company should put most of its resources into customer-value-building marketing investments. Many things marketers do—one-shot sales promotions, cosmetic product changes, direct-response advertising—may raise sales in the short run but add less *value* than would actual

FIGURE | 20.3
Major Marketing Decision Areas That May Be Called into Question under the Law
(photo) wavebreakmedia ltd/Shutterstock.com

Selling decisions
Bribing?
Stealing trade secrets?
Disparaging customers?
Misrepresenting?
Disclosure of customer rights?
Unfair discrimination?

Advertising decisions
False advertising?
Deceptive advertising?
Bait-and-switch advertising?
Promotional allowances and services?

Channel decisions
Exclusive dealing?
Exclusive territorial distributorship?
Tying agreements?
Dealer's rights?

Product decisions
Product additions and deletions?
Patent protection?
Product quality and safety?
Product warranty?

Packaging decisions
Fair packaging and labeling?
Excessive cost?
Scarce resources?
Pollution?

Price decisions
Price fixing?
Predatory pricing?
Price discrimination?
Minimum pricing?
Price increases?
Deceptive pricing?

Competitive relations decisions
Anticompetitive acquisition?
Barriers to entry?
Predatory competition?

improvements in the product's quality, features, or convenience. Enlightened marketing calls for building long-run consumer loyalty and relationships by continually improving the value consumers receive from the firm's market offering. By creating value *for* consumers, the company can capture value *from* consumers in return.

Innovative Marketing

Innovative marketing

A principle of sustainable marketing that requires a company to seek real product and marketing improvements.

The principle of **innovative marketing** requires that the company continuously seek real product and marketing improvements. The company that overlooks new and better ways to do things will eventually lose customers to another company that has found a better way. As we discussed in Chapter 9, an excellent example of an innovative marketer is Samsung:[24]

> Not too many years ago, Samsung was a copycat consumer electronics brand you bought if you couldn't afford Sony. But today, the brand holds a high-end, cutting-edge aura. In 1996, Samsung Electronics turned its back on making cheap knock-offs and set out to overtake rival Sony, not just in size but also in style and innovation. It hired a crop of fresh, young designers who unleashed a torrent of sleek, bold, and beautiful new products targeted to high-end users. Samsung called them "lifestyle works of art"—from brightly colored mobile phones to large-screen TVs that hung on walls like paintings. Every new product had to pass the "Wow!" test: if it didn't get a "Wow!" reaction during market testing, it went straight back to the design studio. Thanks to its strategy of innovation, the company quickly surpassed its lofty goals—and more. Samsung Electronics is now, by far, the world's largest consumer electronics company, with 50 percent greater sales than Sony. It's the world's largest TV and mobile phone producer. And its designs are coveted by consumers. Says a Samsung designer, "We are not el cheapo anymore."[25]

Sense-of-Mission Marketing

Sense-of-mission marketing

A principle of sustainable marketing holding that a company should define its mission in broad social terms rather than narrow product terms.

Sense-of-mission marketing means that the company should define its mission in broad *social* terms rather than narrow *product* terms. When a company defines a social mission, employees feel better about their work and have a clearer sense of direction. Brands linked with broader missions can serve the best long-run interests of both the brand and consumers.

For example, the PEDIGREE Brand makes good dog food, but that's not what the brand is really all about. Instead, five years ago, the brand came up with the manifesto,

Sophie, adopted from the
Nashville Humane Association

Later, shelter.

For a shelter dog, there's no better feeling than going home. And by donating our food to
shelters in need, PEDIGREE is doing more than ever to help keep shelter dogs healthy,
happy, and ready to get adopted. Now you can help too.

When you buy a bag of PEDIGREE, you'll help us feed more shelter dogs.
Learn more at Facebook.com/Pedigree

We're for dogs.

● **For the PEDIGREE Brand, "Everything we do is because we love dogs. It's just so simple." The PEDIGREE Brand's "We're for dogs" mission has helped to make it the world's number-one dog food brand.**

Courtesy of Mars, Incorporated. PEDIGREE® is a registered trademark of Mars. Incorporated.

"We're for dogs." That statement is a perfect encapsulation of everything PEDIGREE stands for. "Everything that we do is because we love dogs," says a PEDIGREE marketer. "It's just so simple." This mission-focused positioning drives everything the brand does—internally and externally. ● One look at a PEDIGREE ad or a visit to the pedigree.com Web site confirms that the people behind the PEDIGREE Brand really do believe the "We're for dogs" mission. Associates are even encouraged to take their dogs to work. To further fulfill the "We're for dogs" brand promise, the company created the PEDIGREE Foundation, which along with the PEDIGREE Adoption Drive campaign, has raised millions of dollars for helping "shelter dogs" find good homes. Sense-of-mission marketing has made PEDIGREE the world's number one dog food brand.[26]

Some companies define their overall corporate missions in broad societal terms. For example, defined in narrow product terms, the mission of sports footwear and apparel maker PUMA might be "to sell sports shoes, clothing, and accessories." However, PUMA states its mission more broadly, as one of producing customer-satisfying products while also contributing to a sustainable future:[27]

> At PUMA, we believe that our position as the creative leader in sport lifestyles gives us the opportunity and the responsibility to contribute to a better world for the generations to come. A better world in our vision—PUMA Vision—would be safer, more peaceful, and more creative than the world we know today. We believe that by staying true to our values, inspiring the passion and talent of our people, working in sustainable, innovative ways, and doing our best to be Fair, Honest, Positive, and Creative, we will keep on making the products our customers love, and at the same time bring that vision of a better world a little closer every day. Through our programs of puma.safe (focusing on environmental and social issues), puma.peace (supporting global peace) and puma.creative (supporting artists and creative organizations), we are providing real and practical expressions of this vision and building for ourselves and our stakeholders, among other things, a more sustainable future.

Under its PUMA Vision mission, the company has made substantial progress in developing more sustainable products, packaging, operations, and supply chains. It has also sponsored many innovative initiatives to carry forward its puma.peace and puma.creative missions. For example, it sponsored a series of "peace starts with me" videos aimed at "fostering a more peaceful world than the one we live in today." Although such efforts may not produce immediate sales, PUMA sees them as an important part of "who we are."

However, having a *double bottom line* of values and profits isn't easy. Over the years, companies such as Patagonia, Ben & Jerry's, The Body Shop, and Burt's Bees—all known and respected for putting "principles before profits"—have at times struggled with less-than-stellar financial returns. In recent years, however, a new generation of social entrepreneurs has emerged, well-trained business managers who know that to *do good*, they must first *do well* in terms of profitable business operations. Moreover, today, socially responsible business is no longer the sole province of small, socially conscious entrepreneurs. Many large, established companies and brands—from Walmart and Nike to Starbucks and PepsiCo—have adopted substantial social and environmental responsibility missions (see Real Marketing 20.2).

Societal marketing
A principle of sustainable marketing holding that a company should make marketing decisions by considering consumers' wants, the company's requirements, consumers' long-run interests, and society's long-run interests.

Societal Marketing

Following the principle of **societal marketing**, a company makes marketing decisions by considering consumers' wants, the company's requirements, consumers' long-run interests, and society's long-run interests. Companies should be aware that neglecting consumer and societal long-run interests is a disservice to consumers and society. Alert companies view societal problems as opportunities.

Real Marketing 20.2

Socially Responsible Marketing:
Making the World a Better Place

Chances are, when you hear the term *socially responsible business*, a handful of companies leap to mind, such as Ben & Jerry's, The Body Shop, Burt's Bees, Stonyfield Farms, Patagonia, Timberland, and TOMS Shoes, to name a few. Such companies pioneered the concept of values-led business or caring capitalism. Their mission: Use business to make the world a better place.

The classic "do good" pioneer is Ben & Jerry's. Ben Cohen and Jerry Greenfield founded the company in 1978 as a firm that cared deeply about its social and environmental responsibilities. Ben & Jerry's bought only hormone-free milk and cream and used only organic fruits and nuts to make its ice cream, which it sold in environmentally friendly containers. It went to great lengths to buy from minority and disadvantaged suppliers. From its early Rainforest Crunch to Imagine Whirled Peace to Chocolate Macadamia (made with sustainably sourced macadamias and fair-trade-certified cocoa and vanilla), Ben & Jerry's has championed a host of social and environmental causes over the years. From the start, Ben & Jerry's donated a whopping 7.5 percent of pretax profits to support projects in line with its social mission to "meet human needs and eliminate injustices [relating to] children and families, the environment and… those who have been denied [economic opportunities]." By the mid-1990s, Ben & Jerry's had become the nation's number two super-premium ice cream brand.

However, as competitors not shackled by Ben & Jerry's "principles before profits" mission invaded its markets, growth and profits flattened. After several years of lackluster financial returns, Ben & Jerry's was acquired by consumer-goods giant Unilever. What happened to the founders' lofty ideals of caring capitalism? Looking back, Ben & Jerry's may have focused too much on social issues at the expense of sound business management. Ben Cohen never really wanted to be a businessperson, and he saw profits as a dirty word. Cohen once commented, "There came a point [when I had to admit] 'I'm a businessman.' And I had a hard time mouthing those words."

Having a "triple bottom line" of people, planet, and profits is no easy proposition. Operating a business is tough enough. Adding social goals to the demands of serving customers and making a profit can be daunting and distracting. You can't take good intentions to the bank. In fact, many of the pioneering values-led businesses have since been acquired by bigger companies. For example, Unilever absorbed Ben & Jerry's, Clorox bought out Burt's Bees, L'Oréal acquired The Body Shop, Dannon ate up Stonyfield Farms, and VFC acquired Timberland.

The experiences of pioneers like Ben & Jerry's, however, taught the socially responsible business movement some hard lessons. As a result, a new generation of mission-driven entrepreneurs emerged—not social activists with big hearts who hate capitalism but well-trained business managers and company builders with a passion for a cause. These new triple-bottom-line devotees know that to do good, they must first do well in terms of viable and profitable business operations.

For example, home and cleaning products company Method is on a mission to "inspire a happy, healthy home revolution." All of Method's products are derived from natural ingredients, such as soy, coconut, and palm oils. The products come in environmentally responsible, biodegradable packaging. But Method knows that just doing good things won't make it successful. In fact, it's the other way around—being successful will let it do good things. "Business is the most powerful agent for positive change on the planet," says Method co-founder and "chief greenskeeper" Adam

Lowry. "Mere sustainability is not our goal. We want to go much farther than that. We want to become restorative and enriching in everything we do so that the bigger we get, the more good we can create. We are striving for sustainable abundance. That's why we've geared our company to be the best at getting better."

Beyond its social responsibility mission, Method is a well-run business and savvy marketer. "We don't run from the green, we just don't make that the lead story," says Eric Ryan, Method's other co-founder. Instead, Method emphasizes product performance, innovation, and style. Its products are "more powerful than a bottle of sodium hypochlorite," yet "gentler than a thousand puppy licks." According to Ryan, "What's worked really well for the brand is people have come in because of the more joyful, fun side [of our products] and then discover that this is actually good for you."

In only a few short years, through smart business practices, Method has become one of the nation's fastest-growing companies, with more than $100 million in annual revenues. The young company has attained mainstream distribution in more than 100 U.S. retailers—including Kroger, Safeway, Target, Whole Foods Market, Bed Bath & Beyond, Staples, and Amazon.com—and a growing list of international retailers. In the process, it's achieving its broader social goals.

Small companies with big social goals are one thing. However, today, socially responsible missions are no longer the exclusive domain of well-intentioned start-ups.

Method's mission is to inspire a happy, healthy home revolution. Says Method co-founder and "chief greenskeeper" Adam Lowry, "business is the most powerful agent for positive change on the planet."

Christopher Schall/Impact Photo

Social responsibility has gone mainstream, with large corporations—from Walmart and Nike to Starbucks and Mars—adopting broad-based "change the world" initiatives. For example, Walmart is fast becoming the world's leading eco-nanny. Likewise, Starbucks created C.A.F.E. practices, guidelines for achieving product quality, economic accountability, social responsibility, and environmental leadership.

Nike supports a broad social and environmental responsibility agenda, everything from eco-friendly product designs and manufacturing processes to improving conditions for the nearly 800,000 workers in its global supply chain to programs that engage the world's youth in the fight against AIDS in Africa. Sounding more like Ben & Jerry's or

Method than a large, uncaring corporation, Nike states "We can use the power of our brand, the energy and passion of our people, and the scale of our business to create meaningful change." Says one Nike manager, "Our customers expect this from us. It's not about two or three green shoes—it's about changing the way our company does things in general."

Whether it's a small start-up with social responsibility in its core or a large corporation looking to embed social responsibility in its mission, it's now clear that doing good and doing well are closely intertwined. As Unilever CEO Paul Polman noted in the chapter-opening story, a company's long-run commercial success depends on how well it manages the social and environmental impact of its actions. But today's social entrepreneurs have learned that it goes both ways: A company's ability to have beneficial long-run social and environmental impact depends on its commercial success as well.

Sources: Quotes and other information from Tilde Herrera, "Want to Sell a Green Product? Don't Call It Green," *GreenBiz*, January 30, 2012, www.greenbiz.com/blog/2012/01/30/want-sell-green-product-don't-call-it-green; David Choi and Edmund Gray, *Values-Centered Entrepreneurs and Their Companies* (Taylor & Francis, 2010), p. 29; Sindya N. Bhanoo, "Products That Are Earth-and-Profit Friendly," *New York Times,* June 12, 2010, p. B3; and www .methodhome.com/behind-the-bottle/, www.benjerry.com/company/history/, and www.nikebiz.com/responsibility/, accessed September 2012.

Deficient products
Products that have neither immediate appeal nor long-run benefits.

Pleasing products
Products that give high immediate satisfaction but may hurt consumers in the long run.

Sustainable marketing calls for products that are not only pleasing but also beneficial. The difference is shown in ● **Figure 20.4**. Products can be classified according to their degree of immediate consumer satisfaction and long-run consumer benefit.

Deficient products, such as bad-tasting and ineffective medicine, have neither immediate appeal nor long-run benefits. **Pleasing products** give high immediate satisfaction but may hurt consumers in the long run. Examples include cigarettes and junk food. **Salutary products** have low immediate appeal but may benefit consumers in the long run, for instance, bicycle helmets or some insurance products. **Desirable products** give both high immediate satisfaction and high long-run benefits, such as a tasty *and* nutritious breakfast food.

Examples of desirable products abound. Philips AmbientLED light bulbs provide good lighting at the same time that they give long life and energy savings. Envirosax reusable shopping bags are stylish and affordable while also eliminating the need for less-eco-friendly disposable paper and plastic store bags. ● And Nau's durable, sustainable urban outdoor apparel fits the "modern mobile lifestyle." Nau clothing is environmentally sustainable—using only sustainable materials such as natural and renewable fibers produced in a sustainable manner and synthetic fibers that contain high recycled content. It's aesthetically sustainable—versatile and designed for lasting beauty. And Nau clothing is also socially sustainable—the company donates 2 percent of every sale to Partners for Change organizations and ensures that its factories adhere to its own strict code of conduct.[28]

Companies should try to turn all of their products into desirable products. The challenge posed by pleasing products is that they sell very well but may end up hurting the consumer. The product opportunity, therefore, is to add long-run benefits without reducing the product's pleasing qualities. The challenge posed by salutary products is to add some pleasing qualities so that they will become more desirable in consumers' minds.

For example, PepsiCo recently hired a team of "idealistic scientists," headed by a former director of

● Desirable products: Nau's urban outdoor apparel products are **environmentally, aesthetically, and socially sustainable. The company donates 2 percent of every sale to Partners for Change organizations chosen by customers.**

Nau Holdings, LLC.

FIGURE | 20.4
Societal Classification
of Products

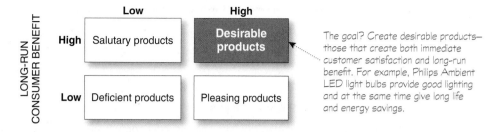

IMMEDIATE SATISFACTION

The goal? Create desirable products—those that create both immediate customer satisfaction and long-run benefit. For example, Philips Ambient LED light bulbs provide good lighting and at the same time give long life and energy savings.

Salutary products

Products that have low immediate appeal but may benefit consumers in the long run.

Desirable products

Products that give both high immediate satisfaction and high long-run benefits.

Objective 5 ┄┄┄►

Explain the role of ethics in marketing.

the World Health Organization, to help the company create attractive new healthy product options while "making the bad stuff less bad." PepsiCo wants healthy products to be a $30-billion business for the company by 2020.[29] The group of physicians, PhDs, and other health advocates, under the direction of PepsiCo's vice president for global health policy, looks for healthier ingredients that can go into multiple products. For example, their efforts led to an all-natural zero-calorie sweetener now featured in several new PepsiCo brands, including the $100-million Trop50 brand, a Tropicana orange juice variation that contains no artificial sweeteners and half the sugar and calories.

Marketing Ethics

Good ethics are a cornerstone of sustainable marketing. In the long run, unethical marketing harms customers and society as a whole. Further, it eventually damages a company's reputation and effectiveness, jeopardizing its very survival. Thus, the sustainable marketing goals of long-term consumer and business welfare can be achieved only through ethical marketing conduct.

Conscientious marketers face many moral dilemmas. The best thing to do is often unclear. Because not all managers have fine moral sensitivity, companies need to develop *corporate marketing ethics policies*—broad guidelines that everyone in the organization must follow. These policies should cover distributor relations, advertising standards, customer service, pricing, product development, and general ethical standards.

The finest guidelines cannot resolve all the difficult ethical situations the marketer faces. ● **Table 20.1** lists some difficult ethical issues marketers could face during their careers. If marketers choose immediate-sales-producing actions in all these cases, their marketing behavior might well be described as immoral or even amoral. If they refuse to go along with *any* of the actions, they might be ineffective as marketing managers and unhappy because of the constant moral tension. Managers need a set of principles that will help them figure out the moral importance of each situation and decide how far they can go in good conscience.

But *what* principle should guide companies and marketing managers on issues of ethics and social responsibility? One philosophy is that the free market and the legal system should decide such issues. Under this principle, companies and their managers are not responsible for making moral judgments. Companies can in good conscience do whatever the market and legal systems allow.

A second philosophy puts responsibility not on the system but in the hands of individual companies and managers. This more enlightened philosophy suggests that a company should have a social conscience. Companies and managers should apply high standards of ethics and morality when making corporate decisions, regardless of "what the system allows." History provides an endless list of examples of company actions that were legal but highly irresponsible.

Each company and marketing manager must work out a philosophy of socially responsible and ethical behavior. Under the societal marketing concept, each manager must look beyond what is legal and allowed and develop standards based on personal integrity, corporate conscience, and long-run consumer welfare.

Dealing with issues of ethics and social responsibility in an open and forthright way helps to build strong customer relationships based on honesty and trust. In fact, many companies now routinely include consumers in the social responsibility process. ● Consider toy maker Mattel In 2007, the company discovered lead paint on many of its top-selling products, forcing it

● Table 20.1 | Some Morally Difficult Situations in Marketing

1. Your R&D department has slightly changed one of your company's products. It is not really "new and improved," but you know that putting this statement on the package and in advertising will increase sales. What would you do?

2. You have been asked to add a stripped-down model to your line that could be advertised to pull customers into the store. The product won't be very good, but salespeople will be able to switch buyers who come into the store up to higher-priced units. You are asked to give the green light for the stripped-down version. What would you do?

3. You are thinking of hiring a product manager who has just left a competitor's company. She would be more than happy to tell you all the competitor's plans for the coming year. What would you do?

4. One of your top dealers in an important territory recently has had family troubles, and his sales have slipped. It looks like it will take him a while to straighten out his family troubles. Meanwhile, you are losing many sales. Legally, on performance grounds, you can terminate the dealer's franchise and replace him. What would you do?

5. You have a chance to win a big account that will mean a lot to you and your company. The purchasing agent hints that a "gift" would influence the decision. Your assistant recommends sending a large-screen television to the buyer's home. What would you do?

6. You have heard that a competitor has a new product feature that will make a big difference in sales. The competitor will demonstrate the feature in a private dealer meeting at the annual trade show. You can easily send a snooper to this meeting to learn about the new feature. What would you do?

7. You have to choose between three advertising campaigns outlined by your agency. The first (a) is a soft-sell, honest, straight-information campaign. The second (b) uses sex-loaded emotional appeals and exaggerates the product's benefits. The third (c) involves a noisy, somewhat irritating commercial that is sure to gain audience attention. Pretests show that the campaigns are effective in the following order: c, b, and a. What would you do?

8. You are interviewing a capable female applicant for a job as salesperson. She is better qualified than the men who have been interviewed. Nevertheless, you know that in your industry some important customers prefer dealing with men, and you will lose some sales if you hire her. What would you do?

● **When the discovery of lead paint on several of its best-selling products forced Mattel to recall millions of toys worldwide, the company's forthright response helped it to maintain customer confidence. Mattel even involved its panel of 400 moms as "brand advisors" to help shape its response.**

Redux Pictures

to issue a massive recall. However, rather than hesitating or hiding the incident, the company's "brand advisors" guided Mattel to a proactive response. This positive response bolstered rather than diminished consumer confidence and even resulted in a sales increase in the months that followed. These brand advisors weren't the high-paid consultants you'd expect. Rather, they were members of Mattel's private online community, The Playground—400 mothers of young children enlisted by Mattel's consumer insights department to provide inputs on the the company's products and practices. Following the recall, The Playground community members helped Mattel develop a positive response plan. Even in times of crisis, brand success hinges on listening to customers and making them a part of the brand. "Brands that engage in a two-way conversation with their customers create stronger, more trusting relationships," says a Mattel executive.[30]

As with environmentalism, the issue of ethics presents special challenges for international marketers. Business standards and practices vary a great deal from one country to the next. For example, bribes and kickbacks are illegal for U.S. firms, and various treaties against bribery and corruption have been signed and ratified by more than 60 countries. Yet these are still standard business practices in many countries. The World Bank estimates that bribes totaling more than $1 trillion per year are paid out worldwide. One study showed that the most flagrant bribe-paying firms were from Indonesia, Mexico, China, and Russia. Other countries where corruption is common include Somalia, Myanmar, and Haiti. The least corrupt were companies from Belgium, Switzerland, and the Netherlands.[31] The question arises as to whether a company must lower its ethical standards to compete effectively in countries with lower standards. The answer is no. Companies should make a commitment to a common set of shared standards worldwide.

Many industrial and professional associations have suggested codes of ethics, and many companies are now adopting their own codes. For example, the American Marketing Association, an international association of marketing managers and scholars, developed a code of ethics that calls on marketers to adopt the following ethical norms:[32]

- *Do no harm.* This means consciously avoiding harmful actions or omissions by embodying high ethical standards and adhering to all applicable laws and regulations in the choices we make.
- *Foster trust in the marketing system.* This means striving for good faith and fair dealing so as to contribute toward the efficacy of the exchange process as well as avoiding deception in product design, pricing, communication, and delivery of distribution.
- *Embrace ethical values.* This means building relationships and enhancing consumer confidence in the integrity of marketing by affirming these core values: honesty, responsibility, fairness, respect, transparency, and citizenship.

Companies are also developing programs to teach managers about important ethical issues and help them find the proper responses. They hold ethics workshops and seminars and create ethics committees. Furthermore, most major U.S. companies have appointed high-level ethics officers to champion ethical issues and help resolve ethics problems and concerns facing employees.

PricewaterhouseCoopers (PwC) is a good example. In 2002, PwC established a global ethics office and comprehensive ethics program, headed by a high-level global ethics officer. The ethics program begins with a code of conduct called "Doing the Right Thing—the PwC Way." PwC employees learn about the code of conduct and about how to handle thorny ethics issues in comprehensive ethics training programs, which start when the employee joins the company and continue throughout the employee's career. The program also includes *ethics champions* around the world and channels such programs as ethics helplines to enable people to raise concerns. "It is obviously not enough to distribute a document," says PwC's former CEO, Samuel DiPiazza. "Ethics is in everything we say and do."[33]

Still, written codes and ethics programs do not ensure ethical behavior. Ethics and social responsibility require a total corporate commitment. They must be a component of the overall corporate culture. PwC's ethics policies are deeply embedded in everything the company does and are every bit as important as other activities such as product development or marketing research. According to DiPiazza, "We ask ourselves every day, 'Are we doing the right things?'"[34]

The Sustainable Company

At the foundation of marketing is the belief that companies that fulfill the needs and wants of customers will thrive. Companies that fail to meet customer needs or that intentionally or unintentionally harm customers, others in society, or future generations will decline.

Says one observer, "Sustainability is an emerging business megatrend, like electrification and mass production, that will profoundly affect companies' competitiveness and even their survival." Says another, "increasingly, companies and leaders will be assessed not only on immediate results but also on . . . the ultimate effects their actions have on societal wellbeing. This trend has been coming in small ways for years but now is surging. So pick up your recycled cup of fair-trade coffee, and get ready."[35]

Sustainable companies are those that create value for customers through socially, environmentally, and ethically responsible actions. Sustainable marketing goes beyond caring for the needs and wants of today's customers. It means having concern for tomorrow's customers in assuring the survival and success of the business, shareholders, employees, and the broader world in which they all live. It means pursuing the mission of a triple bottom line: "people, planet, profits."[36] Sustainable marketing provides the context in which companies can build profitable customer relationships by creating value *for* customers in order to capture value *from* customers in return—now and in the future.

Reviewing the Concepts

MyMarketingLab™

Go to **mymktlab.com** to complete the problems marked with this icon .

Reviewing Objectives and Key Terms

 Objectives Review

In this chapter, we addressed many of the important *sustainable marketing* concepts related to marketing's sweeping impact on individual consumers, other businesses, and society as a whole. Sustainable marketing requires socially, environmentally, and ethically responsible actions that bring value to not only present-day consumers and businesses but also future generations and society as a whole. Sustainable companies are those that act responsibly to create value for customers in order to capture value from customers in return—now and in the future.

Objective 1 **Define sustainable marketing and discuss its importance.**
(pp 582–584)

Sustainable marketing calls for meeting the present needs of consumers and businesses while preserving or enhancing the ability of future generations to meet their needs. Whereas the marketing concept recognizes that companies thrive by fulfilling the day-to-day needs of customers, sustainable marketing calls for socially and environmentally responsible actions that meet both the immediate and future needs of customers and the company. Truly sustainable marketing requires a smooth-functioning marketing system in which consumers, companies, public policy makers, and others work together to ensure responsible marketing actions.

Objective 2 **Identify the major social criticisms of marketing.** (pp 584–591)

Marketing's *impact on individual consumer welfare* has been criticized for its high prices, deceptive practices, high-pressure selling, shoddy or unsafe products, planned obsolescence, and poor service to disadvantaged consumers. Marketing's *impact on society* has been criticized for creating false wants and too much materialism, too few social goods, and cultural pollution. Critics have also denounced marketing's *impact on other businesses* for harming competitors and reducing competition through acquisitions, practices that create barriers to entry, and unfair competitive marketing practices. Some of these concerns are justified; some are not.

Objective 3 **Define consumerism and environmentalism and explain how they affect marketing strategies.** (pp 591–596)

Concerns about the marketing system have led to citizen action movements. *Consumerism* is an organized social movement intended to strengthen the rights and power of consumers relative to sellers. Alert marketers view it as an opportunity to serve consumers better by providing more consumer information, education, and protection. *Environmentalism* is an organized social movement seeking to minimize the harm done to the environment and quality of life by marketing practices. Most companies are now accepting responsibility for doing no environmental harm. They are adopting policies of *environmental sustainability*—developing strategies that both sustain the environment and produce profits for the company. Both consumerism and environmentalism are important components of sustainable marketing.

Objective 4 **Describe the principles of sustainable marketing.**
(pp 596–601)

Many companies originally resisted these social movements and laws, but most now recognize a need for positive consumer information, education, and protection. Under the sustainable marketing concept, a company's marketing should support the best long-run performance of the marketing system. It should be guided by five sustainable marketing principles: *consumer-oriented marketing*, *customer-value marketing*, *innovative marketing*, *sense-of-mission marketing*, and *societal marketing*.

Objective 5 **Explain the role of ethics in marketing.** (pp 601–603)

Increasingly, companies are responding to the need to provide company policies and guidelines to help their managers deal with questions of *marketing ethics*. Of course, even the best guidelines cannot resolve all the difficult ethical decisions that individuals and firms must make. But there are some principles from which marketers can choose. One principle states that the free market and the legal system should decide such issues. A second and more enlightened principle puts responsibility not on the system but in the hands of individual companies and managers. Each firm and marketing manager must work out a philosophy of socially responsible and ethical behavior. Under the sustainable marketing concept, managers must look beyond what is legal and allowable and develop standards based on personal integrity, corporate conscience, and long-term consumer welfare.

Key Terms

Objective 1
Sustainable marketing (p 582)

Objective 3
Consumerism (p 591)
Environmentalism (p 592)
Environmental sustainability (p 592)

Objective 4
Consumer-oriented marketing (p 597)
Customer-value marketing (p 597)
Innovative marketing (p 597)
Sense-of-mission marketing (p 597)
Societal marketing (p 598)

Deficient products (p 600)
Pleasing products (p 600)
Salutary products (p 600)
Desirable products (p 600)

Discussion and Critical Thinking

Discussion Questions

1. What is sustainable marketing? Explain how the sustainable marketing concept differs from the marketing concept and the societal marketing concept. (AACSB: Communication)

2. Critics claim that advertising and promotion result in higher prices for consumers. Discuss the bases for this claim and how marketers refute them. (AACSB: Communication)

3. What is consumerism? What rights do consumers have, and why do some critics feel buyers need more protection? (AACSB: Communication)

4. What is environmental sustainability? How should companies gauge their progress toward achieving it? (AACSB: Communication)

5. Describe the two philosophies regarding what principle should guide companies and marketing managers on issues of ethics and social responsibility. (AACSB: Communication)

Critical Thinking Exercises

1. Conduct an online search for "green awards" to learn about the various awards programs recognizing environmental consciousness and sustainable practices. Select one that recognized a business for a sustainable marketing practice and develop a brief presentation explaining why the company received the award. (AACSB: Communication; Use of IT; Reflective Thinking)

2. Many consumers want to recycle, but varying rules across localities make it difficult for consumers to know if something is

recyclable. Voluntary "How2Recycle" labels are starting to appear on products to help consumers. Visit www.how2recycle .info to learn about these voluntary labels and the types of products that will be carrying them. Will these labels make it easier for consumers to recycle? (AACSB: Communication; Use of IT; Reflective Thinking)

Applications and Cases

Marketing Technology **Compostable Packaging**

Corn-based packaging is hitting the shelves for everything from bottles to bags. But one such endeavor had unintended consequences. Frito-Lay came out with a 100 percent compostable bag for its Sun Chip line of chips. The package, made from 100 percent polylactic acid (PLA), a corn-based biopolymer that fully decomposes within 14 weeks, had one drawback—it was terribly noisy. A U.S. Air Force pilot posted a video on YouTube showing the sound reaching 95 decibels when the bag was touched, leading him to claim it was "louder than the cockpit of my jet." Others likened the sound to "revving motorcycles" or "glass breaking."

The package soon became the butt of jokes, even resulting in a Facebook group called "Sorry But I Can't Hear You Over This Sun Chips Bag." Frito-Lay relented and reintroduced a less-noisy bag.

1. Search the Internet for more examples of compostable packaging. Discuss three of them. (AACSB: Communication; Use of IT)

2. Is corn-based compostable packaging a sustainable solution to replace petroleum-based plastic packaging? Discuss the pros and cons of this alternative. (AACSB: Communication; Reflective Thinking)

Marketing Ethics Mobile Medical Apps

With the explosion of mobile devices and apps, it's not surprising that medical apps are taking off. There are apps to identify pills, track pregnancy, check for melanoma skin cancer, and even teach medical professionals how to read electrocardiograms. Some apps are replacing devices used by health-care professionals in hospitals and doctors' offices. There are more than 40,000 medical applications available, and the market is still in its infancy. The market's growth has caught the attention of the Food and Drug Administration (FDA), the agency responsible for regulating medical devices. So far, medical apps have been unregulated, but that is about to change. The FDA released guidelines requiring developers to apply for FDA approval, which could take years. According to the Government Accountability Office, it

takes the FDA six months to approve a device that is similar to an existing one and up to 20 months for new devices. According to another report, approval costs $24 million to $75 million. Not all apps would require FDA approval—only ones making medical claims. Although many developers think regulation is necessary to protect the public, most believe that the current process is too slow and a new regulatory framework is necessary.

⭐ **1.** Describe two examples of mobile apps for health-care providers. (AACSB: Communication; Use of IT)

2. Is regulatory approval of medical mobile apps necessary? Will the FDA's requirement for approval constrain innovation? Explain. (AACSB: Communication; Ethical Reasoning; Reflective Thinking)

Marketing by the Numbers The Cost of Sustainability

One element of sustainability is organic farming. But if you've priced organic foods, you know they are more expensive. Organic farming costs much more than conventional farming, and those higher costs are passed on to consumers. For example, a dozen conventionally farmed eggs costs consumers $1.50, whereas a dozen organic eggs costs $2.80. However, if prices get too high, consumers will not purchase the organic eggs. Suppose that the average fixed costs per year for conventionally farmed eggs are $1 million per year, and that they are twice that amount for organic eggs. Organic farmers' variable costs per dozen are twice

as much as well, costing $1.80 per dozen. Refer to Appendix 2, Marketing by the Numbers, to answer the following questions.

1. Most large egg farmers sell eggs directly to retailers. What is the farmer's price per dozen to the retailer for both conventional and organic eggs if the retailer's margin is 20 percent based on the retail price? (AACSB: Communication; Analytical Reasoning)

2. How many dozen eggs does a conventional farmer need to sell to break even? How many does an organic farmer need to sell to break even? (AACSB: Communication; Analytical Reasoning)

Video Case Life Is Good

Most companies these days are trying to figure out how they can be more socially responsible in the manufacturing and marketing of the goods and services they produce. But few companies produce goods and services with the primary purpose of making the world a better place. Life Is Good is one of those companies. Most people are familiar with the cheerful logo on Life Is Good products. But few are aware of what the company does with its profits behind the scenes.

This video focuses on Life Is Good Playmakers, a nonprofit organization dedicated to helping children overcome life-threatening challenges. From the time Life Is Good started selling t-shirts in the early 1990s, its founders supported Playmakers. The relationship

between the two organizations progressively became stronger, ultimately leading Life Is Good to make Playmakers an official branch of the company.

After viewing the video featuring Life Is Good, answer the following questions:

1. Give as many examples as you can of how Life Is Good defies the common social criticisms of marketing.

2. Discuss how Life Is Good practices sustainable marketing principles.

3. With all its efforts to do *good*, can Life Is Good continue to do *well*? Explain.

Company Case International Paper: Combining Industry and Social Responsibility

What image comes to mind when you hear "industrial corporation"? Pollution-belching smoke stacks? Strip-mined landscapes? Chemicals seeping into water supplies? Now think about "environmental steward." Although that label might not seem compatible, the truth is that changes in regulations, combined with pressure from environmental and consumer groups, have forced most industrial companies to be more socially responsible. But at least one company has had social responsibility as a core value

since it started business more than 110 years ago. That company is International Paper (IP). Today, IP is considered by many to be one of the most socially responsible companies in the world.

You may not know much about International Paper, but it makes products that you use every day—such as paper for printers, envelopes for mail, cardboard clamshells and paper bags for fast food, and the boxes that hold your cold cereal, to name just a few. And IP makes lots of those products. Last year, it sold over $26 billion worth of paper, packaging, and wood products, placing it 111th on the Fortune 500. With operations all over the world, IP employs more than 62,000 people. Those are pretty big numbers for a company that most people know little about.

But International Paper is more than just big. For many years, it has also ranked consistently among *Fortune* magazine's most admired companies. It grabbed the number one spot on that list in its industry for seven out of the last eight years. And social responsibility was a big part of that score. That's right—a paper and lumber company leading in initiatives to make the world a better place.

At the heart of International Paper's admirable actions, we have to look at the comprehensive, integrated plan that the company labels "sustainability." The company sums up the program with the slogan, "Sustaining a better world for generations: the IP way." That's not just a catchphrase. It lies at the heart of IP's corporate mission statement and has created a culture based on a set of supporting principles. According to company literature, "We have always taken a sustainable approach to business that balances environmental, social, and economic needs. This approach has served our company and society well." IP constantly maintains this balance by adhering to three key pillars that transform the concepts into action: managing natural resources, reducing the environmental footprint, and building strategic partnerships.

Managing Natural Resources

The philosophy at IP is that taking care of the environment and taking care of the business are interdependent concepts. By taking care of the environment, IP has a system in place to ensure that every phase of its corporate global supply chain—manufacturing, distribution, sales, and recycling—is carried out in a way that safely and responsibly cares for natural resources. For example, International Paper has been a leader in promoting the planting and growing of trees. It believes that if forest resources are properly managed, they provide an infinite supply of raw materials for the company's products while supporting clean water, diverse wildlife habitats, recreational opportunities, and aesthetic beauty. To this end, the company actively supports research, innovation, and third-party certification to improve the management of forest resources.

Another way that International Paper manages natural resources is through conservation. It has proven time and time again that conservation doesn't have to be a sunk cost. It can be an investment that provides cost savings for a company.

Pulp and paper mills are complex, energy intensive operations. Finding ways to reduce, reuse, and recycle energy at each of its facilities reduces the consumption of fossil fuels and reduces air emissions, including carbon dioxide.

Typically gas, coal or bark fuels are fired in boilers to produce steam to power operations throughout the mill. Capturing steam in one area and reusing it in another reduces the amount of fresh steam required and reduces the amount of fuel needed to power the plant.

[The IP] mill in Vicksburg, Mississippi, is recovering and reusing 38,000 pounds of steam per hour. A one-time investment of $2.8 million in capital improvements will save an estimated $2.4 million in fuel costs annually. At [an IP] mill in Savannah, Georgia, an investment of $900,000 in capital improvements reduced the demand for steam, and consequently the coal needed to produce it, by 25,000 pounds per hour. The annual savings are estimated at more than $600,000.

Reducing the Environmental Footprint

By reducing its environmental footprint, International Paper means that it is committed to transparently reporting its activities to the public for any of its activities that impact the environment, health, or safety. "At International Paper, we've been routinely sharing our environmental, economic, and social performance with the public

for over a decade," said David Struhs, vice president of Environment, Health, and Safety. "Over the years, these reports have offered a level of transparency unmatched in our industry." This reporting philosophy applies to any company activity that leaves a footprint, including air emissions, environmental performance, health and safety, solid waste, and environmental certifications.

With transparency comes accountability. Because of its reporting practices, International Paper is more motivated to reduce its environmental footprint. As just one example, over the past decade, the company cut its global greenhouse gas emissions by 40 percent, earning IP a Climate Leadership Award from the Environmental Protection Agency. But IP also made improvements in virtually every company footprint area. A recent account of company activities in Brazil illustrates this concept well.

Nature, once tamed, is again growing wild along Brazil's Mogi Guacu River, which means "large river of snakes" in the native language of Tupi. This year, seven constructed lagoons running along the banks of the Mogi Guacu designed to filter used water from the nearby International Paper plant were replaced by a more modern wastewater facility.

Although the lagoons are no longer needed for water treatment, International Paper recognized their potential environmental benefits. Five of the ponds were restored with native vegetation to establish a vast expanse of natural wetland habitat. Two of the ponds were preserved to sustain wildlife that had made their home in the area—snakes included.

To better manage the future impact of mill operations on the lush tropical landscape, the mill also installed technology at the river's edge to continuously measure and report water quality. The results are monitored remotely by facility managers as well as by government regulators. This unprecedented access to information on environmental performance has set a standard for other industries along this large river of snakes.

Building Strategic Partnerships

In order to most efficiently carry out its sustainability efforts, International Paper must enlist the help of numerous organizations. Building strategic partnerships is therefore critical. International Paper has a long tradition of partnering with a broad range of governmental, academic, environmental, and customer organizations. These partnerships are guided by the objectives of making progress in sustainability, providing solutions for customers, making a positive impact on the environment, and supporting social responsibility.

International Paper has partnered with some of the biggest sustainability organizations to make big differences. Partners include the National Park Foundation, the National Recycling Coalition, and the Conservation Fund. But the following story from a company press release illustrates how even a minor partnership oriented around a small product can make a "latte" difference in the world:

Coffee is one of the world's most popular drinks. Coffee houses—long a fixture in cultures and countries around the globe—sprang up across America during the last 20 years. Every year, as many as 15 billion "cups of joe" are served on the go in paper cups and that number is expected to grow to 23 billion by the end of the decade.

While coffee connoisseurs savored the flavors of new varieties of beans and brews, engineers and scientists at International Paper were thinking about how to improve the cup. Though cups are made of fiber grown and harvested from sustainable forests, conventional paper cups are lined with a petroleum-based plastic. The plastic lining is a small part of the cup but is made from non-renewable resources and inhibits the decomposition of the underlying paper. As a result, disposable cups once filled with coffee are filling up our landfills.

But what if disposable coffee cups could join coffee grounds in the compost heap? To achieve that vision, International Paper, with partners DaniMer Scientific and NatureWorks LLC, developed a new type of cup lining made from plants instead of petro-chemicals. The revolutionary new cup, dubbed the ecotainer, is coated with a resin made from modified biopolymer. When discarded in commercial and municipal operations, cups with the new lining become compost, which can then be used for gardening, landscaping, and farming.

Since the launch of the ecotainer with Green Mountain Coffee Roasters in 2006, large and small companies alike have adopted this new cup. More than half a billion cups have eliminated over a million pounds of petrochemical plastic from the marketplace—enough petroleum to heat more than 32,000 homes for one year.

Coffee cups are just the beginning. International Paper is exploring opportunities to expand the technology to other products used in foodservice disposable packaging. So next time you order an espresso with steamed milk, ask for one in an ecotainer and you too can make a "latte" difference in the world.

It is very clear to those who know IP that the company doesn't just pay lip service to concepts of sustainability and social responsibility. Such principles lie at the heart of how the company operates. "At International Paper, we're proud of our legacy of sustainability and environmental stewardship," says John Faraci, IP's chairman and CEO. "Demonstrating our ongoing commitment to these efforts through continuous improvements is important not just for our employees but for our customers, shareowners, and neighbors in the communities where we operate."

International Paper hasn't been one of the high-growth juggernauts of the corporate world. Then again, it operates in a very mature industry. But IP makes innovative products that meet the needs of consumers. It employs tens of thousands of people throughout the world, contributing substantially to the communities in which it does business. It has grown in size to become one of the largest companies in the United States. It has been consistently profitable. And it does all these things while sustaining the world for future generations. Indeed, International Paper proves that good business and good corporate citizenship can go hand in hand.

Questions for Discussion

1. Give as many examples as you can for how International Paper defies the common social criticisms of marketing.

2. Why is International Paper successful in applying concepts of sustainability?

3. Analyze International Paper according to the Environmental Sustainability Portfolio in Figure 20.2.

4. Does International Paper practice enlightened marketing? Support your answer with as many examples as possible.

5. Would International Paper be more financially successful if it were not so focused on social responsibility? Explain.

Sources: Extracts and other case information are from International Paper's corporate Web site, www.internationalpaper.com/US/EN/Company/Sustainability/index.html, accessed August 2012, and International Paper's 2011 Sustainability Report; additional information from money.cnn.com/magazines/fortune/mostadmired/, accessed August 2012.

MyMarketingLab

Go to **mymktlab.com** for Auto-graded writing questions as well as the following Assisted-graded writing questions:

20-1. Discuss the types of harmful impact that marketing practices can have on competition and the associated problems. (AACSB: Communication)

20-2. In a small group, discuss each of the morally difficult situations in marketing presented in Table 20.1. Which ethics philosophy is guiding your decision in each situation? (AACSB: Communication; Ethical Reasoning)

20-3. Mymktlab Only – comprehensive writing assignment for this chapter.

References

1. Quotes and other information from or adapted from Andrew Saunders, "Paul Polman of Unilever," *Management Today,* March 2011, pp. 42–47; Adi Ignatius, "Captain Planet," *Harvard Business Review,* June 2012, pp. 2–8; and www.unilever.com/images/mc_innovation-fact-sheet_tcm13-269251.pdf, www.unilever.com/sustainable-living/customers-suppliers/, www.unilever.com/images/UnileverSustainableLivingPlan_tcm13-284876.pdf, and other reports and documents found at www.unilever.com, accessed October 2012.

2. The figure and the discussion in this section are adapted from Philip Kotler, Gary Armstrong, Veronica Wong, and John Saunders, *Principles of Marketing: European Edition,* 5th ed. (London: Pearson Publishing, 2009), Chapter 2.

3. "McDonald's Launches Marketing for 'Favorites under 400 Calories' Platform," *Advertising Age,* July 24, 2012, http://adage.com/print/236291/.

4. McDonald's financial information and other facts from www.aboutmcdonalds.com/mcd/investors.html and www.aboutmcdonalds.com/mcd, accessed October 2012.

5. Brent Kendall, "Sketchers Settles with FTC over Deceptive-Advertising of Toning Shoes," *Wall Street Journal,* May 17, 2012, p. B3.

6. Based on information from Patrick Corcoran, "Vitaminwater Awash in Accusations of Deceptive Advertising," *FairWarning,* February 14, 2011, www.fairwarning.org/2011/02/vitaminwater-awash-in-accusations-of-deceptive-advertising/; "Consumer Group Urges FTC to Halt Vitaminwater's Outlandish Claims," *International Business Times,* February 4, 2011, http://m.ibtimes.com/coca-cola-vitaminwater-advertising-national-washington-consumers-league-ftc-flu-shots-108891.html; and "NCL Disappointed in FTC Conclusion of Investigation of Misleading Marketing Claims for 'vitaminwater,'" February 3, 2012, www.nclnet.org/newsroom/press-releases/621-ncl-disappointed-in-ftc-conclusion-of-investigation-of-misleading-marketing-claims-for-vitaminwater-.

7. See Ian Cooper, "Obesity in America: What about the 66%?" Examiner.com, June 1, 2012; and "Overweight and Obesity," Centers for Disease Control and Prevention, www.cdc.gov/obesity/data/index.html, accessed October 2012.

8. Elena Ferretti, "Soft Drinks Are the Whipping Boy of Anti-Obesity Campaigns," Fox News, June 1, 2012, www.foxnews.com/leisure/2012/06/01/soda-ban/.

9. For more on perceived obsolescence, see Annie Leonard, *The Story of Stuff* (New York: Free Press, 2010), pp. 162–163; and www.storyofstuff.com, accessed November 2012.

10. Rob Walker, "Replacement Therapy," *Atlantic Monthly*, September 2011, p. 38.

11. See Karen Auge, "Planting Seed in Food Deserts: Neighborhood Gardens, Produce in Corner Stores," *Denver Post*, April 18, 2010, p. 1; Spence Cooper, "National Food Chains Join First Lady to Reach 'Food Deserts,'" *Friends Eat*, July 25, 2011, http://blog.friendseat.com/michelle-obama-program-reaches-food-deserts; and "Supermarket Campaign: Improving Access to Supermarkets in Underserved Communities," The Food Trust, www.thefoodtrust.org/php/programs/super.market.campaign.php, accessed October 2012.

12. Richard J. Varey, "Marketing Means and Ends for a Sustainable Society: A Welfare Agenda for Transformative Change," *Journal of Macromarketing*, June 2010, pp. 112–126.

13. See "The Story of Stuff," www.storyofstuff.com, accessed November 2012.

14. See "The American Dream Has Been Revised Not Reversed," *Business Wire*, March 9, 2009; Connor Dougherty and Elizabeth Holmes, "Consumer Spending Perks Up Economy," *Wall Street Journal*, March 13, 2010, p. A1; John Gerzema, "How U.S. Consumers Are Steering the Spend Shift," *Advertising Age*, October 11, 2010, p. 26; and Gregg Fairbrothers and Catalina Gorla, "The Decline and Rise of Thrift," *Forbes*, April 23, 2012, www.forbes.com.

15. See Texas Transportation Institute, "Traffic Problems Ties to the Economy," September 27, 2011, http://mobility.tamu.edu/ums/media-information/press-release/.

16. See Michael Cabanatuan, "Tolls Thin Traffic in Bay Bridge Carpool Lanes," *San Francisco Chronicle*, November 7, 2011, www.sfgate.com/news/article/Tolls-thin-traffic-in-Bay-Bridge-carpool-lanes-2323670.php#photo-1829296.

17. See Martin Sipkoff, "Four-Dollar Pricing Considered Boom or Bust," *Drug Topics*, August 2008, p. 4S; and Sarah Bruyn Jones, "Economic Survival Guide: Drug Discounts Common Now," *McClatchy-Tribune Business News*, February 23, 2009; and www.walmart.com/cp/PI-4-Prescriptions/1078664, accessed October 2012.

18. Philip Kotler, "Reinventing Marketing to Manage the Environmental Imperative," *Journal of Marketing*, July 2011, pp. 132–135.

19. See "SC Johnson Integrity," www.scjohnson.com/en/commitment/overview.aspx, accessed November 2012.

20. Based on information in Drew Winter, "Honda Workers Eliminate Landfill Waste," WardsAuto, August 1, 2011, http://wardsauto.com/news-amp-analysis/honda-workers-eliminate-landfill-waste; and Kate Bachman, "Manufacturers Gone Zero Landfill," Green Manufacturer, January 31, 2012, www.greenmanufacturer.net/article/facilities/manufacturers-gone-zero-landfill.

21. See Alan S. Brown, "The Many Shades of Green," *Mechanical Engineering*, January 2009, http://memagazine.asme.org/Articles/2009/January/Many_Shades_Green.cfm; www-03.ibm.com/financing/us/recovery/large/disposal.html; www.puma-annual-report.com/en/PUMAAnnualReport2011_ENG.pdf; and www.ibm.com/ibm/environment/products/recycling.shtml, accessed October 2012.

22. Based on information from Simon Houpt, "Beyond the Bottle: Coke Trumpets Its Green Initiatives," *The Globe and Mail (Toronto)*, January 13, 2011; Marc Gunther, "Coca-Cola's Green Crusader," *Fortune*, April 28, 2008, p. 150; "Coca-Cola to Install 1,800 CO_2 Coolers in North America," April 30, 2009, www.r744.com/articles/2009-04-30-coca-cola-to-install-1800-co2-coolers-in-north-america.php; Christina Caldwell, "Coca-Cola Pilots Plant-Based Soda Bottle," Earth911.com, March 9, 2012; "Plant Bottle? Really? Really!" June 5, 2012, http://ccbcu.com/1257-2/; and "The Business of Recycling," www.thecoca-colacompany.com/citizenship/environment_case_studies.html, accessed November 2012.

23. Based on information from "Walmart," *Fast Company*, March 2010, p. 66; "Walmart Eliminates More Than 80 Percent of Its Waste in California That Would Otherwise Go to Landfills," March 17, 2011, http://walmartstores.com/pressroom/news/10553.aspx; Jack Neff, "Why Walmart Has More Green Clout Than Anyone," *Advertising Age*, October 15, 2007, p. 1; Denise Lee Yohn, "A Big, Green, Reluctant Hug for Retailing's 800-lb. Gorilla," *Brandweek*, May 5, 2008, p. 61; Edward Humes, *Force of Nature: The Unlikely Story of Walmart's Green Revolution* (New York: HarperCollins, 2011); and "Sustainability," http://walmartstores.com/sustainability/, accessed November 2012.

24. Based on information found in Chuck Salter, "Fast 50: The World's Most Innovative Companies," *Fast Company*, March 2008, pp. 73+. Also see Yukari Iwatani Kane and Daisuke Wakabayashi, "Nintendo Looks Outside the Box," *Wall Street Journal*, May 27, 2009, p. B5.

25. Information from Mark Borden and Laurie Burkitt, "Samsung's Big Spend," *Forbes*, June 7, 2010, p. 60; Tarun Khanna, Jaeyong Song, and Kyungmook Lee, "The Paradox of Samsung's Rise," *Harvard Business Review*, July–August 2011, pp. 142–147; and Miyoung Kim, "Samsung Group Plans Record $41 Billion Investment in 2012," Reuters, January 17, 2012, www.reuters.com/article/2012/01/17/us-samsung-investment-idUSTRE80G00W20120117.

26. Information from Eleftheria Parpis, "Must Love Dogs," *Adweek*, February 18, 2008, accessed at www.adweek.com; and www.pedigree.com and www.mars.com/global/global-brands/pedigree.aspx, accessed November 2012. PEDIGREE® is a registered trademark of Mars, Incorporated.

27. Based on information found at http://vision.puma.com/us/en/ and http://about.puma.com/sustainability/, accessed November 2012/.

28. Information from www.nau.com, accessed November 2012.

29. Nanette Byrnes, "Pepsi Brings in the Health Police," *Bloomberg Businessweek*, January 25, 2010, pp. 50–51; and Mike Esterl, "You Put What in This Chip?" *Wall Street Journal*, March 24, 2011, p. D1.

30. Based on information from material found in Jeff Heilman, "Rules of Engagement," *The Magazine of Branded Engagement*, Winter 2009, pp. 7–8; "Top Ten Social Media Comebacks," *Marketwire*, September 11, 2011, www.slideshare.net/Marketwire/top-10-social-media-comebacks; and "Mattel's the Playground Community Created by Communispace Helps Them Weather Recall," accessed at www.communispace.com/uploadedFiles/Clients_Section/Forrester_Groundswell/Groundswell_Mattel.pdf, September 2012.

31. See Transparency International, "Bribe Payers Index 2011," http://bpi.transparency.org/results/; and Transparency International, "Global Corruption Barometer 2010/2011," http://archive.transparency.org/policy_research/surveys_indices/gcb/2010_11. Also see Michael Montgomery, "The Cost of Corruption," American RadioWorks, http://americanradioworks.publicradio.org/features/corruption/, accessed August 2012.

32. See www.marketingpower.com/AboutAMA/Pages/Statement%20of%20Ethics.aspx, accessed November 2012.

33. See Samuel A. DiPiazza, Jr., "Ethics in Action," *Executive Excellence*, January 2002, pp. 15–16; "Interview: Why Have a Code?" www.pwc.com/gx/en/ethics-business-conduct/why-have-a-code-interview.jhtml, accessed August 2011; "Doing the Right Thing—the PwC Way," http://download.pwc.com/ie/pubs/2011_code_of_conduct.pdf, accessed November 2012; and "Ethics and Business Conduct," www.pwc.com/ethics, accessed November 2012.

34. DiPiazza, "Ethics in Action," p. 15.

35. David A. Lubin and Daniel C. Esty, "The Sustainability Imperative," *Harvard Business Review*, May 2010, pp. 41–50; and Roasbeth Moss Kanter, "It's Time to Take Full Responsibility," *Harvard Business Review*, October 2010, p. 42.

36. "Why Companies Can No Longer Afford to Ignore Their Social Responsibilities," *Time*, May 28, 2012, http://business.time.com/2012/05/28/why-companies-can-no-longer-afford-to-ignore-their-social-responsibilities/.

Marketing Plan

The Marketing Plan: An Introduction

As a marketer, you will need a good marketing plan to provide direction and focus for your brand, product, or company. With a detailed plan, any business will be better prepared to launch a new product or build sales for existing products. Nonprofit organizations also use marketing plans to guide their fund-raising and outreach efforts. Even government agencies put together marketing plans for initiatives such as building public awareness of proper nutrition and stimulating area tourism.

The Purpose and Content of a Marketing Plan

Unlike a business plan, which offers a broad overview of the entire organization's mission, objectives, strategy, and resource allocation, a marketing plan has a more limited scope. It serves to document how the organization's strategic objectives will be achieved through specific marketing strategies and tactics, with the customer as the starting point. It is also linked to the plans of other departments within the organization. Suppose, for example, a marketing plan calls for selling 200,000 units annually. The production department must gear up to make that many units, the finance department must arrange funding to cover the expenses, the human resources department must be ready to hire and train staff, and so on. Without the appropriate level of organizational support and resources, no marketing plan can succeed.

Although the exact length and layout will vary from company to company, a marketing plan usually contains the sections described in Chapter 2. Smaller businesses may create shorter or less formal marketing plans, whereas corporations frequently require highly structured marketing plans. To guide implementation effectively, every part of the plan must be described in considerable detail. Sometimes a company will post its marketing plans on an intranet site, which allows managers and employees in different locations to consult specific sections and collaborate on additions or changes.

The Role of Research

Marketing plans are not created in a vacuum. To develop successful strategies and action programs, marketers need up-to-date information about the environment, the competition, and the market segments to be served. Often, analysis of internal data is the starting point for assessing the current marketing situation, supplemented by marketing intelligence and research investigating the overall market, the competition, key issues, and threats and opportunities. As the plan is put into effect, marketers use a variety of research techniques to measure progress toward objectives and identify areas for improvement if results fall short of projections.

Finally, marketing research helps marketers learn more about their customers' requirements, expectations, perceptions, and satisfaction levels. This deeper understanding provides a foundation for building competitive advantage through well-informed segmenting, targeting, differentiating, and positioning decisions. Thus, the marketing plan should outline what marketing research will be conducted and how the findings will be applied.

The Role of Relationships

The marketing plan shows how the company will establish and maintain profitable customer relationships. In the process, however, it also shapes a number of internal and external relationships. First, it affects how marketing personnel work with each other and with other departments to deliver value and satisfy customers. Second, it affects how the company works with suppliers, distributors, and strategic alliance partners to achieve the objectives listed in the plan. Third, it influences the company's dealings with other stakeholders, including government regulators, the media, and the community at large. All of these relationships are important to the organization's success, so they should be considered when a marketing plan is being developed.

From Marketing Plan to Marketing Action

Companies generally create yearly marketing plans, although some plans cover a longer period. Marketers start planning well in advance of the implementation date to allow time for marketing research, thorough analysis, management review, and coordination between departments. Then, after each action program begins, marketers monitor ongoing results, compare them with projections, analyze any differences, and take corrective steps as needed. Some marketers also prepare contingency plans for implementation if certain conditions emerge. Because of inevitable and sometimes unpredictable environmental changes, marketers must be ready to update and adapt marketing plans at any time.

For effective implementation and control, the marketing plan should define how progress toward objectives will be measured. Managers typically use budgets, schedules, and performance standards for monitoring and evaluating results. With budgets, they can compare planned expenditures with actual expenditures for a given week, month, or other period. Schedules allow management to see when tasks were supposed to be completed—and when they were actually completed. Performance standards track the outcomes of marketing programs to see whether the company is moving toward its objectives. Some examples of performance standards are market share, sales volume, product profitability, and customer satisfaction.

Sample Marketing Plan: Chill Beverage Company

Executive Summary

The Chill Beverage Company is preparing to launch a new line of vitamin-enhanced water called NutriWater. Although the bottled water market is maturing, the vitamin-enhanced water category is still growing. NutriWater will be positioned by the slogan "Expect more"—indicating that the brand offers more in the way of desirable product features and benefits at a competitive price. Chill Beverage is taking advantage of its existing experience and brand equity among its loyal current customer base of Millennials who consume its Chill Soda soft drink. NutriWater will target similar Millennials who are maturing and looking for an alternative to soft drinks and high-calorie sugared beverages.

The primary marketing objective is to achieve first-year U.S. sales of $30 million, roughly 2 percent of the enhanced water market. Based on this market share goal, the company expects to sell more than 17 million units the first year and break even in the final period of the year.

Current Marketing Situation

The Chill Beverage Company was founded in 2001 by an entrepreneur who had successfully built a company that primarily distributed niche and emerging products in the beverage industry. Its Chill Soda soft drink brand hit the market with six unique flavors in glass bottles. A few years later, the Chill Soda brand introduced an energy drink as well as a line of natural juice drinks. The company now markets dozens of Chill Soda flavors, many unique to the brand. Chill Beverage has grown its business every year since it was founded. In the most recent year, it achieved $185 million in revenue and net profits of $14.5 million. As part of its future growth strategy, Chill Beverage is currently preparing to enter a new beverage category with a line of vitamin-enhanced waters.

As a beverage category, bottled water experienced tremendous growth during the 1990s and 2000s. Currently, the average person in the United States consumes more than 28 gallons of bottled water every year, a number that has increased 20-fold in just 30 years. Bottled water consumption is second only to soft drink consumption, ahead of milk, beer, and coffee. Although bottled water growth has tapered off somewhat in recent years, it is still moderately strong at approximately 3 percent growth annually. Most other beverage categories have experienced declines. In the most recent year, 8.75 billion gallons of bottled water were sold in the United States with a value of more than $7.6 billion.

Competition is more intense now than ever as demand slows, industry consolidation continues, and new types of bottled water emerge. The U.S. market is dominated by three global corporations. With a portfolio of 12 brands (including Poland Spring, Nestlé Pure Life, and Arrowhead), Nestlé leads the market for "plain" bottled water. However, when all subcategories of bottled water are included (enhanced water, flavored water, and so on), Coca-Cola leads the U.S. market with a 22.9 percent share. Nestlé markets only plain waters but is number two at 21.5 percent of the total bottled water market. PepsiCo is third with 16.2 percent of the market. To demonstrate the strength of the vitamin-enhanced water segment, Coca-Cola's Vitaminwater has higher annual sales than any other bottled water brand.

To break into this market, dominated by huge global corporations and littered with dozens of other small players, Chill Beverage must carefully target specific segments with features and benefits valued by those segments.

Market Description

The bottled water market consists of many different types of water. Varieties of plain water include spring, purified, mineral, and distilled. Although these different types of water are sold as consumer products, they also serve as the core ingredient for other types of bottled waters, including enhanced water, flavored water, sparkling water, or any combination of those categories.

Although some consumers may not perceive much of a difference between brands, others are drawn to specific product features and benefits provided by different brands. For example, some consumers may perceive spring water as healthier than other types of water. Some may look for water that is optimized for hydration. Others seek additional nutritional benefits claimed by bottlers that enhance their brands with vitamins, minerals, herbs, and other additives. Still other consumers make selections based on flavor. The industry as a whole has positioned bottled water of all kinds as a low-calorie, healthy alternative to soft drinks, sports drinks, energy drinks, and other types of beverages.

Bottled water brands also distinguish themselves by size and type of container, multipacks, and refrigeration at point of sale. Chill Beverage's market for NutriWater consists of consumers of single-serving-sized bottled beverages who are looking for a healthy yet flavorful alternative. "Healthy" in this context means both low-calorie and enhanced nutritional content. This market includes traditional soft drink consumers who want to improve their health as well as non-soft-drink consumers who want an option other than plain bottled water. Specific segments that Chill Beverage will target during the first year include athletes, the health conscious, the socially responsible, and Millennials who favor independent corporations. The Chill Soda brand has established a strong base of loyal customers, primarily among Millennials. This generational segment is becoming a prime target as it matures and seeks alternatives to full-calorie soft drinks. ● **Table A1.1** shows how NutriWater addresses the needs of targeted consumer segments.

Product Review

Chill Beverage's new line of vitamin-enhanced water—called NutriWater—offers the following features:

- Six new-age flavors: Peach Mango, Berry Pomegranate, Kiwi Dragonfruit, Mandarin Orange, Blueberry Grape, and Key Lime.
- Single-serving-size, 20-ounce, PET recyclable bottles.
- Formulated for wellness, replenishment, and optimum energy.
- Full Recommended Daily Allowance (RDA) of essential vitamins and minerals (including electrolytes).
- Higher vitamin concentration—vitamin levels are 2 to 10 times higher than those of market-leading products, with more vitamins and minerals than any other brand.
- Additional vitamins—vitamins include A, E, and B_2, as well as folic acid—none of which are contained in the market-leading products.
- All natural—no artificial flavors, colors, or preservatives.
- Sweetened with pure cane sugar and Stevia, a natural zero-calorie sweetener.
- Twenty-five cents from each purchase will be donated to Vitamin Angels, a nonprofit organization with a mission to prevent vitamin deficiency in at-risk children.

Competitive Review

As sales of bottled waters entered a strong growth phase in the 1990s, the category began to expand. In addition to the various types of plain water, new categories emerged. These

● **Table A1.1** | **Segment Needs and Corresponding Features/Benefits of NutriWater**

Targeted Segment	Customer Need	Corresponding Features/Benefits
Athletes	• Hydration and replenishment of essential minerals • Energy to maximize performance	• Electrolytes and carbohydrates • B vitamins, carbohydrates
Health conscious	• Maintain optimum weight • Optimize nutrition levels • Avoid harmful chemicals and additives • Desire to consume a tastier beverage than water	• Half the calories of fully sugared beverages • Higher levels of vitamins A, B, C, E, zinc, chromium, and folic acid than other products; vitamins unavailable in other products • All-natural ingredients • Six new-age flavors
Socially conscious	• Support causes that help solve world's social problems	• 25-cent donation from each purchase to Vitamin Angels
Millennials	• Aversion to mass-media advertising/technologically savvy • Counterculture attitude • Diet enhancement due to fast-paced lifestyle	• Less-invasive online and social networking promotional tactics • Small, privately held company • Full Recommended Daily Allowance (RDA) levels of essential vitamins and minerals

included flavored waters—such as Aquafina's Flavorsplash—as well as enhanced waters. Enhanced waters emerged to bridge the gap between soft drinks and waters, appealing to people who knew they should drink more water and less soft drinks but still wanted flavor. Development of brands for this product variation has occurred primarily in start-up and boutique beverage companies. In the 2000s, major beverage corporations acquired the most successful smaller brands, providing the bigger firms with a solid market position in this category and diversification in bottled waters in general. Currently, enhanced water sales account for approximately 18 percent of the total bottled water market.

The fragmentation of this category, combined with domination by the market leaders, has created a severely competitive environment. Although there is indirect competition posed by all types of bottled waters and even other types of beverages (soft drinks, energy drinks, juices, teas), this competitive analysis focuses on direct competition from enhanced water brands. For the purposes of this analysis, enhanced water is bottled water with additives that are intended to provide health and wellness benefits. The most common additives include vitamins, minerals (including electrolytes), and herbs. Most commonly, enhanced waters are sweetened, flavored, and colored. This definition distinguishes enhanced water from sports drinks that have the primary purpose of maximizing hydration by replenishing electrolytes.

Enhanced water brands are typically sweetened with a combination of some kind of sugar and a zero-calorie sweetener, resulting in about half the sugar content, carbohydrates, and calories of regular soft drinks and other sweetened beverages. The types of sweeteners used create a point of differentiation. Many brands, including the market leaders, sell both regular and zero-calorie varieties.

Pricing for this product is consistent across brands and varies by type of retail outlet, with convenience stores typically charging more than grocery stores. The price for a 20-ounce bottle ranges from $1.00 to $1.89, with some niche brands costing slightly more. Key competitors to Chill Beverage's NutriWater line include the following:

• *Vitaminwater:* Created in 2000 as a new product for Energy Brands' Glacéau, which was also the developer of Smartwater (distilled water with electrolytes). Coca-Cola purchased Energy Brands for $4.1 billion in 2007. Vitaminwater is sold in regular and zero-calorie versions. With 28 varieties, Vitaminwater offers more options than any brand on the market. Whereas Vitaminwater varieties are distinguished by flavor, they are named according to functional benefits, such as Stur-D (healthy bones), Defense (strengthens immune system), Focus (mental clarity), and Restore (post-workout recovery). The brand's current slogan is "Hydration for every occasion—morning, noon, and night." Vitaminwater is vapor distilled, de-ionized, and/or filtered and is sweetened with crystalline fructose (corn syrup) and erythritol all-natural sweetener. Available in 20-ounce PET bottles and multipacks, Vitaminwater exceeds $830 million in annual sales and commands 61 percent of the enhanced water market. More notably, it outsells all other bottled water brands, enhanced or otherwise, including Coca-Cola's own Dasani.

- *SoBe Lifewater:* PepsiCo bought SoBe in 2000. SoBe introduced Lifewater in 2008 with a hit Super Bowl ad as an answer to Coca-Cola's Vitaminwater. The Lifewater line includes 17 regular and zero-calorie varieties. Each bottle of Lifewater is designated by flavor and one of six different functional categories: Electrolytes, Lean Machine, B-Energy, C-Boost, Antioxidants, and Pure. Each variety is infused with a formulation of vitamins, minerals, and herbs designed to provide the claimed benefit. The most recent line—Pure—contains only water, a hint of flavor, and electrolytes. Sweetened with a combination of sugar and erythritol, Lifewater makes the claim to be "all natural." It contains no artificial flavors or colors. However, some analysts debate the "natural" designation for erythritol. Lifewater is sold in 20-ounce PET bottles and multipacks as well as one-liter PET bottles. With more than $269 million in annual revenues, Lifewater is the number two enhanced water brand, capturing 20 percent of the market.

- *Propel Zero:* Gatorade created Propel in 2000, just one year prior to PepsiCo's purchase of this leading sports drink marketer. Originally marketed and labeled as "fitness water," it is now available only as Propel Zero. Although the fitness water designation has been dropped, Propel Zero still leans toward that positioning with the label stating "REPLENISH + ENERGIZE + PROTECT." Propel Zero comes in seven flavors, each containing the same blend of B vitamins, vitamin C, vitamin E, antioxidants, and electrolytes. It is sweetened with sucralose. Propel Zero is available in a wider variety of sizes, with 16.9-, 20-, and 24-ounce PET bottles and multipacks. Propel Zero is also marketed in powder form to be added to bottled water. With $165 million in revenues, Propel Zero is the number three enhanced water brand with a 12 percent share of the enhanced water market.

- *RESCUE Water:* The Arizona Beverage Company is best known as the number one producer of ready-to-drink bottled teas. However, it also bottles a variety of other beverages, including smoothies, sports drinks, energy drinks, and juice blends. Its newest brand is RESCUE Water, introduced to the U.S. market in 2010. It sets itself apart from other enhanced waters with green tea extract added to a blend of vitamins and minerals. This provides a significant point of differentiation for those desiring green tea, but rules the brand out for the majority of customers who do not want it. It comes in five flavors, each with its own functional benefit. RESCUE Water touts other points of distinction as well, including branded Twinlab vitamins, all-natural ingredients, and a high-tech plastic bottle that resembles glass and maximizes freshness. Its Blueberry Coconut Hydrate variety contains real coconut water, an emerging alternative beverage category. Although RESCUE Water sales and market share figures are not yet known because of the product's newness, the Arizona Beverage Company is a multi-billion-dollar corporation with a long history of successful new-product introductions.

- *Niche brands:* The market for enhanced water includes at least four companies that market their wares on a small scale through independent retailers: Assure, Ex Aqua Vitamins, Ayala Herbal Water, and Skinny Water. Some brands feature exotic additives and/or artistic glass bottles.

Despite the strong competition, NutriWater believes it can create a relevant brand image and gain recognition among the targeted segments. The brand offers strong points of differentiation with higher and unique vitamin content, all-natural ingredients, and support for a relevant social cause. With other strategic assets, Chill Beverage is confident that it can establish a competitive advantage that will allow NutriWater to grow in the market. ● **Table A1.2** shows a sample of competing products.

Channels and Logistics Review

The purchase of Vitaminwater by Coca-Cola left a huge hole in the independent distributor system. NutriWater will be distributed through an independent distributor to a network of

● **Table A1.2** | **Sample of Competitive Products**

Competitor	Brand	Features
Coca-Cola	Vitaminwater	Regular and zero-calorie versions; 28 varieties; each flavor provides a different function based on blend of vitamins and minerals; vapor distilled, de-ionized, and/or filtered; sweetened with crystalline fructose and erythritol; 20-ounce single-serve or multipack.
PepsiCo	SoBe Lifewater	Regular and zero-calorie versions; 17 varieties; six different functional categories; vitamins, minerals, and herbs; pure—mildly flavored, unsweetened water; sweetened with sugar and erythritol; "all natural"; 20-ounce single-serve and multipacks as well as one-liter bottles.
PepsiCo	Propel Zero	Zero-calorie only; seven flavors; fitness positioning based on "REPLENISH + ENERGIZE + PROTECT"; B vitamins, vitamin C, vitamin E, antioxidants, and electrolytes; sweetened with sucralose; 16.9-ounce, 20-ounce, and 24-ounce PET bottles and multipacks; powdered packets.
Arizona Beverage	RESCUE Water	Full-calorie only; five flavors, each with its own blend of vitamins and minerals; green tea extract (caffeine included); only brand with coconut water; Twinlab-branded vitamins; high-tech plastic bottle.

retailers in the United States. This strategy will avoid some of the head-on competition for shelf space with the Coca-Cola and PepsiCo brands and will also directly target likely Nutri-Water customers. As with the rollout of the core Chill Soda brand, this strategy will focus on placing coolers in retail locations that will exclusively hold NutriWater. These retailers include:

- *Grocery chains:* Regional grocery chains such as HyVee in the Midwest, Wegman's in the East, and WinCo in the West.
- *Health and natural food stores:* Chains such as Whole Foods, as well as local health food co-ops.
- *Fitness centers:* National fitness center chains such as 24 Hour Fitness, Gold's Gym, and other regional chains.

As the brand gains acceptance, channels will expand into larger grocery chains, convenience stores, and unique locations relevant to the target customer segment.

Strengths, Weaknesses, Opportunities, and Threat Analysis

NutriWater has several powerful strengths on which to build, but its major weakness is lack of brand awareness and image. Major opportunities include a growing market and consumer trends targeted by NutriWater's product traits. Threats include barriers to entry posed by limited retail space, as well as image issues for the bottled water industry. ● **Table A1.3** summarizes NutriWater's main strengths, weaknesses, opportunities, and threats.

Strengths

NutriWater can rely on the following important strengths:

1. *Superior quality:* NutriWater boasts the highest levels of added vitamins of any enhanced water, including full RDA levels of many vitamins. It is all natural, with no artificial flavors, colors, or preservatives. It is sweetened with both pure cane sugar and the natural zero-calorie sweetener, Stevia.
2. *Expertise in alternative beverage marketing:* The Chill Soda brand went from nothing to a successful and rapidly growing soft drink brand with fiercely loyal customers in a matter of only one decade. This success was achieved by starting small and focusing on gaps in the marketplace.

● **Table A1.3** | **NutriWater's Strengths, Weaknesses, Opportunities, and Threats**

Strengths	Weaknesses
• Superior quality • Expertise in alternative beverage marketing • Social responsibility • Anti-establishment image	• Lack of brand awareness • Limited budget

Opportunities	Threats
• Growing market • Gap in the distribution network • Health trends • Anti-establishment image	• Limited shelf space • Image of enhanced waters • Environmental issues

3. *Social responsibility:* Every customer will have the added benefit of helping malnourished children throughout the world. Although the price of NutriWater is in line with the prices of other competitors, low promotional costs allow for the substantial charitable donation of 25 cents per bottle while maintaining profitability.
4. *Anti-establishment image:* The big brands have decent products and strong distribution relationships. But they also carry the image of the large, corporate establishments. Chill Beverage has achieved success with an underdog image while remaining privately held. Vitaminwater and SoBe were built on this same image, but both are now owned by major multinational corporations.

Weaknesses

1. *Lack of brand awareness:* As an entirely new brand, NutriWater will enter the market with limited or no brand awareness. The affiliation with Chill Soda will be kept at a minimum in order to prevent associations between NutriWater and soft drinks. This issue will be addressed through promotion and distribution strategies.
2. *Limited budget:* As a smaller company, Chill Beverage has much smaller funds available for promotional and research activities.

Opportunities

1. *Growing market:* Although growth in the overall market for bottled water has slowed to some extent, its current rate of growth in the 3 percent range is relatively strong among beverage categories. Of the top six beverage categories, soft drinks, beer, milk, and fruit drinks experienced declines. The growth for coffee was less than 1 percent. More important than the growth of bottled waters in general, the enhanced water category is experiencing growth in the high single and low double digits.
2. *Gap in the distribution network:* The market leaders distribute directly to retailers. This gives them an advantage in large national chains. However, no major enhanced water brands are currently being sold through independent distributors.
3. *Health trends:* Weight and nutrition continue to be issues for consumers in the United States. The country has the highest obesity rate for developed countries at 34 percent, with well over 60 percent of the population officially "overweight." Those numbers continue to rise. Additionally, Americans get 21 percent of their daily calories from beverages, a number that has tripled in the last three decades. Consumers still desire flavored beverages but look for lower-calorie alternatives.
4. *Anti-establishment image.* Millennials (born between 1977 and 2000) maintain a higher aversion to mass marketing messages and global corporations than do Gen Xers and baby boomers.

Threats

1. *Limited shelf space:* Whereas competition is generally a threat for any type of product, competition in retail beverages is particularly high because of limited retail space. Carrying a new beverage product requires retailers to reduce shelf or cooler space already occupied by other brands.
2. *Image of enhanced waters:* The image of enhanced waters is currently in question, as Coca-Cola recently fought a class-action lawsuit accusing it of violating Food and Drug Administration (FDA) regulations by promoting the health benefits of Vitaminwater. The lawsuit exposed the number one bottled water brand as basically sugar water with minimal nutritional value.
3. *Environmental issues:* Environmental groups continue to educate the public on the environmental costs of bottled water, including landfill waste, carbon emissions from production and transportation, and harmful effects of chemicals in plastics.

Objectives and Issues

Chill Beverage has set aggressive but achievable objectives for NutriWater for the first and second years of market entry.

First-Year Objectives

During the initial year on the market, Chill Beverage aims for NutriWater to achieve a 2 percent share of the enhanced water market, or approximately $30 million in sales, with break-even status achieved in the final period of the year. With an average retail price of $1.69, that equates with a sales goal of 17,751,480 bottles.

Second-Year Objectives

During the second year, Chill Beverage will unveil additional NutriWater flavors, including zero-calorie varieties. The second-year objective is to double sales from the first year, to $60 million.

Issues

In launching this new brand, the main issue is the ability to establish brand awareness and a meaningful brand image based on positioning that is relevant to target customer segments. Chill Beverage will invest in nontraditional means of promotion to accomplish these goals and to spark word-of-mouth interactions. Establishing distributor and retailer relationships will also be critical in order to make the product available and provide point-of-purchase communications. Brand awareness and knowledge will be measured in order to adjust marketing efforts as necessary.

Marketing Strategy

NutriWater's marketing strategy will involve developing a "more for the same" positioning based on extra benefits for the price. The brand will also establish channel differentiation, as it will be available in locations where major competing brands are not. The primary target segment is Millennials. This segment is comprised of tweens (ages 10 to 12), teens (13 to 18), and young adults (19 to 33). NutriWater will focus specifically on the young adult market. Subsets of this generational segment include athletes, the health conscious, and the socially responsible.

Positioning

NutriWater will be positioned on an "Expect more" value proposition. This will allow for differentiating the brand based on product features (expect more vitamin content and all-natural ingredients), desirable benefits (expect greater nutritional benefits), and values (do more for a social cause). Marketing will focus on conveying that NutriWater is more than just a beverage: It gives customers much more for their money in a variety of ways.

Product Strategy

NutriWater will be sold with all the features described in the Product Review section. As awareness takes hold and retail availability increases, more varieties will be made available.

A zero-calorie version will be added to the product line, providing a solid fit with the health benefits sought by consumers. Chill Beverage's considerable experience in brand-building will be applied as an integral part of the product strategy for NutriWater. All aspects of the marketing mix will be consistent with the brand.

Pricing

There is little price variation in the enhanced water category, particularly among leading brands. For this reason, NutriWater will follow a competition-based pricing strategy. Given that NutriWater claims superior quality, it must be careful not to position itself as a lower-cost alternative. Manufacturers do not quote list prices on this type of beverage, and prices vary considerably based on type of retail outlet and whether or not the product is refrigerated. Regular prices for single 20-ounce bottles of competing products are as low as $1.00 in discount-retailer stores and as high as $1.89 in convenience stores. Because NutriWater will not be targeting discount retailers and convenience stores initially, this will allow Chill Beverage to set prices at the average to higher end of the range for similar products in the same outlets. For grocery chains, this should be approximately $1.49 per bottle, with that price rising to $1.89 at health food stores and fitness centers, where prices tend to be higher.

Distribution Strategy

Based on the information presented in the Channels and Logistics Review section, NutriWater will employ a selective distribution strategy with well-known regional grocers, health and natural food stores, and fitness centers. This distribution strategy will be executed through a network of independent beverage distributors, as there are no other major brands of enhanced water following this strategy. Chill Beverage gained success for its core Chill Soda soft drink line using this method. It also placed coolers with the brand logo in truly unique venues such as skate, surf, and snowboarding shops; tattoo and piercing parlors; fashion stores; and music stores—places that would expose the brand to target customers. Then, the soft drink brand expanded by getting contracts with retailers such as Panera, Barnes & Noble, Target, and Starbucks. This same approach will be taken with NutriWater by starting small, then expanding into larger chains. NutriWater will not target all the same stores used originally by Chill Soda, as many of those outlets were unique to the positioning and target customer for the Chill Soda soft drink brand.

Marketing Communication Strategy

As with the core Chill Soda brand, the marketing communication strategy for NutriWater will not be based on traditional mass-communication advertising. Initially, there will be no broadcast or print advertising. Promotional resources for NutriWater will focus on three areas:

- *Online and mobile marketing*: The typical target customer for NutriWater spends more time online than with traditional media channels. A core component for this strategy will be building Web and mobile brand sites and driving traffic to those sites by creating a presence on social networks, including Facebook, Google+, and Twitter. The NutriWater brand will also incorporate location-based services by Foursquare and Facebook to help drive traffic to retail locations. A mobile phone ad campaign will provide additional support to the online efforts.
- *Trade promotions*: Like the core Chill Soda brand, NutriWater's success will rely on relationships with retailers to create product availability. Primary incentives to retailers will include point-of-purchase displays, branded coolers, and volume incentives and contests. This push marketing strategy will combine with the other pull strategies.
- *Event marketing*: NutriWater will deploy teams in brand-labeled RVs to distribute product samples at events such as skiing and snowboarding competitions, golf tournaments, and concerts.

Marketing Research

To remain consistent with the online promotional approach, as well as using research methods that will effectively reach target customers, Chill Beverage will monitor online discussions via services such as Radian6. In this manner, the company will gauge customer perceptions of the brand, the products, and general satisfaction. For future development of the product and new distribution outlets, crowdsourcing methods will be utilized.

Action Programs

NutriWater will be introduced in February. The following are summaries of action programs that will be used during the first six months of the year to achieve the stated objectives.

January: Chill Beverage representatives will work with both independent distributors and retailers to educate them on the trade promotional campaign, incentives, and advantages for selling NutriWater. Representatives will also ensure that distributors and retailers are educated on product features and benefits as well as instructions for displaying point-of-purchase materials and coolers. The brand Web site and other sites such as Facebook will present teaser information about the product as well as availability dates and locations. Buzz will be enhanced by providing product samples to selected product reviewers, opinion leaders, influential bloggers, and celebrities.

February: On the date of availability, product coolers and point-of-purchase displays will be placed in retail locations. The full brand Web site and social network campaign will launch with full efforts on Facebook, Google+, and Twitter. This campaign will drive the "Expect more" slogan, as well as illustrate the ways that NutriWater delivers more than expected on product features, desirable benefits, and values by donating to Vitamin Angels and the social cause of battling vitamin deficiency in children.

March: To enhance the online and social marketing campaign, location-based services Foursquare and Facebook Places will be employed to drive traffic to retailers. Point-of-purchase displays and signage will be updated to support these efforts and to continue supporting retailers. The message of this campaign will focus on all aspects of "Expect more."

April: A mobile phone ad campaign will provide additional support, driving Web traffic to the brand Web site and social network sites, as well as driving traffic to retailers.

May: A trade sales contest will offer additional incentives and prizes to the distributors and retailers that sell the most NutriWater during a four-week period.

June: An event marketing campaign will mobilize a team of NutriWater representatives in NutriWater RVs to concerts and sports events. This will provide additional visibility for the brand as well as give customers and potential customers the opportunity to sample products.

Budgets

Chill Beverage has set a first-year retail sales goal of $30 million with a projected average retail price of $1.69 per unit for a total of 17,751,480 units sold. With an average wholesale price of 85 cents per unit, this provides revenues of just over $15 million. Chill Beverage expects to break even during the final period of the first year. A break-even analysis assumes per-unit wholesale revenue of 85 cents per unit, a variable cost per unit of 14 cents, and estimated first-year fixed costs of $12,500,000. Based on these assumptions, the break-even calculation is:

$$\frac{\$12,500,000}{\$0.85/\text{unit} - \$0.14/\text{unit}} = 17,605,634$$

Controls

Chill Beverage is planning tight control measures to closely monitor product quality, brand awareness, brand image, and customer satisfaction. This will enable the company to react quickly in correcting any problems that may occur. Other early warning signals that will be monitored for signs of deviation from the plan include monthly sales (by segment and channel) and monthly expenses. Given the market's volatility, contingency plans are also in place to address fast-moving environmental changes such as shifting consumer preferences, new products, and new competition.

Sources: Jeffrey Klineman, "Restoring an Icon," *Beverage Spectrum Magazine,* December 2010, pp. 16–18; Ryan Underwood, "Jonesing for Soda," *Fast Company,* December 19, 2007, at www.fastcompany.com; "New Playbook at Jones Soda," *Beverage Spectrum Magazine,* March 2008; Matt Casey, "Enhanced Options Divide a Category," *Beverage Spectrum Magazine,* December 2008, p. 74; and product and market information obtained from www.lifewater.com, www.vitaminwater.com, www.nestlewaters.com, www.drinkarizona.com, and www.jonessoda.com, accessed September 2012.

Marketing by the Numbers

Marketing managers are facing increased accountability for the financial implications of their actions. This appendix provides a basic introduction to measuring marketing financial performance. Such financial analysis guides marketers in making sound marketing decisions and in assessing the outcomes of those decisions.

The appendix is built around a hypothetical manufacturer of consumer electronics products—HD. The company is introducing a device that plays videos and television programming streamed over the Internet on multiple devices in a home, including high-definition televisions, tablets, and mobile phones. In this appendix, we will analyze the various decisions HD's marketing managers must make before and after the new-product launch.

The appendix is organized into *three sections*. The *first section* introduces pricing, break-even, and margin analysis assessments that will guide the introduction of HD's new product. The *second section* discusses demand estimates, the marketing budget, and marketing performance measures. It begins with a discussion of estimating market potential and company sales. It then introduces the marketing budget, as illustrated through a *pro forma* profit-and-loss statement followed by the actual profit-and-loss statement. Next, we discuss marketing performance measures, with a focus on helping marketing managers to better defend their decisions from a financial perspective. In the *third section,* we analyze the financial implications of various marketing tactics.

Each of the three sections ends with a set of quantitative exercises that provide you with an opportunity to apply the concepts you learned to situations beyond HD.

Pricing, Break-Even, and Margin Analysis
Pricing Considerations

Determining price is one of the most important marketing mix decisions. The limiting factors are demand and costs. Demand factors, such as buyer-perceived value, set the price ceiling. The company's costs set the price floor. In between these two factors, marketers must consider competitors' prices and other factors such as reseller requirements, government regulations, and company objectives.

Most current competing Internet-streaming products sell at retail prices between $100 and $500. We first consider HD's pricing decision from a cost perspective. Then, we consider consumer value, the competitive environment, and reseller requirements.

Determining Costs

Fixed costs

Costs that do not vary with production or sales level.

Variable costs

Costs that vary directly with the level of production.

Total costs

The sum of the fixed and variable costs for any given level of production.

Recall from Chapter 10 that there are different types of costs. **Fixed costs** do not vary with production or sales level and include costs such as rent, interest, depreciation, and clerical and management salaries. Regardless of the level of output, the company must pay these costs. Whereas total fixed costs remain constant as output increases, the fixed cost per unit (or average fixed cost) will decrease as output increases because the total fixed costs are spread across more units of output. **Variable costs** vary directly with the level of production and include costs related to the direct production of the product (such as costs of goods sold—COGS) and many of the marketing costs associated with selling it. Although these costs tend to be uniform for each unit produced, they are called variable because their total varies with the number of units produced. **Total costs** are the sum of the fixed and variable costs for any given level of production.

HD has invested $10 million in refurbishing an existing facility to manufacture the new video-streaming product. Once production begins, the company estimates that it will incur fixed costs of $20 million per year. The variable cost to produce each device is estimated to be $125, and is expected to remain at that level for the output capacity of the facility.

Setting Price Based on Costs

Cost-plus pricing (or markup pricing)
A standard markup to the cost of the product.

HD starts with the cost-based approach to pricing discussed in Chapter 10. Recall that the simplest method, **cost-plus pricing** (or **markup pricing**), simply adds a standard markup to the cost of the product. To use this method, however, HD must specify expected unit sales so that total unit costs can be determined. Unit variable costs will remain constant regardless of the output, but *average unit fixed costs* will decrease as output increases.

To illustrate this method, suppose HD has fixed costs of $20 million, variable costs of $125 per unit, and expects unit sales of 1 million players. Thus, the cost per unit is given by:

$$\text{Unit cost} = \text{variable cost} + \frac{\text{fixed costs}}{\text{unit sales}} = \$125 + \frac{\$20,000,000}{1,000,000} = \$145$$

Relevant costs
Costs that will occur in the future and that will vary across the alternatives being considered.

Note that we do *not* include the initial investment of $10 million in the total fixed cost figure. It is not considered a fixed cost because it is not a *relevant* cost. **Relevant costs** are those that will occur in the future and that will vary across the alternatives being considered. HD's investment to refurbish the manufacturing facility was a one-time cost that will not reoccur in the future. Such past costs are *sunk costs* and should not be considered in future analyses.

Break-even price
The price at which total revenue equals total cost and profit is zero.

Also notice that if HD sells its product for $145, the price is equal to the total cost per unit. This is the **break-even price**—the price at which unit revenue (price) equals unit cost and profit is zero.

Suppose HD does not want to merely break even but rather wants to earn a 25% markup on sales. HD's markup price is:[1]

$$\text{Markup price} = \frac{\text{unit cost}}{(1 - \text{desired return on sales})} = \frac{\$145}{1 - 0.25} = \$193.33$$

This is the price at which HD would sell the product to resellers such as wholesalers or retailers to earn a 25% profit on sales.

Return on investment (ROI) pricing (or target-return pricing)
A cost-based pricing method that determines price based on a specified rate of return on investment.

Another approach HD could use is called **return-on-investment (ROI) pricing** (or **target-return pricing**). In this case, the company *would* consider the initial $10 million investment, but only to determine the dollar profit goal. Suppose the company wants a 30% return on its investment. The price necessary to satisfy this requirement can be determined by:

$$\text{ROI price} = \text{unit cost} + \frac{\text{ROI} \times \text{investment}}{\text{unit sales}} = \$145 + \frac{0.3 \times \$10,000,000}{1,000,000} = \$148$$

That is, if HD sells its product for $148, it will realize a 30% return on its initial investment of $10 million.

In these pricing calculations, unit cost is a function of the expected sales, which were estimated to be 1 million units. But what if actual sales were lower? Then the unit cost would be higher because the fixed costs would be spread over fewer units, and the realized percentage markup on sales or ROI would be lower. Alternatively, if sales are higher than the estimated 1 million units, unit cost would be lower than $145, so a lower price would produce the desired markup on sales or ROI. It's important to note that these cost-based pricing methods are *internally* focused and do not consider demand, competitors' prices, or reseller requirements. Because HD will be selling this product to consumers through wholesalers and retailers offering competing brands, the company must consider markup pricing from this perspective.

Setting Price Based on External Factors

Whereas costs determine the price floor, HD also must consider external factors when setting price. HD does not have the final say concerning the final price of its product to consumers—retailers do. So it must start with its suggested retail price and work back. In doing so, HD must consider the markups required by resellers that sell the product to consumers.

Markup
The difference between a company's selling price for a product and its cost to manufacture or purchase it.

In general, a dollar **markup** is the difference between a company's selling price for a product and its cost to manufacture or purchase it. For a retailer, then, the markup is the difference between the price it charges consumers and the cost the retailer must pay for the product. Thus, for any level of reseller:

$$\text{Dollar markup} = \text{selling price} - \text{cost}$$

Markups are usually expressed as a percentage, and there are two different ways to compute markups—on *cost* or on *selling price*:

$$\text{Markup percentage on cost} = \frac{\text{dollar markup}}{\text{cost}}$$

$$\text{Markup percentage on selling price} = \frac{\text{dollar markup}}{\text{selling price}}$$

To apply reseller margin analysis, HD must first set the suggested retail price and then work back to the price at which it must sell the product to a wholesaler. Suppose retailers expect a 30% margin and wholesalers want a 20% margin based on their respective selling prices. And suppose that HD sets a manufacturer's suggested retail price (MSRP) of $299.99 for its product.

Value-based pricing
Offering just the right combination of quality and good service at a fair price.

HD selected the $299.99 MSRP because it is lower than most competitors' prices but is not so low that consumers might perceive the product to be of poor quality. And the company's research shows that it is below the threshold at which more consumers are willing to purchase the product. By using buyers' perceptions of value and not the seller's cost to determine the MSRP, HD is using **value-based pricing**. For simplicity, we will use an MSRP of $300 in further analyses.

Markup chain
The sequence of markups used by firms at each level in a channel.

To determine the price HD will charge wholesalers, we must first subtract the retailer's margin from the retail price to determine the retailer's cost ($300 – [$300 × 0.30] = $210). The retailer's cost is the wholesaler's price, so HD next subtracts the wholesaler's margin ($210 – [$210 × 0.20] = $168). Thus, the **markup chain** representing the sequence of markups used by firms at each level in a channel for HD's new product is:

Suggested retail price:	$300
minus retail margin (30%):	– $90
Retailer's cost/wholesaler's price:	$210
minus wholesaler's margin (20%):	– $ 42
Wholesaler's cost/HD's price:	$168

By deducting the markups for each level in the markup chain, HD arrives at a price for the product to wholesalers of $168.

Break-Even and Margin Analysis

The previous analyses derived a value-based price of $168 for HD's product. Although this price is higher than the break-even price of $145 and covers costs, that price assumed a demand of 1 million units. But how many unit sales and what level of dollar sales must HD achieve to break even at the $168 price? And what level of sales must be achieved to realize various profit goals? These questions can be answered through break-even and margin analysis.

Determining Break-Even Unit Volume and Dollar Sales

Break-even analysis
Analysis to determine the unit volume and dollar sales needed to be profitable given a particular price and cost structure.

Based on an understanding of costs, consumer value, the competitive environment, and reseller requirements, HD has decided to set its price to wholesalers at $168. At that price, what sales level will be needed for HD to break even or make a profit on its product? **Break-even analysis** determines the unit volume and dollar sales needed to be profitable given a particular price and cost structure. At the break-even point, total revenue equals total costs and profit is zero. Above this point, the company will make a profit; below it, the company will lose money. HD can calculate break-even volume using the following formula:

$$\text{Break-even volume} = \frac{\text{fixed costs}}{\text{price} - \text{unit variable cost}}$$

Unit contribution

The amount that each unit contributes to covering fixed costs—the difference between price and variable costs.

The denominator (price – unit variable cost) is called **unit contribution** (sometimes called *contribution margin*). It represents the amount that each unit contributes to covering fixed costs. Break-even volume represents the level of output at which all (variable and fixed) costs are covered. In HD's case, break-even unit volume is:

$$\text{Break-even volume} = \frac{\text{fixed cost}}{\text{price} - \text{variable cost}} = \frac{\$20,000,000}{\$168 - \$125} = 465,116.2 \text{ units}$$

Thus, at the given cost and pricing structure, HD will break even at 465,117 units.

To determine the break-even dollar sales, simply multiply unit break-even volume by the selling price:

$$\text{BE sales} = \text{BE}_{\text{vol}} \times \text{price} = 465,117 \times \$168 = \$78,139,656$$

Contribution margin

The unit contribution divided by the selling price.

Another way to calculate dollar break-even sales is to use the percentage contribution margin (hereafter referred to as **contribution margin**), which is the unit contribution divided by the selling price:

$$\text{Contribution margin} = \frac{\text{price} - \text{variable cost}}{\text{price}} = \frac{\$168 - \$125}{\$168} = 0.256 \text{ or } 25.6\%$$

Then,

$$\text{Break-even sales} = \frac{\text{fixed costs}}{\text{contribution margin}} = \frac{\$20,000,000}{0.256} = \$78,125,000$$

Note that the difference between the two break-even sales calculations is due to rounding.

Such break-even analysis helps HD by showing the unit volume needed to cover costs. If production capacity cannot attain this level of output, then the company should not launch this product. However, the unit break-even volume is well within HD's capacity. Of course, the bigger question concerns whether HD can sell this volume at the $168 price. We'll address that issue a little later.

Understanding contribution margin is useful in other types of analyses as well, particularly if unit prices and unit variable costs are unknown or if a company (say, a retailer) sells many products at different prices and knows the percentage of total sales represented by variable costs. Whereas unit contribution is the difference between unit price and unit variable costs, total contribution is the difference between total sales and total variable costs. The overall contribution margin can be calculated by:

$$\text{Contribution margin} = \frac{\text{total sales} - \text{total variable costs}}{\text{total sales}}$$

Regardless of the actual level of sales, if the company knows what percentage of sales is represented by variable costs, it can calculate contribution margin. For example, HD's unit variable cost is $125, or 74% of the selling price ($125 ÷ $168 = 0.74). That means for every $1 of sales revenue for HD, $0.74 represents variable costs, and the difference ($0.26) represents contribution to fixed costs. But even if the company doesn't know its unit price and unit variable cost, it can calculate the contribution margin from total sales and total variable costs or from knowledge of the total cost structure. It can set total sales equal to 100% regardless of the actual absolute amount and determine the contribution margin:

$$\text{Contribution margin} = \frac{100\% - 74\%}{100\%} = \frac{1 - 0.74}{1} = 1 - 0.74 = 0.26 \text{ or } 26\%$$

Note that this matches the percentage calculated from the unit price and unit variable cost information. This alternative calculation will be very useful later when analyzing various marketing decisions.

Determining the Break-Even Point for Profit Goals

Although it is useful to know the break-even point, most companies are more interested in making a profit. Assume HD would like to realize a $5 million profit in the first year. How many units must it sell at the $168 price to cover fixed costs and produce this profit? To determine this, HD can simply add the profit figure to fixed costs and again divide by the unit contribution to determine unit sales:

$$\text{Unit volume} = \frac{\text{fixed cost} + \text{profit goal}}{\text{price} - \text{variable cost}} = \frac{\$20{,}000{,}000 + \$5{,}000{,}000}{\$168 - \$125} = 581{,}395.3 \text{ units}$$

Thus, to earn a $5 million profit, HD must sell 581,396 units. Multiply by price to determine the dollar sales needed to achieve a $5 million profit:

$$\text{Dollar sales} = 581{,}396 \text{ units} \times \$168 = \$97{,}674{,}528$$

Or use the contribution margin:

$$\text{Sales} = \frac{\text{fixed cost} + \text{profit goal}}{\text{contribution margin}} = \frac{\$20{,}000{,}000 + \$5{,}000{,}000}{0.256} = \$97{,}656{,}250$$

Again, note that the difference between the two break-even sales calculations is due to rounding.

As we saw previously, a profit goal can also be stated as an ROI goal. For example, recall that HD wants a 30% return on its $10 million investment. Thus, its absolute profit goal is $3 million ($10,000,000 × 0.30). This profit goal is treated the same way as in the previous example:[2]

$$\text{Unit volume} = \frac{\text{fixed cost} + \text{profit goal}}{\text{price} - \text{variable cost}} = \frac{\$20{,}000{,}000 + \$3{,}000{,}000}{\$168 - \$125} = 534{,}884 \text{ units}$$

$$\text{Dollar sales} = 534{,}884 \text{ units} \times \$168 = \$89{,}860{,}512$$

Or

$$\text{Dollar sales} = \frac{\text{fixed cost} + \text{profit goal}}{\text{contribution margin}} = \frac{\$20{,}000{,}000 + \$3{,}000{,}000}{0.256} = \$89{,}843{,}750$$

Finally, HD can express its profit goal as a percentage of sales, which we also saw in previous pricing analyses. Assume HD desires a 25% return on sales. To determine the unit and sales volume necessary to achieve this goal, the calculation is a little different from the previous two examples. In this case, we incorporate the profit goal into the unit contribution as an additional variable cost. Look at it this way: If 25% of each sale must go toward profits, that leaves only 75% of the selling price to cover fixed costs. Thus, the equation becomes:

$$\text{Unit volume} = \frac{\text{fixed cost}}{\text{price} - \text{variable cost} - (0.25 \times \text{price})} \text{ or } \frac{\text{fixed cost}}{(0.75 \times \text{price}) - \text{variable cost}}$$

So,

$$\text{Unit volume} = \frac{\$20{,}000{,}000}{(0.75 \times 168) - \$125} = 20{,}000{,}000 \text{ units}$$

$$\text{Dollar sales necessary} = 20{,}000{,}000 \text{ units} \times \$168 = \$3{,}360{,}000{,}000$$

Thus, HD would need more than $3 billion in sales to realize a 25% return on sales given its current price and cost structure! Could it possibly achieve this level of sales? The major point is this: Although break-even analysis can be useful in determining the level of sales needed to cover costs or to achieve a stated profit goal, it does not tell the company whether it is *possible* to achieve that level of sales at the specified price. To address this issue, HD needs to estimate demand for this product.

Before moving on, however, let's stop here and practice applying the concepts covered so far. Now that you have seen pricing and break-even concepts in action as they relate to HD's new product, here are several exercises for you to apply what you have learned in other contexts.

Marketing by the Numbers Exercise Set 1

Now that you've studied pricing, break-even, and margin analysis as they relate to HD's new-product launch, use the following exercises to apply these concepts in other contexts.

1.1. Elkins, a manufacturer of ice makers, realizes a cost of $250 for every unit it produces. Its total fixed costs equal $5 million. If the company manufactures 500,000 units, compute the following:
   a. unit cost
   b. markup price if the company desires a 10% return on sales
   c. ROI price if the company desires a 25% return on an investment of $1 million

1.2. A gift shop owner purchases items to sell in her store. She purchases a chair for $125 and sells it for $275. Determine the following:
   a. dollar markup
   b. markup percentage on cost
   c. markup percentage on selling price

1.3. A consumer purchases a coffee maker from a retailer for $90. The retailer's markup is 30%, and the wholesaler's markup is 10%, both based on selling price. For what price does the manufacturer sell the product to the wholesaler?

1.4. A lawn mower manufacturer has a unit cost of $140 and wishes to achieve a margin of 30% based on selling price. If the manufacturer sells directly to a retailer which then adds a set margin of 40% based on selling price, determine the retail price charged to consumers.

1.5. Advanced Electronics manufactures DVDs and sells them directly to retailers that typically sell them for $20. Retailers take a 40% margin based on the retail selling price. Advanced's cost information is as follows:

DVD package and disc	$2.50/DVD
Royalties	$2.25/DVD
Advertising and promotion	$500,000
Overhead	$200,000

Calculate the following:
   a. contribution per unit and contribution margin
   b. break-even volume in DVD units and dollars
   c. volume in DVD units and dollar sales necessary if Advanced's profit goal is 20% profit on sales
   d. net profit if 5 million DVDs are sold

Demand Estimates, the Marketing Budget, and Marketing Performance Measures

Market Potential and Sales Estimates

HD has now calculated the sales needed to break even and to attain various profit goals on its new product. However, the company needs more information regarding demand in order to assess the feasibility of attaining the needed sales levels. This information is also needed for production and other decisions. For example, production schedules need to be developed and marketing tactics need to be planned.

The **total market demand** for a product or service is the total volume that would be bought by a defined consumer group in a defined geographic area in a defined time period in a defined marketing environment under a defined level and mix of industry marketing effort. Total market demand is not a fixed number but a function of the stated conditions. For example, next year's total market demand for this type of product will depend on how much other producers spend on marketing their brands. It also depends on many

Total market demand
The total volume that would be bought by a defined consumer group in a defined geographic area in a defined time period in a defined marketing environment under a defined level and mix of industry marketing effort.

environmental factors, such as government regulations, economic conditions, and the level of consumer confidence in a given market. The upper limit of market demand is called **market potential**.

Market potential

The upper limit of market demand.

One general but practical method that HD might use for estimating total market demand uses three variables: (1) the number of prospective buyers, (2) the quantity purchased by an average buyer per year, and (3) the price of an average unit. Using these numbers, HD can estimate total market demand as follows:

$$Q = n \times q \times p$$

where

Q = total market demand

n = number of buyers in the market

q = quantity purchased by an average buyer per year

p = price of an average unit

Chain ratio method

Estimating market demand by multiplying a base number by a chain of adjusting percentages.

A variation of this approach is the **chain ratio method**. This method involves multiplying a base number by a chain of adjusting percentages. For example, HD's product is designed to stream high-definition video on high-definition televisions as well as play other video content streamed from the Internet to multiple devices in a home. Thus, consumers who do not own a high-definition television will not likely purchase this player. Additionally, only households with broadband Internet access will be able to use the product. Finally, not all HDTV-owning Internet households will be willing and able to purchase this product. HD can estimate U.S. demand using a chain of calculations like the following:

Total number of U.S. households × The percentage of HDTV-owning U.S. households with broadband Internet access × The percentage of these households willing and able to buy this device

The U.S. Census Bureau estimates that there are approximately 113 million households in the United States.[3] HD's research indicates that 60% of U.S. households own at least one HDTV and have broadband Internet access. Finally, the company's research also revealed that 30% of households possess the discretionary income needed and are willing to buy a product such as this. Then, the total number of households willing and able to purchase this product is:

113 million households × 0.60 × 0.30 = 20.34 million households

Households only need to purchase one device because it can stream content to other devices throughout the household. Assuming the average retail price across all brands is $350 for this product, the estimate of total market demand is as follows:

20.34 million households × 1 device per household × $350 = $7,119,000,000

This simple chain of calculations gives HD only a rough estimate of potential demand. However, more detailed chains involving additional segments and other qualifying factors would yield more accurate and refined estimates. Still, these are only *estimates* of market potential. They rely heavily on assumptions regarding adjusting percentages, average quantity, and average price. Thus, HD must make certain that its assumptions are reasonable and defendable. As can be seen, the overall market potential in dollar sales can vary widely given the average price used. For this reason, HD will use unit sales potential to determine its sales estimate for next year. Market potential in terms of units is 20.34 million (20.34 million households × 1 device per household).

Assuming that HD forecasts it will have a 3.66% market share in the first year after launching this product, then it can forecast unit sales at 20.34 million units × 0.0366 = 744,444 units. At a selling price of $168 per unit, this translates into sales of $125,066,592 (744,444 units × $168 per unit). For simplicity, further analyses will use forecasted sales of $125 million.

This unit volume estimate is well within HD's production capacity and exceeds not only the break-even estimate (465,117 units) calculated earlier, but also the volume necessary to realize a $5 million profit (581,396 units) or a 30% return on investment (534,884 units). However, this forecast falls well short of the volume necessary to realize a 25% return on sales (20 million units!) and may require that HD revise expectations.

To assess expected profits, we must now look at the budgeted expenses for launching this product. To do this, we will construct a pro forma profit-and-loss statement.

The Profit-and-Loss Statement and Marketing Budget

All marketing managers must account for the profit impact of their marketing strategies. A major tool for projecting such profit impact is a **pro forma** (or projected) **profit-and-loss statement** (or **income statement or operating statement**). A pro forma statement shows projected revenues less budgeted expenses and estimates the projected net profit for an organization, product, or brand during a specific planning period, typically a year. It includes direct product production costs, marketing expenses budgeted to attain a given sales forecast, and overhead expenses assigned to the organization or product. A profit-and-loss statement typically consists of several major components (see ● **Table A2.1**):

- *Net sales*— gross sales revenue minus returns and allowances (for example, trade, cash, quantity, and promotion allowances). HD's net sales for 2013 are estimated to be $125 million, as determined in the previous analysis.
- *Cost of goods sold (sometimes called cost of sales)*—the actual cost of the merchandise sold by a manufacturer or reseller. It includes the cost of inventory, purchases, and other costs associated with making the goods. HD's cost of goods sold is estimated to be 50% of net sales, or $62.5 million.
- *Gross margin (or gross profit)*—the difference between net sales and cost of goods sold. HD's gross margin is estimated to be $62.5 million.
- *Operating expenses*—the expenses incurred while doing business. These include all other expenses beyond the cost of goods sold that are necessary to conduct business. Operating expenses can be presented in total or broken down in detail. Here, HD's estimated operating expenses include *marketing expenses* and *general and administrative expenses*.

Marketing expenses include sales expenses, promotion expenses, and distribution expenses. The new product will be sold though HD's sales force, so the company budgets $5 million for sales salaries. However, because sales representatives earn a 10% commission on sales, HD must also add a variable component to sales expenses of $12.5 million (10% of $125 million net sales), for a total budgeted sales expense of $17.5 million. HD sets its advertising and promotion to launch this product at $10 million. However, the company also budgets 4% of sales, or $5 million, for cooperative

---

Pro forma (or projected) profit-and-loss statement (or income statement or operating statement)

A statement that shows projected revenues less budgeted expenses and estimates the projected net profit for an organization, product, or brand during a specific planning period, typically a year.

● **Table A2.1** | **Pro Forma Profit-and-Loss Statement for the 12-Month Period Ended December 31, 2013**

			% of Sales
Net Sales		$125,000,000	100%
Cost of Goods Sold		62,500,000	50%
Gross Margin		$ 62,500,000	50%
Marketing Expenses			
Sales expenses	$17,500,000		
Promotion expenses	15,000,000		
Freight	12,500,000	45,000,000	36%
General and Administrative Expenses			
Managerial salaries and expenses	$2,000,000		
Indirect overhead	3,000,000	5,000,000	4%
Net Profit Before Income Tax		$12,500,000	10%

advertising allowances to retailers who promote HD's new product in their advertising. Thus, the total budgeted advertising and promotion expenses are $15 million ($10 million for advertising plus $5 million in co-op allowances). Finally, HD budgets of net sales, or $12.5 million, for freight and delivery charges. In all, total marketing expenses are estimated to be $17.5 million + $15 million + $12.5 million = $45 million.

General and administrative expenses are estimated at $5 million, broken down into $2 million for managerial salaries and expenses for the marketing function and $3 million of indirect overhead allocated to this product by the corporate accountants (such as depreciation, interest, maintenance, and insurance). Total expenses for the year, then, are estimated to be $50 million ($45 million marketing expenses + $5 million in general and administrative expenses).

* *Net profit before taxes*—profit earned after all costs are deducted. HD's estimated net profit before taxes is $12.5 million.

In all, as Table A2.1 shows, HD expects to earn a profit on its new product of $12.5 million in 2013. Also note that the percentage of sales that each component of the profit-and-loss statement represents is given in the right-hand column. These percentages are determined by dividing the cost figure by net sales (that is, marketing expenses represent 36% of net sales determined by $45 million ÷ $125 million). As can be seen, HD projects a net profit return on sales of 10% in the first year after launching this product.

Marketing Performance Measures

Profit-and-loss statement (or income statement or operating statement)

A statement that shows actual revenues less expenses and net profit for an organization, product, or brand during a specific planning period, typically a year.

Now let's fast-forward a year. HD's product has been on the market for one year and management wants to assess its sales and profit performance. One way to assess this performance is to compute performance ratios derived from HD's **profit-and-loss statement** (or **income statement** or **operating statement**).

Whereas the pro forma profit-and-loss statement shows *projected* financial performance, the statement given in ● **Table A2.2** shows HD's *actual* financial performance based on actual sales, cost of goods sold, and expenses during the past year. By comparing

● **Table A2.2** | **Profit-and-Loss Statement for the 12-Month Period Ended December 31, 2013**

			% of Sales
Net Sales		$100,000,000	100%
Cost of Goods Sold		55,000,000	55%
Gross Margin		$ 45,000,000	45%
Marketing Expenses			
Sales expenses	$15,000,000		
Promotion expenses	14,000,000		
Freight	10,000,000	39,000,000	39%
General and Administrative Expenses			
Managerial salaries and expenses	$2,000,000		
Indirect overhead	5,000,000	7,000,000	7%
Net Profit Before Income Tax		($1,000,000)	(–1%)

the profit-and-loss statement from one period to the next, HD can gauge performance against goals, spot favorable or unfavorable trends, and take appropriate corrective action.

The profit-and-loss statement shows that HD lost $1 million rather than making the $12.5 million profit projected in the pro forma statement. Why? One obvious reason is that net sales fell $25 million short of estimated sales. Lower sales translated into lower variable costs associated with marketing the product. However, both fixed costs and the cost of goods sold as a percentage of sales exceeded expectations. Hence, the product's contribution margin was rather than the estimated 26%. That is, variable costs represented of sales (55% for cost of goods sold, 10% for sales commissions, 10% for freight, and 4% for co-op allowances). Recall that contribution margin can be calculated by subtracting that fraction from 1 (1 − 0.79 = 0.21). Total fixed costs were $22 million, $2 million more than estimated. Thus, the sales that HD needed to break even given this cost structure can be calculated as:

$$\text{Break even sales} = \frac{\text{fixed costs}}{\text{contribution margin}} = \frac{\$22,000,000}{0.21} = \$104,761,905$$

If HD had achieved another $5 million in sales, it would have earned a profit.

Although HD's sales fell short of the forecasted sales, so did overall industry sales for this product. Overall industry sales were only $2.5 billion. That means that HD's **market share** was 4% ($100 million ÷ $2.5 billion = 0.04 = 4%), which was higher than forecasted. Thus, HD attained a higher-than-expected market share but the overall market sales were not as high as estimated.

Market share

Company sales divided by market sales.

Analytic Ratios

Operating ratios

The ratios of selected operating statement items to net sales.

The profit-and-loss statement provides the figures needed to compute some crucial **operating ratios**—the ratios of selected operating statement items to net sales. These ratios let marketers compare the firm's performance in one year to that in previous years (or with industry standards and competitors' performance in that year). The most commonly used operating ratios are the gross margin percentage, the net profit percentage, and the operating expense percentage. The inventory turnover rate and return on investment (ROI) are often used to measure managerial effectiveness and efficiency.

Gross margin percentage

The percentage of net sales remaining after cost of goods sold—calculated by dividing gross margin by net sales.

The **gross margin percentage** indicates the percentage of net sales remaining after cost of goods sold that can contribute to operating expenses and net profit before taxes. The higher this ratio, the more a firm has left to cover expenses and generate profit. HD's gross margin ratio was 45%:

$$\text{Gross margin percentage} = \frac{\text{gross margin}}{\text{net sales}} = \frac{\$45,000,000}{\$100,000,000} = 0.45 = 45\%$$

Note that this percentage is lower than estimated, and this ratio is seen easily in the percentage of-sales column in Table A2.2. Stating items in the profit-and-loss statement as a percent of sales allows managers to quickly spot abnormal changes in costs over time. If there was previous history for this product and this ratio was declining, management should examine it more closely to determine why it has decreased (that is, because of a decrease in sales volume or price, an increase in costs, or a combination of these). In HD's case, net sales were $25 million lower than estimated, and cost of goods sold was higher than estimated (55% rather than the estimated 50%).

Net profit percentage

The percentage of each sales dollar going to profit—calculated by dividing net profits by net sales.

The **net profit percentage** shows the percentage of each sales dollar going to profit. It is calculated by dividing net profits by net sales:

$$\text{Net profit percentage} = \frac{\text{net profit}}{\text{net sales}} = \frac{-\$1,000,000}{\$100,000,000} = 0.01 = -1.0\%$$

This ratio is easily seen in the percent-of-sales column. HD's new product generated negative profits in the first year—not a good situation, given that before the product launch net profits before taxes were estimated at more than $12 million. Later in this appendix, we will discuss further analyses the marketing manager should conduct to defend the product.

Operating expense percentage

The portion of net sales going to operating expenses—calculated by dividing total expenses by net sales.

The **operating expense percentage** indicates the portion of net sales going to operating expenses. Operating expenses include marketing and other expenses not directly related to marketing the product, such as indirect overhead assigned to this product. It is calculated by:

$$\text{Operating expense percentage} = \frac{\text{total expenses}}{\text{net sales}} = \frac{\$46,000,000}{\$100,000,000} = 0.46 = 46\%$$

This ratio can also be quickly determined from the percent-of-sales column in the profit-and-loss statement by adding the percentages for marketing expenses and general and administrative expenses (39% + 7%). Thus, 46 cents of every sales dollar went for operations. Although HD wants this ratio to be as low as possible, and 46% is not an alarming amount, it is of concern if it is increasing over time or if a loss is realized.

Another useful ratio is the **inventory turnover rate** (or **stockturn rate for resellers**). The inventory turnover rate is the number of times an inventory turns over or is sold during a specified time period (often one year). This rate tells how quickly a business is moving inventory through the organization. Higher rates indicate that lower investments in inventory are made, thus freeing up funds for other investments. It may be computed on a cost, selling price, or unit basis. The formula based on cost is:

$$\text{Inventory turnover rate} = \frac{\text{cost of goods sold}}{\text{average inventory at cost}}$$

Assuming HD's beginning and ending inventories were $30 million and $20 million, respectively, the inventory turnover rate is:

$$\text{Inventory turnover rate} = \frac{\$55,000,000}{(\$30,000,000 + \$20,000,000)/2} = \frac{\$55,000,000}{\$25,000,000} = 2.2$$

That is, HD's inventory turned over 2.2 times in 2013. Normally, the higher the turnover rate, the higher the management efficiency and company profitability. However, this rate should be compared to industry averages, competitors' rates, and past performance to determine if HD is doing well. A competitor with similar sales but a higher inventory turnover rate will have fewer resources tied up in inventory, allowing it to invest in other areas of the business.

Companies frequently use **return on investment (ROI)** to measure managerial effectiveness and efficiency. For HD, ROI is the ratio of net profits to total investment required to manufacture the new product. This investment includes capital investments in land, buildings, and equipment (here, the initial $10 million to refurbish the manufacturing facility) plus inventory costs (HD's average inventory totaled $25 million), for a total of $35 million. Thus, HD's ROI for this product is:

$$\text{Return on investment} = \frac{\text{net profit before taxes}}{\text{investment}} = \frac{-\$1,000,000}{\$35,000,000} = 0.286 = 2.86\%$$

ROI is often used to compare alternatives, and a positive ROI is desired. The alternative with the highest ROI is preferred to other alternatives. HD needs to be concerned with the ROI realized. One obvious way HD can increase ROI is to increase net profit by reducing expenses. Another way is to reduce its investment, perhaps by investing less in inventory and turning it over more frequently.

Inventory turnover rate (or stockturn rate for resellers)
The number of times an inventory turns over or is sold during a specified time period (often one year)—calculated based on costs, selling price, or units.

Return on investment (ROI)
A measure of managerial effectiveness and efficiency—net profit before taxes divided by total investment.

Marketing Profitability Metrics

Given the financial results just discussed, you may be thinking that HD should drop this new product. But what arguments can marketers make for keeping or dropping this product? The obvious arguments for dropping the product are that first-year sales were well below expected levels and the product lost money, resulting in a negative ROI.

So what would happen if HD did drop this product? Surprisingly, if the company drops the product, the profits for the total organization will decrease by $4 million! How can that be? Marketing managers need to look closely at the numbers in the profit-and-loss statement to determine the *net marketing contribution* for this product. In HD's case, the net marketing contribution for the product is $4 million, and if the company drops this product, that contribution will disappear as well. Let's look more closely at this concept to illustrate how marketing managers can better assess and defend their marketing strategies and programs.

Net Marketing Contribution

Net marketing contribution (NMC)

A measure of marketing profitability that includes only components of profitability controlled by marketing.

Net marketing contribution (NMC), along with other marketing metrics derived from it, measures *marketing* profitability. It includes only components of profitability that are controlled by marketing. Whereas the previous calculation of net profit before taxes from the profit-and-loss statement includes operating expenses not under marketing's control, NMC does not. Referring back to HD's profit-and-loss statement given in Table A2.2, we can calculate net marketing contribution for the product as:

$$\text{NMC} = \text{net sales} - \text{cost of goods sold} - \text{marketing expenses}$$
$$= \$100 \text{ million} - \$55 \text{ million} - \$41 \text{ million} - \$4 \text{ million}$$

The marketing expenses include sales expenses ($15 million), promotion expenses ($14 million), freight expenses ($10 million), and the managerial salaries and expenses of the marketing function ($2 million), which total $41 million.

Thus, the product actually contributed $4 million to HD's profits. It was the $5 million of indirect overhead allocated to this product that caused the negative profit. Further, the amount allocated was $2 million more than estimated in the pro forma profit-and-loss statement. Indeed, if only the estimated amount had been allocated, the product would have earned a *profit* of $1 million rather than losing $1 million. If HD drops the product, the $5 million in fixed overhead expenses will not disappear—it will simply have to be allocated elsewhere. However, the $4 million in net marketing contribution *will* disappear.

Marketing Return on Sales and Investment

To get an even deeper understanding of the profit impact of marketing strategy, we'll now examine two measures of marketing efficiency—*marketing return on sales* (marketing ROS) and *marketing return on investment* (marketing ROI).[4]

Marketing return on sales (or marketing ROS)

The percent of net sales attributable to the net marketing contribution—calculated by dividing net marketing contribution by net sales.

Marketing return on sales (or **marketing ROS**) shows the percent of net sales attributable to the net marketing contribution. For our product, ROS is:

$$\text{Marketing ROS} = \frac{\text{net marketing contribution}}{\text{net sales}} = \frac{\$4,000,000}{\$100,000,000} = 0.04 = 4\%$$

Thus, out of every $100 of sales, the product returns $4 to HD's bottom line. A high marketing ROS is desirable. But to assess whether this is a good level of performance, HD must compare this figure to previous marketing ROS levels for the product, the ROSs of other products in the company's portfolio, and the ROSs of competing products.

Marketing return on investment (or marketing ROI)

A measure of the marketing productivity of a marketing investment—calculated by dividing net marketing contribution by marketing expenses.

Marketing return on investment (or **marketing ROI**) measures the marketing productivity of a marketing investment. In HD's case, the marketing investment is represented by $41 million of the total expenses. Thus, marketing ROI is:

$$\text{Marketing ROI} = \frac{\text{net marketing contribution}}{\text{marketing expenses}} = \frac{\$4,000,000}{\$41,000,000} = 0.0976 = 9.67\%$$

As with marketing ROS, a high value is desirable, but this figure should be compared with previous levels for the given product and with the marketing ROIs of competitors' products. Note from this equation that marketing ROI could be greater than 100%. This can be achieved by attaining a higher net marketing contribution and/or a lower total marketing expense.

In this section, we estimated market potential and sales, developed profit-and-loss statements, and examined financial measures of performance. In the next section, we discuss methods for analyzing the impact of various marketing tactics. However, before moving on to those analyses, here's another set of quantitative exercises to help you apply what you've learned to other situations.

Marketing by the Numbers Exercise Set 2

2.1. Determine the market potential for a product that has 20 million prospective buyers who purchase an average of 2 per year and price averages $50. How many units must a company sell if it desires a 10% share of this market?

2.2. Develop a profit-and-loss statement for the Westgate division of North Industries. This division manufactures light fixtures sold to consumers through home improvement and hardware stores. Cost of goods sold represents 40% of net sales. Marketing expenses include selling expenses, promotion expenses, and freight. Selling expenses include sales salaries totaling $3 million per year and sales commissions (5% of sales). The company spent $3 million on advertising last year, and freight costs were 10% of sales. Other costs include $2 million for managerial salaries and expenses for the marketing function, and another $3 million for indirect overhead allocated to the division.

    a. Develop the profit-and-loss statement if net sales were $20 million last year.
    b. Develop the profit-and-loss statement if net sales were $40 million last year.
    c. Calculate Westgate's break-even sales.

2.3. Using the profit-and-loss statement you developed in question 2.2b, and assuming that Westgate's beginning inventory was $11 million, ending inventory was $7 million, and total investment was $20 million including inventory, determine the following:

    a. gross margin percentage
    b. net profit percentage
    c. operating expense percentage
    d. inventory turnover rate
    e. return on investment (ROI)
    f. net marketing contribution
    g. marketing return on sales (marketing ROS)
    h. marketing return on investment (marketing ROI)
    i. Is the Westgate division doing well? Explain your answer.

Financial Analysis of Marketing Tactics

Although the first-year profit performance for HD's new product was less than desired, management feels that this attractive market has excellent growth opportunities. Although the sales of HD's product were lower than initially projected, they were not unreasonable given the size of the current market. Thus, HD wants to explore new marketing tactics to help grow the market for this product and increase sales for the company.

For example, the company could increase advertising to promote more awareness of the new product and its category. It could add salespeople to secure greater product distribution. HD could decrease prices so that more consumers could afford its product. Finally, to expand the market, HD could introduce a lower-priced model in addition to the higher-priced original offering. Before pursuing any of these tactics, HD must analyze the financial implications of each.

Increase Advertising Expenditures

HD is considering boosting its advertising to make more people aware of the benefits of this device in general and of its own brand in particular. What if HD's marketers recommend increasing national advertising by 50% to $15 million (assume no change in the variable cooperative component of promotional expenditures)? This represents an increase in fixed costs of $5 million. What increase in sales will be needed to break even on this $5 million increase in fixed costs?

A quick way to answer this question is to divide the increase in fixed costs by the contribution margin, which we found in a previous analysis to be 21%:

$$\text{Increase in sales} = \frac{\text{increase in fixed cost}}{\text{contribution margin}} = \frac{\$5,000,000}{0.21} = \$23,809,524$$

Thus, a 50% increase in advertising expenditures must produce a sales increase of almost $24 million to just break even. That $24 million sales increase translates into an almost 1 percentage point increase in market share (1% of the $2.5 billion overall market equals $25 million). That is, to break even on the increased advertising expenditure, HD would have to increase its market share from 4% to 4.95% ($123,809,524 ÷ $2.5 billion = 0.0495 or 4.95% market share). All of this assumes that the total market will not grow, which might or might not be a reasonable assumption.

Increase Distribution Coverage

HD also wants to consider hiring more salespeople in order to call on new retailer accounts and increase distribution through more outlets. Even though HD sells directly to wholesalers, its sales representatives call on retail accounts to perform other functions in addition to selling, such as training retail salespeople. Currently, HD employs 60 sales reps who earn an average of $50,000 in salary plus 10% commission on sales. The product is currently sold to consumers through 1,875 retail outlets. Suppose HD wants to increase that number of outlets to 2,500, an increase of 625 retail outlets. How many additional salespeople will HD need, and what sales will be necessary to break even on the increased cost?

Workload method

An approach to determining sales force size based on the workload required and the time available for selling.

One method for determining what size sales force HD will need is the **workload method**. The workload method uses the following formula to determine the salesforce size:

$$NS = \frac{NC \times FC \times LC}{TA}$$

where

NS = number of salespeople

NC = number of customers

FC = average frequency of customer calls per customer

LC = average length of customer call

TA = time an average salesperson has available for selling per year

HD's sales reps typically call on accounts an average of 20 times per year for about 2 hours per call. Although each sales rep works 2,000 hours per year (50 weeks per year × 40 hours per week), they each spent about 15 hours per week on nonselling activities such as administrative duties and travel. Thus, the average annual available selling time per sales rep per year is 1,250 hours (50 weeks × 25 hours per week). We can now calculate how many sales reps HD will need to cover the anticipated 2,500 retail outlets:

$$NS = \frac{2,500 \times 20 \times 2}{1,250} = 80 \text{ salespeople}$$

Therefore, HD will need to hire 20 more salespeople. The cost to hire these reps will be $1 million (20 salespeople × $50,000 salary per salesperson).

What increase in sales will be required to break even on this increase in fixed costs? The 10% commission is already accounted for in the contribution margin, so the contribution margin remains unchanged at 21%. Thus, the increase in sales needed to cover this increase in fixed costs can be calculated by:

$$\text{Increase in sales} = \frac{\text{increase in fixed cost}}{\text{contribution margin}} = \frac{\$1,000,000}{0.21} = \$4,761,905$$

That is, HD's sales must increase almost $5 million to break even on this tactic. So, how many new retail outlets will the company need to secure to achieve this sales increase? The average revenue generated per current outlet is $53,333 ($100 million in sales divided by 1,875 outlets). To achieve the nearly $5 million sales increase needed to break even, HD would need about 90 new outlets ($4,761,905 ÷ $53,333 = 89.3 outlets), or about 4.5 outlets per new rep. Given that current reps cover about 31 outlets apiece (1,875 outlets ÷ 60 reps), this seems very reasonable.

Decrease Price

HD is also considering lowering its price to increase sales revenue through increased volume. The company's research has shown that demand for most types of consumer electronics products is elastic—that is, the percentage increase in the quantity demanded is greater than the percentage decrease in price.

What increase in sales would be necessary to break even on a 10% decrease in price? That is, what increase in sales will be needed to maintain the total contribution that HD realized at the higher price? The current total contribution can be determined by multiplying the contribution margin by total sales:[5]

Current total contribution = contribution margin × sales = 0.21 × $100 million = $21 million

Price changes result in changes in unit contribution and contribution margin. Recall that the contribution margin of 21% was based on variable costs representing 79% of sales. Therefore, unit variable costs can be determined by multiplying the original price by this percentage: $168 \times 0.79 = 132.72 per unit. If price is decreased by 10%, the new price is $151.20. However, variable costs do not change just because price decreased, so the contribution and contribution margin decrease as follows:

	Old	**New (reduced 10%)**
Price	$168	$151.20
– Unit variable cost	$132.72	$132.72
= Unit contribution	$35.28	$18.48
Contribution margin	$35.28/$168 = 0.21 or 21%	$18.48/$151.20 = 0.12 or 12%

So, a 10% reduction in price results in a decrease in the contribution margin from 21% to 12%.[6] To determine the sales level needed to break even on this price reduction, we calculate the level of sales that must be attained at the new contribution margin to achieve the original total contribution of $21 million:

New contribution margin $\times$ new sales level = original total contribution

So,

$$\text{New sales level} = \frac{\text{original contribution}}{\text{new contribution margin}} = \frac{\$21,000,000}{0.12} = \$175,000,000$$

Thus, sales must increase by $75 million ($175 million – $100 million) just to break even on a 10% price reduction. This means that HD must increase market share to 7% ($175 million ÷ $2.5 billion) to achieve the current level of profits (assuming no increase in the total market sales). The marketing manager must assess whether or not this is a reasonable goal.

Extend the Product Line

As a final option, HD is considering extending its product line by offering a lower-priced model. Of course, the new, lower-priced product would steal some sales from the higher-priced model. This is called **cannibalization**—the situation in which one product sold by a company takes a portion of its sales from other company products. If the new product has a lower contribution than the original product, the company's total contribution will decrease on the cannibalized sales. However, if the new product can generate enough new volume, it is worth considering.

To assess cannibalization, HD must look at the incremental contribution gained by having both products available. Recall in the previous analysis we determined that unit variable costs were $132.72 and unit contribution was just over $35. Assuming costs remain the same next year, HD can expect to realize a contribution per unit of approximately $35 for every unit of the original product sold.

Assume that the first model offered by HD is called HD1 and the new, lower-priced model is called HD2. HD2 will retail for $250, and resellers will take the same markup percentages on price as they do with the higher-priced model. Therefore, HD2's price to wholesalers will be $140, as follows:

Retail price:	$250
minus retail margin (30%):	– $75
Retailer's cost/wholesaler's price:	$175
minus wholesaler's margin (20%):	– $35
Wholesaler's cost/HD's price:	$140

If HD2's variable costs are estimated to be $120, then its contribution per unit will equal $20 ($140 – $120 = $20). That means for every unit that HD2 cannibalizes from HD1, HD

Cannibalization
The situation in which one product sold by a company takes a portion of its sales from other company products.

will *lose* $15 in contribution toward fixed costs and profit (that is, contribution$_{HD2}$ – contribution$_{HD1}$ = $20 – $35 = –$15). You might conclude that HD should not pursue this tactic because it appears as though the company will be worse off if it introduces the lower-priced model. However, if HD2 captures enough *additional* sales, HD will be better off even though some HD1 sales are cannibalized. The company must examine what will happen to *total* contribution, which requires estimates of unit volume for both products.

Originally, HD estimated that next year's sales of HD1 would be 600,000 units. However, with the introduction of HD2, it now estimates that 200,000 of those sales will be cannibalized by the new model. If HD sells only 200,000 units of the new HD2 model (all cannibalized from HD1), the company would lose $3 million in total contribution (200,000 units × –$15 per cannibalized unit = –$3 million)—not a good outcome. However, HD estimates that HD2 will generate the 200,000 of cannibalized sales plus an *additional* 500,000 unit sales. Thus, the contribution on these additional HD2 units will be $10 million (i.e., 500,000 units × $20 per unit = $10 million). The net effect is that HD will gain $7 million in total contribution by introducing HD2.

The following table compares HD's total contribution with and without the introduction of HD2:

	HD1 Only	HD1 and HD2
HD1 contribution	600,000 units × $35 = $21,000,000	400,000 units × $35 = $14,000,000
HD2 contribution	0	700,000 units × $20 = $14,000,000
Total contribution	$21,000,000	$28,000,000

The difference in the total contribution is a net gain of $7 million ($28 million – $21 million). Based on this analysis, HD should introduce the HD2 model because it results in a positive incremental contribution. However, if fixed costs will increase by more than $7 million as a result of adding this model, then the net effect will be negative and HD should not pursue this tactic.

Now that you have seen these marketing tactic analysis concepts in action as related to HD's new product, here are several exercises for you to apply what you have learned in this section in other contexts.

Marketing by the Numbers Exercise Set 3

3.1. Alliance, Inc. sells gas lamps to consumers through retail outlets. Total industry sales for Alliance's relevant market last year were $100 million, with Alliance's sales representing 5% of that total. Contribution margin is 25%. Alliance's sales force calls on retail outlets, and each sales rep earns $50,000 per year plus 1% commission on all sales. Retailers receive a 40% margin on selling price and generate average revenue of $10,000 per outlet for Alliance.

    a. The marketing manager has suggested increasing consumer advertising by $200,000. By how much would dollar sales need to increase to break even on this expenditure? What increase in overall market share does this represent?

    b. Another suggestion is to hire two more sales representatives to gain new consumer retail accounts. How many new retail outlets would be necessary to break even on the increased cost of adding two sales reps?

    c. A final suggestion is to make a 10% across-the-board price reduction. By how much would dollar sales need to increase to maintain Alliance's current contribution? (See Ref. 6 to calculate the new contribution margin.)

    d. Which suggestion do you think Alliance should implement? Explain your recommendation.

3.2. PepsiCo sells its soft drinks in approximately 400,000 retail establishments, such as supermarkets, discount stores, and convenience stores. Sales representatives call on each retail account weekly, which means each account is called on by a sales rep 52 times per year. The average length of a sales call is 75 minutes (or 1.25 hours). An average salesperson works 2,000 hours per year (50 weeks per year × 40 hours per week), but each spends 10 hours a week on nonselling activities, such as administrative tasks and travel. How many salespeople does PepsiCo need?

3.3. Hair Zone manufactures a brand of hair-styling gel. It is considering adding a modified version of the product—a foam that provides stronger hold. Hair Zone's variable costs and prices to wholesalers are as follows:

	Current Hair Gel	**New Foam Product**
Unit selling price	2.00	2.25
Unit variable costs	.85	1.25

Hair Zone expects to sell 1 million units of the new styling foam in the first year after introduction, but it expects that 60% of those sales will come from buyers who normally purchase Hair Zone's styling gel. Hair Zone estimates that it would sell 1.5 million units of the gel if it did not introduce the foam. If the fixed cost of launching the new foam will be $100,000 during the first year, should Hair Zone add the new product to its line? Why or why not?

References

1. This is derived by rearranging the following equation and solving for price: Percentage markup = (price − cost) ÷ price.

2. Again, using the basic profit equation, we set profit equal to ROI × I: ROI × I = (P × Q) − TFC − (Q × UVC). Solving for Q gives Q = (TFC + [ROI × I]) ÷ (P − UVC).

3. U.S. Census Bureau, www.census.gov/prod/1/pop/p25-1129.pdf, accessed October 26, 2009.

4. See Roger J. Best, *Market-Based Management*, 4th ed. (Upper Saddle River, NJ: Prentice Hall, 2005).

5. Total contribution can also be determined from the unit contribution and unit volume: Total contribution = unit contribution × unit sales. Total units sold in 2013 were 595,238 units, which can be determined by dividing total sales by price per unit ($100 million ÷ $168). Total contribution = $35.28 contribution per unit × 595,238 units = $20,999,996.64 (difference due to rounding).

6. Recall that the contribution margin of 21% was based on variable costs representing 79% of sales. Therefore, if we do not know price, we can set it equal to $1.00. If price equals $1.00, 79 cents represents variable costs and 21 cents represents unit contribution. If price is decreased by 10%, the new price is $0.90. However, variable costs do not change just because price decreased, so the unit contribution and contribution margin decrease as follows:

	Old	**New (reduced 10%)**
Price	$1.00	$0.90
− Unit variable cost	$0.79	$0.79
= Unit contribution	$0.21	$0.11
Contribution margin	$0.21/$1.00 = 0.21 or 21%	$0.11/$0.90 = 0.12 or 12%

Careers in Marketing

You may have decided you want to pursue a marketing career because it offers constant challenge, stimulating problems, the opportunity to work with people, and excellent advancement opportunities. But you still may not know which part of marketing best suits you—marketing is a very broad field offering a wide variety of career options.

This appendix helps you discover what types of marketing jobs best match your special skills and interests, shows you how to conduct the kind of job search that will get you the position you want, describes marketing career paths open to you, and suggests other information resources.

Marketing Careers Today

The marketing field is booming, with nearly a third of all working Americans now employed in marketing-related positions. Marketing salaries may vary by company, position, and region, and salary figures change constantly. In general, entry-level marketing salaries usually are only slightly below those for engineering and chemistry but equal or exceed starting salaries in economics, finance, accounting, general business, and the liberal arts. Moreover, if you succeed in an entry-level marketing position, it's likely that you will be promoted quickly to higher levels of responsibility and salary. In addition, because of the consumer and product knowledge you will gain in these jobs, marketing positions provide excellent training for the highest levels in an organization.

Overall Marketing Facts and Trends

In conducting your job search, consider the following facts and trends that are changing the world of marketing:

Focus on customers: More and more, companies are realizing that they win in the marketplace only by creating superior value for customers. To capture value from customers, they must first find new and better ways to solve customer problems and improve customer brand experiences. This increasing focus on the customer puts marketers at the forefront in many of today's companies. As the primary customer-facing function, marketing's mission is to get all company departments to "think customer."

Technology: Technology is changing the way marketers work. For example, Internet, mobile, and other digital technologies are rapidly changing the ways marketers interact with and service customers. They are also changing everything from the ways marketers create new products and advertise them to how marketers access information and recruit personnel. Whereas advertising firms have traditionally recruited "generalists" in account management, "generalist" has now taken on a whole new meaning—advertising account executives must now have both broad and specialized knowledge.

Diversity: The number of women and minorities in marketing continues to grow, and women and minorities also are advancing rapidly into marketing management. For example, women now outnumber men by nearly two to one as advertising account executives. As marketing becomes more global, the need for diversity in marketing positions will continue to increase, opening new opportunities.

Global: Companies such as Coca-Cola, McDonald's, Google, IBM, Walmart, and Procter & Gamble have become multinational, with manufacturing and marketing operations in hundreds of countries. Indeed, such companies often make more profit from sales outside the United States than from within. And it's not just the big companies that are involved in international marketing. Organizations of all sizes have moved into the global arena. Many new marketing opportunities and careers will be directly linked to the expanding global marketplace. The globalization of business also means that you will need more cultural, language, and people skills in the marketing world of the twenty-first century.

Not-for-profit organizations: Increasingly, colleges, arts organizations, libraries, hospitals, and other not-for-profit organizations are recognizing the need for effectively marketing their "products" and services to various publics. This awareness has led to new marketing positions—with these organizations hiring their own marketing directors and marketing vice presidents or using outside marketing specialists.

Looking for a Job in Today's Marketing World

To choose and find the right job, you will need to apply the marketing skills you've learned in this course, especially marketing analysis and planning. Follow these eight steps for marketing yourself: (1) Conduct a self-assessment and seek career counseling, (2) examine job descriptions, (3) explore the job market and assess opportunities, (4) develop search strategies, (5) prepare résumés, (6) write a cover letter and assemble supporting documents, (7) interview for jobs, and (8) follow up.

Conduct a Self-Assessment and Seek Career Counseling

If you're having difficulty deciding what kind of marketing position is the best fit for you, start out by doing some self-testing or seeking career counseling. Self-assessments require that you honestly and thoroughly evaluate your interests, strengths, and weaknesses. What do you do well (your best and favorite skills) and not so well? What are your favorite interests? What are your career goals? What makes you stand out from other job seekers?

The answers to such questions may suggest which marketing careers you should seek or avoid. For help in completing an effective self-assessment, look for the following books in your local bookstore: Shoya Zichy, *Career Match: Connecting Who You Are with What You Love to Do* (AMACOM Books, 2007) and Richard Bolles, *What Color Is Your Parachute? 2013* (Ten Speed Press, 2012; also see www.eparachute.com/index.webui). Many online sites also offer self-assessment tools, such as the Keirsey Temperament Theory and the Temperament Sorter, a free but broad assessment available at Keirsey.com. For a more specific evaluation, Career-Leader.com offers a complete online business career self-assessment program designed by the Directors of MBA Career Development at Harvard Business School. You can use this for a fee.

For help in finding a career counselor to guide you in making a career assessment, Richard Bolles's *What Color Is Your Parachute? 2013* contains a useful state-by-state sampling. CareerLeader.com also offers personal career counseling. (Some counselors can help you in your actual job search, too.) You can also consult the career counseling, testing, and placement services at your college or university.

Examine Job Descriptions

After you have identified your skills, interests, and desires, you need to see which marketing positions are the best match for them. Two U.S. Labor Department publications available in your local library or online—the *Occupation Outlook Handbook* (www.bls.gov/ooh) and the *Dictionary of Occupational Titles* (www.occupationalinfo.org)—describe the duties involved in various occupations, the specific training and education needed, the availability of jobs in each field, possibilities for advancement, and probable earnings.

Your initial career shopping list should be broad and flexible. Look for different ways to achieve your objectives. For example, if you want a career in marketing management, consider the public as well as the private sector, and local and regional as well as national and international firms. Be open initially to exploring many options, then focus on specific industries and jobs, listing your basic goals as a way to guide your choices. Your list might include "a job in a start-up company, near a big city on the West Coast, doing new-product planning with a computer software firm."

Explore the Job Market and Assess Opportunities

At this stage, you need to look at the market and see what positions are actually available. You do not have to do this alone. Any of the following may assist you.

Career Development Centers

Your college's career development center is an excellent place to start. In addition to checking with your career development center or specific job openings, check the current edition of the National Association of Colleges and Employers *Job Choices* (www.jobchoicesonline .com). It contains a national forecast of hiring intentions of employers as they relate to new college graduates. More and more, college career development centers are also going online. For example, the Web site of the undergraduate career services of Indiana University's Kelley School of Business has a list of career links (http://kelley.iu.edu/UCSO/) that can help to focus your job search.

In addition, find out everything you can about the companies that interest you by consulting company Web sites, business magazine articles and online sites, annual reports, business reference books, faculty, career counselors, and others. Try to analyze the industry's and the company's future growth and profit potential, advancement opportunities, salary levels, entry positions, travel time, and other factors of significance to you.

Job Fairs

Career development centers often work with corporate recruiters to organize on-campus job fairs. You might also use the Internet to check on upcoming career fairs in your region. For example, visit National Career Fairs at www.nationalcareerfairs.com or Coast to Coast Career Fairs listings at www.coasttocoastcareerfairs.com.

Networking

Networking—asking for job leads from friends, family, people in your community, and career centers—is one of the best ways to find a marketing job. Studies estimate that 60 to 90 percent of jobs are found through networking. The idea is to spread your net wide, contacting anybody and everybody.

Internships

An internship is filled with many benefits, such as gaining experience in a specific field of interest and building up a network of contacts. The biggest benefit: the potential of being offered a job shortly before or soon after graduation. According to a recent survey by the National Association of Colleges and Employers, employers converted 58.6 percent of last year's interns into full-time hires. Sixty percent of the seniors who had paid internship experience and applied for a job received at least one job offer. Conversely, only 36 percent of seniors without internship experience who applied for a job received an offer. In addition, survey results show that the median accepted salary offer for seniors with an internship was 31 percent higher than the median accepted salary offered to non-intern seniors.

Many company Internet sites have separate internship areas. For example, check out Internships.com, InternshipPrograms.com, MonsterCollege (http://college.monster.com/ education), CampusCareerCenter.com, InternJobs.com, and GoAbroad.com (www.goabroad .com/intern-abroad). If you know of a company for which you wish to work, go to that company's corporate Web site, enter the human resources area, and check for internships. If none are listed, try e-mailing the human resources department, asking if internships are offered.

Job Hunting on the Internet

A constantly increasing number of sites on the Internet deal with job hunting. You can also use the Internet to make contacts with people who can help you gain information on and research companies that interest you. The Riley Guide offers a great introduction to what jobs are available (www.rileyguide.com). CareerBuilder.com and Monster.com are good general sites for seeking job listings. Other helpful sites are DisabilityInfo.gov and HireDiversity .com, which contain information on opportunities for African Americans, Hispanic Americans, Asian Americans, and Native Americans.

Most companies have their own online sites on which they post job listings. This may be helpful if you have a specific and fairly limited number of companies that you are keeping your eye on for job opportunities. But if this is not the case, remember that to find out what interesting marketing jobs the companies themselves are posting, you may have to visit hundreds of corporate sites.

Professional Networking Sites

Many companies have now begun to take advantage of social networking sites to find talented applicants. From Facebook to LinkedIn, social networking has become professional networking. For example, Ernst & Young has a career page on Facebook (www.facebook.com/ernstandyoungcareers) to find potential candidates for entry-level positions. So do companies ranging from Walmart (www.facebook.com/walmartcareers?v=app_7146470109) to BASF (www.facebook.com/home.php#!/basfcareer) and just about every other potential employer. For job seekers, online professional networking offers more efficient job targeting and reduces associated costs as compared with traditional interaction methods such as traveling to job fairs and interviews, printing résumés, and other expenses.

However, although the Internet offers a wealth of resources for searching for the perfect job, be aware that it's a two-way street. Just as job seekers can search the Internet to find job opportunities, employers can search for information on job candidates. Jobs searches can sometimes be derailed by information mined by potential employers from online social networking sites that reveals unintended or embarrassing anecdotes and photos. Internet searches can sometimes also reveal inconsistencies and résumé inflation.

Develop Search Strategies

Once you've decided which companies you are interested in, you need to contact them. One of the best ways is through on-campus interviews. But not every company you are interested in will visit your school. In such instances, you can write, e-mail, or phone the company directly or ask marketing professors or school alumni for contacts.

Prepare Résumés

A résumé is a concise yet comprehensive written summary of your qualifications, including your academic, personal, and professional achievements, that showcases why you are the best candidate for the job. Because an employer will spend on average only 15 to 20 seconds reviewing your résumé, you want to be sure that you prepare a good one.

In preparing your résumé, remember that all information on it must be accurate and complete. Résumés typically begin with the applicant's full name, telephone number, and mail and e-mail addresses. A simple and direct statement of career objectives generally appears next, followed by work history and academic data (including awards and internships), and then by personal activities and experiences applicable to the job sought.

The résumé sometimes ends with a list of references the employer may contact (at other times, references may be listed separately). If your work or internship experience is limited, nonexistent, or irrelevant, then it is a good idea to emphasize your academic and nonacademic achievements, showing skills related to those required for excellent job performance.

There are three types of résumés. Reverse *chronological* résumés, which emphasize career growth, are organized in reverse chronological order, starting with your most recent job. They focus on job titles within organizations, describing the responsibilities and accomplishments for each job. *Functional* résumés focus less on job titles and work history and more on assets and achievements. This format works best if your job history is scanty or discontinuous. *Mixed,* or *combination,* résumés take from each of the other two formats. First, the skills used for a specific job are listed, then the job title is stated. This format works best for applicants whose past jobs are in other fields or seemingly unrelated to the position. For further explanation and examples of these types of résumés, see the Résumé Resource format page (www.resume-resource.com/format.html).

Your local bookstore or library has many books that can assist you in developing your résumé. A popular guide is Brenda Greene, *Get the Interview Every Time: Proven Résumé and Cover Letter Strategies from Fortune 500 Hiring Professionals* (Kaplan Publishing, 2009). Computer software programs, such as *RésuméMaker* (ResumeMaker.com), provide hundreds of sample résumés and ready-to-use phrases while guiding you through the résumé preparation process. CareerOneStop (www.careeronestop.org/resumeguide/introduction.aspx) offers a step-by-step résumé tutorial, and Monster (http://career-advice.monster.com)

offers résumé advice and writing services. Finally, you can even create your own personalized online résumé at sites such as optimalresume.com.

Online Résumés

The Internet is now a widely used job-search environment, so it's a good idea to have your résumé ready for the online environment. You can forward it to networking contacts or recruiting professionals through e-mail. You can also post it in online databases with the hope that employers and recruiters will find it.

Successful Internet-ready résumés require a different strategy than that for paper résumés. For instance, when companies search résumé banks, they search key words and industry buzz words that describe a skill or the core work required for each job, so nouns are much more important than verbs. Two good resources for preparing electronic résumés are Susan Ireland's Résumé Site (http://susanireland.com/resume/online/email/) and the Riley Guide (www.rileyguide.com/eresume.html).

After you have written your electronic résumé, you need to post it. The following sites may be good locations to start: Monster (www.monster.com) and CareerBuilder.com (www.careerbuilder.com/JobSeeker/Resumes/PostResumeNew/PostYourResume.aspx). However, use caution when posting your résumé on various sites. In this era of identity theft, you need to select sites with care so as to protect your privacy. Limit access to your personal contact information, and don't use sites that offer to "blast" your résumé into cyberspace.

Résumé Tips

- Communicate your worth to potential employers in a concrete manner, citing examples whenever possible.
- Be concise and direct.
- Use active verbs to show you are a doer.
- Do not skimp on quality or use gimmicks. Spare no expense in presenting a professional résumé.
- Have someone critique your work. A single typo can eliminate you from being considered.
- Customize your résumé for specific employers. Emphasize your strengths as they pertain to your targeted job.
- Keep your résumé compact, usually one page.
- Format the text to be attractive, professional, and readable. Times New Roman is often the font of choice. Avoid too much "design" or gimmicky flourishes.

Write Cover Letter, Follow Up, and Assemble Supporting Documents

Cover Letter

You should include a cover letter informing the employer that a résumé is enclosed. But a cover letter does more than this. It also serves to summarize in one or two paragraphs the contents of the résumé and explains why you think you are the right person for the position. The goal is to persuade the employer to look at the more detailed résumé. A typical cover letter is organized as follows: (1) the name and position of the person you are contacting; (2) a statement identifying the position you are applying for, how you heard of the vacancy, and the reasons for your interest; (3) a summary of your qualifications for the job; (4) a description of what follow-ups you intend to make, such as phoning in two weeks to see if the résumé has been received; and (5) an expression of gratitude for the opportunity of being a candidate for the job. CareerOneStop (www.careeronestop.org/ResumeGuide/Writeeffectivecoverletters.aspx) offers a step-by-step tutorial on how to create a cover letter, and Susan Ireland's Web site contains more than 50 cover letter samples (http://susanireland.com/letter/cover-letter-examples). Another popular guide is Kimberly Sarmiento's *Complete Guide to Writing Effective Résumé Cover Letters* (Atlantic Publishing, 2009).

Follow Up

Once you send your cover letter and résumé to perspective employers via the method they prefer—e-mail, their Web site, or regular mail—it's often a good idea to follow up. In today's market, job seekers can't afford to wait for interviews to find them. A quality résumé and an attractive cover letter are crucial, but a proper follow-up may be the key to landing an interview. However, before you engage your potential employer, be sure to research the company. Knowing about the company and understanding its place in the industry will help you shine. When you place a call, send an e-mail, or mail a letter to a company contact, be sure to restate your interest in the position, check on the status of your résumé, and ask employers about any questions they may have.

Letters of Recommendation

Letters of recommendation are written references by professors, former and current employers, and others that testify to your character, skills, and abilities. Some companies may request letters of recommendation, to be submitted either with the résumé or at the interview. Even if letters of recommendation aren't requested, it's a good idea to bring them with you to the interview. A good reference letter tells why you would be an excellent candidate for the position. In choosing someone to write a letter of recommendation, be confident that the person will give you a good reference. In addition, do not assume the person knows everything about you or the position you are seeking. Rather, provide the person with your résumé and other relevant data. As a courtesy, allow the reference writer at least a month to complete the letter and enclose a stamped, addressed envelope with your materials.

In the packet containing your résumé, cover letter, and letters of recommendation, you may also want to attach other relevant documents that support your candidacy, such as academic transcripts, graphics, portfolios, and samples of writing.

Interview for Jobs

As the old saying goes, "The résumé gets you the interview; the interview gets you the job." The job interview offers you an opportunity to gather more information about the organization, while at the same time allowing the organization to gather more information about you. You'll want to present your best self. The interview process consists of three parts: before the interview, the interview itself, and after the interview. If you pass through these stages successfully, you will be called back for the follow-up interview.

Before the Interview

In preparing for your interview, do the following:

1. Understand that interviewers have diverse styles, including the "chitchat," let's-get-to-know-each-other style; the interrogation style of question after question; and the tough-probing "why, why, why" style, among others. So be ready for anything.
2. With a friend, practice being interviewed and then ask for a critique. Or videotape yourself in a practice interview so that you can critique your own performance. Your college placement service may also offer "mock" interviews to help you.
3. Prepare at least five good questions whose answers are not easily found in the company literature, such as "What is the future direction of the firm?" "How does the firm differentiate itself from competitors?" or "Do you have a new-media division?"
4. Anticipate possible interview questions, such as "Why do you want to work for this company?" or "Why should we hire you?" Prepare solid answers before the interview. Have a clear idea of why you are interested in joining the company and the industry to which it belongs.
5. Avoid back-to-back interviews—they can be exhausting, and it is unpredictable how long each will last.
6. Prepare relevant documents that support your candidacy, such as academic transcripts, letters of recommendation, graphics, portfolios, and samples of writing. Bring multiple copies to the interview.
7. Dress conservatively and professionally. Be neat and clean.
8. Arrive 10 minutes early to collect your thoughts and review the major points you intend to cover. Check your name on the interview schedule, noting the name of the interviewer and the room number. Be courteous and polite to office staff.
9. Approach the interview enthusiastically. Let your personality shine through.

During the Interview

During the interview, do the following:

1. Shake hands firmly in greeting the interviewer. Introduce yourself, using the same form of address that the interviewer uses. Focus on creating a good initial impression.

2. Keep your poise. Relax, smile when appropriate, and be upbeat throughout.
3. Maintain eye contact and good posture, and speak distinctly. Don't clasp your hands or fiddle with jewelry, hair, or clothing. Sit comfortably in your chair.
4. Along with the copies of relevant documents that support your candidacy, carry extra copies of your résumé with you.
5. Have your story down pat. Present your selling points. Answer questions directly. Avoid either one-word or too-wordy answers.
6. Let the interviewer take the initiative but don't be passive. Find an opportunity to direct the conversation to things about yourself that you want the interviewer to hear.
7. To end on a high note, make your most important point or ask your most pertinent question during the last part of the interview.
8. Don't hesitate to "close." You might say, "I'm very interested in the position and I have enjoyed this interview."
9. Obtain the interviewer's business card or address and phone number so that you can follow up later.

A tip for acing the interview: Before you open your mouth, find out *what it's like* to be a brand manager, sales representative, market researcher, advertising account executive, or other position for which you're interviewing. See if you can find a "mentor"—someone in a position similar to the one you're seeking, perhaps with another company. Talk with this mentor about the ins and outs of the job and industry.

After the Interview

After the interview, do the following:

1. Record the key points that arose. Be sure to note who is to follow up and when a decision can be expected.
2. Analyze the interview objectively, including the questions asked, the answers to them, your overall interview presentation, and the interviewer's responses to specific points.
3. Immediately send a thank-you letter or e-mail, mentioning any additional items and your willingness to supply further information.
4. If you do not hear from the employer within the specified time, call, e-mail, or write the interviewer to determine your status.

Follow-Up Interview

If your first interview takes place off-site, such as at your college or at a job fair, and if you are successful with that initial interview, you will be invited to visit the organization. The in-company interview will probably run from several hours to an entire day. The organization will examine your interest, maturity, enthusiasm, assertiveness, logic, and company and functional knowledge. You should ask questions about issues of importance to you. Find out about the working environment, job role, responsibilities, opportunities for advancement, current industrial issues, and the company's personality. The company wants to discover if you are the right person for the job, whereas you want to find out if it is the right job for you. The key is to determine if the right *fit* exists between you and the company.

Marketing Jobs

This section describes some of the key marketing positions.

Advertising

Advertising is one of the most exciting fields in marketing, offering a wide range of career opportunities.

Job Descriptions

Key advertising positions include copywriter, art director, production manager, account executive, account planner, and media planner/buyer.

- *Copywriters* write advertising copy and help find the concepts behind the written words and visual images of advertisements.

- *Art directors,* the other part of the creative team, help translate the copywriters' ideas into dramatic visuals called "layouts." Agency artists develop print layouts, package designs, television and video layouts (called "storyboards"), corporate logotypes, trademarks, and symbols. *Production managers* are responsible for physically creating ads, in-house or by contracting through outside production houses.
- *Account development executives* research and understand clients' markets and customers and help develop marketing and advertising strategies to impact them.
- *Account executives* serve as liaisons between clients and agencies. They coordinate the planning, creation, production, and implementation of an advertising campaign for the account.
- *Account planners* serve as the voice of the consumer in the agency. They research consumers to understand their needs and motivations as a basis for developing effective ad campaigns.
- *Media planners (or buyers)* determine the best mix of television, radio, newspaper, magazine, digital, and other media for the advertising campaign.

Skills Needed, Career Paths, and Typical Salaries

Work in advertising requires strong people skills in order to interact closely with an often-difficult and demanding client base. In addition, advertising attracts people with strong skills in planning, problem solving, creativity, communication, initiative, leadership, and presentation. Advertising involves working under high levels of stress and pressure created by unrelenting deadlines. Advertisers frequently have to work long hours to meet deadlines for a presentation. But work achievements are very apparent, with the results of creative strategies observed by thousands or even millions of people.

Positions in advertising sometimes require an MBA. But most jobs only require a business, graphics arts, or liberal arts degree. Advertising positions often serve as gateways to higher-level management. Moreover, with large advertising agencies opening offices all over the world, there is the possibility of eventually working on global campaigns.

Starting advertising salaries are relatively low compared to those of some other marketing jobs because of strong competition for entry-level advertising jobs. Compensation will increase quickly as you move into account executive or other management positions. For more facts and figures, see the online pages of *Advertising Age,* a key ad industry publication (www.adage.com, click on the Jobs link) and the American Association of Advertising Agencies (www.aaaa.org).

Brand and Product Management

Brand and product managers plan, direct, and control business and marketing efforts for their products. They are involved with research and development, packaging, manufacturing, sales and distribution, advertising, promotion, market research, and business analysis and forecasting.

Job Descriptions

A company's brand management team consists of people in several positions:

- *Brand managers* guide the development of marketing strategies for a specific brand.
- *Assistant brand managers* are responsible for certain strategic components of the brand.
- *Product managers* oversee several brands within a product line or product group.
- *Product category managers* direct multiple product lines in the product category.
- *Market analysts* research the market and provide important strategic information to the project managers.
- *Project directors* are responsible for collecting market information on a marketing or product project.
- *Research directors* oversee the planning, gathering, and analyzing of all organizational research.

Skills Needed, Career Paths, and Typical Salaries

Brand and product management requires high problem-solving, analytical, presentation, communication, and leadership skills, as well as the ability to work well in a team. Product management requires long hours and involves the high pressure of running large projects.

In consumer goods companies, the newcomer—who usually needs an MBA—joins a brand team as an assistant and learns the ropes by doing numerical analyses and assisting senior brand people. This person eventually heads the team and later moves on to manage a larger brand, then several brands.

Many industrial goods companies also have product managers. Product management is one of the best training grounds for future corporate officers. Product management also offers good opportunities to move into international marketing. Product managers command relatively high salaries. Because this job category encourages or requires a master's degree, starting pay tends to be higher than in other marketing categories such as advertising or retailing.

Sales and Sales Management

Sales and sales management opportunities exist in a wide range of profit and not-for-profit organizations and in product and service organizations, including financial, insurance, consulting, and government organizations.

Job Descriptions

Key jobs include consumer sales, industrial sales, national account managers, service support, sales trainers, and sales management.

- *Consumer sales* involves selling consumer products and services through retailers.
- *Industrial sales* involves selling products and services to other businesses.
- *National account managers (NAMs)* oversee a few very large accounts.
- *Service support* personnel support salespeople during and after the sale of a product.
- *Sales trainers* train new hires and provide refresher training for all sales personnel.
- *Sales management* includes a sequence of positions ranging from district manager to vice president of sales.

Salespeople enjoy active professional lives, working outside the office and interacting with others. They manage their own time and activities. And successful salespeople can be very well paid. Competition for top jobs can be intense. Every sales job is different, but some positions involve extensive travel, long workdays, and working under pressure. You can also expect to be transferred more than once between company headquarters and regional offices. However, most companies are now working to bring good work–life balance to their salespeople and sales managers.

Skills Needed, Career Paths, and Typical Salaries

Selling is a people profession in which you will work with people every day, all day long. In addition to people skills, sales professionals need sales and communication skills. Most sales positions also require strong problem-solving, analytical, presentation, and leadership abilities as well as creativity and initiative. Teamwork skills are increasingly important.

Career paths lead from salesperson to district, regional, and higher levels of sales management and, in many cases, to the top management of the firm. Today, most entry-level sales management positions require a college degree. Increasingly, people seeking selling jobs are acquiring sales experience in an internship capacity or from a part-time job before graduating. Sales positions are great springboards to leadership positions, with more CEOs starting in sales than in any other entry-level position. This possibly explains why competition for top sales jobs is intense.

Starting base salaries in sales may be moderate but compensation is often supplemented by significant commission, bonus, or other incentive plans. In addition, many sales jobs include a company car or car allowance. Successful salespeople are among most companies' highest paid employees.

Other Marketing Jobs

Retailing

Retailing provides an early opportunity to assume marketing responsibilities. Key jobs include store manager, regional manager, buyer, department manager, and salesperson. *Store managers* direct the management and operation of an individual store. *Regional managers* manage groups of stores across several states and report performance to headquarters.

Buyers select and buy the merchandise that the store carries. The *department manager* acts as store manager of a department, such as clothing, but on the department level. The *salesperson* sells merchandise to retail customers. Retailing can involve relocation, but generally there is little travel, unless you are a buyer. Retailing requires high people and sales skills because retailers are constantly in contact with customers. Enthusiasm, willingness, and communication skills are very helpful for retailers, too.

Retailers work long hours, but their daily activities are often more structured than in some types of marketing positions. Starting salaries in retailing tend to be low, but pay increases as you move into management or a retailing specialty job.

Marketing Research

Marketing researchers interact with managers to define problems and identify the information needed to resolve them. They design research projects, prepare questionnaires and samples, analyze data, prepare reports, and present their findings and recommendations to management. They must understand statistics, consumer behavior, psychology, and sociology. As more and more marketing research goes digital, they must also understand the ins and outs of obtaining and managing online information. A master's degree helps. Career opportunities exist with manufacturers, retailers, some wholesalers, trade and industry associations, marketing research firms, advertising agencies, and governmental and private nonprofit agencies.

New-Product Planning

People interested in new-product planning can find opportunities in many types of organizations. They usually need a good background in marketing, marketing research, and sales forecasting; they need organizational skills to motivate and coordinate others; and they may need a technical background. Usually, these people work first in other marketing positions before joining the new-product department.

Marketing Logistics (Physical Distribution)

Marketing logistics, or physical distribution, is a large and dynamic field, with many career opportunities. Major transportation carriers, manufacturers, wholesalers, and retailers all employ logistics specialists. Increasingly, marketing teams include logistics specialists, and marketing managers' career paths include marketing logistics assignments. Coursework in quantitative methods, finance, accounting, and marketing will provide you with the necessary skills for entering the field.

Public Relations

Most organizations have a public relations staff to anticipate problems with various publics, handle complaints, deal with media, and build the corporate image. People interested in public relations should be able to speak and write clearly and persuasively, and they should have a background in journalism, communications, or the liberal arts. The challenges in this job are highly varied and very people-oriented.

Not-for-Profit Services

The key jobs in not-for-profits include marketing director, director of development, event coordinator, publication specialist, and intern/volunteer. The *marketing director* is in charge of all marketing activities for the organization. The *director of development* organizes, manages, and directs the fund-raising campaigns that keep a not-for-profit in existence. An *event coordinator* directs all aspects of fund-raising events, from initial planning through implementation. The *publication specialist* oversees publications designed to promote awareness of the organization.

Although typically an unpaid position, the *intern/volunteer* performs various marketing functions, and this work can be an important step to gaining a full-time position. The not-for-profit sector is typically not for someone who is money-driven. Rather, most not-for-profits look for people with a strong sense of community spirit and the desire to help others. Therefore, starting pay is usually lower than in other marketing fields. However, the bigger the not-for-profit, the better your chance of rapidly increasing your income when moving into upper management.

Other Resources

Professional marketing associations and organizations are another source of information about careers. Marketers belong to many such societies. You may want to contact some of the following in your job search:

Advertising Women of New York, 25 West 45th Street, New York, NY 10036. (212) 221-7969 (www.awny.org)

American Advertising Federation, 1101 Vermont Avenue, NW, Suite 500, Washington, DC 2005. (202) 898-0089 (www.aaf.org)

American Marketing Association, 311 South Wacker Drive, Suite 5800, Chicago, IL 60606. (800) AMA-1150 (www.marketingpower.com)

The Association of Women in Communications, 3337 Duke Street, Alexandria, VA 22314. (703) 370-7436 (www.womcom.org)

Market Research Association, 1156 15th Street NW, Suite 302, Washington, DC 20005. (202) 800-2545 (www.marketingresearch.org)

National Association of Sales Professionals, 555 Friendly Street, Bloomfield Hills, MI 48302. (866) 365-1520 (www.nasp.com)

National Management Association, 2210 Arbor Boulevard, Dayton, OH 45439. (937) 294-0421 (www.nma1.org)

National Retail Federation, 325 Seventh Street NW, Suite 1100, Washington, DC 20004. (800) 673-4692 (www.nrf.com)

Product Development and Management Association, 401 Michigan Avenue, Chicago, IL 60611. (312) 321-5145 (www.pdma.org)

Public Relations Society of America, 33 Maiden Lane, Eleventh Floor, New York, NY 10038. (212) 460-1400 (www.prsa.org)

Sales and Marketing Executives International, 885 West Georgia Street, Suite 1500, Vancouver, BC, V6C 3E8 Canada. (312) 893-0751 (www.smei.org)

Glossary

Adapted global marketing An international marketing approach that adjusts the marketing strategy and mix elements to each international target market, which creates more costs but hopefully produces a larger market share and return.

Administered VMS A vertical marketing system that coordinates successive stages of production and distribution through the size and power of one of the parties.

Adoption process The mental process through which an individual passes from first hearing about an innovation to final adoption.

Advertising Any paid form of nonpersonal presentation and promotion of ideas, goods, or services by an identified sponsor.

Advertising agency A marketing services firm that assists companies in planning, preparing, implementing, and evaluating all or portions of their advertising programs.

Advertising budget The dollars and other resources allocated to a product or a company advertising program.

Advertising media The vehicles through which advertising messages are delivered to their intended audiences.

Advertising objective A specific communication *task* to be accomplished with a specific *target* audience during a specific period of *time*.

Advertising strategy The strategy by which the company accomplishes its advertising objectives. It consists of two major elements: creating advertising messages and selecting advertising media.

Affordable method Setting the promotion budget at the level management thinks the company can afford.

Age and life-cycle segmentation Dividing a market into different age and life-cycle groups.

Agent A wholesaler who represents buyers or sellers on a relatively permanent basis, performs only a few functions, and does not take title to goods.

Allowance Promotional money paid by manufacturers to retailers in return for an agreement to feature the manufacturer's products in some way.

Alternative evaluation The stage of the buyer decision process in which the consumer uses information to evaluate alternative brands in the choice set.

Approach The sales step in which a salesperson meets the customer for the first time.

Attitude A person's consistently favorable or unfavorable evaluations, feelings, and tendencies toward an object or idea.

Baby boomers The 78 million people born during the years following World War II and lasting until 1964.

Basing-point pricing A geographical pricing strategy in which the seller designates some city as a basing point and charges all customers the freight cost from that city to the customer.

Behavioral segmentation Dividing a market into segments based on consumer knowledge, attitudes, uses, or responses to a product.

Belief A descriptive thought that a person holds about something.

Benchmarking Comparing the company's products and processes to those of competitors or leading firms in other industries to identify best practices and find ways to improve quality and performance.

Benefit segmentation Dividing the market into segments according to the different benefits that consumers seek from the product.

Blogs Online journals where people post their thoughts, usually on a narrowly defined topic.

Brand A name, term, sign, symbol, or design, or a combination of these, that identifies the products or services of one seller or group of sellers and differentiates them from those of competitors.

Brand equity The differential effect that knowing the brand name has on customer response to the product or its marketing.

Brand extension Extending an existing brand name to new product categories.

Break-even analysis Analysis to determine the unit volume and dollar sales needed to be profitable given a particular price and cost structure.

Break-even price The price at which total revenue equals total cost and profit is zero.

Break-even pricing (target return pricing) Setting price to break even on the costs of making and marketing a product, or setting price to make a target return.

Broker A wholesaler who does not take title to goods and whose function is to bring buyers and sellers together and assist in negotiation.

Business analysis A review of the sales, costs, and profit projections for a new product

to find out whether these factors satisfy the company's objectives.

Business buyer behavior The buying behavior of organizations that buy goods and services for use in the production of other products and services that are sold, rented, or supplied to others.

Business buying process The decision process by which business buyers determine which products and services their organizations need to purchase and then find, evaluate, and choose among alternative suppliers and brands.

Business portfolio The collection of businesses and products that make up the company.

Business promotions Sales promotion tools used to generate business leads, stimulate purchases, reward customers, and motivate salespeople.

Business-to-business (B-to-B) online marketing Businesses using online marketing to reach new business customers, serve current customers more effectively, and obtain buying efficiencies and better prices.

Business-to-consumer (B-to-C) online marketing Businesses selling goods and services online to final consumers.

Buyer-readiness stages The stages consumers normally pass through on their way to a purchase, including awareness, knowledge, liking, preference, conviction, and, finally, the actual purchase.

Buyers People in an organization's buying center who make an actual purchase.

Buying center All the individuals and units that play a role in the purchase decision-making process.

Buzz marketing Cultivating opinion leaders and getting them to spread information about a product or a service to others in their communities.

By-product pricing Setting a price for by-products in order to make the main product's price more competitive.

Cannibalization The situation in which one product sold by a company takes a portion of its sales from other company products.

Captive-product pricing Setting a price for products that must be used along with a main product, such as blades for a razor and games for a video-game console.

Catalog marketing Direct marketing through print, video, or digital catalogs that are mailed to select customers, made available in stores, or presented online.

Category killer A giant specialty store that carries a very deep assortment of a particular line.

Causal research Marketing research to test hypotheses about cause-and-effect relationships.

Chain ratio method Estimating market demand by multiplying a base number by a chain of adjusting percentages.

Channel conflict Disagreements among marketing channel members on goals, roles, and rewards—who should do what and for what rewards.

Channel level A layer of intermediaries that performs some work in bringing the product and its ownership closer to the final buyer.

Click-and-mortar companies Traditional brick-and-mortar companies that have added online marketing to their operations.

Click-only companies The so-called dot-coms, which operate online only and have no brick-and-mortar market presence.

Closing The sales step in which a salesperson asks the customer for an order.

Co-branding The practice of using the established brand names of two different companies on the same product.

Cognitive dissonance Buyer discomfort caused by postpurchase conflict.

Commercialization Introducing a new product into the market.

Communication adaptation A global communication strategy of fully adapting advertising messages to local markets.

Competition-based pricing Setting prices based on competitors' strategies, prices, costs, and market offerings.

Competitive advantage An advantage over competitors gained by offering greater customer value, either by having lower prices or providing more benefits that justify higher prices.

Competitive marketing intelligence The systematic collection and analysis of publicly available information about consumers, competitors, and developments in the marketing environment.

Competitive marketing strategies Strategies that strongly position the company against competitors and give the company the strongest possible strategic advantage.

Competitive-parity method Setting the promotion budget to match competitors' outlays.

Competitor analysis Identifying key competitors; assessing their objectives, strategies, strengths and weaknesses, and reaction patterns; and selecting which competitors to attack or avoid.

Competitor-centered company A company whose moves are mainly based on competitors' actions and reactions.

Complex buying behavior Consumer buying behavior in situations characterized by high consumer involvement in a purchase and significant perceived differences among brands.

Concentrated (niche) marketing A market-coverage strategy in which a firm goes after a large share of one or a few segments or niches.

Concept testing Testing new-product concepts with a group of target consumers to find out if the concepts have strong consumer appeal.

Consumer buyer behavior The buying behavior of final consumers—individuals and households that buy goods and services for personal consumption.

Consumer market All the individuals and households that buy or acquire goods and services for personal consumption.

Consumer product A product bought by final consumers for personal consumption.

Consumer promotions Sales promotion tools used to boost short-term customer buying and involvement or enhance long-term customer relationships.

Consumer-generated marketing Brand exchanges created by consumers themselves—both invited and uninvited—by which consumers are playing an increasing role in shaping their own brand experiences and those of other consumers.

Consumer-oriented marketing A principle of sustainable marketing that holds a company should view and organize its marketing activities from the consumer's point of view.

Consumer-to-business (C-to-B) online marketing Online exchanges in which consumers search out sellers, learn about their offers, initiate purchases, and sometimes even drive transaction terms.

Consumer-to-consumer (C-to-C) online marketing Online exchanges of goods and information between final consumers.

Consumerism An organized movement of citizens and government agencies designed to improve the rights and power of buyers in relation to sellers.

Contract manufacturing A joint venture in which a company contracts with manufacturers in a foreign market to produce its product or provide its service.

Contractual VMS A vertical marketing system in which independent firms at different levels of production and distribution join together through contracts.

Contribution margin The unit contribution divided by the selling price.

Convenience product A consumer product that customers usually buy frequently, immediately, and with minimal comparison and buying effort.

Convenience store A small store, located near a residential area, that is open long hours seven days a week and carries a limited line of high-turnover convenience goods.

Conventional distribution channel A channel consisting of one or more independent producers, wholesalers, and retailers, each a separate business seeking to maximize its own profits, perhaps even at the expense of profits for the system as a whole.

Corporate (or brand) Web site A Web site designed to build customer goodwill, collect customer feedback, and supplement other sales channels rather than sell the company's products directly.

Corporate chains Two or more outlets that are commonly owned and controlled.

Corporate VMS A vertical marketing system that combines successive stages of production and distribution under single ownership—channel leadership is established through common ownership.

Cost-based pricing Setting prices based on the costs of producing, distributing, and selling the product plus a fair rate of return for effort and risk.

Cost-plus pricing (markup pricing) Adding a standard markup to the cost of the product.

Creative concept The compelling "big idea" that will bring an advertising message strategy to life in a distinctive and memorable way.

Crowdsourcing Inviting broad communities of people—customers, employees, independent scientists and researchers, and even the public at large—into the new-product innovation process.

Cultural environment Institutions and other forces that affect society's basic values, perceptions, preferences, and behaviors.

Culture The set of basic values, perceptions, wants, and behaviors learned by a member of society from family and other important institutions.

Customer (or market) sales force structure A sales force organization in which salespeople specialize in selling only to certain customers or industries.

Customer database An organized collection of comprehensive data about individual customers or prospects, including geographic, demographic, psychographic, and behavioral data.

Customer equity The total combined customer lifetime values of all of the company's customers.

Customer insights Fresh understandings of customers and the marketplace derived from marketing information that become the basis for creating customer value and relationships.

Customer lifetime value The value of the entire stream of purchases a customer makes over a lifetime of patronage.

Customer relationship management The overall process of building and maintaining profitable customer relationships by delivering superior customer value and satisfaction.

Customer relationship management (CRM) Managing detailed information about individual customers and carefully managing customer touch points to maximize customer loyalty.

Customer satisfaction The extent to which a product's perceived performance matches a buyer's expectations.

Customer value analysis An analysis conducted to determine what benefits target customers value and how they rate the relative value of various competitors' offers.

Customer value-based pricing Setting price based on buyers' perceptions of value rather than on the seller's cost.

Customer-centered company A company that focuses on customer developments in designing its marketing strategies and delivering superior value to its target customers.

Customer-centered new-product development New-product development that focuses on finding new ways to solve customer problems and create more customer-satisfying experiences.

Customer-managed relationships Marketing relationships in which customers, empowered by today's new digital technologies, interact with companies and with each other to shape their relationships with brands.

Customer-perceived value The customer's evaluation of the difference between all the benefits and all the costs of a marketing offer relative to those of competing offers.

Customer-value marketing A principle of sustainable marketing holding that a company should put most of its resources into customer-value-building marketing investments.

Deciders People in an organization's buying center who have formal or informal power to select or approve the final suppliers.

Decline stage The PLC stage in which a product's sales fade away.

Deficient products Products that have neither immediate appeal nor long-run benefits.

Demand curve A curve that shows the number of units the market will buy in a given time period, at different prices that might be charged.

Demands Human wants that are backed by buying power.

Demographic segmentation Dividing the market into segments based on variables such as age, life-cycle stage, gender, income, occupation, education, religion, ethnicity, and generation.

Demography The study of human populations in terms of size, density, location, age, gender, race, occupation, and other statistics.

Department store A retail store that carries a wide variety of product lines, each operated as a separate department managed by specialist buyers or merchandisers.

Derived demand Business demand that ultimately comes from (derives from) the demand for consumer goods.

Descriptive research Marketing research to better describe marketing problems, situations, or markets, such as the market potential for a product or the demographics and attitudes of consumers.

Desirable products Products that give both high immediate satisfaction and high long-run benefits.

Differentiated (segmented) marketing A market-coverage strategy in which a firm decides to target several market segments and designs separate offers for each.

Differentiation Actually differentiating the market offering to create superior customer value.

Direct investment Entering a foreign market by developing foreign-based assembly or manufacturing facilities.

Direct marketing Direct connections with carefully targeted individual consumers to both obtain an immediate response and cultivate lasting customer relationships.

Direct marketing channel A marketing channel that has no intermediary levels.

Direct-mail marketing Marketing that occurs by sending an offer, announcement, reminder, or other item directly to a person at a particular address.

Direct-response television (DRTV) marketing Direct marketing via television, including direct-response television advertising (or infomercials) and interactive television (iTV) advertising.

Discount A straight reduction in price on purchases during a stated period of time or in larger quantities.

Discount store A retail operation that sells standard merchandise at lower prices by accepting lower margins and selling at higher volume.

Disintermediation The cutting out of marketing channel intermediaries by product or service producers or the displacement of traditional resellers by radical new types of intermediaries.

Dissonance-reducing buying behavior Consumer buying behavior in situations characterized by high involvement but few perceived differences among brands.

Distribution center A large, highly automated warehouse designed to receive goods from various plants and suppliers, take orders, fill them efficiently, and deliver goods to customers as quickly as possible.

Diversification Company growth through starting up or acquiring businesses outside the company's current products and markets.

Dynamic pricing Adjusting prices continually to meet the characteristics and needs of individual customers and situations.

E-mail marketing Sending highly targeted, highly personalized, relationship-building marketing messages via e-mail.

E-procurement Purchasing through electronic connections between buyers and sellers—usually online.

Economic community A group of nations organized to work toward common goals in the regulation of international trade.

Economic environment Economic factors that affect consumer purchasing power and spending patterns.

Environmental sustainability A management approach that involves developing strategies that both sustain the environment and produce profits for the company.

Environmental sustainability Developing strategies and practices that create a world economy that the planet can support indefinitely.

Environmentalism An organized movement of concerned citizens, businesses, and government agencies designed to protect and improve people's current and future living environment.

Ethnographic research A form of observational research that involves sending trained observers to watch and interact with consumers in their "natural environments."

Event marketing (or event sponsorships) Creating a brand-marketing event or serving as a sole or participating sponsor of events created by others.

Exchange The act of obtaining a desired object from someone by offering something in return.

Exclusive distribution Giving a limited number of dealers the exclusive right to distribute the company's products in their territories.

Execution style The approach, style, tone, words, and format used for executing an advertising message.

Experience curve (learning curve) The drop in the average per-unit production cost that comes with accumulated production experience.

Experimental research Gathering primary data by selecting matched groups of subjects, giving them different treatments, controlling related factors, and checking for differences in group responses.

Exploratory research Marketing research to gather preliminary information that will help define problems and suggest hypotheses.

Exporting Entering foreign markets by selling goods produced in the company's home country, often with little modification.

Factory outlet An off-price retailing operation that is owned and operated by a manufacturer and normally carries the manufacturer's surplus, discontinued, or irregular goods.

Fad A temporary period of unusually high sales driven by consumer enthusiasm and immediate product or brand popularity.

Fashion A currently accepted or popular style in a given field.

Fixed costs (overhead) Costs that do not vary with production or sales level.

FOB-origin pricing A geographical pricing strategy in which goods are placed free on board a carrier; the customer pays the freight from the factory to the destination.

Focus group interviewing Personal interviewing that involves inviting 6 to 10 people to gather for a few hours with a trained interviewer to talk about a product, service, or organization. The interviewer "focuses" the group discussion on important issues.

Follow-up The sales step in which a salesperson follows up after the sale to ensure customer satisfaction and repeat business.

Franchise A contractual association between a manufacturer, wholesaler, or service organization (a franchisor) and independent businesspeople (franchisees) who buy the right to own and operate one or more units in the franchise system.

Franchise organization A contractual vertical marketing system in which a channel member, called a franchisor, links several stages in the production-distribution process.

Freight-absorption pricing A geographical pricing strategy in which the seller absorbs all or part of the freight charges in order to get the desired business.

Gatekeepers People in an organization's buying center who control the flow of information to others.

Gender segmentation Dividing a market into different segments based on gender.

General need description The stage in the business buying process in which a buyer describes the general characteristics and quantity of a needed item.

Generation X The 49 million people born between 1965 and 1976 in the "birth dearth" following the baby boom.

Geographic segmentation Dividing a market into different geographical units, such as nations, states, regions, counties, cities, or even neighborhoods.

Geographical pricing Setting prices for customers located in different parts of the country or world.

Global firm A firm that, by operating in more than one country, gains R&D, production, marketing, and financial advantages in its costs and reputation that are not available to purely domestic competitors.

Good-value pricing Offering just the right combination of quality and good service at a fair price.

Government market Governmental units—federal, state, and local—that purchase or rent goods and services for carrying out the main functions of government.

Gross margin percentage The percentage of net sales remaining after cost of goods sold—calculated by dividing gross margin by net sales.

Group Two or more people who interact to accomplish individual or mutual goals.

Growth stage The PLC stage in which a product's sales start climbing quickly.

Growth-share matrix A portfolio-planning method that evaluates a company's SBUs in terms of market growth rate and relative market share.

Habitual buying behavior Consumer buying behavior in situations characterized by low consumer involvement and few significant perceived brand differences.

Handling objections The sales step in which a salesperson seeks out, clarifies, and overcomes any customer objections to buying.

Horizontal marketing system A channel arrangement in which two or more companies at one level join together to follow a new marketing opportunity.

Idea generation The systematic search for new-product ideas.

Idea screening Screening new-product ideas to spot good ideas and drop poor ones as soon as possible.

Income segmentation Dividing a market into different income segments.

Independent off-price retailer An off-price retailer that is either independently owned and run or is a division of a larger retail corporation.

Indirect marketing channel A marketing channel containing one or more intermediary levels.

Individual marketing Tailoring products and marketing programs to the needs and preferences of individual customers.

Industrial product A product bought by individuals and organizations for further processing or for use in conducting a business.

Influencers People in an organization's buying center who affect the buying decision; they often help define specifications and also provide information for evaluating alternatives.

Information search The stage of the buyer decision process in which the consumer is motivated to search for more information.

Innovative marketing A principle of sustainable marketing that requires a company to seek real product and marketing improvements.

Inside sales force Salespeople who conduct business from their offices via telephone, the Internet, or visits from prospective buyers.

Institutional market Schools, hospitals, nursing homes, prisons, and other institutions that provide goods and services to people in their care.

Integrated logistics management The logistics concept that emphasizes teamwork—both inside the company and among all the marketing channel organizations—to maximize the performance of the entire distribution system.

Integrated marketing communications (IMC) Carefully integrating and coordinating the company's many communications channels to deliver a clear, consistent, and compelling message about the organization and its products.

Intensive distribution Stocking the product in as many outlets as possible.

Interactive marketing Training service employees in the fine art of interacting with customers to satisfy their needs.

Intermarket (cross-market) segmentation Forming segments of consumers who have similar needs and buying behaviors even though they are located in different countries.

Intermodal transportation Combining two or more modes of transportation.

Internal databases Electronic collections of consumer and market information obtained from data sources within the company network.

Internal marketing Orienting and motivating customer-contact employees and supporting service employees to work as a team to provide customer satisfaction.

Internet A vast public web of computer networks that connects users of all types all around the world to each other and to an amazingly large information repository.

Introduction stage The PLC stage in which a new product is first distributed and made available for purchase.

Inventory turnover rate (or stockturn rate for resellers) The number of times an inventory turns over or is sold during a specified time period (often one year)—calculated based on costs, selling price, or units.

Joint ownership A cooperative venture in which a company creates a local business with investors in a foreign market, who share ownership and control.

Joint venturing Entering foreign markets by joining with foreign companies to produce or market a product or service.

Learning Changes in an individual's behavior arising from experience.

Licensing Entering foreign markets through developing an agreement with a licensee in the foreign market.

Lifestyle A person's pattern of living as expressed in his or her activities, interests, and opinions.

Line extension Extending an existing brand name to new forms, colors, sizes, ingredients, or flavors of an existing product category.

Local marketing Tailoring brands and marketing to the needs and wants of local customer segments—cities, neighborhoods, and even specific stores.

Macroenvironment The larger societal forces that affect the microenvironment—demographic, economic, natural, technological, political, and cultural forces.

Madison & Vine A term that has come to represent the merging of advertising and entertainment in an effort to break through the clutter and create new avenues for reaching customers with more engaging messages.

Management contracting A joint venture in which the domestic firm supplies the management know-how to a foreign company that supplies the capital; the domestic firm exports management services rather than products.

Manufacturers' sales branches and offices Wholesaling by sellers or buyers themselves rather than through independent wholesalers.

Market The set of all actual and potential buyers of a product or service.

Market challenger A runner-up firm that is fighting hard to increase its market share in an industry.

Market development Company growth by identifying and developing new market segments for current company products.

Market follower A runner-up firm that wants to hold its share in an industry without rocking the boat.

Market leader The firm in an industry with the largest market share.

Market nicher A firm that serves small segments that the other firms in an industry overlook or ignore.

Market offerings Some combination of products, services, information, or experiences offered to a market to satisfy a need or want.

Market penetration Company growth by increasing sales of current products to current market segments without changing the product.

Market potential The upper limit of market demand.

Market segment A group of consumers who respond in a similar way to a given set of marketing efforts.

Market segmentation Dividing a market into smaller segments of buyers with distinct needs, characteristics, or behaviors that might require separate marketing strategies or mixes.

Market share Company sales divided by market sales.

Market targeting (targeting) Evaluating each market segment's attractiveness and selecting one or more segments to enter.

Market-centered company A company that pays balanced attention to both customers and competitors in designing its marketing strategies.

Market-penetration pricing Setting a low price for a new product in order to attract a large number of buyers and a large market share.

Market-skimming pricing (price skimming) Setting a high price for a new product to skim maximum revenues layer by layer from the segments willing to pay the high price; the company makes fewer but more profitable sales.

Marketing The process by which companies create value for customers and build strong customer relationships in order to capture value from customers in return.

Marketing channel (or distribution channel) A set of interdependent organizations that help make a product or service available for use or consumption by the consumer or business user.

Marketing channel design Designing effective marketing channels by analyzing customer needs, setting channel objectives, identifying major channel alternatives, and evaluating those alternatives.

Marketing channel management Selecting, managing, and motivating individual channel members and evaluating their performance over time.

Marketing concept A philosophy in which achieving organizational goals depends on knowing the needs and wants of target markets and delivering the desired satisfactions better than competitors do.

Marketing control Measuring and evaluating the results of marketing strategies and plans and taking corrective action to ensure that the objectives are achieved.

Marketing environment The actors and forces outside marketing that affect marketing management's ability to build and maintain successful relationships with target customers.

Marketing implementation Turning marketing strategies and plans into marketing actions to accomplish strategic marketing objectives.

Marketing information system (MIS) People and procedures dedicated to assessing information needs, developing the needed information, and helping decision makers to use the information to generate and validate actionable customer and market insights.

Marketing intermediaries Firms that help the company to promote, sell, and distribute its goods to final buyers.

Marketing logistics (or physical distribution) Planning, implementing, and controlling the physical flow of materials, final goods, and related information from points of origin to points of consumption to meet customer requirements at a profit.

Marketing management The art and science of choosing target markets and building profitable relationships with them.

Marketing mix The set of tactical marketing tools—product, price, place, and promotion—that the firm blends to produce the response it wants in the target market.

Marketing myopia The mistake of paying more attention to the specific products a company offers than to the benefits and experiences produced by these products.

Marketing research The systematic design, collection, analysis, and reporting of data relevant to a specific marketing situation facing an organization.

Marketing return on investment (or marketing ROI) A measure of the marketing productivity of a marketing investment—calculated by dividing net marketing contribution by marketing expenses.

Marketing return on sales (or marketing ROS) The percent of net sales attributable to the net marketing contribution—calculated by dividing net marketing contribution by net sales.

Marketing strategy The marketing logic by which the company hopes to create customer value and achieve profitable customer relationships.

Marketing strategy development Designing an initial marketing strategy for a new product based on the product concept.

Marketing Web site A Web site that interacts with consumers to move them closer to a direct purchase or other marketing outcome.

Markup The difference between a company's selling price for a product and its cost to manufacture or purchase it.

Markup chain The sequence of markups used by firms at each level in a channel.

Maturity stage The PLC stage in which a product's sales growth slows or levels off.

Merchant wholesaler An independently owned wholesale business that takes title to the merchandise it handles.

Microenvironment The actors close to the company that affect its ability to serve its customers—the company, suppliers, marketing intermediaries, customer markets, competitors, and publics.

Micromarketing Tailoring products and marketing programs to the needs and wants of specific individuals and local customer segments; it includes *local marketing* and *individual marketing*.

Millennials (or Generation Y) The 83 million children of the baby boomers born between 1977 and 2000.

Mission statement A statement of the organization's purpose—what it wants to accomplish in the larger environment.

Mobile marketing Marketing to on-the-go consumers through mobile phones, smartphones, tablets, and other mobile communication devices.

Modified rebuy A business buying situation in which the buyer wants to modify product specifications, prices, terms, or suppliers.

Motive (drive) A need that is sufficiently pressing to direct the person to seek satisfaction of the need.

Multichannel distribution system A distribution system in which a single firm sets up two or more marketing channels to reach one or more customer segments.

Natural environment The physical environment and the natural resources that are needed as inputs by marketers or that are affected by marketing activities.

Need recognition The first stage of the buyer decision process, in which the consumer recognizes a problem or need.

Needs States of felt deprivation.

Net marketing contribution (NMC) A measure of marketing profitability that includes only components of profitability controlled by marketing.

Net profit percentage The percentage of each sales dollar going to profit—calculated by dividing net profits by net sales.

New product A good, service, or idea that is perceived by some potential customers as new.

New task A business buying situation in which the buyer purchases a product or service for the first time.

New-product development The development of original products, product improvements, product modifications, and new brands through the firm's own product development efforts.

Nonpersonal communication channels Media that carry messages without personal contact or feedback, including major media, atmospheres, and events.

Objective-and-task method Developing the promotion budget by (1) defining specific promotion objectives, (2) determining the tasks needed to achieve these objectives, and (3) estimating the costs of performing these tasks. The sum of these costs is the proposed promotion budget.

Observational research Gathering primary data by observing relevant people, actions, and situations.

Occasion segmentation Dividing the market into segments according to occasions when buyers get the idea to buy, actually make their purchase, or use the purchased item.

Off-price retailer A retailer that buys at less-than-regular wholesale prices and sells at less than retail.

Online advertising Advertising that appears while consumers are browsing the Internet, including display ads, search-related ads, online classifieds, and other forms.

Online focus groups Gathering a small group of people online with a trained moderator to chat about a product, service, or organization and gain qualitative insights about consumer attitudes and behavior.

Online marketing Efforts to market products and services and build customer relationships over the Internet.

Online marketing research Collecting primary data online through Internet surveys, online focus groups, Web-based experiments, or tracking consumers' online behavior.

Online social networks Online social communities—blogs, social networking sites, and other online communities—where people socialize or exchange information and opinions.

Operating expense percentage The portion of net sales going to operating expenses—calculated by dividing total expenses by net sales.

Operating ratios The ratios of selected operating statement items to net sales.

Opinion leader A person within a reference group who, because of special skills, knowledge, personality, or other characteristics, exerts social influence on others.

Optional-product pricing The pricing of optional or accessory products along with a main product.

Order-routine specification The stage of the business buying process in which the buyer writes the final order with the chosen supplier(s), listing the technical specifications, quantity needed, expected time of delivery, return policies, and warranties.

Outside sales force (or field sales force) Salespeople who travel to call on customers in the field.

Packaging The activities of designing and producing the container or wrapper for a product.

Partner relationship management Working closely with partners in other company departments and outside the company to jointly bring greater value to customers.

Percentage-of-sales method Setting the promotion budget at a certain percentage of current or forecasted sales or as a percentage of the unit sales price.

Perception The process by which people select, organize, and interpret information to form a meaningful picture of the world.

Performance review The stage of the business buying process in which the buyer assesses the performance of the supplier and decides to continue, modify, or drop the arrangement.

Personal communication channels Channels through which two or more people communicate directly with each other, including face to face, on the phone, via mail or e-mail, or even through texting or an Internet chat.

Personal selling Personal presentation by the firm's sales force for the purpose of making sales and building customer relationships.

Personality The unique psychological characteristics that distinguish a person or group.

Pleasing products Products that give high immediate satisfaction but may hurt consumers in the long run.

Political environment Laws, government agencies, and pressure groups that influence and limit various organizations and individuals in a given society.

Portfolio analysis The process by which management evaluates the products and businesses that make up the company.

Positioning Arranging for a market offering to occupy a clear, distinctive, and desirable place relative to competing products in the minds of target consumers.

Positioning statement A statement that summarizes company or brand positioning using this form: To (target segment and need) our (brand) is (concept) that (point of difference).

Postpurchase behavior The stage of the buyer decision process in which consumers take further action after purchase, based on their satisfaction or dissatisfaction.

Preapproach The sales step in which a salesperson learns as much as possible about a prospective customer before making a sales call.

Presentation The sales step in which a salesperson tells the "value story" to the buyer, showing how the company's offer solves the customer's problems.

Price The amount of money charged for a product or service, or the sum of the values that customers exchange for the benefits of having or using the product or service.

Price elasticity A measure of the sensitivity of demand to changes in price.

Primary data Information collected for the specific purpose at hand.

Problem recognition The stage of the business buying pr ocess in which the company recognizes a problem or need that can be met by acquiring a good or a service.

Product Anything that can be offered to a market for attention, acquisition, use, or consumption that might satisfy a want or need.

Product adaptation Adapting a product to meet local conditions or wants in foreign markets.

Product bundle pricing Combining several products and offering the bundle at a reduced price.

Product concept A detailed version of the new-product idea stated in meaningful consumer terms.

Product concept The idea that consumers will favor products that offer the most quality, performance, and features; therefore, the organization should devote its energy to making continuous product improvements.

Product development Company growth by offering modified or new products to current market segments.

Product development Developing the product concept into a physical product to ensure that the product idea can be turned into a workable market offering.

Product invention Creating new products or services for foreign markets.

Product life cycle (PLC) The course of a product's sales and profits over its lifetime.

Product line A group of products that are closely related because they function in a similar manner, are sold to the same customer groups, are marketed through the same types of outlets, or fall within given price ranges.

Product line pricing Setting the price steps between various products in a product line based on cost differences between the products, customer evaluations of different features, and competitors' prices.

Product mix (or product portfolio) The set of all product lines and items that a particular seller offers for sale.

Product position The way a product is defined by consumers on important attributes—the place the product occupies in consumers' minds relative to competing products.

Product quality The characteristics of a product or service that bear on its ability to satisfy stated or implied customer needs.

Product sales force structure A sales force organization in which salespeople specialize in selling only a portion of the company's products or lines.

Product specification The stage of the business buying process in which the buying organization decides on and specifies the best technical product characteristics for a needed item.

Product/market expansion grid A portfolio-planning tool for identifying company growth opportunities through market penetration, market development, product development, or diversification.

Production concept The idea that consumers will favor products that are available and highly affordable; therefore, the organization should focus on improving production and distribution efficiency.

Profit-and-loss statement (or income statement or operating statement) A statement that shows actual revenues less expenses and net profit for an organization, product, or brand during a specific planning period, typically a year.

Pro forma (or projected) profit-and-loss statement (or income statement or operating statement) A statement that shows projected revenues less budgeted expenses and estimates the projected net profit for an organization, product, or brand during a specific planning period, typically a year.

Promotion mix (or marketing communications mix) The specific blend of promotion tools that the company uses to persuasively communicate customer value and build customer relationships.

Promotional pricing Temporarily pricing products below the list price, and sometimes even below cost, to increase short-run sales.

Proposal solicitation The stage of the business buying process in which the buyer invites qualified suppliers to submit proposals.

Prospecting The sales step in which a salesperson or company identifies qualified potential customers.

Psychographic segmentation Dividing a market into different segments based on social class, lifestyle, or personality characteristics.

Psychological pricing Pricing that considers the psychology of prices and not simply the economics; the price is used to say something about the product.

Public Any group that has an actual or potential interest in or impact on an organization's ability to achieve its objectives.

Public relations (PR) Building good relations with the company's various publics by obtaining favorable publicity, building up a good corporate image, and handling or heading off unfavorable rumors, stories, and events.

Pull strategy A promotion strategy that calls for spending a lot on consumer advertising and promotion to induce final consumers to buy the product, creating a demand vacuum that "pulls" the product through the channel.

Purchase decision The buyer's decision about which brand to purchase.

Push strategy A promotion strategy that calls for using the sales force and trade promotion to push the product through channels. The producer promotes the product to channel members, which in turn promote it to final consumers.

Reference prices Prices that buyers carry in their minds and refer to when they look at a given product.

Relevant costs Costs that will occur in the future and that will vary across the alternatives being considered.

Retailer A business whose sales come *primarily* from retailing.

Retailing All the activities involved in selling goods or services directly to final consumers for their personal, nonbusiness use.

Return on advertising investment The net return on advertising investment divided by the costs of the advertising investment.

Return on investment (ROI) A measure of managerial effectiveness and efficiency—net profit before taxes divided by total investment.

Return on investment (ROI) pricing (or target-return pricing) A cost-based pricing method that determines price based on a specified rate of return on investment.

Return on marketing investment (or marketing ROI) The net return from a marketing investment divided by the costs of the marketing investment.

Sales force management Analyzing, planning, implementing, and controlling sales force activities.

Sales promotion Short-term incentives to encourage the purchase or sale of a product or service.

Sales quota A standard that states the amount a salesperson should sell and how sales should be divided among the company's products.

Salesperson An individual who represents a company to customers by performing one or more of the following activities: prospecting, communicating, selling, servicing, information gathering, and relationship building.

Salutary products Products that have low immediate appeal but may benefit consumers in the long run.

Sample A segment of the population selected for marketing research to represent the population as a whole.

Secondary data Information that already exists somewhere, having been collected for another purpose.

Segmented pricing Selling a product or service at two or more prices, where the difference in prices is not based on differences in costs.

Selective distribution The use of more than one but fewer than all of the intermediaries who are willing to carry the company's products.

Selling concept The idea that consumers will not buy enough of the firm's products unless the firm undertakes a large-scale selling and promotion effort.

Selling process The steps that salespeople follow when selling, which include prospecting and qualifying, preapproach, approach, presentation and demonstration, handling objections, closing, and follow-up.

Sense-of-mission marketing A principle of sustainable marketing holding that a company should define its mission in broad social terms rather than narrow product terms.

Service An activity, benefit, or satisfaction offered for sale that is essentially intangible and does not result in the ownership of anything.

Service inseparability Services are produced and consumed at the same time and cannot be separated from their providers.

Service intangibility Services cannot be seen, tasted, felt, heard, or smelled before they are bought.

Service perishability Services cannot be stored for later sale or use.

Service profit chain The chain that links service firm profits with employee and customer satisfaction.

Service retailer A retailer whose product line is actually a service; examples include hotels, airlines, banks, colleges, and many others.

Service variability The quality of services may vary greatly depending on who provides them and when, where, and how they are provided.

Share of customer The portion of the customer's purchasing that a company gets in its product categories.

Shopper marketing Using in-store promotions and advertising to extend brand equity to "the last mile" and encourage favorable in-store purchase decisions.

Shopping center A group of retail businesses built on a site that is planned, developed, owned, and managed as a unit.

Shopping product A consumer product that the customer, in the process of selecting and purchasing, usually compares on such attributes as suitability, quality, price, and style.

Social class Relatively permanent and ordered divisions in a society whose members share similar values, interests, and behaviors.

Social marketing The use of commercial marketing concepts and tools in programs designed to influence individuals' behavior to improve their well-being and that of society.

Societal marketing A principle of sustainable marketing holding that a company should make marketing decisions by considering consumers' wants, the company's requirements, consumers' long-run interests, and society's long-run interests.

Societal marketing concept The idea that a company's marketing decisions should consider consumers' wants, the company's requirements, consumers' long-run interests, and society's long-run interests.

Spam Unsolicited, unwanted commercial e-mail messages.

Specialty product A consumer product with unique characteristics or brand identification for which a significant group of buyers is willing to make a special purchase effort.

Specialty store A retail store that carries a narrow product line with a deep assortment within that line.

Standardized global marketing An international marketing strategy that basically uses the same marketing strategy and mix in all of the company's international markets.

Store brand (or private brand) A brand created and owned by a reseller of a product or service.

Straight product extension Marketing a product in a foreign market without making any changes to the product.

Straight rebuy A business buying situation in which the buyer routinely reorders something without any modifications.

Strategic group A group of firms in an industry following the same or a similar strategy.

Strategic planning The process of developing and maintaining a strategic fit between the organization's goals and capabilities and its changing marketing opportunities.

Style A basic and distinctive mode of expression.

Subculture A group of people with shared value systems based on common life experiences and situations.

Supermarket A large, low-cost, low-margin, high-volume, self-service store that carries a wide variety of grocery and household products.

Superstore A store much larger than a regular supermarket that offers a large assortment of routinely purchased food products, non-food items, and services.

Supplier development Systematic development of networks of supplier-partners to ensure an appropriate and dependable supply of products and materials for use in making products or reselling them to others.

Supplier search The stage of the business buying process in which the buyer tries to find the best vendors.

Supplier selection The stage of the business buying process in which the buyer reviews proposals and selects a supplier or suppliers.

Supply chain management Managing upstream and downstream value-added flows of materials, final goods, and related information among suppliers, the company, resellers, and final consumers.

Survey research Gathering primary data by asking people questions about their knowledge, attitudes, preferences, and buying behavior.

Sustainable marketing Socially and environmentally responsible marketing that meets the present needs of consumers and businesses while also preserving or enhancing the ability of future generations to meet their needs.

SWOT analysis An overall evaluation of the company's strengths (S), weaknesses (W), opportunities (O), and threats (T).

Systems selling (or solutions selling) Buying a packaged solution to a problem from a single seller, thus avoiding all the separate decisions involved in a complex buying situation.

Target costing Pricing that starts with an ideal selling price, then targets costs that will ensure that the price is met.

Target market A set of buyers sharing common needs or characteristics that the company decides to serve.

Team selling Using teams of people from sales, marketing, engineering, finance, technical support, and even upper management to service large, complex accounts.

Team-based new-product development New-product development in which various company departments work closely together, overlapping the steps in the product development process to save time and increase effectiveness.

Technological environment Forces that create new technologies, creating new product and market opportunities.

Telemarketing Using the telephone to sell directly to customers.

Territorial sales force structure A sales force organization that assigns each salesperson to an exclusive geographic territory in which that salesperson sells the company's full line.

Test marketing The stage of new-product development in which the product and its proposed marketing program are tested in realistic market settings.

Third-party logistics (3PL) provider An independent logistics provider that performs any or all of the functions required to get a client's product to market.

Total costs The sum of the fixed and variable costs for any given level of production.

Total market demand The total volume that would be bought by a defined consumer group in a defined geographic area in a defined time period in a defined marketing environment under a defined level and mix of industry marketing effort.

Trade promotions Sales promotion tools used to persuade resellers to carry a brand, give it shelf space, promote it in advertising, and push it to consumers.

Undifferentiated (mass) marketing A market-coverage strategy in which a firm decides to ignore market segment differences and go after the whole market with one offer.

Uniform-delivered pricing A geographical pricing strategy in which the company charges the same price plus freight to all customers, regardless of their location.

Unit contribution The amount that each unit contributes to covering fixed costs—the difference between price and variable costs.

Unsought product A consumer product that the consumer either does not know about or knows about but does not normally consider buying.

Users Members of the buying organization who will actually use the purchased product or service.

Value-added pricing Attaching value-added features and services to differentiate a company's offers and charging higher prices.

Value-based pricing Offering just the right combination of quality and good service at a fair price.

Value chain The series of internal departments that carry out value-creating activities to design, produce, market, deliver, and support a firm's products.

Value delivery network A network composed of the company, suppliers, distributors, and, ultimately, customers who partner with each other to improve the performance of the entire system in delivering customer value.

Value proposition The full positioning of a brand—the full mix of benefits on which it is positioned.

Variable costs Costs that vary directly with the level of production.

Variety-seeking buying behavior Consumer buying behavior in situations characterized by low consumer involvement but significant perceived brand differences.

Vertical marketing system (VMS) A channel structure in which producers, wholesalers, and retailers act as a unified system. One channel member owns the others, has contracts with them, or has so much power that they all cooperate.

Viral marketing The Internet version of word-of-mouth marketing: a Web site, video, e-mail message, or other marketing event that is so infectious that customers will seek it out or pass it along to friends.

Wants The form human needs take as they are shaped by culture and individual personality.

Warehouse club An off-price retailer that sells a limited selection of brand-name grocery items, appliances, clothing, and other goods at deep discounts to members who pay annual membership fees.

Wheel-of-retailing concept A concept that suggests new types of retailers usually begin as low-margin, low-price, low-status operations but later evolve into higher-priced, higher-service operations, eventually becoming like the conventional retailers they replaced.

Whole-channel view Designing international channels that take into account the entire global supply chain and marketing channel, forging an effective global value delivery network.

Wholesaler A firm engaged *primarily* in wholesaling activities.

Wholesaling All the activities involved in selling goods and services to those buying for resale or business use.

Word-of-mouth influence The impact of the personal words and recommendations of trusted friends, associates, and other consumers on buying behavior.

Workload method An approach to determining sales force size based on the workload required and the time available for selling.

Zone pricing A geographical pricing strategy in which the company sets up two or more zones. All customers within a zone pay the same total price; the more distant the zone, the higher the price.

Indexes

Name, Organization, Brand, Company Index

A reference appearing in italic indicates a figure on that page. The letter n indicates the reference note number on the page containing the name listed.

Subject Index

Page numbers in italic indicate an illustration or photo appears on that page.